TABLE 1
EXPONENTIAL FUNCTIONS

x	e^x	e^{-x}	x	e^x	e^{-x}	x	e^x	e^{-x}
0.010	1.0101	0.9901	0.610	1.8404	0.5434	2.050	7.7678	0.1287
0.020	1.0202	0.9802	0.620	1.8589	0.5379	2.100	8.1660	0.1225
0.030	1.0305	0.9704	0.630	1.8776	0.5326	2.150	8.5847	0.1165
0.040	1.0408	0.9608	0.640	1.8965	0.5273	2.200	9.0250	0.1108
0.050	1.0513	0.9512	0.650	1.9155	0.5220	2.250	9.4875	0.1054
0.060	1.0618	0.9418	0.660	1.9348	0.5169	2.300	9.9740	0.1003
0.070	1.0725	0.9324	0.670	1.9542	0.5117	2.350	10.486	0.0954
0.080	1.0833	0.9231	0.680	1.9739	0.5066	2.400	11.023	0.0907
0.090	1.0942	0.9139	0.690	1.9937	0.5016	2.450	11.588	0.0863
0.100	1.1052	0.9048	0.700	2.0138	0.4966	2.500	12.182	0.0821
0.110	1.1163	0.8958	0.710	2.0340	0.4916	2.550	12.807	0.0781
0.120	1.1275	0.8869	0.720	2.0544	0.4868	2.600	13.464	0.0743
0.130	1.1388	0.8781	0.730	2.0751	0.4819	2.650	14.154	0.0707
0.140	1.1503	0.8694	0.740	2.0959	0.4771	2.700	14.880	0.0672
0.150	1.1618	0.8607	0.750	2.1170	0.4724	2.750	15.643	0.0639
0.160	1.1735	0.8521	0.760	2.1383	0.4677	2.800	16.445	0.0608
0.170	1.1853	0.8437	0.770	2.1598	0.4630	2.850	17.287	0.0578
0.180	1.1972	0.8353	0.780	2.1815	0.4584	2.900	18.174	0.0550
0.190	1.2092	0.8270	0.790	2.2034	0.4538	2.950	19.106	0.0523
0.200	1.2214	0.8187	0.800	2.2255	0.4493	3.000	20.086	0.0498
0.210	1.2337	0.8106	0.810	2.2479	0.4449	3.050	21.115	0.0474
0.220	1.2461	0.8025	0.820	2.2705	0.4404	3.100	22.198	0.0451
0.230	1.2586	0.7945	0.830	2.2933	0.4360	3.150	23.336	0.0429
0.240	1.2712	0.7866	0.840	2.3164	0.4317	3.200	24.533	0.0408
0.250	1.2840	0.7788	0.850	2.3396	0.4274	3.250	25.790	0.0388
0.260	1.2969	0.7711	0.860	2.3632	0.4232	3.300	27.113	0.0369
0.270	1.3100	0.7634	0.870	2.3869	0.4190	3.350	28.503	0.0351
0.280	1.3231	0.7558	0.880	2.4109	0.4148	3.400	29.964	0.0334
0.290	1.3364	0.7483	0.890	2.4351	0.4107	3.450	31.500	0.0317
0.300	1.3499	0.7408	0.900	2.4596	0.4066	3.500	33.115	0.0302
0.310	1.3634	0.7334	0.910	2.4843	0.4025	3.550	34.813	0.0287
0.320	1.3771	0.7261	0.920	2.5093	0.3985	3.600	36.598	0.0273
0.330	1.3910	0.7189	0.930	2.5345	0.3946	3.650	38.475	0.0260
0.340	1.4049	0.7118	0.940	2.5600	0.3906	3.700	40.447	0.0247
0.350	1.4191	0.7047	0.950	2.5857	0.3867	3.750	42.521	0.0235
0.360	1.4333	0.6977	0.960	2.6117	0.3829	3.800	44.701	0.0224
0.370	1.4477	0.6907	0.970	2.6379	0.3791	3.850	46.993	0.0213
0.380	1.4623	0.6839	0.980	2.6645	0.3753	3.900	49.402	0.0202
0.390	1.4770	0.6771	0.990	2.6912	0.3716	3.950	51.935	0.0193
0.400	1.4918	0.6703	1.000	2.7183	0.3679	4.000	54.598	0.0183
0.410	1.5068	0.6637	1.050	2.8576	0.3499	4.050	57.397	0.0174
0.420	1.5220	0.6570	1.100	3.0042	0.3329	4.100	60.340	0.0166
0.430	1.5373	0.6505	1.150	3.1582	0.3166	4.150	63.434	0.0158
0.440	1.5527	0.6440	1.200	3.3201	0.3012	4.200	66.686	0.0150
0.450	1.5683	0.6376	1.250	3.4903	0.2865	4.250	70.105	0.0143
0.460	1.5841	0.6313	1.300	3.6693	0.2725	4.300	73.700	0.0136
0.470	1.6000	0.6250	1.350	3.8574	0.2592	4.350	77.478	0.0129
0.480	1.6161	0.6188	1.400	4.0552	0.2466	4.400	81.451	0.0123
0.490	1.6323	0.6126	1.450	4.2631	0.2346	4.450	85.627	0.0117
0.500	1.6487	0.6065	1.500	4.4817	0.2231	4.500	90.017	0.0111
0.510	1.6653	0.6005	1.550	4.7114	0.2122	4.550	94.637	0.0106
0.520	1.6820	0.5945	1.600	4.9530	0.2019	4.600	99.484	0.0101
0.530	1.6989	0.5886	1.650	5.2069	0.1921	4.650	104.58	0.0096
0.540	1.7160	0.5827	1.700	5.4739	0.1827	4.700	109.95	0.0091
0.550	1.7333	0.5770	1.750	5.7545	0.1738	4.750	115.58	0.0087
0.560	1.7507	0.5712	1.800	6.0496	0.1653	4.800	121.51	0.0082
0.570	1.7683	0.5655	1.850	6.3597	0.1572	4.850	127.74	0.0078
0.580	1.7860	0.5599	1.900	6.6858	0.1496			
0.590	1.8040	0.5543	1.950	7.0286	0.1423			
0.600	1.8221	0.5488	2.000	7.3891	0.1353			

(Continued on inside back cover)

APPLIED MATHEMATICS

for Business,
Economics,
and the
Social Sciences

APPLIED MATHEMATICS

for Business, Economics, and the Social Sciences

Second Edition

FRANK S. BUDNICK

University of Rhode Island

McGraw-Hill Book Company

New York | St. Louis | San Francisco | Auckland | Bogotá
Hamburg | Johannesburg | London | Madrid | Mexico
Montreal | New Delhi | Panama | Paris | São Paulo
Singapore | Sydney | Tokyo | Toronto

CHAPTER-OPENING PHOTO CREDITS

1: Dianne Arndt; 2: Bruce Davidson/Magnum; 3: Barrie Rokeach; 4: Jean Gaumy/Magnum; 5: Barrie Rokeach; 6: Barrie Rokeach; 7: Sculpture by Kenneth Snelson; 8: Geisco; 9: J. Kalvar/Magnum; 10: Burk Vzzle/Magnum; 11: Burk Vzzle/Magnum; 12: Reflejo/Nancy Palmer; 13: American Museum of Natural History; 14: Barrie Rokeach; 15: David A. Rahm/McGraw-Hill; 16: Barrie Rokeach; 17: Barrie Rokeach; 18: Barrie Rokeach

APPLIED MATHEMATICS FOR BUSINESS, ECONOMICS, AND THE SOCIAL SCIENCES

Copyright © 1983, 1979 by McGraw-Hill, Inc.
All rights reserved.
Printed in the United States of America.
Except as permitted under the United States Copyright Act of 1976,
no part of this publication may be reproduced or distributed
in any form or by any means, or stored
in a data base or retrieval system, without
the prior written permission of the publisher.

1 2 3 4 5 6 7 8 9 0   VNHVNH   8 9 8 7 6 5 4 3

ISBN 0-07-008858-6

This book was set in Palatino by Progressive Typographers.
The editors were Donald G. Mason and Jonathan Palace;
the designer was Nicholas Krenitsky;
the production supervisor was Dominick Petrellese.
New drawings were done by Fine Line Illustrations, Inc.
Von Hoffmann Press, Inc., was printer and binder.

Library of Congress Cataloging in Publication Data

Budnick, Frank S.
    Applied mathematics for business, economics, and
the social sciences.

    Includes index.
    1. Mathematics—1961-   . I. Title.
QA37.2.B83 1983   510   82-21684
ISBN 0-07-008858-6

TO

CHRIS, SCOTT, and KERRY

CONTENTS

PREFACE

INTRODUCTION

Mathematics is an integral part of the education of students in business, economics, and the social sciences. There is increasingly a desire to improve the level of quantitative sophistication possessed by graduates in these types of programs. The objective is not to make mathematicians of these students, but to make them as comfortable as possible in an environment which increasingly makes use of quantitative analysis and the computer. Students are discovering that they must integrate mathematics, statistical analysis, and the computer in both required and elective courses within their programs. Furthermore, organizations are becoming more effective users of quantitative tools and the computer. Decision makers will be better equipped to operate within this type of environment if they are familiar with the more commonly used types of quantitative analyses and the technology of the computer. Such familiarity can assist them in being better "critics" and "users" of these tools, and hopefully, better decision makers.

DESIGN OF BOOK

This book is an applied mathematics book for students in business, economics, and the social sciences. It provides a comprehensive treatment of selected topics in both finite mathematics and calculus. Although intended principally for students in business and economics, the book is appropriate for students in the social sciences. Designed primarily for a two-term course, the book can be adapted easily for a one-term course. It is appropriate for use in both two-year schools and four-year schools, as well as at the "foundation" level for graduate programs which require some mathematics background. M.B.A. and M.P.A. programs are typical graduate programs having this type of requirement.

The figure on the following page illustrates some *suggested* ways in which this text might be used.

Specific features of this book include:

1   A level of presentation which carefully develops and reinforces topics.

2   A style which appeals to the intuition of students and provides a great deal of visual reinforcement (over 300 figures).

3   An applied orientation which motivates students and provides a sense of purpose for studying mathematics.

4   An approach which first develops the mathematical concept and then reinforces with applications.

5   An approach which minimizes the use of rigorous mathematical proofs. Proofs are included at the end of selected chapters for interested persons.

6   Special aids which address the most universal shortcoming of students entering this type of course: weak algebra skills. These aids include a review of key algebra principles in Chapter 1. A chapter pretest allows the student and

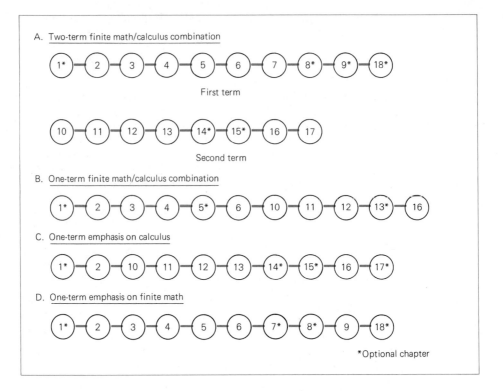

A. Two-term finite math/calculus combination

1^* — 2 — 3 — 4 — 5 — 6 — 7 — 8^* — 9^* — 18^*

First term

10 — 11 — 12 — 13 — 14^* — 15^* — 16 — 17

Second term

B. One-term finite math/calculus combination

1^* — 2 — 3 — 4 — 5^* — 6 — 10 — 11 — 12 — 13^* — 16

C. One-term emphasis on calculus

1^* — 2 — 10 — 11 — 12 — 13 — 14^* — 15^* — 16 — 17^*

D. One-term emphasis on finite math

1^* — 2 — 3 — 4 — 5 — 6 — 7^* — 8^* — 9 — 18^*

*Optional chapter

instructor to identify areas requiring special attention. In addition, "Algebra Flashbacks" are used throughout the book to assist the student in the recall of key rules or concepts. The flashback usually consists of a restatement of a rule or concept with a reference to the appropriate section in Chapter 1.

7   Notes to students which provide them with special insights.

8   "Points for Thought and Discussion" which allow students to pause for a moment and reconsider a concept or example from a different perspective. Their purpose is to reinforce and extend the student's understanding.

9   "Minicases" at the end of many chapters which provide challenging applications.

10   A multitude of other learning aids, including almost 450 solved examples, a wealth of exercises (over 2,200, most of which are new) chapter tests, chapter objectives, lists of key terms and concepts, and summary lists of important formulas.

11   An instructors manual which contains answers for all exercises and tests, suggestions for different course structures, prototype examples for new applications, transparency masters for selected figures, and a bank of questions for constructing quizzes and tests.

Although applications are presented throughout the book, Chapters 5 and 13 are devoted entirely to applications. The intent is that instructors cover as many applications in these chapters as they feel appropriate for their students.

Some exercises in the book are considered to be of a higher level of difficulty than most others. These are preceded by an asterisk (*).

SUMMARY OF NEW FEATURES AND CHANGES FOR THIS EDITION

In preparing this revision I surveyed those who taught from the first edition as well as those who decided not to adopt the first edition. The comments of those surveyed proved extremely valuable. The redesign of the book has resulted in the elimination or reduced coverage of some material and the expansion of other material, as well as some rearrangement of subject matter. I hope that those who continue to use the book find it more satisfactory for their needs; to those who are adopting for the first time, I hope that you and your students will be pleased.

Highlights of the significant changes follow:

■ In this edition, the treatment of *algebra* and *set theory* has been consolidated in one chapter. The algebra treatment is a bit more abbreviated but continues to be as inclusive as in the first edition. The set theory portion of this chapter is also shortened from the chapter status it enjoyed in the first edition.

■ In Chapter 2, the discussion of cartesian products has been eliminated. A new section provides a brief overview of different classes of mathematical functions.

■ In Chapter 5, the material on break-even models has been expanded to include examples of *three-alternative analysis* and *multiproduct break-even analysis*.

■ Chapter 6 represents a repositioning of the material on matrix algebra. Aside from a new subsection on the properties of determinants, the most significant change is an *expanded section on applications*.

■ Chapter 7 represents a major expansion of the material on linear programming. More attention is given to problem formulation, and a new section discusses *computer solution methods*. A sample LP package is illustrated. *Shadow price* and *sensitivity analysis* concepts are introduced and illustrated using the LP package.

■ Chapter 8 is an expanded treatment of the original simplex chapter. A new section discusses *alternative optimal solutions, no feasible solution,* and *unbounded solutions*. Another new section introduces the *dual problem*.

■ Chapter 9 represents a repositioning of the material on probability theory.

■ The material on exponential and logarithmic functions has been separated from other functional forms. Chapter 10 introduces nonlinear functions by discussing quadratic and other polynomial functions and their application. Chapter 14 consolidates the presentation of exponential and logarithmic functions and their application. New sections discuss the *conversion to base-e-functions* and *solving logarithmic and exponential equations*. This chapter also contains an *expanded set of applications*.

■ Chapter 15 represents a significant expansion in the treatment of the calculus of functions of several variables. New (optional) sections examine *n-variable optimization* and *optimization subject to constraints*. This chapter also illustrates *three-dimensional graphics capabilities of computers*.

■ The material on integral calculus has been expanded slightly and repackaged in two chapters. Chapter 16 introduces integral calculus and its methodology. The focus is upon the techniques of integration. A new section discusses *differential equations*. Chapter 17 focuses upon applications of integral calculus.

■ Chapter 18 updates the material on the mathematics of finance by expanding the interest table ranges. A new extension of this material is a section which discusses *cost-benefit analysis*.

■ Another new feature in this edition is the inclusion of *minicases* at the ends of 11 chapters. These provide a challenge to students which goes beyond the regular exercises in the text.

ACKNOWLEDGMENTS

I wish to express my sincere appreciation to those persons who have contributed either directly or indirectly to this project. I wish to thank Professor Emily Bronstein, Prince George's Community College; Professor John Dettman, Oakland University; Professor Benjamin Eichhorn, Temple University; Professor Grace Greenberg, Loyola College; Professor D. Kannan, University of Georgia; Professor Dean C. Morrow, Robert Morris College; and Professor Mustafa R. Yilmaz, Northeastern University. Their comments proved extremely helpful in rewriting.

A very special thanks goes to Professor Robert A. Moreland, Texas Tech University. His detailed comments on the entire manuscript were particularly helpful. Also, special thanks go to Dr. Janet McLeavey, who provided an important final review of the manuscript.

I want to thank the people at McGraw-Hill with whom I worked directly. These persons include Donald Mason, Jon Palace, and Nick Krenitsky. They each provided the kind of support that an author truly appreciates.

I also want to thank Nancy Nakamoto, Sue Rose, and Joe Daly for their assistance in developing problems and solution sets; and Ede Williams and Charlotte Manni for their superb work in typing the manuscript and its revisions. Special thanks also go to my students who served as "guinea pigs" for debugging new exercise sets.

I also wish to thank my parents, Mr. and Mrs. Willard L. Budnick, for their continued support, encouragement, and love during this and all other endeavors.

Finally, I want to thank my precious family—Jane, Chris, Scott, and Kerry—for their patience, understanding, encouragement, and love.

Frank S. Budnick

APPLIED MATHEMATICS

for Business,
Economics,
and the
Social Sciences

A REVIEW OF ALGEBRA AND SET THEORY (OPTIONAL)

CHAPTER OBJECTIVES

- Review the fundamentals of algebra which are necessary for the study of the material in the remainder of this text

- Provide an overview of the nature of sets and their representation, logic, and algebra

- Illustrate the application of set theory

Algebra is the only prerequisite for using this text. The first part of this chapter provides a brief review of the elements of algebra which the author believes are important in studying the material in the remainder of the chapter. To guide you in your review of algebra it is suggested that you take the following self-correcting algebra test. Its purpose is to help you diagnose those areas in which you need more review. The results of the test can guide you in your review of Secs. 1.1 to 1.6.

Algebra Pretest

CORRESPONDING SECTION IN CHAPTER

1 $|-10| =$ 1.1

2 $x^3 \cdot x^4 =$ 1.2

3 $[(x^3)^2]^3 =$ 1.2

4 $x^5/x^3 =$ 1.2

5 $(4x - 2y + z) - (-3x + 4y - 2z) =$ 1.2

6 $\dfrac{2x^2(3x^3)}{(-2x^2)^2} =$ 1.2

7 Factor $2a^3b^2c + 4a^2bc^2$.   1.3

8 Factor $x^2 - 4$.   1.3

9 Factor $x^2 - 5x + 4$.   1.3

10 $\frac{1}{5} + \frac{2}{15} - \frac{1}{6} =$ 1.4

11 $\dfrac{2x^2}{3} \div \dfrac{4x^3}{9} =$ 1.4

12 $x^{1/2}x^{4/3} =$ 1.5

13 $\sqrt[3]{a^2b}\,\sqrt[3]{ab^2} =$ 1.5

14 $3\sqrt{2} - 2\sqrt{8} =$ 1.5

15 $\sqrt{\dfrac{4a^2}{9}} =$ 1.5

16 Express $x^{2/3}$ in radical form.   1.5

17 Determine the roots of the equation $x - 4 = 2x - 6$.   1.6

18 Determine the roots of the equation $3x = 3x + 10$.   1.6

19 Determine the roots of the equation $x^2 - 6x + 9 = 0$. 1.6

20 Solve the inequality $5x - 21 \geq 2x$.   1.6

Answers for Algebra Pretest

1 10;   **2** x^7;   **3** x^{18};   **4** x^2;   **5** $7x - 6y + 3z$;   **6** $3x/2$;
7 $2a^2bc(ab + 2c)$;   **8** $(x + 2)(x - 2)$;   **9** $(x - 4)(x - 1)$;   **10** $\frac{1}{6}$;
11 $3/2x$;   **12** $x^{11/16}$;   **13** ab;   **14** $-\sqrt{2}$;   **15** $2a/3$;
16 $\sqrt[3]{x^2}$;   **17** 2;   **18** no roots;   **19** 3;   **20** $x \geq 7$

1.1   THE REAL NUMBER SYSTEM

Real Numbers

In this book we will be concerned with the mathematics of *real numbers.* As indicated in Fig. 1.1, the real number system consists of rational numbers and irrational numbers. *Rational numbers* are numbers which can be expressed as the *ratio,* or quotient, of two integers with the divisor being a nonzero integer. Thus, a rational number is a number which can be expressed in the form a/b where a and b are integers and b does not equal 0 (stated $b \neq 0$). The numbers $\frac{1}{5}$, $-\frac{2}{7}$, $\frac{23}{455}$, and $137/(-750)$ are all examples of rational numbers.

Because any integer a can be written in the form of the quotient $a/1$, all integers are also rational numbers. Examples include $-5 = -5/1$ and $54 = 54/1$. Zero is also considered to be an integer (neither negative nor positive), and it can be written in the quotient form $0/b = 0$, $b \neq 0$.

Irrational numbers are real numbers which cannot be expressed as the ratio of two integers. Numbers such as $\pi = 3.14159265$ . . . (which is the ratio of the circumference of a circle to its diameter), $\sqrt{2} = 1.4142$ . . . , $\sqrt{3} = 1.7321$ . . . , and $\sqrt{5} = 2.2361$ . . . are all examples of irrational numbers.

The set of real numbers can be represented using a *number line* (see Fig. 1.2). The number line has a zero point, often called the *origin,* which is used to repre-

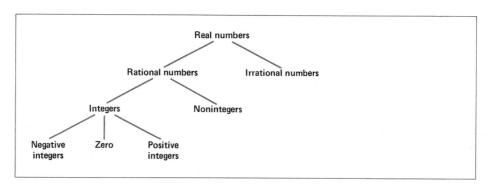

FIGURE 1.1
The real number
system.

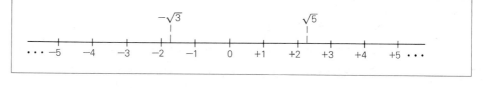

FIGURE 1.2
Number line.

sent the real number 0. To each and every point on the number line there corresponds a real number. The correspondence is that the real number represented by a point equals the *directed distance* traveled in moving from the origin to that point. Movements from left to right along the number line are considered to be in a positive direction. Thus, points to the right of the origin correspond to positive real numbers whereas points to the left correspond to negative real numbers. Note that for each and every real number there corresponds a unique point on the number line.

The *inequality symbols* $>$ or $<$ are used to indicate that two numbers are not equal but they can be compared. When an inequality symbol is placed between two numbers, it "opens" in the direction of the larger number. Given two real numbers a and b, the notation $a > b$ is read "a is greater than b." The statement $a > b$ implies that on the real number line a is located to the right of b.

Absolute Value

The *absolute value* of a real number is the magnitude or size of the number without the sign. The notation $|a|$ denotes the absolute value of a.

DEFINITION: ABSOLUTE VALUE

For any real number a,

$$|a| = \begin{cases} a & \text{if } a \text{ is positive or zero} \\ -a & \text{if } a \text{ is negative} \end{cases}$$

EXAMPLE 1

The absolute value of the number $+5$ is $|+5| = 5$. The absolute value of -20 is $|-20| = 20$. The absolute value of 0 is $|0| = 0$.

1.2 POLYNOMIALS

Positive Integer Exponents

When a real number a is multiplied times itself, we denote this product as $a \cdot a$ or aa. If the same number is multiplied times itself 5 times, the product is denoted by $aaaaa$. A shorthand notation which can be used to express these products is

$$aa = a^2$$

and
$$aaaaa = a^5$$

The number written above and to the right of a is called an *exponent*. The exponent indicates the number of times a occurs as a factor.

DEFINITION

If n is a positive integer and a is any real number,

$$a^n = \underbrace{a \cdot a \cdot a \cdots a}_{n \text{ factors}}$$

The term a^n can be verbalized as "a raised to the nth power" where a is considered the *base* and n is the exponent or *power.*

EXAMPLE 2

(a) $(-2)(-2)(-2)(-2)(-2)(-2) = (-2)^6$
(b) $(5)(5)(5) = (5)^3$
(c) $aaaabbb = a^4b^3$
(d) $aa/(bbbb) = a^2/b^4$

DEFINITION

If n is a positive integer and $a \neq 0$,

$$a^{-n} = \frac{1}{a^n}$$

EXAMPLE 3

(a) $a^{-2} = 1/a^2$
(b) $(2)^{-3} = 1/(2)^3 = \frac{1}{8}$

DEFINITION

If a is real and not equal to 0, $a^0 = 1$.

EXAMPLE 4

(a) $(10)^0 = 1$
(b) $(4x)^0 = 1, x \neq 0$
(c) $-5y^0 = -5(1) = -5, y \neq 0$

The following laws of exponents apply when a and b are any real numbers and m and n are positive integers.

LAWS OF EXPONENTS

I $a^m \cdot a^n = a^{m+n}$

II $(a^m)^n = a^{mn}$

III $(ab)^n = a^n b^n$

IV $\dfrac{a^m}{a^n} = a^{m-n}$ where $a \neq 0$

V $\left(\dfrac{a}{b}\right)^n = \dfrac{a^n}{b^n}$ where $b \neq 0$

EXAMPLE 5

(a) $(b^5)(b) = b^{5+1} = b^6$

(b) $(-2)^3(-2)^2 = (-2)^5$

(c) $(2)(2)^3(2)^{-2} = (2^{1+3})(2^{-2}) = (2^4)(2^{-2}) = 2^2 = 4$

(d) $(a^2)^3 = a^{2 \cdot 3} = a^6$

(e) $[(3)^2]^4 = (3)^{2 \cdot 4} = 3^8$

(f) $[(-1)^3]^5 = (-1)^{3 \cdot 5} = (-1)^{15} = -1$

(g) $(ab)^4 = a^4 b^4$

(h) $(2x)^3 = (2)^3(x)^3 = 8x^3$

(i) $\dfrac{a^6}{a^3} = a^{6-3} = a^3$

(j) $\dfrac{x^2}{x^4} = x^{2-4} = x^{-2} = \dfrac{1}{x^2}$

(k) $(2)^3/(2)^7 = (2)^{3-7} = (2)^{-4} = 1/(2)^4 = \frac{1}{16}$

(l) $(x/y)^5 = x^5/y^5$

(m) $(2a/5b^2)^3 = (2a)^3/(5b^2)^3 = 8a^3/125b^6$

(n) $x^5/x^5 = x^{5-5} = x^0 = 1$

Section 1.2 Follow-up Exercises

In Exercises 1 to 8 express the indicated operations using exponents.

1 $(5)(5)(5)(5)$

2 $(-1)(-1)(-1)(-1)(-1)(-1)(-1)$

3 $(3)(3)(-2)(-2)(-2)$

4 $(7)(7)(7)/[(3)(3)]$

5 $(-x)(-x)(-x)$

6 $aaa/(bb)$

7 $aabbcc$

8 $xxyyyy/(zzz)$

In Exercises 9 to 22 perform the indicated operations

9 $(2)^3(2)^4$

10 $(3)^3(3)^2$

11 $x^3 x^5$

12 $yy^4 y^3$

13 $x^2 y^3 x^3 y$

14 $aa^3 a^2 a$

15 $(x^2)^3$

16 $(a^2)^5$

17 $(x^3)^2(x^2)^4$

18 $a^3(a^3)^4$

19 $[(a^2)^3]^2$

20 $[(-1)^4]^3$

21 $(3x^2)^3$

22 $(5a^3)^2$

In Exercises 23 to 26 rewrite the expression, using positive exponents.

23 a^{-4} 24 $(xy)^{-2}$

25 $(\frac{1}{2})^{-3}$ 26 x^{-1}

In Exercises 27 to 40 perform the indicated operation.

27 x^3/x 28 m^7/m^4

29 $(2)^5/(2)^8$ 30 x^6/x^6

31 $(3)^4/(3)^3$ 32 $(2x^2)^2/2(x^2)$

33 $(xy)^0$ 34 $-(25x^0)^2$

35 $(x/y)^3$ 36 $(\frac{4}{5})^3$

37 $(x^2/y)^4$ 38 $(xy/z)^3$

39 $(a^2b/c^3)^4$ 40 $(2x^2/5yz^3)^3$

Polynomial Expressions

In this section we will discuss some important definitions and terminology. First, *constants* are quantities which do not change in value. A constant may be represented by a letter or by the real number which equals the constant. For example, 5 is a constant, as is the letter b if $b = -20$. *Variables* are quantities whose value may change. These are usually represented by letters. For example, the letter t may be used to represent the temperature each hour in a particular city measured on either the Fahrenheit or Celsius scale. The value of t is likely to be different each hour.

An *algebraic expression* is a collection of constants and variables connected by a series of additions, subtractions, multiplications, divisions, radical signs, and parentheses or other grouping symbols. For example,

$$5x^2y - 10x^3 + 75$$

is an algebraic expression. This algebraic expression consists of the three *terms* $5x^2y$, $10x^3$, and 75. A *term* consists of either a single number or the product of a number and powers of one or more variables. The term $5x^2y$ consists of the *factors* 5, x^2, and y. The constant factor 5 is referred to as the *coefficient* of the term. In this book, *coefficient* will always refer to a constant which is a factor in a term. For instance, 10 is the coefficient on the term $10x^3$. The term 75 in the algebraic expression contains no variables and is referred to as a *constant term.*

A *polynomial* is the sum of one or more terms, with the following restrictions:

The terms of a polynomial consist of a number or the product of a number and *positive integer* powers of one or more variables. This definition excludes terms which have variables under a radical sign and any terms which have variables in the denominator.

A polynomial consisting of one term is called a *monomial.* A polynomial consisting of two terms is called a *binomial.* A polynomial consisting of three terms is called a *trinomial.* Polynomials consisting of more than three terms are referred to simply as polynomials.

EXAMPLE 6

(*a*) The algebraic expression 25 is a polynomial having one term; thus it is called a monomial.

(b) The algebraic expression $5x^2 - 2x + 1$ is a polynomial consisting of three terms; thus it is referred to as a trinomial.

(c) The algebraic expression $2x^2y/z$ is not a polynomial because the variable z appears in the denominator of the term.

(d) The algebraic expression $\sqrt{x}$ is not a polynomial because the variable appears under a radical.

(e) The algebraic expression $x^5 - 2x^4 - x^3 + 2x^2 + x + 9$ is a polynomial consisting of six terms.

The *degree of a term* is the sum of the exponents on the variables contained in the term. For a term involving one variable, the degree is simply the exponent of the variable. The degree of the term $5x^3$ is 3 since the exponent is 3. The degree of the term $5x^2y^3z$ is 6 since the sum of the exponents of x, y, and z equals 6. The degree of a nonzero constant term is 0. To illustrate, the term -20 can be written in the equivalent form $-20x^0$. Thus, the degree of the term equals 0.

In addition to the categorization of terms by degree, polynomials may be classified by their degree. The *degree of a polynomial* is defined as the degree of the highest degree term in the polynomial.

EXAMPLE 7

(a) The polynomial $2x^3 - 4x^2 + x - 10$ has terms of degree 3, 2, 1, and 0, respectively. Therefore, the degree of the polynomial is 3.

(b) The polynomial $4x^2y^3 - 6xy^5 + 2xy$ has terms of degree 5, 6, and 2, respectively. Thus the degree of the polynomial is 6.

Addition and Subtraction of Polynomials

In adding and subtracting polynomials, we combine like terms. *Like terms* are terms which involve the same variables raised to the same powers. The terms $3x$ and $-4x$ are considered to be like terms because each involves the variable x raised (implicitly) to the first power. The fact that their coefficients (3 and -4) are different has no bearing on whether the two terms are like terms. Any real constants are considered to be like terms. The constants -5 and 18 can be envisioned as having the form $-5x^0$ and $18x^0$, which qualifies them as being like terms.

When polynomials are added or subtracted, like terms may be combined into a simpler form. For example, the like terms $4x$ and $3x$ may be added in the following manner:

$$4x + 3x = (4 + 3)x$$
$$= 7x$$

Similarly,

$$5xy^2 - 2xy^2 + 6xy^2 = [5 + (-2) + 6]xy^2$$
$$= 9xy^2$$

Terms which are not like terms cannot be combined into a simpler form (the old "apples and oranges" problem). The sum $5x + 2y$ cannot be written in a simpler form.

To add or subtract polynomials, like terms should be identified and combined. Unlike terms are added or subtracted as indicated. The following examples illustrate this process.

EXAMPLE 8

$$(2x^2 - 5x + 10) + (4x^2 + 3x - 5) = 2x^2 - 5x + 10 + 4x^2 + 3x - 5$$
$$= 2x^2 + 4x^2 - 5x + 3x + 10 - 5$$
$$= 6x^2 - 2x + 5$$

EXAMPLE 9

$$(5x^2y + 2xy^2 - 4y^3) - (-3x^2y + y^3 - 10)$$
$$= 5x^2y + 2xy^2 - 4y^3 + 3x^2y - y^3 + 10$$
$$= 5x^2y + 3x^2y + 2xy^2 - 4y^3 - y^3 + 10$$
$$= 8x^2y + 2xy^2 - 5y^3 + 10$$

Multiplication of Polynomials

All the rules and properties of multiplication for real numbers apply when polynomials are multiplied. We will discuss two different multiplication situations: (1) multiplication of two monomials and (2) multiplication of two polynomials.

MONOMIAL MULTIPLICATION

To multiply two monomials, multiply their coefficients and multiply the variable terms using the rules of exponents.

EXAMPLE 10

(a) $(2x)(3x) = (2)(3)xx = 6x^2$
(b) $(5x^2)(-2x^3) = (5)(-2)x^2x^3 = -10x^5$
(c) $(3ab^2)(6a^3b) = (3)(6)aa^3b^2b = 18a^4b^3$
(d) $(mn^2)(4m^2n^3)(-3m^3n) = -12m^6n^6$

POLYNOMIAL MULTIPLICATION

To multiply two polynomials, multiply *each* term of one polynomial by *every* term of the other polynomial.

EXAMPLE 11

(a) $(2)(4x - 2y) = (2)(4x) + (2)(-2y) = 8x - 4y$
(b) $4x^2y(x^2 + 2x - 1) = 4x^2y(x^2) + (4x^2y)(2x) + (4x^2y)(-1)$
$$= 4x^4y + 8x^3y - 4x^2y$$
(c) $(2x - 6)(4x + 7) = (2x)(4x + 7) + (-6)(4x + 7)$
$$= 8x^2 + 14x - 24x - 42$$
$$= 8x^2 - 10x - 42$$

(d) $(5x^2 - 2x)(x^3 + 2x^2 - 5x) = (5x^2)(x^3 + 2x^2 - 5x) + (-2x)(x^3 + 2x^2 - 5x)$
$$= 5x^5 + 10x^4 - 25x^3 - 2x^4 - 4x^3 + 10x^2$$
$$= 5x^5 + 8x^4 - 29x^3 + 10x^2$$

Division of Polynomials

The only type of polynomial division *explicitly* required in this book will be the division of a polynomial by a monomial. When the division of two polynomials is required, the quotient can be found by simplifying the factored forms of the two polynomials. Factoring of polynomials is reviewed in the next section.

DIVISION OF MONOMIALS

To divide a monomial by a monomial, divide the coefficients of each monomial and divide the variables using the appropriate rule(s) of exponents.

EXAMPLE 12

(a) $\dfrac{12x^5}{3x^2} = \left(\dfrac{12}{3}\right)\left(\dfrac{x^5}{x^2}\right) = 4x^{5-2} = 4x^3$

(b) $\dfrac{-8x^3y^2}{2xy^2} = \left(\dfrac{-8}{2}\right)\left(\dfrac{x^3}{x}\right)\left(\dfrac{y^2}{y^2}\right) = -4x^{3-1}y^{2-2} = -4x^2(1) = -4x^2$

POLYNOMIAL DIVISION BY A MONOMIAL

To divide a polynomial by a monomial, divide each term of the polynomial by the monomial and algebraically sum the individual quotients.

EXAMPLE 13

(a) $\dfrac{4x^3 - 8x^2 + 6x}{2x} = \dfrac{4x^3}{2x} - \dfrac{8x^2}{2x} + \dfrac{6x}{2x} = 2x^2 - 4x + 3$

(b) $\dfrac{24x^4b^5 + 18a^2b^3}{-3a^2b^4} = \dfrac{24a^4b^5}{-3a^2b^4} + \dfrac{18a^2b^3}{-3a^2b^4} = -8a^2b - \dfrac{6}{b}$

NOTE

You can always check your answer in division by multiplying the answer times the divisor. If your answer is correct, this product should equal the dividend.

Section 1.2 Follow-up Exercises (Continued)

In Exercises 1 to 31 perform the indicated operations.

1   $10x + 3x$

2   $5x^2 - 4x^2 + 2x^2$

3   $(5y^3 - 2y^2 + y) + (4y^2 - 5y)$ 4 $(2m^2 - 3m) + (4m^2 + 2m) - (m^2 + 6)$

5   $(40x^3y^2 - 25xy^3) - (15x^3y^2)$ 6 $abc - cab - 4bac$

7   $(x - 2y) - (2x - 3y) + (x - y)$ 8 $(-5x)(4x^2)$

9   $(7x^3)(3xy^2)$ 10 $(3x^2)(2x)(-4x^3)$

11   $(a^2)(4a^5)(-2a^3)$ 12 $5x(x - 10)$

13   $(-2x^2)(x^2 - y)$ 14 $2a(a^2 - 2a + 5)$

15   $x^2y(x^2 - 2xy + y^2)$ 16 $(x - 5)(x + 6)$

17   $(a + b)(a + b)$ 18 $(2x - 3)(2x - 3)$

19   $(a - b)(a - b)$ 20 $(x + 4)(x - 4)$

21   $(x - 2)(x^2 - 4x + 4)$ 22 $21x^5/(3x)$

23   $16x^2y^3/(4xy^2)$ 24 $10a^4b^2/(5ab^2)$

25   $-9xy^2/(3xy^3)$ 26 $25a^2bc^3/(5ab^2c^4)$

27   $(15x^2 - 24x)/(3x)$ 28 $(4x^3y - 2x^2y + 8xy)/(2x)$

29   $(12a^3 - 9a^2 + 6a)/(-3a)$ 30 $(3x^2yz^3 - 4xy^2z)/(-xyz)$

31   $(4x^6 + 6x^3 - 8x^2)/(2x)$

1.3   FACTORING

In this section we discuss *factoring of polynomials.* To factor a polynomial means to express it as the product of two or more other polynomials. The *distributive law of multiplication* is

$$a(b + c) = a \cdot b + a \cdot c$$

The binomial on the right of the equals sign can be expressed as the product of the polynomials a and $b + c$. These two polynomials are considered the factors of the expression $a \cdot b + a \cdot c$. With multiplication of polynomials, we are given the factors and must find the product. With factoring we are given the product and must determine the polynomials which, when multiplied, will yield the product.

Monomial Factors

The distributive law represents an example of *monomial factors.* That is,

$$ab + ac = a(b + c)$$

indicates that the two terms on the left side of the equals sign contain a common factor a. The common factor a may represent any monomial. For example, the polynomial $2x + 2y$ can be rewritten in the *factored form* $2(x + y)$ since each term has a common factor of 2.

EXAMPLE 14

(a) The terms of the polynomial $x^3 - x^2 + x$ have a common factor x. We can rewrite the polynomial as

$$x^3 - x^2 + x = x(x^2 - x + 1)$$

(b) The terms of the polynomial $6x^2y^3 - 10xy^2$ have a common factor $2xy^2$. Factoring $2xy^2$ from each term, we obtain

$$6x^2y^3 - 10xy^2 = 2xy^2(3xy - 5)$$

We are usually interested in factoring polynomials *completely*. That means simply that the factors themselves cannot be factored any further. The right side of the equation

$$x^3y^2 + x^4y^3 = xy(x^2y + x^3y^2)$$

is not factored completely. The term x^2y can be factored from each term inside the parentheses. The polynomial is completely factored when it is written as $x^3y^2(1 + xy)$.

The goal in monomial factoring is usually to identify the *largest* common monomial. The largest common monomial factor is the one containing the largest common numerical factor and the highest powers of variables common to all terms.

Quadratic Polynomials

A second-degree polynomial is often referred to as a *quadratic* polynomial. We will see these types of polynomials frequently, and factoring them will be important. Specifically, we will be interested in expressing quadratic polynomials, if possible, as the product of two first-degree polynomials. The factoring process often involves trial and error. Sometimes it is easy; at other times it can be frustrating. The following cases will help you.

CASE 1

$$x^2 + (a + b)x + ab = (x + a)(x + b)$$

Consider the product $(x + a)(x + b)$. Multiplying these two binomials, we get

$$(x + a)(x + b) = x^2 + ax + bx + ab$$
$$= x^2 + (a + b)x + ab$$

The result of the multiplication is a trinomial having an x^2 term, an x term, and a constant term. Note the coefficients of each term of the trinomial. The x^2 term has a coefficient equal to 1; the x term has a coefficient $a + b$, which is equal to the sum of the constants contained in the **binomial factors;** and the constant term ab is the product of the two constants contained in the binomial factors. In factoring a trinomial of this form, the objective is to determine the values of a and b which generate the coefficient of x, or the middle term of the polynomial, and the constant term.

EXAMPLE 15

To find the factors of $x^2 - 5x + 6$, we seek values for a and b such that

$$(x + a)(x + b) = x^2 - 5x + 6$$

The coefficient of the middle term is -5. From our previous discussion, the values of a and b must be such that $a + b = -5$. And, the third term in the trinomial equals 6, suggesting that $ab = 6$. Using a trial-and-error approach, you should conclude that the values satisfying these two conditions are -2 and -3. It makes no difference which of these two values we assign to a and b. The binomial factors are $(x - 2)(x - 3)$, or $(x - 3)(x - 2)$.

EXAMPLE 16

To find the factors of $m^2 + 6m - 21$, we look for values of a and b such that

$$(m + a)(m + b) = m^2 + 6m - 21$$

Our earlier discussions suggest that the relationships between a and b are

$$a + b = 6$$

and

$$ab = -21$$

Verify that there are no real (integer) values for a and b which satisfy these equations. Thus, this quadratic expression cannot be factored.

CASE 2

$$acx^2 + (ad + bc)x + bd = (ax + b)(cx + d)$$

Consider the product

$$(ax + b)(cx + d) = acx^2 + (ad + bc)x + bd$$

Assuming that a and c are integers, both of which are not equal to 1, the product is a trinomial which differs from Case 1 in that the coefficient of the term x^2 equals an integer other than 1. When a trinomial has an integer coefficient other than 1 on the x^2 term, the binomial factors contain four constants which must be identified. The coefficient of the x^2 term equals the product of a and c, the coefficient of the x term equals $ad + bc$, and the constant term equals the product bd. Identifying the values of the four constants which satisfy these conditions can be difficult. Verify that when $a = 1$ and $c = 1$, Case 2 is simply Case 1.

EXAMPLE 17

To find the factors of $6x^2 - 25x + 25$, we seek values of a, b, c, and d such that

$$6x^2 - 25x + 25 = (ax + b)(cx + d)$$

The conditions which must be satisfied are

$$ac = 6$$
$$ad + bc = -25$$

and

$$bd = 25$$

Verify that the values $a = 3$, $b = -5$, $c = 2$, and $d = -5$ satisfy the conditions. And,

$$(3x - 5)(2x - 5) = 6x^2 - 25x + 25$$

EXAMPLE 18

The first step in factoring is to look for any common monomial factors. Given the trinomial $12x^2 - 27x + 6$, we can factor 3 from each term, or

$$12x^2 - 27x + 6 = 3(4x^2 - 9x + 2)$$

The next step is to determine if the trinomial *factor* can be factored. If so,

$$ac = 4$$
$$ad + bc = -9$$
and
$$bd = 2$$

Values satisfying these conditions are $a = 1$, $b = -2$, $c = 4$, *and* $d = -1$. Thus,

$$12x^2 - 27x + 6 = 3(x - 2)(4x - 1)$$

CASE 3

$$x^2 - a^2 = (x + a)(x - a)$$

This case involves factoring the **difference between perfect squares.** The binomial to be factored is the difference between the squares of two quantities, x and a. This binomial can be factored as the product of the *sum* and *difference* of x and a.

EXAMPLE 19

$$x^2 - 9 = (x)^2 - (3)^2$$
$$= (x + 3)(x - 3)$$

EXAMPLE 20

$$16x^4 - 81 = (4x^2)^2 - (9)^2$$
$$= (4x^2 + 9)(4x^2 - 9)$$

However, the binomial $4x^2 - 9$ is the difference between two squares. Thus,

$$16x^4 - 81 = (4x^2 + 9)(2x + 3)(2x - 3)$$

Other Special Forms

The following rules of factoring are used less frequently in the book.

CASE 4

$$a^3 - b^3 = (a - b)(a^2 + ab + b^2)$$

This case involves factoring the **difference between two cubes.**

EXAMPLE 21

(a) $x^3 - 1 = (x)^3 - (1)^3 = (x - 1)(x^2 + x + 1)$
(b) $8x^3 - 64 = (2x)^3 - (4)^3 = (2x - 4)(4x^2 + 8x + 16)$
(c) $m^3 - n^3 = (m - n)(m^2 + mn + n^2)$

CASE 5

$$a^3 + b^3 = (a + b)(a^2 - ab + b^2)$$

This case involves factoring the *sum of two cubes.*

EXAMPLE 22

(a) $x^3 + 8 = (x)^3 + (2)^3 = (x + 2)(x^2 - 2x + 4)$
(b) $27y^3 + 64 = (3y)^3 + (4)^3 = (3y + 4)(9y^2 - 12y + 16)$

Section 1.3 Follow-up Exercises

Completely factor (if possible) the polynomials in the following exercises. Do not forget to check your answers!

1	$2ax - 8a^3$	2	$21m^2 - 7mn$
3	$4x^3y - 6xy^3 + 8x^2y^2$	4	$65a^3b^2 - 13a^2b^3$
5	$9a^3 - 15a^2 - 27a$	6	$x^2 - 8x + 12$
7	$x^2 + x + 3$	8	$x^2 + 7x + 12$
9	$p^2 + 9p - 36$	10	$x^2 - 2x - 15$
11	$r^2 - 21r - 22$	12	$x^2 - 16x + 48$
13	$x^5 + y^5$	14	$9x^2 + 12x + 4$
15	$6m^2 - 19m + 3$	16	$2x^2 - 7x - 4$
17	$8x^2 - 2x - 3$	18	$2x^3 + 4x^2 - 42x$
19	$x^4 - 81$	20	$100x^2 - 225$
21	$81x^4 - 625$	22	$10x^2 + 13x - 3$
23	$x^2 + 4$	24	$27 - 8m^3$
25	$1 + 8x^3$	26	$a^3 - 125$
27	$x^4 - x^3 - 2x^2$	28	$4x^6 - 4x^2$

1.4 FRACTIONS

Fractions, or *rational numbers,* constitute an important part of the real number system. This section discusses some useful rules for performing computations with fractions.

Addition and Subtraction of Fractions

RULE 1: COMMON DENOMINATORS

If two fractions have the same denominator, their sum (difference) is found by adding (subtracting) their numerators and placing the result over the common denominator.

EXAMPLE 23

(a) $\dfrac{3}{7} + \dfrac{2}{7} = \dfrac{3 + 2}{7} = \dfrac{5}{7}$

(b) $\dfrac{7}{8} - \dfrac{4}{8} = \dfrac{7-4}{8} = \dfrac{3}{8}$

RULE 2: DIFFERENT DENOMINATORS

To add (subtract) two fractions which have different denominators, restate the fractions as equivalent fractions having the same denominator. The sum (difference) is then found by applying Rule 1.

In applying Rule 2, *any* common denominator may be identified when the equivalent fractions are found. However, the usual practice is to identify the *least common multiple (lcm)* of the denominators or the *least common denominator (lcd).*

The procedure for finding the least common denominator is as follows:

1 Write each denominator in a completely factored form.

2 The *lcd* is a product of the factors. To form the *lcd,* each distinct factor is included the greatest number of times it appears in *any* one of the denominators.

EXAMPLE 24

To find the lcd for the fractions $\frac{5}{8}$ and $\frac{3}{20}$, each denominator is factored completely:

$$8 = 8 \cdot 1 = 4 \cdot 2 \cdot 1 = 2 \cdot 2 \cdot 2 \cdot 1$$
$$20 = 20 \cdot 1 = 10 \cdot 2 \cdot 1 = 5 \cdot 2 \cdot 2 \cdot 1$$

These denominators are factored completely since each of the factors can be expressed only as the product of itself and 1 (assuming we are seeking integer-valued factors). Such factors are called *prime factors.*

In forming the lcd, *each distinct prime factor is included the greatest number of times it appears in any one denominator.* The distinct prime factors are 2, 5, and 1. Thus,

$$\text{lcd} = 2 \cdot 2 \cdot 2 \cdot 5 \cdot 1 = 40$$

EXAMPLE 25

Determine the sum $\frac{5}{8} + \frac{3}{20}$.

SOLUTION

Having identified the lcd in the last example, we must restate each fraction with the common denominator 40. Restating the fractions and applying Rule 1, we get

$$\frac{5}{8} + \frac{3}{20} = \frac{5 \cdot 5}{8 \cdot 5} + \frac{3 \cdot 2}{20 \cdot 2} = \frac{25}{40} + \frac{6}{40} = \frac{25 + 6}{40} = \frac{31}{40}$$

EXAMPLE 26

Determine the difference $3/(4x) - 5/(6x^2)$.

SOLUTION
Factoring each denominator, we obtain

$$4x = 4 \cdot x \cdot 1 = 2 \cdot 2 \cdot x \cdot 1$$
$$6x^2 = 6 \cdot x \cdot x \cdot 1 = 3 \cdot 2 \cdot x \cdot x \cdot 1$$

The distinct factors of these denominators are 2, 3, x, and 1, and

$$lcd = 2 \cdot 2 \cdot 3 \cdot x \cdot x \cdot 1$$
$$= 12x^2$$

The fractions, when restated in terms of the lcd, are subtracted yielding

$$\frac{3}{4x} - \frac{5}{6x^2} = \frac{3 \cdot 3x}{4x \cdot 3x} - \frac{5 \cdot 2}{6x^2 \cdot 2}$$
$$= \frac{9x}{12x^2} - \frac{10}{12x^2}$$
$$= \frac{9x - 10}{12x^2}$$

EXAMPLE 27

To find the algebraic sum $3/(x - 1) - 5x/(x + 1) + x^2/(x^2 - 1)$, we first determine the least common denominator, or

$$lcd = (x + 1)(x - 1) \cdot 1 = (x^2 - 1)$$

The three fractions are restated using the lcd yielding

$$\frac{3}{x - 1} - \frac{5x}{x + 1} + \frac{x^2}{x^2 - 1} = \frac{3 \cdot (x + 1)}{(x - 1) \cdot (x + 1)} - \frac{5x(x - 1)}{(x + 1)(x - 1)} + \frac{x^2}{x^2 - 1}$$
$$= \frac{3(x + 1) - 5x(x - 1) + x^2}{x^2 - 1}$$
$$= \frac{3x + 3 - 5x^2 + 5x + x^2}{x^2 - 1}$$
$$= \frac{-4x^2 + 8x + 3}{x^2 - 1}$$

Multiplication and Division

RULE 3: MULTIPLICATION

The product of two or more fractions is found by dividing the product of their numerators by the product of their denominators. That is,

$$\frac{a}{b} \frac{c}{d} = \frac{ac}{bd}$$

EXAMPLE 28

(a) $\dfrac{3}{5} \dfrac{2}{7} = \dfrac{(3)(2)}{(5)(7)} = \dfrac{6}{35}$

(b) $\dfrac{15}{x}\dfrac{x^2}{3} = \dfrac{15x^2}{3x} = \dfrac{5x}{1} = 5x$

(c) $\dfrac{x-1}{10}\dfrac{15}{x^2-1} = \dfrac{(15)\cancel{(x-1)}}{(10)\cancel{(x-1)}(x+1)} = \dfrac{3}{2(x+1)}$

RULE 4: DIVISION

The quotient of two simple fractions can be determined by inverting the divisor fraction and multiplying by the dividend fraction. That is,

$$\frac{a/b}{c/d} = \frac{a}{b}\frac{d}{c} = \frac{ad}{bc}$$

EXAMPLE 29

(a) $\dfrac{-\frac{5}{12}}{\frac{3}{4}} = \left(-\dfrac{5}{12}\right)\left(\dfrac{4}{3}\right) = -\dfrac{20}{36} = -\dfrac{5}{9}$

(b) $\dfrac{\frac{4}{10}}{2} = \dfrac{\frac{4}{10}}{2/1} = \left(\dfrac{4}{10}\right)\left(\dfrac{1}{2}\right) = \dfrac{4}{20} = \dfrac{1}{5}$

(c) $\dfrac{3x^2/4}{9x/2} = \dfrac{3x^2}{4}\dfrac{2}{9x} = \dfrac{6x^2}{36x} = \dfrac{x}{6}$

(d) $\dfrac{1-2/x}{4/x} = \dfrac{x/x-2/x}{4/x} = \dfrac{(x-2)/x}{4/x} = \dfrac{x-2}{x}\dfrac{x}{4} = \dfrac{x-2}{4}$

Section 1.4 Follow-up Exercises

In Exercises 1 to 22 perform the indicated operations.

1 $\frac{1}{5} + \frac{5}{30}$
    2 $\frac{2}{7} - \frac{4}{21}$

3 $\frac{1}{3} - \frac{5}{8} + \frac{5}{12}$
    4 $\frac{4}{25} - \frac{3}{10} + \frac{7}{5}$

5 $\dfrac{1}{x} - \dfrac{2}{x^2}$
    6 $\dfrac{5}{2a} + \dfrac{6}{a^3}$

7 $\dfrac{5x}{x^2-4} + \dfrac{x}{x-2}$
    8 $\dfrac{5}{1} + \dfrac{1}{x}$

9 $\dfrac{10}{1} - \dfrac{2}{x^2}$
    10 $\dfrac{4}{a} + \dfrac{3}{2ab}$

11 $\dfrac{3a}{a+1} - \dfrac{5}{a^2+2a+1}$
    12 $\frac{3}{11}\frac{33}{6}$

13 $(\frac{1}{5})(\frac{10}{3})(-\frac{9}{2})$
    14 $\left(\dfrac{1}{x}\right)\left(\dfrac{2x^3}{3}\right)\left(\dfrac{6}{5}\right)$

15 $\left(\dfrac{ab}{c}\right)\left(\dfrac{c^2}{3a^2b}\right)\left(\dfrac{1}{abc}\right)$
    16 $\left(\dfrac{5}{x-4}\right)\left(\dfrac{x^2-16}{10}\right)\left(\dfrac{x+4}{2}\right)$

17 $\frac{7}{27} \div \frac{5}{9}$
    18 $3x^2/5 \div x/5$

19 $a^2b/(5c) \div 3c^2/(10ab)$
    20 $abc/8 \div 3a^2b/4$

21 $\dfrac{x-1}{x^2-5x-4} \div \dfrac{x-1}{x-4}$
    22 $\dfrac{1-2/(3x)}{3/x+4}$

1.5 EXPONENTS AND RADICALS

In Sec. 1.2 we discussed the following five laws of exponents:

$$\textbf{I} \quad a^m \cdot a^n = a^{m+n}$$

$$\textbf{II} \quad (a^m)^n = a^{mn}$$

$$\textbf{III} \quad (ab)^n = a^n b^n$$

$$\textbf{IV} \quad \frac{a^m}{a^n} = a^{m-n} \qquad a \neq 0$$

$$\textbf{V} \quad \left(\frac{a}{b}\right)^n = \frac{a^n}{b^n} \qquad b \neq 0$$

Recall that the exponents were restricted to integer values.

Fractional Exponents

Occasionally we will need to deal with fractional exponents. The laws of exponents are valid for any real values of m and n. The next example illustrates the application of the laws of exponents when the exponents are fractions.

EXAMPLE 30

(a) $x^{1/2} \cdot x^{1/2} = x^{1/2+1/2} = x$

(b) $x^{3/2} \cdot x^{1/3} = x^{3/2+1/3} = x^{9/6+2/6} = x^{11/6}$

(c) $(x^{1/2})^4 = x^{(1/2)(4)} = x^2$

(d) $(x^{2/3})^{-3} = x^{(2/3)(-3)} = x^{-2} = 1/x^2$

(e) $(2x^{1/4})^4 = (2)^4(x^{1/4})^4 = 16x$

(f) $x^{3/4}/x^{1/2} = x^{3/4-1/2} = x^{3/4-2/4} = x^{1/4}$

(g) $x^{5/8}/x^{3/4} = x^{5/8-3/4} = x^{5/8-6/8}$

$$= x^{-1/8} = 1/x^{1/8}$$

(h) $(x/y)^{1/2} = x^{1/2}/y^{1/2}$

Radicals

Frequently we need to determine the value of x which satisfies an equation of the form

$$x^n = a$$

For example, what values of x satisfy these equations?

$$x^2 = 4 \qquad x^3 = 8 \qquad x^4 = 81$$

In the first equation, we want to determine the value x which, when multiplied times itself, yields a product equal to 4. You should conclude that values of $+2$ and -2 satisfy the equation, i.e., make the left and right sides of the equation equal. Similarly, the second equation seeks the value of x which, when cubed, generates a product of 8. A value of $+2$ satisfies this equation. Verify that $+3$ and -3 satisfy the third equation.

DEFINITION

If $a^n = b$, a is called the nth root of b.

The nth root of b is denoted by $\sqrt[n]{b}$, where the symbol $\sqrt{}$ is the *radical sign,* n is the *index* on the radical sign, and b is the *radicand.* Thus, we can state

$$\boxed{\text{If } a^n = b, \text{ then } a = \sqrt[n]{b}}$$

Referring to the three previous equations,

$$\text{If } x^2 = 4 \qquad x = \sqrt[2]{4} = \sqrt{4}$$

where x is said to equal the **square root** of 4. *If no index appears with the radical sign, the index is implicitly equal to 2.*

For the second equation we can state

$$\text{If } x^3 = 8 \qquad x = \sqrt[3]{8}$$

where x is said to equal the **cube root** of 8. And, for the third equation,

$$\text{If } x^4 = 81 \qquad x = \sqrt[4]{81}$$

where x is said to equal the **fourth root** of 81.

As we have seen with these equations, there may exist more than one nth root of a real number. We usually will be interested in just one of these roots—the **principal nth root.** Given $\sqrt[n]{b}$,

1 The principal nth root is positive if b is positive.

2 The principal nth root is negative if b is negative and n is odd.

The following examples indicate the principal nth root.

EXAMPLE 31

(a) $\sqrt{9} = 3$
(b) $\sqrt[3]{-27} = -3$
(c) $\sqrt[5]{32} = 2$
(d) $\sqrt[5]{-243} = -3$

The following laws apply to computations involving radicals.

LAWS OF RADICALS

I $(\sqrt[n]{a})^n = a$
II $a\sqrt[n]{x} + b\sqrt[n]{x} = (a + b)\sqrt[n]{x}$
III $\sqrt[n]{ab} = \sqrt[n]{a}\sqrt[n]{b}$
IV $\sqrt[n]{\dfrac{a}{b}} = \dfrac{\sqrt[n]{a}}{\sqrt[n]{b}}$ for $b \neq 0$
V $b^{m/n} = (\sqrt[n]{b})^m = \sqrt[n]{b^m}$

EXAMPLE 32

(a) $(\sqrt{4})^2 = (2)^2 = 4$
(b) $(\sqrt[5]{36})^5 = 36$
(c) $(\sqrt[3]{-8})^3 = (-2)^3 = -8$
(d) $\sqrt[3]{a} - 3\sqrt[3]{a} + 5\sqrt[3]{a} = 3\sqrt[3]{a}$
(e) $\sqrt{x} + \sqrt[3]{x}$ cannot be simplified using the laws of radicals because the indices on the two radicals are different

(f) $\sqrt[4]{x^3} + \sqrt[4]{x^2}$ cannot be simplified using the laws of radicals because the radicands are not equal

(g) $\sqrt[3]{128} = \sqrt[3]{(64)(2)} = \sqrt[3]{64}\sqrt[3]{2} = 4\sqrt[3]{2}$

(h) $\sqrt{x^3} = \sqrt{x^2 \cdot x} = \sqrt{x^2}\sqrt{x} = x\sqrt{x},\ x \geq 0$

(i) $\sqrt{\frac{4}{9}} = \sqrt{4}/\sqrt{9} = \frac{2}{3}$

(j) $\sqrt[3]{(-1)/125} = \sqrt[3]{-1}/\sqrt[3]{125} = -\frac{1}{5}$

(k) $x^{1/2} = \sqrt{x}$

(l) $x^{1/3} = \sqrt[3]{x}$

(m) $x^{1/n} = \sqrt[n]{x}$

(n) $(64)^{2/3} = \sqrt[3]{(64)^2} = (\sqrt[3]{64})^2 = 4^2 = 16$

(o) $(49)^{-1/2} = 1/(49)^{1/2} = 1/\sqrt{49} = \frac{1}{7}$

Section 1.5 Follow-up Exercises

In Exercises 1 to 10 perform the indicated operations.

1 $a^{3/2} \cdot a^{4/3}$

2 $b^{1/6} \cdot b^{1/4}$

3 $x^{1/3} \cdot x^{2/5} \cdot x^{3/10}$

4 $(x^{1/2})^{2/3}$

5 $(a^{3/2})^{5/6}$

6 $(2x^{3/4})^4$

7 $(-3x^{2/3})^3$

8 $x^{5/2}/x^{1/2}$

9 $a^{3/2}/a^{1/6}$

10 $(x^4y^2)^{1/2}$

In Exercises 11 to 18 determine the principal nth root.

11 $\sqrt{625}$

12 $\sqrt[4]{625}$

13 $\sqrt[3]{-a^3}$

14 $\sqrt[5]{-1}$

15 $\sqrt[3]{-8x^6}$

16 $\sqrt[3]{27a^9}$

17 $\sqrt{144x^6}$

18 $\sqrt[3]{-64x^3y^6}$

In Exercises 19 to 30 simplify the radical expressions.

19 $2\sqrt{7} + 3\sqrt{7}$

20 $5\sqrt{x} - 3\sqrt{x}$

21 $\sqrt{32} + 3\sqrt{2}$

22 $2\sqrt{45} - 2\sqrt{5}$

23 $4\sqrt{x} - \sqrt{x^3}$

24 $\sqrt{20} - 2\sqrt{5} + 3\sqrt{45}$

25 $\sqrt{2}\sqrt{8}$

26 $\sqrt[3]{5}\sqrt[3]{10}\sqrt[3]{5}$

27 $\sqrt{\frac{64}{9}}$

28 $\sqrt[3]{-\frac{1}{27}}$

29 $\sqrt{625x^2/(49y^4)}$

30 $\sqrt[4]{1/(81a^8)}$

In Exercises 31 to 38 express the term in radical form.

31 $x^{2/3}$

32 $x^{1/5}$

33 $(ab)^{3/5}$

34 $(xy)^{3/4}$

35 $x^{-1/2}$

36 $a^{-2/3}$

37 $(8)^{-1/3}$

38 $(32)^{-1/5}$

In Exercises 39 to 46 express the term using fractional exponents.

39 $\sqrt{45x}$

40 $\sqrt[3]{a^2}$

41 $\sqrt[4]{x^3}$

42 $\sqrt{xy}$

43 $\sqrt[3]{x^5}$

44 $\sqrt[5]{(ab)^3}$

45 $\sqrt{x^4}$

46 $\sqrt[3]{(-1)^9}$

1.6 EQUATIONS

We will work continually with equations in this book. It is absolutely essential that you understand the meaning of equations and their algebraic properties.

Equations and Their Properties

An *equation* is a shorthand way of stating that two algebraic expressions are *equal*. We can distinguish three types of equations. An *identity* is an equation which is true for all values of the letters or variables. An example of an identity is the equation

$$6x + 12 = \frac{12x + 24}{2}$$

Another example is

$$5(x + y) = 5x + 5y$$

In each of these equations, any values that are assigned to the variables will make both sides of the equation equal.

A *conditional equation* is true for only a limited number of values of the variables. For example, the equation

$$x + 3 = 5$$

is true only when x equals 2.

A *false statement* is an equation which is never true. That is, there are no values of the variables which make the two sides of the equation equal. An example is the equation

$$x = x + 5$$

We indicate that the two sides are not equal by using the symbol $\neq$; for this example,

$$x \neq x + 5$$

If an equation contains one variable, any value of the variable which makes the equation true is called a *root of the equation.* We say that roots are values which *satisfy the equation.* "Solving an equation" refers to the process of finding the roots of the equation, if they exist.

We will regularly need to manipulate or rearrange equations in order to solve them. The following rules indicate allowable operations.

SELECTED RULES FOR MANIPULATING EQUATIONS

I Real-valued expressions which are equal can be added to both sides of an equation.

II Both sides of an equation may be multiplied or divided by any nonzero constant.

III Both sides of an equation may be multiplied by a quantity which involves variables.

IV Both sides of an equation may be squared.

V Both sides of an equation may be divided by an expression which involves variables provided the expression is not equal to 0.

Rules I and II lead to the creation of *equivalent equations.* *Equivalent equations are equations which have the same roots.* Rules III and IV can result in roots which are not roots of the original equation. These roots are called *extraneous roots.* Applying Rule V can lead to equations which do not have all the roots contained in the original equation, or equations which are not equivalent to the original equations.

Solving First-Degree Equations

The procedure used for solving equations depends upon the nature of the equation. Let's consider first-degree equations which involve one variable. The following equations are examples.

$$3x = 2x - 5$$
$$5x - 4 = 12 + x$$

Solving equations of this form is relatively easy. By using appropriate rules of manipulation, the approach is simply to isolate the variable on one side of the equation and all constants on the other side of the equation.

EXAMPLE 33

Solve the two first-degree equations given above.

SOLUTION

For the equation $3x = 2x - 5$, we can add $-2x$ to both sides to get

$$3x + (-2x) = 2x - 5 + (-2x)$$

or
$$x = -5$$

The only value of x which satisfies this equation is -5.

For the equation $5x - 4 = 12 + x$, we can add $-x$ and 4 to both sides, getting

$$5x - 4 + 4 + (-x) = 12 + x + 4 + (-x)$$
$$5x - x = 12 + 4$$

or
$$4x = 16$$

Dividing both sides by 4 (or multiplying by $\frac{1}{4}$) gives us the root of the equation:

$$x = 4$$

Solving Second-Degree Equations

A second-degree equation involving the variable x has the generalized form

$$ax^2 + bx + c = 0$$

where a, b, and c are constants with the added provision that $a \neq 0$. If a equals zero, the x^2 term disappears and the equation is no longer of degree 2. Examples of second-degree equations are

$$6x^2 - 2x + 1 = 0$$
$$3x^2 = 12$$
$$2x^2 - 1 = 5x + 9$$

Second-degree equations are usually called *quadratic equations.* A quadratic equation (excluding an identity) can have *no real roots, one real root,* or *two real roots.* A number of different procedures can be used to determine the roots of a quadratic equation. We will discuss two of them. The first step, in either case, is to rewrite the equation in the form $ax^2 + bx + c = 0$.

Factoring Method   If the left side of the quadratic equation can be factored, the roots can be identified very easily. Consider the quadratic equation

$$x^2 - 4x = 0$$

The left side of the equation can be factored, resulting in

$$x(x - 4) = 0$$

The factored form of the equation suggests that the product of the two terms equals 0. The product will equal 0 if either of the two factors equals 0. For this equation the first factor is 0 when $x = 0$, and the second factor is 0 when $x = 4$. Thus, the two roots are 0 and 4.

EXAMPLE 34

Determine the roots of the equation

$$x^2 + 6x + 9 = 0$$

SOLUTION

The left side of the equation can be factored such that

$$(x + 3)(x + 3) = 0$$

Setting each factor equal to 0, we find that there is one root to the equation, and it occurs when $x = -3$.

Quadratic Formula   When the quadratic expression cannot be factored, or if you are unable to identify the factors, you can apply the *quadratic formula.* The quadratic formula will allow you to identify all roots of an equation of the form

$$ax^2 + bx + c = 0$$

The quadratic formula is

$$x = \frac{-b \pm \sqrt{b^2 - 4ac}}{2a}$$

The following examples illustrate the use of the formula

EXAMPLE 35

Given the quadratic equation $x^2 - 2x - 48 = 0$, the coefficients are $a = 1$, $b = -2$, and $c = -48$. By substituting these into the quadratic formula, the roots of the equation are computed as

$$x = \frac{-(-2) \pm \sqrt{(-2)^2 - 4(1)(-48)}}{2(1)}$$

$$= \frac{2 \pm \sqrt{4 + 192}}{2} = \frac{2 \pm \sqrt{196}}{2} = \frac{2 \pm 14}{2}$$

Using the plus sign, we get

$$x = \tfrac{16}{2} = 8$$

Using the minus sign, we obtain

$$x = -\tfrac{12}{2} = -6$$

Thus, these are the only real values of x which satisfy the quadratic equation.

The expression under the radical of the quadratic formula, $b^2 - 4ac$, is called *discriminant*. The value of the discriminant helps us determine the number of roots of a quadratic equation.

INTERPRETATIONS OF THE DISCRIMINANT

For a quadratic equation of the form $ax^2 + bx + c = 0$,

I   If $b^2 - 4ac > 0$, there are two real roots.
II If $b^2 - 4ac = 0$, there is one real root.
III If $b^2 - 4ac < 0$, there are no real roots.

Solving Inequalities

Inequalities express the condition that two quantities are not equal. One way of expressing this condition is by using the *inequality symbols* $<$ and $>$. The following illustrate the use and interpretation of these symbols:

INEQUALITY	INTERPRETATION
(a) $3 < 5$	"3 is less than 5"
(b) $x > 100$	"the value of x is greater than 100"
(c) $0 < y < 10$	"the value of y is greater than zero and less than 10"

These inequalities are *strict inequalities* since the items being compared can never equal one another. Case (*a*) illustrates an *absolute inequality,* which is always true. A *conditional inequality* is true under certain conditions. The inequality in case (*b*) holds when the variable x has a value greater than 100. If $x = 150$, the inequality is true; if $x = -25$, the inequality is not true. Case (*c*) illustrates what is termed a *double inequality.*

Another type of inequality relationship is expressed by the symbols $\geq$ and $\leq$. Such inequality relationships allow for the possibility that two quantities are equal. The following illustrate these types of inequalities.

INEQUALITY	INTERPRETATION
(a) $x + 3 \geq 15$	"the quantity $(x + 3)$ is greater than *or* equal to 15"
(b) $y \leq x$	"the value of y is less than *or* equal to the value of x"

EXAMPLE 36

To determine the values of x which satisfy the inequality $3x + 10 \leq 5x - 4$, 4 may be added to both sides to form

$$3x + 14 \leq 5x$$

Subtracting $3x$ from both sides results in

$$14 \leq 2x$$

Finally, dividing both sides by 2 yields the algebraic definition of the solution set

$$7 \leq x$$

That is, the original inequality is satisfied by any values of x which are greater than or equal to 7.

EXAMPLE 37

To determine the values of x which satisfy the inequality $6x - 10 \geq 6x + 4$, the addition of 10 to both sides yields

$$6x \geq 6x + 14$$

Subtracting $6x$ from both sides results in

$$0 \geq 14$$

which is a false statement. Hence, there are no values for x which satisfy the inequality.

EXAMPLE 38

To determine the values of x which satisfy the inequality $4x + 6 \geq 4x - 3$, 6 is subtracted from both sides to yield

$$4x \geq 4x - 9$$

and subtracting $4x$ from both sides gives us

$$0 \geq -9$$

The variable x has disappeared, and we are left with an inequality which is true all the time. This indicates that *the original inequality is true for any and all (real) values of x.*

EXAMPLE 39

To determine the values of x which satisfy the double inequality $-2x + 1 \leq x \leq 6 - x$ we first find the solution set for each inequality.

The values of x satisfying the left inequality are determined as

$$-2x + 1 \leq x$$
$$1 \leq 3x$$

or

$$\tfrac{1}{3} \leq x$$

Those values satisfying the right inequality are

$$x \leq 6 - x$$
$$2x \leq 6$$

or

$$x \leq 3$$

The values which satisfy the double inequality consist of those values of x which satisfy both inequalities, or $\frac{1}{3} \le x \le 3$.

NOTE

When solving inequalities, if both sides of an inequality are multiplied or divided by the same *negative* value, the *sense* (direction of the inequality sign) must be reversed. For example, to solve the inequality

$$-2x < 6$$

both sides of the inequality are divided by -2 and the sense of the inequality is reversed, yielding the solution

$$x > 3$$

Section 1.6 Follow-up Exercises

Find (if possible) roots to the following equations.

1	$4x = 3x + 6$	2	$-2x + 8 = 2x - 4$
3	$5y = 10y - 30$	4	$4(y - 3) = y + 9$
5	$6x + 20 = 40 + 8x$	6	$15x - 4(2x + 14) = 0$
7	$-3y - 5(y + 4) = 4$	8	$3(x - 4) + 2(2x + 1) = 11$
9	$30x + 50(x - 6) = -20$	10	$4(5 - x) + 2x - 10 = -2x + 10$
11	$x^2 - 36 = 0$	12	$x^2 + 14x + 49 = 0$
13	$x^2 - 5x + 4 = 0$	14	$4x^2 + 2x - 30 = 0$
15	$7x^2 - 70 = 21x$	16	$2x^2 + 3x - 10 = x^2 + 6x + 30$
17	$-6x^2 + 4x - 10 = 0$	18	$-5x^2 + 10x - 20 = 0$
19	$5x^2 - 17.5x - 10 = 0$	20	$x^2 + 64 = 0$
21	$8x^2 + 2x - 15 = 0$	22	$-x^2 - 2x + 35 = 0$

Algebraically solve for the values of x that satisfy the following inequalities.

23	$3x - 2 \le 4x + 8$	24	$x + 6 \ge 10 - x$
25	$x \ge x + 5$	26	$2x \le 2x - 10$
27	$-4x + 10 \ge -10 + x$	28	$3x + 6 \le 3x - 5$
29	$15x + 6 \ge 10x - 24$	30	$-4x + 10 \le x \le 2x + 6$
31	$12 \ge x + 16 \ge -20$	32	$35 \le 2x + 5 \le 80$
33	$50 \le 4x - 6 \le 25$	34	$6x - 9 \le 12x + 9 \le 6x + 81$

1.7 SETS DEFINED

Sets

A *set* is a collection of objects. The objects which belong to a set are called *elements* of the set. Reasons for membership in a set may be obvious—some common property shared by the elements. In some sets, the commonality among elements may be less obvious and in fact may be only their membership in the same set. For a set to be *well defined* and thus a mathematical set, it must be possible to determine whether any object is an element of the set. Examples of sets include the set of real numbers, the set of students enrolled in a course, the set of products sold by a company, and the set of NBA players who average over 20 points and over 12 rebounds per game in a given season.

Sets are usually defined in one of two ways. One method is enumeration. The *enumeration method* simply lists all elements in a set. If we designate a set by a capital letter, we might define the set of positive odd integers having a value less than 10 as

$$A = \{1, 3, 5, 7, 9\}$$

Note the use of *braces* to group the elements or members of the set A.

The enumeration method is convenient when the number of elements in a set is small or when it is not easy or possible to articulate a property defining membership in the set. An alternative approach to defining sets is the *descriptive property method.* With this approach, the set is defined by stating the property required for membership in the set. The set defined in the first example of the enumeration method can be redefined as

$$A = \{x \,|\, x \text{ is a positive odd integer less than 10}\}$$

Verbally, the translation of this equation is "*A is a set consisting of all elements x such that*' (*the vertical line*) *x is a positive odd integer having a value less than 10.*" The x to the left of the vertical line indicates the general notation for an element of the set; the expression to the right of the vertical line states the condition(s) required of an element for membership in the set.

To indicate that an object e is a member of a set S, we use the notation

$$e \in S$$

Verbally, this notation translates as "e is a member of the set S." In the previously defined set A we can say:

$$9 \in A$$

The notation $e \notin S$ means that an object e is not a member of set S.

The number of elements contained in a set B is denoted by n(B). Thus for set A, $n(A) = 5$.

Special Sets

There are certain special sets to which we will refer frequently in discussing the algebra of sets.

DEFINITION: UNIVERAL SET

The **universal set** $\mathcal{U}$ is the set which contains all possible elements within a particular application under consideration.

EXAMPLE 40

If we consider an opinion survey conducted of a random sample of residents within New York City, the universal set might be defined as the residents of New York City.

DEFINITION: COMPLEMENT

The **complement** of a set S is the set which consists of all elements in the universal set that are not members of set S. The complement of set S is denoted by S'.

EXAMPLE 41

If set S consists of all positive integers and the universal set is defined as all integers, the complement S' consists of all negative integers and zero.

If $\mathcal{U} = \{1, 2, 3, 4, 5, 6, 7, 8, 9, 10\}$ and $A = \{1, 3, 5, 7, 9\}$, the complement of set A contains all elements which are members of $\mathcal{U}$ but not A, or $A' = \{2, 4, 6, 8, 10\}$.

DEFINITION: NULL SET

The **empty,** or **null, set** $\varnothing$ is the set consisting of no elements.

Verify for yourself that $\mathcal{U}' = \varnothing$. Also, in Example 37 we determined that the solution set for the inequality $6x \geq 6x + 14$ contained no elements. This is an example of a null set.

DEFINITION: SUBSET

A set A is a **subset** of the set B if and only if every element of set A is also an element of set B. This subset relationship is denoted by $A \subset B$ which may be read "A is a subset of B."

EXAMPLE 42

Given the following sets,

$$A = \{1, 2, 3, 4, 5, 6, 7, 8, 9, 10\} \qquad C = \{x|x \text{ is a real number}\}$$
$$B = \{1, 3, 5, 7, 9\} \qquad D = \{z|z - 1 = 4\}$$

we can identify the following subset relationships: $A \subset C$, $B \subset C$, $D \subset C$, $B \subset A$, $D \subset A$, and $D \subset B$.

NOTE

By definition, the null set is a subset of every set. Consequently, in the previous example $\varnothing \subset A$, $\varnothing \subset B$, $\varnothing \subset C$, and $\varnothing \subset D$.

Venn Diagram Representation

Venn diagrams are a convenient way of envisioning set relationships. To illustrate, Fig. 1.3 depicts a universal set $\mathcal{U}$ within which is another set A, depicted by a circular area. The primary value of these figures is the information they convey about the relationships among sets. For example, if a set B is a subset of another set A, the Venn diagram representation of set B should be contained

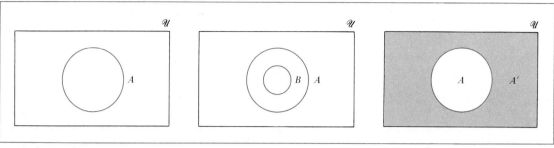

FIGURE 1.3 (left)
Venn diagram.

FIGURE 1.4 (center)
Venn diagram representation of subset relationship.

FIGURE 1.5 (right)
Venn diagram representation of complement.

within set A. In Fig. 1.4, sets A and B are both subsets within the universal set, with set B portrayed as a subset of A.

Figure 1.5 illustrates the complement relationship.

Section 1.7 Follow-up Exercises

In Exercises 1 to 5 redefine each set using the descriptive property method.

1 $A = \{0, 2, 4, 6, 8, 10, 12, 14, 16, 18, 20\}$
2 $S = \{-5, +5, -4, +4, -3, +3, -2, +2, -1, +1, 0\}$
3 $V = \{a, e, i, o, u\}$
4 $S = \{0, 1, 4, 9, 16, 25, 36\}$
5 $C = \{1, 8, 27, 64\}$

In Exercises 6 to 10 redefine each set by enumeration.

6 $A = \{a|a$ is a negative odd integer greater than $-12\}$
7 $B = \{b|b$ is a positive integer less than 5$\}$
8 $C = \{c|c$ is the name of a day of the week$\}$
9 $B = \{b|$ when $a = 2, a + 3b = -7\}$
10 $M = \{m|m$ is the fourth power of a positive integer less than 5$\}$
11 If $\mathcal{U} = \{1, 2, 3, 4, 5, 6, 7, 8, 9, 10\}$ and $B = \{b|b$ is a positive odd integer less than 8$\}$, define B'.
12 If $\mathcal{U}$ equals the set of students in a mathematics class and P is the set of students who fail the course, define P'.
13 If $\mathcal{U} = \{x|x$ is an integer greater than 5 but less than 15$\}$ and $S' = \{7, 9, 10, 12, 13\}$, define S.
14 If $\mathcal{U}$ is the set consisting of all positive integers and T' equals the set consisting of all positive even integers, define T.
15 If $\mathcal{U} = \{x|x$ is a positive integer less than 20$\}$, $A = \{1, 5, 9, 19\}$, $B = \{b|b$ is a positive odd integer less than 11$\}$, and $C = \{c|c$ is a positive odd integer less than 20$\}$, define all subset relationships which exist among $\mathcal{U}$, A, B, and C.
16 Given

$$\mathcal{U} = \{2, 4, 6, 8, 10, 12, 14, 16, 18\}$$
$$A = \{4, 8, 16\}$$
$$B = \{2, 4, 6, 8, 10\}$$

draw a Venn diagram representing the sets.

17 If $\mathcal{U} = \{x|x$ is a negative integer greater than $-11\}$, $A = \{a|a$ is a negative odd integer greater than $-10\}$, and $B = \{b|b$ is a negative integer greater than $-6\}$, draw a Venn diagram representing the sets.

1.8 SET OPERATIONS

Just as there are arithmetic operations which provide the foundation for algebra, trigonometry, and other areas of study in mathematics, there is an arithmetic of set theory which allows for the development of an algebra of sets.

Set Equality

DEFINITION: SET EQUALITY

Two sets A and B are equal if and only if every element of A is an element of B and every element of B is an element of A. Stated symbolically,

$$A = B \quad \text{iff } A \subset B \text{ and } B \subset A$$

EXAMPLE 43

Given the following sets, determine whether any sets are equal.

$$A = \{1, 2\} \qquad\qquad C = \{1, 2, 3\}$$
$$B = \{x|(x - 1)(x - 2)(x - 3) = 0\} \qquad D = \{x|x^2 - 3x + 2 = 0\}$$

Verify that set B can be defined equivalently as $B = \{1, 2, 3\}$. We can make the statement that set B equals set C, or $B = C$. The roots of the quadratic equation in set D are $x = 1$ and $x = 2$. Thus, set D can be redefined as

$$D = \{1, 2\}$$

and we can make the statement that set A equals set D, or $A = D$.

Union of Sets

DEFINITION: UNION OF SETS

The **union** of two sets A and B, denoted by $A \cup B$, is a set which consists of all elements contained in either set A or set B or both A and B.

The Venn diagram representation of $A \cup B$ is shown in Fig. 1.6.

EXAMPLE 44

Given the following sets,

$$A = \{1, 2, 3, 4, 5\}$$
$$B = \{1, 3, 5, 7, 9\}$$
$$C = \{2, 4, 6, 8, 10\}$$

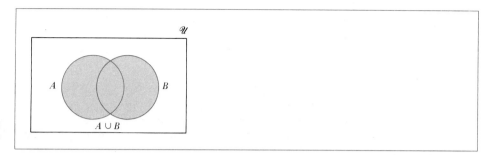

FIGURE 1.6
Union of sets *A*
and *B*.

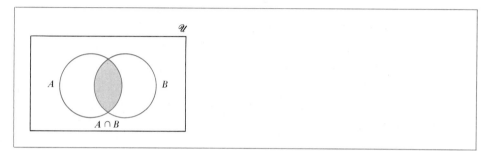

FIGURE 1.7
Intersection of
sets *A* and *B*.

(a) $A \cup B = \{1, 2, 3, 4, 5\} \cup \{1, 3, 5, 7, 9\} = \{1, 2, 3, 4, 5, 7, 9\}$
(b) $A \cup C = \{1, 2, 3, 4, 5\} \cup \{2, 4, 6, 8, 10\} = \{1, 2, 3, 4, 5, 6, 8, 10\}$
(c) $B \cup C = \{1, 3, 5, 7, 9\} \cup \{2, 4, 6, 8, 10\} = \{1, 2, 3, 4, 5, 6, 7, 8, 9, 10\}$

The union of any set *A* and its complement results in the universal set $\mathcal{U}$

Intersection of Sets

DEFINITION: INTERSECTION OF SETS

The **intersection** of two sets *A* and *B*, denoted by $A \cap B$, is a set which consists of all elements which belong to *both A* and *B*.

The Venn diagram representation of the intersection of two sets *A* and *B* is the shaded area in Fig. 1.7. Note in the diagram that the intersection is the area *common to* the two sets.

EXAMPLE 45

Given the sets *A*, *B*, and *C* defined in the last example,

(a) $A \cap B = \{1, 2, 3, 4, 5\} \cap \{1, 3, 5, 7, 9\} = \{1, 3, 5\}$
(b) $A \cap C = \{1, 2, 3, 4, 5\} \cap \{2, 4, 6, 8, 10\} = \{2, 4\}$

(c) $B \cap C = \{1, 3, 5, 7, 9\} \cap \{2, 4, 6, 8, 10\} = \emptyset$

(d) $A \cap A' = \{1, 2, 3, 4, 5\} \cap \{6, 7, 8, 9, 10\} = \emptyset$

(e) $B \cap \mathcal{U} = \{1, 3, 5, 7, 9\} \cap \{1, 2, 3, 4, 5, 6, 7, 8, 9, 10\} = \{1, 3, 5, 7, 9\}$

Other Properties

Some other general properties of sets include:

1 *The intersection of any set A and its complement A' is the null set.* Graphically this is shown in Fig. 1.8. This result was illustrated in Example 45(*d*).

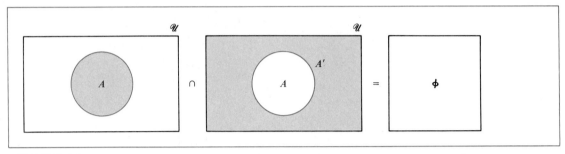

FIGURE 1.8
$A \cap A' = \emptyset.$

2 *The intersection of any set A and itself is the same set A.* Graphically this is shown in Fig. 1.9.

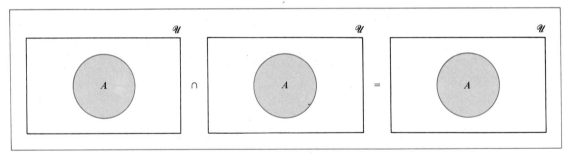

FIGURE 1.9
$A \cap A = A.$

3 *The intersection of any set A and the universal set $\mathcal{U}$ is the set A.* This is shown graphically in Fig. 1.10. This result was illustrated in Example 45(*e*).

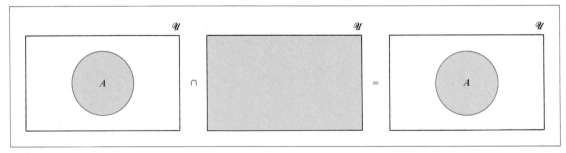

FIGURE 1.10
$A \cap \mathcal{U} = A.$

Section 1.8 Follow-up Exercises

1 Given the following sets, state which, if any, are equal.

$$A = \{3, -4\} \qquad\qquad C = \{x \mid x^3 + x^2 - 12x = 0\}$$
$$B = \{x \mid (x - 3)(x + 4) = 0\} \qquad D = \{0, -4, -3\}$$

2   Given the following sets, state which, if any, are equal.

$$A = \{0, 1, -1\} \qquad C = \{1, 0, -1\}$$
$$B = \{b \mid b^3 - b = 0\} \qquad D = \{d \mid -d + d^3 = 0\}$$

3   Given the sets

$$A = \{-1, -3, -5, -7, -9\}$$
$$B = \{-1, -2, -3, -4, -5, -6, -7, -8, -9\}$$
$$C = \{-2, -4, -6, -8\}$$

find

(a) $A \cup B$ (b) $A \cup C$
(c) $B \cup C$ (d) $A \cap B$
(e) $A \cap C$ (f) $B \cap C$

4   If in Exercise 3 $\mathcal{U} = \{x \mid x \text{ is a negative integer greater than } -12\}$, find

(a) $A \cap A'$ (b) $A' \cap B'$
(c) $B' \cup C$ (d) $A \cap C'$
(e) $B' \cup A$ (f) $C' \cap A'$

1.9   SAMPLE APPLICATIONS

In this section we will examine some sample scenarios which illustrate some applications of set theory. The examples and data are hypothetical, so the conclusions should not be taken too seriously. However, this should not detract from the significance of these examples; they are, indeed, very likely areas for applying the concepts of set theory.

EXAMPLE 46

Vitamin C Research   In recent years there has been much controversy about the possible benefits of using supplemental doses of vitamin C. Claims have been made by proponents of vitamin C that supplemental doses will reduce the incidence of the common cold and influenza (flu). A test group of 1,000 persons received supplemental doses of vitamin C for a period of 1 year. During this period it was found that 300 such people had one or more colds, 100 people suffered from influenza, and 80 people suffered from both colds and influenza. Use a Venn diagram to summarize the results of this study if $\mathcal{U}$ represents all persons in the control group, C is the set of persons incurring colds, and I is the set of persons suffering from influenza during the study period. How many persons suffered from neither colds nor influenza? How many persons suffered colds and not influenza? Influenza but not colds? What conclusions can you draw regarding vitamin C and its effect on these ailments?

SOLUTION

A Venn diagram representation of the sets is provided by Fig. 1.11. The Venn diagram

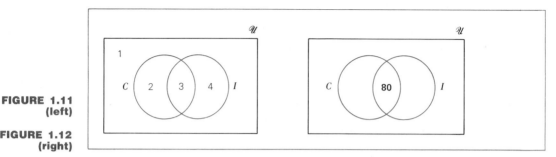

**FIGURE 1.11
(left)**

**FIGURE 1.12
(right)**

provides the *framework* for answering the questions asked about the survey. In order to answer the questions, it is necessary to determine the number of elements in each of the four numbered areas in Fig. 1.11. From the survey data, the only set for which we can immediately identify the number of elements is that represented by area 3, or $C \cap I$. This area represents those 80 people who incurred both colds and influenza during the test period, and this is shown in Fig. 1.12. Area 2 represents those persons who contracted colds *only*. We are told that the number of people having colds during the test period was 300; however, included in this number are those who had *both* colds and influenza. Thus, to determine those who had colds only, we must subtract from the 300 the 80 who had both. Therefore 220 people had colds only. Area 4 represents the set of people who incurred influenza only. The number of people in this set is the 100 identified as having influenza minus the 80 who had both, or 20. The last set of people, represented by area 1, consists of all people who had neither colds nor influenza during the test period. This set is the complement of the union of the other three sets; it contains $1,000 - 220 - 80 - 20 = 680$ members. The numbers of members of each set are indicated in Fig. 1.13.

It is difficult to draw any conclusions about the study without having some comparative data. For example, if there had been a similar control group of 1,000 people who received no vitamin C supplement over the same period, a comparison of health histories during the test period might allow us to reach conclusions about the relative benefits of using or not using vitamin C.

EXAMPLE 47 ▬▬▬▬▬▬▬▬▬▬▬▬▬▬▬▬▬▬▬▬▬▬▬▬

Voter Crossover Immediately following the famed Watergate scandal from 1972 to 1974, many voters became disillusioned with the Republican party and further disillusioned with politics in general. A public opinion research organization wanted to determine the effect that Watergate *might* have had on voters and their political preferences. Therefore, it surveyed 15,000 registered Republicans to determine how they voted during the 1972 and 1976 Presidential elections.

The survey results indicated that of the 15,000 people, 7,500 voted for the Republican candidate in 1972, 4,500 voted for the Republican candidate in 1976, and 4,000 voted for the Republican candidate in both 1972 and 1976. Figure 1.14 is a Venn diagram which summarizes the survey results; R_1 is the set of people who voted for the Republican candidate in 1972, and R_2 the set of people who voted for the Republican candidate in 1976. Determine the number of elements in each of the four subsets represented by the numbered areas 1 to 4, and interpret these answers with respect to voter behavior.

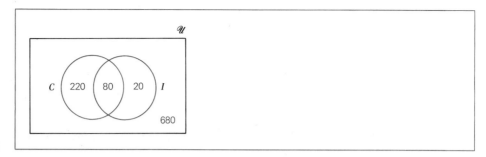

FIGURE 1.13

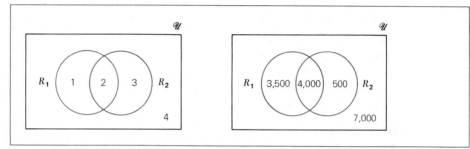

**FIGURE 1.14
(left)**

**FIGURE 1.15
(right)**

SOLUTION

Figure 1.15 indicates the number of members in each subset. As in the last example these numbers are found by first recognizing that $n(R_1 \cap R_2) = 4,000$. Since R_1 contains 7,500 voters in total, the subset represented by area 1 must have 3,500 voters. Similarly, since R_2 contains 4,500 voters, the subset represented by area 3 has 500 voters. The number of people in $R_1 \cup R_2$ can be calculated as

$$n(R_1 \cup R_2) = n(R_1) + n(R_2) - n(R_1 \cap R_2)$$
$$= 7,500 + 4,500 - 4,000 = 8,000$$

Therefore the number of people in the subset represented by area 4 is

$$n(R_1 \cup R_2)' = n(\mathcal{U}) - n(R_1 \cup R_2)$$
$$= 15,000 - 8,000 = 7,000$$

The 3,500 members of the subset represented by area 1 are those who voted for the Republican candidate in 1972 but not in 1976. The 4,000 people represented by area 2 are those who voted for the Republican candidates in both years. The 500 people represented by area 3 voted for the Republican candidate in 1976 but not in 1972. The 7,000 persons represented by area 4 are those Republicans surveyed who did not vote for a Republican candidate during either election. This set could include those persons who (1) did not vote in either election, (2) voted for another candidate in one election and did not vote in the other election, or (3) voted for another candidate in both elections.

The following observations can be made from the survey results:

■ Of the 15,000 registered Republicans, 8,000 voted for a Republican during at least one of the two elections.

■ Of the 15,000, 7,000 did not vote for the Republican candidate during either election.

■ Of the 7,500 Republicans who voted in 1972 for the Republican candidate, 3,500 did not vote Republican in 1976. These 3,500 may indicate a loss attributable to Watergate. Can we state that this loss was caused by Watergate? What else might explain the loss of these votes?

■ The 500 persons represented by area 3 are a measure of gains to the Republican party from 1972. Where might these voters have come from?

EXAMPLE 48

Cancer Research A cancer research team working with the support of the Department of Health and Human Services has gathered statistics related to the deaths of 20,000 cancer victims. Extensive data have been gathered regarding the health histories and living habits of both the victims and their relatives. Three significant variables appear to be associated with victims of cancer: regular smoking, moderate to heavy drinking, and age of 35 or more. The following data were gathered on 20,000 victims:

■ 14,500 victims regularly smoked.

■ 12,500 victims were moderate-to-heavy drinkers of alcohol.

■ 15,000 victims were 35 or more years of age.

■ 11,000 victims smoked regularly and were moderate-to-heavy drinkers.

■ 12,000 victims smoked regularly and were 35 or older.

■ 10,000 victims were moderate-to-heavy drinkers and were 35 or older.

■ 10,000 victims had all three characteristics.

If $\mathcal{U}$ is defined as the set of victims, S the set of victims who were regular smokers, D the set who were moderate-to-heavy drinkers, and A those who were 35 or older, construct a Venn diagram showing the numbers of members having each possible combination of these three attributes. How many victims had none of the three characteristics?

SOLUTION

Since three sets of interest have been identified as being contained within $\mathcal{U}$, the Venn diagram should have the form of Fig. 1.16. Given the information pertaining to the numbers of victims having each combination of attributes, you would very likely conclude that there are far more than 20,000 cancer victims in this group. "Something must be wrong with the data—if you add the 12,500 drinkers to the 14,500 smokers, you already have 27,000 victims." This logic fails to recognize the overlap or intersection property. Many smokers also drink, not all smokers and drinkers are under 35 years of age, and so forth. So what is required is that we sift through the information to identify the eight distinct subsets of interest in the sample.

    If you construct a Venn diagram, identify the eight areas, and review the information presented, you should conclude that the only area for which the number of elements is immediately obvious represents the set of victims who had all three characteristics. These 10,000 victims are denoted in Fig. 1.17. Once this one area is filled in, it becomes a matter of solving some mental equations and filling in a type of jigsaw puzzle. For ex-

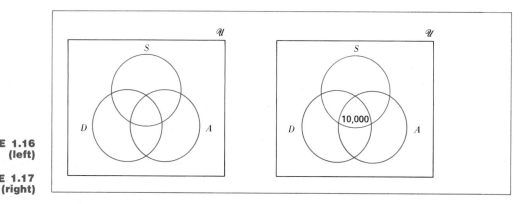

FIGURE 1.16 (left)

FIGURE 1.17 (right)

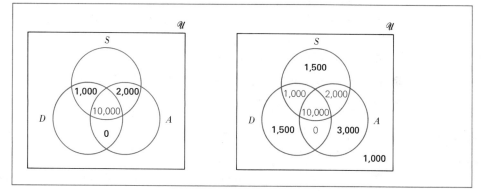

FIGURE 1.18 (left)

FIGURE 1.19 (right)

ample, we are told that the number of victims who were both smokers and drinkers was 11,000, or $n(S \cap D) = 11,000$. In Fig. 1.18 we can see that the set $S \cap D$ is represented by two areas. Since one of these areas represents 10,000 members, the other area must represent the remaining 1,000 elements. Using the information that $n(S \cap A) = 12,000$ and $n(D \cap A) = 10,000$, and applying the same logic, we can complete the Venn diagram to the point shown in Fig. 1.18.

To complete the Venn diagram, we need to use the information that $n(S) = 14,500$, $n(D) = 12,500$, and $n(A) = 15,000$. Since S should contain 14,500 elements, the remaining part of S must contain the other 1,500 elements. Similar reasoning should lead you to agree with the figures in the Venn diagram in Fig. 1.19. Can you verify the figure of 1,000 victims who possessed none of the attributes?

Section 1.9 Follow-up Exercises

1   A survey of 1,500 consumers was conducted to determine their purchasing behavior regarding two leading soft drinks. It was found that during the past month 600 had purchased brand A, 400 had purchased brand B, and 150 had purchased both brand A and brand B.

(*a*) Construct a Venn diagram summarizing the results of the survey.

(*b*) How many respondents purchased A only?

(*c*) How many respondents purchased B only?

(*d*) How many respondents purchased neither *A* nor *B*?

2   A survey of 500 people was conducted to determine the extent to which they attempt to learn the news of the day. It was found that 350 people regularly watch the news on TV, 125 people regularly listen to the news on the radio, and 100 people regularly get the news from both TV and radio.

(*a*) Construct a Venn diagram summarizing the results of the survey.

(*b*) How many of the respondents watch the news only on TV?

(*c*) How many listen to the news only on the radio?

(*d*) How many respondents do not listen to the news on either radio or TV? Describe this group of persons regarding their access to the news.

3   **Energy Conservation**   A group of 2,000 people was surveyed regarding policies which might be enacted to conserve oil. Of the 2,000, 1,000 people said that gas rationing would be acceptable to them, 500 people said that a federal surtax of $0.25 per gallon would be acceptable, and 275 people indicated that both rationing and the surtax would be acceptable.

(*a*) Construct a Venn diagram which summarizes the results of the survey.

(*b*) How many people would willingly accept gas rationing but not the surtax?

(*c*) How many people would willingly accept the surtax but not gas rationing?

(*d*) How many respondents would willingly accept neither policy?

4   A group of 1,000 people was asked if they had purchased three different brands of yogurt. The following data were gathered:

■   175 people had purchased brand *A*.

■   220 had purchased brand *B*.

■   150 had purchased brand *C*.

■   50 had purchased both *A* and *B*.

■   75 had purchased both *A* and *C*.

■   60 had purchased both *B* and *C*.

■   20 had purchased all three.

(*a*) Construct a Venn diagram which summarizes the results of the survey.

(*b*) How many people purchased only *A*? only *B*? Only *C*?

(*c*) How many purchased *A* and *B* only?

(*d*) How many purchased *A* and *C* only?

(*e*) How many people purchased *B* and *C* only?

(*f*) How many had not purchased any of the three?

5   **Public Transportation**   The Department of Transportation surveyed 50,000 people to determine their use of different modes of public transportation during the past year. The results of the survey indicated that

■   12,500 had flown in airplanes.

■   20,500 had ridden buses.

■   10,000 had ridden trains.

■   3,500 had ridden both airplanes and buses.

■ 4,500 had ridden both buses and trains.

■ 4,000 had ridden both airplanes and trains.

■ 2,500 had ridden all three modes.

Determine the percentage of respondents who
(a) Flew airplanes only
(b) Rode only airplanes *and* buses
(c) Rode only airplanes *and* trains
(d) Rode only buses *and* trains
(e) Rode buses only
(f) Did not use any of the three modes

   6   **Criminal Justice System**   The Department of Justice mailed a survey to 2,000 criminal justice system experts to determine where the most immediate needs were— the law enforcement area, the court system, or the corrections area (jails and prisons). All respondents were asked to indicate the sector(s) having the greatest needs. The numbers of experts citing the different areas of need were as follows:

■ 1,250 experts cited the law enforcement area.

■ 1,250 experts cited the court system.

■ 1,050 experts cited the corrections area.

■ 900 experts cited both law enforcement and the courts.

■ 800 experts cited both the courts and corrections areas.

■ 750 experts cited both law enforcement and corrections.

■ 600 experts cited all three areas.

Determine the number of experts who
(a) Cited law enforcement only
(b) Cited the court system only
(c) Cited the corrections sector only
(d) Cited law enforcement and courts only
(e) Cited law enforcement and corrections only
(f) Assuming that each survey returned to the Department of Justice cited at least one of the three areas, how many surveys were not returned?

KEY TERMS AND CONCEPTS

absolute value 5	discriminant 26
algebraic expression 8	element 28
binomial 8	enumeration method 29
complement 30	exponent 6
conditional equation 23	false statement 23
degree of polynomial 9	fractions 16
degree of term 9	identity 23
descriptive property method 29	intersection of sets 33

ADDITIONAL EXERCISES

The following exercises are related to Sec. 1.2.

1   $x^4 x^{-5} =$

2   $a^6 a^3 a^{-4} =$

3   $(x^2)^5 x^{-5} =$

4   $[(x^{-3})^2]^{-4} =$

5   $[(a^2 b^3)^3]^2/(a^4 b^2)^3 =$

6   $(x^2 y^3 z)^3/[(xy^2 z)^{-2}]^{-2} =$

7   $(x^2 y/z)^3/(z^2/xy^3)^2 =$

8   $(2a^3 c/7b^4)^{-2}/(b^3 c^2/a)^{-3} =$

9   $(a^3 b^2 c^4)^0/[(abc)^2]^0 =$

10   $[x^2 (yz^3)^0]/(x^3/y^2 z)^2 =$

The following exercises are related to Sec. 1.3. Completely factor (if possible) the following polynomials.

11   $a^5 b - a^2 b^3 - a^3 b^2$

12   $28x^3 y^2 - 16x^2 y^3 + 8x^4 y$

13   $3x^2 + 16x - 12$

14   $5x^2 + 7x - 6$

15   $12x^2 - 19x - 21$

16   $6x^2 - 44x - 32$

17   $3x^4 - 48$

18   $1250 - 2x^4$

19   $5x^2 + 10x - 40$

20   $18x^4 y + 6x^3 y - 12x^2 y$

The following exercises are related to Sec. 1.4.

21   $\frac{2}{5} - \frac{3}{7} + \frac{1}{3} =$

22   $\frac{2}{9} - \frac{4}{15} + \frac{5}{12} =$

23   $\dfrac{x}{x-3} - \dfrac{3x^2}{x^2 + 2x - 15} =$

24   $\dfrac{3a}{a-5} - \dfrac{1-a}{a+3} =$

25   $\dfrac{x^2 y}{3z} \div \dfrac{9z^3 x}{y} =$

26   $\dfrac{4a^2 b^3}{3c} \div \dfrac{2ab^4}{9c} =$

27   $\dfrac{x}{x^2 - 2x - 15} \div \dfrac{3x}{x+3} =$

28   $\dfrac{5 + 3/(4x^2)}{10 - (1/x)} =$

The following exercises are related to Sec. 1.5.

29   $x^{2/3} \cdot x^{5/2} =$

30   $x^{2/5} \cdot x^{5/2} \cdot x^{3/4} =$

31   $x^{3/4} \div x^{5/3} =$

32   $(x^{1/2} \cdot x^{1/3} \div x^{1/4})^3 =$

33   $(x^4 y^8/z^2)^{1/2} =$

34   $(-64x^6 y^9/z^3)^{1/3} =$

35   $\sqrt{3}\sqrt{9}\sqrt{3} =$

36   $\sqrt[3]{2x^3}\sqrt[3]{8x^5}\sqrt[3]{4x^4} =$

The following exercises are related to Sec. 1.6. Find (if possible) roots to the following equations.

37   $5x - 3 = 4x + 2$

38   $2x + 15 = 2x - 21$

39	$x^2 + 2x - 15 = 0$		**40**	$x^2 - 4x - 12 = 0$
41	$3x^2 - 14x - 5 = 0$		**42**	$2x^2 - 3x - 20 = 0$
43	$x^2 - 10x + 25 = 0$		**44**	$9 - 6a + a^2 = 0$
45	$6x^2 - 2x + 4 = 0$		**46**	$10x^2 - 4x + 15 = 0$

Algebraically solve for the values of x that satisfy the following inequalities.

47	$5x - 10 \le 3x + 20$		**48**	$-3x + 25 \ge x - 40$
49	$45 \le 2x - 5 \le 80$		**50**	$2x \le 3x + 10 \le 4x - 5$

The following exercises are related to Secs. 1.7 to 1.9.

51   Redefine set A using the descriptive property method if
(a) $A = \{2, 4, 8, 16, 32, 64\}$
(b) $A = \{3, 9, 27, 81, 243\}$
(c) $A = \{-1, 4, -9, 16, -25, 36, -49, 64\}$
(d) $A = \{10, 100, 1{,}000, 10{,}000, 100{,}000\}$

52   Given

$$\mathcal{U} = \{x | x \text{ is an integer greater than } -6 \text{ but less than } +11\}$$
$$A = \{a | a \text{ is an even positive integer less than } 12\}$$
$$B = \{b | b \text{ is an odd integer greater than } -4 \text{ but less than } +6\}$$

(a) Define A'.
(b) Define B'.

53   If $\mathcal{U}$ consists of all students enrolled in courses at a university, A consists of all male students, B consists of all students aged 35 years or over, and C consists of all engineering students, (a) define the set A', (b) define the set B', and (c) define the set C'.

54   If $\mathcal{U}$ consists of the different total scores possible on the roll of a pair of dice and B' consists of the scores of 5, 7, and 9, define B.

55   If

$$\mathcal{U} = \{1, 2, 3, 4, 5, 6, 7, 8, 9, 10\} \qquad B = \{1, 3, 5, 7, 9\}$$
$$A = \{1, 5, 9\} \qquad\qquad\qquad C = \{2, 4, 6, 8, 10\}$$

define all subset relationships which exist for these sets.

56   Draw a Venn diagram representing all the sets in Exercise 55.

57   Ten residents of a city were surveyed regarding their use of public transportation in that city. They were asked whether they had ridden the subway (S), the bus (B), or neither (N) during the past year. The responses were as follows:

Resident	1	2	3	4	5	6	7	8	9	10
Response	N	N	B	B,S	S	B,S	B,S	B,S	B	S

Draw a Venn diagram which shows how each resident responded to the survey.

58   Given the following sets, determine if any sets are equal.

$$A = \{x | x^3 + 6x^2 + 9x = 0\} \qquad B = \{x | x^2 + 3x = 0\}$$
$$C = \{-3, 0] \qquad\qquad\qquad D = \{-3, \quad 0, \quad 3\}$$

59   Given the sets

$$\mathcal{U} = \{x|x \text{ is a positive integer less than 20}\} \qquad A = \{5, 10, 15\}$$
$$B = \{2, 4, 6, 8, 10\} \qquad\qquad\qquad\qquad C = \{1, 5, 9, 15, 17\}$$

find

(a) $A \cap B$

(b) $A \cup B \cup C$

(c) $A' \cap B'$

(d) $A' \cup C'$

(e) $A \cap B \cap C$

(f) $A' \cup B$

(g) $A' \cap B$

(h) $(A \cap B \cap C)'$

60   In Fig. 1.20, the numbers represent the elements contained in the various subsets. Determine

(a) $n(A)$

(b) $n(A \cup B)$

(c) $n(A \cup B \cup C)$

(d) $n(\mathcal{U})$

(e) $n(A' \cup B)$

(f) $n(B' \cap C')$

(g) $n(B \cap C)$

(h) $n(A' \cap B' \cap C')$

61   **Victimization Survey**   Figure 1.21 is a Venn diagram used to represent the results of a survey. Set A represents those respondents who have been victims of robbery, set B represents those respondents who have been victims of automobile theft, set C represents those respondents who have been victims of burglary, and $\mathcal{U}$ consists of all respondents. Give a verbal interpretation of the elements contained in areas 1 to 8.

62   **Child Abuse**   A survey of 1000 high school seniors was conducted to determine the extent to which child abuse exists. It was found that 300 respondents recalled having been physically abused by their fathers, 210 recalled having been physically abused by their mothers, and 160 recalled having been physically abused by both parents. What percentage of respondents was

(a) Physically abused by fathers only?

(b) Physically abused by mothers only?

(c) Physically abused by both parents?

(d) Physically abused?

(e) Not physically abused?

63   A major TV network surveyed 5,000 viewers to determine their viewing habits during the past week. They found that

■   3,000 viewers had watched a sports event.

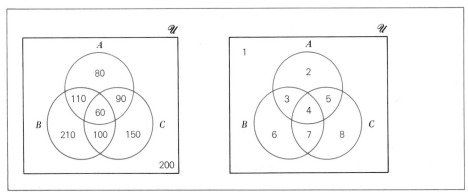

FIGURE 1.20 (left)

FIGURE 1.21 (right)

- 2,500 viewers had watched a news show.

- 2,000 viewers had watched a TV movie.

- 1,750 viewers had watched both sports and news shows.

- 1,000 viewers had watched both news shows and TV movies.

- 1,250 viewers had watched both sports shows and TV movies.

- 500 viewers had watched all three types of shows.

What percentage of viewers watched
(*a*) News shows only?
(*b*) Sports shows only?
(*c*) TV movies only?
(*d*) None of the three types of programs?

64 A group of 2,500 citizens was surveyed to see how many had been robbery or burglary victims. It was found that 500 had been victims of burglary, 350 had been robbery victims, and 220 had been victims of both types of crime.
(*a*) Construct a Venn diagram which summarizes the results of the survey.
(*b*) How many persons were victims of robbery but not burglary?
(*c*) How many persons were victims of burglary but not robbery?
(*d*) How many persons were victims of neither crime?

65 A state criminal justice agency has conducted a survey of the incidence of serious crimes within the state. One area of particular concern is residential crime. As a part of the survey, the heads of family from 2,000 households were interviewed to determine whether their families had been victims of burglary, robbery, or auto theft during the preceding year. The Venn diagram in Fig. 1.22 indicates the results of the survey. The universal set represents all families interviewed, *B* is the set of all households having been burglary victims, *R* is the set of all households having been robbery victims, and *A* is the set of households which were victims of auto theft.
Determine the *percentages* of households which were victims of
(*a*) Burglary   (*b*) Robbery
(*c*) Auto theft   (*d*) Burglary and robbery
(*e*) Burglary and auto theft   (*f*) Robbery and auto theft
(*g*) All three crimes   (*h*) None of the crimes

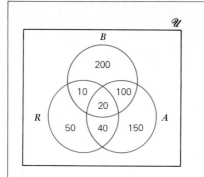

FIGURE 1.22

CHAPTER TEST

1 Completely factor the expression $2x^2 - 9x + 9$.

2 $\frac{5}{6} - \frac{7}{12} + \frac{8}{15} =$

3 $(4x^2y/5z) \div (2xy^2/7z^2) =$

4 $[(x^2yz^3)^3(xy^2z)]^2 =$

5 Express $(ab)^{4/5}$ in radical form.

6 Find any roots to the equation $15x^2 - 2x^2 + 10 = 0$.

7 Algebraically solve for the values of x which satisfy the inequality $14 \leq 6x + 2 \leq 80$.

8 Given the sets $A = \{1, 2, 3, 4, 5, 6, 7, 8\}$, $B = \{-2, 0, 2, 4, 6, 8, 10\}$, and $C = \{-3, -2, -1, 0, 1, 2, 3\}$, determine the sets
(a) $A \cap B$
(b) $A \cap B \cap C$
(c) $A \cup B \cup C$

9 The Venn diagram in Fig. 1.23 is used to represent the results of a survey. Set S consists of all respondents who smoke, set D consists of all respondents who drink, and $\mathcal{U}$ consists of all respondents. Give a verbal interpretation of the elements represented by the numbered areas 1 to 4.

10 One thousand registered Democrats were surveyed regarding whether they had voted for the party candidate in the last three gubernatorial elections. The results of the survey indicated that:

■ 570 had in the first election

■ 550 had in the second election.

■ 510 had in the third election.

■ 400 had in *both* the first and second elections.

■ 400 had in *both* the second and third elections.

■ 420 had in *both* the first and third elections.

■ 350 had in all three elections.

(a) Construct a Venn diagram summarizing the survey results
(b) How many persons voted for the party candidate in the first election only?
(c) How many of the registered Democrats did not vote for the party candidate in any of the three elections?

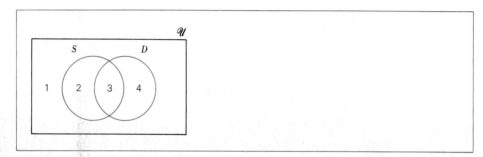

FIGURE 1.23

2

MATHEMATICAL FUNCTIONS

2.1 FUNCTIONS

2.2 TYPES OF FUNCTIONS

2.3 GRAPHICAL REPRESENTATION OF FUNCTIONS

KEY TERMS AND CONCEPTS

IMPORTANT FORMULAS

ADDITIONAL EXERCISES

CHAPTER TEST

CHAPTER OBJECTIVES

- Enable the reader to understand the nature and notation of mathematical functions

- Provide illustrations of the application of mathematical functions

- Provide a brief overview of important types of functions and their characteristics

- Discuss the graphical representation of functions and methods of generating these representations

The application of mathematics rests upon the ability to identify a relevant mathematical representation of a real-world phenomenon. This representation is often called a *mathematical model.* A model is relevant if it successfuly captures those attributes of the phenomenon which are significant to the model builder. Just as a model airplane portrays the physical likeness of an actual airplane, a mathematical model of a demand function represents the significant interrelationships between, say, the price of a commodity and the quantity demanded.

2.1 FUNCTIONS

In mathematical models, the significant relationships typically are represented by *mathematical functions,* or, more simply, *functions.* Functions form a cornerstone of much of what follows in this book. It is the purpose of this chapter to introduce this important topic.

Functions Defined

A function essentially is an input/output device. An input is provided to a mathematical rule which transforms (manipulates) the input into a specific output. (See Fig. 2.1.) Consider the equation $y = x^2 - 2x + 1$. If selected values of x are *input*, the equation yields corresponding values of y as outputs. To illustrate,

$$\text{If } x = 1 \qquad y = (1)^2 - 2(1) + 1 = 0$$
$$\text{If } x = -5 \qquad y = (-5)^2 - 2(-5) + 1 = 36$$
$$\text{If } x = 10 \qquad y = (10)^2 - 2(10) + 1 = 81$$

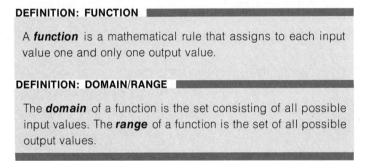

FIGURE 2.1
Input/output
representation
of function.

The equation provides the *rule* which allows one to transform a value of x into a corresponding value of y. The rule for *this* equation might be verbalized as "take the input value and square it, subtract two times the input value, and add 1." Note that for any input value, a unique output value is determined.

DEFINITION: FUNCTION

A *function* is a mathematical rule that assigns to each input value one and only one output value.

DEFINITION: DOMAIN/RANGE

The *domain* of a function is the set consisting of all possible input values. The *range* of a function is the set of all possible output values.

The assigning of output values to corresponding input values is often referred to as a *mapping*. The notation

$$f: x \rightarrow y$$

represents the mapping of the set of input values x into the set of output values y, using the mapping rule f.

Figure 2.2 illustrates some important points regarding functions. The mapping indicated in Fig. 2.2a complies with the definition of a function. For each indicated value in the domain there corresponds a unique value in the range of the function. Similarly, the mapping in Fig. 2.2b complies with the definition. The fact that two different values in the domain "transform" into the same value in the range does not violate the definition. However, the mapping in Fig. 2.2c does not represent a function since one value in the domain results in two different values in the range.

The Nature and Notation of Functions

Functions, as we will treat them, suggest that the value of something depends upon the value of *one or more* other things. There are uncountable numbers of functional relationships in the world about us. The size of the crowds at a beach may depend upon the temperature and the day of the week, quantities sold of a product may depend upon the price charged for the product and the prices of competing brands, grades may depend upon the amount of time that a student studies, city tax rates may depend upon the level of municipal spending, and the length of a person's hair may depend upon the length of time since it was last cut.

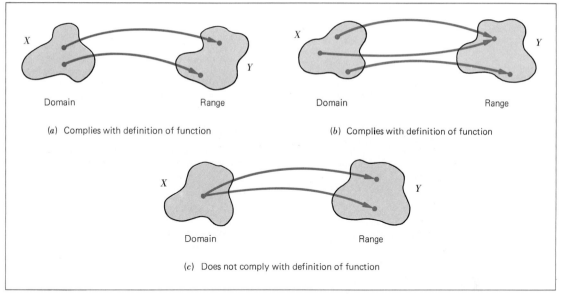

X

Domain   Range   Domain   Range

(a) Complies with definition of function   (b) Complies with definition of function

X   Y

Domain   Range

(c) Does not comply with definition of function

FIGURE 2.2
Sample
mappings.

The language of mathematics provides a succinct way of describing how variables are functionally related. The equation

$$y = f(x)$$

denotes a functional relationship between the variables x and y. A verbal translation of this equation is *"y equals f of x"* or *"y is a function of x." This equation is not to be interpreted as "y equals f times x."* When we say that y is *a function of x,* we mean that the value of the variable y *depends upon* and is uniquely determined by the value of the variable x; x is the input variable and y the output variable. The respective roles of the two variables result in the variable x being called the **independent variable** and the variable y being called the **dependent variable.** Alternatively, y is often referred to as the **value** of the function. "f" is the **name** of the function or mapping rule.

EXAMPLE 1

Suppose that you have taken a job as a salesperson. Your employer has stated that your salary will depend upon the number of units you sell each week. If we let

$$y = \text{weekly salary in dollars}$$
$$x = \text{number of units sold each week}$$

the dependency stated by your employer can be represented by the equation

$$y = f(x)$$

where f is the name of the salary function.

Although y usually represents the dependent variable, x the independent variable, and f the name of the function, *any* letter may be used to represent the dependent and independent variables and the function name. The equation

$$u = g(v)$$

is a way of stating that the value of a dependent variable u is determined by the value of an independent variable v. And the name of the function or rule relating the two variables is g.

Suppose your employer in the previous example has given you the following equation for determining your weekly salary.

$$y = f(x) = 3x + 25 \qquad \textbf{(2.1)}$$

The specific rule which determines y is

$$f(x) = 3x + 25$$

Given any value for x, substitution of this value into f will result in the corresponding value of y. For instance, if we want to compute your weekly salary when 100 units are sold, substitution of $x = 100$ into Eq. (2.1) yields

$$y = 3(100) + 25$$
$$= \$325$$

> For the function $y = f(x)$, the value of y which corresponds to the input value $x = b$ is denoted by $f(b)$.

In Eq. (2.1), the salary associated with selling 75 units can be denoted by $f(75)$. To evaluate $f(75)$, simply substitute the value $x = 75$ into Eq. (2.1) wherever the letter x appears, or

$$f(75) = 3(75) + 25$$
$$= \$250$$

Similarly, the value of y corresponding to $x = 0$ is denoted as $f(0)$ and computed as $f(0) = 3(0) + 25 = \$25$.

EXAMPLE 2

Given the functional relationship

$$z = h(t)$$
$$= t^2 + t - 10$$

(*a*) $h(0) = (0)^2 + (0) - 10 = -10$

(*b*) $h(-5) = (-5)^2 + (-5) - 10 = 25 - 5 - 10 = 10$

(*c*) $h(u + v) = (u + v)^2 + (u + v) - 10$
$$= u^2 + 2uv + v^2 + u + v - 10 = u^2 + u + 2uv + v + v^2 - 10$$

Note in c that the input value for t is the sum $u + v$. To evaluate $h(u + v)$ the procedure is exactly the same as for parts a and b. Wherever t appears in the function, we substitute the quantity $u + v$.

EXAMPLE 3

A small city police department is contemplating the purchase of an additional patrol car. Police analysts estimate the purchase cost of a fully equipped car to be $18,000. They also have estimated an average operating cost of $0.40 per mile. (*a*) Determine the mathematical function which represents the total cost *C* of owning and operating the car in terms of the number of miles *x* it is driven. (*b*) What are projected total costs if the car is driven 50,000 miles during its lifetime? (*c*) If it is driven 100,000 miles?

SOLUTION

(*a*) In this example, we are asked to determine the function which relates total cost *C* to miles driven *x*. The first question is: Which variable depends upon the other? A rereading of the problem and some thought about the two variables should lead to the conclusion that total cost is dependent upon the number of miles driven, or

$$C = f(x)$$

At this stage you may be able to write the cost function as

$$C = f(x) = 0.40x + 18,000$$

For those who cannot write the cost function, mentally or on paper, determine the value of the dependent variable, given arbitrary values of the independent variable. Examine the respective values of the variables and see if a pattern begins to emerge. If it does, then *articulate your mental model* (or more simply, write out the function).

Let's try this approach. What would total cost equal if the car were driven 0 miles (assuming it was purchased)? Your mental model should respond "$18,000." What would the total cost equal if the car were driven 10,000 miles? $22,000. What if it were driven 20,000 miles? $26,000. If you are having no difficulty arriving at these answers, indeed you have some mental cost model. Now is the time to express that model mathematically. The total cost of owning and operating the police car is the sum of two component costs—purchase cost and operating cost. And the type of computation you should have been making when responding to each question was to multiply the number of miles by $0.40 and add this result to the $18,000 purchase cost. Or,

$$C = f(x)$$
$$= \text{total operating cost} + \text{purchase cost}$$
$$= (\text{operating cost per mile})(\text{number of miles}) + \text{purchase cost}$$

or $\quad C = 0.40x + 18,000$

(*b*) If the car is driven 50,000 miles, total costs are estimated to equal

$$C = f(50,000)$$
$$= 0.40(50,000) + 18,000$$
$$= \$38,000$$

(*c*) Similarly, at 100,000 miles

$$C = f(100,000)$$
$$= 0.40(100,000) + 18,000$$
$$= \$58,000$$

Domain and Range Considerations

Earlier, the domain of a function was defined as the set of all possible input values. Because we will focus upon real-valued functions, the domain consists of all real values of the independent variable for which the dependent variable is defined and real. To determine the domain, it is usually easier to identify those values *not* included in the domain (i.e., find the exceptions). Given the domain, the range of a function is the corresponding set of values for the dependent variable. Defining the range can be more difficult than defining the domain. We will have less concern with this process now. We will discuss the range in more detail when we examine the graphical representation of functions later in this chapter.

EXAMPLE 4

Given the function

$$y = f(x)$$
$$= x^2 - 2x + 1$$

any real value may be substituted for x with a corresponding and unique value of y resulting. If D is defined as the domain of f,

$$D = \{x \mid x \text{ is real}\}$$

EXAMPLE 5

The function

$$u = f(v)$$
$$= \frac{1}{v^2 - 4}$$

has the form of a quotient. Any values of v which result in the denominator equalling 0 would be excluded from the domain. The denominator equals 0 when $v^2 - 4 = 0$ or when v assumes a value of either $+2$ or -2. The domain of the function includes all real numbers *except* $+2$ and -2, or $D = \{v \mid v \text{ is real and } v \neq \pm 2\}$.

EXAMPLE 6

For the function

$$y = f(x)$$
$$= \sqrt{x - 5}$$

x can assume any value for which the expression under the square root sign is positive or zero. To determine these values,

$$x - 5 \geq 0$$

when

$$x \geq 5$$

Thus the domain of the function includes all real numbers which are greater than or equal to 5, or $D = \{x \mid x \text{ is real and } x \geq 5\}$.

Restricted Domain and Range

We have discussed the concepts of domain and range in a purely mathematical sense. In a practical sense there may be conditions within an application which further restrict the domain and range of a function. Returning again to the patrol car example, the mathematical domain of the cost function $C = 0.40x + 18,000$ includes any real value for x. However, within the context of the application we would have to restrict x from assuming negative values (there is no such thing as negative miles traveled). In addition, if the department has a policy that no patrol car will be driven over 150,000 miles, then x would be restricted to values no greater than 150,000. Thus the *restricted domain* of the function in this application is

$$0 \leq x \leq 150,000$$

The *restricted range* for this cost function, in light of the restrictions on x, would be

$$\$18,000 \leq C \leq \$78,000$$

assuming that the car is purchased. What would be the effect on the restricted range if a value of $x = 0$ implies a decision not to purchase the car?

In applied problems, it is quite common for independent variables to be restricted to *integer values*. In the salary function

$$\begin{aligned} y &= f(x) \\ &= 3x + 25 \end{aligned}$$

presented earlier, it is likely that the number of units sold each week, x, would be restricted to integer or whole units. Thus, the domain of $f(x)$ might be defined as

$$D = \{x | x \text{ is an integer } and \ 0 \leq x \leq u\}$$

The lower limit on x is zero, excluding the possibility of negative sales, and u is an upper limit on sales which might reflect such considerations as maximum sales potential within the salesperson's district.

Note that for this function the integer restriction on the domain of f logically results in an integer-valued range. We can also state that the range has a lower limit of 25 and an upper limit equal to $3u + 25$, or

$$R = \{25, 28, 31, 34, \ldots , 3u + 25\}$$

Multivariate Functions

For many mathematical functions the value of a dependent variable depends upon more than one independent variable. Functions which contain more than one independent variable are called *multivariate functions*. In most real-world applications, multivariate functions are the most appropriate to use. For example, stating that profit is dependent only upon the number of units sold probably oversimplifies the situation. Many variables usually interact with one another in order to determine the profit for a firm.

One class of multivariate functions is that of *bivariate functions*. Bivariate functions (as compared with *univariate functions*) have two independent variables. The notation

$$z = f(x, y)$$

suggests that the dependent variable z depends upon the values of the two independent variables x and y. An example of a bivariate function is

$$z = f(x, y) = x^2 - 2xy + y^2 - 5$$

The notation for evaluating multivariate functions is very similar to that of functions of one independent variable. If we wish to evaluate $f(x, y)$ when $x = 0$ and $y = 0$, this is denoted by $f(0, 0)$. For the previous function

$$f(0, 0) = (0)^2 - 2(0)(0) + (0)^2 - 5$$
$$= -5$$
$$f(-10, 5) = (-10)^2 - 2(-10)(5) + 5^2 - 5$$
$$= 100 + 100 + 25 - 5$$
$$= 220$$
$$f(u, v) = u^2 - 2uv + v^2 - 5$$

As the number of independent variables increases, the convention of using a different letter to represent each independent variable can become cumbersome. Consequently, a convenient way of representing multivariate functions is the use of *subscripted variables.* A general way of denoting a function where the value of a dependent variable y depends on the value of n independent variables is

$$y = f(x_1, x_2, x_3, \ldots, x_n)$$

The *subscript* is the positive integer index located to the right of and below each x. The index simply numbers the independent variables and enables you to distinguish one from another. We will frequently make use of subscripted notation in this book.

EXAMPLE 7

Given the function

$$y = f(x_1, x_2, x_3, x_4)$$
$$= x_1^2 - 2x_1x_2 + x_3^2x_4 - 25$$
$$f(-2, 0, 1, 4) = (-2)^2 - 2(-2)(0) + (1)^2(4) - 25$$
$$= 4 - 0 + 4 - 25$$
$$= -17$$

For the remainder of this chapter, the functions discussed will contain one independent variable. Later in the book we will return to functions involving more than one independent variable.

Section 2.1 Follow-up Exercises

In Exercises 1 to 8 determine (a) $f(0)$, (b) $f(-3)$, (c) $f(2)$, (d) $f(p)$.

1. $f(x) = -4x + 5$ 2. $f(x) = \dfrac{5x}{2} - 1$

3. $f(x) = 3x^2 - x + 4$ 4. $f(x) = 25 - x^2$

5. $f(x) = (x - 1)^3$ 6. $f(x) = x^3 + 30$

7. $f(x) = 10$ 8. $f(t) = t^4 - 5t^2 + 10$

9.   Given $f(x) = x^2 - 2x + 5$, determine $f(-1)$ and $f(a + b)$.

10.   Given $f(x) = 25 - 3x + 2x^2$, determine $f(0)$ and $f(a - b)$.

In Exercises 11 to 20 determine the domain of the function.

11. $f(x) = 5$ 12. $f(x) = 25 - x^2$

13. $f(x) = \sqrt{25 - x^2}$ 14. $f(x) = 3x - 5$

15 $f(x) = (x - 3)/(x^3 - 27)$

16 $f(x) = (x^2 - 25)/(x^2 - 9)$

17 $f(x) = |x|$

18 $f(x) = \sqrt{x - 9}/(x^3 - 4x)$

19 $f(x) = \sqrt{x^2 - 4}/(x^3 + x^2 - 6x)$

20 $f(x) = \sqrt{x}/(x - 5)$

21 The function $C(x) = 25x + 50,000$ expresses the total cost $C(x)$ (in dollars) of manufacturing x units of a product. If the maximum number of units which can be produced equals 20,000, state the restricted domain and range for this cost function.

22 The function $q = f(p) = 200,000 - 25p$ is a *demand function* which expresses the quantity demanded of a product q as a function of the price charged for the product p, stated in dollars. Determine the restricted domain and range for this function.

23 The function $q = f(p) = 150,000 - 30p$ is a demand function which expresses the quantity demanded of a product q as a function of the price charged for the product p, stated in dollars. Determine the restricted domain and range for this function.

24 An insurance company has a simplified method for determining the annual premium for a term life insurance policy. A flat annual fee of $25 is charged for all policies *plus* $2 for each thousand dollars of the amount of the policy. For example, a $20,000 policy would cost $25 for the fixed fee plus $40 which corresponds to the face value of the policy. If p equals the annual premium in dollars and x equals the face value of the policy (stated in thousands of dollars), determine the function which can be used to compute annual premiums.

25 In Exercise 24, assume that the smallest policy which will be issued is a $10,000 policy and the largest is a $200,000 policy. Determine the restricted domain and range for the function found in Exercise 24.

26 The local electric company uses the following method for computing monthly electric bills for one class of customers. A monthly service charge of $3 is assessed for each customer. In addition, the company charges $0.08 per kilowatt hour. If c equals the monthly charge stated in dollars and k equals the number of kilowatt hours used during a month, (*a*) determine the function which expresses a customer's monthly charge as a function of the number of kilowatt hours, and (*b*) use this function to compute the monthly charge for a customer who uses 725 kilowatt hours.

27 Referring to Exercise 26, assume that the method for computing customer bills applies for customers who use between 200 and 1,500 kilowatt hours per month. Determine the restricted domain and range for the function in that exercise.

28 Given $f(x_1, x_2, x_3) = x_1^3 + 3x_1^2x_2 - 4x_2x_3 - 10$, determine (*a*) $f(0, 2, -3)$, (*b*) $f(-2, 1, 5)$.

29 Given $f(x_1, x_2) = x_1^2 - 2x_1x_2 + 2x_2^2 + 5$, determine (*a*) $f(-2, 4)$, (*b*) $f(3, 4)$, (*c*) $f(a + b, a - b)$.

30 Given $f(x_1, x_2, x_3, x_4) = 3x_1x_2 - 5x_2x_4 - x_1x_3x_4$, determine (*a*) $f(0, 1, 0, 1)$, (*b*) $f(2, 1, 2, -3)$.

31 Given $f(a, b, c, d) = 3ab - a^2bd + 3c^2d$, determine (*a*) $f(1, 2, 3, 4)$, (*b*) $f(2, 0, 1, 5)$.

2.2 TYPES OF FUNCTIONS

Functions can be classified according to their structural characteristics. A discussion of some of the more common functions follows. A more thorough treatment of these functions is provided in Chaps. 5, 11, and 15.

Constant Functions

A *constant function* has the general form

$$y = f(x) = a_0 \qquad (2.2)$$

where a_0 is real. For example, the function

$$y = f(x) = 20$$

is a constant function. Regardless of the value of x, the range consists of the single value 20. That is,

$$f(-10) = 20$$
$$f(1{,}000) = 20$$
$$f(a + b) = 20$$

As shown in Fig. 2.3, every value in the domain maps into the same value in the range for constant functions.

Linear Functions

A *linear function* has the general form

$$y = f(x) = a_1 x + a_0 \qquad (2.3)$$

where a_0 and a_1 are real. The function

$$y = f(x) = -2x + 15$$

is a linear function with $a_1 = -2$ and $a_0 = 15$. We will focus upon this important class of functions in Chap. 5.

Quadratic Functions

A *quadratic function* has the general form

$$y = a_2 x^2 + a_1 x + a_0 \qquad (2.4)$$

where a_2, a_1, and a_0 are real and $a_2 \neq 0$. The function

$$y = f(x) = 3x^2 - 20x + 100$$

is a quadratic function with $a_2 = 3$, $a_1 = -20$, and $a_0 = 100$. The function

$$y = f(x) = -\frac{x^2}{2}$$

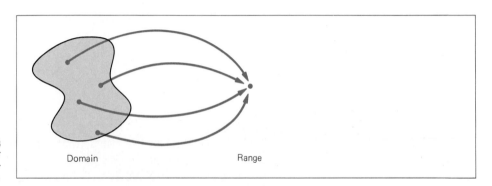

FIGURE 2.3 Mapping for constant function.

Domain   Range

is a quadratic function with $a_0 = a_1 = 0$ and $a_2 = -\frac{1}{2}$. This class of functions will be examined in detail in Chap. 11.

> **NOTE**
>
> In generalizing these first three classes of functions, subscripted coefficients a_0, a_1, and a_2 have been used. The letters a, b, and c (or any other set of letters) could have been used. However, the subscripted notation has been chosen to conserve on the number of different letters needed. There also is a relationship between a subscript and the exponent on each term; the subscript corresponds to the exponent. (The constant a_0 can be rewritten as $a_0 x^0$ for $x \neq 0$. Agree?)

Cubic Functions

A *cubic function* has the general form

$$y = f(x) = a_3 x^3 + a_2 x^2 + a_1 x + a_0 \tag{2.5}$$

where a_3, a_2, a_1, and a_0 are real and $a_3 \neq 0$. The function

$$y = f(x) = x^3 - 40x^2 + 25x - 1{,}000$$

is a cubic function with $a_3 = 1$, $a_2 = -40$, $a_1 = 25$, and $a_0 = -1{,}000$.

Polynomial Functions

Each of the previous functions is an example of a polynomial function. A *polynomial function of degree n* has the general form

$$y = f(x) = a_n x^n + a_{n-1} x^{n-1} + \cdots + a_1 x + a_0 \tag{2.6}$$

where a_n, a_{n-1}, . . . , a_1, a_0 are real and $a_n \neq 0$. The exponent on each x must be a *nonnegative integer* and the degree of the polynomial is the highest power (exponent) in the function. The function

$$y = f(x) = x^5$$

is a polynomial function of degree 5 with $a_0 = a_1 = a_2 = a_3 = a_4 = 0$ and $a_5 = 1$.

You should observe that constant, linear, quadratic, and cubic functions are polynomial functions of degree 0, 1, 2, and 3, respectively.

Rational Functions

A *rational function* has the general form

$$y = f(x) = \frac{g(x)}{h(x)} \tag{2.7}$$

where g and h are both polynomial functions. Rational functions are so named because of their ratio structure. The function

$$y = f(x) = \frac{2x}{5x^3 - 2x + 10}$$

is an illustration of a rational function where $g(x) = 2x$ and $h(x) = 5x^3 - 2x + 10$.

Exponential Functions

An *exponential function* is one in which the independent variable appears in the exponent. If an exponential function has the form $y = f(x)$, x appears as either an exponent or part of an exponent. There are different classes of exponential functions, each having unique structural characteristics. The following are examples of exponential functions:

$$y = f(x) = \left(\frac{1}{2}\right)^x$$
$$y = f(x) = 5e^x \quad \text{where } e = 2.71828 \ldots$$

Exponential functions have many important applications in business and economics. These functions will be examined in detail in Chapter 15.

Logarithmic Functions

A *logarithmic function* expresses the value of the dependent variable in terms of the logarithm of a function the independent variable. The following are examples of logarithmic functions:

$$y = f(x) = \log_{10} x$$
$$y = f(x) = 5 \log_e x$$

As is true of exponential functions, logarithmic functions have many important applications in business and economics. We will revisit these functions in Chapter 15.

Combinations of Functions

Aside from the functional forms mentioned thus far, functions may be combined algebraically to form a resultant function. If

$$f(x) = 3x - 5 \qquad g(x) = x^2 - 2x + 1 \qquad h(x) = 2^x \qquad \text{and} \qquad j(x) = \log_e x$$

these functions can be combined in the following ways to form new functions:

1 $p(x) = f(x) + g(x) = (3x - 5) + (x^2 - 2x + 1) = x^2 + x - 4$

2 $q(x) = h(x) - j(x) = 2^x - \log_e x$

3 $r(x) = f(x)h(x) = (3x - 5)(2^x) = 3x(2^x) - 5(2^x)$

4 $s(x) = h(x)/j(x) = 2^x/\log_e x$

Composite Functions

In addition to combining functions algebraically to form new functions, component functions can be related in another way. A *composite function* exists when one function can be viewed as a function of another function.

If $y = g(u)$ and $u = h(x)$, the composite function $y = f(x) = g(h(x))$ is created by substituting $h(x)$ into the function $g(u)$ wherever u appears. *And, for $f(x) = g(h(x))$ to be defined, x must be in the domain of h and $h(x)$ must be in the domain of g.* That is, the input value x must allow for a unique and definable output value u and the resulting u when input to $g(u)$ must yield a unique and definable output y. Figure 2.4 illustrates schematically the nature of composite functions.

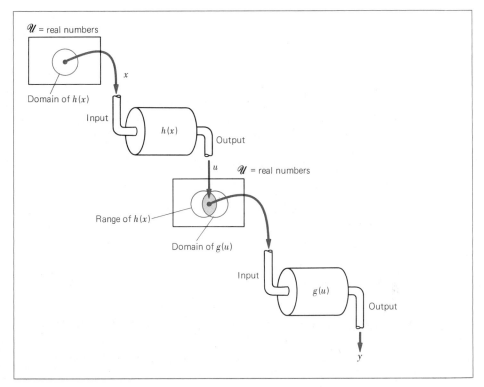

FIGURE 2.4
The nature of composite functions.

To illustrate these functions, assume that the function

$$y = g(x) = 2x + 50$$

indicates that a salesperson's weekly salary y is determined by the number of units x sold each week. Suppose that an analysis has revealed that the quantity sold each week by a salesperson is dependent upon the price charged for the product. This function h is given by the rule

$$x = h(p) = 150 - 2.5p$$

where p equals the price, stated in dollars.

Thus, to compute a salesperson's salary, the initial *input* is the selling price for the given week. This will determine the *output* for $h(p)$, the number of units expected to be sold. This output becomes an input which can be substituted into $g(x)$ to determine the weekly salary. These relationships are illustrated in Fig. 2.5a. For example, suppose that the price during a given week is \$30. The number of units expected to be sold during the week is

$$x = h(30)$$
$$= 150 - 2.5(30) = 150 - 75 = 75 \text{ units}$$

Since the number of units expected to be sold is known, the weekly salary is computed as

$$y = g(75)$$
$$= 2(75) + 50 = \$200$$

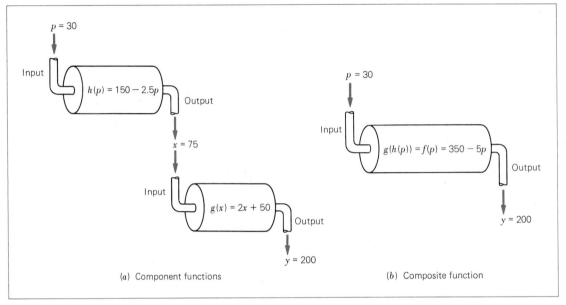

(a) Component functions   (b) Composite function

FIGURE 2.5

Since weekly salary depends upon the number of units sold each week and the number of units sold depends upon the price per unit, weekly salary actually can be stated directly as a function of the price per unit. Or,

$$y = f(p) = g(h(p))$$

To define this function, we substitute $h(p)$ into $g(x)$ wherever x appears. That is,

$$y = 2(150 - 2.5p) + 50$$
$$= 300 - 5p + 50$$

or $\qquad\qquad y = f(p) = 350 - 5p$

The function $f(p)$ is a composite function, having been formed by combining $g(x)$ and $h(p)$. We can compute the expected weekly salary directly from $f(p)$ if we know the selling price for a given week as shown in Fig. 2.5b. At a price of \$30,

$$y = f(30)$$
$$= 350 - 5(30) = 350 - 150 = \$200$$

which is the same value as determined before.

EXAMPLE 8

If $y = g(u) = u^2 - 2u + 10$ and $u = h(x) = x + 1$, the composite function $y = f(x) = g(h(x))$ is found by substituting $h(x)$ into $g(u)$ wherever u appears.

$$y = f(x) = g(h(x))$$
$$= g(x + 1)$$
$$= (x + 1)^2 - 2(x + 1) + 10$$
$$= x^2 + 2x + 1 - 2x - 2 + 10$$
$$= x^2 + 9$$

EXAMPLE 9

If $y = g(u) = 2u^3$ and $u = h(x) = x^2 - 2x + 5$, determine (a) $g(h(x))$, (b) $g(h(2))$, and (c) $g(h(-3))$

SOLUTION

(a) $y = g(h(x)) = 2(x^2 - 2x + 5)^3$

(b) $g(h(2)) = 2[(2)^2 - 2(2) + 5]^3 = 2(5)^3 = 2(125) = 250$

(c) $g(h(-3)) = 2[(-3)^2 - 2(-3) + 5]^3 = 2(20)^3 = 2(8,000) = 16,000$

Implicit Functions

In this chapter we have suggested that functions portray a dependence between two or more variables. For a function of the form $y = f(x)$, y can be said to be an *explicit function* of the independent variable x. The functional notation suggests the nature of the dependency. An example is the function

$$y = f(x)$$
$$y = 5x + 100$$

or

However, if this equation is rearranged to yield

$$y - 5x - 100 = 0 \qquad \textbf{(2.8)}$$

a relationship between x and y is suggested, but it is not explicit that y depends on x. Equation (2.8) can be thought of as having the general form

$$f(x, y) = 0 \qquad \textbf{(2.9)}$$

An *implicit function* is defined if a functional relationship is implied by an equation of the form (2.9). Equation (2.8) might suggest that y is an implicit function of x or that x is an implicit function of y. In a given application, knowledge of the application itself can make it more obvious which variable is to be thought of as the dependent variable.

Some implicit functions can be rewritten in explicit form. For example, the implicit function

$$2xy + 3y - 100 = 0$$

can be rewritten as

$$y(2x + 3) = 100$$
$$y = f(x) = 100/(2x + 3)$$

or

In other cases, the implied function cannot be stated in explicit form. The function

$$x^3 - xy - 3y^3 = 0$$

cannot be rewritten in the explicit form

$$y = f(x) \text{ or } x = g(y)$$

EXAMPLE 10

Economists and consumers alike recognize that there usually is a relationship between the price charged for certain commodities and the quantity demanded. The relationship between the two variables typically is an *inverse relationship;* that is, the higher the unit price, the lower the demand for the commodity (there are exceptions to this, of course, depending upon such factors as the type of commodity, the income of the consumer, etc.).

Consider the relation

$$3p + 6q - 500 = 0 \tag{2.10}$$

where p = unit price, dollars
$\quad\quad q$ = quantity demanded units

Depending on your perspective, Eq. (2.10) can imply that price p is an implicit function of quantity demanded q or that quantity demanded is an implicit function of price. The explicit forms of these functions are easily derived from Eq. (2.10) as

$$p = f(q) = \frac{500 - 6q}{3} \tag{2.11}$$

and

$$q = h(p) = \frac{500 - 3p}{6} \tag{2.12}$$

When an implicit function $f(x, y) = 0$ yields two explicit functions of the form

$$y = f(x)$$

and
$$x = g(y)$$

$f(x)$ and $g(y)$ are said to be *inverse functions.* Note that x is the independent variable for the function f but x is the dependent variable for the function g. Inverse functions of this form have the property that each value of x yields a unique value of y *and* each value of y yields a unique value of x. Using the notation of inverse functions we can say that the function f has an inverse, $x = f^{-1}(y)$, which is read "x is an inverse function of y" (be advised that f^{-1} *does not mean* $1/f$ in this situation). Similarly we can say that the function g has an inverse $y = g^{-1}(x)$. In Example 10 $f(q)$ and $h(p)$ are inverse functions.

Section 2.2 Follow-up Exercises

In the following exercises, classify each function by type.

1 $f(x) = -\frac{1}{2}$ 	2 $f(x) = \frac{1}{2}x - \frac{1}{4}$
3 $f(x) = 35 - 4.5x$ 	4 $f(x) = x^2$
5 $f(x) = (5 - x)/x$ 	6 $f(x) = x^3 - 15$
7 $f(x) = 45 + 3x^2 - 5x$ 	8 $f(b) = b^3/10$
9 $g(h) = \frac{1}{4}$ 	10 $f(n) = (\frac{1}{2})^n$
11 $f(x) = \log_{10}x$ 	12 $f(x) = (3)^{x^2}$
13 $f(x) = x^5 - 4x^2$ 	14 $f(v) = v/2$
15 $h(u) = \log_2(u^2 - 5)$ 	16 $g(h) = 5h/(1 - h^3)$
17 $f(x) = 1/(3x^2 - 4x + 6)$ 	18 $f(x) = (2)^{20}$

19 Given the general form of a constant function stated by Eq. (2.2), determine the domain for these functions.

20 Given the general form of polynomial functions stated by Eq. (2.6), determine the domain for these functions.

21   Given the general form of a rational function stated by Eq. (2.7), determine the domain for these functions.

22   If $y = g(u) = 3u + 5$ and $u = h(x) = x - 3$, determine (a) $g(h(x))$, (b) $g(h(3))$, (c) $g(h(0))$.

23   Given $y = g(u) = u^2 - 2u + 1$ and $u = h(x) = x + 5$, determine (a) $g(h(x))$, (b) $g(h(-2))$, (c) $g(h(1))$.

24   If $y = g(u) = u^3 - 2u$ and $u = h(x) = u^2$, determine (a) $g(h(x))$, (b) $g(h(0))$, (c) $g(h(2))$.

25   Given $c = h(s) = s^2 + 5s - 3$ and $s = f(t) = 20$, determine (a) $h(f(t))$, (b) $h(f(3))$, (c) $h(f(-2))$.

26   Given the implicit function $3x - 2y + 15 = 0$, determine (if possible) the explicit functions $y = f(x)$ and $x = g(y)$.

27   Given the implicit function $3xy^2 + 4y = 0$, determine (if possible) the explicit functions $y = f(x)$ and $x = g(y)$.

28   Given the implicit function $25x^2y^2 - xy^2 - 10 = 0$, determine (if possible) the explicit functions $y = f(x)$ and $x = g(y)$.

29   Given the implicit function $x^2y - 20 = 0$, determine (if possible) the explicit functions $y = f(x)$ and $x = g(y)$.

30   **Demand Functions**   Consider the relation $5p + 10q - 25,000 = 0$, where p equals the price of a product in dollars and q equals the quantity demanded in units. Determine the corresponding explicit demand functions $q = f(p)$ and $p = h(q)$.

31   **Supply Functions**   Supply functions convey information about the quantity of a commodity that suppliers are willing to bring to the marketplace and the price the marketplace is willing to pay for the commodity. Consider the relation $-20p + 5q + 2,000 = 0$, where p equals the price the market will pay for a unit of a commodity (stated in dollars) and q equals the quantity (in units) that a supplier is willing to bring to the market at price p. Determine the corresponding explicit supply functions $q = f(p)$ and $p = h(q)$.

2.3   GRAPHICAL REPRESENTATION OF FUNCTIONS

Throughout this book the visual model will be used as often as possible to reinforce your understanding of different mathematical concepts. The visual model will most frequently take the form of a graphical representation. In this section we discuss the graphical representation of functions involving two variables.

Rectangular Coordinate System

Consider a plane onto which are drawn a horizontal line and a vertical line as in Fig. 2.6. The two lines are *real number lines,* and they intersect at their respective zero points. The horizontal line is called the *horizontal axis.* As labeled in Fig. 2.6 it is more commonly referred to as the *x axis.* The vertical line is the *vertical axis* and in this figure would be called the *y axis.* The two axes together are referred to as *coordinate axes.* Note that the horizontal axis is scaled with positive values to the right of the vertical axis and negative values to the left. Similarly the vertical axis is scaled with positive values above the horizontal axis and negative values below.

The plane containing the coordinate axes is often called a *coordinate plane* or *cartesian plane.* The coordinate plane can be thought of as consisting of an infi-

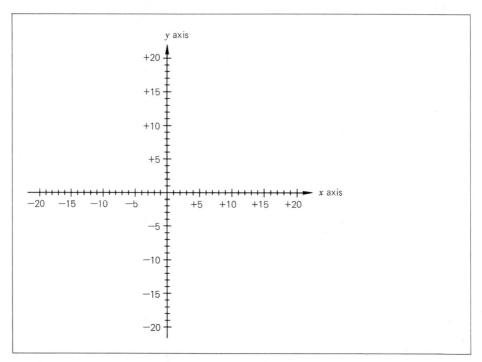

FIGURE 2.6
Cartesian plane.

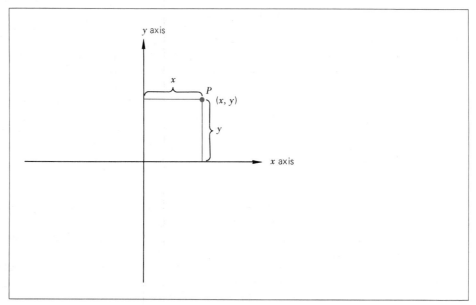

FIGURE 2.7
Rectangular
coordinate
system.

nite number of points, each point specified by its location relative to the two axes. The location of any point p is specified by the *ordered pair* of values (x, y). The first member of the ordered pair is known as the *abscissa,* or more commonly as the *x coordinate.* As indicated in Fig. 2.7 the abscissa is the *directed distance* along a horizontal line drawn from the vertical axis to P. The second

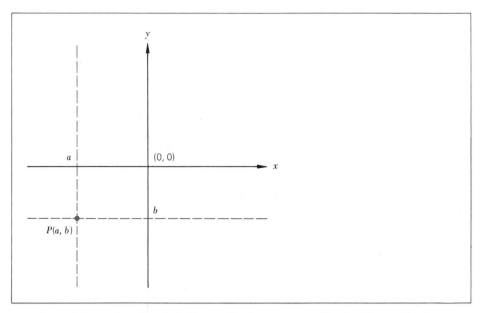

FIGURE 2.8
Locating point P
with coordinates
(a, b).

member of the ordered pair is the *ordinate, or y coordinate.* The ordinate represents the directed distance along a vertical line drawn from the horizontal axis to P. Together, the *coordinates (x, y)* specify the location or address of a point P in a coordinate plane. The system of coordinates used in a coordinate plane is called a *cartesian,* or *rectangular, coordinate system.*

To locate a point P having coordinates (a, b), first draw an imaginary vertical line through the horizontal axis at a. Then draw an imaginary horizontal line through the vertical axis at b. Point P occurs at the intersection of these two lines, as shown in Fig. 2.8. Notice for P that $a < 0$ and $b < 0$.

Figure 2.9 is a graphical representation of several sample points. The point of intersection of the two axes has coordinates $(0, 0)$ and is known as the *origin.* Also convince yourself that *the x coordinate of any point on the y axis is 0 and the y coordinate of any point on the x axis is 0.* Finally, note that the axes divide the coordinate plane into *quadrants.* Indicated are the sign conditions for coordinates of points located in each quadrant.

Graphing Functions in Two Dimensions

Functions of one or two independent variables can be represented graphically. This graphical portrayal brings an added dimension to the understanding of mathematical functions. You will come to appreciate the increased understanding and insight that graphs provide.

Graphical representation requires a dimension for each independent variable contained in a function and one for the functional value, or dependent variable. Thus, functions of one independent variable are graphed in two dimensions, or *2-space.* Functions of two independent variables can be graphed in three dimensions, or *3-space.* However, it is considerably more difficult to graph in three dimensions than in two. When a function contains more than three variables, the graphical representation is lost. Unless you have some unusual sixth sense, you will not be able to conceptualize or graph in four or more dimensions.

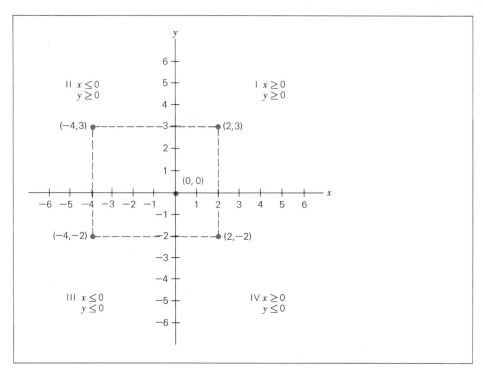

FIGURE 2.9
Sample points
in the four
quadrants.

Functions which contain two variables are graphed on a set of rectangular coordinate axes. Typically the vertical axis is selected to represent the dependent variable in the function; the horizontal axis is usually selected to represent the independent variable.

To graph a mathematical function, one can simply *assign* different values for the independent variable and *compute* the corresponding value for the dependent variable. Each ordered pair of values for the two variables represents values of x and y which satisfy the function. It also specifies the coordinates of a single point which lies on the graph of the function. To *sketch* the function, determine an *adequate number of ordered pairs* of values which satisfy the function; locate their coordinates relative to a pair of axes. *Connect these points by a smooth curve to determine a sketch of the graph of the function.* (Although this approach will suffice for now, later we learn more efficient ways of sketching functions).

NOTE

The most orderly way to generate the pairs of points which satisfy a function is to set up a table with one row or column containing selected values for the independent variable and another containing the computed values for the dependent variable.

EXAMPLE 11

To sketch the graph of the *linear* function

$$y = f(x) = 2x - 4$$

TABLE 2.1

x	−4	−3	−2	−1	0	+1	+2	+3	+4
y	−12	−10	−8	−6	−4	−2	0	2	4

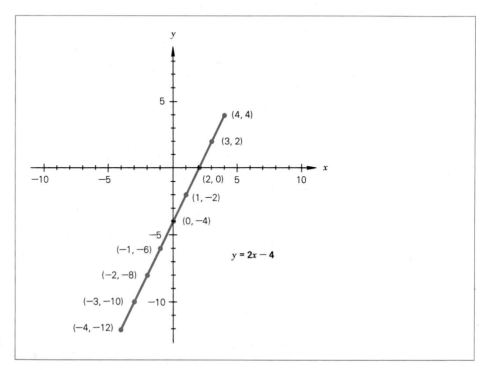

FIGURE 2.10
Sketch of
$f(x) = 2x - 4$.

the first step is to arbitrarily select values for x and compute the corresponding values for y. A set of sample values is shown in Table 2.1. Next, if these values of x and y are envisioned as coordinates, the points associated with each pair of coordinates should be located as in Fig. 2.10. Once the points have been plotted, they are connected with a smooth curve, which in this case is suspiciously straight. If we wish to know how the function appears for values of x less than -4 or greater than $+4$, we should compute values of y for selected values of x within those regions of the domain.

POINT FOR THOUGHT AND DISCUSSION

Earlier we said that the graph of a function can assist in reaching conclusions about the range of that function. By observation, you should conclude that the domain of $f(x) = 2x - 4$ is the set of real numbers. It appears from the set of sample data points in Fig. 2.10 that y can be made as large as we wish by choosing an appropriately large value for x. And, it seems that y can be made as negative as desired by choosing an appropriately large negative value for x. Thus, we can conclude that *the range of $f(x)$ is the set of real numbers*.

TABLE 2.2

v	−6	−5	−4	−3	−2	−1	0	1	2	3	4
u	140	50	−20	−70	−100	−110	−100	−70	−20	50	140

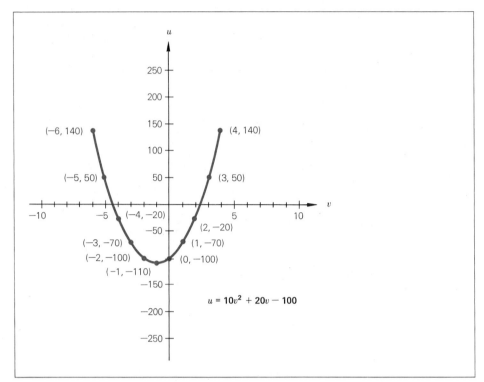

FIGURE 2.11
Sketch of
$f(v) = 10v^2 + 20v − 100$.

EXAMPLE 12

To sketch the *quadratic function*

$$u = f(v)$$
$$= 10v^2 + 20v − 100$$

sample pairs of values for u and v are computed as shown in Table 2.2. These points are plotted in Fig. 2.11, and have been connected to provide a sketch of the function. Note that the horizontal axis is labeled with the independent variable v and the vertical axis with the dependent variable u. As opposed to the linear function in the previous example, this quadratic function obviously cannot be represented by a straight line.

NOTE

A few points should be made regarding the graphing of functions. First, it is always useful to determine the set of sample points you want to graph prior to scaling the axes. By doing this, you determine the range of values which you wish to graph for the two variables. Once you have determined these ranges, you can determine the appropriate scale to use on each axis. A second point is that the two axes need not be scaled the same. The units on one axis may represent millions and those on the other axis single units. Similarly, the intervals used to scale each axis need not be the same width. Examine the scaling in Fig. 2.11. If you overlook this possibility, your graph may run beyond the boundaries of your paper. (The author has had situations during class in which graphs required points below the floor or above the ceiling.) Finally, the unit of measurement for one variable does not have to be the same as that of the other variable. The cost function in the patrol car example would show cost *in dollars* on one axis and miles driven on the other axis.

POINT FOR THOUGHT AND DISCUSSION

What would be the effect on the shape of the graph in the last example if the vertical axis is scaled the same as the horizontal axis? What if the horizontal axis is scaled the same as the vertical axis? Given Fig. 2.11, determine the range of $f(v)$.

EXAMPLE 13

To sketch the *cubic function*

$$y = f(x) = x^3$$

sample points are computed as shown in Table 2.3.

These points are plotted, resulting in the sketch of f in Fig. 2.12.

EXAMPLE 14

In some instances, the functional relationship existing between variables is described by more than one equation. To illustrate, assume that y equals a salesperson's weekly salary in dollars and that x equals the number of units of a product sold during the week. Given that the weekly salary depends upon the number of units sold, assume that the following function applies.

$$y = f(x) = \begin{cases} 2x + 50 & \text{where } 0 \leq x < 40 \\ 2.25x + 75 & \text{where } x \geq 40 \end{cases}$$

If the number of units sold during a week is less than 40, the salesperson receives a base salary of $50 and a commission of $2 per unit sold. If the number of units sold during a week is 40 or more, a bonus of $25 raises the base portion of the salary to $75. In addition, the commission on *all* units increases to $2.25 per unit.

Figure 2.13 illustrates the graph of the function. Note that the graph uses quadrant I only, where x and y are both nonnegative. The sketch of the function is in two linear "pieces." Each piece of the graph is valid for a certain portion of the domain of the function. The open circle (○) at the end of the first segment is used to indicate that that point is *not* part of the graph. It corresponds to the break in the function at $x = 40$. The point

TABLE 2.3

x	0	1	2	3	−1	−2	−3
y	0	1	8	27	−1	−8	−27

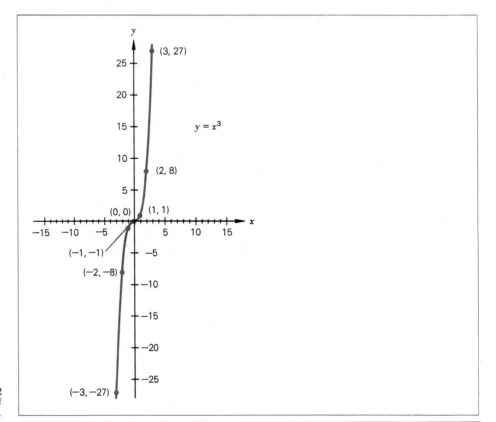

FIGURE 2.12
Sketch of
$f(x) = x^3$.

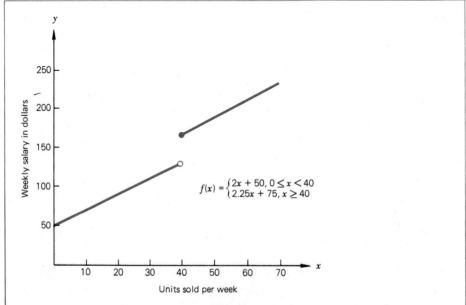

FIGURE 2.13
Piecewise linear
function.

corresponding to $x = 40$ is the first point on the second segment of the function, and this is denoted by the solid circle ($\bullet$).

By the definition of a function, to each element in the domain there should correspond one and only one element in the range. This property allows for a simple graphical check to determine whether a graph represents a mathematical function. If a vertical line is drawn through any value in the domain, it will intersect the graph of the function at one point only. In contrast, if a vertical line intersects a curve at more than one point, the curve is not the graph of a function. The curve in Fig. 2.14 does not represent a function since the dashed vertical line intersects the curve at two points.

In this section we have been introduced to the graphical representation of mathematical functions. The procedure which has been presented must be called a "brute force" method in that it is necessary to determine an "adequate" number of points in order to get a reasonable idea of the shape of the graph of a function. However, it does work! The question of how many points are adequate will be answered with experience. Throughout the text we will continue to gain knowledge about mathematical functions. You will soon come to recognize the structural differences between linear functions and the various nonlinear functions, and with this knowledge will come greater facility and ease in determining a visual or graphical counterpart.

Section 2.3 Follow-up Exercises

Sketch each of the following functions.

1 $f(x) = x - 5$
3 $f(x) = -3x$
5 $f(x) = x^2 - 2x + 1$

2 $f(x) = -4$
4 $f(x) = x^2 - 4$
6 $f(x) = x^3 - 5$

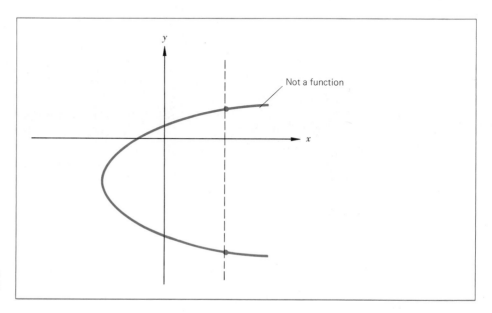

FIGURE 2.14
Graphical test for functions.

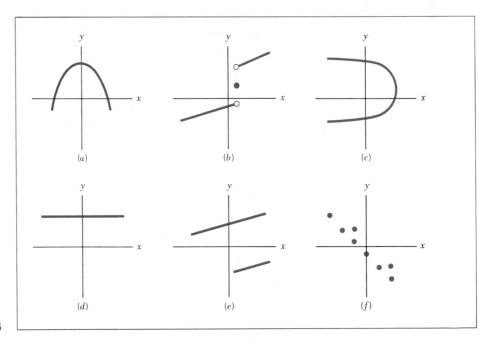

FIGURE 2.15

7 $f(x) = x^3 + 5$ 8 $f(x) = -x^3$

9 $f(x) = \begin{cases} x + 3 & \text{when } x \geq 0 \\ -x + 3 & \text{when } x < 0 \end{cases}$

10 $f(x) = \begin{cases} 2x & \text{when } 0 \leq x \leq 4 \\ x^2 & \text{when } x < 0 \\ 5 & \text{when } x > 4 \end{cases}$

11 In Figure 2.15, identify those graphs which represent functions.

KEY TERMS AND CONCEPTS

abscissa (x coordinate) 66
bivariate function 55
cartesian (rectangular) coordinate
 system 67
composite function 60
constant function 58
coordinate or cartesian plane 65
cubic function 59
dependent variable 51
domain 50
explicit function 63
exponential function 60
function 50
implicit function 63
independent variable 51

linear function 58
logarithmic function 60
mapping 50
multivariate functions 55
ordinate (y coordinate) 67
origin 67
polynomial function 59
quadratic function 58
range 50
rational function 59
real number line 65
restricted domain 55
subscripted variables 56
univariate functions 55

IMPORTANT FORMULAS

$y = f(x) = a_0$ **Constant function**   (2.2)

$y = f(x) = a_1 x + a_0$ **Linear function**   (2.3)

$y = f(x) = a_2 x^2 + a_1 x + a_0$ **Quadratic function**   (2.4)

$y = f(x) = a_3 x^3 + a_2 x^2 + a_1 x + a_0$ **Cubic function**   (2.5)

$y = f(x) = a_n x^n + a_{n-1} x^{n-1} + \cdots + a_1 x + a_0$ **Polynomial function**   (2.6)

$y = f(x) = \dfrac{g(x)}{h(x)}$ for g, h polynomials   **Rational function**   (2.7)

ADDITIONAL EXERCISES

The following exercises are related to Sec. 2.1. In Exercises 1 to 6 determine (a) $f(1)$, (b) $f(-2)$, (c) $f(a - b)$.

1   $f(x) = \frac{1}{2}x - 5$ 2 $f(x) = 5x^2 - 2x + 10$

3   $f(u) = u^3 - 2u^2 + 3u - 3$ 4 $f(t) = \frac{1}{4}$

5   $f(x) = x^2/(1 - x)$ 6 $f(s) = s^4$

In Exercises 7 to 12 determine the domain of the function.

7   $f(x) = \sqrt{x + 6}/(x^2 + x - 12)$ 8 $f(x) = 1/\sqrt{x^2 - 1}$

9   $f(x) = \sqrt{(x - 2)/(x^2 - 16)}$ 10 $f(x) = \sqrt{x^3 - 8}$

11   $f(x) = (2)^x$ 12 $f(x) = e^{x^2}$, where $e = 2.718 \cdots$

13   Given $f(a, b) = 3a^2 - 2ab + 5b^2$, determine (a) $f(-2, 3)$, (b) $f(x + y, x - y)$.

14   Given $f(a, b, c, d) = a^3 - 2abc + cd^2 - 5$, determine (a) $f(-1, 2, 0, 1)$, (b) $f(0, 0, 0, 0)$.

15   A local radio station has been given the exclusive right to promote a concert in the city's civic arena, which seats 22,000 persons. The commission for the radio station is $5,000 plus $0.50 for each ticket sold to the concert.
(a) Determine the function $C = f(n)$, where C equals the commission paid to the radio station, stated in dollars, and n equals the number of tickets sold.
(b) Determine the restricted domain and range for this function.

16   A salesperson has been hired to sell three products. The salesperson is paid on a commission basis, earning $2.50, $3.00, and $2.00 per unit, respectively, for products 1, 2, and 3. In addition, the salesperson receives a base salary of $40 per week. x_j equals the number of units sold per week of product j and s equals the weekly salary in dollars.
(a) Determine the salary function $s = f(x_1, x_2, x_3)$.
(b) If maximum weekly sales for the three products are estimated at 20, 35, and 25 units, respectively, determine the restricted domain and range for the salary function.

The following exercises are related to Sec. 2.2. In Exercises 17 to 24, classify each function by type.

17   $g(u) = u^2/5$ 18 $f(x) = \log_{10} 100$

19   $f(x) = (3x^2 - 5)/(x^3 - 4x + 5)$ 20 $f(x) = (10)^x$

21   $f(t) = t^4 - t^3 - t^2 + t$ 22 $g(h) = \sqrt[3]{h}$

23   $f(x) = (x^3 - 4x^2 + 3x - 10)/5$ 24 $f(x) = 4/(x^3 - 2x + 8)$

25   If $y = g(u) = u^3 - 5u$ and $u = h(x) = x^2 - 4$, determine (a) $g(h(x))$, (b) $g(h(2))$.

26   If $y = g(u) = u - 5$ and $u = h(x) = x^2 - 3x + 6$, determine (a) $g(h(x))$, (b) $g(h(-2))$.

*27   If $y = f(r) = r^2$ and $r = g(s) = s^2 - 4$ and $s = h(x) = x - 3$, determine the composite functions (a) $g(h(x))$, (b) $f(g(h(x)))$.

28   Given the implicit function $10x - 5y + 25 = 0$, determine (if possible) the explicit functions $y = f(x)$ and $x = g(y)$.

29   Given the implicit function $4x^2y - 5y^3 + xy - 5x + 100 = 0$, determine (if possible) the explicit functions $y = f(x)$ and $x = g(y)$.

The following exercises are related to Sec. 2.3. Sketch each of the following functions.

30   $f(x) = 6$ 31 $f(x) = 10 - 2x$

32   $f(x) = -x^2 + 10$ 33 $f(x) = x^4$

34   $f(x) = x^5$

35   $f(x) = \begin{cases} |x| \text{ when} & -2 < x \le 2 \\ x \text{ when} & x \le -2 \text{ and } x > 2 \end{cases}$

CHAPTER TEST

1   Given $f(x) = x^2 - 2x + 9$, determine $f(-3)$ and $f(a + b)$.

2   Determine the domain of the function

$$f(x) = \sqrt{x + 2}/(x^3 - 2x^2 - 3x)$$

3   Define what is meant by the *domain* and *range* of a function.

4   Given the function $y = f(x) = 4x^2 - 3x + 1$, rewrite this function in the implicit form.

5   If $y = g(u) = u^2/(1 - 2u)$ and $u = h(x) = x + 5$, determine the composite functions (a) $g(h(x))$, (b) $g(h(-2))$.

6   Classify each of the following functions by type.
(a) $f(x) = x^6$ (b) $f(x) = (25)^{1/2}$

7   Sketch the function

$$f(x) = \begin{cases} x^2 & \text{when } x \geq 0 \\ -x & \text{when } x < 0 \end{cases}$$

3

LINEAR EQUATIONS

CHAPTER OBJECTIVES

- Provide a thorough understanding of the algebraic and graphical characteristics of linear equations

- Provide the tools which will allow one to determine the equation which represents a linear relationship

- Illustrate a variety of applications of linear equations

When you consider all the areas of study within mathematics, it is possible to distinguish between two major *subsets* — linear mathematics and nonlinear mathematics. In this book we will distinguish between the two areas, and we will spend a good portion of our time examining areas of study within each. In this chapter we begin a discussion of linear mathematics which will be continued in the following five chapters.

Linear mathematics is significant for a number of reasons:

1 Many of the real-world phenomena which we might be interested in representing mathematically either are linear or can be approximated reasonably well by using linear relationships. As a result, linear mathematics is widely used.

2 Given that some method of mathematical analysis, i.e., finding a solution, is needed, the analysis of linear relationships is generally easier than for nonlinear relationships.

3 The methods used in nonlinear mathematics are often similar to, or extensions of, those used in linear mathematics. Consequently, having a good understanding of linear mathematics is of benefit in the study of nonlinear mathematics.

3.1 CHARACTERISTICS OF LINEAR EQUATIONS

General Form

DEFINITION:

LINEAR EQUATION WITH TWO VARIABLES

A linear equation involving two variables x and y has the standard form

$$ax + by = c \qquad (3.1)$$

where a, b, and c are real numbers *and* a and b cannot both equal zero.

Notice that the exponents are (implicitly) 1 for each variable in a linear equation. The presence of terms having exponents other than 1 (for example, x^2) would exclude an equation from being considered linear. The presence of terms involving a product of the two variables (for example, $2xy$) would also exclude an equation from being considered linear.

The following are all examples of linear equations involving two variables:

	Eq. (3.1) Parameters		
	a	b	c
$2x + 5y = -5$	2	5	-5
$-x + \frac{1}{2}y = 0$	-1	$\frac{1}{2}$	0
$x/3 = 25$	$\frac{1}{3}$	0	25
(*Note:* $x/3 = \frac{1}{3}x$)			
$2s - 4t = -\frac{1}{2}$	2	-4	$-\frac{1}{2}$

(*Note:* The names of the variables may be different from x and y.)

The following are examples of equations which are *not* linear. Can you explain why?

$$2x + 3xy - 4y = 10$$
$$x + y^2 = 6$$
$$\sqrt{u} + \sqrt{v} = -10$$

In attempting to identify the form of an equation (linear versus nonlinear), an equation is linear if it *can be* written in the form of Eq. (3.1). A quick glance at the equation

$$2x = \frac{5x - 2y}{4} + 10$$

might lead to the false conclusion that it is not linear. However, multiplying both sides of the equation by 4 and moving all variables to the left-hand side yields $3x + 2y = 40$, which is in the form of Eq. (3.1).

DEFINITION:

LINEAR EQUATION WITH n VARIABLES

A linear equation involving n variables $x_1, x_2, x_3, \ldots, x_n$ has the general form

$$a_1x_1 + a_2x_2 + a_3x_3 + \cdots + a_nx_n = b \qquad (3.2)$$

where $a_1, a_2, a_3, \ldots, a_n$ and b are real numbers and *not all* $a_1, a_2, a_3, \ldots, a_n$ equal zero.

We will spend much of our time in this book discussing equations and mathematical functions that involve two variables. Aside from the fact that the arithmetic is a little easier, another important reason for concentrating on the two-variable situation is that these functions can be graphed to provide a visual frame of reference. Equation (3.2), however, generalizes the definition of a linear equation for those instances when we venture beyond two variables.

Representation Using Linear Equations

Given a linear equation having the form $ax + by = c$, the **solution set** for the equation is the set of all ordered pairs (x, y) which satisfy the equation. Using set notation the solution set S can be defined by

$$\boxed{S = \{(x, y) \mid ax + by = c\}} \qquad (3.3)$$

Verbally, this equation states that the solution set S consists of elements (x, y) such that $ax + by = c$. For any linear equation, S is an infinite set; that is, *there are an infinite number of pairs of values (x, y) which satisfy any linear equation involving two variables.*

To determine any pair of values which satisfy a linear equation, assume *any* value for one of the variables, substitute this value into the equation, and solve for the corresponding value of the other variable.

EXAMPLE 1 ▬▬▬▬▬▬▬▬▬▬▬▬▬▬▬▬▬

Given the equation

$$2x + 4y = 16$$

(*a*) Determine *any* pair of values which satisfies the equation.
(*b*) Determine the pair of values which satisfies the equation when $x = -2$.
(*c*) Determine the pair of values which satisfies the equation when $y = 0$.

SOLUTION

(*a*) According to the procedure specified, we might let $x = 0$. Substituting this value into the equation, we get

$$2(0) + 4y = 16$$
or
$$4y = 16$$
and
$$y = 4$$

Thus, one pair of values satisfying the equation is $x = 0$ and $y = 4$, or $(0, 4)$.
(*b*) Substituting $x = -2$ into the equation, we have

$$2(-2) + 4y = 16$$
$$4y = 20$$
and
$$y = 5$$

When $x = -2$, the pair of values satisfying the equation is $x = -2$ and $y = 5$, or $(-2, 5)$.

(c) Substituting $y = 0$ into the equation gives

$$2x + 4(0) = 16$$
$$2x = 16$$

and

$$x = 8$$

When $y = 0$, the pair of values satisfying the equation is $(8, 0)$. If $S = \{(x, y)|2x + 4y = 16\}$, we can make the statement that

$$\{(0, 4), (-2, 5), (8, 0)\} \subset S$$

EXAMPLE 2

Product Mix   A company manufactures two different products. For the coming week 120 hours of labor are available for manufacturing the two products. Work-hours can be allocated for production of either product. In addition, since both products generate a good profit, management is interested in using all 120 hours during the week. Each unit produced of product A requires 3 hours of labor and each unit of product B requires 2.5 hours.

(a) Define an equation which states that total work-hours used for producing x units of product A and y units of product B equal 120.

(b) How many units of product A can be produced if 30 units of product B are produced?

(c) If management decides to produce one product only, what is the maximum quantity which can be produced of product A? The maximum of product B?

SOLUTION

(a) We can define our variables as follows:

x = number of units produced of product A
y = number of units produced of product B

The desired equation has the following structure.

| Total hours used in producing products A and B = 120 | (3.4)

What we need, then, is the expression for the left-hand side of the equation.

NOTE

Do you remember the discussion of mental models in Chap. 2? You may well have a mental model for the left side of this equation—it is simply a matter of recognizing its form and stating it. Try it by asking yourself how many hours would be used if you produced 1 unit of each product? 2 units of each? 10 units of product A and 20 of product B? Look back at the definitions of x and y and state the model that allows you to answer these questions.

As you reason through the structure of the let side of Eq. (3.4), the final equation might evolve as follows:

$$\boxed{\begin{array}{ccc} \text{Total hours used} & & \text{total hours used} \\ \text{in producing} & + & \text{in producing} \\ \text{product } A & & \text{product } B \end{array} = 120}$$ (3.5)

Since the total hours required to produce either product equals hours required per unit produced times number of units produced, Eq. (3.5) reduces to

$$\boxed{3x + 2.5y = 120}$$ (3.6)

Is that the answer you reached?

(b) If 30 units of product B are produced, then $y = 30$. Therefore

$$3x + 2.5(30) = 120$$
$$3x = 45$$
$$x = 15 \text{ units}$$

A pair of values satisfying Eq. (3.6) is (15, 30). In other words, *one combination* of the two products which will fully utilize the 120 hours is 15 units of product A and 30 units of product B.

(c) If management decides to manufacture product A only, no units of product B are produced, or $y = 0$. If $y = 0$,

$$3x + 2.5(0) = 120$$
$$3x = 120$$
$$x = 40$$

Therefore 40 is the maximum number of units of product A which can be produced using the 120 hours.

If management decides to manufacture product B only, $x = 0$ and

or
$$3(0) + 2.5y = 120$$
$$y = 48 \text{ units}$$

EXAMPLE 3 ▬▬▬▬▬▬▬▬▬▬▬▬▬▬▬▬▬▬▬▬▬▬▬

We stated earlier that there are an infinite number of pairs of values (x, y) which satisfy any linear equation. In Example 2, are there any members of the solution set which might not be realistic in terms of what the equation represents?

SOLUTION

In Example 2, x and y represent the number of units produced of the two products. Since *negative* production is not possible, negative values of x and y are not meaningful. There are negative values which satisfy Eq. (3.5). For instance, if $y = 60$, then

$$3x + 2.5(60) = 120$$
$$3x = -30$$
$$x = -10$$

In addition to negative values, it is possible to have decimal or fractional values for x

and y. For example, if $y = 40$,

$$3x + 2.5(40) = 120$$
$$3x = 20$$
$$x = 6\tfrac{2}{3}$$

Given all the pairs of *nonnegative* values for x and y which satisfy Eq. (3.6), noninteger values may not be meaningful given the nature of the products.

POINT FOR THOUGHT AND DISCUSSION

Give examples of types of products where only integer values would be reasonable. Give an example of a product for which noninteger values are reasonable.

Generalizing for *n*-Variable Linear Equations

Given a linear equation involving n variables, as defined by Eq. (3.2), the solution set S can be specified as

$$S = \{(x_1, x_2, x_3, \ldots, x_n) | a_1x_1 + a_2x_2 + a_3x_3 + \cdots + a_nx_n = b\} \quad (3.7)$$

As with the two-variable case, there are an infinite number of elements in the solution set. An element in S is represented by a collection of values $(x_1, x_2, x_3, \ldots, x_n)$, one for each of the n variables in the equation. One way of identifying specific elements in S is to assume values for $n - 1$ of the variables, substitute these into the equation, and solve for the value of the remaining variable.

EXAMPLE 4

Given the equation

$$2x_1 + 3x_2 - x_3 + x_4 = 16$$

(*a*) determine one set of values for x_1, x_2, x_3, and x_4 which satisfies the equation.
(*b*) What values satisfy the equation when $x_1 = 2$, $x_2 = -1$, and $x_3 = 0$?
(*c*) Determine all members of the solution set which have values of 0 for three of the four variables.

SOLUTION

(*a*) Let's assume that $x_1 = x_2 = x_3 = 1$ and substitute these into the equation to determine the value of x_4.

$$2(1) + 3(1) - (1) + x_4 = 16$$

or

$$x_4 = 12$$

Therefore one element of the solution set is $x_1 = 1$, $x_2 = 1$, $x_3 = 1$, and $x_4 = 12$, or (1, 1, 1, 12).

(*b*) Substituting the given values for x_1, x_2, and x_3 into the equation yields

$$2(2) + 3(-1) - (0) + x_4 = 16$$

or

$$x_4 = 15$$

The corresponding element of the solution set is $(2, -1, 0, 15)$.

(c) If $x_1 = x_2 = x_3 = 0$, then

$$2(0) + 3(0) - (0) + x_4 = 16$$

or

$$x_4 = 16$$

If $x_1 = x_2 = x_4 = 0$,

$$2(0) + 3(0) - x_3 + 0 = 16$$

or

$$x_3 = -16$$

If $x_1 = x_3 = x_4 = 0$, then

$$2(0) + 3x_2 - 0 + 0 = 16$$

or

$$3x_2 = 16$$

and

$$x_2 = \tfrac{16}{3}$$

If $x_2 = x_3 = x_4 = 0$,

$$2x_1 + 3(0) - 0 + 0 = 16$$

or

$$2x_1 = 16$$

and

$$x_1 = 8$$

Therefore, the elements of the solution set which have three of the four variables equaling 0 are $(0, 0, 0, 16)$, $(0, 0, -16, 0)$, $(0, \tfrac{16}{3}, 0, 0)$, and $(8, 0, 0, 0)$.

Section 3.1 Follow-up Exercises

Determine which of the following equations are linear.

1 $4y - 11x = 0$

2 $3y = 4x^2 - x/2$

3 $3y = 1$

4 $\sqrt{2}x + y/2 = 10$

5 $3y^2 = x + 10$

6 $25 + x = \sqrt{5}$

7 $x = 2$

8 $2x_1 + 3x_2 + x_3 = 15$

9 $(x + y)/3 - y/2 = 5x - y$

10 $(x_1 + x_2 + x_3 + x_4 + x_5)/2 = x_6$

11 Use set notation to specify membership in the solution set S for the equation $3x + 7y = 21$.

12 Use set notation to specify membership in the solution set P for the equation $4a - 5b = -10$.

13 Given the equation $3x + 4y = 20$, (a) determine a pair of values which satisfy the equation. (b) What pair of values satisfies the equation when $y = -4$? When $x = 0$? When $y = 0$?

14 Consider the equation $5x = 75$ as a two-variable equation having the form of Eq. (3.1)

(a) Define a, b, and c.

(b) What pair of values satisfies the equation when $y = 12$?

(c) What pair of values satisfies the equation when $x = 20$?

(d) Can you generalize a statement about the nature of the values of x and y which belong to the solution set for this equation?

15 Rework Example 2 if product A requires 4 hours per unit and product B requires 2 hours per unit.

16 Given the equation $5x_1 - 2x_2 + 6x_3 = 0$,

(a) What values satisfy the equation when $x_1 = 2$ and $x_3 = 1$?

(b) Define the elements of the solution set in which the values of two variables equal 0.

17 Given the equation $2x_1 - 2x_2 - 6x_3 - 4x_4 = 32$

(a) Determine one set of values for x_1, x_2, x_3, and x_4 which satisfies the equation.

(b) What values satisfy the equation when $x_1 = 0$, $x_3 = 1$, and $x_4 = -2$?

(c) Determine all elements of the solution set for which the values of three variables equal zero.

18 The equation $x_4 = 20$ is one of a set of related equations involving four variables x_1, x_2, x_3, and x_4.

(a) Determine one set of values (x_1, x_2, x_3, x_4) which satisfies the equation.

(b) What values satisfy the equation when $x_1 = 4$, $x_2 = 2$, and $x_3 = 10$?

(c) What values satisfy the equation when $x_4 = 10$?

(d) Determine all elements of the solution set for which the values of three variables equal zero.

19 A company manufactures two products, A and B. Each unit of A requires 4 labor hours and each unit of B requires 5 labor hours. Daily manufacturing capacity is 120 labor hours.

(a) If x units of product A and y units of product B are manufactured each day and all labor hours are to be used, determine the appropriate linear equation expressing this relationship.

(b) How many units of A can be made each day if 8 units of B are manufactured each day?

(c) How many units of A can be made each *week* if 16 units of B are manufactured each day? (Assume a 5-day work week.)

3.2 GRAPHICAL CHARACTERISTICS

Graphing Two-Variable Equations

A linear equation involving two variables has a graph which is a straight line in two dimensions. In order to graph a linear equation involving two variables, you only need to (1) *identify the coordinates of any two points which lie on the line*, (2) *connect the two points with a straight line, and* (3) *extend the straight line in both directions as far as necessary or desirable for your purposes.* The coordinates of the two points are found by identifying any two members of the solution set. The graphical representation (counterpart) of each element in the solution set is a point in 2-space. The location of this point is described by coordinates (x, y) where x and y are the respective values of the two variables. For example, if the values of $x = 1$ and $y = 3$ satisfy an equation, the graphical representation of this member of the solution set is a point located at (1, 3).

EXAMPLE 5

The graph of the equation

$$2x + 4y = 16$$

is found by first identifying any two pairs of values for x and y which satisfy the equation.

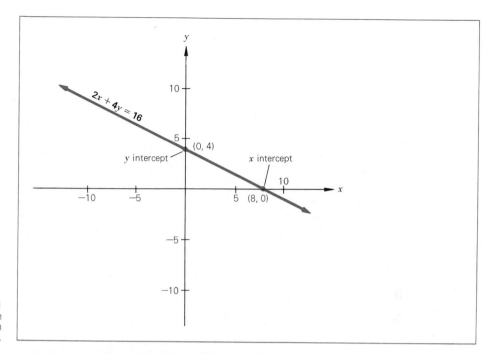

FIGURE 3.1
Graph of the
linear equation
$2x + 4y = 16$.

NOTE

Aside from the case where the right side of the equation equals 0, the easiest points to identify (algebraically) are those found by setting one variable equal to 0 and solving for the value of the other variable. That is, let $x = 0$ and solve for the value of y; then let $y = 0$ and solve for the value of x. Observe that the resulting ordered pairs, $(0, y)$ and $(x, 0)$, are points on the y and x axes, respectively.

Letting $x = 0$, the corresponding value for y is 4, and letting $y = 0$ results in $x = 8$. Thus $(0, 4)$ and $(8, 0)$ are two members of the solution set, and their graphical representation is indicated by the two points in Fig. 3.1. The two points have been connected by a straight line, and the line has been extended in both directions.

Just as $(0, 4)$ and $(8, 0)$ are members of the solution set for the equation $2x + 4y = 16$, the coordinates of every point lying on the line represent other members of the solution set. How many unique points are there on the line? There are an infinite number, which is entirely consistent with our earlier statement that there are an infinite number of pairs of values for x and y which satisfy any linear equation. In summary, if there are any pairs of values (x, y) that satisfy an equation, they can be identified by the coordinates of points lying on the line representing the equation. In Fig. 3.1, the coordinates of any point *not* lying on the line will not satisfy the equation.

EXAMPLE 6

Graph the linear equation $4x - 7y = 0$.

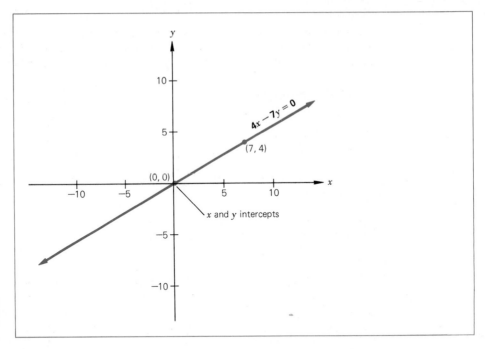

FIGURE 3.2
Graph of the
linear equation
$4x - 7y = 0$.

SOLUTION

This equation is an example of the situation where two points will not be found by setting each variable equal to 0 and solving for the remaining variable. Watch what happens! If $x = 0$,

$$4(0) - 7y = 0 \quad \text{or} \quad y = 0$$

If $y = 0$,

$$4x - 7(0) = 0 \quad \text{or} \quad x = 0$$

Both cases have yielded the same point, $(0, 0)$. Therefore another value must be assumed for one of the variables. If we let $x = 7$,

$$4(7) - 7y = 0$$
$$-7y = -28$$
$$y = 4$$

Two members of the solution set, then, are $(0, 0)$ and $(7, 4)$. Figure 3.2 illustrates the graph of the equation.

NOTE

The graph of any two-variable linear equation having the form $ax + by = 0$ is a straight line which *passes through the origin*.

Intercepts

In describing the graphical appearance of a mathematical function, two characteristics of frequent interest are the *x intercepts* and *y intercepts* of the function.
These can be described both in a graphical sense and algebraically.

DEFINITION: x INTERCEPT ▬▬▬▬▬▬▬▬▬

The *x* intercepts of an equation are the points where the graph
of the equation crosses the *x* axis. Algebraically, the *x* intercepts represent the ordered pairs found by setting $y = 0$.

DEFINITION: y INTERCEPT ▬▬▬▬▬▬▬▬▬

The *y* intercepts of an equation are the points where the graph
of the equation crosses the *y* axis. Algebraically, the *y* intercepts represent the ordered pairs found by setting $x = 0$.

For a two-variable linear equation there exist (except for two special cases) one *x*
intercept and one *y* intercept. In Fig. 3.1, the *x* intercept is (8, 0), and the *y* intercept is (0, 4) for the equation $2x + 4y = 16$. In Fig. 3.2, the *x* and *y* intercepts
both occur at the same point, the origin. The *x* intercept is (0, 0), and the *y* intercept is (0, 0). Look at both figures carefully and verify that the *x* intercept represents the point whose *y* value is 0 and that the *y* intercept represents the point
whose *x* value is 0.

NOTE ▬▬▬▬▬▬▬▬▬

The procedure for identifying two points suggested in Example
5 determines the *x* and *y* intercepts.

The Equation x = k

A linear equation of the form $ax = c$ is a special case of Eq. (3.1) where $b = 0$.
For this equation there is no *y*-term. Dividing both sides of the equation by *a*
yields the simplified form

$$x = c/a$$

Since *c* and *a* are constants we can let $c/a = k$ and write the equation in the
equivalent form

$$\boxed{x = k} \tag{3.8}$$

where *k* is a real number. This linear equation is special in the sense that *x*
equals *k* regardless of the value of *y*. The variable *y* may assume any value as
long as $x = k$. That is the only condition required by the equation. As a result,
any equation of this form graphs as a vertical line crossing the x axis at x = k. Figure
3.3 illustrates two equations of this type. *Note that for these equations there is an x
intercept (k, 0) but no y intercept (unless k = 0).* What happens when $k = 0$?

The Equation y = k

A linear equation of the form $by = c$ is a special case of Eq. (3.1) where $a = 0$,

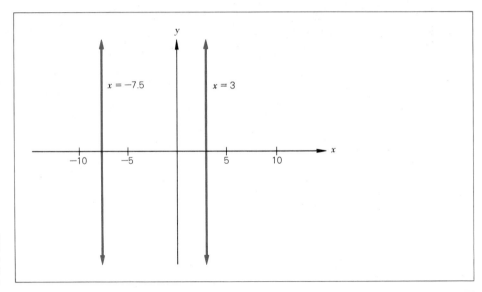

FIGURE 3.3
Graphs of
sample equa-
tions of the form
$x = k$.

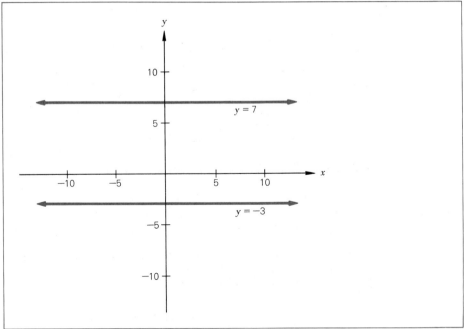

FIGURE 3.4
Graphs of
sample equa-
tions of the form
$y = k$.

i.e., where there is no x term. After both sides of the equation are divided by b, the general reduced form of this case is

$$y = k \qquad\qquad (3.9)$$

where k is a real number. This equation suggests that y equals k regardless of the value of x. The variable x may assume any value as long as $y = k$. *Any equation of this form graphs as a horizontal line crossing the y axis at $y = k$.* Figure 3.4 illustrates two such equations. *Note that equations of this form have no x intercepts (unless $k = 0$).* What happens when $k = 0$?

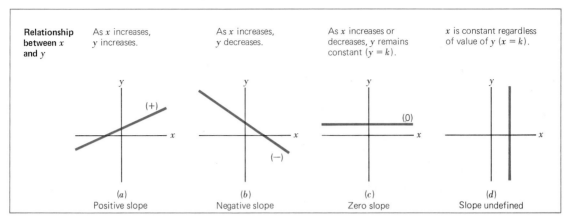

Relationship between x and y	As x increases, y increases.	As x increases, y decreases.	As x increases or decreases, y remains constant $(y = k)$.	x is constant regardless of value of y $(x = k)$.
	(+)	(−)	(0)	
	(a) Positive slope	(b) Negative slope	(c) Zero slope	(d) Slope undefined

FIGURE 3.5
Slope conditions for straight lines.

Slope

Any straight line, with the exception of vertical lines, can be characterized by its *slope.* By "slope" we mean basically the *inclination of a line* — whether it rises or falls as you move from left to right along the x axis — and *the rate at which the line rises or falls* (in other words, how steep the line is).

*The slope of a line may be **positive, negative, zero,** or **undefined.*** A line with a positive slope rises from left to right, or runs uphill. For such a line the value of y increases as x increases (or y decreases as x decreases). A line having a negative slope falls from left to right, or runs downhill. For such a line the value of y decreases as x increases (or y increases as x decreases). This means that x and y behave in an **inverse** manner; as one increases, the other decreases and vice versa. A line having a zero slope is horizontal. As x increases or decreases, y stays constant (the special case: $y = k$). Vertical lines (of the form $x = k$) have a slope which is undefined. These slope relationships are illustrated in Fig. 3.5.

The slope of a line is quantified by a real number. The sign of the slope (number) indicates whether the line is rising or falling. The magnitude (absolute value) of the slope indicates the relative steepness of the line. The slope tells us the rate at which the value of y changes *relative to* changes in the value of x. The larger the absolute value of the slope, the steeper the angle at which the line rises or falls. In Fig. 3.6a lines AB and CD both have positive slopes, but the slope of CD is larger than that for AB. Similarly, in Fig. 3.6b lines MN and OP both have negative slopes, but OP would have the larger slope in an absolute value sense.

Given any two points which lie on a straight line *that is not vertical,* the slope can be computed as a ratio of the change in the value of y while moving from one point to the other divided by the corresponding change in the value of x, or

$$\text{Slope} = \frac{\text{change in } y}{\text{change in } x} = \frac{\Delta y}{\Delta x}$$

where Δ (delta) means "change in." Thus Δy denotes "the change in the value of y" and Δx "the change in the value of x." The *two-point formula* is one way of determining the slope of a straight line connecting two points.

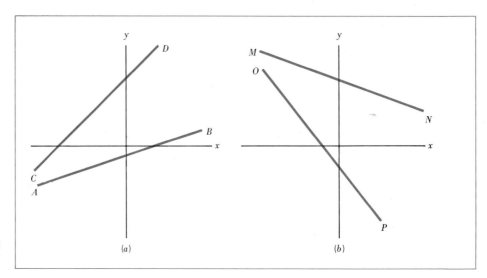

FIGURE 3.6
Comparing rela-
tive steepness.

TWO-POINT FORMULA

The slope m of the straight line connecting two points having coordinates (x_1, y_1) and (x_2, y_2), respectively, is

$$m = \frac{\Delta y}{\Delta x} = \frac{y_2 - y_1}{x_2 - x_1} \qquad (3.10)$$

where $x_1 \neq x_2$

Figure 3.7 illustrates the computation of Δx and Δy for the line segment PQ.

EXAMPLE 7

To compute the slope of the line connecting points located at (2, 4) and (5, 12), arbitrarily identify one point as (x_1, y_1) and the other as (x_2, y_2). Given the location of the two points in Fig. 3.8, let's label (5, 12) as (x_1, y_1) and (2, 4) as (x_2, y_2).

In moving from (5, 12) to (2, 4)

$$\Delta y = y_2 - y_1 = 4 - 12 = -8$$
and
$$\Delta x = x_2 - x_1 = 2 - 5 = -3$$

Hence,

$$m = \frac{\Delta y}{\Delta x} = \frac{-8}{-3} = \frac{8}{3}$$

The slope is positive indicating that the line segment rises from left to right. The sign combined with the magnitude indicate that in moving along the line segment y increases at a rate of 8 units for every 3 units that x increases.

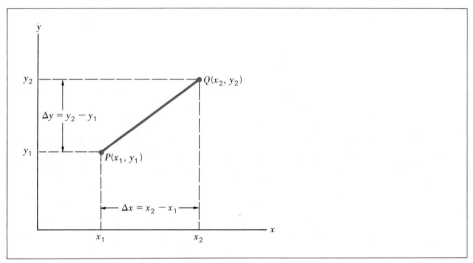

FIGURE 3.7
Measuring Δx
and Δy.

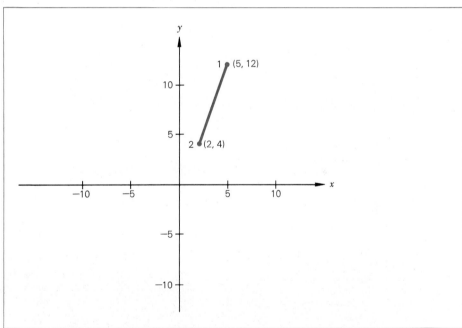

FIGURE 3.8

Another way of interpreting the slope is given by the following definition.

DEFINITION: SLOPE

The **slope** is the change in the value of y if x increases by 1 unit.

According to this definition, the value of $m = \frac{8}{3}$ indicates that if x increases by 1 unit, then y will *increase* by $\frac{8}{3}$ or $2\frac{2}{3}$ units.

NOTE

Along any straight line the slope is constant. That is, if a line is said to have a slope of -2, the slope of the line segment connecting any two points on the line will always equal -2.

EXAMPLE 8

We have already seen that the slope of a linear equation having the form $y = k$ is 0. For a horizontal line, the value of y is always the same, and the numerator of the two-point formula, $y_2 - y_1$, always equals 0. We also examined the other special case of a linear equation, $x = k$. We verified that any linear equation having this form graphs as a vertical line crossing the x axis at $x = k$. *The slope of any vertical line is undefined.* This can be verified by attempting to use the two-point formula to determine the slope of the line represented by $x = 5$. If we choose the two points $(x_1, y_1) = (5, 0)$ and $(x_2, y_2) = (5, -1)$, substitution into Eq. (3.10) gives

$$m = \frac{-1 - 0}{5 - 5}$$

$$= \frac{-1}{0}$$

which is not defined. Remember, Eq. (3.10) is not defined when $x_1 = x_2$.

Section 3.2 Follow-up Exercises

In Exercises 1 to 10 identify the x and y intercepts for the given linear equation.

1	$3x - 4y = 24$	2	$4x - y = -16$
3	$-2x + 3y = 18$	4	$x - 12 = -2y$
5	$15x = 120$	6	$-2y + 20 = 0$
7	$x - 4 = (x + y)/2$	8	$x + 4 = -(x - y)/3$
9	$4x - 3y = 0$	10	$3x - 5y = x + 3y$

For Exercises 11 to 20, graph the given linear equation.

11	$3x - 2y = -12$	12	$2x - y = 0$
13	$-x - y = -8$	14	$x - 2y = -10$
15	$5x - 2y = 0$	16	$2x = (x + y)/3$
17	$-x + y = 0$	18	$-3y = 21$
19	$-4y = 0$	20	$-5x = 0$

21 What is the equation of the x axis? The y axis?

22 In Example 7, recompute the slope if the points are labeled as $(x_1, y_1) = (2, 4)$ and $(x_2, y_2) = (5, 12)$. Is the answer the same as obtained before?

In Exercises 23 to 30, compute the slope of the line segment connecting the two points. Interpret the meaning of the slope in each case.

23	$(2, 8)$ and $(5, 20)$	24	$(-3, 10)$ and $(-5, 18)$
25	$(5, 8)$ and $(10, -12)$	26	$(-2, -4)$ and $(-6, -20)$

27   (5, 3) and $(-15, 3)$ 28 $(-6, 10)$ and $(-6, 12)$
29   (a, b) and (c, d) 30 $(a, -b)$ and $(-a, b)$

3.3   SLOPE-INTERCEPT FORM

From a Different Vantage Point

In this section we discuss another form of expressing linear equations. In Sec. 3.1 we stated the general form of a two-variable linear equation as

$$ax + by = c \qquad (3.1)$$

Solving Eq. (3.1) for the variable y, we get

$$by = c - ax$$

or

$$y = \frac{c}{b} - \frac{ax}{b} \qquad (3.11)$$

For any linear equation the terms c/b and $-a/b$ on the right side of Eq. (3.11) have special significance. The term c/b represents the y coordinate of the y intercept for the equation, and $-a/b$ represents the slope of the equation. This information is obtained from any linear equation of the form of Eq. (3.1) *if it can be solved for y.*

The form of (Eq. 3.11) is called the ***slope-intercept form*** of a linear equation. Equation (3.11) can be generalized in a simpler form as

$$y = mx + k \qquad (3.12)^*$$

where m *represents the slope* of the equation and k *equals the y coordinate of the y intercept*. There could be some temporary confusion here in going from Eq. (3.11) to Eq. (3.12), so look closely at the structure of the right side of Eq. (3.12). In solving any linear equation for y, *the slope is the coefficient of x*. And, *the y coordinate of the y intercept is the isolated constant (sign included) on the same side of the equation.*

To illustrate this form, the equation

$$5x + y = 10$$

can be rewritten in the slope-intercept form as

$$y = -5x + 10$$

Hence, the slope is -5 and the y intercept equals $(0, 10)$. Choose two points which satisfy the original equation and verify that the slope equals -5 using Eq. (3.10).

EXAMPLE 9

The equation $y = 2x/3$ is a linear equation having a slope of $+\frac{2}{3}$ and a y intercept of $(0, 0)$. The absence of the isolated constant implicitly suggests that $k = 0$ in Eq. (3.12).

EXAMPLE 10

The special case of a linear equation $y = k$ is in the slope-intercept form. To realize this,

---

* Note that this equation has the same form as that of a linear function $y = f(x) = a_1 x + a_0$, as mentioned in Chap. 2.

you must recognize that this equation can be written in the form $y = k + 0x$. The absence of the x term on the right side implicitly suggests that $m = 0$, i.e., the slope of the line having this form equals zero. We confirmed this in Sec. 3.2 when we discussed the graphical characteristics of this case. The y intercept is $(0, k)$ for such equations.

EXAMPLE 11

For the special case $x = k$, it is impossible to solve for the slope-intercept form of the linear equation. The variable y is not a part of the equation. Our conclusion is that it is impossible to determine the slope and y intercept for equations having this form. Look back at Fig. 3.3 to see if this conclusion is consistent with our earlier findings.

Interpreting the Slope and y Intercept

In many applications of linear equations, the slope and y intercept have interpretations which are of interest. Take, for example, the salary equation

$$y = 25 + 3x$$

where y = *weekly salary, dollars*
x = *number of units sold during one week*

The salary equation is linear and is written in the slope-intercept form. Graphically, the equation is represented by the line in Fig. 3.9, which has a slope of $+3$ and y intercept equal to $(0, 25)$. Notice that this equation has been graphed only for nonnegative values of x and y. Can you suggest why this would be appropriate?

Think back to the definition of *slope*. Since the slope represents the change in y associated with a unit increase in x, the slope of $+3$ means that weekly salary y increases by \$3 for each additional unit sold. The y coordinate of the y inter-

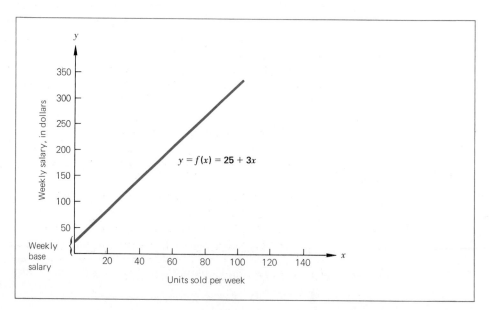

FIGURE 3.9
Salary function.

cept represents the value of y when $x = 0$, or the salary which would be earned if no units were sold. This is the base salary per week.

EXAMPLE 12

In Example 3 of Chap. 2, we developed an estimated total cost function associated with owning and operating a police patrol car. The cost equation was

$$C = 0.40x + 18,000$$

where C = *total cost, dollars*

x = *number of miles driven*

This equation is also in the slope-intercept form with a slope of 0.40 and y intercept of (0, 18,000). The slope suggests that total cost increases at a rate of $0.40 for each additional mile driven. The 18,000 implies a fixed cost of $18,000 which is incurred whether or not the car is driven. Although we might speculate about what makes up this $18,000, it is likely to be mainly the purchase cost of the car. Can you think of other costs which might be a part of this $18,000? How about the cost of a life-time maintenance policy purchased from the manufacturer or from a local garage?

Section 3.3 Follow-up Exercises

For Exercises 1 to 8 rewrite each equation in the slope-intercept form and determine the slope and y intercept.

1   $2x - 4y = 24$ 2 $-3x + 4y = 48$

3   $x - y = 10$ 4 $2x - y = -8$

5   $(x + y)/2 = 5$ 6 $(x - y)/3 = 2x$

7   $-2x - 4y = 0$ 8 $3y - 15 = -2y$

9   **Women in the Labor Force**   The number of women in the labor force is expected to increase during the 1980s, but not as dramatically as occurred during the 1970s. One forecasting consultant uses the linear equation $n = 8.8 + 0.25t$ to predict the number of women between the ages of 35 and 44 who will be in the labor force. In this equation, n equals the number of women (aged 35 to 44) in the labor force (measured in millions) and t equals time measured in years *since* 1981 ($t = 0$ corresponds to 1981). If n is plotted on the vertical axis,

(*a*) Graph the equation.

(*b*) Identify the slope and y intercept (n intercept, here).

(*c*) Interpret the meaning of the slope and n intercept in this application.

(*d*) Predict the number of women in this age group who will be in the labor force in 1990.

10   The chamber of commerce for a resort town is trying to determine how many tourists will be visiting each season over the coming years. A marketing research firm has estimated that the number of tourists can be predicted by the equation $p = 60,000 + 3,000t$, where p = number of tourists per year and t = years (measured *from* this current season). Thus $t = 0$ identifies the current season, $t = 1$ is the next season, etc. Let p be the dependent variable (plotted on the vertical axis).

(*a*) Graph the equation.

(b) Identify the slope and y intercept (p intercept, here).

(c) Interpret the meaning of the slope and p intercept in this application.

11   Think metric! $C = \frac{5}{9}F - \frac{160}{9}$ is an equation relating temperature in Celsius units to temperature measured on the Fahrenheit scale. Let $C =$ degrees Celsius and $F =$ degrees Fahrenheit; assume the equation is graphed with C measured on the vertical axis.

(a) Identify the slope and y intercept.

(b) Interpret the meaning of the slope and y intercept for purposes of converting from Fahrenheit to Celsius temperatures.

(c) Solve the equation for F and rework parts a and b if F is plotted on the vertical axis.

3.4   DETERMINING THE EQUATION OF A STRAIGHT LINE

In applying mathematics, usually we must begin our analysis by determining the true or approximate relationship among the variables of interest. For instance, the cost equation for the patrol car in Example 12 had to be derived from information available to department analysts. We will look at this preliminary stage of analysis continually as we move through the book. This is a very important stage with which you should be familiar and comfortable.

In this section we will show how to determine the equation for a linear relationship. The way in which you determine the equation depends upon the information available. The following sections discuss different possibilities.

Slope and Intercept

The easiest situation is one in which you know the slope m and y intercept $(0, k)$ of the line representing an equation. To determine the linear equation in this almost trivial case, simply substitute m and k into the slope-intercept form, Eq. (3.12). If you are interested in stating the equation in the standard form of Eq. (3.1), simply rearrange the terms in the slope-intercept equation.

EXAMPLE 13

Determine the equation of the straight line which has a slope of -5 and a y intercept of $(0, 15)$.

SOLUTION

Substituting values of $m = -5$ and $k = 15$ into Eq. (3.12) gives

$$y = -5x + 15$$

Restated in the form of Eq. (3.1), an equivalent form of this equation is

$$5x + y = 15$$

EXAMPLE 14

Determine the equation of the straight line which has a slope of $+\frac{1}{2}$ and a y intercept equal to $(0, 0)$.

SOLUTION

Substituting $m = \frac{1}{2}$ and $k = 0$ into Eq. (3.12) gives

$$y = \tfrac{1}{2}x + 0$$

or
$$y = \tfrac{1}{2}x$$

verify that the equation can be stated in the form of Eq. (3.1) as $\tfrac{1}{2}x - y = 0$, or as $x - 2y = 0$.

POINT FOR THOUGHT AND DISCUSSION

Is the equation $y - \tfrac{1}{2}x = 0$ an equivalent form of the equation in this example? Why? Graph the two to see if they are the same.

Slope and One Point

Another possibility for a line is that you may know the slope and also one member of the solution set (i.e., the coordinates of one point on the line). If you consider the slope-intercept form [Eq. (3.12)], any member of the solution set should satisfy this equation. That is, we can define the values of x and y which satisfy an equation by the set S, where

$$\boxed{S = \{(x, y) | y = mx + k\}} \qquad (3.13)$$

Now follow this carefully! In the last section we said that knowing the slope and the y intercept of an equation allows you to write out the slope-intercept form directly. In this section we talk of knowing the slope and one point—but not the y intercept. From Eq. (3.13), any point which lies on a line should satisfy the slope-intercept equation. If we substitute the known slope m and the coordinates of the point into Eq. (3.12) we can solve for k. At this stage we would have m, the slope, and k, the y coordinate of the y intercept; the equation of the line would follow directly. Let's illustrate this with a few examples.

EXAMPLE 15

Given that the slope of a straight line is -2 and one point lying on the line is $(2, 8)$, we can substitute these values into Eq. (3.12), yielding

$$8 = (-2)(2) + k$$

or
$$12 = k$$

Knowing that $m = -2$ and $k = 12$ leads directly to the slope-intercept equation

$$y = -2x + 12$$

And, as before, we can rewrite this equation in the equivalent form

$$2x + y = 12$$

NOTE

You may be wondering which form of the linear equation—Eq. (3.1) or Eq. (3.12)—is the correct one. The answer depends on what you intend to do with the equation. Depending on the type of analysis to be conducted, one of these forms may be more appropriate than the other.

EXAMPLE 16

If the slope of a straight line is zero and one point lying on the line is $(5, -30)$ the equation of the line can be found by first substituting the zero slope and coordinates $(5, -30)$ into Eq. (3.12).

$$-30 = (0)(5) + k$$

or

$$-30 = k$$

Since we know that $m = 0$ and $k = -30$, the slope-intercept equation is

$$y = 0x + (-30)$$

or

$$y = -30$$

EXAMPLE 17

Given the linear equation $3x - 6y = 24$.
(a) What is the slope of the line represented by the given equation?
(b) What is the slope of any line perpendicular to the given line?
(c) How many different lines are perpendicular to this line?
(d) Find the equation of the line which is perpendicular to the given line *and* which passes through the point $(2, 5)$.

SOLUTION

(a) The given equation can be restated in slope-intercept form as

$$-6y = 24 - 3x$$

or

$$y = -4 + \tfrac{1}{2}x$$

From this equation the slope can be seen to equal $+1/2$.

If a line has a slope m_1 ($m_1 \neq 0$), the slope of any line which is perpendicular to the given line has a slope equal to the negative reciprocal of the given line, or $m_2 = -1/m_1$.

(b) Since $m_1 = \tfrac{1}{2}$, the slope of any line perpendicular to the line $3x - 6y = 24$ is

$$m_2 = -\frac{1}{\tfrac{1}{2}}$$

$$= -2$$

(c) Because there is an infinite set of lines with $m = -2$, an infinite number of lines are perpendicular to this line.
(d) The line we are interested in has a slope equal to -2 and one point on the line is $(2, 5)$. Substituting these three values into Eq. (3.12) yields

$$5 = (-2)(2) + k$$

or
$$9 = k$$

Therefore the equation of the line is

$$y = -2x + 9$$

or, alternatively,

$$2x + y = 9$$

Two Points

A more likely situation is that some data points have been gathered which lie on a line and we wish to determine the equation of the line. Assume that we are given the coordinates of two points which lie on a straight line. We can determine the slope of the line by using the two-point formula [Eq. (3.10)]. As soon as we know the slope, the y intercept can be determined by using *either* of the two data points, and proceeding as we did in the last section.

EXAMPLE 18

To determine the equation of the straight line which passes through $(-4, 2)$ and the origin, we substitute the coordinates into the two-point formula, resulting in

$$m = \frac{0 - 2}{0 - (-4)}$$

$$= \frac{-2}{4} = -\frac{1}{2}$$

Substituting $m = -\frac{1}{2}$ and the coordinates $(-4, 2)$ into Eq. (3.12) yields

$$2 = (-\tfrac{1}{2})(-4) + k$$
$$2 = 2 + k$$
$$0 = k$$

Thus, the slope-intercept form of the equation is

$$y = -\tfrac{1}{2}x$$

Let's check ourselves and solve for the y coordinate of the y intercept k by substituting $(0, 0)$ into Eq. (3.12) as opposed to $(-4, 2)$. Doing this,

$$0 = (-\tfrac{1}{2})(0) + k$$
or $$0 = k$$

which is consistent with our original result.

NOTE

If you are on top of things you might have realized that the origin is the y intercept. How would this have simplified the analysis?

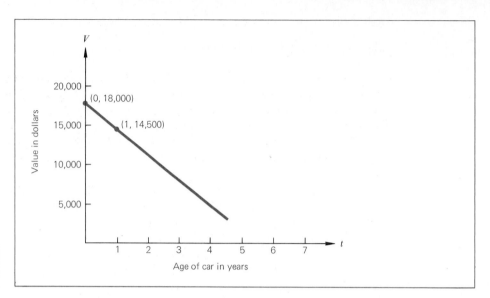

FIGURE 3.10
Value of patrol
car as function
of its age t.

EXAMPLE 19

Depreciation The value of the police patrol car in Example 12 is expected to decrease at a linear rate over time. Figure 3.10 shows two data points on the line which represents the value V of the car as a function of its age t, where V is measured in dollars and t is measured in years from the time of purchase. The two data points indicate that the value of the car at $t = 0$ (time of purchase) is $18,000 and its value in one year will equal $14,500.

Determine the slope-intercept equation which relates the value of the patrol car V to its age t.

SOLUTION

The slope can be determined using the two-point formula, resulting in

$$m = \frac{14{,}500 - 18{,}000}{1 - 0}$$

$$= \frac{-3{,}500}{1} = -3{,}500$$

Substituting $m = -3{,}500$ and $(0, 18{,}000)$ into Eq. (3.12)—with V and t replacing y and x, respectively—we get

$$18{,}000 = (-3{,}500)(0) + k$$

or $18{,}000 = k$

(That was obvious from Fig. 3.10, wasn't it?) Consequently, the slope-intercept equation is

$$V = -3{,}500t + 18{,}000$$

EXAMPLE 20

(*a*) For the last example, interpret the meaning of the slope.

(b) At what time is the value of the car expected to equal zero?

SOLUTION

(a) The slope of $-3,500$ implies that with each additional year of ownership the value of the patrol car decreases by $3,500. (The term *depreciation* is often used by accountants to describe the rate at which an asset, i.e., something of value, declines in value over time.)
(b) V will equal zero when the line crosses the t axis (equivalent to the x intercept); algebraically, we are searching for the value of t when $V = 0$. By setting V equal to 0 in the equation developed in Example 19 and solving for t, we find the car will have a value of zero when

$$0 = -3,500t + 18,000$$
$$3,500t = 18,000$$
$$t = \frac{18,000}{3,500}$$

$$\text{or} \quad t = 5.142 \text{ years}$$

Section 3.4 Follow-up Exercises

In Exercises 1 to 20 determine the slope-intercept form of the linear equation characterized by the indicated attributes.

1   Slope $= 3$, y intercept $= (0, 5)$ 2   Slope $= -2.5$, y intercept $= (0, 5)$
3   Slope $= \frac{1}{2}$, y intercept $= (0, -3)$ 4   Slope $= -4$, y intercept $= (0, -12)$
5   Slope $= 2.8$, intercept $= (0, \frac{1}{2})$ 6   Slope $= 0$, y intercept $= (0, 0)$
7   Slope undefined, infinite number of y intercepts.
8   Slope $= \frac{1}{2}$, $(2, 4)$ lies on the line
9   Slope $= -2$, $(0, 0)$ lies on the line
10   Slope $= 3$, $(6, 0)$ lies on the line
11   Slope $= -\frac{1}{4}$, $(-2, -4)$ lies on the line
12   Slope $= a$, $(0, 0)$ lies on the line
13   Slope $= -a$, $(2, 4)$ lies on the line
14   Slope undefined, $(6, -4)$ lies on the line
15   $(-4, 2)$ and $(-2, -6)$ lie on the line
16   $(2, 1)$ and $(4, 9)$ lie on the line
17   $(-1, 3)$ and $(2, -9)$ lie on the line
18   (a, b) and (c, d) lie on the line
19   $(a, 5)$ and $(a, -3)$ lie on the line
20   $(3, b)$ and $(7, b)$ lie on the line
21   Without graphing, determine whether the points $(3, 8)$, $(-1, 4)$, and $(-4, 0)$ are all on the same straight line. (*Hint:* One approach is to find the equation of the line connecting two of the points and substitute the coordinates of the third point into the equation to see if they satisfy it.)
22   *Parallel lines have slopes which are equal to one another.* Find the equation of the line which passes through $(6, 4)$ and is also parallel to the line $x + y = 0$.
23   Find the equation of the line which is perpendicular to the line $x + y = 0$ and passes through $(6, 4)$.

24 In Exercise 10 in Sec. 3.3 the chamber of commerce was trying to forecast the number of tourists who would be visiting in the coming years. Some students from the local university have examined the problem as part of a class project. They estimated this current year's volume at 60,000 tourists, or that one data point is (0, 60,000). They have also projected that the volume next year will be 67,500 people and that the volume in the future will continue to grow at the same rate according to a linear relationship. Determine the slope-intercept equation which relates number of tourists P to years t as measured from this current year.

25 If F denotes degrees Fahrenheit and C denotes degrees Celsius, assume that the relationship between these two temperature scales is being graphed with F on the vertical axis. Two data points on the line relating C and F are (5, 41) and (25, 77). Using these points, determine the slope-intercept equation which allows you to transform from Celsius into Fahrenheit.

3.5 LINEAR EQUATIONS INVOLVING MORE THAN TWO VARIABLES

When linear equations involve more than two variables, the algebraic properties remain basically the same but the visual or graphical characteristics change considerably or are lost altogether.

Three-Dimensional Coordinate Systems

Three-dimensional space can be described using a *three-dimensional coordinate system.* In three dimensions we use three coordinate axes which are all perpendicular to one another, intersecting at their respective zero points. Figure 3.11 illustrates a set of axes which are labeled by the variables x_1, x_2, and x_3. The point of intersection of the three axes is referred to as the *origin.* And, using three-component coordinates **(ordered triples)**, (x_1, x_2, x_3), the coordinates of the origin are (0, 0, 0).

Observe that graphing three dimensions on paper (two dimensions) requires a certain perspective that may be difficult to see at first. We might have drawn Fig. 3.11 such that we were looking right "down the barrel" of the x_2 axis. In

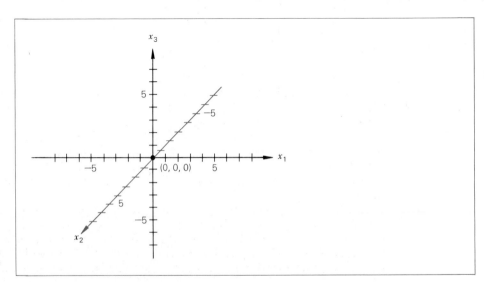

FIGURE 3.11
Coordinate axis system in three dimensions.

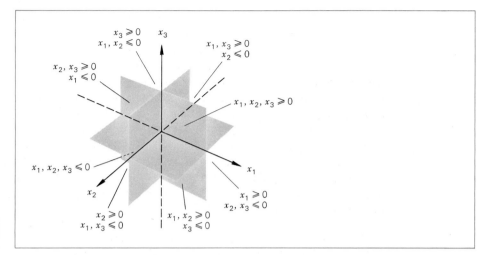

FIGURE 3.12
Octants of 3
space.

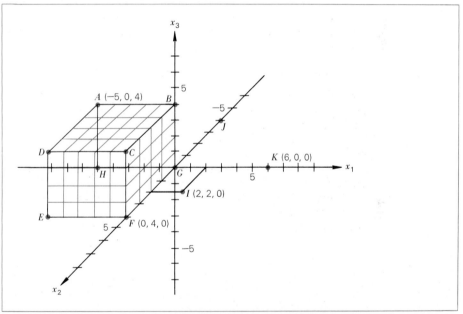

FIGURE 3.13
Sample loca-
tions in
3-space.

that case we would have no sense of depth or location relative to the x_2 axis. Therefore, we rotate the coordinate axes by turning the x_3 axis clockwise. This allows us to have a sense of depth when the x_2 axis is drawn at an angle.

Just as the coordinate axes in two dimensions divide 2-space into quadrants, the axes in three dimensions divide 3-space into **octants.** This is illustrated in Fig. 3.12. Note the sign characteristics in each octant. The three-component coordinates allow for specifying the location or address of any point in three dimensions.

As with two-dimensional coordinates, each component of (x_1, x_2, x_3) specifies the location of a point relative to each axis. Carefully examine Fig. 3.13. In order to assist in understanding this figure, a *rectangular polyhedron* has been sketched. Along with several other points, we are interested in the locations of the corner points of this polyhedron. Obviously G occurs at the origin, having coordinates $(0, 0, 0)$. Point F lies directly on the x_2 axis, four units out. Its coordinates are $(0, 4, 0)$. Point A forms the upper left corner of one end $(ABHG)$ of the polyhedron. Since H lies on the x_1 axis and A is vertically above H, we can conclude that the x_1 coordinate of A is -5 *and* the x_2 coordinate of A is 0. Finally, points A, B, C, and D all seem to be at the same *height* (relative to the x_3 axis). Because point B lies on the x_3 axis at a height of 4, we conclude that A has the same x_3 coordinate. Thus, A is located at $(-5, 0, 4)$. See if you agree with the coordinates of I and k. Test your skills and define the coordinates of points B, C, D, E, and J.*

Equations Involving Three Variables

Equations having the form

$$a_1 x_1 + a_2 x_2 + a_3 x_3 = b$$

graph as *planes* in three dimensions. The number of variables in an equation determines the number of dimensions required to graphically represent the equation. Three variables require three dimensions. It is not so important that you actually be able to graph in three dimensions. It is more important that (1) you be aware that linear equations involving three variables graph as planes in three dimensions, (2) you know what a *plane* is, and (3) you have some feeling for how planes can be represented graphically. A plane, of course, is a flat surface like the ceiling, walls, and floor of the room in which you are currently sitting or lying. Instead of the two points needed to graph a line, three points are necessary to define a plane. The three points must not be *collinear;* i.e., they must not lie on the same line. Take, for example, the equation

$$2x_1 + 4x_2 + 3x_3 = 12 \tag{3.14}$$

If we can identify three members of the solution set for this equation, they will specify the coordinates of three points lying on the plane. Three members which are identified easily are the intercepts. These are found by setting any two of the three variables equal to 0 and solving for the remaining variable. Verify that when $x_1 = x_2 = 0$, $x_3 = 4$, or $(0, 0, 4)$ is a member of the solution set. Similarly, verify that $(6, 0, 0)$ and $(0, 3, 0)$ are members of the solution set and thus are points lying on the plane representing Eq. (3.14). Figure 3.14 shows these points and a portion of the plane which contains them.

When graphing equations involving two variables, we identified two points and connected them with a straight line. However, we saw that in order to represent *all* members of the solution set, the line must extend an infinite distance in each direction. The same is true with the solution set for three-variable equations. To represent all members of the solution set for the equation $2x_1 + 4x_2 + 3x_3 = 12$, the plane in Fig. 3.14 must extend an infinite distance in all directions.

EXAMPLE 21 ▬▬▬▬▬▬▬▬▬▬▬▬▬▬▬▬▬▬▬▬▬▬▬

Graph the linear equation $x_1 = 0$ in three dimensions.

SOLUTION

In later chapters we will see that problems often involve the use of more than one equation. In a problem which involves n variables, a subset of the equations may involve

---

* B $(0, 0, 4)$, C $(0, 4, 4)$, D $(-5, 4, 4)$, E $(-5, 4, 0)$, J $(0, -4, 0)$.

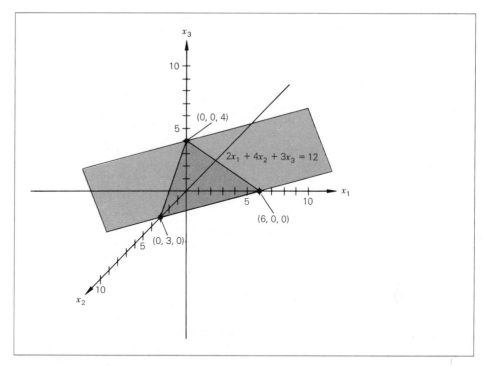

FIGURE 3.14
Graph of plane
representing the
linear equation
$2x_1 + 4x_2 + 3x_3 = 12$

fewer than n variables. Being asked to graph the equation $x_1 = 0$ in 3-space suggests that the equation represents information in a three-variable problem. The given equation may be one of a group of equations which deal with x_1, x_2, and x_3.

In order to graph the equation, we again need to identify three noncollinear points which satisfy the equation. We see that as long as $x_1 = 0$, x_2 and x_3 can equal *any* values. For example, (0, 0, 0), (0, 2, 0), and (0, 0, 4) all satisfy the equation. Figure 3.15 illustrates the graph of the equation. The equation $x_1 = 0$ graphs as a plane perpendicular to the x_1 axis and passing through $x_1 = 0$. This plane is the x_2x_3 *plane*.

Any equation of the form $x_1 = k$ graphs in 3-space as a plane perpendicular to the x_1 axis, intersecting it at $x_1 = k$.

Any equation of the form $x_j = k$, where $j = 1, 2,$ *or* 3, will graph as a plane which is perpendicular to the x_j axis at $x_j = k$. Figures 3.16 to 3.18 illustrate this property.

Equations Involving More than Three Variables

When more than three variables exist ($n > 3$), graphing requires more than three dimensions. To the author's knowledge no one has ever provided a visual representation or graph of a linear equation in four or more dimensions. Even though we cannot envision the graphical representation of such equations, the term *hyperplane* is used to describe the geometric representation of the equa-

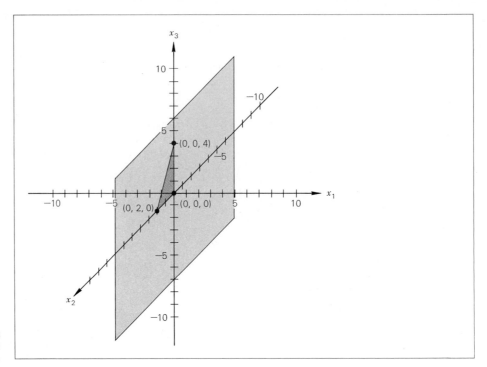

FIGURE 3.15
The plane
$x_1 = 0$.

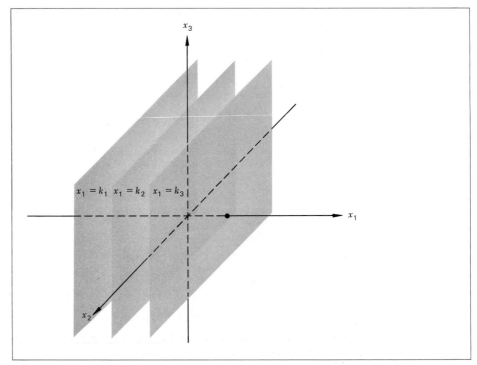

FIGURE 3.16
Planes of the
form $x_1 = k$.

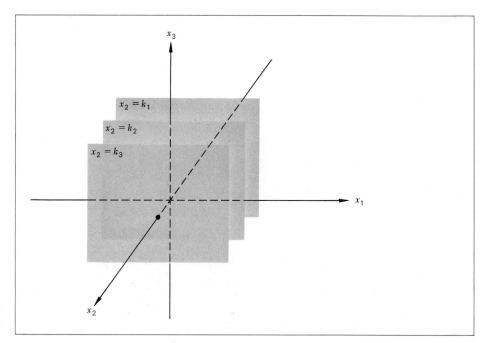

FIGURE 3.17
Planes of the
form $x_2 = k$.

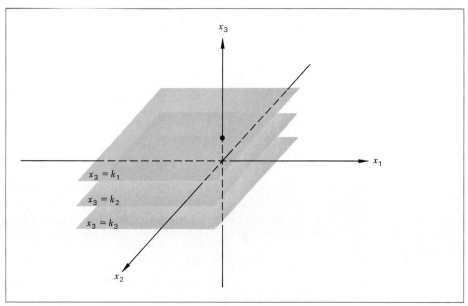

FIGURE 3.18
Planes of the
form $x_3 = k$.

tion. Mathematicians would, for instance, say that the equation

$$x_1 + x_2 + x_3 + x_4 = 10$$

is represented by a hyperplane in 4-space or four dimensions. Or, in general, an equation of the form

$$a_1x_1 + a_2x_2 + \cdots + a_nx_n = b$$

where $n > 3$ would be represented by a hyperplane in **n-space.**

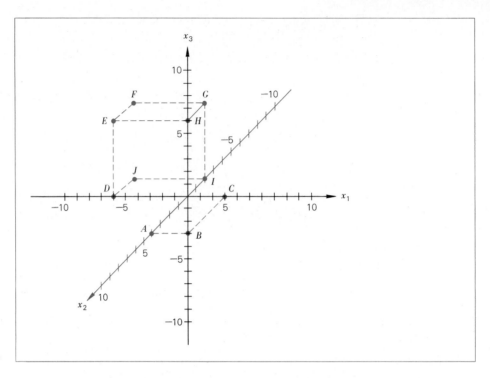

FIGURE 3.19

Section 3.5 Follow-up Exercises

    1   Given Figure 3.19, determine the coordinates of points A through I.

    2   Given the equation $x_1 - 2x_2 + 4x_3 = 10$, determine the coordinates of the x_1, x_2, and x_3 intercepts.

    3   Given the equation $-2x_1 + 3x_2 - x_3 = -15$, determine the coordinates of the x_1, x_2, and x_3 intercepts.

    4   Sketch the plane $3x_1 = 9$.   5   Sketch the plane $-2x_2 = -8$.

    6   Sketch the plane $x_3 = -2$.

    *7   Can you draw any general conclusions about the characteristics of planes which represent linear equations involving two of the three variables? For example, the equation $x_1 + x_2 = 5$ does not contain the variable x_3 but can be graphed in three dimensions. How does this equation graph? How about equations which involve x_1 and x_3? x_2 and x_3?

3.6 ADDITIONAL APPLICATIONS

The more exposure you have to word problems, the more skilled you will become in formulating them. The following examples illustrate the formulation of linear equations for different types of applications. Study these carefully and try as many of these types of problems as you can, both at the end of this section and at the end of the chapter.

EXAMPLE 22

Emergency Airlift The International Red Cross is making plans to airlift emergency food and medical supplies into a large South American city which has recently suffered from extensive flooding. The four items needed immediately and their respective volumes per container are shown below. The first plane to be sent into the area has a volume capacity of 6,000 cubic feet. Determine an equation whose solution set contains all possible combinations of the four items which will fill the plane to its volume capacity.

ITEM	VOLUME/CONTAINER, ft³
Blood	20
Medical supply kits	30
Food	8
Water	6

SOLUTION

As mentioned in Chap. 2, the first step in almost every word problem is to define the unknowns or variables which are to be used. It is useful to ask yourself what decisions need to be made in the problem. If these decisions can be identified, they hold the key to defining the variables.

In this example the decision facing the Red Cross personnel deals with how many containers of each item should be sent on the first plane. Since the Red Cross wishes to ship as many supplies as possible on this first plane, they are interested in identifying the different combinations which will fill the plane to capacity (volumewise).

Verbally, the equation we are seeking should have the form

$$\boxed{\text{Volume of supplies shipped} = 6{,}000 \text{ cubic feet}}$$

We can be more specific by rewriting the equation as

$$\boxed{\begin{array}{l}\text{Volume of blood} + \text{volume of medical supply kits} \\ \qquad\qquad\qquad + \text{volume of food} + \text{volume of water} = 6{,}000\end{array}}$$

If we let

$x_1 =$ *number of containers of blood*
$x_2 =$ *number of containers of medical supply kits*
$x_3 =$ *number of containers of food*
$x_4 =$ *number of containers of water*

the equation can be stated in its correct mathematical form as

$$20x_1 + 30x_2 + 8x_3 + 6x_4 = 6{,}000$$

Verify that *each term* on the left side of the equation is formed by using the relationship

$$\boxed{\begin{array}{c}\text{Total volume} \\ \text{of item } j\end{array} = \left(\begin{array}{c}\text{volume per container} \\ \text{of item } j\end{array}\right)\left(\begin{array}{c}\text{number of containers} \\ \text{of item } j\end{array}\right)}$$

Follow-up Exercises

1   In a realistic sense, what are the ranges of possible values for *each* of the four variables? What are the maximum and minimum possible quantities of each item?

2   Assume that the plane can only carry 40,000 pounds of cargo and that the items weigh 150, 100, 60, and 70 pounds per container, respectively. State the equation whose solution set contains all combinations of the four items which will add up to equal the weight capacity of the plane.

EXAMPLE 23 ▮▬▬▬▬▬▬▬▬▬▬▬▬▬▬▬▬▬▬▬▬

Investment Portfolio A local university has $5 million to invest in stocks. The board of trustees has approved six different types of stocks in which the university may invest. The current prices per share for each type of stock are indicated below. Determine the equation for which the solution set includes all the different combinations of the six stocks which could be purchased for exactly $5 million.

STOCK	PRICE PER SHARE
1	$ 35
2	60
3	125
4	100
5	500
6	250

SOLUTION

The general form of the equation should be total dollars spent on the six stocks equals $5 million, or more specifically

> Total dollars spent on stock 1 + total dollars spent on stock 2
> $+ \cdots +$ total dollars spent on stock 6 = $5 million

The basic decision to be made concerns the number of shares of each security to be purchased so as to expend the full $5 million. Therefore let's generalize our variables as

$$x_j = \text{number of shares purchased of stock } j$$

where j = 1, 2, 3, 4, 5, or 6
   Using these variables, we state the equation as

$$35x_1 + 60x_2 + 125x_3 + 100x_4 + 500x_5 + 250x_6 = 5 \text{ million}$$

Note that each term on the left side of the equation has the form

> Total dollars spent on stock j = (price per share)(number of shares purchased)

▬▬▬▬▬▬▬▬▬▬▬▬▬▬▬▬▬▬▬▬▬▬▬▬▬▬▬▬

Follow-up Exercises

   1   In a realistic sense, what are the maximum and minimum allowable values for each variable in the equation developed above?
   2   The expected annual dividends per share of each of the above stocks are shown below. Assume that the board of trustees desires to earn annual dividends of $1,000,000 from its investments. Using the same variables as in the example, develop the equation whose solution set includes all possible combinations of the six stocks which will generate annual dividends equal to $1,000,000.

STOCK	1	2	3	4	5	6
Expected annual dividend	$5	$8	$4	$7.50	$30	$40

EXAMPLE 24

Court Scheduling A metropolitan district court sorts its cases into three categories. Court records have enabled the court clerk to provide estimates of the average number of hours required to process each type of case. Type 1 cases average 16 hours, type 2 average 8 hours, and type 3 average 4.5 hours. For the coming month 850 hours are available in the six different courtrooms in the building. Determine an equation whose solution set includes all the different combinations of the three types of cases which would schedule the courts to their capacity.

SOLUTION

The general form of the equation should be

$$\boxed{\text{Total court hours scheduled} = 850}$$

Letting x_1, x_2, and x_3 equal the number of cases scheduled of Types 1, 2, and 3, respectively, the equation is

$$16x_1 + 8x_2 + 4.5x_3 = 850$$

EXAMPLE 25

Nutrition Planning A dietician at a local school is planning luncheon menus. He has eight choices of items which may be served at any one meal. One concern of the dietician is meeting various nutritional requirements. Our dietician is interested in determining the various quantities of each of the eight foods which would provide exactly 45 milligrams of a required vitamin. The vitamin content of each of the eight food items is shown below. Determine the equation whose solution set satisfies this requirement.

FOOD TYPE	1	2	3	4	5	6	7	8
mg/serving	5	7.5	3	4.5	9	10	2.5	6

SOLUTION

Letting x_j = number of servings of food j, where j = 1, 2, 3, 4, 5, 6, 7, or 8, the equation is

$$5x_1 + 7.5x_2 + 3x_3 + 4.5x_4 + 9x_5 + 10x_6 + 2.5x_7 + 6x_8 = 45$$

Section 3.6 Follow-up Exercises

1 In which of the last four examples should there be concern only with integer values for the variables?

2 A student is taking five courses and is facing the crunch of final exams. She estimates that she has 40 hours available to study. If x_j = the number of hours allocated to studying for course j, state the equation whose solution set specifies all possible allocations of time among the five courses which will exhaust the 40 hours available.

3 **Product-Mix** A firm produces three products. Product A requires 8 hours of production time, product B requires 5.5 hours, and product C requires 6.5 hours for each unit produced. If 600 hours are available during the coming week, determine the equation whose solution set specifies all possible amounts or quantities of the three products which can be produced using the 600 hours.

4   Transportation   A manufacturer distributes its product to four different whole-salers. The monthly capacity is 34,000 units of the product. Decisions need to be made about how many units should be shipped to each of the wholesalers. Determine the equation whose solution set specifies the different quantities which might be shipped if all 34,000 units are to be distributed.

5   Advertising   A national firm is beginning an advertising campaign using televi-sion, radio, and newspapers. The goal is to have 10 million people see their adver-tisements. Past experience indicates that for every $1,000 allocated to TV, radio, and newspaper advertising, 25,000, 18,000, and 15,000 people, respectively, will see the ad-vertisement. The decisions that need to be made involve how much money should be allocated to each form of advertising in order to reach 10 million people. Determine the equation whose solution set specifies all the different advertising allocations which will result in the achievement of this goal.

6   Agricultural Planning   An argicultural company has a goal of harvesting 500,000 bushels of soybeans during the coming year. The company has three farms available to meet this goal. Because of climate differences and other factors, the yields per acre in the different locations are 25, 23, and 27 bushels, respectively, for farms 1, 2, and 3. The deci-sion which needs to be made concerns how many acres should be planted in soybeans at each farm in order to meet the company's goal. State the equation which allows for speci-fying the different possibilities for meeting the 500,000-bushel goal.

KEY TERMS AND CONCEPTS

hyperplane 107	slope relationship for
linear equation 80	perpendicular lines 100
n-space 109	solution set 81
plane 106	three-space 104
slope 91	two-point formula 92
slope-intercept form of	x-intercept 89
linear equation 95	y intercept 89

IMPORTANT FORMULAS

$ax + by = c$ **Linear equation: two variables**   **(3.1)**

$a_1x_1 + a_2x_2 + a_3x_3 + \cdots + a_nx_n = b$ **Linear equation: n variables**   **(3.2)**

$m = \dfrac{y_2 - y_1}{x_2 - x_1}$ **Two-point formula**   **(3.10)**

$y = mx + k$ **Slope-intercept form of linear equation**   **(3.12)**

ADDITIONAL EXERCISES

Exercises 1 to 8 are related to Sec. 3.1.

In Exercises 1 to 6, determine whether the equation is linear.

1	$x - \frac{1}{4}y = 6$	2	$\frac{1}{2}(x - 3y) = 5$
3	$x + 2y = xy$	4	$x_1 + x_1x_2 - x_2 = 13$

5    $x_1 - x_2 + x_3 = \frac{1}{4}x_4 + \sqrt{2}$ 6 $(a - 5)2 - b = -3(b - a)$

7   A company manufactures two different products, A and B. Each unit of product A costs \$5 to produce, and each unit of product B costs \$3. The company insists that total costs for the two products be \$300.

(a) Define the cost equation which states that the total cost of producing x units of product A and y units of product B equals \$300.

(b) Identify a pair of values for x and y which satisfies this equation.

(c) Assuming the company has agreed to fill an order for 30 units of product A, how many units of product B should be produced if total costs are to be kept at \$300?

(d) Use set notation to specify membership in the solution set P for the equation defined in part a.

8   A local travel agent has been authorized to sell three new vacation packages for a major airline. The three packages are priced at \$500, \$750, and \$1,000, respectively. The airline has promised a sizeable bonus commission if total sales by the travel agent equal \$50,000 or more. If x_1, x_2, and x_3 equal the number of packages sold of types 1, 2, and 3, respectively,

(a) Define the equation which states that total sales equal \$50,000.

(b) If the airline specifies that the agent must sell 10 of the \$1,000 packages and 30 of the \$750 packages in order to qualify for the bonus, how many of the \$500 packages will be necessary to qualify?

(c) One strategy being considered by the agent is to sponsor a charter flight where all persons would select the same package. Given that three different charters could be planned, how many persons would have to sign up for each in order to qualify for the bonus?

Exercises 9 to 18 are related to Sec. 3.2.

In Exercises 9 to 14, identify the x and y intercepts if they exist and graph the linear equation.

9    $-2x = \frac{1}{2}y$ 10 $-\frac{1}{4}x = 2$
11    $(y - 3)/2 = -x$ 12 $2(y - 4) = y - 3$
13    $x - 2y = 0$ 14 $3x - 4y + 4 = -3y - x + 3$

In Exercises 15 to 18, compute the slope of the line segment connecting the two points. Interpret the meaning of the slope in each case.

15    $(-3, 2)$ and $(-1, -6)$ 16 $(-a, -a)$ and (a, a)
17   (a, b) and $(a, 3b)$ 18 $(3, c)$ and $(-4, c)$

Exercises 19 to 24 are related to Sec. 3.3.

In Exercises 19 to 22 rewrite each equation in the slope-intercept form and determine the slope and y intercept.

19    $5x - 2y = -x + 15$ 20 $-\frac{1}{2}x = \frac{1}{4}y - 3$
21    $rx - sy = p$ 22 $-cx + cy = 5c$

23   A local dairy association enlists the help of a marketing research firm to predict the demand for milk. The research firm finds that the local demand for milk can be predicted by the equation $q = -2,000p + 4,200$, where p represents the price per quart (in dollars) and q represents the number of quarts purchased per week.

(a) Graph the equation.

(b) Identify the slope and y intercept.

(c) Interpret the meaning of the slope and y intercept in this application.

   24   A manufacturing firm has 40 hours per week available in one of its departments. Two products are processed through this department. Product A requires 2.5 hours per unit and product B 5 hours per unit in this department. If x equals the number of units of product A produced per week and y equals the number of units of product B produced per week,

(a) Determine the equation which states that total time expended for producing these two products equals 40 hours per week.

(b) Rewrite this equation in slope-intercept form and identify the slope and y intercept.

(c) Interpret the meaning of the slope and y intercept in this application.

Exercises 25 to 34 are related to Sec. 3.4.

In Exercises 25 to 30 use the given information to determine the slope-intercept form of the linear equation.

   25   m undefined and line passes through $(-3, 5)$
   26   Slope equals $\frac{1}{2}$, y intercept occurs at $(0, -5)$
   27   Slope equals 0, $(a, -b)$ lies on the line
   28   $(-1, 3)$ and $(2, -6)$ lie on the line
   29   $(2, -b)$ and $(-4, -b)$ lie on the line
   30   $(0, 0)$ and (b, b) lie on the line
   31   Determine the equation of the line which is parallel to the line representing the equation $2x - y = 5$ and which passes through the point $(3, 6)$.
   32   Determine the equation of the line which is perpendicular to the line $x - 2y = 20$ and which passes through the point $(3, 0)$.
   33   An economist believes there is a linear relationship which exists between the market price of a particular commodity and the number of units suppliers of the commodity are willing to bring to the marketplace. Two sample observations indicate that when the price equals $10 per unit, the weekly supply equals 30,000 units and when the price equals $12 per unit, the weekly supply equals 40,000 units.

(a) If price per unit, p, is plotted on the horizontal axis and the quantity supplied, q, is plotted on the vertical axis, determine the equation of the line which passes through these two points.

(b) Determine the slope-intercept form of the equation.

(c) Interpret the slope of the equation in this application.

(d) Predict the weekly supply if the market price equals $15 per unit.

   34   In attempting to predict the demand for a particular style of shoe, a retail shoe store finds that 60 pairs are sold per week if the price per pair is $25; and when the price rises to $30 per pair, only 40 pairs are sold.

(a) If price is to be plotted on the horizontal axis, determine the slope-intercept form of the equation for demand. Restate the equation in the standard form of Eq. (3.1).

(b) Using this equation, predict how many pairs of shoes will be sold if the price is lowered to $15.

Exercises 35 to 37 are related to Sec. 3.6.

35   A retail store sells four products. Let x_1, x_2, x_3, and x_4 represent the number of units sold, respectively, of the four products. The profits earned from each unit sold of the four products are $20, $5, $8, and $2, respectively. Target profits for the firm are $40,000.

(a) Using x_1, x_2, x_3, and x_4, define an equation which states that total profit from selling the four products equals $40,000.

(b) Give the range of values (maximum and minimum) possible for each variable in the equation developed in part a.

36   A woman who has recently inherited $100,000 decides to invest her inheritance in stocks. She is considering eight stocks, the prices of which are given below.

STOCK	1	2	3	4	5	6	7	8
Price per share	$12	$150	$76.50	$25	$8	$57	$200	$42

Determine the equation whose solution set contains all possible combinations of the eight stocks which can be purchased for $100,000. (Be sure to define your variables.)

37   **Personnel Management**   The head of personnel has been given a budget allotment of $250,000 to staff an engineering department. Four types of employees are needed: senior engineers at an annual salary of $35,000 each, junior engineers at an annual salary of $20,000 each, drafters at an annual salary of $15,000 each, and secretaries at a salary of $9,000 each. Write an equation whose solution set contains the possible combinations of employees which could be hired for $250,000. (Be sure to define your variables.)

CHAPTER TEST

1   Given the equation $3x - 5y = 30$,
(a) Determine the x and y intercepts.
(b) Graph the equation.

2   Given the equation $(x + y)/2 = 10 - (2x - 3y)/3$,
(a) Rewrite the equation in the slope-intercept form.
(b) Identify the slope and y intercept.
(c) Interpret the meaning of the slope.

3   Given two points $(2, 8)$ and $(-2, -4)$,
(a) Determine the equation of the straight line which passes through these two points.
(b) Identify the slope and y intercept.

4   Determine the equation of the straight line which is perpendicular to the line represented by the equation $4x - y = 5$ and which passes through the point $(-2, 0)$.

5   A manufacturer has a monthly supply of 300,000 pounds of a raw material for use in making four products. The number of pounds required to manufacture a unit of each product equals 3,000, 4,000, 1,000, and 1,500, respectively. If x_1, x_2, x_3, and x_4 equal the number of units produced of each product, define the equation whose solution set includes the possible combinations of the four products which would exhaust the monthly supply of the raw material.

4

SYSTEMS OF LINEAR EQUATIONS

CHAPTER OBJECTIVES

- Provide an understanding of the nature of systems of equations and their graphical representation (where appropriate)

- Provide an understanding of the different solution set possibilities for different types of systems of equations

- Provide an appreciation of the graphical interpretation of solution sets

- Present procedures for determining solution sets for systems of equations

4.1 INTRODUCTION

Systems of Equations

A *system of equations* is a set consisting of more than one equation. One way to characterize a system of equations is by its *dimensions.* If a system of equations consists of m equations and n variables, we say that this system is an *"m by n" system,* or that it has dimensions *(m × n).* A system of equations involving two equations and two variables is described as having dimensions (2×2). A system consisting of 15 equations and 10 variables is said to be a (15×10) system.

Many applications in business and economics deal with systems of equations. As such, we are often concerned with analyzing the interactions among equations. For example, in the last chapter, Example 22 was concerned with airlifting emergency supplies into a South American city. An equation was formulated to represent the various quantities of each item which would fill the plane to its volume capacity:

$$20x_1 + 30x_2 + 8x_3 + 6x_4 = 6,000 \tag{4.1}$$

Exercise 2 on page 111 introduced data concerning the weight capacity of the same plane and the weight per container of each item. Your answer to that exercise should have been the equation

$$120x_1 + 180x_2 + 80x_3 + 95x_4 = 40,000 \qquad \textbf{(4.2)}$$

The solution set for this equation contains values for the four variables which represent all quantities of the various items which would fill the plane to its weight capacity of 40,000 pounds. Given these two equations, it may be of interest to determine whether there are combinations of the four items which would fill the plane to both its weight and volume capacities. How to go about answering this type of question is the subject of this chapter.

Solution Sets

In solving systems of equations, we are interested in identifying values of the variables that satisfy all equations in the system simultaneously. For example, given the two equations

$$5x + 10y = 20$$
$$3x + 4y = 10$$

we may wish to identify any values of x and y which satisfy both equations at the same time. Stated in set notation, we would want to identify the *solution set* S where

$$S = \{(x, y) | 5x + 10y = 20 \text{ and } 3x + 4y = 10\}$$

As you will see in this chapter, the solution set S for a system of linear equations may be a *null set*, a *finite set*, or an *infinite set*.*

There are quite a few solution procedures which may be used in solving systems of equations. We will concentrate on two different procedures. Other procedures will be presented in either examples or appendices. The most important consideration is that we have the ability to solve a system of equations when a solution is required.

In this chapter we will develop solution procedures starting with the simplest systems, two equations and two variables. Our discussions will emphasize both the graphical and algebraic aspects of each situation. These procedures will be extended later in the chapter to acquaint us with how larger systems of equations are handled. We will also discuss a variety of applications of systems of equations.

4.2 TWO-VARIABLE SYSTEMS OF EQUATIONS

Graphical Analysis

From Chap. 3 we know that a linear equation involving two variables graphs as a straight line. Thus a (2×2) system of equations is represented by two straight lines in two dimensions. In solving for the values of the two variables which satisfy *both* equations, we are graphically trying to determine if the two lines representing the equations have any points in common.

For (2×2) systems of equations three different types of solution sets might exist. Given that two lines are graphed in a plane, Fig. 4.1 illustrates the three

---

* A finite set consists of a limited number of elements; an infinite set consists of an infinite number of elements.

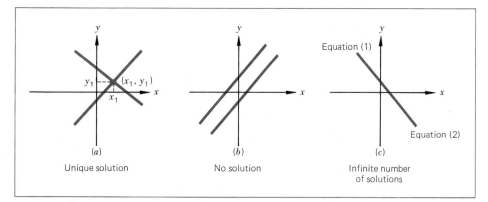

FIGURE 4.1
Solution set possibilities for a (2 × 2) system of equations.

(a) Unique solution

(b) No solution

(c) Infinite number of solutions

possibilities. In Fig. 4.1*a*, the two lines intersect. The *coordinates* of the point of intersection (x_1, y_1) represent the solution for the system of equations; that is, the pair of values for x and y which satisfy *both* equations. When there is just one pair of values for the variables which satisfy the system of equations, the system is said to have a ***unique solution.***

In Fig. 4.1*b*, the two lines are parallel to each other. You should remember from the last chapter that parallel lines have the same slope; and provided that they have different y intercepts, the lines have no points in common. Graphically the lines never intersect. If a (2 × 2) system of equations has these characteristics, the system is said to have ***no solution.*** That is, there are no values for the variables which satisfy both equations. The equations in such a system are said to be *inconsistent.*

The final possibility for a (2 × 2) system is illustrated in Fig. 4.1*c*. In this case both equations graph as the same line, and they are considered to be *equivalent equations.* An infinite number of points are common to the two lines and the system is said to have an ***infinite number of solutions.*** Being represented by the same line implies that both lines have the same slope *and* the same y intercept. Although this situation is relatively uncommon in an application, two equations *can* look very different from each other and still be equivalent to one another. For example, the two equations

$$-6x + 12y = -24$$

and

$$1.5x - 3y = 6$$

are equivalent. Verify that the slope and the y intercept are the same for both.

Another way of summarizing the three cases illustrated in Fig. 4.1 is as follows:

In a (2 × 2) system of linear equations let m_1 and m_2 represent the respective slopes of the two lines and k_1 and k_2 represent the respective y intercepts.

I There is a *unique solution* to the system if $m_1 \neq m_2$.

II There is *no solution* to the system if $m_1 = m_2$ but $k_1 \neq k_2$.

III There are an *infinite number of solutions* if $m_1 = m_2$ and $k_1 = k_2$.

Graphical Solutions

Graphical solution approaches are possible for two-variable systems of equations. However, you must be accurate in your graphics. The following example illustrates a graphical solution.

EXAMPLE 1

Graphically determine the solution to the system of equations

$$2x + 4y = 20 \tag{4.3}$$
$$3x + y = 10 \tag{4.4}$$

The x and y intercepts are, respectively, (10, 0) and (0, 5) for Eq. (4.3). Similarly, the intercepts for Eq. (4.4) are $(\frac{10}{3}, 0)$ and (0, 10). When these are plotted in Fig. 4.2 and connected, the two lines appear to cross at (2, 4).

A problem with graphical solutions is that it may be difficult to read the precise coordinates of the points of intersection. This is especially true when the coordinates are not integers. This is why algebraic solution procedures are generally viewed as being superior from the standpoint of identifying *exact* solutions. However, whether you use graphical or algebraic procedures, there is always a check on your answer: substitute your answer into the original equations to see if they are satisfied by the values. Substituting $x = 2$ and $y = 4$ into Eqs. (4.3) and (4.4), we get

$$2(2) + 4(4) = 20$$

or

$$20 = 20$$

and

$$3(2) + (4) = 10$$

or

$$10 = 10$$

Therefore our solution checks.

The Elimination Procedure

One popular solution method is the *elimination procedure,* which uses the operations of multiplication and addition. Given a (2×2) system of equations, the two equations, or multiples of the two equations, are added so as to *eliminate* one of the two variables. The resultant equation is stated in terms of the remaining variable. This equation can be solved for the remaining variable, the value of which can be substituted back into one of the original equations to solve for the value of the eliminated variable. The solution process is demonstrated in the following example, after which the procedure will be formalized.

EXAMPLE 2

Solve the system of equations in Example 1.

SOLUTION

The original system was

$$2x + 4y = 20 \tag{4.3}$$
$$3x + y = 10 \tag{4.4}$$

The objective of the elimination procedure is to eliminate one of the two variables by adding (multiples of) the equations. If we *multiply* Eq. (4.4) by -4 and *add* the resulting

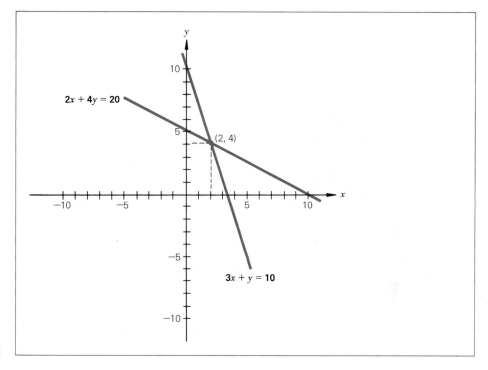

FIGURE 4.2

equation to Eq. (4.3), we get Eq. (4.5):

$$
\begin{array}{rl}
2x + 4y = & 20 \qquad\qquad\qquad \textbf{(4.3)}\\
-12x - 4y = & -40 \qquad\qquad\quad \textbf{(4.4}a\textbf{)}\\
\hline
-10x \quad\;\; = & -20 \qquad\qquad\quad \textbf{(4.5)}
\end{array}
$$

Equation (4.5) contains the variable x only, and we can solve this equation to find the value of $x = 2$. Substituting this value for x into one of the original equations—let's select Eq. (4.3)—we find that

$$
\begin{aligned}
2(2) + 4y &= 20\\
4y &= 16\\
y &= 4
\end{aligned}
$$

or

Therefore the unique solution to the system, as we determined earlier, occurs when $x = 2$ and $y = 4$.

NOTE

It is advisable always to substitute back into one of the *original* equations to guard against careless arithmetic errors. If, for example, we had failed to multiply the right side of Eq. (4.4) by -4, the following would have occurred:

$$
\begin{array}{rl}
2x + 4y = 20 \qquad\qquad\quad \textbf{(4.3)}\\
-12x - 4y = 10 \qquad\qquad\quad \textbf{(4.4}a\textbf{)}\\
\hline
-10x \quad\;\; = 30 \qquad\qquad\quad \textbf{(4.5)}
\end{array}
$$

and

$$
x = -3
$$

If we had substituted $x = -3$ *back into Eq. (4.4a)*, which is not one of the original equations, the value for y would have been computed as

$$-12(-3) - 4y = 10$$
$$-4y = -26$$
$$y = 6.5$$

This is not the solution to the original system. It *is* the solution to the system consisting of Eqs. (4.3) and (4.4a). Because of the multiplication error, this system is not equivalent to the original system.

Checking your solution values in *all* the original equations is the best check on your answer.

EXERCISE

Verify that the solution is exactly the same if x is selected for elimination. To eliminate x multiply Eqs. (4.3) and (4.4) by -3 and 2, respectively.

The elimination procedure can be generalized as follows for a (2×2) system of equations:

ELIMINATION PROCEDURE FOR 2× 2 SYSTEMS

I Multiply (if necessary) the equations by constants so that the coefficients on one of the variables are the negatives of one another in the two equations.
II Add the two resulting equations.
III (a) If adding the equations results in a new equation having one variable, there is a **unique solution** to the system. Solve for the value of the remaining variable, and substitute this value back into one of the original equations to determine the value of the variable that was originally eliminated.
(b) If adding the equations results in an identity, (i.e., an equation that is always true, such as 0 = 0), the two original equations are **equivalent** to each other and there are an **infinite number of solutions** to the system.
(c) If adding the equations results in a false statement, say, 0 = 5, the equations are **inconsistent** and there is **no solution set.** See Fig. 4.3.

EXAMPLE 3

Solve the following system of equations by the elimination procedure.

$$3x - 2y = \quad 6 \qquad \qquad \textbf{(4.6)}$$
$$-15x + 10y = -30 \qquad \textbf{(4.7)}$$

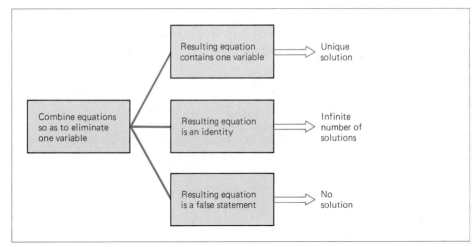

FIGURE 4.3
Elimination pro-
cedure for
(2 × 2)
systems.

SOLUTION

Choosing x as the variable to eliminate, let's multiply Eq. (4.6) by 5 and add the resulting equations:

$$
\begin{array}{rl}
15x - 10y = & 30 \qquad \textbf{(4.6}a\textbf{)} \\
-15x + 10y = & -30 \qquad \textbf{(4.7)} \\
\hline
0 = & 0
\end{array}
$$

When Eqs. (4.6a) and (4.7) are added, both variables are eliminated on the left side of the equation and we are left with the identity $0 = 0$. From step IIIb of the solution procedure we conclude that the two equations are equivalent and there are an infinite number of solutions.

In order to specify sample members of the solution set, we could assume an arbitrary value for either x or y and substitute this value into one of the original equations, solving for the corresponding value of the other variable. For example, verify that if we let $x = 4$, substitution of this value into either Eq. (4.6) or (4.7) will result in the corresponding value $y = 3$. Thus, one member of the solution set is (4, 3). A more general way of specifying the solution set is to solve either of the original equations for one of the variables. The result is an equation which states the value of one variable as a function of the value of the second variable. To illustrate, if Eq. (4.7) is solved for y, the result is

$$10y = 15x - 30$$

or

$$y = \tfrac{3}{2}x - 3$$

Therefore, one way of specifying the solution set is

$$\boxed{\begin{array}{l} x \text{ arbitrary} \\ y = \tfrac{3}{2}x - 3 \end{array}}$$

or, alternatively

$$S = \{(x,y) \mid x \text{ is real}, y = \tfrac{3}{2}x - 3\}$$

EXAMPLE 4 ▆▆▆▆▆▆▆▆▆▆▆▆▆▆▆▆▆▆▆▆▆▆▆▆▆▆▆▆▆▆▆▆▆▆▆▆

Solve the following system of equations by the elimination procedure.

$$6x - 12y = 24 \qquad\qquad\qquad \textbf{(4.8)}$$
$$-1.5x + 3y = 9 \qquad\qquad\qquad \textbf{(4.9)}$$

SOLUTION

Multiplying Eq. (4.9) by 4 and adding this multiple to Eq. (4.8) yields

$$
\begin{array}{ll}
6x - 12y = 24 & \textbf{(4.8)} \\
\underline{-6x + 12y = 36} & \textbf{(4.9}a\textbf{)} \\
 0 = 60 &
\end{array}
$$

Since $0 = 60$ is a false statement, there is no solution to the system of equations.

▆▆

EXERCISE ▆▆▆▆▆▆▆▆▆▆▆▆▆▆▆▆▆▆▆▆▆▆▆

Rewrite Eqs. (4.8) and (4.9) in slope-intercept form and confirm
that they have the same slope but different y intercepts.

(*m* × 2) Systems

When there are more than two equations ($m > 2$) involving two variables, each
equation still graphs as a line in two dimensions. For example, Fig. 4.4 illustrates two (3 × 2) systems. In Fig. 4.4*a* the three lines all intersect at the same
point, and there is a unique solution. In Fig. 4.4*b* there are points which are
common to different pairs of lines, but there is no point common to all three,
which means that there is no solution. A possible, but unlikely, situation is that
the *m* equations are all equivalent to one another and all graph as the same line.
    The solution procedure is relatively simple for these systems.

SOLUTION PROCEDURE FOR *m* × 2 SYSTEMS ▆▆▆▆▆▆▆▆▆▆▆▆▆
(*m* > 2)

I Select any two of the *m* equations and solve them simultaneously.
II (*a*) If in step I there is a unique solution, substitute the values found into the remaining equations in the system. If each
remaining equation is satisfied by these values, they represent
a unique solution. If the values fail to satisfy *any* of the remaining equations, there is no solution to the system.

---

* y arbitrary, $x = \frac{2}{3}y + 2$.

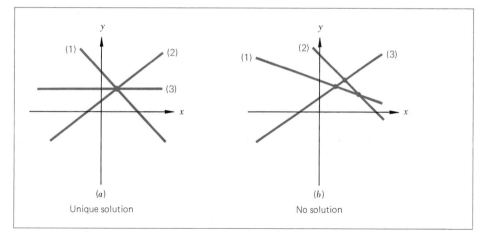

FIGURE 4.4
Solution possibilities for (3×2) systems.

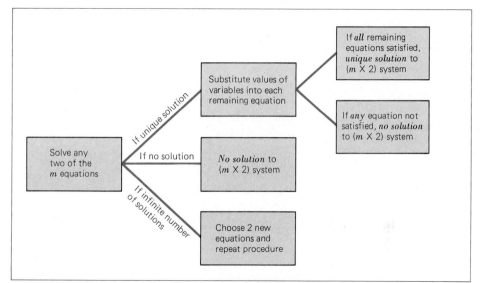

FIGURE 4.5
Elimination procedure for $(m \times 2)$ systems where $m > 2$.

(*b*) If in step I there is no solution, there is no solution for the system.
(*c*) If in step I there are an infinite number of solutions, two different equations should be selected and step 1 should be repeated. See Fig. 4.5.

EXAMPLE 5

Determine the solution set for the following system of equations:

$$x + 2y = 8 \tag{4.10}$$
$$2x - 3y = -5 \tag{4.11}$$
$$-5x + 6y = 8 \tag{4.12}$$
$$x + y = 7 \tag{4.13}$$

SOLUTION

The (2 × 2) system consisting of Eqs. (4.10) and (4.11) is solved by multiplying Eq. (4.10) by −2 and adding it to Eq. (4.11), or

$$
\begin{array}{r}
-2x - 4y = -16 \\
\underline{2x - 3y = -5} \\
-7y = -21 \\
y = 3
\end{array}
$$

Substituting back into Eq. (4.10) yields

$$x + 2(3) = 8$$

or

$$x = 2$$

The solution (2, 3) is tested by substituting into Eq. (4.12). Since

$$-5(2) + 6(3) = 8$$

the point (2, 3) satisfies the first three equations. Substituting into Eq. (4.13) gives

$$2 + 3 \neq 7$$

or

$$5 \neq 7$$

Since (2, 3) does not satisfy Eq. (4.13), there is no unique solution to the system of equations. Figure 4.6 illustrates the situation. Note that the lines representing Eqs. (4.10) to (4.12) intersect at the point (2, 3); however (2, 3) does not lie on the line representing Eq. (4.13).

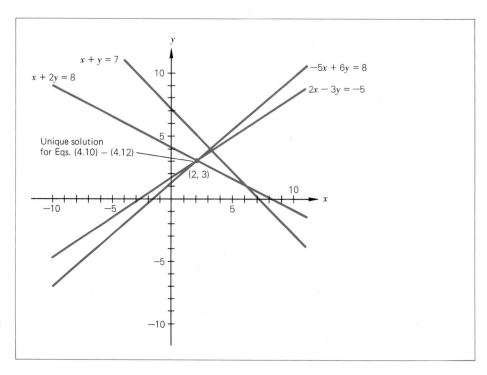

FIGURE 4.6
No solution set
for (4 × 2)
system.

Section 4.2 Follow-up Exercises

In Exercises 1 to 4, determine the nature of the solution set—unique, infinite, or no solution—by comparing the slope and y coordinates of the y intercepts for the lines representing the two equations.

1 $2x - 9y = 108$
   $8x + 6y = 48$

2 $5x + 5y = 0$
   $x \qquad = -y$

3 $3x - 9y = 24$
   $-x + 3y = 0$

4 $4x - 2y = 8$
   $x + 2y = 12$

In Exercises 5 to 8, solve graphically and check your answer algebraically.

5 $3x + 2y = 8$
   $x - y = 1$

6 $2x - 3y = -13$
   $4x + 2y = -2$

7 $x - 2y = 0$
   $-3x + 6y = 5$

8 $-x + 2y = -2$
   $3x \qquad = 6y + 6$

Solve each of the following systems of equations. For any system having an infinite number of solutions, specify the generalized form of the solution.

9 $4x - y = 17$
   $5x + 3y = 0$

10 $4x - 2y = 20$
    $-2x \qquad = -y + 15$

11 $6x - 8y = 4$
    $6 + 12y = 9x$

12 $-2x + 5y = 20$
    $4x + y = 4$

13 $2x + 4y = -8$
    $-3x + 2y = 4$

14 $2x - y = 9$
    $x + 3y = -6$

15 $2x - y = 4$
    $-6x + 3y = -12$

16 $12x - 4y = 18$
    $-4x + y = 6$

17 $x - 2y = -7$
    $3x + y = 0$
    $2x + 3y = 7$

18 $x - y = 2$
    $2x + y = 1$
    $7x - 5y = 6$

19 $x + y = 4$
    $2x - 3y = 3$
    $4x - 2y = 10$
    $-x + 3y = 0$

20 $x + y = 3$
    $2x - y = 12$
    $x - 4y = 13$
    $-2x + 5y = 0$

21 $x - y = 8$
    $2x + y = 4$
    $3x + 2y = 4$
    $x + 2y = -4$
    $5x - 2y = 20$

22 $x - y = 1$
    $x + 2y = -8$
    $3x - 2y = 0$
    $2x - 5y = 11$
    $-4x + 3y = -1$

4.3 THREE-VARIABLE SYSTEMS

Graphical Analysis

With three variables each linear equation graphs as a *plane* in three dimensions. In solving a system of three-variable equations, we are looking for any points common to the planes. Let's first consider (2 × 3) systems, or those represented by two planes. For (2 × 3) systems there cannot be a unique solution. There is no way in which two planes can intersect at only one point. Think about it! *The*

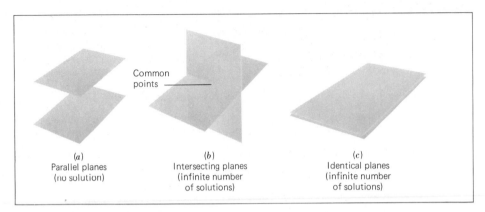

FIGURE 4.7
Possible solution sets for
(2×3)
systems.

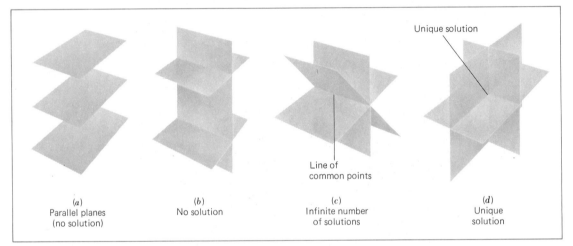

FIGURE 4.8
Possible solution sets for
(3×3)
systems.

solution sets for (2×3) systems contain either no elements (no solution) or an infinite number of solutions. Figure 4.7 illustrates different possibilities for these types of systems.

For $(m \times 3)$ systems, where $m \geq 3$, it is possible to have a unique solution, no solution, or an infinite number of solutions. Figure 4.8 illustrates different solution possibilities for (3×3) systems.

Elimination Procedure for (3×3) Systems

The elimination procedure for (3×3) systems is similar to that for (2×2) systems. The aim is to start with the (3×3) system and to reduce this to an equivalent system having two variables and two equations. With one of the three variables eliminated, the same procedure as used for (2×2) systems is employed to eliminate a second variable, resulting in a (1×1) system. After you solve for the remaining variable, its value is substituted sequentially back through the (2×2) system and finally the (3×3) system to determine the values of the other two variables. Figure 4.9 illustrates the process schematically. In Fig. 4.9, x_1 is eliminated first, followed by x_2. This order is not required; it is simply illustrative.

The elimination procedure for a (3×3) system is as follows:

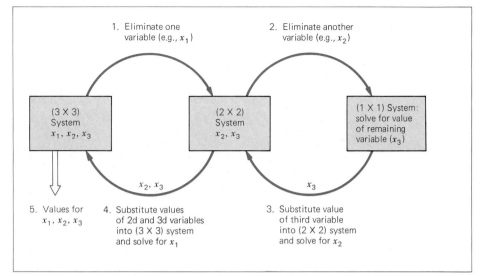

FIGURE 4.9
Elimination pro-
·cedure for
(3 × 3)
systems.

ELIMINATION PROCEDURE FOR 3 × 3 SYSTEMS

I Add multiples of any two of the three equations in order to eliminate one of the three variables. The result should be an equation involving the other two variables.

II Repeat step I with *another* pair of the original equations, eliminating the same variable as in step I. This second pair of equations will include *one* of the two equations used in step I and the equation not used in step I.

III The results of steps I and II should be a (2 × 2) system. Use the procedure for (2 × 2) systems (page 124) to determine the values for the remaining two variables.

IV Substitute the values of these two variables into one of the original equations. Solve for the value of the third variable.

If during any phase of the elimination procedure an identity results [see step III*b* of the (2 × 2) procedure], then the solution set contains an infinite number of elements. An exception to this is the case where step I results in an identity and step II a false statement. What is the graphical implication of these two results? *If at any stage a false statement results [step IIIc of the (2 × 2) procedure], then there is no solution to the original system of equations.*

EXAMPLE 6

Unique Solution   Determine the solution set for the following system of equations.

$$x_1 + x_2 + x_3 = 6 \tag{4.14}$$
$$2x_1 - x_2 + 3x_3 = 4 \tag{4.15}$$
$$4x_1 + 5x_2 - 10x_3 = 13 \tag{4.16}$$

SOLUTION

Although it makes no difference which variable is eliminated first, let's eliminate x_2. If Eqs. (4.14) and (4.15) are added, the resultant Eq. (4.17) is stated in terms of x_1 and x_3:

$$\begin{array}{r} x_1 + x_2 + x_3 = 6 \\ 2x_1 - x_2 + 3x_3 = 4 \\ \hline 3x_1 \phantom{{}- x_2} + 4x_3 = 10 \end{array} \qquad \text{(4.17)}$$

Multiplying Eq. (4.15) by $+5$ and adding it to Eq. (4.16) yields the new Eq. (4.18) as follows:

$$\begin{array}{r} 10x_1 - 5x_2 + 15x_3 = 20 \\ 4x_1 + 5x_2 - 10x_3 = 13 \\ \hline 14x_1 \phantom{{}+ 5x_2} + 5x_3 = 33 \end{array} \qquad \text{(4.18)}$$

Since x_2 has been eliminated, the system has been reduced to the (2×2) system

$$\begin{array}{ll} 3x_1 + 4x_3 = 10 & \text{(4.17)} \\ 14x_1 + 5x_3 = 33 & \text{(4.18)} \end{array}$$

By proceeding as we did in Sec. 4.2, x_3 can be eliminated if we multiply Eq. (4.17) by $+5$ and Eq. (4.18) by -4. When the two equations are added, x_3 is eliminated and Eq. (4.19) is formed:

$$\begin{array}{r} 15x_1 + 20x_3 = 50 \\ -56x_1 - 20x_3 = -132 \\ \hline -41x_1 \phantom{{}- 20x_3} = -82 \end{array} \qquad \text{(4.19)}$$

Solving Eq. (4.19) for x_1, we get $x_1 = 2$. If this value is substituted into Eq. (4.17), the value of x_3 is determined in the following manner:

$$\begin{array}{r} 3(2) + 4x_3 = 10 \\ 4x_3 = 4 \\ x_3 = 1 \end{array}$$

Substituting the values of $x_1 = 2$ and $x_3 = 1$ into Eq. (4.14) yields

$$2 + x_2 + 1 = 6$$

or

$$x_2 = 3$$

Verify that the solution set consists of one point where $x_1 = 2$, $x_2 = 3$, and $x_3 = 1$ by substituting these values into Eqs. (4.15) and (4.16).

EXAMPLE 7

No Solution Determine the solution set for this system of equations:

$$\begin{array}{rl} -2x_1 + x_2 + 3x_3 = 12 & \text{(4.20)} \\ x_1 + 2x_2 + 5x_3 = 10 & \text{(4.21)} \\ 6x_1 - 3x_2 - 9x_3 = 24 & \text{(4.22)} \end{array}$$

SOLUTION

Variable x_1 can be eliminated by multiplying Eq. (4.21) by $+2$ and adding it to Eq. (4.20) as follows:

$$\begin{array}{rcl} -2x_1 + x_2 + 3x_3 &=& 12 \\ 2x_1 + 4x_2 + 10x_3 &=& 20 \\ \hline 5x_2 + 13x_3 &=& 32 \end{array}$$ (4.23)

Similarly, x_1 can be eliminated by multiplying Eq. (4.21) by -6 and adding the resulting equation to Eq. (4.22), or

$$\begin{array}{rcl} -6x_1 - 12x_2 - 30x_3 &=& -60 \\ 6x_1 - 3x_2 - 9x_3 &=& 24 \\ \hline -15x_2 - 39x_3 &=& -36 \end{array}$$ (4.24)

Eliminating x_1 leaves the (2 × 2) system

$$5x_2 + 13x_3 = 32$$ (4.23)
$$-15x_2 - 39x_3 = -36$$ (4.24)

To eliminate x_2, Eq. (4.23) is multiplied by $+3$ and added to Eq. (4.24), or

$$\begin{array}{rcl} 15x_2 + 39x_3 &=& 96 \\ -15x_2 - 39x_3 &=& -36 \\ \hline 0 &=& 60 \end{array}$$ (4.25)

Note that Eq. (4.25) is a false statement, meaning that there is no solution to the original system of equations.

EXAMPLE 8

Infinite Number of Solutions Determine the solution set for the system of equations

$$x_1 + x_2 + x_3 = 20$$ (4.26)
$$2x_1 - 3x_2 + x_3 = -5$$ (4.27)
$$6x_1 - 4x_2 + 4x_3 = 30$$ (4.28)

SOLUTION

Verify that x_3 can be eliminated and Eq. (4.29) can be found by multiplying Eq. (4.26) by -1 and adding this new equation to Eq. (4.27):

$$x_1 - 4x_2 = -25$$ (4.29)

Also verify that Eq. (4.30) is formed by multiplying Eq. (4.26) by -4 and adding this to Eq. (4.28):

$$2x_1 - 8x_2 = -50$$ (4.30)

To eliminate x_1 from Eqs. (4.29) and (4.30), Eq. (4.29) may be multiplied by -2 and added to Eq. (4.30). When these operations are performed, Eq. (4.31) is an identity:

$$\begin{array}{rcl} -2x_1 + 8x_2 &=& 50 \\ 2x_1 - 8x_2 &=& -50 \\ \hline 0 &=& 0 \end{array}$$ (4.31)

This is the signal that there are an infinite number of solutions to the original system.

To determine particular members of the solution set, return to one of the last meaningful equations generated during the elimination procedure [Eqs. (4.29) and (4.30)]. Arbitrarily assume a value for one of the variables and solve for the corresponding value of the other variable in the equation. The corresponding value for the third variable can be found by substituting the two known values into one of the original equations.

In our example, if x_1 is assumed to equal -5 in Eq. (4.29),

$$-5 - 4x_2 = -25$$
$$-4x_2 = -20$$

and

$$x_2 = 5$$

Substituting $x_1 = -5$ and $x_2 = 5$ into Eq. (4.26), we get

$$-5 + 5 + x_3 = 20$$

or

$$x_3 = 20$$

Verify that $x_1 = -5$, $x_2 = 5$, and $x_3 = 20$ satisfy Eqs. (4.27) and (4.28).

NOTE

Generating sample members of an infinite solution set can be performed in an orderly manner as was shown in Example 3. In this example we can begin with *either* Eq. (4.29) or (4.30) and solve for one of the variables in terms of the other. For example, we can solve for x_1 in Eq. (4.29), yielding

$$\boxed{x_1 = 4x_2 - 25} \qquad (4.32)$$

Similarly, we can substitute the right side of Eq. (4.32) into one of the original equations in the problem in place of x_1 and solve for the remaining variable, x_3. If we substitute into Eq. (4.26), we get

$$(4x_2 - 25) + x_2 + x_3 = 20$$
$$5x_2 - 25 + x_3 = 20$$

or

$$\boxed{x_3 = 45 - 5x_2} \qquad (4.33)$$

Equations (4.32) and (4.33) state the values of x_1 and x_3 as functions of x_2.

The solution can be generalized as

$$x_2 \text{ arbitrary}$$
$$x_1 = 4x_2 - 25$$
$$x_3 = 45 - 5x_2$$

or

$$S = \{(x_1, x_2, x_3) \mid x_2 \text{ is real}, x_1 = 4x_2 - 25, x_3 = 45 - 5x_2\}$$

Fewer than Three Equations

In the section on graphical analysis we concluded that a (2×3) system either has no solution or an infinite number of solutions. The following examples illustrate solution identification using the elimination procedure.

EXAMPLE 9 ▰▰▰▰▰▰▰▰▰▰▰▰▰▰▰▰▰▰▰▰▰▰

Determine the solution set for the system of equations

$$-4x_1 + 6x_2 + 2x_3 = \quad 8 \tag{4.34}$$
$$2x_1 - 3x_2 - \quad x_3 = -14 \tag{4.35}$$

SOLUTION

To eliminate x_1, we multiply Eq. (4.35) by $+2$ and add to Eq. (4.34), or

$$
\begin{array}{r}
-4x_1 + 6x_2 + 2x_3 = \quad 8 \\
\underline{4x_1 - 6x_2 - 2x_3 = -28} \\
0 = -20
\end{array}
\tag{4.36}
$$

This process leads to Eq. (4.36) which is a false statement, and we conclude that the original system has no solution.

EXAMPLE 10 ▰▰▰▰▰▰▰▰▰▰▰▰▰▰▰▰▰▰▰▰▰

Determine the solution set for the system

$$4x_1 - 2x_2 + \quad x_3 = 10 \tag{4.37}$$
$$-3x_1 + 2x_2 + 4x_3 = 20 \tag{4.38}$$

SOLUTION

If Eqs. (4.37) and (4.38) are added, x_2 will be eliminated and Eq. (4.39) will result:

$$x_1 + 5x_3 = 30 \tag{4.39}$$

Since we are left with one equation and two variables, the system cannot be reduced any further. If for a (2×3) system, the elimination of one variable leads to a new equation involving two variables, there are an infinite number of solutions to the system. If you are interested in specifying different members of the solution set, Eq. (4.39) can be solved for x_1, yielding

$$x_1 = 30 - 5x_3 \tag{4.40}$$

If the right side of Eq. (4.40) is substituted into Eq. (4.38),

$$-3(30 - 5x_3) + 2x_2 + 4x_3 = 20$$
$$2x_2 = 90 - 19x_3$$
or $$x_2 = 45 - 9.5x_3 \tag{4.41}$$

Thus, a generalized statement of the solution is

$$x_3 \text{ arbitrary}$$
$$x_1 = 30 - 5x_3$$
$$x_2 = 45 - 9.5x_3$$

or $$S = \{(x_1, x_2, x_3) \mid x_3 \text{ is real}, x_1 = 30 - 5x_3, x_2 = 45 - 9.5x_3\}$$

EXAMPLE 11 ▬▬▬▬▬▬▬▬▬▬▬▬▬▬▬▬▬▬▬▬▬

Determine the solution set for the system

$$-10x_1 + 25x_2 - 15x_3 = 35 \qquad \text{(4.42)}$$
$$2x_1 - 5x_2 + 3x_3 = -7 \qquad \text{(4.43)}$$

SOLUTION

To eliminate x_1, Eq. (4.43) is multiplied by $+5$ and added to Eq. (4.42) to yield the equation

$$0 = 0$$

The identity implies that there are an infinite number of solutions to the original system. *To determine members of the solution set, assume arbitrary values for any two of the three variables in one of the original equations and then solve for the corresponding value of the third variable.* For example, if in Eq. (4.42) x_2 and x_3 are assigned values of 0,

$$-10x_1 + 25(0) - 15(0) = 35$$
or
$$-10x_1 = 35$$
and
$$x_1 = -3.5$$

Thus one member of the solution set is the point $(-3.5, 0, 0)$. Verify that this point satisfies Eq. (4.43).

Again, the solution set can be generalized by solving for one variable in either of the original equations. If Eq. (4.42) is solved for x_1, the resulting general solution is

$$x_2 \text{ arbitrary}$$
$$x_3 \text{ arbitrary}$$
$$x_1 = -3.5 + 2.5x_2 - 1.5x_3$$

or $\qquad S = \{(x_1, x_2, x_3) \mid x_2 \text{ is real}, x_3 \text{ is real}, x_1 = -3.5 + 2.5x_2 - 1.5x_3\}$

Notice that we could have solved Eq. (4.42) for x_2 or x_3.

NOTE ▬▬▬▬▬▬▬▬▬▬▬▬▬▬▬▬▬▬▬▬▬

See Exercise 18 regarding graphical differences between Examples 10 and 11.

More than Three Equations

For $(m \times 3)$ systems, where $m > 3$, we concluded that there may be a unique solution, no solution, or an infinite number of solutions. Solving by the elimination procedure is basically the same as for $(m \times 2)$ systems, where $m > 2$. The procedure is as follows:

SOLUTION PROCEDURE FOR $m \times 3$ SYSTEMS ($m > 3$) ▬▬▬▬

I Select and solve any (3×3) subset of the original system.
II (a) If there is a unique solution to the (3×3) system, sub-

stitute the solution values into the remaining $m - 3$ equations to see if they are satisfied. If they are, a unique solution has been found. If any of the remaining equations is not satisfied, there is no solution to the original system.

(b) If there is no solution to the (3×3) system, there is no solution to the original system.

(c) If there are an infinite number of solutions to the (3×3) system, there may be a unique solution, no solution, or an infinite number of solutions to the entire $(m \times 3)$ system. Determining which situation exists can be complex and time-consuming; the procedures for resolving this type of situation will not be discussed here.

EXAMPLE 12

Determine the solution set for the system of equations

$$x_1 + x_2 + x_3 = 6 \tag{4.44}$$
$$2x_1 - x_2 + x_3 = 7 \tag{4.45}$$
$$2x_1 + 4x_2 - 3x_3 = 4 \tag{4.46}$$
$$x_1 + 2x_2 + 3x_3 = 11 \tag{4.47}$$
$$4x_1 + 2x_2 - 5x_3 = 10 \tag{4.48}$$

SOLUTION

If the (3×3) subset of Eqs. (4.44) to (4.46) is solved, a unique solution is found when $x_1 = 3$, $x_2 = 1$, and $x_3 = 2$. (Verify this, if you wish.) Upon substituting these values into Eq. (4.47) we find

$$3 + 2(1) + 3(2) = 11$$

or

$$11 = 11$$

and this equation is satisfied. Substituting into Eq. (4.48), however, we find that

$$4(3) + 2(1) - 5(2) \neq 10$$

or

$$4 \neq 10$$

and consequently there is no solution to the original (5×3) system.

n-Variable Systems

With more than three variables $(n > 3)$, the graphical frame of reference disappears. However, aside from the cumbersome arithmetic, the elimination procedure is a valid solution method for these systems. And the possible solution sets are similar to the cases studied for three variables. For example if $m = n$ (the number of variables and equations are equal), it is possible to have a unique solution, an infinite number of solutions, or no solution. The indications of each of these cases are exactly the same as with (3×3) systems. The occurrence of a false statement at any stage indicates no solution; the occurrence of an identity implies an infinite number of solutions.

When the number of equations is less than the number of variables ($m < n$), there will be either no solution or an infinite number of solutions. And when the number of equations is greater than the number of variables ($m > n$), there may be no solution, an infinite number of solutions, or a unique solution.

The objectives, aspects of interpretation, and general nature of the elimination procedure are the same for each of these situations. However, the steps of the procedure vary slightly depending on the dimensions of the system of equations. Beyond three-variable systems manual computation procedures are impractical. Computerized solution procedures are readily available to solve larger systems.

Section 4.3 Follow-up Exercises

Determine the solution set for each of the following systems of equations. For any system having an infinite number of solutions, specify the generalized form of the solution.

1
$$x_1 + x_2 + x_3 = 2$$
$$x_1 - 3x_2 + 2x_3 = 7$$
$$4x_1 - 2x_2 - x_3 = 9$$

2
$$-2x_1 + x_2 + 3x_3 = 10$$
$$10x_1 - 5x_2 - 15x_3 = 30$$
$$x_1 + x_2 - 3x_3 = 25$$

3
$$-4x_1 - 12x_2 + 4x_3 = -40$$
$$x_1 + x_2 - 6x_3 = 10$$
$$x_1 + 3x_2 - x_3 = 10$$

4
$$x_1 - x_2 + x_3 = -5$$
$$3x_1 + x_2 - x_3 = 25$$
$$2x_1 + x_2 + 3x_3 = 20$$

5
$$x_1 + x_2 + x_3 = 0$$
$$3x_1 - x_2 + 2x_3 = -1$$
$$x_1 + 2x_2 + 3x_3 = -5$$

6
$$x_1 - 3x_2 + x_3 = 2$$
$$2x_1 - 4x_2 + 3x_3 = 7$$
$$-3x_1 + x_2 + 2x_3 = 9$$

7
$$2x_1 + 4x_2 - 2x_3 = 10$$
$$3x_1 - x_2 + 4x_3 = 12$$
$$-x_1 - 2x_2 + x_3 = 0$$

8
$$x_1 + x_2 + x_3 = 3$$
$$2x_1 - x_2 + 3x_3 = 13$$
$$3x_1 - 2x_2 + x_3 = 17$$

9
$$-2x_1 + 4x_2 - 2x_3 = 20$$
$$x_1 - 2x_2 + x_3 = 30$$

10
$$3x_1 - 6x_2 + 3x_3 = -30$$
$$-5x_1 + 10x_2 - 5x_3 = 50$$

11
$$x_1 + x_2 + x_3 = 25$$
$$-x_1 + 3x_2 + x_3 = 15$$

12
$$8x_1 - 4x_2 + 16x_3 = 50$$
$$-2x_1 + x_2 - 4x_3 = 20$$

13
$$x_1 + x_2 + x_3 = 6$$
$$x_1 - x_2 + x_3 = 2$$
$$4x_1 + 2x_3 = 14$$
$$-x_1 + 2x_2 + 3x_3 = 4$$

14
$$4x_1 - 2x_2 + x_3 = 8$$
$$3x_1 + x_2 - 2x_3 = 3$$
$$x_1 + x_2 + x_3 = 5$$
$$x_1 - 4x_2 + x_3 = 0$$

15 In Example 8, restate the generalized solution with x_1 assumed arbitrary.

16 In Example 10, restate the generalized solution with x_1 assumed arbitrary.

17 In Example 11, restate the generalized solution with (a) x_1 and x_2 assumed arbitrary and (b) x_1 and x_3 assumed arbitrary.

18 In Examples 10 and 11, describe the graphical representation. Are there any differences in the graphical representations of the two systems of equations?

19 What solution set possibilities exist for (a) a (5×3) system of equations, (b) a (4×8) system, (c) a (25×25) system, (d) a (100×75) system, and (e) a ($4{,}000 \times 1{,}000$) system?

$$\begin{bmatrix} a_1x_1 + b_1x_2 = c_1 \\ a_2x_1 + b_2x_2 = c_2 \end{bmatrix} \text{ Original system}$$

} Gauss-Jordan transformation

$$\begin{bmatrix} \textcircled{1}x_1 + \textcircled{0}x_2 = v_1 \\ \textcircled{0}x_1 + \textcircled{1}x_2 = v_2 \end{bmatrix} \text{ Transformed system}$$

or

$$\begin{bmatrix} x_1 \qquad\; = v_1 \\ \quad x_2 = v_2 \end{bmatrix} \{(v_1, v_2)\} \text{ is the Solution set}$$

FIGURE 4.10
Gauss-Jordan
transformation
for (2 × 2)
systems.

4.4 GAUSS–JORDAN PROCEDURE

In this section we will discuss another solution procedure which has very important value in the solution of linear programming problems (Chap. 7). This procedure is somewhat tedious for manual computations. However, one advantage is that the steps of the solution procedure remain the same regardless of the dimensions of the system. And, the procedure is easily programmed for computer use.

The General Idea

The *Gauss–Jordan procedure* is a type of elimination method. The procedure begins with the original system of equations and transforms it, using *row operations,* into an equivalent* system from which the solution may be read directly. Figure 4.10 shows the transformation, i.e., change in form, which is desired in solving a (2 × 2) system. In contrast to the elimination procedure, the transformed system still has dimensions of 2 × 2. The row operations, however, have transformed the coefficients on the variables so that only one variable remains in each equation; and the value of that variable (v_1 or v_2 in Fig. 4.10) is given by the right side of the equation. Note the coefficients on each variable in the "transformed system."

The following row operations are all that are needed in the Gauss–Jordan procedure. Given an original system of equations, the application of these operations results in an equivalent system of equations.

SOME BASIC ROW OPERATIONS ▮▮▮▮▮▮▮

   I Both sides of an equation may be multiplied by a nonzero constant,
   II Nonzero multiples of one equation may be added to another equation.
   III The order of equations may be interchanged.

---

* Remember that an *equivalent* system is one which has the same solution set as the original system.

Let's work a simple example and then generalize and streamline the procedure.

EXAMPLE 13 ▬▬▬▬▬▬▬▬▬▬▬▬▬▬▬▬▬▬▬▬▬▬▬

Solve the following system of equations by the Gauss–Jordan elimination method:

$$2x - 3y = -7 \tag{4.49}$$
$$x + y = 4 \tag{4.50}$$

SOLUTION
If we multiply Eq. (4.49) by $\frac{1}{2}$, the coefficient on the variable x becomes 1, resulting in the equivalent system of equations

$$x - \tfrac{3}{2}y = -\tfrac{7}{2} \tag{4.49a}$$
$$x + y = 4 \tag{4.50}$$

The coefficient of x can be transformed to zero in Eq. (4.50) if Eq. (4.49a) is multiplied by -1 and added to Eq. (4.50). This results in the equivalent system

$$x - \tfrac{3}{2}y = -\tfrac{7}{2} \tag{4.49a}$$
$$0x + \tfrac{5}{2}y = \tfrac{15}{2} \tag{4.50a}$$

By multiplying Eq. (4.50a) by $+\frac{2}{5}$, the coefficient on y becomes 1:

$$x - \tfrac{3}{2}y = -\tfrac{7}{2} \tag{4.49a}$$
$$0x + y = 3 \tag{4.50b}$$

Finally, the coefficient of y can be transformed to zero in Eq. (4.49a) if Eq. (4.50b) is multiplied by $\frac{3}{2}$ and added to Eq. (4.49a), or

$$x + 0y = 1 \tag{4.49b}$$
$$0x + y = 3 \tag{4.50b}$$

There is a reason for carrying these zero coefficients through the transformation. You will see why very shortly. However, when these zero terms are dropped from Eqs. (4.49b) and (4.50b), the final system has the form

$$x = 1$$
$$y = 3$$

which gives the solution to the system.

NOTE ▬▬▬▬▬▬▬▬▬▬▬▬▬▬▬▬▬▬▬▬▬▬▬

To create a coefficient of 1 on x in Eq. (4.49), we could have begun the solution process by interchanging Eqs. (4.49) and (4.50).

The Method
This procedure can be streamlined if we use a type of shorthand notation to represent the system of equations. The approach eliminates the variables and represents a system of equations using the variable coefficients and right-side con-

$$\begin{array}{cc|c} a_1 & b_1 & c_1 \\ a_2 & b_2 & c_2 \end{array} \quad \text{Original system}$$

↓ Gauss–Jordan transformation

$$\begin{array}{cc|c} 1 & 0 & v_1 \\ 0 & 1 & v_2 \end{array} \quad \text{Transformed system}$$

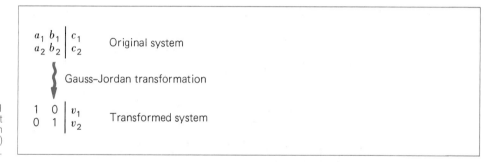

FIGURE 4.11 Coefficient transformation for (2 × 2) system.

$$\begin{array}{ccc|c} a_1 & b_1 & c_1 & d_1 \\ a_2 & b_2 & c_2 & d_2 \\ a_3 & b_3 & c_3 & d_3 \end{array} \quad \text{Original system}$$

↓ Gauss–Jordan transformation

$$\begin{array}{ccc|c} 1 & 0 & 0 & v_1 \\ 0 & 1 & 0 & v_2 \\ 0 & 0 & 1 & v_3 \end{array} \quad \text{Transformed system}$$

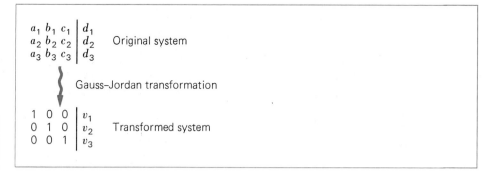

FIGURE 4.12 Coefficient transformation for (3 × 3) system.

stants only. For example, the system of equations

$$\begin{aligned} 2x + 5y &= 10 \\ 3x - 4y &= -5 \end{aligned}$$

would be written as

$$\begin{array}{cc|c} 2 & 5 & 10 \\ 3 & -4 & -5 \end{array}$$

The vertical line is used to separate the left and right sides of the equations.

For the general (2 × 2) system portrayed in Fig. 4.10, the Gauss–Jordan procedure would appear as in Fig. 4.11. The primary objective is to change the array of coefficients $\begin{pmatrix} a_1 & b_1 \\ a_2 & b_2 \end{pmatrix}$ into the form of $\begin{pmatrix} 1 & 0 \\ 0 & 1 \end{pmatrix}$.

In a (3 × 3) system of the form

$$\begin{aligned} a_1x_1 + b_1x_2 + c_1x_3 &= d_1 \\ a_2x_1 + b_2x_2 + c_2x_3 &= d_2 \\ a_3x_1 + b_3x_2 + c_3x_3 &= d_3 \end{aligned}$$

the Gauss-Jordan transformation would proceed as in Fig. 4.12.

Although there are variations on this procedure, and for any given problem you may be tempted to *try* a shortcut, the following procedure will always work.

A GAUSS–JORDAN APPROACH

I *Transform the coefficients one column at a time starting with column 1.* For example, in a (2 × 2) system begin by transforming $\begin{pmatrix} a_1 \\ a_2 \end{pmatrix}$ into $\begin{pmatrix} 1 \\ 0 \end{pmatrix}$. Then transform column 2 so that it looks like $\begin{pmatrix} 0 \\ 1 \end{pmatrix}$. In a (3 × 3) system first transform $\begin{pmatrix} a_1 \\ a_2 \\ a_3 \end{pmatrix}$ into $\begin{pmatrix} 1 \\ 0 \\ 0 \end{pmatrix}$; then move to column 2 followed by column 3.

II *In any column transformation, first create the element which equals 1. This is accomplished by multiplying the row (equation) in which the 1 is desired by the reciprocal of the coefficient currently in that position.*

III *The zeros in a column are created by first multiplying the row created in step II by the negative of the value currently in the position where the 0 is desired. This row multiple is added to the row in which the 0 is desired to create the new row.*

Let's illustrate step III, since it tends to be confusing. Assume in the following system

$$
\begin{array}{cc|c}
1 & 6 & 10 \\
\circled{5} & 3 & 12
\end{array}
\qquad \begin{array}{l} \textbf{(1)} \\ \textbf{(2)} \end{array}
$$

we desire a zero where the $\circled{5}$ appears in column 1. We can create the zero by multiplying row 1 by the negative of $\circled{5}$, or -5, and adding this multiple of row 1 to row 2, or

$$
\begin{array}{cc|c}
-5 & -30 & -50 \\
5 & 3 & 12 \\
\hline
0 & -27 & -38
\end{array}
\qquad
\left.\begin{array}{r}
-5 \cdot \text{row 1} \\
\text{row 2} \\
\hline
\text{new row 2 or } 2a
\end{array}\right\} \text{Step III}
$$

The revised system would be

$$
\begin{array}{cc|c}
1 & 6 & 10 \\
0 & -27 & -38
\end{array}
\qquad \begin{array}{l} \textbf{row 1} \\ \textbf{row 2a (new row 2)} \end{array}
$$

The following examples illustrate the entire procedure.

EXAMPLE 14

Solve the following system by the Gauss–Jordan method:

$$
\begin{aligned}
5x + 20y &= 25 \\
4x - 7y &= -26
\end{aligned}
$$

SOLUTION

Let's rewrite the system without the variables. (See Fig. 4.13a.)

$$
\begin{array}{cc|c}
5 & 20 & 25 \\
4 & -7 & -26
\end{array}
\qquad \begin{array}{l} R_1 \\ R_2 \end{array}
$$

Note the labeling of rows 1 and 2 by R_1 and R_2. This will be convenient for summarizing the row operations used in the transformation process.

A $\circled{1}$ is created in row 1 by multiplying that row by $\frac{1}{5}$, and the new system (see Fig. 4.13b) becomes

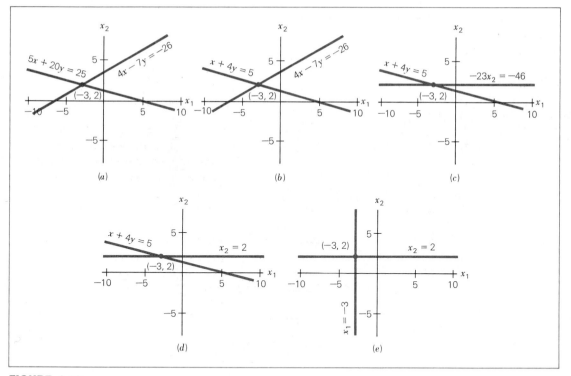

FIGURE 4.13
Equivalent
systems of
equations using
Gauss-Jordan
procedure.

$$
\begin{array}{cc|c}
\boxed{1} & 4 & 5 \\
4 & -7 & -26
\end{array}
\quad
\begin{array}{l}
R_{1a} = \tfrac{1}{5}R_1 \\
R_2
\end{array}
\qquad \textbf{(Step II)}
$$

A $\boxed{0}$ is created in row 2 by multiplying row 1 by -4 and adding this row multiple to row 2. The new system (see Fig. 4.13c) is

$$
\begin{array}{cc|c}
1 & 4 & 5 \\
\boxed{0} & -23 & -46
\end{array}
\quad
\begin{array}{l}
R_{1a} \\
R_{2a} = -4R_{1a} + R_2
\end{array}
\qquad \textbf{(Step III)}
$$

Moving to the second column, a $\boxed{1}$ is created in row 2 by multiplying the row by $-\tfrac{1}{23}$. The resulting system (see Fig. 4.13d) is

$$
\begin{array}{cc|c}
1 & 4 & 5 \\
0 & \boxed{1} & 2
\end{array}
\quad
\begin{array}{l}
R_{1a} \\
R_{2b} = -\tfrac{1}{23}R_{2a}
\end{array}
\qquad \textbf{(Step II)}
$$

Finally, a $\boxed{0}$ is created in the second column of row 1 by multiplying row 2 by -4 and adding this to row 1 (see Fig. 4.13e), or

$$
\begin{array}{cc|c}
1 & \boxed{0} & -3 \\
0 & 1 & 2
\end{array}
\quad
\begin{array}{l}
R_{1b} = -4R_{2b} + R_{1a} \\
R_{2b}
\end{array}
\qquad \textbf{(Step III)}
$$

Remember that at any stage in the Gauss–Jordan process we have a system of equations which is equivalent to the original system. By this, we mean that the modified system of equations has the same solution set as the original system.

This is illustrated in Figs. 4.13a to 4.13e. These show the graphical representation of each intermediate system in this example.

Also, remember that at any step in the solution process, the rows of constants represent the equivalent system of equations. The intermediate result

$$\begin{array}{cc|c} 1 & 4 & 5 \\ 0 & 1 & 2 \end{array}$$

is an efficient way of writing

$$\begin{aligned} x + 4y &= 5 \\ y &= 2 \end{aligned}$$

when the Gauss–Jordan transformation is completed, the equivalent system of equations has the form

$$\begin{aligned} x &= -3 \\ y &= 2 \end{aligned}$$

which is the solution to the original system.

EXAMPLE 15

Solve the system in Example 6 using the Gauss–Jordan procedure.

SOLUTION

For this example, the successive transformations will simply be listed with the corresponding row equations indicated to the right of each row.

$$\begin{array}{ccc|cl} \textcircled{1} & 1 & 1 & 6 & R_1 \quad \text{(Step II, unnecessary)} \\ 2 & -1 & 3 & 4 & R_2 \\ 4 & 5 & -10 & 13 & R_3 \end{array}$$

$$\begin{array}{ccc|cl} 1 & 1 & 1 & 6 & R_1 \\ \textcircled{0} & -3 & 1 & -8 & R_{2a} = -2R_1 + R_2 \quad \text{(Step III)} \\ 4 & 5 & -10 & 13 & R_3 \end{array}$$

$$\begin{array}{ccc|cl} 1 & 1 & 1 & 6 & R_1 \\ 0 & -3 & 1 & -8 & R_{2a} \\ \textcircled{0} & 1 & -14 & -11 & R_{3a} = -4R_1 + R_3 \quad \text{(Step III)} \end{array}$$

$$\begin{array}{ccc|cl} 1 & 1 & 1 & 6 & R_1 \\ 0 & \textcircled{1} & -\frac{1}{3} & \frac{8}{3} & R_{2b} = -\frac{1}{3}R_{2a} \quad \text{(Step II)} \\ 0 & 1 & -14 & -11 & R_{3a} \end{array}$$

$$\begin{array}{ccc|cl} 1 & \textcircled{0} & \frac{4}{3} & \frac{10}{3} & R_{1a} = -R_2 + R_1 \quad \text{(Step III)} \\ 0 & 1 & -\frac{1}{3} & \frac{8}{3} & R_{2b} \\ 0 & 1 & -14 & -11 & R_{3a} \end{array}$$

$$\begin{array}{ccc|cl} 1 & 0 & \frac{4}{3} & \frac{10}{3} & R_{1a} \\ 0 & 1 & -\frac{1}{3} & \frac{8}{3} & R_{2b} \\ 0 & \textcircled{0} & -\frac{41}{3} & -\frac{41}{3} & R_{3b} = -R_{2b} + R_{3a} \quad \text{(Step III)} \end{array}$$

$$
\begin{array}{ccc|c}
1 & 0 & \frac{4}{3} & \frac{10}{3} \\
0 & 1 & -\frac{1}{3} & \frac{8}{3} \\
0 & 0 & \textcircled{1} & 1
\end{array}
\quad
\begin{array}{l}
R_{1a} \\
R_{2b} \\
R_{3c} = -\frac{3}{41}R_{3b}
\end{array}
\qquad \text{(Step II)}
$$

$$
\begin{array}{ccc|c}
1 & 0 & \frac{4}{3} & \frac{10}{3} \\
0 & 1 & \textcircled{0} & 3 \\
0 & 0 & 1 & 1
\end{array}
\quad
\begin{array}{l}
R_{1a} \\
R_{2c} = \frac{1}{3}R_{3c} + R_{2b} \\
R_{3c}
\end{array}
\qquad \text{(Step III)}
$$

$$
\begin{array}{ccc|c}
1 & 0 & \textcircled{0} & 2 \\
0 & 1 & 0 & 3 \\
0 & 0 & 1 & 1
\end{array}
\quad
\begin{array}{l}
R_{1b} = -\frac{4}{3}R_{3c} + R_{1a} \\
R_{2c} \\
R_{3c}
\end{array}
\qquad \text{(Step III)}
$$

The system has a unique solution when $x_1 = 2$, $x_2 = 3$, and $x_3 = 1$.

The Gauss–Jordan procedure works in exactly the same manner for determining the solution set for (4×4), (5×5), . . . , $(n \times n)$ systems although writer's cramp can be a problem. *The indications of no solution or an infinite number of solutions are the same as with the elimination procedure.* You will be asked to verify this in the Follow-up Exercises.

Section 4.4 Follow-up Exercises

Determine the solution sets for each of the following systems of equations using the Gauss–Jordan procedure.

1. $2x + 4y = -16$
   $x - 2y = 16$

2. $3x - 2y = 7$
   $2x + 4y = 10$

3. $5x - 2y = -12$
   $-3x + y = 7$

4. $-2x + 5y = 40$
   $3x - 2y = -5$

5. $6x - 8y = 14$
   $-x + 4y = -7$

6. $-x + 2y = 4$
   $5x - 10y = -20$

7. $-x + 2y = -1$
   $5x - 10y = 6$

8. $24x - 15y = 30$
   $-8x + 5y = -20$

9. $-x_1 + 3x_2 + x_3 = 7$
   $3x_1 - 9x_2 - 3x_3 = 14$
   $4x_1 + 2x_2 - 2x_3 = 24$

10. $5x_1 - 4x_2 + 6x_3 = 24$
    $3x_1 - 3x_2 + x_3 = 54$
    $-2x_1 + x_2 - 5x_3 = 30$

11. $4x_1 + 2x_2 - 5x_3 = 13$
    $x_1 + x_2 + x_3 = 2$
    $2x_1 - x_2 - 3x_3 = 3$

12. $2x_1 + x_2 - 2x_3 = 3$
    $3x_1 - x_2 - 2x_3 = 4$
    $x_1 + x_2 + x_3 = 6$

13. $x_1 - x_2 + x_3 = 10$
    $-3x_1 + x_2 - 2x_3 = 17$
    $-4x_1 + 2x_2 - 3x_3 = 7$

14. $10x_1 + 5x_2 - 15x_3 = 60$
    $6x_1 + 4x_2 + x_3 = 48$
    $-4x_1 - 2x_2 + 6x_3 = -36$

4.5 SUMMARY

In this chapter we have discussed solving systems of linear equations. We have examined the graphical characteristics of solution sets for two- and three-variable systems, we have looked at the elimination procedure for solving systems of equations, and finally we examined the Gauss–Jordan procedure for solving systems of equations.

In the next chapter we will discuss applications of linear functions and systems of linear equations. Be sure that you are comfortable with the concepts presented in this and the preceding chapter before moving on.

KEY TERMS AND CONCEPTS

basic row operations 139

dimensions 119

elimination procedure 122, 130

equivalent equations 121

Gauss–Jordan procedure 139

inconsistent equations 121

infinite number of solutions 121

no solution 121

solution set 120

system of equations 119

unique solution 121

ADDITIONAL EXERCISES

Exercises 1 to 16 are related to Sec. 4.2.

In Exercises 1 to 4 compare the y intercepts and slopes of the lines representing each equation and determine the nature of the solution set.

$$\begin{array}{ll}
1 & 4x - 2y = 12 \\
& x - 2y = 18
\end{array}$$

$$\begin{array}{ll}
2 & -x + 2y = -3 \\
& 3x - 6y = 9
\end{array}$$

$$\begin{array}{ll}
3 & 16x - 4y = 24 \\
& -4x + y = 10
\end{array}$$

$$\begin{array}{ll}
4 & x - 2y = 0 \\
& 3x + 4y = 0
\end{array}$$

5–8 Solve the systems in Exercises 1 to 4 graphically.

Solve the following systems of equations. For any questions having an infinite number of solutions, specify the generalized form of the solution.

$$\begin{array}{ll}
9 & x + y = 6 \\
& 3x - 2y = 3
\end{array}$$

$$\begin{array}{ll}
10 & 4x - 2y = -40 \\
& 3x + 4y = 25
\end{array}$$

$$\begin{array}{ll}
11 & 5x - 2y = 18 \\
& 3x + y = 2
\end{array}$$

$$\begin{array}{ll}
12 & 6x + 3y = 6 \\
& 2x + 4y = 14
\end{array}$$

$$\begin{array}{ll}
13 & x - 2y = -8 \\
& -4x + 8y = 10
\end{array}$$

$$\begin{array}{ll}
14 & 2x - 3y = -1 \\
& -10x + 15y = 5
\end{array}$$

$$\begin{array}{ll}
15 & x + y = 0 \\
& 2x - 3y = -10 \\
& x + 2y = 2 \\
& -5x + y = 12 \\
& 3x - 2y = 10
\end{array}$$

$$\begin{array}{ll}
16 & x + y = 1 \\
& 3x - 2y = 18 \\
& -x + 3y = -13 \\
& 5x - y = 23 \\
& -x - 4y = 8
\end{array}$$

Exercises 17 to 26 are related to Sec. 4.3.

Solve the following systems of equations. For any system having an infinite number of solutions, specify the generalized form of the solution.

$$\begin{array}{ll}
17 & x_1 + x_2 + x_3 = 1 \\
& 3x_1 - 2x_2 + x_3 = -1 \\
& x_1 + 3x_2 - x_3 = 11
\end{array}$$

$$\begin{array}{ll}
18 & 2x_1 - x_2 + x_3 = -2 \\
& x_1 + 4x_2 - x_3 = 5 \\
& x_1 + x_2 + x_3 = 6
\end{array}$$

19 $\quad -x_1 + 2x_2 + x_3 = 10$
$\qquad x_1 - 4x_2 + x_3 = 6$
$\qquad 3x_1 - 6x_2 - 3x_3 = 25$

20 $\quad 3x_1 - x_2 + 2x_3 = 6$
$\qquad x_1 + x_2 + x_3 = 10$
$\qquad -9x_1 + 3x_2 - 6x_3 = -18$

21 $\quad x_1 + x_2 + x_3 = 1$
$\qquad x_1 - x_2 - x_3 = 7$
$\qquad 2x_1 + x_2 + x_3 = 5$
$\qquad 4x_1 - 2x_2 + 3x_3 = 7$

22 $\quad 4x_1 - x_2 + 3x_3 = 15$
$\qquad x_1 - 2x_2 + x_3 = 8$
$\qquad x_1 + x_2 + x_3 = 2$
$\qquad 6x_1 - x_2 + 2x_3 = 16$

*23   Suppose that a (3 × 3) system of equations is represented by three planes which intersect along a common line. How many variables would be specified as arbitrary in the generalized solution?

*24   Suppose in Exercise 23 the three planes are identical. How many variables would be specified as arbitrary?

*25   Suppose that a (2 × 4) system of equations can be thought of as being represented by identical hyperplanes in 4-space. How many variables would be specified as arbitrary in the generalized solution?

*26   Suppose that a (m × n) system of equations can be thought of as being represented by m identical hyperplanes in n-space. How many variables would be specified as arbitrary in the generalized solution?

Exercises 27 to 32 are related to Sec. 4.4.

Determine the solution for each of the following systems of equations using the Gauss–Jordan procedure.

27 $\quad 5x - 8y = 1$
$\qquad 4x + 2y = 26$

28 $\quad -3x + 2y = 22$
$\qquad 5x + 4y = 0$

29 $\quad x - 2y = 4$
$\qquad -5x + 10y = 10$

30 $\quad 5x - 3y = -2$
$\qquad -25x + 15y = 10$

31 $\quad 3x - x_2 + 2x_3 = 4$
$\qquad 2x_1 - 3x_2 + x_3 = -5$
$\qquad x_1 - x_2 + x_3 = -3$

32 $\quad 4x_1 - 2x_2 + x_3 = -11$
$\qquad x_1 + x_2 + x_3 = 1$
$\qquad 3x_1 - x_2 + 2x_3 = -6$

CHAPTER TEST

1   Solve the following system of equations graphically.

$$x + 5y = -4$$
$$-3x + 2y = -5$$

2   Solve the following system of equations.

$$5x - 2y = 25$$
$$4x + y = 7$$
$$2x - 5y = 31$$
$$x + y = -2$$

3   (a) What are the solution set possibilities for a (20 × 15) system of equations? (b) For a (15 × 20) system?

4   Solve the following system of equations.

$$x_1 - 2x_2 + x_3 = 10$$
$$3x_1 - 2x_2 + 4x_3 = 20$$
$$-3x_1 + 6x_2 - 3x_3 = -30$$

5   Using the Gauss–Jordan procedure, complete the solution for an unknown
(3 × 3) system of equations, given the following intermediate solution.

$$\begin{array}{ccc|c} 1 & 0 & 3 & 12 \\ 0 & 1 & -2 & -10 \\ 0 & 0 & 6 & 18 \end{array}$$

6   Interpret the meaning of the following Gauss–Jordan results.

$$(a)\ \begin{array}{ccc|c} 1 & 6 & 4 & 10 \\ 0 & 1 & -2 & -5 \\ 0 & 0 & 0 & 16 \end{array} \qquad (b)\ \begin{array}{cccc|c} 1 & 0 & 0 & 0 & 4 \\ 0 & 1 & 0 & 0 & -2 \\ 0 & 0 & 1 & 0 & 1 \\ 0 & 0 & 0 & 1 & 3 \end{array}$$

MINICASE A

XYZ MANUFACTURING COMPANY

The XYZ Manufacturing Company manufactures five different products. Each of the products must be processed through five different departments A through E. The following table indicates the number of hours required to produce a unit of each product in each department. Also indicated is the number of production hours available each week in each of the departments.

DEPARTMENT	Product 1	2	3	4	5	HOURS AVAILABLE PER WEEK
A	2	1	4	3	2	330
B	4	2	3	2	1	330
C	5	4	2	4	3	440
D	3	2	2	2	3	320
E	1	1	1	1	1	130

The company wants to determine whether there are any quantities of the five products which can be produced each week that will result in total utilization of the hours available in all departments.

1   Formulate the appropriate system of linear equations.

2   Locate a computer package (if possible) which solves systems of linear equations and use it to solve the system of equations determined in part 1. Are there any combinations of the five products? If so, what are they? How will each department's weekly capacity be allocated among the five products?

MINICASE B

GAUSS–JORDAN PROCEDURE: COMPUTERIZED VERSION

Using an appropriate computer language (e.g., FORTRAN, BASIC, PASCAL),

1   Write a short program which will solve (2×2) systems of equations using the Gauss–Jordan procedure. The program should print results when a unique solution occurs. When no solution or an infinite number of solutions occur, the program should print a message indicating "no solution" or "infinite number of solutions."

*2   Write a program which will solve ($m \times n$) systems of linear equations using the Gauss–Jordan procedure, where $m = n$. The requirements for output are the same as in part 1.

5

APPLICATIONS OF LINEAR FUNCTIONS AND SYSTEMS OF EQUATIONS

5.1 LINEAR FUNCTIONS

5.2 OTHER EXAMPLES
OF LINEAR FUNCTIONS

5.3 BREAK-EVEN MODELS

5.4 OTHER APPLICATIONS

KEY TERMS AND CONCEPTS

IMPORTANT FORMULAS

ADDITIONAL EXERCISES

MINICASE: AUTOMOBILE
REPLACEMENT DECISION

CHAPTER OBJECTIVES

■ Provide a review of the structure of linear functions

■ Present a wide variety of applications of linear functions and systems of
linear equations

In this chapter we extend the material presented in Chap. 2 by presenting a
discussion of linear functions. After reviewing the form and assumptions underlying these functions, we will see examples which illustrate the applications
of these models in business, economics, and other areas. The remainder of the
chapter will illustrate a variety of applications of systems of linear equations.

5.1 LINEAR FUNCTIONS

General Form and Assumptions

In Chap. 2 we discussed mathematical functions.

DEFINITION:

LINEAR FUNCTION INVOLVING 1 INDEPENDENT VARIABLE

A *linear function* f involving one independent variable x and a
dependent variable y has the general form

$$y = f(x) = ax + b \qquad (5.1)*$$

You should recognize Eq. (5.1) as being the slope-intercept form of a linear
equation. The parameters have been named differently, but they represent the
same characteristics. That is, a is the slope of the line that represents the function, and b represents the y coordinate of the y intercept.

---

* This equation is of the same form as Eq. (2.2); only the constants have been named differently.

For a linear function having the form of Eq. (5.1), a change in the value of y is directly proportional to a change in the value of x. Stated differently, the *rate* of change in the value of y, given a change in the value of x, is *constant*. This rate of change is represented by the slope of the function, or by the constant a in Eq. (5.1).

The salary function on page 52 is of the form

$$y = f(x) = 3x + 25$$

where *y is defined as weekly salary in dollars* and *x represents number of units sold per week.* This is an example of a linear function. Graphically, the function appears as in Fig. 5.1. Note that the equation is graphed in the first quadrant only, restricting x and y to nonnegative values. Does this make sense?

DEFINITION:

LINEAR FUNCTION INVOLVING 2 INDEPENDENT VARIABLES

A linear function f involving two independent variables x_1 and x_2 and a dependent variable y has the general form

$$y = f(x_1, x_2) = a_1 x_1 + a_2 x_2 + b \qquad (5.2)$$

where a_1, a_2, and b are real-valued constants.

For a linear function of the form of Eq. (5.2) the variable y depends jointly on the values of x_1 and x_2. The value of y varies in direct proportion to changes in the values of x_1 and x_2. Specifically, if x_1 increases by 1 unit, y will change by a_1 units. And if x_2 increases by 1 unit, y will change by a_2 units.

EXAMPLE 1

Assume that a salesperson's salary depends on the number of units sold of each of two products. More specifically, assume that the salary function

$$y = f(x_1, x_2)$$

is

$$y = 5x_1 + 3x_2 + 25$$

where y = *weekly salary*, x_1 = *number of units sold of product 1*, and x_2 = *number of units sold of product 2.* An interpretation of this salary function is that there is a base weekly salary of $25 and that commissions earned per unit sold are $5 and $3, respectively, for products 1 and 2.

DEFINITION:

LINEAR FUNCTION INVOLVING n INDEPENDENT VARIABLES

A linear function f involving n independent variables x_1, x_2, . . . , x_n and a dependent variable y has the general form

$$y = f(x_1, x_2, . . . , x_n)$$

where $y = a_1 x_1 + a_2 x_2 + \cdots + a_n x_n + b \qquad (5.3)$

where a_1, a_2, . . . , a_n and b are real-valued constants.

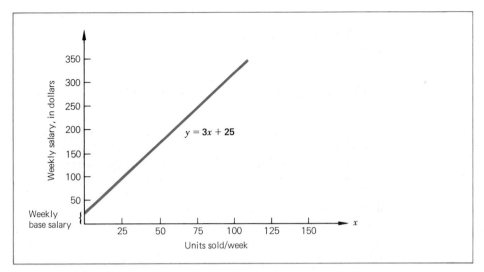

FIGURE 5.1
Linear salary
function.

Linear Cost Functions

Organizations are concerned with *costs* because they reflect dollars flowing out of the organization. These outflows usually pay for salaries, raw materials, supplies, rent, heat, utilities, and so forth. As mentioned earlier, accountants and economists often define total cost in terms of two components: *total variable cost* and *total fixed cost.* These two components must be added to determine total cost. The cost function for owning and operating the patrol car in Example 3 of Chap. 2 was an example of a linear cost function. The cost function,

$$C(x) = 0.40x + 18{,}000$$

had variable costs which varied with the number of miles driven and fixed costs of $18,000.

Total variable costs vary with the level of output and are computed as the product of variable cost per unit of output and the level of output. In a production setting, variable cost per unit is usually composed of raw material and labor costs. In the example of the patrol car, variable cost per mile consisted of operating costs per mile such as gasoline, oil, maintenance costs, and depreciation.

Linear cost functions are very often realistic although they ignore the possibility of *economies* or *diseconomies of scale.* That is, linear cost functions imply *constant returns to scale.* Constant returns to scale imply that regardless of the number of units produced, the variable cost for each unit is the same. This assumption ignores the possibility that the elements of the production process, laborers or machines, may become more efficient as the number of units produced increases or that buying raw materials in large quantities may result in quantity discounts which in turn may lower the variable cost per unit produced. The cost function for the patrol car assumes that operating costs per mile will be $0.40 regardless of the number of miles driven. We might expect that over the life of a piece of equipment, such as the patrol car, it will become less efficient and will require greater maintenance. This should translate into a higher variable cost per unit. Some cost models recognize these potential "nonlinearities" by using some measure of *average variable cost per unit*. In other situations a set of linear cost functions might be developed, each appropriate in certain cases depending on the level of output selected.

The following example illustrates the formulation of a linear cost function.

EXAMPLE 2

A firm which produces a single product is interested in determining the function that expresses annual total cost y as a function of the number of units produced x. Accountants indicate that fixed expenditures each year are $50,000. They also have estimated that raw material costs for each unit produced are $5.50, and labor costs per unit are $1.50 in the assembly department, $0.75 in the finishing room, and $1.25 in the packaging and shipping department.

The total cost function will have the form

$$y = C(x)$$
$$= \text{total variable cost} + \text{total fixed cost}$$

Total variable costs consist of the two components: raw material costs and labor costs. Labor costs are determined by summing the respective labor costs for the three departments. Total cost is defined by the function

$$y = \text{total raw material cost} + \text{total labor cost} + \text{total fixed cost}$$

$$= \begin{array}{l} \text{total raw} \\ \text{material cost} \end{array} + \begin{array}{l} \text{labor cost} \\ \text{(assembly dept.)} \end{array} + \begin{array}{l} \text{labor cost} \\ \text{(finishing room)} \end{array}$$
$$+ \begin{array}{l} \text{labor cost} \\ \text{(shipping dept.)} \end{array} + \begin{array}{l} \text{total fixed} \\ \text{cost} \end{array}$$

or $\qquad y = 5.50x + (1.50x + 0.75x + 1.25x) + 50{,}000$

which simplifies to

$$y = 9x + 50{,}000$$

The 9 represents the combined variable cost per unit produced of $9.00.

EXAMPLE 3

Linear Approximation of Nonlinear Cost Function Figure 5.2 illustrates a nonlinear cost function f. As indicated earlier, circumstances may exist where it is reasonable to approximate nonlinear functions with one or more linear functions. Suppose, for the situation portrayed in Fig. 5.2, that analysts believe the linear functions f_1 and f_2 approximate f reasonably well. Specifically, they wish to approximate f with f_1 when $x \le 8{,}000$ and with f_2 when $8{,}000 < x \le 20{,}500$. Based upon historical sales figures, analysts believe it is unlikely that annual production will exceed 20,500 units.

EXERCISE

Using the data points (0, 300,000), (8,000, 1,300,000), and (20,500, 1,900,000), verify that the approximating functions are

$$f_1(x) = 125x + 300{,}000 \qquad 0 \le x \le 8{,}000 \qquad \textbf{(5.4)}$$
$$f_2(x) = 48x + 916{,}000 \qquad 8{,}000 < x \le 20{,}500 \qquad \textbf{(5.5)}$$

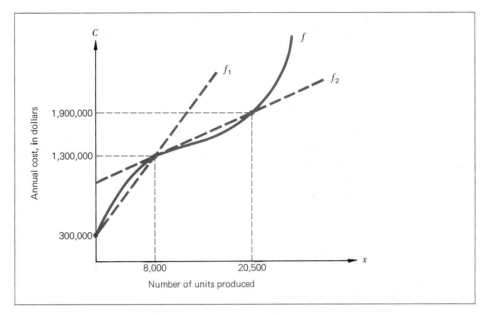

FIGURE 5.2
Linear approxi-
mation of non-
linear cost func-
tion.

POINTS FOR THOUGHT AND DISCUSSION

How are economies of scale reflected by the graph of f? How
do Eqs. (5.4) and (5.5) reflect these economies of scale? If f_1
and f_2 are used to approximate f, comment on the approximation as compared with the actual value when $x < 8,000$.
When $8,000 < x < 20,500$? When $x = 8,000$?

Linear Revenue Functions

The money which flows into an organization from either selling products or
providing services is often referred to as *revenue*. The most fundamental way of
computing total revenue from selling a product (or service) is

$$\boxed{\text{Total revenue} = (\text{price})(\text{quantity sold})}$$

An assumption in this relationship is that the selling price is the same for all
units sold.

If a firm sells n products, where x_i equals the number of units sold of product
i and p_i equals the price of product i, the function which allows you to compute
total revenue from the n products is

$$\boxed{R = p_1 x_1 + p_2 x_2 + p_3 x_3 + \cdots + p_n x_n} \tag{5.6}$$

This revenue function can be stated more concisely using *summation notation** as

$$\boxed{R = \sum_{i=1}^{n} p_i x_i} \tag{5.7}$$

---

* If you are unfamiliar with summation notation, see Appendix A.

EXAMPLE 4

A local car rental agency, Hurts Renta-Lemon, is trying to compete with some of the larger national firms. Management realizes that many travelers are not concerned about frills such as windows, hubcaps, radios, and heaters. I. T. Hurts, owner and president of Hurts, has been recycling used cars to become part of the fleet. Hurts has also simplified the rental rate structure by charging a flat $9.95 per day for the use of a car. Total revenue for the year is a linear function of the number of car-days rented out by the agency, or *if* R = *annual revenue* and d = *number of car-days rented during the year,*

$$R = f(d) = 9.95d$$

Linear Profit Functions

Profit for an organization is the difference between total revenue and total cost. Stated in equation form,

$$\boxed{\text{Profit} = \text{total revenue} - \text{total cost}} \tag{5.8}$$

When total revenue exceeds total cost, profit is positive. In such cases the profit may be referred to as a *net gain,* or *net profit.* When total cost exceeds total revenue, profit is negative and it may be called a *net loss,* or *deficit.*

When *both* total revenue and total cost are linear functions of the same variable(s), the profit function is also a linear function of the same variable(s). That is, if

$$\text{Total revenue} = R(x)$$
and
$$\text{Total cost} = C(x)$$

profit is defined as

$$\boxed{P(x) = R(x) - C(x)} \tag{5.9}$$

EXAMPLE 5

A firm sells a single product for $65 per unit. Variable costs per unit are $20 for materials and $27.50 for labor. Annual fixed costs are $100,000. Construct the profit function stated in terms of x, the number of units produced and sold. What profit is earned if annual sales are 20,000 units?

SOLUTION

If the product sells for $65 per unit, total revenue is computed by using the function

$$R(x) = 65x$$

Is this consistent with your mental model? Similarly, total annual cost is made up of material costs, labor costs, and fixed costs:

$$C(x) = 20x + 27.50x + 100,000$$

which reduces to

$$C(x) = 47.50x + 100,000$$

TABLE 5.1

FARM	CROP	COST/ACRE (c_j)	REVENUE/ACRE (r_j)	FIXED COST (F_j)
1	Soybeans	$ 900	$1,300	$150,000
2	Corn	1,100	1,650	175,000
3	Potatoes	750	1,200	125,000

Thus the profit function is computed as

$$P(x) = R(x) - C(x)$$
$$= 65x - (47.50x + 100,000)$$
$$= 17.50x - 100,000$$

Notice that $P(x)$ is a linear function. If the firm sells 20,000 units during the year, then

$$P(20,000) = 17.50(20,000) - 100,000$$
$$= 350,000 - 100,000 = \$250,000$$

EXAMPLE 6

Agricultural Planning A corporate agricultural organization has three separate farms which are to be used during the coming year. Each farm has unique characteristics which make it most suitable for raising one crop only. Table 5.1 indicates the crop selected for each farm, the annual cost of planting 1 acre of the crop, the expected revenue to be derived from each acre, and the fixed costs associated with operating each farm. In addition to the fixed costs associated with operating each farm, there are annual fixed costs of $75,000 for the corporation as a whole. Determine the profit function for the three-farm operation if x_j = *the number of acres planted at farm j, r_j = revenue per acre at farm j, c_j = cost per acre at farm j, and F_j = fixed cost at farm j.*

SOLUTION

Total revenue comes from the sale of crops planted at each of the three farms, or

$$R(x_1, x_2, x_3) = r_1x_1 + r_2x_2 + r_3x_3$$
$$= 1,300x_1 + 1,650x_2 + 1,200x_3$$

Total costs are the sum of those at the three farms plus the corporate fixed costs, or

$$C(x_1, x_2, x_3) = c_1x_1 + F_1 + c_2x_2 + F_2 + c_3x_3 + F_3 + 75,000$$
$$= 900x_1 + 150,000 + 1,100x_2 + 175,000 + 750x_3 + 125,000 + 75,000$$
$$= 900x_1 + 1,100x_2 + 750x_3 + 525,000$$

Total profit is a linear function computed as

$$P(x_1, x_2, x_3) = R(x_1, x_2, x_3) - C(x_1, x_2, x_3)$$
$$= 1,300x_1 + 1,650x_2 + 1,200x_3 - (900x_1 + 1,100x_2 + 750x_3 + 525,000)$$
$$= 400x_1 + 550x_2 + 450x_3 - 525,000$$

Section 5.1 Follow-up Exercises

1   Write the general form of a linear function involving 5 independent variables.

2   Assume that the salesperson in Example 1 has a salary goal of $400 per week. If product B is not available one week, how many units of product A must be sold to meet the salary goal? If product A is unavailable, how many units must be sold of product B?

3   Assume in Example 1 that the salesperson receives a bonus when combined sales from the two products exceed 50 units. The bonus is $2.50 per unit for each unit over 50. With this incentive program, the salary function must be described by two different linear functions. What are they, and when are they valid?

4   For Example 4, how many units must be produced and sold in order to (a) earn a profit of $2.2 million, (b) earn zero profit (break even)?

5   A manufacturer of microcomputers produces three different models. The table below summarizes wholesale prices, material cost per unit, and labor cost per unit. Annual fixed costs are $25 million.

	Microcomputer		
	MODEL 1	MODEL 2	MODEL 3
Wholesale price/unit	$400	$1,000	$1,750
Material cost/unit	200	450	795
Labor cost/unit	100	150	225

(a) Determine a joint total revenue function for sales of the three different microcomputer models.

(b) Determine an annual total cost function for manufacturing the three models.

(c) Determine the profit function for sales of the three models.

(d) What is annual profit if the firm sells 20,000, 40,000 and 10,000 pairs, respectively, of the three models?

6   For Example 5, the board of directors has voted on the following planting program for the coming year: 1,000 acres will be planted at farm 1, 1,600 at farm 2, and 1,550 at farm 3. (a) What are the expected profits for the program? (b) A summer drought has resulted in the revenue yields per acre being reduced by 20, 30, and 10 percent, respectively, at the three farms. What is the profit expected from the previously mentioned planting program?

7   Figure 5.3 illustrates a nonlinear cost function f. Analysts have suggested that the nonlinear function can be approximated reasonably well by one of two linear functions; either f_1 or f_2. Using the sample data points, determine the linear function $y = f_1(x)$ and $y = f_2(x)$. From Fig. 5.3, comment on the relative accuracy of the approximations by f_1 and f_2.

5.2   OTHER EXAMPLES OF LINEAR FUNCTIONS

In this section we will see, by example, other applications of linear functions.

EXAMPLE 7 ▓▓▓▓▓▓▓▓▓▓▓▓▓▓▓▓▓▓▓▓▓▓▓▓▓▓▓▓▓▓▓▓▓▓▓

Straight-Line Depreciation   When organizations purchase equipment, vehicles, buildings, and other types of "capital assets," accountants usually allocate the cost of the item

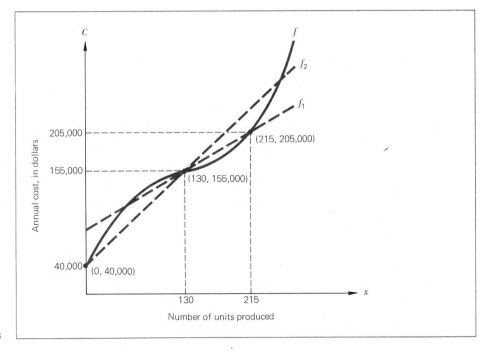

FIGURE 5.3

over the period the item is used. For a truck costing $10,000 and having a useful life of 5 years, accountants might allocate $2,000 a year as a cost of owning the truck. The cost allocated to any given period is called *depreciation.* Accountants also keep records of each major asset and it current, or "book," value. For instance, the value of the truck may appear on accounting statements as $10,000 at the time of purchase, $10,000 − $2,000 = $8,000 one year from the date of purchase, and so forth. Depreciation can also be thought of as the amount by which the book value of an asset has decreased.

Although there are a variety of depreciation methods, one of the simplest is *straight-line depreciation.* Under this method the rate of depreciation is constant. This implies that the book value declines as a linear function over time. *If V equals the book value (in dollars) of an asset and t equals time (in years) measured from the purchase date* for the previously mentioned truck,

$$V = f(t)$$
$$= \text{purchase cost} - \text{depreciation}$$
or $$= 10{,}000 - 2{,}000t$$

The graph of this function appears in Fig. 5.4.

EXERCISE

Define the restricted domain and range for this function.*

---

* Domain = $\{t|0 \le t \le 5\}$; range = $\{V|0 \le V \le 10{,}000\}$.

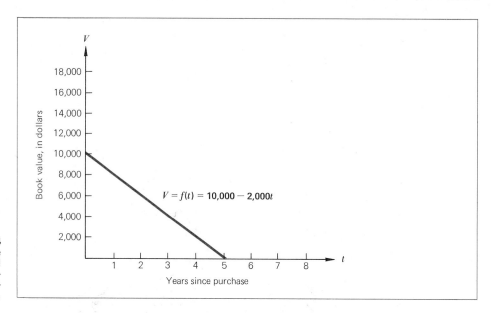

FIGURE 5.4
Book value
function based
upon straight-
line deprecia-
tion.

EXAMPLE 8

Straight-Line Depreciation with Salvage Value   Many assets have a *resale,* or *salvage value* even after they have served the purposes for which they were originally purchased. In such cases the allocated cost over the life of the asset is the difference between the purchase cost and the salvage value. The cost allocated each time period is the allocated cost divided by the useful life. Assume that the truck in the last example has a useful life of 5 years, after which it can be sold for $1,000. The total cost which will be allocated over the life of the truck is $10,000 − $1,000, or $9,000. If the truck is to be depreciated on a straight-line basis, the annual depreciation will be

$$\frac{\text{Purchase cost} - \text{salvage value}}{\text{Useful life (in years)}} = \frac{\$10,000 - \$1,000}{5}$$

$$= \frac{\$9,000}{5} = \$1,800$$

The function which expresses the book value V as a function of time t is

$$V = f(t) = 10,000 - 1,800t \qquad 0 \leq t \leq 5$$

EXAMPLE 9

Crime Deterrence   There continues to be a debate as to whether police patrol activities have any effect on crime levels. The research in this area has provided inconsistent results. Researchers generally agree that the effectiveness of patrols varies depending upon a variety of factors including the type of crime. For example, it is likely that police patrol has little effect on the incidence of shoplifting, which is more of an indoor crime. One might expect that there would be a greater effect on crimes such as automobile theft and armed robbery.

A number of police departments believe that the level of serious crime is influenced

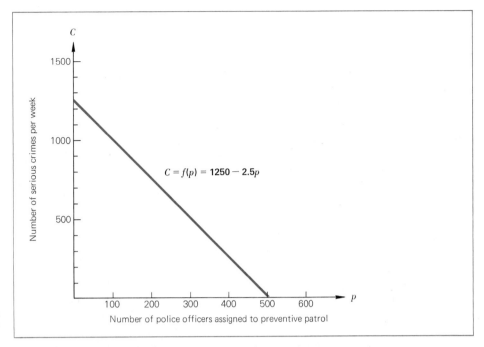

FIGURE 5.5
Crime deter-
rence function.

by police patrol activities. One city has gathered data on crime rates while varying the number of police officers assigned to preventive patrol activities. The data indicate a linear functional relationship where

$$\text{Number of serious crimes per week} = f \begin{pmatrix} \text{average number of police officers} \\ \text{assigned to preventive patrol} \end{pmatrix}$$

Their data indicate that with no preventive patrol activities the expected number of serious crimes is 1,250 per week. The data also indicate that the expected number of serious crimes per week will decrease by 2.5 for each additional police officer. This relationship is represented by the linear function

$$c = f(p) = 1{,}250 - 2.5p$$

where c equals the expected number of serious crimes per week and p equals the average number of officers assigned to preventive patrol. Figure 5.5 illustrates this relationship.

POINTS FOR THOUGHT AND DISCUSSION
Interpret the meaning of the slope of this linear function. Interpret the meaning of the x and y intercepts. Do these interpretations seem valid? Does *linearity* seem to be a reasonable assumption for this relationship?

EXAMPLE 10

Linear Demand Functions A *demand function* is a mathematical relationship expressing the way in which the quantity demanded of an item varies with the price charged for it.

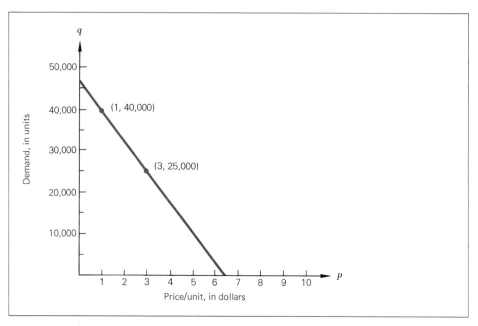

FIGURE 5.6
Linear demand
function.

The relationship between these two variables—*quantity demanded* and *price per unit*—is usually *inverse*. For most products, a decrease in price results in an increase in demand. The purpose of special sales is almost always to stimulate demand. If supermarkets reduced the price of filet mignon to $0.75 per pound, there would likely be a significant increase in the demand for that item. On the other hand, increases in the price of a product usually result in a decrease in the demand. The phrase *pricing people out of the market* refers to the customers lost as a result of price increases. If filet mignon were to suddenly triple in price with all other things such as income levels held constant, many people currently capable of purchasing it would be priced out of the market.

There are exceptions to this behavior, of course. The demand for products or services which are considered *necessities* is likely to fluctuate less with moderate changes in price. Items such as prescription medical drugs, medical services, and certain food items are examples of this class of products.

Although most demand functions are nonlinear, there are situations in which the demand relationship either is, or can be approximated by, a linear function. Figure 5.6 illustrates a linear demand function with two sample data points. Although most economics books measure price on the vertical axis and quantity demanded on the horizontal axis, we will reverse the labeling of the axes, as illustrated in Fig. 5.6. The reason for this is that most consumers view the demand relationship as having the form

$$\text{Quantity demanded} = f(\text{price per unit})$$

That is, consumers respond to price. Thus, quantity demanded, the dependent variable, is plotted on the vertical axis.

Verify, using the methods of the last chapter, that the demand function in Fig. 5.6 has the form

$$q = f(p) = 47{,}500 - 7{,}500p$$

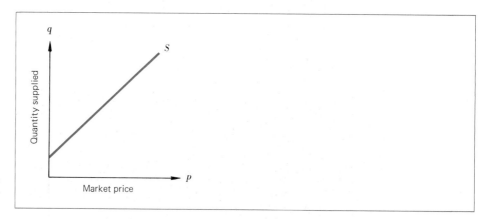

FIGURE 5.7
Linear supply
function.

POINTS FOR THOUGHT AND DISCUSSION ▬▬▬▬▬▬

Interpret the meaning of the y intercept in this example. Does this seem valid? What is the interpretation of the x intercept? What is the interpretation of the slope in this function? The restricted domain of the function seems to be $0 \le p \le 6.333$. Would you be tempted to restrict the domain any further?

EXAMPLE 11 ▬▬▬▬▬▬▬▬▬▬▬▬▬▬▬▬▬▬▬▬▬▬▬▬

Linear Supply Functions A *supply function* relates market price to the quantities that suppliers are willing to produce and sell. The implication of supply functions is that what is brought to the market depends upon the price people are willing to pay. As opposed to the inverse nature of price and demand in demand functions, the quantity which suppliers are willing to provide usually varies directly with the market price. *All other things being equal,* the higher the market price, the more a supplier would like to produce and sell; and the lower the price people are willing to pay, the less the incentive to produce and sell. Assume that you own a lobster boat. All other things considered equal, how much incentive is there to take your boat and crew out if lobster is wholesaling at $0.25 per pound? How much incentive is there if it is wholesaling at $10 per pound?

As with demand functions, supply functions can be approximated sometimes using linear functions. Figure 5.7 illustrates a sample supply function. Note that by labeling the vertical axis q, it is suggested that

$$\text{Quantity supplied} = f(\text{market price})$$

POINTS FOR THOUGHT AND DISCUSSION ▬▬▬▬▬▬

What does the y intercept in Fig. 5.7 suggest about the relationship between supply and demand? If the supply curve appears as in Fig. 5.8, what does the x intercept suggest about the relationship? Which figure do you believe is the most representative of an actual supply function relationship? Why?

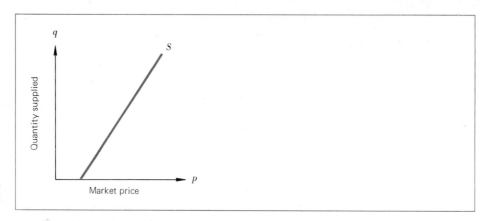

FIGURE 5.8
Linear supply
function.

Section 5.2 Follow-up Exercises

1   A piece of machinery is purchased for $50,000. Accountants have decided to use a straight-line depreciation method with the machine being fully depreciated after 8 years. Letting V equal the book value of the machine and t the age of the machine, determine the function $V = f(t)$. (Assume no salvage value.)

2   In Exercise 1 assume that the machine will have a salvage value of $10,000 at the end of 8 years. Determine the function $V = f(t)$ for this situation.

3   A piece of machinery is purchased for $400,000. Accountants have decided to use a straight-line depreciation method with the machine being fully depreciated after 20 years. Letting V equal the book value of the machine and t the age of the machine, determine the function $V = f(t)$. Assume there is no salvage value.

4   A company purchases cars for use by its executives. The purchase cost this year is $8,000. The cars are kept 3 years after which they are expected to have a resale value of $2,600. If accountants use straight-line depreciation, determine the function which describes the book value V as a function of the age of the car t.

5   A police department believes that arrest rates R are a function of the number of plainclothes officers n assigned. The arrest rate is defined as the percentage of cases in which arrests have been made. It is believed that the relationship is linear and that each additional officer assigned to the plainclothes detail results in an increase in the arrest rate of 0.75 percent. If the current plainclothes force consists of 20 officers and the arrest rate is 36 percent,
(a) Define the function $R = f(n)$.
(b) Interpret the meaning of the y intercept.

6   Two points on a linear demand function are ($20, 50,000) and ($30, 42,500).
(a) Determine the demand function $g = f(p)$.
(b) Determine what price would result in demand of 65,000 units.
(c) Interpret the slope of the function.

7   Two points (p, q) on a linear demand function are ($25, 40,000) and ($35, 32,500).
(a) Determine the demand function $q = f(p)$.
(b) What price would result in demand of 55,000 units?
(c) Interpret the slope of the function.
(d) Sketch the function.

8   Two points on a linear supply function are ($5.00, 28,000) and ($6.50, 37,000).

(a) Determine the supply function $q = f(p)$.

(b) What price would result in suppliers offering 20,500 units?

9   Two points (p, q) on a linear supply function are ($5.50, 45,000) and ($7.50, 80,000).

(a) Determine the supply function $q = f(p)$.

(b) What price would result in suppliers offering 155,000 units for sale?

(c) Interpret the slope of the function.

(d) Interpret the x intercept.

(e) Sketch the function.

10   **Gun Control**   With crime rates on the rise, the number of handguns in circulation appears to be increasing. A 10-year survey of citizens within one U.S. city indicated a surprisingly linear increase in the number of handguns over time. In 1970 the estimated number of handguns was 250,000; in 1980 the estimated number was 375,000. Let n equal the number of handguns possessed by the residents of the city and let t represent time measured in years since 1970 ($t = 0$ for 1970).

(a) Using the two data points, determine the linear function $n = f(t)$.

(b) Interpret the meaning of the slope.

(c) If the number of guns continues to increase at the same rate, when will the number of guns surpass 500,000?

11   **Sports Attendance**   Prior to the strike in 1981, major league baseball continued to be one of the leading spectator sports in the United States.* Attendance in 1978 was 54,881,009 fans, compared with 53,004,141 in 1977. If attendance has been increasing linearly over time since 1975,

(a) Determine the function $y = f(t)$, where y equals annual attendance and t is time measured in years ($t = 0$ for 1975).

(b) Estimate the attendance in 1975.

(c) Assuming the strike had no unfavorable impact on attendance, what is it expected to equal in 1985?

(d) Comment on the factors which might influence the upper limit on the range of this function over the years.

5.3   BREAK-EVEN MODELS

In this section we will discuss *break-even models,* a set of planning tools which can be, and has been, very useful in managing organizations. One significant indication of the performance of the companies is reflected by the so-called "bottom line" of the income statement for the firm, that is, how much profit is earned! Break-even analysis focuses upon the profitability of a firm. Of specific concern in break-even analysis is identifying the level of operation or level of output that would result in a zero profit. This level of operation or output is called the *break-even point.* The break-even point is a useful reference point in the sense that it represents the level of operation at which total revenue equals total cost. Any changes from this level of operation will result in either a profit or a loss.

---

* Surprisingly, horse racing is the number one spectator sport by quite a large margin.

Break-even analysis is valuable particularly as a planning tool when firms are contemplating expansions such as offering new products or services. Similarly, it is useful in evaluating the pros and cons of beginning a new business venture. In each instance the analysis allows for a projection of profitability.

Assumptions

In this discussion we will focus upon situations in which both the total cost function and the total revenue function are linear. The use of a linear total cost function implies that variable costs per unit either are constant or can be assumed to be constant. The linear cost function assumes that total variable costs depend upon the level of operation or output. It is also assumed that the fixed-cost portion of the cost function is constant over the level of output being considered.

The linear total revenue function assumes that the selling price per unit is constant. Where the selling price is not constant, average price is sometimes chosen for purposes of conducting the analysis.

Another assumption is that price per unit is greater than variable cost per unit. Think about that for a moment. If price per unit is less than variable cost per unit, a firm will lose money on every unit produced and sold. A break-even condition could never exist.

Break-Even Analysis

In break-even analysis the primary objective is to determine the break-even point. The break-even point may be expressed in terms of (1) *volume of output* (or level of activity), (2) *total dollar sales,* or possibly (3) *percentage of production capacity.* For example, it might be stated that a firm will break even at 100,000 units of output, when total sales equal $2.5 million or when the firm is operating at 60 percent of its plant capacity. We will focus primarily on the first of these three ways, although on occasion expressing the break-even point in an alternative form is desirable.

The methods of performing break-even analysis are rather straight-forward, and there are alternative ways of determining the break-even point. The usual approach is as follows:

1 Formulate total cost as a function of x, the level of output.

2 Formulate total revenue as a function of x.

3 Set $C(x)$ equal to $R(x)$ and solve for x. The resulting value of x is the break-even level of output and might be denoted by x_{BE}.

An alternative to step 3 is to construct the profit function $P(x) = R(x) - C(x)$, set $P(x)$ equal to zero, and solve for x_{BE}.

The following example illustrates both approaches.

EXAMPLE 12

A group of engineers is interested in forming a company to produce smoke detectors. They have developed a design and estimate that variable costs per unit, including materials, labor, and marketing costs, are $22.50. Fixed costs associated with the formation, operation, and management of the company and the purchase of equipment and machinery total $250,000. They estimate that the selling price will be $30 per detector.

(*a*) Determine the number of smoke detectors which must be sold in order for the firm to break even on the venture.

(*b*) Preliminary marketing data indicate that the firm can expect to sell approximately 30,000 smoke detectors over the life of the project if the detectors are sold for $30 per unit. Determine expected profits at this level of output.

SOLUTION

(*a*) The total revenue function is represented by the equation

$$R(x) = 30x$$

The total cost function is represented by the equation

$$C(x) = 22.50x + 250,000$$

The break-even condition occurs when total revenue equals total cost, or when

$$\boxed{R(x) = C(x)} \tag{5.10}$$

For this problem the break-even point is computed as

$$30x = 22.50x + 250,000$$

or
$$7.50x = 250,000$$

and
$$x_{BE} = 33,333.33 \text{ units}$$

The alternative approach is to first write the profit function and set it equal to 0 as follows:

$$\begin{aligned}
P(x) &= R(x) - C(x) \\
&= 30x - (22.50x + 250,000) \\
&= 7.50x - 250,000
\end{aligned}$$

Setting the profit function P equal to 0, we have

$$7.50x - 25,000 = 0$$
$$7.50x = 250,000$$

or
$$x_{BE} = 33,333.33 \text{ units}$$

This is the same result, and our conclusion is that *given the assumed cost and price parameters (values)*, the firm must sell 33,333.33 units in order to break even.

EXERCISE

Verify that total revenue and total costs both equal $1,000,000 (taking rounding into account) at the break-even point.

(*b*) With sales projected at 30,000 smoke detectors,

$$\begin{aligned}
P(30,000) &= 7.5(30,000) - 250,000 \\
&= 225,000 - 250,000 = -25,000
\end{aligned}$$

This suggests that if all estimates hold true—price, cost, and demand—the firm can expect to lose $25,000 on the venture.

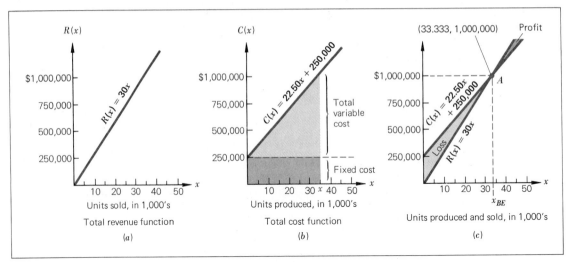

FIGURE 5.9

EXAMPLE 13

Graphical Approach The essence of break-even analysis is illustrated quite effectively by graphical analysis. Figure 5.9a illustrates the total revenue function, Fig. 5.9b the total cost function, and Fig. 5.9c a composite graph showing both functions, for Example 12. Note in Fig. 5.9b that the fixed-cost component is distinguished from the variable-cost component. At *any* level of output x, the vertical distance within the darker shaded area indicates the fixed cost of $250,000. To this is added the total variable cost, which is represented by the vertical distance at x within the lighter area. The sum of these two vertical distances represents the total cost $C(x)$.

In Fig. 5.9c the two functions are graphed on the same set of axes. The point where the two functions intersect represents the one level of output where total revenue and total cost are equal. This is the break-even point. For all points to the left of the break-even point the cost function C has a value greater than the revenue function R. In this region the vertical distance separating the two functions represents the loss which would occur at a given level of output. To the right of $x = 33.333$, $R(x)$ is higher than $C(x)$, or $R(x) > C(x)$. For levels of output greater than $x = 33.333$ the vertical distance separating $R(x)$ and $C(x)$ represents the profit at a given level of output.

Figure 5.10 illustrates the profit function P for this example. The break-even point is identified by the x coordinate of the x intercept. Note that to the left of the break-even point the profit function is below the x axis, indicating a negative profit, or loss. To the right, $P(x)$ is above the x axis, indicating a positive profit.

POINT FOR THOUGHT AND DISCUSSION

Discuss any changes in Fig. 5.10 and the break-even point if (a) the price per unit increases (decreases), (b) the fixed cost increases (decreases), and (c) the variable cost per unit increases (decreases).

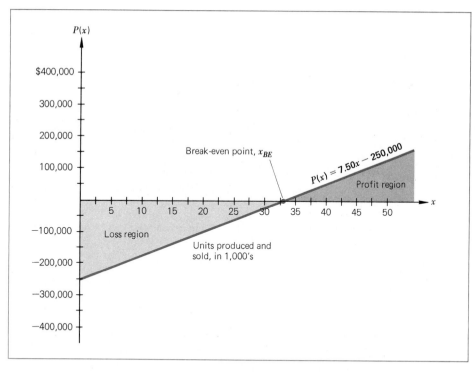

FIGURE 5.10
Profit function.

An alternative way of viewing break-even analysis is in terms of *profit contribution.* As long as the price per unit p exceeds the variable cost per unit v, the sale of each unit results in a contribution to profit. The difference between p and v is called the *profit margin.* Or, stated in equation form,

$$\text{Profit margin} = p - v \qquad p > v$$

The profit margin generated from the sale of units must first be allocated to recover any fixed costs which exist. At lower levels of output, the *total profit contribution* (profit margin for all units sold) is typically less than fixed costs, meaning that total profit is negative (see Fig. 5.10). Only when *total* profit contribution exceeds fixed cost will a positive profit exist. Because of this orientation—that the profit margin per unit contributes first to recovering fixed costs after which it contributes to profit—profit margin is often called the *contribution to fixed cost and profit.*

With this perspective in mind, the computation of the break-even point can be thought of as determining the number of units to produce and sell in order to recover the fixed costs. The calculation of the break-even point is thus

$$\frac{\text{Break-even level}}{\text{of output}} = \frac{\text{fixed cost}}{\substack{\text{contribution to} \\ \text{fixed cost and profit}}}$$

or

$$x_{\text{BE}} = \frac{FC}{p - v} \qquad \text{(5.11)}$$

EXAMPLE 14 ▬▬▬▬▬▬▬▬▬▬▬▬▬▬▬▬▬▬▬▬

Convention Planning A professional organization is planning its annual convention to be held in San Francisco. Arrangements are being made with a large hotel in which the convention will be held. Registrants for the 3-day convention will be charged a flat fee of $250 per person which includes registration fee, room, all meals, and tips. The hotel charges the organization $20,000 for the use of the facilities such as meeting rooms, ballroom, and recreational facilities. In addition, the hotel charges $145 per person for room, meals, and tips. The professional organization appropriates $25 of the $250 fee as annual dues to be deposited in the treasury of the national office. Determine the number of registrants necessary for the organization to cover the fixed cost of $20,000.

SOLUTION

The contribution to fixed cost and profit is the registration fee (price) per person less the cost per person charged by the hotel less the national organization's share per registrant, or

$$\text{Contribution per registrant} = \text{registration fee} - \frac{\text{hotel charge}}{\text{per person}} - \text{annual dues}$$
$$= 250 - 145 - 25 = \$80$$

Therefore, according to Eq. (5.11), the number of registrants required to cover the fixed cost is

$$x_{BE} = \frac{20,000}{80} = 250 \text{ persons}$$

EXAMPLE 15 ▬▬▬▬▬▬▬▬▬▬▬▬▬▬▬▬▬▬▬▬

In-House Computer vs. Service Bureau Decision A large medical group practice has 30 full-time physicians. Currently, all billing of patients is done manually by clerks. Due to the heavy volume of billing the business manager believes it is time to convert from manual to computerized patient billing. The two options being considered are (1) the group practice can lease its own computer and software and do the billing itself (the *make* option) or (2) the group can contract with a computer service bureau which would do the patient billing (the *buy* option).

The costs of each alternative are a function of the number of patient bills. The lowest bid submitted by a service bureau would result in an annual flat fee of $3,000 plus $0.95 per bill processed. With the help of a computer consultant, the business manager has estimated that the group can lease a small business computer system and the required software at a cost of $15,000 per year. Variable costs of doing the billing in this manner are estimated at $0.65 per bill.

If *x equals the number of patient bills per year,* the annual billing cost using a service bureau is represented by the function

$$S(x) = 3,000 + 0.95x$$

The annual cost of leasing a computer system and software is expressed by the function

$$L(x) = 15,000 + 0.65x$$

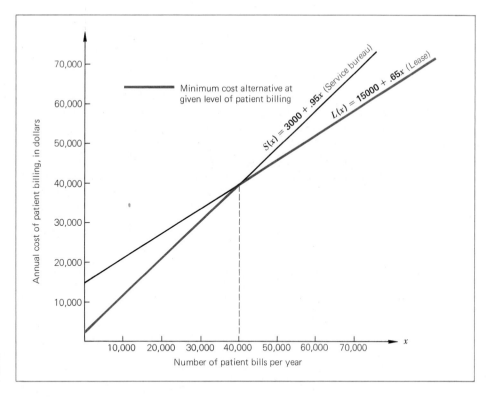

FIGURE 5.11
Patient billing
cost functions.

These two alternatives are equally costly when

$$S(x) = L(x)$$

or

$$3{,}000 + 0.95x = 15{,}000 + 0.65x$$
$$0.30x = 12{,}000$$
$$x = 40{,}000$$

Thus, if the expected number of patient bills per year exceeds 40,000, the lease option is the least costly. If the number of patient bills is expected to be less than 40,000, the service bureau option is the least costly. Figure 5.11 illustrates the two cost functions.

POINT FOR THOUGHT AND DISCUSSION

Suppose the patient billing volume is expected to be 35,000 per year. What reasons could you present to the business manager favoring the *lease* option? Discuss potential advantages and disadvantages which are not quantifiable for the *lease* and *service bureau* options.

EXAMPLE 16

Patient Billing Revisited: Three Alternatives Suppose in the last example that the business manager is not convinced that computer processing is the most cost-effective means

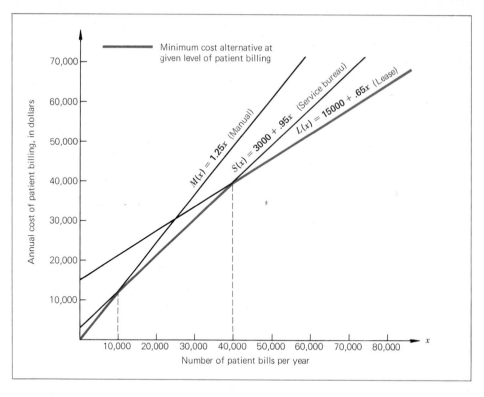

FIGURE 5.12
Patient billing
cost functions.

of handling patient billing. She estimates that processing bills manually costs the group practice $1.25 per bill, or

$$M(x) = 1.25x$$

If this method is considered as a third option, let's examine the implications. The three cost functions are graphed together in Fig. 5.12. If you study this figure carefully you should reach the following conclusions:

1 The least cost option at any level of patient bills is highlighted by the heavy line segments.

2 If the number of patient bills per year is expected to be less than 10,000, the manual system is the least costly.

3 If the number of patient bills is expected to be between 10,000 and 40,000, the service bureau arrangement is the least costly.

4 If the number is expected to exceed 40,000, the lease arrangement is the least costly.

EXAMPLE 17

Multiproduct Analysis Our discussion in this section has been limited to single-product/service situations. For multiproduct situations, break-even analysis can be performed when a *product-mix* is known. The product-mix expresses the ratio of output levels for the different products. For example, a firm having three products might pro-

TABLE 5.2

	Product		
	A	B	C
Price/unit	$40	$30	$55
Variable cost/unit	30	21	43
Profit margin	$10	$ 9	$12

duce 3 units of product A and 2 units of product B for each unit of product C. In this situation we might define *1 unit of product mix* as consisting of 3 units of product A, 2 units of B, and 1 unit of C. If a product-mix unit can be defined we can conduct break-even analysis using this as the measure of output.

Suppose that these three products have the price and cost attributes shown in Table 5.2. Combined fixed cost for the three products is $240,000. Since *1 unit of the product-mix* consists of 3 units of A, 2 units of B, and 1 unit of C the *profit contribution per unit of product-mix equals*

$$3(\$10) + 2(\$9) + 1(\$12) = \$60$$

If we *let x equal the number of units of product-mix,* the profit function for the three products is

$$P(x) = 60x - 240,000$$

The break-even point occurs when $P(x) = 0$, or

$$60x - 240,000 = 0$$
$$60x = 240,000$$
$$x = 4,000$$

The firm will break even when it produces 4,000 product-mix units, or 12,000 units of A, 8,000 units of B, and 4,000 units of C.

The analysis presented in Example 17 presumes that a product-mix is known. If the product-mix is not known exactly, but can be approximated, this analysis can still be of value as a planning tool.

Section 5.3 Follow-up Exercises

1   A firm sells a product for $20 per unit. Variable costs per unit are $8 and fixed costs equal $90,000. How many units must be sold in order to break even?

2   An enterprising college student has decided to purchase a local car wash business. The purchase cost is $20,000. Car washes will be priced at $1.50 and variable cost per car (soap, water, labor, etc.) is expected to equal $0.70. How many cars must be washed in order to recover the $20,000 purchase price?

3   A charitable organization is planning a raffle to raise $10,000. Five hundred chances will be sold on a new car. The car will cost the organization $7,500. How much should each ticket cost if the organization wishes to net a profit of $10,000?

4   **Make or Buy Decision** Assume that a manufacturer can purchase a needed

component from a supplier at a cost of $8 per unit, or it can invest $20,000 in equipment and produce the item at a cost of $5.50 per unit.

(*a*) Determine the quantity for which total costs are equal for the *make* and *buy* alternatives.

(*b*) What is the minimum cost alternative if 6,000 units are required? What is the minimum cost?

5 Advertising Campaign A firm is developing a TV advertising campaign. Development costs (fixed costs) are $150,000, and the firm must pay $15,000 per minute for television spots. The firm estimates that for each minute of advertising additional sales of $70,000 result. Of this $70,000, $47,500 is absorbed to cover the variable cost of producing the items and $15,000 must be used to pay for the minute of advertising. Any remainder is the contribution to fixed cost and profit.

(*a*) How many minutes of advertising are necessary to recover the development costs of the advertising campaign?

(*b*) If the firm uses 15 one-minute spots, determine total revenue, total costs (production and advertising), and total profit (or loss) resulting from the campaign.

6 A local civic arena is negotiating a contract with a touring ice skating show, Icey Blades. Icey Blades charges a flat fee of $30,000 per night plus 50 percent of the gate receipts. The civic arena plans to charge one price for all seats, $7.50 per ticket.

(*a*) Determine the number of tickets which must be sold each night in order to break even.

(*b*) If the civic arena has a goal of clearing $15,000 each night, how many tickets must be sold?

(*c*) What would nightly profit equal if average attendance is 7,500 per night?

7 In the previous exercise, assume that past experience with this show indicates that average attendance should equal 7,500 persons.

(*a*) What ticket price would allow the civic arena to break even?

(*b*) What ticket price would allow them to earn a profit of $15,000?

8 Automobile Leasing A car leasing agency purchases new cars each year for use in the agency. The cars cost $7,500 new. They are used for 2 years, after which they are sold for $2,000. The owner of the agency estimates that the variable costs of operating the cars, exclusive of gasoline, are $0.22 per mile. Cars are leased at a flat rate of $0.32 per mile (gasoline not included).

(*a*) What is the break-even mileage for the 2-year period?

(*b*) What are total revenue, total cost, and total profit for the 2-year period if a car is leased for 40,000 miles?

(*c*) What price per mile must be charged in order to break even if a car is leased for 40,000 miles for 2 years?

(*d*) What price per mile must be charged in order to earn a profit of $2,000 per car over its 2-year lifetime if it is leased for 40,000 miles?

9 Computer Software Development A firm has a computer which it uses for a variety of purposes. One of the major costs associated with the computer is software development (writing computer programs). The vice president for Information Systems wants to evaluate whether it is less costly to have his own programming staff or to have programs developed by a software development firm. The costs of both options are a function of the number of lines of code (program statements). The vice president estimates that in-house development costs $1.25 per line of code. In addition, annual over-head costs for supporting the programmers equal $12,500. Software developed outside the firm costs, on average, $2 per line of code.

(a) How many lines of code per year make costs of the two options equal?

(b) If programming needs are estimated at 20,000 lines per year, what are the costs of the two options?

(c) In part (b) what would the in-house cost per line of code have to equal for the two options to be equally costly?

10   Sensitivity Analysis   Because the parameters (constants) used in mathematical models are frequently estimates, actual results may differ from those projected by the mathematical analysis. To account for some of the uncertainties which may exist in a problem, analysts often conduct *sensitivity analysis*. The objective is to assess how much a solution might change if there are changes in model parameters.

Assume in the last exercise that software development costs by outside firms might actually fluctuate by ±20 percent from the $2 per line estimate.

(a) Recompute the break-even point if costs are 20 percent higher or lower and compare your result with the original answer.

(b) Along with the uncertainty in part (a), in-house variable costs might increase by as much as 30 percent due to a new union contract. Compute the combined effects of these uncertainties.

11   A high-technology electronics firm needs a special microprocessor for use in a microcomputer it manufactures. Three alternatives have been identified for satisfying its needs. It can purchase the microprocessors from a supplier at a cost of $10 each. The firm also could purchase one of two pieces of automated equipment and manufacture the microprocessors. One piece of equipment costs $80,000 and would have variable costs per microprocessor of $8. A more highly automated piece of equipment costs $120,000 and would result in variable costs of $5 per unit. Determine the minimum cost alternatives for different ranges of output (as determined in Example 16). Also, graph the cost functions for the three alternatives.

12   A new entrant to the "designer jeans" market is Françoise Strauss, a French cousin of Levi's great-grandnephew. Françoise plans on marketing three styles of jeans. The following table summarizes price and cost data.

	Style		
	A	B	C
Selling price	$45	$36	$28
Variable cost/pair	19	17	14

Combined fixed costs equal $7.5 million. A market research study projects a product-mix such that for each pair of style A, two pairs of B and four pairs of C will be sold. How many pairs of each style must be sold in order to break even?

5.4   OTHER APPLICATIONS

In this section we will see some additional applications of linear functions and simultaneous equations. Further applications are contained in the Follow-up Exercises and end-of-chapter problems.

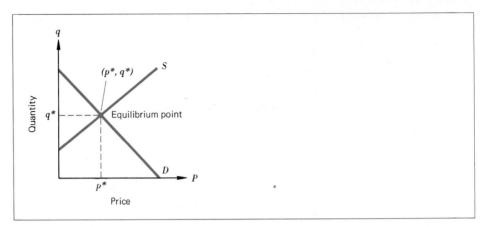

FIGURE 5.13
Equilibrium
between supply
and demand.

Equilibrium between Supply and Demand

In Examples 10 and 11 we discussed linear supply and demand functions. One of the concerns of economists is whether the consumers and suppliers will ever have a meeting of the minds and reach agreement about the quantities which will be supplied and purchased and the market price at which this will occur. When agreement is reached, the market is said to be in *equilibrium.* That is, at the equilibrium price the amount demanded by consumers is exactly equal to the quantity suppliers are willing to bring to the market. This equilibrium condition is defined by the coordinates of the point where the graphs of the supply and demand functions intersect. Figure 5.13 illustrates this condition, where p^* is the *equilibrium price* and q^* is the *equilibrium quantity.*

EXAMPLE 18

Suppose that the demand function for a particular product is $q_a = 10,000 - 50p$, where p is the price stated in dollars and q_a is *the quantity demanded in thousands of units.* The supply function is $q_s = 2,000 + 30p$, where q_s is *the quantity supplied, in thousands of units.* Determine the equilibrium price and quantity.

SOLUTION

Equilibrium occurs if there is a price which equates supply and demand, or when

$$q_s = q_a$$

or
$$2,000 + 30p = 10,000 - 50p$$

Solving for p, we find that equilibrium occurs when

$$80p = 8,000$$

or
$$p = 100$$

The equilibrium price is $100. At a price of $100 the quantity supplied and demanded equals 5,000 (thousands), or 5 million units which is the equilbrium quantity. Figure 5.14 illustrates the functions.

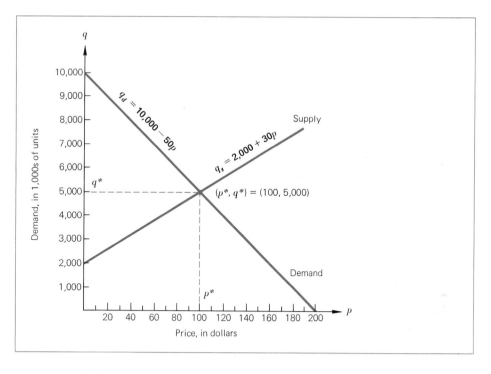

FIGURE 5.14

Defining Mathematical Functions

Simultaneous equations provide another approach to defining mathematical functions. A linear function involving two variables has the form of Eq. (5.1), or

$$y = f(x) = ax + b \qquad \textbf{(5.1)}$$

In order to define a linear function of this form, values must be determined for a and b. If the coordinates of two points which lie on the graph of the function are known, the values of a and b can be determined by the procedures presented in Sec. 3.4. Another approach is to substitute *each pair* of coordinates into Eq. (5.1), resulting in two equations. These two equations can be solved simultaneously to determine a and b.

EXAMPLE 19 ▮▮▮▮▮▮▮▮▮▮▮▮▮▮▮▮

To determine the linear function which is satisfied by $(4, 8)$ and $(7, -4)$, we can substitute $(4, 8)$ and $(7, -4)$ into Eq. (5.1). This yields

$$8 = 4a + b \qquad \textbf{(5.12)}$$
$$-4 = 7a + b \qquad \textbf{(5.13)}$$

Multiplying Eq. (5.12) by -1 and adding to Eq. (5.13) yields

$$\begin{aligned} -8 &= -4a - b \\ \underline{-4} &= \underline{7a + b} \\ -12 &= 3a \\ -4 &= a \end{aligned}$$

or

Substituting this result into Eq. (5.12) gives

$$8 = 4(-4) + b$$

or

$$24 = b$$

With a and b defined as -4 and 24 respectively, the function can be specified as

$$y = f(x) = -4x + 24$$

Product-Mix Problem

A variety of applications are concerned with determining the quantities of different products which satisfy specific requirements. In the following example we are interested in determining the quantities of three products which will fully utilize available production capacity.

EXAMPLE 20

A company produces three products, each of which must be processed through three different departments. Table 5.3 summarizes the hours required per unit of each product in each department. In addition, the weekly capacities are stated for each department in terms of work-hours available. What is desired is to determine whether there are any combinations of the three products which would exhaust the weekly capacities of the three departments.

TABLE 5.3

DEPARTMENT	Product 1	2	3	HOURS AVAILABLE PER WEEK
A	2	3.5	3	1,200
B	3	2.5	2	1,150
C	4	3	2	1,400

If we let x_j = *number of units produced per week of product j,* the conditions to be satisfied are expressed by the following system of equations.

$$
\begin{aligned}
2x_1 + 3.5x_2 + 3x_3 &= 1,200 && \text{(department A)} \\
3x_1 + 2.5x_2 + 2x_3 &= 1,150 && \text{(department B)} \\
4x_1 + 3x_2 + 2x_3 &= 1,400 && \text{(department C)}
\end{aligned}
$$

EXERCISE

Verify that by solving these equations simultaneously, the solution set consists of one solution which is $x_1 = 200$, $x_2 = 100$, and $x_3 = 150$, or (200, 100, 150). Interpret the solution set for the production supervisor of this company.

EXAMPLE 21

Emergency Airlift Revisited In Example 22 (Chap. 3, page 110) and at the very beginning of Chap. 4, we discussed a problem involving the airlift of emergency supplies into a South American city. Two restrictions were imposed—a volume capacity of 6,000 cubic feet and a weight capacity of 40,000 pounds. The two equations whose solution sets contain quantities of the different items which fill the plane to its respective capacities were

$$20x_1 + 30x_2 + 8x_3 + 6x_4 = 6,000 \quad \text{(volume)}$$
$$150x_1 + 100x_2 + 60x_3 + 70x_4 = 40,000 \quad \text{(weight)}$$

(Refer to page 111 for a definition of the variables.)

To determine quantities of the various items which will fill the plane to *both* its volume and its weight capacities, we must define the solution set for the system. From Chap. 4 we should conclude that there is either no solution or, more likely, an infinite number of solutions for the system. Sample solutions may be found by assuming values for two of the four variables and solving for the values of the remaining two. As an example, if $x_3 = x_4 = 0$, then $x_1 = 240$ and $x_2 = 40$.

EXERCISE

Interpret the meaning of the sample solution. If only food and water are to go on the first plane, determine the appropriate quantities.*

Portfolio Model

A *portfolio* of stocks is simply the set of stocks owned by an investor. In selecting the portfolio for a particular investor, consideration is often given to such things as the amount of money to be invested, the attitude the investor has about risk (is he or she a risk taker?), and whether the investor is interested in long-term growth or short-run return. This type of problem is similar to the product-mix example. The products are the stocks or securities available for investment.

EXAMPLE 22

When people invest money, there are professionals, such as stockbrokers, who may be consulted for advice about the portfolio which best meets an investor's needs. Suppose that an investor has consulted with a local investment expert. After talking with the client, the investment expert determines that the client is interested in a portfolio which will have the following attributes: (1) total value of the portfolio at the time of purchase is $50,000, (2) expected annual growth in market value equals 12 percent, and (3) average risk factor is 10 percent. Three investment alternatives have been identified with relative growth and risk rates shown in Table 5.4.

To determine the portfolio, *let's define x_j as the number of dollars invested in investment j.* The first attribute can be stated in equation form as

$$x_1 + x_2 + x_3 = 50,000 \tag{5.14}$$

---

* $x_3 = 900$ and $x_4 = -200$. Since a negative number of containers of water is meaningless, we conclude that there is no combination of containers of only food and water which will fill the plane *exactly* to its volume and weight capacities.

TABLE 5.4

INVESTMENT	EXPECTED ANNUAL GROWTH IN MARKET VALUE	EXPECTED RISK
1	16%	12%
2	8	9
3	12	8

Attribute (2) little more difficult to formulate. Let's precede the formulation by looking at a simple example. Suppose that you put $100 in a bank and it earns interest of 8 percent per year. Also suppose you put $200 in a certificate of deposit which earns interest at a rate of 14 percent per year. To determine the *average* percent return on your $300 investment, we must compute total interest and divide by the original investment, or

$$\text{Average percent return} = \frac{\text{dollars of interest earned}}{\text{total dollars invested}}$$

For this example, the average annual percent return is computed as

$$\frac{0.08(100) + 0.14(200)}{100 + 200} = \frac{8 + 28}{300} = \frac{36}{300} = 0.12, \text{ or } 12\%$$

To compute the average percent growth in our example, we must determine the annual interest (in dollars) for each investment, sum these, and divide by the total dollars invested, or

$$\text{Average percent growth} = \frac{0.16x_1 + 0.08x_2 + 0.12x_3}{x_1 + x_2 + x_3}$$

Since Eq. (5.14) specifies that $x_1 + x_2 + x_3 = 50{,}000$ and since the investor desires an average percent growth of 12 percent, we can rewrite the equation as

$$\frac{0.16x_1 + 0.08x_2 + 0.12x_3}{50{,}000} = 0.12$$

or, multiplying both sides of the equation by 50,000, we get

$$0.16x_1 + 0.08x_2 + 0.12x_3 = 6{,}000 \tag{5.15}$$

This equation states that the total annual increase in market value for the three investments must equal $6,000 (or 12 percent of $50,000).

The weighted risk condition is determined in exactly the same manner. To calculate average risk per dollar invested, each dollar must be multiplied by the risk factor associated with the investment of that dollar. These must be summed for all different investments and divided by the total investment. This relationship is generalized by the equation

$$\text{Average risk} = \frac{\text{sum of weighted risks for all investments}}{\text{total dollars invested}}$$

This equation can be stated in our example as

$$\frac{0.12x_1 + 0.09x_2 + 0.08x_3}{50{,}000} = 0.10$$

or

$$0.12x_1 + 0.09x_2 + 0.08x_3 = 5{,}000 \tag{5.16}$$

EXERCISE

Verify that when Eqs. (5.14) to (5.16) are solved simultaneously, $x_1 = 20,000$, $x_2 = 20,000$, and $x_3 = 10,000$. Interpret this solution for the investor.

Blending Model

Some applications involve the mixing of ingredients or components to form a final blend having specific characteristics. Examples include the blending of gasoline and other petroleum products, the blending of coffee beans, and the blending of whiskeys. Very often the blending requirements and relationships are defined by linear equations or linear inequalities. The following example illustrates a simple application.

EXAMPLE 23

A coffee manufacturer is interested in blending three different types of coffee beans into a final coffee blend. The three component beans cost the manufacturer $1.20, $1.60, and $1.40 per pound, respectively. The manufacturer wants to blend a batch of 40,000 pounds of coffee and has a coffee purchasing budget of $57,600. In blending the coffee, one restriction is that the amount used of component 2 should be twice that of component 1 (the brewmaster believes this to be critical in avoiding a bitter flavor).

The objective is to determine whether there is a combination of the three components which will lead to a final blend (1) consisting of 40,000 pounds (2) costing $57,600 and (3) satisfying the blending restriction on components 1 and 2.

If x_j equals the number of pounds of component j used in the final blend, Eq. (5.17) specifies that the total blend should weigh 40,000 pounds:

$$x_1 + x_2 + x_3 = 40,000 \tag{5.17}$$

Equation (5.18) specifies that the total cost of the three components should equal $57,600:

$$1.20x_1 + 1.60x_2 + 1.40x_3 = 57,600 \tag{5.18}$$

The recipe restriction is stated as

$$x_2 = 2x_1$$

or alternatively,
$$-2x_1 + x_2 = 0 \tag{5.19}$$

EXERCISE

Verify that when Eqs. (5.17) to (5.19) are solved simultaneously, the solution is $x_1 = 8,000$, $x_2 = 16,000$, and $x_3 = 16,000$. Interpret this solution for the brewmaster.

Section 5.4 Follow-up Exercises

1   Determine the equilibrium price and quantity if

$$q_d = 60,000 - 50p \quad \text{and} \quad q_s = 10,000 + 30p$$

where p is stated in dollars.

2   Determine the equilibrium price and quantity if

$$q_d = 40{,}000 - 25p \quad \text{and} \quad q_s = 6000 + 15p$$

3   **Income Shifts**   Economists believe that if there is a general shift in income levels, demand will change at all price levels. For instance, if everyone's income increased by 10 percent, all other things remaining unchanged, at any given price level greater quantities of a product would be demanded. Tax rebates are often employed to stimulate greater demand. Similarly, it is believed that decreases in income levels will result in smaller quantities being demanded at any given price. These income shifts can be represented by a shift in the demand curve. Figure 5.15 indicates the nature of the demand curve movements. Note the changes in demand at a price p_1 for the different curves. Assume in Example 18 that income levels have increased such that the demand curve has shifted outward. The slope is the same, but the y coordinate of the y intercept is 12,500 instead of 10,000. Determine the new equilibrium price and quantity.

4   Referring to the discussion of income shifts in Exercise 3, assume in Exercise 1 that income levels have decreased sufficiently to cause a downward shift in the demand curve. The slope is the same, but the y coordinate of the y intercept is now 50,000. Determine the new equilibrium price and quantity.

5   **Supply Shifts**   Just as changes in income levels can cause shifts of the demand curve, there are factors which can cause shifts in supply functions. For example, severe weather conditions may lead to general shortages of crops, which may be evidenced by a *downward* shift in the supply curve. Similarly, exceptionally good years may result in a more abundant supply and an upward shift in the supply function. These shifts in the supply curve reflect the fact that when more is available, suppliers are willing to supply larger quantities at any given price. And when less is available, they are willing to supply smaller quantities at any given price.

Assume in Exercise 1 that poor weather conditions have resulted in a downward shift of the supply function such that it is described by

$$q_s = 6{,}000 + 30p$$

Determine the new equilibrium price and quantity.

6   Using simultaneous equations, determine the linear function which contains the points (20, 50) and (40, 10).

7   Using simultaneous equations, determine the linear function which contains the points (−10, 5) and (10, 75).

8   **Quadratic Functions**   As discussed in Sec. 2.2 a quadratic function is a nonlinear function having the general form $y = a_0 + a_1x + a_2x^2$, where $a_2 \neq 0$. If a_0, a_1, and a_2 can be specified, the function is defined. Since three parameters define a quadratic function, three data points are needed to define their values. A quadratic function contains the points (0, 10), (10, −70), and (−5, −25). Substitute these coordinates into the general quadratic equation and solve the three resulting linear equations for a_0, a_1, and a_2. What is the equation of the quadratic function containing these points?

9   A company produces three products, each of which must be processed through one department. Table 5.5 summarizes the labor hour and raw material requirements per unit of each product. Each month there are 1,500 labor hours and 3,800 pounds of the raw material available. If combined monthly production for the three products should equal 500 units, determine whether there are any combinations of the three products which

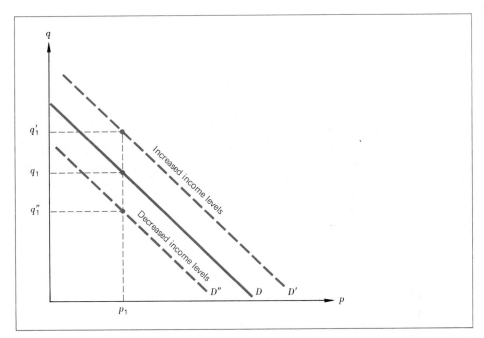

FIGURE 5.15
Demand curve
shifts.

TABLE 5.5

	Product		
	1	2	3
Labor hours/unit	3	2	4
Pounds of raw material/unit	10	8	6

would exhaust the monthly availabilities of labor and raw material and meet the production goal of 500 units.

10 A coffee manufacturer is interested in blending three types of coffee beans into 10,000 pounds of a final coffee blend. The three component beans cost $2.40, $2.60, and $2 per pound, respectively. The manufacturer wants to blend the 10,000 pounds at a total cost of $21,000. In blending the coffee, one restriction is that the amounts used of component beans 1 and 2 be the same. Determine whether there is a combination of the three types of beans which will lead to a final blend of 10,000 pounds costing $21,000 and satisfying the blending restriction.

11 An investor has $500,000 to spend. Three investments are being considered, each having an expected annual interest rate. The interest rates are 15, 10, and 18 percent, respectively. The investor's goal is an average return of 15 percent in the three investments. Because of the high return on investment alternative 3, the investor wants the amount in this alternative to equal 40 percent of the total investment. Determine whether there is a meaningful investment strategy which will satisfy these requirements.

12 In Example 21, specify the generalized solution if x_3 and x_4 are considered arbitrary. Is it appropriate to state that x_3 and x_4 are arbitrary, or should other conditions be stated?

KEY TERMS AND CONCEPTS

IMPORTANT FORMULAS

$$y = f(x) = ax + b \tag{5.1}$$

$$y = f(x_1, x_2) = a_1x_1 + a_2x_2 + b \tag{5.2}$$

$$y = f(x_1, x_2, \ldots, x_n) = a_1x_1 + a_2x_2 + \cdots + a_nx_n + b \tag{5.3}$$

$$\left. R(x) = C(x) \right\} \quad \text{Break-even conditions} \tag{5.10}$$

$$\left. x_{BE} = \frac{FC}{p - v} \right\} \tag{5.11}$$

ADDITIONAL EXERCISES

1   A firm sells a product for $60 per unit. Raw material costs are $12.50 per unit, labor costs are $17.50 per unit, and annual fixed costs are $120,000.
(a) Determine the profit function $P(x)$ where x equals the number of units sold.
(b) How many units would have to be sold to earn an annual profit of $150,000.

2   A firm produces three products which sell, respectively, for $15, $25, and $10. Labor requirements for each product are respectively, 3.0, 4.0, and 3.5 hours per unit. Assume labor costs are $3 per hour and annual fixed costs are $50,000.
(a) Construct a joint total revenue function for the sales of the three products.
(b) Determine an annual total cost function for production of the three products.
(c) Determine the profit function for the three products. Is there anything unusual about this function?
(d) What is annual profit if 20,000, 10,000 and 30,000 units are sold, respectively, of the three products?

3   A city has purchased a new asphalt paving machine for $120,000. The city comptroller states that the machine will be depreciated using a straight-line method. At the end of 8 years, the machine will be sold with an expected salvage value of $24,000.
(a) Determine the function $V = f(t)$ which expresses the book value of the machine V as a function of its age t.
(b) What is the book value expected to be when the machine is 6 years old?

4   The birthrate in a particular country has been declining linearly in recent years. In 1975 the birthrate was 32.4 births per 1,000 people. In 1980 the birthrate was 30.6

births per 1,000 people. Assume R equals the birthrate per 1,000 and t equals time measured in years since 1975 ($t = 0$ for 1975).

(a) Determine the linear birthrate function $R = f(t)$.

(b) Interpret the meaning of the slope.

(c) If the linear pattern continues, what is the expected birthrate in 1990?

(d) What is the restricted domain for this function?

   5   Two points (p, q) on a linear demand function are ($4.50, 45,000) and ($4.75, 40,500).

(a) Determine the demand function $q = f(p)$.

(b) What price would result in a demand of 67,500 units?

(c) Determine the y intercept and interpret its meaning.

(d) Determine the x intercept and interpret its meaning.

   6   Two points (p, q) on a linear supply function are ($10, 450,000) and ($13, 630,000).

(a) Determine the supply function $q = f(p)$.

(b) What price would result in suppliers offering 750,000 units for sale?

(c) Interpret the slope of the supply function.

(d) What is the x intercept? Interpret the meaning of this point.

   7   **Alcoholism**   Since 1970 there has been a seemingly linear increase in the percentage of the population of one European city who are alcoholics. In 1970 the percentage was 10.5 percent. In 1976 the percentage had risen to 12.9 percent. If p equals the percentage of the population who are alcoholics and t represents time in years since 1970 ($t = 0$ for 1970),

(a) Determine the linear growth function $p = f(t)$.

(b) Interpret the meaning of the slope.

(c) If the pattern of growth continues, forecast the percentage of alcoholics expected in 1985. What is the forecast for 1995?

   8   A publisher has a fixed cost of $150,000 associated with the production of a college mathematics book. The contribution to profit and fixed cost from the sale of each book is $3.75.

(a) Determine the number of books which must be sold in order to break even.

(b) What is the expected profit if 30,000 books are sold?

   9   A local university football team has added a national power to next year's schedule. The other team has agreed to play the game for a guaranteed fee of $75,000 plus 25 percent of the gate receipts. Assume ticket prices are $8.

(a) Determine the number of tickets which must be sold to recover the $75,000 guarantee.

(b) If college officials hope to net a profit of $180,000 from the game, how many tickets must be sold?

(c) If a sellout of 50,000 fans is assured, what ticket price would allow the university to earn the desired profit of $180,000?

(d) Again assuming a sellout, what would total profit equal if the $8 price is charged?

   10   **Equipment Selection**   A firm has two equipment alternatives it can choose from in producing a new product. One automated piece of equipment costs $200,000 and produces items at a cost of $4 per unit. Another semi-automated piece of equipment costs $75,000 and produces items at a cost of $5.25 per unit.

(a) What volume of output makes the two pieces of equipment equally costly?

(b) If 80,000 units are to be produced, which piece of equipment is the least costly? What is the minimum cost?

11 Robotics A manufacturer is interested in introducing the robotics technology into one of its production processes. The process is one which would provide a "hostile environment" for humans. To be more specific, the process involves exposure to extremely high temperatures as well as to potentially toxic fumes. Two robots have been identified which appear to have the capabilities for executing the functions of the production process. There appear to be no significant differences in the speeds at which the two models work. One robot costs $180,000 and has estimated maintenance costs of $100 per hour of operation. The second type of robot costs $250,000 with maintenance costs estimated at $80 per hour of operation.

(a) At what level of operation (total production hours) are the two robots equally costly? What is the associated cost?

(b) Define the levels of operation for which each robot would be the least costly.

12 Video Games A leading manufacturer of video games is about to introduce four new games. Table 5.6 summarizes price and cost data. Combined fixed costs equal $500,000.

TABLE 5.6

	Game			
	PACPERSON	ASTERVOIDS	HALEY'S COMET	BLACK HOLE
Selling price	$50	$45	$30	$20
Variable cost/unit	20	15	10	10

A marketing research study predicts that for each unit sold of Black Hole, 1.5 units of Haley's Comet, 3 units of Astervoids, and 4 units of PacPerson will be sold.

(a) How many product-mix units must be sold to break even?

(b) How does this translate into sales of individual games?

13 Using simultaneous equations, determine the linear function which is satisfied by the points $(10, -5)$ and $(-5, 40)$.

14 Using simultaneous equations, determine the quadratic function which is satisfied by the points $(1, 4)$, $(-5, 40)$, and $(2, 5)$.

***15** Using simultaneous equations, determine the linear function having the form $y = f(x_1, x_2) = a_1x_1 + a_2x_2 + b$ which is satisfied by the points $(1, 3, -2)$, $(2, -2, 15)$, and $(1, 1, 4)$.

16 Diet-Mix Problems A dietician is planning the menu for the evening meal at a university dining hall. Three main items will be served, each having different nutritional content. The goal is that the nutritional content of the meal meet the minimum daily levels for three different vitamins. Table 5.7 summarizes the vitamin content *per ounce* of each food. In addition, the minimum daily levels of the three vitamins are indicated. Determine the number of ounces of each food to be included in the meal such that minimum daily vitamin levels are met for the three vitamins.

17 Soviet Arms Buildup In recent years there has been great concern expressed about the nuclear arms capabilities of the United States and the Soviet Union. In the period from 1966 to 1980, the Soviet Union increased the number of submarine-launched ballistic missiles (SLBMs) at an estimated linear rate. The number of such missiles in 1966 was 75. The estimated number in 1975 was 700.

TABLE 5.7

VITAMIN	MDR	FOOD 1	FOOD 2	FOOD 3
			mg/oz	
1	29	5	3	2
2	20	2	1	3
3	21	1	5	2

(a) Determine the linear function which estimates the number of SLBMs held by the Soviets. ($t = 0$ corresponds to 1966.)

(b) Interpret the slope and y intercept of the function.

(c) Estimate the number of SLBMs held by the Soviets in 1980.

*18 **Generalized Equilibrium Model** Given the generalized demand and supply functions $q_d = a - bp$ $(a, b > 0)$ and $q_s = -c + dp$ $(c, d > 0)$, determine the generalized expressions for (a) the equilibrium price and (b) the equilibrium quantity, stated in terms of the parameters a, b, c, and d.

CHAPTER TEST

1 **Grade Inflation** Since 1973 there has been evidence of grade inflation at a large Midwestern university. The cumulative grade-point average for all undergraduate students was 2.42 in 1973. In 1977 the average was 2.66. Assuming the trend is linear, let g represent the cumulative grade-point average for all undergraduate students and t represent time measured in years since 1973.

(a) Determine the function $g = f(t)$.

(b) According to this function, when will the grade-point average reach 3.0?

(c) Forecast the grade-point average for 1980.

(d) Interpret the meaning of the slope in this function.

2 A company sells a product for $100 per unit. Raw material costs are $40 per unit, labor costs are $25 per unit, shipping costs are $10 per unit, and annual fixed costs are $100,000.

(a) Determine the profit function $P = f(x)$, where x equals the number of units sold.

(b) How many units must be sold in order to earn an annual profit of $150,000?

3 A local charity organization is planning a chartered flight and one-week vacation to the Caribbean. The venture is a fund-raising effort. A package deal has been worked out with a commercial airline in which the charity will be charged a fixed cost of $10,000 plus $300 per person. The $300 covers the flight cost, transfers, hotel, meals, and tips. The organization is planning to price the package at $450 per person.

(a) Determine the number of persons necessary to break even on the venture.

(b) The goal of the organization is to net a profit of $10,000. How many people must participate for the goal to be realized?

4 Determine the equilibrium price and quantity if

$$q_d = 100,000 - 1,500p \quad \text{and} \quad q_s = 10,000 + 3,000p$$

where p is stated in dollars.

TABLE 5.8

DEPARTMENT	Product			HOURS AVAILABLE PER WEEK
	A	B	C	
1	6	2	2	80
2	7	4	1	60
3	5	5	3	100

5 A company produces three products, each of which must be processed through three different departments. Table 5.8 summarizes the hours required per unit of each product in each department as well as the weekly capacities in each department. Formulate, *but do not solve,* the system of equations which, when solved, would indicate whether there are any combinations of the three products that would consume the weekly labor availability in all departments.

MINICASE

AUTOMOBILE REPLACEMENT DECISION

Given the high cost of gasoline, automobile owners are constantly searching for ways of economizing on driving expenses. One costly alternative for many persons is to purchase a car which gets significantly better gasoline mileage than does their present car. Robert G. Chamberlain, a systems analyst at the Jet Propulsion Laboratory in Pasadena, California, developed a mathematical formula to calculate how many years a person would have to drive a new car to make the gasoline savings offset the cost of trading in the old car and buying a new one.* The variables to be used in this analysis are:

y = number of years to justify the purchase of a new car
m = gasoline mileage of present car, mi/gal
n = gasoline mileage of new car, mi/gal
c = net cost of new car (purchase cost less proceeds from sale of present car)
d = average number of miles driven per year
p = gasoline price per gallon

Chamberlain determines this "break-even" period using the general relationship:

$$\begin{matrix} \text{Cost of gasoline} \\ \text{for present car} \\ \text{during break-even period} \end{matrix} = \begin{matrix} \text{cost of gasoline} \\ \text{for new car during} \\ \text{break-even period} \end{matrix} + \begin{matrix} \text{net cost} \\ \text{of new car} \end{matrix}$$

or
$$f_{\text{old}}(y) = f_{\text{new}}(y)$$

1 Using the variables defined above, determine the expressions for $f_{\text{old}}(y)$ and $f_{\text{new}}(y)$.

2 Set $f_{\text{old}}(y)$ equal to $f_{\text{new}}(y)$ and derive the general formula for the break-even period y.

3 Determine the break-even period if the present car has a value of $2,500 and gets 20 miles per gallon. The new car has a purchase cost of $9,500 and gets an estimated 54 miles per gallon. Gasoline prices are currently $1.80 per gallon.

4 Examine the sensitivity of the break-even period to changes in the price of gasoline. To test this, assume that the actual price may vary by ± 25 percent from the $1.80 figure. Is there much of a change in the break-even period?

5 List assumptions of this model. What assumptions are unrealistic? Why? What cost factors have not been considered?

* "Should the Gas Guzzler Go?" (letter), *Science*, vol. 207, p. 1028, March 1980.

6

MATRIX ALGEBRA

CHAPTER OBJECTIVES

■ Provide an understanding of the nature of a matrix and matrix representation of data

■ Provide an understanding of the algebra of matrices

■ Present a variety of applications of matrices and matrix algebra

This chapter discusses matrix algebra and its applications. The nature of matrices is presented, followed by a discussion of different types of matrices, the algebra of matrices, and some specialized matrix concepts. The last section in the chapter presents several applications of matrix algebra.

6.1 INTRODUCTION TO MATRICES

What Is a Matrix?

Whenever one is dealing with data, there should be concern for organizing them in such a way that they are meaningful and can be readily identified. Summarizing data in tabular form serves this function. Income tax tables are an example of this type of organization. A *matrix* is a common device for summarizing and displaying numbers or data.

DEFINITION: MATRIX

A **matrix** is a rectangular array of elements.

The elements of a matrix are usually, but not always, real numbers. Consider the test scores for five students on three examinations. These could be displayed in the following matrix.

Test

		1	2	3
	1	75	82	86
	2	91	95	100
Student	3	65	70	68
	4	59	80	99
	5	75	76	74

The matrix is the array of test scores enclosed by the large parentheses. The array is rectangularly shaped, having five rows (one for each student) and three columns (one for each test). Each row contains the three test scores for a particular student. Each column contains the five scores on a particular test.

GENERALIZED FORM

A matrix **A** containing elements a_{ij} has the general form

$$\mathbf{A} = \begin{pmatrix} a_{11} & a_{12} & \cdots & a_{1n} \\ a_{21} & a_{22} & \cdots & a_{2n} \\ \cdots & \cdots & \cdots & \cdots \\ a_{m1} & a_{m2} & \cdots & a_{mn} \end{pmatrix}$$

This generalized matrix is represented as having m rows and n columns. The subscripts on an element a_{ij} indicate that the element is located at the intersection of row i and column j of the matrix. For example, a_{21} is located at the intersection of row 2 and column 1. The element a_{35} would be located in row 3 and column 5 of the matrix.

EXERCISE

If the student test score matrix is named **S** and the elements are denoted by s_{ij}, what are the elements s_{12}, s_{32}, s_{43}, and s_{16}?*

Matrix names are usually represented by capital letters and the elements of a matrix by lowercase, subscripted letters.

A matrix is characterized further by its *dimension*. The dimension or *order* indicates the number of rows and the number of columns contained within the matrix. If a matrix has m rows and n columns, it is said to have dimension $m \times n$, which is read *"m by n."* The student test score matrix has dimension 5×3, or it is a "5 by 3" matrix.

Purpose of Studying Matrix Algebra

Given that we know what a matrix is, matrices provide a convenient medium for the storage, display, and manipulation of data. The test score data are stored conveniently in the previous matrix and the matrix provides a clear and compact method for displaying this data.

---

* 82, 70, 99, no s_{16} element.

Computer programs regularly use matrices or "arrays" for storage of information. In the FORTRAN language you reserve storage space for arrays in the memory of the computer by use of the DIMENSION statement. The statement "DIMENSION $A(20, 30)$" reserves space for a matrix **A** which has dimension of 20×30.

When data are stored within matrices, there is often a need to display them. If the data are stored within a matrix in some logical pattern, the retrieval of individual items or groups of items can be relatively easy. Frequently there is a need to manipulate data which is stored in a matrix. For instance, an instructor may want to determine a class average on a given test or a student average for the three tests using the student test score data in the previously defined matrix. Matrix algebra allows for manipulating data and for performing computations while keeping the data in a matrix form. This is convenient, especially in computerized applications.

EXAMPLE 1

U.S. Energy Consumption The matrix **E** below displays average daily energy consumption by energy source for four different regions of the country during 1980. The figures are in millions of barrels per day and represent the amount of oil that would yield the equivalent energy. They have been rounded to the nearest 100,000 barrels.

American oil and gas	Coal	Imported oil and gas	Hydroelectric, solar, geothermal, and synthetic fuels	Nuclear	
6.5	2.8	3.0	0.2	0.5	Northeast
3.2	1.1	0.5	0.5	0.2	South
3.4	2.0	1.1	0.1	0.4	Midwest
5.5	1.5	3.3	0.6	0.2	West

$$\mathbf{E} =$$

The following sections discuss different types of matrices and their manipulation.

6.2 SPECIAL TYPES OF MATRICES

Vectors

One special class of matrices is called a *vector.* A vector is a matrix having only one row or one column.

DEFINITION: ROW VECTOR

A *row vector* is a matrix having only one row. A row vector **R** having n elements r_{1j} has dimension $1 \times n$ and the general form

$$\mathbf{R} = (r_{11}\ r_{12}\ r_{13} \cdots r_{1n})$$

The three test scores for student 1 might be represented by the (1×3) row vector **A** as

$$\mathbf{A} = (75 \quad 82 \quad 86)$$

The matrix **B** below is a (1×8) row vector.

$$\mathbf{B} = (3 \quad 4 \quad 7 \quad -6 \quad 2 \quad 0 \quad 1 \quad -2)$$

DEFINITION: COLUMN VECTOR

A **column vector** is a matrix having only one column. A column vector **C** having m elements c_{i_1} has dimension $m \times 1$ and the general form

$$\mathbf{C} = \begin{pmatrix} c_{11} \\ c_{21} \\ \vdots \\ c_{m1} \end{pmatrix}$$

For the previous test score matrix the scores of the five students on the first examination might be represented by the (5×1) column vector

$$\mathbf{T} = \begin{pmatrix} 75 \\ 91 \\ 65 \\ 59 \\ 75 \end{pmatrix}$$

Square Matrices

DEFINITION: SQUARE MATRIX

A **square matrix** is a matrix having the same number of rows and columns.

If the dimension of a matrix is $m \times n$, a square matrix is such that $m = n$. The following matrices are square.

$$\mathbf{A} = (3) \qquad \mathbf{B} = \begin{pmatrix} 1 & 3 \\ -5 & 4 \end{pmatrix} \qquad \mathbf{C} = \begin{pmatrix} 2 & 0 & -3 \\ 1 & -4 & 5 \\ 0 & 2 & 6 \end{pmatrix}$$

If a matrix **A** is square, we might concern ourselves with a subset of elements a_{ij} which lie along the **primary diagonal** of the matrix. These elements are located in positions where $i = j$, for example, $a_{11}, a_{22}, a_{33}, a_{44}, \ldots, a_{nn}$. The elements on the primary diagonal of matrix **B** are $b_{11} = 1$ and $b_{22} = 4$. The elements on the primary diagonal of matrix **C** are $c_{11} = 2$, $c_{22} = -4$, and $c_{33} = 6$.

DEFINITION: IDENTITY MATRIX

An **identity matrix I,** sometimes called a **unit matrix,** is a square matrix for which the elements along the primary diagonal all equal 1 while all other elements equal 0.

If e_{ij} denotes a generalized element within an identity matrix, then

$$e_{ij} = \begin{cases} 1 & \text{if } i = j \\ 0 & \text{if } i \neq j \end{cases}$$

The matrices

$$\mathbf{I} = \begin{pmatrix} 1 & 0 \\ 0 & 1 \end{pmatrix} \quad \text{and} \quad \mathbf{I} = \begin{pmatrix} 1 & 0 & 0 \\ 0 & 1 & 0 \\ 0 & 0 & 1 \end{pmatrix}$$

are (2×2) and (3×3) identity matrices.

Although we will see different applications of the identity matrix, one important property involves the multiplication of an identity matrix and another matrix. Multiplication of matrices is a legitimate algebraic operation under certain circumstances. Given a matrix $\mathbf{A}$ and an identity matrix $\mathbf{I}$, *if the product AI is defined, AI = A.* Similarly, *if the product IA is defined, then IA = A.* The identity matrix $\mathbf{I}$ is to matrix multiplication as the number 1 is to multiplication in the real number system; that is, $(a)(1) = (1)(a) = a$.

Transpose of a Matrix

There are times when the data elements in a matrix need to be rearranged. The rearrangement may be simply to see the array of numbers from a different perspective or to manipulate the data in a later stage. One rearrangement is to form the *transpose* of a matrix.

DEFINITION: TRANSPOSE

Given the $m \times n$ matrix $\mathbf{A}$ with elements a_{ij}, the **transpose** of $\mathbf{A}$, denoted by $\mathbf{A}^t$, is an $n \times m$ matrix which contains elements a_{ij}^t where $a_{ij}^t = a_{ji}$.

EXAMPLE 2

To find the transpose of the matrix

$$\mathbf{A} = \begin{pmatrix} 3 & 2 \\ 4 & 0 \\ 1 & -2 \end{pmatrix}$$

we first determine the dimension of $\mathbf{A}^t$. Since $\mathbf{A}$ is a (3×2) matrix, $\mathbf{A}^t$ will be a (2×3) matrix having the form

$$\mathbf{A}^t = \begin{pmatrix} a_{11}^t & a_{12}^t & a_{13}^t \\ a_{21}^t & a_{22}^t & a_{23}^t \end{pmatrix}$$

Using the previous definition, we get

$$a_{11}^t = a_{11} = 3 \qquad a_{21}^t = a_{12} = 2$$

$$a_{12}^t = a_{21} = 4 \qquad a_{22}^t = a_{22} = 0$$
$$a_{13}^t = a_{31} = 1 \qquad a_{23}^t = a_{32} = -2$$

or
$$\mathbf{A}^t = \begin{pmatrix} 3 & 4 & 1 \\ 2 & 0 & -2 \end{pmatrix}$$

Study the matrices $\mathbf{A}$ and $\mathbf{A}^t$ in Example 2. Do you notice any pattern? What you should observe is that the rows of $\mathbf{A}$ become the columns of $\mathbf{A}^t$ and the columns of $\mathbf{A}$ become the rows of $\mathbf{A}^t$. These relationships will be true for any matrix and its transpose, and they provide an easy method for determining the transpose.

EXAMPLE 3

Let's apply this logic in finding the transpose of

$$\mathbf{B} = \begin{pmatrix} 3 & 0 & 6 \\ 5 & 1 & 3 \\ 2 & -1 & 4 \end{pmatrix}$$

To form the transpose of $\mathbf{B}$, rows 1, 2, and 3 become columns 1, 2, and 3 of $\mathbf{B}^t$, or

$$\mathbf{B}^t = \begin{pmatrix} 3 & 5 & 2 \\ 0 & 1 & -1 \\ 6 & 3 & 4 \end{pmatrix}$$

You might also have envisioned this in terms of columns 1, 2, and 3 of $\mathbf{B}$ becoming rows 1, 2, and 3 of $\mathbf{B}^t$. Both perspectives are valid.

Section 6.2 Follow-up Exercises

Determine the dimension of each of the following matrices and find the transpose.

1 $(6 \quad -8 \quad 2)$

2 $\begin{pmatrix} 3 & 5 \\ -1 & 8 \end{pmatrix}$

3 $\begin{pmatrix} 0 \\ 4 \\ -5 \\ 1 \end{pmatrix}$

4 $\begin{pmatrix} 2 & 0 \\ -3 & -5 \\ 1 & -6 \end{pmatrix}$

5 $\begin{pmatrix} 1 & 0 & 0 \\ 0 & 1 & 0 \\ 0 & 0 & 1 \end{pmatrix}$

6 $\begin{pmatrix} -6 & 3 & 2 & 1 & 4 \\ 2 & 3 & 1 & 4 & 6 \\ 2 & -1 & 5 & 8 & 3 \end{pmatrix}$

7 Find a (2×4) matrix $\mathbf{A}$ for which

$$a_{ij} = \begin{cases} i + j & \text{if } i = j \\ 0 & \text{if } i \neq j \end{cases}$$

6.3 MATRIX OPERATIONS

In this section we will discuss some of the operations of matrix algebra.

Matrix Addition and Subtraction

PROPERTY OF MATRIX ADDITION (SUBTRACTION)

Two matrices may be added or subtracted if and only if they have the same dimension.

If matrices A and B are added to form a new matrix C, C will have the same dimension as A and B and the elements of C are found by adding the corresponding elements of A and B. That is,

$$c_{ij} = a_{ij} + b_{ij} \qquad \text{for all } i \text{ and } j$$

EXAMPLE 4

Given

$$A = \begin{pmatrix} 1 & 3 \\ 4 & -2 \end{pmatrix} \quad \text{and} \quad B = \begin{pmatrix} -3 & 2 \\ 0 & 4 \end{pmatrix}$$

$$A + B = \begin{pmatrix} 1 & 3 \\ 4 & -2 \end{pmatrix} + \begin{pmatrix} -3 & 2 \\ 0 & 4 \end{pmatrix}$$

$$= \begin{pmatrix} 1 + (-3) & 3 + 2 \\ 4 + 0 & -2 + 4 \end{pmatrix} = \begin{pmatrix} -2 & 5 \\ 4 & 2 \end{pmatrix}$$

EXAMPLE 5

Using the same matrices

$$B - A = \begin{pmatrix} -3 - (1) & 2 - 3 \\ 0 - (4) & 4 - (-2) \end{pmatrix}$$

$$= \begin{pmatrix} -4 & -1 \\ -4 & 6 \end{pmatrix}$$

EXAMPLE 6

The Department of Energy has projected energy consumption figures for the year 1990. The matrix P displays average daily energy consumption by energy source for the same regions of the U.S. as indicated in Example 1. As before, these figures are in millions of barrels of oil per day that would yield the equivalent energy.

	American oil and gas	Coal	Imported oil and gas	Hydroelectric, solar, geothermal, and synthetic fuels	Nuclear	
	5.9	4.8	2.0	0.7	1.2	Northeast
	2.9	1.9	0.2	0.9	0.5	South
$P =$	2.3	2.4	0.5	0.5	0.9	Midwest
	6.0	1.9	2.9	1.0	0.6	West

The matrix computation $P - E$ reflects the estimated change in average daily energy consumption by energy source between 1980 and 1990.

$$P - E = \begin{pmatrix} 5.9 & 4.8 & 2.0 & 0.7 & 1.2 \\ 2.9 & 1.9 & 0.2 & 0.9 & 0.5 \\ 2.3 & 2.4 & 0.5 & 0.5 & 0.9 \\ 6.0 & 1.9 & 2.9 & 1.0 & 0.6 \end{pmatrix} - \begin{pmatrix} 6.5 & 2.8 & 3.0 & 0.2 & 0.5 \\ 3.2 & 1.1 & 0.5 & 0.5 & 0.2 \\ 3.4 & 2.0 & 1.1 & 0.1 & 0.4 \\ 5.5 & 1.5 & 3.3 & 0.6 & 0.2 \end{pmatrix}$$

$$= \begin{pmatrix} -0.6 & 2.0 & -1.0 & 0.5 & 0.7 \\ -0.3 & 0.8 & -0.3 & 0.4 & 0.3 \\ -1.1 & 0.4 & -0.6 & 0.4 & 0.5 \\ 0.5 & 0.4 & -0.4 & 0.4 & 0.4 \end{pmatrix}$$

EXERCISE

Interpret the meaning of the values in the difference matrix
$\mathbf{P} - \mathbf{E}$.

Scalar Multiplication

A *scalar* is a real number. *Scalar multiplication* of a matrix is the multiplication of a matrix by a scalar. The product is found by multiplying each element in the matrix by the scalar. For example, if k is a scalar and $\mathbf{A}$ the (3×2) matrix below, then

$$k\mathbf{A} = k \cdot \begin{pmatrix} 5 & 3 \\ -2 & 1 \\ 0 & 4 \end{pmatrix} = \begin{pmatrix} 5k & 3k \\ -2k & k \\ 0 & 4k \end{pmatrix}$$

EXAMPLE 7

One private policy research foundation projects that energy consumption will increase by 20 percent in each region and for each energy source between 1980 and 1985. The projected consumption in 1985 can be determined by the scalar multiplication 1.2$\mathbf{E}$, or

$$\mathbf{R} = 1.2 \begin{pmatrix} 6.5 & 2.8 & 3.0 & 0.2 & 0.5 \\ 3.2 & 1.1 & 0.5 & 0.5 & 0.2 \\ 3.4 & 2.0 & 1.1 & 0.1 & 0.4 \\ 5.5 & 1.5 & 3.3 & 0.6 & 0.2 \end{pmatrix} = \begin{pmatrix} 7.80 & 3.36 & 3.60 & 0.24 & 0.60 \\ 3.84 & 1.32 & 0.60 & 0.60 & 0.24 \\ 4.08 & 2.40 & 1.32 & 0.12 & 0.48 \\ 6.50 & 1.80 & 3.96 & 0.72 & 0.24 \end{pmatrix}$$

The Inner Product

DEFINITION: INNER PRODUCT

Let $\mathbf{A} = (a_{11}, a_{12}, \ldots, a_{1n})$ and $\mathbf{B} = \begin{pmatrix} b_{11} \\ b_{21} \\ \cdot \\ \cdot \\ \cdot \\ b_{n1} \end{pmatrix}$; then we shall de-

fine the **inner product**, written $\mathbf{A} \cdot \mathbf{B}$, *as*

$$\mathbf{A} \cdot \mathbf{B} = a_{11}b_{11} + a_{12}b_{21} + \cdots + a_{1n}b_{n1}$$

The *inner product* results when a row vector is multiplied by a column vector. *The resulting product is a scalar quantity.* As you will see, the inner product is a significant operation in matrix multiplication.

The inner product is defined only if the row and column vectors contain the same number of elements. Consider the multiplication of the following vectors:

$$\mathbf{AB} = (5 \quad -2) \begin{pmatrix} 4 \\ 6 \end{pmatrix}$$

The inner product is computed by multiplying corresponding elements in the two vectors and algebraically summing. To find the inner product, the first element in the row vector is multiplied by the first element in the column vector; the resulting product is added to the product of element 2 in the row vector and element 2 in the column vector. For the vectors indicated, the inner product is computed as $a_{11}b_{11} + a_{12}b_{21}$, or

$$= (5)(4) + (-2)(6) = 8$$

The inner product of a $(1 \times n)$ row vector $\mathbf{A}$ and an $(n \times 1)$ column vector $\mathbf{B}$ can be represented using summation notation as

$$\mathbf{A} \cdot \mathbf{B} = \sum_{j=1}^{n} a_{1j}b_{j1}$$

(6.1)

EXAMPLE

Given the row and column vectors

$$\mathbf{M} = (5 \quad -2 \quad 0 \quad 1 \quad 3) \quad \text{and} \quad \mathbf{N} = \begin{pmatrix} -2 \\ -4 \\ 10 \\ 20 \\ 6 \end{pmatrix}$$

the inner product is computed as

$$\mathbf{M} \cdot \mathbf{N} = (5 \quad -2 \quad 0 \quad 1 \quad 3) \begin{pmatrix} -2 \\ -4 \\ 10 \\ 20 \\ 6 \end{pmatrix}$$

$$= (5)(-2) + (-2)(-4) + (0)(10) + (1)(20) + (3)(6) = 36$$

Matrix Multiplication

Assume that a matrix $\mathbf{A}$ having dimension $m_A \times n_A$ is to be multiplied by a matrix $\mathbf{B}$ having dimension $m_B \times n_B$:

PROPERTIES OF MATRIX MULTIPLICATION

I The matrix product **AB** is defined if and only if the number of columns of **A** equals the number of rows of **B**, or if $n_A = m_B$.

II If the multiplication can be performed (that is, $n_A = m_B$), the resulting product will be a matrix having dimension $m_A \times n_B$.

The first multiplication property states the *necessary and sufficient condition* for matrix multiplication. If $n_A \neq m_B$, the matrices cannot be multiplied.

$$
\begin{array}{ccc}
\mathbf{A} & \cdot & \mathbf{B} \\
(m_A \times n_A) & & (m_B \times n_B) \\
& n_A = m_B &
\end{array}
$$
?

Test for necessary and sufficient condition

Property II defines the dimension of a product matrix.

$$
\begin{array}{ccccc}
\mathbf{A} & \cdot & \mathbf{B} & = & \mathbf{C} \\
(\boldsymbol{m_A} \times n_A) & & (m_B \times \boldsymbol{n_B}) & & (\boldsymbol{m_A} \times \boldsymbol{n_B}) \\
& n_A = m_B & & &
\end{array}
$$

Product matrix dimension

To determine elements of the product matrix, the following rule applies.

COMPUTATIONAL RULE

If **AB** = **C,** an element c_{ij} of the product matrix is equal to the *inner product* of row i in matrix **A** and column j of matrix **B**. (See Fig. 6.1.)

FIGURE 6.1
Matrix multiplication: computation of c_{ij} using inner product.

$$
\begin{array}{ccccc}
& \mathbf{A} & \mathbf{B} & = & \mathbf{C} \\
& & \text{Column } j & & \\
\text{Row } i & \left(\text{—} \right) & \left(\text{|} \right) & = & \left(c_{ij} \right)
\end{array}
$$

EXAMPLE 8

To find the matrix product **AB,** where

$$
\mathbf{A} = \begin{pmatrix} 2 & 4 \\ 3 & 1 \end{pmatrix} \quad \text{and} \quad \mathbf{B} = \begin{pmatrix} -4 \\ 2 \end{pmatrix}
$$

the first check is to determine whether the multiplication is possible. **A** is a (2 × 2) matrix and **B** is a (2 × 1) matrix.

$$
\begin{array}{ccc}
\mathbf{A} & \cdot\ \mathbf{B} & \mathbf{C} \\
(2 \times \mathbf{2}) & (\mathbf{2} \times 1) & = (2 \times 1)
\end{array}
$$

The product is defined because the number of columns of **A** equals the number of rows of **B**. The resulting product matrix will be of dimension 2×1 and will have the general form

$$
\mathbf{C} = \begin{pmatrix} c_{11} \\ c_{21} \end{pmatrix}
$$

To find c_{11}, the inner product is found by multiplying row 1 of **A** times column 1 of **B**, or

$$
\begin{pmatrix} 2 & 4 \\ 3 & 1 \end{pmatrix} \begin{pmatrix} -4 \\ 2 \end{pmatrix} = \begin{pmatrix} 0 \\ \end{pmatrix}
$$

Similarly, c_{21} is found by computing the inner product between row 2 of **A** and column 1 of **B**, or

$$
\begin{pmatrix} 2 & 4 \\ 3 & 1 \end{pmatrix} \begin{pmatrix} -4 \\ 2 \end{pmatrix} = \begin{pmatrix} 0 \\ -10 \end{pmatrix}
$$

NOTE

As you first attempt matrix multiplication problems, you may find it helpful to write out the general form of the product matrix. We did this by first stating the general form of **C** as $\begin{pmatrix} c_{11} \\ c_{21} \end{pmatrix}$.

With the elements identified in this manner, the subscripts of each element indicate how each element can be computed.

EXAMPLE 9

Determine the matrix product **BA** for the matrices in Example 8.

SOLUTION

The product **BA** involves multiplying a (2×1) matrix times a (2×2) matrix, or

$$
\begin{array}{cc}
\mathbf{B} & \cdot\quad \mathbf{A} \\
(2 \times 1) & (2 \times 2) \\
1 & \neq\ 2
\end{array}
$$

Since the number of columns of **B** does not equal the number of rows of **A**, the product **BA** is not defined.

NOTE

This example illustrates that the commutative property which holds for the multiplication of real numbers *does not necessarily* hold for matrix multiplication. We *cannot* state that **AB** = **BA** for any two matrices **A** and **B**.

EXAMPLE 10 ▮▮▮▮▮▮▮▮▮▮▮▮▮▮▮▮▮▮▮▮▮▮▮▮▮

Find, if possible, the product $\mathbf{PI} = \mathbf{T}$ where

$$\mathbf{P} = \begin{pmatrix} 1 & 0 & -1 \\ 2 & 6 & -2 \\ 0 & 10 & 1 \\ 3 & 4 & 5 \end{pmatrix} \quad \text{and} \quad \mathbf{I} = \begin{pmatrix} 1 & 0 & 0 \\ 0 & 1 & 0 \\ 0 & 0 & 1 \end{pmatrix}$$

SOLUTION

$\mathbf{P}$ is a (4×3) matrix, and $\mathbf{I}$ is a (3×3) identity matrix. Since the number of columns of $\mathbf{P}$ equals the number of rows of $\mathbf{I}$, the multiplication can be performed and the product matrix $\mathbf{T}$ will have dimension 4×3. Thus,

$$\begin{array}{ccccc} \mathbf{P} & \cdot & \mathbf{I} & = & \mathbf{T} \\ (4 \times 3) & & (3 \times 3) & & (4 \times 3) \end{array}$$

$\mathbf{T}$ will have the general form

$$\mathbf{T} = \begin{pmatrix} t_{11} & t_{12} & t_{13} \\ t_{21} & t_{22} & t_{23} \\ t_{31} & t_{32} & t_{33} \\ t_{41} & t_{42} & t_{43} \end{pmatrix}$$

Some sample elements are computed below.

$$t_{11} = (1 \quad 0 \quad -1) \begin{pmatrix} 1 \\ 0 \\ 0 \end{pmatrix} = (1)(1) + (0)(0) + (-1)(0) = 1$$

$$t_{12} = (1 \quad 0 \quad -1) \begin{pmatrix} 0 \\ 1 \\ 0 \end{pmatrix} = (1)(0) + (0)(1) + (-1)(0) = 0$$

$$t_{13} = (1 \quad 0 \quad -1) \begin{pmatrix} 0 \\ 0 \\ 1 \end{pmatrix} = (1)(0) + (0)(0) + (-1)(1) = -1$$

Verify that the product matrix $\mathbf{T}$ is

$$\mathbf{T} = \begin{pmatrix} 1 & 0 & -1 \\ 2 & 6 & -2 \\ 0 & 10 & 1 \\ 3 & 4 & 5 \end{pmatrix}$$

NOTE ▮▮▮▮▮▮▮▮▮▮▮▮▮▮▮▮▮▮▮▮▮▮▮▮▮

This example illustrates the property mentioned earlier concerning identity matrices. That is, if an identity matrix is multiplied by another matrix, the product will be the other matrix. In this example $\mathbf{PI} = \mathbf{T}$. But $\mathbf{P} = \mathbf{T}$; thus $\mathbf{PI} = \mathbf{P}$.

EXAMPLE 11

The instructor who gave the three tests to five students is preparing course averages. She has decided to weight the first two tests at 30 percent each and the third at 40 percent. The instructor wishes to compute the final averages for the five students using matrix multiplication. The matrix of grades is

$$\mathbf{G} = \begin{pmatrix} 74 & 82 & 86 \\ 91 & 95 & 100 \\ 65 & 70 & 68 \\ 59 & 80 & 99 \\ 75 & 76 & 74 \end{pmatrix}$$

and the examination weights are placed in the row vector

$$\mathbf{W} = (0.30 \quad 0.30 \quad 0.40)$$

The instructor needs to multiply these matrices in such a way that the first examination score for *each* student is multiplied by 0.30, the second examination score by 0.30, and the last score by 0.40. Verify for yourself that the products **GW** and **WG** are not defined. If, however, **W** had been stated as a column vector, the matrix product **GW** would lead to the desired result.

We can transform **W** into a column vector by simply finding its transpose. The product $\mathbf{GW}^t$ is defined, it leads to a (5×1) product matrix, and most important it performs the desired computations.

$$\underset{(5 \times 3)}{\mathbf{G}} \quad \cdot \quad \underset{(3 \times 1)}{\mathbf{W}^t} \quad = \quad \underset{(5 \times 1)}{\mathbf{A}}$$

The final averages are computed as

$$\begin{pmatrix} 75 & 82 & 86 \\ 91 & 95 & 100 \\ 65 & 70 & 68 \\ 59 & 80 & 99 \\ 75 & 76 & 74 \end{pmatrix} \begin{pmatrix} 0.30 \\ 0.30 \\ 0.40 \end{pmatrix} = \begin{pmatrix} 75(0.3) + 82(0.3) + 86(0.4) \\ 91(0.3) + 95(0.3) + 100(0.4) \\ 65(0.3) + 70(0.3) + 68(0.4) \\ 59(0.3) + 80(0.3) + 99(0.4) \\ 75(0.3) + 76(0.3) + 74(0.4) \end{pmatrix} = \begin{pmatrix} 81.5 \\ 95.8 \\ 67.7 \\ 81.3 \\ 74.9 \end{pmatrix}$$

The averages are 81.5, 95.8, 67.7, 81.3, and 74.9, respectively, for the five students.

EXERCISE

Compute the product $\mathbf{WG}^t$. Doesn't this yield the same result as $\mathbf{GW}^t$?

Representation of an Equation

An equation may be represented using the inner product. The expression

$$3x_1 + 5x_2 - 4x_3$$

can be represented by the inner product

$$(3 \quad 5 \quad -4) \begin{pmatrix} x_1 \\ x_2 \\ x_3 \end{pmatrix}$$

where the row vector contains the coefficients for each variable in the expression and the column vector contains the variables. Multiply the two vectors to verify that the inner product does result in the original expression.

To represent the *equation*

$$3x_1 + 5x_2 - 4x_3 = 25$$

we can equate the inner product with a (1×1) matrix containing the right-side constant, or

$$(3 \quad 5 \quad -4) \begin{pmatrix} x_1 \\ x_2 \\ x_3 \end{pmatrix} = (25)$$

Remember that for two matrices to be equal, they must have the same dimension. The inner product always results in a (1×1) matrix, which in this case contains one element—the expression $3x_1 + 5x_2 - 4x_3$.

A linear equation of the form $a_1x_1 + a_2x_2 + a_3x_3 + \cdots + a_nx_n = b$ can be represented in matrix form as

$$(a_1 \quad a_2 \quad a_3 \quad \cdots \quad a_n) \begin{pmatrix} x_1 \\ x_2 \\ x_3 \\ \cdot \\ \cdot \\ \cdot \\ x_n \end{pmatrix} = b \qquad \textbf{(6.2)}$$

Representation of Systems of Equations

When single equations may be represented using the inner product, a system of equations can be represented using matrix multiplication. The system

$$5x_1 + 3x_2 = 15$$
$$4x_1 - 2x_2 = 12$$

can be represented as

$$\begin{pmatrix} 5 & 3 \\ 4 & -2 \end{pmatrix} \begin{pmatrix} x_1 \\ x_2 \end{pmatrix} = \begin{pmatrix} 15 \\ 12 \end{pmatrix}$$

If we perform the matrix multiplication on the left side of the matrix equation, the result is

$$\begin{pmatrix} 5x_1 + 3x_2 \\ 4x_1 - 2x_2 \end{pmatrix} = \begin{pmatrix} 15 \\ 12 \end{pmatrix}$$

For these two (2×1) matrices to be equal, the corresponding elements must be equal (i.e., $5x_1 + 3x_2 = 15$ and $4x_1 - 2x_2 = 12$, the original pair of equations).

An $(m \times n)$ system of equations having the form

$$
\begin{aligned}
a_{11}x_1 + a_{12}x_2 + \cdots + a_{1n}x_n &= b_1 \\
a_{21}x_1 + a_{22}x_2 + \cdots + a_{2n}x_n &= b_2 \\
\cdots \cdots \cdots \cdots \cdots \cdots \cdots & \\
a_{m1}x_1 + a_{m2}x_2 + \cdots + a_{mn}x_n &= b_m
\end{aligned}
$$

can be represented by the matrix equation

$$\mathbf{AX} = \mathbf{B}$$

where $\mathbf{A}$ is an $(m \times n)$ matrix containing the variable coefficients on the left side of the set of equations, $\mathbf{X}$ is an n-component column vector containing the n variables, and $\mathbf{B}$ is an m-component column vector containing the right-side constants for the m equations. This representation appears as

$$
\begin{pmatrix}
a_{11} & a_{12} & \cdots & a_{1n} \\
a_{21} & a_{22} & \cdots & a_{2n} \\
& & & \\
\cdots & \cdots & \cdots & \cdots \\
a_{m1} & a_{m2} & \cdots & a_{mn}
\end{pmatrix}
\begin{pmatrix}
x_1 \\
x_2 \\
\cdot \\
\cdot \\
\cdot \\
x_n
\end{pmatrix}
=
\begin{pmatrix}
b_1 \\
b_2 \\
\cdot \\
\cdot \\
\cdot \\
b_m
\end{pmatrix}
\qquad \textbf{(6.3)}
$$

EXAMPLE 12

The system of equations

$$
\begin{aligned}
x_1 - 2x_2 \phantom{{}- 3x_3} + 3x_4 + x_5 &= 100 \\
2x_1 \phantom{{}- 2x_2} - 3x_3 + x_4 \phantom{{}+ x_5} &= 60 \\
4x_2 - x_3 + 2x_4 + x_5 &= 125
\end{aligned}
$$

can be represented in the matrix form $\mathbf{AX} = \mathbf{B}$ as

$$
\begin{pmatrix}
1 & -2 & 0 & 3 & 1 \\
2 & 0 & -3 & 1 & 0 \\
0 & 4 & -1 & 2 & 1
\end{pmatrix}
\begin{pmatrix}
x_1 \\
x_2 \\
x_3 \\
x_4 \\
x_5
\end{pmatrix}
=
\begin{pmatrix}
100 \\
60 \\
125
\end{pmatrix}
$$

Verify that this representation is valid and that the 0s must be included in the $\mathbf{A}$ matrix when a variable does not appear in a particular equation.

Section 6.3 Follow-up Exercises

Perform the following matrix operations wherever possible.

1. $-\begin{pmatrix} 2 & 7 \\ 5 & 6 \end{pmatrix} - \begin{pmatrix} 1 & 2 \\ 3 & 4 \end{pmatrix}$

2. $\begin{pmatrix} 1 & 3 \\ 2 & 4 \end{pmatrix} + \begin{pmatrix} 6 & -2 \\ 1 & 4 \end{pmatrix} - \begin{pmatrix} -1 & 4 \\ 2 & -3 \end{pmatrix}$

3   $-2 \begin{pmatrix} 1 & -2 \\ -1 & 4 \end{pmatrix} + 3 \begin{pmatrix} 1 & 0 \\ -2 & 4 \end{pmatrix}$ 4 $k \begin{pmatrix} a & b \\ -b & 2a \end{pmatrix} - 2k \begin{pmatrix} a & b \\ b & a \end{pmatrix}$

5   $(2 \ -3) \begin{pmatrix} 4 \\ 2 \end{pmatrix}$ 6 $(1 \ 2 \ 3) \begin{pmatrix} 3 \\ 2 \\ 1 \end{pmatrix}$

7   $(3 \ 1) \begin{pmatrix} 1 \\ -2 \\ 3 \end{pmatrix}$ 8 $(1 \ -4 \ 3) \begin{pmatrix} 2 \\ 3 \end{pmatrix}$

9   $(a \ b) \begin{pmatrix} x \\ y \end{pmatrix}$ 10 $(a_1 \ a_2 \ a_3) \begin{pmatrix} x_1 \\ x_2 \\ x_3 \end{pmatrix}$

11   $\begin{pmatrix} 4 & 0 \\ -2 & 1 \end{pmatrix} \begin{pmatrix} 2 & 6 \\ -1 & 0 \end{pmatrix}$ 12 $\begin{pmatrix} 3 & 1 \\ -2 & 0 \end{pmatrix} \begin{pmatrix} 5 \\ -3 \end{pmatrix}$

13   $(2 \ -3) \begin{pmatrix} 1 & 0 \\ 0 & 1 \end{pmatrix}$ 14 $\begin{pmatrix} 2 & 1 \\ -1 & 3 \end{pmatrix} \begin{pmatrix} 1 & 0 \\ 0 & 1 \end{pmatrix}$

15   $\begin{pmatrix} 1 & -2 \\ 0 & 3 \end{pmatrix} \begin{pmatrix} 1 & 0 & 1 \\ 0 & 1 & 0 \end{pmatrix}$ 16 $\begin{pmatrix} 2 & 0 \\ 1 & 0 \\ -2 & 5 \end{pmatrix} \begin{pmatrix} 1 & 2 \\ 3 & -4 \end{pmatrix}$

17   $\begin{pmatrix} 4 & 1 \\ -2 & 3 \end{pmatrix} \begin{pmatrix} 1 & -2 \\ 4 & 0 \\ 3 & 1 \end{pmatrix}$ 18 $(1 \ 3 \ -2) \begin{pmatrix} 0 & 2 & 1 \\ 3 & -1 & 0 \\ 1 & 2 & 3 \end{pmatrix}$

19   $\begin{pmatrix} 2 & -1 & 3 \\ 1 & 0 & -4 \\ 3 & 1 & -1 \end{pmatrix} \begin{pmatrix} 1 & 0 & 0 \\ 0 & -1 & 0 \\ 1 & 1 & 1 \end{pmatrix}$ 20 $\begin{pmatrix} 1 & 0 & 0 \\ 0 & 1 & 0 \\ 0 & 0 & 1 \end{pmatrix} \begin{pmatrix} 1 & 2 & 3 \\ 3 & 2 & 1 \end{pmatrix}$

21   $\begin{pmatrix} a_{11} & a_{12} \\ a_{21} & a_{22} \end{pmatrix} \begin{pmatrix} x_1 \\ x_2 \end{pmatrix}$ 22 $\begin{pmatrix} a_{11} & a_{12} & a_{13} \\ a_{21} & a_{22} & a_{23} \end{pmatrix} \begin{pmatrix} x_1 \\ x_2 \\ x_3 \end{pmatrix}$

Rewrite the following systems of equations in matrix form.

23   $x - y = 5$
     $2x + 3y = -10$

24   $x = 4$
     $3x + y = 15$

25   $x_1 - 2x_2 + x_3 = 12$
     $3x_1 - x_2 - 2x_3 = 5$

26   $x_1 - 3x_2 = 40$
     $2x_1 - 4x_3 = 15$

27   $ax_1 + bx_2 = c$
     $dx_1 + ex_2 = f$
     $gx_1 + hx_2 = i$

28   $ax_1 + bx_2 + cx_3 + dx_4 + ex_5 = f$
     $gx_1 \qquad - hx_3 \qquad + ix_5 = j$

29   $a_1x^2 + a_2x + a_3 = b_1$
     $a_4x^2 + a_5x + a_6 = b_2$

30   $a_{11}x^2 + a_{12}x + a_{13} = b_1$
     $a_{21}x^2 + a_{22}x + a_{23} = b_2$
     $a_{31}x^2 + a_{32}x + a_{33} = b_3$

6.4   THE DETERMINANT

An important concept in matrix algebra is that of the **determinant.** *If a matrix is square, the elements of the matrix may be combined to compute a real-valued number called the determinant.* The determinant concept is of particular interest in solving simultaneous equations. We will discuss its significance in the next section.

The determinant of the matrix

$$\mathbf{A} = \begin{pmatrix} 2 & 5 \\ 3 & -2 \end{pmatrix}$$

can be denoted by either enclosing vertical lines around the matrix name or by placing vertical lines around the elements of the matrix. The determinant of $\mathbf{A}$ can be denoted by either

$$|\mathbf{A}| \qquad \text{or} \qquad \begin{vmatrix} 2 & 5 \\ 3 & -2 \end{vmatrix}$$

There are different ways of finding the value of a determinant. First let's discuss specific techniques for handling (1×1), (2×2), and (3×3) matrices and follow with the more generalized *cofactor procedure.*

The Determinant of a (1 × 1) Matrix

The determinant of a (1×1) matrix is simply the value of the one element contained in the matrix. If $\mathbf{A} = (5)$, $|\mathbf{A}| = 5$. If $\mathbf{M} = (-10)$, $|\mathbf{M}| = -10$.

The Determinant of a (2 × 2) Matrix

Given a (2×2) matrix having the form

$$\mathbf{A} = \begin{pmatrix} a_{11} & a_{12} \\ a_{21} & a_{22} \end{pmatrix}$$

$$\boxed{|\mathbf{A}| = a_{11}a_{22} - a_{21}a_{12}} \tag{6.4}$$

The computation involves a cross multiplication of elements on the two diagonals, as indicated:

$$|\mathbf{A}| = \begin{pmatrix} a_{11} \\ \quad \times \\ \quad a_{22} \end{pmatrix} - \begin{pmatrix} \quad \times \quad a_{12} \\ a_{21} \end{pmatrix}$$

EXAMPLE 13

If

$$\mathbf{A} = \begin{pmatrix} 1 & -2 \\ 3 & 4 \end{pmatrix}$$

then

$$|\mathbf{A}| = (1)(4) - (3)(-2)$$
$$= 4 + 6 = 10$$

The Determinant of a (3 × 3) Matrix

Given the (3×3) matrix

$$\mathbf{A} = \begin{pmatrix} a_{11} & a_{12} & a_{13} \\ a_{21} & a_{22} & a_{23} \\ a_{31} & a_{32} & a_{33} \end{pmatrix}$$

the determinant may be found by the following process:

1 Rewrite the first two columns of the matrix to the right of the original matrix.

2 Locate the elements on the three primary diagonals (P_1, P_2, P_3) and those on the three secondary diagonals (S_1, S_2, S_3).

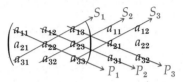

3 Multiply the elements on *each* primary and *each* secondary diagonal.

4 The determinant equals the sum of the products for the three primary diagonals minus the sum of the products for the three secondary diagonals.

Algebraically the determinant is computed as

$$|\mathbf{A}| = a_{11}a_{22}a_{33} + a_{12}a_{23}a_{31} + a_{13}a_{21}a_{32} - a_{31}a_{22}a_{13} - a_{32}a_{23}a_{11} - a_{33}a_{21}a_{12}$$

(6.5)

EXAMPLE 14

To find the determinant of the matrix

$$\mathbf{A} = \begin{pmatrix} 3 & 1 & 2 \\ -1 & 2 & 4 \\ 3 & -2 & 1 \end{pmatrix}$$

the first two columns are rewritten to the right of the original (3×3) matrix:

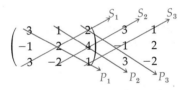

The three primary and secondary diagonals are identified and the determinant is computed as

$$\begin{aligned}|\mathbf{A}| &= [(3)(2)(1) + (1)(4)(3) + (2)(-1)(-2)] - [(3)(2)(2) + (-2)(4)(3) \\ &\quad + (1)(-1)(1)] \\ &= (6 + 12 + 4) - (12 - 24 - 1) = 22 - (-13) = 35\end{aligned}$$

NOTE

The methods examined for (1×1), (2×2), and (3×3) matrices apply only for matrices of those dimensions. We cannot extend the (3×3) procedure to deal with (4×4), (5×5), or square matrices of a higher order. The following optional section discusses a more generalized procedure.

The Method of Cofactors (Optional)

This section discusses an alternative computational procedure which can be applied for all square matrices of size 2×2 or higher. For any square matrix **A** there can be found a *matrix of cofactors* which we will denote as A_c. The matrix of cofactors will have the same dimension as A and will consist of elements a'_{ij} which are called *cofactors.* For each element a_{ij} contained in A there will be a corresponding cofactor a'_{ij}.

The cofactor associated with an element a_{ij} is determined as follows:

1 Either mentally or with a pencil, cross off row i and column j in the original matrix. Focus upon the remaining elements in the matrix. The remaining elements form a *submatrix* of the original matrix.

2 Find the determinant of the remaining submatrix. This determinant is called the *minor* of the element a_{ij}.

3 The cofactor a'_{ij} is found by multiplying the minor by either $+1$ or -1 depending on the position of the element a_{ij}. A formula for computing the cofactor is

$$a'_{ij} = (-1)^{i+j}(\text{the minor})$$

(The essence of this formula is that if $i + j$ is an *even* number, the minor is multiplied by $+1$ retaining its sign; if $i + j$ is *odd,* the minor is multiplied by -1 changing its sign.)

EXAMPLE 15

To find the matrix of cofactors for the (2×2) matrix

$$A = \begin{pmatrix} 5 & -4 \\ 2 & -2 \end{pmatrix}$$

let's begin with the cofactor corresponding to element a_{11}. Crossing off row 1 and column 1 leaves the (1×1) submatrix (-2). The determinant of this submatrix

$$\begin{pmatrix} 5 & -4 \\ 2 & -2 \end{pmatrix} \rightarrow \quad (-2)$$
$$\text{Submatrix}$$

equals -2 and is therefore the *minor.* The cofactor is computed as

$$a'_{11} = (-1)^{1+1}(-2) = (-1)^2(-2)$$
$$= (1)(-2) = -2$$

For the remaining elements,

$$\begin{pmatrix} 5 & -4 \\ 2 & -2 \end{pmatrix} \quad \begin{aligned} a'_{12} &= (-1)^{1+2}(2) \\ &= (-1)(2) \quad = -2 \end{aligned}$$

$$\begin{pmatrix} 5 & -4 \\ 2 & -2 \end{pmatrix} \quad \begin{aligned} a'_{21} &= (-1)^{2+1}(-4) \\ &= (-1)(-4) \quad = 4 \end{aligned}$$

$$\begin{pmatrix} 5 & -4 \\ 2 & -2 \end{pmatrix} = \quad \begin{aligned} a'_{22} &= (-1)^{2+2}(5) \\ &= (1)(5) \quad = 5 \end{aligned}$$

The matrix of cofactors is

$$A_c = \begin{pmatrix} -2 & -2 \\ 4 & 5 \end{pmatrix}$$

EXAMPLE 16

To find the matrix of cofactors for the (3 × 3) matrix in Example 14 let's begin with the element a_{11}. Crossing off row 1 and column 1, we are left with a (2 × 2) submatrix:

$$\mathbf{A} = \begin{pmatrix} 3 & 1 & 2 \\ -1 & 2 & 4 \\ 3 & -2 & 1 \end{pmatrix} \rightarrow \begin{pmatrix} 2 & 4 \\ -2 & 1 \end{pmatrix}$$
$$\text{Submatrix}$$

The cofactor is computed as

$$a'_{11} = (-1)^{1+1} \begin{vmatrix} 2 & 4 \\ -2 & 1 \end{vmatrix}$$
$$= (-1)^2[(2)(1) - (-2)(4)] = 1(10) = 10$$

For element a_{12}, row 1 and column 2 are crossed off resulting in

$$\begin{pmatrix} 3 & 1 & 2 \\ -1 & 2 & 4 \\ 3 & -2 & 1 \end{pmatrix} \rightarrow \begin{pmatrix} -1 & 4 \\ 3 & 1 \end{pmatrix}$$
$$\text{Submatrix}$$

The cofactor a'_{12} is computed as

$$a'_{12} = (-1)^{1+2} \begin{vmatrix} -1 & 4 \\ 3 & 1 \end{vmatrix}$$
$$= (-1)^3[(-1)(1) - (3)(4)] = -1(-13) = 13$$

Now it is your turn! Verify that the matrix of cofactors is

$$\mathbf{A}_c = \begin{pmatrix} 10 & 13 & -4 \\ -5 & -3 & 9 \\ 0 & -14 & 7 \end{pmatrix}$$

The Determinant and Cofactors We began this section with the objective of finding a generalized approach for computing the determinant. The *method of cofactor expansion* allows you to compute the determinant of a matrix as follows:

1 Select *any* row or column of the matrix.

2 Multiply each element in the row (column) by its corresponding cofactor and sum these products.

For the (*m* × *m*) matrix **A,** the determinant can be found by expanding along any *row i* according to the equation

$$|\mathbf{A}| = a_{i1}a'_{i1} + a_{i2}a'_{i2} + \cdots + a_{im}a'_{im} \tag{6.6}$$

By using summation notation, Eq. (6.6) can be rewritten as

$$|\mathbf{A}| = \sum_{j=1}^{m} a_{ij}a'_{ij} \qquad i = 1, 2, 3, \ldots, m \tag{6.7}$$

Similarly, the determinant can be found by expanding in any column j according to the equation

$$|\mathbf{A}| = a_{1j}a'_{1j} + a_{2j}a'_{2j} + \cdots + a_{mj}a'_{mj} \tag{6.8}$$

or

$$|\mathbf{A}| = \sum_{i=1}^{m} a_{ij}a'_{ij} \qquad j = 1, 2, 3, \ldots, m \tag{6.9}$$

NOTE

If your objective is to find the determinant, it is not necessary to compute the entire matrix of cofactors! You need to determine only the cofactors for the row or column selected for expansion.

EXAMPLE 17

Matrix $\mathbf{A}$ and its matrix of cofactors $\mathbf{A}_c$ from Example 15 are repeated below.

$$\mathbf{A} = \begin{pmatrix} 5 & -4 \\ 2 & -2 \end{pmatrix} \qquad \mathbf{A}_c = \begin{pmatrix} -2 & -2 \\ 4 & 5 \end{pmatrix}$$

The determinant of $\mathbf{A}$ can be found by expanding along row 1 as

$$|\mathbf{A}| = a_{11}a'_{11} + a_{12}a'_{12}$$
$$= (5)(-2) + (-4)(-2) = -2$$

or down column 2 as

$$|\mathbf{A}| = a_{12}a'_{12} + a_{22}a'_{22}$$
$$= (-4)(-2) + (-2)(5) = -2$$

EXAMPLE 18

The matrices $\mathbf{A}$ and $\mathbf{A}_c$ from Example 16 are repeated below.

$$\mathbf{A} = \begin{pmatrix} 3 & 1 & 2 \\ -1 & 2 & 4 \\ 3 & -2 & 1 \end{pmatrix} \qquad \mathbf{A}_c = \begin{pmatrix} 10 & 13 & -4 \\ -5 & -3 & 9 \\ 0 & -14 & 7 \end{pmatrix}$$

The determinant of $\mathbf{A}$ is computed by expanding down column 3 as

$$|\mathbf{A}| = (2)(-4) + (4)(9) + (1)(7)$$
$$= -8 + 36 + 7 = 35$$

EXERCISE

Verify that the value of the determinant is the same if you expand down the other two columns or across any of the rows.

EXAMPLE 19

The selection of a row of column for expanding by cofactors shouldn't always be arbitrary. Often you can take advantage of the content or form of a matrix. For example, let's find the determinant of the (4 × 4) matrix

$$\mathbf{A} = \begin{pmatrix} 3 & 0 & 1 & 2 \\ 6 & -2 & -5 & 4 \\ -1 & 0 & 2 & 4 \\ 3 & 0 & -2 & 1 \end{pmatrix}$$

If we select column 2 for expansion, we will have to find only one cofactor—that corresponding to a_{22}. That is,

$$\begin{aligned} |\mathbf{A}| &= (0)a'_{12} + (-2)a'_{22} + (0)a'_{32} + (0)(a'_{42}) \\ &= (-2)a'_{22} \end{aligned}$$

Crossing off row 2 and column 2, we are left with the (3 × 3) submatrix

$$\begin{pmatrix} 3 & 1 & 2 \\ -1 & 2 & 4 \\ 3 & -2 & 1 \end{pmatrix}$$

Compare this matrix with the one in the last example. Since probably you have just about reached your limit, this problem has been "doctored." We have already computed the determinant of this submatrix as 35. Thus,

$$a'_{22} = (-1)^{2+2}(35) = 35$$

and

$$\begin{aligned} |\mathbf{A}| &= (-2)a'_{22} \\ &= (-2)(35) = -70 \end{aligned}$$

Properties of Determinants

Certain properties hold for matrices and their determinants. *Given the square matrix A:*

Property 1   If all elements of any row or column equal zero, $|\mathbf{A}| = 0$.

EXERCISE

Verify for the matrix $\mathbf{A} = \begin{pmatrix} 5 & 0 \\ 10 & 0 \end{pmatrix}$ that $|\mathbf{A}| = 0$.

Property 2   If any two rows (or columns) are interchanged, the sign of the determinant changes.

EXERCISE

Given the matrix $\mathbf{A} = \begin{pmatrix} 1 & 5 \\ -6 & 15 \end{pmatrix}$, interchange columns 1 and 2 to form the matrix **B**. Compute $|\mathbf{A}|$ and $|\mathbf{B}|$ and compare.

Property 3 If all elements in any row or column are multiplied by a constant k, the value of the determinant equals $k|A|$.

EXERCISE

Given the matrix $A = \begin{pmatrix} 3 & -6 \\ 5 & 12 \end{pmatrix}$, multiply each element in column 2 by -5 to form the matrix **B**. Compute $|A|$ and $|B|$ and compare.

Property 4 If any multiple of one row (column) is added to another row (column), the value of the determinant is unchanged.

EXERCISE

Given the matrix $A = \begin{pmatrix} 1 & 2 \\ 3 & 4 \end{pmatrix}$, multiply row 2 by -3 and add the result to row 1 forming a new matrix **B**. Compute $|A|$ and $|B|$ and compare.

Property 5 If any row (column) is a multiple of another row (column), the determinant equals zero.*

EXERCISE

In the matrix $A = \begin{pmatrix} 3 & -2 & 4 \\ 6 & 8 & 1 \\ -9 & 6 & -12 \end{pmatrix}$, note that row 3 equals (-3) times row 1. Compute $|A|$.

These properties can be useful in computing the value of the determinant. For example, the magnitude of the numbers being manipulated can be reduced if all elements in a row or column have a common factor. This can be achieved also by adding (subtracting) multiples of one row (column) to another. Significant efficiencies can be introduced if, prior to using the method of cofactors, multiples of rows (columns) are combined to create a row (column) containing mostly zeros (as occurred in Example 19).

Section 6.4 Follow-up Exercises

Find the determinant of each of the following matrices.

1. $A = (-2)$

2. $A = (a)$

3. $T = \begin{pmatrix} 3 & 1 \\ -2 & 4 \end{pmatrix}$

4. $S = \begin{pmatrix} -1 & 2 \\ -4 & 3 \end{pmatrix}$

---

* A special case of this property occurs when two rows (columns) are equal to one another.

5 $\quad \mathbf{B} = \begin{pmatrix} 1 & 0 \\ 0 & 1 \end{pmatrix}$

6 $\quad \mathbf{A} = \begin{pmatrix} a & a \\ a & a \end{pmatrix}$

7 $\quad \mathbf{C} = \begin{pmatrix} 2 & 6 & 0 \\ 4 & 0 & 2 \\ 1 & 2 & 3 \end{pmatrix}$

8 $\quad \mathbf{B} = \begin{pmatrix} 1 & 3 & 0 \\ -2 & 0 & -1 \\ 1 & 2 & 3 \end{pmatrix}$

9 $\quad \mathbf{D} = \begin{pmatrix} 1 & -2 & 3 \\ 2 & 0 & 5 \\ 4 & -8 & 12 \end{pmatrix}$

10 $\quad \mathbf{A} = \begin{pmatrix} 3 & 0 & 9 \\ 2 & 6 & 6 \\ 1 & -3 & 3 \end{pmatrix}$

Find the matrix of cofactors for each of the following matrices.

11 $\quad \begin{pmatrix} 3 & -2 \\ 1 & 4 \end{pmatrix}$

12 $\quad \begin{pmatrix} -1 & 2 \\ 4 & 0 \end{pmatrix}$

13 $\quad \begin{pmatrix} 1 & 0 \\ 0 & 1 \end{pmatrix}$

14 $\quad \begin{pmatrix} a & b \\ c & d \end{pmatrix}$

15 $\quad \begin{pmatrix} 2 & 4 & -2 \\ 2 & 0 & 4 \\ 1 & 2 & 3 \end{pmatrix}$

16 $\quad \begin{pmatrix} 1 & 0 & 0 \\ 0 & 1 & 0 \\ 0 & 0 & 1 \end{pmatrix}$

17 $\quad \begin{pmatrix} 1 & 0 & 1 \\ 0 & 1 & 0 \\ 1 & 0 & 1 \end{pmatrix}$

18 $\quad \begin{pmatrix} 2 & 1 & 4 \\ 0 & 3 & 0 \\ 1 & 2 & -2 \end{pmatrix}$

19–26 Using the matrix of cofactors found, respectively, in exercises 11 to 18, find the determinant of the original matrix.

27 Find the determinant of

$$\mathbf{A} = \begin{pmatrix} 2 & 1 & -2 & 0 \\ 1 & -2 & 3 & 0 \\ 3 & 2 & 4 & 7 \\ 6 & -3 & -2 & 0 \end{pmatrix}$$

28 Find the determinant of

$$\mathbf{A} = \begin{pmatrix} 0 & 0 & 3 & 0 & 0 \\ 3 & 0 & 1 & 0 & 9 \\ 2 & 6 & -2 & 0 & 6 \\ 1 & -3 & 4 & 0 & 3 \\ 2 & 3 & 2 & 1 & 4 \end{pmatrix}$$

6.5 THE INVERSE OF A MATRIX

For *some* matrices there can be identified another matrix called the *multiplicative-inverse matrix,* or more simply, the *inverse.* The relationship between a matrix $\mathbf{A}$ and its inverse (denoted by $\mathbf{A}^{-1}$) is that the product of $\mathbf{A}$ and $\mathbf{A}^{-1}$, in either order, results in the identity matrix, or

$$\boxed{\mathbf{A}\mathbf{A}^{-1} = \mathbf{A}^{-1}\mathbf{A} = \mathbf{I}} \tag{6.10}$$

The inverse is similar to the reciprocal in the algebra of real numbers. Multiplying a quantity b by its reciprocal $1/b$ results in a product of 1. In matrix algebra multiplying a matrix by its inverse results in the identity matrix.

I For a matrix **A** to have an inverse, it must be square.

II The inverse of **A** will also be square and of the same dimension as **A**.

III Not every square matrix has an inverse.

A square matrix will have an inverse provided that all rows or columns are *linearly independent;* that is, no row (or column) is a linear combination of the remaining rows (or columns). If any rows (or columns) are linearly dependent [are linear combinations of other rows (columns),] the matrix will not have an inverse. If a matrix has an inverse, it is said to be a *nonsingular matrix.* If a matrix does not have an inverse, it is said to be a *singular matrix.*

EXAMPLE 20

We can verify that matrix **B** below is the inverse of matrix **A** by finding the products **AB** and **BA**.

$$A = \begin{pmatrix} 3 & 7 \\ 2 & 5 \end{pmatrix} \qquad B = \begin{pmatrix} 5 & -7 \\ -2 & 3 \end{pmatrix}$$

$$AB = \begin{pmatrix} 3 & 7 \\ 2 & 5 \end{pmatrix} \begin{pmatrix} 5 & -7 \\ -2 & 3 \end{pmatrix} = \begin{pmatrix} 1 & 0 \\ 0 & 1 \end{pmatrix}$$

$$BA = \begin{pmatrix} 5 & -7 \\ -2 & 3 \end{pmatrix} \begin{pmatrix} 3 & 7 \\ 2 & 5 \end{pmatrix} = \begin{pmatrix} 1 & 0 \\ 0 & 1 \end{pmatrix}$$

Because both products result in a (2 × 2) identity matrix, we can state that matrix **B** is the inverse of **A**, or

$$B = A^{-1}$$

and **A** is the inverse of **B**, or

$$A = B^{-1}$$

Determining the Inverse

There are several methods for determining the inverse of a matrix. One method is based on the Gauss-Jordan procedure discussed in Sec. 4.4. Let's develop the general procedure by using an example. If you are fuzzy on the Gauss-Jordan procedure, a rereading of Sec. 4.4, is advised.

EXAMPLE 21

Let's return to the matrix **A** in the last example. If there is another matrix **B** which is the inverse of **A**, it will have dimension 2 × 2. Let's label the elements of **B** as below

$$B = \begin{pmatrix} b_{11} & b_{12} \\ b_{21} & b_{22} \end{pmatrix}$$

If $A^{-1} = B,$

$$\mathbf{AB = I} \quad \text{or} \quad \begin{pmatrix} 3 & 7 \\ 2 & 5 \end{pmatrix} \begin{pmatrix} b_{11} & b_{12} \\ b_{21} & b_{22} \end{pmatrix} = \begin{pmatrix} 1 & 0 \\ 0 & 1 \end{pmatrix}$$

If we multiply on the left side of the equation, the result is

$$\begin{pmatrix} 3b_{11} + 7b_{21} & 3b_{12} + 7b_{22} \\ 2b_{11} + 5b_{21} & 2b_{12} + 5b_{22} \end{pmatrix} = \begin{pmatrix} 1 & 0 \\ 0 & 1 \end{pmatrix}$$

For these two matrices to be equal, their respective elements must equal one another; that is,

$$3b_{11} + 7b_{21} = 1 \tag{6.11}$$

$$2b_{11} + 5b_{21} = 0 \tag{6.12}$$

$$3b_{12} + 7b_{22} = 0 \tag{6.13}$$

$$2b_{12} + 5b_{22} = 1 \tag{6.14}$$

To determine the values of b_{11} and b_{21} we need to solve Eqs. (6.11) and (6.12) simultaneously. To determine b_{12} and b_{22} we must solve Eqs. (6.13) and (6.14).

If we were to solve these two systems individually by the Gauss-Jordan method, the transformations would proceed as shown in Fig. 6.2. For each system we would perform row operations to transform the array of coefficients $\begin{pmatrix} 3 & 7 \\ 2 & 5 \end{pmatrix}$ into a (2 × 2) identity matrix. Since *both* systems have the same matrix of coefficients on the left side, the same row operations will be used to solve *both* systems. The process can be streamlined by augmenting the right-side coefficients for the first system with those for the second system of equations, as shown below.

$$\begin{pmatrix} 3 & 7 & | & 1 & 0 \\ 2 & 5 & | & 0 & 1 \end{pmatrix}$$

The row operations need to be performed one time only. Upon transforming the matrix of coefficients on the left side into a (2 × 2) identity matrix, the first column of values on the right side would contain the solution for the first system of equations (b_{11} and b_{21}) and the second column the solution for the second system of equations (b_{12} and b_{22}). The transformed matrices would appear as

$$\begin{pmatrix} 1 & 0 & | & b_{11} & b_{12} \\ 0 & 1 & | & b_{21} & b_{22} \end{pmatrix}$$

and the (2 × 2) matrix to the right of the vertical line is the matrix **B**, or the inverse of **A**.

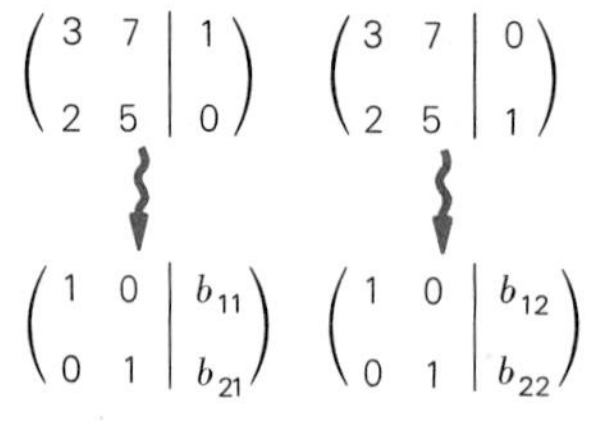

FIGURE 6.2
Gauss-Jordan transformation.

GAUSSIAN REDUCTION PROCEDURE

To determine the inverse of an $(m \times m)$ matrix **A**:

I Augment the matrix **A** with an $(m \times m)$ identity matrix.

$$(\mathbf{A}|\mathbf{I})$$

II Perform row operations on the entire augmented matrix so as to transform A into an $(m \times m)$ identity matrix. The resulting matrix will have the form

$$(\mathbf{I}|\mathbf{A}^{-1})$$

where $\mathbf{A}^{-1}$ can be read to the right of the vertical line.

EXAMPLE 22

Continuing the last example, we can find $\mathbf{A}^{-1}$ by the following steps:

$$\begin{pmatrix} 3 & 7 & | & 1 & 0 \\ 2 & 5 & | & 0 & 1 \end{pmatrix}$$

$$\begin{pmatrix} \boxed{1} & \frac{7}{3} & | & \frac{1}{3} & 0 \\ 2 & 5 & | & 0 & 1 \end{pmatrix} \qquad \text{(multiplying row 1 by } \tfrac{1}{3})$$

$$\begin{pmatrix} 1 & \frac{7}{3} & | & \frac{1}{3} & 0 \\ \boxed{0} & \frac{1}{3} & | & -\frac{2}{3} & 1 \end{pmatrix} \qquad \begin{array}{l} \text{(multiplying row 1 by } -2 \\ \text{and adding to row 2)} \end{array}$$

$$\begin{pmatrix} 1 & \frac{7}{3} & | & \frac{1}{3} & 0 \\ 0 & \boxed{1} & | & -2 & 3 \end{pmatrix} \qquad \text{(multiplying row 2 by 3)}$$

$$\begin{pmatrix} 1 & \boxed{0} & | & 5 & -7 \\ 0 & 1 & | & -2 & 3 \end{pmatrix} \qquad \begin{array}{l} \text{(multiplying row 2 by } -\tfrac{7}{3} \\ \text{and adding to row 1)} \end{array}$$

The inverse of **A** is

$$\mathbf{A}^{-1} = \begin{pmatrix} 5 & -7 \\ -2 & 3 \end{pmatrix}$$

as was indicated in Example 20.

NOTE

If the matrix does not have an inverse, it will not be possible to transform **A** into an identity matrix.

EXAMPLE 23

Consider the matrix

$$\mathbf{B} = \begin{pmatrix} 2 & -4 & 6 \\ 6 & 1 & 5 \\ 1 & -2 & 3 \end{pmatrix}$$

Note the linear dependence between rows 1 and 3. Row 1 equals 2 times row 3. From our previous discussion we can anticipate that **B** will not have an inverse. Let's test this hypothesis by applying the Gaussian procedure.

$$\begin{pmatrix} 2 & -4 & 6 & | & 1 & 0 & 0 \\ 6 & 1 & 5 & | & 0 & 1 & 0 \\ 1 & -2 & 3 & | & 0 & 0 & 1 \end{pmatrix}$$

$$\begin{pmatrix} ① & -2 & 3 & | & \frac{1}{2} & 0 & 0 \\ 6 & 1 & 5 & | & 0 & 1 & 0 \\ 1 & -2 & 3 & | & 0 & 0 & 1 \end{pmatrix}$$ (multiplying row 1 by $\frac{1}{2}$)

$$\begin{pmatrix} 1 & -2 & 3 & | & \frac{1}{2} & 0 & 0 \\ ⓪ & 13 & -13 & | & -3 & 1 & 0 \\ 1 & -2 & 3 & | & 0 & 0 & 1 \end{pmatrix}$$ (multiplying row 1 by -6 and adding to row 2)

$$\begin{pmatrix} 1 & -2 & 3 & | & \frac{1}{2} & 0 & 0 \\ 0 & 13 & -13 & | & -3 & 1 & 0 \\ ⓪ & 0 & 0 & | & -\frac{1}{2} & 0 & 1 \end{pmatrix}$$ (multiplying row 1 by -1 and adding to row 3)

$$\begin{pmatrix} 1 & -2 & 3 & | & \frac{1}{2} & 0 & 0 \\ 0 & ① & -1 & | & -\frac{3}{13} & \frac{1}{13} & 0 \\ 0 & 0 & 0 & | & -\frac{1}{2} & 0 & 1 \end{pmatrix}$$ (multiplying row 2 by $\frac{1}{13}$)

$$\begin{pmatrix} 1 & ⓪ & 1 & | & \frac{1}{26} & \frac{2}{13} & 0 \\ 0 & 1 & -1 & | & -\frac{3}{13} & \frac{1}{13} & 0 \\ 0 & 0 & 0 & | & -\frac{1}{2} & 0 & 1 \end{pmatrix}$$ (multiplying row 2 by 2 and adding to row 1)

At this point it becomes impossible to generate a 1 in the third column of row 3. A 1 could be placed in this position by adding a multiple of row 1 or 2 to row 3. However, this would result in nonzero values in columns 1 or 2 of row 3. Try it if you need convincing. Our conclusion is that **B** has no inverse.

Finding the Inverse Using Cofactors (Optional)
Another method for determining the inverse of a matrix utilizes the matrix of cofactors.

THE COFACTOR METHOD

The cofactor procedure for finding the inverse of a square matrix **A** is as follows.

I Determine the matrix of cofactors $\mathbf{A}_c$ for the matrix **A**.
II Determine the **adjoint matrix** $\mathbf{A}_j$ which is the transpose of $\mathbf{A}_c$:

$$\mathbf{A}_j = \mathbf{A}_c^t$$

III The inverse of **A** is found by multiplying the adjoint matrix by the reciprocal of the determinant of **A**, or

$$\mathbf{A}^{-1} = \frac{1}{|\mathbf{A}|}\mathbf{A}_j \qquad (6.15)$$

EXAMPLE 24

Let's determine the inverse of the (2 × 2) matrix in Example 22:

$$\mathbf{A} = \begin{pmatrix} 3 & 7 \\ 2 & 5 \end{pmatrix}$$

The cofactor matrix $\mathbf{A}_c$ is

$$\mathbf{A}_c = \begin{pmatrix} 5 & -2 \\ -7 & 3 \end{pmatrix}$$

The adjoint matrix is the transpose of $\mathbf{A}_c$, or

$$\mathbf{A}_j = \begin{pmatrix} 5 & -7 \\ -2 & 3 \end{pmatrix}$$

The determinant of **A** is

$$|\mathbf{A}| = (3)(5) - (2)(7)$$
$$= 1$$

Therefore

$$\mathbf{A}^{-1} = \frac{1}{1} \begin{pmatrix} 5 & -7 \\ -2 & 3 \end{pmatrix}$$
$$= \begin{pmatrix} 5 & -7 \\ -2 & 3 \end{pmatrix}$$

EXAMPLE 25

To determine the inverse of the (3 × 3) matrix **B** in Example 23

$$\mathbf{B} = \begin{pmatrix} 1 & 2 & 0 \\ 1 & 0 & -1 \\ -1 & 3 & 2 \end{pmatrix}$$

the matrix of cofactors $\mathbf{B}_c$ is

$$\mathbf{B}_c = \begin{pmatrix} 3 & -1 & 3 \\ -4 & 2 & -5 \\ -2 & 1 & -2 \end{pmatrix}$$

The adjoint matrix $\mathbf{B}_j$ is the transpose of $\mathbf{B}_c$, or

$$\mathbf{B}_j = \begin{pmatrix} 3 & -4 & -2 \\ -1 & 2 & 1 \\ 3 & -5 & -2 \end{pmatrix}$$

Verify that the determinant of **B** equals 1.
    Therefore,

$$\mathbf{B}^{-1} = \frac{1}{1} \begin{pmatrix} 3 & -4 & -2 \\ -1 & 2 & 1 \\ 3 & -5 & -2 \end{pmatrix}$$
$$= \begin{pmatrix} 3 & -4 & -2 \\ -1 & 2 & 1 \\ 3 & -5 & -2 \end{pmatrix}$$

The Inverse and Systems of Equations

In Sec. 6.3 we discussed the matrix representation of systems of equations. The matrix inverse can be used to determine the solution set for a system of equations. Given a system of equations of the form $\mathbf{AX} = \mathbf{B}$ where $\mathbf{A}$ is a *square* matrix of coefficients, both sides of the matrix equation may be multiplied by $\mathbf{A}^{-1}$, yielding

$$\mathbf{A}^{-1}\mathbf{AX} = \mathbf{A}^{-1}\mathbf{B} \tag{6.16}$$

Because $\mathbf{A}^{-1}\mathbf{A} = \mathbf{I}$, Eq. (6.16) can be written as

$$\mathbf{IX} = \mathbf{A}^{-1}\mathbf{B}$$

or

$$\boxed{\mathbf{X} = \mathbf{A}^{-1}\mathbf{B}} \tag{6.17}$$

That is, the solution vector for the system of equations can be found by multiplying the inverse of the matrix of coefficients $\mathbf{A}$ by the vector of right-side constants $\mathbf{B}$. If $\mathbf{A}^{-1}$ does not exist, the equations (more specifically, the matrix of coefficients) are linearly dependent and there is either no solution or an infinite number of solutions.

EXAMPLE 26

Consider the system of equations

$$3x_1 + 7x_2 = 27$$
$$2x_1 + 5x_2 = 19$$

This system of equations may be written in matrix form as

$$\mathbf{AX} = \mathbf{B}$$

or

$$\begin{pmatrix} 3 & 7 \\ 2 & 5 \end{pmatrix} \begin{pmatrix} x_1 \\ x_2 \end{pmatrix} = \begin{pmatrix} 27 \\ 19 \end{pmatrix}$$

To solve this system of equations by the inverse method we must determine $\mathbf{A}^{-1}$. Conveniently, $\mathbf{A}$ is the matrix examined in Examples 22 and 24 and $\mathbf{A}^{-1}$ has been computed. Therefore, the solution vector $\mathbf{X}$ is calculated as

$$\mathbf{X} = \mathbf{A}^{-1}\mathbf{B}$$

$$= \begin{pmatrix} 5 & -7 \\ -2 & 3 \end{pmatrix} \begin{pmatrix} 27 \\ 19 \end{pmatrix} = \begin{pmatrix} 2 \\ 3 \end{pmatrix}$$

The solution to the system of equations is $x_1 = 2$ and $x_2 = 3$.

EXAMPLE 27

Consider the system of equations

$$x_1 + 2x_2 \qquad = 5$$
$$x_1 \qquad - x_3 = -15$$
$$-x_1 + 3x_2 + 2x_3 = 40$$

The matrix of coefficients is

$$\mathbf{A} = \begin{pmatrix} 1 & 2 & 0 \\ 1 & 0 & -1 \\ -1 & 3 & 2 \end{pmatrix}$$

and again the example has been contrived (see Example 25). The solution vector is calculated as

$$\mathbf{X} = \begin{pmatrix} 3 & -4 & -2 \\ -1 & 2 & 1 \\ 3 & -5 & -2 \end{pmatrix} \begin{pmatrix} 5 \\ -15 \\ 40 \end{pmatrix}$$

$$= \begin{pmatrix} -5 \\ 5 \\ 10 \end{pmatrix}$$

or $x_1 = -5$, $x_2 = 5$, and $x_3 = 10$.

Section 6.5 Follow-up Exercises

Determine the inverse, if it exists, for the following matrices, using the Gaussian procedure.

1 $\begin{pmatrix} 1 & -1 \\ 2 & -3 \end{pmatrix}$ 2 $\begin{pmatrix} 2 & 3 \\ 4 & 7 \end{pmatrix}$

3 $\begin{pmatrix} 4 & 2 \\ -2 & -1 \end{pmatrix}$ 4 $\begin{pmatrix} 40 & 8 \\ 30 & 6 \end{pmatrix}$

5 $\begin{pmatrix} 1 & 0 \\ 0 & 1 \end{pmatrix}$ 6 $\begin{pmatrix} -1 & 3 \\ 2 & -4 \end{pmatrix}$

7 $\begin{pmatrix} 0 & 3 & 1 \\ 1 & 1 & 0 \\ 2 & 3 & 3 \end{pmatrix}$ 8 $\begin{pmatrix} 1 & 0 & -1 \\ -1 & 1 & -1 \\ -1 & 0 & 2 \end{pmatrix}$

Determine the inverse of the following matrices using the matrix of cofactors approach.

9 $\begin{pmatrix} 3 & 7 \\ 2 & 5 \end{pmatrix}$ 10 $\begin{pmatrix} 3 & -15 \\ 5 & 25 \end{pmatrix}$

11 $\begin{pmatrix} 3 & 5 & 2 \\ 4 & 1 & 0 \\ -9 & -15 & -6 \end{pmatrix}$ 12 $\begin{pmatrix} -5 & 6 & -7 \\ 10 & -11 & 13 \\ -1 & 1 & -1 \end{pmatrix}$

Using the results of Exercises 1 to 12, determine the solutions for the following systems of equations.

13    $x_1 - x_2 = -1$
       $2x_1 - 3x_2 = -5$

15    $-x_1 + 3x_2 = 5$
       $2x_1 - 4x_2 = 0$

17    $x_1 \quad - x_3 = -10$
       $-x_1 + x_2 - x_3 = -40$
       $-x_1 \quad + 2x_3 = 40$

14    $2x_1 + 3x_2 = 1$
       $4x_1 + 7x_2 = 3$

16    $3x_2 + x_3 = 1$
       $x_1 + x_2 = 2$
       $2x_1 + 3x_2 + 3x_3 = 7$

18    $3x_1 + 7x_2 = -3$
       $2x_1 + 5x_2 = -3$

19   $3x_1 - 15x_2 = 25$
     $5x_1 + 25x_2 = 40$

20   $3x_1 + 5x_2 + 2x_3 = 20$
     $4x_1 + x_2 = 40$
     $-9x_1 - 15x_2 - 6x_3 = 30$

21   $-5x_1 + 6x_2 - 7x_3 = 25$
     $10x_1 - 11x_2 + 13x_3 = -45$
     $-x_1 + x_2 - x_3 = 4$

22   The solution to a system of equations having the form $\mathbf{AX} = \mathbf{B}$ can be found by the matrix multiplication

$$\mathbf{X} = \begin{pmatrix} 2 & -3 \\ -1 & 2 \end{pmatrix} \begin{pmatrix} 17 \\ 10 \end{pmatrix}$$

What was the original system of equations?

23   The solution to a system of equations having the form $\mathbf{AX} = \mathbf{B}$ can be found by the matrix multiplication

$$\mathbf{X} = \begin{pmatrix} 0 & -1 & 1 \\ -1 & 1 & 2 \\ 1 & 0 & -2 \end{pmatrix} \begin{pmatrix} 3 \\ 2 \\ 4 \end{pmatrix}$$

What was the original system of equations?

6.6   SELECTED APPLICATIONS

EXAMPLE 28

Election Projection   A political pollster is watching a closely contested mayoral race in a particular city. Recent surveys indicate voters' preferences in the city's six voting districts. The matrix $\mathbf{P}$ displays these preferences.

District

	1	2	3	4	5	6	
$\mathbf{P} =$	0.40	0.35	0.30	0.50	0.30	0.36	Democrat
	0.42	0.40	0.25	0.30	0.30	0.32	Republican
	0.18	0.25	0.45	0.20	0.40	0.32	Independent

Each column indicates the percentages of voters in each district who expect to vote for the different mayoral candidates. For example, column 3 indicates that in district 3, 30 percent of voters are expected to vote for the Democratic candidate, 25 percent for the Republican candidate, and 45 percent for the Independent candidate.

Given these voter preferences, it is possible to project the election outcome if the number of citizens expecting to vote in each district is known. The vector $\mathbf{V}$ contains current estimates of these numbers.

$$\mathbf{V} = \begin{pmatrix} 30{,}000 \\ 60{,}000 \\ 70{,}000 \\ 45{,}000 \\ 55{,}000 \\ 40{,}000 \end{pmatrix}$$

The election outcome can be projected by the matrix multiplication **PV**, or

$$
\begin{pmatrix}
0.40 & 0.35 & 0.30 & 0.50 & 0.30 & 0.36 \\
0.42 & 0.40 & 0.25 & 0.30 & 0.30 & 0.32 \\
0.18 & 0.25 & 0.45 & 0.20 & 0.40 & 0.32
\end{pmatrix}
\begin{pmatrix}
30,000 \\
60,000 \\
70,000 \\
45,000 \\
55,000 \\
40,000
\end{pmatrix}
=
\begin{pmatrix}
107,400 \\
96,900 \\
95,700
\end{pmatrix}
$$

These results suggest that the Democratic candidate has an edge of more than 10,000 votes over the other two candidates.

EXERCISE

The pollster believes that the relative voting preferences within each district will not change significantly by the time of the election. Thus, changes in the projected outcome will be influenced primarily by voter turnout in each district. The campaign manager for the Independent candidate believes that voter turnout in districts 3 and 5 can be increased significantly with an intensified campaign which emphasizes the importance of voting. Since districts 3 and 5 have a decided preference for the Independent candidate, the hope is that the election can be swung. A survey organization estimates that the proposed "voter awareness" campaign is likely to increase turnout to levels of 35,000, 66,000, 82,000, 48,000, 70,000, and 45,000 voters, respectively, in each district. Project the election outcome under these circumstances.*

EXAMPLE 29

Parts Requirements Planning   Matrix algebra can be helpful in planning the future operations of a firm. One specific area is production planning. Matrix techniques are regularly used to calculate and display the parts requirements for a production schedule. The process begins by determining the number of units of finished products that are to be produced. Given that each final product is produced from component parts, a parts matrix may be formed which displays the quantity of each component part required in each final product. Matrix multiplications may be used to determine the quantities of each component part required for the entire production run as well as other information such as the costs of components.

Suppose that the national office of a car rental corporation is planning its maintenance program for the next year. Executives are interested in determining the company's needs for certain repair parts and expected costs for these categories of parts. The company rents midsized, compact, and subcompact cars. The matrix **N** indicates the number of each size car available for renting in four regions of the country.

---

* Democrat (122,900), Republican (111,400), Independent (117,700).

$$\mathbf{N} = \begin{array}{c} \text{Midsized} \quad \text{Compact} \quad \text{Subcompact} \\ \begin{pmatrix} 16{,}000 & 40{,}000 & 50{,}000 \\ 15{,}000 & 30{,}000 & 20{,}000 \\ 10{,}000 & 10{,}000 & 15{,}000 \\ 12{,}000 & 40{,}000 & 30{,}000 \end{pmatrix} \begin{array}{l} \text{East} \\ \text{Midwest} \\ \text{South} \\ \text{West} \end{array} \end{array}$$

Four repair parts of particular interest because of their cost and frequency of replacement are fan belts, spark plugs, batteries, and tires. Based upon studies of maintenance records in different parts of the country, analysts have determined the average number of repair parts needed per car during a year. These are summarized in the matrix **R:**

$$\mathbf{R} = \begin{array}{c} \text{Midsized} \quad \text{Compact} \quad \text{Subcompact} \\ \begin{pmatrix} 1.7 & 1.6 & 1.5 \\ 12.0 & 8.0 & 5.0 \\ 0.9 & 0.75 & 0.5 \\ 4.0 & 6.5 & 6.0 \end{pmatrix} \begin{array}{l} \text{Fan belts} \\ \text{Plugs} \\ \text{Batteries} \\ \text{Tires} \end{array} \end{array}$$

Executives want to determine what quantity of each repair part will be needed in each region. These can be calculated by performing the matrix multiplication $\mathbf{NR}^t$. These regional needs are shown in the matrix **P.** Verify the elements of this matrix.

$$\mathbf{P} = \mathbf{NR}^t = \begin{array}{c} \text{Fan belts} \quad \text{Plugs} \quad \text{Batteries} \quad \text{Tires} \\ \begin{pmatrix} 166{,}200 & 762{,}000 & 69{,}400 & 624{,}000 \\ 103{,}500 & 520{,}000 & 46{,}000 & 375{,}000 \\ 55{,}500 & 275{,}000 & 24{,}000 & 195{,}000 \\ 129{,}400 & 614{,}000 & 55{,}800 & 488{,}000 \end{pmatrix} \begin{array}{l} \text{East} \\ \text{Midwest} \\ \text{South} \\ \text{West} \end{array} \end{array}$$

The column vector **C** contains the cost per unit for fan belts, plugs, batteries, and tires:

$$\mathbf{C} = \begin{pmatrix} \$1.25 \\ \$0.80 \\ \$30.00 \\ \$35.00 \end{pmatrix}$$

Executives can compute annual repair parts cost for each region by performing the multiplication

$$\mathbf{T} = \mathbf{PC} = \begin{pmatrix} \$24{,}739{,}350 \\ \$15{,}050{,}375 \\ \$ 7{,}834{,}375 \\ \$19{,}406{,}950 \end{pmatrix} \begin{array}{l} \text{East} \\ \text{Midwest} \\ \text{South} \\ \text{West} \end{array}$$

Expected annual costs of the four parts for the company are the sum of the four elements in **T,** or $67,031,050.

EXAMPLE 30

Brand-switching analysis concerns itself with the purchasing behavior of consumers who make repeated purchases of a product or service. Examples of such products or services are gasoline, detergents, soft drinks, fast-food meals, etc. Brand-switching analysis focuses upon brand loyalty and the degree to which consumers are willing to switch to competing products. Firms often try to project the effects promotion campaigns, such as rebates or advertising programs, will have on the sales of their products. If information is available concerning the rates of gains from and losses to all competitors, a firm can (a) predict its market share at some time in the future, (b) predict the rate at which the firm will increase or decrease its market share in the future, and (c) determine whether market shares will ever reach equilibrium levels (each firm, or brand, retains a constant share of the market).

Using consumer surveys, it may be possible to determine a *matrix of transition probabilities* (or *transition matrix*) which reflects the chance that a company will retain its customers, the chance that a company will gain customers from other companies, and the chance that it will lose customers to competing companies. Consider the following matrix of transition probabilities for two competing brands:

$$T = \begin{pmatrix} p_{11} & p_{12} \\ p_{21} & p_{22} \end{pmatrix}$$

Let p_{ij} equal the percentage of brand i consumers who will purchase brand j during the next period. This definition implies that a consumer purchases brand i in one period, and then purchases brand j during the next period. A period may be defined as any appropriate time interval such as a week or month. When $i = j$, p_{ij} represents the percentage of brand i consumers who remain loyal to brand i and purchase it again. Thus, p_{11} and p_{22} represent the percentage of original customers retained in the next period by brands 1 and 2, respectively, p_{12} represents the percentage of customers purchasing brand 1 in the previous period who purchase brand 2 in the next period, and p_{21} represents the percentage of customers purchasing brand 2 in the last period who purchase brand 1 in the next period.

The transition matrix T indicates that brand 1 retains 80 percent of its customers but loses 20 percent to brand 2. Brand 2 retains 90 percent of its customers and loses 10 percent of its customers to brand 1.

$$T = \begin{pmatrix} 0.80 & 0.20 \\ 0.10 & 0.90 \end{pmatrix}$$

If market shares are known for the two brands, it is possible to use the transition matrix to project market shares in the next period. Suppose that these are the only two brands on the market and that in the last period brand 1 had 40 percent of the market and brand 2 had 60 percent of the market. If these market shares are represented in the (1×2) share vector S, the expected market shares in the next period can be computed by the product ST, or

$$(0.40 \quad 0.60) \begin{pmatrix} 0.80 & 0.20 \\ 0.10 & 0.90 \end{pmatrix}$$

$$= [0.40(0.80) + 0.60(0.10) \quad 0.40(0.20) + 0.60(0.90)] = (0.38 \quad 0.62)$$

Carefully note how the new market shares are calculated. The 38 percent for brand 1 results from brand 1 retaining 80 percent of its previous share and from gaining 10 percent of the previous share of brand 2 customers.

If the switching behavior is constant for a number of periods, the matrix of transition probabilities will remain the same. Under these conditions the vector of market shares after n periods, S_n, can be computed as

$$S_n = S\overbrace{\text{TTT} \cdots \cdot \text{T}}^{n}$$
$$= S \cdot T^n$$

or

Given the most recent market shares S and the matrix of transition probabilities T for three competing brands, we can determine the market shares at the end of each of the next two periods as follows:

$$S = (0.30 \quad 0.40 \quad 0.30) \qquad T = \begin{pmatrix} 0.90 & 0.05 & 0.05 \\ 0.05 & 0.85 & 0.10 \\ 0.05 & 0.15 & 0.80 \end{pmatrix}$$

For the next period,

$$S_1 = (0.30 \quad 0.40 \quad 0.30) \begin{pmatrix} 0.90 & 0.05 & 0.05 \\ 0.05 & 0.85 & 0.10 \\ 0.05 & 0.15 & 0.80 \end{pmatrix}$$

$$= [0.30(0.90) + 0.40(0.05) + 0.30(0.05)$$
$$0.30(0.05) + 0.40(0.85) + 0.30(0.15)$$
$$0.30(0.05) + 0.40(0.10) + 0.30(0.80)]$$
$$= (0.305 \quad 0.400 \quad 0.295)$$

For the second period,

$$S_2 = (0.305 \quad 0.400 \quad 0.295) \begin{pmatrix} 0.90 & 0.05 & 0.05 \\ 0.05 & 0.85 & 0.10 \\ 0.05 & 0.15 & 0.80 \end{pmatrix}$$

$$= (0.30925 \quad 0.39950 \quad 0.29125)$$

After two periods, brands 2 and 3 will have experienced slight decreases in their market shares while brand 1 will have increased its share.

EXAMPLE 31

Population Migration—Equilibrium Conditions An application similar to brand-switching analysis deals with *population migration.* The population may consist of persons, wildlife, etc. The migration patterns might be represented by a *transition matrix* similar to that characterizing brand-switching behavior. Given such a transition matrix along with a *population vector* describing the population totals for each relevant region, it becomes possible to project the dynamics of population shifts over time. If the migration patterns are stable over time (the transition matrix does not change), an equilibrium condition can ultimately occur where the population of each region becomes stable. At equilibrium the population increases in each region are offset by the decreases during each time period. The following simplified example illustrates this condition.

Because of the increasing cost of energy, the population within one European country seems to be shifting from the north to the south, as shown in Fig. 6.3. The transition matrix S describes the migration behavior observed between the two regions.

$$S = \begin{pmatrix} \text{To north} & \text{To south} \\ 0.95 & 0.05 \\ 0.02 & 0.98 \end{pmatrix} \begin{matrix} \text{From north} \\ \text{From south} \end{matrix}$$

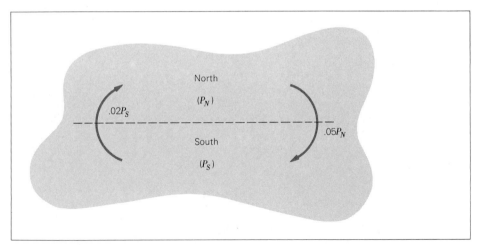

FIGURE 6.3
Population
shifts.

The value of 0.95 in **S** indicates that 95 percent of those living in the north during one year will still be living in the north the following year. The 0.05 represents the remaining 5 percent who would move from the north to the south. The 0.02 indicates annual migration to the north of 2 percent of the population living in the south.

NOTE

To simplify the analysis we will assume that the population of the country is constant or that the 0.95 and 0.98 parameters reflect net effects which account for births, deaths, immigration, and emigration during the year.

If P_N represents the population of the northern region of the country and P_S the population of the southern region in any given year, the projected population for each region in the following year is found by the matrix multiplication

$$\mathbf{PS} = \mathbf{P'} \tag{6.18}$$

or
$$(P_N \quad P_S) \begin{pmatrix} 0.95 & 0.05 \\ 0.02 & 0.98 \end{pmatrix} = (P'_N \quad P'_S) \tag{6.19}$$

Equilibrium occurs when $P_N = P'_N$ and $P_S = P'_S$. If we expand Eq. (6.19), equilibrium will occur when

$$0.95P_N + 0.02P_S = P_N \tag{6.20}$$

and
$$0.05P_N + 0.98P_S = P_S \tag{6.21}$$

We have yet to specify any population figures for this country. In order to determine the equilibrium condition we only need the total population. Let's assume that the population of the country is 70 million persons, or

$$P_N + P_S = 70 \tag{6.22}$$

Thus, Eq. (6.22) must be included with Eqs. (6.20) and (6.21). To solve this (3×2)

system it can be shown that only two of the three equations are needed—Eq. (6.22) and either (6.20) or (6.21). Thus, the solution to the system

$$0.95P_N + 0.02P_S = P_N \tag{6.20}$$

$$P_N + P_S = 70 \tag{6.22}$$

will yield the equilibrium populations. Solve (by matrix or nonmatrix methods) the system and verify that $P_N = 20$ and $P_S = 50$.

To prove that equilibrium exists at these values, we can project the population for the next year using Eq. (6.18), or

$$(20 \quad 50) \begin{pmatrix} 0.95 & 0.05 \\ 0.02 & 0.98 \end{pmatrix} = (19 + 1 \quad 1 + 49) = (20 \quad 50)$$

POINTS FOR THOUGHT AND DISCUSSION

Recall that we did not specify initial population distributions for the country. It turns out that equilibrium *values* are independent of these initial conditions. Given the initial figures, however, an interesting question is how long is required to reach equilibrium. This is an issue we will not address. However, we would speculate that the nearer the initial population distribution to the equilibrium distribution, the shorter the *time to equilibrium*.

Discuss the assumptions of this model. Which assumptions do you have reservations about? Does there seem to be any value in using a model such as this?

EXAMPLE 32

Input-Output Analysis A Nobel Prize recipient, Wassily Leontief, is most noted for his input-output model of an economy. An assumption of the model is that whatever is produced will be consumed. Demand for an industry's output can come from two sources: (1) demand from different industries and (2) demand from sources other than industries. To illustrate this, consider the energy sector. Power companies generate energy which is (1) needed to operate their own plants, (2) needed to supply other industries with their electrical needs, and (3) needed for other consumers like ourselves.

The first two of these are examples of *interindustry demand* and the last is *nonindustry demand.* The objective of input-output analysis is typically to determine how much an industry should produce so that both types of demand are satisfied exactly. That is, how much should be produced in order to bring supply and demand into balance?

(Read this paragraph very carefully.) The interindustry demand is usually summarized in a *technological* or **input-output matrix.** An example is the (3×3) matrix **A** below. Assume that the output of an industry is measured in dollars. If a_{ij} is the general

$$\begin{array}{c} \\ \text{Supplier} \\ \begin{matrix} 1 \\ 2 \\ 3 \end{matrix} \end{array} \overset{\begin{matrix} & \text{User} & \\ 1 & 2 & 3 \end{matrix}}{\begin{pmatrix} 0.3 & 0.3 & 0.2 \\ 0.1 & 0.2 & 0.3 \\ 0.2 & 0.1 & 0.4 \end{pmatrix}} = \mathbf{A}$$

element in the input-output matrix, a_{ij} *represents the amount of industry i's output required in producing one dollar of output in industry j.* This matrix represents a three-industry situation. The element $a_{11} = 0.3$ suggests that of every dollar of output *from* industry 1, 30 percent of this value is contributed by industry 1. The element a_{12} suggests that for every dollar of output *from* industry 2, 30 percent is contributed by industry 1. The element a_{13} indicates that every dollar of output from industry 3 requires 20 cents of output from industry 1. The element $a_{21} = 0.1$ indicates that for every dollar of output *from* industry 1, 10 percent is contributed by industry 2. The element $a_{31} = 0.2$ indicates that for every dollar of output *from* industry 1, 20 percent is provided by industry 3. Try to interpret the remaining elements.

Let x_j *equal the output from industry j (in dollars) and let d_j equal the nonindustry demand (in dollars) for the output of industry j.* A set of simultaneous equations may be formulated which when solved would determine the levels of output x_j at which total supply and demand would be in equilibrium. The equations in this system would have the general form

$$\boxed{\text{Industry output} = \text{interindustry demand} + \text{nonindustry demand}}$$

For the three-industry example the system would be

$$
\begin{array}{ccc}
 & \overbrace{\text{Interindustry}}^{} & \overbrace{\text{Nonindustry}}^{} \\
 & \text{demand} & \text{demand} \\
x_1 = & \overbrace{0.3x_1 + 0.3x_2 + 0.2x_3} + & \overbrace{d_1} \\
x_2 = & 0.1x_1 + 0.2x_2 + 0.3x_3 + & d_2 \\
x_3 = & 0.2x_1 + 0.1x_2 + 0.4x_3 + & d_3
\end{array}
\tag{6.23}
$$

Rearranging these equations

$$
\begin{aligned}
0.7x_1 - 0.3x_2 - 0.2x_3 &= d_1 \\
-0.1x_1 + 0.8x_2 - 0.3x_3 &= d_2 \\
-0.2x_1 - 0.1x_2 + 0.6x_3 &= d_3
\end{aligned}
$$

Given a set of nonindustry demand values d_j, these equations may be solved to determine the equilibrium levels of output.

Note for a moment the structure of Eq. (6.23). If $\mathbf{X}$ is a column vector containing elements x_1, x_2, and x_3, and $\mathbf{D}$ is a column vector containing elements d_1, d_2, and d_3, Eq. (6.23) has the form

$$\mathbf{X} = \mathbf{AX} + \mathbf{D}$$

This matrix equation can be simplied as follows:

$$
\begin{aligned}
\mathbf{X} - \mathbf{AX} &= \mathbf{D} \\
\mathbf{IX} - \mathbf{AX} &= \mathbf{D} \\
(\mathbf{I} - \mathbf{A})\mathbf{X} &= \mathbf{D}
\end{aligned}
$$

$$\boxed{\mathbf{X} = (\mathbf{I} - \mathbf{A})^{-1}\mathbf{D}} \tag{6.24}$$

That is, assuming a square input-output matrix $\mathbf{A}$, the equilibrium levels of output may be found by (1) forming the matrix $(\mathbf{I} - \mathbf{A})$, (2) finding $(\mathbf{I} - \mathbf{A})^{-1}$ if it exists, and (3) multiplying $(\mathbf{I} - \mathbf{A})^{-1}$ times the nonindustry demand vector $\mathbf{D}$.

You should verify that for the three-industry example, $|\mathbf{I} - \mathbf{A}| = 0.245$ and

$$(\mathbf{I} - \mathbf{A})^{-1} = \begin{pmatrix} 1.837 & 0.816 & 1.020 \\ 0.490 & 1.551 & 0.939 \\ 0.694 & 0.531 & 2.163 \end{pmatrix}$$

Giving the input-output matrix for the three-industry example, suppose that the levels for nonindustry demands are

$$d_1 = \$50{,}000{,}000$$
$$d_2 = \$30{,}000{,}000$$
$$d_3 = \$60{,}000{,}000$$

The equilibrium levels can be determined as

$$\mathbf{X} = \begin{pmatrix} 1.837 & 0.816 & 1.020 \\ 0.490 & 1.551 & 0.939 \\ 0.694 & 0.531 & 2.163 \end{pmatrix} \begin{pmatrix} 50{,}000{,}000 \\ 30{,}000{,}000 \\ 60{,}000{,}000 \end{pmatrix}$$

$$= \begin{pmatrix} 177{,}530{,}000 \\ 127{,}370{,}000 \\ 180{,}410{,}000 \end{pmatrix}$$

Industry 1 should produce \$177,530,000 worth of output, industry 2 \$127,370,000, and industry 3 \$180,410,000.

Using the coefficients in the original input-output matrix, the interindustry demand can be calculated (in millions of dollars) as

		User 1	User 2	User 3
Supplier	1	53.259	38.211	36.082
	2	17.753	25.474	54.123
	3	35.506	12.737	72.164

If you add the interindustry demand plus the nonindustry demand, you will find the totals slightly different than the computed equilibrium values. These differences may be attributed to rounding errors in calculating $(\mathbf{I} - \mathbf{A})^{-1}$.

EXAMPLE 33

Network Applications A *network* consists of a set of *nodes* and a set of *arcs* which connect nodes. The nodes can represent cities, highway intersections, computers, water reservoirs, or less tangible items such as project milestones. Nodes typically represent points where some type of flow originates, is relayed, or terminates. Arcs in a network can represent roads, air routes, power lines, pipelines, and so forth. Figure 6.4 illustrates different representations of nodes and arcs. In 6.4*a* no specific flow orientation is indicated. The arc in this case is called an *undirected arc.* In 6.4*b* the arc is called a *directed arc* because flow is in one direction. In 6.4*c* the arc is *bidirected* because flows can be in both directions.

Figure 6.5 is a network diagram which illustrates the route structure for a small regional commuter airline servicing four cities. The nodes represent the different cities and the arcs represent the routes servicing the cities. The bidirected arc connecting nodes A and B indicates that the airline flies from A to B and from B to A.

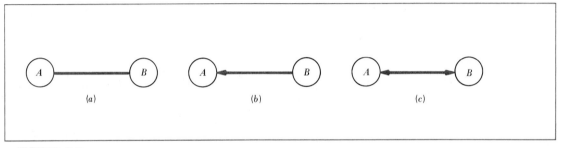

FIGURE 6.4
Node-arc
representation.

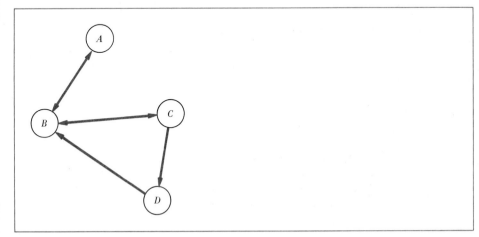

FIGURE 6.5
Commuter air-
line routes.

The essence of these node-arc relationships can be summarized in what is called an *adjacency matrix.* The adjacency matrix has a row and a column for each node. The elements of the matrix consist of 0s or 1s, depending on whether there is a directed arc from one node to another. In this example, an element in position (i, j) is assigned a value of 1 if there is service from city i to city j; otherwise, a value of 0 is assigned. Compare the

$$
\begin{array}{c}
\text{To} \\
\begin{array}{cccc}
 & A & B & C & D
\end{array} \\
\text{From}\ \begin{array}{c} A \\ B \\ C \\ D \end{array}
\begin{pmatrix}
0 & 1 & 0 & 0 \\
1 & 0 & 1 & 0 \\
0 & 1 & 0 & 1 \\
0 & 1 & 0 & 0
\end{pmatrix}
\end{array}
\qquad \text{Adjacency matrix}
$$

adjacency matrix with Fig. 6.5. The adjacency matrix summarizes all *nonstop service* between cities on the airline's routes.

Now, if the adjacency matrix is multiplied times itself, an interesting result occurs.

$$
\begin{pmatrix}
0 & 1 & 0 & 0 \\
1 & 0 & 1 & 0 \\
0 & 1 & 0 & 1 \\
0 & 1 & 0 & 0
\end{pmatrix}
\begin{pmatrix}
0 & 1 & 0 & 0 \\
1 & 0 & 1 & 0 \\
0 & 1 & 0 & 1 \\
0 & 1 & 0 & 0
\end{pmatrix}
=
\begin{array}{c}
\text{To} \\
\begin{array}{cccc}
 & A & B & C & D
\end{array} \\
\text{From}\ \begin{array}{c} A \\ B \\ C \\ D \end{array}
\begin{pmatrix}
1 & 0 & 1 & 0 \\
0 & 2 & 0 & 1 \\
1 & 1 & 1 & 0 \\
1 & 0 & 1 & 0
\end{pmatrix}
\end{array}
$$

The product matrix summarizes the *one-stop service* between all cities. For example, the product matrix indicates that there is a one-stop route from city C to city A. A check of Fig. 6.5 confirms that service is available from C to A with a stop at city B.

Let's see if this makes sense. If we examine the inner product resulting in element (3, 1) of the product matrix, row 3 of the first matrix indicates the presence (absence) of direct flights *from* city C to other cities. Column 1 of the second matrix indicates the presence (absence) of flights *to* city A from other cities. The multiplication seeks matches of pairs of flights.

$$
\begin{array}{c}
\text{From}
\end{array}
\begin{array}{c}
 \\ A \\ B \\ C \\ D
\end{array}
\begin{array}{cccc}
 & \text{To} & & \\
A & B & C & D
\end{array}
\left(
\boxed{\begin{array}{cccc} 0 & 1 & 0 & 1 \end{array}}
\right)
\begin{array}{cccc}
 & \text{To} & & \\
A & B & C & D
\end{array}
\left(
\boxed{\begin{array}{c} 1 \\ 0 \\ 1 \\ 1 \end{array}}
\right)
=
\begin{array}{c}
A \\ B \\ C \\ D
\end{array}
\begin{array}{cccc}
 & \text{To} & & \\
A & B & C & D
\end{array}
\left(
\boxed{1}
\right)
$$

In this case we look for matches between flights *from* city C to another city with flights *from* that destination city *to* city A. Perhaps we can illustrate this by expanding the inner product computation as shown in Fig. 6.6. Note in this figure that the only pairs of flights which match are C to D and D to A. Study the multiplication procedure until you understand how (and why) each element is calculated.

Although not particularly meaningful, the matrix indicates two one-stop routes from city B to city B. These reflect the round-trip routes to cities A and C.

Cubing the matrix will result in a product matrix which summarizes the number of "two-stop" routes between all cities. For example, our results thus far have indicated no nonstop or one-stop service from A to D. This product matrix suggests that there is a two-stop route ($A \rightarrow B \rightarrow C \rightarrow D$).

$$
\begin{pmatrix}
0 & 1 & 0 & 0 \\
1 & 0 & 1 & 0 \\
0 & 1 & 0 & 1 \\
0 & 1 & 0 & 0
\end{pmatrix}
\begin{pmatrix}
1 & 0 & 1 & 0 \\
0 & 2 & 0 & 1 \\
1 & 1 & 1 & 0 \\
1 & 0 & 1 & 0
\end{pmatrix}
=
\begin{array}{c}
A \\ B \\ C \\ D
\end{array}
\begin{array}{cccc}
 & \text{To} & & \\
A & B & C & D
\end{array}
\begin{pmatrix}
0 & 2 & 0 & 1 \\
2 & 1 & 2 & 0 \\
1 & 2 & 1 & 1 \\
0 & 2 & 0 & 1
\end{pmatrix}
$$

In this particular example, two-stop routes are not always meaningful. To illustrate, the 2 two-stop routes indicated from city A to city B are $A \rightarrow B \rightarrow A \rightarrow B$ and $A \rightarrow B \rightarrow C \rightarrow B$. Another example is that a two-stop route can occur when flying from city C to city A. The route is from $C \rightarrow D \rightarrow B \rightarrow A$. The more direct route, though, is $C \rightarrow B \rightarrow A$.

This example is very simple, not really justifying matrix methods. However, it is simplified for purposes of illustration. These methods, especially when executed on a computer, bring considerable efficiencies for larger-scale problems, such as might occur for major airlines like United, Eastern, TWA, and Delta.

Section 6.6 Follow-up Exercises

1 Regarding the election discussed in Example 28, the Independent candidate

FIGURE 6.6
Inner product
computation for
row 3 and
column 1.

Inner product components	(0)	(1)	+	(1)	(0)	+	(0)	(1)	+	(1)	(1) · = 1
Corresponding flight pairs	$C \to A$	$A \to A$		$C \to B$	$B \to A$		$C \to C$	$C \to A$		$C \to D$	$D \to A$

made a particularly strong showing in a recent televised debate among the three candidates. The political pollster has observed a shift in voter preferences as indicated in the matrix below.

$$
\begin{array}{c}
\text{District} \\
\begin{array}{cccccc}
1 & 2 & 3 & 4 & 5 & 6
\end{array}
\end{array}
$$

$$
\mathbf{P} = \begin{pmatrix}
0.35 & 0.33 & 0.30 & 0.44 & 0.25 & 0.30 \\
0.40 & 0.38 & 0.27 & 0.35 & 0.28 & 0.35 \\
0.25 & 0.29 & 0.43 & 0.21 & 0.47 & 0.35
\end{pmatrix}
\begin{array}{l}
\text{Democrat} \\
\text{Republican} \\
\text{Independent}
\end{array}
$$

Assuming the original estimates of voter turnout in the six districts, project the outcome of the election. Does it seem that the debate has had any effect on the outcome?

2 The following matrix is a matrix of transition probabilities related to a market dominated by two firms.

$$
\mathbf{T} = \begin{pmatrix}
0.70 & 0.30 \\
0.25 & 0.75
\end{pmatrix}
$$

Assume brand 1 currently has 70 percent of the market and brand 2 has the remaining 30 percent.
(a) Predict market shares in the next period.
(b) Predict market shares after four periods.
*(c) Assuming that the transition matrix remains stable, will a market equilibrium be reached? If so, what are the expected equilibrium shares? (*Hint:* If p_1 and p_2 represent the market shares for brands 1 and 2, $p_1 + p_2 = 1$.)

3 Examine the following matrices of transition for two different market situations. For each matrix, it is assumed that there are three brands dominating the market. By observation, see if you can predict (without formal computation) what equilibrium conditions will be.

$$
\mathbf{T}_1 = \begin{pmatrix}
0.80 & 0.15 & 0.05 \\
0.20 & 0.70 & 0.10 \\
0 & 0 & 1.00
\end{pmatrix}
\qquad
\mathbf{T}_2 = \begin{pmatrix}
0.80 & 0.10 & 0.10 \\
0 & 0.50 & 0.50 \\
0 & 0.50 & 0.50
\end{pmatrix}
$$

4 The following matrix illustrates the transition probabilities associated with a market dominated by three brands.

$$
\mathbf{T} = \begin{pmatrix}
0.2 & 0.6 & 0.2 \\
0.1 & 0.5 & 0.4 \\
0.2 & 0.3 & 0.5
\end{pmatrix}
$$

Assume brand 1 currently has 40 percent of the market, brand 2 has 40 percent, and brand 3 has 20 percent.
(a) Predict market shares after the next period.
*(b) Assuming the transition matrix remains stable, will a market equilibrium be reached? If so, what are the expected equilibrium shares?

5   In Example 31 assume that the transition matrix describing migration behavior is

$$\begin{array}{cc} & \text{To north} \quad \text{To south} \\ \mathbf{S} = \begin{pmatrix} 0.90 & 0.10 \\ 0.05 & 0.95 \end{pmatrix} & \begin{array}{l} \text{From north} \\ \text{From south} \end{array} \end{array}$$

Determine if the populations will attain an equilibrium condition, and if so, the populations of the two regions.

6   Referring to Example 32, assume that the nonindustry demands are $80 million, $40 million, and $100 million, respectively. Determine the equilibrium levels of output for the three industries. Also, determine the interindustry demands for the three industries.

7   Figure 6.7 is a network diagram which illustrates the route structure for a small regional commuter airline which services four cities. Using this figure, construct an adjacency matrix. Square the adjacency matrix and summarize the one-stop service which exists between all cities.

8   Figure 6.8 is a network diagram which illustrates the route structure for a small commuter airline which services five cities. Using this figure, construct an adjacency matrix. Square the adjacency matrix and summarize the one-stop service which exists between all cities.

KEY TERMS AND CONCEPTS

ADDITIONAL EXERCISES

Exercises 1 to 5 are related to Sec. 6.3.

1   The matrices $\mathbf{S}_1$ and $\mathbf{S}_2$ represent annual sales for a firm's three products by region, stated in millions of dollars. $\mathbf{S}_1$ represents sales for the firm's first year of operation and $\mathbf{S}_2$ the sales for the second year of operation.

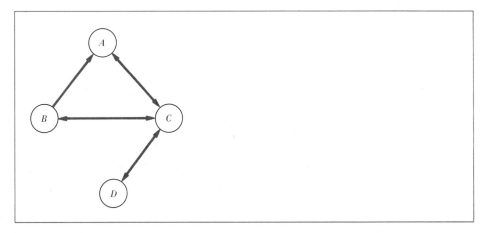

FIGURE 6.7

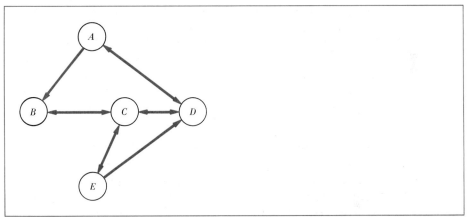

FIGURE 6.8

$$
\begin{array}{c}
\text{Region} \\
\begin{array}{cccc}
1 & 2 & 3 & 4
\end{array} \\
S_1 = \begin{pmatrix}
2.5 & 1.8 & 1.5 & 0.9 \\
3.2 & 4.1 & 2.5 & 1.8 \\
2.4 & 3.6 & 3.0 & 2.5
\end{pmatrix}
\end{array}
\qquad
\begin{array}{c}
\text{Region} \\
\begin{array}{cccc}
1 & 2 & 3 & 4
\end{array} \\
S_2 = \begin{pmatrix}
3.0 & 2.5 & 3.0 & 1.5 \\
4.5 & 6.0 & 3.5 & 3.0 \\
2.9 & 3.0 & 4.5 & 4.0
\end{pmatrix}
\end{array}
$$

(a) Compute $S_2 - S_1$ and interpret the meaning of the resulting matrix.

(b) Compute $S_1 + S_2$ and interpret the meaning of the resulting matrix.

(c) Management had projected a 20 percent increase in sales for all products in all regions for the second year of operation. Using matrix operations, compute the difference between the projected sales levels and the actual levels for the second year and interpret the results. Identify the regions and products which were below management's expectations.

2 Given the following matrices

$$
A = \begin{pmatrix} 2 & -3 \\ 4 & 1 \end{pmatrix}
\qquad
B = \begin{pmatrix} 1 & 0 & 0 \\ 0 & 1 & 0 \\ 0 & 0 & 1 \end{pmatrix}
\qquad
C = \begin{pmatrix} 2 & -1 & 3 \\ 3 & 0 & -2 \end{pmatrix}
\qquad
D = \begin{pmatrix} 3 & 2 & 1 \\ 0 & 1 & 0 \\ 2 & 3 & 1 \end{pmatrix}
$$

compute (if possible) (*a*) **AB**, (*b*) **BC**, (*c*) **BC'**, (*d*) **CD**, (*e*) **DC'B**, (*f*) **ACBD**.

3   Given the following matrices

$$A = \begin{pmatrix} -1 & 1 \\ 1 & -1 \end{pmatrix} \quad B = \begin{pmatrix} 0 & 0 & 1 \\ 0 & 1 & 0 \\ 1 & 0 & 0 \end{pmatrix} \quad C = \begin{pmatrix} 2 & -3 \\ 1 & 0 \\ 3 & -1 \end{pmatrix} \quad D = \begin{pmatrix} 1 & 2 & 3 \\ 3 & 2 & 1 \\ 1 & 0 & 1 \end{pmatrix}$$

Compute (if possible) (*a*) **B** + **C**, (*b*) **B** − **D**, (*c*) **BC**, (*d*) **CA**, (*e*) **C'BD**, (*f*) **DBCA**.

4   State the following matrix equation in algebraic form.

$$\begin{pmatrix} 1 & 3 & -2 & 0 & 4 \\ 2 & 0 & 1 & -1 & 0 \end{pmatrix} \begin{pmatrix} x_1 \\ x_2 \\ x_3 \\ x_4 \\ x_5 \end{pmatrix} = \begin{pmatrix} 300 \\ 175 \end{pmatrix}$$

5   State the following matrix equation in algebraic form.

$$\begin{pmatrix} 3 & -2 & 1 \\ 4 & 0 & -2 \\ 5 & -3 & 0 \\ 3 & 1 & -2 \\ 0 & 4 & 2 \\ 1 & -1 & 1 \end{pmatrix} \begin{pmatrix} x_1 \\ x_2 \\ x_3 \end{pmatrix} = \begin{pmatrix} 25 \\ 100 \\ 55 \\ 75 \\ 250 \\ 15 \end{pmatrix}$$

Exercises 6 to 16 are related to Sec. 6.4.

Find the matrix of cofactors for each of the following matrices.

6 $\begin{pmatrix} 5 & 10 \\ -5 & 20 \end{pmatrix}$ **7** $\begin{pmatrix} 4 & -4 \\ -2 & 2 \end{pmatrix}$

8 $\begin{pmatrix} 3 & 2 & 1 \\ 2 & 0 & 2 \\ 3 & -1 & 0 \end{pmatrix}$ **9** $\begin{pmatrix} 4 & 2 & 1 \\ 3 & 0 & 0 \\ 1 & -2 & -3 \end{pmatrix}$

Find the determinant for each of the following matrices.

10 $\begin{pmatrix} 5 & 15 \\ -10 & 20 \end{pmatrix}$ **11** $\begin{pmatrix} -2 & -2 \\ 3 & -5 \end{pmatrix}$

12 $\begin{pmatrix} 1 & -1 & 1 \\ -1 & 1 & -1 \\ 1 & -1 & 1 \end{pmatrix}$ **13** $\begin{pmatrix} 2 & 0 & 1 \\ 1 & -1 & -2 \\ 0 & 2 & 1 \end{pmatrix}$

14   Find the determinant of the matrix   **15**   Find the determinant of the matrix

$$C = \begin{pmatrix} 3 & -1 & 2 & 0 \\ 4 & 6 & 0 & 1 \\ 7 & -1 & 0 & 5 \\ 0 & 1 & 0 & 1 \end{pmatrix} \qquad D = \begin{pmatrix} 1 & 0 & 0 & 0 \\ 0 & 1 & 0 & 0 \\ 0 & 0 & 1 & 0 \\ 0 & 0 & 0 & 1 \end{pmatrix}$$

16   **Cramer's Rule**   Given a system of linear equations of the form

$$AX = B$$

where **A** is a *square* matrix of coefficients, Cramer's rule provides a method of solving the system using determinants. To solve for the value of the jth variable, we use the formula

$$x_j = \frac{|\mathbf{A}_j|}{|\mathbf{A}|}$$

where $\mathbf{A}_j$ is the matrix $\mathbf{A}$ with one modification. $\mathbf{A}_j$ is formed by replacing the jth column of $\mathbf{A}$ with the column vector $\mathbf{B}$. Notice that if $\mathbf{A}$ is singular, $|\mathbf{A}| = 0$ and x_j is undefined. Thus, if $|\mathbf{A}| = 0$, the system of equations has either no solution or an infinite number of solutions. If $|\mathbf{A}| \neq 0$, a unique solution exists. Use Cramer's rule to solve the following systems of equations.

(a) $x_1 + x_2 = -1$
$2x_1 - x_2 = 7$

(b) $-x_1 + 2x_2 = 24$
$3x_1 - 6x_2 = 10$

(c) $2x_1 - 3x_2 + x_3 = 1$
$x_1 + x_2 + x_3 = 2$
$3x_1 \quad\quad - 4x_3 = 17$

Exercises 17 to 28 are related to Sec. 6.5.

For the following matrices, find the inverse (if it exists).

17 $\begin{pmatrix} 0 & 1 \\ 8 & 3 \end{pmatrix}$

18 $\begin{pmatrix} 4 & 8 \\ 7 & 2 \end{pmatrix}$

19 $\begin{pmatrix} 1 & 8 & 7 \\ 2 & 3 & 5 \\ 7 & 4 & -1 \end{pmatrix}$

20 $\begin{pmatrix} 4 & -4 & 3 \\ -3 & 2 & -2 \\ 1 & -1 & 0 \end{pmatrix}$

For the following matrices, determine the inverse using the method of cofactors.

21 $\begin{pmatrix} 8 & 10 \\ 11 & 13 \end{pmatrix}$

22 $\begin{pmatrix} 4 & 2 & 6 \\ 9 & 3 & 7 \\ -1 & 0 & 5 \end{pmatrix}$

Using the results from Exercises 17 to 22, determine the solution of the following systems of equations.

23 $\quad\quad x_2 = 4$
$8x_1 + 3x_2 = 12$

24 $4x_1 + 8x_2 = 12$
$7x_1 + 2x_2 = 9$

25 $x_1 + 8x_2 + 7x_3 = 0$
$2x_1 + 3x_2 + 5x_3 = 4$
$7x_1 + 4x_2 - x_3 = 2$

26 $4x_1 - 4x_2 + 3x_3 = 7$
$-3x_1 + 2x_2 - 2x_3 = -7$
$x_1 - x_2 = 1$

27 $8x_1 + 10x_2 = 4$
$11x_1 + 13x_2 = 4$

28 $4x_1 + 2x_2 + 6x_3 = 2$
$9x_1 + 3x_2 + 7x_3 = 20$
$-x_1 \quad\quad + 5x_3 = -10$

Exercises 29 to 36 are related to Sec. 6.6.

29 **College Admissions** The admissions office for a large university plans on admitting 7,500 students next year. The column vector $\mathbf{M}$ indicates the expected breakdown of the new students into the categories of in-state males (ISM), in-state females (ISF), out-of-state males (OSM), and out-of-state females (OSF):

$$\mathbf{M} = \begin{pmatrix} 3,000 \\ 2,750 \\ 1,000 \\ 750 \end{pmatrix} \begin{matrix} \text{ISM} \\ \text{ISF} \\ \text{OSM} \\ \text{OSF} \end{matrix}$$

Admissions personnel expect the students to choose their majors within the colleges of business (B), engineering (E), and arts and sciences (A&S) according to the percentages given in the matrix **P**:

$$
\begin{array}{cccc}
\text{ISM} & \text{ISF} & \text{OSM} & \text{OSF}
\end{array}
$$

$$
\mathbf{P} = \begin{pmatrix} 0.30 & 0.30 & 0.30 & 0.24 \\ 0.20 & 0.10 & 0.30 & 0.06 \\ 0.50 & 0.60 & 0.40 & 0.70 \end{pmatrix} \quad \begin{matrix} \text{B} \\ \text{E} \\ \text{A\&S} \end{matrix}
$$

Using matrix operations, compute the expected number of students to enter each college.

30   Refer to Exercise 29. The housing office estimates that students will select housing alternatives according to the percentages in **H**:

$$
\begin{array}{ccc}
 & \text{Fraternity} & \\
\text{Dorm} & \text{or sorority} & \text{Off campus}
\end{array}
$$

$$
\mathbf{H} = \begin{pmatrix} 0.40 & 0.30 & 0.30 \\ 0.60 & 0.20 & 0.20 \end{pmatrix} \quad \begin{matrix} \text{IS} \\ \text{OS} \end{matrix}
$$

Perform a matrix multiplication which will compute the number of new students expected to choose the different housing options.

31   A company manufactures three products, each of which requires certain amounts of raw materials and labor. The matrix **R** summarizes the requirements per unit of each product.

$$
\begin{array}{c}
\text{Raw material} \\
\begin{array}{cccc}
1 & 2 & 3 & \text{Labor}
\end{array}
\end{array}
$$

$$
\mathbf{R} = \begin{pmatrix} 2 & 4 & 5 & 5 \\ 3 & 2 & 3 & 8 \\ 1 & 3 & 5 & 4 \end{pmatrix} \quad \begin{matrix} \text{Product } A \\ \text{Product } B \\ \text{Product } C \end{matrix}
$$

Raw material requirements are stated in pounds per unit and labor requirements in hours per unit. The three raw materials cost $2, $3, and $1.50 per pound, respectively. Labor costs are $5 per hour. Assume 500, 1,000, and 400 units of products A, B, and C are to be produced.

(*a*) Perform a matrix multiplication which computes total quantities of the four resources required to produce products A, B, and C.

(*b*) Using your answer from part *a*, perform a matrix multiplication which calculates the combined total cost of production.

32   **Hospital Administration**   A local hospital has gathered data regarding people admitted for in-patient services. The vector **P** indicates the percentages of all patients admitted to different hospital units. The vector **S** indicates the average length of patient stay (in days) for each hospital unit.

$$
\mathbf{P} = \begin{pmatrix} 0.18 \\ 0.10 \\ 0.24 \\ 0.48 \end{pmatrix} \quad \begin{matrix} \text{Obstetrical} \\ \text{Cardiac} \\ \text{Pediatric} \\ \text{Other} \end{matrix} \qquad \mathbf{S} = (4 \quad 14 \quad 3 \quad 5)
$$

The vector **C** summarizes current daily patient cost for the different hospital units:

$$
\mathbf{C} = (\$280 \quad \$400 \quad \$240 \quad \$260)
$$

If 200 new patients are admitted, perform a matrix multiplication to compute:

(a) The numbers of patients admitted to each hospital unit

(b) The total number of patient-days expected

(c) Total cost per day for the 200 patients

33   Social Interaction   A group of executives has been surveyed regarding the persons who have direct influence over their decision making. The matrix below summarizes their responses.

Person whose
opinion is sought

	A	B	C	D	E	F
A	0	1	0	1	0	0
B	1	0	0	0	1	0
C	1	0	0	0	0	1
D	0	1	1	0	0	1
E	0	0	0	1	0	0
F	1	0	0	0	1	0

An entry of 1 indicates that the person represented by the corresponding column has some direct influence over the decision making of the person represented by the row. An entry of 0 indicates no direct influence. As with Example 33, this matrix is similar to the adjacency matrix. The square of the matrix would indicate indirect influences on decision making involving an intermediary. Square the matrix and summarize the indirect influences.

34   The technological matrix for a three-industry input-output model is

$$\mathbf{A} = \begin{pmatrix} 0.5 & 0 & 0.2 \\ 0.2 & 0.8 & 0.12 \\ 1 & 0.4 & 0 \end{pmatrix}$$

If the nonindustry demand for the output of these industries is d_1 = $5 million, d_2 = $3 million, and d_3 = $4 million, determine the equilibrium output levels for the three industries.

35   Wildlife Migration   Scientists have been studying the migration habits of a particular species of wildlife. An annual census is conducted in three different regions inhabited by the species. A stable pattern of changes has been observed in their movements. This is reflected in the transition matrix below.

To region

From region	1	2	3
1	0.90	0.05	0.05
2	0.10	0.80	0.10
3	0.05	0.10	0.85

Assume the populations of the three regions were 40,000, 20,000, and 30,000 during the last census.

(a) Predict the populations of each region at the time of the next census. Two years from now?

(b) If the migration patterns remain constant, will an equilibrium be reached in terms of

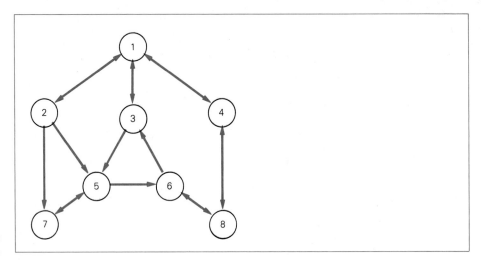

FIGURE 6.9
Bus routes.

the populations of the three regions? If so, what are the equilibrium populations?

36 Figure 6.9 is a network diagram which illustrates the route structure for a commercial bus company which services eight cities. Using this figure, construct an adjacency matrix. Square the adjacency matrix and summarize the one-stop service which exists between all cities.

CHAPTER TEST

1 Find the transpose of **A** if

$$A = \begin{pmatrix} 1 & -3 & 0 & 5 \\ 6 & -2 & 4 & 9 \end{pmatrix}$$

2 Find the inner product

$$(a \quad b \quad c \quad d)\begin{pmatrix} e \\ f \\ g \\ h \end{pmatrix}$$

3 Given the matrices

$$A = \begin{pmatrix} 2 & -1 \\ 3 & 4 \end{pmatrix} \quad B = \begin{pmatrix} 2 & -5 \\ 1 & 0 \\ 7 & 4 \end{pmatrix} \quad C = \begin{pmatrix} -1 & 0 & 0 \\ 0 & -1 & 0 \\ 0 & 0 & -1 \end{pmatrix}$$

determine, if possible, (a) **AB,** (b) **BA,** (c) **BC.**

4 Write the following system of equations as a matrix product:

$$\begin{aligned} x_1 \quad\quad - x_4 &= 20 \\ x_2 + x_3 \quad\quad &= 15 \\ x_3 + x_4 &= 18 \\ x_4 &= 9 \end{aligned}$$

5 Find the determinant for the matrix

$$\mathbf{A} = \begin{pmatrix} 0 & 0 & -2 \\ 0 & 5 & 0 \\ -3 & 0 & 0 \end{pmatrix}$$

6   Find $\mathbf{A}^{-1}$ if

$$\mathbf{A} = \begin{pmatrix} 20 & -8 \\ -5 & 2 \end{pmatrix}$$

7   The solution to a system of equations having the form $\mathbf{AX} = \mathbf{B}$ can be found by the matrix multiplication

$$\mathbf{X} = \begin{pmatrix} 5 & -7 \\ -2 & 3 \end{pmatrix}\begin{pmatrix} 15 \\ 11 \end{pmatrix}$$

What was the original system of equations?

MINICASE A

BRAND SWITCHING

A marketing research organization has recently completed a survey of purchasing behavior in a market dominated by four different brands. The table below summarizes total purchases during the current purchasing period. Note that each row indicates the brand purchased during the previous purchasing period and each column the brand purchased during this period.

		Brand purchased this period				
		1	2	3	4	
	1	47,500	500	1,000	1,000	50,000
Brand purchased in previous period	2	400	38,000	0	1,600	40,000
	3	0	4,500	54,000	1,500	60,000
	4	5,000	1,000	4,000	40,000	50,000

The marketing research organization believes that the switching behavior occurring during the current period is representative of that which normally occurs in this market. They also believe that these patterns are stable.

1 What were the relative market shares for these brands during the previous period? During the current period?

2 Construct the matrix of transition probabilities for these four brands.

3 Predict the market shares at the end of the next purchasing period and at the end of the following period.

4 Assuming stability in the matrix of transition probabilities, will a market equilibrium ever occur? If so, what will the equilibrium shares equal?

*5 Write a computer program which can be used to predict market shares in each successive period. Using the program, determine the number of periods which must elapse before market equilibrium is reached. You may use any programming language you like. However, BASIC, with its specialized matrix commands, is suggested.

MINICASE B

MATRIX INVERSION COMPUTERIZED

Using a language such as BASIC, write a program which can be used to solve systems of linear equations having the form AX = B, where A is a square matrix of coefficients. Test your program by solving the following system of equations.

$$
\begin{array}{r}
x_1 + x_2 + x_3 + x_4 + x_5 + x_6 + x_7 + x_8 + x_9 + x_{10} = 8 \\
2x_1 - x_2 + x_3 \qquad\quad - 4x_5 + 2x_6 \qquad\quad - x_8 \qquad\qquad = -8 \\
3x_2 \qquad\quad - x_4 + 5x_5 \qquad\quad - 2x_7 \qquad\quad + 3x_9 \qquad = 6 \\
x_1 \qquad\qquad\qquad + x_5 \qquad\qquad\quad - 3x_8 \qquad\quad + 4x_{10} = -9 \\
5x_1 - 2x_2 + 4x_3 \qquad\qquad\qquad\qquad\qquad\qquad\qquad = 0 \\
3x_6 - 5x_7 + 2x_8 - x_9 + x_{10} = 5 \\
5x_3 - 2x_4 + 6x_5 - 4x_6 \qquad\qquad\qquad\qquad = 1 \\
x_1 - x_2 + 3x_3 + 2x_4 - 5x_5 \qquad\qquad\qquad\qquad = -9 \\
3x_1 + 5x_2 - x_3 + 2x_4 + x_5 - x_6 + 2x_7 - 5x_8 - x_9 + x_{10} = 7 \\
x_2 \qquad\quad - x_4 \qquad\quad + x_6 \qquad\quad - 2x_8 \qquad\quad + x_{10} = -5
\end{array}
$$

LINEAR PROGRAMMING: AN INTRODUCTION

CHAPTER OBJECTIVES

- ■ Provide an understanding of the structure of and assumptions underlying linear programming models

- ■ Illustrate a variety of applications of linear programming models

- ■ Provide an understanding of graphical solution procedures

- ■ Illustrate the nature and significance of special phenomena which can arise with linear programming models

- ■ Discuss the nature of computer solution methods and illustrate a sample computer package

This chapter introduces the topic of *linear programming,* a topic which integrates much of the material we have discussed in the previous chapters. Linear programming is a powerful and widely applied mathematical modeling technique. Also, the technique provides an important framework which is relevant to the more generalized area of modeling techniques called *mathematical programming.*

In this chapter we will discuss the nature and structure of linear programming problems; we will see sample applications and graphical solution procedures for the two-variable situation. Also, since most linear programming problems are solved by computer methods, we will discuss computer-based solution procedures. In the last section we will discuss various forms of postoptimality analysis. This topic is particularly relevant in any applied mathematical analysis. Chapter 8 discusses the *simplex method,* a solution procedure which is algebraically based and which is appropriate when graphical methods are not. Most computer packages used to solve linear programming problems are based on the simplex method.

7.1 LINEAR PROGRAMMING

Introduction

Linear programming (*LP*) is a mathematical optimization technique. By "optimization" technique we are usually referring to a method which attempts to maximize or minimize some objective, e.g., maximize profits, minimize costs, etc. Linear programming is a subset of a larger area of mathematical optimization procedures called *mathematical programming.* Although the application of these mathematical programming methods usually requires the use of computers, none of the methods is directly concerned with computer "programming." They are concerned with making an optimal set of decisions. Linear programming is a powerful and widely applied technique. There have been extensive applications of linear programming within the military and the oil industry. Although these sectors have been perhaps the heaviest users of linear programming, the services sector and public sector of the economy have applied the methods increasingly.

In any linear programming problem certain decisions need to be made. These decisions are represented by *decision variables x_j* used in the formulation of the linear programming model. The basic structure of a linear programming problem is either to maximize or to minimize an *objective function* while satisfying a set of *constraining conditions,* or *constraints.* The objective function is a mathematical representation of the overall goal stated as a function of the decision variables x_j. The objective function may represent goals such as profit level, total revenue, total cost, pollution levels, percent return on investment, and so forth. The set of constraints, also stated in terms of x_j, represents conditions which must be satisfied when determining levels for the decision variables. For example, in attempting to maximize profits from the production and sale of a group of products, sample constraints might reflect limited labor resources, limited raw materials, and limited demand for the products. The constraints in an LP problem can be represented by equations or by inequalities ($\le$ and/or $\ge$ types).

These problems are called *linear* programming problems because the objective function and constraints are all linear. A simple linear programming problem is stated below.

$$\text{Maximize} \quad z = 4x_1 + 2x_2 \tag{7.1}$$

$$\text{subject to} \quad x_1 + 2x_2 \le 24 \tag{7.2}$$

$$4x_1 + 3x_2 \ge 30 \tag{7.3}$$

The objective is to maximize z, which is stated as a linear function of the two decision variables x_1 and x_2. In choosing values for x_1 and x_2, however, two constraints must be satisfied. The constraints are represented by the two linear inequalities (7.2) and (7.3).

A Scenario

Product-mix problems represent an important group of applications of mathematical modeling. We discussed product-mix examples in Chaps. 4 and 5. Let's illustrate the LP treatment of this type of problem in a simplified example. A

TABLE 7.1

	PRODUCT A	PRODUCT B	WEEKLY LABOR CAPACITY
Department 1	3 h per unit	2 h per unit	120 h
Department 2	4 h per unit	6 h per unit	260 h
Selling price	$25	$30	
Labor cost per unit	16	20	
Raw material cost per unit	4	4	

firm manufacturers two products, each of which must be processed through departments 1 and 2. Table 7.1 summarizes labor hour requirements per unit for each product in each department. Also presented are weekly labor hour capacities in each department, price per unit, labor cost per unit, and raw material cost per unit. The problem is to determine the number of units to produce of each product so as to maximize total contribution to fixed cost and profit.

If we define x_1 and x_2 to equal the number of units produced and sold, respectively, of products A and B, then total profit contribution can be found by adding the contributions from both products. The contribution from each product would be computed by multiplying the profit margin per unit times the number of units produced and sold. Verify from Table 7.1 that the profit margins are $5 and $6, respectively, for the two products. *If z is defined as the total contribution to fixed cost and profit,* we have

$$z = 5x_1 + 6x_2$$

From the information given in the statement of the problem, the only restrictions in deciding the number of units to produce are the weekly labor capacities in the two departments. From our earlier discussions you should be able to verify that these restrictions can be represented by the inequalities

$$3x_1 + 2x_2 \le 120 \qquad \text{department 1}$$
$$4x_1 + 6x_2 \le 260 \qquad \text{department 2}$$

Although there is no formal statement of such a restriction, implicitly we know that x_1 and x_2 cannot be negative. We must account for this type of restriction in formulating the model.

By combining these components, the LP model which represents the problem is stated as follows:

Maximize	$z = 5x_1 + 6x_2$	
subject to	$3x_1 + 2x_2 \le 120$	**(7.4)**
	$4x_1 + 6x_2 \le 260$	**(7.5)**
	$x_1 \ge 0$	**(7.6)**
	$x_2 \ge 0$	**(7.7)**

Structural Constraints and Nonnegativity Constraints

The linear programming model is concerned with maximizing or minimizing a linear objective function subject to two types of constraints: (1) *structural constraints* and (2) *nonnegativity constraints,* one for each decision variable. Structural constraints reflect such things as resource limitations and other conditions imposed by the problem setting. Inequalities (7.4) and (7.5) in the previous formulation are structural constraints. Nonnegativity constraints guarantee that each decision variable will not be negative. Constraints (7.6) and (7.7) are non-negativity constraints. In almost all problems this restriction makes sense. Techniques are available to handle those unusual cases where a variable is allowed to assume negative values.

The Generalized LP Model

A generalized (symbolic) statement of the LP model follows. Given the definitions

$$x_j = \text{jth decision variable}$$
$$c_j = \text{coefficient on jth decision variable in the objective function}$$
$$a_{ij} = \text{coefficient in the ith constraint for the jth variable}$$
$$b_i = \text{right-hand-side constant for the ith constraint}$$

the generalized LP model can be stated as:

$$
\begin{aligned}
&\text{Optimize (maximize or minimize)}\\
&\quad z = c_1 x_1 + c_2 x_2 + \cdots + c_n x_n\\
&\text{subject to}\\
&\quad a_{11} x_1 + a_{12} x_2 + \cdots + a_{1n} x_n \ (\le, \ge, =) \ b_1 \quad (1)\\
&\quad a_{21} x_1 + a_{22} x_2 + \cdots + a_{2n} x_n \ (\le, \ge, =) \ b_2 \quad (2)\\
&\qquad\qquad\qquad\qquad\vdots\\
&\quad a_{m1} x_1 + a_{m2} x_2 + \cdots + a_{mn} x_n \ (\le, \ge, =) \ b_m \quad (m)\\
&\qquad\qquad\qquad\qquad\qquad\quad x_1 \ \ge \ 0\\
&\qquad\qquad\qquad\qquad\qquad\quad x_2 \ \ge \ 0\\
&\qquad\qquad\qquad\qquad\qquad\qquad \vdots\\
&\qquad\qquad\qquad\qquad\qquad\quad x_n \ \ge \ 0
\end{aligned}
$$

(7.8)

This generalized model has n decision variables and m structural constraints. Note that each structural constraint has only one of the $(\le, \ge, =)$ conditions assigned to it.

Those of you familiar with **summation notation** (Appendix A) will appreciate the compactness and efficiency of the following alternative statement of the generalized model:

$$
\begin{aligned}
&\text{Maximize (or minimize)}\\
&\qquad\qquad\qquad z = \sum_{j=1}^{n} c_j x_j\\
&\text{subject to}\\
&\qquad \sum_{j=1}^{n} a_{ij} x_j \ (\le, \ge, =) \ b_i \qquad i = 1, \ldots, m\\
&\qquad\qquad x_j \ge 0 \qquad\qquad\quad j = 1, \ldots, n
\end{aligned}
$$

(7.9)

7.2 SOME APPLICATIONS OF LINEAR PROGRAMMING

In the last section a simple product-mix problem was discussed. In this section, we will present several other areas of application.

TABLE 7.2

FOOD	Vitamin 1	Vitamin 2	Vitamin 3	COST PER OZ, $
1	50 mg	20 mg	10 mg	0.10
2	30 mg	10 mg	50 mg	0.15
3	20 mg	30 mg	20 mg	0.12
Minimum daily requirement (MDR)	290 mg	200 mg	210 mg	

Diet-Mix Models

A diet-mix problem was discussed earlier in Chap. 3 (Example 2). The classic diet-mix problem involves determining the items which should be included in a meal so as to (1) minimize the cost of the meal while (2) satisfying certain nutritional requirements. The nutritional requirements usually take the form of numerous daily vitamin requirements, restrictions encouraging variety in the meal (e.g., do not serve each person 10 pounds of boiled potatoes), and restrictions which consider taste and logical companion foods. The following example illustrates a simple diet-mix problem.

EXAMPLE 1

A dietician is planning the menu for the evening meal at a university dining hall. Three main items will be served, each having different nutritional content. The dietician is interested in providing at least the minimum daily requirement of each of three vitamins in this one meal. Table 7.2 summarizes the *vitamin content per ounce of each type of food,* the cost per ounce of each food, and minimum daily requirements (MDR) for the three vitamins. Any combination of the three foods may be selected as long as the total serving size is at least 9 ounces.

The problem is to determine the number of ounces of each food to be included in the meal. The objective is to minimize the cost of each meal subject to satisfying minimum daily requirements of the three vitamins as well as the restriction on minimum serving size.

To formulate the linear programming model for this problem, *let x_j equal the number of ounces of food j.* The objective function should represent the total cost of the meal. Stated in dollars

$$z = 0.10x_1 + 0.15x_2 + 0.12x_3 \tag{7.10}$$

Since we are interested in providing *at least* the minimum daily requirement of the three vitamins, there will be three "greater than or equal to" constraints. The constraint for each vitamin will have the form

> Milligrams of vitamin intake $\geq$ MDR

or

milligrams from food 1 + milligrams from food 2 + milligrams from food 3 $\geq$ MDR

The constraints are, respectively,

$$50x_1 + 30x_2 + 20x_3 \geq 290 \tag{7.11}$$

$$20x_1 + 10x_2 + 30x_3 \geq 200 \tag{7.12}$$

$$10x_1 + 50x_2 + 20x_3 \geq 210 \tag{7.13}$$

The restriction that the serving size be at least 9 ounces is stated as

$$x_1 + x_2 + x_3 \geq 9 \tag{7.14}$$

The complete formulation of the problem is as follows:

$$
\begin{aligned}
\text{Minimize} \quad & z = 0.10x_1 + 0.15x_2 + 0.12x_3 \\
\text{subject to} \quad & 50x_1 + 30x_2 + 20x_3 \geq 290 \\
& 20x_1 + 10x_2 + 30x_3 \geq 200 \\
& 10x_1 + 50x_2 + 20x_3 \geq 210 \\
& x_1 + x_2 + x_3 \geq 9 \\
& x_1, x_2, x_3 \geq 0
\end{aligned}
$$

Note that the nonnegativity constraint has been included in the formulation. This ensures that negative quantities of any of the foods will not be recommended.

This is a very simplified problem involving the planning of one meal, the use of just three food types, and consideration of three vitamins. In actual practice models have been formulated which consider: (1) menu planning over longer periods of time (daily, weekly, etc.), (2) the interrelationships among all meals served during a given day, (3) the interrelationships among meals served over the entire planning period, (4) many food items, and (5) many nutritional requirements. The number of variables and number of constraints for such models can become extremely large.

Transportation Models

Transportation models are possibly the most widely used linear programming models. Oil companies commit tremendous resources to the implementation of such models. The typical transportation problem involves the shipment of some *homogeneous commodity* from *m sources of supply*, or *origins*, to *n points of demand*, or *destinations*. By *homogeneous* we mean that there are no significant differences in the quality of the item provided by the different sources of supply. The product characteristics are essentially the same.

In the classic problem each origin can supply any of the destinations. And the demand at each destination may be supplied jointly from a combination of the origins or totally from one origin. Each origin usually has a specific capacity which represents the maximum number of units it can supply. Each destination has a specified demand which represents the number of units needed.

Given that each origin can supply units to each destination, some measure of the cost or effort of shipping a unit is specified for each *origin-destination combination*. This may take the form of a dollar cost, distance between the two points, or time required to move from one point to another. A typical problem is concerned with determining the number of units which should be supplied from each origin to each destination. The objective is to minimize the total transportation or delivery costs while ensuring that (1) the number of units shipped from any origin does not exceed the number of units available at that origin and

(2) the demand at each destination is satisfied. Example 2 illustrates a simple transportation model.

EXAMPLE 2 ▮▮▮▮▮▮▮▮▮▮▮▮▮▮▮▮▮▮▮▮▮▮▮▮▮▮▮▮

Highway Maintenance   A medium-sized city has two locations in the city at which salt and sand stockpiles are maintained for use during winter icing and snow storms. During a storm, salt and sand are distributed from these two locations to four different city zones. Usually additional salt and sand are needed. However, it is usually impossible to get additional supplies during a storm since they are stockpiled at a central location some distance outside the city. City officials hope that there will not be back-to-back storms.

The director of public works is interested in determining the minimum cost of allocating salt and sand supplies during a storm. Table 7.3 summarizes the cost of supplying 1 ton of salt or sand from each stockpile to each city zone. In addition, stockpile capacities and normal levels of demand for each zone are indicated (in tons).

In formulating the linear programming model for this problem, there are eight decisions to make—how many tons should be shipped from each stockpile to each zone. In some cases the best decision may be to ship no units from a particular stockpile to a given zone. Let's define our variables a little differently. *Let x_{ij} equal the number of tons supplied from stockpile i to zone j.* For example, x_{11} equals the number of tons supplied by stockpile 1 to zone 1. Similarly, x_{23} equals the number of tons supplied by stockpile 2 to zone 3. This *double-subscripted variable* conveys more information to the user than simply defining the variables in this problem as $x_1, x_2, \ldots, x_8$. Given this definition of the variables, the total cost of distributing salt and sand has the form

$$\text{Total cost} = 2x_{11} + 3x_{12} + 1.5x_{13} + 2.5x_{14} + 4x_{21} + 3.5x_{22} + 2.5x_{23} + 3x_{24} \quad \textbf{(7.15)}$$

This is the function we wish to minimize. Does its structure look right? Use your mental model to compute the total cost of shipping 200 tons from stockpile 1 to zone 3 and 100 tons from stockpile 2 to zone 1. Are we using the same function?

One class of constraints deals with the different stockpiles. For each stockpile a constraint should be formulated specifying that total shipments not exceed available supply. For stockpile 1, the sum of the shipments to all zones cannot exceed 900 tons, or

$$x_{11} + x_{12} + x_{13} + x_{14} \leq 900 \quad \textbf{(7.16)}$$

The same constraint for stockpile 2 is

$$x_{21} + x_{22} + x_{23} + x_{24} \leq 750 \quad \textbf{(7.17)}$$

The final class of constraints should guarantee that each zone receives its demanded quantity. For zone 1, the sum of the shipments from stockpiles 1 and 2 should equal 300 tons, or

$$x_{11} + x_{21} = 300 \quad \textbf{(7.18)}$$

TABLE 7.3

	Zone				
	1	2	3	4	MAXIMUM SUPPLY (TONS)
Stockpile 1	$2.00	$3.00	$1.50	$2.50	900
Stockpile 2	4.00	3.50	2.50	3.00	750
Demand, tons	300	450	500	350	

The same constraints for the other three zones are, respectively,

$$x_{12} + x_{22} = 450 \tag{7.19}$$

$$x_{13} + x_{23} = 500 \tag{7.20}$$

$$x_{14} + x_{24} = 350 \tag{7.21}$$

The complete formulation of the linear programming model is as follows:

$$
\begin{array}{ll}
\text{Minimize} \quad z = 2x_{11} + 3x_{12} + 1.5x_{13} + 2.5x_{14} + 4x_{21} + 3.5x_{22} + 2.5x_{23} + 3x_{24} \\
\text{subject to} \\
\qquad x_{11} + x_{12} + x_{13} + x_{14} \leq 900 \\
\qquad x_{21} + x_{22} + x_{23} + x_{24} \leq 750 \\
\qquad x_{11} + x_{21} = 300 \\
\qquad x_{12} + x_{22} = 450 \\
\qquad x_{13} + x_{23} = 500 \\
\qquad x_{14} + x_{24} = 350 \\
x_{11}, x_{12}, x_{13}, x_{14}, x_{21}, x_{22}, x_{23}, x_{24} \geq 0
\end{array}
$$

Capital Budgeting Models

Capital budgeting (rationing) decisions involve the allocation of limited investment funds among a set of competing investment alternatives. The alternatives available in any given time period are usually (but not necessarily) mutually exclusive, each characterized by an investment cost and some estimated benefit. The determination of investment costs usually is relatively easy. Estimating benefits can be more difficult, especially when projects are characterized by less tangible returns (e.g., programs having social benefits). The problem is to select the set of alternatives which will maximize overall benefits subject to budgetary constraints and other constraints which may affect the choice of projects.

EXAMPLE 3

Grant Awards   A federal agency has a budget of $1 billion to award in the form of grants for innovative research in the area of energy alternatives. A management review team consisting of scientists and economists has made a preliminary review of 200 applications, narrowing the field to six finalists. Each of the six finalist's projects has been evaluated and scored relative to potential benefits expected over the next 10 years. These benefits are expressed by a benefit-cost ratio, as shown in Table 7.4. The benefit-cost ratio equals the estimated 10-year benefits divided by the cost of generating the benefits. To make the expected benefits more comparable to the cost figures, the benefit-cost ratio is estimated in terms of current dollars.* That is, all projected dollar benefits over the next 10 years have been expressed in terms of the value of a dollar today. Thus, the benefit-cost ratio of 5.4 for project 1 suggests that for each dollar invested, the expected 10-year return is equivalent to $5.40 today.

Table 7.4 also shows the requested level of funding (in millions of dollars). These figures represent the maximum amount which can be awarded to any project. The agency can award any amount up to the indicated maximum for a given project. Along these lines, the President has mandated that the nuclear project should be funded to at least 50

---

* The appropriate term is *present value,* a concept discussed in Chap. 18.

TABLE 7.4

PROJECT	PROJECT CLASSIFICATION	BENEFIT-COST RATIO	REQUESTED LEVEL OF FUNDING, $ MILLIONS
1	Solar	5.4	220
2	Solar	4.8	180
3	Synthetic Fuels	5.1	250
4	Coal	4.5	150
5	Nuclear	6.1	400
6	Geothermal	4.2	120

percent of the requested amount. The agency's administrator has a strong interest in solar projects and has requested that the combined amount awarded to the two solar projects be at least $300 million.

The problem is to determine the amounts of money to award to each project in order to maximize total *net benefits,* measured in dollars. The net benefit from any project equals total benefit minus total cost. In the case of project 1, the net benefit *per dollar invested* equals $5.40 - $1.00 = $4.40. If we *let x_j equal the number of dollars (in millions) awarded to project j,* the objective function is

$$\text{Maximize} \quad z = 4.4x_1 + 3.8x_2 + 4.1x_3 + 3.5x_4 + 5.1x_5 + 3.2x_6 \qquad (7.22)$$

Structural constraints include the following types. First, the budget equals $1 billion and the total sum awarded cannot exceed this amount. Stated mathematically,

$$x_1 + x_2 + x_3 + x_4 + x_5 + x_6 \leq 1{,}000 \qquad (7.23)$$

There must be a constraint for *each* project which reflects the maximum possible award. For project 1 the constraint is

$$x_1 \leq 220 \qquad (7.24)$$

To assure the President's concern about the nuclear project we must include the constraint

$$x_5 \geq 0.5(400)$$
$$\geq 200 \qquad (7.25)$$

Finally, the administrator's interest in the solar projects is assured by the constraint

$$x_1 + x_2 \geq 300 \qquad (7.26)$$

The complete formulation for this problem is

$$
\begin{array}{llr}
\text{Maximize} & z = 4.4x_1 + 3.8x_2 + 4.1x_3 + 3.5x_4 + 5.1x_5 + 3.2x_6 & \\
\text{subject to} & x_1 + x_2 + x_3 + x_4 + x_5 + x_6 & \leq \quad 1{,}000 \\
& x_1 & \leq \quad 220 \\
& x_2 & \leq \quad 180 \\
& x_3 & \leq \quad 250 \\
& x_4 & \leq \quad 150 \\
& x_5 & \leq \quad 400 \\
& x_6 & \leq \quad 120 \\
& x_5 & \geq \quad 200 \\
& x_1 + x_2 & \geq \quad 300 \\
& x_1, \quad x_2, \quad x_3, \quad x_4, \quad x_5, \quad x_6 & \geq \quad 0
\end{array}
$$

Blending Models

Linear programming has found wide application in an area referred to as *blending models.* Blending models are formulated to determine an optimal combination of component ingredients to be blended into a final product. Blending models have been used in the blending of petroleum products, feed mixes for agricultural use, fertilizers and grass seeds, spirits, teas and coffees, and so forth. The objective with such models usually is to minimize the cost of the blend. Typical constraints include lot size requirements for each blend, technological (or recipe) requirements, and limited availability of component ingredients. The following example illustrates a blending model.

EXAMPLE 4

Petroleum Blending A small refinery is about to blend four petroleum products into three final blends of gasoline. Although the blending formulas are not precise, there are some restrictions which must be adherred to in the blending process. These blending restrictions are:

1 Component 2 should constitute no more than 40 percent of the volume of blend 1.

2 Component 3 should constitute at least 25 percent of the volume of blend 2.

3 Component 1 should be exactly 30 percent of blend 3.

4 Components 2 and 4, together, should constitute at least 60 percent of the volume of blend 1.

There is a limited availability of components 2 and 3, 1,500,000 liters and 1,000,000 liters, respectively. The production manager wants to blend a total of 5,000,000 liters. Of this total at least 2,000,000 liters of final blend 1 should be produced. The wholesale price per liter from the sale of each final blend equals $0.26, $0.22, and $0.20, respectively. The input components cost $0.15, $0.18, $0.12, and $0.14 per liter, respectively. The problem is to determine the number of liters of each component to be used in each final blend so as to maximize the total profit contribution from the production run.

In formulating this problem we will use the double subscripted variable x_{ij} *to represent the number of liters of component i used in final blend j.* A major assumption in this model is that there is no volume loss in the blending process. That is, if three liters of component products are combined, the result is a final blend of exactly three liters.

The objective function has the form

Total profit contribution
    = total revenue − total cost
        from all 3   of the 4
        blends   components

    = profit contri- + profit contri- + profit contri- − cost of   − cost of
        bution from   bution from   bution from   component   component
        blend 1   blend 2   blend 3   1   2

                                             − cost of   − cost of
                                             component   component
                                             3   4

= $0.26 (# of liters of blend 1)	+ $0.22 (# of liters of blend 2)	+ $0.20 (# of liters of blend 3)	− $0.15 (# of liters of component 1)	− $0.18 (# of liters of component 2)
			− $0.12 (# of liters of component 3)	− $0.14 (# of liters of component 4)

Examine the expressions in parentheses in the following equations and verify that the objective function is

$$z = 0.26(x_{11} + x_{21} + x_{31} + x_{41}) + 0.22(x_{12} + x_{22} + x_{32} + x_{42})$$
$$+ 0.20(x_{13} + x_{23} + x_{33} + x_{43}) - 0.15(x_{11} + x_{12} + x_{13})$$
$$- 0.18(x_{21} + x_{22} + x_{23}) - 0.12(x_{31} + x_{32} + x_{33})$$
$$- 0.14(x_{41} + x_{42} + x_{43})$$

which can be simplified by combining like terms to yield

$$z = 0.11x_{11} + 0.07x_{12} + 0.05x_{13} + 0.08x_{21} + 0.04x_{22} + 0.02x_{23} + 0.14x_{31}$$
$$+ 0.10x_{32} + 0.08x_{33} + 0.12x_{41} + 0.08x_{42} + 0.06x_{43} \quad \textbf{(7.27)}$$

Regarding structural constraints, the total production run must equal 5,000,000 liters, or

$$x_{11} + x_{12} + x_{13} + x_{21} + x_{22} + x_{23} + x_{31} + x_{32} + x_{33} + x_{41} + x_{42} + x_{43} = 5,000,000 \quad \textbf{(7.28)}$$

Recipe restriction (*a*) is represented by the inequality

$$x_{21} \leq 0.40(x_{11} + x_{21} + x_{31} + x_{41})$$

which simplifies to the form

$$-0.4x_{11} + 0.6x_{21} - 0.4x_{31} - 0.4x_{41} \leq 0 \quad \textbf{(7.29)}$$

Recipe restriction (*b*) is stated as

$$x_{32} \geq 0.25(x_{12} + x_{22} + x_{32} + x_{42})$$
or
$$-0.25x_{12} - 0.25x_{22} + 0.75x_{32} - 0.25x_{42} \geq 0 \quad \textbf{(7.30)}$$

Restrictions (*c*) and (*d*) are represented by Eqs. (7.31) and (7.32):

$$x_{13} = 0.3(x_{13} + x_{23} + x_{33} + x_{43})$$
or
$$0.7x_{13} - 0.3x_{23} - 0.3x_{33} - 0.3x_{43} = 0 \quad \textbf{(7.31)}$$

and
$$x_{21} + x_{41} \geq 0.6(x_{11} + x_{21} + x_{31} + x_{41})$$
or
$$-0.6x_{11} + 0.4x_{21} - 0.6x_{31} + 0.4x_{41} \geq 0 \quad \textbf{(7.32)}$$

The limited availabilities of components 2 and 3 are represented by Eqs. (7.33) and (7.34).

$$x_{21} + x_{22} + x_{23} \leq 1,500,000 \quad \textbf{(7.33)}$$

$$x_{31} + x_{32} + x_{33} \leq 1,000,000 \quad \textbf{(7.34)}$$

Finally, the minimum production requirement for final blend 1 is represented by

$$x_{11} + x_{21} + x_{31} + x_{41} \geq 2{,}000{,}000 \qquad (7.35)$$

The complete formulation of this blending model is

Maximize $z = 0.11x_{11} + 0.07x_{12} + 0.05x_{13} + 0.08x_{21} + 0.04x_{22} + 0.02_{23}$
$\qquad\qquad + 0.14x_{31} + 0.10x_{32} + 0.08x_{33} + 0.12x_{41} + 0.08x_{42} + 0.06x_{43}$

subject to

$$x_{11} + x_{12} + x_{13} + x_{21} + x_{22} + x_{23} + x_{31} + x_{32} + x_{33} + x_{41} + x_{42} + x_{43} = 5{,}000{,}000$$
$$-0.4x_{11} \qquad\qquad +0.6x_{21} \qquad\qquad -0.4x_{31} \qquad\qquad -0.4x_{41} \qquad\qquad \leq 0$$
$$-0.25x_{12} \qquad\qquad -0.25x_{22} \qquad\qquad +0.75x_{32} \qquad\qquad -0.25x_{42} \qquad\qquad \geq 0$$
$$0.7x_{13} \qquad\qquad -0.3x_{23} \qquad\qquad -0.3x_{33} \qquad\qquad -0.3x_{43} = 0$$
$$-0.6x_{11} \qquad\qquad +0.4x_{21} \qquad\qquad -0.6x_{31} \qquad\qquad +0.4x_{41} \qquad\qquad \geq 0$$
$$x_{21} + x_{22} + x_{23} \qquad\qquad \leq 1{,}500{,}000$$
$$x_{31} + x_{32} + x_{33} \qquad\qquad \leq 1{,}000{,}000$$
$$x_{11} \qquad\qquad + x_{21} \qquad\qquad + x_{31} \qquad\qquad + x_{41} \qquad\qquad \geq 2{,}000{,}000$$
$$x_{11}, x_{12}, x_{13}, x_{21}, x_{22}, x_{23}, x_{31}, x_{32}, x_{33}, x_{41}, x_{42}, x_{43} \geq 0$$

Section 7.2 Follow-up Exercises

1 For Example 3, modify the formulation if the following are true.
(a) Each project should receive at least 10 percent of the requested level of funding.
(b) The amount awarded for the coal project should be at least as much as that awarded for the synthetic fuels project.
(c) Combined funding for the geothermal project and the synthetic project should be at least $40 million.

2 For Example 4, modify the formulation if the following additional conditions must be satisfied.
(a) No more than 3 million liters should be made of final blend 1.
(b) Components 1 and 3 should constitute at least 50 percent of final blend 3.
(c) Components 1 and 4 should constitute no more than 60 percent of final blend 1.
(d) Total revenue from blend 2 should exceed $200,000.

3 A dietician is planning the menu for the noon meal at an elementary school. He plans to serve three main items, each having different nutritional content. The dietician is interested in providing at least the minimum daily requirement of each of three vitamins in this one meal. Table 7.5 summarizes the vitamin content per ounce of each type of food, the cost per ounce, and the minimum daily requirement for each vitamin.

Any combination of the three foods may be selected as long as the total serving size is at least 7.5 ounces.

Formulate the linear programming problem which when solved would determine the number of ounces of each food to serve. The objective is to minimize the cost of the meal while satisfying minimum daily requirement levels of the three vitamins as well as the restriction on the minimum serving size.

4 A leading processor of sugar has two plants which supply four warehouses. Table 7.6 summarizes weekly capacities at each plant, weekly requirements at each warehouse,

TABLE 7.5

FOOD	Vitamin 1	2	3	COST/OUNCE, $
1	30 mg	10 mg	40 mg	0.15
2	20 mg	15 mg	30 mg	0.10
3	40 mg	5 mg	20 mg	0.12
MDR	300 mg	120 mg	210 mg	

TABLE 7.6

	Warehouse 1	2	3	4	WEEKLY SUPPLY, TONS
Plant 1	20	15	10	25	1,200
Plant 2	30	25	20	15	1,500
Weekly demand, tons	400	600	1,000	500	

TABLE 7.7

	Depot 1	2	3	SUPPLY, 1000 GAL
Plant 1	50	40	35	1,000
Plant 2	30	45	40	1,400
Demand, 1000 gal	800	750	650	

TABLE 7.8

	Product A	B	C	WEEKLY AVAILABILITY
Department 1	3.5	4	2	120 h
Department 2		2	2	100 h
Department 3	4	1		80 h
Department 4	2	3	6	150 h
Pounds of raw material per unit	5.5	4.0	3.5	250
Selling price	$50	$60	$65	
Labor cost per unit	30	32	36	
Material cost per unit	11	8	7	

and the shipping cost per ton (in dollars) between any plant and any warehouse. If x_{ij} equals the number of tons shipped from plant i to depot j, formulate the linear programming model which allows for determining the distribution schedule which results in minimum shipping cost. Weekly plant capacities are not to be violated and warehouse requirements are to be satisfied.

5   A chemical company manufactures liquid oxygen at two different locations in the South. It must supply three storage depots in the same region. Table 7.7 summarizes shipping cost per 1,000 gallons between any plant and any depot as well as monthly capacity at each plant and monthly demand at each depot. If x_{ij} equals the number of gallons (in thousands) shipped from plant i to depot j, formulate the linear programming model which allows for determining the minimum cost allocation schedule. Plant capacities are not to be violated, and depot demands are to be satisfied by the schedule.

6   A firm manufactures three products which must be processed through some or all of four departments. Table 7.8 indicates the number of hours a unit of each product requires in the different departments and the number of pounds of raw material required. Also listed are labor and material costs per unit, selling price, and weekly capacities of both labor-hours and raw materials. If the objective is to maximize total weekly profit, formulate the linear programming model for this exercise.

TABLE 7.9

	Shortage Area				SURPLUS OF TRUCKS
	1	2	3	4	
Surplus city 1	$100	$250	$300	$150	150
Surplus city 2	400	75	100	200	125
Surplus city 3	300	100	50	400	180
Shortage of trucks	40	80	90	150	

7 Referring to Exercise 6, write the constraints associated with each of the following conditions.

(a) Combined weekly production must be at least 40 units.

(b) The number of units of product A must be no more than twice the quantity of product C.

(c) Since products B and C are usually sold together, production levels of both should be the same.

8 A regional truck rental agency is planning for a heavy demand during the summer months. The agency has taken truck counts at different cities and has compared these with projected needs for each city (all trucks are the same size). Three metropolitan areas are expected to have more trucks than will be needed during the summer, while four cities are expected to have fewer trucks than will be demanded. To prepare for these months, trucks can be relocated from surplus areas to shortage areas by hiring drivers. Drivers are paid a flat fee which depends on the distance between the two cities. In addition, they receive per diem (daily) expenses. Table 7.9 summarizes costs of having a truck delivered between two cities. Also shown are the projected surpluses for each city which has an oversupply and projected shortages for each city needing additional trucks. (Note that total surplus exceeds total shortage.)

If the objective is to minimize the cost of reallocating the trucks, formulate the linear programming model which would allow for solving the problem. (*Hint:* Let x_{ij} equal the number of trucks delivered from surplus area i to shortage area j.)

9 A coffee manufacturer blends four component coffee beans into three final blends of coffee. The four component beans cost the manufacturer $0.55, $0.70, $0.60, and $0.80 per pound, respectively. The weekly availabilities of the four components are 30,000, 40,000, 25,000, and 20,000 pounds, respectively. The manufacturer sells the three blends at wholesale prices of $1.25, $1.40, and $1.80 per pound, respectively. Weekly output should include at least 40,000 pounds of final blend 1.

The following are blending restrictions which must be followed by the brewmaster.

(a) Component 2 should constitute at least 30 percent of final blend 1 and no more than 20 percent of final blend 3.

(b) Component 3 should constitute exactly 20 percent of final blend 3.

(c) Component 4 should constitute at least 40 percent of final blend 3 and no more than 10 percent of final blend 1.

The objective is to determine the number of pounds of each component which should be used in each final blend so as to maximize weekly profit. Formulate this as an LP model, carefully defining your decision variables.

7.3 GRAPHICAL SOLUTIONS

When a linear programming model is stated in terms of two decision variables, it can be solved by graphical procedures. The graphical approach provides an effective visual frame of reference, and it is extremely helpful in understanding

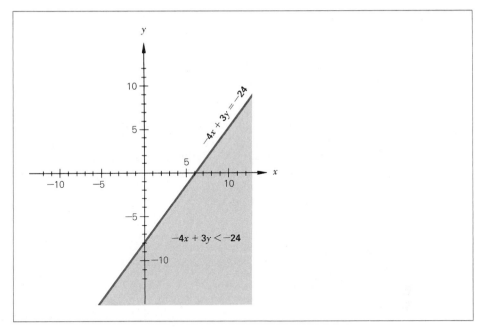

FIGURE 7.1
Solution for
$-4x + 3y$
≤ -24.

the kinds of phenomena which can occur in solving linear programming problems. In this section we will develop the graphical solution approach. Before discussing the graphical solution method, we will discuss the graphics of linear inequalities.

The Graphics of Linear Inequalities

When a linear inequality involves two variables, the solution set can be described graphically. For example, the inequality

$$-4x + 3y \leq -24$$

has a solution set represented by the shaded *half-space* in Fig. 7.1. The solution set can be divided into two subsets. One subset consists of all pairs of values (x, y) which satisfy the *equality part* or the equation $-4x + 3y \,\textcircled{=}\, -24$. This subset is represented by the straight line in Fig. 7.1. The other subset consists of all pairs of values (x, y) which satisfy the *inequality part,* or the inequality $-4x + 3y \,\textcircled{<}\, -24$. This subset is represented by the shaded area below and to the right of the straight line in Fig. 7.1.

Our conclusion is as follows: (*a*) Linear inequalities which involve two variables can be represented graphically in two dimensions by a half-space of the cartesian plane, and (*b*) the half-space consists of the line representing the equality part of the inequality and all points on one side of the straight line (representing the strict inequality). The procedure for determining the appropriate half-space is:

1 Graph the line which represents the equation.

2 Determine the side of the line satisfying the strict inequality. To make this determination, a point can be selected arbitrarily on either side of the straight line (the *origin* is often a convenient choice if it does not lie on the line) and its coordinates substituted into the inequality. If the coordinates *satisfy* the inequality, *that* side of the line is included in the **permissible half-space.** If the coordinates do not satisfy the inequality, the permissible half-space lies on the other side of the line.

EXAMPLE 5

A firm manufactures two products. The products must be processed through one department. Product A requires 4 hours per unit, and product B requires 2 hours per unit. Total production time available for the coming week is 60 hours. A restriction in planning the production schedule, therefore, is that total hours used in producing the two products cannot exceed 60; or, *if x_1 equals the number of units produced of product A and x_2 equals the number of units produced of product B,* the restriction is represented by the inequality

$$4x_1 + 2x_2 \le 60$$

There are two other restrictions implied by the variable definitions. Since each variable represents a production quantity, neither variable can be negative. These restrictions are represented by the inequalities $x_1 \ge 0$ and $x_2 \ge 0$.

The solution set of the original inequality portrays the different combinations of the two products which can be manufactured while not exceeding the 60 hours. Figure 7.2 illustrates the solution set graphically. Check to see whether the half-space has been identified correctly. The points satisfying the inequality $4x_1 + 2x_2 \le 60$ would be the half-space including all points on and to the left of the line. However, the restriction that both variables not be negative confines us to the portion of the half-space in the first quadrant. Thus, the shaded area represents the combinations of products A and B which can be produced. A further distinction can be made in Fig. 7.2. All combinations of the two products represented by points on $\overline{AB}$ would use all 60 hours. Any points in the interior of the shaded area represent combinations of the two items which will require fewer than 60 hours. Is the origin a possible decision?

Systems of Linear Inequalities

In linear programming problems, we will be dealing with *systems* of linear inequalities. Our first interest will be in determining the solution set which satisfies all the inequalities. If S_j is the solution set for linear inequality j, the set of points S which satisfies n different linear inequalities can be represented by

$$S = S_1 \cap S_2 \cap S_3 \cap \cdots \cap S_n \qquad (7.36)$$

EXAMPLE 6

Assume that the products in the last example also need to be processed through another department in addition to the original department. Assume that product A requires 3 hours per unit and that product B requires 5 hours per unit. If the second department has 75 hours available each week, the inequality describing production possibilities in this department is

$$3x_1 + 5x_2 \le 75$$

The solution set for this inequality is illustrated in Fig. 7.3. As with Fig. 7.2, the shaded area represents all combinations of products A and B which can be manufactured in the second department while not exceeding the 75 hours available.

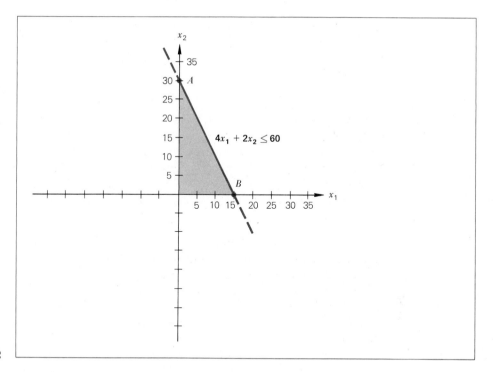

FIGURE 7.2

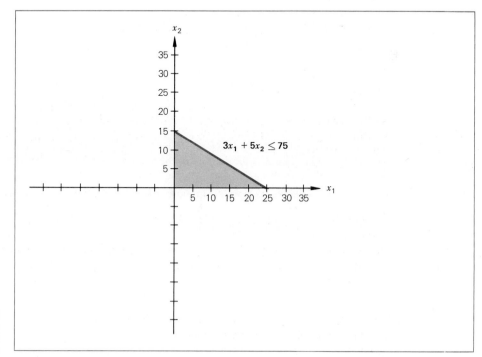

FIGURE 7.3
Production
possibilities:
Department 2.

If our objective is to determine the combinations of the two products which can be processed through *both* departments, we are looking for the solution set for the system of linear inequalities

$$4x_1 + 2x_2 \leq 60 \tag{7.37}$$

$$3x_1 + 5x_2 \leq 75 \tag{7.38}$$

$$x_1 \geq 0 \tag{7.39}$$

$$x_2 \geq 0 \tag{7.40}$$

Figure 7.4 illustrates the composite of the two solution sets. Remember that the solution set for the system is the intersection of the solution sets for each inequality. And in Fig. 7.4 the solution set for the system is the shaded area *ABCD* which is common to the two individual solution sets.

POINTS FOR THOUGHT AND DISCUSSION

Why are combinations of the two products within area *AEB* not possible? Why are combinations within *BFC* not possible? Is there any unique production characteristic associated with the combination of products represented by point *B*? How about the combinations along $\overline{AB}$? Those along $\overline{BC}$?

EXAMPLE 7

Graphically determine the solution set for the following system.

$$2x_1 + 5x_2 \leq 20 \tag{7.41}$$

$$2x_1 + 2x_2 \geq 24 \tag{7.42}$$

$$2x_1 + x_2 = 10 \tag{7.43}$$

$$x_1 \geq 0 \tag{7.44}$$

$$x_2 \geq 0 \tag{7.45}$$

SOLUTION

Figure 7.5 illustrates the system. Several observations should be noted. First, the third member of this system is an equation whose solution set is represented by a line. Second, inequalities (7.44) and (7.45) have been accounted for by graphing in the first quadrant. Third, there are no points common to Eqs. (7.41) to (7.45). Therefore the solution set contains no elements.

Area of Feasible Solutions

In Sec. 7.1 we formulated a two-variable, product-mix LP problem. The formulation is rewritten below:

$$\text{Maximize} \quad z = 5x_1 + 6x_2 \tag{7.46}$$

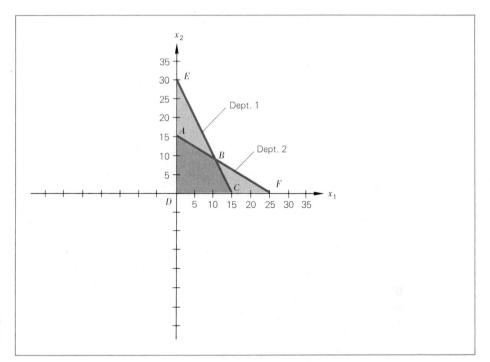

FIGURE 7.4
Production pos-
sibilities: both
departments.

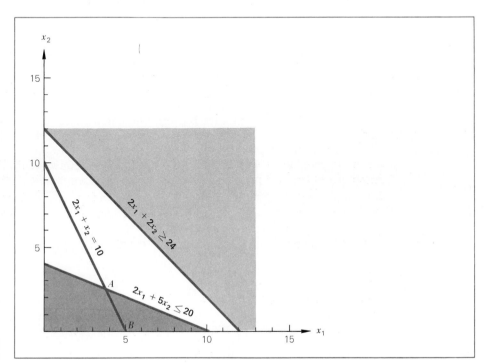

FIGURE 7.5
No solution set.

$$\text{subject to} \quad 3x_1 + 2x_2 \leq 120 \qquad \qquad \textbf{(7.47)}$$

$$4x_1 + 6x_2 \leq 260 \qquad \qquad \textbf{(7.48)}$$

$$x_1, \, x_2 \geq \quad 0 \qquad \qquad \textbf{(7.49)}$$

where x_1 and x_2 represent the number of units produced of products A and B. Since the problem involves two decision variables, we can determine the optimal solution graphically. *The first step in the graphical procedure is to identify the solution set for the system of constraints.* This solution set is often called the *area of feasible solutions.* It identifies all combinations of the decision variables which satisfy the structural and nonnegativity constraints. These combinations can be thought of as *candidates* for the optimal solution. The solution set for inequalities (7.47) to (7.49) is indicated in Fig. 7.6. This is the area of feasible solutions for the linear programming problem.

NOTE

The coordinates of points *A* and *C* are identified as the intercept values. Because of inaccuracies in the graph it may be difficult to read the exact coordinates of some points such as point *B*. To determine the exact coordinates of such points, the *equations* of the lines intersecting at the point must be solved simultaneously. To determine the coordinates (20, 30), the equality portions of (7.47) and (7.48) are solved simultaneously.

Each point within the area of feasible solutions in Fig. 7.6 represents a combination of the two products which can be produced. The problem is to determine the combination(s) which maximize the objective function.

Incorporating the Objective Function

The LP solution procedure involves a search of the area of feasible solutions for the optimal solution. Before we present the search procedure, let's first examine some characteristics of objective functions. In the product-mix problem, let's identify combinations of the two products which would generate some predetermined profit level. For instance, if we wanted to determine the different combinations of the two products which would generate a profit of $120, we would set the objective function equal to 120:

$$5x_1 + 6x_2 = 120$$

The solution set for this equation is indicated in Fig. 7.7. If we are interested in determining the combinations yielding a profit of $180, we would determine the solution set for the equation

$$5x_1 + 6x_2 = 180$$

This is also shown in Fig. 7.7. Similarly, the $240 profit line is indicated in Fig. 7.7. These three lines are often referred to as *isoprofit lines* because each point on a given line represents the same profit.

Note that for these three profit lines we are interested in the portions which

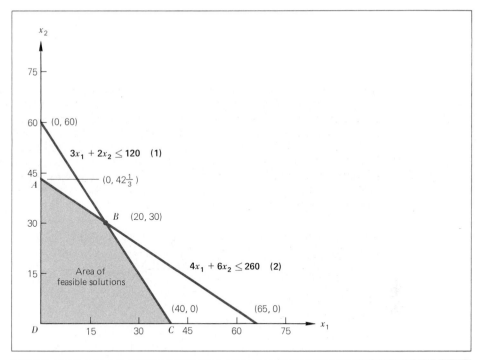

FIGURE 7.6

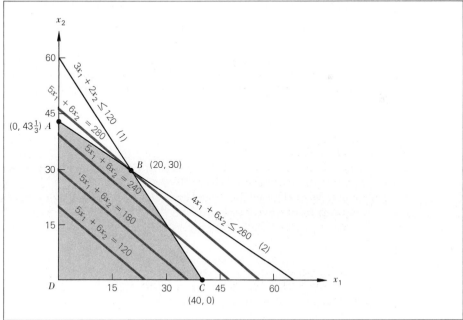

FIGURE 7.7
Isoprofit lines.

lie within the area of feasible solutions. For the \$240 line there are some combinations of the two products which would generate a combined profit of \$240 but are not within the area of feasible solutions. An example of such a combination is 48 units of product A and no units of product B.

Observe from the three profit lines that profit levels increase as the lines move outward from the origin. It also appears that the three profit lines are parallel to one another. This can be verified quickly by rewriting the profit function

$$z = 5x_1 + 6x_2 \qquad\qquad (7.50)$$

in the slope-intercept form. In Fig. 7.7 x_2 is equivalent to y (if we had named our variables x and y). If we solve Eq. (7.50) for x_2, we get

$$x_2 = \frac{-5}{6} x_1 + \frac{z}{6} \qquad\qquad (7.51)$$

The slope for the objective function is $-5/6$, and it is not influenced by the value of z. It is determined solely by the coefficients of the two variables in the objective function.

The x_2 (or y) intercept is defined by $(0, z/6)$. It is apparent that as z changes in value, so does the x_2 intercept. If z increases in value, so does the x_2 intercept, meaning that the isoprofit line moves up and to the right. If we are interested in maximizing profit, we want to move the profit line as far outward as possible while still touching a point within the area of feasible solutions. In sliding outward from the $240 line, the last point to be touched is B, with coordinates (20, 30). This point lies on the $280 profit line. *Our conclusion: Profit is maximized at a value of $280 when 20 units and 30 units are manufactured, respectively, of products A and B.*

EXAMPLE 8

Minimization Problem Determine the optimal solution to the linear programming problem

$$
\begin{aligned}
\text{Minimize} \quad & z = 3x_1 + 6x_2 \\
\text{subject to} \quad & 4x_1 + x_2 \geq 20 \\
& x_1 + x_2 \leq 20 \\
& x_1 + x_2 \geq 10 \\
& x_1, x_2 \geq 0
\end{aligned}
$$

SOLUTION

Figure 7.8*a* indicates the area of feasible solutions. In an effort to determine the optimal solution, let's determine the orientation of the objective function. Let's assume an arbitrary value for z, say 60. The equation

$$3x_1 + 6x_2 = 60$$

is graphed in Fig. 7.8*b*. To determine the direction of movement of the objective function, we can choose a point on either side of the line. If we select the origin, we find the value of the objective function at $(0, 0)$ is

$$
\begin{aligned}
z &= 3(0) + 6(0) \\
&= 0
\end{aligned}
$$

The value at the origin is less than 60, and our conclusion is that movement of the objective function toward the origin results in *lower* values of z. Since we want to minimize z, we will want to move the objective function, parallel to itself, as close to the origin as

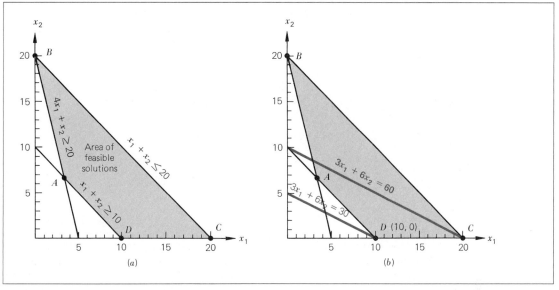

FIGURE 7.8

possible while still having it touch a point in the area of feasible solutions. The last point touched before the function moves entirely out of the area of feasible solutions is D, or $(10, 0)$. The minimum value of z is computed as

$$z = 3(10) + 6(0)$$
$$= 30$$

Corner-Point Solutions

The search procedure can be simplified if we take advantage of the joint characteristics of the area of feasible solutions and the objective function. A *convex set* is a set of points such that if any two arbitrarily selected points within the set are connected by a straight line, all elements on the line segment are also members of the set. Figure 7.9 illustrates the difference between a convex set and a nonconvex set. The set of points in Fig. 7.9*b* represents a convex set. If any two points within the set are connected by a line segment, each point on the line segment will also be a member of the set. In contrast to this, Fig. 7.9*a* illustrates a nonconvex set. For this set there are many pairs of points like A and B for which the connecting line segment contains points that are *not* members of the set.

This leads us to the following statements which are of fundamental importance in linear programming.

1   The solution set for a group of linear inequalities is a convex set. Therefore, the area of feasible solutions (if one exists) for a linear programming problem is a convex set.

2   Given a linear objective function in a linear programming problem, the optimal solution will always include a corner point on the area of feasible solutions. This is true regardless of the slope of the objective function and for either maximization or minimization problems.

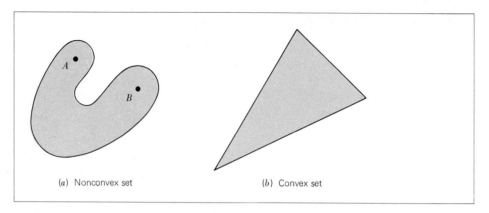

FIGURE 7.9

(a) Nonconvex set   (b) Convex set

The second statement simply implies that when a linear objective function is shifted through a convex area of feasible solutions, the last point touched before it moves entirely outside the area will include at least one corner point.

Therefore, the *corner-point method* for solving linear programming problems is as follows:

CORNER-POINT METHOD

I Graphically identify the area of feasible solutions.
II Determine the coordinates of each corner point on the area of feasible solutions.
III Substitute the coordinates of the corner points into the objective function to determine the corresponding value of z.
IV An optimal solution occurs in a maximization problem at the corner point yielding the highest value of z and in a minimization problem at the corner point yielding the lowest value of z.

EXAMPLE 9

In the product-mix example in this section, the objective function to be maximized is $z = 5x_1 + 6x_2$. Corner points on the area of feasible solutions were $(0, 0)$, $(0, 43\frac{1}{3})$, $(20, 30)$, and $(40, 0)$. Substituting these into the objective function, we arrive at the figures in Table 7.10. Note that an optimal solution occurs at $x_1 = 20$ and $x_2 = 30$, resulting in a maximum value for z of 280.

EXAMPLE 10

For Example 8, Fig. 7.8 indicates four corner points on the area of feasible solutions. By using the corner-point method, the corner points and respective values of the objective function are summarized in Table 7.11. Given that the objective is to minimize z, the optimal solution occurs when $x_1 = 10$ and $x_2 = 0$ and $z = 30$.

Had the objective been to maximize z in this problem, the maximum value of 120 would have resulted when $x_1 = 0$ and $x_2 = 20$.

TABLE 7.10

CORNER POINT	(x_1, x_2)	$z = 5x_1 + 6x_2$
A	$(0, 0)$	$5(0) + 6(0)\ \ = 0$
B	$(0, 43\frac{1}{3})$	$5(0) + 6(43\frac{1}{3}) = 260$
C	$(20, 30)$	$5(20) + 6(30) = 280*$
D	$(40, 0)$	$5(40) + 7(0)\ \ = 200$

TABLE 7.11

CORNER POINT	(x_1, x_2)	$z = 3x_1 + 6x_2$
A	$(3\frac{1}{3}, 6\frac{2}{3})$	$3(3\frac{1}{3}) + 6(6\frac{2}{3}) = 50$
B	$(0, 20)$	$3(0) + 6(20)\ \ = 120$
C	$(20, 0)$	$3(20) + 6(0)\ \ = 60$
D	$(10, 0)$	$3(10) + 6(0)\ \ = 30*$

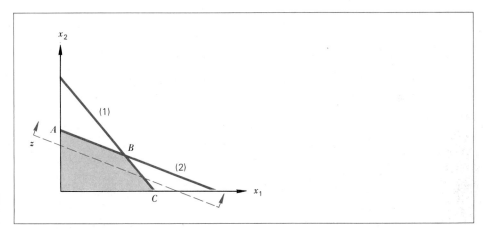

FIGURE 7.10
Alternative optimal solutions.

Alternative Optimal Solutions

In the corner-point method it was stated that an optimal solution will always occur at a corner point on the area of feasible solutions. There is the possibility of more than one optimal solution. Figure 7.10 illustrates a case where the objective function has the same slope as constraint (2). If the objective function is improved by moving out, away from the origin, the last points touched <u>before</u> the function moves outside the area of feasible solutions are all points on $\overline{AB}$. In this situation there would exist an infinite number of points, each resulting in the same maximum value of z. For situations such as this, we say that there are *alternative optimal solutions* to the problem.

Two conditions need to be satisfied in order for alternative optimal solutions to exist: (1) *the objective function must be parallel to a constraint which forms an edge or boundary on the area of feasible solutions;* (2) *the constraint must form a boundary on the area of feasible solutions in the direction of optimal movement of the objective function; that is, the constraint must be a binding constraint.* This second condition would be violated in Fig. 7.10 if the problem were one of minimization, i.e., if we desired to shift the objective function in the other direction.

When using the corner-point method, alternative optimal solutions are indicated if a *tie* occurs for the optimal value of the objective function. The alternative optimal solutions occur at the "tying" corner points, as well as along the entire line segment connecting the two points.

EXAMPLE 11 ▰▰▰▰▰▰▰▰▰▰▰▰▰▰▰▰▰▰▰▰▰▰▰▰▰▰

Solve the following linear programming problem by the corner-point method.

$$\text{Maximize} \quad z = 20x_1 + 15x_2 \tag{7.52}$$

$$\text{subject to} \quad 3x_1 + 4x_2 \le 60 \tag{7.53}$$

$$4x_1 + 3x_2 \le 60 \tag{7.54}$$

$$x_1 \le 10 \tag{7.55}$$

$$x_2 \le 12 \tag{7.56}$$

$$x_1, \, x_2 \ge 0 \tag{7.57}$$

SOLUTION

The area of feasible solutions is shown in Fig. 7.11. The corner points and their respective values for z are summarized in Table 7.12.

Note that there is a tie for the highest value of z between points D and E. The slope of the objective function, is the same as for constraint (7.54). In Fig. 7.11 there are infinitely many alternative optimal solutions along $\overline{DE}$.

POINTS FOR THOUGHT AND DISCUSSION ▰▰▰▰▰▰▰▰▰▰▰▰▰

There are several implications of alternative optimal solutions. One issue is the set of criteria which might be chosen to select the solution to implement. These criteria can include tangible as well as intangible factors. To serve as a basis for discussion, return to the product-mix problem on pages 262–264 [Eqs. (7.46) to (7.49)] and re-solve using the new objective function $z = 4x_1 + 6x_2$. You should verify that alternative optimal solutions exist along $\overline{AB}$ in Fig. 7.6. Discuss the implications of selecting point A versus point B. Consider such issues as the number of production hours consumed in each department and the *mix* of products to be offered to consumers.

No Feasible Solution

The system of constraints in a linear programming problem may have no points which satisfy all constraints. In such cases, there are no points in the solution set, and the linear programming problem is said to have *no feasible solution*. Figure 7.12 illustrates a problem having no feasible solution. Constraint 1 is a "less than or equal to" type while constraint 2 is a "greater than or equal to" type. A problem can certainly have both types of constraints. In this case the set of points satisfying one constraint includes none of the points satisfying the other.

Unbounded Solutions

Figure 7.13 illustrates what is termed an *unbounded solution space.* The two constraints appear to be ($\ge$) types with the resulting solution space extending

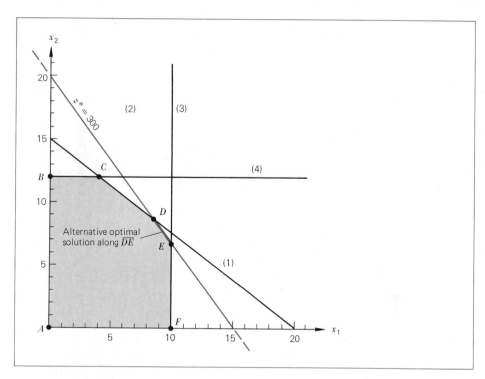

FIGURE 7.11
Alternative optimal solutions.

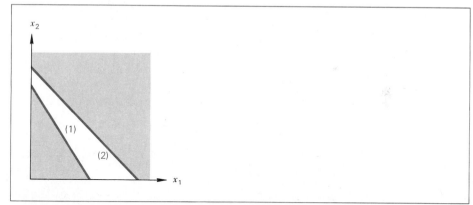

FIGURE 7.12
No feasible solution.

TABLE 7.12

CORNER POINT	(x_1, x_2)	$z = 20x_1 + 15x_2$
A	(0, 0)	$20(0) + 15(0) = 0$
B	(0, 12)	$20(0) + 15(12) = 180$
C	(4, 12)	$20(4) + 15(12) = 260$
D	$(\frac{60}{7}, \frac{60}{7})$	$20(\frac{60}{7}) + 15(\frac{60}{7}) = 300^*$
E	$(10, \frac{20}{3})$	$20(10) + 15(\frac{20}{3}) = 300^*$
F	(10, 0)	$20(10) + 15(0) = 200$

outward an infinite distance—having no bound. Given an unbounded solution space, the optimal value of the objective function may be bounded or unbounded. If in Fig. 7.13 the *direction of improvement* in the objective function is toward the origin—typically a minimization objective—there would be a

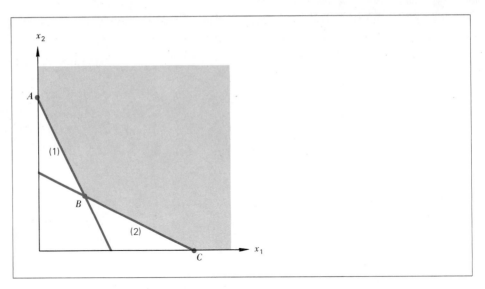

FIGURE 7.13
Unbounded so-
lution space.

bound on the value of z and it would be realized at corner point A, B, or C. However, if the direction of improvement is outward, away from the origin—typically maximization—the objective function can be shifted out an infinite distance. Thus, there is no bound on the value of z and the problem is said to have an ***unbounded solution.***

NOTE

An unbounded solution space is a *necessary condition*, but not a sufficient condition, for the occurrence of an unbounded solution.

Section 7.3 Follow-up Exercises

In Exercises 1 to 6, graphically determine the permissible half-space which satisfies the inequality.

1	$2x + 3y \le 15$	2	$-4x + 2y \ge 24$
3	$0.5x - y \ge -5$	4	$-x + 2.5y \le 10$
5	$1.5x + 3y \le -18$	6	$-x - 2y \ge 7$

In Exercises 7 to 10, graphically determine the solution space (if one exists).

7	$2x - 4y \le 20$	8	$3x + 2y \le 18$
	$3x + 2y \ge 18$		$x + 4y \le 8$
9	$4x - 2y \ge 12$	10	$2x + 2y \le 16$
	$x \le 15$		$3x - y \ge 18$
	$y \le 6$		$x + 2y = 10$
			$x \ge 0$
			$y \ge 0$

For the following LP problems, graph the area of feasible solutions (if one exists) and solve by the corner-point method.

11　Maximize　$z = 9x_1 + 3x_2$
　　subject to　$x_1 + x_2 \leq 20$
　　　　　　　　$2x_1 + x_2 \leq 32$
　　　　　　　　$x_1, x_2 \geq 0$

12　Minimize　$z = 3x_1 + 6x_2$
　　subject to　$3x_1 + 2x_2 \geq 36$
　　　　　　　　$4x_1 + 5x_2 \geq 90$
　　　　　　　　$x_1, x_2 \geq 0$

13　Maximize　$z = 30x_1 + 20x_2$
　　subject to　$3x_1 + x_2 \leq 18$
　　　　　　　　$x_1 + x_2 \leq 12$
　　　　　　　　$x_1 \geq 2$
　　　　　　　　$x_2 \geq 2$
　　　　　　　　$x_1, x_2 \geq 0$

14　Minimize　$z = 10x_1 + 16x_2$
　　subject to　$x_1 \leq 400$
　　　　　　　　$x_2 \geq 200$
　　　　　　　　$x_1 + x_2 = 500$
　　　　　　　　$x_1, x_2 \geq 0$

15　Maximize　$z = 10x_1 + 15x_2$
　　subject to　$x_1 + x_2 \geq 20$
　　　　　　　　$2x_1 + x_2 \leq 48$
　　　　　　　　$x_1 \leq 20$
　　　　　　　　$x_1 + x_2 \leq 30$
　　　　　　　　$x_1, x_2 \geq 0$

16　Maximize　$z = 2x_1 + 5x_2$
　　subject to　$x_1 + x_2 \leq 16$
　　　　　　　　$x_1 \leq 12$
　　　　　　　　$x_1 \geq 8$
　　　　　　　　$x_2 \leq 10$
　　　　　　　　$x_2 \geq 4$
　　　　　　　　$x_1, x_2 \geq 0$

17　Maximize　$z = 16x_1 + 8x_2$
　　subject to　$2x_1 + x_2 \leq 30$
　　　　　　　　$x_1 + 2x_2 \leq 24$
　　　　　　　　$x_1, x_2 \geq 0$

18　Maximize　$z = 6x_1 + 5x_2$
　　subject to　$2x_1 + 4x_2 \leq 40$
　　　　　　　　$x_1 + 2x_2 \leq 30$
　　　　　　　　$1.5x_1 + x_2 \geq 50$
　　　　　　　　$x_1, x_2 \geq 0$

19　Maximize　$z = 5x_1 + 4x_2$
　　subject to　$20x_1 + 10x_2 \leq 60$
　　　　　　　　$40x_1 + 32x_2 \leq 160$
　　　　　　　　$x_1 \leq 2.5$
　　　　　　　　$x_2 \leq 4$
　　　　　　　　$x_1, x_2 \geq 0$

20　Minimize　$z = 20x_1 + 5x_2$
　　subject to　$x_1 + x_2 \geq 12$
　　　　　　　　$4x_1 + x_2 \geq 24$
　　　　　　　　$x_1 \geq 3$
　　　　　　　　$x_2 \leq 18$
　　　　　　　　$5x_1 + 4x_2 \leq 120$
　　　　　　　　$x_1, x_2 \geq 0$

21　Maximize　$z = 15x_1 + 20x_2$
　　subject to　$x_1 + x_2 \geq 48$
　　　　　　　　$6x_1 + 9x_2 \leq 216$
　　　　　　　　$15x_1 + 10x_2 \leq 360$
　　　　　　　　$x_1, x_2 \geq 0$

22　Minimize　$z = 4x_1 + 2x_2$
　　subject to　$4x_1 + 6x_2 \leq 48$
　　　　　　　　$x_1 + x_2 \geq 15$
　　　　　　　　$x_1, x_2 \geq 0$

23　A firm manufactures two products. Each product must be processed through two departments. Product A requires 2 hours per unit in department 1 and 4 hours per unit in department 2. Product B requires 3 hours per unit in department 1 and 2 hours per unit in department 2. Departments 1 and 2 have, respectively, 60 and 80 hours available each week. Profit margins for the two products are, respectively, $3 and $4 per unit. If x_j equals the number of units produced of product j, (a) formulate the linear programming model for determining the product-mix which maximizes total profit and (b) solve using the corner-point method. (c) Fully interpret the results indicating the recommended product-mix. What percentage of daily capacity will be utilized in each department?

24　The dietician at a local penal institution is preparing the menu for tonight's *light*

TABLE 7.13

	FOOD 1	FOOD 2	MINIMUM DAILY REQUIREMENT
Vitamin 1	2 mg/oz	3 mg/oz	18 mg
Vitamin 2	4 mg/oz	2 mg/oz	22 mg
Cost per oz	$0.12	$0.15	

meal. Two food items will be served at the meal. The dietician is concerned about achieving minimum daily requirement of two vitamins. Table 7.13 summarizes vitamin content per ounce of each food, the minimum daily requirements of each, and cost per ounce of each food. If x_j equals the number of ounces of food j (a) formulate the linear programming model for determining the quantities of the two foods which will minimize the cost of the meal while ensuring that at least minimum levels of both vitamins will be satisfied. (b) Solve using the corner-point method indicating what the minimum-cost meal will consist of and its cost. What percentages of the minimum daily requirements for each vitamin will be realized?

7.4 COMPUTER SOLUTION METHODS

The graphical approach is obviously limited to two-variable problems. The sample applications discussed earlier (Examples 1 to 4) are quite modest in size when compared with typical applications in today's organizations. These examples could be solved manually by algebraic procedures such as the *simplex method* presented in the next chapter. However, the author would recommend solving these examples by such procedures only to the masochistically inclined.

In actual applications, LP problems are solved by computer methods. There are many efficient computer codes available today through computer manufacturers, software "houses," and universities. As a user of LP models, one need not always be concerned about the internal nuts and bolts of the solution method.* Rather, effective use of these models can be made if a person (1) fully understands the LP model and its assumptions, (2) is skillful in recognizing an LP problem, (3) is skillful in problem formulation, (4) can arrange for solution by a computer package, and (5) is capable of interpreting the output from such packages.

Requirements of the Simplex Method

Before discussing computer solution methods we need to mention some preliminaries. Most computer methods are based upon algebraic solution procedures. The simplex method is the most popular algebraic procedure and it is discussed in Chap. 8. There are three requirements in solving a linear programming problem by the simplex method:

REQUIREMENTS OF SIMPLEX METHOD

   I All constraints must be stated as equations.
   II The right side of a constraint cannot be negative.
  III All variables are restricted to nonnegative values.

---

* However, there is no question that one *can* be a better user of these packages if one *does* understand the nuts and bolts.

Regarding the *first requirement,* the simplex method is a special routine for solving systems of simultaneous equations. Most linear programming problems contain constraints which are inequalities. Before we solve by the simplex method, these inequalities must be restated as equations. The transformation from inequalities to equations varies depending on the nature of the inequality.

For each "less than or equal to" ($\leq$) constraint a nonnegative variable, called a **slack variable,** is added to the left side of the constraint. This variable serves the function of balancing the two sides of the equation.

EXAMPLE 12

Consider the two constraints

$$2x_1 + 3x_2 \leq 50 \qquad \text{(department 1)}$$
$$4x_1 + 2x_2 \leq 60 \qquad \text{(department 2)}$$

where x_1 and x_2 equal, respectively, the number of units produced of products A and B. Assume that the two constraints represent limited labor availability in two departments; the coefficients on the variables represent the number of hours required to produce a unit of each product, and the right sides of the constraints equal the number of hours available in each department.

The treatment of these constraints is to add a slack variable to the left side of each. Or, the constraints are rewritten as

$$2x_1 + 3x_2 + S_1 = 50 \qquad \text{(department 1)}$$
$$4x_1 + 2x_2 + S_2 = 60 \qquad \text{(department 2)}$$

The slack variables S_1 and S_2 keep the two sides of their respective equations in balance. They also have a meaning which is easy to understand. They represent, in this problem, the number of unused hours in each department. For example, $x_1 = 5$ and $x_2 = 10$ suggests producing 5 units of product A and 10 units of product B. If these values are substituted into the two constraints, we have

$$2(5) + 3(10) + S_1 = 50$$
$$4(5) + 2(10) + S_2 = 60$$

or

$$40 + S_1 = 50 \qquad \text{(department 1)}$$
$$40 + S_2 = 60 \qquad \text{(department 2)}$$

In other words, 40 hours would be used for production in each department. The slack variables would have to assume respective values of $S_1 = 10$ and $S_2 = 20$ to balance the equations. The interpretation of these values is that producing 5 units of product A and 10 units of product B will result in 10 hours being left over in department 1 and 20 hours being left over in department 2.

Note that slack variables become additional variables in the problem and must be treated like any other variables. This means that they are subject to requirement 3; that is, they cannot assume negative values.

For each "greater than or equal to" ($\geq$) constraint a nonnegative variable, called a **surplus variable,** is subtracted from the left side of the constraint. This variable serves the same function as a slack variable: it keeps the two sides of the equation in balance.

EXAMPLE 13

Assume in Example 12 that combined production of the two products must be at least 25 units. The constraint representing this third condition is

$$x_1 + x_2 \geq 25$$

Before we solve by the simplex method, the inequality must be transformed into the equivalent equation

$$x_1 + x_2 - E_3 = 25.$$

The subscript on the surplus variable indicates the constraint number; it does not indicate that this is the third surplus variable. If $x_1 = 20$ and $x_2 = 35$, the surplus variable E_3 must equal 30 for the equation to be satisfied. The interpretation of the surplus variable is that combined production exceeds the minimum quantity by 30 units.

For each ($\geq$) constraint and each ($=$) constraint, a nonnegative variable, called an **artificial variable,** is added to the left side of the constraint.

The artificial variable has no real meaning in the problem; its only function is to provide a convenient starting point (initial solution) for the simplex. And yes—*for ($\geq$) constraints you add the artificial variable in addition to subtracting a surplus variable.*

EXAMPLE 14

Transform the following constraint set into the standard form required by the simplex method:

$$\begin{aligned}
x_1 + x_2 &\leq 100 \\
2x_1 + 3x_2 &\geq 40 \\
x_1 - 2x_2 &= 25 \\
x_1, x_2 &\geq 0
\end{aligned}$$

SOLUTION

The transformed constraint set is

$$x_1 + x_2 + S_1 \qquad\qquad\qquad = 100 \qquad\qquad (1)$$

$$2x_1 + 3x_2 \qquad - E_2 + A_2 \quad = 40 \qquad\qquad (2)$$

$$x_1 - 2x_2 \qquad\qquad\qquad + A_3 = 25 \qquad\qquad (3)$$

$$x_1, x_2, S_1, E_2, A_2, A_3 \geq 0$$

Note that each supplemental variable (slack, surplus, artificial) is assigned a subscript which corresponds to the constraint number. *

Slack and surplus variables usually are assigned objective function coefficients of 0. This usually makes sense when their meaning is considered, although there can be exceptions. Since artificial variables have no real meaning in a problem, they are usually assigned objective function coefficients which make them extremely undesirable. *For maximization problems artificial variables should be assigned objective function coefficients of* $-M$, *where* M *is assumed to be a very large number, much larger than any other coefficient in the objective function. For minimization problems artificial variables should be assigned objective function coefficients of* $+M$. The very large negative (positive) contribution in a maximization (minimization) problem creates no incentive for an artificial variable to be positive. In fact, there is a very great incentive to make each artificial variable 0. Think about it!

EXAMPLE 15

If the original objective function in Example 14 had been

$$\text{Maximize} \quad z = 5x_1 + 10x_2$$

then it would be revised to have the form

$$\text{Maximize} \quad z = 5x_1 + 10x_2 + 0S_1 + 0E_1 - MA_1 - MA_2$$

The *second requirement* of the simplex method is that the right side of any constraint equation not be negative. If a constraint has a negative right side, the constraint can be multiplied by -1 to make the right side positive.

EXAMPLE 16

For the following constraints, make the right side positive.

(a) $2x_1 - 5x_2 \leq -10$ (b) $x_1 + 6x_2 \geq -100$ (c) $5x_1 - 2x_2 = -28$

SOLUTION

(a) Multiplying the constraint by -1 results in

$$-2x_1 + 5x_2 \geq 10$$

(b) Multiplying the constraint by -1 results in

$$-x_1 - 6x_2 \leq 100$$

(c) Multiplying the constraint by -1 results in

$$-5x_1 + 2x_2 = 28$$

---

* The labeling of supplemental variables may vary slightly with different textbooks.

The *third requirement* of the simplex method is that all variables be restricted to nonnegative values. There are specialized techniques for dealing with variables which *can* assume negative values; however, we will not examine these methods. The only point which should be mentioned is that slack, surplus, and artificial variables are also restricted to being nonnegative.

Basic Feasible Solutions and the Simplex

When LP problems have been converted to the *standard form* where all constraints are restated as equalities and supplemental variables have been added, the resulting system of equations has more variables than equations. Consider a generalized LP problem having the form of Eq. (7.8) on page 248. Once this problem has been transformed into the standard form, there will be m structural constraints and n' variables (real variables plus supplemental variables) where $n' > m$.* Recall from Chap. 4 that *if there is a solution to such a system of equations,* there is an infinite number of solutions.

Let's cite some definitions which are significant to later discussions. Given the standard form of an LP problem having m structural constraints and n' real and supplemental variables:

DEFINITION: FEASIBLE SOLUTION ▰▰▰▰▰▰▰▰▰

A **feasible solution** is any set of values for the n' variables which satisfies both the structural and nonnegativity constraints.

DEFINITION: BASIC SOLUTION ▰▰▰▰▰▰▰▰▰

A **basic solution** is any solution obtained by setting $(n' - m)$ variables equal to 0 and solving the system of equations for the values of the remaining m variables. The m variables solved for are called **basic variables.** These variables are said to constitute a **basis.** The remaining $(n' - m)$ variables, or those which have been assigned values of 0, are called **nonbasic variables.**

DEFINITION: BASIC FEASIBLE SOLUTION ▰▰▰▰▰▰▰▰▰

A **basic feasible solution** is a basic solution which also satisfies the nonnegativity constraints.

It can be proven that the optimal solution to a linear programming problem is a member of the set of basic feasible solutions. Thus, the optimal solution can be found by performing a search of the set of basic feasible solutions. This is what the simplex method accomplishes. It begins with a basic feasible solution consisting of two pools of variables—m basic variables and $(n' - m)$ nonbasic variables. The simplex method determines whether the objective function can be improved by exchanging a basic variable and a nonbasic variable. If an exchange will result in an improvement, an existing basic variable is set equal to 0 (becoming a nonbasic variable), an existing nonbasic variable is included in the

---

* The nonnegativity constraints are assumed for all problems and are usually not included when counting constraints.

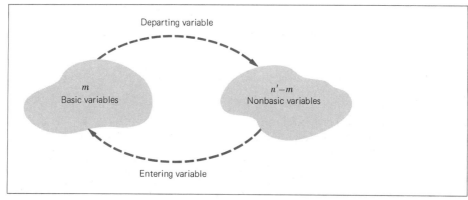

FIGURE 7.14
Simplex exchange of variables.

Maximize

$$z = 4.4x_1 + 3.8x_2 + 4.1x_3 + 3.5x_4 + 5.1x_5 + 3.2x_6$$

subject to

$x_1 + x_2 + x_3 + x_4 + x_5 + x_6$	≤ 1000	(1)
x_1	≤ 220	(2)
x_2	≤ 180	(3)
x_3	≤ 250	(4)
x_4	≤ 150	(5)
x_5	≤ 400	(6)
x_6	≤ 120	(7)
x_5	≥ 200	(8)
$x_1 + x_2$	≥ 300	(9)
$x_1, x_2, x_3, x_4, x_5, x_6$	$\geq \quad 0$	

FIGURE 7.15
Formulation of Example 3.

pool of basic variables, and the system of equations is re-solved with the new set of basic variables to form a new basic feasible solution. A determination is made again regarding whether a better solution exists. If so, another exchange takes place and the process repeats itself. The simplex method is termed an *iterative process* because a specified set of solution steps are repeated until an optimal solution is identified. The exchange of variables which takes place at each iteration is summarized in Fig. 7.14.

An Illustration of an LP Package

As mentioned previously, many LP computer packages are available, both in batch mode and online. You should check with your computer center to see which ones are available on your system. This section illustrates one interactive LP package. As you read this section you should realize that the input requirements and general format for output (results) are specific to this computer package and will differ from other packages you might use. However, the general principles illustrated are the same.

The problem solved by the package is Example 3 (grant awards). To facilitate following the example, the formulation of the problem is repeated in Fig. 7.15.

Problem Input Figure 7.16 illustrates the input and output for this problem. Note the interactive nature of the package and the way in which it prompts the user for input. The user responses are highlighted in color to distinguish them from the computer responses. The following observations should be made regarding problem input:

1 The user must initially characterize the *problem structure,* indicating by a five-digit code (*a*) whether the problem is a maximization or minimization type, (*b*) the number of real variables, (*c*) the number of (≤) constraints, (*d*) the number of (≥) constraints, and (*e*) the number of (=) constraints.

2 Once the problem structure is specified the package prompts the user for constraint parameters. This package always prompts by type of constraint; that is, information is requested first for all (≤) constraints followed by all (≥) constraints, and finally all (=) constraints. Right-hand-side constants are requested first for each constraint, followed by the variable coefficients.

3 Note that supplemental (slack, surplus, or artificial) variables do not need to be added by the user. For each constraint type the package automatically inputs the supplemental variables and assigns the appropriate objective function coefficient to each.

4 The nonnegativity restriction for all variables is assumed by the package (which is usually the case) and does not need to be explicitly accounted for during input.

5 Once the constraint parameters have been input, the package requests objective function parameters.

6 Upon completion of the objective function input, this package allows for changing data in the event that input errors have been identified.

Interpretation of Results The output section summarizes the solution. The total net benefit of the grant award program is maximized at a value of $4,526.9961 million. The optimal solution was achieved after seven simplex iterations. The section entitled "INCLUDED VARIABLES" summarizes the values of the ($m = 9$) basic variables. This section indicates the variable number, its solution value, the type of variable, and for supplemental variables the associated constraint number. The solution recommends:

1 An award of $220 million to project 1 (solar)

2 An award of $130 million to project 2 (solar)

3 An award of $250 million to project 3 (synthetic fuels)

4 An award of $400 million to project 5 (nuclear)

The values for the slack and surplus variables can be interpreted as follows:

5 The award of $130 million to project 2 is $50 million less than could have been authorized according to constraint 3

6 The award of no funds to project 4 is $150 million less than could have been authorized according to constraint 5

7 The award of no funds to project 6 is $120 million less than could have been authorized according to constraint 7

```
   SUPPLY THE FOLLOWING INFORMATION BY
   ENTERING FIVE INTEGER NUMBERS ON ONE LINE
   SEPARATED BY COMMAS.


      (1) TYPE: (MAX = 1)   (MIN = 2)

   NO. OF:

      (2)  REAL VARIABLES
      (3)  <= CONSTRAINTS
      (4)  >= CONSTRAINTS
      (5)   = CONSTRAINTS
   ?1,6,7,2,0

   CONSTRAINT INPUT
   ..........  .....

   THE RIGHT-HAND-SIDE CONSTANT AND COEFFICIENT VALUES WILL BE
   REQUESTED FOR EACH CONSTRAINT.   TO ENTER THE COEFFICIENT
   VALUES, TYPE THE VARIABLE NO. AND THE COEFF. VALUE,
   SEPARATED BY A COMMA.   ZERO COEFF. NEED NOT BE ENTERED.
   EXIT TO NEXT CONSTRAINT BY ENTERING 0,0


   CONSTRAINT NO.      1       (<= TYPE)

   RIGHT-HAND SIDE
   ?1000

   COEFFICIENTS
   ?1,1

   ?2,1

   ?3,1

   ?4,1

   ?5,1

   ?6,1

   CONSTRAINT NO.      2       (<= TYPE)

   RIGHT-HAND SIDE
   ?220

   COEFFICIENTS
   ?1,1

   ?0,0
```

FIGURE 7.16
Computer
input/output for
Example 3.

```
CONSTRAINT NO.      3     (<= TYPE)

RIGHT-HAND SIDE
?180

COEFFICIENTS
?2,1

?0,0

CONSTRAINT NO.      4     (<= TYPE)

RIGHT-HAND SIDE
?250

COEFFICIENTS
?3,1

?0,0

CONSTRAINT NO.      5     (<= TYPE)

RIGHT-HAND SIDE
?150

COEFFICIENTS
?4,1

?0,0

CONSTRAINT NO.      6     (<= TYPE)

RIGHT-HAND SIDE
?400

COEFFICIENTS
?5,1

?0,0

CONSTRAINT NO.      7     (<= TYPE)

RIGHT-HAND SIDE
?120

COEFFICIENTS
?6,1

?0,0
```

FIGURE 7.16
Continued

```
CONSTRAINT NO.     8      (>= TYPE)

RIGHT-HAND SIDE
?200

COEFFICIENTS
?5,1

?0,0

CONSTRAINT NO.     9      (>= TYPE)

RIGHT-HAND SIDE
?300

COEFFICIENTS
?1,1

?2,1

?0,0


OBJECTIVE FUNCTION INPUT

.........  .........  .....

ENTER THE VARIABLE NUMBER AND THE COEFFICIENT VALUE IN
A SIMILAR MANNER.

?1,4.4

?2,3.8

?3,4.1

?4,3.5

?5,5.1

?6,3.2

DO YOU WISH TO CHANGE ANY DATA?

  (YES=1, NO=2)
?2

OBJECTIVE FUNCTION MAXIMIZED AT      4526.9961

     7  ITERATIONS REQUIRED
```

FIGURE 7.16
Continued

```
INCLUDED VARIABLES
• • • • • • •   • • • • • • • •

VARIABLE          QUANTITY OF       VARIABLE          ASSOCIATED WITH
 NUMBER          THIS VARIABLE        TYPE           CONSTRAINT NUMBER

    1               220.00000        REAL
    2               130.00000        REAL
    3               250.00000        REAL
    5               400.00000        REAL
   11                50.00000        SLACK                 3
   13               150.00000        SLACK                 5
   15               120.00000        SLACK                 7
    7               200.00000        SURPLUS               8
    8                50.00000        SURPLUS               9
```

FIGURE 7.16
Continued

8 The award of $400 million to project 5 is $200 million greater than the $200 million minimum requested by the President

9 The combined award to projects 1 and 2 of $350 million is $50 million greater than the $300 million minimum specified by the agency's administrator

Any real or supplemental variables not listed in the "INCLUDED VARI-ABLES" section are nonbasic variables and by definition have a value of 0 in the optimal solution.

Shadow Prices

The solution to an LP problem is based upon certain assumptions and esti-mates. Once a solution is obtained, it should be analyzed carefully in light of these assumptions and estimates. This phase of the solution process is called *postoptimality analysis.* An important type of postoptimality analysis is the examination of shadow prices.

DEFINITION: SHADOW PRICE

A *shadow price* is the amount the optimal value of the objec-tive function would change if the right-hand-side of a con-straint were increased by one unit.

Since many ($\leq$) constraints represent limited resources, shadow prices are often thought of as representing the economic value of having an additional unit of a resource. Figure 7.17 illustrates the results section showing shadow prices for the grant awards example. This LP package summarizes shadow prices for all ($\leq$) constraints. Other LP packages may or may not include shadow price analysis. Those which do might include the analysis for *all types* of constraints; not just ($\leq$) types.

If you examine the original formulation in Figure 7.15 it will help in under-standing the shadow price analysis. The shadow price of 3.8 for constraint (1) suggests that if the total amount of money available for grants was increased

```
DO YOU WANT SHADOW PRICES?

(YES=1, NO=2)
?1



SHADOW PRICES
++++++ ++++++

      ASSOCIATED                          SHADOW
    WITH CONSTRAINT                        PRICE

         1                                3.8000
         2                                0.6000
         3                                0.0
         4                                0.3000
         5                                0.0
         6                                1.3000
         7                                0.0
```

FIGURE 7.17
Shadow prices
for Example 3.

from $1,000 million to $1,001 million, total net benefits would be increased by $3.8 million, increasing from the original maximum of $4,526.9961 million to $4,530.7961 million.

The shadow price of 0.6000 for constraint 2 suggests that total net benefits would be increased by $0.6000 million if the maximum investment allowed in project 1 was increased from $220 to $221 million. Remember in the optimal solution that the maximum of $220 million was awarded to project 1.

The shadow price of 0 associated with constraint 3 indicates that the value of the objective function would not change if the maximum investment allowed in project 2 was increased from $180 to $181 million. This makes sense since the optimal solution currently recommends an award of $130 million, $50 million less than the original maximum.

Interpret the remaining shadow prices for yourself. You should also make the following observations. *The shadow prices are positive for any constraint which has been satisfied as an equality in the optimal solution (no slack exists).* The optimal solution has pushed these constraints to their limits, suggesting potential value from being able to increase these limits. *The shadow prices equal 0 for any constraint which is not satisfied as an equality (slack exists).* The optimal solution has not pushed these constraints to their respective limits. Increasing these limits farther results in no additional improvement to the objective function.

Another point to be made is that shadow prices represent *marginal returns.* They indicate the change in the value of the objective function, given a unit increase in the right-hand-side constant of the corresponding constraint. The shadow price is valid for a particular range of changes in the right-hand-side constant. The shadow price of 3.8 does not suggest that an increase of $100 million in the right-hand-side constant of constraint (1) will result in an increase of 3.8 (100) = $380 million in total net benefits. The valid range for each shadow price can be determined by another type of postoptimality analysis discussed in the next section.

Sensitivity Analysis

The parameters (c_j's, b_i's, and a_{ij}'s) in LP problems frequently are best estimates of their actual values. For example, the profit contribution (c_j) assumed for a product may be based upon best estimates of selling price and variable cost per unit, which assume certain wage rates, expected processing times, and material costs. As another example, estimates of labor availability in different departments may not reflect uncertainties associated with absenteeism and personnel shifts. The point is that the parameters used to derive an optimal solution frequently cannot be determined with certainty.

Therefore, once a solution has been derived using these "assumed" values, it should be examined to determine the effects if the parameters take on values other than those used in the original formulation. This postsolution analysis is called *sensitivity analysis.* If the analysis reveals that the optimal *basis* and/or *objective function value* are affected only slightly by significant changes in the values of parameters, we say that the solution is *insensitive.* If, however, the basis and/or objective function do vary significantly with relatively minor changes in parameters, the solution is judged to be *sensitive* and probably deserves additional scrutiny.

Many LP packages provide for sensitivity analysis. Figure 7.18 illustrates this section of the results for the grant awards example. This particular package conducts sensitivity analysis for objective function coefficients (c_j's) of all real variables and right-hand-side constants (b_i's). It does not evaluate technological coefficients (a_{ij}'s).

Let's focus first on the analysis for the objective function coefficients. The actual computational procedures used to perform the sensitivity analysis vary depending upon whether a variable is a *basic variable* or *nonbasic variable*. Thus, the results are presented separately for the two types of variables.

> For c_j values, sensitivity analysis determines by how much each c_j value can change and have the current basis remain the same; that is, the same pool of basic variables remains optimal and their values are unchanged. Another way of thinking about this is that we are concerned with how much c_j values can change and still have the same corner point on the area of feasible solutions remain optimal.

In the "NON-BASIC VARIABLES" section of Fig. 7.18 "DELTA" represents the maximum allowable change in the parameter. The "LIMIT" column indicates the corresponding c_j value if the maximum change occurs. For variable 4, $c_4 = 3.5$ can change by a maximum of 0.30000 before a new optimal basis would occur. If c_4 *increases* by more than 0.30000, or exceeds the LIMIT of 3.80000, a new optimal basis will result. Another way of interpreting this value is as follows: variable 4 is a nonbasic variable, suggesting that with its original net return coefficient of 3.5, project 4 was not sufficiently attractive to get an award. This sensitivity analysis implies that if the net return coefficient is increased beyond a value of 3.8, project 4 will be more attractive and will likely be awarded a grant.

```
DO YOU WANT A SENSITIVITY ANALYSIS?

(YES=1, NO=2)
?1



SENSITIVITY ANALYSIS
+ + + + + + + + + +  + + + + + + +

OBJECTIVE FUNCTION
+ + + + + + + + +  + + + + + + +


*** NON-BASIC VARIABLES ***

VARIABLE        DELTA          LIMIT

    4          0.30000        3.80000
    6          0.60000        3.80000


*** BASIC VARIABLES ***

VARIABLE  LOWER DELTA  UPPER DELTA  LOWER LIMIT  UPPER LIMIT

   1.       -0.60000   ***********    3.80000    ***********
   3.       -0.30000   ***********    3.80000    ***********
   5.       -1.30000   ***********    3.80000    ***********
   2.       -0.30000     0.30000      3.50000      4.10000


RIGHT-HAND-SIDE CONSTANTS
+ + + + + + + + +  + + + +  + + + + + + + +

CONSTRAINT NO.  LOWER DELTA  UPPER DELTA  LOWER LIMIT  UPPER LIMIT

      1          -50.00000    50.00000     950.00000   1050.00000
      2          -50.00000   130.00000     170.00000    350.00000
      3          -50.00000  ***********    130.00000   ***********
      4          -50.00000    50.00000     200.00000    300.00000
      5         -150.00000  ***********      0.0       ***********
      6          -50.00000    50.00000     350.00000    450.00000
      7         -120.00000  ***********      0.0       ***********
      8         ***********   200.00000   ***********    400.00000
      9         ***********    50.00000   ***********    350.00000
```

FIGURE 7.18
Sensitivity
analysis for
Example 3.

EXERCISE

Interpret the sensitivity analysis for c_6.

In the "BASIC VARIABLES" section, the "LOWER DELTA" and "UPPER DELTA" columns suggest that the optimal solution can be sensitive to *decreases* and/or *increases* in the c_j value. The "LOWER LIMIT" and "UPPER LIMIT" columns express the corresponding values of c_j if it decreases by the LOWER DELTA value or increases by the UPPER DELTA value. For variable 1, the LOWER DELTA of -0.60000 says the value of c_1 (originally 4.4) can decrease by as much as 0.60000 to a LOWER LIMIT of 3.8 and the pool of basic variables and their values will remain the same. The ∗∗∗∗∗∗∗∗∗∗∗∗ in the "UPPER DELTA" column suggests that c_1 can increase by an infinite amount to an UPPER LIMIT equal to infinity (∗∗∗∗∗∗∗∗∗∗∗∗) and the optimal pool of basic variables will remain the same. To summarize this discussion in other words, the original value of $c_1 = 4.4$ was sufficiently high to result in an award of \$220 million, the maximum possible for that project. The sensitivity analysis suggests that a decrease in c_1 might eventually make other competing projects more attractive, resulting in either no award to project 1 or a reduced award. However, if c_1 increases, the attractiveness of project 1 is greater and the decision to award the maximum of \$220 million is further reinforced. We can say that the current optimal solution is somewhat *sensitive* to decreases in c_1, but *insensitive* to increases.

EXERCISE

Interpret the sensitivity analysis for c_2. Why do you think the solution is sensitive to *both* increases and decreases?

The final section of sensitivity analysis in Fig. 7.18 pertains to the right-hand-side constants ($b_i's$).

For b_i values, sensitivity analysis determines by how much each b_i value can change and have the optimal basis remain *feasible*.

For constraint (1), the sensitivity analysis indicates that $b_1 = 1,000$ can *decrease* by as much as 50 to a lower limit of 950 or increase by as much as 50 to an upper limit of 1,050 and the optimal basis will remain feasible. If b_1 falls below 950 or exceeds 1,050, the optimal basis will no longer be feasible. Stated differently, the optimal basis will remain feasible as long as the total amount to be awarded is between \$950 million and \$1,050 million. For this parameter, the optimal solution is relatively sensitive to both decreases and increases.

The b_i sensitivity analysis provides a second type of information. The range of permissible variation for the b_i parameter also indicates the range over which the corresponding shadow price is valid. For example, Fig. 7.18 suggests that the shadow price of 3.8 assigned to constraint 1 is valid for decreases of as much as 50 and increases up to 50. In other words, b_1 can increase to 1,050 and the optimal value of z will equal $4,526.9961 + 50(3.8) = 4,716.9961$. By the same token, if b_1 decreases to 950, the optimal value of z will equal $4,526.9961 - 50(3.8) = 4,336.9961$.

EXERCISE

Interpret the sensitivity analysis for b_3 and b_7.

Section 7.4 Follow-up Exercises

1 Given the formulation of the diet-mix application (Example 1) on page 249, rewrite it in standard form incorporating all supplemental variables.

2 Given the formulation of the highway maintenance application (Example 2) on page 252, rewrite it in standard form incorporating all supplemental variables.

3 Given the formulation of the grant awards application (Example 3) on page 252, rewrite it in standard form incorporating all supplemental variables.

4 Given the formulation of the petroleum blending application (Example 4) on page 256, rewrite it in standard form incorporating all supplemental variables.

5 Given the following LP problem, rewrite it in standard form incorporating all supplemental variables.

$$\text{Minimize} \quad z = 3x_1 - 5x_2 + 2x_3 + 7x_4$$
$$\text{subject to} \quad x_1 + x_2 + x_3 + x_4 \geq 25$$
$$-x_1 + 3x_2 - 2x_4 \leq -20$$
$$3x_1 - 4x_4 = 10$$
$$5x_1 - x_2 + 3x_3 + 8x_4 \leq 125$$
$$x_1 \geq 5$$
$$x_3 \leq 30$$
$$x_1, x_2, x_3, x_4 \geq 0$$

6 An LP problem has 10 decision variables, 15 ($\leq$) constraints, 24 ($\geq$) constraints, and 6 (=) constraints. When rewritten in standard form, how many variables will be included? How many supplemental variables of each type?

The following exercises are contingent upon the availability of a computerized LP package.

7 In Sec. 7.3 the LP problem on page 262 was solved using the corner-point method. Verify this result by solving with an LP package.

8 In Sec. 7.3 the LP problem in Example 8 (page 266) was solved. Verify the result by solving with an LP package.

9 Example 11 on page 270 solved an LP problem and found alternative optimal solutions. Solve using an LP package. Does your package explicitly signal alternative optimal solutions?

10 The LP problem

$$\text{Maximize} \quad z = 6x_1 + 4x_2$$
$$\text{subject to} \quad x_1 + x_2 \geq 10$$
$$3x_1 + 2x_2 \geq 15$$
$$x_1, x_2 \geq 0$$

has an unbounded solution. Solve using an LP package and determine whether your package explicitly signals this result.

11 Solve the LP problem

$$\text{Maximize} \quad z = 2x_1 + 12x_2 + 8x_3$$
$$\text{subject to} \quad 2x_1 + 2x_2 + x_3 \leq 100$$
$$x_1 - 2x_2 + 5x_3 \leq 80$$
$$10x_1 + 5x_2 + 4x_3 \leq 300$$
$$x_1, x_2, x_3 \geq 0$$

If the LP package has the capabilities, determine the shadow prices for the three constraints and conduct sensitivity analysis on the objective function coefficients and the right-hand-side constants.

12 Given the formulation of the diet-mix application (Example 1) on page 250, determine the optimal solution and interpret the results.

13 Given the formulation of the highway maintenance application (Example 2) on page 252, determine the optimal solution and interpret the results.

14 Given the formulation of the petroleum blending application (Example 4) on page 256, determine the optimal solution and interpret the results.

KEY TERMS AND CONCEPTS

ADDITIONAL EXERCISES

Exercises 1 to 7 are related to Sec. 7.2.

1 A producer of machinery wishes to maximize the profits from producing two products, product *A* and product *B*. The three major inputs for each product are steel, electricity, and work-hours. Table 7.14 summarizes the inputs per unit, available resources, and profit margin per unit. Formulate the linear programming model for this situation. Which constraint is the most restrictive?

2 In a certain area there are two warehouses which supply food to four grocery stores. Table 7.15 summarizes the delivery cost per truckload from each warehouse to each store, the required number of truckloads per store per week, and the maximum number of truckloads available per week per warehouse. Formulate a linear programming model that would determine the number of deliveries from each warehouse to each store which would minimize total delivery cost.

3 **Capital Expansion** A company is considering the purchase of some additional machinery as part of a capital expansion program. Four types of machines are being con-

TABLE 7.14

| | PRODUCT | | |
	A	B	MONTHLY TOTAL AVAILABLE
Energy	200 kWh	400 kWh	20,000 kWh
Steel	100 lb	120 lb	10,000 lb
Labor	5 h	8 h	400 h
Profit per unit	$20	$50	

TABLE 7.15

| | STORE | | | | MAXIMUM NUMBER OF TRUCKLOADS |
	1	2	3	4	
Warehouse A	$25	$50	$25	$ 75	15
Warehouse B	$75	$25	$50	$100	25
Required number of truckloads	10	15	5	10	

TABLE 7.16

| | MACHINE | | | |
	A	B	C	D
Cost	$20,000	$25,000	$18,000	$30,000
Square footage required	150	180	200	190
Daily output, units	10,000	13,000	8,000	20,000

TABLE 7.17

| | SHORTAGE AREA | | | | SURPLUS OF CARS |
	1	2	3	4	
Surplus city 1	$30	$40	$20	$55	150
Surplus city 2	45	35	30	40	120
Surplus city 3	65	30	40	50	100
Shortage of cars	80	100	75	60	

sidered. Table 7.16 indicates relevant attributes of the four machines.

The total budget for this program is $400,000. The maximum available floor space is 10,000 square feet. The company wants to maximize the output resulting from the purchase of the new machines. Define your decision variables carefully and formulate the LP model for this problem.

4   A national car rental firm is planning for the summer season. An analysis of current inventories of subcompact cars in seven cities along with projections of demands during the summer in these same cities indicate that three of these areas will be short of their needs while four of the cities will have surplus numbers of subcompact automobiles. In order to prepare for the summer season, company officials have decided to relocate cars from those cities expected to have surpluses to those expected to have shortages. The cars can be relocated by contracting with an auto transport firm. Bids have been received from the trucking firm which indicate the cost of relocating a car from a given surplus city to a given shortage city. Table 7.17 summarizes these costs along with the surpluses and shortages for the mentioned cities.

Let x_{ij} equal the number of cars relocated from surplus area i to shortage area j. If the objective is to minimize the cost of relocating these cars such that each shortage area will have its needs satisfied, formulate the LP model for this problem.

5   **Financial Portfolio**   A person is interested in investing $200,000 in a mix of investments. Table 7.18 indicates the investment choices and estimated rates of return for each. The investor wants at least 20 percent of her investment to be in government bonds. Because of the higher perceived risk of the two stocks, she has specified that the

TABLE 7.18

INVESTMENT	PROJECTED RATE OF RETURN
Mutual fund A	0.12
Mutual fund B	0.14
Money market fund	0.15
Government bonds	0.125
Stock A	0.16
Stock B	0.18

combined investment in these not exceed $30,000. The investor also has a hunch that interest rates are going to remain high and has specified that at least 30 percent of the investment should be in the money market fund. Her final investment condition is that the amount invested in mutual fund A should be no more than the amount invested in mutual fund B. The problem is to decide the amount of money to invest in each alternative so as to maximize total annual return (in dollars). Carefully define your variables and formulate the LP model for this problem.

6 **Assignment Model** A company is interested in assigning five sales representatives to five different sales districts. Management has estimated the total sales each representative would generate if assigned to the different districts for a 1-year period. Table 7.19 summarizes these sales estimates (in $1,000 units). The desire is to assign each representative to one sales district in such a way that annual sales are maximized. Let $x_{ij} = 1$ if representative i is assigned to district j and let $x_{ij} = 0$ if representative i is not assigned to district j. Formulate the LP model for this problem (remembering that each representative must be assigned and each district must be assigned a representative).

7 **Cargo Loading** The owner of a cargo ship is considering the nature of the next shipment. Four different commodities are being offered for shipment. Table 7.20 summarizes their weight, volume, and revenue-generating characteristics. The cargo ship has three cargo holds, each characterized by weight and volume capacities. The forward hold has a weight capacity of 100 tons and volume capacity of 6,000 cubic feet. The center hold has a weight capacity of 140 tons and volume capacity of 8,000 cubic feet. The aft hold has a weight capacity of 80 tons and volume capacity of 5,000 cubic feet. The problem is to decide how much of each commodity should be accepted for shipment if the objective is to maximize total revenue. Specifically, it must be decided how many tons of each commodity should be placed in each hold while not exceeding the weight and volume capacities. Let x_{ij} equal the number of tons of commodity i placed in hold j and formulate the LP model for this problem.

Exercises 8 to 13 are related to Sec. 7.3

For the following LP problems, graph the area of feasible solutions (if one exists) and solve by the corner-point method.

8   Maximize $z = 8x_1 + 3x_2$
     subject to $x_1 = x_2$
            $2x_1 + 5x_2 \leq 40$
            $x_1, x_2 \geq 0$

9   Minimize $z = 15x_1 + 6x_2$
     subject to $x_1 + x_2 \geq 24$
            $x_2 \geq 4$
            $3x_1 + 2x_2 \leq 30$
            $x_1 \geq 0$

10   Maximize $z = 2x_1 + 4x_2$
     subject to $2x_1 + 2x_2 \leq 10$
            $-x_1 + x_2 \geq 8$
            $x_1, x_2 \geq 0$

11   Maximize $z = 3x_1 + 3x_2$
     subject to $4x_1 + 3x_2 \geq 12$
            $2x_1 + 3x_2 \geq -6$
            $x_1, x_2 \geq 0$

TABLE 7.19

SALES REP.	DISTRICT				
	1	2	3	4	5
1	100	120	80	95	140
2	90	100	110	105	75
3	150	140	120	130	100
4	120	140	100	100	120
5	90	100	105	95	80

TABLE 7.20

COMMODITY	WEIGHT OFFERED, TONS	VOLUME, FT³/TON	REVENUE, $ PER TON
1	200	70	$1,250
2	100	50	900
3	80	60	1,000
4	150	75	1,200

12 Minimize $z = 4x_1 + 4x_2$
    subject to $x_1 + 3x_2 \le 24$
    $3x_1 + x_2 \ge 26$
    $x_1 - x_2 = 6$
    $x_1, x_2 \ge 0$

13 Maximize $z = 3x_1 + 2x_2$
    subject to $x_1 + 2x_2 \ge 6$
    $9x_1 + 6x_2 \le 108$
    $x_1 \ge 8$
    $x_2 \ge 4$

Exercises 14 to 22 are related to Sec. 7.4.

14 Given the following LP problem, rewrite it in standard form incorporating all supplemental variables.

$$\text{Maximize} \quad z = 4x_1 - 2x_2 + 5x_3$$
$$\text{subject to} \quad x_1 + x_2 + x_3 \ge 30$$
$$2x_1 - 3x_2 \le -15$$
$$x_1 + 4x_2 + 5x_3 \ge 40$$
$$x_1 \ge 5$$
$$-2x_2 \le -4$$
$$x_1, x_2, x_3 \ge 0$$

15 Given the following LP problem, rewrite it in standard form incorporating all supplemental variables.

$$\text{Minimize} \quad z = 3x_1 + 2x_2 + 4x_3$$
$$\text{subject to} \quad 5x_1 - 3x_2 + 2x_3 \le 50$$
$$x_1 + x_2 + x_3 \ge 24$$
$$3x_1 - 2x_3 \ge -15$$
$$x_2 \le 20$$
$$x_1 = 2x_3$$
$$x_1, x_2, x_3 \ge 0$$

16 An LP problem has 50 decision variables, 70 ($\le$) constraints, 30 ($\ge$) constraints, and 10 ($=$) constraints. When rewritten in standard form, how many variables will be included? How many supplemental variables of each type?

17 An LP problem has 200 decision variables, 150 ($\le$) constraints, 100 ($\ge$) constraints, and 25 ($=$) constraints. When rewritten in standard form, how many variables will be included? How many supplemental variables of each type?

18   Using a computerized LP package, solve the following problem:

$$\text{Maximize} \quad z = 3x_1 + 10x_2 + 4x_3 + 6x_4$$
$$\text{subject to} \quad 2x_1 + 2x_2 + 5x_3 + x_4 \leq 50$$
$$x_1 - 2x_2 + x_3 + 5x_4 \leq 40$$
$$10x_1 + 5x_2 + 2x_3 + 4x_4 \leq 150$$
$$x_1, x_2, x_3, x_4 \geq 0$$

19   Using a computerized LP package, solve the LP problem stated in Exercise 14.
20   Using a computerized LP package, solve the LP problem stated in Exercise 15.
21   Using a computerized LP package, solve the financial portfolio problem in Exercise 5. Fully interpret the results.
22   Using a computerized LP package, solve the cargo loading problem in Exercise 7. Fully interpret the results.

CHAPTER TEST

1   Graphically determine the solution, if one exists, for this system of inequalities:

$$x_1 - x_2 \geq 5$$
$$x_1 + x_2 \leq 15$$
$$x_1 \qquad \leq 20$$
$$x_1, x_2 \geq 0$$

2   A company manufactures and sells five products. Costs per unit and selling price are given in Table 7.21. If the objective is to maximize total profit, formulate a linear programming model having the following constraints: at least 20 units of product A and at least 10 units of product B must be produced; sufficient raw materials are not available for total production in excess of 75 units; the number of units produced of products C and E must be equal.

3   Solve the following problem using the corner-point method.

$$\text{Maximize} \quad z = 1.5x_1 + 3x_2$$
$$\text{subject to} \quad x_1 + x_2 \geq 10$$
$$5x_1 + 10x_2 \leq 120$$
$$x_1 \qquad \leq 8$$
$$x_2 \leq 6$$
$$x_1, x_2 \geq 0$$

4   Discuss the meaning and significance of (a) shadow prices and (b) sensitivity analysis.

5   Rewrite the following problem in standard form incorporating all supplemental variables.

$$\text{Minimize} \quad z = 10x_1 + 5x_2 + 15x_3$$
$$\text{subject to} \quad x_1 + x_2 + x_3 \leq 40$$
$$3x_1 - 5x_2 + 4x_3 \geq 25$$
$$2x_1 \qquad - 3x_3 \leq -10$$
$$x_1 + x_2 \qquad = 24$$
$$x_1, x_2, x_3 \geq 0$$

TABLE 7.21	Product				
	A	B	C	D	E
Cost per unit	$50	$80	$300	$25	$10
Selling price	$70	$90	$350	$50	$12

MINICASE:

CONTRACT AWARDS

The purchasing department for a state agency has requested bids for four different products. Three suppliers have submitted bids on the products. Table 7.22 summarizes the prices bid per unit for each product. Notice that suppliers did not necessarily submit bids for all four products. Also shown in Table 7.22 is the agency's required quantity for each item.

Some suppliers have indicated maximum quantities they can provide of particular products. Supplier 1 indicates that it can provide no more than 20,000 units of product 3, supplier 2 can provide no more than 12,000 units of product 2, and supplier 3 can provide no more than 18,000 units of product 1. State purchasing regulations do not require that all units of a given product be purchased from one supplier. Similarly, they do not require that contracts be awarded to the lowest bidder.

The purchasing department wants to determine how many units of each product it should purchase from each supplier so as to satisfy agency requirements at a minimum total cost.

1   Formulate the LP model for this problem, carefully defining your variables.

2   Solve the problem using a computerized LP package and fully interpret the results. Indicate the quantities of each product purchased from and the dollar amounts awarded to each supplier. Also indicate what the minimum total costs equal.

*3   Assume that the purchasing department wishes not to award more than $300,000 in contracts to any one supplier. Also, assume that supplier 3 stipulated that it should be awarded contracts of at least $200,000; if this requirement is not met, the supplier will withdraw all bids. Modify the original formulation and solve using a computerized LP package. Interpret your results and compare with the answer in part 2. (*Hint:* Formulate and solve two separate models—one which assumes that supplier 3 will have its requirement met, the other assuming that supplier 3 has withdrawn its bids.)

TABLE 7.22	PRODUCT			
SUPPLIER	1	2	3	4
1	$5.00	$7.50	$3.00	—
2	—	$7.25	$3.20	$8.75
3	$4.80	$7.75	$3.10	$9.00
Agency requirement	20,000	15,000	30,000	25,000

8

THE SIMPLEX METHOD

CHAPTER OBJECTIVES

■ Provide an understanding of the simplex method of solving LP problems

■ Illustrate the ways in which special LP phenomena evidence themselves when using the simplex method

■ Provide an understanding of the dual problem and the way in which it is formulated from a primal problem

■ Illustrate key primal-dual properties which allow the solution of one problem to be read from the solution of another problem

In this chapter we will examine the *simplex method* of solving linear programing problems. First, we will overview the nature of and requirements for using the simplex method. Following this, the technique will be presented and illustrated for solving maximization problems which contain all "less than or equal to" constraints. Next, the procedure for solving minimization problems and problems containing other types of constraints will be presented. This will be followed by a discussion of the way in which special LP phenomena, such as alternative optimal solutions, are identified through the simplex method. Finally, we will discuss the *dual* LP problem and its significance.

8.1 THE SIMPLEX PROCEDURE

Overview of the Simplex Procedure

As indicated in Chap. 7, graphical solution procedures are applicable only for linear programming problems involving two variables. We can discuss the geometry of three-variable problems; however, most of us are not skilled at three-dimensional graphics. And beyond three variables, there is no geometric frame of reference. Since most realistic applications of linear programming involve far more than two variables, there is a need for a solution procedure other than the graphical method.

The most popular nongraphical procedure is called the *simplex method.* The simplex method is a sophisticated algebraic procedure for solving systems of simultaneous equations where an objective function is to be optimized. It is an *iterative* process, which identifies a feasible starting solution. The procedure

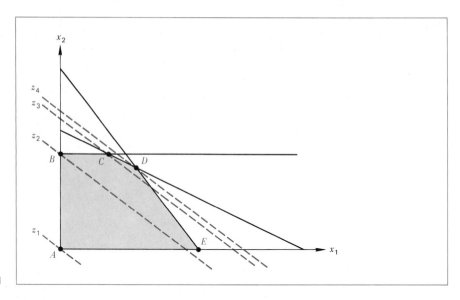

FIGURE 8.1

then searches to see whether there exists a better solution. "Better" is measured by whether the value of the objective function can be improved. If a better solution is identified, the search resumes. The generation of each successive solution requires solving a system of linear equations. The search continues until no further improvement is possible in the objective function. An important characteristic of the simplex method is that *it guarantees that each successive solution will be feasible and that the value of the objective function will be at least as good as the value in the previous solution.*

Graphically, you may envision the procedure as searching different corner points on the area of feasible solutions. The solutions found at each iteration of the simplex method represent such corner points. Not all corner points are examined, however. The search chooses only a subset of these corner points, selecting a new one if and only if the objective function is at least as good as the current corner point. This idea is illustrated by Fig. 8.1. If we assume an objective of maximization, the simplex method might move from an initial solution at corner point A to points B, C, and finally point D. Note the *isoprofit lines* z_1, z_2, z_3, and z_4. The isoprofit line moves outward, away from the origin, with each successive corner point. This illustrates a situation in which the value of z is increasing at each successive solution.

In a minimization problem successive solutions would have objective function values which are typically decreasing.

Recall from Chap. 7 that there are three requirements which must be satisfied in order to solve an LP problem by the simplex method. They are:

1 All constraints must be stated as equations.

2 The right-hand-side constant for a constraint cannot be negative.

3 All variables are restricted to nonnegative values.

Before reading on, it is suggested that you review the meaning of the terms *basis, basic variable, nonbasic variable, basic solution,* and *basic feasible solution* beginning on page 278.

Solution By Enumeration

Consider a problem having $m \leq$ constraints and n variables. Prior to solving by the simplex method, the m constraints would be changed into equations by adding m slack variables. This restatement results in a constraint set consisting of m equations and $m + n$ variables.

In Sec. 7.3 we examined the following linear programming problem:

$$\begin{aligned}
\text{Maximize} \quad & z = 5x_1 + 6x_2 \\
\text{subject to} \quad & 3x_1 + 2x_2 \leq 120 \\
& 4x_1 + 6x_2 \leq 260 \\
& x_1, x_2 \geq 0
\end{aligned}$$

Before we solve this problem by the simplex method, the constraint set must be transformed into the equivalent set

$$\begin{aligned}
3x_1 + 2x_2 + S_1 &= 120 \\
4x_1 + 6x_2 + S_2 &= 260 \\
x_1, x_2, S_1, S_2 &\geq 0
\end{aligned}$$

The constraint set involves two equations and four variables. Note that the slack variables, in addition to the real variables, are restricted to being nonnegative.

Of all the possible solutions to the constraint set, it can be proved that an optimal solution occurs when two of the four variables in this problem are set equal to zero and the system is solved for the other two variables. The question is, Which two variables should be set equal to 0 (should be *nonbasic variables*)? Let's enumerate the different possibilities. If S_1 and S_2 are set equal to 0, the constraint equations become

$$\begin{aligned}
3x_1 + 2x_2 &= 120 \\
4x_1 + 6x_2 &= 260
\end{aligned}$$

Solving for the corresponding *basic variables* x_1 and x_2 results in $x_1 = 20$ and $x_2 = 30$.

If S_1 and x_1 are set equal to 0, the system becomes

$$\begin{aligned}
2x_2 &= 120 \\
S_2 + 6x_2 &= 260
\end{aligned}$$

Solving for the corresponding basic variables x_2 and S_2 results in $x_2 = 60$ and $S_2 = -100$.

Table 8.1 summarizes the *basic solutions* (see Sec. 7.4, page 278); that is, all the solution possibilities given that two of the four variables are assigned values of 0. Solutions 2 and 5 (denoted by asterisks) have received special attention because they are not feasible. They each contain a variable which has a negative value, violating the nonnegativity restriction. However, solutions 1, 3, 4, and 6 are *basic feasible solutions* to the linear programming problem and are candidates for the optimal solution.

TABLE 8.1

SOLUTION	NONBASIC VARIABLES	BASIC VARIABLES
1	S_1, S_2	$x_1 = 20, x_2 = 30$
*2	x_1, S_1	$x_2 = 60, S_2 = -100$
3	x_1, S_2	$x_2 = 43\frac{1}{3}, S_1 = 33\frac{1}{3}$
4	x_2, S_1	$x_1 = 40, S_2 = 100$
*5	x_2, S_2	$x_1 = 65, S_1 = -75$
6	x_1, x_2	$S_1 = 120, S_2 = 260$

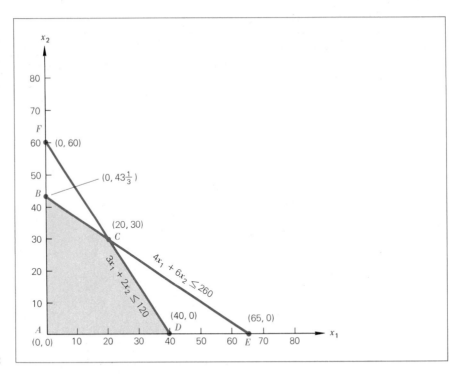

FIGURE 8.2

Figure 8.2 is the graphical representation of the set of constraints. In this figure the points of intersection (A, B, C, D, E, F) between the structural constraint lines and the nonnegativity constraints (x_1 and x_2 axes) represent the set of basic solutions. Solutions 1, 3, 4, and 6 in Table 8.1 are the basic feasible solutions and correspond to the four corner points on the area of feasible solutions in Fig. 8.2. Specifically, solution 1 corresponds to corner point C, solution 3 corresponds to corner point B, solution 4 corresponds to corner point D, and solution 6 corresponds to corner point A. Solutions 2 and 5, which are infeasible, correspond to points E and F in Fig. 8.2.

The important thing to note is that by setting all combinations of two different variables equal to 0 and solving for the remaining variables, a set of potential solutions (basic solutions) was identified for the LP problem. A subset of these solutions was automatically disqualified because it contained infeasible solutions (2 and 5). However, the remaining basic feasible solutions corresponded to the corner points on the area of feasible solutions. Since we know that an optimal solution will occur at at least one of these corner points, further examination of these will reveal an optimal solution.

For a maximization problem having $m \leq$ constraints and n variables, the addition of m slack variables results in m constraint equations containing $m + n$ variables. *An optimal solution to this problem can be found by setting n of the variables equal to 0 and solving for the remaining m variables.* In the process of selecting different combinations of n variables to be set equal to 0, the simplex (1) *will never select a combination which will result in an infeasible solution* and (2) *will ensure that each new combination selected will result in a solution which has an objective function value at least as good as the current solution.*

The Algebra of the Simplex Procedure

Before presenting the simplex method formally, let's discuss the algebra upon which the method is based. The simplex arithmetic is based upon the Gauss-Jordan procedure discussed in Sec. 4.4. A rereading of this section is suggested if you are a little rusty with this method.

Let's return to the following maximization problem:

$$\text{Maximize} \quad z = 5x_1 + 6x_2 + 0S_1 + 0S_2$$
$$\text{subject to} \quad 3x_1 + 2x_2 + S_1 \qquad\quad = 120$$
$$4x_1 + 6x_2 \qquad\quad + S_2 = 260$$
$$x_1, x_2, S_1, S_2 \geq 0$$

Note that the slack variables have been assigned objective function coefficients of 0. *Although there can be exceptions, slack and surplus variables are usually assigned coefficients of 0 in the objective function.* The reason is that these variables typically contribute nothing to the value of the objective function.

Let's illustrate how the Gauss-Jordan procedure can be used to identify the set of basic solutions. If we represent the system of equations by showing only the variable coefficients and right-hand-side constraints, we have

x_1	x_2	S_1	S_2		
3	2	1	0	120	(8.1)
4	6	0	1	260	(8.2)

Remember that the Gauss-Jordan procedure uses *row operations* to transform the original system of equations into an equivalent system. The equivalent system has the properties that only one variable remains in each equation and that the right side of the equation equals the value of that variable. In looking at the variable coefficients for this system of equations, a convenient starting point would be to declare x_1 and x_2 as nonbasic variables, setting them equal to 0. The variable coefficients for S_1 and S_2 are already in the desired form. If x_1 and x_2 both equal 0, the corresponding values of the basic variables S_1 and S_2 are $S_1 = 120$ and $S_2 = 260$.

Assume that we wish to set x_1 and S_1 equal to 0 and solve for x_2 and S_2. Compared with the original solution, we wish to replace S_1 with x_2 as a basic variable. And we would like the coefficients for x_2 and S_2 to have the form

x_1	x_2	S_1	S_2		
■	①	■	0	■	(8.3)
■	⓪	■	1	■	(8.4)

Since the coefficients for S_2 are already in the desired form, we need only to change those for x_2 from $\binom{2}{6}$ to $\binom{1}{0}$. To create the ①, we multiply Eq. (8.1) by $\frac{1}{2}$, resulting in

x_1	x_2	S_1	S_2		
$\frac{3}{2}$	1	$\frac{1}{2}$	0	60	$(8.1a) = \frac{1}{2}(8.1)$
4	6	0	1	260	(8.2)

The 6 is transformed into ⓪ by multiplying Eq. (8.1a) by -6 and adding this multiple to Eq. (8.2), or

$$
\begin{array}{cccc}
x_1 & x_2 & S_1 & S_2 \\
\end{array}
$$

x_1	x_2	S_1	S_2		
$\frac{3}{2}$	1	$\frac{1}{2}$	0	60	(8.1a)
-5	0	-3	1	-100	$(8.2a) = (8.2) + (-6) \cdot (8.1a)$

Because x_1 and S_1 were set equal to 0, the values of x_2 and S_2 can be read directly as $x_2 = 60$ and $S_2 = -100$. If you refer to Table 8.1, you will see that this solution is the same as solution 2.

If we set S_1 and S_2 equal to 0, x_1 will replace S_2 as a basic variable. For the new basis we would like the coefficients on x_1 and x_2 to have the form

x_1	x_2	S_1	S_2	
⓪	1	▮	▮	(8.5)
①	0	▮	▮	(8.6)

Starting with the last basic solution, the coefficients on x_2 are in the desired form, and we need to change those for x_1 from $\begin{pmatrix} \frac{3}{2} \\ -5 \end{pmatrix}$ to $\begin{pmatrix} 0 \\ 1 \end{pmatrix}$. The ① is created by multiplying the Eq. (8.2a) by $-\frac{1}{5}$, resulting in

x_1	x_2	S_1	S_2		
$\frac{3}{2}$	1	$\frac{1}{2}$	0	60	(8.1a)
1	0	$\frac{3}{5}$	$-\frac{1}{5}$	20	$(8.2b) = -\frac{1}{5} \cdot (8.2a)$

The ⓪ is created by multiplying Eq. (8.2b) by $-\frac{3}{2}$ and adding this multiple to Eq. (8.1a), or

x_1	x_2	S_1	S_2		
0	1	$-\frac{2}{5}$	$\frac{3}{10}$	30	$(8.1b) = (8.1a) + (-\frac{3}{2})(8.2a)$
1	0	$\frac{3}{5}$	$-\frac{1}{5}$	20	$(8.2a)$

With S_1 and S_2 set equal to 0, the values of x_1 and x_2 are read directly as $x_1 = 20$ and $x_2 = 30$, which corresponds to solution 1 in Table 8.1.

Incorporating the Objective Function

When solving by the simplex method, the objective function and constraints are combined to form a system of equations. The objective function is one of the equations, and z becomes an additional variable in the system. In rearranging the variables in the objective function so that they are all on the left side of the equation, the problem is represented by the system of equations

$$
\begin{aligned}
z - 5x_1 - 6x_2 - 0S_1 - 0S_2 &= 0 & (0) \\
3x_1 + 2x_2 + S_1 \quad\quad &= 120 & (1) \\
4x_1 + 6x_2 \quad\quad + S_2 &= 260 & (2)
\end{aligned}
$$

Note that the objective function is labeled as Eq. (0).

The objective is to solve this (3×5) system of equations so as to maximize

TABLE 8.2

BASIC VARIABLES	z	x_1	x_2	S_1	S_2	b_i	ROW NUMBER
	1	−5	−6	0	0	0	(0)
S_1	0	3	2	1	0	120	(1)
S_2	0	4	6	0	1	260	(2)

the value of z. Since we are particularly concerned about the value of z and will want to know its value for any solution, z will always be a basic variable. The standard practice, however, is not to refer to z as a basic variable. The terms *basic variable* and *nonbasic variable* are usually reserved for the other variables in the problem.

The simplex operations are usually performed in a tabular format. The initial table, or *tableau,* for our problem is shown in Table 8.2. Note that there is one row for each equation and the table contains the coefficients of each variable in the equations. The b_i *column* contains the right-hand-side constants of the equations; b_i is the right-hand-side constant for equation i or row i.

In a maximization problem having all ≤ constraints, the starting solution will have a set of basic variables consisting of the slack variables in the problem. By setting x_1 and x_2 equal to 0 in our problem, the initial solution is $S_1 = 120$, $S_2 = 260$, and $z = 0$. The basic variables and the rows in which their values are read are noted in the first column of the tableau.

Given any intermediate solution, the simplex method compares the nonbasic variables with the set of basic variables. The purpose is to determine whether any nonbasic variable should replace a basic variable. *A nonbasic variable will replace a basic variable only if (1) the objective function will be improved and (2) the new solution is feasible.*

RULE 1:

OPTIMALITY CHECK IN MAXIMIZATION PROBLEM

In a maximization problem, the optimal solution has been found if all row (0) coefficients for the basic and nonbasic variables are greater than or equal to 0.

Since the row (0) coefficients for x_1 and x_2 are −5 and −6, respectively, the optimal solution has not been found.

A negative row (0) coefficient for a nonbasic variable indicates that the objective function will increase in value if a positive quantity is assigned to the variable.

This point can be seen more easily if we rewrite Eq. (0) so that z is written as a function of the nonbasic variables. The result is

$$z = 0 + 5x_1 + 6x_2 \qquad (0a)$$

In this form, we can determine the effects of changes in the nonbasic variables. Equation $(0a)$ indicates that the current value of z is 0, but assigning x_1 a value of 1 will result in z increasing by 5. Similarly, assigning x_2 a value of 1 will result in z increasing by 6. Thus, introducing positive values for either x_1 or x_2 would result in a better value for z.

RULE 2: NEW BASIC VARIABLE IN MAXIMIZATION PROBLEM ■

In a maximization problem the nonbasic variable which will replace a basic variable is the one having the **most negative** row (0) coefficient. "Ties" may be broken arbitrarily.

In selecting a nonbasic variable to become a basic variable, the simplex method chooses the one which will result in the largest *marginal* (per unit) improvement in z. Since an improvement of 6 units is better than an improvement of 5 units, the simplex would choose x_2 to become a basic variable in the next solution. *In the simplex tableau the column representing the new basic variable will be called the* **key column.**

If z will increase by 6 units for *each* unit of x_2, we would like x_2 to become as large as possible. The simplex method will allow x_2 to increase in value until one of the current basic variables is driven to a value of 0 (becoming a nonbasic variable). If Eqs. (1) and (2) are rewritten in terms of the nonbasic variables, we can observe the effects that changes in x_2 will have on the values of the current basic variables:

$$S_1 = 120 - 3x_1 - 2x_2 \qquad \textbf{(1a)}$$

$$S_2 = 260 - 4x_1 - 6x_2 \qquad \textbf{(2a)}$$

Equation (1a) indicates that S_1 currently equals 120, but will decrease in value by 2 units for each unit that x_2 increases. If x_2 is allowed to grow to a value of 120/2, or 60 units, S_1 will be driven to a value of 0. Equation (2a), indicates that S_2 currently equals 260 but will decrease in value by 6 units for each unit that x_2 increases. S_2 will be driven to a value of 0 if x_2 is allowed to grow to a value of 260/6, or $43\frac{1}{3}$ units. The question is, Which basic variable will be driven to a value of 0 (will become nonbasic) first as x_2 is allowed to increase? The answer is S_2, when $x_2 = 43\frac{1}{3}$. If x_2 were allowed to grow to a value of 60, substitution into Eq. (2a) would result in

$$S_2 = 260 - 6(60)$$
$$= -100$$

Since S_2 would be negative, this solution is not feasible. Our conclusion is that x_2 should replace S_2 as a basic variable in the next solution.

Using the tableau structure, the decision of which basic variable to replace is made by focusing upon the key column and the b_i column. The partial tableau in Table 8.3 illustrates a column which is supposed to repesent the *key column* for an intermediate solution. The key column element a_{ik} represents the constant appearing in row i of the key (k) column. Similarly, b_i values represent the right side constants for row i.

RULE 3: DEPARTING BASIC VARIABLE

The basic variable to be replaced is found by determining the row i associated with

$$\min \frac{b_i}{a_{ik}} \qquad i = 1, \ldots, m$$

where $a_{ik} > 0$.

TABLE 8.3

		KEY COLUMN		
...	x_k	...	b_i	ROW NUMBER
...	a_{0k}	...	b_0	(0)
...	a_{1k}	...	b_1	(1)
...	a_{mk}	...	b_m	(m)

TABLE 8.4

KEY COLUMN → x_2

BASIC VARIABLES	z	x_1	x_2	S_1	S_2	b_i	ROW NUMBER	b_i/a_{ik}
	1	-5	-6	0	0	0	(0)	
S_1	0	3	②	1	0	120	(1)	$120/2 = 60$
S_2	0	4	⑥	0	1	260	(2)	$260/6 = 43\frac{1}{3}$*

(DEPARTING VARIABLE) S_2

TABLE 8.5

BASIC VARIABLES	z	x_1	x_2	S_1	S_2	b_i	ROW NUMBER	
	1	-1	0	0	1	260	(0)	$R_0' = R_0 + 6R_2'$
S_1	0	$\frac{10}{6}$	0	1	$-\frac{1}{3}$	$33\frac{1}{3}$	(1)	$R_1' = R_1 - 2R_2'$
x_2	0	$\frac{4}{6}$	1	0	$\frac{1}{6}$	$43\frac{1}{3}$	(2)	$R_2' = \frac{1}{6}R_2$

Rule 3 suggests that the ratio b_i/a_{ik} should be determined for rows (1) to (m) *where $a_{ik} > 0$.* The minimum ratio should be identified and the corresponding row i noted. The departing basic variable is the one whose value is currently read from this row. Table 8.4 illustrates this process for our example.

In Table 8.4 attention is focused on the key column. The ratios b_i/a_{ik} are computed for rows (1) and (2). The minimum ratio is $43\frac{1}{3}$, associated with row (2). Since the value of S_2 is currently read from row (2), S_2 is the departing basic variable.

In the next solution we will want to read the value of the new basic variable x_2 from row (2). Thus, we need to apply the Gauss-Jordan procedures to transform the column of coefficients under x_2 from $\begin{pmatrix} -6 \\ 2 \\ 6 \end{pmatrix}$ to $\begin{pmatrix} 0 \\ 0 \\ 1 \end{pmatrix}$. The ① is created by multiplying row (2) by $\frac{1}{6}$. The two ⓪s are created by multiplying the *new* row (2) by $+6$ and -2 and adding these multiples, respectively, to rows (0) and (1). The next solution appears in Table 8.5. Note in Table 8.5 that a shorthand notation to the right of each row indicates how the elements of that row were computed. The notation R_j is used to represent row j.

Note also in Table 8.5 that x_2 has replaced S_2 in the column of basic variables. Since x_1 and S_2 are nonbasic variables, we can read the values of z, S_1, and x_2 from the b_i column as $z = 260$, $S_1 = 33\frac{1}{3}$, and $x_2 = 43\frac{1}{3}$.

EXERCISE

Substitute the values $x_1 = 0$ and $x_2 = 43\frac{1}{3}$ back into the original formulation and verify (a) that the first constraint has slack equal to $33\frac{1}{3}$ units, (b) that the second constraint is satisfied as an equality ($S_2 = 0$), and (c) that the value of z equals 260.

With this new solution, the first thing to check is whether it is optimal. Applying Rule 1, we conclude that the solution is not optimal because of the -1 coefficient for x_1 in row (0). Since x_1 has the only negative coefficient in row (0), it will become the new basic variable. To determine the departing basic variable, we focus on the elements in the x_1 column. As shown in Table 8.6, the minimum b_i/a_{ik} ratio is 20, and this minimum ratio is associated with row (1). Since the value of S_1 is currently read from row (1), S_1 is identified as the departing variable.

In the next solution we will want to read the value of the new basic variable x_1 from row (1). As such, the column of coefficients under x_1 should be transformed from $\begin{pmatrix} -1 \\ \frac{10}{6} \\ \frac{4}{6} \end{pmatrix}$ to $\begin{pmatrix} 0 \\ 1 \\ 0 \end{pmatrix}$.

The $\textcircled{1}$ is created by multiplying row (1) by $\frac{6}{10}$. The two $\textcircled{0}$s are created by multiplying the new row (1) by $+1$ and $-\frac{4}{6}$ and adding these multiples, respectively, to rows (0) and (2) (see equations to the right of Table 8.7). The new solution appears in Table 8.7.

Note in Table 8.7 that x_1 has replaced S_1 in the column of basic variables. With S_1 and S_2 being nonbasic the values of z, x_1, and x_2 are read from the b_i column as $z = 280$, $x_1 = 20$, and $x_2 = 30$. Our next step is to check for optimality. Applying Rule 1, we conclude that this solution is optimal because *all row (0) coefficients are greater than or equal to 0*. This answer agrees with the one we found when solving graphically in Sec. 7.3. The objective function is maximized at a value of 280 when $x_1 = 20$, $x_2 = 30$, $S_1 = 0$, and $S_2 = 0$.

Summary of Simplex Procedure

Let's generalize the *simplex procedure for maximization problems having all $\leq$ constraints.* First, add slack variables to each constraint and place the variable coefficients and right-hand-side constants in a simplex tableau. Then:

1 Identify the initial solution by declaring each of the slack variables as basic variables in the solution. All other variables are nonbasic in the initial solution.

2 Determine if the current solution is optimal by applying Rule 1. If it is optimal, stop! If it is not optimal, proceed to step 3.

3 Determine the nonbasic variable which should become a basic variable in the next solution by applying Rule 2.

4 Determine the basic variable which should be replaced in the next solution by applying Rule 3.

5 Apply the Gauss-Jordan operations to generate the new solution (or new tableau). Go to step 2.

EXAMPLE 1

Let's solve the following linear programming problem using the simplex method.

$$\begin{aligned}
\text{Maximize} \quad & z = 2x_1 + 12x_2 + 8x_3 \\
\text{subject to} \quad & 2x_1 + 2x_2 + x_3 \leq 100 \\
& x_1 - 2x_2 + 5x_3 \leq 80 \\
& 10x_1 + 5x_2 + 4x_3 \leq 300 \\
& x_1, x_2, x_3 \geq 0
\end{aligned}$$

TABLE 8.6

KEY COLUMN

	z	x_1	x_2	S_1	S_2	b_i	ROW NUMBER	b_i/a_{ik}
BASIC VARIABLES	1	−1	0	0	1	260	(0)	
S_1	0	$\frac{10}{6}$	0	1	$-\frac{1}{3}$	$33\frac{1}{3}$	(1)	$33\frac{1}{3} \div \frac{10}{6} = 20^{*}$
x_2	0	$\frac{4}{6}$	1	0	$\frac{1}{6}$	$43\frac{1}{3}$	(2)	$43\frac{1}{3} \div \frac{4}{6} = 65$

(DEPARTING VARIABLE) — S_1

TABLE 8.7

	z	x_1	x_2	S_1	S_2	b_i	ROW NUMBER	
BASIC VARIABLES	1	0	0	$\frac{6}{10}$	$\frac{24}{30}$	280	(0)	$R_0'' = R_0' + R_1''$
x_1	0	1	0	$\frac{6}{10}$	$-\frac{6}{30}$	20	(1)	$R_1'' = \frac{6}{10} R_1'$
x_2	0	0	1	$-\frac{24}{60}$	$\frac{3}{10}$	30	(2)	$R_2'' = R_2' - \frac{4}{6} R_1''$

TABLE 8.8

KEY COLUMN

	z	x_1	x_2	x_3	S_1	S_2	S_3	b_i	ROW NUMBER	b_i/a_{ik}
BASIC VARIABLES	1	−2	−12	−8	0	0	0	0	(0)	
S_1	0	2	2	1	1	0	0	100	(1)	$100/2 = 50^{*}$
S_2	0	1	−2	5	0	1	0	80	(2)	
S_3	0	10	5	4	0	0	1	300	(3)	$300/5 = 60$

Rewriting the problem in standard form with slack variables added in, we have the following.

$$\text{Maximize} \quad z = 2x_1 + 12x_2 + 8x_3 + 0S_1 + 0S_2 + 0S_3$$

$$
\begin{aligned}
\text{subject to} \quad 2x_1 + 2x_2 + x_3 + S_1 \qquad\qquad &= 100 \\
x_1 - 2x_2 + 5x_3 \qquad + S_2 \qquad &= 80 \\
10x_1 + 5x_2 + 4x_3 \qquad\qquad + S_3 &= 300 \\
x_1, x_2, x_3, S_1, S_2, S_3 &\geq 0
\end{aligned}
$$

The objective function should be restated by moving all variables to the left side of the equation. The initial simplex tableau is shown in Table 8.8.

Step 1 In the initial solution x_1, x_2, and x_3 are nonbasic variables having values of 0. The basic variables are the slack variables with $S_1 = 100$, $S_2 = 80$, $S_3 = 300$, and $z = 0$.

Step 2 Since all row (0) coefficients are *not* greater than or equal to 0, the initial solution is not optimal.

Step 3 The most negative coefficient in row (0) is −12, and it is associated with x_2. Thus, x_2 will become a basic variable in the next solution and its column of coefficients becomes the key column.

Step 4 In computing the b_i/a_{ik} ratios, the minimum ratio is 50, and it corresponds to row (1). Thus S_1 will become a nonbasic variable in the next solution. Note that no ratio was computed for row (2) because the a_{ik} value was negative.

Step 5 The new solution is found by transforming the coefficients in the x_2 column

$$\text{from} \begin{pmatrix} -12 \\ 2 \\ -2 \\ 5 \end{pmatrix} \text{to} \begin{pmatrix} 0 \\ 1 \\ 0 \\ 0 \end{pmatrix}.$$

TABLE 8.9

BASIC VARIABLES	z	x_1	x_2	x_3 KEY COLUMN	S_1	S_2	S_3	b_i	ROW NUMBER		b_i/a_{ik}
	1	10	0	-2	6	0	0	600	(0)	$R_0' = R_0 + 12R_1'$	
x_2	0	1	1	$\frac{1}{2}$	$\frac{1}{2}$	0	0	50	(1)	$R_1' = \frac{1}{2}R_1$	$50 \div \frac{1}{2} = 100$
S_2	0	3	0	6	1	1	0	180	(2)	$R_2' = R_2 + 2R_1'$	$\mathbf{180 \div 6 = 30^*}$
S_3	0	5	0	$\frac{3}{2}$	$-\frac{1}{2}$	0	1	50	(3)	$R_3' = R_3 - 5R_1'$	$50 \div \frac{3}{2} = 33\frac{1}{3}$

TABLE 8.10

BASIC VARIABLES	z	x_1	x_2	x_3	S_1	S_2	S_3	b_i	ROW NUMBER	
	1	11	0	0	$\frac{38}{6}$	$\frac{2}{6}$	0	660	(0)	$R_0'' = R_0' + 2R_2''$
x_2	0	$\frac{3}{4}$	1	0	$\frac{5}{12}$	$-\frac{1}{12}$	0	35	(1)	$R_1'' = R_1' - \frac{1}{2}R_2''$
x_3	0	$\frac{1}{2}$	0	1	$\frac{1}{6}$	$\frac{1}{6}$	0	30	(2)	$R_2'' = \frac{1}{6}R_2'$
S_3	0	$\frac{17}{4}$	0	0	$-\frac{11}{4}$	$-\frac{1}{4}$	1	5	(3)	$R_3'' = R_3' - \frac{3}{2}R_2''$

Table 8.9 indicates the next solution. The shorthand notation to the right of each row indicates how the elements of that row were computed. In this solution the basic variables and their values are $x_2 = 50$, $S_2 = 180$, $S_3 = 50$, and $z = 600$. Continuing the simplex procedure we next return to step 2.

Step 2 Since the row (0) coefficient for x_3 is negative, this solution is not optimal.

Step 3 The variable x_3 will become a basic variable in the next solution since it has the only negative coefficient in row (0). The x_3 column becomes the new key column.

Step 4 In computing the b_i/a_{ik} ratios, the minimum ratio is 30, and it corresponds to row (2). Thus, S_2 will become a nonbasic variable in the next solution.

Step 5 The new solution is found by transforming the coefficients in the x_3 column

$$\text{from} \begin{pmatrix} -2 \\ \frac{1}{2} \\ 6 \\ \frac{3}{2} \end{pmatrix} \text{ to } \begin{pmatrix} 0 \\ 0 \\ 1 \\ 0 \end{pmatrix}.$$

Table 8.10 indicates the next solution. The basic variables and their values in this solution are $x_2 = 35$, $x_3 = 30$, and $S_3 = 5$. The value of z is 660. We return to step 2.

Step 2 Since all row (0) coefficients are greater than or equal to 0 in Table 8.10, the current solution is the optimal solution.

The objective function is maximized at a value of 660 when $x_1 = 0$, $x_2 = 35$, $x_3 = 30$, $S_1 = 0$, $S_2 = 0$, and $S_3 = 5$.

Maximization Problems with Mixed Constraints

We chose the simplest problem structure to illustrate the simplex method: a maximization problem with all ($\leq$) constraints. For a maximization problem having a mix of ($\leq$, $\geq$, and =) constraints the simplex method itself does not change. The only change is in transforming constraints to the standard equation form with appropriate supplemental variables. This was discussed in Sec. 7.4 on page 275. *For each ($\geq$) constraint a surplus variable is subtracted and an artificial* *variable is added to the left side of the constraint. For each* (=) *constraint, an artificial variable is added to the left side.* An additional column is added to the simplex tableau for each supplemental variable. Also, surplus and artificial variables must be assigned appropriate objective function coefficients (c_j values). As discussed in Chap. 7, surplus variables usually are assigned a c_j value of 0: For maximization problems, artificial variables are assigned a large negative c_j value, which we will denote by $-M$, where $|M|$ is assumed to be much larger than any other coefficient.

Computationally, the simplex method proceeds exactly as discussed in the last section. The only difference which will be noted is the identification of the initial basis.

> In any linear programming problem, the initial set of basic variables will consist of all the slack variables and all the artificial variables which appear in the problem.

Minimization Problems

The simplex procedure changes only slightly when minimization problems are solved. Aside from assigning artificial variables objective function coefficients of $+M$, the only difference relates to the interpretation of row (0) coefficients. The following two rules are modifications of Rule 1 and Rule 2. These apply for minimization problems.

RULE 1A:

OPTIMALITY CHECK IN MINIMIZATION PROBLEM

In a minimization problem, the optimal solution has been found if all row (0) coefficients for the basic and nonbasic variables are less than or equal to 0.

RULE 2A:

NEW BASIC VARIABLE IN MINIMIZATION PROBLEM

In a minimization problem, the nonbasic variable which will replace a current basic variable is the one having the largest positive row (0) coefficient. Ties may be broken arbitrarily.

EXAMPLE 2

Solve the following linear programming problem using the simplex method.

$$\text{Minimize} \quad z = 5x_1 + 6x_2$$
$$\text{subject to} \quad x_1 + x_2 \geq 10$$
$$2x_1 + 4x_2 \geq 24$$
$$x_1, x_2 \geq 0$$

SOLUTION

This problem is first rewritten with the constraints expressed as equations as follows:

$$\begin{aligned}
\text{Minimize} \quad & z = 5x_1 + 6x_2 + 0E_1 + 0E_2 + MA_1 + MA_2 \\
\text{subject to} \quad & x_1 + x_2 - E_1 \qquad\quad + A_1 \qquad\quad = 10 \\
& 2x_1 + 4x_2 \qquad - E_2 \qquad\quad + A_2 = 24 \\
& x_1, x_2, E_1, E_2, A_1, A_2 \geq 0
\end{aligned}$$

If all variables in the objective function are moved to the left side of the equation, the initial tableau for this problem appears in Table 8.11. Note that the artificial variables are the basic variables in this initial solution. However, in any problem containing artificial variables, the row (0) coefficients for the artificial variables will not equal 0 in the initial tableau. As a consequence, we do not have the desired columns of an identity matrix in the basic variable columns. These $-M$ coefficients must be changed to 0 using row operations if the value of z is to be read from row (0). In Table 8.11 we can accomplish this by multiplying rows (1) and (2) by $+M$ and adding these multiples to row (0). Table 8.12 shows the resulting tableau.

In this initial solution the nonbasic variables are x_1, x_2, E_1, and E_2. The basic variables are the two artificial variables with $A_1 = 10$, $A_2 = 24$, and $z = 34M$.

Applying Rule 1A, we conclude that this solution is not optimal. The row (0) coefficients for x_1 and x_2 are both positive (remember that M is an extremely large number). In applying Rule 2A, x_2 is identified as the new basic variable. The x_2 column becomes the new key column. The minimum b_i/a_{ik} value equals 6 and is associated with row (2). Thus, A_2 will be the departing basic variable. Table 8.13 indicates the next solution. In Table 8.13 the nonbasic variables are x_1, E_1, E_2, and A_2. For this solution $A_1 = 4$, $x_2 = 6$, and $z = 36 + 4M$.

Applying Rule 1A, we see that this solution is not optimal. The row (0) coefficients for x_1 and E_2 are both positive. In applying Rule 2A, x_1 is identified as the new basic variable. The x_1 column becomes the new key column. The b_i/a_{ik} ratios are $4 \div \frac{1}{2} = 8$ and $6 \div \frac{1}{2} = 12$ for rows (1) and (2). Since the minimum ratio is associated with row (1), A_1 is identified as the departing basic variable. Table 8.14 indicates the new solution. The solution in Table 8.14 has $x_1 = 8$, $x_2 = 2$, and $z = 52$.

Applying Rule 1A, we conclude that this solution is optimal. All row (0) coefficients are less than or equal to 0 for the basic and nonbasic variables. Therefore, z is minimized at a value of 52 when $x_1 = 8$ and $x_2 = 2$.

Section 8.1 Follow-up Exercises

1 Given the linear programming problem:

$$\begin{aligned}
\text{Maximize} \quad & z = 14x_1 + 10x_2 \\
\text{subject to} \quad & 5x_1 + 4x_2 \leq 48 \\
& 2x_1 + 5x_2 \leq 26 \\
& x_1, x_2 \geq 0
\end{aligned}$$

(a) Transform the $\leq$ constraints into equations.
(b) Enumerate all solutions for which two variables have been set equal to 0.
(c) From part b identify the basic feasible solutions.
(d) Graph the original constraint set and confirm that the basic feasible solutions are corner points on the area of feasible solutions.
(e) What is the optimal solution?

TABLE 8.11

need to be transformed to zero

BASIC VARIABLES	z	x_1	x_2	E_1	E_2	A_1	A_2	b_i	ROW NUMBER
	1	-5	-6	0	0	$-M$	$-M$	0	(0)
A_1	0	1	1	-1	0	1	0	10	(1)
A_2	0	2	4	0	-1	0	1	24	(2)

TABLE 8.12

KEY COLUMN

BASIC VARIABLES	z	x_1	x_2	E_1	E_2	A_1	A_2	b_i	ROW NUMBER		b_i/a_{ik}
	1	$-5+3M$	$-6+5M$	$-M$	$-M$	0	0	$34M$	(0)	$R_0' = R_0 + MR_1 + MR_2$	
A_1	0	1	1	-1	0	1	0	10	(1)	R_1	$10/1 = 10$
A_2	0	2	4	0	-1	0	1	24	(2)	R_2	$24/4 = 6^*$

TABLE 8.13

KEY COLUMN

BASIC VARIABLES	z	x_1	x_2	E_1	E_2	A_1	A_2	b_i	ROW NUMBER		b_i/a_{ik}
	1	$-2+\frac{M}{2}$	0	$-M$	$-\frac{3}{2}+\frac{M}{4}$	0	$\frac{3}{2}-\frac{5M}{4}$	$36+4M$	(0)	$R_0'' = R_0' + (6-5M)R_2'$	
A_1	0	$\frac{1}{2}$	0	-1	$\frac{1}{4}$	1	$-\frac{1}{4}$	4	(1)	$R_1' = R_1 - R_2'$	$4/\frac{1}{2} = 8^*$
x_2	0	$\frac{1}{2}$	1	0	$-\frac{1}{4}$	0	$\frac{1}{4}$	6	(2)	$R_2' = \frac{1}{4}R_2$	$6/\frac{1}{2} = 12$

TABLE 8.14

BASIC VARIABLES	z	x_1	x_2	E_1	E_2	A_1	A_2	b_i	ROW NUMBER	$R_0''' = R_0'' + \left(2 - \frac{M}{2}\right)R_1''$
	1	0	0	-4	$-\frac{1}{2}$	$4-M$	$\frac{1}{2}-M$	52	(0)	
x_1	0	1	0	-2	$\frac{1}{2}$	2	$-\frac{1}{2}$	8	(1)	$R_1'' = 2R_1'$
x_2	0	0	1	1	$-\frac{1}{2}$	-1	$\frac{1}{2}$	2	(2)	$R_2'' = R_2' - \frac{1}{2}R_1''$

2 Given the linear programming problem:

$$\text{Maximize} \quad z = 6x_1 + 4x_2$$
$$\text{subject to} \quad 6x_1 + 10x_2 \le 90$$
$$12x_1 + 8x_2 \le 96$$
$$x_1, x_2 \ge 0$$

(a) Transform the $\le$ constraints into equations.
(b) Enumerate all solutions for which two variables have been set equal to 0.
(c) From part b identify the basic feasible solutions.
(d) Graph the original constraint set and confirm that the basic feasible solutions are corner points on the area of feasible solutions.
(e) What is the optimal solution?

For Exercises 3 to 8 solve by the simplex method.

3 Maximize $\quad z = 4x_1 + 2x_2$
$\quad$ subject to $\quad x_1 + x_2 \le 50$
$\quad\quad\quad\quad\quad 6x_1 \quad\quad \le 240$
$\quad\quad\quad\quad\quad\quad x_1, x_2 \ge 0$

4 Maximize $z = 4x_1 + 4x_2$

subject to $4x_1 + 8x_2 \le 24$

$24x_1 + 16x_2 \le 96$

$x_1, x_2 \ge 0$

5 Maximize $z = 10x_1 + 12x_2$

subject to $x_1 + x_2 \le 150$

$3x_1 + 6x_2 \le 300$

$4x_1 + 2x_2 \le 160$

$x_1, x_2 \ge 0$

6 Maximize $z = 6x_1 + 8x_2 + 10x_3$

subject to $x_1 + 2.5x_2 \le 1,200$

$2x_1 + 3x_2 + 4x_3 \le 2,600$

$x_1, x_2, x_3 \ge 0$

7 Maximize $z = 10x_1 + 3x_2 + 4x_3$

subject to $8x_1 + 2x_2 + 3x_2 \le 400$

$4x_1 + 3x_2 \le 200$

$x_3 \le 40$

$x_1, x_2, x_3 \ge 0$

8 Maximize $z = 4x_1 - 2x_2 + x_3$

subject to $6x_1 + 2x_2 + 2x_3 \le 240$

$2x_1 - 2x_2 + 4x_3 \le 40$

$2x_1 + 2x_2 - 2x_3 \le 80$

$x_1, x_2, x_3 \ge 0$

9 (a) Solve the following linear programming problem using the simplex method.

$$\text{Minimize} \quad z = 3x_1 + 6x_2$$
$$\text{subject to} \quad 4x_1 + x_2 \ge 20$$
$$x_1 + x_2 \le 20$$
$$x_1 + x_2 \ge 10$$
$$x_1, x_2, \ge 0$$

(b) Verify the solution in part a by solving graphically.

10 (a) Solve the following linear programming problem using the simplex method.

$$\text{Minimize} \quad z = 6x_1 + 10x_2$$
$$\text{subject to} \quad x_1 \le 12$$
$$2x_2 = 36$$
$$3x_1 + 2x_2 \ge 54$$
$$x_1, x_2 \ge 0$$

(b) Verify the solution in part a by solving graphically.

11 Rule 3 discussed the identification of the departing basic variable in the simplex procedure. Why is consideration not given to the b_i/a_{ik} ratios which have $a_{ik} \le 0$?

12 Rule 3 also indicated that the departing basic variable is associated with the row corresponding to the minimum ratio b_i/a_{ik}. Why is the departing variable identified by the *minimum* ratio?

8.2 SPECIAL PHENOMENA

In Sec. 7.3 certain phenomena were discussed which can arise when solving LP problems. Specifically, the phenomena of *alternative optimal solutions, no fea-*

sible solution, and *unbounded solutions* were presented. In this section we discuss the manner in which these phenomena occur when solving by the simplex method.

Alternative Optimal Solutions

In Sec. 7.3 we described circumstances where there can be more than one optimal solution to an LP problem. This situation, termed *alternative optimal solutions,* results when the objective function is parallel to a constraint which binds in the direction of optimization. In two-variable problems we are made aware of alternative optimal solutions with the *corner-point method* when a "tie" occurs for the optimal corner point.

When using the simplex method, alternative optimal solutions are indicated when:

1 An optimal solution has been identified, and

2 The row (0) coefficient for a nonbasic variable equals zero.

The first condition confirms that there is no better solution than the present solution. The presence of a 0 in row (0) for a nonbasic variable indicates that the nonbasic variable can become a basic variable (can become positive) and the current value of the objective function (known to be optimal) will not change.

EXAMPLE 3

Consider the LP problem

$$\begin{aligned} \text{Maximize} \quad & z = 6x_1 + 4x_2 \\ \text{subject to} \quad & x_1 + x_2 \leq 5 \\ & 3x_1 + 2x_2 \leq 12 \\ & x_1, x_2 \geq 0 \end{aligned}$$

Table 8.15 presents the initial simplex solution with $S_1 = 5$ and $S_2 = 12$ being the basic variables; x_1 and x_2 are nonbasic variables.

By Rule 1 we see that a better solution exists. Using Rule 2, x_1 is selected as the new basic variable and the x_1 column becomes the key column. The b_i/a_{ik} ratios are computed with S_2 identified as the departing variable. The elements in the x_1 column are transformed from $\begin{pmatrix} -6 \\ 1 \\ 3 \end{pmatrix}$ to $\begin{pmatrix} 0 \\ 0 \\ 1 \end{pmatrix}$ using row operations, with the resulting simplex tableau shown in Table 8.16. In this new solution, x_1 has replaced S_2 in the basis; the basic variables are $S_1 = 1$ and $x_1 = 4$ with a resulting objective function value of $z = 24$.

Applying Rule 1 we see that this is the optimal solution since all row (0) coefficients are greater than or equal to 0. However, for the nonbasic variable x_2, the row (0) coeffi-

TABLE 8.15

BASIC VARIABLES	z	x_1	x_2	S_1	S_2	b_i	ROW NUMBER	b_i/a_{ik}
	1	−6	−4	0	0	0	(0)	
S_1	0	1	1	1	0	5	(1)	5/1 = 5
S_2	0	3	2	0	1	12	(2)	12/3 = 4*

KEY COLUMN (over x_1)

TABLE 8.16

alternative optimal solution indication

BASIC VARIABLES	z	x_1	x_2	S_1	S_2	b_i	ROW NUMBER		b_i/a_{ik}
	1	0	⓪	0	2	24	(0)	$R_0' = R_0 + 6R_2'$	
S_1	0	0	$\frac{1}{3}$	1	$-\frac{1}{3}$	1	(1)	$R_1' = R_1 - R_2'$	$1/\frac{1}{3} = 3^*$
x_1	0	1	$\frac{2}{3}$	0	$\frac{1}{3}$	4	(2)	$R_2' = \frac{1}{3}R_2$	$4/\frac{2}{3} = 6$

TABLE 8.17

BASIC VARIABLES	z	x_1	x_2	S_1	S_2	b_i	ROW NUMBER	
	1	0	0	0	2	24	(0)	$R_0'' = R_0'$
x_2	0	0	1	3	-1	3	(1)	$R_1'' = 3R_1'$
x_1	0	1	0	-2	1	2	(2)	$R_2'' = R_2' - \frac{2}{3}R_1''$

cient equals 0. This suggests that x_2 can assume positive values (become a basic variable) and the current (optimal) value of z will not change.

> When alternative optimal solutions are indicated by the simplex method, the other optimal corner point alternatives can be generated by treating the nonbasic variable with the zero coefficient as if it is a new basic variable.

If in Table 8.16 we treat the x_2 column as a key column associated with the entry of the new basic variable x_2, b_i/a_{ik} ratios are computed as usual and S_1 is identified as the departing variable. Table 8.17 indicates the new solution. The optimality check (Rule 1) indicates that the current solution is optimal with $x_1 = 2$, $x_2 = 3$, and $z = 24$. And, for the nonbasic variable S_1, the coefficient of 0 in row (0) indicates that there is an alternative optimal solution in which S_1 would be a basic variable. If we were to treat the S_1 column as the key column and iterate to a new solution, we would return to the first optimal solution found in Table 8.16.

EXERCISE

Verify the two corner-point alternative optimal solutions found in this example by solving the problem graphically.

Multiple alternative optimal (corner-point) solutions may exist in a problem. This situation may be indicated by (1) more than one nonbasic variable having a 0 coefficient in row (0) of an optimal tableau, or (2) during the course of generating successive alternative optimal solutions using the simplex method, 0 coefficients appear in row (0) for nonbasic variables which have not appeared previously in an optimal basis.

No Feasible Solution

In Sec. 7.3 we indicated that a problem has *no feasible solution* if there are no values for the variables which satisfy all the constraints in a problem. While such a

TABLE 8.18

		z	x_1	x_2	S_1	E_2	A_2	b_i	ROW NUMBER	
		1	−10	−20	0	0	M	0	(0)	R_0
S_1		0	1	1	1	0	0	5	(1)	R_1
A_2		0	1	1	0	−1	1	20	(2)	R_2

TABLE 8.19

			KEY COLUMN								
BASIC VARIABLES	z	x_1	x_2	S_1	E_2	A_2	b_i	ROW NUMBER		b_i/a_{ik}
	1	$-10 - M$	$-20 - M$	0	M	0	$-20M$	(0)	$R_0' = R_0 - MR_2$	
S_1	0	1	1	1	0	0	5	(1)	R_1	$5/1 = 5^*$
A_2	0	1	1	0	−1	1	20	(2)	R_2	$20/1 = 20$

TABLE 8.20

BASIC VARIABLES	z	x_1	x_2	S_1	E_2	A_2	b_i	ROW NUMBER	
	1	10	0	$M + 20$	M	0	$-15M + 100$	(0)	$R_0'' = R_0' + (M + 20)R_1'$
x_2	0	1	1	1	0	0	5	(1)	$R_1' = R_1$
A_2	0	0	0	−1	−1	1	15	(2)	$R_2' = R_2 - R_1'$

condition may be obvious by inspection in small problems, it is considerably more difficult to identify in large-scale problems.

The condition of no feasible solution is indicated in the simplex method when an artificial variable appears in an optimal basis at a positive level (value). The following example illustrates this condition.

EXAMPLE 4

Let's solve the following LP problem which, by inspection, has no feasible solution.

$$\text{Maximize} \quad z = 10x_1 + 20x_2$$
$$\text{subject to} \quad x_1 + x_2 \leq 5$$
$$x_1 + x_2 \geq 20$$
$$x_1, x_2 \geq 0$$

Tables 8.18 to 8.20 present the simplex iterations in solving this problem. In Table 8.20, all row (0) coefficients are greater than or equal to 0 indicating an optimal solution. However, one of the basic variables is A_2 and it has a value of 15; that is, the optimal solution is $x_2 = 5$, $A_2 = 15$, and $z = -15M + 100$. Artificial variables have no meaning in an LP problem, and the assignment of $A_2 = 15$ signals no feasible solution to the problem.

Unbounded Solutions

Unbounded solutions exist when (1) there is an *unbounded solution space* and (2) improvement in the objective function occurs with movement in the direction of the unbounded portion of the solution space.

If at any iteration of the simplex method the a_{ik} values are all 0 or negative for the variable selected to become the new basic variable, there is an unbounded so-

TABLE 8.21

	z	x_1	x_2	S_1	S_2	b_i
			KEY COLUMN			
BASIC VARIABLES	1	2	−3	0	0	0
S_1	0	1	0	1	0	10
S_2	0	2	−1	0	1	30

lution for the LP problem. This will require a little explanation. The a_{ik} values indicate the marginal changes in the values of current basic variables for each unit introduced of the new basic variable. Positive a_{ik} values indicate *marginal decreases* in the values of the corresponding basic variables, negative a_{ik} values indicate *marginal increases,* and a_{ik} values of 0 indicate *no change.* Once a new basic variable is identified (Rule 2), the departing basic variable is found by computing the minimum b_i/a_{ik} value, where $a_{ik} > 0$ (Rule 3). When applying Rule 3, we are focusing upon those basic variables which will decrease in value ($a_{ik} > 0$) as the new basic variable is introduced. We wish to determine the maximum number of units to introduce before an existing basic variable is driven to 0. If the a_{ik} values are all 0 or negative, none of the current basic variables will decrease in value and there is no limit on the number of units of the new variable which can be entered. Since the new variable was selected on the basis of a promised improvement in z and there is no limit on the number of units which can be entered, there is no limit on how much the objective function can be improved; hence, there is an unbounded solution.

EXAMPLE 5

Consider the following problem:

$$\text{Maximize} \quad z = -2x_1 + 3x_2$$
$$\text{subject to} \quad x_1 \leq 10$$
$$2x_1 - x_2 \leq 30$$
$$x_1, x_2 \geq 0$$

Table 8.21 presents the initial simplex tableau. Row (0) indicates that the nonbasic variable x_2 will result in an improved value of z. However, the a_{ik} values are 0 and −1. These suggest that for *each unit* introduced of x_2, S_1 will not change and S_2 will *increase* by 1 unit. Neither of these basic variables will be driven to zero. This signals an unbounded solution.

EXERCISE

Verify that this problem has an unbounded solution by solving graphically.

Section 8.2 Follow-up Exercises

In the following exercises, solve by the simplex method.

1 Maximize $z = 4x_1 + 2x_2$
   subject to $x_1 + x_2 \leq 15$
   $2x_1 + x_2 \leq 20$
   $x_1, x_2 \geq 0$

2 Minimize $z = 4x_1 + 6x_2$
   subject to $3x_1 + x_2 \geq 15$
   $2x_1 + 3x_2 \geq 17$
   $x_1, x_2 \geq 0$

3 Maximize $z = 6x_1 + 3x_2$
   subject to $x_1 + 2x_2 \le 20$
   $4x_1 + 2x_2 \le 32$
   $x_1 \le 8$
   $x_1, x_2 \ge 0$

4 Maximize $z = 5x_1 + 3x_2$
   subject to $4x_1 + 3x_2 \le 24$
   $3x_1 + x_2 \ge 20$
   $x_1, x_2 \ge 0$

5 Minimize $z = 4x_1 - 3x_2$
   subject to $2x_1 - 4x_2 \ge 20$
   $4x_1 + 3x_2 \le 12$
   $x_1, x_2 \ge 0$

6 Maximize $z = 5x_1 + 3x_2$
   subject to $-x_1 + 2x_2 \le 10$
   $x_2 \le 5$
   $x_1, x_2 \ge 0$

8.3 THE DUAL PROBLEM

Every LP problem has a related problem called the *dual problem* or, simply, the *dual*. Given an original LP problem, referred to as the *primal problem,* or *primal,* the dual can be formulated from information contained in the primal. The dual problem is significant for numerous theoretical reasons and also for practical purposes. One property of the dual is that when it is solved, it provides all essential information about the solution to the primal problem. Similarly, the solution to the primal provides all essential information about the solution to the dual problem. Given an LP problem, its solution can be determined by solving *either* the original problem or its dual. The structural properties of the two problems may result in a decided preference regarding which problem should be solved. Even with computer-based solution methods, computational efficiencies can arise from solving one form of the problem.

Formulation of the Dual

The parameters and structure of the primal provide all the information necessary to formulate the dual. Figure 8.3 illustrates the formulation of a maximization problem and the dual of the problem. Let's make some observations regarding the relationships between these primal and dual problems.

1 The primal is a maximization problem and the dual is a minimization problem. *The sense of optimization is always opposite for corresponding primal and dual problems.*

2 The primal consists of two variables and three constraints and the dual consists of three variables and two constraints. *The number of variables in the primal always equals the number of constraints in the dual. The number of constraints in the primal always equals the number of variables in the dual.*

3 The objective function coefficients for x_1 and x_2 in the primal equal the right-hand-side constants for constraints (1) and (2) in the dual. *The objective function coefficient for the jth primal variable equals the right-hand-side constant for the jth dual constraint.*

4 The right-hand-side constants for constraints (1)–(3) in the primal equal the objective function coefficients for the dual variables y_1, y_2, and y_3. *The right-hand-side constant for the ith primal constraint equals the objective function coefficient for the ith dual variable.*

5 The variable coefficients for constraint (1) of the primal equal the column coefficients for the dual variable y_1. The variable coefficients for constraints (2) and (3) of the primal equal the column coefficients of the dual variables y_2 and

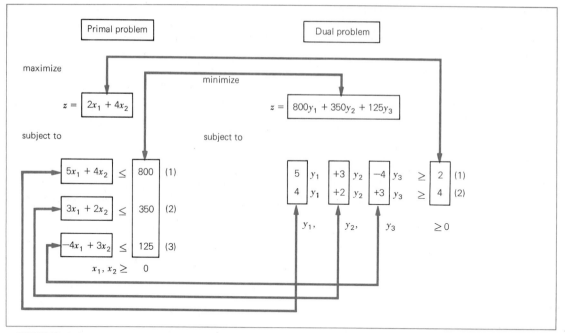

FIGURE 8.3
Some primal-
dual relation-
ships.

y_3. *The technological coefficients a_{ij} in the primal are the transpose of those in the dual. That is, the row coefficients in the primal become column coefficients in the dual, and vice-versa.*

Even though this problem has a primal which is a maximization type, the primal may be a minimization problem. The rules of transformation actually should be stated in terms of how to transform from a maximization problem to the corresponding minimization problem, or vice versa. Table 8.22 summarizes the symmetry of the two types of problems and their relationships.

Relationships 4 and 8 indicate that an equality constraint in one problem corresponds to an *unrestricted variable* in the other problem. An unrestricted variable can assume a value which is positive, negative, or 0. Similarly, relationships 3 and 7 indicate that a problem may have *nonpositive variables* (for example, $x_j \le 0$). Unrestricted and nonpositive variables appear to violate the third requirement of the simplex method, the nonnegativity restriction. Although this is true, for problems containing any of these special types of variables there are methods which allow us to adjust the formulation to satisfy the third requirement.

EXAMPLE 6

Given the primal problem:

$$\text{Minimize} \quad z = 10x_1 + 20x_2 + 15x_3 + 12x_4$$
$$\text{subject to} \quad x_1 + x_2 + x_3 + x_4 \ge 100 \quad \textbf{(1)}$$
$$2x_1 \qquad - x_3 + 3x_4 \le 140 \quad \textbf{(2)}$$

TABLE 8.22

MAXIMIZATION PROBLEM		MINIMIZATION PROBLEM
Number of constraints	$\xleftrightarrow{(1)}$	Number of variables
($\leq$) constraint	$\xleftrightarrow{(2)}$	Nonnegative variable
($\geq$) constraint	$\xleftrightarrow{(3)}$	Nonpositive variable
($=$) constraint	$\xleftrightarrow{(4)}$	Unrestricted variable
Number of variables	$\xleftrightarrow{(5)}$	Number of constraints
Nonnegative variable	$\xleftrightarrow{(6)}$	($\geq$) constraint
Nonpositive variable	$\xleftrightarrow{(7)}$	($\leq$) constraint
Unrestricted variable	$\xleftrightarrow{(8)}$	($=$) constraint
Objective function coefficient for jth variable	$\xleftrightarrow{(9)}$	Right-hand-side constant for jth constraint
Right-hand-side constant for ith constraint	$\xleftrightarrow{(10)}$	Objective function coefficient for ith variable
Technological coefficient in constraint i for variable j	$\xleftrightarrow{(11)}$	Technological coefficient in constraint j for variable i

$$x_1 + 4x_2 \quad - 2x_4 = \ 50 \qquad\qquad (3)$$
$$x_1,\, x_3,\, x_4 \geq \ \ 0$$
$$x_2 \quad \text{unrestricted}$$

verify that the corresponding dual is:

$$\text{Maximize} \quad z = 100y_1 + 140y_2 + 50y_3$$
$$\text{subject to} \quad y_1 + 2y_2 + \ y_3 \leq 10$$
$$y_1 \qquad\quad + 4y_3 = 20$$
$$y_1 - \ y_2 \qquad\quad \leq 15$$
$$y_1 + 3y_2 - 2y_3 \leq 12$$
$$y_1 \geq \ \ 0$$
$$y_2 \leq \ \ 0$$
$$y_3 \quad \text{unrestricted}$$

Primal-Dual Solutions

It was indicated earlier that the solution to the primal problem can be obtained from the solution to the dual problem and vice versa. Let's illustrate this by example. Consider the primal problem:

$$\text{Maximize} \quad z = 5x_1 + 6x_2$$
$$\text{subject to} \quad 3x_1 + 2x_2 \leq 120 \qquad\qquad (1)$$
$$4x_1 + 6x_2 \leq 260 \qquad\qquad (2)$$
$$x_1,\, x_2 \geq \ \ 0$$

The corresponding dual is:

$$\text{Minimize} \quad z = 120y_1 + 260y_2$$
$$\text{subject to} \quad 3y_1 + 4y_2 \geq 5$$
$$2y_1 + 6y_2 \geq 6$$
$$y_1,\, y_2 \geq 0$$

TABLE 8.23

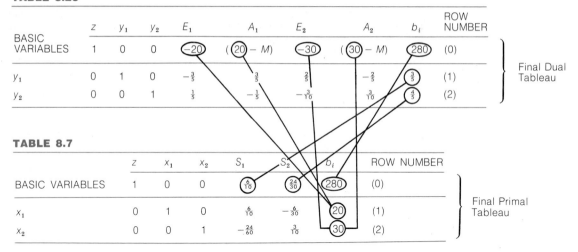

TABLE 8.7

Table 8.23 presents the final (optimal) tableau for the dual problem. Note from this tableau that z is minimized at a value of 280 when $y_1 = \frac{3}{5}$ and $y_2 = \frac{4}{5}$.

The primal problem was solved earlier in the chapter. Table 8.7, which summarizes the optimal solution, is repeated for convenience. Let's illustrate how the solution to each problem can be read from the optimal tableau of the corresponding dual problem.

PRIMAL-DUAL PROPERTY 1

If feasible solutions exist for both the primal and dual problems, then both problems have an optimal solution for which the objective function values are equal. A peripheral relationship is that if one problem has an unbounded solution, its dual has no feasible solution

For this primal-dual pair of problems, note that the optimal values for their respective objective functions both equal 280.

PRIMAL-DUAL PROPERTY 2

The optimal values for decision variables in one problem are read from row (0) of the optimal tableau for the other problem.

The optimal values $y_1 = \frac{3}{5}$ and $y_2 = \frac{4}{5}$ are read from Table 8.7 as the row (0) coefficients for the slack variables S_1 and S_2. The optimal values $x_1 = 20$ and $x_2 = 30$ are read from Table 8.23 as the negatives of the row (0) coefficients for the surplus variables E_1 and E_2. These values can be read, alternatively, under the respective artificial variables, as the portion (term) of the row (0) coefficient *not* involving M.

Epilogue

The dual is a slippery, but significant, topic in linear programming. The purpose has been to acquaint you with the topic and to overview some important properties of the dual. If you choose to take a course in linear or mathematical programming, you will probably receive a more detailed treatment of the dual and its implications.

Section 8.3 Follow-up Exercises

For the following primal problems, formulate the corresponding dual problem.

1   Maximize $z = 3x_1 + 4x_2 + 2x_3$
    subject to $x_1 + x_2 + x_3 \leq 45$
    $4x_1 + 5x_2 - 3x_2 \leq 30$
    $-x_1 + 3x_2 - 4x_3 \leq 50$
    $x_1, x_2, x_3 \geq 0$

2   Minimize $z = 4x_1 + 3x_2 + 5x_3$
    subject to $2x_1 + x_2 - 5x_3 \geq 300$
    $x_1 + x_2 + x_3 \geq 75$
    $x_1, x_2, x_3 \geq 0$

3   Maximize $z = 20x_1 + 15x_2 + 18x_3 + 10x_4$
    subject to $5x_1 - 3x_2 + 10x_3 + 4x_4 \leq 60$
    $x_1 + x_2 + x_3 \qquad = 25$
    $- x_2 + 4x_3 + 7x_4 \geq 35$
    $x_1, x_2, x_3 \geq 0$
    $x_4 \qquad$ unrestricted

4   Minimize $z = 6x_1 + 4x_2$
    subject to $x_1 + x_2 \leq 45$
    $5x_1 - 4x_2 = 10$
    $-3x_1 + 5x_2 \geq 75$
    $3x_1 + 6x_2 \geq 30$
    $x_1 \qquad$ unrestricted
    $x_2 \geq 0$

5   Minimize $z = 4x_1 + 5x_2 + 2x_3 + 3x_4 + x_5$
    subject to $x_1 + x_2 + x_3 + x_4 + x_5 = 45$
    $3x_1 + 5x_2 \qquad - 2x_4 \qquad \leq 24$
    $7x_3 - 5x_4 + 3x_5 \geq 20$
    $x_1, x_2, x_4 \geq 0$
    $x_3, x_5 \qquad$ unrestricted

6   Maximize $z = x_1 + 4x_2 + 6x_3 + 2x_4 + 3x_5 + 2x_6$
    subject to $x_1 + \qquad x_3 + \qquad x_5 \qquad = 40$
    $3x_1 + 5x_2 + 2x_3 - x_4 + 3x_5 - 3x_6 = 70$
    $4x_2 - 5x_3 \qquad + 2x_5 - 4x_6 = 35$
    $x_1, x_3, x_4, x_6 \geq 0$
    $x_2, x_5 \qquad$ unrestricted

7   Given the following primal problem:

Maximize $z = 5x_1 + 3x_2$

$$\text{subject to} \quad 2x_1 + 4x_2 \leq 32$$
$$3x_1 + 2x_2 \leq 24$$
$$x_1, x_2 \geq 0$$

(a) Formulate the corresponding dual problem.
(b) Solve the primal problem using the simplex method.
(c) Determine the optimal solution to the dual problem from the optimal tableau of the primal problem.
(d) Solve the dual problem using the simplex method to verify the result obtained in part (c). Read the optimal solution to the primal problem from the optimal tableau of the dual.

8 Given the following primal problem:

$$\text{Minimize} \quad z = 4x_1 + 3x_2$$
$$\text{subject to} \quad 4x_1 + 2x_2 \geq 80$$
$$3x_1 + x_2 \geq 50$$
$$x_1, x_2 \geq 0$$

(a) Formulate the corresponding dual problem.
(b) Solve the primal problem using the simplex method.
(c) Determine the optimal solution to the dual problem from the optimal tableau of the primal problem.
(d) Solve the dual problem using the simplex method to verify the result obtained in part (c). Read the optimal solution to the primal problem from the optimal tableau of the dual.

KEY TERMS AND CONCEPTS

alternative optimal solution   313
basic feasible solution   299
basic solution   299
basic variable   299
dual (problem)   317
Gauss-Jordan procedure   301
key column   304
nonbasic variable   299
no feasible solution   314

nonpositive variables   318
primal (problem)   317
simplex method   297
solution by enumeration   299
tableau   303
unbounded solution   315
unbounded solution space   315
unrestricted variable   318

ADDITIONAL EXERCISES

Exercises 1 to 8 are related to Sec. 8.1.

Solve the following problems using the simplex method.

1 Maximize $z = 5x_1 + 9x_2$
subject to $4x_1 + 8x_2 \leq 600$
$12x_1 + 8x_2 \leq 960$
$x_1, x_2 \geq 0$

2   Minimize $z = 100x_1 + 75x_2$
    subject to $x_1 + x_2 \geq 200$
    $x_2 \geq 100$
    $x_1 \qquad \geq 80$
    $x_1, x_2 \geq 0$

3   Maximize $z = 4x_1 + 2x_2 + 6x_3$
    subject to $x_1 + 2x_2 + x_3 \leq 100$
    $3x_1 + 2x_2 + 3x_3 \leq 120$
    $x_1, x_2, x_3 \geq 0$

4   Minimize $z = 4x_1 + 4x_2$
    subject to $2x_1 + 4x_2 \geq 160$
    $2x_1 \qquad \geq 60$
    $2x_2 \geq 40$
    $x_1, x_2 \geq 0$

5   Maximize $z = 6x_1 + 12x_2 + 5x_3 + 2x_4$
    subject to $3x_1 + 4x_2 + 8x_3 + 6x_4 \leq 1{,}100$
    $8x_1 + 2x_2 + 4x_3 + 2x_4 \leq 1{,}400$
    $4x_1 + 6x_2 + 2x_3 + 4x_4 \leq 400$
    $x_1, x_2, x_3, x_4 \geq 0$

6   Maximize $z = 5x_1 + 8x_2 + x_3$
    subject to $x_1 + x_2 + 3x_3 \leq 70$
    $x_1 + 2x_2 + x_3 \leq 100$
    $2x_1 + x_2 + x_3 \leq 80$
    $x_1, x_2, x_3 \geq 0$

7   Minimize $z = 8x_1 + 4x_2 + 7x_3$
    subject to $4x_1 + 6x_2 + 2x_3 \geq 120$
    $4x_1 + 2x_2 + 2x_3 \geq 80$
    $2x_1 + 2x_2 + 4x_3 \geq 80$
    $x_1, x_2, x_3 \geq 0$

8   Maximize $z = 7x_1 + 2x_2 + 5x_3$
    subject to $x_1 + 3x_2 + x_3 = 35$
    $2x_1 + x_2 + x_3 \leq 50$
    $x_1 + x_2 + 2x_3 \leq 40$
    $x_1, x_2, x_3 \geq 0$

Exercises 9 to 12 are related to Sec. 8.2.

In the following exercises, solve by the simplex method.

9   Maximize $z = 5x_1 + 10x_2$
    subject to $4x_1 + x_2 \leq 53$
    $x_1 + 2x_2 \leq 22$
    $x_1, x_2 \geq 0$

10   Minimize $z = 15x_1 + 25x_2$
     subject to $5x_1 + 3x_2 \geq 80$
     $6x_1 + 10x_2 \geq 160$
     $x_1, x_2 \geq 0$

11   Minimize $z = 6x_1 + 4x_2$

     subject to $3x_1 + 2x_2 \le 24$

              $x_1 + 2x_2 \ge 30$

                  $x_1,\ x_2 \ge 0$

12   Maximize $z = 2x_1 + 3x_2$

     subject to $-x_1 + 3x_2 \ge 12$

            $x_1 \qquad\quad \le 5$

                $x_1,\ x_2 \ge 0$

Exercises 13 to 17 are related to Sec. 8.3.

For the following problems, formulate the corresponding dual problem.

13   Minimize $z = 8x_1 + 4x_2 + 5x_3 + 6x_4$

     subject to $3x_1 - 2x_2 + 4x_3 + x_4 \le 125$

            $x_1 \qquad + x_3 + x_4 = 75$

         $2x_1 + x_2 - 3x_3 \qquad \le 150$

                 $x_1,\ x_2,\ x_3 \ge 0$

                      x_4 unrestricted

14   Maximize $z = x_1 + 6x_2 + 5x_3 + 3x_4 + 2x_5$

     subject to $3x_1 + 4x_2 \qquad\qquad\qquad \le 35$

         $5x_1 + 3x_2 + 7x_3 - 2x_4 + x_5 \ge 130$

          $x_1 + x_2 + x_3 \qquad\qquad = 50$

                  $x_4 + x_5 \le 20$

            $x_1,\ x_2,\ x_3,\ x_4,\ x_5 \ge 0$

15   Formulate the dual of the highway maintenance problem (Example 2 on page 252) presented in Chap. 7.

16   Formulate the dual of the grant awards problem (Example 3 on page 253) presented in Chap. 7.

17   Formulate the dual of the petroleum blending problem (Example 4 on page 256) presented in Chap. 7.

CHAPTER TEST

1   Given the following linear programming problem:

         Maximize $z = 10x_1 + 8x_2 + 12x_3$

         subject to $4x_1 - 2x_2 + x_3 \le 25$

                $x_1 + 3x_2 \qquad \ge -10$

              $2x_1 \qquad + 3x_3 = -20$

                 $x_1,\ x_2,\ x_3 \ge 0$

transform the constraint set into an equivalent system of constraint equations suitable for the simplex method.

2   Solve the following linear programming problem using the simplex method.

         Maximize $z = 20x_1 + 24x_2$

         subject to $3x_1 + 6x_2 \le 60$

                $4x_1 + 2x_2 \le 32$

                  $x_1,\ x_2 \ge 0$

3 You are given the linear programming problem

$$\text{Minimize} \quad z = 5x_1 + 4x_2$$
$$\text{subject to} \quad x_1 + x_2 \geq 10$$
$$2x_1 - x_2 = 15$$
$$x_1, x_2 \geq 0$$

(a) Set up the initial simplex tableau and revise it, if necessary, so that the row (0) coefficients equal 0 for all basic variables.
(b) Which basic variable will leave first?
(c) Which nonbasic variable will enter first?

4 Describe the way in which alternative optimal solutions are indicated when using the simplex method. How is an unbounded solution indicated?

5 Given the following primal problem, formulate the corresponding dual problem.

$$\text{Minimize} \quad z = 8x_1 + 5x_2 + 6x_3$$
$$\text{subject to} \quad x_1 + x_2 + x_3 = 25$$
$$4x_1 - 5x_2 \geq 10$$
$$x_1 - x_2 + 2x_3 \leq 48$$
$$x_2 \leq 12$$
$$x_1, x_2 \geq 0$$
$$x_3 \quad \text{unrestricted}$$

INTRODUCTION TO PROBABILITY THEORY

CHAPTER OBJECTIVES

- Provide an understanding of the counting methods of permutations and combinations

- Introduce the notion of probability and the computation of probabilities for selected statistical environments

- Provide an understanding of probability distributions and their attributes

- Introduce the notion of expected monetary value and discuss its application to decision making

- Acquaint readers with the characteristics and usage of the binomial and normal probability distributions

Much in life is characterized by uncertainty. Many phenomena in our world seem to be characterized by random behavior. Most decisions are made in an environment characterized by an absence of complete knowledge. A decision about the number of units of a product to produce is based upon *estimates* of the number of units expected to be sold. If the number to be sold was known in advance, the decision would be to manufacture precisely this quantity, incurring neither shortages nor overages. However, in actual decision-making situations exact information is rarely obtainable.

Probability concepts can be very useful in dealing with the uncertainty which characterizes most decision-making environments. Probability theory takes advantage of the fact that, for many uncertain phenomena, there are "long run" patterns. For instance, on the single flip of a fair coin it is uncertain whether a head or a tail will occur. However, with many flips of the same coin—over the long run—approximately half of the outcomes should be "heads" and approximately half "tails."

Medical research heavily relies upon long-run observations to generalize re-

TABLE 9.1

NUMBER OF PERSONS RECEIVING THE DRUG	NUMBER OF PERSONS HAVING NO RECURRENCE OF HEART ATTACK	PERCENTAGE HAVING NO RECURRENCE
100	64	64
300	196	65.3
500	317	63.4
1,000	636	63.6
5,000	3,177	63.54
10,000	6,351	63.51

sults. Table 9.1 shows the results of a study which examined the effectiveness of a new drug in reducing the recurrence of heart attacks. Persons who survived a first heart attack were given the drug for a period of 5 years. Table 9.1 summarizes the results of the study as the sample of persons increases. Notice how the percentage having no recurrence fluctuates, yet tends to stabilize, as the sample increases in size. The evidence after 10,000 observations suggests that approximately 63.5 percent of heart attack victims using this particular drug will not have another attack in the 5 years following a first heart attack. These results have greater meaning when compared with those for a second sample of heart attack victims who were not given the same drug. For 10,000 persons in this group, the percentage having no recurrence was 45.26. These results are encouraging regarding the potential for the new drug.

The purpose of this chapter is to introduce the fundamentals of probability theory. The first section discusses some special counting methods which are useful in probability theory. The next section introduces fundamental concepts of probability and the computation of probabilities. This is followed by a discussion of the use of probability in determining *expected values*. The last two sections discuss two of the more frequently used probability distributions—the *binomial* and the *normal distributions*.

9.1 PERMUTATIONS AND COMBINATIONS

Before we introduce probability theory, the special counting methods of *permutations* and *combinations* will be discussed.

Permutations

A *permutation* is an ordered arrangement of a set of items. Consider the three numerals 1, 2, and 3. One permutation of these numerals is 123. Another permutation is 132. All the different permutations of these three numerals are

123   132   213   231   312   321

PERMUTATION COUNTING: RULE 1

The number of permutations of n different items *taken n at a time* is denoted by $_nP_n$ where

$$_nP_n = n(n-1)(n-2) \cdots 2 \cdot 1 \qquad (9.1)$$

The logic underlying Eq. (9.1) is that in selecting the first of the n items, there are n choices. Once the first item is selected, there are $n - 1$ choices for the second item, or $(n)(n - 1)$ possible choices for the first two items. Following selection of the second item there are $n - 2$ choices for the third item, or

$(n)(n - 1)(n - 2)$ possible choices for the first three items. This logic concludes that having selected the first $(n - 1)$ items, there remains but one choice for the nth item. Equation (9.1) can be rewritten by using *factorial* notation as

$$\boxed{_nP_n = n!} \tag{9.2}$$

The notation $n!$ (read "n factorial") is a shorthand way of representing the product on the right side of Eq. (9.1). For example, "5 factorial" is expressed as

$$5! = 5 \cdot 4 \cdot 3 \cdot 2 \cdot 1$$

and

$$10! = 10 \cdot 9 \cdot 8 \cdot 7 \cdot 6 \cdot 5 \cdot 4 \cdot 3 \cdot 2 \cdot 1$$

By definition

$$0! = 1$$

The number of different permutations of the three numerals 1, 2, and 3 taken three at a time is $_3P_3 = 3! = 3 \cdot 2 \cdot 1 = 6$. Note that this equals the number of different permutations enumerated previously.

EXAMPLE 1

Six football teams compete in a particular conference. Assuming no ties, how many different end-of-season rankings are possible in the conference?

SOLUTION

The number of different rankings is

$$_6P_6 = 6!$$
$$= 6 \cdot 5 \cdot 4 \cdot 3 \cdot 2 \cdot 1 = 720$$

PERMUTATION COUNTING: RULE 2

The number of permutations of n different objects *taken r at a time* is denoted by $_nP_r$ where

$$_nP_r = \underbrace{n(n - 1)(n - 2) \cdots (n - r + 1)}_{r \text{ factors}} \tag{9.3}$$

The logic underlying Eq. (9.3) is similar to that for Eq. (9.1). However, once $r - 1$ items have been selected, the number of different choices for the rth item equals $n - (r - 1)$, or $n - r + 1$.

An alternative statement of Eq. (9.3) is

$$\boxed{_nP_r = \frac{n!}{(n - r)!}} \tag{9.4}$$

This is obtained by multiplying the right side of Eq. (9.3) by $(n - r)!/(n - r)!$.

EXAMPLE 2

A person wishes to place a bet which selects the first three horses to finish a race in their correct order of finish. If eight horses are in the race, how many different possibilities exist for the first three horses (assuming no ties)?

SOLUTION

The number of possibilities is

$$_8P_3 = 8 \cdot 7 \cdot 6 = 336$$

or, according to Eq. (9.4),

$$_8P_3 = \frac{8!}{(8-3)!}$$

$$= \frac{8 \cdot 7 \cdot 6 \cdot 5 \cdot 4 \cdot 3 \cdot 2 \cdot 1}{5 \cdot 4 \cdot 3 \cdot 2 \cdot 1} = 8 \cdot 7 \cdot 6 = 336$$

The logic underlying this computation is that there are eight possibilities for first place. Given these eight, there remain seven possibilities for second place; and, given the selection of first and second places, there are six choices for third place.

Combinations

With permutations we are concerned with the number of different ways in which a set of items can be arranged. In many situations there is an interest in the number of ways in which a set of items can be selected without any particular concern for the order or arrangement of the items. For example, one may be interested in determining the number of different committees of three people which can be formed from six candidates. In this instance, the committee consisting of (A, B, C) is the same committee as (B, A, C), where A, B, and C represent three of the candidates. Order of selection is not significant in determining the number of different committees.

A *combination* is a set of items with no consideration given to the order or arrangement of the items. A combination of r items selected from a set of n items is a *subset* of the set of n items.

COMBINATIONS COUNTING RULE

The number of different combinations of r items which can be selected from n different items is denoted by $_nC_r$ where

$$_nC_r = \frac{n!}{r!(n-r)!} \tag{9.5}$$

To return to the committee example, the number of different combinations of six persons taken three at a time equals

$$_6C_3 = \frac{6!}{3!(6-3)!}$$

$$= \frac{6!}{3!3!} = \frac{6 \cdot 5 \cdot 4 \cdot 3 \cdot 2 \cdot 1}{3 \cdot 2 \cdot 1 \cdot 3 \cdot 2 \cdot 1} = 20$$

EXAMPLE 3

Super Bowl organizers are selecting game officials. From 12 officials who are eligible, 5 will be selected. How many different teams of 5 officials can be selected from the 12?

SOLUTION

The number of different teams of officials is

$$_{12}C_5 = \frac{12!}{5!(12-5)!}$$

$$= \frac{12!}{5!7!} = \frac{12 \cdot 11 \cdot 10 \cdot 9 \cdot 8}{5 \cdot 4 \cdot 3 \cdot 2 \cdot 1} = 792$$

Section 9.1 Follow-up Exercises

In Exercises 1 to 8, evaluate each symbol.

1   $_4P_4$

2   $_6P_4$

3   $_8P_5$

4   $_{10}P_2$

5   $_4C_4$

6   $_6C_4$

7   $_{10}C_5$

8   $_4C_3$

9   Ten horses are to be placed within a starting gate for a major sweepstakes race. How many different starting arrangements are possible?

10   A political candidate wishes to visit eight different states. In how many different orders can she visit these states?

11   The same political candidate in Exercise 10 has time and funds to visit only five cities. How many different combinations of five cities can she visit?

12   A credit card company issues credit cards which have a three-letter prefix as part of the card number. A sample card number is ABC1234.

(a) If each letter of the prefix is to be different, how many prefixes are possible?

(b) If each of the four numerals following the prefix is to be different, how many different four-digit sequences are possible?

13   Twelve astronauts are being considered for the next flight team. If a flight team consists of three members, how many different combinations of astronauts could be considered?

14   A portfolio management expert is considering 25 stocks for investment. Only 10 stocks will be selected for inclusion in a portfolio. How many different combinations of stocks can be considered?

9.2 BASIC PROBABILITY CONCEPTS

This section will introduce the notion of probability and some basic probability concepts.

Experiments, Outcomes, and Events

The notion of probability is associated with *random processes,* or *random experiments.* A *random experiment* (or, more simply, *experiment*) is a process which results in one of a number of possible *outcomes.*

Classic random experiments include flipping a coin, rolling a die, drawing a card from a well-shuffled deck, and selecting a ball from an urn which contains a certain number of balls. There are many random processes around us which are less obvious. Many manufacturing processes produce defective products in a random manner. The time between the arrivals of telephone calls at a telephone exchange, cars at toll booths, and customers at supermarkets have been described as random processes. The process by which the sex of a child is determined is also random.

Each repetition of an experiment can be thought of as a *trial* which has an observable outcome. If we assume in the coin-flipping experiment that the coin cannot come to rest on its edge, the two possible outcomes for a trial are the occurrence of a head or the occurrence of a tail. The set which includes all possible outcomes for an experiment is called the *sample space* for the experiment. For the coin flipping example, the sample space S is defined as

$$S = \{head, tail\}$$

For an experiment which measures the time between arrivals of telephone calls at a telephone exchange the sample space might be defined as

$$S = \{t \mid t \text{ is measured in seconds and } t \geq 0\}$$

In the coin flipping experiment we have a *finite sample space;* in the telephone call experiment we have an *infinite sample space.*

Given an experiment, outcomes are frequently classified into *events.* An event E for an experiment is a subset of a sample space, as shown in Fig. 9.1 The way in which events are defined depends upon the combinations of outcomes for which probabilities are to be computed. For the coin-flipping experiment events and outcomes are likely to be defined identically as shown in Fig. 9.2. This is because there are only two possible outcomes and we are likely to be interested either in the probability of a head or the probability of a tail.

The relationship between an outcome and an event can be illustrated better when considering the experiment involving the time between arrivals of telephone calls. Events may be defined in different ways depending on the purpose of the experiment. In Fig. 9.3, the infinite sample space has been transformed into an infinite set of events using a one-for-one mapping of outcomes and events. For the same experiment, Fig. 9.4 shows a mapping of the infinite sample space into two events. Thus, it is possible that an event can be defined in such a way as to consist of multiple outcomes.

EXAMPLE 4

Suppose that an experiment consists of selecting three manufactured parts from a production process and observing whether they are *acceptable* (satisfy all production specifications) or *defective* (do not satisfy all specifications).

(*a*) Determine the sample space S.

(*b*) What outcomes are included in the event "exactly two acceptable parts"?

(*c*) What outcomes are included in the event "at least one defective part"?

SOLUTION

(*a*) If we denote "acceptable" by A and "defective" by D, the outcome of any trial will be denoted by a sequence of three As and Ds. The possible experiment outcomes are represented by the solution space

$$S = \{AAA, AAD, ADA, ADD, DAA, DAD, DDA, DDD\}$$

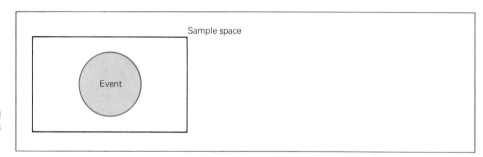

FIGURE 9.1
An event is a subset of the sample space.

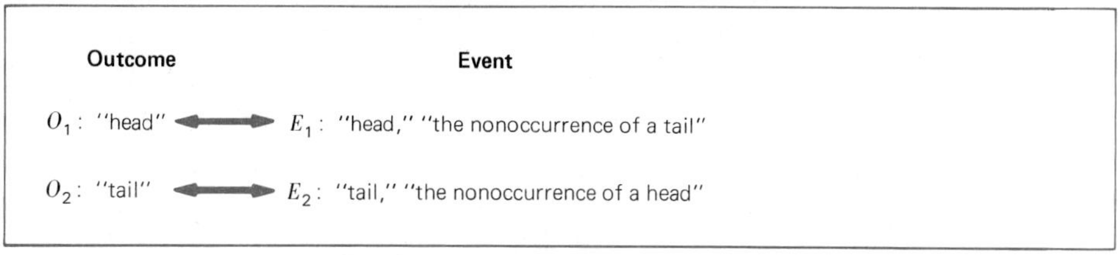

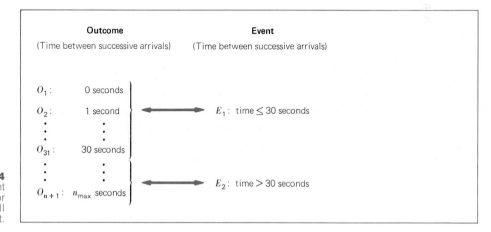

FIGURE 9.2
Outcome/event mapping for coin flip experiment.

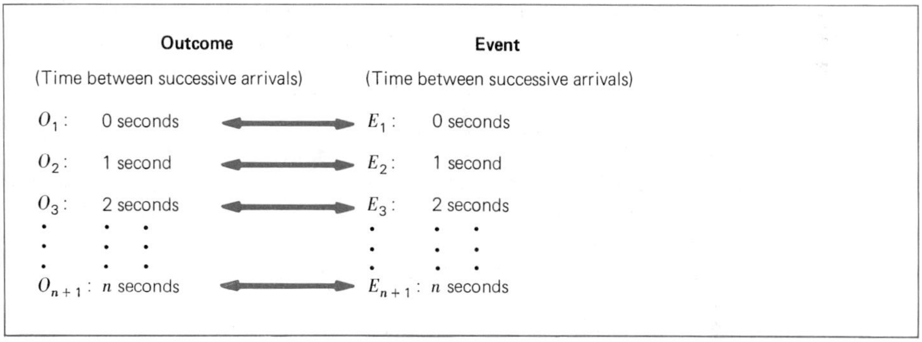

FIGURE 9.3
Outcome/event mapping for telephone call experiment.

FIGURE 9.4
Outcome/event mapping for telephone call experiment.

(b) The event "exactly two acceptable parts" is the subset of S

$$E = \{AAD, ADA, DAA\}$$

(c) The event "at least one defective part" is the subset of S

$$E = \{AAD, ADA, ADD, DAA, DAD, DDA, DDD\}$$

Probabilities and Odds

Although we can guess about the outcome of an experiment, we cannot know for certain what outcome will occur. We can guess head or tail for the flip of a coin, but we cannot know for sure. With many random processes, however, there is long-run regularity. As mentioned earlier, the long-run expectation in flipping a coin is that approximately half of the outcomes will be heads and half tails. In the roll of a die, the long-run expectation is that each side of the die will occur approximately one-sixth of the time. These values reflect the expectation of the *relative frequency* of an event. The relative frequency of an event is the proportion of the time that the event occurs. It is computed by dividing the number of times m the event occurs by the number of times n the experiment is conducted. *The probability of an event can be thought of as the relative frequency m/n of the event over the long run.*

Since the probability of an event is a proportion, we can state the following rule.

RULE 1

The probability of an event E, denoted by $P(E)$, is a number between 0 and 1, inclusive, or

$$0 \leq P(E) \leq 1 \qquad (9.6)$$

Two special cases of Eq. (9.6) are $P(E) = 0$ and $P(E) = 1$. *If $P(E) = 0$, it is certain that event E will not occur.* For example, if a coin is two-headed, $P(\text{tail}) = 0$ in a single flip of the coin. *If $P(E) = 1$, it is certain that event E will occur.* With the same coin, $P(\text{head}) = 1$. If $0 < P(E) < 1$, there is uncertainty about the occurrence of event E. For example, if $P(E) = .4$, we can state that there is a 40 percent chance that event E will occur.

EXAMPLE 5

Table 9.2 indicates some characteristics of the first-year class at a junior college. Assume that a student will be selected at random from the freshman class and that each person has an equal chance of being selected. Using the relative frequency concept of probability, we can estimate the likelihood that the selected student will have certain characteristics. For example, the probability that the selected student will be a male is

$$P(M) = \frac{\text{number of males}}{\text{total number of first-year students}}$$

$$= \frac{750}{1,500} = .50$$

The probability that the selected student will be a preengineering student is

TABLE 9.2

SEX \ MAJOR	(B) BUSINESS	(L) LIBERAL ARTS	(E) PREENGINEERING	TOTAL
Male (M)	350	300	100	750
Female (F)	250	450	50	750
Total	600	750	150	1,500

TABLE 9.3

SEX \ MAJOR	(B) BUSINESS	(L) LIBERAL ARTS	(E) PREENGINEERING	TOTAL
Male (M)	.233	.200	.067	.500
Female (F)	.167	.300	.033	.500
Total	.400	.500	.100	1.000

$$P(E) = \frac{\text{number of preengineering students}}{\text{total number of first-year students}}$$

$$= \frac{150}{1,500} = .10$$

The probability that the selected student will be a female majoring in business is

$$P(F \text{ and } B) = \frac{250}{1,500} = .167$$

Table 9.3 summarizes the probabilities of various events associated with selecting a student. Notice that the sum of the probabilities for the events M and F equals 1. Similarly, the sum of the probabilities for the events B, L, and E equals 1.

POINT FOR THOUGHT AND DISCUSSION

Why do the probabilities for the two different sets of events $\{M, F\}$ and $\{B, L, E\}$ each total 1?

Probabilities may be classified in several ways. One classification is the distinction between *objective* and *subjective probabilities.* Objective probabilities are based upon definite historical experience or general knowledge. For example, probabilities assigned to the events associated with flipping a fair coin or rolling a die are based upon much historical and generally known experience. Other objective probabilities are assigned because of actual experimentation. For instance, if one has been told that a die is "loaded," one method of determining the probability of any side occurring is to roll the die many times while keeping a record of the relative frequency for each side.

Subjective probabilities are assigned in the absence of wide historical experience. They are based upon personal experiences and intuition. They are really expressions of personal judgment. A subjective probability would be the probability that you would assign to your receiving a grade of A in this course. Such an estimate would reflect your personal assessment of such factors as your aptitude in this type of course, your perception of the degree of difficulty of this course, and your assessment of the instructor and the way in which he or she will conduct the course and evaluate performance.

When *odds* are given in association with some event, they reflect someone's assessment of the likelihood of occurrence (or nonoccurrence) of the event. If an oddsmaker states odds of 3 to 1 that team A will win a football game, the oddsmaker is stating a belief that if the game were played four times, team A would win three of the four times. Or, these odds assign a probability of $3/(1 + 3) = \frac{3}{4}$ or .75 that team A will win. The odds of 3 to 1 favoring team A are equivalent to stating odds of 1 to 3 that the opponent team will win. Odds of 1 to 3 are equivalent to assigning a probability of $1/(1 + 3) = \frac{1}{4} = .25$.

Some Additional Rules of Probability

RULE 2

If $P(E)$ represents the probability that an event E will occur, the probability that E will not occur, denoted by $P(\overline{E})$, is

$$P(\overline{E}) = 1 - P(E) \qquad (9.7)$$

If the probability that a business will earn a profit during its first year of operation is estimated at .85, the probability that it will not earn a profit during the first year is $1 - .85 = .15$. Given a "fair" die, the probability of rolling a "one" equals $\frac{1}{6}$. The probability of not rolling a "one" equals $1 - \frac{1}{6} = \frac{5}{6}$.

DEFINITION: MUTUALLY EXCLUSIVE EVENTS

A set of events is said to be ***mutually exclusive*** if the occurrence of any one of the events precludes the occurrence of any of the other events.

In flipping a coin, the two possible outcomes are *heads* and *tails*. Since the occurrence of a head precludes any possibility of a tail, and vice versa, the events "heads" and "tails" are mutually exclusive events. Suppose for the roll of a die, two events are defined as E_1 ("one") and E_2 ("a value less than three"). E_1 and E_2 are not mutually exclusive because the occurrence of one event does not necessarily preclude the other. For a single trial, the outcome "one" implies that both E_1 and E_2 have occurred. Figure 9.5 is a Venn diagram representation of mutually exclusive and nonmutually exclusive events.

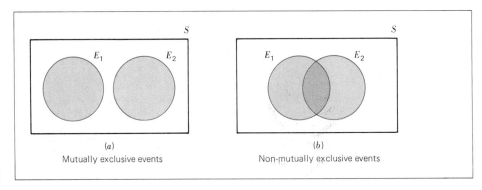

(a)
Mutually exclusive events

(b)
Non-mutually exclusive events

FIGURE 9.5

EXAMPLE 6

Consider a survey of political preferences in which a random sample of registered voters is selected. The events "Democrat" and "woman" are not mutually exclusive because the selection of a Democrat does not preclude the possibility that the person is also a woman. The two events "man" and "woman" would be mutually exclusive, as would the events "Democrat," "Republican," and "Independent."

RULE 3

If events E_1 and E_2 are mutually exclusive, the probability of either E_1 or E_2 occurring is

$$P(E_1 \cup E_2) = P(E_1) + P(E_2) \qquad (9.8)$$

Note the use of the union operator from set theory in the statement of this rule.

EXAMPLE 7

Public Works The department of public works for a community is gearing up for winter. The department is planning its sand and salt needs for maintaining roads during and after snowstorms. An analysis of past winters has resulted in the following probability estimates regarding the expected number of major snowstorms. What is the probability of three of more major snowstorms during the coming year?

TABLE 9.4

n (NUMBER OF MAJOR STORMS)	$P(n)$
0	.10
1	.25
2	.30
3	.20
more than 3	.15

SOLUTION

The events in Table 9.4 which correspond to "3 or more" major snowstorms are $n = 3$ and $n =$ more than 3. These two events are mutually exclusive. Therefore, the probability of three or more major snowstorms is

$$P(3 \text{ or more}) = P(3) + P(\text{more than 3})$$
$$= .20 + .15 = .35$$

RULE 4

Given n mutually exclusive events $E_1, E_2, \ldots, E_n$, the probability of occurrence of one of the n events is

$$P(E_1 \cup E_2 \cup \cdots \cup E_n)$$
$$= P(E_1) + P(E_2) + \cdots + P(E_n) \quad (9.9)$$

EXAMPLE 8

Given the information in Example 7, what is the probability of having fewer than three major snowstorms?

SOLUTION

The events corresponding to "fewer than three" storms are 0, 1, or 2 storms. Therefore

$$P(\text{less than 3}) = P(0 \cup 1 \cup 2)$$
$$= P(0) + P(1) + P(2) = .10 + .25 + .30 = .65$$

NOTE

This problem could have been solved using our result in Example 7 and applying Rule 2. That is,

$$P(\text{less than 3}) = 1 - P(3 \text{ or more})$$
$$= 1 - .35 = .65$$

When a set of events is not mutually exclusive, Rule 3 must be modified to reflect the possibility that two events may occur at the same time.

RULE 5

The probability of occurrence of event E_1, event E_2, or both E_1 and E_2 is

$$P(E_1 \cup E_2) = P(E_1) + P(E_2) - P(E_1 \cap E_2) \qquad \textbf{(9.10)}$$

Note that the intersection operator is used to denote the joint or simultaneous occurrence of events E_1 and E_2.

Rule 3 is the special case of Rule 5 where $P(E_1 \cap E_2) = 0$. This is because E_1 and E_2 are assumed to be mutually exclusive in Rule 3, meaning that the events can never occur together. Figure 9.6 illustrates these rules using Venn diagrams. In these diagrams, areas represent probabilities with the area of the sample space S assumed to equal 1.0.

FIGURE 9.6

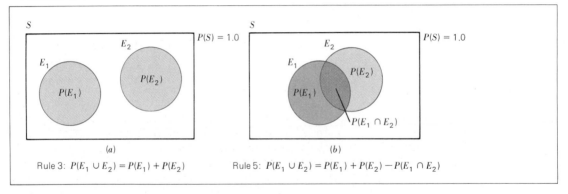

(a)
Rule 3: $P(E_1 \cup E_2) = P(E_1) + P(E_2)$

(b)
Rule 5: $P(E_1 \cup E_2) = P(E_1) + P(E_2) - P(E_1 \cap E_2)$

EXAMPLE 9

In an experiment consisting of selecting one card at random from a deck of 52 cards, the events "king" and "spade" are not mutually exclusive. The probability of selecting a king, a spade, or both a king and a spade is determined by applying Rule 5, or

$$P(\text{king} \cup \text{spade}) = P(\text{king}) + P(\text{spade}) - P(\text{king} \cap \text{spade})$$
$$= P(\text{king}) + P(\text{spade}) - P(\text{king of spades})$$
$$= \tfrac{4}{52} + \tfrac{13}{52} - \tfrac{1}{52}$$
$$= \tfrac{16}{52} = \tfrac{4}{13}$$

Note that $P(\text{king} \cap \text{spade})$ must be subtracted to offset the double counting of the event (king $\cap$ spade). When $P(\text{king})$ is computed, the king of spades is included; and when $P(\text{spade})$ is computed, the king of spades is included. Thus, double counting has occurred, and $P(\text{king of spades})$ must be subtracted.

DEFINITION: COLLECTIVELY EXHAUSTIVE EVENTS

A set of events is said to be **collectively exhaustive** if their union accounts for all possible outcomes of an experiment.

The events "head" and "tail," associated with the flip of a coin, are collectively exhaustive since their union accounts for all possible outcomes. For an experiment which involves flipping a coin two times, the events H_1H_2, H_1T_2, and T_1T_2 describe possible outcomes. This set of events is not collectively exhaustive since the union of the events does not include the outcome T_1H_2.

For the same experiment, the set of events H_1H_2, H_1T_2, T_1T_2, and T_1H_2 is *both* mutually exclusive and collectively exhaustive.

Statistical Independence

Events may be classified as *independent* or *dependent.*

DEFINITION: INDEPENDENT EVENTS

Two events are independent if the occurrence or nonoccurrence of one event in no way affects the likelihood (or probability) of occurrence of the other event. Otherwise they are said to be dependent.

Successive flips of a fair coin are an example of independent events. The occurrence of a head or tail on any one toss of the coin has no effect on the probability of a head or tail on the next or succeeding tosses of the coin. Drawing cards from a deck or balls from an urn *with replacement* is an experiment characterized by independent events. "*With replacement*" means that the item selected is put back in the deck or the urn before the next item is selected. In the case of a deck of cards, the probability of drawing a heart on each draw is $\tfrac{13}{52}$ as long as the previously drawn card is replaced in the deck.

The random generation of *acceptable* or *defective* products from a production process is another example of events which may be statistically independent.

For such processes, the probability of generating an acceptable (defective) unit is assumed to remain the same for a given trial regardless of previous outcomes.

The simple probability of an event is often called a **marginal probability.** The marginal probability of a head is .5 when a fair coin is tossed. Assuming a random draw, the marginal probability of selecting a spade from a deck of cards equals $\frac{13}{52}$. Very often there is an interest in computing the probability of two or more events occurring at the same time or in succession. For example, we may be interested in the probability of rolling a pair of dice and having a 5 occur on one die and a 2 on the other; or, we may be interested in the likelihood that five heads would occur in five successive tosses of a coin. *The probability of the joint occurrence of two or more events is called a* **joint probability.**

RULE 6

The joint probability that two independent events E_1 and E_2 will occur together or in succession equals the product of the marginal probabilities of E_1 and E_2, or

$$P(E_1 \cap E_2) = P(E_1) \cdot P(E_2) \tag{9.11}$$

EXAMPLE 10

The probability that a machine will produce a defective part equals .05. The production process is characterized by statistical independence. That is, the probability of any item being defective is .05, regardless of the quality of previous units. Suppose we wish to determine the probability that two consecutive parts will be defective. If the event D represents the occurrence of a defective item, then according to Rule 6,

$$
\begin{aligned}
P(D_1 \cap D_2) &= P(D_1)P(D_2) \\
&= (.05)(.05) = .0025
\end{aligned}
$$

RULE 7

The joint probability that n independent events E_1, E_2, . . . , E_n will occur together or in succession is

$$P(E_1 \cap E_2 \cap \cdots \cap E_n) = P(E_1)P(E_2) \cdots P(E_n) \tag{9.12}$$

EXAMPLE 11

The Internal Revenue Service (IRS) estimates the probability of an error on personal income tax returns to be .4. Suppose that an experiment is conducted in which three returns are selected at random for purposes of an audit, and we wish to determine all possible outcomes and the probabilities of these outcomes.

A tool which is useful in problems such as this is a *probability tree.* A probability tree provides a logical method for enumerating and displaying all possible outcomes in an experiment. Figure 9.7 illustrates the probability tree for this experiment. Let E represent the outcome "error" for the ith trial and N the outcome "no error." For the first return selected, the two circles indicate the marginal probabilities of the two simple events which are possible.

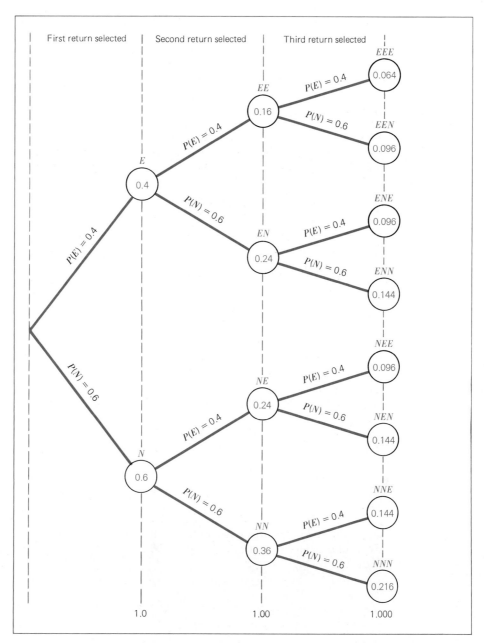

First return selected | Second return selected | Third return selected

$P(E) = 0.4$
$P(N) = 0.6$

EEE 0.064
EEN 0.096
ENE 0.096
ENN 0.144
NEE 0.096
NEN 0.144
NNE 0.144
NNN 0.216

EE 0.16
EN 0.24
NE 0.24
NN 0.36

E 0.4
N 0.6

1.0   1.00   1.000

FIGURE 9.7
Probability tree
for IRS
example.

For the second return selected, the four circles indicate the joint probabilities of the different outcomes possible when selecting two returns. If we assume that the outcomes for successive selections (trials) are independent, the probabilities of the different joint events for two selected returns can be computed using Rule 6. For example,

$$P(E \cap N) = P(E)P(N)$$
$$= (.4)(.6) = .24$$

For the third return selected, the eight circles indicate the joint probabilities of the different outcomes possible when selecting three returns. These probabilities can be computed using Rule 7. For example,

$$P(E \cap N \cap E) = P(E)P(N)P(E)$$
$$= (.4)(.6)(.4) = .096$$

Note in Fig. 9.7 that for each trial the sum of the joint probabilities equals 1. This is so because the set of events identified is collectively exhaustive and mutually exclusive.

EXERCISE

Using the probability tree in Figure 9.7, determine the probability that (1) two of three returns contain errors and (2) the three returns contain at least one error.*

In addition to marginal and joint probabilities, another type of probability is a *conditional probability. The notation $P(E_1|E_2)$ represents the conditional probability of event E_1 given that event E_2 has occurred.* The probability of a head on the third toss of a coin, given that the first two tosses both resulted in a head, is a conditional probability.

By definition, however, independent events have the property that the occurrence or nonoccurrence of one event has no influence on the probability of another event.

RULE 8

Given two independent events E_1 and E_2, the conditional probability of event E_1 given that event E_2 has occurred is the marginal probability of E_1, or

$$P(E_1|E_2) = P(E_1) \qquad \textbf{(9.13)}$$

The conditional probability of a 6 on the roll of a die given that no 6s have occurred in the last 20 rolls equals $\frac{1}{6}$. For the IRS example, the probability that the next return selected contains an error equals .4, regardless of the outcomes from previous income tax returns examined.

Statistical Dependence

In contrast to the state of statistical independence, many events are characterized as being *statistically dependent.*

DEFINITION: DEPENDENT EVENTS

Two events are **dependent** if the probability of occurrence of one event is affected by the occurrence or nonoccurrence of the other event.

---

* Answer: (*a*) .288, (*b*) .784

TABLE 9.5

	NO EXERCISE (NE)	SOME EXERCISE (SE)	REGULAR EXERCISE (RE)	TOTAL
Heart disease (HD)	700	300	100	1,100
No heart disease ($\overline{HD}$)	1,300	6,600	1,000	8,900
Total	2,000	6,900	1,100	10,000

Examples of experiments consisting of dependent events include drawing cards from a deck or balls from an urn *without replacement*. If a card is selected which is not a heart and the card is kept out of the deck, the probability of selecting a heart on the next draw is not the same as it was for the first draw. Given the following events related to weather conditions:

Event E_1 = it will snow
Event E_2 = the temperature will be below freezing

the probability of event E_1 is affected by the occurrence or nonoccurrence of event E_2.

EXAMPLE 12

A nationwide survey of 10,000 middle-aged men resulted in the data shown in Table 9.5. It is believed that the results from this survey of 10,000 men are representative of these particular attributes for the average middle-aged man in this country. We can estimate probabilities related to heart disease and exercise habits based upon relative frequencies of occurrence in the survey. For example, the probability that a middle-aged man gets no exercise is

$$P(NE) = \frac{\text{number of respondents who do no exercise}}{\text{number of men surveyed}}$$

$$= \frac{2,000}{10,000} = .20$$

The probability that a middle-aged man has heart disease is

$$P(HD) = \frac{\text{number of respondents having heart disease}}{\text{number of men surveyed}}$$

$$= \frac{1,100}{10,000} = .11$$

The joint probability that a middle-aged man exercises regularly and has heart disease is

$$P(HD \cap RE) = \frac{100}{10,000} = .01$$

Suppose we are interested in the conditional probability that a man will suffer from heart disease *given* that he does not exercise. The *given* information focuses our attentions upon the first column in Table 9.5, those respondents who do not exercise. Of the 2,000 surveyed who do not exercise, 700 suffer heart disease. Therefore, the conditional probability is computed as

$$P(HD|NE) = \frac{\text{number of respondents who do not exercise } and \text{ suffer heart disease}}{\text{number of respondents who do not exercise}}$$

$$= \frac{700}{2,000} = .35$$

The conditional probability that a man exercises regularly given that he suffers heart disease is

$$P(RE|HD) = \frac{\text{number of respondents who exercise}}{\text{number of respondents who suffer heart disease}}$$

$$= \frac{100}{1{,}100} = .09$$

Conditional probabilities under conditions of statistical dependence can be computed by using the following rule.

RULE 9

The conditional probability of event E_1 given the occurrence of event E_2 is

$$P(E_1|E_2) = \frac{P(E_1 \cap E_2)}{P(E_2)} \qquad (9.14)$$

The conditional probability is found by dividing the joint probability of events E_1 and E_2 by the marginal probability of E_2.

Indirectly, we were using Eq. (9.14) when computing the conditional probabilities in Example 12. Applying Eq. (9.14) in that example, we get

$$P(HD|NE) = \frac{P(HD \cap NE)}{P(NE)}$$

$$= \frac{700/10{,}000}{2{,}000/10{,}000} = \frac{.07}{.20} = .35$$

and

$$P(RE|HD) = \frac{P(RE \cap HD)}{P(HD)}$$

$$= \frac{100/10{,}000}{1{,}100/10{,}000} = \frac{.01}{.11} = .09$$

EXAMPLE 13

Suppose that a person selects a card at random from a deck of 52 cards and tells us that the selected card is red. The probability that the card is the king of hearts *given* that it is red can be determined using Eq. (9.14).

$$P(\text{king of hearts} \mid \text{red}) = \frac{P(\text{king of hearts} \cap \text{red})}{P(\text{red})}$$

$$= \frac{1/52}{26/52} = \frac{1}{26}$$

If both sides of Eq. (9.14) are multiplied by $P(E_2)$, the resulting equation provides an expression for the joint probability $P(E_1 \cap E_2)$, or

$$\boxed{P(E_1 \cap E_2) = P(E_2)P(E_1|E_2)} \qquad (9.15)$$

EXAMPLE 14

The joint probability of selecting two aces in a row from a deck without replacement of the first card can be found using Eq. (9.15) as

$$P(A_1 \cap A_2) = P(\text{ace on first draw}) \cdot P(\text{ace on second draw } given \text{ an ace on first draw})$$
$$= P(A_1)P(A_2|A_1)$$

$$= \frac{4}{52} \cdot \frac{3}{51} = \frac{12}{2{,}652}$$

EXAMPLE 15

Terrorist Activities   A terrorist group operating within a foreign country has made a threat to destroy certain airplanes unless its demands are met. They claim to have placed bombs on 3 of 20 planes currently on the ground at a major airport. All passengers and crews have been evacuated and a bomb squad is about to begin its search of the planes. Of interest is the probability that the first 3 planes searched will be the 3 affected planes.

If A denotes the selection of an affected plane and N the selection of a nonaffected plane, we are interested in $P(A_1 \cap A_2 \cap A_3)$. The probability that the first two planes selected are affected is computed as

$$P(A_1 \cap A_2) = P(A_1) \cdot P(A_2|A_1)$$
$$= \frac{3}{20} \cdot \frac{2}{19} = \frac{6}{380} = \frac{3}{190}$$

The probability that the first three planes selected are the affected ones is found as

$$P(A_1 \cap A_2 \cap A_3) = P(A_1 \cap A_2) \cdot P(A_3|A_1 \cap A_2)$$
$$= \frac{3}{190} \cdot \frac{1}{18} = \frac{3}{3{,}420}$$

EXERCISE

What is the probability that a random selection of four planes will result in the outcome $A_1 N_2 A_3 A_4$?*

EXAMPLE 16

Space Shuttle Simulation   While the space shuttle flights are being prepared, one contingency anticipated is replacement of defective components while in space. One scenario simulated suggests that of 10 fuel cells of a particular type used on a mission, three become defective while in flight. Suppose that it is impossible to know which three are defective. The only way of identifying the defective cells is to remove them and test them with on-board equipment. If the cells are selected at random, (*a*) construct a probability tree which summarizes the possible outcomes from selecting three cells and testing them. (*b*) What is the probability that none of the defective cells will be included in the sample of three? One defective cell? Two defective cells? All three?

SOLUTION

(*a*) If we let D_j and N_j represent defective and nondefective outcomes for the jth cell se-

---

* Answer: $\frac{102}{116{,}280} = \frac{1}{1{,}140}$

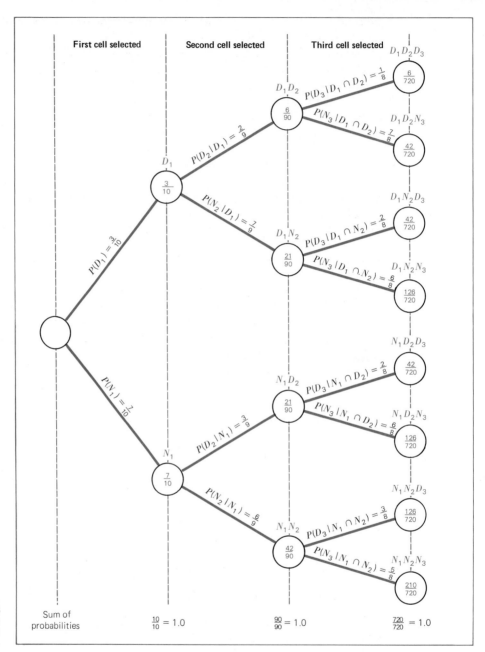

FIGURE 9.8
Probability tree
for space
shuttle example.

lected, Fig. 9.8 presents the probability tree summarizing the possible outcomes from selecting three cells. Note that the events described in this problem are statistically
dependent. Also, note that the sum of the probabilities for all outcomes associated with
each trial equals 1. Finally, in an experiment consisting of three trials (three fuel cells selected), there are eight different outcomes possible.

(*b*) The probability that none of the defective cells will be selected corresponds to the outcome $N_1N_2N_3$ which has a probability of $\frac{210}{720}$. The probability of one defective cell being selected corresponds to the outcomes $D_1N_2N_3$, $N_1D_2N_3$, and $N_1N_2D_3$. The sum of the probabilities for these outcomes equals $3(\frac{126}{720}) = \frac{378}{720}$. The probability of two defective cells being selected corresponds to the outcomes $D_1D_2N_3$, $D_1N_2D_3$, and $N_1D_2D_3$. The sum of the probabilities for these outcomes equals $3(\frac{42}{720}) = \frac{126}{720}$. Finally, the probability of all three defective cells being identified corresponds to outcome $D_1D_2D_3$ which has a probability of $\frac{6}{720}$.

Section 9.2 Follow-up Exercises

1   Table 9.6 indicates some characteristics of a pool of 500 applicants for an administrative position. Applicants are classified by sex and by *highest* educational degree received. If one applicant is selected at random (each having an equal chance of being selected), what is the probability that the applicant selected will (*a*) be a female, (*b*) have a high school diploma as the highest degree, (*c*) be a male with no degrees, (*d*) be a female with a college degree?

2   Table 9.7 indicates some characteristics of 20,000 borrowers from a major financial institution. Borrowers are classified according to the type of loan (personal or business) and level of risk. If one borrower's account is to be selected at random (each having an equal chance of selection) for purposes of review, what is the probability that the account selected will (*a*) be in the good risk category, (*b*) be a personal loan, (*c*) be a business loan in the poor risk category, (*d*) be a personal loan with an excellent risk?

3   Convert the following odds to equivalent probabilities:
   (*a*) 1 to 4   (*b*) 7 to 3
   (*c*) 2 to 1   (*d*) 100 to 1

4   Convert the following probabilities to equivalent odds:
   (*a*) .8   (*b*) .1
   (*c*) .6   (*d*) .25

5   Preseason odds that the New York Yankees will win the World Series have been stated as 1 to 4. According to the odds, what is the probability that the Yankees will win the World Series? What are the odds that some other team will win the World Series?

6   A student, having finished a final exam, subjectively estimates with a probability of .90 that she has earned an A in the course. What are the equivalent odds? What subjective probability is she assigning to not earning an A?

TABLE 9.6

SEX	HIGHEST DEGREE → COLLEGE DEGREE (C)	HIGH SCHOOL DIPLOMA (H)	NO DEGREE (N)	TOTAL
Male (*M*)	175	70	20	265
Female (*F*)	150	80	5	235
Total	325	150	25	500

TABLE 9.7

TYPE OF LOAN	CREDIT RISK → EXCELLENT RISK (E)	GOOD RISK (G)	POOR RISK (P)	TOTAL
Personal (*P*)	4,000	9,500	2,500	16,000
Business (*B*)	1,000	2,500	500	4,000
Total	5,000	12,000	3,000	20,000

TABLE 9.8

NUMBER OF VICTIMS TREATED (n)	P(n)
Fewer than 5	.05
5	.15
6	.30
7	.25
More than 7	.25

TABLE 9.9

NUMBER OF ALARMS PULLED (n)	P(n)
Fewer than 10	.30
10	.20
11	.25
12	.15
More than 12	.10

7 In order to support its request for a cardiac intensive care unit, the emergency room at a major urban hospital has gathered data on the number of heart attack victims seen. Table 9.8 indicates the probabilities of different numbers of heart attack victims being treated in the emergency room on a typical day. For a given day, what is the probability that (a) five or fewer victims will be seen, (b) five or more victims will be seen, (c) no more than seven victims will be seen?

8 The number of fire alarms pulled each hour fluctuates in a particular city. Analysts have estimated the probability of different numbers of alarms per hour as shown in Table 9.9. In any given hour, what is the probability that (a) more than 10 alarms will be pulled, (b) between 10 and 12 alarms (inclusive) will be pulled, (c) no more than 11 alarms will be pulled?

9 A card is to be drawn at random from a well-shuffled deck. What is the probability that the card will be (a) a king or queen, (b) a face card (jack, queen, or king), (c) a 9 or a spade, (d) a face card or a card from a black suit?

10 The probability that a machine will produce a defective part equals 15. If the process is characterized by statistical independence, what is the probability that (a) two items in succession will not be defective, (b) the first three items are not defective and the fourth is defective, (c) five consecutive items will not be defective?

11 An income tax return can be audited by the federal government and/or by the state. The probability that an individual tax return will be audited by the federal government is .04. The probability that it will be audited by the state is .03. Assume that audit decisions are made independent of one another at the federal and state levels.
(a) What is the probability of being audited by both agencies?
(b) What is the probability of a state audit but not a federal audit?
(c) What is the probability of not being audited?

12 A coin is weighted such that $P(H) = .4$ and $P(T) = .6$. Construct a probability tree denoting all possible outcomes if the coin is tossed three times. What is the probability of two tails in three tosses? Two heads?

13 Five cards are selected at random from a deck of 52. If the drawn cards are not replaced in the deck, what is the probability of selecting an ace, king, queen, jack, and 10 in that order?

14 Table 9.10 summarizes the results of a recent survey of attitudes regarding nuclear war. The question asked was "How likely do you believe it is that a nuclear war will occur during the next 10 years?"

TABLE 9.10

RESPONDENT AGE	Response VERY LIKELY	LIKELY	UNLIKELY	TOTAL
20–29	550	1,300	150	2,000
30–39	350	900	250	1,500
40 and over	100	300	1,100	1,500
Total	1,000	2,500	1,500	5,000

If a respondent is selected at random from the sample of 5,000, what are the following probabilities?

(*a*) The respondent is 30 years or older.

(*b*) The respondent believes nuclear war is "likely."

(*c*) The respondent is between the ages of 30 and 39 and believes that nuclear war is "very likely."

(*d*) The respondent is between the ages of 20 and 39 and believes that nuclear war is "unlikely."

(*e*) The respondent believes that nuclear war is "unlikely" given that he or she is between the ages of 20 and 29.

(*f*) The respondent is 40 years of age or older given that they believe nuclear war is "unlikely."

15   A television game show contestant has earned the opportunity to win some prizes. The contestant is shown 10 boxes, five of which contain prizes. If the contestant is allowed to select any four of the boxes, what is the probability that (*a*) four prizes will be selected, (*b*) no prizes will be selected, (*c*) the first three boxes selected contain no prizes but the fourth box does?

16   For the previous exercise, draw a probability tree which summarizes the different outcomes possible when selecting four boxes at random and their associated probabilities. What is the probability that at least one prize will be won? Exactly one prize?

9.3   MATHEMATICAL EXPECTATION

This section discusses random variables, probability distributions, and mathematical expectation.

Random Variables

A *random variable* is a function which assigns a numerical value to each outcome of an experiment. The numerical value fluctuates in no predictable manner. Very often the results or outcomes of an experiment are described by random variables. For instance, events in an experiment may be the number of heads which occur in three tosses of a coin. In an experiment concerned with crime prevention techniques, the outcomes may reflect the number of crimes per day. An experiment comparing lawn fertilizers may describe outcomes in terms of growth per week or perhaps density or thickness of grass. In each of these experiments, a value of the random variable corresponds to each possible outcome in the experiment.

If a random variable can assume only a finite number of distinct values or a countably infinite subset of the set of real numbers, it is called a *discrete random variable.* The outcomes of an experiment which measures the number of units of a product demanded each day can be represented by a discrete random vari-

TABLE 9.11

NUMBER OF DEFECTIVE FUEL CELLS (n)	$P(n)$
0	$\frac{210}{720}$
1	$\frac{378}{720}$
2	$\frac{126}{720}$
3	$\frac{6}{720}$
	$\frac{720}{720} = 1$

able. The outcomes of an experiment which measures the number of cars passing through a toll booth each hour can be represented by a discrete random variable.

A random variable which can assume any value within some interval of real numbers is called a *continuous random variable.* In an experiment which selects people at random and records some attribute such as height or weight, the outcomes can be represented by a continuous random variable. The outcomes of an experiment which measures the length of time that a transistor will operate before burning out can be described by a continuous random variable.

Probability Distributions

A *probability distribution* is a complete listing of all possible outcomes of an experiment along with the probabilities of each outcome When the outcomes are described by a discrete random variable, the probability distribution lists all possible values of the random variable and the probabilities of each value. Since all possible outcomes are included, the sum of their probabilities should total 1.

Table 9.11 is a discrete probability distribution associated with Example 16. The discrete random variable x represents the number of defective fuel cells identified in a random sample of three.

With continuous probability distributions, the number of possible values for the random variable is infinite. For these distributions, probabilities are assigned only to intervals of values for the random variable. To illustrate this, think of the random variable x which equals the annual rainfall in an area, measured in inches. The number of possible amounts of rain is infinite. For example, one possible value for x is 24.000056 inches. With an infinite number of possible values for x, the likelihood of any one value is extremely small. Thus, with continuous probability distributions, statements are not made regarding the probability that the random variable will assume a specific value. Rather, statements are usually made regarding the probability that the random variable will assume a value within a defined interval. In the rainfall example, we may want to know the probability that annual rainfall will be between 24 and 25 inches.

Mean and Standard Deviation

The *arithmetic mean,* or more simply the *mean,* of a random variable is one measure of the *central tendency* of the value of the random variable. The mean is a single value which is most frequently referred to as the *average* of the random variable. We have all heard and used the term *average* to describe the value of some attribute in our daily lives. Average temperature, Environmental Protection Agency estimates of average gasoline mileage for a new car, and average age of a set of persons are examples.

TABLE 9.12

QUANTITY DEMANDED (x)	$P(x)$
25	.10
26	.20
27	.25
28	.30
29	.10
30	.05
	1.00

TABLE 9.13

x_1	$P(x_1)$	x_2	$P(x_2)$
49	.05	0	.05
50	.90	50	.90
51	.05	100	.05

The mean of a discrete probability distribution is found by multiplying each value of the random variable by its probability of occurring and algebraically summing these products for each value.

MEAN OF DISCRETE PROBABILITY DISTRIBUTION

If a discrete random variable x can assume n values x_1, $x_2, \ldots , x_n$ having respective probabilities of occurrence p_1, $p_2, \ldots , p_n$, the **mean value** μ (mu) of the random variable is

$$\mu = x_1 p_1 + x_2 p_2 + \cdots + x_n p_n \qquad (9.16)$$

EXAMPLE 17

Analysis has revealed that demand for a product varies randomly on a day-to-day basis. Table 9.12 presents a discrete probability distribution based on the study of historical data. The mean value for this random variable is

$$\mu = 25(.10) + 26(.20) + (27)(.25) + (28)(.30) + (29)(.10) + (30)(.05)$$
$$= 27.25$$

Note that the quantity demanded on any given day cannot equal the mean. However, *on the average*, daily demand will equal 27.25 units.

Whereas the mean of a random variable provides information about central tendency, the *standard deviation* yields information about the degree of variability in the value of a random variable. Consider the two probability distributions in Table 9.13. Both these distributions have the same mean $\mu = 50$. However, the possible variation in the values of the two random variables is quite different.

STANDARD DEVIATION: DISCRETE PROBABILITY DISTRIBUTION

Given a discrete random variable x which can assume n values $x_1, x_2, \ldots , x_n$ having respective probabilities of occurrence $p_1, p_2, \ldots , p_n$, the **standard deviation** σ **(sigma)** of the random variable is

$$\sigma = \sqrt{(x_1 - \mu)^2 p_1 + (x_2 - \mu)^2 p_2 + \cdots + (x_n - \mu)^2 p_n} \quad \text{(9.17)}$$

or, using summation notation,

$$\sigma = \sqrt{\sum_{j=1}^{n} (x_j - \mu)^2 p_j} \quad \text{(9.18)}$$

EXAMPLE 18

Let's compute the standard deviations for the two distributions in Table 9.13. For the first distribution,

$$\sigma = \sqrt{(49 - 50)^2(.05) + (50 - 50)^2(.90) + (51 - 50)^2(.05)}$$
$$= \sqrt{.05 + 0 + .05} = \sqrt{.10} = 0.3162$$

For the second distribution,

$$\sigma = \sqrt{(0 - 50)^2(.05) + (50 - 50)^2(.90) + (100 - 50)^2(.05)}$$
$$= \sqrt{125 + 0 + 125} = \sqrt{250} = 15.81$$

From this example we can conclude that the greater the variability in the value of a random variable, the greater the value of the standard deviation. Later we will see that the standard deviation has some very useful interpretations.

Expected Monetary Value

Consider a game in which a fair die is rolled. The participant in the game pays $3 to play and receives a payoff of x dollars where x equals the number which comes up on the die. The question is whether it is worthwhile monetarily to participate in the game. *Expected monetary value,* or average dollar payoff, may be used to help make a decision about participating in the game. Table 9.14 presents a probability distribution showing the possible outcomes on a roll of the die, the corresponding dollar payoffs, and their probabilities of occurrence. Note that payoffs, being dependent upon the roll of the die, become the random variable. The mean of this distribution is

$$\mu = \$1(\tfrac{1}{6}) + \$2(\tfrac{1}{6}) + \$3(\tfrac{1}{6}) + \$4(\tfrac{1}{6}) + \$5(\tfrac{1}{6}) + \$6(\tfrac{1}{6})$$
$$= \frac{\$21}{6} = \$3.50$$

Thus, the *expected payoff* associated with this game is $3.50. This represents the average dollar payoff over many plays of the game and when compared with the $3 cost of playing the game, the *expected profit per play* is 50 cents.

TABLE 9.14	OUTCOME OF ROLL	PAYOFF x	$P(x)$
	1	$1	$\frac{1}{6}$
	2	$2	$\frac{1}{6}$
	3	$3	$\frac{1}{6}$
	4	$4	$\frac{1}{6}$
	5	$5	$\frac{1}{6}$
	6	$6	$\frac{1}{6}$
			$\overline{1}$

TABLE 9.15

DAILY DEMAND (x)	NUMBER OF DAYS OBSERVED	P(x)
21	20	.10
22	60	.30
23	100	.50
24	20	.10
	200	1.00

TABLE 9.16 **CONDITIONAL PROFIT TABLE**

	Possible Stock Decision			
POSSIBLE DEMAND	21	22	23	24
21	63	58	53	48
22	63	66	61	56
23	63	66	69	64
24	63	66	69	72

EXAMPLE 19

Expected monetary value can assist in deciding which alternative is best in a given situation. Consider a situation in which a retailer sells a single product. The retailer purchases the product from a supplier at a cost of $5 per unit and sells each unit at a price of $8. The item is perishable; if it is not sold on the first day, it has no value. That is, it cannot be sold, and there is no salvage value. When this occurs, the retailer must absorb the cost of the item as a $5 loss.

Historical data has been gathered which confirm that daily demand for the product assumes four possible values. Table 9.15 summarizes this demand information in terms of a discrete probability distribution.

The retailer is trying to decide how many units to stock on a given day. She has decided that rather than try to second-guess the market each day, she would prefer to determine one quantity which will be stocked each day. Her goal is to select the quantity which maximizes expected daily profit.

Table 9.16 presents a *conditional profit table* which summarizes the daily profit which would result *given* any quantity demanded and the corresponding stock decision. Note that the possible stock decisions and the different discrete demand possibilities are exactly the same.

The conditional profit values are determined by computing the total profit from units sold and subtracting from this any loss which would have to be absorbed because of overstocking. For example, the decision to stock 21 units always results in a conditional profit of $63. The $63 results from selling all 21 units stocked with a profit per unit of $8 − $5 = $3. If demand equals 22 units or more, the 21 units stocked will always be sold. However, at these levels of demand, the retailer has understocked.

Let's consider the decision to stock 22 units. If 21 units are demanded, 21 units will be sold, earning a profit of $63. However, since the retailer overstocked by 1 unit, the cost of the leftover unit must be absorbed, reducing the conditional profit to $63 − $5 = $58. If 22 units are stocked and 22 units are demanded, conditional profits of $66 result. And if more than 22 units are demanded, the 22 units stocked will be sold, resulting in conditional profits of $66.

TABLE 9.17 **EXPECTED DAILY PROFIT COMPUTATION**

Stock 21

CONDITIONAL PROFIT	PROBABILITY OF OCCURRENCE	EXPECTED DAILY PROFIT
$63	× .10	= $ 6.30
63	× .30	= 18.90
63	× .50	= 31.50
63	× .10	= 6.30
		$63.00

Stock 22

CONDITIONAL PROFIT	PROBABILITY OF OCCURRENCE	EXPECTED DAILY PROFIT
$58	× .10	= $ 5.80
66	× .30	= 19.80
66	× .50	= 33.00
66	× .10	= 6.60
		$65.20

Stock 23

CONDITIONAL PROFIT	PROBABILITY OF OCCURRENCE	EXPECTED DAILY PROFIT
$53	× .10	= $ 5.30
61	× .30	= 18.30
69	× .50	= 34.50
69	× .10	= 6.90
		$65.00

Stock 24

CONDITIONAL PROFIT	PROBABILITY OF OCCURRENCE	EXPECTED DAILY PROFIT
$48	× .10	= $ 4.80
56	× .30	= 16.80
64	× .50	= 32.00
72	× .10	= 7.20
		$60.80

The conditional profits for the stock decisions of 23 and 24 units are computed in a similar manner. For example, the $53 conditional profit from stocking 23 units and having demand for 21 units results from 21 units being sold at a profit of $63, but this is reduced by $2 \cdot \$5 = \$10$ because of the overstocking of 2 units.

The expected daily profit for each stock decision can be determined by weighting each conditional profit by its likelihood of occurrence (which is the probability of the corresponding level of demand). Table 9.17 illustrates the computation for each stock decision.

Based on expected daily profit, the best stock decision is to stock 22 items each day, resulting in an expected (average) daily profit of $65.20.

POINT FOR THOUGHT AND DISCUSSION

Why would the retailer not consider stocking fewer than 21 units or more than 24 units?

Section 9.3 Follow-up Exercises

1 Construct the discrete probability distribution which corresponds to the experiment of tossing a *fair* coin three times. Let the random variable x equal the number of heads occurring in three tosses.

TABLE 9.18

NUMBER DEMANDED PER DAY (x)	P(x)
10	.05
20	.18
30	.32
40	.30
50	.15
	1.00

TABLE 9.19

NUMBER OF COMPONENTS FAILING (x)	P(x)
0	.04
1	.12
2	.18
3	.30
4	.30
5	.06
	1.00

TABLE 9.20

x_1	$P(x_1)$	x_2	$P(x_2)$
500	1	0	.050
		100	.125
		300	.200
		500	.250
		700	.200
		900	.125
		1000	.050
			1.000

2 Construct the discrete probability distribution which corresponds to the experiment of rolling a *pair* of dice. Assume equal likelihood of occurrence of each side of a die, and let the random variable x equal the sum of the dots which come up on the pair.

3 Table 9.18 presents a discrete probability distribution associated with the daily demand for a product.

(a) Determine the mean daily demand.

(b) What is the standard deviation of daily demand?

4 A manufactured product consists of five electrical components. Each of the components has a limited lifetime. The company has tested the product to determine the reliability of the components. Table 9.19 presents a probability distribution where the random variable x indicates the number of components which fail during the first 100 hours of operation.

(a) What is the mean number of components which fail during the first 100 hours of operation?

(b) What is the standard deviation of the random variable x?

(c) If the product will continue to operate if no more than two components fail, what percentage of the manufactured parts will continue to operate during the first 100 hours?

5 Compute the respective means and standard deviations for the two distributions in Table 9.20.

6 A game involves tossing a coin for which $P(H) = .4$. If a head occurs, the participant receives a payoff of $10. If a tail occurs, the participant receives no payoff. If it costs $6 to participate in the game, what is the expected profit associated with playing the game? Would you play?

7 A single card will be selected from a well-shuffled deck of 52 cards. A payoff will be made based upon the rank of the card. A 2 will result in payment of $2, a 10 in a pay-

TABLE 9.21

DAILY DEMAND (x)	P(x)
10	.10
11	.30
12	.40
13	.20
	1.00

ment of $10, and so forth. Jack, queen, king, and ace will result in payments of $15, $20, $25, and $30, respectively. What is the expected payoff associated with a single draw?

8 A perishable product is purchased by a retailer for $15 and sold at a price of $25. Daily demand varies at random according to the distribution in Table 9.21. If an item is stocked but not sold, the retailer must absorb the $15 cost as a loss. The retailer wishes to determine the level to stock each day so as to maximize expected daily profit.

(a) Set up the conditional profit table.

(b) What stock decision results in the maximum expected daily profit?

(c) What is the maximum expected daily profit?

9 **Salvage Value** Rework Exercise 8 with the assumption that units unsold after the first day have a salvage value of $5.

10 Rework Example 19 if there is a salvage value of $3 for any units not sold on the first day.

11 **Expected profit with perfect information** Assume in Example 19 that there is a way of predicting exactly how many units will be demanded on a given day (an order-ahead system might achieve this). When demand is known ahead of time, the prudent stock decision is to stock the quantity demanded. This prevents overstocking and understocking. In Example 19, for instance, 21 units would be stocked whenever 21 units are demanded, 22 units stocked whenever 22 are demanded, and so forth. Using the appropriate conditional profits in Table 9.16, compute the expected profit (*expected profit with perfect information*) for this situation. How does it compare with the maximum expected profit (without perfect information) of $65.20 from stocking 22 units?

12 Compute the expected profit with perfect information (see previous exercise) for the situation in Exercise 8.

9.4 THE BINOMIAL PROBABILITY DISTRIBUTION

This section discusses one of the more commonly used discrete probability distributions—the *binomial probability distribution.* First is a discussion of the characteristics of random processes which can be represented by the binomial distribution. This will be followed by a discussion of the binomial distribution and its applications.

Bernoulli Process

Many random processes are characterized by trials in which there are just two mutually exclusive outcomes possible. Manufactured parts may be sampled to determine whether they are of an acceptable quality or defective; the toss of a coin results in either head or tail; patients arriving at an emergency room might be classified as male or female; survey questionnaires mailed to potential respondents may be classified as returned or not returned; and questions on a multiple-choice test may be judged as answered correctly or incorrectly.

Frequently the two possible outcomes in these situations are characterized as "successful" or "unsuccessful." The occurrence of a head in the toss of a coin may be declared a successful outcome. This assignment of labels, though, is completely arbitrary. The occurrence of a tail might just as easily, and appropriately, be termed a success (it depends on the side for which you are rooting).

Random experiments such as tossing a fair coin care examples of *Bernoulli processes.* Bernoulli processes have the the following characteristics:

CHARACTERISTICS OF BERNOULLI PROCESSES

I There are n trials, each of which has two mutually exclusive outcomes that can be classified as either *success* or *failure*.

II The probability of a *success* p remains fixed for each trial.

III The probability of *failure* q remains fixed for each trial and $q = 1 - p$.

IV The random variable x is the total number of successes in n trials.

EXAMPLE 20

A single die is rolled 25 times. A successful outcome is the occurrence of a 6. This is an example of a Bernoulli process. If a fair die is assumed, the probability of a success for each trial is $\frac{1}{6}$, or $p = \frac{1}{6}$. If the probability of success equals $\frac{1}{6}$, the probability of a failure q is $q = 1 - p$ or $q = 1 - \frac{1}{6} = \frac{5}{6}$. Successive rolls of a die are statistically independent. The random variable x is the number of times a 6 occurs in the 25 rolls.

EXAMPLE 21

One hundred parts will be selected from a manufacturing process which is judged to produce defective parts at random with a probability of .05. The process resulting in defective parts is characterized by statistical independence. The probability of a nondefective part, the production of such being deemed a successful outcome, is $p = .95$. The probability of a failure (defective part) is $q = 1 - .95 = .05$. The random variable x is the number of nondefective items identified in the 100 trials.

The Binomial Distribution

Consider a student who is taking a true-false quiz consisting of five questions. Assume that the probability of answering any one of the questions correctly is .8. Suppose we are interested in the probability that the student will answer exactly four questions correctly. This situation is a Bernoulli process where the probability of success on any trial is $p = .8$, the probability of a failure is $q = .2$, the number of trials is $n = 5$, and the random variable x equals the number of questions answered correctly.

One way of answering four questions correctly is to answer the first four correctly and the last incorrectly; or, stated in terms of success (S) or failure (F), the sequence of outcomes is $S_1 S_2 S_3 S_4 F_5$. The probability of this joint event is a joint probability for independent events computed by applying Rule 7 from Sec. 9.2, or

$$P(S_1 \cap S_2 \cap S_3 \cap S_4 \cap F_5) = (.8)(.8)(.8)(.8)(.2)$$
$$= .08192$$

Another way of getting four correct answers is the sequence $F_1 S_2 S_3 S_4 S_5$ and

$$P(F_1 \cap S_2 \cap S_3 \cap S_4 \cap S_5) = (.2)(.8)(.8)(.8)(.8)$$
$$= .08192$$

which is the same probability as computed for the joint event $S_1 S_2 S_3 S_4 F_5$. There are, in fact, five different ways in which four questions can be answered correctly. They are $S_1 S_2 S_3 S_4 F_5$, $S_1 S_2 S_3 F_4 S_5$, $S_1 S_2 F_3 S_4 S_5$, $S_1 F_2 S_3 S_4 S_5$, and $F_1 S_2 S_3 S_4 S_5$. Note that in applying Rule 7 to compute the probability of each of these sequences, the probability of success, $p = .8$, will be a factor 4 times and the probability of a failure will be a factor once. The only difference is the order of multiplication, which has no effect on the product. Thus, the probability of answering four questions correctly is

$$p(x = 4) = \left(\begin{array}{c} \text{number of different ways} \\ \text{in which four questions can} \\ \text{be answered correctly} \end{array} \right) \left(\begin{array}{c} \text{probability of answering} \\ \text{four questions correctly} \\ \text{in any one order} \end{array} \right)$$

$$= 5(.08192) = .4096$$

An alternative to enumerating the different ways in which four successes can occur in five trials is to recognize that this is a combinations question. The number of ways in which x successes can occur in n trials is found by applying Eq. (9.5), or

$$_nC_x = \frac{n!}{x!(n-x)!}$$

The number of ways in which four successes can occur in five trials is

$$_5C_4 = \frac{5!}{4!(5-4)!}$$

$$= \frac{5!}{4!1!} = 5$$

The *binomial probability distribution* is used to represent experiments which are Bernoulli processes. The following computational rule is fundamental to determining *binomial probabilities.*

COMPUTATION OF BINOMIAL PROBABILITIES

Given a Bernoulli process where the probability of success in any trial equals p and the probability of a failure equals q, the probability of x successes in n trials is

$$P(x,n) = {_nC_x}(\overbrace{p \cdot p \cdot p \cdots p}^{x \text{ times}})(\overbrace{q \cdot q \cdot q \cdots q}^{n-x \text{ times}})$$

or $\quad P(x,n) = {_nC_x}p^x q^{n-x}$ \hfill (9.19)

If we continue with the quiz example, the possible outcomes for the quiz are zero, one, two, three, four, or five questions correct (successes). Let's compute the probabilities for the other outcomes. The probability of zero successes (correct answers) in five trials is

$$P(0, 5) = {}_5C_0(.8)^0(.2)^5$$
$$= \frac{5!}{0!(5-0)!}(.00032) = (1)(.00032) = .00032$$

The probability of one success in five trials is

$$P(1, 5) = {}_5C_1(.8)^1(.2)^4$$
$$= \frac{5!}{1!(5-1)!}(.00128) = 5(.00128) = .0064$$

The probability of two successes in five trials is

$$P(2, 5) = {}_5C_2(.8)^2(.2)^3$$
$$= \frac{5!}{2!(5-2)!}(.00512) = 10(.00512) = .0512$$

The probability of three successes in five trials is

$$P(3, 5) = {}_5C_3(.8)^3(.2)^2$$
$$= \frac{5!}{3!(5-3)!}(.02048) = 10(.02048) = .2048$$

The probability of five successes in five trials is

$$P(5, 5) = {}_5C_5(.8)^5(.2)^0$$
$$= \frac{5!}{0!(5-0)!}(.32768) = .32768$$

Table 9.22 summarizes the binomial distribution for this experiment. Note that the set of values for the random variable is mutually exclusive and collectively exhaustive; the sum of the probabilities equals 1.0.

Figure 9.9 presents a graphical representation of the distribution called a *histogram.* Each bar corresponds to an event, and the height of the bar equals the probability of the event.

TABLE 9.22　BINOMIAL DISTRIBUTION FOR QUIZ RESULTS

NUMBER OF SUCCESSES (CORRECT ANSWERS ON QUIZ) (x)	P(x)
0	.00032
1	.00640
2	.05120
3	.20480
4	.40960
5	.32768
	1.00000

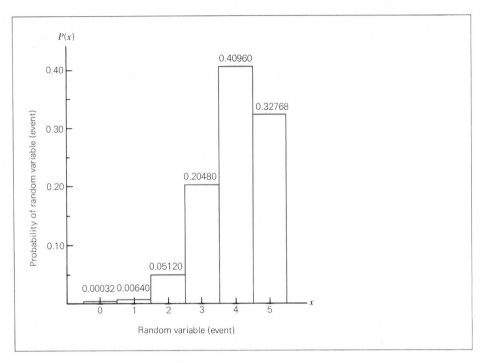

FIGURE 9.9
Histogram representation of a binomial distribution.

EXAMPLE 22

A major bank issues credit cards under the name of VISACARD. It has determined that 40 percent of all credit card accounts are paid in full following the first bill. That is, 40 percent of all accounts never incur interest charges. If a sample of six accounts is selected at random from the previous years' records, construct the binomial distribution where the random variable x equals the number of accounts found to have incurred no interest expense.

SOLUTION

This experiment can be considered to be a Bernoulli process where an account incurring no interest charges is considered a success and one incurring interest charges is considered a failure. For this experiment $p = .40$, $q = .60$, and $n = 6$.

The probability that none of the six accounts will have incurred no interest charges is

$$P(0, 6) = {}_6C_0(.4)^0(.6)^6$$

$$= \frac{6!}{0!(6 - 0)!} (.046656) = (1)(.046656) = .046656$$

The probability that exactly one account will have incurred no interest charge is

$$P(1, 6) = {}_6C_1(.4)^1(.6)^5$$

$$= \frac{6!}{1!(6 - 1)!} (.031104) = (6)(.031104) = .186624$$

The probability that exactly two accounts will have incurred no interest charge is

$$P(2, 6) = {}_6C_2(.4)^2(.6)^4$$

$$= \frac{6!}{2!(6-2)!} (.020736) = (15)(.020736) = .31104$$

The probability that exactly three accounts will have incurred no interest charges is

$$P(3, 6) = {}_6C_3(.4)^3(.6)^3$$

$$= \frac{6!}{3!(6-3)!} (.013824) = (20)(.013824) = .27648$$

By continuing this process, the result is the probability distribution shown in Table 9.23.

TABLE 9.23 **BINOMIAL DISTRIBUTION FOR CONSUMER CREDIT REVIEW**

NUMBER OF SUCCESSES (ACCOUNTS FOUND TO HAVE INCURRED NO INTEREST CHARGES) (x)	$P(x)$
0	.046656
1	.186624
2	.311040
3	.276480
4	.138240
5	.036864
6	.004096
	1.000000

EXERCISE

In Example 22, what is the probability that no more than three accounts will have incurred no interest charges? More than four accounts?*

POINT FOR THOUGHT AND DISCUSSION

Is the process in Example 16 (space shuttle simulation) a Bernoulli process? Why or why not?

Mean and Standard Deviation of the Binomial Distribution

MEAN OF A BINOMIAL DISTRIBUTION

The mean value μ for a binomial distribution equals

$$\mu = np \tag{9.20}$$

If the binomial distribution relates to the number of heads occurring in 500 flips of a fair coin, the mean is

---

* Answers: .8208, .04096

$$\mu = 500(.5)$$
$$= 250$$

which suggests that on the average we would expect to get 250 heads in 500 flips of a fair coin.

EXAMPLE 23 ▇▇▇▇▇▇▇▇▇▇▇▇▇▇▇▇▇▇▇▇▇▇▇▇▇▇▇▇

In Example 22, the probability that an account incurred no interest charges was .4. In the selection of six accounts, the mean is

$$\mu = 6(.4)$$
$$= 2.4$$

or on the average a selection of six accounts at random should result in 2.4 being identified as having incurred no interest charges.

STANDARD DEVIATION OF A BINOMIAL DISTRIBUTION ▇▇▇▇

The standard deviation of a binomial probability distribution equals

$$\sigma = \sqrt{npq} \qquad\qquad (9.21)$$

For Example 22, the standard deviation is

$$\sigma = \sqrt{6(.4)(.6)}$$
$$= \sqrt{1.44} = 1.2$$

Section 9.4 Follow-up Exercises

1   Determine which of the following random variables are not variables in a Bernoulli process.
(a) x = the number of heads in the toss of a coin 20 times
(b) x = the heights of 10 students selected at random
(c) x = the number of 6s which appear in five rolls of a *pair* of dice
(d) x = scores earned by 100 different students on a standardized test
(e) x = the closing price of a stock for 10 randomly selected days
(f) x = the number of arrivals per hour at an emergency room observed for 20 randomly selected hours of operation
(g) x = the number of false alarms in a sample of 10 fire alarms where the probability that any alarm is a false alarm equals .18
2   A fair coin is to be flipped 4 times. What is the probability that exactly three heads will occur? Four heads? One or more heads?
3   A fair die will be rolled 4 times. What is the probability that exactly two 1s will occur? Less than two 1s?
4   **Drunken Driving**   A state has determined that of all traffic accidents in which a fatality occurs, 75 percent involve situations in which at least one driver has been

drinking. If a sample of four fatal accidents is selected at random, construct the binomial distribution where the random variable x equals the number of accidents in which at least one driver was drinking.

5   It has been determined that 90 percent of all American households have at least one television set. If five residences are selected at random, construct the binomial distribution where the random variable x equals the number of residences having at least one television.

6   A firm which conducts consumer surveys by mail has found that 30 percent of those families receiving a questionnaire will return it. In a survey of 20 families, what is the probability that exactly eight families will return the questionnaire? Exactly 12 families?

7   A student takes a true-false examination which consists of 10 questions. The student knows nothing about the subject and chooses answers at random. Assuming independence between questions and a probability of .6 of answering any question correctly, what is the probability that the student will pass the test (assume that passing means getting seven or more correct)? If the test contains 20 questions does the probability of passing change (14 or more correct)?

8   **Immunization**   A particular influenza vaccine has been found to be 98 percent effective in providing immunity. In a random sample of five vaccinated people who have been exposed to this strain of influenza, what is the probability that none of the five will come down with the disease?

9   An urn contains five red balls, two green balls, and three blue balls. If 10 balls are selected at random with replacement between each draw, what is the probability that no red balls will be selected? What is the probability that four green balls will be selected?

10   A manufacturing process produces defective parts randomly at a rate of 20 percent. In a sample of 10 parts, what is the probability that fewer than 2 will be defective?

11   In Exercise 10, what is the mean number of defective parts expected? What is the interpretation of this value? What is the standard deviation for this distribution?

12   In a local hospital 48 percent of all babies born are males. On a particular day five babies are born. What is the probability that three or more of the babies are males? What is the mean of this distribution for $n = 5$? What is the standard deviation?

9.5 CONTINUOUS PROBABILITY DISTRIBUTIONS

As mentioned in Sec. 9.3, continuous probability distributions are characterized by random variables which can assume any value within some interval of real numbers. This section discusses one of the most familiar and most widely applied continuous probability distributions—the *normal probability distribution.*

The Normal Probability Distribution

The normal probability distribution is one of the most important distributions in modern-day probability theory. The normal probability distribution is represented by the classic *bell-shaped curve,* or *normal curve,* shown in Fig. 9.10. The bell-shaped curve in Fig. 9.10 is typical of a family of bell-shaped curves which represent normal probability distributions, each different with regard to its mean and standard deviation. Figure 9.11 illustrates the graphs of two

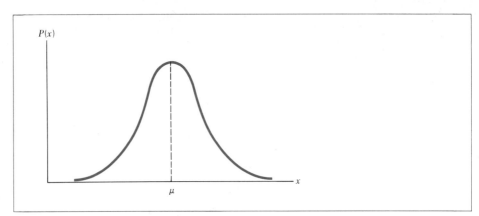

FIGURE 9.10
Normal curve.

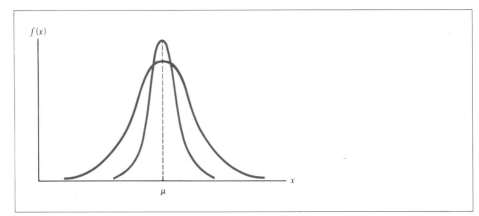

FIGURE 9.11
Normal distributions with equal means.

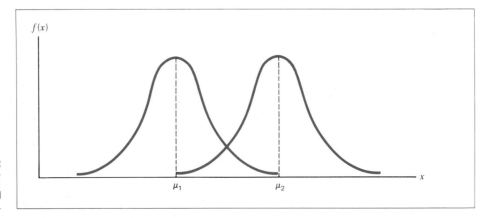

FIGURE 9.12
Normal distributions with equal standard deviations.

normal distributions having the same mean but different standard deviations. Figure 9.12 illustrates the graphs of two normal distributions which have different means but the same standard deviation.

The normal curve is symmetrical about an imaginary vertical line which passes through the mean μ. This symmetry means the height of the curve is the same if one moves equal distances to the left and right of the mean. The "tails"

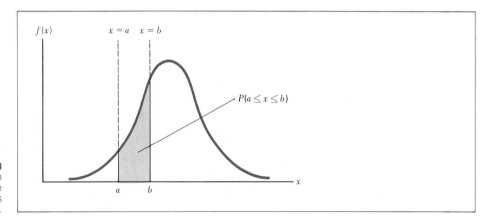

FIGURE 9.13
Area beneath
normal curve
represents
probability.

of the curve come closer and closer to the horizontal axis without ever reaching it, no matter how far one moves to the left or the right. If μ equals the mean and σ the standard deviation of a normal probability distribution, the mathematical function describing the normal curve is

$$f(x) = \frac{1}{\sqrt{2\pi\sigma}}\, e^{-1/2[(x-\mu)/\sigma]^2} \qquad\qquad \textbf{(9.22)}$$

where $\pi \doteq 3.14159$, $e \doteq 2.71828$, and $f(x)$ is the height of the normal curve corresponding to a given value of the random variable x.

Areas under the curve representing a probability distribution represent probabilities. If the total area under a normal curve is considered to equal 1, the probability that the random variable x will assume a value between a and b equals the area beneath the curve and bounded on the left and right by the vertical lines $x = a$ and $x = b$. This is illustrated in Fig. 9.13.

Consider a situation in which the scores on a standardized aptitude test have been found to be *normally distributed* with a mean of 70 and standard deviation of 7.5. Suppose we are interested in determining the probability that a student will score between 70 and 85 on the test. In order to determine this probability, we take advantage of a very useful property of normal probability distributions. *Any normal probability distribution with mean μ and standard deviation σ can be transformed into an equivalent* **standard (unit) normal distribution** *which has a mean equal to 0 and standard deviation equal to 1. The transformation redefines each value of the random variable x in terms of its distance from the mean, stated as a multiple of the standard deviation.*

Figure 9.14 illustrates this transformaton of x in terms of another variable z which equals the distance from the mean in multiples of the standard deviation. Note that z values to the right of the mean are positive, and those to the left of the mean are negative. A value of x which is one standard deviation to the right of the mean would be defined equivalently by a z value of 1. A point located three standard deviations to the left of the mean would be defined equivalently by a z value of -3.

Table 9.24 at the end of this section provides areas under the standard normal curve. *Note that the areas given are areas under the curve between the mean and another point located z standard deviations from the mean.* The normal curve is such

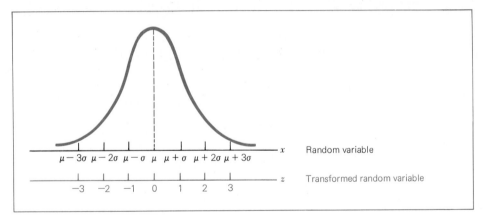

FIGURE 9.14
Transformation
to standard
(unit) normal
distribution.

that 50 percent of the area is to the left of the mean and 50 percent to the right. That is, there is a 50 percent chance that the value of the random variable x will be less than the mean and a 50 percent chance it will be greater than the mean. The symmetry of the normal curve suggests that Table 9.24 can be used to determine areas between the mean and another point when the second point is to the left *or* right of the mean. A z value of 1 in Table 9.24 suggests that the area under the curve between $z = 0$ and $z = 1$ is 0.3413. *The area is the same between $z = 0$ and $z = -1$.* Figure 9.15 illustrates these areas. Note also that we can make the statement that the area under the standard normal curve *between $z = -1$ and $z = 1$* equals 0.6826.

Let's return to the original problem concerning the standardized aptitude test. Scores had been found to be normally distributed with a mean of 70 and standard deviation of 7.5. The problem was to determine the probability that a student selected at random will score between 70 and 85. To determine this probability, we must transform the original distribution into the standard normal distribution. In order to do this, equivalent z values must be identified for pertinent x values. The formula enabling one to transform values of the random variable x into equivalent z values is

$$z = \frac{x - \mu}{\sigma}$$

(9.23)

The z value corresponding to the mean is always 0. Thus, in this case, the z value corresponding to an x of 70 is

$$z = \frac{70 - 70}{7.5} = 0$$

The z value corresponding to an x value of 85 is

$$z = \frac{85 - 70}{7.5}$$

$$= \frac{15}{7.5} = 2$$

This means that a score of 85 is two standard deviations above (to the right of) the mean score of 70.

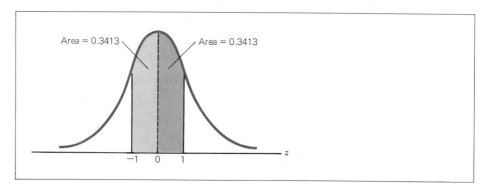

FIGURE 9.15

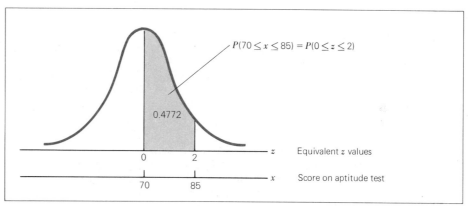

FIGURE 9.16

Thus, the probability that a student will score between 70 and 85 is equal to the area under the standard normal curve between $z = 0$ and $z = 2$. This area, illustrated in Fig. 9.16, is read directly from Table 9.24 as 0.4772. Therefore, the probability that a student will score between 70 and 85 equals .4772. Note in Fig. 9.16 that an equivalent x scale has been drawn below the z scale to show the corresponding value of x. This is not necessary, but it helps to remind us of the pertinent values for the random variable x.

Suppose we are interested in the probability that a student will score between 0 and 85 on the examination. This probability is equal to the probability that z will be less than 2 for the standard normal distribution. The probability is the area under the standard normal distribution, illustrated in Fig. 9.17. This area consists of the 50 percent to the left of the mean and the .4772 we identified previously, or

$$P(z \leq 2) = P(z \leq 0) + P(0 < z \leq 2)$$
$$= .5000 + .4772 = .9772$$

NOTE

In any problems requiring the identification of probabilities for a normally distributed variable, it is strongly advised that you make a rough sketch which identifies the equivalent area or areas under the standard normal curve.

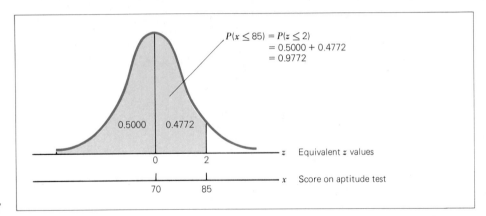

$P(x \le 85) = P(z \le 2)$
$= 0.5000 + 0.4772$
$= 0.9772$

0.5000 | 0.4772

0

2

— z Equivalent z values

70

85

— x Score on aptitude test

FIGURE 9.17

EXAMPLE 24

A survey of per capita income indicated that the annual income for people in one state is normally distributed with a mean of $9,800 and a standard deviation of $1,600. If a person is selected at random, what is the probability that the person's annual income is (*a*) greater than $5,000, (*b*) greater than $12,200, (*c*) between $8,520 and $12,200, (*d*) between $11,400 and $13,000?

SOLUTION

(*a*) The z value corresponding to an income of $5,000 is

$$z = \frac{5,000 - 9,800}{1,600}$$

$$= \frac{-4,800}{1,600} = -3$$

From Fig. 9.18 we can conclude that the probability that a person's salary is greater than $5,000 is equal to the probability that z is greater than -3 for the standard normal distribution. From Table 9.24,

$$P(z > -3) = P(-3 < z \le 0) + P(z > 0)$$
$$= .49865 + .5000 = .99865$$

(*b*) The z value corresponding to an income of $12,200 is

$$z = \frac{12,200 - 9,800}{1,600}$$

$$= \frac{2,400}{1,600} = 1.5$$

From Fig. 9.19 we can conclude that the probability that a person's salary is greater than $12,200 is equal to the probability that z is greater than 1.5. From Table 9.24 we can determine that $P(0 < z \le 1.5) = .4332$. Since

$$P(z > 0) = .5000$$
$$P(z > 1.5) = P(z > 0) - P(0 < z \le 1.5)$$
$$= .5000 - .4332 = .0668$$

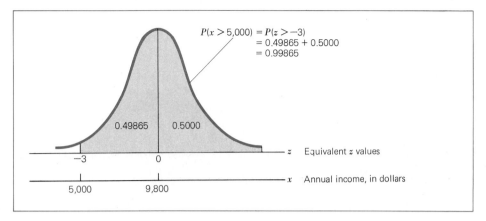

$P(x > 5,000) = P(z > -3)$
$= 0.49865 + 0.5000$
$= 0.99865$

0.49865   0.5000

−3   0 z Equivalent z values

x Annual income, in dollars

5,000   9,800

FIGURE 9.18

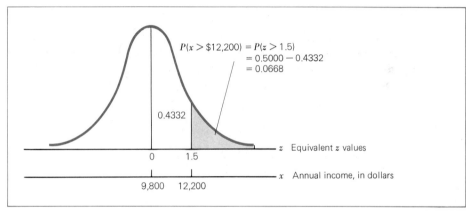

$P(x > \$12,200) = P(z > 1.5)$
$= 0.5000 - 0.4332$
$= 0.0668$

0.4332

0   1.5 z Equivalent z values

x Annual income, in dollars

9,800   12,200

FIGURE 9.19

(c) The z value corresponding to an income of \$8,520 is

$$z = \frac{8,520 - 9,800}{1,600}$$

$$= \frac{-1,280}{1,600} = -.8$$

From Fig. 9.20, the probability that a person's salary is between \$8,520 and \$12,200 is equal to the probability that z is between $-.8$ and 1.5, or

$$P(-0.8 \le z \le 1.5) = P(-0.8 \le z < 0) + P(0 \le z \le 1.5)$$

$$= .2881 + .4332 = .7213$$

(d) The z value corresponding to an income of \$11,400 is

$$z = \frac{11,400 - 9,800}{1,600}$$

$$= \frac{1,600}{1,600} = 1$$

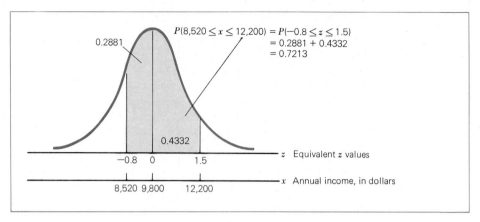

FIGURE 9.20

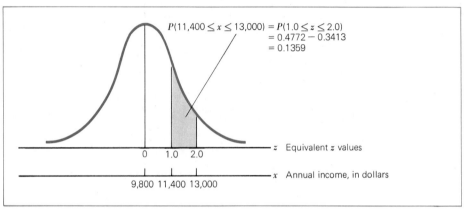

FIGURE 9.21

The z value corresponding to an income of \$13,000 is

$$z = \frac{13,000 - 9,800}{1,600}$$

$$= \frac{3,200}{1,600} = 2$$

From Fig. 9.21, the probability that a person's salary is between \$11,400 and \$13,000 is equal to the probability that z is between 1 and 2. To determine this probability, we must find the area between $z = 0$ and $z = 2$ and subtract from this the area between $z = 0$ and $z = 1$. Or,

$$P(1 \leq z \leq 2) = P(0 \leq z \leq 2) - P(0 \leq z \leq 1)$$
$$= .4772 - .3413 = .1359$$

One point should be made regarding the use of Table 9.24. It was mentioned earlier that for continuous variables, the probability of occurrence of any specific value of the variable equals 0. That is, for any point a,

$$P(x = a) = 0$$

Thus, for any two constants $a < b$,

$$P(a \leq x \leq b) = P(a < x \leq b) = P(a \leq x < b) = P(a < x < b)$$

The practical implication of this is that the values in Table 9.24 represent the probabilities that z will assume values between two points z_1 and z_2 where the exact values of z_1 and z_2 may or may not be included. In Example 24(a), the probabilities that a person's salary is greater than $5,000 or greater than or equal to $5,000 are both the same—.99865.

One final observation about normally distributed random variables is that of all the possible outcomes of the random variable x, about 68 percent are expected to occur within plus or minus one standard deviation from the mean (that is, $\mu \pm 1\sigma$), about 95 percent are expected to occur within plus or minus two standard deviations of the mean ($\mu \pm 2\sigma$), and about 99 percent within plus or minus three standard deviations of the mean ($\mu \pm 3\sigma$). This is a useful set of properties when attempting to reach generalizations about random variables.

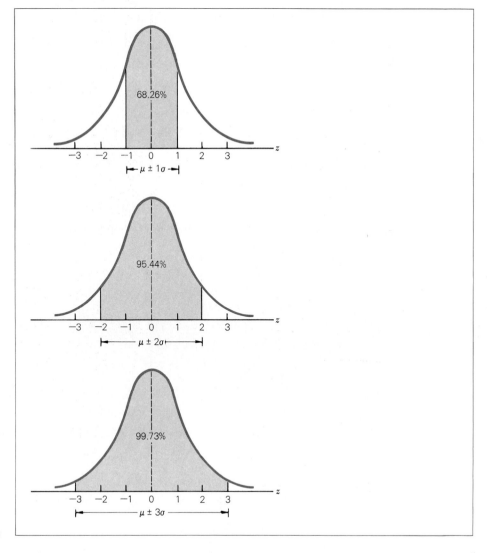

FIGURE 9.22

Section 9.5 Follow-up Exercises

1　For the standard normal distribution determine
(a) $P(z > 1.2)$　　　　　　　　　　　　(b) $P(z < 1.0)$
(c) $P(0.8 < z < 1.9)$　　　　　　　　　(d) $P(-2.1 \leq z \leq 2.7)$

2　For the standard normal distribution determine
(a) $P(z > -1.3)$　　　　　　　　　　　(b) $P(z < -1.6)$
(c) $P(-1.9 < z < -0.5)$　　　　　　　(d) $P(-0.5 \leq z \leq 1.9)$

3　Given a random variable x which is normally distributed with a mean of 15 and standard deviation of 2.5, determine
(a) $P(x \geq 10.9)$　　　　　　　　　　(b) $P(x \leq 15.3)$
(c) $P(7.6 \leq x \leq 13.1)$　　　　　　(d) $P(9.8 \leq x \leq 10.9)$

4　Given a random variable x which is normally distributed with a mean of 75 and standard deviation of 5, determine
(a) $P(x \geq 80)$　　　　　　　　　　　(b) $P(x < 72.5)$
(c) $P(70 \leq x \leq 77.5)$　　　　　　(d) $P(80 < x < 82.5)$

5　The weights of newborn babies at a particular hospital have been observed to be normally distributed with a mean of 7.3 pounds and a standard deviation of 0.5 pounds. What is the probability that a baby born in this hospital will weigh more than 8 pounds? Less than 6 pounds?

6　The annual income of workers in one state is normally distributed with a mean of $10,000 and a standard deviation of $2,000. If a worker is chosen at random, what is the probability that the worker earns more than $15,000? Less than $7,500?

7　A manufacturer has conducted a study of the lifetime of a particular type of light bulb. The study concluded that the lifetime, measured in hours, is a random variable with a normal distribution. The mean lifetime is 800 hours with a standard deviation of 100 hours. What is the probability that a bulb selected at random would have a lifetime between 700 and 900 hours? Greater than 1,000 hours?

8　Grades on a national aptitude test have been found to be normally distributed with a mean of 430 and a standard deviation of 75. What is the probability that a student selected at random will score between 400 and 520? Greater than 550?

9　In a large city the number of calls for police service during a 24-hour period seems to be random. The number of calls has been found to be normally distributed with a mean of 325 and a standard deviation of 50. What is the probability that for a randomly selected day the number of calls will be fewer than 300? More than 400?

KEY TERMS AND CONCEPTS

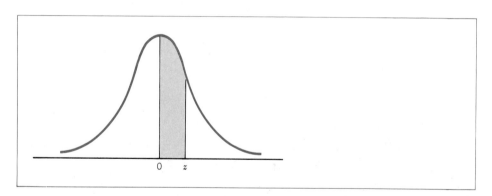

TABLE 9.24   **AREA UNDER THE STANDARD NORMAL CURVE**

x	.00	.01	.02	.03	.04	.05	.06	.07	.08	.09
0.0	.0000	.0040	.0080	.0120	.0160	.0199	.0239	.0279	.0319	.0359
0.1	.0398	.0438	.0478	.0517	.0557	.0596	.0636	.0675	.0714	.0753
0.2	.0793	.0832	.0871	.0910	.0948	.0987	.1026	.1064	.1103	.1141
0.3	.1179	.1217	.1255	.1293	.1331	.1368	.1406	.1443	.1480	.1517
0.4	.1554	.1591	.1628	.1664	.1700	.1736	.1772	.1808	.1844	.1879
0.5	.1915	.1950	.1985	.2019	.2054	.2088	.2123	.2157	.2190	.2224
0.6	.2257	.2291	.2324	.2357	.2389	.2422	.2454	.2486	.2518	.2549
0.7	.2580	.2612	.2642	.2673	.2704	.2734	.2764	.2794	.2823	.2852
0.8	.2881	.2910	.2939	.2967	.2995	.3023	.3051	.3078	.3106	.3133
0.9	.3159	.3186	.3212	.3238	.3264	.3289	.3315	.3340	.3365	.3389
1.0	.3413	.3438	.3461	.3485	.3508	.3531	.3554	.3577	.3599	.3621
1.1	.3643	.3665	.3686	.3708	.3729	.3749	.3770	.3790	.3810	.3830
1.2	.3849	.3869	.3888	.3907	.3925	.3944	.3962	.3980	.3997	.4015
1.3	.4032	.4049	.4066	.4082	.4099	.4115	.4131	.4147	.4162	.4177
1.4	.4192	.4207	.4222	.4236	.4251	.4265	.4279	.4292	.4306	.4319
1.5	.4332	.4345	.4357	.4370	.4382	.4394	.4406	.4418	.4429	.4441
1.6	.4452	.4463	.4474	.4484	.4495	.4505	.4515	.4525	.4535	.4545
1.7	.4554	.4564	.4573	.4582	.4591	.4599	.4608	.4616	.4625	.4633
1.8	.4641	.4649	.4656	.4664	.4671	.4678	.4686	.4693	.4699	.4706
1.9	.4713	.4719	.4726	.4732	.4738	.4744	.4750	.4756	.4761	.4767
2.0	.4772	.4778	.4783	.4788	.4793	.4798	.4803	.4808	.4812	.4817
2.1	.4821	.4826	.4830	.4834	.4838	.4842	.4846	.4850	.4854	.4857
2.2	.4861	.4864	.4868	.4871	.4875	.4878	.4881	.4884	.4887	.4890
2.3	.4893	.4896	.4898	.4901	.4904	.4906	.4909	.4911	.4913	.4916
2.4	.4918	.4920	.4922	.4925	.4927	.4929	.4931	.4932	.4934	.4936
2.5	.4938	.4940	.4941	.4943	.4945	.4946	.4948	.4949	.4951	.4952
2.6	.4953	.4955	.4956	.4957	.4959	.4960	.4961	.4962	.4963	.4964
2.7	.4965	.4966	.4967	.4968	.4969	.4970	.4971	.4972	.4973	.4974
2.8	.4974	.4975	.4976	.4977	.4977	.4978	.4979	.4979	.4980	.4981
2.9	.4881	.4982	.4982	.4983	.4984	.4984	.4985	.4985	.4986	.4986
3.0	.49865	.4987	.4987	.4988	.4988	.4989	.4989	.4989	.4990	.4990

IMPORTANT FORMULAS

$$_nP_n = n!$$ (9.2)

$$_nP_r = n(n - 1)(n - 2) \cdots (n - r + 1)$$ (9.3)

$$_nP_r = \frac{n!}{(n - r)!}$$ (9.4)

$$_nC_r = \frac{n!}{r!(n - r)!}$$ (9.5)

$$0 \leq P(E) \leq 1$$ (9.6)

$$P(\bar{E}) = 1 - P(E)$$ (9.7)

$$P(E_1 \cup E_2) = P(E_1) + P(E_2) \quad \text{(mutually exclusive)}$$ (9.8)

$$P(E_1 \cup E_2 \cup \cdots \cup E_n) = P(E_1) + P(E_2) + \cdots + P(E_n)$$
$$\text{(mutually exclusive)}$$ (9.9)

$$P(E_1 \cup E_2) = P(E_1) + P(E_2) - P(E_1 \cap E_2)$$ (9.10)

$$P(E_1 \cap E_2) = P(E_1)P(E_2) \quad \text{(independence)}$$ (9.11)

$$P(E_1 \cap E_2 \cap \cdots \cap E_n) = P(E_1)P(E_2) \cdots P(E_n)$$
$$\text{(independence)}$$ (9.12)

$$P(E_1|E_2) = P(E_1) \quad \text{(independence)}$$ (9.13)

$$P(E_1|E_2) = \frac{P(E_1 \cap E_2)}{P(E_2)} \quad \text{(dependence)}$$ (9.14)

$$P(E_1 \cap E_2) = P(E_2)P(E_1|E_2)$$ (9.15)

$$\mu = x_1p_1 + x_2p_2 + \cdots + x_np_n$$ (9.16)

$$\sigma = \sqrt{\sum_{j=1}^{n} (x_j - \mu)^2 p_j}$$ (9.18)

$$P(x, n) = {}_nC_x p^x q^{n-x} \quad \text{(binomial)}$$ (9.19)

$$\mu = np \quad \text{(binomial)}$$ (9.20)

$$\sigma = \sqrt{npq} \quad \text{(binomial)}$$ (9.21)

$$z = \frac{x - \mu}{\sigma} \quad \text{(normal)}$$ (9.23)

ADDITIONAL EXERCISES

Exercises 1 to 8 are related to Sec. 9.1.

1   $_6P_3 =$

2   $_7P_4 =$

3   $_7C_4 =$

4   $_8C_5 =$

5   A basketball coach has been frustrated in not being able to find the best five players to have in his starting lineup. If there are 10 players on the team, how many different combinations of players may be selected for the starting lineup? If we assume that any of the 10 players can be selected for any of the five different positions in the starting lineup, how many different lineups are possible?

6   A political candidate wishes to visit seven different cities. In how many different orders can the candidate visit these cities?

7   How many different telephone numbers can be dialed (or pushed) with a three-digit area code and a seven-digit regional number?

8   An automobile dealer has eight different car models. The dealer can display only five in the showroom. How many different combinations of cars could the dealer select for the showroom?

Exercises 9 to 17 are related to Sec. 9.2.

9   Table 9.25 indicates some data gathered on a group of 1,000 victims of robbery, burglary, or both.

TABLE 9.25

	ROBBERY VICTIM	BURGLARY VICTIM	ROBBERY AND BURGLARY VICTIM	TOTAL
Residence	50	500	100	650
Business	150	75	125	350
Total	200	575	225	1000

If one victim is selected at random from this group, what is the probability that the victim will (a) be a residential victim, (b) be a victim of robbery only, (c) be a commercial victim of both robbery and burglary?

10   Odds for a sporting event have been fixed at 3 to 5 that a given team will win. What is the probability the team will win according to the given odds? What are the odds that the opponents will win?

11   The probability that an applicant for pilot school will be admitted is .4. If three applicants are selected at random, what is the probability that (a) all three will be admitted, (b) none will be admitted, (c) only one will be admitted?

12   A student estimates the probability of receiving an A in a course at .3 and the probability of receiving a B at .2. What is the probability that the student (a) will not receive an A, (b) will not receive a B, (c) will receive neither an A nor a B?

13   An urn contains eight green-dotted balls, four green-striped balls, six blue-dotted balls, and two blue-striped balls. If a ball is selected at random from the urn, what is the probability that the ball will be (a) green or striped, (b) dotted, (c) blue or dotted?

14   The probability that a customer entering a particular store will make a purchase is .15. If two customers enter the store, what is the probability that (a) they will both make a purchase, (b) neither will make a purchase, (c) precisely one of the two will make a purchase?

15   A single die is rolled where each side has an equal chance of occurring. What is the probability of rolling three consecutive 6s?

16   A ball is selected at random from an urn containing four red-striped balls, six solid red balls, eight yellow-striped balls, four solid yellow balls, and three blue-striped balls. (a) What is the probability that the ball is yellow given that it is striped?

(*b*) What is the probability that the ball is striped given that it is red?

(*c*) What is the probability that the ball is blue given that it is solid colored?

    17   The probability that the price of a particular stock will increase during a business day is .3. If the nature of the change in price on any day is independent of what has happened on previous days, what is the probability that the price will (*a*) increase three days in a row, (*b*) remain the same or decrease three days in a row, (*c*) increase two days out of three?

Exercises 18 to 23 are related to Sec. 9.3.

    18   Construct the discrete probability distribution which corresponds to the experiment of tossing a coin three times. Assume $P(H) = .6$ and let the random variable x equal the number of tails in three tosses.

    19   The following table presents a discrete probability distribution.

x	$P(x)$
10	.10
20	.20
30	.30
40	.30
50	.10
	1.00

(*a*) Determine the mean of the distribution.

(*b*) Determine the standard deviation.

    20   A single card will be selected from a well-shuffled deck of 52 cards. A payoff of $5 will be made if a jack or higher is selected. A payoff of $2 will be made otherwise. What is the expected payoff associated with a single draw?

    21   A retailer buys an item for $2 and sells it for $5. Because the product is perishable, it has no value if not sold on the first day. Daily demand (*x*) varies at random according to the following distribution.

x	$P(x)$
10	.10
11	.20
12	.40
13	.30

The retailer wishes to determine the level to stock each day so as to maximize expected daily profit.

(*a*) What stock decision results in the maximum expected daily profit?

(*b*) What is the maximum expected daily profit?

    22   **Expected Profit with Perfect Information** Assume that the retailer in Exercise 21 knows ahead of time the exact number which will be demanded each day. Determine the expected daily profit associated with having this perfect information about demand. How does this compare with the expected daily profit found in Exercise 21?

    23   A perishable product is purchased by a retailer for $10 and sold at a price of $15. Daily demand (*x*) varies at random according to the following distribution.

x	$P(x)$
20	.10
21	.20
22	.40
23	.30

If an item is stocked but not sold on the first day, it can be salvaged for $5. The retailer wishes to determine the level to stock each day so as to maximize expected daily profit.
(a) What stock decision results in the maximum expected daily profit?
(b) What is the maximum expected daily profit?

Exercises 24 to 29 are related to Sec. 9.4.

24 A fair coin is to be flipped five times. What is the probability that exactly two heads will occur? five heads?

25 A turnpike authority released data which indicates that 70 percent of the vehicles which travel on the turnpike are cars. Assume that arrivals at the entrance to the turnpike occur at random with regard to the type of vehicle. If 10 vehicles arrive at the entrance, what is the probability that nine will be cars?

26 A U.S. Customs official estimates that 30 percent of all persons returning from Europe fail to declare all purchases which are subject to duty. If six persons are randomly selected upon their return from Europe, determine the probabilities that 0, 1, 2, 3, 4, 5, or 6 of these persons will fail to declare all their purchases which are subject to duty. Construct a histogram which summarizes these results.

27 A test consists of 20 true-false questions. Find the probability that a student who knows the correct answer to 10 of the questions, but guesses at the remaining questions by tossing a coin, will score 85 percent or higher on the test (assume the probability of a correct guess = .5).

28 The IRS has determined that 60 percent of all personal income tax returns contain at least one error. If a sample of 10 returns is selected at random, what is the probability that exactly 6 will be found to contain at least one error?

29 A binomial distribution is characterized by $p = 0.8$, $q = 0.2$, and $n = 50$.
(a) Determine the mean of the distribution.
(b) Determine the standard deviation?

Exercises 30 to 33 are related to Sec. 9.5.

30 **Blood Pressure Screening** A study of blood pressures for a group of women aged 25 to 34 years is normally distributed with a mean of 121 mmHg and a standard deviation of 12.5 mmHg. If a person is selected at random from this age group of women, what is the probability that (a) her blood pressure is between 96 and 133.5 mmHg, (b) her blood pressure is less than 96 mmHg, (c) her blood pressure is higher than 146 mmHg?

31 The entering students for one law school class averaged 720 on the LSAT with a standard deviation of 40. The LSAT scores for this class also appear to be normally distributed.
(a) What percentage of the class is likely to have scored above 750 on the test? Between 700 and 750? Above 700? Below 650?
(b) One student was 1 standard deviation below the mean on the test. About what percentage of his classmates scored lower on the test than him?

32 **Cigarette Smoking** A recent study conducted by the Public Health Service found that males who smoke average 24 cigarettes per day. The number of cigarettes smoked per day is normally distributed with a standard deviation of 8. If a male smoker is selected at random, what is the probability that he smokes (a) more than two packs (40 cigarettes) per day, (b) less than one pack per day, (c) less than half a pack?

33   A manufacturing process produces a circular metal part. The diameters of the manufactured parts have been found to be normally distributed with a mean of 18 centimeters and a standard deviation of 0.05 centimeters. If a metal part is selected at random, what is the probability that it will have a diameter between 17.925 and 18.075 centimeters?

CHAPTER TEST

1   (a) What is the difference between the states of statistical independence and statistical dependence?
(b) What are the characteristics of a Bernoulli process?

2   A grocer has display space for three products. He has six products that he would like to display.
(a) How many different arrangements of three products can be made?
(b) How many different combinations of the six products could he put on display?

3   What is the probability of drawing three cards, without replacement, from a deck of cards and getting three kings?

4   An urn contains 18 red balls, 14 red-striped balls, 16 yellow balls, and 12 yellow-striped balls.
(a) Given that a ball selected from the urn is striped, what is the probability it is yellow?
(b) Given that a ball selected from the urn is not striped, what is the probability it is red?

5   A perishable product is purchased by a retailer for $3 per unit and is sold at a price of $5 per unit. Daily demand has been observed to be random with the following distribution. If an item is not sold on the first

Demand (x)	P(x)
6	.30
7	.25
8	.18
9	.15
10	.12
	1.00

day, the retailer must absorb the $3 cost as a loss. The retailer wishes to determine the number of units to stock each day so as to maximize expected daily profit.
(a) Set up the conditional profit table.
(b) What stock decision results in maximum expected daily profit?
(c) What is the maximum expected daily profit?

6   A fair coin is to be flipped 6 times. What is the probability of getting exactly four tails in the six flips?

7   A random variable x is normally distributed with a mean of 180 and a standard deviation of 40. Determine (a) $P(x \le 172)$, (b) $P(192 \le x \le 204)$.

MINICASE

THE BIRTHDAY PROBLEM

A classic application of probability theory relates to the likelihood, within a group of persons, that two or more have the same birthday. The probability that two or more persons have the same birthday obviously depends upon the size of the group of persons considered. The larger the group, the higher the probability. Let's make some assumptions related to this problem. Assume that there are 365 different birthday possibilities (which ignores leap year) and that for any given person, the 365 days are equally likely to be the person's birthday.

To determine the probability that two or more persons within a group have the same birthday, it is easier to compute the probability that no two persons have the same birthday. Think about this for a moment. The event "two or more persons have the same birthday" consists of many possibilities. These possibilities must account for "three or more," "four or more," etc. They must also account for subsets of persons having the same birthdays (e.g., two persons born on January 5 and three persons born on April 26). Thus, if one can determine the probability p that no two persons have the same birthday, the desired probability can be computed as $1 - p$.

Given a group of n persons, selected at random, the number of different birthday outcomes is

$$T = \overbrace{(365)(365)(365) \cdots (365)}^{n} = (365)^n$$

If, within this group of n persons, no two have the same birthday, there must be n different birth dates. The number of different outcomes which satisfy this event is computed as

$$O = (365)(364)(363) \cdots (365 - n + 1)$$

Thus, the probability that, within the group of persons, *no two persons have the same birthday* equals

$$p = \frac{O}{T} = \frac{(365)(364)(363) \cdots (365 - n + 1)}{(365)^n}$$

Required:
(*a*) Discuss the logic behind the computation of T.
(*b*) Discuss the logic behind the computation of O.
(*c*) Compute the probability that two or more persons will have the same birthday in a group of five randomly selected persons.
(*d*) Compute the same probability for groups of 10, 20, 30, 40, and 50 persons.
(*e*) What is the smallest group of persons for which the probability of two or more having the same birthday exceeds .50? Exceeds .75?

10

NONLINEAR FUNCTIONS

CHAPTER OBJECTIVES

■ Distinguish between the characteristics of linear and nonlinear functions

■ Provide an understanding of the algebraic and graphical characteristics of quadratic functions

■ Illustrate a variety of applications of quadratic functions

■ Overview some of the algebraic and graphical characteristics of polynomial functions

Until this point, our attentions have been focused primarily on linear (versus nonlinear) mathematics. However, as useful and convenient as the linear mathematics has been, there are a variety of phenomena which do not behave in a linear manner and cannot be adequately approximated using linear functions. In this chapter we will be introduced to some of the more common nonlinear functions. The purposes of this chapter are to acquaint you with these nonlinear functions, to create insights which will allow you to anticipate the behavior of these types of functions, and to illustrate a few areas of application in which nonlinear functions are appropriate.

10.1 WHEN LINEAR FUNCTIONS ARE INAPPROPRIATE

Any function of one variable which does not graph as a straight line in two dimensions or any function of two variables which does not graph as a plane in three dimensions can be thought of as being nonlinear. For our purposes, *nonlinear functions* of one or two variables can be thought of as mathematical functions which graph as curved lines in two dimensions and as curved surfaces in three dimensions. Aside from this geometric point of view, we can think of the differences between linear and nonlinear functions in terms of "response." Given

$$y = f(x) \qquad \qquad \textbf{(10.1)}$$

if f is a linear function, the dependent variable y changes in direct proportion to the change in the independent variable x. For example, in the linear function

$$y = -6x + 10 \qquad (10.2)$$

y *decreases* by 6 units for every unit that x increases. The slope of a linear function is the *constant* rate of change in the dependent variable given a unit increase in the independent variable.

For nonlinear functions, the response of the dependent variable is not in direct or exact proportion to changes in the independent variable. To illustrate, if

$$y = x^2 \qquad (10.3)$$

the dependent variable y is computed by squaring the value of the independent variable x. Substituting a few values for x into Eq. (10.3), we can see from Table 10.1 that as x increases from 0 to 1, the change in x, Δx (read "delta x"), and the change in y, Δy (read "delta y"), are the same. But as x increases from 1 to 2, $\Delta x = 1$ and $\Delta y = 3$. Similarly, as x increases from 2 to 3, y increases by 5 units. The changes in y are neither constant nor in *direct* proportion to the changes in x. Figure 10.1 illustrates these responses.

There are many situations in which the relationship between variables is nonlinear. A good example of this from economics is the *law of diminishing returns*.

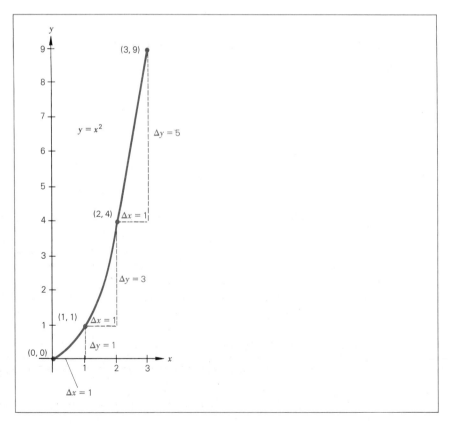

FIGURE 10.1

TABLE 10.1 $y = f(x) = x^2$

x	y	Δx	Δy
0	0		
1	1	1	1
2	4	1	3
3	9	1	5

*An increase in some inputs relative to other fixed inputs will cause total output to increase; but after a point the extra output resulting from the same additions of extra inputs is likely to become less and less.**

EXAMPLE 1

Law of Diminishing Returns   An example of the law of diminishing returns might be the response of sales of a product to changes in the number of salespeople employed or to the level of advertising expenditures. Suppose that a new company has defined a certain geographic area to be a pilot sales district for testing new products. One of their concerns is the number of salespeople to assign to the district. Company analysts suspect that sales (in dollars), s, will depend upon the number of salespeople, n, assigned to the district. This relationship might be represented by the notation $S = f(n)$. Company analysts have projected sales for different numbers of salespeople, as indicated in Table 10.2.

TABLE 10.2

NUMBER OF SALESPEOPLE (n)	Δn	DOLLAR SALES (S)	ADDITIONAL SALES (ΔS)
0		0	0
1	1	$100,000	$100,000
2	1	210,000	110,000
3	1	330,000	120,000
4	1	430,000	100,000
5	1	500,000	70,000
6	1	530,000	30,000
7	1	540,000	10,000

If we think of the number of salespersons as being the *input* and sales as the *output*, sales increase with each additional salesperson. However, if we examine the additional sales associated with each additional salesperson, the *additional sales* increase up to the third salesperson but begin to decrease thereafter. We can state that the point at which the fourth salesperson is added to the district is the point of *diminishing returns*, the point at which the extra or marginal output (sales) associated with additional inputs (salespeople) decreases compared with the marginal returns of previous inputs.

EXAMPLE 2

Economists have spent much time studying the laws and behavior of *supply* and *demand*.

---

* Paul A. Samuelson, *Economics*, 11th ed., McGraw-Hill Book Company, New York, 1980, p. 25.

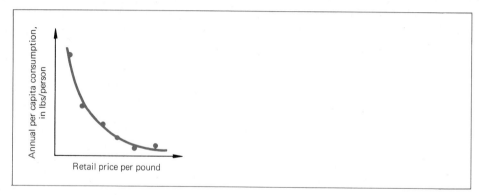

FIGURE 10.2
Demand
relationship
for lobster.

As discussed in Chap. 5, one theory states that a primary determinant of the quantity demanded of certain commodities is the price charged for the commodity. A general functional representation of this relationship is

$$q = f(p) \qquad (10.4)$$

where q = *number of units demanded*
p = *price per unit*

In some cases the relationship between price and quantity demanded is linear, or it can be reasonably approximated by a linear function. We discussed this case in Chap. 5. In other instances, the relationship is nonlinear and cannot be adequately approximated using a linear function. Figure 10.2 illustrates a demand function for the sale of lobsters in the New England region. The smooth curve is an approximation to data points which were gathered in a consumer expenditure poll. The relationship between retail price and annual per capita consumption is obviously nonlinear.

The question you should be asking yourself is, When do you use a linear function and when do you use a nonlinear function to represent the relationship between variables? The answer to this question depends on whether the logical structure of how the variables are interrelated is clear and explicit. In the case where the structure is clear, the mathematical representation should take the exact form of the relationship. A good example of this situation is the determination of the total revenue function associated with selling a product. If the firm sells each unit for the same price p, the total revenue R from selling q units is determined as

$$R = pq$$

In many other cases, the way in which variables are interrelated is not exactly known. In these instances, it is first necessary to collect relevant data by using an appropriate sampling procedure. An example of this type of data gathering occurred in Example 2. Sample data points were found by surveying consumers about the quantities of lobster they expected to purchase given different retail prices. Once the data have been gathered, the objective is to identify the mathematical function which best "fits" the data. Different functional forms, linear and

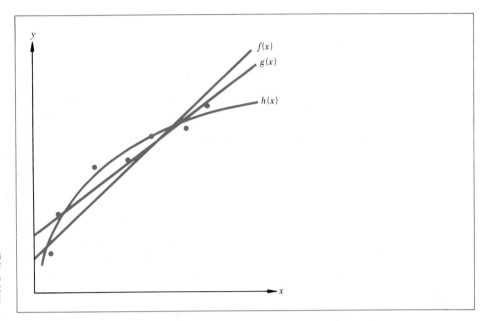

nonlinear, may be fit to the same set of data points and some determination reached as to which form most accurately approximates the relationship suggested by the data points. Figure 10.3 illustrates a set of data points which have been fit with three different functions, two linear and one nonlinear. There are different criteria which may be used to determine which function is "best." The methods can vary from simply "eyeballing" a curve to fit the data points to more rigorous statistical procedures such as regression analysis. Once the mathematical function (model) has been identified, the analysis of the model can begin.

10.2 QUADRATIC FUNCTIONS AND THEIR CHARACTERISTICS

One of the more common nonlinear functions is the quadratic function.

Mathematical Form

DEFINITION: QUADRATIC FUNCTION

A **quadratic function** involving the independent variable x and the dependent variable y has the general form

$$y = f(x) = ax^2 + bx + c \qquad (10.5)$$

where a, b, and c are constants and $a \neq 0$.

Can you see the reason why the coefficient of x^2 cannot equal 0? If $a = 0$ and b and c are nonzero, Eq. (10.5) becomes

$$y = bx + c$$

which is a linear function. As long as $a \neq 0$, b and c can assume any values.

EXAMPLE 3

Which of the following functions are quadratic functions?

(a) $y = f(x) = 5x^2$

(b) $u = f(v) = -10v^2 - 6$

(c) $y = f(x) = 7x - 2$

(d) $g = f(h) = -6$

(e) $y = f(x) = x^2 + 10x$

(f) $y = f(x) = 6x^2 - 40x + 15$

(g) $y = f(x) = 2x^3 + 4x^2 - 2x + 5$

SOLUTION

(a) $y = 5x^2$ is a quadratic function. According to the general form of Eq. (10.5), $a = 5$, $b = 0$, and $c = 0$.

(b) $u = -10v^2 - 6$ is a quadratic function where, according to Eq. (10.5), $a = -10$, $b = 0$, and $c = -6$.

(c) $y = 7x - 2$ is *not* a quadratic function since there is no x^2 term, or $a = 0$.

(d) $g = -6$ is not a quadratic function for the same reason as presented in (c).

(e) $y = x^2 + 10x$ is a quadratic function where $a = 1$, $b = 10$, and $c = 0$.

(f) $y = 6x^2 - 40x + 15$ is a quadratic function where $a = 6$, $b = -40$, and $c = 15$.

(g) $y = 2x^3 + 4x^2 - 2x + 5$ is not a quadratic function because it does not have the form of Eq. (10.5). It is not a quadratic because it contains a third-degree term—$2x^3$.

NOTE

Equation (10.5) has the same form as that presented in Chap. 2. In Chap. 2, we stated the general form of a quadratic function as

$$y = a_2x^2 + a_1x + a_0 \qquad a_2 \neq 0 \qquad \text{(2.3)}$$

You should observe that the two statements [Eqs. (2.3) and (10.5)] are equivalent. Only the names of the coefficients have been changed. This is a matter of author preference in order to conform with the notation often used to generalize quadratic functions in other texts.

Graphical Representation

All quadratic functions having the form of Eq. (10.5) graph as *parabolas.* Figure 10.4 illustrates two parabolas which have different orientations. A parabola which "opens" upward, such as that in Fig. 10.4a, is said to be *concave up.* A parabola which "opens" downward, such as that in Fig. 10.4b, is said to be *concave down.** The point at which a parabola either "bottoms out" when it is concave up or "peaks out" when it is concave down is called the *vertex* of the parabola. Points A and B are the respective *vertices* for the two parabolas in Fig. 10.4.

---

* A more detailed discussion of the *concavity* of functions will be presented in Chap. 12.

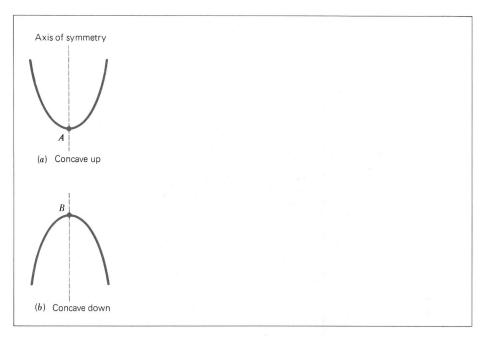

FIGURE 10.4
Parabolas.

NOTE

It can be shown that the coordinates of the vertex of a parabola are

$$\left(\frac{-b}{2a}, \frac{4ac - b^2}{4a}\right)$$

where a, b, and c are the parameters of Eq. (10.5).*

The dashed vertical line which passes through the vertex of each parabola is an imaginary line called the *axis of symmetry.* The parabola is divided into two halves which are symmetrical about the axis of symmetry. That is, if you fold one side of the parabola using the axis of symmetry as a hinge, you will find that the two halves are mirror images of each other.

POINT FOR THOUGHT AND DISCUSSION

Given the general form of a quadratic function stated by Eq. (10.5), what equation represents the axis for symmetry? *Hint:* Examine the general form of the coordinates of the vertex.

EXAMPLE 4

Sketch the graph of the quadratic function $y = f(x) = x^2$.

---

* See Exercise 6 at the end of the chapter.

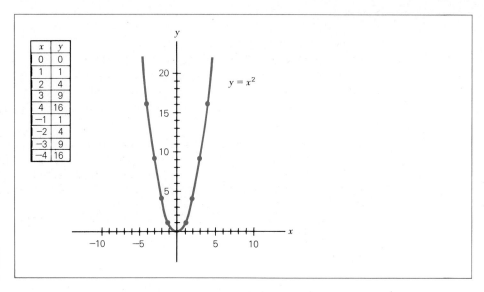

SOLUTION

To sketch any mathematical function which involves two variables, it is necessary to determine the set of points which satisfy the function. Sample values for x and the corresponding values for y are shown in Fig. 10.5 along with the sketch of the parabola.

For this quadratic function, $a = 1$, $b = 0$, and $c = 0$. The x coordinate of the vertex is

$$x = \frac{-b}{2a} = -\frac{0}{2(1)} = 0$$

and the y coordinate is

$$y = \frac{4ac - b^2}{4a} = \frac{4(1)(0) - (0)^2}{4(1)} = 0$$

Given that $(0, 0)$ is the vertex, the y axis is the axis of symmetry. You can verify the symmetry about the y axis by noting that equal movements along the x axis to either side of the vertex result in the same values for y. For example, note that the value of y is the same when x equals $+1$ or -1, $+2$ or -2, $+3$ or -3, and $+4$ or -4.

Figure 10.5 is only a *sketch* of the function. The more data points identified and plotted, the more accurate the sketch will be for any function.

Special Insights to Sketching Quadratic Functions

Given the general quadratic form of Eq. (10.5), the concavity of the parabola can be determined by the sign of the coefficient on the x^2 term. If *a is positive,* the function will graph as a parabola which is *concave up.* If *a is negative,* the parabola is *concave down.*

EXAMPLE 5

What is the concavity of the parabola representing each quadratic function identified in Example 3?

SOLUTION

(a) The graph of $y = 5x^2$ is concave *up* since $a = +5$.
(b) The graph of $u = -10v^2 - 6$ is concave *down* since $a = -10$.
(c) The graph of $y = x^2 + 10x$ is concave *up* since $a = +1$.
(d) The graph of $y = 6x^2 - 40x + 15$ is concave *up* since $a = +6$.

Knowing the concavity and a few other key data points can allow for a quick and easy sketch of the parabola which represents a quadratic function. If we know the concavity, also knowing (1) the location of the vertex, (2) the y intercept, and (3) the x intercept(s) can allow for a rough sketch of the function.

The **y intercept** for a function was defined in Chap. 3 as the point at which the function crosses the y axis. The y coordinate of the y intercept is the value of y when x equals 0, or $f(0)$.

EXAMPLE 6

What are the y intercepts for the quadratic functions in Example 3?

SOLUTION

(a) For $y = 5x^2$, $f(0) = 0$, or the y intercept occurs at $(0, 0)$.
(b) For $u = -10v^2 - 6$, $f(0) = -6$, or the u intercept occurs at $(0, -6)$.
(c) For $y = x^2 + 10x$, $f(0) = 0$, or the y intercept occurs at $(0, 0)$.
(d) For $y = 6x^2 - 40x + 15$, $f(0) = 15$, or the y intercept occurs at $(0, 15)$.

The **x intercept** for a function was also defined in Chap. 3 as the point(s) at which the function crosses the x axis. Equivalently, the x intercept represents the value(s) of x when y equals 0. For quadratic functions, there may be one x intercept, two x intercepts, or *no* x intercept. These possibilities are shown in Fig. 10.6.

There are a number of ways of determining the x intercepts for a quadratic function if any exist. The x intercepts are found by determining the roots of the equation

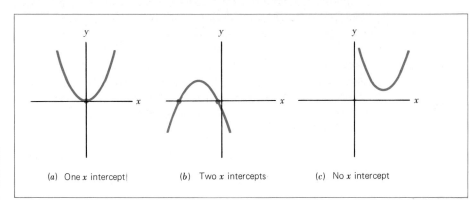

FIGURE 10.6
x intercept possibilities for quadratic functions.

(a) One x intercept

(b) Two x intercepts

(c) No x intercept

$$ax^2 + bx + c = 0 \qquad\qquad \textbf{(10.6)}$$

Two methods of determining the roots to Eq. (10.6) were discussed in Sec. 1.6. These methods are illustrated in the following example.

EXAMPLE 7

Determining Roots by Factoring Some quadratic functions can be factored (Sec. 1.3) into either two binomials or a binomial and a monomial. If a quadratic function can be factored, it is an easy matter to determine the roots of Eq. (10.6). For example, the values of x which satisfy the quadratic equation

$$6x^2 - 2x = 0 \qquad\qquad \textbf{(10.7)}$$

can be determined by first factoring $2x$ from the expression on the left-hand side of the equation, yielding

$$(2x)(3x - 1) = 0 \qquad\qquad \textbf{(10.8)}$$

By setting each factor equal to 0, the roots of the equation are identified as

$$2x = 0 \quad \text{or} \quad x = 0$$

and

$$3x - 1 = 0 \quad \text{or} \quad x = \tfrac{1}{3}$$

Similarly, the values of x satisfying the equation

$$x^2 + 6x + 9 = 0$$

are found by factoring the left side of the equation, yielding

$$(x + 3)(x + 3) = 0$$

When the factors are set equal to 0, it is found that the only value which satisfies the equation is $x = -3$.

When a quadratic function cannot be factored, the approach illustrated in Example 7 fails to identify the roots of the quadratic equation. Applying the *quadratic formula* will *always* identify the real roots of a quadratic equation *if any exist.*

ALGEBRA FLASHBACK

The *quadratic formula,* which is used to identify roots of equations of the form of Eq. (10.6), is

$$x = \frac{-b \pm \sqrt{b^2 - 4ac}}{2a}$$

Recall from Sec. 1.6 that (1) if $b^2 - 4ac > 0$, there will be two real roots; (2) if $b^2 - 4ac = 0$, there will be one real root; and (3) if $b^2 - 4ac < 0$, there will be no real roots

EXAMPLE 8

Given the quadratic function $f(x) = x^2 - x - 3.75$, the x intercepts occur when $x^2 - x - 3.75 = 0$. Referring to Eq. (10.6), we get $a = 1$, $b = -1$, $c = -3.75$. Substituting these values of a, b, and c into the quadratic formula, the roots of the equation are computed as

$$x = \frac{-(-1) \pm \sqrt{(-1)^2 - 4(1)(-3.75)}}{2(1)}$$

$$= \frac{1 \pm \sqrt{1 + 15}}{2} = \frac{1 \pm \sqrt{16}}{2} = \frac{1 \pm 4}{2}$$

or, using the plus sign, we have

$$x = \tfrac{5}{2} = 2.5$$

Using the minus sign gives

$$x = -\tfrac{3}{2} = -1.5$$

Thus, there are two values of x which satisfy the quadratic equation. The parabola representing the quadratic function will cross the x axis at $(2.5, 0)$ and $(-1.5, 0)$. This case is similar to that of Fig. 10.6b.

Let's use the information developed thus far to illustrate how the sketch of a quadratic function can be made when its concavity, the location of the vertex, the y intercept, and the x intercept(s) are known.

EXAMPLE 9

Suppose we want to sketch the quadratic function $f(x) = 3x^2 + 6x - 45$. Since $a = 3$ is greater than 0, we can immediately state that the graph is a parabola which is *concave up*. The y coordinate of the y *intercept* equals $f(0)$, or -45. The x *intercepts* can be identified by factoring as

$$3x^2 + 6x - 45 = 0$$
or
$$(3x - 9)(x + 5) = 0$$

Setting each factor equal to 0 yields

when
$$3x - 9 = 0$$
$$x = 3$$
and
$$x + 5 = 0$$
when
$$x = -5$$

Thus, the parabola crosses the x axis at $(-5, 0)$ and $(3, 0)$. The coordinates of the vertex are $(-1, -48)$ as computed below.

$$x = \frac{-b}{2a} = \frac{-6}{2(3)} = -1$$

and
$$y = \frac{4ac - b^2}{4a} = \frac{4(3)(-45) - (6)^2}{4(3)}$$

$$= \frac{-540 - 36}{12} = \frac{-576}{12} = -48$$

The parabola is sketched in Fig. 10.7.

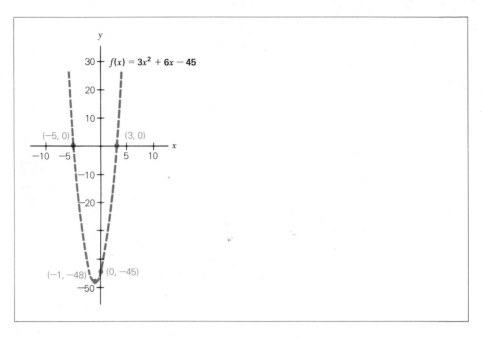

FIGURE 10.7
Sketch of
$f(x) = 3x^2 +$
$6x - 45$.

NOTE

Because of the symmetry of parabolas, whenever a parabola has two x intercepts, the x coordinate of the vertex will always be midway between the x intercepts. Whenever the parabola has one x intercept, the vertex occurs at that point.

In Example 9 the x coordinate of the vertex will lie halfway between $x = -5$ and $x = 3$, or at $x = -1$, which is the same value as determined by formula.

Determining the Equation of Quadratic Functions

In Exercise 8 on page 390 we saw that the parameters a, b, and c of a quadratic function can be determined if the coordinates are known for three points which lie on the graph of the function. When the coordinates of the three points are substituted into Eq. (10.5), the result is a system of three equations stated in terms of a, b, and c. The values for these parameters can be found by solving the equations simultaneously.

EXAMPLE 10

Determine the equation of the quadratic function which passes through the points (1, 8), (3, 20), and (−2, 5).

SOLUTION

Substituting the coordinates of the three points into Eq. (10.5) yields

$$8 = a(1)^2 + b(1) + c \qquad or \qquad a + b + c = 8 \qquad\qquad \textbf{(10.9)}$$

$$20 = a(3)^2 + b(3) + c \qquad or \qquad 9a + 3b + c = 20 \qquad\qquad \textbf{(10.10)}$$

$$5 = a(-2)^2 + b(-2) + c \qquad or \qquad 4a - 2b + c = 5 \qquad\qquad \textbf{(10.11)}$$

Verify that the solution of the resulting system of equations is $a = 1$, $b = 2$, and $c = 5$. By substituting this result into Eq. (10.5) it can be determined that the function which passes through the three given points is

$$y = x^2 + 2x + 5$$

POINT FOR THOUGHT AND DISCUSSION

Suppose that three points (x_1, y_1), (x_2, y_2), and (x_3, y_3) are given. Upon substituting these into Eq. (10.5) to solve for a, b, and c, what conclusion would you reach if there is no solution to the system of three equations?

Section 10.2 Follow-up Exercises

In Exercises 1 to 8, determine which functions are quadratic and identify values for the parameters a, b, and c.

1   $f(x) = 5x^3 - 4x^2 - 20$ 2 $f(w) = w^2 - 5w + 100$
3   $f(t) = -t^2/100$ 4 $f(x) = x^{1/2} - 2x + 5$
5   $f(n) = (n^2 - 2n + 4)/5$ 6 $f(u) = u^2 - u$
7   $f(r) = (16r^4)^{1/2} - r + 1$ 8 $f(x) = \sqrt{x^2 - 2x + 1}$

In Exercises 9 to 16, determine the concavity of the quadratic function, its y intercept, its x intercepts if any exist, and the coordinates of the vertex. Sketch the parabola.

9   $f(x) = -3x^2$ 10 $f(x) = -x^2 + 5x - 4$
11   $f(x) = 5x^2 - 2x + 6$ 12 $f(x) = x^2 + 10$
13   $f(x) = -x^2 - 6x - 9$ 14 $f(x) = x^2 - 4x + 4$
15   $f(x) = x^2 - 0.5x - 5$ 16 $f(x) = 15x^2 + 8x - 12$

17   Sketch the following three quadratic functions, making note of the values of $|a|$ for each and the relative steepness of the three parabolas.

$$y = x^2 \qquad y = 0.01x^2 \qquad y = 100x^2$$

18   Determine the equation of the quadratic function which passes through the points $(0, 10)$, $(1, 6)$, and $(-2, 24)$.

19   Determine the equation of the quadratic function which passes through the points $(1, -1)$, $(-3, 33)$, and $(2, -8)$.

20   Determine the equation of the quadratic function which passes through the points $(-3, 3)$, $(0, 0)$, and $(4, -4)$.

10.3   QUADRATIC FUNCTIONS: APPLICATIONS

In this section examples will be presented which illustrate a few areas of application of quadratic functions.

EXAMPLE 11

Quadratic Revenue Functions Often the demand for the product of a firm can be described as a function of the price which the firm charges for the product. Assume that a firm has determined that the quantity demanded of one of its products depends on the price charged. The function describing this relationship is

$$q = f(p)$$

or
$$q = 1,500 - 50p$$

where q equals the quantity demanded in thousands of units and p equals the price in dollars.
Total revenue R from selling q units is stated as the product of p and q, or

$$R = pq$$

Because q is stated as a function of p, total revenue can be stated as a function of price, or

$$R = h(p)$$
$$= p \cdot f(p)$$
$$= p(1,500 - 50p)$$
$$= 1,500p - 50p^2$$

You should recognize this as a quadratic function. The total revenue function is sketched in Fig. 10.8. Notice that the restricted domain (see Chap. 2) of the function consists of nonnegative values of p. Does this make sense?

The total revenue expected from charging a particular price can be computed by substituting the value of p into the total revenue function. For example, the total revenue which corresponds to a price of $10 is

$$h(10) = 1,500(10) - 50(10)^2$$
$$= 15,000 - 5,000 = \$10,000$$

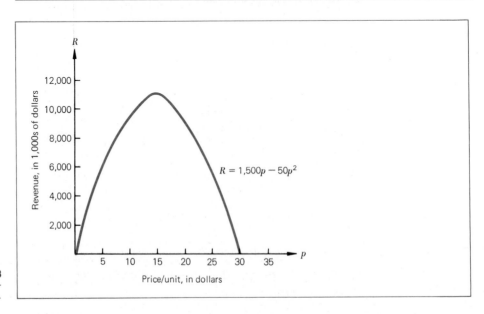

FIGURE 10.8
Quadratic revenue function.

EXAMPLE 12

Quadratic Supply Functions Market surveys of suppliers of a particular product have resulted in the conclusion that the form of the supply function (see Chap. 5) is quadratic. Suppliers were asked what quantities they would be willing to supply at different market prices. Results of the survey indicated that at market prices of $25, $30, and $40 the quantities which suppliers would be willing to offer to the market were 112.5, 250.0, and 600.0 (thousand) units, respectively. Using the procedure discussed in Example 10, we can determine the equation of the quadratic supply function by substituting the three price-quantity combinations into the general equation

$$q_s = f(p)$$

or

$$q_s = ap^2 + bp + c$$

The resulting system of equations is

$$625a + 25b + c = 112.5$$
$$900a + 30b + c = 250$$
$$1,600a + 40b + c = 600$$

which, when solved, yields values of $a = 0.5$, $b = 0$, and $c = -200$. Thus the quadratic supply function, shown in Fig. 10.9, is represented by the equation

$$q_s = f(p) = 0.5p^2 - 200$$

The quantity supplied at any market price can be determined by substituting the price into the supply function. For example, the quantity supplied at a price of $50 is

$$f(50) = 0.5(50)^2 - 200$$
$$= 0.5(2,500) - 200 = 1,250 - 200 = 1,050 \text{ (thousand) units}$$

EXAMPLE 13

Quadratic Demand Functions Related to the previous example, a consumer survey was conducted to determine the demand function for the same product. Researchers asked consumers if they would purchase the product at various prices and from their responses constructed estimates of market demand at various market prices. After sample data

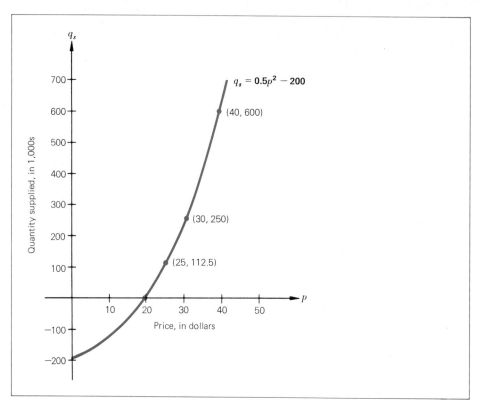

$q_s = 0.5p^2 - 200$

(40, 600)

(30, 250)

(25, 112.5)

FIGURE 10.9
Quadratic
supply function.

points were plotted, it was concluded that the demand relationship was represented best by a quadratic function. Researchers concluded that the quadratic representation was valid for prices between $5 and $45.

Three data points chosen for "fitting" the curve were (5, 2,025.0)(10, 1,600.0), and (20, 900.0). Substituting these data points into the general equation for a quadratic function and solving the resulting system simultaneously gives the demand function

$$q_d = g(p)$$

or

$$q_d = p^2 - 100p + 2,500$$

where p equals the selling price in dollars and q_d equals demand stated in thousands of units. Figure 10.10 illustrates the demand function.

The quantity demanded at any price can be calculated by substituting the price into the demand function. For example, at a price of $30, the quantity demanded is

$$q(30) = (30)^2 - 100(30) + 2,500$$
$$= 900 - 3,000 + 2,500 = 400 \text{ (thousand) units}$$

EXAMPLE 14

Supply-Demand Equilibrium   Market equilibrium between supply and demand can be estimated for the supply and demand functions in the last two examples by determining the market price which equates quantity supplied and quantity demanded. This condition is expressed by the equation

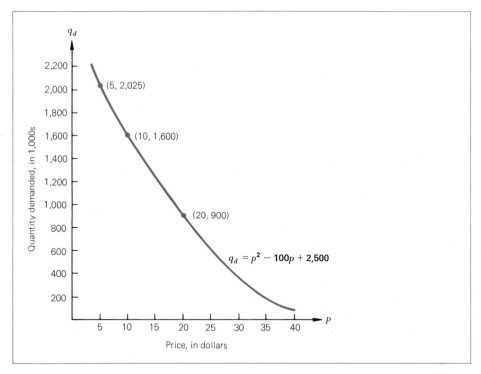

FIGURE 10.10
Quadratic demand function.

$$q_s = q_d$$
or
$$0.5p^2 - 200 = p^2 - 100p + 2,500$$

The equation can be rearranged so that

$$0.5p^2 - 100p + 2,700 = 0 \qquad \textbf{(10.12)}$$

The quadratic formula can be used to determine the roots to Eq. (10.12) as follows:

$$p = \frac{-(-100) \pm \sqrt{(-100)^2 - 4(0.5)(2,700)}}{2(0.5)}$$

$$= \frac{100 \pm \sqrt{4,600}}{1} = 100 \pm 67.82$$

The two values of p which satisfy Eq. (10.12) are $p = \$32.18$ and $p = \$167.82$. The second root is outside the relevant domain of the demand function and is therefore meaningless. However, $q_s = q_d$ when the selling price is $32.18. Substitution of $p = 32.18$ into the supply and demand functions results in values of $q_s = 317.77$ and $q_d = 317.55$. (Rounding is the reason for the difference between these two values.) Thus market equilibrium occurs when the market price equals $32.18 and the quantity supplied and demanded equals 317,770 units. Figure 10.11 illustrates the two functions.

POINT FOR THOUGHT AND DISCUSSION
Why were there two roots to Eq. (10.12)?

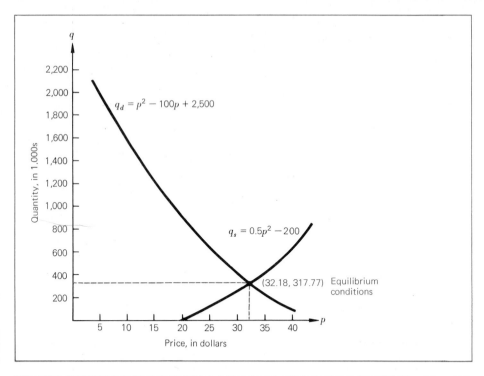

FIGURE 10.11
Supply-demand
equilibrium.

FIGURE 10.12
Relative loca-
tion of cities.

EXAMPLE 15

Emergency Response: Location Model   Figure 10.12 illustrates the relative locations of three cities along a coastal highway. The three cities are popular resorts, and their populations swell during the summer months. The three cities believe their emergency rescue and health treatment capabilities are inadequate during the vacation season. They have decided to support jointly an emergency response facility which dispatches rescue trucks and trained paramedics. A key question concerns the location of the facility.

In choosing the location, it has been agreed that the distance from the facility to each city should be kept as short as possible to ensure quick response times. Another consideration is the size of the summer population of each city, since this is one measure of the potential need for emergency response services. The larger the summer population of a city, the greater the desire to locate the facility close to the city. Analysts have decided that the criterion for selecting the location is to minimize the sum of the products of the summer populations of each town and the square of the distance between the town and the facility. This can be stated more succinctly as

$$\text{Minimize} \quad S = \sum_{j=1}^{3} p_j d_j^2$$

where p_j equals the summer population for city j, stated in thousands, and d_j is the distance between city j and the rescue facility.

If the summer populations are, respectively, 150,000, 100,000, and 200,000 for the three cities, compute the general expression for S. (*Hint: Let x equal the location of the facility relative to the zero point of the scale in Fig. 10.12, and let x_j equal the location of city j. The distance between the facility and city j is calculated by the equation $d_j = x - x_j$.*)

SOLUTION

With x defined as the unknown location of the proposed facility, S can be stated as a function of x. The function is defined as

$$S = f(x)$$
$$= \sum_{j=1}^{3} p_j(x - x_j)^2$$
$$= 150(x - 12)^2 + 100(x - 20)^2 + 200(x - 30)^2$$
$$= 150x^2 - 3,600x + 21,600 + 100x^2 - 4,000x$$
$$+ 40,000 + 200x^2 - 12,000x + 180,000$$

or
$$S = 450x^2 - 19,600x + 241,600$$

Note that this function is quadratic in form, and it will graph as a parabola which is concave up. S will be minimized at the vertex of the parabola, or where

$$x = \frac{-b}{2a} = \frac{-(-19,600)}{2(450)}$$
$$= \frac{19,600}{900} = 21.77$$

According to Fig. 10.13 the emergency response facility will be located 21.77 miles to the right of the zero point, or 1.77 miles to the right of city 2.

We will reconsider this example in Chap. 13 and solve it by another method.

FIGURE 10.13
Optimal location
of emergency
response
facility.

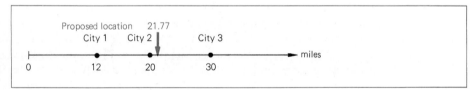

Section 10.3 Follow-up Exercises

1 The demand function for a particular product is

$$q = f(p) = 400,000 - 2,000p$$

where q is stated in units and p is stated in dollars. Determine the quadratic total revenue function where R is a function of p, or $R = g(p)$. What is the concavity of the function? What is the y intercept? What does total revenue equal at a price of $20? How many units will be demanded at this price?

2 The demand function for a particular product is

$$q = f(p) = 1,500 - 7.5p$$

where q is stated in units and p is stated in dollars. Determine the quadratic total revenue function where R is a function of p, or $R = g(p)$. What is the concavity of the function? What is the y intercept? What does total revenue equal at a price of $50? How many units will be demanded at this price?

3 Total revenue in Exercise 2 can be stated in terms of either price p or demand q. Restate total revenue as a function of q rather than p. That is, determine the function $R = h(q)$. (*Hint:* Solve for p in the demand function and multiply this expression by q.)

4 In Exercise 2, restate the function for total revenue as a function of q. (See Exercise 3 for a hint.)

5 The supply function $q_s = f(p)$ for a product is quadratic. Three points which lie on the supply function are (60, 2,750), (70, 6,000), and (80, 9,750).
(*a*) Determine the equation for the function.
(*b*) Make any observations you can about the relevant domain of the function.
(*c*) Compute and interpret the x intercept.
(*d*) What quantity will be supplied at a price of $75.

6 The supply function $q_s = f(p)$ for a product is quadratic. Three points which lie on the function are (30, 1,500), (40, 3,600) and (50, 6,300).
(*a*) Determine the equation for the supply function.
(*b*) Make any observations you can about the relevant domain of the function.
(*c*) Compute and interpret the x intercept.
(*d*) What quantity will be supplied at a price of $60?

7 The demand function $q_d = f(p)$ for a product is quadratic. Three points which lie on the function are (10, 2,700), (20, 1,200) and (30, 300). Determine the equation for the demand function. What quantity will be demanded at a market price of $25?

8 The demand function $q_d = f(p)$ for a product is quadratic. Three points which lie on the function are (5, 1,600), (10, 900), and (20, 100). Determine the equation for the demand function. What quantity will be demanded at a market price of $15?

9 The supply and demand functions for a product are $q_s = p^2 - 400$ and $q_d = p^2 - 40p + 2,600$. Determine the market equilibrium price and quantity.

10 The supply and demand functions for a product are $q_s = 4p^2 - 500$ and $q_d = 3p^2 - 20p + 1,000$. Determine the market equilibrium price and quantity.

11 In Example 15, assume that the criterion is to minimize the sum of the squares of the distances separating the emergency response facility and the three cities; that is,

$$S = \sum_{j=1}^{3} d_j^2$$

(*a*) Determine the distance function $S = f(x)$.
(*b*) Determine the location which minimizes S.

10.4 OTHER NONLINEAR FUNCTIONS

Polynomial Functions

Linear and quadratic functions are examples of the general set of functions called *polynomial functions.*

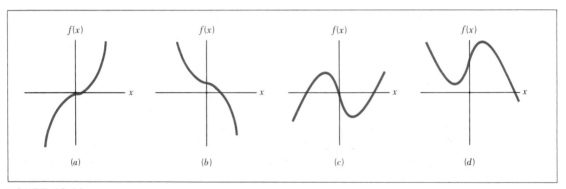

FIGURE 10.14
Graphical char-
acteristics of
cubic functions.

DEFINITION: POLYNOMIAL FUNCTION

A **polynomial function** of degree n involving the independent
variable x and the dependent variable y has the general form

$$y = f(x)$$

where $\quad f(x) = a_n x^n + a_{n-1} x^{n-1} + \cdots + a_1 x + a_0 \quad$ **(10.13)**

a_j equals a real number for each j, n is a positive integer, and
$a_n \neq 0$.

The degree of a polynomial is the exponent of the highest powered term in the
expression. A linear function is a *first-degree polynomial function,* whereas a
quadratic function is a *second-degree function.* A *third-degree function* such as

$$y = x^3 - 2x^2 + 5x + 10$$

is referred to as a *cubic function.*

Cubic functions of the form $y = f(x)$ tend to exhibit a behavior similar to
those portrayed in Fig. 10.14. Although we will learn more about the graphical
characteristics of functions in the coming chapters, let's explore one attribute of
polynomial functions.

ULTIMATE DIRECTION ATTRIBUTE

The **ultimate direction** of a function f refers to the behavior of
$f(x)$ as x assumes larger and larger positive values and as x assumes larger and larger negative values. For polynomial functions the ultimate behavior of $f(x)$ is determined by the behavior
of the highest-powered term in the function. This is based
on the observation that as x becomes more positive (or negative), eventually the highest-powered term will contribute more
to the value of $f(x)$ than all other terms in the function.

For polynomial functions of the form

$$f(x) = a_n x^n + a_{n-1} x^{n-1} + \cdots + a_1 x + a_0$$

the ultimate behavior depends on the term $a_n x^n$. Figure 10.15
illustrates the different possibilities. The sign of a_n as well as
whether n is odd or even are the significant factors in deter-

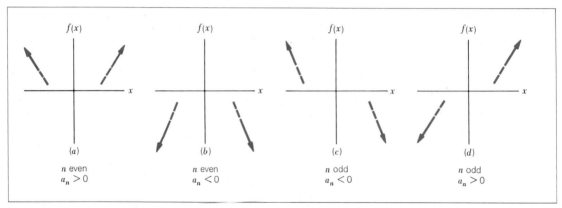

FIGURE 10.15
Ultimate direction attributes for polynomial functions of the form $f(x) = a_n x^n + a_{n-1} x^{n-1} + \cdots + a_1 x + a_0$.

mining the ultimate direction. When *n is even*, $x^n > 0$ for positive or negative x; for these cases the coefficient a_n determines the sign on $a_n x^n$. When *n is odd*, $x^n > 0$ if $x > 0$ and $x^n < 0$ if $x < 0$. Again, a_n determines the sign of $a_n x^n$; however, $f(x)$ ultimately heads in different directions for $x > 0$ and $x < 0$.

If we refer back to Fig. 10.14, cases (*a*) and (*c*) represent cubic functions where $a_3 > 0$, while cases (*b*) and (*d*) represent those where $a_3 < 0$.

EXAMPLE 16

For the following polynomial functions, determine the ultimate direction of $f(x)$ and sketch f.

(*a*) $f(x) = \dfrac{x^5}{5} + \dfrac{x^4}{8} - 2.5x^3$ (*b*) $g(x) = \dfrac{x^4}{4} - 8x^2 + 10$

SOLUTION

(*a*) The ultimate direction for $f(x)$ is determined by the term $x^5/5$. As x assumes larger and larger (positive and negative) values, this term will eventually become dominant in determining the value of $f(x)$. Because the exponent on this term is odd and the coefficient ($\frac{1}{5}$) is positive, the ultimate direction will correspond to the situation in Fig. 10.15*d*.

If sufficient numbers of values of x are substituted into f and the resulting ordered pairs plotted, the sketch of f should appear as shown in Fig. 10.16.

(*b*) The ultimate direction of $g(x)$ is determined by the term $x^4/4$. Since the degree of this term is even and the coefficient ($\frac{1}{4}$) is positive, the ultimate direction will correspond to the situation in Fig. 10.15*a*. If enough ordered pairs of values satisfying g are identified and plotted, the graph of g should appear as shown in Fig. 10.17.

NOTE

The behavior of polynomial functions between the "tails" of ultimate direction can be determined more easily than by the "brute force" method of plotting many ordered pairs. We will examine this in greater detail in Chap. 12.

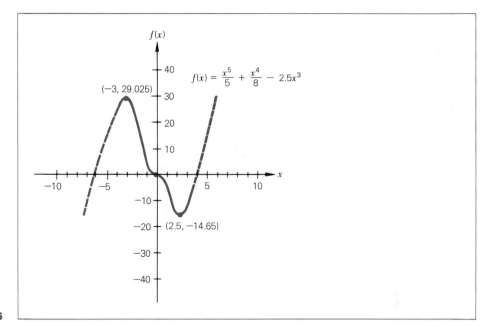

$$f(x) = \frac{x^5}{5} + \frac{x^4}{8} - 2.5x^3$$

(−3, 29.025)

(2.5, −14.65)

FIGURE 10.16

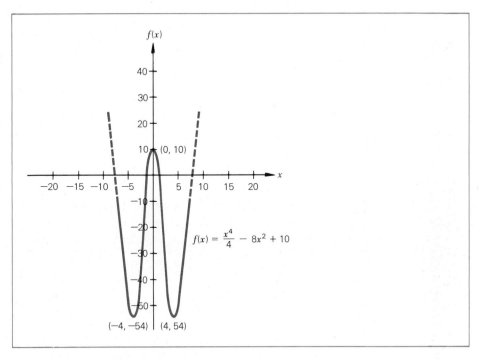

(0, 10)

$$f(x) = \frac{x^4}{4} - 8x^2 + 10$$

(−4, −54) | (4, 54)

FIGURE 10.17

Rational Functions

As mentioned in Chap. 2, *rational functions* are functions expressed as the *ratio* or quotient of two polynomials.

DEFINITION: RATIONAL FUNCTION

A *rational function* has the general form

$$f(x) = \frac{g(x)}{h(x)} = \frac{a_n x^n + a_{n-1} x^{n-1} + \cdots + a_1 x + a_0}{b_m x^m + b_{m-1} x^{m-1} + \cdots + b_1 x + b_0}$$

where g is an nth degree polynomial function and h is a non-zero mth degree polynomial function.

Two examples of rational functions are

$$f(x) = \frac{x}{x^2 - 4} \qquad x \neq 2, -2$$

$$g(x) = \frac{x^3 - 5x + 10}{x} \qquad x \neq 0$$

EXAMPLE 17

Disability Rehabilitation Physical therapists often find that the rehabilitation process is characterized by a diminishing returns effect. That is, regained functionality usually increases with the length of a therapy program but eventually in decreased amounts relative to additional program efforts. For one particular disability, therapists have developed a mathematical function which describes the cost C of a therapy program as a function of the percentage of functionality recovered, x. The function is a rational function having the form

$$C = f(x)$$

or

$$C = \frac{5x}{120 - x} \qquad 0 \leq x \leq 100$$

where C is measured in thousands of dollars. For example, the therapy cost to gain a 10 percent recovery is estimated to equal

$$f(10) = \frac{5(10)}{120 - 10}$$

$$= \frac{50}{110} = 0.454 \text{ (thousand dollars)}$$

The cost to gain a 60 percent recovery is estimated to equal

$$f(60) = \frac{5(60)}{120 - 60}$$

$$= \frac{300}{60} = 5.0 \text{ (thousand dollars)}$$

A sketch of this cost function appears in Fig. 10.18.

Section 10.4 Follow-up Exercises

In Exercises 1 to 8, (a) determine the degree of the function and (b) determine the ultimate direction for the function.

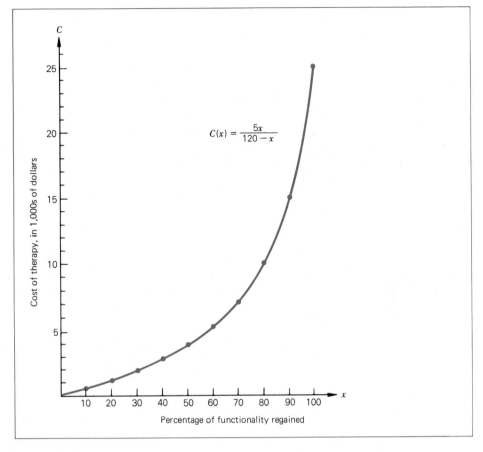

FIGURE 10.18
Cost of
rehabilitation.

1 $f(x) = -x^3$

2 $f(x) = -x^5$

3 $f(x) = x^6$

4 $f(x) = -x^4$

5 $f(x) = x^5 - 4x^4 + 3x^2$

6 $f(x) = x^7 - 2x^5 + x^3 - 10x$

7 $f(x) = x^4 - x^3 + x^2$

8 $f(x) = x^{10} - 5x^4 - 100$

9 Sketch the function $f(x) = -x^3$.

10 Sketch the function $f(x) = -x^5$.

11 Sketch the function $f(x) = x^6$.

12 Sketch the function $f(x) = -x^4$.

*13 Sketch the rational function $f(x) = 3x/(100 - x)$.

*14 Sketch the rational function $f(x) = 1/(x - 1)$.

KEY TERMS AND CONCEPTS

IMPORTANT FORMULAS

$y = f(x) = ax^2 + bx + c, \ a \neq 0$ **Quadratic function**   (10.5)

$\left(\dfrac{-b}{2a}, \ \dfrac{4ac - b^2}{4a}\right)$ **Vertex of parabola**

$x = \dfrac{-b \pm \sqrt{b^2 - 4ac}}{2a}$ **Quadratic formula**

$f(x) = a_n x^n + a_{n-1} x^{n-1} + \cdots + a_1 x + a_0$ **Polynomial function**   (10.13)

$f(x) = \dfrac{g(x)}{h(x)} = \dfrac{a_n x^n + a_{n-1} x^{n-1} + \cdots + a_1 x + a_0}{b_m x^m + b_{m-1} x^{m-1} + \cdots + b_1 x + b_0}$ **Rational function**

ADDITIONAL EXERCISES

Exercises 1 to 7 are related to Sec. 10.2.

In Exercises 1 to 4, determine the concavity of the corresponding parabola, its y intercept, its x intercepts if any exist, and the coordinates of the vertex.

1 $f(x) = 2x^2 - x - 10$ 2 $f(x) = -5 - 10x^2$

3 $f(x) = ex^2 + fx + g,$ $e, f, g > 0$ 4 $f(x) = -x^2/d$, where $d > 0$

5 Determine the equation of the quadratic function which passes through the points $(0, -20)$, $(5, -120)$, and $(-3, -56)$.

*6 Verify that the coordinates of the vertex of a parabola are $\left(\dfrac{-b}{2a}, \ \dfrac{4ac - b^2}{4a}\right)$ where $f(x) = ax^2 + bx + c$.

*7 Given the quadratic equation $ax^2 + bx + c = 0$, show (prove) that the roots (if any exist) can be determined using the quadratic formula

$$x = \dfrac{-b \pm \sqrt{b^2 - 4ac}}{2a}$$

Exercises 8 to 16 are related to Sec. 10.3.

8 A ball is thrown straight up into the air. The height of the ball can be described as a function of time according to the function $h(t) = -16t^2 + 128t$, where $h(t)$ is height measured in feet and t is time measured in seconds. (a) What is the height 3 seconds after the ball is thrown? (b) When will the ball attain its greatest height? (c) When will the ball hit the ground $(h = 0)$?

9 An object is dropped from a bridge which is 400 feet high. The height of the object can be determined as a function of time (since being dropped) according to the function $h(t) = 400 - 16t^2$, where $h(t)$ is height measured in feet and t is time measured in seconds. (a) What is the height of the ball after 3 seconds? (b) How long does it take for the ball to hit the water?

10 The demand function for a particular product is

$$q = f(p) = 50{,}000 - 20p$$

where q is stated in units and p is stated in dollars. Determine the quadratic total revenue function $R = g(p)$. What does total revenue equal when $p = \$30$?

11   The demand function for a particular product is

$$q = f(p) = 50,000 - 20p$$

where q is stated in units and p is stated in dollars. Determine the quadratic total revenue function $R = h(q)$ (note that q is the independent variable).

12   The supply function $q_s = f(p)$ for a product is quadratic. Three points which lie on the graph of the supply function are (20, 150), (30, 400), and (40, 750). Determine the equation of the supply function.

13   The demand function for a product is

$$q_d = p^2 - 70p + 1,225$$

(a) How many units will be demanded if a price of $20 is charged?
(b) Determine the y intercept and interpret its meaning.
(c) Determine the x intercept(s) and interpret.

14   The supply and demand functions for a product are $q_s = p^2 - 525$ and $q_d = p^2 - 70p + 1,225$. Determine the market equilibrium price and quantity.

*15   A local travel agent is organizing a charter flight to a well-known resort. The agent has quoted a price of $300 per person if 100 or fewer sign up for the flight. For every person over the 100, the price for *all* will decrease by $2.50. For instance, if 101 people sign up, each will pay $297.50. Let x equal the number of persons above 100.
(a) Determine the function which states price per person p as a function of x, or $p = f(x)$.
(b) In part a, is there any restriction on the domain?
(c) Formulate the function $R = h(x)$, which states total ticket revenue R as a function of x.
(d) What value of x results in the maximum value of R?
(e) What is the maximum value of R?
(f) What price per ticket results in maximum R?

*16   **Wage Incentive Plan**   A producer of a perishable product offers a wage incentive to the drivers of its trucks. A standard delivery route takes an average of 20 hours. Drivers are paid at the rate of $10 per hour up to a *maximum* of 20 hours (if the trip requires 30 hours, the drivers receive payment for only 20 hours). There is an incentive for drivers to make the trip in less than 20 hours. For each hour under 20, the hourly wage increases by $1. Assume x equals the number of hours required to complete the trip.
(a) Determine the function $w = f(x)$ where w equals the hourly wage in dollars.
(b) Determine the function which state the driver's salary for the trip as a function of x.
(c What trip time x will maximize the driver's salary for the trip?
(d) What hourly wage is associated with this trip time?
(e) What is the maximum salary?

Exercises 17 to 26 are related to Sec. 10.4.
In Exercises 17 to 22, (a) determine the degree of the function and (b) determine the ultimate direction of the function.

17   $f(x) = 3x^6 - 4x^3$ 18 $f(x) = -x^3/25$
19   $f(x) = -x^5 + 5x^3 - 2x$ 20 $f(x) = x^9 - 5x^7 + 6x^3 - 50$
21   $f(x) = -x^6 + 40,000x^5$
22   $f(x) = (x^7 - 5x^6 + 3x^5 - 5x^4)/100$

23 Sketch the function $f(x) = x^8$.

24 Sketch the function $f(x) = -x^7$.

*25 Sketch the rational function $f(x) = 5x/(200 - x)$.

*26 Sketch the rational function $f(x) = 3/(x - 3)$.

CHAPTER TEST

1 For the quadratic function

$$f(x) = x^2 + 10x + 25$$

determine (a) the concavity, (b) the y intercept, (c) the x intercept(s), and (d) coordinates of the vertex of the parabola. (e) Sketch the function.

2 The demand function for a product is

$$q = f(p) = 400{,}000 - 30p$$

where q equals the quantity demanded and p equals the selling price in dollars. Determine the quadratic total revenue function $R = g(p)$.

3 Three points (p, q) on a quadratic supply function are $(20, 400)$, $(25, 850)$, and $(30, 1{,}400)$. Set up (only) the system of equations which, when solved, would provide the parameters of the supply function $q_s = ap^2 + bp + c$.

4 Determine (a) the degree and (b) the ultimate direction of the function

$$f(x) = \frac{x^9 - 5x^6 + 7x^4 - 3x}{150}$$

MINICASE

NONLINEAR BREAK-EVEN AND PROFIT ANALYSIS

The I. M. Handy Corporation is a major producer of microcomputers. It is currently planning a new entry to the micro market. I. M. Handy needs some assistance in analyzing this new product. Manufacturing engineers estimate that variable production costs per unit will be $50. Fixed costs for setting up the production line are estimated at $1 million. Market researchers conducted some preliminary studies and have concluded that the demand function for the new product will be approximately linear. That is, the number of units demanded, q, will vary with the price charged, p, in a linear manner. Two data points (p, q) to be used in defining the demand function are (100, 17,500) and (500, 7,500).

I.M. Handy is requesting from you the following:

(a) Formulation of the demand function $q = f(p)$.

(b) Formulation of the quadratic total revenue function $R = g(q)$.

(c) Formulation of the total cost function $C = h(q)$.

(d) Determination of the break-even level(s) of output.

(e) A graphical representation of the revenue and cost functions illustrating the break-even point(s).

(f) Determination of the price(s) which must be charged at the break-even point(s).

(g) Discussion of why there is more than one break-even point (if this is, in fact, true).

(h) Formulation of the quadratic total profit function $p = r(q)$.

(i) Determination of the number of units which should be sold in order to maximize total profit.

(j) Determination of the price which should be charged at the profit-maximizing level of output.

Your results are needed as soon as possible!

11

DIFFERENTIATION

CHAPTER OBJECTIVES

■ Introduce the important concepts of limits and continuity

■ Provide an understanding of average rate of change and the manner in
which it is determined for functions

■ Provide an understanding of the derivative; its meaning, computation, and
interpretation

■ Present selected rules of differentiation and illustrate their use

■ Introduce the nature of higher-order derivatives and their interpretation,
where appropriate

This is the first of seven chapters which examine the *calculus* and its application
to business, economics, and other areas of problem solving. Two major areas of
study within the calculus are *differential calculus* and *integral calculus.* Differential calculus focuses on *rates of change* in analyzing a situation. Graphically, differential calculus solves the following problem: *Given a function whose
graph is a smooth curve and given a point in the domain of the function, what is the
slope of the line tangent to the curve at this point?* You will see later that this
"slope" expresses the instantaneous rate of change of the function.

Integral calculus involves summation of a special type. Graphically, the concepts of *area* in two dimensions or *volume* in three dimensions are important in
integral calculus. In two dimensions, integral calculus solves the following
problem: *Given a function whose graph is a smooth curve and two points in the domain of the function, what is the area of the region bounded by the curve and the x
axis between these two points?*

This chapter and the following four will discuss differential calculus and its
applications. Chapter 16 will introduce integral calculus and Chap. 17 will
discuss applications of integral calculus. The goal in these chapters is to provide

an appreciation for what the calculus is and where it can be applied. Though it would take several semesters of intensive study to understand most of the finer points of the calculus, your coverage will enable you to understand the tools for conducting analyses at elementary levels.

This chapter is concerned with laying foundations for the remaining chapters. First, two concepts which are important in the theory of differential calculus—*limits* and *continuity*—will be presented. This discussion will be followed by an intuitive development of the concept of the *derivative*. The remainder of the chapter will provide the tools for finding derivatives as well as insights into interpreting the meaning of the derivative. Although proofs of the rules of differentiation are not presented in the main part of the chapter, selected proofs are presented in the appendix at the end of the chapter.

11.1 LIMITS AND CONTINUITY

Two concepts which are important in the theory of differential and integral calculus are the *limit of a function* and *continuity*. These concepts are discussed in this section. Since these concepts are frequently misunderstood, take care in reading these discussions.

Limits of Functions

In the calculus there is often a concern about the limiting value of a function as the independent variable approaches some specific value. This limiting value, when it exists, is called a *limit*. The notation

$$\lim_{x \to a} f(x) = L \qquad\qquad (11.1)$$

is used to express the limiting values of a function. Equation (11.1) is read "the limit of $f(x)$, as x approaches the value a, equals L." When investigating a limit, one is actually asking whether $f(x)$ approaches a specific value L as the value of x gets closer and closer to a.

There are different procedures for determining the limit of a function. The temptation is simply to substitute the value $x = a$ into f and determine $f(a)$. This is actually a valid way of determining the limit for many but not all functions.

One approach that can be used is to substitute values of the independent variable into the function while observing the behavior of $f(x)$ as the value of x comes closer and closer to a. An important point in this procedure is that the value of the function is observed as the value of a is approached from both sides of a. The notation $\lim_{x \to a^-} f(x)$ represents the limit of $f(x)$ as x approaches a from the left (*left-hand limit*) or from below. The notation $\lim_{x \to a^+} f(x)$ represents the limit of $f(x)$ as x approaches a from the right (*right-hand limit*) or from above. *If the value of the function approaches the same number L as x approaches a from either direction, then the limit exists.* To state it more precisely,

TEST FOR EXISTENCE OF A LIMIT

If $\lim_{x \to a^-} f(x) = L$ and $\lim_{x \to a^+} f(x) = L$, then

$$\lim_{x \to a} f(x) = L$$

TABLE 11.1   Approaching $x = 2$ from the Left

x	1	1.5	1.9	1.95	1.99	1.995	1.999
$f(x) = x^3$	1	3.375	6.858	7.415	7.881	7.94	7.988

Approaching $x = 2$ from the Right

x	3	2.5	2.1	2.05	2.01	2.005	2.001
$f(x) = x^3$	27	15.625	9.261	8.615	8.121	8.060	8.012

If the limiting values of $f(x)$ are different when x approaches a from each direction, then the function does not approach a limit as x approaches a. The following examples are illustrative.

EXAMPLE 1 ▬▬▬▬▬▬▬▬▬▬▬▬▬▬▬▬▬▬▬▬▬▬▬▬▬▬

In order to determine $\lim\limits_{x \to 2} x^3$ (if it exists), let's construct a table of assumed values for x and corresponding values for $f(x)$. Table 11.1 indicates these values. Note that the value of $x = 2$ has been approached from both the left and the right. And, from either direction, $f(x)$ is approaching the same value of 8. Since

$$\lim_{x \to 2^-} x^3 = 8 \text{ and } \lim_{x \to 2^+} x^3 = 8$$

then
$$\lim_{x \to 2} x^3 = 8$$

Note that this limit could have been determined by simply substituting $x = 2$ into f.

Figure 11.1 confirms our result. The closer we get to a value of $x = 2$, the closer the value of $f(x)$ comes to 8.

EXAMPLE 2 ▬▬▬▬▬▬▬▬▬▬▬▬▬▬▬▬▬▬▬▬▬▬▬▬▬▬

Given the function

$$f(x) = \begin{cases} 2x & \text{when } x \leq 4 \\ 2x + 3 & \text{when } x > 4 \end{cases}$$

Let's determine if $\lim\limits_{x \to 4} f(x)$ exists. A table is constructed with values for $f(x)$ determined as x approaches a value of 4 from both the left and right (Table 11.2). As x approaches a value of 4 from the left, $f(x)$ approaches a value of 8, or

$$\lim_{x \to 4^-} f(x) = 8$$

As x approaches 4 from the right, $f(x)$ approaches a value of 11, or

TABLE 11.2   Approaching $x = 4$ from the Left

x	3	3.5	3.8	3.9	3.95	3.99
$f(x) = 2x$	6.0	7.0	7.6	7.8	7.9	7.98

Approaching $x = 4$ from the Right

x	5	4.5	4.3	4.1	4.05	4.01
$f(x) = 2x + 3$	13.0	12.0	11.6	11.2	11.1	11.02

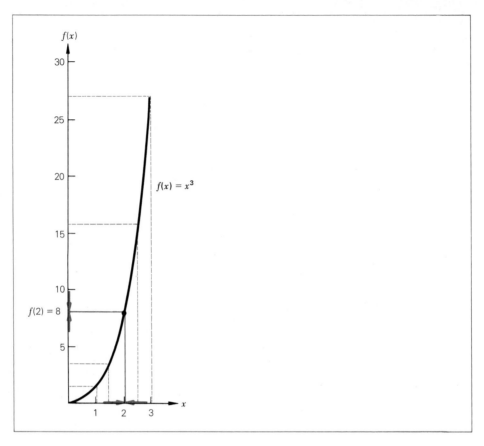

FIGURE 11.1
$\lim_{x \to 2^-} x^3 =$
$\lim_{x \to 2^+} x^3 = 8.$

$$\lim_{x \to 4^+} f(x) = 11$$

Since

$$\lim_{x \to 4^-} f(x) \neq \lim_{x \to 4^+} f(x)$$

the function does not approach a limiting value as $x \to 4$, and $\lim_{x \to 4} f(x)$ does not exist. Figure 11.2 shows the graph of this function. Recall from Chap. 2 that the solid circle (●) indicates that $x = 4$ is included in the domain for the lower line segment, and the open circle (○) indicates that $x = 4$ is not included in the domain for the upper line segment. The break in the function at $x = 4$ is the reason that the limit does not exist. An important point, regarding this function, is that $f(x)$ does approach a limit for values other than $x = 4$.

EXAMPLE 3

Let's determine if $\lim_{x \to 3} f(x)$ exists if

$$f(x) = \frac{x^2 - 9}{x - 9}$$

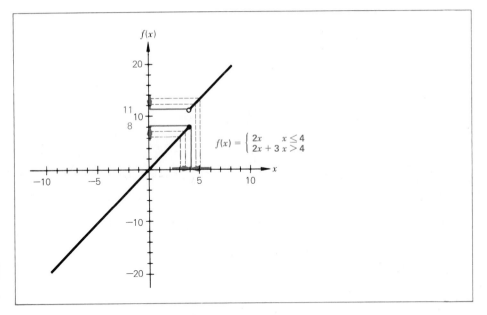

$$f(x) = \begin{cases} 2x & x \le 4 \\ 2x + 3 & x > 4 \end{cases}$$

FIGURE 11.2
$\lim_{x \to 4^-} f(x) \ne$
$\lim_{x \to 4^+} f(x).$

Since the denominator equals 0 when $x = 3$, we can conclude that the function is undefined at this point. And, it would be tempting to conclude that no limit exists when $x = 3$. However, this function does approach a limit as x approaches (gets closer to) 3, even though the function is not defined at $x = 3$.

Table 11.3 contains values of $f(x)$ as x approaches 3 from both the left and the right. Since

$$\lim_{x \to 3^-} f(x) = 6 \qquad \text{and} \qquad \lim_{x \to 3^+} f(x) = 6$$

then

$$\lim_{x \to 3} \frac{x^2 - 9}{x - 3} = 6$$

Even though the function is undefined when $x = 3$, the function approaches a value of 6 as the value of x comes closer to 3. Figure 11.3 presents the graph of the function.

One special case is that of limits at an endpoint on the domain of a function. Consider the function $f(x) = \sqrt{x}$. The domain for this function is $x \ge 0$. If we are interested in $\lim_{x \to 0} \sqrt{x}$, we cannot determine both the left-hand and the right-

TABLE 11.3

Approaching $x = 3$ from the Left

x	2	2.5	2.9	2.95	2.99
$f(x) = \dfrac{x^2 - 9}{x - 3}$	5.0	5.5	5.9	5.95	5.99

Approaching $x = 3$ from the Right

x	4	3.5	3.1	3.05	3.01
$f(x) = \dfrac{x^2 - 9}{x - 3}$	7.0	6.5	6.1	6.05	6.01

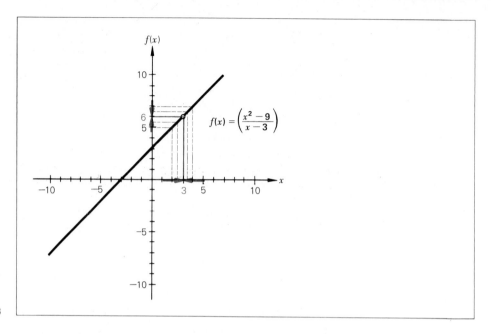

FIGURE 11.3

hand limits. We can determine $\lim_{x \to 0^+} \sqrt{x}$, but not $\lim_{x \to 0^-} \sqrt{x}$. *Our concern always will be in determining limits from within the domain of a function. In this instance, the limit must be determined based on the right-hand limit only. Since* $\lim_{x \to 0^+} \sqrt{x} = 0$, then $\lim_{x \to 0} \sqrt{x} = 0.$

A key point with the limit concept is that we are not interested in the value of $f(x)$ when $x = a$. We are interested in the behavior of the values of $f(x)$ as x comes closer and closer to a value of a. And, the notation

$$\lim_{x \to a} f(x) = L$$

means that as x gets close to a, for $x \neq a$, $f(x)$ gets close to L.

Section 11.1 Follow-up Exercises

For the following exercises, determine the limit (if it exists) by constructing a table of values for $f(x)$ and examining left and right-hand limits (where appropriate).

1   $\lim_{x \to 2} 3x^2$

2   $\lim_{x \to -1} (5x + 5)$

3   $\lim_{x \to 5} f(x)$ where $f(x) = \begin{cases} 2x & \text{for } x < 5 \\ 20 - 2x & \text{for } x \geq 5 \end{cases}$

4   $\lim_{x \to 3} f(x)$ where $f(x) = \begin{cases} 2x^2 & \text{for } x < 3 \\ 2 - x & \text{for } x \geq 3 \end{cases}$

5   $\lim_{x \to 2} g(x)$ where $g(x) = \begin{cases} 5 - 2x & \text{for } x < 2 \\ 2x & \text{for } x \geq 2 \end{cases}$

6   $\lim_{x \to 3} h(x)$ where $h(x) = \begin{cases} x^2 & \text{for } x < 3 \\ 0.5x^2 & \text{for } x \geq 3 \end{cases}$

7    $\lim\limits_{x\to 8} \dfrac{x^2 - 64}{x - 8}$

8    $\lim\limits_{x\to -3} \dfrac{x^2 - 9}{x + 3}$

9    $\lim\limits_{x\to -1} \dfrac{3x^2 - 9x - 12}{3x + 3}$

10    $\lim\limits_{x\to 1/2} \dfrac{2x^2 + x - 1}{2x - 1}$

11    $\lim\limits_{x\to 0} \dfrac{2}{x}$

12    $\lim\limits_{x\to -4} \dfrac{1}{x + 4}$

Some Properties of Limits

This section discusses some properties of limits which are useful in determining the limiting value of a function. We will soon see that the process of determining limits need not always involve evaluation of $f(x)$ at a series of points on either side of $x = a$.

1   If $f(x) = c$, where c is real,

$$\lim_{x\to a} (c) = c$$

Example:

$$\lim_{x\to 3} 100 = 100$$

2   If $f(x) = x^n$, where n is a positive integer, then

$$\lim_{x\to a} x^n = a^n$$

Example:

$$\lim_{x\to -2} x^3 = (-2)^3 = -8$$

3   If $f(x)$ has a limit as $x \to a$ and c is real, then

$$\lim_{x\to a} c \cdot f(x) = c \cdot \lim_{x\to a} f(x)$$

Example:

$$\lim_{x\to 10} 5x^2 = 5 \lim_{x\to 10} x^2$$
$$= 5(10)^2 = 500$$

4   If $\lim\limits_{x\to a} f(x)$ and $\lim\limits_{x\to a} g(x)$ exist, then

$$\lim_{x\to a} [f(x) \pm g(x)] = \lim_{x\to a} f(x) \pm \lim_{x\to a} g(x)$$

Example:

$$\lim_{x\to -1} (x^5 - 10) = \lim_{x\to -1} x^5 - \lim_{x\to -1} 10$$
$$= (-1)^5 - 10 = -1 - 10 = -11$$

5   If $\lim\limits_{x\to a} f(x)$ and $\lim\limits_{x\to a} g(x)$ exist, then

$$\lim_{x\to a} [f(x) \cdot g(x)] = \lim_{x\to a} f(x) \cdot \lim_{x\to a} g(x)$$

Example:

$$\lim_{x\to 4} [(x^2 - 5)(x + 1)] = \lim_{x\to 4} (x^2 - 5) \cdot \lim_{x\to 4} (x + 1)$$
$$= [(4)^2 - 5][4 + 1]$$
$$= 11(5) = 55$$

6 If $\lim\limits_{x \to a} f(x)$ and $\lim\limits_{x \to a} g(x)$ exist, then

$$\lim_{x \to a} \frac{f(x)}{g(x)} = \frac{\lim\limits_{x \to a} f(x)}{\lim\limits_{x \to a} g(x)} \qquad \text{provided } \lim_{x \to a} g(x) \neq 0$$

Example:

$$\lim_{x \to -5} \frac{x}{x^2 + 10} = \frac{\lim\limits_{x \to -5} x}{\lim\limits_{x \to -5} (x^2 + 10)}$$

$$= \frac{-5}{(-5)^2 + 10} = \frac{-5}{35} = \frac{-1}{7}$$

As you will see in the following examples, evaluating a limit frequently requires the use of more than one of these properties.

EXAMPLE 4

$$\lim_{x \to -1} x^4 = (-1)^4 = 1 \qquad \textbf{(Property 2)}$$

EXAMPLE 5

$$\lim_{x \to 5} (x^2 - x + 10) = \lim_{x \to 5} x^2 - \lim_{x \to 5} x + \lim_{x \to 5} 10 \qquad \textbf{Property 4)}$$
$$= 5^2 - 5 + 10 \qquad \textbf{(Properties 1 and 2)}$$
$$= 30$$

EXAMPLE 6

$$\lim_{x \to -2} 5x^3 = 5 \cdot \lim_{x \to -2} x^3 \qquad \textbf{(Property 3)}$$
$$= (5)(-2)^3 \qquad \textbf{(Property 2)}$$
$$= (5)(-8) = -40$$

EXAMPLE 7

$$\lim_{x \to 0} [(x^5 - 1)(x^3 + 4)] = \lim_{x \to 0} (x^5 - 1) \cdot \lim_{x \to 0} (x^3 + 4) \qquad \textbf{(Property 5)}$$
$$= (\lim_{x \to 0} x^5 - \lim_{x \to 0} 1)(\lim_{x \to 0} x^3 + \lim_{x \to 0} 4) \qquad \textbf{(Property 4)}$$
$$= (0 - 1)(0 + 4) \qquad \textbf{(Properties 1 and 2)}$$
$$= (-1)(4) = -4$$

EXAMPLE 8

$$\lim_{x \to 2} \frac{x^3 - 1}{x^2} = \frac{\lim\limits_{x \to 2} (x^3 - 1)}{\lim\limits_{x \to 2} x^2} \qquad \textbf{(Property 6)}$$

$$= \frac{\lim\limits_{x \to 2} x^3 - \lim\limits_{x \to 2} 1}{\lim\limits_{x \to 2} x^2} \qquad \textbf{(Property 4)}$$

$$= \frac{2^3 - 1}{2^2} = \frac{8 - 1}{4} = \frac{7}{4} \qquad \textbf{(Properties 1 and 2)}$$

The properties make the process of evaluating limits considerably easier for certain classes of functions. Limits of these types of functions may be evaluated by **substitution** to determine $f(a)$. For these classes of functions

$$\lim_{x \to a} f(x) = f(a) \qquad (11.2)$$

Polynomial functions are a commonly used class of functions for which Eq. (11.2) is valid. This follows from Properties 1 through 4.

EXAMPLE 9

$$\lim_{x \to -2} (3x^2 - 4x + 10) = f(-2)$$

$$= 3(-2)^2 - 4(-2) + 10 = 12 + 8 + 10 = 30$$

In Example 3 we determined the

$$\lim_{x \to 3} \frac{x^2 - 9}{x - 3} = 6$$

Even though the function is not defined at $x = 3$, the value of the function approaches 6 as x approaches 3. This function is an example of a family of "quotient" functions which can be simplified by factoring.

$$f(x) = \frac{x^2 - 9}{x - 3}$$

$$= \frac{(x + 3)(x - 3)}{x - 3}$$

$$= x + 3 \qquad \text{for all } x \neq 3$$

Even though $f(x) = [(x + 3)(x - 3)]/(x - 3)$ and $g(x) = x + 3$ are *not* the same function, *they are the same everywhere $f(x)$ is defined.* As illustrated in Fig. 11.4, g graphs as a line, and f graphs as a line with a "hole" at $x = 3$. However, since we do not care what happens at $x = 3$, we can determine the behavior of $f(x)$ by studying the behavior of $g(x)$.

This simplification has reduced the function to a form for which the substitution approach is valid. That is,

$$\lim_{x \to 3} \frac{x^2 - 9}{x - 3} = \lim_{x \to 3} (x + 3)$$

$$= 3 + 3 = 6$$

EXAMPLE 10

$$\lim_{x \to -1} \frac{4x^2 + x - 3}{x + 1} = \lim_{x \to -1} \frac{(4x - 3)(x + 1)}{x + 1}$$

$$= \lim_{x \to -1} (4x - 3)$$

$$= 4(-1) - 3 = -7$$

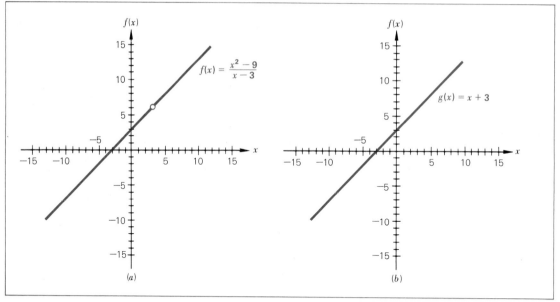

FIGURE 11.4

Limits and Infinity

Frequently there is an interest in the behavior of a function as the independent variable becomes large without limit (positively or negatively). We say that the independent variable "approaches infinity." Examine the two functions sketched in Fig. 11.5. In Fig. 11.5*a*, as *x* approaches negative infinity, *f*(*x*) approaches but never quite reaches a value of 4. Using limit notation, we state

$$\lim_{x \to -\infty} f(x) = 4$$

We can also state that *f*(*x*) has a *horizontal asymptote* of *y* = 4 as *x* approaches −∞. Again, this suggests that *f*(*x*) approaches but never quite reaches a value of 4 as *x* approaches −∞.

Similarly, in Fig. 11.5*b*, *g* approaches but never quite reaches the *x* axis as *x* approaches ∞. We can state this behavior by the notation

$$\lim_{x \to \infty} g(x) = 0$$

As with *f*, *g* has a horizontal asymptote of *y* = 0 as *x* approaches ∞.
A more formal definition for a horizontal asymptote follows:

DEFINITION: HORIZONTAL ASYMPTOTE

The line *y* = *a* is a ***horizontal asymptote*** of the graph of *f* if and only if

$$\lim_{x \to \infty} f(x) = a$$

or

$$\lim_{x \to -\infty} f(x) = a$$

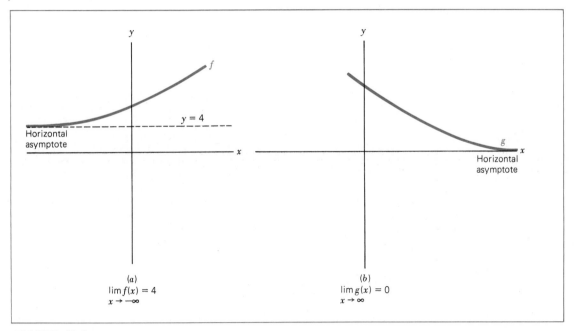

FIGURE 11.5
Limits at infinity.

EXAMPLE 11

To evaluate $\lim\limits_{x \to \infty} (1/x^2)$, consider what happens to the denominator. As x approaches ∞, the denominator increases without bound and the quotient $1/x^2$ approaches a value of 0. Therefore

$$\lim_{x \to \infty} \frac{1}{x^2} = 0$$

EXAMPLE 12

To evaluate $\lim\limits_{x \to -\infty} [(1 - 3x)/(1 + x)]$, let's first rewrite the numerator and denominator by dividing each by x.

$$\lim_{x \to -\infty} \frac{1 - 3x}{1 + x} = \lim_{x \to -\infty} \frac{1/x - 3x/x}{1/x + x/x}$$

$$= \lim_{x \to -\infty} \frac{1/x - 3}{1/x + 1}$$

As x approaches $-\infty$, the terms $1/x$ both approach 0 with the following result:

$$\lim_{x \to -\infty} \frac{1 - 3x}{1 + x} = \frac{0 - 3}{0 + 1}$$

$$= -3$$

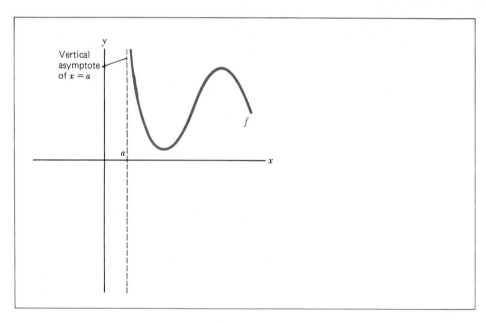

FIGURE 11.6
Vertical
asymptote.

Another limit possibility is illustrated in Fig. 11.6. In this figure $f(x)$ becomes arbitrarily large as x approaches a value of a. For this situation we state that $f(x)$ has a *vertical asymptote* of $x = a$ because as x approaches the value a, $f(x)$ gets large without limit. Visually, the ordinate of the curve representing f becomes large without limit as it gets closer to a line at $x = a$, never quite touching it. A more formal definition of this phenomenon is:

DEFINITION: VERTICAL ASYMPTOTE

The line $x = a$ is a **vertical asymptote** of the graph of f if and only if

$$\lim_{x \to a^-} f(x) = \infty \qquad (\text{or} -\infty)$$

or
$$\lim_{x \to a^+} f(x) = \infty \qquad (\text{or} -\infty)$$

EXAMPLE 13

To evaluate $\lim_{x \to 0} (1/x^2)$, we must take left- and right-hand limits as x approaches 0. Table 11.4 presents selected values. We should conclude that $\lim_{x \to 0} (1/x^2) = \infty$. Graphically, f appears as in Fig. 11.7. Note that $f(x) = 1/x^2$ has a vertical asymptote of $x = 0$ and horizontal asymptotes of $y = 0$.

Continuity

In an informal sense, a function is described as *continuous* if it can be sketched without lifting your pen or pencil from the paper. Most of the functions that we

TABLE 11.4

Approaching $x = 0$ from the Left					
x	-1	-0.5	-0.1	-0.01	-0.001
$f(x) = \dfrac{1}{x^2}$	1	4	100	10,000	1,000,000

Approaching $x = 0$ from the Right					
x	1	0.5	0.1	0.01	0.001
$f(x) = \dfrac{1}{x^2}$	1	4	100	10,000	1,000,000

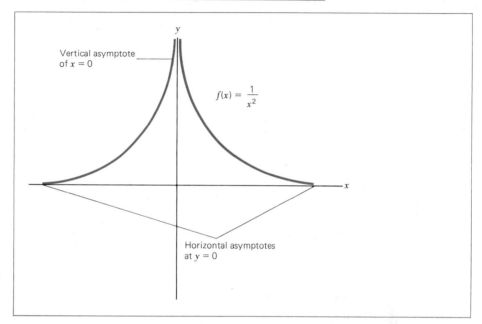

FIGURE 11.7
Horizontal
asymptote at
$y = 0$.

will examine in the calculus will be continuous functions. Figure 11.8 indicates the sketches of four different functions. Those depicted in Fig. 11.8*a* and 11.8*b* are continuous since they can be drawn without lifting your pencil. Those in Fig. 11.8*c* and 11.8*d* are not continuous because of the "breaks" in the functions. A function which is not continuous is termed *discontinuous*. A more formal definition of the property of continuity follows:

DEFINITION: CONTINUITY AT A POINT

A function f is said to be **continuous** at $x = a$ if (1) the function is defined at $x = a$ and (2)

$$\lim_{x \to a} f(x) = f(a) \qquad (11.3)$$

EXAMPLE 14

In Example 1 we determined that for $f(x) = x^3$

$$\lim_{x \to 2} x^3 = 8$$

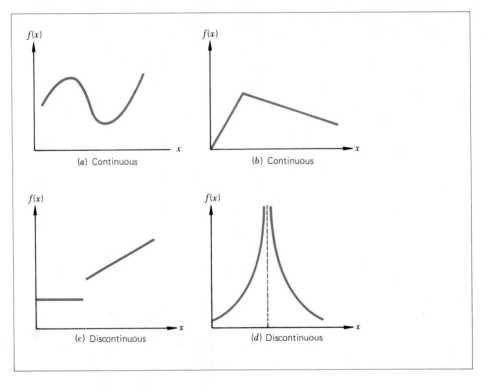

Because $f(x) = x^3$ is defined at $x = 2$ and $\lim\limits_{x \to 2} x^3 = f(2) = 8$, we can state that the function $f(x) = x^3$ is continuous when $x = 2$.

EXAMPLE 15 ▬▬▬▬▬▬▬▬▬▬▬▬▬▬▬▬▬▬▬▬▬▬

In Example 3 we determined that

$$\lim_{x \to 3} \frac{x^2 - 9}{x - 3} = 6$$

Because $x = 3$ is not in the domain of the function, $f(3)$ is not defined and we can state that the function $(x^2 - 9)/(x - 3)$ is *discontinuous* at $y = 3$.

DEFINITION: CONTINUITY OVER AN INTERVAL ▬▬▬▬▬▬▬

A function f is continuous over an interval $[a, b]$ if it is continuous at every point within the interval.

NOTE ▬▬▬▬▬▬▬▬▬▬▬▬▬▬▬▬▬▬▬

If a and b are real and $a < b$, the ***closed interval*** $[a, b]$ is the set $\{x|a \leq x \geq b\}$. The ***open interval*** (a, b) is the set $\{x|a < x < b\}$. Similarly, $(a, b] = \{x|a < x \leq b\}$ and $[a, b) = \{x|a \leq x < b\}$ are termed ***half-open intervals***.

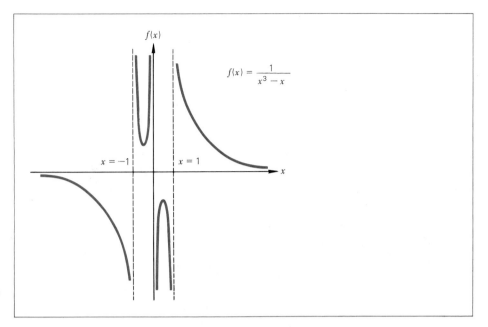

FIGURE 11.9
Discontinuities
at $x = 0, -1, 1$.

EXAMPLE 16

The function $f(x) = x^2 - 2x + 5$ is continuous when x is real-valued because

$$\lim_{x \to a} (x^2 - 2x + 5) = f(a)$$

$$= a^2 - 2a + 5 \qquad \text{for all real } a$$

EXAMPLE 17

The rational function

$$f(x) = \frac{1}{x^3 - x}$$

is not defined when

$$x^3 - x = 0$$

or

$$x(x^2 - 1) = 0$$

or

$$x(x + 1)(x - 1) = 0$$

The product on the left side of the equation equals 0 when $x = 0$, $x = -1$, or $x = +1$. Thus, the function is discontinuous at these three points. Figure 11.9 presents a sketch of the function. Note that this function has vertical asymptotes described by the equations $x = 1$, $x = -1$, and $x = 0$.

Section 11.1 Follow-up Exercises (Continued)

For the following exercises, find the indicated limit.

1   $\lim\limits_{x\to 0} (5x^2 - 2x + 1)$

2   $\lim\limits_{x\to 2} (2x^3 - 5x)$

3   $\lim\limits_{x\to 1} \left(\dfrac{x^3}{3} - 2x^2 + \dfrac{2}{3}\right)$

4   $\lim\limits_{x\to 3} \dfrac{x - 5}{x - 4}$

5   $\lim\limits_{x\to 0} \dfrac{x^2 - 4}{x^3 - 4x - 2}$

6   $\lim\limits_{x\to -2} 25$

7   $\lim\limits_{x\to 0} 125$

8   $\lim\limits_{x\to -5} \dfrac{x^2 - 25}{x}$

9   $\lim\limits_{x\to -3} (6x^3 - 2x)(5x - 10)$

10   $\lim\limits_{x\to 4} \left[\left(\dfrac{x + 1}{x + 6}\right)(x^2 - 12)\right]$

11   $\lim\limits_{x\to -7} \dfrac{x^2 + 5x - 14}{x + 7}$

12   $\lim\limits_{x\to 3} \dfrac{x^2 + 5x - 24}{x - 3}$

13   $\lim\limits_{x\to -4} \dfrac{x^2 - 16}{x + 4}$

14   $\lim\limits_{x\to -9} \dfrac{81 - x^2}{9 + x}$

15   $\lim\limits_{x\to c} (4x^3 - 3x^2 + 10)$

16   $\lim\limits_{x\to -d} (x^2 - 2x + 1)$

For the following exercises, find the indicated limit and comment on the existence of any asymptotes.

17   $\lim\limits_{x\to \infty} \dfrac{1}{x^3}$

18   $\lim\limits_{x\to -\infty} \dfrac{2x - 3}{x + 10}$

19   $\lim\limits_{x\to \infty} \dfrac{x}{4x + 100}$

20   $\lim\limits_{x\to -\infty} \dfrac{2x + 8}{-4x}$

21   $\lim\limits_{x\to -\infty} 5x$

22   $\lim\limits_{x\to \infty} \dfrac{x^2}{x - 1}$

In the following exercises, determine whether there are any discontinuities and, if so, where they occur.

23   $f(x) = 5x^2 - x + 10$

24   $f(x) = \dfrac{1}{x}$

25   $f(x) = x^5$

26   $f(x) = \dfrac{x}{x - 5}$

27   $f(x) = \dfrac{10}{6 + x}$

28   $f(x) = |x|$

29   $f(x) = \dfrac{x}{x^2 - 4x - 21}$

30   $f(x) = \dfrac{6x - 2}{x^2 - 5x}$

31   $f(x) = \dfrac{4}{x^3 + x^2 - 6x}$

32   $f(x) = \dfrac{5/x}{2x^2 - 7x - 15}$

11.2   AVERAGE RATE OF CHANGE

Average Rate of Change and Slope

As discussed in Chap. 3, the slope of a straight line can be determined by applying the two-point formula:

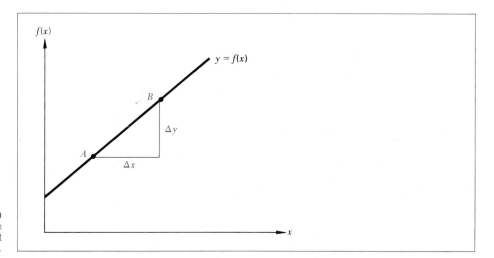

FIGURE 11.10
Linear function
with constant
slope.

TWO-POINT FORMULA

$$m = \frac{\Delta y}{\Delta x} = \frac{y_2 - y_1}{x_2 - x_1} \qquad (11.4)$$

Figure 11.10 illustrates the graph of a linear function. With linear functions the slope is constant over the domain of the function. The slope provides an *exact measure* of the rate of change in the value of y with respect to a change in the value of x. If the function in Fig. 11.10 represents a linear cost function and x equals the number of units produced, the slope indicates the rate at which total cost increases with respect to changes in the level of output.

With nonlinear functions the rate of change in the value of y with respect to a change in x is not constant. However, one way of partially describing nonlinear functions is by the *average rate of change* over some interval.

EXAMPLE 18

Assume that a person takes a leisurely automobile trip and that the distance traveled d can be described as a function of time t by the nonlinear function

$$d = f(t) = 8t^2 + 8t$$

where d is measured in miles, t is measured in hours, and $0 \le t \le 5$. During this 5-hour journey the speed of the car may change continuously (e.g., because of traffic lights, rest stops, etc.).

After 1 hour, the total distance traveled is

$$f(1) = 8(1)^2 + 8(1)$$
$$= 16 \text{ miles}$$

The average rate of change in the distance traveled with respect to a change in time during a time interval (better known as *average velocity*) is computed as

$$\frac{\text{Distance traveled}}{\text{Time traveled}}$$

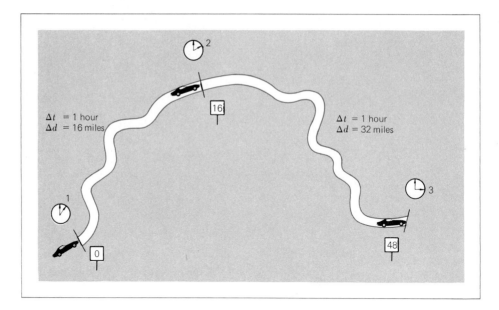

For the first hour of this trip, the average velocity equals

$$\frac{\Delta d}{\Delta t} = \frac{f(1) - f(0)}{1 - 0} = \frac{16 - 0}{1} = 16 \text{ mph}$$

The distance traveled at the end of 2 hours is

$$f(2) = 8(2)^2 + 8(2)$$
$$= 32 + 16 = 48 \text{ miles}$$

The distance traveled *during* the second hour is

$$\Delta d = f(2) - f(1)$$
$$= 48 - 16 = 32 \text{ miles}$$

The average velocity *for the second hour* equals

$$\frac{\Delta d}{\Delta t} = \frac{32}{1} = 32 \text{ mph}$$

And, the average velocity is different compared with that for the first hour.

The average velocity *during the first 2 hours* is the total distance traveled during that period divided by the time traveled, or

$$\frac{\Delta d}{\Delta t} = \frac{f(2) - f(0)}{2 - 0} = \frac{48 - 0}{2} = 24 \text{ mph}$$

EXERCISE

What is the average velocity for the entire 5-hour trip?*

* Answer: 48 mph.

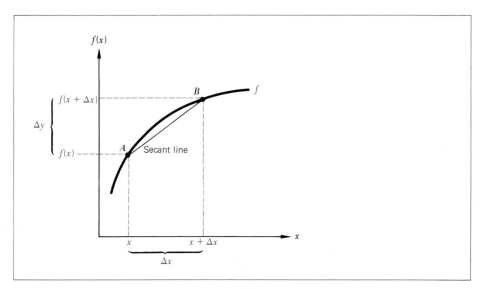

FIGURE 11.11
Secant line
AB.

POINT FOR THOUGHT AND DISCUSSION

Consider the function

$$d = f(t) = 55t$$

which expresses the distance traveled d (in miles) as a function of time t (in hours). Compare this function with the function in Example 18. What is the difference with regard to average velocity for the 5-hour trip?

Consider two points A and B in Fig. 11.11. The straight line connecting these two points on f is referred to as a *secant line.* At point A the independent variable has a value of x, and the corresponding value of the dependent variable can be determined by evaluating $f(x)$. At point B the independent variable has changed in value to $x + \Delta x$, and the corresponding value of the dependent variable can be determined by evaluating $f(x + \Delta x)$. In moving from point A to point B, the change in the value of x is $(x + \Delta x) - x$, or Δx. The associated change in the value of y is $\Delta y = f(x + \Delta x) - f(x)$. The ratio of these changes is

$$\boxed{\frac{\Delta y}{\Delta x} = \frac{f(x + \Delta x) - f(x)}{\Delta x}}$$

11.5

Equation (11.5) is sometimes referred to as the *difference quotient.*

THE DIFFERENCE QUOTIENT

Given any two points on a function f having coordinates $[x, f(x)]$ and $[(x + \Delta x), f(x + \Delta x)]$, the difference quotient provides a general expression which

I Represents the *average rate of change* in the value of y with respect to the change in x while moving from $[x, f(x)]$ to $[(x + \Delta x), f(x + \Delta x)]$.

II Computes the slope of the secant line connecting the two points.

EXAMPLE 19

(a) Find the general expression for the difference quotient of the function $y = f(x) = x^2$.

(b) Find the slope of the line connecting $(-2, 4)$ and $(3, 9)$ using the two-point formula.

(c) Find the slope in part b using the expression for the difference quotient found in part a.

SOLUTION

(a) Given two points on the function $f(x) = x^2$ which have coordinates $(x, f(x))$ and $(x + \Delta x, f(x + \Delta x))$, we have

$$\frac{\Delta y}{\Delta x} = \frac{f(x + \Delta x) - f(x)}{\Delta x} = \frac{(x + \Delta x)^2 - x^2}{\Delta x}$$

$$= \frac{[x^2 + x(\Delta x) + x(\Delta x) + (\Delta x)^2] - x^2}{\Delta x}$$

$$= \frac{[x^2 + 2x(\Delta x) + (\Delta x)^2] - x^2}{\Delta x}$$

$$= \frac{2x(\Delta x) + (\Delta x)^2}{\Delta x}$$

Factoring Δx from each term in the numerator and canceling with Δx in the denominator, we get

$$\frac{\Delta y}{\Delta x} = \frac{f(x + \Delta x) - f(x)}{\Delta x} = \frac{\cancel{\Delta x}(2x + \Delta x)}{\cancel{\Delta x}}$$

$$= 2x + \Delta x \qquad \qquad \textbf{(11.6)}$$

NOTE

When finding the difference quotient, the evaluation of $f(x + \Delta x)$ and $f(x)$ for a specific function causes the greatest difficulty for students. If, for this function, you were asked to find $f(3)$, you would substitute the value of 3 into the function wherever the independent variable appears, or $f(3) = 3^2 = 9$. When asked to find $f(x + \Delta x)$ in this example, we substituted $x + \Delta x$ into the function where the independent variable appeared and evaluated $(x + \Delta x)^2$. Similarly, when finding $f(x)$, we substituted the value x where the independent variable appeared and evaluated x^2. *Whenever you are asked to determine the difference quotient, $f(x)$ will always be the specific function with which you are working.*

(b) Using the two-point slope formula, we get

$$\frac{\Delta y}{\Delta x} = \frac{f(3) - f(-2)}{3 - (-2)}$$

$$= \frac{9 - 4}{3 - (-2)} = \frac{5}{5} = 1$$

The slope of the secant line connecting $(-2, 4)$ and $(3, 9)$ on f equals 1.

(c) Let $(x, f(x))$ and $(x + \Delta x, f(x + \Delta x))$ correspond to the points $(-2, 4)$ and $(3, 9)$ on the function. Assume that x corresponds to the coordinate -2 and $x + \Delta x$ corresponds to the coordinate of 3. Thus,

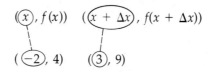

So $\qquad\qquad x = -2$

and $\qquad\qquad x + \Delta x = 3$

Therefore $\qquad (-2) + \Delta x = 3$

or $\qquad\qquad \Delta x = 5$

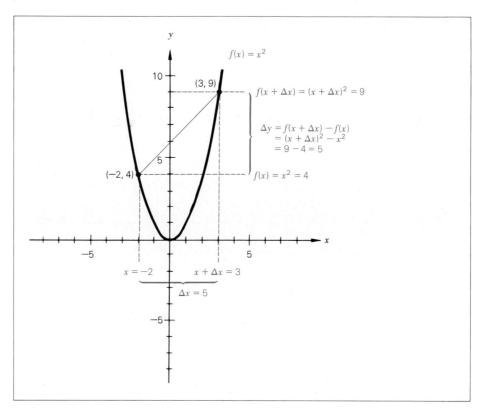

FIGURE 11.12

This value for Δx simply means that the distance separating these two points along the x axis is 5 units.

If we substitute the values of $x = -2$ and $\Delta x = 5$ into Eq. (11.6), the difference quotient for these two points equals $2(-2) + 5 = 1$. This is exactly the same result as we got in part b.

EXERCISE

In the last example, let $x = 3$ and $(x + \Delta x) = -2$. Evaluate the difference quotient and see if you arrive at the same result as in the example. Conclusions?

Section 11.2 Follow-up Exercises

For each of the following functions, determine the average rate of change in the value of y in moving from $x = -1$ to $x = 3$.

1. $y = f(x) = 5x^2$
2. $y = f(x) = 2x^3$
3. $y = f(x) = x^2 - 2x + 1$
4. $y = f(x) = x^3 - 2x^2 + x - 5$
5. $y = f(x) = x^2/(x + 4)$
6. $y = f(x) = x^5/10$

7. A ball is thrown straight up into the air. The height of the ball can be described as a function of time according to the function

$$h(t) = -16t^2 + 128t$$

where $h(t)$ is height measured in feet and t is time measured in seconds.
(a) Determine the average rate of change in height between $t = 0$ and $t = 2$. Between $t = 0$ and $t = 4$. Between $t = 0$ and $t = 8$.
(b) How long does it take for the ball to hit the ground ($h = 0$)?

8. An object is dropped from a bridge which is 400 feet high. The height of the object can be determined as a function of time (since being dropped) according to the func-

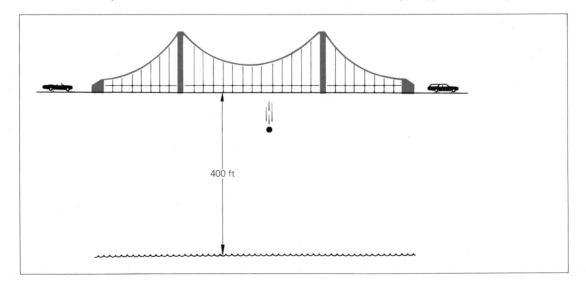

400 ft

tion

$$h(t) = 400 - 16t^2$$

where $h(t)$ is height measured in feet and t is time measured in seconds.

(a) Determine the average rate of change in height between $t = 0$ and $t = 1$. Between $t = 0$ and $t = 2$. Between $t = 0$ and $t = 4$.

(b) How long does it take for the ball to hit the water ($h = 0$)?

9   The following table indicates annual sales (in dollars) for a company during a selected period. At what average rate did annual sales increase between 1979 and 1981? Between 1979 and 1980? Between 1980 and 1981? Between 1980 and 1982?

Year	1979	1980	1981	1982
Annual Sales (millions)	$40.0	$46.0	$51.5	$56.0

10   Annual attendance at professional baseball games has been increasing in recent years (up until the players strike of 1981). Figures for the years 1977 to 1981 are shown in the table. Determine the average rate of change in annual attendance between 1977 and 1981, 1977 and 1980, and 1979 and 1981.

Year	1977	1978	1979	1980	1981
Annual Attendance (millions)	53.1	54.8	56.0	57.8	53.0

11   Figure 11.13 indicates data points which have been gathered regarding the annual demand for timber from commercial forest land. Demand is measured in billions of cubic feet. Demand is increasing but not at a constant rate. Determine the average rate of change in demand between 1970 and 1975, 1970 and 1973, and 1973 and 1975.

12   A person takes an automobile trip. The distance traveled d (in miles) is described as a function of time t (in hours):

$$d = f(t) = 5t^2 + 12t \qquad \text{where } 0 \le t \le 4$$

(a) What is the average speed during the first hour? Fourth hour?

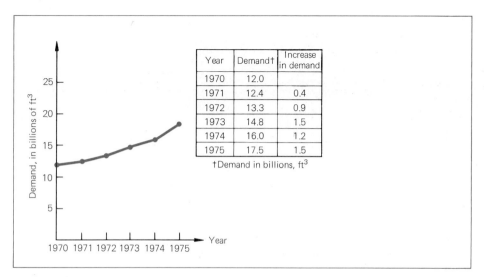

Year	Demand†	Increase in demand
1970	12.0	
1971	12.4	0.4
1972	13.3	0.9
1973	14.8	1.5
1974	16.0	1.2
1975	17.5	1.5

†Demand in billions, ft³

FIGURE 11.13
Annual demand
for commercial
forestland.

(b) What is the average speed for the 4-hour trip?

For Exercises 13 to 20, (a) determine the general expression for the difference quotient, and (b) use the difference quotient to compute the slope of the secant line connecting points at $x = 1$ and $x = 3$.

13 $y = f(x) = 2x^2 + 5$	14 $y = f(x) = 3x^2 + 9x$
15 $y = f(x) = 20x^2 + 6x + 10$	16 $y = f(x) = 50$
*17 $y = f(x) = x^3$	*18 $y = f(x) = -2x^3$
*19 $y = f(x) = 1/x$	*20 $y = f(x) = 5/x$

11.3 THE DERIVATIVE

In this section the concept of the *derivative* will be developed. This concept is fundamental to all that follows, so study this material carefully.

Instantaneous Rate of Change

A distinction needs to be made between the concepts of *average rate of change* and *instantaneous rate of change.* Example 18 discussed a situation in which the distance traveled d was described as a function of time t by the function

$$d = f(t) = 8t^2 + 8t \qquad \text{where } 0 \le t \le 5$$

Suppose that we are interested in determining how fast the car is moving at the *instant* that $t = 1$. We might determine this instantaneous velocity by examining the average velocity during time intervals near $t = 1$.

For instance, the average velocity during the second hour (between $t = 1$ and $t = 2$) can be determined as

$$\frac{\Delta d}{\Delta t} = \frac{f(2) - f(1)}{2 - 1}$$
$$= \frac{[8(2^2) + 8(2)] - [8(1^2) + 8(1)]}{1} = \frac{48 - 16}{1} = 32 \text{ mph}$$

The average velocity between $t = 1$ and $t = 1.5$ can be determined as

$$\frac{\Delta d}{\Delta t} = \frac{f(1.5) - f(1)}{1.5 - 1}$$
$$= \frac{[8(1.5)^2 + 8(1.5)] - [8(1^2) + 8(1)]}{0.5} = \frac{30 - 16}{0.5} = 28 \text{ mph}$$

The average velocity between $t = 1$ and $t = 1.1$ can be determined as

$$\frac{\Delta d}{\Delta t} = \frac{f(1.1) - f(1)}{1.1 - 1}$$
$$= \frac{[8(1.1)^2 + 8(1.1)] - [8(1^2) + 8(1)]}{0.1} = \frac{18.48 - 16}{0.1} = 24.8 \text{ mph}$$

The average velocity between $t = 1$ and $t = 1.01$ can be determined as

$$\frac{\Delta d}{\Delta t} = \frac{f(1.01) - f(1)}{1.01 - 1}$$
$$= \frac{[8(1.01)^2 + 8(1.01)] - [8(1^2) + 8(1)]}{0.01} = \frac{16.2408 - 16}{0.01} = 24.08 \text{ mph}$$

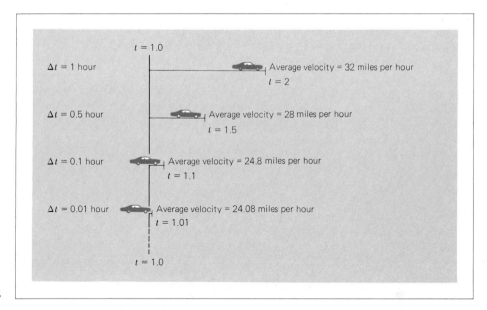

FIGURE 11.14

These computations have been determining the average velocity over shorter and shorter time intervals measured *from t* = 1. As the time interval becomes shorter (or as the second value of *t* is chosen closer and closer to 1), the average velocity $\Delta d/\Delta t$ is approaching a limiting value. The *instantaneous velocity* at *t* = 1 can be defined as this limiting value. To determine this limiting value, we could compute

$$\lim_{t \to 1} \frac{f(t) - f(1)}{t - 1} = \lim_{t \to 1} \frac{(8t^2 + 8t) - [8(1)^2 + 8(1)]}{t - 1}$$

$$= \lim_{t \to 1} \frac{(8t^2 + 8t) - 16}{t - 1}$$

$$= \lim_{t \to 1} \frac{8(t^2 + t - 2)}{t - 1}$$

$$= \lim_{t \to 1} \frac{8(t + 2)(t - 1)}{t - 1}$$

$$= \lim_{t \to 1} 8(t + 2)$$

$$= 8 \lim_{t \to 1} (t + 2)$$

$$= 8(1 + 2) = 24$$

Thus, the *instantaneous* velocity of the automobile at *t* = 1 is 24 mph. Note that the average velocity is measured over a time interval and the instantaneous velocity is defined for a particular point in time. The instantaneous velocity is a "snapshot" of what is happening at a particular instant.

GEOMETRIC REPRESENTATION OF
INSTANTANEOUS RATE OF CHANGE

The instantaneous rate of change of a smooth, continuous

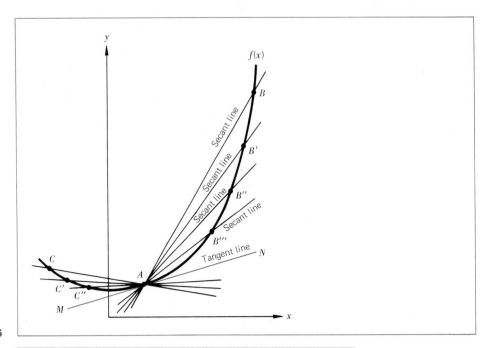

FIGURE 11.15

function can be represented geometrically by the slope of the line drawn tangent to the curve at the point of interest.

Let's first determine the meaning of ***tangent line.*** Consider Fig. 11.15. *The tangent line at A is the limiting position of the secant line AB as point B comes closer and closer to A.* Note how the position of the secant line rotates in a clockwise manner as B is drawn closer to A(AB, AB', AB'', and AB'''). The limiting position of AB is the line segment MN. This same limiting position results whether A is approached with secant lines from the left or right of A. The sequence of secant lines AC, AC', and AC'' have the same limiting position MN as C is drawn closer to A. *Since MN is the limiting position whether the approach is from the left or right, MN is the tangent line at point A.*

Not all continuous functions have unique tangent lines at each point on the function. For example, the function $y = f(x) = \sqrt{|x|}$, shown in Fig. 11.16, does not have a tangent at (0, 0). The secant lines drawn from (0, 0) to points on the left or right do not converge to the same limiting position.

DEFINITION: SLOPE OF CURVE

The slope of a curve at $x = a$ is the slope of the tangent line at $x = a$.

Later we will have a particular interest in determining the instantaneous rate of change in functions. Since the instantaneous rate of change is represented by the slope of the tangent line at the point of interest, we will need a way of determining these slopes of tangent lines. Suppose in Fig. 11.17 that we are inter-

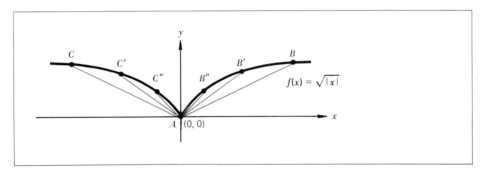

FIGURE 11.16
No tangent line
at point *A*.

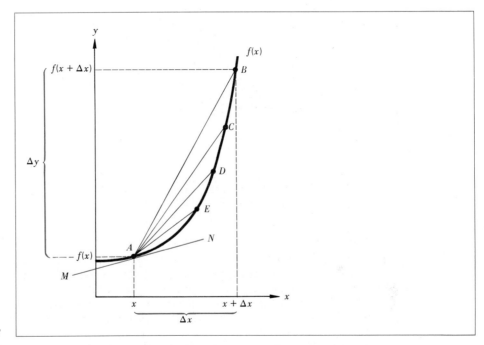

FIGURE 11.17

ested in finding the slope of the tangent line at *A*. There are several different methods we might use to determine this slope. If we were good at mechanical drawing, we might construct a tangent line at point *A* using graph paper, read from the line coordinates of any two points, and substitute these coordinates into the two-point formula.

An alternative approach would be to pick another point *B* on the curve. If we connect *A* and *B* with a secant line, the slope of the line segment *AB* can be computed and used as an "approximation" to the slope of *MN*. Obviously, the slope of *AB* is not a good approximation. However, let's continue, still referring to Fig. 11.17. At point *B* the value of the independent variable is $x + \Delta x$; the distance between *A* and *B* along the *x* axis is Δx. If the two-point formula is applied, the slope of *AB* is computed by using the difference quotient:

$$\frac{\Delta y}{\Delta x} = \frac{f(x + \Delta x) - f(x)}{\Delta x} \qquad (11.5)$$

Now, let's observe what happens to our approximation if a second point is chosen closer to point A. If point C is chosen as the second point, the slope of the secant line AC is still a poor approximation, but better than that of AB. And, if you look at the slopes of AD and AE, you should conclude that *as the second point is chosen closer and closer to A, the approximation becomes better.* In fact, as the value of Δx gets close to 0, the slope of the tiny line segment connecting A with the second point becomes an excellent approximation. The exact tangent slope can be determined by finding the limit of the difference quotient as $\Delta x \to 0$.

DEFINITION: THE DERIVATIVE

Given a function of the form $y = f(x)$, the **derivative** of the function is

$$\frac{dy}{dx} = \lim_{\Delta x \to 0} \frac{f(x + \Delta x) - f(x)}{\Delta x} \qquad \textbf{(11.7)}$$

The following points should be made regarding this definition.

COMMENTS ABOUT THE DERIVATIVE

I Equation (11.7) is the general expression for the *derivative* of the function f.

II The derivative is an expression which represents the *instantaneous rate of change* in the dependent variable given a change in the independent variable. The notation dy/dx is used to represent the *instantaneous* rate of change in y with respect to a change in x. This notation is distinguished from $\Delta y/\Delta x$ which represents the average rate of change.

III The derivative is a general expression for the slope of the graph of a function at any point x in the domain of the function.

IV If the limit in Eq. (11.7) does not exist, the derivative does not exist.

The Limit Approach to Finding the Derivative

FINDING THE DERIVATIVE (LIMIT APPROACH)

Step 1: Determine the difference quotient for f using Eq. (11.5).

Step 2: Find the limit of the difference quotient as $\Delta x \to 0$.

NOTE

If
$$\lim_{\Delta x \to 0} \frac{f(x + \Delta x) - f(x)}{\Delta x}$$

does not exist for a function at x, the function does not have a derivative at x.

The following examples illustrate the *limit approach* for determining the deriva-tive.

EXAMPLE 20 ▰▰▰▰▰▰▰▰▰▰▰▰▰▰▰▰▰▰▰▰

Given the function $f(x) = -5x + 9$, we should observe that f is linear with a slope of -5. With the slope always -5, we should find that the derivative equals -5.

Step 1: The difference quotient is

$$\frac{\Delta y}{\Delta x} = \frac{f(x + \Delta x) - f(x)}{\Delta x}$$

$$= \frac{[-5(x + \Delta x) + 9] - (-5x + 9)}{\Delta x}$$

$$= \frac{-5x - 5\Delta x + 9 + 5x - 9}{\Delta x}$$

$$= \frac{-5\Delta x}{\Delta x}$$

or

$$\frac{\Delta y}{\Delta x} = -5$$

Step 2: The derivative is the limit of the difference quotient, or

$$\frac{dy}{dx} = \lim_{\Delta x \to 0} (-5)$$

$$= -5$$

Thus, the derivative is exactly what we anticipated.

EXAMPLE 21 ▰▰▰▰▰▰▰▰▰▰▰▰▰▰▰▰▰▰▰▰

In Example 19 we found that the difference quotient for $f(x) = x^2$ was

$$\frac{\Delta y}{\Delta x} = 2x + \Delta x$$

To find the derivative of f, the limit of the difference quotient is determined.

$$\frac{dy}{dx} = \lim_{\Delta x \to 0} (2x + \Delta x)$$

or

$$\frac{dy}{dx} = 2x$$

USING AND INTERPRETING THE DERIVATIVE ▰▰▰▰▰▰▰▰

To determine the instantaneous rate of change (or equiva-lently, the slope) at any point on the graph of a function f, sub-stitute the value of the independent variable into the expres-sion for dy/dx. The derivative, evaluated at $x = c$, can be denoted by $\dfrac{dy}{dx}\bigg|_{x=c}$, which is read "the derivative of y with respect to x evaluated at $x = c$."

EXAMPLE 22

For the function $f(x) = x^2$
(a) Determine the instantaneous rate of change in $f(x)$ at $x = -3$.
(b) Determine the instantaneous rate of change in $f(x)$ at $x = 0$.
(c) Determine the instantaneous rate of change in $f(x)$ at $x = +3$.

SOLUTION

In Exercise 21 we determined that $dy/dx = 2x$. Answers to parts (a) to (c) are found by substitution into this expression.

(a) $\dfrac{dy}{dx}\Big|_{x=-3} = 2(-3) = -6$

(b) $\dfrac{dy}{dx}\Big|_{x=0} = 2(0) = 0$

(c) $\dfrac{dy}{dx}\Big|_{x=3} = 2(3) = +6$

POINTS FOR THOUGHT AND DISCUSSION

From Chap. 10 we know that the function $y = x^2$ is quadratic. Sketch the function and confirm that the values which we found in Example 22 a, b, and c seem reasonable as representing the slope at $x = -3$, 0, and 3. The derivative expression $dy/dx = 2x$ suggests that as x becomes more negative, the slope becomes more negative and as x becomes more positive, the slope becomes more positive. Does this seem correct in light of your sketch?

EXAMPLE 23

For the function $f(x) = -2x^2 + 3x - 10$
(a) Determine the derivative.
(b) Determine the instantaneous rate of change in $f(x)$ at $x = 5$.
(c) Determine where on the function the slope equals 0.

SOLUTION

(a) **Step I:** The difference quotient for f is

$$\frac{\Delta y}{\Delta x} = \frac{f(x + \Delta x) - f(x)}{\Delta x}$$

$$= \frac{[-2(x + \Delta x)^2 + 3(x + \Delta x) - 10] - (-2x^2 + 3x - 10)}{\Delta x}$$

$$= \frac{[-2(x^2 + 2x\Delta x + \Delta x^2) + 3x + 3\Delta x - 10] + 2x^2 - 3x + 10}{\Delta x}$$

$$= \frac{-2x^2 - 4x\Delta x - 2\Delta x^2 + 3x + 3\Delta x - 10 + 2x^2 - 3x + 10}{\Delta x}$$

Simplifying the numerator gives

$$\frac{\Delta y}{\Delta x} = \frac{-4x\Delta x - 2(\Delta x)^2 + 3\Delta x}{\Delta x}$$

Factoring Δx from the numerator and simplifying yield

$$\frac{\Delta y}{\Delta x} = \frac{\cancel{\Delta x}(-4x - 2\Delta x + 3)}{\cancel{\Delta x}} = -4x - 2\Delta x + 3$$

Step II: The derivative of the function is

$$\frac{dy}{dx} = \lim_{\Delta x \to 0} (-4x - 2\Delta x + 3)$$

or

$$\frac{dy}{dx} = -4x + 3$$

(b) $\left. \dfrac{dy}{dx} \right|_{x=5} = -4(5) + 3$

$$= -17$$

(c) The slope will equal 0 whenever $dy/dx = 0$, or for this function when $-4x + 3 = 0$. Solving for x, we have

$$-4x = -3$$

or

$$x = \tfrac{3}{4}$$

The only point where the slope equals 0 occurs where $x = \tfrac{3}{4}$.

EXERCISE

Verify that $x = \tfrac{3}{4}$ is the x coordinate of the vertex of the parabola representing the function $f(x) = -2x^2 + 3x - 10$ using the appropriate formula in Sec. 10.2.

If a function is not continuous at a point, it cannot have a derivative at that point. However, some functions are continuous and yet there are some points within the domain at which the derivative does not exist.

EXAMPLE 24

Consider $f(x) = |2x|$ shown in Fig. 11.18. Suppose we wish to find the derivative of f at $x = 0$. Evaluating Eq. 11.7 at $x = 0$ gives us

$$\frac{dy}{dx} = \lim_{\Delta x \to 0} \frac{f(0 + \Delta x) - f(0)}{\Delta x}$$

$$= \lim_{\Delta x \to 0} \frac{|2(0 + \Delta x)| - |2(0)|}{\Delta x}$$

$$= \lim_{\Delta x \to 0} \frac{|2\Delta x|}{\Delta x}$$

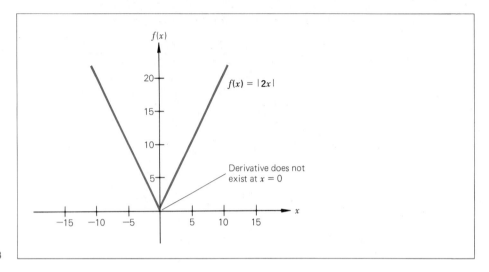

FIGURE 11.18

Evaluating both the left- and right-hand limits, we have

$$\lim_{\Delta x \to 0^-} \frac{|2\Delta x|}{\Delta x} = -2 \quad and \quad \lim_{\Delta x \to 0^+} \frac{|2\Delta x|}{\Delta x} = 2$$

Since these two limits are not the same,

$$\lim_{\Delta x \to 0} \frac{|2\Delta x|}{\Delta x}$$

does not exist. Therefore, for the function $f(x) = |2x|$, which is continuous over its domain, the derivative does not exist *at the point* $x = 0$.

Instantaneous Rate of Change Revisited

In the last section we found that the derivative dy/dx can be interpreted as a measure of the instantaneous rate of change in y with respect to a change in x. Using this interpretation, the derivative can be used to approximate changes which would occur in y given a change in the value of x. The following example illustrates the use of dy/dx in approximating these changes.

EXAMPLE 25

In Example 22 we evaluated the derivative of the function $f(x) = x^2$ at different values of x. We determined that the slope at $x = 3$ is $+6$. Using the instantaneous rate of change interpretation, we can state that "at the instant" when $x = 3$, y is increasing at a rate of 6 units for each unit that x increases. And this provides an approximation of what will happen if x increases from the value of 3. The value of the derivative at $x = 3$ suggests that for each unit that x increases beyond 3, y will increase by approximately 6 units. To test this approximation, we can compare the values of $f(x)$ when x increases by 1 unit from a value of 3 to 4.

TABLE 11.5

x	Δx	$f(x)$	ACTUAL CHANGE $f(x) - f(3)$	PROJECTED CHANGE $6(\Delta x)$	ACTUAL CHANGE − PROJECTED CHANGE
3.1	0.1	9.61	0.61	$6(0.1) = 0.6$	0.01
3.5	0.5	12.25	3.25	$6(0.5) = 3.0$	0.25
4.0	1.0	16.00	7.00	$6(1.0) = 6.0$	1.00
5.0	2.0	25.00	16.00	$6(2.0) = 12.0$	4.00
6.0	3.0	36.00	27.00	$6(3.0) = 18.0$	9.00

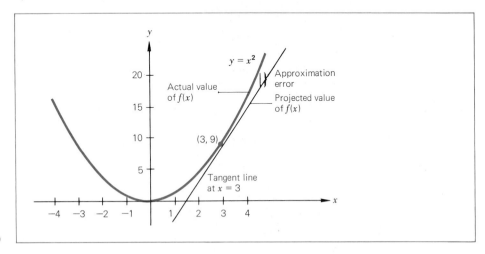

FIGURE 11.19

In moving from $x = 3$ to $x = 4$

$$\Delta y = f(4) - f(3)$$
$$= 4^2 - 3^2 = 16 - 9 = 7$$

The difference between the "actual" change in y and the approximated or "projected" change based on the derivative is $7 - 6 = 1$ unit. The derivative provides an *approximation* of the actual change.

Table 11.5 presents similar comparisons for values of x closer to 3 and for values of x greater than 4. A close examination of this table reveals that *the smaller the change in x (Δx) the better the approximation provided by dy/dx*. This is illustrated by Fig. 11.19. For any value of x, the vertical separation between the curve representing $y = x^2$ and the tangent line at $x = 3$ represents the difference between the actual value of $f(x)$ and the projected value. Note that for values of x close to 3 the vertical separation is small; however, it increases as one moves farther from $x = 3$.

The tangent line can be used as an approximation for $f(x)$ near the point of tangency. The accuracy of this approximation depends on the distance from the point of tangency (as illustrated above), as well as upon the nature of the function itself and its behavior in the vicinity of the tangent. This is illustrated in Fig. 11.20. The behavior of $f(x)$ near A in Fig. 11.20b is such that the tangent line is less accurate for approximation purposes than in Fig. 11.20a.

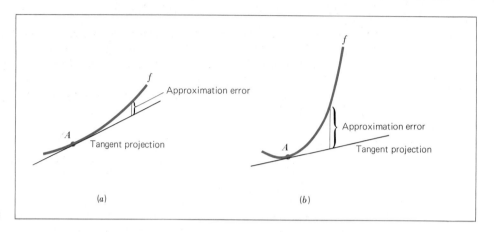

(a)

(b)

FIGURE 11.20

Section 11.3 Follow-up Exercises

In Exercises 1 to 14, (a) determine the derivative of f using the limit approach and (b) determine the slope at $x = -1$ and $x = 2$.

1 $f(x) = 2x + 5$ 2 $f(x) = 25$
3 $f(x) = 8x^2$ 4 $f(x) = -x^2$
5 $f(x) = 3x^2 - 10$ 6 $f(x) = -5x^2 + 10x$
7 $f(x) = x^2 - 2x + 3$ 8 $f(x) = 10x^2 - 7x + 6$
*9 $f(x) = 3/x$ *10 $f(x) = 2x^3$
*11 $f(x) = x^3$ *12 $f(x) = 1/x^2$
*13 $f(x) = x^3 - 3x^2$ *14 $f(x) = x^4$

In Exercises 15 to 22 the function f and its derivative dy/dx are given. (a) Determine the slope when $x = 0$ and $x = -2$, (b) verbalize the instantaneous rate of change interpretation for your results in part (a), and (c) determine any values of x for which the slope equals 0.

15 $f(x) = 4x^2 - 2x + 1$ 16 $f(x) = 3x^2 + 24x - 10$
    $dy/dx = 8x - 2$ $dy/dx = 6x + 24$
17 $f(x) = 20x - 250$ 18 $f(x) = -x/2 + 5$
    $dy/dx = 20$ $dy/dx = -\frac{1}{2}$
19 $f(x) = -24$ 20 $f(x) = 4x^3 - 2x^2 - 5x + 10$
    $dy/dx = 0$ $dy/dx = 12x^2 - 4x - 5$
21 $f(x) = x^5/5 - 16x + 3$ 22 $f(x) = 16x^5 - 5x$
    $dy/dx = x^4 - 16$ $dy/dx = 80x^4 - 5$

23 Given the function in Exercise 15, (a) determine the instantaneous rate of change in $f(x)$ when $x = 2$. (b) Using this result, estimate the value of $f(x)$ when $x = 2.5$ and $x = 3$. (c) Compute $f(2)$, $f(2.5)$, and $f(3)$, and determine how accurate your estimates were in part (b).

24 Given the function in Exercise 16, (a) determine the instantaneous rate of change in $f(x)$ when $x = 2$. (b) Using this result, estimate the value of $f(x)$ when $x = 2.5$ and $x = 3$. (c) Compute $f(2)$, $f(2.5)$, and $f(3)$ and determine how accurate your estimates were in part (b).

11.4 DIFFERENTIATION

The process of finding a derivative is called *differentiation.* Fortunately, for us, the process does not have to be as laborious as it may have seemed when we used the limit approach. A set of rules of differentiation exists for finding the derivatives of many common functions. Although there are many functions for which the derivative does not exist, *our concern will be with functions which are differentiable.*

Rules of Differentiation

The rules of differentiation presented in this section have been developed using the limit approach. The mathematics involved in proving these rules can be fairly complicated. For our purposes it will suffice to present the rules without proof. The appendix at the end of the chapter presents proofs of selected differentiation rules for anyone interested.

The rules of differentiation apply to functions which have specific structural characteristics. A rule will state that if a function has specific characteristics, then the derivative of the function will have a resulting form. As you study these rules, remember that each function can be graphed and that the derivative is a general expression for the slope of the function. An alternative to the dy/dx notation is to let $f'(x)$ (read "*f* **prime of** x") represent the derivative of the function f at x. That is, given $f(x)$,

$$\frac{dy}{dx} = f'(x)$$

This notation will be used in presenting the rules.

RULE 1: CONSTANT FUNCTION

If $f(x) = c$, where c is any constant,

$$f'(x) = 0$$

EXAMPLE 26

Consider the function $f(x) = 5$. This function has the form indicated in Rule 1. Thus, $f'(x) = 0$. If you consider what the function looks like graphically, this result seems reasonable. The function $f(x) = 5$ graphs as a horizontal line crossing the y axis at 5. The slope at all points along such a function equals 0.

RULE 2: POWER RULE

If $f(x) = x^n$, where n is a real number,

$$f'(x) = nx^{n-1}$$

EXAMPLE 27

Consider the function $f(x) = x$. This function is the same as $f(x) = x^1$. Applying Rule 2, we know $n = 1$ and

$$f'(x) = 1 \cdot x^{1-1}$$
$$= x^0$$
$$= 1$$

This implies that for the function $f(x) = x$, the slope equals 1 at all points. You should recognize that $f(x) = x$ is a linear function with slope of 1.

EXAMPLE 28

Consider the function $f(x) = x^5$. Applying Rule 2, we have $n = 5$ and

$$f'(x) = 5x^{5-1}$$
$$= 5x^4$$

EXAMPLE 29

Consider the function $f(x) = 1/x^3$.

ALGEBRA FLASHBACK

$$\frac{1}{x^n} = x^{-n}$$

Rewriting f as $f(x) = x^{-3}$, we have $n = -3$ and

$$f'(x) = -3x^{-3-1}$$
$$= -3x^{-4}$$
$$= \frac{-3}{x^4}$$

EXAMPLE 30

Consider the function $f(x) = \sqrt[3]{x^2}$.

ALGEBRA FLASHBACK

$$\sqrt[n]{x^m} = x^{m/n}$$

Rewriting f as $f(x) = x^{2/3}$ gives us $n = \frac{2}{3}$ and

$$f'(x) = \tfrac{2}{3}x^{2/3-1}$$
$$= \frac{2x^{-1/3}}{3}$$

Rewriting with a positive exponent yields

$$f'(x) = \frac{2}{3x^{1/3}}$$

which can be written, using a radical, as

$$f'(x) = \frac{2}{3\sqrt[3]{x}}$$

RULE 3: CONSTANT TIMES A FUNCTION

If $f(x) = c \cdot g(x)$, where c is a constant and g is a differentiable function,

$$f'(x) = c \cdot g'(x)$$

EXAMPLE 31

Consider the function $f(x) = 10x^2$. Applying Rule 3 gives us $g(x) = x^2$ and $c = 10$, and

$$f'(x) = 10(2x)$$
$$= 20x$$

EXAMPLE 32

Consider the function $f(x) = -3/x$. This function can be rewritten as

$$f(x) = -3\left(\frac{1}{x}\right) = -3x^{-1}$$

Applying Rules 2 and 3 gives

$$f'(x) = (-3)(-1)(x^{-1-1})$$
$$= 3x^{-2}$$
$$= \frac{3}{x^2}$$

RULE 4: SUM OR DIFFERENCE OF FUNCTIONS

If $f(x) = u(x) \pm v(x)$, where u and v are differentiable,

$$f'(x) = u'(x) \pm v'(x)$$

This rule implies that the derivative of a function formed by the sum (difference) of two or more component functions is the sum (difference) of the derivatives of the component functions.

EXAMPLE 33

Consider the function $f(x) = x^2 - 5x + 10$. Applying Rules 1 through 4, we have

$$f'(x) = 2x - 5 + 0$$
$$= 2x - 5$$

RULE 5: PRODUCT RULE

If $f(x) = u(x) \cdot v(x)$, where u and v are differentiable, then

$$f'(x) = u'(x) \cdot v(x) + v'(x) \cdot u(x)$$

EXAMPLE 34

Consider the function $f(x) = (x^2 - 5)(x - x^3)$. Applying Rule 5, we have $u(x) = x^2 - 5$ and $v(x) = x - x^3$. Therefore

$$\begin{aligned} f'(x) &= (2x)(x - x^3) + (1 - 3x^2)(x^2 - 5) \\ &= 2x^2 - 2x^4 + x^2 - 5 - 3x^4 + 15x^2 \\ &= -5x^4 + 18x^2 - 5 \end{aligned}$$

EXAMPLE 35

In the last example the function could have been rewritten in the equivalent form

$$\begin{aligned} f(x) &= (x^2 - 5)(x - x^3) \\ &= x^3 - x^5 - 5x + 5x^3 \\ &= -x^5 + 6x^3 - 5x \end{aligned}$$

Finding the derivative of this form of the function does not require the use of Rule 5. The derivative is

$$f'(x) = -5x^4 + 18x^2 - 5$$

which is the same result as obtained before.

NOTE

As with the last two examples, many functions can be algebraically manipulated into an equivalent form. This can be useful for two reasons. *First*, rewriting a function in an equivalent form can allow the use of derivative rules which are more efficient or easier to remember. *Second*, finding the derivative of both the original function and an equivalent form of the function provides a check on your answer.

RULE 6: QUOTIENT RULE

If $f(x) = u(x)/v(x)$, where u and v are differentiable and $v(x) \neq 0$, then

$$f'(x) = \frac{v(x) \cdot u'(x) - u(x) \cdot v'(x)}{[v(x)]^2}$$

Verbally, this rule states that the derivative is found by multiplying the denominator by the derivative of the numerator, then subtracting the product of the numerator and the derivative of the denominator, and finally dividing the result by the square of the denominator.

EXAMPLE 36

In Example 29 we used the power rule to determine that the derivative of $f(x) = 1/x^3$ is $f'(x) = -3/x^4$. Since f has the form of a quotient, we can, as an alternative approach, apply Rule 6 as follows:

$$f'(x) = \frac{x^3(0) - (1)(3x^2)}{(x^3)^2}$$

$$= \frac{-3x^2}{x^6}$$

$$= \frac{-3}{x^4}$$

EXAMPLE 37

Consider the function $f(x) = (3x^2 - 5)/(1 - x^3)$. Applying Rule 6 gives us

$$f'(x) = \frac{(1 - x^3)(6x) - (3x^2 - 5)(-3x^2)}{(1 - x^3)^2}$$

$$= \frac{6x - 6x^4 + 9x^4 - 15x^2}{(1 - x^3)^2}$$

$$= \frac{3x^4 - 15x^2 + 6x}{(1 - x^3)^2}$$

RULE 7: POWER OF A FUNCTION*

If $f(x) = [u(x)]^n$, where u is a differentiable function,

$$f'(x) = n \cdot [u(x)]^{n-1} \cdot u'(x)$$

This rule looks very similar to the power rule (Rule 2). In fact, the power rule is the special case of this rule where $u(x)$ equals x. When $u(x) = x$, $u'(x) = 1$ and applying Rule 7 results in

$$f'(x) = n(x)^{n-1}(1)$$
$$= nx^{n-1}$$

EXAMPLE 38

Consider the function $f(x) = \sqrt{7x^4 - 5x - 9}$. Rewriting the function gives $f(x) = (7x^4 - 5x - 9)^{1/2}$. In this form, Rule 7 applies, where $u(x) = 7x^4 - 5x - 9$. Applying Rule 7 yields

$$f'(x) = \tfrac{1}{2}(7x^4 - 5x - 9)^{(1/2)-1}(28x^3 - 5)$$
$$= (14x^3 - \tfrac{5}{2})(7x^4 - 5x - 9)^{-1/2}$$

which can rewritten as

$$f'(x) = \frac{14x^3 - \frac{5}{2}}{(7x^4 - 5x - 9)^{1/2}}$$

or

$$f'(x) = \frac{14x^3 - \frac{5}{2}}{\sqrt{7x^4 - 5x - 9}}$$

---

* We will revisit this rule later with discussion in chain-rule terminology.

EXAMPLE 39 ▮▬▬▬▬▬▬▬▬▬▬▬▬▬▬▬▬▬▬▬▬▬

Consider the function

$$f(x) = \left(\frac{3x}{1 - x^2}\right)^5$$

This function has the form stated in Rule 7 where u is the rational function $3x/(1 - x^2)$. Applying Rule 7 gives

$$f'(x) = 5\left(\frac{3x}{1 - x^2}\right)^4 \frac{(1 - x^2)(3) - (3x)(-2x)}{(1 - x^2)^2}$$

$$= 5\left(\frac{3x}{1 - x^2}\right)^4 \frac{3 - 3x^2 + 6x^2}{(1 - x^2)^2}$$

$$= 5\left(\frac{3x}{1 - x^2}\right)^4 \frac{3 + 3x^2}{(1 - x^2)^2}$$

▬▬▬▬▬▬▬▬▬▬▬▬▬▬▬▬▬▬▬▬▬▬▬▬▬▬▬▬▬▬▬▬▬▬▬▬

Instantaneous Rate of Change—Again

In Example 18 the function

$$d = f(t) = 8t^2 + 8t$$

described the distance (in miles) an automobile traveled as a function of time (in hours). The instantaneous velocity of the car at any point in time is found by evaluating the derivative at that value of t. To determine the instantaneous velocity at $t = 3$, the derivative

$$f'(t) = 16t + 8$$

must be evaluated at $t = 3$, or

$$f'(3) = 16(3) + 8$$
$$= 56 \text{ mph}$$

EXAMPLE 40 ▮▬▬▬▬▬▬▬▬▬▬▬▬▬▬▬▬▬▬▬▬▬

An object is dropped from a cliff which is 1,296 feet above the ground. The height of the object is described as a function of time. The function is

$$h = f(t) = -16t^2 + 1,296$$

where h equals the height in feet and t equals time measured in seconds from the time the object is dropped.
(*a*) How far will the object drop in 2 seconds?
(*b*) What is the instantaneous velocity of the object at $t = 2$?
(*c*) What is the velocity of the object at the instant it hits the ground?

SOLUTION

(*a*) The change in the height is

$$\Delta h = f(2) - f(0)$$
$$= [-16(2)^2 + 1,296] - [-16(0)^2 + 1,296]$$
$$= (-64 + 1,296) - 1,296 = -64$$

Thus, the object drops 64 feet during the first 2 seconds.

(*b*) Since $f'(t) = -32t$, the object will have a velocity equal to

$$f'(2) = -32(2)$$
$$= -64 \text{ feet/second}$$

at $t = 2$. The minus sign indicates the direction of velocity (down).

(*c*) In order to determine the velocity of the object when it hits the ground, we must know *when* it will hit the ground. The object will hit the ground when $h = 0$, or

$$-16t^2 + 1,296 = 0$$

If we solve for t,

$$t^2 = \frac{1,296}{16} = 81$$

and $t = \pm 9$. Since a negative root is meaningless, we can conclude that the object will hit the ground after 9 seconds. The velocity at this time will be

$$f'(9) = 32(9)$$
$$= 288 \text{ feet/second}$$

Section 11.4 Follow-up Exercises

For Exercises 1 to 36, find the expression for $f'(x)$.

1	$f(x) = 140$	2	$f(x) = -55$
3	$f(x) = x^3 - 4x$	4	$f(x) = -3x/4 + 9$
5	$f(x) = \sqrt[5]{x^3}$	6	$f(x) = \sqrt[4]{x^3}$
7	$f(x) = x^{10}$	8	$f(x) = x^{5/3}$
9	$f(x) = x^6/3 - 2x$	10	$f(x) = x^4/2 - 3x^2 + 10$
11	$f(x) = 5/x^2$	12	$f(x) = 3/6x^3$
13	$f(x) = x - 1/\sqrt{x}$	14	$f(x) = 1/\sqrt[6]{x^5}$
15	$f(x) = (x^3 - 2x)(x^5 + 6x^2)$	16	$f(x) = (x^2/2 - 10)(x^3 - 2x^2 + 1)$
17	$f(x) = (6x^2 - 2x + 1)(x^3/4 + 5)$	18	$f(x) = [(x + 3)/2](x^2 - 4x + 9)$
19	$f(x) = x/(1 - x^2)$	20	$f(x) = 4x/(6x^2 - 5)$
21	$f(x) = 1/(4x^5 - 3x^2 + 1)$	22	$f(x) = (-x^3 + 1)/(x^5 - 20)$
23	$f(x) = (1 - 4x^3)^5$	24	$f(x) = (7x^2 - 3x + 1)^3$
25	$f(x) = \sqrt{1 - 5x^3}$	26	$f(x) = \sqrt[3]{x^2 - 2x + 5}$
27	$f(x) = 1/\sqrt{x^2 - 1}$	28	$f(x) = \sqrt{1/(x^2 + 9)}$
*29	$f(x) = \sqrt[3]{[x^2/(5x - 1)]^2}$	*30	$f(x) = \sqrt{(x - 1)^5(6x - 5)}$
*31	$f(x) = \sqrt[3]{(1 - x^3)^5 x^3/(9 - 2x^2)}$	*32	$f(x) = (6x - 2)\sqrt{x^2 - 5x + 3}$
33	$f(x) = ax^2 + bx + c$	34	$f(x) = mx + b$
35	$f(x) = a_3 x^3 + a_2 x^2 + a_1 x + a_0$	36	$f(x) = (mx + b)/(cx + d)$

For Exercises 37 to 46, (*a*) find $f'(2)$ and (*b*) determine the values of x for which the slope of the graph of f equals 0.

37 $f(x) = 10x - 5$

38 $f(x) = 8x^2 - 2x + 1$

39 $f(x) = x^3/3 - 6x + 8$

40 $f(x) = 16x^4/4 - x$

41 $f(x) = a_2 x^2 + a_1 x + a_0$

42 $f(x) = -1/x$

43 $f(x) = x^2/(1 - x^2)$

44 $f(x) = (8x - 4)^{5/2}$

45 $f(x) = (x - 2)(x + 15)$

46 $f(x) = 4/x^3$

47 The function $h = f(t) = 2.5t^3$, where $0 \le t \le 30$, describes the height h (in hundreds of feet) of a rocket t seconds after it has been launched.
(a) What is the average velocity during the time interval $0 \le t \le 4$?
(b) What is the instantaneous velocity at $t = 10$? At $t = 20$?

48 An object is launched from ground level with an initial velocity of 256 feet per second. The function which describes the height h of the ball is

$$h = f(t) = 256t - 16t^2$$

where h is measured in feet and t is time measured in seconds since the ball was thrown.
(a) What is the velocity of the ball at $t = 1$ second?
(b) When will the ball return to the ground?
(c) What is the velocity of the ball when it hits the ground?

49 A ball is dropped from the roof of a building which is 256 feet high. The height of the ball is described by the function

$$h = f(t) = -16t^2 + 256$$

where h equals the height in feet and t equals time measured in seconds from when the ball was dropped.
(a) What is the average velocity during the time interval $1 \le t \le 2$?
(b) What is the instantaneous velocity at $t = 1$?
(c) What is the velocity of the ball at the instant it hits the ground?

50 **Epidemic Control** An epidemic is spreading through a large Western state. Health officials estimate that the number of persons who will be afflicted by the disease is a function of time since the disease was first detected. Specifically, the function is

$$n = f(t) = 300t^3 - 20t^2$$

where n equals the number of persons and $0 \le t \le 60$, measured in days.
(a) How many persons are expected to have caught the disease after 10 days? 30 days?
(b) What is the average rate at which the disease is expected to spread between $t = 10$ and $t = 20$?
(c) What is the instantaneous rate at which the disease is expected to be spreading at $t = 30$?

11.5 HIGHER-ORDER DERIVATIVES

Given a function f, there are other derivatives which can be defined. This section discusses these *higher-order derivatives* and their interpretation.

The Second Derivative

The derivative f' of the function f is often referred to as the *first derivative* of the function. The adjective *first* is used to distinguish this derivative from other derivatives associated with a function. The *order* of the first derivative is 1.

TABLE 11.6

$f(x)$	$f'(x)$	$f''(x)$
x^5	$5x^4$	$20x^3$
$x^2 - 3x + 10$	$2x - 3$	2
$mx + b$	m	0
$x^3 - 2x^2 + 5x$	$3x^2 - 4x + 5$	$6x - 4$
$x^{3/2}$	$\frac{3}{2}x^{1/2}$	$\frac{3}{4}x^{-1/2}$

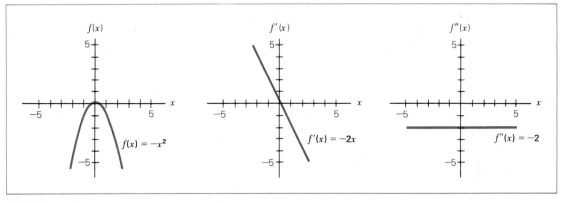

FIGURE 11.21

The *second derivative f″* of a function is the derivative of the first derivative. At x, it is denoted by either d^2y/dx^2 or $f''(x)$. The second derivative is found by applying the same rules of differentiation as were used in finding the first derivative. Table 11.6 illustrates the computation of first and second derivatives for several functions.

Just as the first derivative is a measure of the instantaneous rate of change in the value of y with respect to a change in x, the *second derivative* is a measure of the instantaneous rate of change in the value of the first derivative with respect to a change in x. Described differently, the second derivative is a *measure of the instantaneous rate of change in the slope with respect to a change in x.*

Consider the function $f(x) = -x^2$. The first and second derivatives of this function are

$$f'(x) = -2x \qquad f''(x) = -2$$

Figure 11.21 illustrates the graphs of f, f', and f''. These graphs have been sketched directly above one another so that some important observations can be made more easily. The function f is a parabola which is concave down with the vertex at $(0, 0)$. Looking at the sketch of f, we see the tangent slope is positive to the left of the vertex but becomes *less positive* as x approaches 0. To the right of the vertex the tangent slope is negative and becomes *more negative* (decreases) as x increases. The graph of f' indicates the value of the slope at any point on f. Note that values of $f'(x)$ are positive, but becoming less positive, as x approaches 0 from the left. And, $f'(x)$ becomes more and more negative as the value of x becomes more positive. Thus, the graph of f' is consistent with our observations of the sketch of f.

The second derivative is a measure of the instantaneous rate of change in the first derivative or in the slope of the graph of a function. Since $f''(x) = -2$, this suggests that the rate of change in the first derivative is constant over the entire function. Specifically $f''(x) = -2$ suggests that everywhere on the function the slope is *decreasing* at an instantaneous rate of 2 units for each unit that x increases. If you look at f' and its graph, f' is a linear function with slope of -2.

Some earlier examples in this chapter discussed functions having the form $d = f(t)$ where d represents the distance traveled after time t. We concluded that the instantaneous velocity at any time t was represented by the first derivative $f'(t)$. The second derivative of this type of function $f''(t)$ provides a measure of the instantaneous rate of change *in the velocity* with respect to a change in time. Measured in units of distance per unit of time squared (for example, ft/sec² and km/hr²), this second derivative represents the instantaneous *acceleration* of an object. If

$$d = f(t) = t^3 - 2t^2 + 3t$$

the expression representing the *instantaneous velocity* is

$$f'(t) = 3t^2 - 4t + 3$$

and the expression representing the *instantaneous acceleration* is

$$f''(t) = 6t - 4$$

Third and Higher-Order Derivatives

Further derivatives can be determined for functions. These derivatives become less easy to understand from an intuitive standpoint. However, they will be useful to us later, and they have particular value at higher levels of mathematical analysis.

DEFINITION: nth-ORDER DERIVATIVE

The **nth order derivative** of f denoted by $f^{(n)}$ is found by differentiating the derivative of order $n - 1$. That is, at x,

$$f^{(n)}(x) = \frac{d}{dx} [f^{(n-1)}(x)]$$

EXAMPLE 41

Given

$$f(x) = x^6 - 2x^5 + x^4 - 3x^3 + x^2 - x + 1$$

the derivatives of f are

$$f'(x) = 6x^5 - 10x^4 + 4x^3 - 9x^2 + 2x - 1$$
$$f''(x) = 30x^4 - 40x^3 + 12x^2 - 18x + 2$$
$$f'''(x) = 120x^3 - 120x^2 + 24x - 18$$
$$f^{(4)}(x) = 360x^2 - 240x + 24$$
$$f^{(5)}(x) = 720x - 240$$
$$f^{(6)}(x) = 720$$
$$f^{(7)}(x) = 0$$

All additional higher-order derivatives will also equal 0.

Section 11.5 Follow-up Exercises

For Exercises 1 to 10, (*a*) find $f'(x)$ and $f''(x)$, (*b*) evaluate $f'(1)$ and $f''(1)$, and (*c*) verbalize the meaning of $f'(1)$ and $f''(1)$.

1 $f(x) = 15$

2 $f(x) = 24 - 10x$

3 $f(x) = 4x^2 - x + 5$

4 $f(x) = x^2 - 15x + 10$

5 $f(x) = 5x^3$

6 $f(x) = 7x^3 - 2x^2 + 5x + 1$

7 $f(x) = x^4/4 - x^3/3 + 10x$

8 $f(x) = x^5/5 - x^3/3 + 100$

9 $f(x) = 1/x$

10 $f(x) = (x^2 - 2)^5$

11 The height of a falling object dropped from a height of 1,000 feet is described by the function

$$h = 1,000 - 16t^2$$

where h is measured in feet and t is measured in seconds.
(*a*) What is the velocity at $t = 4$?
(*b*) What is the acceleration at $t = 4$?

12 A ball thrown upward from the roof of a building which is 600 feet high will be at a height of h feet after t seconds as described by the function

$$h = f(t) = -16t^2 + 50t + 600$$

(*a*) What is the height of the ball after 3 seconds?
(*b*) What is the velocity of the ball after 3 seconds? (A negative sign implies a downward direction.)
(*c*) What is the acceleration of the ball at $t = 0$? $t = 5$?

In Exercises 13 to 20, find all higher-order derivatives.

13 $f(x) = 16x^3 - 4x^2$

14 $f(x) = 2,500$

15 $f(x) = mx + b$

16 $f(x) = -x/4 + 10$

17 $f(x) = x^5 - 5x^4 - 30x^2$

18 $f(x) = (x - 10)^3$

19 $f(x) = a_3 x^3 + a_2 x^2 + a_1 x + a_0$

20 $f(x) = (a_1 x + b_1)(a_2 x + b_2)$

11.6 DIFFERENTIATION OF SPECIAL FUNCTIONAL FORMS (OPTIONAL)

This section discusses techniques for differentiating some functional forms not covered by Rules 1 through 7.

Chain Rule

Rule 7 (power of a function) was presented expeditiously and without the attention it should have been given. As stated in Sec. 11.5, Rule 7 is a special case of the more general *chain rule*.

RULE 8: CHAIN RULE

If $y = f(u)$ is a differentiable function and $u = g(x)$ is a differentiable function, then

$$\frac{dy}{dx} = \frac{dy}{du} \cdot \frac{du}{dx}$$

Recall that in Chap. 2 we examined composite functions—functions whose values depend upon other functions. The chain rule specifically applies to composite functions. Consider the two functions

$$y = f(u) = 20 - 3u$$

and

$$u = g(x) = 5x - 4$$

Note that the value of y ultimately depends upon x. We can see this by observing that if x increases by 1 unit, u increases by 5 units. And an increase in u of 5 units results in a *decrease* in y of $(3)(5) = 15$ units. If we are interested in determining how the value of y responds to changes in x, we can apply the chain rule.

Since

$$\frac{dy}{du} = -3$$

and

$$\frac{du}{dx} = 5$$

then

$$\frac{dy}{dx} = \frac{dy}{du} \cdot \frac{du}{dx} = (-3)(5)$$

$$= -15$$

EXAMPLE 42

Given $y = f(u) = u^2 - 2u + 1$ and $u = g(x) = x^2 - 1$,

$$\frac{dy}{dx} = \frac{dy}{du} \cdot \frac{du}{dx}$$

$$= (2u - 2)(2x)$$

We can rewrite dy/dx strictly in terms of x by substituting $u = x^2 - 1$. This results in

$$\frac{dy}{dx} = [2(x^2 - 1) - 2](2x)$$

$$= (2x^2 - 4)(2x)$$

$$= 4x^3 - 8x$$

Rule 7 would approach this problem by first restating $f(u)$ in terms of x. That is, because $u = x^2 - 1$

$$y = u^2 - 2u + 1$$

$$= (x^2 - 1)^2 - 2(x^2 - 1) + 1$$

The expression for dy/dx is found directly as

$$\frac{dy}{dx} = 2(x^2 - 1)(2x) - 4x$$

$$= 4x^3 - 8x$$

which again is the same result obtained before.

EXAMPLE 43

Given $y = f(u) = u^3 - 5u$ where $u = g(x) = x^4 + 3x$,

$$\frac{dy}{dx} = \frac{dy}{du} \cdot \frac{du}{dx}$$

$$= (3u^2 - 5)(4x^3 + 3)$$

Rewriting this as a function of x gives

$$\frac{dy}{dx} = [3(x^4 + 3x)^2 - 5](4x^3 + 3)$$

$$= [3(x^8 + 6x^5 + 9x^2) - 5](4x^3 + 3)$$
$$= (3x^8 + 18x^5 + 27x^2 - 5)(4x^3 + 3)$$
$$= 12x^{11} + 72x^8 + 108x^5 - 20x^3 + 9x^8 + 54x^5$$
$$+ 81x^2 - 15$$
$$= 12x^{11} + 81x^8 + 162x^5 - 20x^3 + 81x^2 - 15$$

Other Derivatives

The derivative dx/dy is a measure of the instantaneous rate of change in x with respect to a change in y. With many functions we may have a real interest in knowing the value of dx/dy. In some cases a function of the form $y = f(x)$ can be solved explicitly for x, creating an inverse function of the form $x = g(y)$. In other cases it may be possible to solve explicitly for x. The following derivative property is useful in determining dx/dy.

RULE 9

Given a differentiable function of the form $y = f(x)$,

$$\frac{dx}{dx} = \frac{1}{dy/dx} \qquad \text{provided } \frac{dy}{dx} \neq 0 \qquad \textbf{(11.8)}$$

EXAMPLE 44

Given $y = f(x) = 5x - 20$, we can solve for x in terms of the variable y, creating the inverse function

$$x = g(y)$$

or

$$x = 4 + \frac{y}{5}$$

Differentiating g with respect to y yields

$$\frac{dx}{dy} = \frac{1}{5}$$

Checking our answer with the property stated by Eq. (11.8), let's differentiate f with respect to x

$$\frac{dy}{dx} = 5$$

According to Eq. (11.8)

$$\frac{dx}{dy} = \frac{1}{dy/dx} = \frac{1}{5}$$

which agrees with our original answer.

EXAMPLE 45

Given the function $y = f(x) = x^3 - 3x^2 + 5$; it is extremely difficult to solve for the inverse function $x = g(y)$. However, we can determine dx/dy because f is differentiable and

$$\frac{dy}{dx} = 3x^2 - 6x$$

According to Eq. (11.8)

$$\frac{dx}{dy} = \frac{1}{3x^2 - 6x} \qquad x \neq 0 \text{ or } 2$$

RULE 10: THREE-FACTOR PRODUCT RULE

If $f(x) = u(x) \cdot v(x) \cdot w(x)$, where u, v, and w are differentiable, then

$$f'(x) = u'(x)v(x)w(x) + v'(x)u(x)w(x) + w'(x)u(x)v(x)$$

EXAMPLE 46

Given $f(x) = x^3(x^2 - 1)(x^3 + 1)$, the application of Rule 10 yields

$$f'(x) = 3x^2(x^2 - 1)(x^3 + 1) + 2x(x^3)(x^3 + 1) + 3x^2(x^3)(x^2 - 1)$$

When $f'(x)$ is multiplied through and simplified algebraically, the result is

$$f'(x) = 8x^7 - 6x^5 + 5x^4 - 3x^2$$

To check this version of the product rule, we could simplify f before differentiating. If we multiply through on the right side of f, we get

$$f(x) = x^8 - x^6 + x^5 - x^3$$

which when differentiated yields the same result

$$f'(x) = 8x^7 - 6x^5 + 5x^4 - 3x^2$$

RULE 11: CHAIN RULE EXTENDED

If $y = f(u)$, where $u = g(v)$, $v = h(x)$, and f, g, and h are differentiable functions, then

$$\frac{dy}{dx} = \frac{dy}{du} \cdot \frac{du}{dv} \cdot \frac{dv}{dx}$$

EXAMPLE 47

Given the functions

$$y = f(u) = u^2 - 3$$
$$u = g(v) = 2v + 5$$

and

$$v = h(x) = 3x^2 - 6x + 1$$

then application of Rule 11 yields

$$\frac{dy}{dx} = (2u)(2)(6x - 6)$$

To restate this result in terms of x we can substitute through the composite functions as follows:

$$\frac{dy}{dx} = 4u(6x - 6)$$

$$= 4(2v + 5)(6x - 6)$$
$$= (8v + 20)(6x - 6)$$
$$= [8(3x^2 - 6x + 1) + 20](6x - 6)$$
$$= (24x^2 - 48x + 28)(6x - 6)$$
$$= 144x^3 - 432x^2 + 456x - 168$$

Section 11.6 Follow-up Exercises

For the following exercises, find dy/dx.

1   $y = f(u) = 5u + 3$ and $u = g(x) = -3x + 10$
2   $y = f(u) = u^2 - 5$ and $u = g(x) = 10x - 3$
3   $y = f(u) = u^2 - 2u + 1$ and $u = g(x) = x^2$
4   $y = f(u) = u^3$ and $u = g(x) = x^2 + 3x + 1$
5   $y = f(u) = 10 - 5u^3$ and $u = g(x) = -x + x^3$
6   $y = f(u) = u^4 - u^2 + 1$ and $u = g(x) = x^2 - 4$
7   $y = f(u) = \sqrt{u}$ and $u = g(x) = x^2/2$
8   $y = f(u) = \sqrt{u^2 - 1}$ and $u = g(x) = x^4$
9   $y = f(u) = (u - 3)^5$ and $u = g(x) = x^2 - 2x$
10 $y = f(u) = \sqrt{u^3}$ and $u = g(x) = \sqrt{x}$

For Exercises 11 to 16, determine dx/dy and state the values for which dx/dy is not defined.

11   $f(x) = 4x^3 - 12x^2 + 12x$ 12 $f(x) = 25 - x/2$

13   $f(x) = 7x^2 - 5x + 12x$ 14 $f(x) = 2x^4 - 4x^2$

15   $f(x) = (2x - 6)^5$ 16 $f(x) = 1/(x^2 - 2x)^3$

For Exercises 17 to 20, find dy/dx.

17   $x = g(y) = a_2 y^2 + a_1 y + a_0$ 18 $x = g(y) = y^2 - 5y + 3$

19   $x = g(y) = 5y^3 - 2y^2 + y$ 20 $x = g(y) = (y^4 - 2y^3)^5$

For Exercises 21 to 28, find dy/dx.

*21 $y = f(x) = x^3 \sqrt{x^2 - 1}(1 - x^3)^2$

*22 $y = f(x) = (x - 1)^5(x^2 + 5)^3 x^4$

*23 $y = f(x) = x^5 \sqrt[3]{x^2 - 3x}(x - 5)^4$

*24 $y = f(x) = (x - 3)^4(x^2 - 5x)^3(x^3)$

*25 $y = f(u) = 5u - 3$, where $u = g(v) = v^2$ and $v = h(x) = 5x^3$

*26 $y = f(u) = u^2 - 2u$, where $u = g(v) = 10 - 3v$ and $v = h(x) = x^2/2$

*27 $y = f(u) = u^3$, where $u = g(v) = v^2$ and $v = h(x) = x^4$

*28 $y = f(u) = \sqrt{u}$, where $u = g(v) = \sqrt[3]{v}$ and $v = h(x) = x^2$

KEY TERMS AND CONCEPTS

average rate of change   427   instantaneous rate of change   434

chain rule   455   limit of a function   412

closed interval   424 nth-order derivative   454

continuity   412   open interval   424

derivative   434   secant line   429

difference quotient   429   second derivative   453

differentiation   445   slope of a curve   436

half-open interval   424   tangent line   436

horizontal asymptote   420   vertical asymptote   422

IMPORTANT FORMULAS

$$\frac{\Delta y}{\Delta x} = \frac{f(x + \Delta x) - f(x)}{\Delta x} \qquad \text{Difference quotient} \qquad (11.5)$$

$$\frac{dy}{dx} = \lim_{\Delta x \to 0} \frac{f(x + \Delta x) - f(x)}{\Delta x} \qquad \text{Derivative} \qquad (11.7)$$

Rules of Differentiation

1 If $f(x) = c$, $f'(x) = 0$ (Constant function)

2 If $f(x) = x^n$, $f'(x) = nx^{n-1}$ (Power rule)

3 If $f(x) = c \cdot g(x)$, $f'(x) = c \cdot g'(x)$ (Constant times a function)

4 If $f(x) = u(x) \pm v(x)$, $f'(x) = u'(x) \pm v'(x)$ (Sum or difference)

5   If $f(x) = u(x)v(x)$, $f'(x) = u'(x)v(x) + v'(x)u(x)$ **(Product rule)**

6   If $f(x) = u(x)/v(x)$, $f'(x) = \dfrac{v(x)u'(x) - u(x)v'(x)}{[v(x)]^2}$ **(Quotient rule)**

7   If $f(x) = [u(x)]^n$, $f'(x) = n[u(x)]^{n-1}u'(x)$ **(Power of a function)**

8   $\dfrac{dy}{dx} = \dfrac{dy}{du}\dfrac{du}{dx}$ **(Chain rule)**

9   $\dfrac{dx}{dy} = \dfrac{1}{dy/dx}$ $\dfrac{dy}{dx} \neq 0$ **(Inverse-function rule)**

10   If $f(x) = u(x) \cdot v(x) \cdot w(x)$, $f'(x) = u'(x)v(x)w(x)$
$\qquad\qquad + v'(x)u(x)w(x) + w'(x)u(x)v(x)$

(Three-factor product rule)

11   If $y = f(u)$, where $u = g(v)$ and $v = h(x)$
$$\frac{dy}{dx} = \frac{dy}{du} \cdot \frac{du}{dv} \cdot \frac{dv}{dx}$$ **(Chain rule extended)**

ADDITIONAL EXERCISES x^2

Exercises 1 to 18 are related to Sect. 11.1
For the following exercises, find the indicated limit if it exists.

1   $\lim\limits_{x \to 3}\left[x^2\left(4x - 2 + \dfrac{1}{x}\right)\right]$

2   $\lim\limits_{x \to 1} \dfrac{x^5 - 2x + 6}{x^4 - 6x}$

3   $\lim\limits_{x \to 5} \dfrac{2x^2 + 7x - 15}{x + 5}$

4   $\lim\limits_{x \to -1} (x^5 + x^4 + x^3 + x^2 + x + 1)$

5   $\lim\limits_{x \to -2} \dfrac{x^2 - 3}{x + 3}$

6   $\lim\limits_{x \to -3} \dfrac{2x^2 + x - 15}{x + 3}$

7   $\lim\limits_{x \to \infty} \dfrac{1}{x - 5}$

8   $\lim\limits_{x \to -\infty} \dfrac{-x^2 + 1}{x + 1}$

9   $\lim\limits_{x \to \infty} \dfrac{5x^3 + 2x^2 + 1}{x^2 - x + 7}$

10   $\lim\limits_{x \to -\infty} \dfrac{2x + 1}{x}$

11   $\lim\limits_{x \to -\infty} \dfrac{4x - 5}{-x + 3}$

12   $\lim\limits_{x \to \infty} \dfrac{1/x}{1/2x}$

In the following exercises, determine whether there are any discontinuities and, if so, where they occur.

13   $f(x) = x^7/(x^2 - 1)$

14   $f(x) = (x^2 - 9)/(16 - x^4)$

15   $f(x) = |x^2 - 3x + 2|$

16   $f(x) = (x^2 - 9)/(16 - x^4)$

17   $f(x) = \begin{cases} 2/x^2 & \text{if } x \neq 6 \\ 10 & \text{if } x = 6 \end{cases}$

18   $f(x) = \begin{cases} x^2 - 5 & \text{if } x > 5 \\ -x^2 & \text{if } x < 5 \end{cases}$

Exercises 19 to 33 are related to Sec. 11.2.
For each of the following functions, determine the average rate of change in the value of y in moving from $x = 1$ to $x = 4$.

19   $y = f(x) = x^2 + 2x - 3$

20   $y = f(x) = x^3 - 3x^2 + 1$

21   $y = f(x) = (x - 1)/(1 - x^2)$ 22 $y = f(x) = -x^3$

23   The population of a city has increased annually as indicated in the following table.

YEAR	POPULATION (IN MILLIONS)
1970	2.55
1971	2.70
1972	2.80
1973	2.88
1974	2.90
1975	3.01

At what average rate did the population change between 1970 and 1975? Between 1971 and 1973?

For the following exercises, (a) determine the general expression for the difference quotient and (b) use the difference quotient to compute the slope of the secant line connecting points at $x = 1$ and $x = 2$.

24   $f(x) = -3x^2 + 5x$ 25 $f(x) = -3/x$
26   $f(x) = -10$ 27 $f(x) = 2x - 5$
28   $f(x) = 2x^2 - x + 3$ 29 $f(x) = x^2/4$
*30 $f(x) = x^3 - 1$ *31 $f(x) = 10/x$
*32 $f(x) = ax + b$ *33 $f(x) = ax^2 + bx + c$

Exercises 34 to 39 are related to Sec. 11.3.

For the following functions, (a) find the derivative using the limit approach and (b) determine any values of x for which the slope equals 0.

34   $f(x) = -3x^2 + 5x$ 35 $f(x) = -3/x$
36   $f(x) = cx^2$ 37 $f(x) = -4x^2$
*38 $f(x) = x^4$ *39 $f(x) = x^4 - 4x$

Exercises 40 to 59 are related to Sec. 11.4.

For the following exercises, find the derivative.

40   $f(x) = 11/13$ 41 $f(x) = 25x - 15$
42   $f(x) = 3(x - 1/x)$ 43 $f(x) = 15x/(1 - x^2)$
44   $f(x) = 12x^4 - 5x^3 + 100$ 45 $f(x) = 5x^3/3 + 2x^2$
46   $f(x) = (x^3 - 1)^4$ 47 $f(x) = \sqrt{x^7}$
48   $f(x) = 1/\sqrt[3]{x}$ 49 $f(x) = x^2/\sqrt{x}$
50   $f(x) = \sqrt{x^3 - 2x^2 + 10}$ 51 $f(x) = (x - 7)(x^3 - 3x^2 + 2x)$
52   $f(x) = 8x^2/(7 - x^3)$ 53 $f(x) = (9 - x^2)(x + 3)^4$
54   $f(x) = 7/\sqrt{x - 1}$ 55 $f(x) = (3x^2 - 4x + 5)/(1 - x)$
*56 $f(x) = [(x - 5)\sqrt{x + 4}]/(1 - x)$ *57 $f(x) = [(x^2 + 3)/(4 - x)]^3$
*58 $f(x) = (x\sqrt{x^2 + 7})^{1/2}$ *59 $f(x) = [(x^2)^3]^4/(x^3)^2$

Exercises 60 to 72 are related to Sec. 11.5.

For the following exercises, find (a) $f''(x)$ and (b) $f''(2)$.

60   $f(x) = 45$ 61 $f(x) = 30 - 5x$
62   $f(x) = x^2 - 20x$ 63 $f(x) = 5x^3 - 4x^2 + x - 25$
64   $f(x) = (x^2 - 5)/x^3$ 65 $f(x) = (x^2 + 3x)^{1/2}$
66   $f(x) = \frac{1}{2}(10 - x^3)^{1/4}$ 67 $f(x) = ax^2 + bx + c$

68   A ball thrown upward from the roof of a building which is 900 feet high will be at a height of h feet after t seconds as described by the function

$$h = f(t) = -16t^2 + 80t + 900$$

(*a*) What is the height of the ball after 4 seconds?
(*b*) What is the velocity of the ball after 4 seconds?
(*c*) What is the acceleration of the ball at $t = 0$? At $t = 4$?

For the following exercises, find all higher-order derivatives.

69   $f(x) = x^5 - 5x^2$ 70 $f(x) = 4x^3 - 5x^2 + 3x + 50$
71   $f(x) = (x - 15)^5$ 72 $f(x) = (ax - b)^3$

Exercises 73 to 87 are related to Sec. 11.6.
For the following exercises, find dy/dx.

73   $y = f(u) = u^3 - 4$ and $u = g(x) = x^3$
74   $y = f(u) = (2u + 3)^2$ and $u = g(x) = 2x + 3$
75   $y = f(u) = u^{1/3}$ and $u = g(x) = x^2 + 2$

76   $y = f(u) = \dfrac{5u + 1}{2 - u}$ and $u = g(x) = x^2$

77   $y = f(u) = \sqrt{u^2 + 3u}$ and $u = g(x) = \dfrac{1}{x}$

For the following exercises, find dx/dy and state the values for which dx/dy is not defined.

78   $y = f(x) = 2x^3 + 4x^2 - 3x/2 + 1$ 79 $y = f(x) = 3x^4 - 5x^2$
80   $y = f(x) = ax^2 + bx + c$ 81 $y = f(x) = ax^3 + bx^2 + cx + d$

For the following exercises, find dy/dx.

*82 $y = f(x) = x^2(5 - x^2)^{1/4}(x - 4)^4$
*83 $y = f(x) = \sqrt{x - 1}(x^3 + 5)(x + 1)^3$
*84 $y = f(x) = (x + 20)^2(x^2 - 3)^3/x^2$
*85 $y = f(u) = u - 5$, where $u = g(v) = 3v^2$ and $v = h(x) = 3x - 1$
*86 $y = f(u) = 3u^2 - u + 5$, where $u = g(v) = v + 3$ and $v = h(x) = 3x^3$
*87 $y = f(u) = u^{3}$, where $u = g(v) = \sqrt{v}$ and $v = h(x) = x^2 - 4$

CHAPTER TEST

1   Determine

(*a*) $\lim\limits_{x \to 3} \dfrac{x^2 - x - 6}{x - 3}$

(*b*) $\lim\limits_{x \to \infty} \dfrac{4}{(2x - 1)/x}$

2   Determine whether there are any discontinuities on f and, if so, where they occur if

$$f(x) = \dfrac{x^2 - 25}{4x^2 - 2x + 5}$$

3 Determine dy/dx using the limit approach if

$$f(x) = -3x^2 + x + 10$$

4 Find $f'(x)$ if

(a) $f(x) = 4/\sqrt[5]{x^2}$
(b) $f(x) = x^8 - 7x^4 - x^2 + 9$
(c) $f(x) = (12 - x^2)/(x^3 + 5)^2$

5 Given $f(x) = 5x^2 - 5x - 35$, determine the locations of any points on the graph of $f(x)$ where the slope equals $+5$.

6 Find all higher-order derivatives of f if

$$f(x) = \frac{x^3}{3} - \frac{4x^2}{2} + 5x - 1$$

7 Find dy/dx if

$$y = f(u) = u^4 - 2u \qquad \text{and} \qquad u = g(x) = x^2 - 15$$

8 Find dx/dy if $f(x) = 10x - 15$.

APPENDIX:
PROOFS OF SELECTED RULES
OF DIFFERENTIATION

The first proof is a "partial" proof in that it proves Rule 2 when n is a positive integer. The proof of this rule for all other values of n is beyond the scope of this text.

RULE 2 MODIFIED

If $f(x) = x^n$, where n is a positive integer, then $f'(x) = nx^{n-1}$.

PROOF

$$f(x) = x^n$$
$$f(x + \Delta x) = (x + \Delta x)^n$$
$$f(x + \Delta x) - f(x) = (x + \Delta x)^n - x^n$$

By the *binomial theorem*, for $n =$ a positive integer,

$$(x + \Delta x)^n = x^n + nx^{n-1}(\Delta x) + \frac{n(n - 1)}{2} x^{n-2}(\Delta x)^2 + \cdots + (\Delta x)^n$$

Substituting into $f(x + \Delta x) - f(x)$ yields

$$f(x + \Delta x) - f(x) = x^n + nx^{n-1}(\Delta x) + \frac{n(n - 1)}{2} x^{n-2}(\Delta x)^2$$

$$+ \cdots + (\Delta x)^n - x^n$$

Dividing by Δx and taking the limit as $\Delta x \to 0$, we get

$$\lim_{\Delta x \to 0} \frac{f(x + \Delta x) - f(x)}{\Delta x} = \lim_{\Delta x \to 0} \left[x^n + nx^{n-1}\Delta x + \frac{n(n-1)}{2} x^{n-2}(\Delta x)^2 \right. $$
$$\left. + \cdots + (\Delta x)^n - x^n \right] \bigg/ \Delta x$$

$$= \lim_{\Delta x \to 0} \left[nx^{n-1} + \frac{n(n-1)}{2} x^{n-2}(\Delta x) \right. $$
$$\left. + \cdots + (\Delta x)^{n-1} \right]$$

or

$$f'(x) = nx^{n-1}$$

RULE 3

If $f(x) = c \cdot g(x)$, where c is a constant and g is a differentiable function, then $f'(x) = c \cdot g'(x)$.

PROOF

$$f(x) = c \cdot g(x)$$
$$f(x + \Delta x) = c \cdot g(x + \Delta x)$$
$$f(x + \Delta x) - f(x) = c \cdot g(x + \Delta x) - c \cdot g(x)$$
$$= c[g(x + \Delta x) - g(x)]$$
$$\frac{f(x + \Delta x) - f(x)}{\Delta x} = \frac{c[g(x + \Delta x) - g(x)]}{\Delta x}$$
$$= c \frac{g(x + \Delta x) - g(x)}{\Delta x}$$
$$\lim_{\Delta x \to 0} \frac{f(x + \Delta x) - f(x)}{\Delta x} = \lim_{\Delta x \to 0} c \frac{g(x + \Delta x) - g(x)}{\Delta x}$$
$$= c \cdot \lim_{\Delta x \to 0} \frac{g(x + \Delta x) - g(x)}{\Delta x}$$

or

$$f'(x) = c \cdot g'(x)$$

RULE 4

If $f(x) = u(x) \pm v(x)$, where u and v are differentiable, then $f'(x) = u'(x) \pm v'(x)$. The proof presented is for the "sum" of $u(x)$ and $v(x)$.

PROOF

$$f(x) = u(x) + v(x)$$
$$f(x + \Delta x) = u(x + \Delta x) + v(x + \Delta x)$$
$$f(x + \Delta x) - f(x) = [u(x + \Delta x) + v(x + \Delta x)] - [u(x) + v(x)]$$
$$\frac{f(x + \Delta x) - f(x)}{\Delta x} = \frac{[u(x + \Delta x) + v(x + \Delta x)] - [u(x) + v(x)]}{\Delta x}$$
$$= \left[\frac{u(x + \Delta x) - u(x)}{\Delta x} + \frac{v(x + \Delta x) - v(x)}{\Delta x} \right]$$

$$\lim_{\Delta x \to 0} \frac{f(x + \Delta x) - f(x)}{\Delta x} = \lim_{\Delta x \to 0} \left[\frac{u(x + \Delta x) - u(x)}{\Delta x} + \frac{v(x + \Delta x) - v(x)}{\Delta x} \right]$$

$$= \lim_{\Delta x \to 0} \frac{u(x + \Delta x) - u(x)}{\Delta x} + \lim_{\Delta x \to 0} \frac{v(x + \Delta x) - v(x)}{\Delta x}$$

or
$$f'(x) = u'(x) + v'(x)$$

RULE 5

If $f(x) = u(x) \cdot v(x)$, where u and v are differentiable, then

$$f'(x) = u'(x) \cdot v(x) + v'(x) \cdot u(x)$$

PROOF

$$f(x) = u(x) \cdot v(x)$$
$$f(x + \Delta x) = u(x + \Delta x) \cdot v(x + \Delta x)$$
$$f(x + \Delta x) - f(x) = u(x + \Delta x) \cdot v(x + \Delta x) - u(x) \cdot v(x)$$

Adding *and* subtracting the quantity $u(x + \Delta x) \cdot v(x)$ to the right side gives

$$f(x + \Delta x) - f(x) = u(x + \Delta x) \cdot v(x + \Delta x) - u(x + \Delta x) \cdot v(x)$$
$$+ u(x + \Delta x) \cdot v(x) - u(x)v(x)$$
$$= u(x + \Delta x)[v(x + \Delta x) - v(x)]$$
$$+ v(x)[u(x + \Delta x) - u(x)]$$

$$\frac{f(x + \Delta x) - f(x)}{\Delta x} = \frac{u(x + \Delta x)[v(x + \Delta x) - v(x)] + v(x)[u(x + \Delta x) - u(x)]}{\Delta x}$$

$$= u(x + \Delta x) \frac{v(x + \Delta x) - v(x)}{\Delta x} + v(x) \frac{u(x + \Delta x) - u(x)}{\Delta x}$$

$$\lim_{\Delta x \to 0} \frac{f(x + \Delta x) - f(x)}{\Delta x} = \lim_{\Delta x \to 0} u(x + \Delta x) \frac{v(x + \Delta x) - v(x)}{\Delta x}$$

$$+ \lim_{\Delta x \to 0} v(x) \frac{u(x + \Delta x) - u(x)}{\Delta x}$$

$$= \lim_{\Delta x \to 0} u(x + \Delta x) \cdot \lim_{\Delta x \to 0} \frac{v(x + \Delta x) - v(x)}{\Delta x}$$

$$+ \lim_{\Delta x \to 0} v(x) \cdot \lim_{\Delta x \to 0} \frac{u(x + \Delta x) - u(x)}{\Delta x}$$

or
$$f'(x) = u(x) \cdot v'(x) + v(x) \cdot u'(x)$$
$$= v'(x) \cdot u(x) + u'(x) \cdot v(x)$$

RULE 6

If $f(x) = u(x)/v(x)$, where u and v are differentiable and $v(x) \neq 0$, then

$$f'(x) = \frac{v(x) \cdot u'(x) - u(x) \cdot v'(x)}{[v(x)]^2}$$

PROOF

$$f(x) = \frac{u(x)}{v(x)}$$

$$f(x + \Delta x) = \frac{u(x + \Delta x)}{v(x + \Delta x)}$$

$$f(x + \Delta x) - f(x) = \frac{u(x + \Delta x)}{v(x + \Delta x)} - \frac{u(x)}{v(x)}$$

which can be rewritten as

$$f(x + \Delta x) - f(x) = \frac{u(x + \Delta x) \cdot v(x) - u(x) \cdot v(x + \Delta x)}{v(x + \Delta x) \cdot v(x)}$$

Adding *and* subtracting the quantity $[u(x)v(x)]/[v(x + \Delta x)v(x)]$ yields

$$f(x + \Delta x) - f(x) = \frac{u(x + \Delta x) \cdot v(x) - u(x) \cdot v(x + \Delta x)}{v(x + \Delta x) \cdot v(x)}$$

$$+ \frac{u(x) \cdot v(x)}{v(x + \Delta x) \cdot v(x)} - \frac{u(x) \cdot v(x)}{v(x + \Delta x) \cdot v(x)}$$

Rearranging gives

$$f(x + \Delta x) - f(x) = \frac{u(x + \Delta x) \cdot v(x) - u(x) \cdot v(x) - v(x + \Delta x) \cdot u(x) + u(x) \cdot v(x)}{v(x + \Delta x) \cdot v(x)}$$

$$= \frac{v(x)[u(x + \Delta x) - u(x)] - u(x)[v(x + \Delta x) - v(x)]}{v(x + \Delta x) \cdot v(x)}$$

$$\frac{f(x + \Delta x) - f(x)}{\Delta x} = \frac{v(x)[u(x + \Delta x) - u(x)] - u(x)[v(x + \Delta x) - v(x)]}{v(x + \Delta x) \cdot v(x)} \bigg/ \Delta x$$

$$= \frac{v(x)\dfrac{u(x + \Delta x) - u(x)}{\Delta x} - u(x)\dfrac{v(x + \Delta x) - v(x)}{\Delta x}}{v(x + \Delta x) \cdot v(x)}$$

$$\lim_{\Delta x \to 0} \frac{f(x + \Delta x) - f(x)}{\Delta x}$$

$$= \lim_{\Delta x \to 0} \frac{v(x)\dfrac{u(x + \Delta x) - u(x)}{\Delta x} - u(x)\dfrac{v(x + \Delta x) - v(x)}{\Delta x}}{v(x + \Delta x) \cdot v(x)}$$

$$= \frac{\lim\limits_{\Delta x \to 0} v(x) \cdot \lim\limits_{\Delta x \to 0} \dfrac{u(x + \Delta x) - u(x)}{\Delta x} - \lim\limits_{\Delta x \to 0} u(x) \cdot \lim\limits_{\Delta x \to 0} \dfrac{v(x + \Delta x) - v(x)}{\Delta x}}{\lim\limits_{\Delta x \to 0} v(x + \Delta x) \cdot \lim\limits_{\Delta x \to 0} v(x)}$$

or

$$f'(x) = \frac{v(x) \cdot u'(x) - u(x) \cdot v'(x)}{v(x) \cdot v(x)}$$

$$= \frac{v(x) \cdot u'(x) - u(x) \cdot v'(x)}{[v(x)]^2}$$

12

OPTIMIZATION: METHODOLOGY

12.1 DERIVATIVES: ADDITIONAL INTERPRETATIONS	12.4 CURVE SKETCHING
12.2 IDENTIFICATION OF MAXIMA AND MINIMA	KEY TERMS AND CONCEPTS
	ADDITIONAL EXERCISES
12.3 RESTRICTED-DOMAIN CONSIDERATIONS	CHAPTER TEST

CHAPTER OBJECTIVES

■ Enhance understanding of the meaning of first and second derivatives

■ Reinforce understanding of the nature of concavity

■ Provide a methodology for determining optimization conditions for mathematical functions

■ Illustrate methods for sketching the general shape of mathematical functions

In this chapter the tools developed in Chap. 11 will be extended. We will further our understanding of the first and second derivatives. We will see how these derivatives can be useful in describing the behavior of mathematical functions. A major objective of the chapter is to develop a method for determining where a function achieves maximum or minimum values. We will discuss calculus-based *optimization* procedures used to locate maximum and minimum values of a function. Finally, we will examine an approach which can facilitate the sketching of functions.

12.1 DERIVATIVES: ADDITIONAL INTERPRETATIONS

In this section we will continue to expand our understanding of derivatives.

The First Derivative

As mentioned in the last chapter, the first derivative represents the instantaneous rate of change in $f(x)$ with respect to a change in x.

DEFINITION: INCREASING FUNCTION

The function f is said to be an ***increasing function*** on an interval I if for any x_1 and x_2 within the interval, $x_1 < x_2$ implies that $f(x_1) < f(x_2)$.*

---

* Technically speaking, these are definitions for *strictly* increasing (decreasing) functions.

Increasing functions can also be identified by slope conditions. *If the first derivative of f is positive throughout an interval, then the slope is positive and f is an increasing function on the interval.* That is, at any point within the interval, a slight increase in the value of x will be accompanied by an increase in the value of $f(x)$. The curves in Fig. 12.1a and Fig. 12.1b are the graphs of increasing functions of x because the tangent slope at any point is positive.

DEFINITION: DECREASING FUNCTION

The function f is said to a **decreasing function** on an interval I if for any x_1 and x_2 within the interval, $x_1 < x_2$ implies that $f(x_1) > f(x_2)$.*

As with increasing functions, decreasing functions can be identified by tangent slope conditions. *If the first derivative of f is negative throughout an interval, then the slope is negative and f is a decreasing function on the interval.* That is, at any point within the interval a slight increase in the value of x will be accompanied by a decrease in the value of $f(x)$. The curves in Fig. 12.1c and d are the graphs of decreasing functions of x.

---

* Technically speaking, the last two definitions are for *strictly* increasing (decreasing) functions.

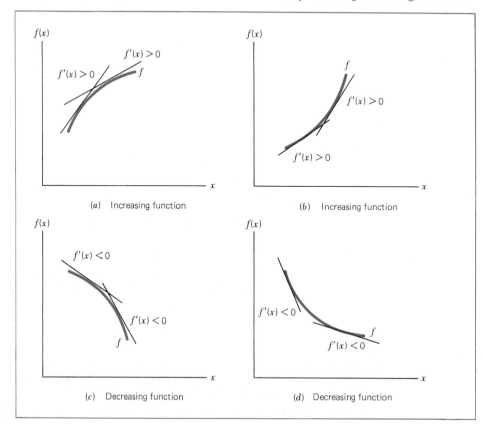

(a)   Increasing function

(b)   Increasing function

(c)   Decreasing function

(d)   Decreasing function

FIGURE 12.1

NOTE

If a function is increasing (decreasing) on an interval, the function is increasing (decreasing) at every point within the interval.

EXAMPLE 1

Given $f(x) = 5x^2 - 20x + 3$, determine the intervals over which f can be described as (a) an increasing function, (b) a decreasing function, and (c) neither increasing or decreasing.

SOLUTION

To determine whether f is increasing or decreasing, we should first find f':

$$f'(x) = 10x - 20$$

f will be an increasing function when $f'(x) > 0$, or when

$$10x - 20 > 0$$
or
$$10x > 20$$
or
$$x > 2$$

f will be a decreasing function when $f'(x) < 0$, or when

$$10x - 20 < 0$$
or
$$10x < 20$$
or
$$x < 2$$

f will be neither increasing or decreasing when $f'(x) = 0$, or when

$$10x - 20 = 0$$
or
$$10x = 20$$
or
$$x = 2$$

Summarizing, f is a decreasing function when $x < 2$, neither increasing or decreasing at $x = 2$, and an increasing function when $x > 2$. Sketch the graph of f to see if these conclusions seem reasonable.

The Second Derivative

The second derivative is the derivative of the first derivative. Although we will almost always use $f''(x)$ to represent the second derivative, we might express it using the notation

$$\frac{d^2y}{dx^2}$$

The second derivative is a measure of the instantaneous rate of change in dy/dx with respect to a change in x. In other words, it indicates the rate at which the slope of the function is changing with respect to a change in x—whether the slope of the function is increasing or decreasing at a particular instant.

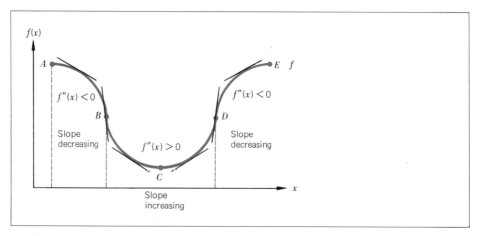

FIGURE 12.2

If f"(x) is negative on an interval I of f, the first derivative is decreasing on I. Graphically, the slope is decreasing in value on the interval. If f"(x) is positive on an interval I of f, the first derivative is increasing on I. Graphically, the slope is increasing on the interval.

Examine Fig. 12.2. Either mentally construct tangent lines or lay a straight-edge on the curve to represent the tangent line at various points. Along the curve from A to B the slope is slightly negative near A and becomes more and more negative as we get closer to B. In fact, the slope of the tangent line goes from a value of 0 at A to its most negative value at point B. Thus the slope is decreasing in value over the interval between A and B, and we would expect $f"(x)$ to be negative on this interval (that is, $f"(x) < 0$).

Having reached its most negative value at point B, the slope continues to be negative on the interval between B and C; but the slope becomes less and less negative, eventually equaling 0 at C. If the slope assumes values which are becoming *less negative* (for example, $-5, -4, -3, -2, -1, 0$), the slope is increasing in value. As such, we would expect $f"(x)$ to be positive on this interval (that is, $f"(x) > 0$).

Between C and D the slope becomes more and more positive assuming its largest positive value at D. Since the slope is increasing in value on this interval, we would expect $f"(x)$ to be positive.

Between D and E the slope continues to be positive, but it is becoming less and less positive, eventually equaling 0 at E. If the slope is assuming values which are positive but becoming smaller (for example, $5, 4, 3, 2, 1, 0$), it is decreasing in value and we would expect $f"(x)$ to be negative on the interval.

Figure 12.3 summarizes the first- and second-derivative conditions for the four regions of the function. These relationships can be difficult to understand. Take your time studying these figures and retrace the logic if necessary.

Concavity and Inflection Points

In Chap. 10 the notion of concavity was briefly introduced. A more formal definition of concavity follows.

DEFINITION: CONCAVITY

The graph of a function f is **concave up (down)** on an interval if f' increases (decreases) on the entire interval.

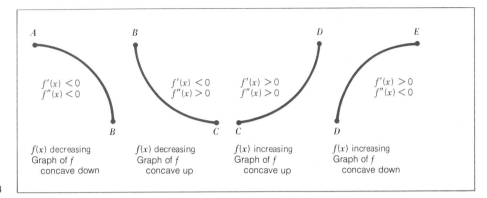

FIGURE 12.3

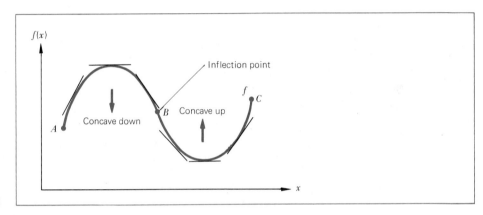

FIGURE 12.4

This definition suggests that the graph of a function is concave up on an interval if the slope *increases* over the entire interval. For any point within such an interval *the curve representing f will lie above the tangent line drawn at the point.* Similarly, the graph of a function is concave down on an interval if the slope *decreases* over the entire interval. For any point within such an interval *the curve representing f will lie below the tangent line drawn at the point.*

In Fig. 12.4 the graph of f is *concave down* between A and B, and it is *concave up* between B and C. Note that between A and B the curve lies below its tangent lines and between B and C the curve lies above its tangent lines. Point B is where the concavity changes from concave down to concave up. A point at which the concavity changes is called an ***inflection point.*** Thus, point B is an inflection point.

There are relationships between the second derivative and the concavity of the graph of a function which are going to be of considerable value later in this chapter. These relationships are as follows:

RELATIONSHIPS BETWEEN CONCAVITY
AND THE SECOND DERIVATIVE

I If $f''(x) < 0$ on an interval $a \le x \le b$, the graph of f is *concave down* over that interval. For any point $x = c$ within the interval, f is said to be concave down at $[c, f(c)]$.

II If $f''(x) > 0$ on any interval $a \le x \le b$, the graph of f is *con-*

cave up over that interval. For any point $x = c$ within the interval, f is said to be concave up at $[c, f(c)]$.

III If $f''(x) = 0$ at any point $x = c$ in the domain of f, no conclusion can be drawn about the concavity at $[c, f(c)]$.

Be very careful not to reverse the logic of these relationships! Because of relationship III we *cannot* make statements about the sign of the second derivative knowing the concavity of the graph of a function. For example, we cannot state that if the graph of a function is concave down at $x = a$, $f''(a) < 0$.

EXAMPLE 2

To determine the concavity of the graph of the generalized quadratic function $f(x) = ax^2 + bx + c$, let's find the first and second derivatives.

$$f'(x) = 2ax + b \qquad \text{and} \qquad f''(x) = 2a$$

If $a > 0$, then $f''(x) = 2a > 0$. From relationship II, the graph of f is concave up whenever $a > 0$. If $a < 0$, then $f''(x) = 2a < 0$. From relationship I, the graph of f is concave down whenever $a < 0$. This is entirely consistent with our discussions in Chap. 10 which concluded that if $a > 0$, f graphs as a parabola which is concave up. And, if $a < 0$, f graphs as a parabola which is concave down.

EXAMPLE 3

For $f(x) = x^3 - 2x^2 + x - 1$ determine the concavity of the graph of f at $x = -2$ and $x = 3$.

SOLUTION

$$f'(x) = 3x^2 - 4x + 1$$
and
$$f''(x) = 6x - 4$$

Evaluating $f''(x)$ at $x = -2$ gives

$$f''(-2) = 6(-2) - 4 = -16$$

Since $f''(-2) < 0$, the graph of f is concave down at $x = -2$. To determine the concavity at $x = 3$, we find

$$f''(3) = 6(3) - 4 = 14$$

Since $f''(3) > 0$, the graph of f is concave up at $x = 3$.

EXAMPLE 4

Determine the concavity of the graph of $f(x) = x^4$ at $x = 0$.

SOLUTION

$$f'(x) = 4x^3$$
$$f''(x) = 12x^2$$
$$f''(0) = 12(0)^2 = 0$$

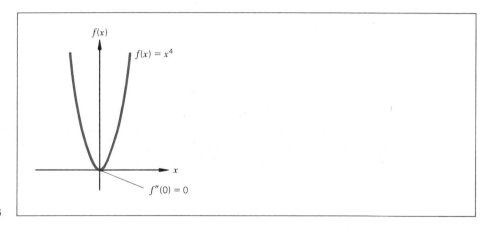

FIGURE 12.5

Because $f''(0) = 0$, according to relationship III we can make no statement about the concavity at $x = 0$. However, substituting a sufficient number of values for x into f and plotting these ordered pairs, we see that f has the shape shown in Fig. 12.5. And from this sketch it is obvious that the graph is concave up at $x = 0$.

At times we may have a need to locate points of inflection on the graph of a function. *A necessary condition (something which must be true) for the existence of an inflection point at $x = a$ is that $f''(a) = 0$.* That is, by finding all values of x for which $f''(x) = 0$, you will identify *candidate locations* for inflection points.* For many functions, all values satisfying this condition will, in fact, be inflection points. For some functions, such as $f(x) = x^4$ in the last example, the condition $f''(a) = 0$ does not guarantee that an inflection point exists at $x = a$.

Therefore a practical test to identify inflection points is the following:

A TEST FOR INFLECTION POINTS

I Find all points a where $f''(a) = 0$.
II If $f''(x)$ changes sign when passing through $x = a$, there is an inflection point at $x = a$.

The essence of this test is to choose points slightly to the left and right of $x = a$ and determine if the concavity is different on each side. If $f''(x)$ is positive to the left and negative to the right, or vice versa, an inflection point exists at $x = a$.

EXAMPLE 5

To verify that an inflection point does *not* exist at $x = 0$ for $f(x) = x^4$, $f''(x)$ is evaluated to the left at $x = -0.1$ and to the right at $x = +0.1$.

$$f''(-0.1) = 12(-0.1)^2$$
$$= 0.12 > 0$$

---

* Other candidates for inflection points occur where $f''(x)$ is discontinuous. However, we will not encounter such candidates in this book.

and
$$f''(+0.1) = 12(+0.1)^2$$
$$= 0.12 > 0$$

Since the second derivative has the same sign to the left and right of $x = 0$, there is no inflection point at $x = 0$.

EXAMPLE 6

To determine the location(s) of all inflection points on the graph of

$$f(x) = \frac{x^4}{12} - \frac{x^3}{2} + x^2 + 10$$

we find

$$f'(x) = \frac{4x^3}{12} - \frac{3x^2}{2} + 2x$$

$$= \frac{x^3}{3} - \frac{3x^2}{2} + 2x$$

and
$$f''(x) = \frac{3x^2}{3} - \frac{6x}{2} + 2$$

$$= x^2 - 3x + 2$$

Next, $f''(x)$ is set equal to 0 in order to find candidate locations:

$$x^2 - 3x + 2 = 0$$

or
$$(x - 1)(x - 2) = 0$$

Therefore, $f''(x) = 0$ when $x = 1$ and $x = 2$. For $x = 1$, $f''(x)$ is evaluated to the left and right of $x = 1$ at $x = 0.9$ and $x = 1.1$.

$$f''(0.9) = 0.11 > 0$$
$$f''(1.1) = -0.09 < 0$$

Since the sign of $f''(x)$ changes, an inflection point exists at $x = 1$. Values of $x = 1.9$ and $x = 2.1$ are chosen for evaluating $f''(x)$ to the left and right of $x = 2$.

$$f''(1.9) = -0.09 < 0$$
$$f''(2.1) = 0.11 > 0$$

Because $f''(x)$ changes sign, we conclude that an inflection point also exists at $x = 2$.

Concavity from a Different Perspective

We will use the terms "concave up" and "concave down" to describe the curvature attribute which we call concavity. Other terminology may be used to describe this attribute. For example, many writers distinguish between *strictly concave functions* and *strictly convex functions*.

DEFINITION: STRICTLY CONCAVE (CONVEX) FUNCTION

A function which is strictly concave (convex) has the following graphical property: Given any two points A and B which lie on

> the curve representing the function, if the two points are connected by a straight line, the entire line segment AB will lie below (above) the curve except at points A and B.

This definition can be loosened somewhat to define a *concave function* and a *convex function* (as opposed to *strictly* concave (convex) functions). If the line segment AB is allowed to lie below (above) the curve, *or to lie on the curve*, the function is termed a concave (convex) function. Figure 12.6 illustrates these definitions.

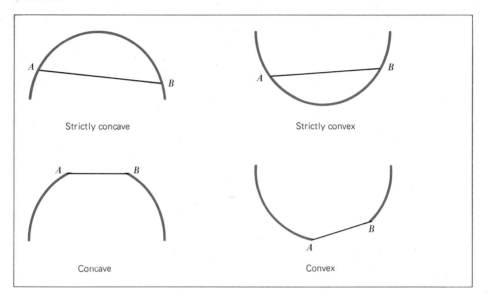

FIGURE 12.6
Concave and convex functions.

Section 12.1 Follow-up Exercises

For each of the following functions, (a) determine whether f is increasing or decreasing at $x = 1$. Determine the values of x for which f is (b) an increasing function, (c) a decreasing function, and (d) neither increasing nor decreasing.

1 $f(x) = 20 - 4x$ 2 $f(x) = 5x - 15$
3 $f(x) = x^2 - 5x + 20$ 4 $f(x) = 3x^2 - 7x - 9$
5 $f(x) = x^3/3 - x^2/2$ 6 $f(x) = x^3/3 - x^2/2 - 6x + 10$
7 $f(x) = x^4 - 2x^2$ 8 $f(x) = 5x^5$
9 $f(x) = (x - 5)^{3/2}$ 10 $f(x) = 3x^2/(x^2 - 1)$

For each of the following functions, use $f''(x)$ to determine the concavity conditions at $x = -1$ and $x = +4$.

11 $f(x) = -4x^2 + 5x - 3$ 12 $f(x) = x^3 - 2x + 1$
13 $f(x) = x^6 - 4x^5 + 9$ 14 $f(x) = -x^3 + 5x$
15 $f(x) = \sqrt{x^3 - 10}$ 16 $f(x) = (x + 1)^5$
17 $f(x) = x^5 - 3x^2$ 18 $f(x) = x^3/(1 - x)$

If $a > 0$, $b > 0$, and $c > 0$, determine the values of x for which f is (a) increasing, (b) decreasing, (c) concave up, and (d) concave down, if

*19 $f(x) = ax + b$	*20 $f(x) = b - ax$
*21 $f(x) = ax^2 + bx + c$	*22 $f(x) = -ax^2 - bx - c$
*23 $f(x) = ax^3$	*24 $f(x) = ax^4$

For each of the following functions identify the locations of any inflection points.

25 $f(x) = x^3 - 9x^2$	26 $f(x) = -x^3 + 24x^2$
27 $f(x) = x^4/12 - x^3/3 - 7.5x^2$	28 $f(x) = (3 - x)^4$
29 $f(x) = (x - 5)^5$	30 $f(x) = x^5/20 - x^3/6 + 25$
31 $f(x) = -10x^4 + 100$	32 $f(x) = (x - 1)/x$

33   Given the function shown in Fig. 12.7, indicate the values of x for which f is (a) increasing, (b) decreasing, and (c) neither increasing or decreasing.

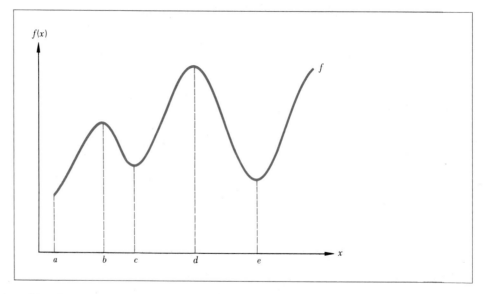

FIGURE 12.7

34   Given the function shown in Fig. 12.8, indicate the values of x for which f is (a) increasing, (b) decreasing, and (c) neither increasing or decreasing.

35   Given the function shown in Fig. 12.8, indicate the values of x for which f is (a) concave up, (b) concave down, (c) changing concavity, (d) concave, and (e) convex.

36   Given the function shown in Fig. 12.8, indicate the values of x for which f is (a) increasing at an increasing rate, (b) increasing at a decreasing rate, (c) decreasing at a decreasing rate, and (d) decreasing at an increasing rate.

12.2 IDENTIFICATION OF MAXIMA AND MINIMA

In applications of mathematics, a nonlinear function can represent some decision criterion. For example, a function may represent profit, revenue, cost, or pollution levels, stated as a function of a variable which is at least partially under the control of the decision maker. For instance, profit may be stated as a function of the number of dollars spent on advertising. If the decision maker can determine, within certain limits, how much to spend on advertising, a goal might be to determine the amount to spend so as to maximize profit. If x equals

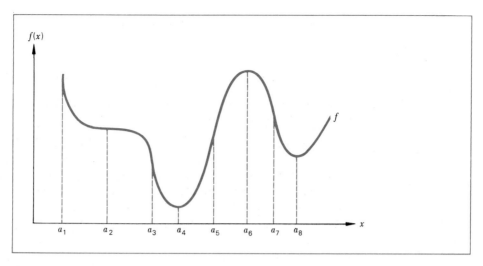

FIGURE 12.8

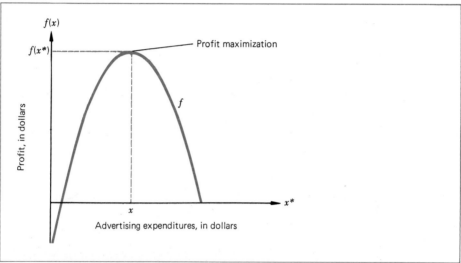

FIGURE 12.9
Profit =
f (advertisting
expenditures).

the number of dollars spent on advertising and $f(x)$ equals the associated profit, the graph of the profit function might have the general form shown in Fig. 12.9. If the decision maker desires to locate the greatest value of $f(x)$, it occurs at $[x^*, f(x^*)]$.

In this section we will examine functions with the purpose of locating maximum and minimum values.

Relative Extrema

DEFINITION: RELATIVE MAXIMUM

If f is defined on an interval (b, c) which contains $x = a$, f is said to reach a **relative (local) maximum** at $x = a$ if $f(a) \geq f(x)$ for all x within the interval (b, c).

DEFINITION: RELATIVE MINIMUM

If f is defined on an interval (b, c) which contains $x = a$, f is said to reach a **relative (local) minimum** at $x = a$ if $f(a) \le f(x)$ for all x within the interval (b, c).

Both definitions focus upon the value of $f(x)$ within an interval. A relative maximum refers to a point where the value of $f(x)$ is greater than the value of $f(x)$ for points which are nearby. A relative minimum refers to a point where the value of $f(x)$ is lower than the value of $f(x)$ for points which are nearby. If we use these definitions and examine Fig. 12.10, f has **relative maxima** at $x = a$ and $x = c$. Similarly, f has **relative minima** at $x = b$ and $x = d$. Collectively, relative maxima and minima are called **relative extrema**.

DEFINITION: ABSOLUTE MAXIMUM

A function f is said to reach an **absolute maximum** at $x = a$ if $f(a) > f(x)$ for any other x in the domain of f.

DEFINITION: ABSOLUTE MINIMUM

A function f is said to reach an **absolute minimum** at $x = a$ if $f(a) < f(x)$ for any other x in the domain of f.

If we refer again to Fig. 12.10, $f(x)$ reaches an absolute maximum at $x = c$. It reaches an absolute minimum at $x = b$. It should be noted that *a point on the graph of a function can be both a relative maximum (minimum) and an absolute maximum (minimum)*.

Critical Points

We will have a particular interest in relative maxima and minima. It will be important to know how to identify and distinguish between them.

NECESSARY CONDITIONS FOR RELATIVE MAXIMA (MINIMA)

Given the function f, necessary conditions for the existence of a relative maximum or minimum at $x = a$ (a contained in the domain of f) are

$$1.\ f'(a) = 0$$

or

$$2.\ f'(a) \text{ is undefined.}$$

Points which satisfy either of the conditions in this definition are *candidates* for, relative maxima (minima). Such points are often referred to as **critical points.** Points which satisfy condition 1 are those on the graph of f where the slope equals 0. The locations of these points are found by setting $f'(x)$ equal to 0 and solving for the values of x (if any exist) which satisfy the equation. Points satisfying condition 2 are exemplified by discontinuities on f or points where

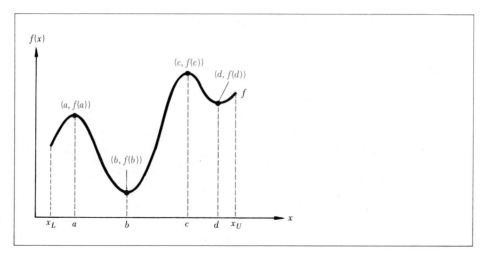

FIGURE 12.10
Relative extrema.

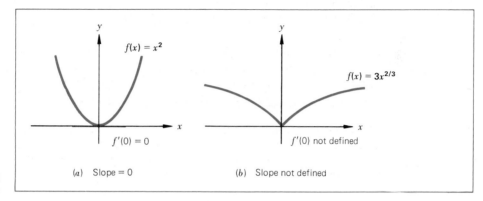

FIGURE 12.11
Critical points.

$f'(x)$ cannot be evaluated. Values of x in the domain of f which satisfy either condition 1 or condition 2 are called *critical values.* These are often denoted as x^* in order to distinguish them from other values of x. Given a critical value for f, the corresponding critical point is $[x^*, f(x^*)]$.

Figure 12.11 illustrates the graphs of two functions which have critical points at $(0, 0)$. For the function $f(x) = x^2$, shown in Fig. 12.11a, $f'(x) = 2x$ and a critical value occurs when $x = 0$. At the critical point $(0, 0)$ the slope equals 0 and the function achieves a relative minimum.

For the function $f(x) = 3x^{2/3}$, $f'(x) = 2/x^{1/3}$. Note that condition 1 can never be satisfied since there are no points where the tangent slope equals 0. However, a critical value of $x = 0$ exists according to condition 2. The derivative is undefined (there is no unique tangent line) at $x = 0$. However, $f(0)$ is defined and the critical point $(0, 0)$ is a relative minimum, as shown in Fig. 12.11b.

EXAMPLE 7

In order to determine the location(s) of any critical points on the graph of

$$f(x) = \frac{x^3}{3} - \frac{x^2}{2} - 6x + 100$$

the derivative f' is found.

$$f'(x) = \frac{3x^2}{3} - \frac{2x}{2} - 6$$

$$= x^2 - x - 6$$

If f' is set equal to 0,

$$x^2 - x - 6 = 0$$

when

$$(x - 3)(x + 2) = 0$$

When the two factors are set equal to 0, two critical values are $x = 3$ and $x = -2$. When these values are substituted into f, the resulting critical points are $(-2, 107\frac{1}{3})$ and $(3, 86\frac{1}{2})$.

The only statements we can make about the behavior of f at these points is that the slope equals 0. And furthermore, nowhere else on the graph of f is the slope equal to 0. Additional testing is necessary to determine whether there is a relative maximum or minimum at $x = 3$ and $x = -2$.

POINT FOR THOUGHT AND DISCUSSION

What comment can be made regarding the existence of critical points on constant functions [for example, $f(x) = 10$]?

Figure 12.12 illustrates different critical points where $f'(x) = 0$. Figures 12.12a and b illustrate relative maximum and minimum points, whereas Figs. 12.12c and d illustrate two different types of inflection points. In Fig. 12.12c the graph of the function has a slope of 0 at point a, and it is also changing from being concave down to concave up. In Fig. 12.12d the graph has a slope of 0 and is changing from being concave up to concave down.

In summary, any critical point where $f'(x) = 0$ will be a relative maximum, a relative minimum, or an inflection point.

POINT FOR THOUGHT AND DISCUSSION

For polynomial functions f of degree n, the largest possible number of critical points where $f'(x) = 0$ is $n - 1$. Thus, a function f of degree 5 can have *as many as* four points of zero slope. Why is this so?

The First Derivative Test

In an effort to locate relative maximum or minimum points, the first step is to locate all critical points on the graph of the function. Given that a critical point may be either a relative maximum or minimum or an inflection point, some test must be devised to distinguish among these. There are a number of tests available. One test which is easy to understand intuitively is the *first-derivative test.*

After the locations of critical points are identified, the first-derivative test requires an examination of slope conditions to the left and right of the critical point. Figure 12.13 illustrates the four critical point possibilities and their slope

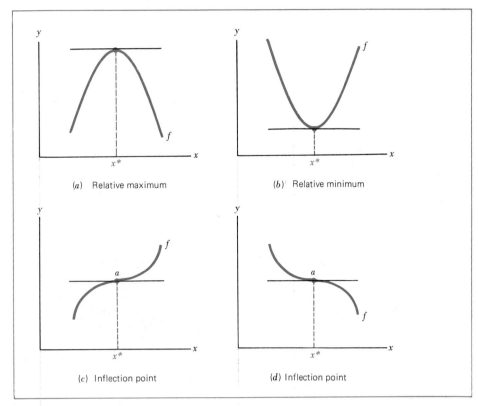

FIGURE 12.12
Critical points
where $f'(x) = 0$.

(a) Relative maximum

(b) Relative minimum

(c) Inflection point

(d) Inflection point

conditions to either side of x^*. *For a relative maximum,* the slope is positive to the left (x_l) and negative to the right (x_r). *For a relative minimum,* the slope is negative to the left and positive to the right. *For the inflection points,* the slope has the *same sign* to the left or the right of the critical point.

Another way of describing this test is the following.

1   For a relative maximum, the value of the function is increasing to the left and decreasing to the right.

2   For a relative minimum, the value of the function is decreasing to the left and increasing to the right.

3   For inflection points, the value of the function is either increasing both to the left *and* right or decreasing both to the left and right.

The first-derivative test is summarized below.

FIRST-DERIVATIVE TEST
  I   Locate all critical values x^*.
  II   For any critical value x^* determine the value of $f'(x)$ to the left (x_l) and right (x_r) of x^*.
   i   If $f'(x_l) > 0$ and $f'(x_r) < 0$, there is a relative maximum for f at $[x^*, f(x^*)]$.

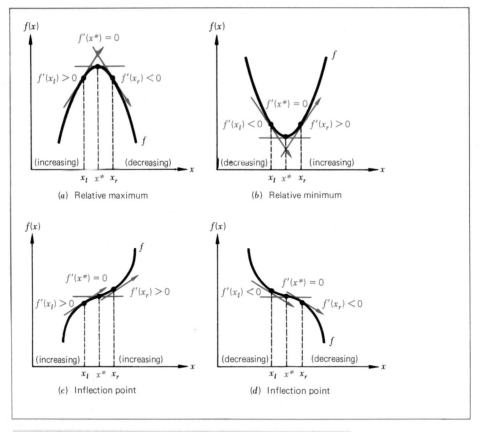

FIGURE 12.13
First derivative
test.

   ii If $f'(x_l) < 0$ and $f'(x_r) > 0$, there is a relative minimum for f
at $[x^*, f(x^*)]$.
   iii If $f'(x)$ has the same sign both at x_l and x_r an inflection point
exists at $[x^*, f(x^*)]$.

EXAMPLE 9

Determine the location(s) of any critical points on the graph of $f(x) = 2x^2 - 12x - 10$,
and determine their nature.

SOLUTION

The first derivative is

$$f'(x) = 4x - 12$$

When the first derivative is set equal to 0,

$$4x - 12 = 0$$
or
$$4x = 12$$

and there is a critical value at

$$x = 3$$

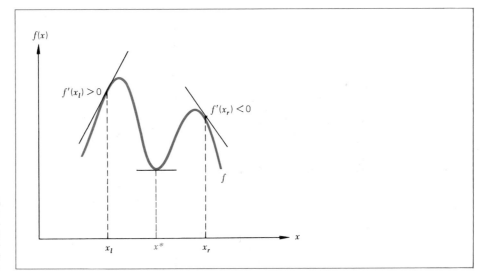

Since $f(3) = 2(3^2) - 12(3) - 10 = -28$, there is a critical point located at $(3, -28)$.

To test the critical point, let's select $x_l = 2.9$ and $x_r = 3.1$.

$$f'(2.9) = 4(2.9) - 12$$
$$= 11.6 - 12 = -0.4$$
$$f'(3.1) = 4(3.1) - 12$$
$$= 12.4 - 12 = +0.4$$

Because the first derivative is negative (-0.4) to the left of $x = 3$ and positive $(+0.4)$ to the right, the point $(3, -28)$ is a relative minimum on f. Note that f is a quadratic function which graphs as a parabola that is concave up.

A CAVEAT

When selecting x_l and x_r, one must stay reasonably close to the critical value x^*. If you stray too far left or right, you may reach an erroneous result as in Fig. 12.14 where a relative minimum could be judged to be a relative maximum. Some latitude does exist in selecting x_l and x_r. However, when more than one critical point exists, x_l and x_r should be chosen in such a way that they fall between the critical value being examined and any adjacent critical values.

EXAMPLE 10

In Example 8 we determined that the graph of the function

$$f(x) = \frac{x^3}{3} - \frac{x^2}{2} - 6x + 100$$

has critical points at $(3, 86\frac{1}{2})$ and $(-2, 107\frac{1}{3})$. To determine the nature of these critical points, we examine the first derivative

$$f'(x) = x^2 - x - 6$$

In testing the critical point at $x = 3$, let's select $x_l = 2$ and $x_r = 4$.

$$f'(2) = (2)^2 - 2 - 6$$
$$= -4$$
$$f'(4) = (4)^2 - 4 - 6$$
$$= 6$$

Since $f'(x)$ is negative (f is decreasing) to the left of $x = 3$ and positive (f is increasing) to the right, a relative minimum occurs for f when $x = 3$.

In testing the critical point at $x = -2$, let's select $x_l = -3$ and $x_r = 2$.

$$f'(-3) = (-3)^2 - (-3) - 6$$
$$= 6$$

From the previous test, we know that $f'(2) = -4$. Since $f'(x)$ is positive (f is increasing) to the left of $x = -2$ and negative (f is decreasing) to the right, a relative maximum occurs for $f(x)$ when $x = -2$.

EXAMPLE 11

The first derivative test also is valid for those critical points where $f'(x)$ is undefined. Consider the function $f(x) = 3x^{2/3}$, the graph of which is shown in Fig. 12.11*b*. For this function, $f'(x) = 2/x^{1/3}$ and a critical value of $x = 0$ exists according to condition 2. Using the first derivative test, let's select $x_l = -1$ and $x_r = 1$.

$$f'(-1) = \frac{2}{\sqrt[3]{-1}} = \frac{2}{-1} = -2$$

$$f'(1) = \frac{2}{\sqrt[3]{1}} = \frac{2}{1} = 2$$

Since $f'(x)$ is negative to the left of $x = 0$ and positive to the right, a relative minimum occurs at the critical point $(0, 0)$.

The Second-Derivative Test

The most expedient test of critical points where $f'(x) = 0$ is the *second-derivative test.* Intuitively, the second-derivative test attempts to determine the concavity of the function at a critical point $[x^*, f(x^*)]$. We concluded in Sec. 12.1 that if $f''(x) < 0$ at a point on the graph of f the curve is *concave down* at that point. If $f''(x) > 0$ at a point on the graph of f, the curve is *concave up* at that point. Thus, the second-derivative test suggests finding the value of $f''(x^*)$. Of greater interest, though, is the *sign* of $f''(x^*)$. If $f''(x^*) > 0$, we know that not only is the slope equal to 0 at x^* but also the function f is concave up at x^*. If we refer to the four critical point possibilities in Fig. 12.12, only one is concave up at x^*, that being the relative minimum in Fig. 12.12*b*.

If $f''(x^*) < 0$, the function is concave down at x^*. Again referring to Fig. 12.12, we find that the only critical point accompanied by concave-down conditions is the relative maximum in Fig. 12.12*a*.

As stated in Sec. 12.1, if $f''(x^*) = 0$, no conclusions can be drawn regarding the concavity at $[x^*, f(x^*)]$. Another test such as the first-derivative test is required to determine the nature of these critical points.

SECOND-DERIVATIVE TEST

I Find all critical values x^*, such that $f'(x^*) = 0$.

II For any critical value x^* determine the value of $f''(x^*)$.

i If $f''(x^*) > 0$, the function is concave up at x^* and there is a *relative minimum* for f at $[x^*, f(x^*)]$.

ii If $f''(x^*) < 0$, the function is concave down at x^* and there is a *relative maximum* for f at $[x^*, f(x^*)]$.

iii If $f''(x^*) = 0$, no conclusions can be drawn about the critical point. Another test such as the first-derivative test is necessary.

EXAMPLE 12

Examine the following function for any critical points and determine their nature.

$$f(x) = -\tfrac{3}{2}x^2 + 6x - 20$$

SOLUTION

We should recognize this as a quadratic function which graphs as a parabola that is concave down. There should be one critical point which is a relative maximum. To confirm this, we find the first derivative

$$f'(x) = -3x + 6$$

If $f'(x)$ is set equal to 0,

$$-3x + 6 = 0$$
$$-3x = -6$$

and one critical value occurs when

$$x = 2$$

The value of $f(x)$ when $x = 2$ is

$$f(2) = -\tfrac{3}{2}(2^2) + 6(2) - 20$$
$$= -6 + 12 - 20 = -14$$

The only critical point occurs at $(2, -14)$.

If we continue with the second-derivative test,

$$f''(x) = -3$$

and

$$f''(2) = -3 < 0$$

Since the second derivative is negative at $x = 2$, we can conclude that the graph of f is concave down at this point, and the critical point is a relative maximum. Figure 12.15 presents a sketch of the function.

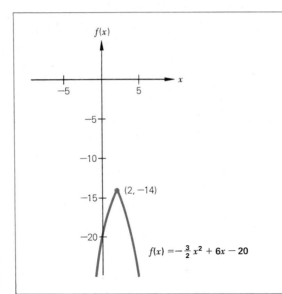

FIGURE 12.15
Relative
minimum at
$(2, -14)$.

EXAMPLE 13

Examine the following function for any critical points and determine their nature if

$$f(x) = \frac{x^4}{4} - \frac{9x^2}{2}$$

SOLUTION

If f' is identified and set equal to 0,

$$f'(x) = \frac{4x^3}{4} - \frac{18x}{2}$$

$$= x^3 - 9x$$

$$x^3 - 9x = 0$$

when $$x(x^2 - 9) = 0$$

or when $$x(x + 3)(x - 3) = 0$$

If the three factors are set equal to 0, critical values are found when

$$x = 0 \qquad x = -3 \qquad \text{and} \qquad x = 3$$

Upon substituting these critical values into f we can state that critical points occur on the graph of f at $(0, 0)$, $(-3, -81/4)$, and $(3, -81/4)$.

The second derivative is

$$f''(x) = 3x^2 - 9$$

To test the critical point $(0, 0)$,

$$f''(0) = 3(0^2) - 9$$

$$= -9 < 0$$

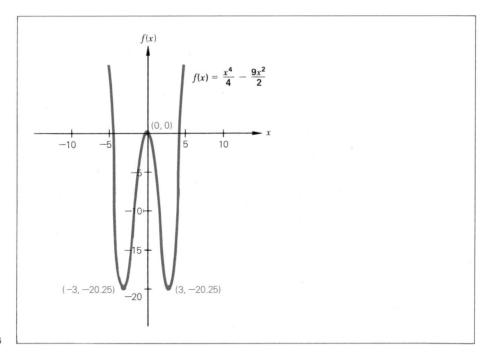

FIGURE 12.16

Since $f''(0)$ is negative, the function is concave down at $x = 0$ and a *relative maximum* occurs at $(0, 0)$. To test the critical point $(-3, -81/4)$,

$$f''(-3) = 3(-3)^2 - 9$$
$$= 27 - 9 = 18 > 0$$

The graph of f is concave up when $x = -3$ and a *relative minimum* occurs at $(-3, -81/4)$.
   To test the critical point $(3, -81/4)$,

$$f''(3) = 3(3^2) - 9$$
$$= 27 - 9 = 18 > 0$$

The graph of f is concave up when $x = 3$ and a *relative minimum* occurs at $(3, -81/4)$.
   To summarize, relative minima occur on f at the points $(-3, -81/4)$ and $(3, -81/4)$ and a relative maximum occurs at $(0, 0)$. Figure 12.16 is a sketch of the graph of f.

When the Second-Derivative Test Fails

As indicated in the description of the second-derivative test, if $f''(x^*) = 0$, the second derivative does not allow for any conclusion about the behavior of f at x^*. Consider the following example.

EXAMPLE 14

Examine the following function for any critical points and determine their nature.

$$f(x) = -x^5$$

SOLUTION

Given f,

$$f'(x) = -5x^4$$

Setting f' equal to 0,

$$-5x^4 = 0$$

when

$$x = 0$$

Thus, a critical value exists for f when $x = 0$ and there is a critical point at $(0, 0)$. Continuing with the second-derivative test, we get

$$f''(x) = -20x^3$$

At $x = 0$

$$f''(0) = -20(0)^3$$
$$= 0$$

Given this result, there is no conclusion about the nature of the critical point. We can use the first-derivative test to determine the nature of the critical point. If $x_l = -1$ and $x_r = 1$, then

$$f'(-1) = -5(-1)^4$$
$$= -5$$
$$f'(1) = -5(1)^4$$
$$= -5$$

Since $f'(-1)$ and $f'(1)$ are both negative, an inflection point occurs at $x = 0$. Figure 12.17 presents a sketch of the graph of the function.

Higher-Order Derivative Test (Optional)

There are several ways to reach a conclusion about the nature of a critical point when the second-derivative test fails. One method which is efficient but not easy to understand intuitively is the *higher-order derivative test.* This test will always be conclusive.

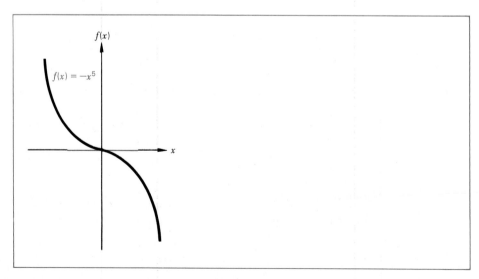

FIGURE 12.17

HIGHER-ORDER DERIVATIVE TEST

I Given a critical point $[x^*, f(x^*)]$ on f, find the lowest-order derivative whose value is nonzero *at the critical value* x^*. Denote this derivative as $f^{(n)}(x)$ where n is the order of the derivative.

II If the order n of this derivative is *even*, $f(x^*)$ is a *relative maximum* if $f^{(n)}(x^*) < 0$ and a *relative minimum* if $f^{(n)}(x^*) > 0$

III If the order n of this derivative is *odd*, the critical point is an *inflection point*.

EXAMPLE 15

Identify any critical points and determine their nature if

$$f(x) = (x - 2)^4$$

SOLUTION

First we find f'.

$$f'(x) = 4(x - 2)^3(1)$$
$$= 4(x - 2)^3$$

If we set f' equal to 0

$$4(x - 2)^3 = 0$$

when

$$x = 2$$

At this critical value

$$f(2) = (2 - 2)^4$$
$$= (0)^4 = 0$$

Thus a critical point occurs at (2, 0).

To determine the nature of the critical point, the second derivative is

$$f''(x) = 4(3)(x - 2)^2$$
$$= 12(x - 2)^2$$

Evaluating f'' at the critical value

$$f''(2) = 12(2 - 2)^2$$
$$= 0$$

There is no conclusion based upon the second-derivative test. If we proceed using the higher-order derivative test, the third derivative is

$$f'''(x) = 24(x - 2)$$

and

$$f'''(2) = 24(2 - 2) = 0$$

Since $f'''(2) = 0$, there is no conclusion based on the third derivative.

The fourth derivative is

$$f^{(4)}(x) = 24$$

and

$$f^{(4)}(2) = 24$$

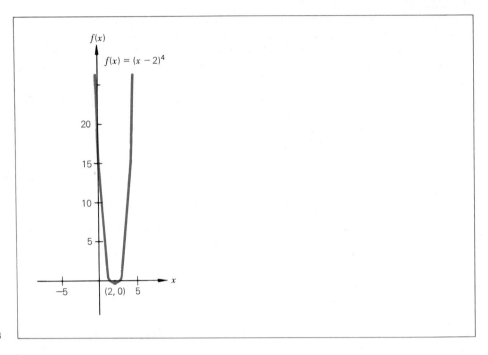

FIGURE 12.18

This is the lowest-order derivative not equaling 0 when $x = 2$. Since the order of the derivative ($n = 4$) is even, a relative maximum or minimum exists at $(2, 0)$. To determine which is the case, we look at the sign of $f^{(4)}(2)$. Because $f^{(4)}(2) > 0$, we can conclude that there is a relative minimum at $x = 2$, and $f(2) = 0$ is a relative minimum value of $f(x)$. Figure 12.18 contains a sketch of the function.

NOTE

The second-derivative test is actually a special case of the higher-order derivative test—the case where the lowest-order derivative not equaling 0 is the second derivative ($n = 2$).

Section 12.2 Follow-up Exercises

For each of the following functions determine the location of all critical points and determine their nature.

1   $f(x) = 5x^2 - 40x + 10$
2   $f(x) = x^3/3 - 5x^2 + 16x - 100$
3   $f(x) = 10x^3 - 25$
4   $f(x) = x^2 - 10x + 8$
5   $f(x) = x^5 + 12$
6   $f(x) = x^3/3 - 2.5x^2 + 4x$
7   $f(x) = x^4/4 - 9x^2/2$
8   $f(x) = x^4/4 - 25x^2/2$
9   $f(x) = 2x^3 + 10.5x^2 - 12x$
10 $f(x) = x^5/5 - x$
11 $f(x) = x^3/3 + 5x^2/2$
12 $f(x) = x^6/6 - 8x^2 - 10$
13 $f(x) = (4x - 10)^3$
14 $f(x) = (x^2 - 9)^4$
15 $f(x) = -(x - 6)^3$
16 $f(x) = x^9/9 - x + 25$
*17 $f(x) = x/(x^2 + 1)$
*18 $f(x) = x(x + 2)^3$

*19 $f(x) = ax^2 + bx + c$, where $a > 0$, $b < 0$, $c > 0$

*20 $f(x) = ax^2 + bx + c$, where $a < 0$, $b < 0$, $c < 0$

*21 **Original Equation Test** It was mentioned in the last section that other techniques exist for determining the nature of critical points. One test involves comparing the value of $f(x^*)$ with the values of $f(x)$ just to the left and right of x^*. Refer to Fig. 12.12, and determine a set of rules which would allow one to distinguish among the four critical point possibilities.

*22 Compare the relative efficiencies associated with performing the original equation test and the first-derivative test of critical points.

*23 Compare the relative efficiencies associated with performing the first-derivative, second-derivative, and higher-order derivative tests of critical points.

12.3 RESTRICTED-DOMAIN CONSIDERATIONS

The last section concentrated on procedures for identifying relative maxima and minima. This section will examine procedures for identifying absolute maxima and minima when the domain of a function is restricted.

When the Domain Is Restricted

Very often in applied problems the domain is restricted. For example, if profit P is stated as a function of the number of units produced x, it is likely that x will be restricted to values such that $0 \leq x \leq x_C$. In this case x is restricted to nonnegative values (there is no production of negative quantities) which are less than or equal to some upper limit x_C. The value of x_C may reflect production capacity, as defined by limited labor, limited raw materials, or by the physical capacity of the plant itself.

In searching for the absolute maximum or absolute minimum of a function, consideration must be given not only to the relative maxima and minima of the function but also to the *endpoints* of the domain of the function. For example, look at the function graphed in Fig. 12.19. Note that the domain of the function is restricted to values between 0 and x_u and that the absolute maximum for f,

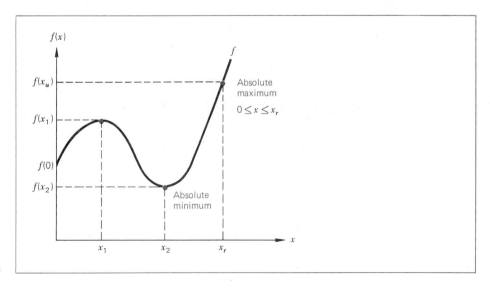

FIGURE 12.19

occurs at x_r, the right endpoint of the domain. The absolute minimum occurs at x_2, which is also a relative minimum on the function. The procedure for identifying absolute extrema follows.

PROCEDURE FOR IDENTIFYING ABSOLUTE MAXIMUM AND MINIMUM POINTS

Given the continuous function f defined over the closed interval $[x_l, x_r]$:

I Locate all critical points $[x^*, f(x^*)]$ which lie within the domain of the function.* Exclude from consideration any critical values x^* which lie outside the domain.

II Compute the values of $f(x)$ at the two endpoints of the domain $[f(x_l)$ and $f(x_r)]$.

III Compare the values of $f(x^*)$ for all relevant critical points with $f(x_l)$ and $f(x_r)$. The absolute maximum is the largest of these values. The absolute minimum is the smallest of these values.

EXAMPLE 16

Determine the locations and values of the absolute maximum and minimum for the function

$$f(x) = \frac{x^3}{3} - \frac{7x^2}{2} + 6x + 5$$

where $2 \le x \le 10$.

SOLUTION

Step I: Finding the first derivative, we have

$$f'(x) = \frac{3x^2}{3} - \frac{14x}{2} + 6$$

$$= x^2 - 7x + 6$$

If f' is set equal to 0,

$$x^2 - 7x + 6 = 0$$

or

$$(x - 6)(x - 1) = 0$$

Thus,

$$x = 6 \quad \text{and} \quad x = 1$$

The only critical value within the domain of the function is $x = 6$.

$$f(6) = \frac{6^3}{3} - \frac{7(6^2)}{2} + 6(6) + 5$$

$$= 72 - 126 + 36 + 5 = -13$$

---

* Recall that critical points satisfy the condition $f'(x) = 0$ or $f'(x)$ undefined.

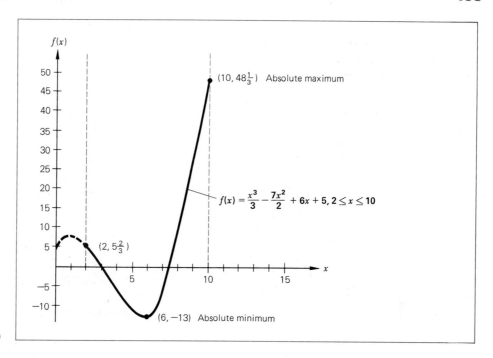

FIGURE 12.20

Thus, a critical point occurs at $(6, -13)$.

The second derivative is

$$f''(x) = 2x - 7$$

To test $x = 6$,

$$f''(6) = 2(6) - 7$$
$$= 5 > 0$$

Since $f''(6) > 0$, a relative minimum occurs at $(6, -13)$. Because $f'(x)$ is defined for all real x, no other critical values exist.

Step II: The values of $f(x)$ at the endpoints of the domain are

$$f(2) = \frac{2^3}{3} - \frac{7(2^2)}{2} + 6(2) + 5$$

$$= \tfrac{8}{3} - 14 + 12 + 5 = 5\tfrac{2}{3}$$

and

$$f(10) = \frac{(10)^3}{3} - \frac{7(10)^2}{2} + 6(10) + 5$$

$$= \frac{1,000}{3} - \frac{700}{2} + 65 = 48\tfrac{1}{3}$$

Step III: Comparing $f(2)$, $f(6)$, and $f(10)$, we find the absolute minimum of -13 occurs when $x = 6$ and the absolute maximum of $48\tfrac{1}{3}$ occurs when $x = 10$. Figure 12.20 presents a sketch of the function.

Section 12.3 Follow-up Exercises

In the following exercises, determine the locations and values of the absolute maximum and absolute minimum for f.

1   $f(x) = 2x^2 - 4x + 5$, where $0 \leq x \leq 6$
2   $f(x) = -x^2 + 8x - 100$, where $-4 \leq x \leq 2$
3   $f(x) = x^3 - 12x^2$, where $0 \leq x \leq 10$
4   $f(x) = -2x^3 - 15x^2 + 10$, where $-5 \leq x \leq -1$
5   $f(x) = x^5/5 - x - 25$, where $0 \leq x \leq 5$
6   $f(x) = x^5/5 - 3x^4/4 + 2x^3/3 - 20$, where $2 \leq x \leq 5$
7   $f(x) = x^6/6 - x^5 + 2.5x^4$, where $0 \leq x \leq 2$
8   $f(x) = x^{2/3}$, where $0 \leq x \leq 4$
9   $f(x) = x^{1/2}$, where $1 < x \leq 16$
10 $f(x) = (x - 2)^{1/3}$, where $0 \leq x \leq 10$

12.4   CURVE SKETCHING

Sketching functions is facilitated with the information we have acquired in this chapter. One can get a feeling for the general shape of the graph of a function without determining and plotting a large number of ordered pairs. This section discusses some of the key determinants of the shape of the graph of a function and illustrates curve-sketching procedures.

Key Data Points

In determining the general shape of the graph of a function, the following attributes are the most significant:

■   Relative maxima and minima

■   Inflection points

■ x and y intercepts

■   Ultimate direction

To illustrate this, consider the function

$$f(x) = \frac{x^3}{3} - 4x^2 + 12x + 5$$

1   Relative Maxima and Minima   To locate relative extrema on f we find the first derivative

$$f'(x) = x^2 - 8x + 12$$

Setting f' equal to 0 yields

$$x^2 - 8x + 12 = 0$$

or $$(x - 2)(x - 6) = 0$$

Critical values occur at $x = 2$ and $x = 6$. If we substitute these critical values into f

$$f(2) = \frac{2^3}{3} - 4(2^2) + 12(2) + 5$$

$$= \tfrac{8}{3} - 16 + 24 + 5 = 15\tfrac{2}{3}$$

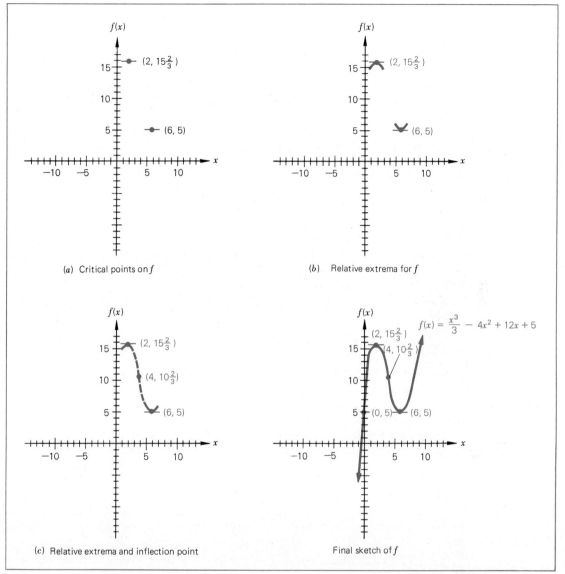

FIGURE 12.21 Development of sketch of $f(x) = \dfrac{x^3}{3} - 4x^2 + 12x + 5$.

and
$$f(6) = \frac{6^3}{3} - 4(6^2) + 12(6) + 5$$
$$= 72 - 144 + 72 + 5 = 5$$

Thus, critical points exist at $(2, 15\frac{2}{3})$ and $(6, 5)$. Graphically, we know that zero slope conditions exist at these points, as shown in Fig. 12.21a.

The second derivative of f is
$$f''(x) = 2x - 8$$

To test the nature of the critical point $(2, 15\frac{2}{3})$,
$$f''(2) = 2(2) - 8 = -4 < 0$$

Therefore, a relative maximum occurs at $(2, 15\frac{2}{3})$. To test the nature of the critical point $(6,5)$,

$$f''(6) = 2(6) - 8$$
$$= 4 > 0$$

Therefore a relative minimum occurs at $(6, 5)$. The information we have developed thus far allows us to develop the sketch of f to the degree shown in Fig. 12.21b.

2 Inflection Points Inflection point candidates are found when f'' is set equal to 0, or when

$$2x - 8 = 0$$
or $$x = 4$$

If we substitute $x = 4$ into f, we can state that the only candidate for an inflection point occurs at $(4, 10\frac{1}{3})$. And, without checking the sign of f'' to the left and right of $x = 4$, we can conclude that the point $(4, 10\frac{1}{3})$ is the only inflection point on the graph of f. The reason for this is that there *must be* an inflection point between the relative maximum at $(2, 15\frac{2}{3})$ and the relative minimum at $(6, 5)$. *For a continuous function, the concavity of the function must change between any adjacent critical points.* The only candidate identified lies between the two critical points; thus, it must be an inflection point. The information developed to this point allows us to enhance the sketch of $f(x)$ as shown in Fig. 12.21c.

3 Intercepts The y intercept is usually an easy point to locate. In this case

$$f(0) = 5$$

The y intercept occurs at $(0, 5)$.

   Depending on the function, the x intercepts may or may not be easy to find. For this function they would be rather difficult to identify. Our sketch of f will not be affected significantly by not knowing the precise location of the one x intercept which exists for f.

4 Ultimate Direction For f, the highest-powered term is $x^3/3$. To determine the behavior of f as x becomes more and more positive, we need to observe the behavior of $x^3/3$ as x becomes more and more positive.

As $x \to +\infty$ $\dfrac{x^3}{3} \to +\infty$

Therefore,

as $x \to +\infty$ $f(x) = \dfrac{x^3}{3} - 4x^2 + 12x + 5 \to +\infty$

Similarly,

as $x \to -\infty$ $\dfrac{x^3}{3} \to -\infty$

and $f(x) = \dfrac{x^3}{3} - 4x^2 + 12x + 5 \to -\infty$

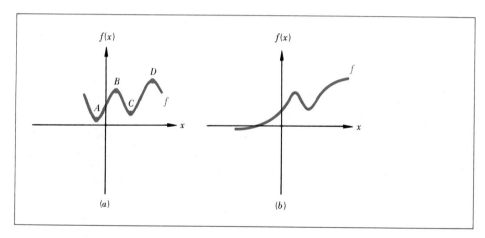

(a)   (b)

FIGURE 12.22

Figure 12.21d incorporates the intercepts and the ultimate directions into our sketch.

POINTS FOR THOUGHT AND DISCUSSION

Given the function in the previous illustration, what information do we have that would exclude the two sketches in Fig. 12.22 from being the sketches of $f(x) = x^3/3 - 4x^2 + 12x + 5$?

EXAMPLE 17

Sketch the graph of the function

$$f(x) = \frac{x^4}{4} - \frac{8x^3}{3} + 8x^2$$

SOLUTION

1 Relative Maxima and Minima   To locate relative extrema on f we find the first derivative

$$f'(x) = x^3 - 8x^2 + 16x$$

Setting f' equal to 0 yields

$$x^3 - 8x^2 + 16x = 0$$
$$x(x^2 - 8x + 16) = 0$$

or
$$x(x - 4)(x - 4) = 0$$

If the factors are set equal to 0, critical values are found at $x = 0$ and $x = 4$. If we substitute these critical values into f

$$f(0) = 0$$

and
$$f(4) = \frac{4^4}{4} - \frac{8(4^3)}{3} + 8(4^2)$$

$$= 64 - 170\tfrac{2}{3} + 128 = 21\tfrac{1}{3}$$

Therefore, critical points occur at $(0, 0)$ and $(4, 21\frac{1}{3})$.

Testing $x = 0$, we find

$$f''(x) = 3x^2 - 16x + 16$$

and

$$f''(0) = 16 > 0$$

A relative minimum occurs at $(0, 0)$.

Testing $x = 4$,

$$f''(4) = 3(4)^2 - 16(4) + 17$$
$$= 48 - 64 + 16 = 0$$

No conclusion can be drawn about $x = 4$ based upon the second derivative. Continuing with the higher-order derivative test,

and

$$f'''(x) = 6x - 16$$
$$f'''(4) = 6(4) - 16$$
$$= 8 > 0$$

Since the order of the derivative is odd, an inflection point occurs at $(4, 21\frac{1}{3})$.

2   Inflection Points   Candidates for inflection points are found by setting f'' equal to 0, or when

$$3x^2 - 16x + 16 = 0$$
$$(3x - 4)(x - 4) = 0$$
$$x = \tfrac{4}{3} \quad \text{and} \quad x = 4$$

We have already verified that an inflection point occurs at $(4, 21\frac{1}{3})$. Confirm for yourself that $(\frac{4}{3}, 8.69)$ is also an inflection point.

3   Intercepts   By computing $f(0) = (0)^4/4 - 8(0)^3/3 + 8(0)^2 = 0$, we conclude that the y intercept occurs at $(0, 0)$. To locate the x intercepts,

$$\frac{x^4}{4} - \frac{8x^3}{3} + 8x^2 = 0$$

when

$$x^2 \left(\frac{x^2}{4} - \frac{8x}{3} + 8 \right) = 0$$

One root to this equation is $x = 0$, suggesting that one x intercept is located at $(0, 0)$ (earlier, we should have observed that the y intercept is also an x intercept). Use the quadratic formula to verify that there are no roots for the equation

$$\frac{x^2}{4} - \frac{8x}{3} + 8 = 0$$

For f, the point $(0, 0)$ represents the only intercept.

4   Ultimate Direction   The ultimate behavior of $f(x)$ is linked to the behavior of the term $x^4/4$.

As $\qquad\qquad x \to +\infty \qquad \dfrac{x^4}{4} \to +\infty \qquad \text{and} \qquad f(x) \to +\infty$

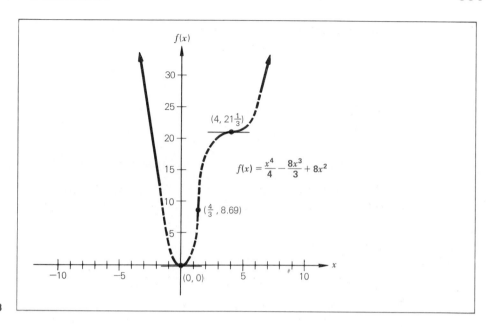

FIGURE 12.23

As $\qquad\qquad x \to -\infty \quad \dfrac{x^4}{4} \to +\infty \quad$ and $\quad f(x) \to +\infty$

Using the information gathered, we can sketch the approximate shape of f as shown in Fig. 12.23.

Section 12.4 Follow-up Exercises

Sketch the graphs of the following functions.

1　$f(x) = x^2 - 5x + 6$　　　　　　　　　　2　$f(x) = x^3/3 - 5x^2 + 16x - 100$
3　$f(x) = x^3/3 - 2.5x^2 + 4x$　　　　　　4　$f(x) = x^4/4 - 25x^2/2$
5　$f(x) = x^6/6 - 8x^2 - 10$　　　　　　　6　$f(x) = (6x - 12)^3$
7　$f(x) = (x^2 - 16)^4$　　　　　　　　　8　$f(x) = -(x - 5)^3$
9　$f(x) = -(x - 2)^4$　　　　　　　　　　10　$f(x) = x^3/3 - 7x^2/2 - 30x$

KEY TERMS AND CONCEPTS

absolute maximum
　(minimum)　480
concave functions　476
concavity　472
convex functions　476
critical points　480
critical values　481
decreasing function　470
first-derivative test　482

higher-order derivative test　490
increasing function　469
inflection point　473
relative maximum (minimum)　479
restricted-domain
　considerations　493
second derivative test　486
ultimate direction　498

ADDITIONAL EXERCISES

Exercises 1 to 14 are related to Sec. 12.1

For the following exercises, determine the intervals over which f is (a) increasing, (b) decreasing, (c) neither increasing or decreasing, (d) concave up, and (e) concave down.

1 $f(x) = x^2 - 5x + 6$ 2 $f(x) = 20 - 4x$

3 $f(x) = x^3 - 27x$ 4 $f(x) = -x^5$

5 $f(x) = b$ 6 $f(x) = 5x^2 - 25x + 150$

For the following exercises, identify the locations of any inflection points.

7 $f(x) = x^5$ 8 $f(x) = -x^4/2$

9 $f(x) = 4x^3 - 2x^2 + 15$ 10 $f(x) = x^4/12 + x^3 + 4x^2$

11 $f(x) = x^5/20 - x^3/6$ 12 $f(x) = (x - 4)^3$

13 $f(x) = (x - \frac{1}{2})^5$ 14 $f(x) = x^4/12 + x^3/6 - 3x^2 + 120$

Exercises 15 to 26 are related to Sec. 12.2.

For the following functions, determine the location of all critical points and determine their nature.

15 $f(x) = 2x^2 - 5x + 3$ 16 $f(x) = -x^2/2 + 6x - 7$

17 $f(x) = 2x^4$ 18 $f(x) = x^4 - 9x^2/2$

19 $f(x) = x^3 - 2x^2 + 4$ 20 $f(x) = -2x^3 + 3x^2/2 + 3x + 1$

21 $f(x) = x^5 - x^4 - x^3/3$ 22 $f(x) = (-x + 2)^5$

23 $f(x) = 3x^4 - 16x^3 + 24x^2 + 10$ 24 $f(x) = x^4 - 20x^3 + 100x^2 + 80$

25 $f(x) = 2x + 98/x$ 26 $f(x) = 96\sqrt{x} - 6x$

Exercises 27 to 33 are related to Sec. 12.3.

27 $f(x) = 3x^2 - 48x + 30$, where $5 \le x \le 10$

28 $f(x) = 2x^2 - 5x + 15$, where $-1 \le x \le 1$

29 $f(x) = 2x^3/3 + 3x^2 + 4x - 1$, where $-3 \le x \le 0$

30 $f(x) = x^3/3 - 7x^2/2 - 30x$, where $0 \le x \le 5$

31 $f(x) = 2x^5/5 - 27x^2$, where $-2 \le x \le 1$

32 $f(x) = -x^6 + x^4 + 2x^3/3$, where $-1 \le x \le 2$

33 $f(x) = x^4 + 5x^3 + 5.5x^2 + 6$, where $-2 \le x \le 0$

Exercises 34 to 37 are related to Sec. 12.4.

Sketch the graphs of the following functions.

34 $f(x) = x^3/3 - 7x^2/2 + 12x$

35 $f(x) = (10 - x)^3$

36 $f(x) = (x + 5)^3$

37 $f(x) = 2x^5/5 + x^4/4 - x^3 + 1$

CHAPTER TEST

1 Given $f(x) = -3x^2 + 24x - 15$, for what values of x is f an increasing function?

2 Sketch a portion of a function which has the characteristics that $f'(x) > 0$ and $f''(x) > 0$.

3 Given $f(x) = x^3/3 - 2x^2 - 21x + 1$, determine the location of all critical points and determine their nature.

4 Given $f(x) = x^4/12 - x^2$, identify the locations of any inflection points.

5 The function $f(x) = -x^3/3 - x^2/2 + 2x$ has critical points at $x = 1$ and $x = -2$. If the domain of f is $-1 \le x \le 2$, determine the locations and values of the absolute maximum and absolute minimum.

6 Sketch the function $f(x) = (x - 4)^3$.

13

OPTIMIZATION: APPLICATIONS

13.1 REVENUE, COST,
AND PROFIT APPLICATIONS

13.2 MARGINAL APPROACH
TO PROFIT MAXIMIZATION

13.3 ADDITIONAL APPLICATIONS

ADDITIONAL EXERCISES

MINICASE: THE EOQ MODEL

CHAPTER OBJECTIVE

■ Provide a wide variety of applications of optimization procedures

Chapter 12 provided the tools of classical optimization. That is, it gave us a method for examining functions in order to locate maximum and minimum points. This chapter, as with Chap. 5, is devoted entirely to applications. Specifically, this chapter presents applications of optimization methods. As in Chap. 5 applied problems require a translation from the verbal statement to an appropriate mathematical representation. Care must be taken to define variables (unknowns) precisely. And once a mathematically derived solution has been found, an essential element in the process is the translation of the mathematical result into a meaningful recommendation within the application setting.

13.1 REVENUE, COST, AND PROFIT APPLICATIONS

Revenue Applications

The following applications focus on revenue maximization. Recall from Chap. 5 that the money which flows *into* an organization from either selling products or providing services is referred to as *revenue.* And, the most fundamental way of computing total revenue from selling a product (or service) is

$$\boxed{\text{Total revenue} = (\text{price})(\text{quantity sold})}$$

An assumption in this relationship is that the selling price is the same for all units sold.

EXAMPLE 1

The demand for the product of a firm varies with the price that the firm charges for the product. The firm has determined that annual total revenue R (stated in \$1,000s) is a function of the price p (stated in dollars). Specifically,

$$R = f(p) = -50p^2 + 500p$$

(a) Determine the price which should be charged in order to maximize total revenue.

(b) What is the maximum value of annual total revenue?

SOLUTION

(a) From Chap. 10 we know that the revenue function is quadratic, and it graphs as a parabola which is concave down. Thus the maximum value of R will occur at the vertex. The first derivative of the revenue function is

$$f'(p) = -100p + 500$$

If we set f' equal to 0,

$$-100p + 500 = 0$$
$$-100p = -500$$

or a critical value occurs when

$$p = 5$$

There is one critical point on the graph of f, and it occurs when $p = 5$. Although we know that a relative maximum occurs when $p = 5$, let's formally verify this using the second-derivative test:

$$f''(p) = -100 \quad \text{and} \quad f''(5) = -100 < 0$$

Therefore, a relative maximum occurs on f at $p = 5$.

(b) The maximum value of R is found by substituting $p = 5$ into f, or

$$f(5) = -50(5^2) + 500(5)$$
$$= -1,250 + 2,500 = 1,250$$

Thus, annual total revenue is expected to be maximized at $1,250 (1,000s) or $1.25 million when the firm charges $5 per unit. Figure 13.1 presents a sketch of the revenue function.

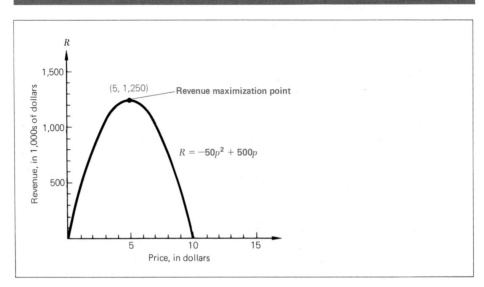

FIGURE 13.1
Quadratic reve-
nue function.

NOTE

This has been mentioned earlier in the text when we have dealt with applications; however, it is worth repeating. It is quite common for students to work through a word problem, find the solution, but have no ability to interpret the results within the framework of the application. If you become caught up in the mechanics of finding a solution and temporarily lose your frame of reference regarding the original problem, reread the problem, making special note of how the variables are defined. Also review the specific questions asked in the problem. This should assist in reminding you of the objectives and the direction in which you should be heading.

EXAMPLE 2

Public Transportation Management   The transit authority for a major metropolitan area has experimented with the fare structure for the city's public bus system. It has abandoned the zone fare structure in which the fare varies depending on the number of zones through which a passenger passes. The new system is a fixed-fare system in which a passenger may travel between any two points in the city for the same fare.

The transit authority has surveyed citizens to determine the number of persons who would use the bus system if the fixed fare were equal to different amounts. From the survey results, systems analysts have determined an approximate demand function which expresses the daily ridership as a function of the fare charged. Specifically, the demand function is

$$q = 10{,}000 - 125p$$

where q equals the number of riders per day and p equals the fare in cents.
(*a*) Determine the fare which should be charged in order to maximize daily bus fare revenue.
(*b*) What is the expected maximum revenue?
(*c*) How many riders per day are expected under this fare?

SOLUTION

(*a*) The first step is to determine a function which states daily revenue as a function of the fare p. The reason for selecting p as the independent variable is that the question was to determine the fare which would result in maximum total revenue. Also, the fare is a *decision variable*—a variable whose value can be decided by the transit authority management.

The general expression for total revenue is, as stated before,

$$\boxed{R = pq}$$

But in this form, R is stated as a function of two variables—p and q. *At this time* we cannot deal with the optimization of functions involving more than one independent variable. The demand function, however, establishes a relationship between the variables p and q which allows us to transform the revenue function into one where R is stated as a function of one independent variable p. The right side of the demand function is an expression, stated in terms of p, which is equivalent to q. If we substitute this expression for q in the revenue function, we get

$$R = f(p)$$
$$= p(10{,}000 - 125p)$$

or

$$R = 10{,}000p - 125p^2$$

The first derivative is

$$f'(p) = 10{,}000 - 250p$$

If the derivative is set equal to 0,

$$10{,}000 - 250p = 0$$
$$10{,}000 = 250p$$

and a critical value occurs when

$$40 = p$$

The second derivative is found and evaluated at $p = 40$ to determine the nature of the critical point:

$$f''(p) = -250$$
$$f''(40) = -250 < 0$$

Thus, a relative maximum occurs for f when $p = 40$. The interpretation of this result is that daily revenue will be maximized when a fixed fare of \$0.40 is charged.

(b)
$$f(40) = 10{,}000(40) - 125(40)^2$$
$$= 400{,}000 - 200{,}000 = 200{,}000$$

Since the fare is stated in cents, the maximum expected daily revenue is 200,000 cents, or \$2,000.

(c) The number of riders expected each day with this fare is found by substituting the fare into the demand function, or

$$q = 10{,}000 - 125(40)$$
$$= 10{,}000 - 5{,}000$$
$$= 5{,}000 \text{ riders per day}$$

Figure 13.2 presents a sketch of the daily revenue function.

Cost Applications

As mentioned earlier, costs represent cash *outflows* for an organization. Most organizations seek ways to minimize these outflows. This section presents applications which deal with the minimization of some measure of cost.

EXAMPLE 3

Inventory Management A common problem in organizations is determining how much of a needed item should be kept on hand. For retailers, the problem may relate to

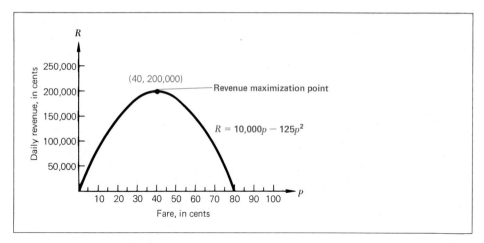

FIGURE 13.2
Quadratic revenue function.

how many units of each product should be kept in stock. For producers, the problem may involve how much of each raw material should be kept available. This problem is identified with an area called *inventory control,* or *inventory management.* Concerning the question of how much "inventory" to keep on hand, there may be costs associated with having too little or too much inventory on hand.

A retailer of motorized bicycles has examined cost data and has determined a cost function which expresses the annual cost of purchasing, owning, and maintaining inventory as a function of the size (number of units) of each order it places for the bicycles. The cost function is

$$C = f(q) = \frac{4,860}{q} + 15q + 750,000$$

where C equals annual inventory cost, stated in dollars, and q equals the number of cycles ordered each time the retailer replenishes the supply.

(*a*) Determine the order size which minimizes annual inventory cost.

(*b*) What is minimum annual inventory cost expected to equal?

SOLUTION

(*a*) The first derivative is

$$f'(q) = -4,860q^{-2} + 15$$

If f' is set equal to 0,

$$-4,860q^{-2} + 15 = 0$$

when

$$\frac{-4,860}{q^2} = -15$$

Multiplying both sides by q^2 and dividing both sides by -15 yields

$$\frac{4,860}{15} = q^2$$

$$324 = q^2$$

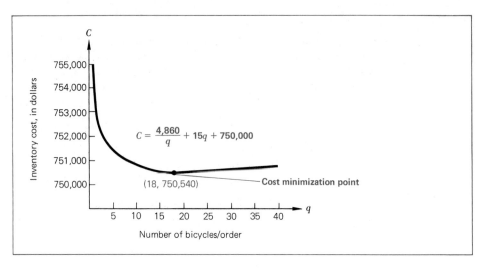

FIGURE 13.3
Inventory cost
function.

and a critical value exists at

$$18 = q$$

The nature of the critical point is checked by finding f'':

$$f''(q) = 9,720q^{-3}$$
$$= \frac{9,720}{q^3}$$

Evaluating at the critical value,

$$f''(18) = \frac{9,720}{(18)^3}$$
$$= 1.667 > 0$$

Thus, a relative minimum occurs for f when $q = 18$. Annual inventory costs will be minimized when 18 cycles are ordered each time the retailer replenishes the supply. (*b*) Minimum annual inventory costs are determined by calculating $f(18)$, or

$$f(18) = \frac{4,860}{18} + 15(18) + 750,000$$
$$= 270 + 270 + 750,000 = \$750,540$$

Figure 13.3 presents a sketch of the cost function.

EXAMPLE 4 ▰▰▰▰▰▰▰▰▰▰▰▰▰▰▰▰▰▰▰▰▰▰▰

Minimizing Average Cost per Unit The total cost of producing q units of a certain product is described by the function

$$C = 100,000 + 1,500q + 0.2q^2$$

where C is the total cost stated in dollars. Determine how many units q should be produced in order to minimize the *average cost per unit*.

SOLUTION

Average cost per unit is calculated by dividing the total cost by the number of units produced. For example, if the total cost of producing 10 units of a product equals \$275, the average cost per unit is \$275/10 = \$27.50. Thus, the function representing average cost per unit in this example is

$$\overline{C} = f(q) = \frac{C}{q} = \frac{100{,}000}{q} + 1{,}500 + 0.2q$$

The first derivative of the average cost function is

$$f'(q) = -100{,}000q^{-2} + 0.2$$

If f' is set equal to 0,

$$0.2 = \frac{100{,}000}{q^2}$$

or

$$q^2 = \frac{100{,}000}{0.2}$$

$$= 500{,}000$$

Finding the square root of both sides, we have a critical value of

$$q = 707.11 \text{ (units)}$$

The nature of the critical point is tested with the second-derivative test:

$$f''(q) = 200{,}000q^{-3}$$

$$= \frac{200{,}000}{q^3}$$

$$f''(707.11) = \frac{200{,}000}{(707.11)^3}$$

$$= 0.00056 > 0$$

Thus, a relative minimum occurs for f when $q = 707.11$. This minimum average cost per unit is

$$f(707.11) = \frac{100{,}000}{707.11} + 1500 + 0.2(707.11)$$

$$= 141.42 + 1500 + 141.42 = \$1782.84$$

Figure 13.4 is a sketch of the average cost function.

EXERCISE

For Example 4, what is the total cost of production at this level of output?* What are the two ways in which this figure can be computed?

* Answer: \$1,260,663.90

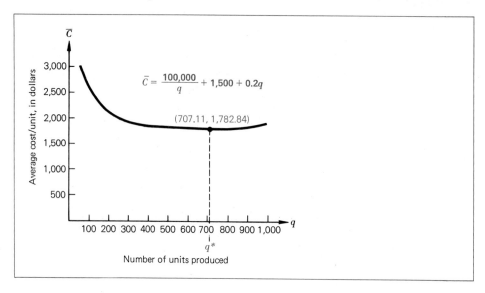

FIGURE 13.4
Average cost
function.

Profit Applications

This section contains two examples which deal with profit maximization.

EXAMPLE 5

Sales Force Allocation   Example 1 in Chap. 10 discussed the *law of diminishing returns* as an illustration of a nonlinear function. A major cosmetic and beauty supply firm, which specializes in a door-to-door sales approach, has found that the response of sales to the allocation of additional sales representatives behaves according to the law of diminishing returns. For one regional sales district, the company has determined that *annual profit P, stated in hundreds of dollars, is a function of the number of sales representatives x assigned to the district.* Specifically, the function relating these two variables is

$$P = f(x) = -12.5x^2 + 1{,}375x - 1{,}500$$

(*a*) What number of representatives will result in maximum profit for the district?
(*b*) What is the expected maximum profit?

SOLUTION

(*a*) The derivative of the profit function is

$$f'(x) = -25x + 1{,}375$$

If f' is set equal to 0,

$$-25x = -1375$$

or, a critical value occurs at

$$x = 55$$

Checking the nature of the critical point, we find

$$f''(x) = -25 \quad \text{and} \quad f''(55) = -25 < 0$$

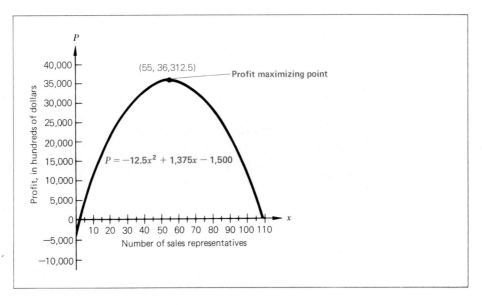

FIGURE 13.5
Profit function.

Thus, a relative maximum occurs for f when $x = 55$.

(b) The expected maximum profit is

$$f(55) = -12.5(55)^2 + 1,375(55) - 1,500$$
$$= -37,812.5 + 75,625 - 1,500 = 36,312.5$$

We can conclude that annual profit will be maximized at a value of $36,312.5 (100s), or $3,631,250 if 55 representatives are assigned to the district. Figure 13.5 presents a sketch of the profit function.

POINTS FOR THOUGHT AND DISCUSSION

What do the x intercepts represent in Fig. 13.5? Interpret the meaning of the y intercept. Discuss the law of diminishing returns as it pertains to the shape of this profit function.

EXAMPLE 6

Solar Energy   A manufacturer has developed a new design for solar collection panels. Marketing studies have indicated that annual demand for the panels will depend on the price charged. The demand function for the panels has been estimated as

$$q = 100,000 - 200p \tag{13.1}$$

where q equals the number of units demanded each year and p equals the price in dollars. Engineering studies indicate that the total cost of producing q panels is represented well by the function

$$C = 150,000 + 100q + 0.003q^2 \tag{13.2}$$

Formulate the profit function $P = f(q)$ which states the annual profit P as a function of the number of units q which are produced and sold.

SOLUTION

We have been asked to develop a function which states profit P as a function of q. As opposed to Example 5, *we must construct* the profit function. Equation (13.2) is a total cost function stated in terms of q; so, that component of the profit function is already available. However, we need to formulate a total revenue function stated in terms of q.

Again it is necessary to remember the basic structure for computing total revenue;

$$\boxed{R = pq} \tag{13.3}$$

Because we want R to be stated in terms of q, we need to replace p in Eq. (13.3) by an equivalent expression which can be derived from the demand function. Solving for p in Eq. (13.1), we find

$$200p = 100{,}000 - q$$

or

$$\boxed{p = 500 - 0.005q} \tag{13.4}$$

We can substitute the right side of this equation into Eq. (13.3) to yield the revenue function

$$R = (500 - 0.005q)q$$
$$= 500q - 0.005q^2$$

Now that both the revenue and cost functions have been stated in terms of q, the profit function can be defined as

$$P = f(q)$$
$$= R - C$$
$$= 500q - 0.005q^2 - (150{,}000 + 100q + 0.003q^2)$$
$$= 500q - 0.005q^2 - 150{,}000 - 100q - 0.003q^2$$

or
$$P = -0.008q^2 + 400q - 150{,}000$$

EXERCISE

For Example 6, determine (1) how many units q should be produced to maximize annual profit; (2) what price should be charged for each panel to generate a demand equal to the answer in part (1); and (3) the maximum annual profit.*

EXAMPLE 7

Restricted Domain   Assume in the last example that the manufacturer's annual production capacity is 20,000 units. Re-solve Example 6 with this added restriction.

---

* Answer: (1) $q = 25{,}000$ units, (2) $p = \$375$, (3) \$4,850,000.

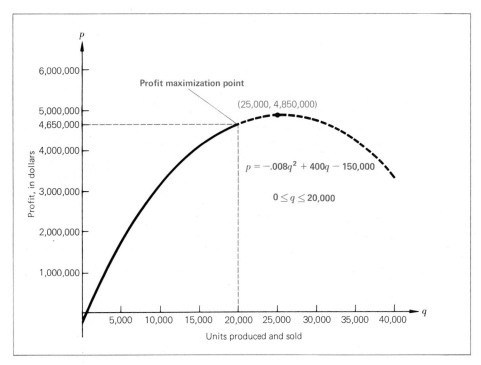

FIGURE 13.6
Profit function/restricted domain.

SOLUTION

With the added restriction, the domain of the function is defined as $0 \leq q \leq 20{,}000$. From Chap. 12, it should be recalled that we must compare the values of $f(q)$ at the endpoints of the domain with the values of $f(q^*)$ for any q^* value where $0 \leq q^* \leq 20{,}000$.

The only critical point on the profit function occurs at $q = 25{,}000$, which is outside the domain. Thus, profit will be maximized at one of the endpoints. Evaluating $f(q)$ at the endpoints, we find

$$f(0) = -150{,}000$$

and
$$f(20{,}000) = -0.008(20{,}000)^2 + 400(20{,}000) - 150{,}000$$
$$= -3{,}200{,}000 + 8{,}000{,}000 - 150{,}000 = 4{,}650{,}000$$

Profit is maximized at a value of \$4,650,000 when $q = 20{,}000$, or when the manufacturer operates at capacity.

The price which should be charged is found by substituting $q = 20{,}000$ into Eq. (13.4) or

$$p = 500 - 0.005(20{,}000)$$
$$= 500 - 100 = \$400$$

Figure 13.6 presents a sketch of the profit function.

Section 13.1 Follow-up Exercises

1 A firm has determined that total revenue is a function of the price charged for its

product. Specifically, the total revenue function is

$$R = f(p) = -10p^2 + 1,750p$$

where p equals the price in dollars.

(a) Determine the price p which results in maximum total revenue.

(b) What is the maximum value for total revenue?

2   The demand function for a firm's product is

$$q = 150,000 - 75p$$

where q equals the number of units demanded and p equals the price in dollars.

(a) Determine the price which should be charged to maximize total revenue

(b) What is the maximum value of total revenue?

(c) How many units are expected to be demanded?

3   The annual profit for a firm depends upon the number of units produced. Specifically, the function which describes the relationship between profit p (stated in dollars) and the number of units produced x is

$$p = -0.01x^2 + 5,000x - 250,000$$

(a) Determine the number of units x which will result in maximum profit.

(b) What is the expected maximum profit?

4   **Beach Management**   A community which is located in a resort area is trying to decide on the parking fee to charge at the town-owned beach. There are other beaches in the area, and there is competition for bathers among the different beaches. The town has determined the following function which expresses the average number of cars per day q as a function of the parking fee p stated in cents.

$$q = 6,000 - 12p$$

(a) Determine the fee which should be charged to maximize daily beach revenues.

(b) What is the maximum daily beach revenue expected to be?

(c) How many cars are expected on an average day?

5   **Import Tax Management**   The United States government is studying the import tax structure for color television sets imported from other countries into the United States. The government is trying to determine the amount of the tax to charge on each TV set. The government realizes that the demand for imported TV sets will be affected by the tax. It estimates that the demand for imported sets D, measured in hundreds of TV sets, will be related to the import tax t, measured in cents, according to the function

$$D = 60,000 - 12.5t$$

(a) Determine the import tax which will result in maximum tax revenues from importing TV sets.

(b) What is the maximum revenue?

(c) What will the demand for imported color TV sets equal with this tax?

6   A manufacturer has determined a cost function which expresses the annual cost of purchasing, owning, and maintaining its raw material inventory as a function of the size of each order. The cost function is

$$C = \frac{51,200}{q} + 8q + 750,000$$

where q equals the size of each order (in tons) and C equals the annual inventory cost.

(a) Determine the order size q which minimizes annual inventory cost.

(b) What are minimum inventory costs expected to equal?

    7   In Exercise 6 assume that the maximum amount of the raw material which can be accepted in any one shipment is 75 tons.

(a) Given this restriction, determine the order size q which minimizes annual inventory cost.

(b) What are the minimum annual inventory costs?

(c) How do these results compare with those in Exercise 6?

    8   A major distributor of racquetballs is thriving because racquetball has taken over as one of the country's most popular participant sports. One of the distributor's major problems is keeping up with the demand for racquetballs. Balls are purchased periodically from a sporting goods manufacturer. The annual cost of purchasing, owning, and maintaining the inventory of racquetballs is described by the function

$$C = \frac{280,000}{q} + 0.15q + 2,000,000$$

where q equals the order size (in dozens of racquetballs) and C equals the annual inventory cost.

(a) Determine the order size q which minimizes annual inventory cost.

(b) What are the minimum inventory costs expected to equal?

    9   The distributor in Exercise 8 has storage facilities to accept up to 1,200 dozens of balls in any one shipment.

(a) Determine the order size q which minimizes annual inventory costs.

(b) What are the minimum inventory costs?

(c) How do these results compare with those in Exercise 9?

    10   The total cost of producing q units of a certain product is described by the function

$$C = 5,000,000 + 250q + 0.002q^2$$

where C is the total cost stated in dollars.

(a) How many units should be produced in order to minimize the *average cost per unit?*

(b) What is the minimum average cost per unit?

(c) What is the total cost of production at this level of output?

    11   The total cost of producing q units of a certain product is described by the function

$$C = 350,000 + 7,500q + 0.25q^2$$

where C is the total cost stated in dollars.

(a) Determine how many units q should be produced in order to minimize the *average cost per unit.*

(b) What is the minimum average cost per unit?

(c) What is the total cost of production at this level of output?

    12   Re-solve Exercise 11 if the maximum production capacity is 1,000 units.

    13   **Public Utilities** A cable TV antenna company has determined that its profitability depends upon the monthly fee it charges its customers. Specifically, the relationship

which describes annual profit P (stated in dollars) as a function of the monthly rental fee r (stated in dollars) is

$$P = -40{,}000r^2 + 720{,}000r - 300{,}000$$

(*a*) Determine the monthly rental fee r which will lead to maximum profit.
(*b*) What is the expected maximum profit?

14 In Exercise 13 assume that the local public utility commission has restricted the CATV company to a monthly fee not to exceed $8.50.
(*a*) What fee leads to a maximum profit for the company?
(*b*) What is the effect of the utility commission's ruling on the profitability of the firm?

15 A company estimates that the demand for its product fluctuates with the price it charges. The demand function is

$$q = 180{,}000 - 250p$$

where q equals the number of units demanded and p equals the price in dollars. The total cost of producing q units of the product is estimated by the function

$$C = 350{,}000 + 300q + 0.001q^2$$

(*a*) Determine how many units q should be produced in order to maximize annual profit.
(*b*) What price should be charged?
(*c*) What is the annual profit expected to equal?

16 If annual capacity is 40,000 units in Exercise 15, how many units q will result in maximum profit?

17 An equivalent way of solving Example 2 is to state total revenue as a function of q, the number of riders per day. Formulate the function $R = g(q)$ and determine the number of riders q which will result in maximum total revenue. Verify that the maximum value of R and the price which should be charged are the same as obtained in Example 2.

13.2 MARGINAL APPROACH TO PROFIT MAXIMIZATION

An alternative approach to finding the profit maximization point involves *marginal analysis.* Popular among economists, marginal analysis examines *incremental effects* on profitability. Given that a firm is producing a certain number of units each year, marginal analysis would be concerned with the effect on profit if *one* additional unit is produced and sold.

To utilize the marginal approach to profit maximization, the following conditions must hold:

REQUIREMENTS FOR USING THE MARGINAL APPROACH

I It must be possible to identify the total revenue function *and* the total cost function, separately.
II The revenue and cost functions must be stated in terms of the level of output or number of units produced and sold.

TABLE 13.1   **COMPUTATION OF MARGINAL REVENUE**

LEVEL OF OUTPUT q	TOTAL REVENUE $f_1(q)$	MARGINAL REVENUE $\Delta R = f_1(q) - f_1(q-1)$
100	$49,950.00	
101	$50,448.995	$498.995
102	$50,947.98	$498.985
103	$51,446.955	$498.975

Marginal Revenue

One of the two important concepts in marginal analysis is marginal revenue. *Marginal revenue is the additional revenue derived from selling one more unit of a product or service.* If each unit of a product sells at the same price, the marginal revenue is always equal to the price. For example, the linear revenue function

$$R = 10q$$

represents a situation where each unit sells for $10. The marginal revenue from selling one additional unit is $10 at any level of output q.

In Example 6 a demand function for solar panels was stated as

$$q = 100,000 - 200p$$

From this demand function we formulated the nonlinear total revenue function

$$R = f_1(q) = 500q - 0.005q^2 \qquad (13.5)$$

Marginal revenue for this example is not constant. We can illustrate this by computing total revenue for different levels of output. Table 13.1 illustrates these calculations for selected values of q. The third column represents the marginal revenue associated with moving from one level of output to another. Note that although the differences are slight, the marginal revenue values are changing at each different level of output.

For a total revenue function $R(q)$, the derivative $R'(q)$ represents the instantaneous rate of change in total revenue given a change in the number of units sold. R' also represents a general expression for the slope of the graph of the total revenue function. For purposes of marginal analysis, the derivative is used to represent the marginal revenue, or

$$MR = R'(q) \qquad (13.6)$$

The derivative, as discussed in Chap. 11, provides an approximation to actual changes in the value of a function. As such, R' can be used to approximate the marginal revenue from selling the next unit. If we find R' for the revenue function in Eq. (13.5)

$$R'(q) = 500 - 0.010q$$

To approximate the marginal revenue from selling the 101st unit, we evaluate R' at $q = 100$, or

$$R'(100) = 500 - 0.010(100)$$
$$= 500 - 1 = 499$$

TABLE 13.2 **COMPUTATION OF MARGINAL COST**

LEVEL OF OUTPUT q	TOTAL COST $f_2(q)$	MARGINAL COST $\Delta C = f_2(q) - f_2(q - 1)$
100	$160,030.00	
101	$160,130.603	$100.603
102	$160,231.212	$100.609
103	$160,331.827	$100.615

And this is a very close approximation to the actual value ($498.995) for marginal revenue shown in Table 13.1.

Marginal Cost

The other important concept in marginal analysis is marginal cost. *Marginal cost is the additional cost incurred as a result of producing and selling one more unit of a product or service.* Linear cost functions assume that the variable cost per unit is constant; for such functions the marginal cost is the same at any level of output. An example of this is the cost function

$$C = 150,000 + 3.5q$$

where variable cost per unit is $3.50.

A nonlinear cost function is characterized by variable marginal costs. This can be illustrated by the cost function

$$C = f_2(q) = 150,000 + 100q + 0.003q^2 \qquad (13.7)$$

which was used in Example 6. We can illustrate that the marginal costs do fluctuate at different levels of output by computing marginal cost values for selected values of q. This computation is illustrated in Table 13.2.

For a total cost function C, the derivative $C'(q)$ represents the instantaneous rate of change in total cost given a change in the number of units produced. $C'(q)$ also represents a general expression for the slope of the graph of the total cost function. For purposes of marginal analysis, the derivative is used to represent the marginal cost, or

$$MC = C'(q) \qquad (13.8)$$

As with R', C' can be used to approximate the marginal cost associated with producing the next unit. The derivative of the cost function in Eq. (13.7) is

$$C'(q) = 100 + 0.006q$$

To approximate the marginal cost from producing the 101st unit, we evaluate C' at $q = 100$, or

$$C'(100) = 100 + 0.006(100)$$
$$= \$100.60$$

If we compare this value with the actual value ($100.603) in Table 13.2, we see that the two values are very close.

Marginal Profit Analysis

As indicated earlier, the marginal profit analysis is concerned with the effect on profit if one additional unit of a product is produced and sold. As long as the additional revenue brought in by the next unit exceeds the cost of producing and selling that unit, there is a net profit from producing and selling that unit and total profit increases. If, however, the additional revenue from selling the next unit is exceeded by the cost of producing and selling the additional unit, there is a net loss from that next unit and total profit decreases. Here is a rule of thumb concerning whether or not to produce an additional unit (assuming profit is of greatest importance).

RULE OF THUMB:

SHOULD AN ADDITIONAL UNIT BE PRODUCED?

I If $MR > MC$, produce the next unit.

II If $MR < MC$, do not produce the next unit.

For many production situations, the marginal revenue exceeds the marginal cost at lower levels of output. As the level of output (quantity produced) increases, the amount by which marginal revenue exceeds marginal cost becomes smaller. Eventually a level of output is reached at which $MR = MC$. Beyond this point $MR < MC$, and total profit begins to decrease with added output. Thus, from a theoretical standpoint, if the point can be identified where for the last unit produced and sold $MR = MC$, total profit will be maximized. This profit maximization level of output can be identified by the following condition.

PROFIT MAXIMIZATION CRITERION

Produce to the level of output where

$$MR = MC \qquad\qquad \textbf{(13.9)}$$

Stated in terms of derivatives, this criterion suggests producing to the point where

$$\boxed{R'(q) = C'(q)} \qquad\qquad \textbf{(13.10)}$$

This equation is a natural result of differentiating the profit equation

$$P(q) = R(q) - C(q)$$

and setting the derivative equal to 0:

$$P'(q) = R'(q) - C'(q)$$
and
$$P'(q) = 0$$
when
$$R'(q) - C'(q) = 0$$
or
$$R'(q) = C'(q)$$

SUFFICIENT CONDITION

FOR PROFIT MAXIMIZATION

Given a level of output q^* where $R'(q) = C'(q)$ (or, $MR = MC$), producing q^* will result in profit maximization if

$$R''(q^*) < C''(q^*) \qquad\qquad (13.11)$$

EXAMPLE 8

Re-solve Example 6 using the marginal approach.

SOLUTION

In Example 6

$$R = 500q - 0.005q^2$$

and

$$C = 150,000 + 100q + 0.003q^2$$

Because the revenue and cost functions are distinct, and both are stated in terms of the level of output q, the two requirements for conducting marginal analysis are satisfied. We have already determined that

$$R'(q) = 500 - 0.01q$$

and

$$C'(q) = 100 + 0.06q$$

Therefore,

$$R'(q) = C'(q)$$

when

$$500 - 0.01q = 100 + 0.006q$$

$$-0.016q = -400$$

or

$$q = 25,000$$

Since

$$R''(q) = -0.01 \quad\text{and}\quad C''(q) = 0.007$$

$$R''(q^*) < C''(q^*)$$

or

$$-0.01 < 0.006$$

and there is a relative maximum on the profit function when $q = 25,000$. Figure 13.7 presents the graphs of $R(q)$ and $C(q)$.

Take a moment to examine Fig. 13.7. The following observations are worth noting:

1 Points C and D represent points where the revenue and cost functions intersect. These represent break-even points.

2 Between points C and D the revenue function is above the cost function, indicating that total revenue is greater than total cost and a profit will be earned within this interval. For levels of output to the right of D, the cost function lies above the revenue function, indicating that total cost exceeds total revenue and a negative profit (loss) will result.

3 The *vertical* distance separating the graphs of the two functions represents the profit or loss, depending on the level of output.

4 In the interval $0 \le q \le 25,000$, the slope of the revenue function is positive and greater than the slope of the cost function. Stated in terms of MR and MC, $MR > MC$ in this interval.

5 Also, in the interval $0 \le q \le 25,000$, the vertical distance separating the two curves becomes greater, indicating that profit is increasing on the interval.

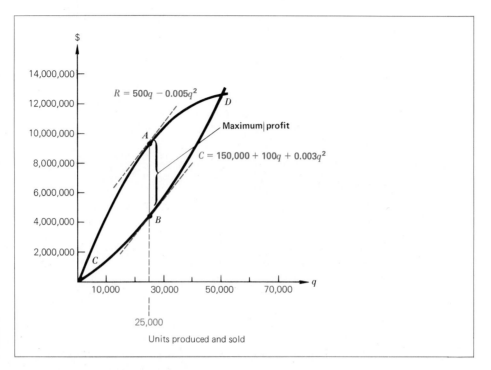

FIGURE 13.7
Marginal
analysis: profit
maximization.

6 At $q = 25,000$ the slopes at points A and B are the same, indicating that $MR = MC$. Also at $q = 25,000$ the vertical distance separating the two curves is greater than at any other point in the profit region; thus, this is the point of profit maximization.

7 For $q > 25,000$ the slope of the revenue function is positive but less positive than that for the cost function. Thus, $MR < MC$ and for each additional unit profit decreases, actually resulting in a loss beyond point D.

EXAMPLE 9

In Example 5 we were asked to determine the number of sales representatives x which would result in maximum profit P for a cosmetic and beauty supply firm. The profit function was stated as

$$P = f(x) = -12.5x^2 + 1,375x - 1,500$$

Using the marginal approach, determine the number of representatives which will result in maximum profit for the firm.

SOLUTION

We cannot use the marginal approach in this example because we cannot identify the total revenue and total cost functions which were combined to form the profit function! Requirement 1 for using marginal analysis is not satisfied.

EXAMPLE 10

Figure 13.8 illustrates a sketch of a linear revenue function and a nonlinear cost function.

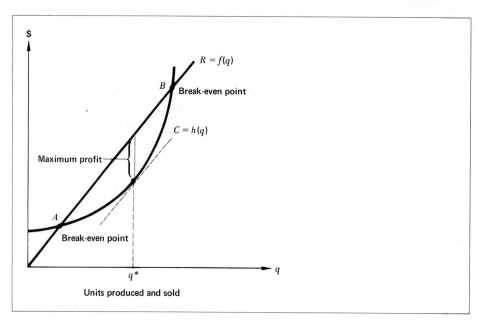

FIGURE 13.8
Linear
revenue/
quadratic cost
functions.

To the left of q^*, the slope of the revenue function exceeds the slope of the cost function, indicating that $MR > MC$. At q^* the slopes of the two functions are the same. And the vertical distance separating the two functions is greater at q^* than for any other value of q between points A and B. Points A and B are break-even points.

Section 13.2 Follow-up Exercises

1   The total cost and total revenue functions for a product are

$$C(q) = 500 + 100q + 0.5q^2$$
$$R(q) = 500q$$

(a) Using the marginal approach, determine the profit maximizing level of output.
(b) What is the maximum profit?
2   A firm sells each unit of a product for $50. The total cost of producing x (thousand) units is described by the function

$$C(x) = 10 - 2.5x^2 + x^3$$

where $C(x)$ is measured in thousands of dollars.
(a) Use the marginal approach to determine the profit maximizing level of output.
(b) What is total revenue at this level of output? Total cost? Total profit?
3   The profit function for a firm is

$$P(q) = -4.5q^2 + 36{,}000q - 45{,}000$$

(a) Using the marginal approach, determine the profit-maximizing level of output.
(b) What is the maximum profit?
4   The total cost and total revenue functions for a product are

$$C(q) = 500{,}000 + 250q + 0.002q^2$$
$$R(q) = 1{,}250q - 0.005q^2$$

(a) Using the marginal approach, determine the profit-maximizing level of output.

(b) What is the maximum profit?

    5   The total cost and total revenue functions for a product are

$$C(q) = 40{,}000 + 25q + 0.002q^2$$
$$R(q) = 75q - 0.008q^2$$

(a) Using the marginal approach, determine the profit-maximizing level of output.

(b) What is the maximum profit?

    6   Portrayed in Fig. 13.9 is a total cost function $C(q)$ and a total revenue function $R(q)$. Discuss the economic significance of the four levels of output q_1, q_2, q_3, and q_4.

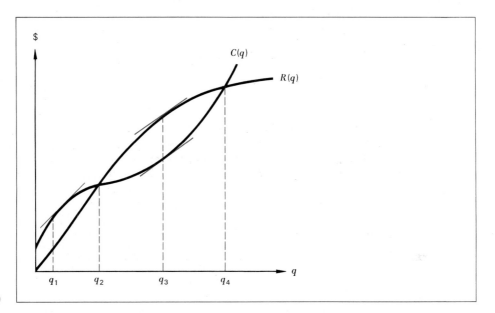

FIGURE 13.9

13.3 ADDITIONAL APPLICATIONS

The following examples are additional applications of optimization procedures.

EXAMPLE 11

Real Estate A large multinational conglomerate is interested in purchasing some prime boardwalk real estate at a major ocean resort. The conglomerate is interested in acquiring a rectangular lot which is located on the boardwalk. The only restriction is that the lot have an area of 100,000 square feet. Figure 13.10 presents a sketch of the layout with x equaling the boardwalk frontage for the lot and y equaling the depth of the lot (both measured in feet).

    The seller of the property is pricing the lots at $500 per foot of frontage along the boardwalk and $200 per foot of depth away from the boardwalk. The conglomerate is

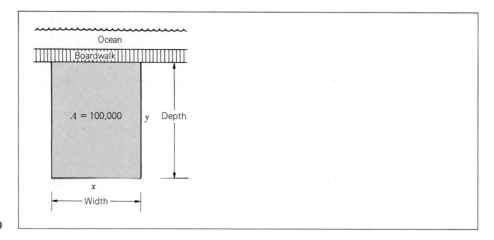

FIGURE 13.10

interested in determining the dimensions of the lot which will minimize the total purchase cost.

Refer to Fig. 13.10. Total purchase cost for a lot having dimensions of x feet by y feet is

$$C = 500x + 200y \qquad \text{(13.12)}$$

where C is cost in dollars.

The problem is to determine the values of x and y which minimize C. However, C is stated as a function of two variables, and we are unable, as yet, to handle functions which have two independent variables.

Because the conglomerate has specified that the area of the lot must equal 100,000 square feet, a relationship which exists between x and y is

$$xy = 100,000 \qquad \text{(13.13)}$$

Given this relationship, we can solve for either variable in terms of the other. For instance,

$$y = \frac{100,000}{x} \qquad \text{(13.14)}$$

We can substitute the right side of this equation into the cost function wherever the variable y appears, or

$$C = f(x)$$

$$= 500x + 200\,\frac{100,000}{x}$$

$$= 500x + \frac{20,000,000}{x} \qquad \text{(13.15)}$$

Equation (13.15) is a restatement of Eq. (13.12), only in terms of one independent variable. We can now seek the value of x which minimizes the purchase cost C.

The first derivative is

$$C'(x) = 500 - 20,000,000x^{-2}$$

If C' is set equal to 0,

$$500 = \frac{20,000,000}{x^2}$$

$$x^2 = \frac{20,000,000}{500}$$

$$= 40,000$$

or critical values occur at

$$x = \pm 200$$

The critical point at $x = -200$ is meaningless. To test $x = 200$,

$$C''(x) = 40,000,000x^{-3}$$

$$= \frac{40,000,000}{x^3}$$

$$C''(200) = \frac{40,000,000}{(200)^3}$$

$$= \frac{40,000,000}{8,000,000} = 5 > 0$$

Thus, a relative minimum occurs for C at $x = 200$.

Total costs will be minimized when the width of the lot equals 200 feet. The depth of the lot can be found by substituting $x = 200$ into Eq. (13.14), or

$$y = \frac{100,000}{200}$$

$$= 500$$

If the lot is 200 feet by 500 feet, total cost will be minimized at a value of

$$C = \$500(200) + \$200(500)$$
$$= \$200,000$$

EXAMPLE 12

Emergency Response: Location Model   Example 15 in Chap. 10 discussed a problem in which three resort cities had agreed jointly to build and support an emergency response facility which would house rescue trucks and trained paramedics. The key question dealt with the location of the facility. The criterion selected was to choose the location so as to minimize S, the sum of the products of the summer populations of each town and the square of the distance betweeen the town and the facility. Figure 13.11 shows the relative locations of the three cities.

The criterion function to be minimized was determined to be

$$S = f(x) = 450x^2 - 19,600x + 241,600$$

where x is the location of the facility relative to the zero point in Fig. 13.11 (You may want to reread Example 15 on page 398). Given the criterion function, the first derivative is

$$f'(x) = 900x - 19,600$$

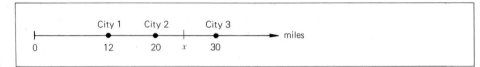

FIGURE 13.11

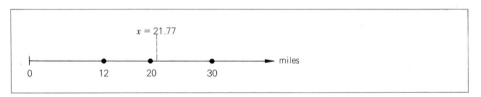

FIGURE 13.12

If f' is set equal to 0,

$$900x = 19,600$$

and a critical value occurs at

$$x = 21.77$$

Checking the nature of the critical point, we find

$$f''(x) = 900$$
$$f''(21.77) = 900 > 0$$

Thus, a relative minimum occurs for f when $x = 21.77$. The criterion S is minimized at $x = 21.77$, and the facility should be located as shown in Fig. 13.12.

EXAMPLE 13 ▮▮▮▮▮▮▮▮▮▮▮▮▮▮▮▮▮▮▮▮▮▮▮▮▮▮▮

Equipment Replacement A decision faced by many organizations is determining the optimal point in time to replace a major piece of equipment. Major pieces of equipment are often characterized by two cost components—*capital cost* and *operating cost*. **Capital cost** is purchase cost less any salvage value. If a machine costs $10,000 and is later sold for $2,000, the capital cost is $8,000. **Operating cost** includes costs of owning and maintaining a piece of equipment. Gasoline, oil, insurance, and repair costs associated with owning and operating a vehicle would be considered operating costs.

Some organizations focus on the *average capital cost* and *average operating cost* when they determine when to replace a piece of equipment. These costs tend to trade off against one another. That is, as one cost increases, the other decreases. Average capital cost for a piece of equipment tends to decrease over time. For a new automobile which decreases in value from $6,000 to $5,000 in the first year, the average capital cost for that year is $1,000. If the automobile decreases in value to $2,000 after 5 years, the average capital cost is

$$\frac{\$6,000 - \$2,000}{5} = \frac{\$4,000}{5} = \$800 \text{ per year}$$

Average operating cost tends to increase over time as equipment becomes less efficient and more maintenance is required. For example, the average annual operating cost of a car tends to increase as the car ages.

A taxi company in a major city wants to determine how long it should keep its cabs. Each cab comes fully equipped at a cost of $12,000. The company estimates average capital cost and average operating cost to be a function of x, the number of miles the car is driven. The salvage value of the car, in dollars, is expressed by the function

$$S(x) = 10,000 - 0.06x$$

This means that the car decreases $2,000 in value as soon as the cab is driven, and it decreases in value at the rate of $0.06 per mile.

The average operating cost, stated in dollars per mile, is estimated by the function

$$O(x) = 0.0000003x + 0.15$$

Determine the number of miles the car should be driven prior to replacement if the objective is to minimize the *sum* of average capital cost and average operating cost.

SOLUTION

Average capital cost per mile equals the purchase cost less the salvage value, all divided by the number of miles driven, or

$$C(x) = \frac{12,000 - (10,000 - 0.06x)}{x}$$

$$= \frac{2,000 + 0.06x}{x}$$

$$= \frac{2,000}{x} + 0.06$$

The sum of average capital cost and average operating cost is

$$f(x) = O(x) + C(x)$$

$$= 0.0000003x + 0.15 + \frac{2,000}{x} + 0.06$$

$$= 0.0000003x + 0.21 + \frac{2,000}{x}$$

$$f'(x) = 0.0000003 - 2,000x^{-2}$$

If f' is set equal to 0,

$$0.0000003 = \frac{2,000}{x^2}$$

$$x^2 = \frac{2,000}{0.0000003}$$

$$= 6,666,666,666.67$$

or a critical value occurs when

$$x = 81,649.6$$

Checking this critical point, we have

$$f''(x) = 4,000x^{-3}$$

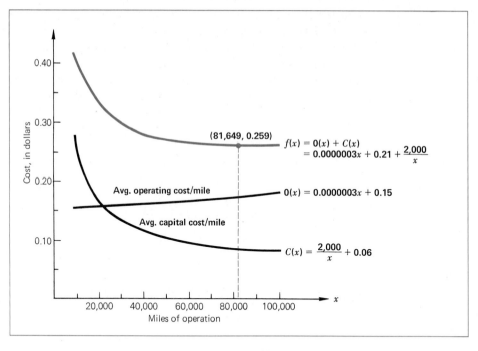

FIGURE 13.13

$$= \frac{4,000}{x^3}$$

$$f''(81,649.6) = \frac{4,000}{81,649.6} > 0$$

Therefore, a relative minimum occurs for f when $x = 81,649.6$,

$$f(81,649.6) = 0.0000003(81,649.6) + 0.21 + \frac{2,000}{81,649.6}$$

$$= 0.02450 + 0.21 + 0.02450 = 0.259$$

Average capital and operating costs are minimized at a value of $0.259 per mile when a taxi is driven 81,649.6 miles. Total capital and operating costs will equal (cost/mile) · (number of miles), or

$$(\$0.259)(81,649.6) = \$21,147.25$$

Figure 13.13 illustrates the two component cost functions and the total cost function. Notice that the average operating cost per mile $O(x)$ increases with increasing values of x and that average capital cost per mile $C(x)$ decreases with increasing values of x.

POINT FOR THOUGHT AND DISCUSSION

Does $f(x)$ exhibit any asymptotic behavior? If so, how?

EXAMPLE 14

Compensation Planning   A producer of a perishable product offers a wage incentive to drivers of its trucks. A standard delivery takes an average of 20 hours. Drivers are paid at the rate of $10 per hour up to a *maximum* of 20 hours. If the trip requires more than 20 hours, the drivers receive compensation for only 20 hours. There is an incentive for drivers to make the trip in less (but not too much less!) than 20 hours. For each hour under 20, the hourly wage increases by $1.

(a) Determine the function $w = f(x)$ where w equals the hourly wage in dollars and x equals the number of hours required to complete the trip.

(b) What trip time x will maximize the driver's salary for a trip?

(c) What is the hourly wage associated with this trip time?

(d) What is the maximum salary?

(e) How does this salary compare with that received for a 20-hour trip?

SOLUTION

(a) The hourly wage function must be stated in two parts.

$$\text{Hourly wage} = \begin{cases} \$10 + \$1 \times \text{(no. of hours trip time is less than 20)} \\ \qquad \text{(when trip time is less than 20 hours)} \\ \$10 \qquad \text{(when trip time is 20 hours or more)} \end{cases}$$

Given the variable definitions for x and w, this function can be restated as

$$w = f(x) = \begin{cases} 10 + 1(20 - x) & 0 \le x < 20 & \textbf{(13.16a)} \\ 10 & x \ge 20 & \textbf{(13.16b)} \end{cases}$$

(b) A driver's salary S for a trip will equal $10/hour $\times$ 20 hours = $200 if trip time is greater than or equal to 20 hours. If the trip time is less than 20 hours,

$$\begin{aligned} S &= g(x) \\ &= wx \\ &= [10 + 1(20 - x)] \, x \\ &= (30 - x) \, x \\ &= 30x - x^2 \qquad\qquad \textbf{(13.17)} \end{aligned}$$

To examine g for a relative maximum, we find the derivative

$$g'(x) = 30 - 2x$$

Setting g' equal to 0,

$$30 - 2x = 0$$
$$30 = 2x$$

and a critical value occurs when

$$15 = x$$

To check the behavior of $g(x)$ when $x = 15$,

$$g''(x) = -2$$

and
$$g''(15) = -2 < 0$$

Therefore, a relative maximum occurs on g when $x = 15$, or when a trip takes 15 hours.

(c) The hourly wage associated with a 15-hour trip is

$$w = 10 + 1(20 - 15)$$
$$= 10 + 5 = \$15$$

(*d*) The driver salary associated with a 15-hour trip is found by evaluating $g(15)$. If we substitute $x = 15$ into Eq. (13.17),

$$S = 30(15) - 15^2$$
$$= 450 - 225 = \$225$$

We also could have arrived at this answer by multiplying the hourly wage of $15 times the trip time of 15 hours.

(*e*) The $225 salary for a 15-hour trip is $25 more than the salary for a trip time of 20 hours or more.

EXAMPLE 15

Pipeline Construction   A major oil company is planning to construct a pipeline to deliver crude oil from a major well site to a point where the crude will be loaded on tankers and shipped to refineries. Figure 13.14 illustrates the relative locations of the well site A and the destination point C. Points A and C are on opposite sides of a river which is 25 miles wide. Point C is also 100 miles south of A along the river. The oil company is proposing a pipeline which will run south along the east side of the river, and at some point x will cross the river to point C. Construction costs are $100,000 per mile along the bank of the river and $200,000 per mile for the section crossing the river. Determine the crossing point x which will result in minimum construction costs for the pipeline.

SOLUTION

Construction costs will be computed according to the formula

$$
\boxed{
\begin{aligned}
\text{Cost} = \ &\$100{,}000/\text{mile (miles of pipeline along the river)}\\
&+ \$200{,}000/\text{mile (miles of pipeline crossing the river)}
\end{aligned}
}
\qquad \textbf{(13.18)}
$$

The distance from point A to the crossing point x is $(100 - x)$ miles.

PYTHAGOREAN THEOREM

Given a right triangle with base a, height b, and hypotenuse c,

$$c^2 = a^2 + b^2$$

or

$$c = \sqrt{a^2 + b^2}$$

See Fig. 13.15.

Using the Pythagorean theorem, the length of the underwater section of the pipeline from C to x is

$$\sqrt{x^2 + (25)^2}$$

Using Eq. (13.18), the total cost of construction of the pipeline, C (stated in thousands of dollars), is

$$
\begin{aligned}
C = f(x)\\
= \ &100(100 - x) + 200\sqrt{x^2 + (25)^2}\\
= \ &10{,}000 - 100x + 200\sqrt{x^2 + 625}\\
= \ &10{,}000 - 100x + 200(x^2 + 625)^{1/2}
\end{aligned}
\qquad \textbf{(13.19)}
$$

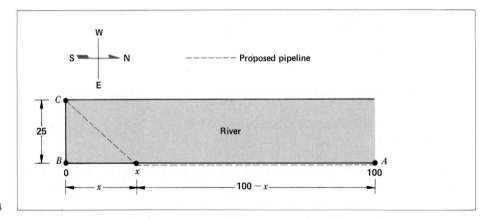

FIGURE 13.14

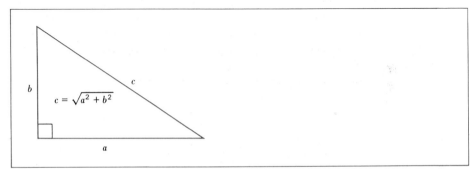

FIGURE 13.15
Pythagorean
theorem.

To examine f for any relative minima, we find the derivative

$$f'(x) = -100 + 200(\tfrac{1}{2})(x^2 + 625)^{-1/2}\,(2x)$$
$$= -100 + 200x(x^2 + 625)^{-1/2}$$
$$= -100 + \frac{200x}{(x^2 + 625)^{1/2}}$$

Setting f' equal to zero,

$$-100 + \frac{200x}{(x^2 + 625)^{1/2}} = 0$$
$$\frac{200x}{(x^2 + 625)^{1/2}} = 100$$
$$\frac{200x}{100} = (x^2 + 625)^{1/2}$$
$$2x = \sqrt{x^2 + 625} \qquad\qquad \textbf{(13.20)}$$

If we square both sides of Eq. (13.20),

$$4x^2 = x^2 + 625$$
$$3x^2 = 625$$
$$x^2 = 208.33$$

and a (relevant) critical value occurs when $x = 14.43$ (a negative root is meaningless).

The exercise above should verify that a relative minimum occurs when $x = 14.43$, or
the pipeline should cross the river after the pipeline has come south 85.57 miles. Total
construction costs (in thousands of dollars) can be calculated by substituting $x = 14.43$
into Eq. (13.19), or

$$
\begin{aligned}
C &= 10{,}000 - 100(14.43) + 200\sqrt{(14.43)^2 + 625} \\
&= 10{,}000 - 1443 + 200\sqrt{833.22} \\
&= 10{,}000 - 1443 + 200(28.86) \\
&= 10{,}000 - 1443 + 5772 \\
&= 14{,}329(\$1{,}000\text{s}) \\
&= \$14{,}329{,}000
\end{aligned}
$$

Section 13.3 Follow-up Exercises

1 A person wishes to fence in a rectangular garden which is to have an area of
2,025 square feet. Determine the dimensions which will create the desired area but will
require the minimum length of fencing.

2 An owner of a ranch wishes to build a rectangular riding corral having an area of
5,000 square meters. If the corral appears as in Fig. 13.16 determine the dimensions x and
y which will require the minimum length of fencing. (*Hint:* Set up a function for the total
length of fencing required, stated in terms of x and y. Then, remembering that $xy = 5{,}000$, restate the length function in terms of either x or y.)

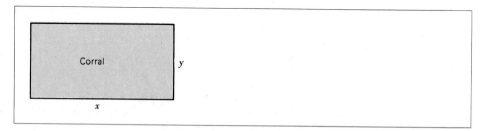

FIGURE 13.16

3 A small beach club has been given 300 meters of flotation barrier to enclose a
swimming area. The desire is to create the largest rectangular swim area given the 300
meters of flotation barrier. Figure 13.17 illustrates the proposed layout. Note that the flotation barrier is required on only three sides of the swimming area. Determine the dimensions x and y which result in the largest swim area. What is the maximum area?
(*Hint:* Remember that $x + 2y = 300$.)

FIGURE 13.17

4 An automobile distributor wishes to create a parking area near a major U.S. port for storing new cars from Japan. The parking area is to have a total area of 1,000,000 square meters and will have dimensions as indicated in Fig. 13.18. Because of security concerns, the section of fence across the front of the lot will be more heavy-duty and taller than the fence used along the sides and rear of the lot. The cost of fence for the front is $20 per running meter and that used for the other three sides costs $12 per running meter. Determine the dimensions x and y which result in a minimum total cost of fence. What is the minimum cost? (*Hint:* $xy = 1,000,000.$)

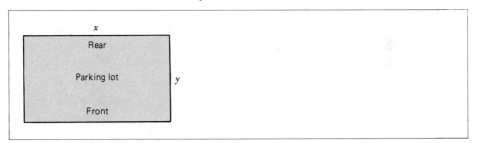

FIGURE 13.18

5 Figure 13.19 illustrates a recreation yard which is to be fenced within a prison. In addition to enclosing the area, a section of fence should divide the total area in half. If 3,600 feet of fence are available, determine the dimensions x and y which result in the maximum enclosed area. What is the maximum area? (*Hint:* $2x + 3y = 3,600.$)

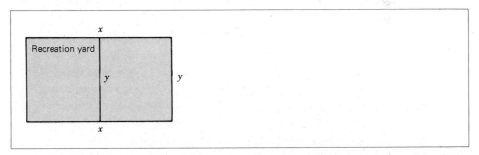

FIGURE 13.19

6 A manufacturer wishes to locate a warehouse between three cities. The relative locations of the cities are shown in Fig. 13.20. The objective is to locate the warehouse so as to minimize the sum of the squares of the distances separating each city and the warehouse. How far from the reference point should the warehouse be located?

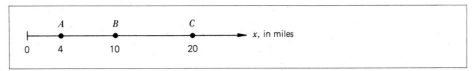

FIGURE 13.20

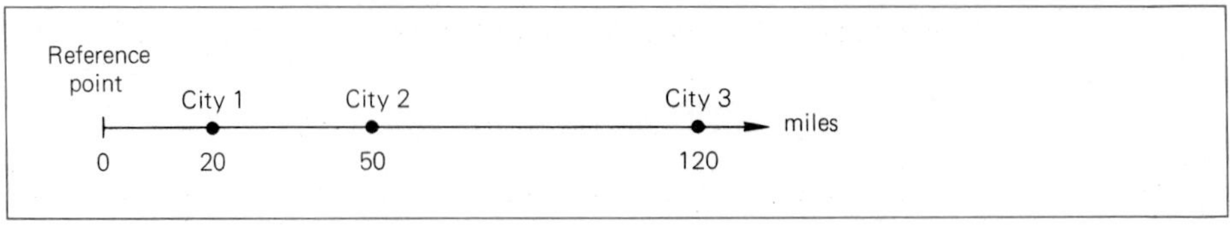

FIGURE 13.21

7 **Health Maintenance Organization** Figure 13.21 illustrates the relative locations of three cities. A large health maintenance organization (HMO) wishes to build a satellite clinic to service the three cities. The location of the clinic x should be such that the sum of the squares of the distances between the clinic and each city is minimized. This criterion can be stated as

Minimize
$$S = \sum_{j=1}^{3} (x_j - x)^2$$

where x_j is the location of the city j and x is the location of the clinic. Determine the location x which minimizes S.

*8 In Exercise 7, suppose that cities 1, 2, and 3 have 10,000, 5,000, and 3,000 persons, respectively, who are members of the HMO. Assume that the HMO has established its location criterion as the minimization of

$$\sum_{j=1}^{3} \begin{pmatrix} \text{HMO membership} \\ \text{in city } j \end{pmatrix} \begin{pmatrix} \text{square of distance} \\ \text{separating city } j \\ \text{and the clinic} \end{pmatrix}$$

or
$$S = \sum_{j=1}^{3} n_j (x_j - x)^2$$

where n_j equals the number of members residing in city j. Determine the location x which minimizes S.

9 A police department purchases new patrol cars for $15,000. The department estimates average capital cost and average operating cost to be a function of x, the number of miles the car is driven. The salvage value of a patrol car (in dollars) is expressed by the function

$$S(x) = 12,000 - 0.06x$$

Average operating cost, stated in dollars per mile, is estimated by the function

$$O(x) = 0.0000006x + 0.18$$

(a) Determine how many miles the car should be driven prior to replacement if the objective is to minimize the sum of average capital cost and average operating cost per mile.
(b) What is the minimum cost per mile?
(c) What is the salvage value expected to equal?

10 A major airline purchases a particular type of plane at a cost of $25,000,000. The company estimates that average capital cost and average operating cost are a function of x, the number of hours of flight time. The salvage value of a plane (in dollars) is expressed by the function

$$S(x) = 21,000,000 - 5,000x$$

Average operating cost, stated in dollars per hour of flight time, is estimated by the function

$$O(x) = 400 + 0.20x$$

(a) Determine how many hours a plane should be flown before replacement if the objective is to minimize the sum of average capital and average operating cost per hour?
(b) What is the minimum cost per hour?
(c) What is the salvage value expected to equal?

   11   A university ski club is organizing a weekend trip to a ski lodge. The price for the trip is $100 if 50 or fewer persons sign up for the trip. For every traveler in excess of 50, the price for *all* will decrease by $1. For instance, if 51 persons sign up, each will pay $99. Let x equal the number of travelers in excess of 50.
(a) Determine the function which states price per person p as a function of x.
(b) In part (a) is there any restriction on the domain?
(c) Formulate the function $R = h(x)$, which states total revenue R as a function of x.
(d) What value of x results in the maximum value of R?
(e) How many persons should sign up for the trip?
(f) What is the maximum value of R?
(g) What price per ticket results in the maximum revenue?
(h) Could the club generate more revenue by taking 50 or fewer persons?

   12   **Wage Incentive Plan**   A manufacturer offers a wage incentive to persons who work on one particular product. The standard time to complete one unit of the product is 15 hours. Laborers are paid at the rate of $6 per hour up to a maximum of 15 hours for each unit they work on (if a laborer takes 20 hours to complete a unit, he or she is only paid for the 15 hours the unit should have taken). There is an incentive for laborers to complete a unit in less than 15 hours. For each hour under 15 the hourly wage increases by $1.50. Let x equal the number of hours required to complete a unit
(a) Determine the function $w = f(x)$ where w equals the hourly wage in dollars.
(b) What length of time x will maximize a laborer's total wages for completing one unit?
(c) What is the hourly wage associated with this time per unit x?
(d) What is maximum salary per unit?
(e) How does this salary compare with the wages earned by taking 15 or more hours per unit?

   13   **Pipeline Construction**   A major oil company is planning to construct a pipeline to deliver crude oil from a major well site to a point where the crude will be loaded on tankers and shipped to refineries. Figure 13.22 illustrates the relative locations of the well site A and the destination point C. Points A and C are on opposite sides of a river which is 20 miles wide. Point C is also 200 miles south of A along the river.

   The oil company is proposing a pipeline which will run south along the east side of the river and at some point, x, will cross the river to point C. Construction costs are $50,000 per mile along the bank of the river and $100,000 per mile for the section crossing the river. There are tradeoffs between taking a route from A to B to C versus a route which crosses the river prior to reaching point B. The former route only has a 20-mile section across the river at the higher construction cost per mile, but the total length of the pipeline is longer. A route which crosses prior to reaching point B is shorter in total but has a greater length across the river. Determine the crossing point x which leads to minimum construction costs. What is the minimum construction cost?

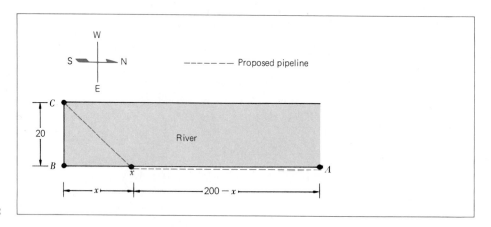

FIGURE 13.22

ADDITIONAL EXERCISES

1   A firm sells each unit of a product for $250. The cost function which describes the total cost C as a function of the number of units produced and sold x is

$$C(x) = 50x + 0.1x^2 + 150$$

(a) Formulate the profit function $P = f(x)$.
(b) How many units should be produced and sold in order to maximize total profit?
(c) What is total revenue at this level of output?
(d) What is total cost at this level of output?

2   Re-solve Exercise 1 using the marginal approach.

3   A local travel agent is organizing a charter flight to a well-known resort. The agent has quoted a price of $300 per person if 100 or fewer sign up for the flight. For every person over the 100, the price for *all* will decrease by $2.50. For instance, if 101 people sign up, each will pay $297.50. Let x equal the number of persons above 100.
(a) Determine the function which states price per person p as a function of x, or $p = f(x)$.
(b) In part a, is there any restriction on the domain?
(c) Formulate the function $R = h(x)$, which states total ticket revenue R as a function of x.
(d) What value of x results in the maximum value of R?
(e) What is the maximum value of R?
(f) What price per ticket results in the maximum R?

4   The total cost of producing q units of a certain product is described by the function

$$C = 12{,}500{,}000 + 100q + 0.02q^2$$

(a) Determine how many units q should be produced in order to minimize the *average cost per unit*.
(b) What is the minimum average cost per unit?
(c) What is the total cost of production at this level of output?

5   A law of economics states that the average cost per unit is minimized when the marginal cost equals the average cost. Show that this is true for the cost function in Exercise 4.

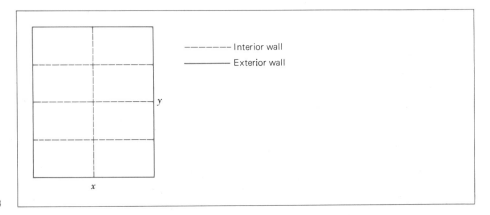

— — — — — Interior wall

———————— Exterior wall

FIGURE 13.23

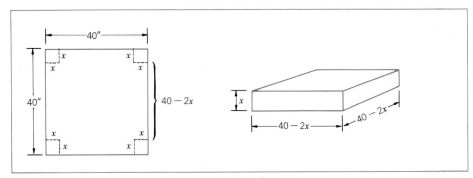

FIGURE 13.24

6 The quadratic total cost function for a product is

$$C = ax^2 + bx + c$$

where x equals the number of units produced and sold and C is stated in dollars. The product sells at a price of p dollars per unit.

(a) Construct the profit function stated in terms of x.

(b) What value of x results in maximum profit?

(c) What restriction assures that a relative maximum occurs at this value of x?

(d) What restrictions on a, b, c, and p assure that $x > 0$?

7 An oil field currently has 10 wells, each producing 300 barrels of oil per day. For each new well drilled, it is estimated that the yield per well will decrease by 10 barrels per day. Determine the number of new wells to drill in order to maximize total daily output for the oil field. What is the maximum output?

8 A small warehouse is to be constructed which is to have a total area of 10,000 square feet. The building is to be partitioned as shown in Fig. 13.23. Costs have been estimated based on exterior and interior wall dimensions. The costs are $200 per running foot of exterior wall plus $100 per running foot of interior wall. (a) Determine the dimensions which will minimize the construction costs. (b) What are the minimum costs?

9 An open rectangular box is to be constructed by cutting square corners from a 40- × 40-inch piece of cardboard and folding up the flaps as shown in Fig. 13.24. (a) Determine the value of x which will yield the box of maximum volume. (b) What is the maximum volume?

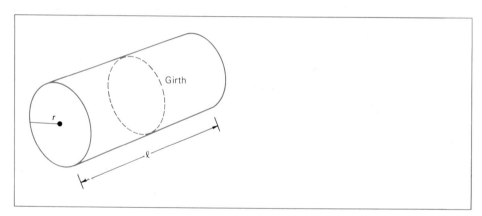

FIGURE 13.25

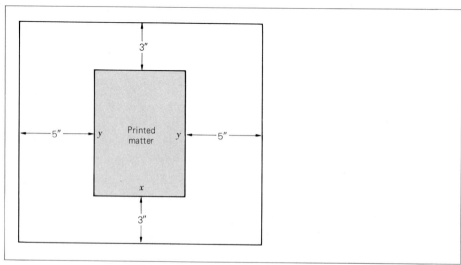

FIGURE 13.26

*10   The U.S. Parcel Post requires that packages conform to specified dimensions. Specifically, the length plus girth must be no greater than 84 inches. (*a*) Find the dimensions (*r* and *l*) of a cylindrical package which maximize the volume of the package. (*Hint:* See Fig. 13.25 and remember that $V = \pi r^2 l$). (*b*) What is the girth of the package? (*c*) What is the maximum volume?

*11   **Poster Problem**   Figure 13.26 is a sketch of a poster which is being designed for a political campaign. The printed area should contain 1,500 square inches. A margin of 5 inches should appear on each side of the printed matter and a 3-inch margin on the top and bottom.

(*a*) Determine the dimensions of the printed area which minimize the *area* of the poster.
(*b*) What are the optimal dimensions of the poster?
(*c*) What is the minimum poster area?

*12   A person wants to purchase a rectangular piece of property in order to construct a warehouse. The warehouse should have an area of 10,000 square feet. Zoning ordinances specify that there should be at least 30 feet between the building and the side boundaries of the lot and at least 40 feet between the building and the front and rear boundaries of the lot. Figure 13.27 is a sketch of the proposed lot.

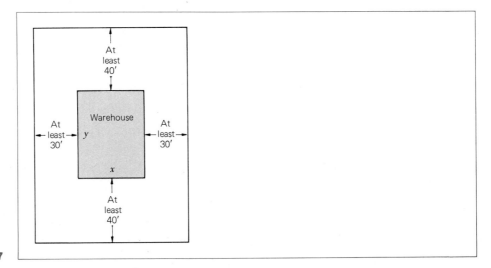

FIGURE 13.27

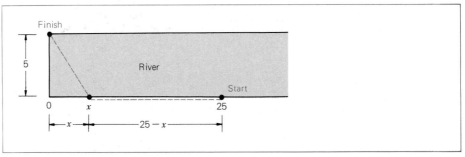

FIGURE 13.28

(*a*) Determine the dimensions of the warehouse which will minimize the area of the lot.

(*b*) What are the optimal dimensions of the lot?

(*c*) What is the minimum lot area?

13 Determine two numbers x and y whose sum is 50 and whose product is as large as possible. What is the maximum product of the two numbers?

14 Determine two positive numbers whose product equals 40 and whose sum is as small as possible. What is the minimum sum?

*15 Biathalon A woman is going to participate in a run-swim biathalon. The course is of variable length and is shown in Fig. 13.28. Each participant must run (or walk) from the starting point along the river. They must cross the river by swimming; however, the crossing point x may be chosen by each participant.

This contestant estimates that she will average 5 miles per hour for the running portion of the biathalon and 1 mile per hour for the swimming portion. She wishes to minimize her time in the event.

(*a*) Determine the crossing point x which will result in the minimum time.

(*b*) What is the minimum time expected to equal?

(*c*) How does this time compare with that if she chose to run the full 25 miles (crossing point is at $x = 0$?).

Hint: Time = distance ÷ speed or hours = miles ÷ miles/hour; also

$$t_{\text{total}} = t_{\text{run}} + t_{\text{swim}}$$

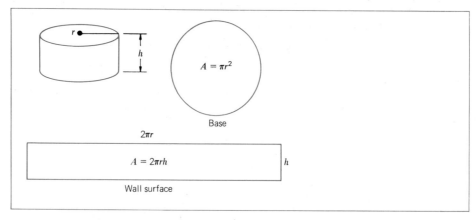

FIGURE 13.29

*16 **Solid Waste Management** A local city is planning to construct a solid waste treatment facility. One of the major components of the plant is a solid waste agitation pool. This pool is to be circular in shape and is supposed to have a volume capacity of 2 million cubic feet. Municipal engineers have estimated construction costs as a function of the surface area of the base and wall of the pool. Construction costs are estimated at $20 per square foot for the base of the pool and $30 per square foot of wall surface. Figure 13.29 presents a sketch of the pool. Note that r equals the radius of the pool in feet and h equals the depth of the pool in feet. Determine the dimensions r and h which provide a capacity of 2 million cubic feet at a minimum cost of construction. (*Hint:* The area A of a circle having radius r is $A = \pi r^2$, the surface area A of a circular cylinder having radius r and height h is $A = 2\pi rh$ and the volume V is $V = \pi r^2 h$.)

*17 **Elasticity of Demand** Given the demand function for a product and a specified point (p, q) on the demand function, the *elasticity of demand* is the ratio

$$\eta = \frac{\text{percent change in quantity demanded}}{\text{percent change in price}}$$

This ratio indicates the response of demand to changes in price at the point (p, q). It can be shown (and will in Example 27 of Chap. 14) that at (p, q)

$$\eta = -\frac{p}{q}\frac{dq}{dp}$$

If $\eta > 1$, demand is said to be *elastic* at (p, q), meaning that the percentage change in demand is greater than the percentage change in price (e.g., a 1 percent change in price results in a greater than 1 percent change in demand). If $\eta < 1$, demand is said to be *inelastic*. If $\eta = 1$, demand is *unit elastic*. (*a*) Interpret what is meant if $\eta < 1$. (*b*) Interpret what is meant if $\eta = 1$. (*c*) Given the demand function $q = 400 - 2.5p$, determine the general expression for η. (*d*) What is the elasticity when $p = 50$?

*18 Related to Exercise 17, (*a*) determine the value of p which results in $\eta = 1$. (*b*) What values of p result in *elastic demand*? (*c*) What values of p result in *inelastic demand*?

CHAPTER TEST

1 The demand function for a product is

$$q = f(p) = 50,000 - 7.5p$$

where q equals the quantity demanded and p equals the price in dollars. Formulate the total revenue function $R = g(p)$.

2   The total revenue function for a product is

$$R = f(x) = -3x^2 + 200x$$

where R is measured in hundreds of dollars and x equals the number of units sold (in 100s). The total cost of producing x (hundred) units is described by the function

$$C = g(x) = 2x^2 - 150x + 5,000$$

where C is measured in hundreds of dollars.
(a) Formulate the profit function $P = h(x)$.
(b) How many units should be produced and sold in order to maximize total profit?
(c) What is the maximum profit?

3   An importer wants to fence in a storage area near the local shipping docks. The area will be used for temporary storage of shipping containers. The area is to be rectangular with an area of 100,000 square feet. The fence will cost $10 per running foot.
(a) Determine the dimensions of the area which will result in fencing costs being minimized.
(b) What is the minimum cost?

4   A retailer has determined that the annual cost C of purchasing, owning, and maintaining one of its products behaves according to the function

$$C = f(q) = \frac{20,000}{q} + 0.5q + 50,000$$

where q is the size (in units) of each order purchased from suppliers.
(a) What order quantity q results in minimum annual cost?
(b) What is the minimum annual cost?

MINICASE:

THE EOQ MODEL

   The economic order quantity (EOQ) model is a classic inventory model. The purpose of the EOQ model is to find the quantity of an item to order which minimizes total inventory costs. The model assumes three different cost components; *ordering cost, carrying cost,* and *purchase cost.* Ordering costs are those associated with placing and receiving an order. These costs are largely for salaries of persons involved in requisitioning goods, processing paperwork, receiving goods, and placing goods into inventory. Ordering costs are assumed to be incurred each time an order is placed.

   Carrying costs, sometimes referred to as *holding costs,* are the costs of owning and maintaining inventory. Carrying costs include such components as cost of storage space, insurance, salaries of inventory control personnel, obsolescence, and opportunity costs associated with having the investment in inventory. Carrying costs are often expressed as a percentage of the average value of inventory on hand (e.g., 25 percent per year). Purchase cost is simply the cost of the inventory items.

Although there are variations on the EOQ model, the basic model makes the following assumptions: (1) demand for items is known and is at a constant (or near constant) rate, (2) time between placing and receiving an order (*lead time*) is known with certainty, (3) order quantities are always the same size, and (4) inventory replenishment is instantaneous (that is, the entire order is received in one batch).

If we assume a time frame of 1 year, total inventory costs are

TC = annual ordering cost + annual carrying cost
   + annual purchase cost

$$= \left(\begin{array}{c}\text{number of}\\ \text{orders per year}\end{array}\right)\left(\begin{array}{c}\text{ordering}\\ \text{cost per order}\end{array}\right)$$

$$+ \left(\begin{array}{c}\text{average}\\ \text{inventory}\\ \text{in units}\end{array}\right)\left(\begin{array}{c}\text{value}\\ \text{per unit}\end{array}\right)\left(\begin{array}{c}\text{carrying}\\ \text{cost in percent}\end{array}\right)$$

$$+ \left(\begin{array}{c}\text{annual}\\ \text{demand}\end{array}\right)\left(\begin{array}{c}\text{purchase price}\\ \text{per unit}\end{array}\right)$$

If

$\qquad\qquad D$ = *annual demand in units*
$\qquad\qquad C_o$ = *ordering cost per order*
$\qquad\qquad C_h$ = *carrying cost (stated as a percentage of average*
$\qquad\qquad\qquad$ *value of inventory on hand)*
$\qquad\qquad p$ = *purchase price per unit*
$\qquad\qquad q$ = *order quantity*

annual inventory costs can be expressed as a function of the order quantity q as follows:

$$TC = f(q) = \frac{D}{q}\,C_o + \frac{q}{2}\,p\,C_h + pD$$

Requirements:
(*a*) For a given inventory item, $D = 5{,}000$, $C_o = \$125$, $p = \$100$, and $C_h = 0.20$. Determine the value of q which minimizes total annual inventory costs. What are minimum annual inventory costs? How many orders must be placed each year? What are annual ordering costs? Annual carrying costs?
(*b*) The order quantity which minimizes annual inventory costs is termed the "economic order quantity" or EOQ. Using the generalized cost function, determine the general expression for the order quantity q which minimizes annual inventory cost. (*Hint:* Find the derivative with respect to q, assuming that D, C_o, p, and C_h are constant.)
(*c*) Prove that the critical value for q does result in a relative minimum on the cost function.
(*d*) Using the expression for q found in part (*b*), show that annual or-

dering cost equals annual carrying cost when operating at the EOQ level. (*e*) Annual inventory costs can be expressed in terms of the number of orders placed per year, N, recognizing that $N = D/q$. Rewrite the generalized cost function in terms of N rather than q. Determine the general expression for the value of N which minimizes annual inventory costs. Confirm that the critical value for N does result in a relative minimum on the cost function.

14

EXPONENTIAL AND LOGARITHMIC FUNCTIONS

CHAPTER OBJECTIVES

- Discuss the nature of exponential functions: their structural characteristics and graphical behavior

- Present the derivative rules for exponential functions and illustrate their use

- Present a variety of applications of exponential functions

- Discuss the nature of logarithms and the equivalence between exponential and logarithmic forms

- Present the characteristics of logarithmic functions and their derivatives

- Present a variety of applications of logarithmic functions

Two classes of mathematical functions which have important applications in business, economics, and the sciences are *exponential functions* and *logarithmic functions.* In this chapter we will examine the nature of these functions and illustrations of their application.

14.1 CHARACTERISTICS OF EXPONENTIAL FUNCTIONS

ALGEBRA FLASHBACK

Some important properties of exponents and radicals are repeated here for your review. Assume that a and b are positive numbers and m and n are real valued.

$$\text{Property 1:} \quad b^m \cdot b^n = b^{m+n}$$

Examples:
$$2^2 2^3 = 2^{2+3} = 2^5 = 32$$
$$x^5 x^{-3} = x^{5-3} = x^2$$

Property 2: $\dfrac{b^m}{b^n} = b^{m-n}$ $b \neq 0$

Examples:
$$\frac{3^6}{3^3} = (3)^{6-3} = 3^3 = 27$$

$$\frac{x^4}{x} = x^{4-1} = x^3$$

Property 3: $(b^m)^n = b^{mn}$

Examples:
$$(10^3)^2 = 10^{(3)(2)} = 10^6 = 1,000,000$$
$$(x^{-2})^5 = x^{(-2)(5)} = x^{-10}$$

Property 4: $a^m b^m = (ab)^m$

Examples:
$$3^4 2^4 = [(3)(2)]^4 = 6^4 = 1,296$$
$$x^2 y^2 = (xy)^2$$

Property 5: $b^{m/n} = \sqrt[n]{b^m}$

Examples:
$$8^{2/3} = \sqrt[3]{8^2} = \sqrt[3]{64} = 4$$
$$x^{1/4} = \sqrt[4]{x}$$

Property 6: $b^0 = 1$ $b \neq 0$

Examples:
$$5,000^0 = 1$$
$$(xy)^0 = 1 \qquad \text{provided } xy \neq 0$$

Property 7: $b^{-m} = \dfrac{1}{b^m}$ $b \neq 0$

Examples:
$$(2)^{-3} = \frac{1}{2^3} = \frac{1}{8}$$

$$\frac{1}{x^{-2}} = \frac{1}{1/x^2} = 1\frac{x^2}{1} = x^2$$

If you are a little rusty on exponents, radicals, and their properties, you are urged to review Sec. 1.5.

Characteristics of Exponential Functions

DEFINITION: EXPONENTIAL FUNCTION

An **exponential function** of the form $y = f(x)$ is one in which the independent variable x appears as either an exponent or part of an exponent.

Examples of exponential functions include

$$f(x) = 10^x$$
$$g(x) = (2)^{x^2-5}$$
and
$$h(x) = 10(3)^{x/2}$$

There are different classes of exponential functions. One important class is that having the form

$$y = f(x) = ab^{mx} \qquad (14.1)$$

where a, b, and m are real-valued constants. One restriction is that $b > 0$ but $b \neq 1$.

In order to get a feeling for the behavior of exponential functions, let's examine some of the form $y = b^x$ [assuming $a = m = 1$ in Eq. (14.1)].

EXAMPLE 1

Let's sketch the exponential function $f(x) = 2^x$. This function can be sketched by determining a set of ordered pairs which satisfy the function. Table 14.1 indicates a sample of values assumed for x and the corresponding values for $f(x)$.

ALGEBRA FLASHBACK

Property 7 $(b^{-m} = 1/b^m,\ b \neq 0)$ must be used to evaluate 2^x when x is negative.

Note from Fig. 14.1 that f is an increasing function. That is, any increase in the value of x results in an increase in the value of $f(x)$. Another way to note this is to observe that the slope of any tangent line on the curve is positive. Finally, the graph of f is asymptotic to the negative x axis. As x approaches negative infinity $(x \rightarrow -\infty)$, $f(x)$ approaches but never quite reaches a value of 0.

EXAMPLE 2

$f(x) = b^x$ **where** $b > 1$ Figure 14.2 illustrates graphs of the three exponential functions f, g, and h.

$$f(x) = 2^x$$
$$g(x) = 2.5^x$$
$$h(x) = 3^x$$

TABLE 14.1

x	0	1	2	3	−1	−2	−3
$f(x) = 2^x$	1	2	4	8	0.5	0.25	0.125

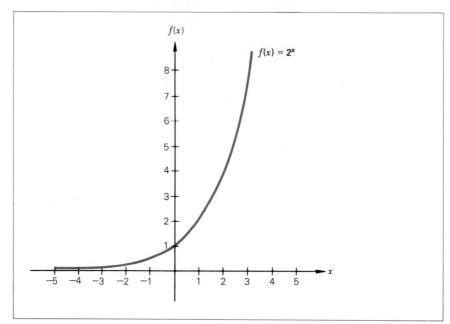

FIGURE 14.1

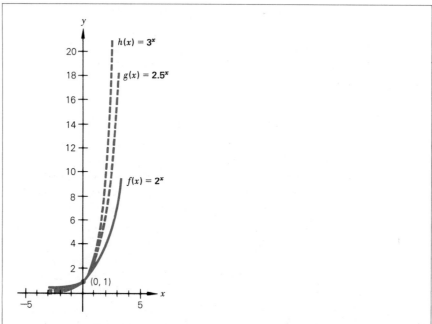

FIGURE 14.2
$f(x) = b^x$,
$b > 1$.

Notice that each function has a positive base b with the only difference between them being the size of b. These are graphed together to illustrate some characteristics of the set of functions

$$f(x) = b^x \qquad \text{where } b > 1$$

Examine Fig. 14.2 and confirm the following characteristics of this set of functions.

CHARACTERISTICS OF FUNCTIONS $f(x) = b^x$ **where** $b > 1$

I Each function is defined for all values of x. The domain of f is the set of real numbers.

II The graph of f lies entirely *above* the x axis (the range is the set of positive real numbers).

III The graph of f is *asymptotic* to the x axis. That is, the value of y approaches but never reaches a value of 0 as x approaches negative infinity.

IV The y intercept occurs at $(0,1)$.

V y is an increasing function of x; that is, over the domain of the function any increase in x is accompanied by an increase in y. More precisely, this property suggests that for $x_1 < x_2$, $f(x_1) < f(x_2)$.

VI The larger the magnitude of the base b, the greater the rate of increase in $f(x)$ as x increases in value.

This class of functions is particularly useful in modeling *growth processes*. We will see examples of these types of applications in the next section.

EXAMPLE 3

$f(x) = b^x$ **where** $0 < b < 1$ Figure 14.3 illustrates the graphs of the three exponential functions

$$f(x) = (0.2)^x$$
$$g(x) = (0.6)^x$$
$$h(x) = (0.9)^x$$

These functions are representative of the set of exponential functions $f(x) = b^x$ where $0 < b < 1$. The three functions illustrated differ only in the magnitude of b. Examine Fig. 14.3 and confirm the following characteristics for this set of functions.

CHARACTERISTICS OF FUNCTIONS $f(x) = b^x, 0 < b < 1$

I Each function is defined for all values of x (the domain is the set of real numbers).

II The graph of f is entirely above the x axis (the range is the set of positive real numbers).

III The graph of f is asymptotic to the x axis. That is, the value of y approaches but never reaches a value of 0 as x approaches positive infinity.

IV The y intercept occurs at $(0, 1)$.

V y is a decreasing function of x; that is, any increase in the

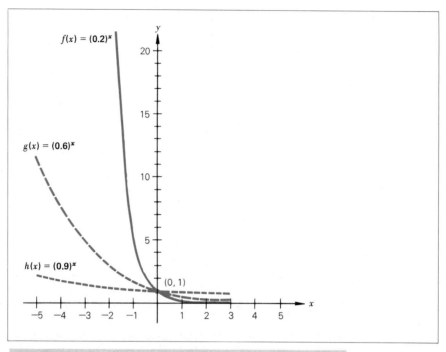

FIGURE 14.3
$f(x) = b^x$,
$0 < b < 1$.

value of x is accompanied by a decrease in the value of y. More precisely, this property suggests that for $x_1 < x_2$, $f(x_1) > f(x_2)$.

VI The smaller the magnitude of the base b, the greater the rate of decrease in $f(x)$ as x increases in value

This class of functions is particularly useful in modeling *decay processes*. We will see examples of these applications in the next section.

POINT FOR THOUGHT AND DISCUSSION

What are the graphical characteristics of the exponential function $f(x) = b^x$, where $b = 1$?

Base-e Exponential Functions

A special class of exponential functions is of the form

$$y = f(x) = ae^{mx}$$ (14.2)

The base of this exponential function is e, which is an irrational number approximately equal to 2.71828. The exact value of e is defined by

$$e = \lim_{n \to \infty} \left(1 + \frac{1}{n}\right)^n$$

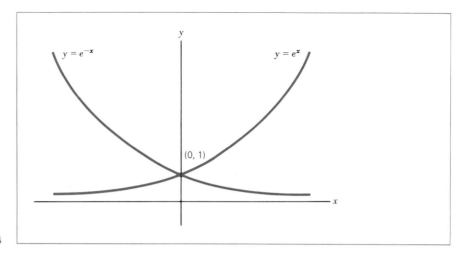

FIGURE 14.4

Although we will not dwell on the origin of this constant, you will gain insights as we go along as to why such an unusual constant is used as the base for such a popular class of exponential functions. And, indeed, base-e exponential functions are more widely applied than any other class of exponential functions.

Two special exponential functions in this class are $y = e^x$ and $y = e^{-x}$. Figure 14.4 illustrates the graphs of these two functions. In order to sketch these functions, values for $(2.71828 \ldots)^x$ or $(2.71828 \ldots)^{-x}$ must be computed. This could be a very tedious process. However, since these calculations are performed frequently, values of e^x and e^{-x} are readily available. Most pocket calculators have e^x or e^{-x} functions. Values are also available from tables like Table 1 inside the front book cover.

EXAMPLE 4

Modified Exponential Functions   Certain applications of exponential functions involve functions of the form

$$y = f(x) = 1 - e^{-mx}$$ (14.3)

In order to illustrate these modified exponential functions, let's graph the function $f(x) = 1 - e^{-x}$ where $x \geq 0$. Table 14.2 contains some sample data points for this function. The graph of the function is shown in Fig. 14.5. Notice that the graph of the function is asymptotic to the line $y = 1$. As x increases in value, the value of y approaches but never quite reaches a value of 1. This is because the second term e^{-x} approaches but never quite reaches a value of 0 as x increases in value. Perhaps the behavior of e^{-x} can be understood better if e^{-x} is rewritten as $1/e^x$. As x increases in value the denominator becomes larger and the quotient $1/e^x$ approaches but never quite reaches 0.

Conversion to Base-e Functions

It was mentioned earlier that base-e exponential functions are preferred to those having another base b. Again, you will understand the reason for this shortly.

TABLE 14.2

x	0	1	2	3	4
e^{-x}	1	0.3679	0.1353	0.0498	0.0183
$1 - e^{-x}$	0	0.6321	0.8647	0.9502	0.9817

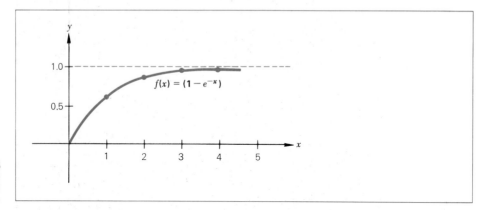

FIGURE 14.5
Modified
exponential
function.

Interestingly, we will see in this section that exponential functions having a base other than e can be transformed into equivalent base-e functions. This is because any positive number b can be expressed equivalently as some power of the base e; that is, we can find an exponent n such that $e^n = b$.

To illustrate, suppose we have an exponential function

$$f(x) = 3^x$$

where the base equals 3. To convert f to an equivalent base-e function we must express the base in terms of e. We want to determine the exponent n which results in

$$e^n = 3$$

From Table 1 (inside the front cover) we find that

$$e^{1.1} = 3.0042$$
or
$$e^{1.1} \doteq 3$$

Therefore, the original function can be expressed as

$$f(x) = 3^x \doteq (e^{1.1})^x$$
or
$$f(x) \doteq e^{1.1x}$$

To test the equivalence of these functions, let's compute $f(2)$ using the base-3 and base-e forms.

Base 3: $\qquad$ $f(2) = 3^2 = 9$
Base e: $\qquad$ $f(2) = e^{1.1(2)} = e^{2.2}$
From Table 1, $\qquad$ $e^{2.2} = 9.0250$

The difference ($9.0250 - 9 = 0.0250$) can be attributed to the fact that we were unable to find the precise value of n resulting in $e^n = 3$ from Table 1. Our value of $n = 1.1$ is close, but approximate. More detailed tables, a hand calculator with an e^x function, or the use of logarithms could have assisted in making our approximation a better one.

Section 14.1 Follow-up Exercises

1 Which of the following functions can be considered to be exponential functions? For those which are not, indicate why.

(a) $y = f(x) = (\pi)^{x^2}$, where $\pi = 3.14$ . . .

(b) $y = h(x) = \sqrt[x]{0.50}$

(c) $y = v(t) = (4)^{t^2 - 2t + 1}$

(d) $u = v(t) = \sqrt[3]{t^2}$

(e) $g = h(x) = 1/e^{2x}$

(f) $y = f(x) = \sqrt{2}x^5$

2 (a) Sketch the functions

$$y = f(x) = 2^x$$
$$y = g(x) = 2^{1.5x}$$
$$y = h(x) = 2^{2x}$$

(b) If these functions are compared with Eq. (14.1), the differences are in the values of the parameter m. Examine the sketches from part (a). What conclusions can be drawn regarding the behavior of exponential functions and the value of m?

3 (a) Sketch the functions

$$y = f(x) = 2^x$$
$$y = g(x) = 0.5(2)^x$$
$$y = h(x) = 2(2)^x$$

(b) If these functions are compared with Eq. (14.1), the differences are in the values of the parameter a. From the sketches in part (a), what conclusions can be drawn regarding the behavior of exponential functions and the value of a?

For each of the following exponential functions, compute $f(0)$, $f(-2)$, and $f(2)$.

4 $f(x) = 2^{x^2}$ 　　　　　　　　　　　　**5** $f(x) = 3^{x/2}$

6 $f(x) = e^x$ 　　　　　　　　　　　　　**7** $f(x) = e^{-x/2}$

8 $f(x) = e^{x-2}$ 　　　　　　　　　　　**9** $f(x) = e^{x^2/2}$

10 $f(x) = 1 - e^{0.5x}$ 　　　　　　　　**11** $f(x) = 10(1 - e^{2x})$

Sketch the following functions.

12 $f(x) = e^{x/2}$ 　　　　　　　　　　**13** $f(x) = e^x/2$

14 $f(x) = 0.5e^{x^2}$ 　　　　　　　　　**15** $f(x) = -2e^x$

16 $f(x) = 5(1 - e^x)$ 　　　　　　　　**17** $f(x) = -2(1 - e^x)$

Convert each of the following exponential functions into equivalent base-e exponential functions.

18 $f(x) = (1.6)^x$ 　　　　　　　　　　**19** $f(x) = (2)^{x^2}$

20 $f(x) = (0.6)^x$ 　　　　　　　　　　**21** $f(x) = (2.25)^{x/2}$

22 $f(t) = 5(1.6)^{t^2}$ 　　　　　　　　**23** $f(t) = 10(.3)^t$

24 $f(t) = 2.5(20)^t$ 　　　　　　　　**25** $f(t) = -2(90)^t$

14.2 APPLICATIONS OF EXPONENTIAL FUNCTIONS

Exponential functions have particular application to *growth processes* and *decay processes*. Examples of growth processes include population growth, appreciation in the value of assets, inflation, growth in the rate at which particular resources are used (such as energy), and growth in the gross national product (GNP). Examples of decay processes include the declining value of certain assets such as machinery, the decline in the rate of incidence of certain diseases as medical research and technology improve, the decline in the purchasing power of a dollar, and the decline in the efficiency of a machine as it ages.

When a growth process is characterized by a constant percent increase in value, it is referred to as an *exponential growth process.* When a decay process is characterized by a constant percent decline in value, it is referred to as an *exponential decay process.* If the population of a country is growing constantly at a rate of 8 percent, the growth process can be described by an *exponential growth function.* If the incidence of infant mortality is declining continually at a rate of 5 percent, the decay process can be described by an *exponential decay function.*

Although exponential growth and decay functions are usually stated as a function of time, the independent variable may represent something other than time. Regardless of the nature of the independent variable, the effect is that *equal increases in the independent variable result in constant percent changes (increases or decreases) in the value of the dependent variable.*

The following examples illustrate some of the areas of application of exponential functions.

EXAMPLE 5 ▬▬▬▬▬▬▬▬▬▬▬▬▬▬▬▬▬▬▬▬▬▬▬▬▬▬▬

Compound Interest   The equation

$$S = P(1 + i)^n \qquad (14.4)$$

can be used to determine the amount S that an investment of P dollars will grow to if it receives interest of i percent per compounding period for n compounding periods.* S is referred to as the *compound amount* and p as the *principal.* If S is considered to be a function of n, Eq. (14.4) can be viewed as having the form of Eq. (14.1). That is,

$$S = f(n)$$
or
$$S = ab^{mn}$$

where $a = P$, $b = 1 + i$, and $m = 1$.

Assume that $P = \$1,000$, and $i = 0.08$ per year. Equation (14.4) becomes $S = f(n)$, or

$$S = (1,000)(1.08)^n$$

To determine the value of S given any value of n, it is necessary to evaluate the exponential term $(1.08)^n$. If we want to know to what sum $\$1,000$ will grow after 25 years, we must evaluate $(1.08)^{25}$. Because this type of calculation is so common, values for the expression $(1 + i)^n$ can be determined by special function keys on many hand calculators or by tables. Table I on page T.0 can be used to evaluate $(1 + 0.08)^{25}$. From Table I,

$$(1 + 0.08)^{25} = 6.8485$$

and

$$f(25) = 1,000(1.08)^{25} = 1,000(6.8485) = \$6,848.50$$

---

* Assuming reinvestment of any accrued interest.

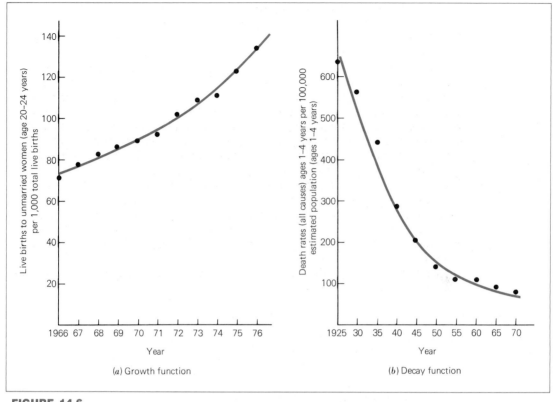

FIGURE 14.6
Source: Division
of Vital
Statistics,
National Center
for Health
Statistics.

EXAMPLE 6

Compound Interest: Continuous Compounding   When compounding of interest occurs more than once a year, we can restate Eq. (14.4) as

$$S = P\left(1 + \frac{i}{m}\right)^{mt}$$ (14.5)

where *i equals the annual interest rate, m equals the number of compounding periods per year, and t equals the number of years.* The product *mt* equals the number of compounding periods over *t* years.

Banks often use *continuous compounding* schemes on savings accounts as a way of promoting business. Continuous compounding means that compounding is occurring all the time. Another way of thinking of continuous compounding is that there are an infinite number of compounding periods each year. In Eq. (14.5), continuous compounding would suggest that we determine the value of S as m approaches $+\infty$. Since i/m can be written as $1/(m/i)$, Eq. (14.5) can be rewritten as

$$S = P\left(1 + \frac{1}{m/i}\right)^{mt}$$ (14.6)

And since *mt* can be rewritten in the form $(m/i)(it)$, Eq. (14.6) can be restated as

$$S = P\left[\left(1 + \frac{1}{m/i}\right)^{m/i}\right]^{it}$$

(14.7)

When we discussed base-e exponential functions, we stated that

$$e = \lim_{n \to \infty}\left(1 + \frac{1}{n}\right)^n$$

(14.8)

Confirm that the expression in brackets has the same structure as Eq. (14.8) and that as m, the number of compounding periods per year, approaches $+\infty$,

$$\left[1 + \frac{1}{m/i}\right]^{m/i} \to e = 2.718 \ldots$$

or

$$\lim_{m \to \infty}\left[1 + \frac{1}{m/i}\right]^{m/i} = e$$

Therefore, for continuous compounding, Eq. (14.7) simplifies to

$$S = Pe^{it}$$

(14.9)

EXAMPLE 7

In Example 5, we computed the amount that a $1,000 investment would grow to if invested at 8 percent per year for 25 years compounded annually. If the $1,000 earns 8 percent per year compounded continuously, it will grow to a sum

$$S = \$1{,}000e^{0.08(25)}$$
$$= 1{,}000e^{2.0}$$

From Table 1 at the front of the book, we have

$$e^{2.0} = 7.3891$$

and

$$S = \$1{,}000(7.3891)$$
$$= \$7{,}389.10$$

By comparing this value with that found in Example 5, continuous compounding results in additional interest of $7,389.10 − $6,848.50 = $540.60 over the 25-year period. A sketch of the investment function appears in Fig. 14.7.

EXAMPLE 8

Exponential Growth Process: Population As mentioned at the beginning of this section, *exponential growth processes* are characterized by a constant percent increase in value over time. Such processes may be described by the general function

$$V = f(t)$$

or

$$V = V_0 e^{kt}$$

(14.10)

where V equals the value of the function at time t, V_0 equals the value of the function at $t = 0$,

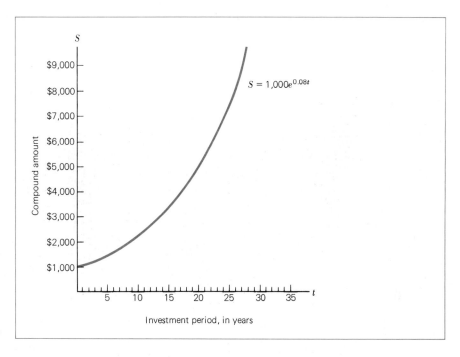

FIGURE 14.7

k is the percent rate of growth, and t is time measured in the appropriate units (hours, days, weeks, years, etc.).

The population of a country was 100 million in 1970. It has been growing since that time exponentially at a constant rate of 4 percent per year. The function which describes the size of the population P (in millions) is

$$P = f(t)$$
$$= 100e^{0.04t}$$

where 100 (million) is the population at $t = 0$ (1970) and 0.04 is the percent rate of exponential growth.

The projected population for 1995 (assuming continued annual growth at the same rate) is found by evaluating $f(25)$, where $t = 25$ corresponds to 1995. The projected population for the country is

$$P = f(25)$$
$$= 100e^{0.04(25)}$$
$$= 100e$$
$$= 271.83 \text{ (millions)}$$

A sketch of the population function appears in Fig. 14.8.

EXAMPLE 9

Exponential Growth Processes Continued   A question of interest in growth functions is, How long will it take for the value of the function to increase by some multiple? In Example 8 there may be a question concerning how long it will take for the population to double. In Eq. (14.10), the value V_0 will double when

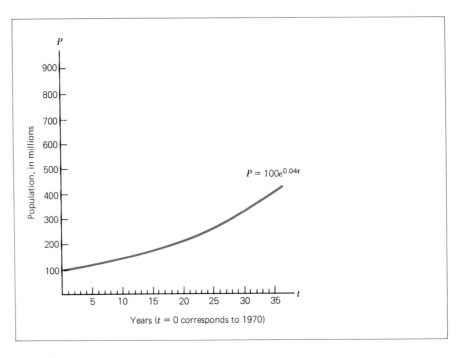

FIGURE 14.8

$$\frac{V}{V_0} = 2$$

Dividing both sides of Eq. (14.10) by V_0, we get

$$\frac{V}{V_0} = e^{kt}$$

Therefore the value will double when

$$e^{kt} = 2$$

To illustrate this, the population in Example 8 will double when $V = 200$, or

$$200 = 100e^{0.04t}$$

Dividing both sides by 100 yields

$$2 = e^{0.04t}$$

From Table 1 we see that

$$e^{0.69} \doteq 2$$

A better approximation is

$$e^{0.69314} \doteq 2$$

In order to determine how long it takes the population of 100 million to double, we must find the value of t which makes

$$e^{0.69314} \doteq e^{0.04t}$$

These expressions will be equal when their exponents are equal, or when

$$0.04t = 0.69314$$

or

$$t = 17.33 \text{ years}^*$$

EXAMPLE 10

Exponential Decay Functions   An *exponential decay process* is one characterized by a constant percent decrease in value over time. Such processes may be described by the general function

$$V = f(t)$$

or

$$\boxed{V = V_0 e^{-kt}}$$ **(14.11)**

where V equals the value of the function at time t, V_0 equals the value of the function at $t = 0$ and k is the percentage rate of decay (sometimes called the *decay constant*). Compare Eq. (14.11) with Eq. (14.10) and note the differences.

   The resale value V (stated in dollars) of a certain piece of industrial equipment has been found to behave according to the function $V = f(t) = 100,000e^{-0.1t}$ where $t =$ years since original purchase.

(*a*) What is the original value of a piece of the equipment?

(*b*) What is the expected resale value after 5 years? After 10 years?

SOLUTION

(*a*) The original value is the value of V when $t = 0$. At $t = 0$

$$V = 100,000e^{-0.1(0)}$$
$$= 100,000e^0$$
$$= 100,000$$

Thus, the original value $V_0 = \$100,000$.

(*b*) $f(5) = 100,000e^{-0.1(5)}$
$$= 100,000e^{-0.5}$$
$$= 100,000(0.6065) \quad \text{(from Table 1)}$$
$$= \$60,650$$
$f(10) = 100,000e^{-0.1(10)}$
$$= 100,000e^{-1}$$
$$= 100,000(0.3679) \quad \text{(from Table 1)}$$
$$= \$36,790$$

---

* Solving for t can be easier if you understand logarithms. An alternative and equivalent approach would be to find the natural logarithms (Sec. 14.4) of both sides of the equation $2 = e^{0.04t}$ and equate these, solving for t.

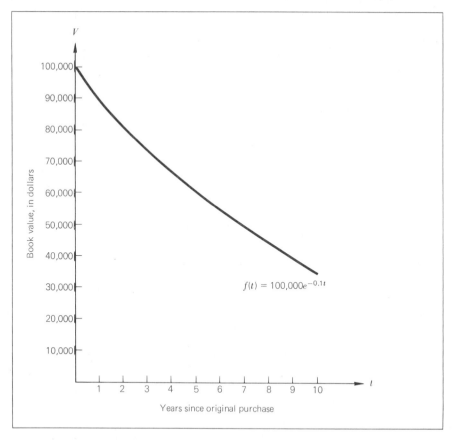

FIGURE 14.9
Depreciation
function.

Figure 14.9 presents a graph of this decay function.

EXAMPLE 11 ▰▰▰▰▰▰▰▰▰▰▰▰▰▰▰▰▰▰▰▰▰▰▰▰▰▰▰▰

Bill Collection   A major financial institution offers a credit card which can be used in-
ternationally. The question arose among executives as to how long it takes to collect the
accounts receivable for credit issued in any given month. Data gathered over a number
of years have indicated that the collection percentage for credit issued in any month is an
exponential function of the time since the credit was issued. Specifically, the function
which approximates this relationship is

$$P = f(t)$$
or $$P = 0.95(1 - e^{-0.7t}) \qquad t \geq 0$$

where *P equals the percentage of accounts receivable (in dollars) collected t months after the
credit is granted.* Sample data points for this function are shown in Table 14.3. The values
for $e^{-0.7t}$ can be found in Table 1 inside the front cover. The function is sketched in Fig.
14.10. Note the figures in Table 14.3. For $t = 0$, $f(t) = 0$, which suggests that no accounts
will have been collected at the time credit is issued. When $t = 1$, the function has a value
of 0.4782. This indicates that after 1 month 47.82 percent of accounts receivable (in
dollars) will have been collected. After 2 months, 71.56 percent will have been collected.

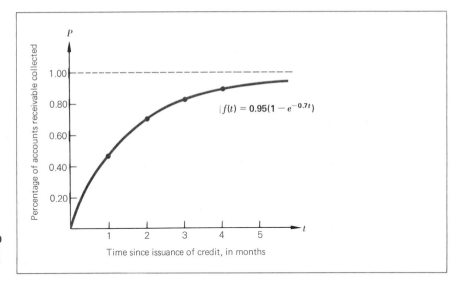

FIGURE 14.10
Collection
response
function.

TABLE 14.3

t	0	1	2	3	4
$e^{-0.7t}$	1	0.4966	0.2466	0.1225	0.0608
$1 - e^{-0.7t}$	0	0.5034	0.7534	0.8775	0.9392
$0.95(1 - e^{-0.7t})$	0	0.4782	0.7156	0.8336	0.8922

POINTS FOR THOUGHT AND DISCUSSION

What value does P approach as t increases without limit? Why will the value of P never equal 1? Do you think that a restricted domain would apply in this type of application?

Section 14.2 Follow-up Exercises

1   An investment of $250,000 is made which earns interest at the rate of 15 percent per year. If interest is compounded continuously,
(a) Determine the exponential function which states the compound amounts as a function of years of investment t.
(b) What will the $250,000 grow to if it is invested for 4 years? 10 years?

2   An investment of $500,000 is made which earns interest at the rate of 12 percent per year. If interest is compounded continuously,
(a) Determine the exponential function which states the compound amount S as a function of years of investment t.
(b) What will the $500,000 grow to if it is invested for 10 years? 20 years?

3   In Exercise 1, determine the length of time required for the investment to double in value? To quadruple?

4   In Exercise 2, determine the length of time required for the investment to double in value? To triple?

5 Population Growth The population P of a South American country has been growing exponentially at a constant rate of 3.2 percent per year. The population on January 1, 1975, was 40 million.

(a) Write the general exponential growth function $P = f(t)$ for the population of the country.

(b) If the rate and pattern of growth continue, what is the population expected to equal at the beginning of 1990? In the beginning of the year 2000?

6 In Exercise 5, determine the year in which the population can be expected to double. In what year will the population have increased by 50 percent?

7 Solid Waste Within a major United States city, the annual tonnage of solid waste (garbage) has been increasing at an exponential rate of 6 percent per year. Assume the current daily tonnage is 3,000 tons and the rate and pattern of growth continue.

(a) What daily tonnage will be expected 10 years from now?

(b) Current capacity for handling solid waste is 6,000 tons per day. When will this capacity no longer be sufficient?

8 The resale value V of a piece of industrial equipment has been found to behave according to the function

$$V = 250{,}000e^{-0.05t}$$

where t = years since original purchase.

(a) What was the original value of the piece of equipment?

(b) What is the expected resale value after 8 years?

9 In Exercise 8, how long does it take for the resale value of the asset to reach 50 percent of its original value?

10 Endangered Species The Department of the Interior for the U.S. estimated that the number of deer of a particular species was 50,000 at the beginning of 1980. Scientists estimate that the population of the species is decreasing exponentially at a rate of 5 percent per year.

(a) Write the decay function $P = f(t)$ where P equals the number of deer and t equals time (in years) measured from 1980.

(b) What is the population expected to equal in the year 2000 if the decay rate remains constant?

11 In Exercise 10, when is it expected that the population will equal 25,000?

12 For the past 3 years, real estate prices in one area of the country have been increasing at an exponential rate of 8 percent per year. A home was purchased 3 years ago for $80,000.

(a) What is its estimated value today?

(b) Assuming appreciation continues at the same rate, what will its value be 5 years from today?

13 A national charity is planning a fund-raising campaign. Past experience indicates that total contributions raised are a function of the length of time that a campaign is conducted. Within one city a response function has been determined which indicates the percentage of the population R who will make a donation as a function of the number of days t of the campaign. The function is

$$R = 0.6(1 - e^{-0.04t})$$

(a) What percentage of the population will make a donation after 5 days? After 10 days?

(b) What is the upper bound on the value of R?

14 **Advertising Response** A large record company sells tapes and albums by direct mail only. Advertising is done through network television. Much experience with this type of sales approach has allowed analysts to determine the expected response to an advertising program. Specifically, the response function for classical music albums and tapes is $R = f(t) = 1 - e^{-0.04t}$, where R is the percentage of customers in the target market actually purchasing the album or tape and t is the number of times an advertisement is run on national TV.

(a) What percentage of the target market is expected to buy a classical music offering if advertisements are run one time on TV? 10 times? 20 times?

(b) Sketch the response function $R = f(t)$.

14.3 DERIVATIVES AND THEIR APPLICATION

Derivatives of Exponential Functions

Since any base-b exponential function ($b > 0$) can be expressed in an equivalent base-e form, our focus will be upon base-e functions and their derivatives, exclusively. In order to find derivatives of these functions, the following rule is required.

RULE 1

If $f(x) = e^{u(x)}$, where u is differentiable, then

$$f'(x) = u'(x)e^{u(x)}$$

EXAMPLE 12

Consider the function $f(x) = e^x$. If we refer to Rule 1, the exponent $u(x) = x$. Applying Rule 1,

$$f'(x) = 1e^x$$
$$= e^x$$

This result is a significant reason for focusing upon base-e functions. The unique result is that *the function e^x and its derivative are identical.* That is, $f(x) = f'(x) = e^x$. Graphically, the interpretation is that for any value of x, the slope of the graph of $f(x) = e^x$ is exactly equal to the value of the function. Finding the derivative of $f(x) = e^x$ is very easy compared with base-b functions.*

EXAMPLE 13

Consider the function $f(x) = e^{-x^2+2x}$. If Rule 1 is applied

$$f'(x) = (-2x + 2)e^{-x^2+2x}$$

EXAMPLE 14

In Example 8, we discussed exponential growth processes. The generalized exponential

---

* To illustrate this, consider the following derivative rule: If $f(x) = b^x$, $f'(x) = b^x \ln b$, where $\ln b$ is the natural (base-e) logarithm of b.

growth function was presented in Eq. (14.10) as

$$V = f(t) = V_0e^{kt}$$

We indicated that these processes are characterized by a constant percentage rate of growth. To verify this, let's find the derivative

$$f'(t) = V_0(k)e^{kt}$$

which can be written as

$$f'(t) = kV_0e^{kt}$$

The derivative represents the instantaneous rate of change in the value V with respect to a change in t. The *percentage rate of change* would be found by the ratio

$$\frac{\text{Instantaneous rate of change}}{\text{Value of the function}} = \frac{f'(t)}{f(t)}$$

For this function,

$$\frac{f'(t)}{f(t)} = \frac{kV_0e^{kt}}{V_0e^{kt}}$$

$$= k$$

This confirms that for an exponential growth function of the form of Eq. (14.10), k represents the percentage rate of growth. Given that k is a constant, the percentage rate of growth is the same for all values of t.

EXAMPLE 15

Examine the following function for any critical points and determine their nature.

$$f(x) = -10{,}000e^{-0.03x} - 120x + 10{,}000$$

SOLUTION

If we find f' and set it equal to 0,

$$f'(x) = -10{,}000(-0.03)e^{-0.03x} - 120$$
$$= 300e^{-0.03x} - 120$$
$$300e^{-0.03x} - 120 = 0$$

when $\qquad 300e^{-0.03x} = 120$

or when $\qquad e^{-0.03x} = \frac{120}{300} = 0.4$

If we refer to Table 1 we find

$$e^{-0.92} \doteq 0.4$$

Therefore, $\qquad e^{-0.03x} \doteq 0.4$

when $\qquad -0.03x = -0.92$

or a critical value occurs when $\qquad x = 30.67$

The only critical point occurs when $x = 30.67$.

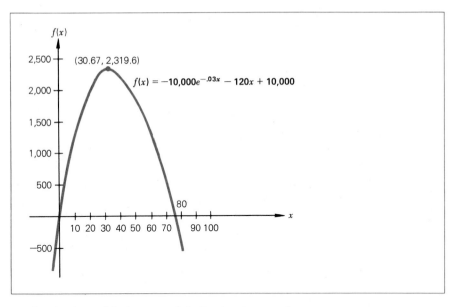

$$(30.67, 2{,}319.6)$$

$$f(x) = -10{,}000e^{-.03x} - 120x + 10{,}000$$

FIGURE 14.11

Continuing with the second-derivative test, we have

$$
\begin{aligned}
f''(x) &= -0.03(300)e^{-0.03x} \\
&= -9e^{-0.03x} \\
f''(30.67) &= -9e^{-0.03(30.67)} \\
&= -9e^{-0.92} \\
&= -9(0.4) \\
&= -3.6 < 0
\end{aligned}
$$

Therefore, a *relative maximum* occurs when $x = 30.67$. The corresponding value for $f(x)$ is

$$
\begin{aligned}
f(30.67) &= -10{,}000e^{-0.03(30.67)} - 120(30.67) + 10{,}000 \\
&= -10{,}000(0.4) - 3{,}680.4 + 10{,}000 = 2{,}319.6
\end{aligned}
$$

The relative maximum occurs at $(30.67, 2{,}319.6)$. Figure 14.11 contains a sketch of the function.

EXAMPLE 16

Bill Collection Example 11 discussed the collection of accounts receivable for credit issued to people who use a major credit card. The financial institution determined that the percentage of accounts receivable P (in dollars) collected t months after the credit was issued is

$$P = 0.95(1 - e^{-0.7t})$$

The average credit issued in any one month is $100 million. The financial institution estimates that *for each $100 million in new credit* issued in any month, collection efforts cost $1 million per month. That is, if credit of $100 million is issued today, it costs $1 million for every month the institution attempts to collect these accounts receivable. Determine the number of months that collection efforts should be continued if the objective is to maximize the *net collections N* (dollars collected minus collection costs).

SOLUTION

Given that $100 million of credit is issued, the amount of receivables collected (in millions of dollars) equals

(Amount of credit issued)(percentage of accounts collected)

or
$$(100)(0.95)(1 - e^{-0.7})$$

Therefore, net collections N are described by the function

Net collections = amount collected − collection costs

or
$$
\begin{aligned}
N &= f(t) \\
&= (100)(0.95)(1 - e^{-0.7t}) - (1)t \\
&= 95(1 - e^{-0.7t}) - t \\
&= 95 - 95e^{-0.7t} - t
\end{aligned}
$$

The first derivative is

$$f'(t) = 66.5e^{-0.7t} - 1$$

If f' is set equal to 0,

$$
\begin{aligned}
66.5e^{-0.7t} &= 1 \\
e^{-0.7t} &= 0.01503
\end{aligned}
$$

From Table 1 at the front of the book

$$e^{-4.2} = 0.0150$$

Thus, $e^{-0.7t} \doteq 0.01503$ when

$$-0.7t = -4.2$$

and a critical value occurs at

$$t = 6$$

The only critical point on f occurs when $t = 6$. As an exercise, we leave to you the confirmation that a relative maximum occurs at $t = 6$. Maximum net collections are

$$
\begin{aligned}
f(6) &= 95 - 95e^{-0.7(6)} - 6 \\
&= 95 - 95(0.0150) - 6 = 95 - 1.425 - 6 = 87.575
\end{aligned}
$$

or $87.575 million.

For each $100 million of credit issued, net collections will be maximized at a value of $87.575 million if collection efforts continue for 6 months.

EXERCISE

(1) Verify that the critical point at $t = 6$ is a relative maximum; and (2) What is the total (gross) amount collected over the six-month period?*

---

* Answer: $93.575 million.

Section 14.3 Follow-up Exercises

Find f' for each of the following exponential functions.

1	$f(x) = e^x$	2	$f(x) = e^{x^3}$
3	$f(x) = 10e^{x^2}$	4	$f(x) = -5e^{x/2}$
5	$f(x) = (5e^x)^3$	6	$f(x) = 3x^2e^x$
7	$f(x) = 4xe^{x^2}$	8	$f(x) = (e^x - 5)^4$
9	$f(x) = e^x/x$	10	$f(x) = 2x^2/e^x$
11	$f(x) = (e^x)^3$	12	$f(x) = \sqrt{e^{2x}}$

For each of the following functions, determine the location of all critical points and determine their nature.

13	$f(x) = e^x$	14	$f(x) = e^{-x}$
15	$f(x) = 1,000e^{-0.05x} + 100x - 150$	16	$f(x) = -4,000e^{-0.02x} - 40x + 1,000$
17	$f(x) = e^{3x+10}$	18	$f(x) = -500e^{-0.09x} + 30x$
19	$f(x) = -1,500e^{-0.05x} - 100x + 4,500$	20	$f(x) = xe^{-x}$

21 A national charity is planning a fund raising campaign in a major United States city having a population of 2 million. The percentage of the population who will make a donation is estimated by the function

$$R = 1 - e^{-0.02x}$$

where R equals the percentage of the population and x equals the number of days the campaign is conducted.

Past experience indicates that the average contribution in this city is $2 per donor. Costs of the campaign are estimated at $10,000 per day.
(a) How many days should the campaign be conducted if the objective is to maximize net proceeds (total contributions minus total costs) from the campaign?
(b) What are maximum net proceeds expected to equal? What percentage of the population is expected to donate?

22 A national record distribution company sells records and tapes by mail only. Advertising is done on local TV stations. A promotion program is being planned for a major metropolitan area for a new country western album. The target audience—those who might be interested in this type of album—is estimated at 600,000. Past experience indicates that for this city and this type of album the percentage of the target market R actually purchasing an album or tape is a function of the length of the advertising campaign t. Specifically, this *sales response function* is

$$R = 1 - e^{-0.025t}$$

The profit margin on each album is $1.50. Advertising costs include a fixed cost of $15,000 and a variable cost of $2,000 per day.
(a) Determine how long the campaign should be conducted if the goal is to maximize *net profit* (gross profit minus advertising costs).
(b) What is the expected maximum net profit?
(c) What percentage of the target market is expected to purchase the album?

23 Assume in Example 16 that the average amount of credit issued each month is $50 million instead of $100 million and monthly collection costs equal $0.5 million. Re-solve the problem.

24 A police department has determined that the average daily crime rate in the city depends upon the number of officers assigned to each shift. Specifically, the function describing this relationship is

$$N = f(x) = 250 - 10xe^{-0.025x}$$

where N equals the average daily crime rate and x equals the number of officers assigned to each shift. Determine the number of officers which will result in a minimum average daily crime rate. What is the minimum average daily crime rate?

25 A firm's annual profit is stated as a function of the number of salespersons employed. The profit function is

$$P = 20(x)e^{-0.002x}$$

where P equals profit stated in thousands of dollars and x equals the number of salespersons.

(*a*) Determine the number of salespersons which will maximize annual profit.

(*b*) What is the maximum profit expected to equal?

14.4 LOGARITHMIC FUNCTIONS AND THEIR DERIVATIVES

This section discusses another class of functions which are directly related to exponential functions.

Logarithms

A **logarithm** is the *power* to which a *base* must be raised in order to yield a given number (i.e., a logarithm is an exponent). Consider the equation

$$2^3 = 8$$

The exponent 3 can be considered as the logarithm, to the base 2, of the number 8. That is, *3 is the power to which 2 must be raised in order to generate the number 8.* We can state this logarithm property as

$$3 = \log_2 8$$

In general,

$$\boxed{y = b^x \Leftrightarrow x = \log_b y \qquad \text{for } b > 0}$$

We will concern ourselves with situations where the base b is restricted to positive values other than 1.

EXAMPLE 17

Following are statements of equivalent pairs of exponential and logarithmic equations.

Logarithmic Equation	Exponential Equation
$4 = \log_2 16$	$\Leftrightarrow \quad 2^4 = 16$
$2 = \log_{10} 100$	$\Leftrightarrow \quad 10^2 = 100$
$3 = \log_3 27$	$\Leftrightarrow \quad 3^3 = 27$
$-1 = \log_{10} 0.1$	$\Leftrightarrow \quad 10^{-1} = 0.1$

Exponential Equation		Logarithmic Equation
$10^4 = 10{,}000$	$\Leftrightarrow$	$4 = \log_{10} 10{,}000$
$4^3 = 64$	$\Leftrightarrow$	$3 = \log_4 64$
$5^2 = 25$	$\Leftrightarrow$	$2 = \log_5 25$
$10^{-2} = 0.01$	$\Leftrightarrow$	$-2 = \log_{10} 0.01$

The two most commonly used bases for logarithms are base 10 and base e. Most of us have probably had some experience with *base-10*, or *common logarithms*.† Logarithms which use $e = 2.718 \ldots$ as the base are called *natural logarithms*.‡ Logarithms of this form arise from the use of exponential functions which employ e as the base.

Common logarithms can be denoted by

$$x = \log_{10} y$$

However, because most logarithm computations involve the base 10, a more common way of expressing such logarithms is

$$x = \log y$$

where the base, though not indicated, is implicitly 10. Base-e or natural logarithms can be denoted by

$$x = \log_e y$$

but are more commonly denoted by

$$x = \ln y$$

A logarithm having a base b other than 10 or e would be expressed as

$$x = \log_b y$$

Procedures for determining values of common logarithms will not be presented. The examples in this book will deal solely with natural logarithms. Table 2 (inside the back cover) contains values of natural logarithms. As an alternative to tables, most scientific hand calculators have a natural logarithm function key for determining these values.

Properties of Logarithms

The use of logarithms can result in certain efficiencies when computations of very large or very small numbers are required. These efficiencies can be attributed partly to certain properties of logarithms. Some of the more important properties follow.

$$\boxed{\text{Property 1:} \quad \log_b uv = \log_b u + \log_b v}$$

Examples: $\log_{10}[(100)(1{,}000)] = \log_{10} 100 + \log_{10} 1{,}000$
$$= 2 + 3 = 5$$

---

† These are sometimes referred to as *briggsian* logarithms (after H. Briggs, who first used them).
‡ Natural logs are named after John Napier, the Scot, as *napierian* logarithms.

$$\ln 8{,}000 = \ln[(40)(200)]$$
$$= \ln 40 + \ln 200$$
$$= 3.6889 + 5.2983 \qquad \text{(from Table 2)}$$
$$= 8.9872$$

Property 2: $\log_b \dfrac{u}{v} = \log_b u - \log_b v$

Examples: $\qquad \log_{10} \dfrac{10{,}000}{100} = \log_{10} 10{,}000 - \log_{10} 100$

$$= 4 - 2 = 2$$

$$\ln 37.5 = \ln \dfrac{75}{2}$$

$$= \ln 75 - \ln 2$$
$$= 4.3175 - 0.6931 \qquad \text{(from Table 2)}$$
$$= 3.6244$$

Property 3: $\log_b u^n = n \log_b u$

Examples: $\qquad \log_{10} 100^2 = 2 \log_{10} 100$

$$= 2(2) = 4$$
$$\ln 10{,}000 = \ln(100)^2$$
$$= 2 \ln 100$$
$$= 2(4.6052) \qquad \text{(from Table 2)}$$
$$= 9.2104$$

Property 4: $\log_b b = 1$

Examples: $\qquad \log_{10} 10 = 1 \qquad (10^1 = 10)$
$$\ln e = 1 \qquad (e^1 = e)$$

Property 5: $\log_b 1 = 0$

Examples: $\qquad \log_{10} 1 = 0 \qquad (10^0 = 1)$
$$\ln 1 = 0 \qquad (e^0 = 1)$$

Property 6: $b^{\log_b x} = x$

Example: $\qquad 10^{\log_{10} 100} = 10^2 = 100$

Property 7: $\log_b b^x = x$

Example: $\qquad \log_2 2^5 = 5$

Solving Logarithmic and Exponential Equations

Throughout the book we have had to solve for the roots of equations. Usually, these equations have been of the polynomial form (most frequently linear, quadratic, or cubic). The following examples illustrate the solution of logarithmic and exponential equations.

EXAMPLE 18

To solve the logarithmic equation.

$$\ln x^2 + \ln x = 9$$

Property 3 is applied resulting in

$$2 \ln x + \ln x = 9$$
$$3 \ln x = 9$$
$$\ln x = 3$$

From Table 2, ln 20 = 2.9957. Therefore we can state that $x \doteq 20$ is the root of the given equation.

EXAMPLE 19

To solve the logarithmic equation

$$\ln(x^2 + 2) - \ln x^2 = 2$$

Property 2 is applied to the left side of the equation, resulting in

$$\ln \frac{x^2 + 2}{x^2} = 2$$

Our understanding of logarithm relationships allows us to rewrite this equation in the equivalent exponential form

$$e^2 = \frac{x^2 + 2}{x^2}$$

or, from Table 1,

$$7.3891 = \frac{x^2 + 2}{x^2}$$

$$7.3891 \, x^2 = x^2 + 2$$
$$6.3891 \, x^2 = 2$$

$$x^2 = \frac{2}{6.3891}$$

$$x^2 = 0.3130$$

and $$x = \pm 0.5595$$

EXAMPLE 20

To solve the exponential equation

$$e^{2x} = 5$$

the natural logarithm is taken of both sides of the equation yielding

$$\ln e^{2x} = \ln 5$$

or
$$2x = \ln 5$$

From Table 2, ln 5 equals 1.6094 and

$$2x = 1.6094$$
$$x = 0.8047$$

EXAMPLE 21

In Example 15 we solved the equation

$$e^{-0.03x} = 0.4$$

using Table 1. An alternative approach would be to find the natural logarithm of both sides of the equation, yielding

$$\ln e^{-0.03x} = \ln 0.4$$

or
$$-0.03x = \ln 0.4$$

From Table 2, ln 0.4 equals -0.9163 and

$$-0.03x = -0.9163$$
$$x = \frac{-0.9163}{-0.03} = 30.54$$

which is a more accurate solution than that obtained in Example 15.

Logarithmic Functions

When a variable is expressed as a function of the logarithm of another variable, the function is referred to as a *logarithmic function.*

A *logarithmic function* has the form

$$y = f(x) = \log_b u(x) \qquad \text{(14.12)}$$

where $b > 0$ but $b \neq 1$.

The following are examples of logarithmic functions:

$$f(x) = \log x$$
$$f(x) = \ln x$$
$$f(x) = \log(x - 1)$$
$$f(x) = \ln(x^2 - 2x + 1)$$

EXAMPLE 22

Suppose we want to graph the function $y = \ln x$ where $x > 0$. The function $y = \ln x$ can be graphed using two procedures. If values of ln x are available (from tables or a hand

TABLE 14.4

x	0.1	0.5	1	10	100	200	300
ln x	−2.3026	−0.6932	0	2.3026	4.6052	5.2983	5.7038

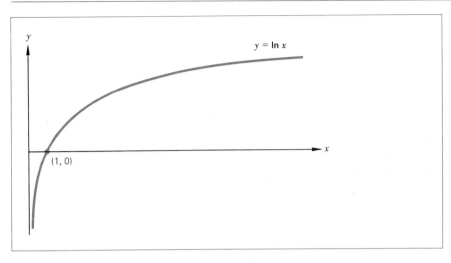

FIGURE 14.12

calculator), the function can be graphed directly. Using Table 2 at the end of the book, sample values of ln x are shown in Table 14.4. The general shape of this function is indicated in Fig. 14.12.

An alternative procedure for graphing a logarithmic function is to rewrite the function in its equivalent exponential form. The equivalent exponential form of $y = \ln x$ is

$$e^y = x$$

By *assuming values for* y and computing the corresponding values of x, a set of data points may be generated. Table 1 inside the front cover can be used to evaluate e^y. Sample data points are shown in Table 14.5. If these points are graphed (remembering that x is the independent variable in the function of interest $y = \ln x$), the sketch will be identical to that of Fig. 14.12.

TABLE 14.5

y	−1	−0.5	0	1	2	3	4
$x = e^y$	0.3679	0.6065	1.000	2.7183	7.3891	20.086	54.598

An examination of Fig. 14.12 indicates that the natural logarithm function $y = \ln x$ is an increasing function; also, $y > 0$ when $x > 1$, $y = 0$ when $x = 1$, and $y < 0$ when $0 < x < 1$.

EXAMPLE 23

To sketch the logarithmic function

$$y = 5 - 3\ln(x + 1) \qquad x > -1$$

ordered pairs of values (x, y) are determined. Table 14.6 presents sample values. Figure

TABLE 14.6

x	−0.5	0	1	2	5	10
y = 5 − 3 ln (x + 1)	7.0796	5	2.9204	1.7042	−0.3754	−2.1937

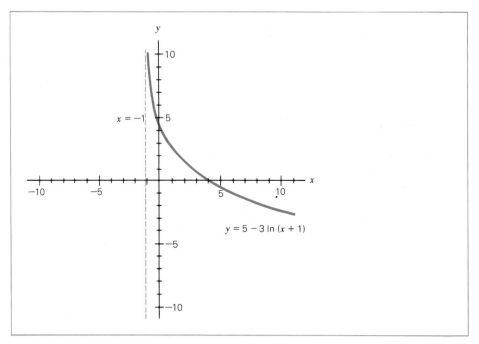

FIGURE 14.13

14.13 presents a sketch of the function. Note that the function is monotonically decreasing and that the curve has a vertical asymptote of $x = -1$.

Derivatives of Logarithmic Functions

RULE 2

If $f(x) = \ln u(x)$, where u is differentiable, then

$$f'(x) = \frac{u'(x)}{u(x)}$$

EXAMPLE 24

Consider the function

$$f(x) = \ln x$$

If we let $u(x) = x$,

$$f'(x) = \frac{1}{x}$$

The derivative of $f(x) = \ln x$ is

$$f'(x) = \frac{1}{x}$$

EXAMPLE 25

Consider the function $f(x) = \ln(5x^2 - 2x + 1)$. Application of Rule 2 results in

$$u(x) = 5x^2 - 2x + 1$$

and

$$f'(x) = \frac{10x - 2}{5x^2 - 2x + 1}$$

EXAMPLE 26

Let's examine the function

$$f(x) = x \ln x$$

for any extrema. First, the derivative is found using the product rule as

$$f'(x) = 1 \ln x + \frac{1}{x} x$$

$$= \ln x + 1$$

If f' is set equal to 0

$$\ln x + 1 = 0 \qquad \text{when} \qquad \ln x = -1$$

The equivalent exponential equation is

$$x = e^{-1}$$

From Table 1

$$e^{-1} = 0.3679$$

Therefore a critical value occurs when $x = 0.3679$.

To determine the nature of the critical point at $x = 0.3679$, the second derivative is

$$f''(x) = \frac{1}{x}$$

and

$$f''(0.3679) = \frac{1}{0.3679} = 2.7181 > 0$$

Therefore, a relative minimum occurs on f when $x = 0.3679$.

Section 14.4 Follow-up Exercises

For each of the following exponential equations, write the equivalent logarithmic equation.

1	$2^4 = 16$	2	$5^3 = 125$
3	$6^3 = 216$	4	$4^5 = 1,024$
5	$2^{-4} = \frac{1}{16}$	6	$5^{-2} = 0.04$
7	$(0.5)^{-4} = 16$	8	$(0.2)^{-3} = 125$
9	$(0.1)^{-3} = 1,000$	10	$(0.4)^{-2} = 6.25$

For each of the following logarithmic equations, write the equivalent exponential equation.

11	$\log_2 128 = 7$	12	$\log_4 64 = 3$
13	$\log_3 81 = 4$	14	$\log_2 0.125 = -3$
15	$\log_5 125 = 3$	16	$\log_{0.1} 10,000 = -4$
17	$\log_{0.2} 25 = -2$	18	$\ln 3 = 1.0986$
19	$\ln 100 = 4.6052$	20	$\ln e^x = x$

Using Table 2, determine the values of the following natural logarithms.

21	$\ln 10$	22	$\ln 300$
23	$\ln 350$	24	$\ln 20,000$
25	$\ln 475$	26	$\ln 0.75$
27	$\ln 0.15$	28	$\ln 4.75$
29	$\ln 160$	30	$\ln 0.01$

Solve the following equations.

31	$\ln x^3 - \ln x = 2$	32	$3 \ln 2x - 4 = 2 \ln 2x$
33	$x \ln x - \ln x = 0$	34	$x^2 \ln x - 4 \ln x = 0$
35	$\ln(x + 1) - \ln x = 0.5$	36	$\ln(x^2 + 3) - \ln x^2 = 1$
37	$e^{3x} = 20$	38	$e^{-2x} = 40$
39	$5e^{x^2} = 400$	40	$e^{-0.25x} = 16$

Sketch the following logarithmic functions.

41	$y = \ln(x/2)$	42	$y = \ln x^3$
43	$y = -2 \ln(x + 4)$	44	$y = 20 - 5 \ln x$

*45 Given the general logarithmic function

$$y = a \ln(x + b) - c$$

where a, b, and c are constants, determine the expression for (a) the x intercept, (b) the y intercept.

*46 Given the general exponential function

$$y = -e^{kx} + c$$

where k and c are constants, determine the expression for (a) the x intercept, (b) the y intercept.

For each of the following logarithmic functions, find f'.

47	$f(x) = \ln(5x)$	48	$f(x) = \ln(x/2)$
49	$f(x) = \ln(x^2 - 3)$	50	$f(x) = \ln(x^3 - 2x^2 + 5)$
51	$f(x) = x^2 \ln x$	52	$f(x) = (x + 3) \ln x^2$
53	$f(x) = 10x/\ln x$	54	$f(x) = [\ln x]^3$

55 $f(x) = (x - 1)/\ln 3x$ **56** $f(x) = [5x - \ln x]^5$

For each of the following logarithmic functions locate any critical points and determine their nature.

57 $f(x) = \ln 30x - 3x$ **58** $f(x) = 2 + \ln x$
59 $f(x) = \ln x - x^2/2$ **60** $f(x) = \ln(x^2 + 1) - x$
61 $f(x) = -4 \ln x - x^2/2 + 5x$ **62** $f(x) = -10 \ln x - x^2/2 + 7x$
63 $f(x) = x^2 \ln x$ **64** $f(x) = 5x \ln x$

14.5   APPLICATIONS OF LOGARITHMIC FUNCTIONS

The following examples illustrate applications of logarithmic functions.

EXAMPLE 27

Bacterial Growth   Many types of bacteria are believed to grow exponentially according to functions of the form

$$P = f(t) = P_0 e^{kt} \tag{14.13}$$

where P equals the population at time t, P_0 gives the population at t = 0, and k is the growth constant (percentage rate of growth). Exponential growth functions were discussed in Sec. 14.3. Determine the period of time required for an initial population to double in size.

SOLUTION

If an initial population doubles,

$$\frac{P}{P_0} = 2$$

If we divide both sides of Eq. (14.13) by P_0,

$$\frac{P}{P_0} = e^{kt}$$

The population will double when

$$e^{kt} = 2$$

Taking the natural logarithm of both sides of this equation

$$kt = \ln 2$$

and the time required for doubling is

$$t = \frac{\ln 2}{k} \tag{14.14}$$

If for a given bacteria the growth constant equals 0.4 and t is stated in hours, the time required for the population to double is

$$t = \frac{\ln 2}{0.4}$$

$$= \frac{0.6932}{0.4} = 1.733 \text{ hours}$$

POINT FOR THOUGHT AND DISCUSSION

Is the doubling time determined by Eq. (14.14) appropriate only for the initial population to double in size, or is this generalized, given the population at *any* time?

EXAMPLE 28

Half-Life   An exponential decay function has the general form

$$V = V_0 e^{-kt} \tag{14.15}$$

where *V equals the value of the function at time t, V_0 equals the value of the function at t = 0, and k is the decay constant (percentage rate of decay)*. Many natural processes are characterized by exponential decay behavior. One such process is the decay of certain radioactive substances. One measure frequently cited when examining a radioactive substance is its *half-life.* This is the time required for the amount of a substance to be reduced by a factor of $\frac{1}{2}$. For exponential decay functions of the form of Eq. (14.15), the half-life is a function of the decay constant.

Suppose the amount of a radioactive substance is determined by Eq. (14.15). The amount of the substance will halve itself when

$$\frac{V}{V_0} = 0.5$$

or when $e^{-kt} = 0.5$

Taking the natural logarithm of both sides of this equation,

$$-kt = \ln 0.5$$

and $$t = \frac{\ln 0.5}{-k} \tag{14.16}$$

The decay constant for strontium 90 is $k = 0.0244$, where *t* is measured in years. An amount of strontium 90 will decay to one-half its size when

$$t = \frac{\ln 0.5}{0.0244}$$

$$= \frac{-0.6932}{-0.0244} \doteq 28.40 \text{ years}$$

EXAMPLE 29

Welfare Management   A newly created state welfare agency is attempting to determine the number of analysts to hire to process welfare applications. Efficiency experts estimate that the average cost C of processing an application is a function of the number of analysts x. Specifically, the cost function is

$$C = f(x) = 0.001x^2 - 5 \ln x + 60$$

Determine the number of analysts who should be hired in order to minimize the average cost per application

The derivative of f is

$$f'(x) = 0.002x - 5\frac{1}{x}$$

$$= 0.002x - \frac{5}{x}$$

If f' is set equal to 0,

$$0.002x = \frac{5}{x}$$

$$0.002x^2 = 5$$

$$x^2 = \frac{5}{0.002}$$

$$x^2 = 2,500$$

and a critical value occurs when

$$x = 50$$

The value of $f(x)$ at the critical point is

$$f(50) = 0.001(50)^2 - 5 \ln 50 + 60$$
$$= 0.001(2,500) - 5(3.912) + 60 = 2.5 - 19.56 + 60 = \$42.94$$

To check the nature of the critical point,

$$f''(x) = 0.002 + 5x^{-2}$$

$$= 0.002 + \frac{5}{x^2}$$

$$f''(50) = 0.002 + \frac{5}{(50)^2}$$

$$= 0.002 + \frac{5}{2,500} = 0.002 + 0.002 = 0.004 > 0$$

Therefore, a relative minimum occurs for f when $x = 50$. Average processing cost per application is minimized at a value of \$42.94 when 50 analysts are employed. Figure 14.14 presents a sketch of the average cost function.

EXAMPLE 30 ▰▰▰▰▰▰▰▰▰▰▰▰▰▰▰▰▰▰▰▰▰▰▰▰

Elasticity of Demand   An important concept in economics and price theory is the *price elasticity of demand,* or, more simply, the *elasticity of demand.* Given the *demand func-*

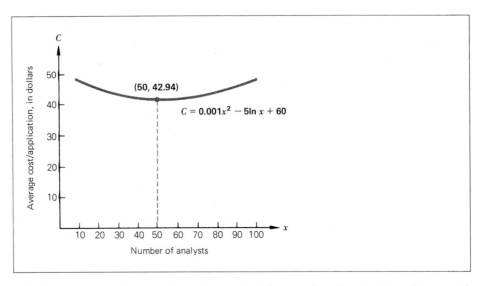

FIGURE 14.14

tion for a product and a particular point (p,q) on the function, the elasticity of demand is the ratio

$$\frac{\text{Percent change in quantity demanded}}{\text{Percent change in price}}$$

This ratio is a measure of the relative response of demand to changes in price. For non-linear demand functions, the relative response varies from point to point on the function. Given the computation of the elasticity of demand at a particular point, it represents an *instantaneous measure* of the relative response.

Equation (14.17) is the formula for computing the elasticity of demand η.

$$\eta = -\frac{\Delta q/q}{\Delta p/p} = -\frac{dq/q}{dp/p} = -\frac{p}{q}\frac{dq}{dp} \qquad (14.17)$$

For typical functions the following interpretations are assigned to different values of η.

■ *Case 1* $(\eta > 1)$: The percentage change in demand is greater than the percentage change in price (e.g., a 1 percent change in price results in a greater than 1 percent change in demand). In these regions of a demand function, demand is said to be *elastic.*

■ *Case 2* $(\eta < 1)$: The percentage change in demand is less than the percentage change in price. In these regions of the demand function, demand is said to be *inelastic.*

■ *Case 3* $(\eta = 1)$: The percentage change in demand equals the percentage change in price. In these regions of the demand function, demand is said to be *unit elastic.*

Consider the demand relationship

$$p = 200 - 25 \ln q \qquad (14.18)$$

To determine the value for η, we must find dq/dp. It would be somewhat difficult to solve for q in Eq. (14.18). However, from Eq. (11.8), if we find dp/dq, we know that

$$\frac{dq}{dp} = \frac{1}{dp/dq} \qquad \frac{dp}{dq} \neq 0$$

From Eq. (14.18)

$$\frac{dp}{dq} = -\frac{25}{q}$$

Therefore,

$$\frac{dq}{dp} = \frac{1}{-25/q}$$

$$= -q/25$$

Given a demand level of 100, the corresponding price is

$$p = 200 - 25 \ln 100$$
$$= 200 - 25(4.6052) \qquad \text{(from Table 2)}$$
$$= 84.87$$

At this point on the demand function the elasticity of demand is

$$\eta = \left(-\frac{84.87}{100}\right)\left(-\frac{100}{25}\right)$$

$$= 3.3948$$

The interpretation of this result is that the instantaneous, relative response of demand to a change in price is at a rate of 3.3948 to 1. That is, a 1 percent increase (decrease) in price will result in (approximately) a 3.3948 percent decrease (increase) in demand. Demand is elastic at this point.

Section 14.5 Follow-up Exercises

1   A company is hiring persons to work in its plant. For the job the persons will perform, efficiency experts estimate that the average cost C of performing the task is a function of the number of persons hired x. Specifically,

$$C = f(x) = 0.003x^2 - 0.216 \ln x + 5$$

(a) Determine the number of persons who should be hired to minimize the average cost.
(b) What is the minimum average cost?
2   Given the demand relationship in Example 30,

$$p = 200 - 25 \ln q$$

(a) determine the elasticity of demand when demand equals 50, and
(b) determine the elasticity of demand when demand equals 200.
3   Given the demand relationship

$$p = 500 - 50 \ln q$$

determine the elasticity of demand when demand equals 300.
4   A culture of bacteria E. coli is being grown in a medium consisting of inorganic salts and glucose. The bacteria has an initial population of 10^6 per milliliter and it grows at an exponential rate with growth constant $k = 0.7$.
(a) Determine the exponential growth function $f(t)$ where t is stated in hours.
(b) What is the doubling time?

(c) What is the tripling time?

    5   A particular bacteria grows at an exponential rate with growth constant $k = 0.45$.

(a) Determine the exponential growth function $f(t)$ where t is stated in hours.

(b) What is the doubling time?

(c) What is the tripling time?

    6   A yeast culture grows at an exponential rate. The population of the culture doubles after 2 hours. Determine the growth constant k.

    7   A radioactive substance has a decay constant $k = 0.325$. If t is measured in hours, determine the half-life for the substance. What is the quarter-life (time to reduce the amount by $\frac{1}{4}$)?

    8   A radioactive isotope used to check the thyroid gland has a decay constant $k = 0.125$. If a tracer of 4 units of the isotope is introduced into the bloodstream,

(a) Determine the exponential decay function $f(t)$ where t is stated in days.

(b) What amount of radioactivity is expected to be in the blood after 10 days?

(c) What is the half-life for the isotope?

    9   A radioactive substance has a half-life of 10,000 years. Determine the decay constant k.

    10   The amount of a particular drug contained in the bloodstream can be described by an exponential decay function where t is stated in hours. If the half-life of the drug is 3 hours, what is the decay constant k?

KEY TERMS AND CONCEPTS

base-e exponential functions   552
common logarithm   571
continuous compounding   557
conversion to base-e functions   553
elasticity of demand   581
exponential decay process   556
exponential function   547

exponential growth process   556
logarithm   570
modified exponential function   553
natural logarithm   571
solving logarithmic and exponential
   equations   573

IMPORTANT FORMULAS

$S = P(1 + i)^n$ Compound amount   (14.4)

$$e = \lim_{n \to \infty} \left(1 + \frac{1}{n}\right)^n \tag{14.8}$$

$S = Pe^{it}$ Compound amount (continuous compounding)   (14.9)

$V = V_0 e^{kt}$ Exponential growth process   (14.10)

$V = V_0 e^{-kt}$ Exponential decay process   (14.11)

$$t = \frac{\ln 2}{k} \qquad \text{Doubling time (exponential growth)} \tag{14.14}$$

$$t = \frac{\ln 0.5}{-k} \qquad \text{Half-life (exponential decay)} \tag{14.16}$$

$$\eta = -\frac{p}{q}\frac{dq}{dp} \qquad \textbf{Elasticity of demand} \tag{14.17}$$

If $f(x) = e^{u(x)}$, $f'(x) = u'(x)e^{u(x)}$

$y = b^x \Leftrightarrow x = \log_b y$

If $y = \ln u(x)$, $f'(x) = u'(x)/u(x)$

ADDITIONAL EXERCISES

Exercises 1 to 8 are related to Sec. 14.1.

For each of the following exponential functions, compute $f(-1)$, $f(0)$, and $f(2)$.

1 $f(x) = e^{x/3}$ **2** $f(x) = e^{x^2/4}$

3 $f(x) = 5(1 - e^x)$ **4** $f(x) = 4(1 - e^{2x})$

Convert each of the following into base-e exponential functions.

5 $f(x) = (1.7)^x$ **6** $f(x) = 10(2.56)^{x^2}$

7 $f(x) = 5(.1)^{x/2}$ **8** $f(x) = -3(.35)^{x/3}$

Exercises 9 to 16 are related to Sec. 14.2.

9 **Present Value: Continuous Compounding** Assuming continuous compounding, the present value P of S dollars t years in the future can be expressed by the function

$$P = f(t) = Se^{-it}$$

Assuming interest of 8 percent per year compounded continuously, what sum should be deposited today if $100,000 is desired 15 years from now?

10 The population of a particular species of fish has been estimated at 200 million. Scientists suspect that the population is growing exponentially at a rate of 4.5 percent per year. If the rate and pattern of growth continue, what is the fish population expected to equal in 20 years?

11 **Public Utilities** The number of new telephones installed each day in a particular city is currently 200. Telephone company officials believe that the number of new telephones installed each day will continue to increase exponentially at a rate of 8 percent per year. If this pattern holds true, what is the daily rate of installation expected to be 10 years from today?

12 The population of a particular class of endangered species has been *decreasing* exponentially at a rate of 4 percent per year. If the current population of the species is 900,000, what is the population expected to equal in 10 years?

13 **Police Patrol Allocation** A police department has determined that the average daily crime rate depends on the number of officers assigned to each shift. The function describing this relationship is

$$N = f(x)$$
$$= 300 - 8xe^{-0.03x}$$

where N equals the average daily crime rate and x equals the number of officers assigned to each shift. What is the average daily crime rate if 20 officers are assigned? If 30 officers are assigned?

14   Product Reliability   A manufacturer of batteries used in portable radios, toys, flashlights, etc., estimates that the percentage P of manufactured batteries having a useful life of at least t hours is described by the function

$$P = f(t) = e^{-0.2t}$$

What percentage of batteries is expected to last at least 6 hours? At least 12 hours?

15   Learning Curves   Exponential functions can be used to describe the learning process. One such exponential function has the form

$$y = f(x) = a - be^{-kx} \qquad\qquad (14.19)$$

where a, b, and k are positive. For this general *learning curve* function, y represents some measure of the degree of learning and x the number of learning reinforcements.

Industrial engineers have studied a particular job on an assembly line. The function

$$y = f(x) = 100 - 75e^{-0.40x}$$

is the learning curve function which describes the number of units completed per hour y for a typical employee as a function of the number of hours experience x the employee has with the job. (*a*) What is the hourly rate after 1 hour of experience? (*b*) After 10 hours?

16   Given the learning curve function in the last exercise, sketch $f(x)$. Is there an upper limit on the value of y?

Exercises 17 to 28 are related to Sec. 14.3.
Find f' for each of the following functions.

17   $f(x) = 5e^{x^2-2x}$ 18 $f(x) = 2x^3e^{x^2}$
19   $f(x) = x/e^{x^3}$ 20 $f(x) = (2x^2 - 5x)^5e^{x/2}$
21   $f(x) = (10 - 5e^{x^2})^4$ 22 $f(x) = (a - be^{-x})^c$

For each of the following functions, find the location of all critical points and determine their nature.

23   $f(x) = 50x - e^x$ 24 $f(x) = 0.5x + e^{-0.5x}$
25   $f(x) = e^{(x-0.2x^2)}$ 26 $f(x) = 20x - e^{0.1x} + 50$

27   The demand function for a product is

$$q = f(p) = 25{,}000e^{-0.05p}$$

where q is quantity demanded (in units) and p is the price (in dollars). (*a*) Determine the value of p which will result in maximum total revenue. (*b*) What is the maximum total revenue?

28   A marketing research organization believes that if a company spends x million dollars on TV advertising, total profit can be estimated by the function

$$P = f(x) = 40x^2e^{-0.5x}$$

where P is measured in millions of dollars. (*a*) How much should be spent on TV advertising in order to maximize total profit? (*b*) What is the maximum profit?

Exercises 29 to 44 are related to Sec. 14.4.

Solve the following equations.

29 $\ln x^4 - \ln x^2 = 3$

30 $x^2 \ln x - 9 \ln x = 0$

31 $x \ln x - 4 \ln x = 0$

32 $e^{x^2} = 100$

33 $e^{-5x} = 50$

34 $5e^{-0.2x} = 2$

For the following functions, find f'.

35 $f(x) = \ln ax^2$

36 $f(x) = \ln(ax^2 + bx + c)$

37 $f(x) = x \ln(x - 5)$

38 $f(x) = (\ln x - 3x)^3$

39 $f(x) = e^x/\ln 6x$

40 $f(x) = e^{x^3}/\ln x$

For the following functions locate any critical points and determine their nature.

41 $f(x) = \ln 50x - 5x$

42 $f(x) = 5x^2 \ln x$

43 $f(x) = 40x - 20 \ln x$

44 $f(x) = 0.5x^2 - 4x - 5 \ln x + 50$

Exercises 45 to 51 are related to Sec. 14.5.

45 Given the demand relationship

$$p = 1,000 - 80 \ln q$$

determine the elasticity of demand when demand equals 100.

46 A bacterial culture grows at an exponential rate. The population of the culture doubles after 4 hours. Determine the growth constant k.

47 A radioactive isotope used to check the thyroid gland has a decay constant $k = 0.100$. If a tracer of 10 units of the isotope is introduced into the bloodstream, (a) determine the exponential decay function $f(t)$ where t is stated in days. (b) What amount of the isotope is expected to be in the blood after 10 days? (c) What is the half-life of the isotope?

48 A radioactive substance has a half-life of 20,000 years. Determine the decay constant k.

49 **Memory Retention** An experiment was conducted to determine the effects of elapsed time on a person's memory. Subjects were asked to look at a picture which contained many different objects. After studying the picture, they were asked to recall as many of the objects as they could. At different time intervals following this, they would be asked to recall as many objects as they could. Based on the experiment, the following function was developed.

$$\overline{R} = f(t) = 84 - 25 \ln t \qquad t \geq 1$$

For this function $\overline{R}$ represents the average percent recall as a function of time since studying the picture (measured in hours). A value of $\overline{R} = 50$ would indicate that at the corresponding time t the average recall for the study group was 50 percent. (a) What is the average percent recall after 1 hour? (b) After 10 hours? (c) Find the expression for the rate of change in $\overline{R}$ with respect to time. (d) What is the maximum percent recall? Minimum?

50 A new state welfare agency wants to determine how many analysts to hire for processing of welfare applications. It is estimated that the average cost C of processing an application is a function of the number of analysts x. Specifically, the cost function is

$$C = 0.005x^2 - 16 \ln x + 70$$

(*a*) If the objective is to minimize the average cost per application, determine the number of analysts who should be hired.

(*b*) What is the minimum average cost of processing an application expected to equal?

   51   A firm has estimated that the average production cost per unit $\overline{C}$ fluctuates with the number of units produced x. The average cost function is

$$\overline{C} = 0.002x^2 - 1{,}000 \ln x + 7{,}500$$

where $\overline{C}$ is stated in dollars per unit and x is stated in hundreds of units.

(*a*) Determine the number of units which should be produced in order to minimize the average production cost per unit.

(*b*) What is the minimum average cost expected to equal?

(*c*) What are total production costs expected to equal?

CHAPTER TEST

1   Given $f(x) = 1{,}000e^{-x}$, determine $f(2.5)$.

2   An investment of \$10,000 receives interest of 7 percent per year compounded continuously. What is the compound amount S if the investment is for a period of 20 years? How much interest will be earned during this period?

3   Given

$$4^8 = 65{,}536$$

write the equivalent logarithmic equation.

4   Determine the location and nature of any critical points for

$$f(x) = e^{-x^2+3}$$

5   Determine the location and nature of any critical points for

$$f(x) = x(\ln x)$$

6   A national charity is planning a fund raising campaign in a major city. The population of the city is 1.5 million. The percentage of the population who will make a donation is described by the function

$$R = 1 - e^{-0.06x}$$

where R equals the percentage of the population and x equals the number of days the campaign is conducted. Past experience indicates that the average contribution per donor is \$1. Costs of the campaign are estimated at \$5,000 per day. Formulate the function $N = f(x)$ which expresses net proceeds N(total contributions minus total costs) as a function of x. (*Note:* This is a formulation problem.)

MINICASE

TIME OF DEATH?

If an object is placed in a cooler environment, the temperature of the object decreases toward the temperature of the surrounding environment. The mathematical model which describes this process is

$$T = f(t) = ae^{-kt} + C \qquad (14.20)$$

where T equals the temperature of the object t time units after it is placed in the cooler environment, which is of temperature C. Figure 14.15 is a sketch of the function.

The laws of physics underlying this process have many important applications. One important application involves determining the time of death of a person, a function typically performed by a coroner. Suppose that a person's body is discovered in an apartment. The coroner arrives at 1:00 p.m. and finds that the temperature of the body is 88.7°F and the temperature of the apartment is 68°F. The coroner waits 1 hour and then retakes the temperature of the body, finding it to be 86.0°F. The requirement is to determine the time of death. *Hints:* First, assume that the body temperature at the time of death was 98.6°F and that in Eq. (14.20) $t = 0$ corresponds to the time of death. This information, along with the room temperature, allows for determining a and C in Eq. (14.20). Second, we know that t hours after death the body temperature was 88.7°F and $t + 1$ hours after death it was 86.0°F.

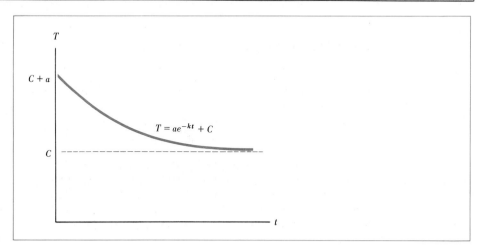

FIGURE 14.15

15

OPTIMIZATION: FUNCTIONS OF SEVERAL VARIABLES

CHAPTER OBJECTIVES

- Provide an understanding of the calculus of functions which contain two independent variables
- Illustrate the graphical representation of functions in three dimensions
- Overview the optimization procedures for functions which contain more than two independent variables
- Introduce the nature of and procedures for optimization of functions subject to constraining conditions

Chapters 11 to 14 have provided a methodology for examining functions which involve one independent variable. In actual applications a decision criterion or objective frequently depends on more than one variable. When functions involve more than one independent variable, they are referred to as *multivariate functions*, or *functions of several variables.* Methods of differential calculus are available for examining such functions and for determining optimal values (maxima and minima). As we examine some of these procedures in this chapter, you will see that they are very similar to those we used for functions of one independent variable.

This chapter will concentrate initially on **bivariate functions** (functions involving two independent variables). The graphics of these functions will be illustrated and a discussion of the derivatives of these functions and their interpretation will follow. Next, procedures for determining optimal values of these functions will be developed. This will be followed by a section which discusses applications of bivariate functions. The discussion of bivariate functions will be extended to the optimization of n-variable functions. The final section in the chapter examines the topic of *constrained optimization*.

15.1 GRAPHICAL REPRESENTATION OF BIVARIATE FUNCTIONS

Graphical Representation

A function involving a dependent variable z and two independent variables x and y may be represented by using the notation

$$z = f(x, y)$$ (15.1)

We established a long time ago that the number of variables in a function determines the number of dimensions required to graph the function. Whereas two dimensions are required to graph single-variable functions, three dimensions are required to graph bivariate functions.

We established earlier in the book that linear functions involving one independent variable graph as *straight lines* in two dimensions. Linear functions involving two independent variables graph as *planes* in three dimensions. Generally speaking, nonlinear functions involving one independent variable graph as *curves* in two dimensions. And, nonlinear functions containing two independent variables graph as *curved surfaces* in three dimensions. Examples of nonlinear surfaces include the undulating surface of a golf green, a mogul-laden ski slope, and a billowing sail on a sailboat. An important point is that these functions are represented by *surfaces*, not solids.

Sketching Bivariate Functions

Although graphing in three dimensions is difficult, there are procedures that can be used in some instances to sketch the general shape of the graph of a bivariate function. An understanding of the graphics of these functions can assist with the material which follows.

Consider the bivariate function

$$z = f(x, y) = 25 - x^2 - y^2$$ (15.2)

where $0 \le x \le 5$ and $0 \le y \le 5$. In order to sketch this function, let's fix the value of one of the independent variables and graph the resulting function. For example, if we let $y = 0$, the function f becomes

$$z = 25 - x^2 - 0^2$$

or
$$z = 25 - x^2$$ (15.3)

By fixing the value of one of the variables, the function is restated in terms of one independent variable. That is, once the value of one independent variable is specified, the value of the dependent variable varies with the value of the remaining independent variable. Given Eq. (15.3), Table 15.1 indicates selected values for x and resulting values of z.

Figure 15.1 is a partial sketch of the function with the value of y fixed at 0. If we let $y = 0$, the sketch of Eq. (15.3) must be in the xz plane. A close examination of Eq. (15.3) reveals that the relationship between z and x is quadratic. And the sketch in Fig. 15.1 is part of a parabola which is concave down.

If we let $x = 0$ in the original function, f becomes

$$z = 25 - 0^2 - y^2$$

or
$$z = 25 - y^2$$ (15.4)

TABLE 15.1

x	0	1	2	3	4	5
$z = 25 - x^2$	25	24	21	16	9	0

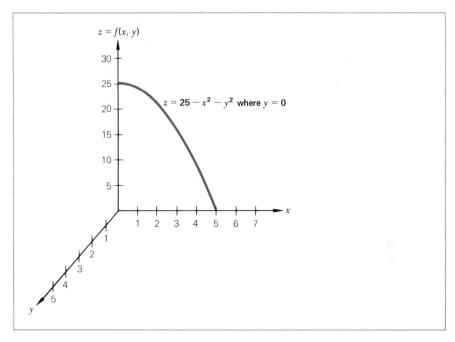

FIGURE 15.1
Partial sketch of $f(x, y) = 25 - x^2 - y^2$.

TABLE 15.2

y	0	1	2	3	4	5
$z = 25 - y^2$	25	24	21	16	9	0

Table 15.2 indicates selected values of y and the resulting values of z.

Figure 15.2 is a partial sketch of $f(x, y)$. With $x = 0$, the sketch of Eq. (15.4) is in the yz plane. Equation (15.4) indicates a quadratic relationship between y and z. And, if you were to look at Fig. 15.2 in a direction parallel to the x axis, you would see that this equation graphs as a portion of a parabola which is concave down. Figure 15.3 indicates what you would see if sighting along the x axis.

DEFINITION: TRACE

Given $z = f(x, y)$, a ***trace*** is the graph of f when one variable is held constant.

Refer to Fig. 15.2. The two portions of f which are illustrated are *traces*. One is a trace where $y = 0$, and the other is a trace where $x = 0$. Each trace represents a *rib* on the surface which represents the function.

Figure 15.4 presents a sketch of the function which includes four additional traces. By letting $y = 1$, the function becomes

$$f(x, y) = 25 - x^2 - 1^2$$
$$= 24 - x^2$$

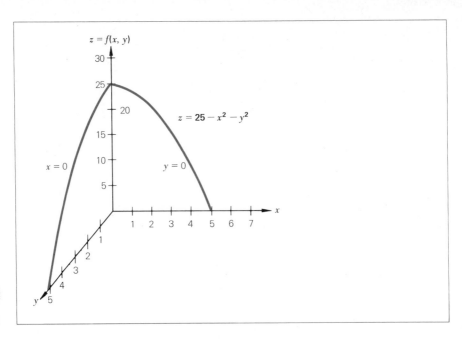

FIGURE 15.2
Partial sketch of
$f(x, y) = 25 - x^2 - y^2$.

The trace representing this function is parallel to the xz plane and 1 unit out along the positive y axis. Similarly, letting $y = 3$, we have

$$f(x, y) = 25 - x^2 - 3^2$$
$$= 16 - x^2$$

The trace representing this function graphs parallel to the xz plane and 3 units out along the y axis.

Traces have also been sketched by letting $x = 1$ and $x = 3$. These six traces in combination begin to resemble a skeletal structure of the surface. And if we were to graph more traces associated with other assumed values for x and y, we would get a more accurate representation of the surface representing f.

Therefore, a procedure which can sometimes provide a rough sketch of a function of the form $z = f(x, y)$ is to assume selected values for x and y and graph the traces which represent the resulting functions.

NOTE

An important observation should be made regarding the graphics of a function $f(x, y)$. *Whenever x is held constant, the resulting trace graphs in a plane which is parallel to the yz plane. Whenever y is held constant, the resulting trace graphs in a plane which is parallel to the xz plane.*

Section 15.1 Follow-up Exercises

Sketch the following functions.

1    $f(x, y) = 16 - x^2 - y^2$, where $0 \le x \le 4$ and $0 \le y \le 4$

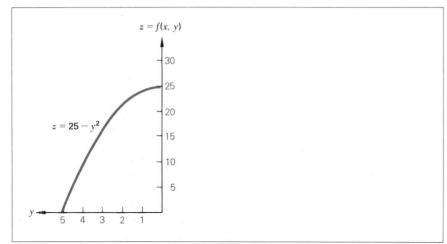

FIGURE 15.3
Trace with
$x = 0$ viewed
along the x
axis.

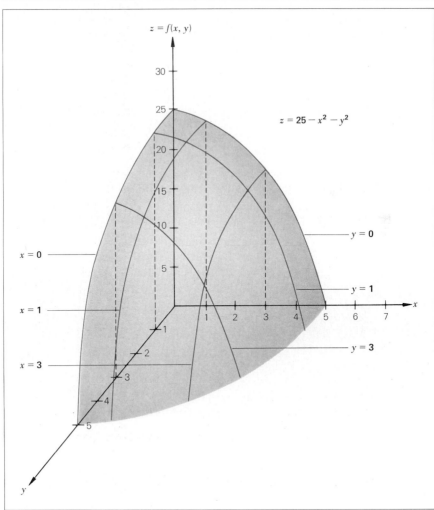

FIGURE 15.4
Sketch of
$f(x, y) = 25 - x^2 - y^2$.

2　$f(x, y) = 9 - x^2 - y^2$, where $0 \le x \le 3$ and $0 \le y \le 3$

3　$f(x, y) = 4 - x^2 - y^2$, where $0 \le x \le 2$ and $0 \le y \le 2$

4　$f(x, y) = 25 - x^2/4 - y^2/4$, where $0 \le x \le 10$ and $0 \le y \le 10$

5　$f(x, y) = x^2 + y^2$, where $0 \le x \le 5$ and $0 \le y \le 5$

15.2 PARTIAL DERIVATIVES

Although more involved, the calculus of bivariate functions is very similar to that of single-variable functions. In this section we will discuss derivatives of bivariate functions and their interpretation.

Derivatives of Bivariate Functions

With single-variable functions, the derivative represents the instantaneous rate of change in the dependent variable with respect to a change in the independent variable. For bivariate functions, derivatives can also be defined. We will focus on *partial derivatives* which represent the instantaneous rate of change in the dependent variable, but with respect to changes in the two independent variables, separately. Given a function $z = f(x, y)$, a partial derivative can be found with respect to each independent variable. The partial derivative taken with respect to x is denoted by

$$\frac{\partial z}{\partial x} \quad \text{or} \quad f_x$$

The partial derivative taken with respect to y is denoted by

$$\frac{\partial z}{\partial y} \quad \text{or} \quad f_y$$

Although both forms are used to denote the partial derivative, we will use the subscripted notation f_x or f_y in this chapter.

DEFINITION: PARTIAL DERIVATIVE

Given the function $z = f(x, y)$, the **partial derivative** of z with respect to x at (x, y) is

$$\frac{\partial z}{\partial x} = \lim_{\Delta x \to 0} \frac{f(x + \Delta x, y) - f(x, y)}{\Delta x}$$

provided the limit exists. The partial derivative of z with respect to y at (x, y) is

$$\frac{\partial z}{\partial y} = \lim_{\Delta y \to 0} \frac{f(x, y + \Delta y) - f(x, y)}{\Delta y}$$

provided the limit exists.

EXAMPLE 1

Consider the function

$$f(x, y) = 3x^2 + 5y^3$$

To find the partial derivative with respect to x, let's use the *limit approach* from Sec. 11.3.

First, the difference quotient is formed as

$$\frac{\Delta f(x, y)}{\Delta x} = \frac{f(x + \Delta x, y) - f(x, y)}{\Delta x}$$

$$= \frac{3(x + \Delta x)^2 + 5y^3 - (3x^2 + 5y^3)}{\Delta x}$$

$$= \frac{3(x^2 + 2x\Delta x + \Delta x^2) + 5y^3 - 3x^2 - 5y^3}{\Delta x}$$

which simplifies to

$$\frac{\Delta f(x, y)}{\Delta x} = \frac{6x\Delta x + 3\Delta x^2}{\Delta x}$$

$$= \frac{\cancel{\Delta x}(6x + 3\Delta x)}{\cancel{\Delta x}}$$

$$= 6x + 3\Delta x$$

The partial derivative is

$$f_x = \lim_{\Delta x \to 0} \frac{\Delta f(x, y)}{\Delta x}$$

$$= \lim_{\Delta x \to 0} (6x + 3\Delta x)$$

$$= 6x$$

Note that in finding f_x, we are examining the effects of changes in x (i.e., Δx); the other independent variable y is held constant.

The partial derivative taken with respect to y can be found in a similar manner.

$$\frac{\Delta f(x, y)}{\Delta y} = \frac{f(x, y + \Delta y) - f(x, y)}{\Delta y}$$

$$= \frac{3x^2 + 5(y + \Delta y)^3 - (3x^2 + 5y^3)}{\Delta y}$$

$$= \frac{3x^2 + 5(y^3 + 3y^2\Delta y + 3y\Delta y^2 + \Delta y^3) - 3x^2 - 5y^3}{\Delta y}$$

$$= \frac{\cancel{3x^2} + \cancel{5y^3} + 15y^2\Delta y + 15y\Delta y^2 + 5\Delta y^3 - \cancel{3x^2} - \cancel{5y^3}}{\Delta y}$$

$$= \frac{\cancel{\Delta y}(15y^2 + 15y\Delta y + 5\Delta y^2)}{\cancel{\Delta y}}$$

$$= 15y^2 + 15y\Delta y + 5\Delta y^2$$

The partial derivative is

$$f_y = \lim_{\Delta y \to 0} \frac{\Delta f(x, y)}{\Delta y}$$

$$= \lim_{\Delta y \to 0} (15y^2 + 15y\Delta y + 5\Delta y^2)$$

$$= 15y^2$$

In determining $f_{y,}$, we are examining the effects of changes in y (i.e., Δy); the other independent variable x is held constant.

EXAMPLE 2 ▐▬▬▬▬▬▬▬▬▬▬▬▬▬▬▬▬▬▬▬▬▬▬▬▬▬▬▬▬

Consider the function

$$f(x, y) = 5x^2 y$$

Using the limit approach to find the partial derivatives,

$$\frac{\Delta f(x, y)}{\Delta x} = \frac{f(x + \Delta x, y) - f(x, y)}{\Delta x}$$

$$= \frac{5(x + \Delta x)^2 - 5x^2 y}{\Delta x}$$

$$= \frac{5(x^2 + 2x\Delta x + \Delta x^2)y - 5x^2 y}{\Delta x}$$

$$= \frac{5x^2 y + 10xy\Delta x + 5y\Delta x^2 - 5x^2 y}{\Delta x}$$

$$= \frac{\Delta x(10xy + 5y\Delta x))}{\Delta x}$$

$$= 10xy + 5y\Delta x$$

Thus,

$$f_x = \lim_{\Delta x \to 0} \frac{\Delta f(x, y)}{\Delta x}$$

$$= \lim_{\Delta x \to 0} (10xy + 5y\Delta x)$$

$$= 10xy$$

To find f_y

$$\frac{\Delta f(x, y)}{\Delta y} = \frac{f(x, y + \Delta y) - f(x, y)}{\Delta y}$$

$$= \frac{5x^2(y + \Delta y) - 5x^2 y}{\Delta y}$$

$$= \frac{5x^2 y + 5x^2 \Delta y - 5x^2 y}{\Delta y}$$

$$= 5x^2$$

And

$$f_y = \lim_{\Delta y \to 0} \frac{\Delta f(x, y)}{\Delta y}$$

$$= \lim_{\Delta y \to 0} 5x^2$$

$$= 5x^2$$

Fortunately, partial derivatives are found more easily using the same differentiation rules we used in the last four chapters. The only exception is that *when a partial derivative is found with respect to one independent variable, the other independent variable is assumed to be held constant.* For instance, in finding the partial derivative with respect to x, y is assumed to be constant. And a very important point is that *the variable which is assumed constant must be treated like a constant in applying the rules of differentiation.*

EXAMPLE 3

Find the partial derivatives with respect to x and y for the function

$$f(x, y) = 5x^2 + 6y^3$$

SOLUTION

First, to find the partial derivative with respect to x, the variable y must be assumed held constant. Differentiating term by term, we find that the derivative of $5x^2$ with respect to x is $10x$. In differentiating the second term, remember that y is assumed to be constant. Thus, this term has the general form of

$$6(\text{constant})^3$$

which is simply a constant. Since a constant does not change in value as other variables change in value—or, remember from Chap. 11 that the derivative of a constant equals 0—the derivative of the second term equals 0. Thus,

$$f_x = 10x + 0$$
$$= 10x$$

In finding the partial derivative with respect to y, the variable x is assumed held constant. In differentiating term by term, $5x^2$ is viewed as being a constant since x is assumed constant and the derivative equals 0. The derivative of $6y^3$ with respect to y is $18y^2$. Thus,

$$f_y = 0 + 18y^2$$
$$= 18y^2$$

EXAMPLE 4

Find f_x and f_y for the function

$$f(x, y) = 4xy$$

SOLUTION

To find f_x, y is assumed to be constant. The term $4xy$ is in the form of a product. To differentiate such product terms, you can use two approaches. The first approach is simply to apply the product rule. In viewing $4xy$ as the product of $4x$ and y, the product rule yields

$$f_x = (4)(y) + (0)(4x)$$
or
$$f_x = 4y$$

An *alternative approach* is to remember which variable is assumed constant. When y is held constant, we can rearrange $4xy$ to have the form

$$(4y)x$$

By grouping the 4 and y, this term has the general form of a constant $4y$ times x. And the derivative of a constant times x is the constant, or

$$f_x = 4y$$

To find f_y, x is assumed constant. Applying the product rule, we find

$$f_y = (0)(y) + (1)(4x)$$

or
$$f_y = 4x$$

Or, by using the alternative approach, the factor $4x$ is constant (with x held constant) and f can be viewed as having the form

$$f(x, y) = \text{constant} \cdot y$$

The derivative with respect to y is the constant, or

$$f_y = 4x$$

EXAMPLE 5

Find f_x and f_y if

$$f(x, y) = -10xy^3$$

SOLUTION

To find f_x, y must be assumed constant. This function can be rearranged (mentally or explicitly) to have the form

$$(-10y^3)x$$

where $-10y^3$ is constant. The derivative is

$$f_x = -10y^3$$

For f_y the function can be viewed as having the form

$$(-10x)y^3 \qquad \text{or} \qquad (\text{constant})(y^3)$$

The derivative with respect to y is

$$(\text{constant})(3y^2)$$

or
$$f_y = -30xy^2$$

Remember, the product rule also can be used to find the derivatives of product forms.

EXAMPLE 6

Find f_x and f_y if

$$f(x, y) = e^{x^2+y^2}$$

SOLUTION

Using the differentiation rules for exponential functions,

$$f_x = 2xe^{x^2+y^2}$$
$$f_y = 2ye^{x^2+y^2}$$

EXAMPLE 7

Find f_x and f_y if

$$f(x, y) = (3x - 2y^2)^3$$

SOLUTION

Remembering the power of a function rule, we have

$$f_x = 3(3x - 2y^2)^2(3)$$
$$= 9(3x - 2y^2)^2$$
$$f_y = 3(3x - 2y^2)^2(-4y)$$
$$= -12y(3x - 2y^2)^2$$

Interpreting Partial Derivatives

One interpretation of partial derivatives is the instantaneous rate-of-change interpretation. As with single-variable functions, partial derivatives can be used to approximate changes in the value of the dependent variable, given a change in *one* of the independent variables. For example, f_x can be used to approximate the change in $f(x, y)$, given a change in x with y assumed constant. The partial derivative f_y can be used to approximate the change in $f(x, y)$, given a change in y with x assumed constant. The following examples illustrate this interpretation.

EXAMPLE 8

Multiproduct Demand Interrelationships Until this point, we have assumed that the demand for a product only depends on the price of that product. Thus, the *demand functions* we have examined have had the form

$$q = f(p)$$

Frequently, the demand for a product or service is influenced not only by its own price but also by the prices of other products or services. Equation (15.5) is a demand function which expresses the quantity demanded of product 1 (q_1) as a function of its price (p_1) as well as the prices of two other products (p_2 and p_3), all stated in dollars.

$$q_1 = f(p_1, p_2, p_3) = 10,000 - 2.5p_1 + 3p_2 + 1.5p_3 \qquad (15.5)$$

Partial derivatives of this demand function can provide a measure of the instantaneous response of demand to changes in the prices of the three goods. For example,

$$f_{p_1} = -2.5$$

suggests that if p_2 and p_3 are held constant, the demand for product 1 will *decrease* at an instantaneous rate of 2.5 units for every unit (dollar) that p_1 increases. Similarly, the partial derivatives

$$f_{p_2} = 3 \qquad \text{and} \qquad f_{p_3} = 1.5$$

indicate the instantaneous rates of change in demand associated with changes in the prices of the other two products. $f_{p_2} = 3$ suggests that demand for product 1 will *increase* at an instantaneous rate of 3 units for every unit (dollar) that p_2 increases (p_1 and p_3 held constant), and $f_{p_3} = 1.5$ indicates that demand for product 1 will *increase* at an instantaneous rate of 1.5 units for each unit (dollar) that p_3 increases (p_1 and p_2 held constant).

Let's make a couple of observations. First, this demand function is linear and the corresponding partial derivatives are constant. That is, the instantaneous rates of change are really the same anywhere in the domain of the demand function. Second, the fact that the demand for product 1 *increases* with an increase in the prices of both product 2 and product 3 suggests an interdependence among the three products. This is the type of relationship we would expect to exist among *competing products.* Examples of competing products are different brands of the same product (e.g., steel-belted radial tires) or different products which can be used to satisfy a particular need (e.g., margarine vs. butter and chicken vs. beef). For competing products we would expect that as the price of one product increases, demand for it will decrease and demand for competing products will increase. Equivalently, as the price for a product decreases, we would expect demand for it to increase and demand for competing products to decrease. This is the type of behavior illustrated by the demand function in Eq. (15.5) and its partial derivatives.

EXERCISE

Given the demand function

$$q_1 = f(p_1, p_2, p_3) = 120,000 - 0.5p_1^2 - 0.4p_2^2 - 0.2p_3^2$$

(1) Find all partial derivatives. (2) If current prices for the three products are $p_1 = 10$, $p_2 = 20$, and $p_3 = 30$, evaluate the partial derivatives and interpret their meaning. (3) What does the demand function and its partial derivatives suggest about the interdependence among the three products?*

EXAMPLE 9

Advertising Expenditures   A national manufacturer estimates that the number of units it sells each year is a function of its expenditures on radio and TV advertising. The function specifying this relationship is

$$z = 50,000x + 40,000y - 10x^2 - 20y^2 - 10xy$$

where *z equals the number of units sold annually, x equals the amount spent for TV advertising, and y equals the amount spent for radio advertising (both in $1,000s).*

Assume that the firm is currently spending $40,000 on TV advertising ($x = 40$) and $20,000 on radio advertising ($y = 20$). With these expenditures,

$$f(40, 20) = 50,000(40) + 40,000(20) - 10(40)^2 - 20(20)^2 - 10(40)(20)$$
$$= 2,000,000 + 800,000 - 16,000 - 8,000 - 8,000 = 2,768,000$$

or it is projected that 2,768,000 units will be sold.

Suppose we are interested in determining the effect on annual sales if $1,000 more is spent on TV advertising. The partial derivative f_x should provide us with an approximation of this effect: This partial derivative is

$$f_x = 50,000 - 20x - 10y$$

---

* Answer: (1) $f_{p_1} = -p_1$, $f_{p_2} = -0.8p_2$, $f_{p_3} = -0.4p_3$; (2) $f_{p_1}(10, 20, 30) = -10$, $f_{p_2}(10, 20, 30) = -16$, $f_{p_3}(10, 20, 30) = -12$; (3) they are complementary products.

Because we are interested in the instantaneous rate of change, given that expenditures are currently \$40,000 and \$20,000, we evaluate f_x at $x = 40$ and $y = 20$:

$$f_x(40, 20) = 50,000 - 20(40) - 10(20)$$
$$= 50,000 - 800 - 200 = 49,000$$

Evaluating the partial derivative, we can state that an increase in TV expenditures of \$1,000 should result in additional sales of approximately 49,000 units.

To determine how accurate this approximation is, let's evaluate $f(41, 20)$:

$$f(41, 20) = 50,000(41) + 40,000(20) - 10(41)^2 - 20(20)^2 - 10(41)(20)$$
$$= 2,050,000 + 800,000 - 16,810 - 8,000 - 8,200 = 2,816,990$$

The *actual increase* in sales is projected as

$$f(41, 20) - f(40, 20) = 2,816,990 - 2,768,000$$
$$= 48,990 \text{ units}$$

The difference between the actual increase and the increase estimated by using f_x is $48,990 - 49,000 = -10$ units. The minus sign indicates that the partial derivative *overestimated* the actual change.

Now suppose that we are interested in determining the effect if an additional \$1,000 is spent on radio, rather than TV, advertising. The partial derivative taken with respect to y will approximate this change:

$$f_y = 40,000 - 40y - 10x$$

Evaluating f_y at $x = 40$ and $y = 20$, we get

$$f_y(40, 20) = 40,000 - 40(20) - 10(40)$$
$$= 40,000 - 800 - 400 = 38,800$$

Thus an increase of \$1,000 in radio advertising expenditures will lead to an approximate increase of 38,800 units.

With an increase of \$1,000 in radio advertising expenses, actual sales are estimated at

$$f(40, 21) = 50,000(40) + 40,000(21) - 10(40)^2 - 20(21)^2 - 10(40)(21)$$
$$= 2,000,000 + 840,000 - 16,000 - 8,820 - 8,400 = 2,806,780 \text{ units}$$

The *actual increase* in sales is

$$f(40, 21) - f(40, 20) = 2,806,780 - 2,768,000$$
$$= 38,780 \text{ units}$$

Again, the approximate change estimated by using f_y is in error by only 20 units.

From a comparative standpoint, if \$1,000 is to be allocated to either TV or radio, it appears that the greater return will come from TV.

The other interpretation of partial derivatives deals with the tangent slope. As with single-variable functions, the partial derivatives f_x and f_y have a tangent slope interpretation.

SLOPE INTERPRETATION OF f_x AND f_y

I f_x is a general expression for the tangent slope of the family of traces which are parallel to the xz plane.

‖ f_y is a general expression for the tangent slope of the family of traces which are parallel to the yz plane.

The partial derivative f_x estimates the change in z given a change in x, assuming y is held constant. In Sec. 15.1, we saw that when y is held constant, the corresponding traces are graphed parallel to the xz plane. f_x represents the slope of these traces.

Similarly, f_y assumes that x is held constant. When x was held constant in Sec. 15.1, the result was a family of traces which were parallel to the yz plane. And, f_y represents the slope of these traces. Figure 15.5 illustrates the slope representation.

Second-Order Derivatives

As with single-variable functions, we can determine second-order derivatives for bivariate functions. These will be of considerable importance to us in the next section when we seek to optimize the value of a function.

For functions of the form $f(x, y)$, there are *four* different second-order derivatives. These are divided into two types: *pure second-order partial derivatives* and *mixed partial derivatives*. The two pure partial derivatives are denoted by f_{xx} and f_{yy}. The pure second-order partial derivative with respect to x, f_{xx}, is found by first finding f_x and then differentiating f_x with respect to x. Similarly, f_{yy} is found by determining the expression for f_y and then differentiating f_y with respect to y.

The two mixed partial derivatives are denoted by f_{xy} and f_{yx}. The mixed partial derivative f_{xy} is found by determining f_x and then differentiating f_x with respect to y. Similarly, f_{yx} is found by determining f_y and then differentiating f_y with respect to x.

EXAMPLE 10 ▮

Determine all first and second-order derivatives for the function

$$f(x, y) = 8x^3 - 4x^2y + 10y^3$$

SOLUTION

We start with the first derivatives:

$$f_x = 24x^2 - 8xy$$
$$f_y = -4x^2 + 30y^2$$

The pure partial derivative f_{xx} is found by differentiating f_x with respect to x, or

$$f_{xx} = 48x - 8y$$

f_{yy} is found by differentiating f_y with respect to y, or

$$f_{yy} = 60y$$

The mixed partial derivative f_{xy} is found by differentiating f_x with respect to y, or

$$f_{xy} = -8x$$

f_{yx} is found by differentiating f_y with respect to x, or

$$f_{yx} = -8x$$

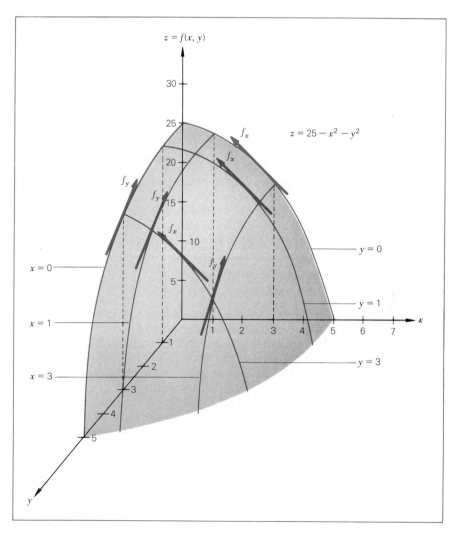

FIGURE 15.5
Tangent slope
representation
of partial deriv-
atives.

NOTE

A proposition known as Young's theorem states that the mixed partial derivatives f_{xy} and f_{yx} will equal one another provided that f_{xy} and f_{yx} are both continuous. Notice that this was true in Example 10. This property provides a possible check on errors which may have been made in finding f_x, f_y, f_{xy}, and f_{yx}.

We will not dwell on the interpretation of these second-order derivatives. However, a few points should be made. The pure partial derivatives f_{xx} and f_{yy} convey information about the concavity of a function (just as the second derivative does for single-variable functions). Specifically, *f_{xx} offers information about the concavity of traces which are parallel to the xz plane. Similarly, f_{yy} provides information about the concavity of traces which are parallel to the yz plane.*

The interpretation of the mixed partial derivatives f_{xy} and f_{yx} is less intuitive than with the pure partial derivatives. However, they will be significant in the next section.

Section 15.2 Follow-up Exercises

In Exercises 1 to 20, determine f_x and f_y.

1. $f(x, y) = 5x^2 - 6y^3$
2. $f(x, y) = -3x + 5y$
3. $f(x, y) = 10x^2 - 3xy + 5y^2$
4. $f(x, y) = x^3 - 4y^2$
5. $f(x, y) = x^3y^2$
6. $f(x, y) = 15xy^3$
7. $f(x, y) = 3x^2 - xy + 10y^3$
8. $f(x, y) = 20x^3 - 4x^3y^2 + 5y^4$
9. $f(x, y) = 1/xy$
10. $f(x, y) = 2x/5y$
11. $f(x, y) = (x^2 - 3y)(5x + 2y^5)$
12. $f(x, y) = (1/x)(y^4 - 3y^2)$
13. $f(x, y) = (x - y)^3$
14. $f(x, y) = (x^2 - 3y^3)^5$
15. $f(x, y) = \sqrt{x^2 - y^2}$
16. $f(x, y) = 10/\sqrt[3]{x + y}$
17. $f(x, y) = \ln(x + 5)[\ln(y - 1)]$
18. $f(x, y) = e^{3x-2y}$
19. $f(x, y) = e^{5x^3-2y^2}$
20. $f(x, y) = e^x \ln y$

In Exercises 21 to 30, find all second-order partial derivatives

21. $f(x, y) = 3x^2 - 5y^3 - 100$
22. $f(x, y) = x^2 - 2x + 4y^3 - 3y$
23. $f(x, y) = x^3 - 3xy + 7y^2$
24. $f(x, y) = -40x^5 + 10xy + 5y^3$
25. $f(x, y) = x^3y^2$
26. $f(x, y) = -10xy^3$
27. $f(x, y) = e^{x+y}$
28. $f(x, y) = \ln(x + y)$
29. $f(x, y) = e^{xy}$
30. $f(x, y) = e^y \ln x$

31. Given $f(x, y) = 100x^2 + 200y^2 - 10xy$:

(a) Determine $f(10, 20)$.

(b) Using partial derivatives, estimate the change expected in $f(x, y)$ if x increases by 1 unit.

(c) Compare the actual change with the estimated change.

(d) Repeat parts b and c assuming a possible increase in y of 1 unit.

32. Given $f(x, y) = 20x^3 - 30y^3 + 10x^2y$:

(a) Determine $f(20, 10)$.

(b) Using partial derivatives, estimate the change expected in $f(x, y)$ if x increases by 1 unit.

(c) Compare the actual change with the estimated change.

(d) Repeat parts b and c assuming a possible increase in y of 1 unit.

33. A firm estimates that the number of units it sells each year is a function of the advertising expenditures for TV and radio. The function expressing this relationship is

$$z = 2{,}000x + 5{,}000y - 20x^2 - 10y^2 - 50xy$$

where z equals the number of units sold, x equals the amount spent on TV advertising, and y equals the amount spent on radio advertising (the latter two variables expressed in $1,000s). The firm is presently allocating $50,000 to TV and $30,000 to radio.

(a) What are annual sales expected to equal?

(b) Using partial derivatives, estimate the effect on annual sales if an additional $1,000 is allocated to TV.

(c) Using partial derivatives, estimate the effect on annual sales if an additional $1,000 is allocated to radio.

(d) Where does it seem that the $1,000 is better spent?

   34   Given the demand function

$$q_1 = f(p_1, p_2) = 25{,}000 - 0.1p_1^2 - 0.5p_2^2$$

(a) Determine the partial derivatives f_{p_1} and f_{p_2}.

(b) If $p_1 = 20$ and $p_2 = 10$, evaluate f_{p_1} and f_{p_2} and interpret their meaning.

(c) How are the two products interrelated?

   35   Given the demand function

$$q_1 = f(p_1, p_2, p_3) = 250{,}000 - 0.5p_1^2 + p_2^2 - 0.4p_3^2$$

(a) Determine the partial derivatives f_{p_1}, f_{p_2}, and f_{p_3}.

(b) If $p_1 = 30$, $p_2 = 10$, and $p_3 = 20$, evaluate the partial derivatives and interpret their meaning.

(c) How are the three products interrelated?

15.3 OPTIMIZATION OF BIVARIATE FUNCTIONS

The process of finding optimum values of bivariate functions is very similar to that used for single-variable functions. This section discusses the process.

Critical Points

As with single-variable functions, we will have a particular interest in identifying relative maximum and minimum points on the surface representing a function $f(x, y)$. Relative maximum and minimum points have the same meaning in three dimensions as in two dimensions.

DEFINITION: RELATIVE MAXIMUM

A function $z = f(x, y)$ is said to have a **relative maximum** at $x = a$ and $y = b$ if for all points (x, y) "sufficiently close" to (a, b)

$$f(a, b) \geq f(x, y)$$

A relative maximum usually appears as the top or peak of a mound on the surface representing $f(x, y)$.

DEFINITION: RELATIVE MINIMUM

A function $z = f(x, y)$ is said to have a **relative minimum** at $x = a$ and $y = b$ if for all points (x, y) "sufficiently close" to (a, b)

$$f(a, b) \leq f(x, y)$$

A relative minimum usually appears as the bottom of a valley on the surface representing $f(x, y)$.

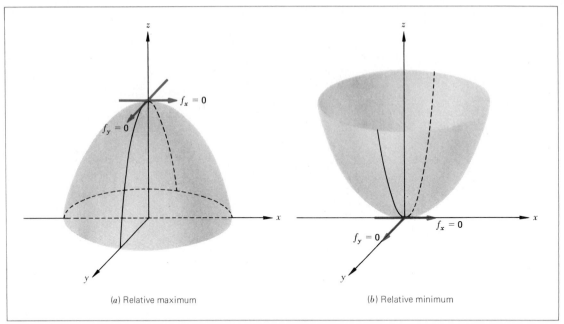

(a) Relative maximum   (b) Relative minimum

FIGURE 15.6
Relative extrema in 3-space.

Figure 15.6 illustrates both a relative maximum point and a relative minimum point. If you examine the slope conditions of a smooth surface at a relative maximum or at a relative minimum, you should conclude that a line drawn tangent at the point in any direction has a slope equal to 0. Given that the first partial derivatives f_x and f_y represent general expressions for the tangent slope of traces which are parallel, respectively, to the xz and yx planes, we can state the following.

NECESSARY CONDITION FOR RELATIVE EXTREMA

A *necessary condition* for the existence of a relative maximum or a relative minimum of a function f whose partial derivatives f_x and f_y both exist is that

$$f_x = 0 \quad \text{and} \quad f_y = 0 \qquad \text{(15.6)}$$

An important part of this definition is that *both* f_x and f_y equal 0. As illustrated in Fig. 15.7, there can be an infinite number of points on a surface where f_x equals 0. In Fig. 15.7 a tangent line drawn parallel to the xz plane anywhere along the trace AB will have a slope of 0 ($f_x = 0$). However, the only point where *both* f_x and f_y equal zero is at A. At the other points along AB, a tangent line drawn parallel to the yz plane has a negative slope ($f_y < 0$).

Similarly, Fig. 15.8 illustrates a trace AC along which $f_y = 0$ but $f_x < 0$ except at point A.

The values x^* and y^* at which Eq. (15.6) is satisfied are **critical values.** The corresponding point $(x^*, y^*, f(x^*, y^*))$ is a candidate for a relative maximum or minimum on f and is called a **critical point.**

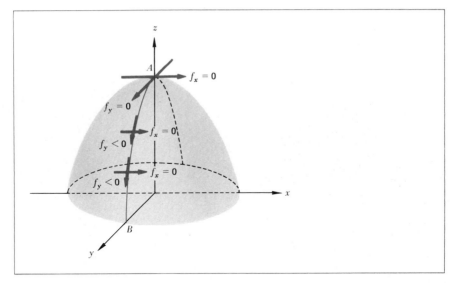

FIGURE 15.7
$f_x = 0$ along
trace AB.

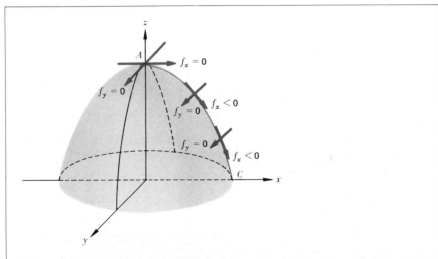

FIGURE 15.8
$f_y = 0$ along
trace AC.

EXAMPLE 11

Locate any critical points on the graph of the function

$$f(x, y) = 4x^2 - 12x + y^2 + 2y - 10$$

SOLUTION

First, find the expressions for f_x and f_y

$$f_x = 8x - 12$$
$$f_y = 2y + 2$$

To determine the values of x and y at which f_x and f_y both equal 0,

$$f_x = 0 \quad \text{when } 8x - 12 = 0$$

or a critical value for x is
$$x = \tfrac{3}{2}$$
$$f_y = 0 \quad \text{when } 2y + 2 = 0$$
or the corresponding critical value for y is
$$y = -1$$

Substituting these values into f,

$$f(\tfrac{3}{2}, -1) = 4(\tfrac{3}{2})^2 - 12(\tfrac{3}{2}) + (-1)^2 + 2(-1) - 10$$
$$= 9 - 18 + 1 - 2 - 10 = -20$$

The only critical point for f occurs at $(\tfrac{3}{2}, -1, -20)$.

EXAMPLE 12

To locate any critical points on the graph of the function

$$f(x, y) = -2x^2 - y^2 + 8x + 10y - 5xy$$

we find the first partial derivatives,

$$f_x = -4x + 8 - 5y$$
$$f_y = -2y + 10 - 5x$$

The values of x and y which make f_x and $f_y = 0$ are found by solving the following equations

$$-4x + 8 - 5y = 0 \tag{15.7}$$
$$-2y + 10 - 5x = 0 \tag{15.8}$$

Rewriting these equations, we have

$$4x + 5y = 8 \tag{15.9}$$
$$5x + 2y = 10 \tag{15.10}$$

Multiplying both sides of Eq. (15.9) by -2 and both sides of Eq. (15.10) by 5 and adding the resulting equations, we get

$$-8x - 10y = -16$$
$$\underline{25x + 10y = 50}$$
$$17x = 34$$

and a critical value for x is
$$x = 2$$

If $x = 2$ is substituted into Eq. (15.10) we find

$$5(2) + 2y = 10$$
$$2y = 0$$
and the corresponding critical value for y is
$$y = 0$$

If we substitute these values into f,

$$f(2, 0) = -2(2)^2 - (0)^2 + 8(2) + 10(0) - 5(2)(0)$$
$$= -8 + 16$$
$$= 8.$$

Thus, a critical point occurs at $(2, 0, 8)$.

EXAMPLE 13

To determine any critical points on the graph of the function

$$f(x, y) = 2x^2 + 4xy - x^2y - 4x$$

the first partial derivatives are identified and set equal to 0.

$$f_x = 4x + 4y - 2xy - 4 = 0 \qquad\qquad \textbf{(15.11)}$$

$$f_y = 4x - x^2 = 0 \qquad\qquad \textbf{(15.12)}$$

These two equations must be solved simultaneously. However, the equations are not linear. In Eq. (15.12), f_y will equal 0 when

$$4x - x^2 = 0$$
$$x(4 - x) = 0$$

or two critical values for x are

$$x = 0 \qquad \text{and} \qquad x = 4$$

To determine the values of y which correspond to these critical values of x and which make f_x equal 0, let's substitute these values, one at a time, into Eq. (15.11).
For x = 0,

$$4(0) + 4y - 2(0)y - 4 = 0$$
$$4y = 4$$
$$y = 1$$

Thus, one critical point occurs on the graph of f when $x = 0$ and $y = 1$. When $x = 0$ and $y = 1$,

$$f(0, 1) = 2(0)^2 + 4(0)(1) - (0)^2(1) - 4(0)$$
$$= 0$$

Thus one critical point occurs at $(0, 1, 0)$.

For x = 4, $\qquad\qquad 4(4) + 4y - 2(4)y - 4 = 0$
$$16 + 4y - 8y - 4 = 0$$
$$-4y = -12$$
$$y = 3$$

Since

$$f(4, 3) = 2(4)^2 + 4(4)(3) - (4)^2(3) - (4)(4)$$
$$= 32 + 48 - 48 - 16 = 16$$

another critical point occurs on f at $(4, 3, 16)$.

Distinguishing among Critical Points

Once a critical point has been identified, it is necessary to determine its nature. Aside from relative maximum and minimum points, there is one other situation in which f_x and f_y both equal 0. Figure 15.9 illustrates this situation which is referred to as a *saddle point.* A saddle point is a portion of a surface which has the shape of a saddle. At point A—"where you sit on the horse"—the values of f_x and f_y both equal 0. However, the function does not

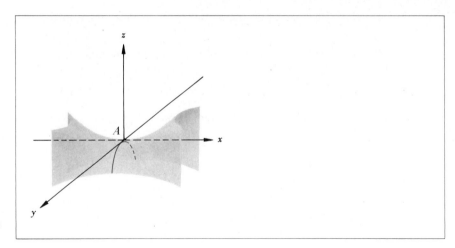

FIGURE 15.9
Saddle point.

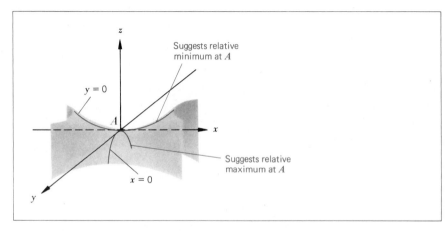

FIGURE 15.10
Conflicting con-
cavity signals
for saddle point.

reach either a relative maximum or a relative minimum at A. If you slice through the surface at point A with the plane having the equation $x = 0$, the resulting edge or trace indicates a relative maximum at A. However, in slicing through the surface with the plane having the equation $y = 0$, the resulting trace indicates a relative minimum at A. Figure 15.10 illustrates these observations.

The conditions which allow you to distinguish among relative maximum, relative minimum, or saddle points follow. The test of a critical point is a second-derivative test (as used in single-variable problems) which, from an intuitive standpoint, investigates the concavity conditions at the critical point.

TEST OF CRITICAL POINT ▐▬▬▬▬▬

Given that a critical point of f is located at (x^*, y^*, z) where all second partial derivatives are continuous, determine the value of $D(x^*, y^*)$ where

$$D(x^*, y^*) = f_{xx}(x^*, y^*)f_{yy}(x^*, y^*) - [f_{xy}(x^*, y^*)]^2 \qquad \textbf{(15.13)}$$

▌ If $D(x^*, y^*) > 0$, the critical point is a ***relative maximum*** if *both* $f_{xx}(x^*, y^*)$ and $f_{yy}(x^*, y^*)$ are negative and the critical point is a **relative minimum** if both $f_{xx}(x^*, y^*)$ and $f_{yy}(x^*, y^*)$ are positive.

II If $D(x^*, y^*) < 0$, the critical point is a **saddle point.**

III If $D(x^*, y^*) = 0$, other techniques (beyond the scope of this text) are required to determine the nature of the critical point.

EXAMPLE 14

In Example 11 we determined that a critical point occurs on the graph of the function

$$f(x, y) = 4x^2 - 12x + y^2 + 2y - 10$$

Determine the nature of the critical point at $(\frac{3}{2}, -1, -20)$.

SOLUTION

In Example 11 we determined that

$$f_x = 8x - 12$$
$$f_y = 2y + 2$$

The four second-order derivatives are

$$f_{xx} = 8 \qquad f_{xy} = 0$$
$$f_{yy} = 2 \qquad f_{yx} = 0$$

Evaluating $D(x^*, y^*)$, we have

$$D(\tfrac{3}{2}, -1) = (8)(2) - 0^2$$
$$= 16 > 0$$

Since $D(x^*, y^*) > 0$ and $f_{xx}(\frac{3}{2}, -1) = 8$ and $f_{yy}(\frac{3}{2}, -1) = 2$, both of which are greater than 0, we can conclude that a relative minimum occurs at $(\frac{3}{2}, -1, -20)$. Figure 15.11 is a sketch of the function. This graph, as well as a number of the following, is computer generated using the SAS Graph package and plotted on the Calcomp plotter.*

EXAMPLE 15

To determine the location and nature of any critical points for the function

$$f(x, y) = -2x^2 + 24x - y^2 + 30y$$

the first derivatives are found and set equal to 0.

$$f_x = 4x + 24 = 0$$

A critical value for x is

$$x = 6$$
$$f_y = -2y + 30 = 0$$

The corresponding critical value for y is

$$y = 15$$

---

* Statistical Analysis System, G3D subroutine.

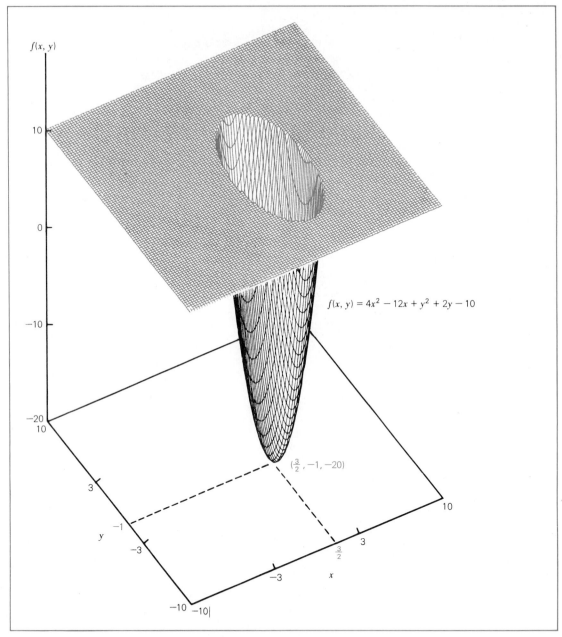

FIGURE 15.11
Relative minimum on $f(x, y) = 4x^2 - 12x + y^2 + 2y - 10$.

The second-order derivatives are

$$f_{xx} = -4 \qquad f_{xy} = 0$$
$$f_{yy} = -2 \qquad f_{yx} = 0$$

Evaluating $D(x^*, y^*)$, we get

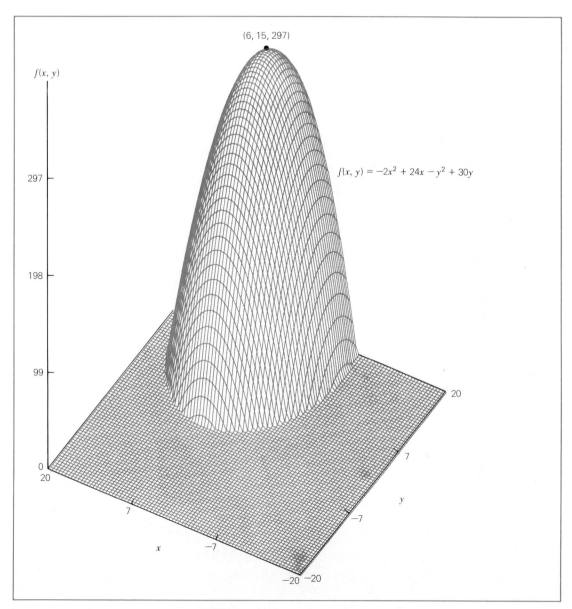

$(6, 15, 297)$

$f(x, y)$

297

198

99

$f(x, y) = -2x^2 + 24x - y^2 + 30y$

20

7

y

-7

0

20

7

-7

x

-7

-20 -20

FIGURE 15.12
Relative maximum on $f(x, y) = -2x^2 + 24x - y^2 + 30y$.

$$D(6, 15) = (-4)(-2) - 0^2$$
$$= 8 > 0$$

Since $D(6, 15)$ is positive and both f_{xx} and f_{yy} are negative, a relative maximum occurs when $x = 6$ and $y = 15$. The value of $f(x, y)$ at the relative maximum is

$$f(6, 15) = -2(6^2) + 24(6) - (15)^2 + 30(15)$$
$$= -72 + 144 - 225 + 450 = 297$$

Thus, a relative maximum occurs at $(6, 15, 297)$. Figure 15.12 is a sketch of the function.

EXAMPLE 16 ▮▬▬▬▬▬▬▬▬▬▬▬▬▬▬▬▬▬▬▬▬▬▬▬

In Example 13 we determined that critical points occur on the graph of the function

$$f(x, y) = 2x^2 + 4xy - x^2y - 4x$$

at $(0, 1, 0)$ and $(4, 3, 16)$. To determine the nature of the two critical points, we must find all second derivatives. From Example 13

$$f_x = 4x + 4y - 2xy - 4$$
$$f_y = 4x - x^2$$

The second-order derivatives are

$$f_{xx} = 4 - 2y \qquad f_{xy} = 4 - 2x$$
$$f_{yy} = 0 \qquad f_{yx} = 4 - 2x$$

Evaluation of $(0, 1, 0)$:

$$D(0, 1) = [4 - 2(1)](0) - [4 - 2(0)]^2$$
$$= (2)(0) - 4^2$$
$$= -16 < 0$$

Since $D(0, 1) < 0$, a saddle point occurs on f at $(0, 1, 0)$.

Evaluation of $(4, 3, 16)$:

$$D(4, 3) = [4 - 2(3)](0) - [4 - 2(4)]^2$$
$$= (-2)(0) - (-4)^2$$
$$= -16 < 0$$

A second saddle point occurs on f, this one at $(4, 3, 16)$. Figure 15.13 presents a sketch of the function.

EXAMPLE 17 ▮▬▬▬▬▬▬▬▬▬▬▬▬▬▬▬▬▬▬▬▬▬▬▬

Given the function

$$f(x, y) = -x^2 - y^3 + 12y^2$$

determine the location and nature of all critical points.

SOLUTION

Finding the first partial derivatives and setting them equal to 0 gives us

$$f_x = -2x = 0 \qquad \text{or} \qquad \text{a critical value occurs at } x = 0$$
$$f_y = -3y^2 + 24y = 0$$
$$3y(-y + 8) = 0$$

Or critical values occur at

$$y = 0 \qquad \text{and} \qquad y = 8$$

There are two critical points on f—one associated with the critical values $x = 0$ and $y = 0$ and the other associated with the critical values $x = 0$ and $y = 8$. Verify that the two stationary points occur at $(0, 0, 0)$ and $(0, 8, 256)$.

The second-order derivatives are

$$f_{xx} = -2 \qquad\qquad f_{xy} = 0$$
$$f_{yy} = -6y + 24 \qquad f_{yx} = 0$$

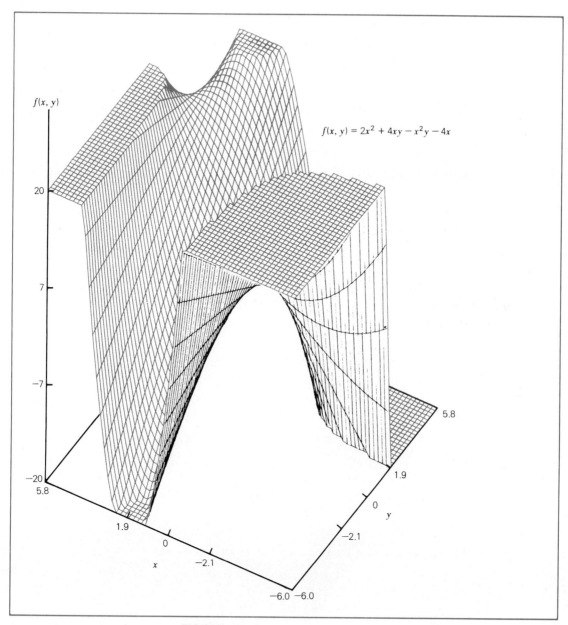

$$f(x, y) = 2x^2 + 4xy - x^2y - 4x$$

FIGURE 15.13
Two saddle points on $f(x, y) = 2x^2 + 4xy - x^2y - 4x$.

Evaluation of (0, 0, 0):

$$D(0, 0) = (-2)[-6(0) + 24] - 0^2$$
$$= (-2)(24) - 0$$
$$= -48 < 0$$

Therefore, a saddle point occurs at (0, 0, 0).

Evaluation of (0, 8, 256):

$$D(0, 8) = (-2)[-6(8) + 24] - 0^2$$
$$= (-2)(-24)$$
$$= 48 > 0$$

The values of the two pure partial derivatives at the critical point are $f_{xx}(0, 8) = -2$ and $f_{yy}(0, 8) = -6(8) + 24 = -24$. Since both are negative, we conclude that a relative

FIGURE 15.14
Relative maximum and saddle point on $f(x, y) = -x^2 - y^3 + 12y^2$

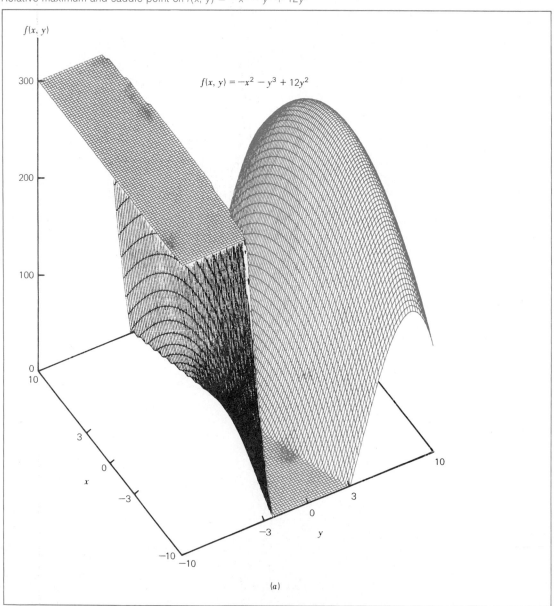

$f(x, y)$

$f(x, y) = -x^2 - y^3 + 12y^2$

(a)

maximum occurs on the graph of f at $(0, 8, 256)$. Figure 15.14 is a sketch of f which provides two different views of the surface.

FIGURE 15.14 Continued.

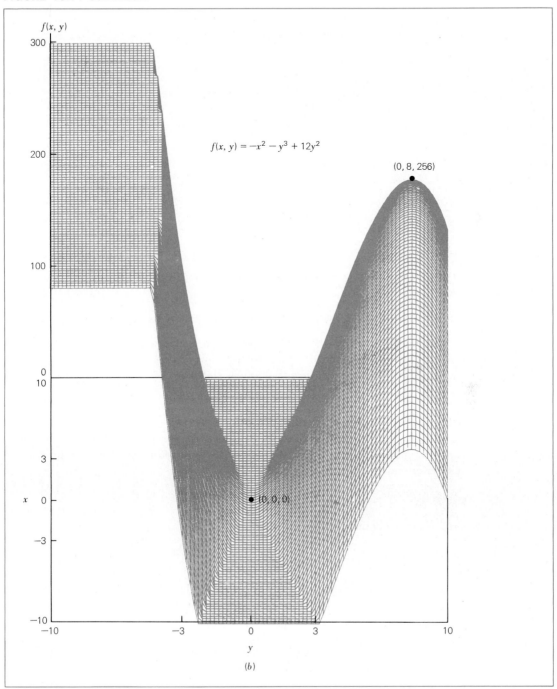

$f(x, y) = -x^2 - y^3 + 12y^2$

$(0, 8, 256)$

$(0, 0, 0)$

(b)

Section 15.3 Follow-up Exercises

In the following exercises, determine the location of all critical points and their nature.

1   $f(x, y) = 4x^2 - y^2 + 80x + 20y - 10$
2   $f(x, y) = x^2 + xy - 5x - 2y^2 + 2y$
3   $f(x, y) = x^3/3 - 5x^2/2 + 3y^2 - 12y$
4   $f(x, y) = -8x^2 + 12xy + 44x - 12y^2 + 12y$
5   $f(x, y) = 3x^2 - 4xy + 3y^2 + 8x - 17y + 5$
6   $f(x, y) = -x^2 + 6x - 12y + y^3 + 5$
7   $f(x, y) = x^3 + y^2 - 3x + 6y + 10$
8   $f(x, y) = x^2 - 2xy + 3y^2 + 4x - 16y + 22$
9   $f(x, y) = x^3 + y^3 - 3xy$
10   $f(x, y) = x^3 + y^3 + 3xy$
11   $f(x, y) = xy + \ln x + y^2 - 10, \ x > 0$
12   $f(x, y) = 25x - 25xe^{-y} - 50y - x^2$

15.4   APPLICATIONS OF BIVARIATE OPTIMIZATION

This section presents some applications of the optimization of bivariate functions.

EXAMPLE 18

Advertising Expenditures   Example 9 involved a manufacturer who estimated annual sales (in units) to be a function of the expenditures made for radio and TV advertising. The function specifying this relationship was stated as

$$z = 50{,}000x + 40{,}000y - 10x^2 - 20y^2 - 10xy$$

where *z equals the number of units sold each year, x equals the amount spent for TV advertising, and y equals the amount spent for radio advertising (x and y both in $1,000s)*. Determine how much money should be spent on TV and radio in order to maximize the number of units sold.

SOLUTION

The first partial derivatives are

$$f_x = 50{,}000 - 20x - 10y$$
$$f_y = 40{,}000 - 40y - 10x$$

Rearranging the derivatives and setting them equal to 0, we have

$$20x + 10y = 50{,}000$$
$$10x + 40y = 40{,}000$$

If both sides of the second equation are multiplied by -2 and the result is added to the first equation, then

$$20x + 10y = 50{,}000$$
$$\underline{-20x - 80y = -80{,}000}$$
$$-70y = -30{,}000$$

and a critical value for y is
$$y = 428.57$$

Substituting y into one of the original equations yields

$$20x + 10(428.57) = 50{,}000$$
$$20x = 50{,}000 - 4{,}285.7$$
$$20x = 45{,}714.3$$

and the corresponding critical value for x is

$$x = 2{,}285.72$$

Total sales associated with $x = 2{,}285.72$ and $y = 428.57$ equals

$$f(2{,}285.72, 428.57) = 50{,}000(2{,}285.72) + 40{,}000(428.57)$$
$$- 10(2{,}285.72)^2 - 20(428.57)^2 - 10(2{,}285.72)(428.57)$$
$$= 65{,}714{,}296.00 \text{ units}$$

Thus a critical point occurs on the graph of f at (2285.72, 428.57, 65,714,296). To determine the nature of the critical point, the second derivatives are

$$f_{xx} = -20 \qquad f_{xy} = -10$$
$$f_{yy} = -40 \qquad f_{yx} = -10$$

Testing the critical point, we find

$$D(2{,}285.72, 428.57) = (-20)(-40) - (-10)^2$$
$$= 800 - 100 = 700 > 0$$

Since $D > 0$ and both f_{xx} and f_{yy} are negative, we can conclude that annual sales are maximized at 65,714,296 units when 2,285.72 ($1,000s) is spent for TV advertising and 428.57 ($1,000s) is spent for radio advertising. Figure 15.15 is a sketch of the sales surface.

EXAMPLE 19

Pricing Model   A manufacturer sells two related products, the demand for which is characterized by the following two demand functions:

$$q_1 = 150 - 2p_1 - p_2 \qquad\qquad \textbf{(15.14)}$$

$$q_2 = 200 - p_1 - 3p_2 \qquad\qquad \textbf{(15.15)}$$

where p_j equals the price (in dollars) of product j and q_j equals the demand (in thousands of units) for product j. Examination of these demand functions indicates that the two products are related. The demand for one product depends not only on the price charged for the product itself but also on the price charged for the other product.

The firm wants to determine the price it should charge for each product in order to maximize total revenue from the sale of the two products.

SOLUTION

This problem is exactly like the single-product problems discussed in Chap. 13. The only difference is that there are two products and two pricing decisions to be made.

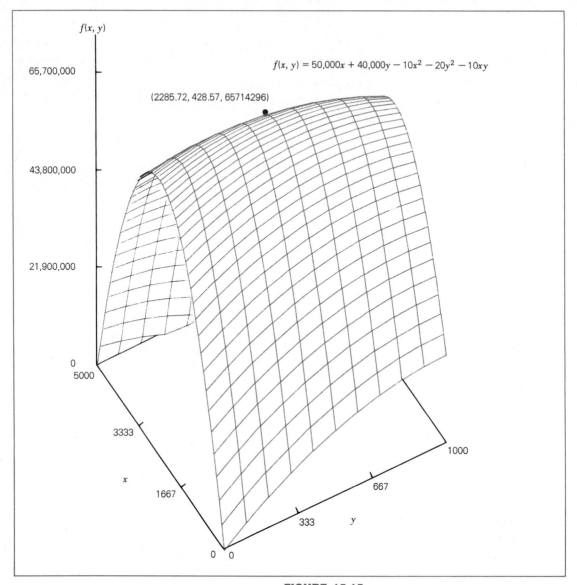

FIGURE 15.15

Relative maximum on $f(x, y) = 50,000x + 40,000y - 10x^2 - 20y^2 - 10xy$.

Total revenue from selling the two products is determined by the equation

$$\boxed{R = p_1q_1 + p_2q_2} \qquad (15.16)$$

This equation, however, is stated in terms of four variables. As with the single-product problems, we can substitute the right side of Eqs. (15.14) and (15.15) into Eq. (15.16) to yield

$$R = f(p_1, p_2)$$
$$= p_1(150 - 2p_1 - p_2) + p_2(200 - p_1 - 3p_2)$$
$$= 150p_1 - 2p_1^2 - p_1p_2 + 200p_2 - p_1p_2 - 3p_2^2$$
$$= 150p_1 - 2p_1^2 - 2p_1p_2 + 200p_2 - 3p_2^2$$

We can now proceed to examine the revenue surface for relative maximum points.
The first partial derivatives are

$$f_{p_1} = 150 - 4p_1 - 2p_2$$
$$f_{p_2} = -2p_1 + 200 - 6p_2$$

Rearranging these derivative expressions and setting them equal to 0, we have

$$4p_1 + 2p_2 = 150 \tag{15.17}$$

$$2p_1 + 6p_2 = 200 \tag{15.18}$$

If Eq. (15.18) is multiplied by -2 and added to Eq. (15.17), we get

$$4p_1 + 2p_2 = 150$$
$$\underline{-4p_1 - 12p_2 = -400}$$
$$-10p_2 = -250$$

or, a critical value for p_2 is $\qquad p_2 = 25$

Substituting $p_2 = 25$ into Eq. (15.17) yields

$$4p_1 + 2(25) = 150$$
$$4p_1 = 100$$

or, a critical value for p_1 is $\qquad p_1 = 25$

If these values are substituted into f,

$$f(25, 25) = 150(25) - 2(25)^2 - 2(25)(25) + 200(25) - 3(25)^2$$
$$= 4375$$

A critical point occurs on f at (25, 25, 4375).
The second derivatives are

$$f_{p_1p_1} = -4 \qquad f_{p_1p_2} = -2$$
$$f_{p_2p_2} = -6 \qquad f_{p_2p_1} = -2$$

And $\qquad\qquad D(25, 25) = (-4)(-6) - (-2)^2$
$$= 24 - 4 = 20 > 0$$

Since $D(x^*, y^*) > 0$ and $f_{p_1p_1}$ and $f_{p_2p_2}$ are both negative, a relative maximum exists on f when $p_1 = 25$ and $p_2 = 25$. Revenue will be maximized at a value of \$4,375 (thousands) when each product is sold for \$25. Expected demand at these prices can be determined by substituting p_1 and p_2 into the demand equations, or

$$q_1 = 150 - 2(25) - (25) = 75 \text{ (thousand units)}$$
$$q_2 = 200 - (25) - 3(25) = 100 \text{ (thousand units)}$$

Figure 15.16 is a sketch of the revenue surface.

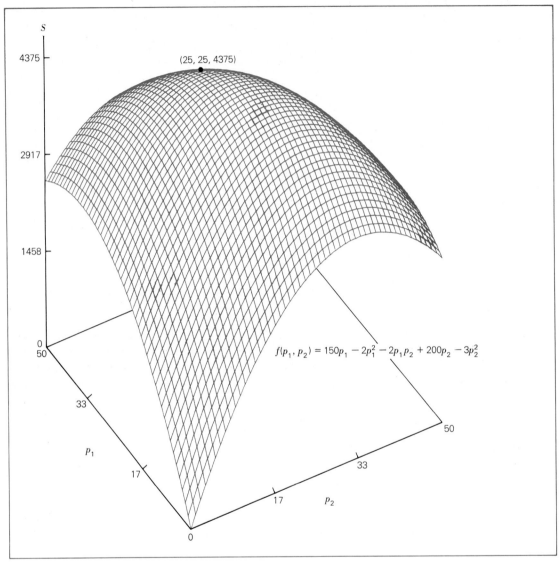

$f(p_1, p_2) = 150p_1 - 2p_1^2 - 2p_1p_2 + 200p_2 - 3p_2^2$

FIGURE 15.16

Relative maximum on revenue surface $f(p_1, p_2) = 150p_1 - 2p_1^2 - 2p_1p_2 + 200p_2 - 3p_2^2$.

EXAMPLE 20

Satellite Clinic Location   A large health maintenance organization (HMO) is planning to locate a satellite clinic in a location which is convenient to three suburban townships, the relative locations of which are indicated in Fig. 15.17. The HMO wants to select a preliminary site by using the following criterion: determine the location (x, y) which minimizes the *sum of the squares* of the distances from each township to the satellite clinic.

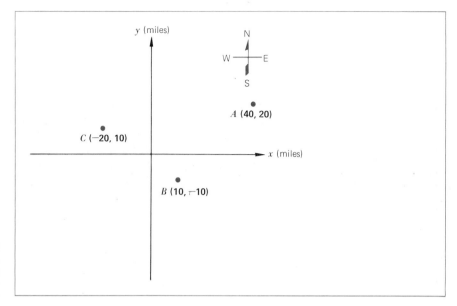

FIGURE 15.17
Relative locations on three suburban townships.

SOLUTION

The unknowns in this problem are x and y, the coordinates of the satellite clinic location. We need to determine an expression for the square of the distance separating the clinic and each of the towns. The Pythagorean theorem* provides this for us. Given two points (x_1, y_1) and (x_2, y_2), the square of the distance d separating these two points is found using the equation

$$d^2 = (x_2 - x_1)^2 + (y_2 - y_1)^2 \qquad (15.19)$$

To illustrate, the square of the distance separating the clinic with location (x, y) and township A located at $(40, 20)$ is

$$d^2 = (x - 40)^2 + (y - 20)^2$$

Finding similar expressions for the square of the distance separating townships B and C and the clinic and summing for the three townships, we get

$$
\begin{aligned}
s &= f(x, y) \\
&= [(x - 40)^2 + (y - 20)^2] + [(x - 10)^2 + (y + 10)^2] \\
&\quad + [(x + 20)^2 + (y - 10)^2]
\end{aligned}
$$

The right side of this function can be expanded or left in this form for purposes of finding derivatives. Let's leave it as it is. The first partial derivatives are

$$
\begin{aligned}
f_x &= 2(x - 40)(1) + 2(x - 10)(1) + 2(x + 20)(1) \\
&= 2x - 80 + 2x - 20 + 2x + 40 \\
&= 6x - 60 \\
f_y &= 2(y - 20)(1) + 2(y + 10)(1) + 2(y - 10)(1) \\
&= 2y - 40 + 2y + 20 + 2y - 20 \\
&= 6y - 40
\end{aligned}
$$

---

* See Chap. 13, page 532.

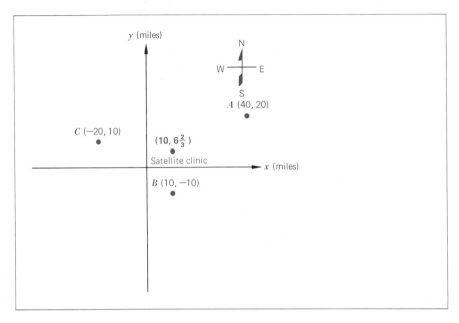

FIGURE 15.18
Proposed loca-
tion of satellite
clinic.

If the two partial derivatives are set equal to 0, we find critical values at $x = 10$ and $y = 6\frac{2}{3}$. The second partial derivatives are

$$f_{xx} = 6 \qquad f_{xy} = 0$$
$$f_{yy} = 6 \qquad f_{yx} = 0$$
$$D(10, 6\tfrac{2}{3}) = (6)(6) - 0^2 = 36 > 0$$

Since $D > 0$ and f_{xx} and f_{yy} are both greater than 0, we conclude that a relative minimum occurs on f when $x = 10$ and $y = 6\frac{2}{3}$, or when the satellite clinic is located as indicated in Fig. 15.18.

EXAMPLE 21

Least-Squares Model Organizations gather data regularly on a multitude of variables which are related to their operation. One major area of analysis deals with determining whether there are any patterns to the data—are there any apparent relationships among the variables of interest? For example, the demand functions to which we have contin-ually referred, have most likely been determined by gathering data on the demand for a product at different prices. And, analysis of this data translates into a formal statement of the demand function.

Consider the four data points (x_1, y_1), (x_2, y_2), (x_3, y_3), and (x_4, y_4) in Fig. 15.19, which have been gathered for the variables x and y. Suppose there is evidence suggesting that x and y are related and that the nature of the relationship is linear. And, suppose that we would like to fit a straight line to these points, the equation of which would be used as an approximation of the actual relationship existing between x and y. The question becomes, What line best fits the data points? There are an infinite number of straight lines which can be fit to these data points, each having the general form

$$\boxed{y_p = ax + b}$$ (15.20)

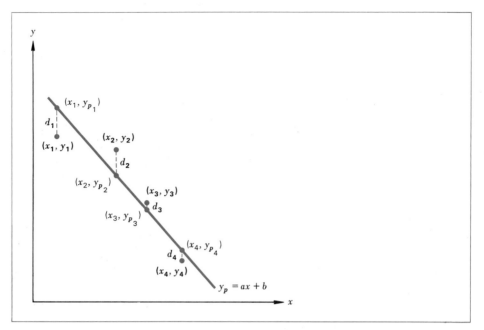

FIGURE 15.19
Four sample
data points.

The difference between each line would be differences in the slope a and/or the y coordinate of the y intercept b. Note that y has a subscript of p in Eq. (15.20). This is because the line fit to the data points can be used to *predict* values of y, given a known value of x.

In Fig. 15.19, the predicted values of y, given the x coordinates of the four data points, are indicated on the line. The vertical distance separating the actual data point and the corresponding point on the line is a measure of the error introduced by using the line to predict the location of the data point. The error, indicated by the d_j values in Fig. 15.19, is called the **deviation** between the actual value of y and the predicted value of y for the jth data point, or

$$d_j = y_j - y_{p_j} \tag{15.21}$$

Given that we wish to find the "best" line to fit to the data points, the next question is, How do you define *best*? One of the most popular methods of finding the line of best fit is the **least-squares model.** The least-squares model defines *best* as the line which minimizes the sum of the squared deviations for all the data points. In Fig. 15.19 we would seek the line which minimizes

$$S = d_1^2 + d_2^2 + d_3^2 + d_4^2$$

$$= \sum_{j=1}^{4} d_j^2$$

or

$$S = \sum_{j=1}^{4} (y_j - y_{p_j})^2 \tag{15.22}$$

For any line $y_{p_j} = ax_j + b$ chosen to fit the data points, Eq. (15.22) can be rewritten as

$$S = f(a, b)$$

or

$$S = \sum_{j=1}^{4} [y_j - (ax_j + b)]^2 \tag{15.23}$$

For any straight line having slope a and y intercept b, the sum of the squared deviations S can be determined. *The least-squares model seeks the values of a and b which result in a minimum value for S.*

Consider the simple case where a firm has collected three price-demand data points. Table 15.3 indicates the price-quantity combinations. Figure 15.20 is a graph of their locations. Suppose that we wish to determine the line of best fit to these data points using the least-squares model. The least-squares function is generated by using Eq. (15.23).

$$S = f(a, b)$$

$$= \sum_{j=1}^{3} [y_j - (ax_j + b)]^2$$

$$= [50 - (5a + b)]^2 + [30 - (10a + b)]^2 + [20 - (15a + b)]^2$$

To determine the values of a and b which minimize S, we find the partial derivatives with respect to a and b.

$$\begin{aligned}
f_a &= 2[50 - (5a + b)](-5) + 2[30 - (10a + b)](-10) \\
&\quad + 2[20 - (15a + b)](-15) \\
&= -500 + 50a + 10b - 600 + 200a + 20b - 600 + 450a + 30b \\
&= 700a + 60b - 1{,}700 \\
f_b &= 2[50 - (5a + b)](-1) + 2[30 - (10a + b)](-1) \\
&\quad + 2[20 - (15a + b)](-1) \\
&= -100 + 10a + 2b - 60 + 20a + 2b - 40 + 30a + 2b \\
&= 60a + 6b - 200
\end{aligned}$$

If these two derivatives are set equal to 0, these two equations result:

$$700a + 60b = 1{,}700 \tag{15.24}$$

$$60a + 6b = 200 \tag{15.25}$$

Multiplying Eq. (15.25) by -10 and adding it to Eq. (15.24) yields

$$\begin{aligned}
700a + 60b &= 1{,}700 \\
-600a - 60b &= -2{,}000 \\
\hline
100a &= -300 \\
a &= -3
\end{aligned}$$

Substituting $a = 3$ into Eq. (15.25) yields

$$\begin{aligned}
60(-3) + 6b &= 200 \\
6b &= 380 \\
b &= 63\tfrac{1}{3}
\end{aligned}$$

To verify that the critical point results in a minimum value for S,

$$f_{aa} = 700 \qquad f_{ab} = 60$$

TABLE 15.3

y (Demand in thousands of units)	50	30	20
x (Price in dollars)	5	10	15

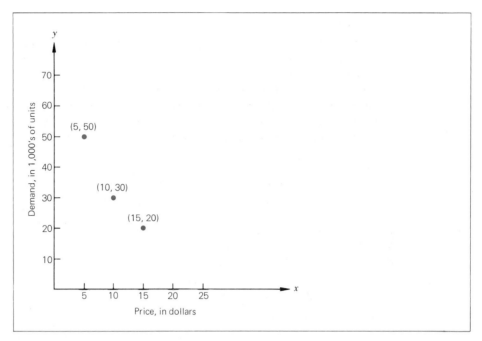

FIGURE 15.20
Three sample
price/quantity
data points.

$$f_{bb} = 6 \qquad f_{ba} = 60$$
$$D(-3, 63\tfrac{1}{3}) = (700)(6) - (60)^2$$
$$= 4{,}200 - 3{,}600$$
$$= 600 > 0$$

Since $D > 0$ and both f_{aa} and f_{bb} are positive, we can conclude that the sum of the squares of the deviations S is minimized when $a = -3$ and $b = 63\tfrac{1}{3}$, or when the data points are fit with a straight line having a slope of -3 and y intercept of $63\tfrac{1}{3}$. The equation of this line is

$$y_p = -3x + 63\tfrac{1}{3}$$

The minimum sum of squared deviations can be determined by substituting $a = -3$ and $b = 63\tfrac{1}{3}$ into f if that value is of interest.

Section 15.4 Follow-up Exercises

1   A manufacturer estimates that annual sales (in units) are a function of the expenditures made for TV and radio advertising. The function specifying the relationship is

$$z = 40{,}000x + 60{,}000y - 5x^2 - 10y^2 - 10xy$$

where z equals the number of units sold each year, x equals the amount spent for TV ad-

vertising, and y equals the amount spent for radio advertising (both x and y in \$1,000s).
(a) Determine how much should be spent for radio and TV advertising in order to maximize the number of units sold.
(b) What is the maximum number of units expected to equal?

2   A company sells two products. Total revenue from the two products is estimated to be a function of the numbers of units sold of the two products. Specifically, the function is

$$R = 30{,}000x + 15{,}000y - 10x^2 - 10y^2 - 10xy$$

where R equals total revenue and x and y equal the numbers of units sold of the two products.
(a) How many units of each product should be produced in order to maximize total revenue?
(b) What is the maximum revenue?

3   A firm sells two products. The demand functions for the two products are

$$q_1 = 110 - 4p_1 - p_2$$
$$q_2 = 90 - 2p_1 - 3p_2$$

where p_j equals the price of product j and q_j equals the demand (in thousands of units) for product j.
(a) Determine the price which should be charged for each product in order to maximize total revenue from the two products.
(b) How many units will be demanded of each product at these prices?
(c) What is maximum total revenue expected to equal?

4   A company is planning to locate a warehouse which will supply three major department stores. The relative locations of the three department stores on a set of coordinate axes are (30, 10), (0, 40), and (−30, −10) where the coordinates are stated in miles. Figure 15.21 indicates the relative locations of the department stores. Determine the warehouse location (x, y) which minimizes the sum of the squares of the distances from each city to the warehouse.

5   **Airport Location**   A new airport is being planned to service four metropolitan areas. The relative locations of the metropolitan areas on a set of coordinate axes are (20, 5), (0, 30), (−30, 10), and (−5, −5), where the coordinates are stated in miles. Figure 15.22 indicates the relative locations of the four cities. Determine the airport location (x, y) which minimizes the sum of the squares of the distances from the airport to each metropolitan area.

6   In Example 20, assume that the number of HMO members living in the three townships equals 20,000, 10,000, and 30,000, respectively, for townships A, B, and C. Also assume that the HMO wishes to determine the location (x, y) which minimizes the sum of the products of the number of members in each township and the square of the distance separating the towns and the clinic. This objective can be stated as

Minimize $$\sum_{j=1}^{3} n_j d_j^2$$

where n_j equals the number of members living in township j and d_j equals the distance from township j to the clinic. Determine the location of the clinic.

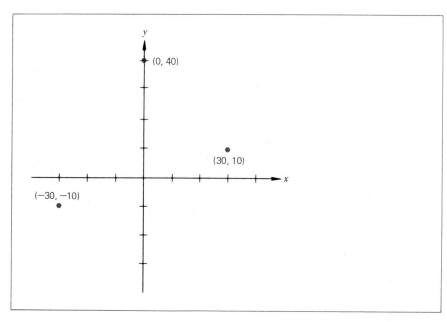

FIGURE 15.21
Department
store locations.

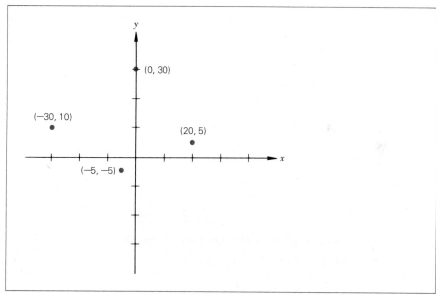

FIGURE 15.22
Relative loca-
tions of four
metropolitan
areas.

TABLE 15.4

y (Demand in thousands of units)	200	160	120
x (Price in dollars)	30	40	50

7   Given the data points (2, 2), (−3, 17), and (10, −22), determine the equation of the line of best fit using the least squares model.

8   Given the price-demand data points in Table 15.4, determine the equation of the line of best fit to these data points using the least-squares model.

15.5   *n*-VARIABLE OPTIMIZATION (OPTIONAL)

When a function contains more than two independent variables, the process for identifying relative maxima and relative minima is very similar to that used for functions having two independent variables. Before discussing the process, let's define these relative extrema.

DEFINITION: RELATIVE MAXIMUM ▉▉▉▉▉▉▉▉

A function $y = f(x_1, x_2, \ldots, x_n)$ is said to have a **relative maximum** at $x_1 = a_1$, $x_2 = a_2$, $\ldots$, $x_n = a_n$ if for all points $(x_1, x_2, \ldots, x_n)$ sufficiently close to $(a_1, a_2, \ldots, a_n)$,
$$f(a_1, a_2, \ldots, a_n) \geq f(x_1, x_2, \ldots, x_n)$$

DEFINITION: RELATIVE MINIMUM ▉▉▉▉▉▉▉▉

A function $y = f(x_1, x_2, \ldots, x_n)$ is said to have a **relative minimum** at $x_1 = a_1$, $x_2 = a_2$, $\ldots$, $x_n = a_n$ if for all points $(x_1, x_2, \ldots, x_n)$ sufficiently close to $(a_1, a_2, \ldots, a_n)$,

$$f(a_1, a_2, \ldots, a_n) \leq f(x_1, x_2, \ldots, x_n)$$

With more than two independent variables it is not possible to graph a function. However, we may say that the function $f(x_1, x_2, \ldots, x_n)$ is represented by a **hypersurface** in $(n+1)$ dimensions. Our interest with these functions is to identify the $(n + 1)$ dimensional equivalents to *peaks* (relative maxima) and *valleys* (relative minima) on a three-dimensional surface.

Necessary Condition for Relative Extrema

A necessary condition for a relative maximum or a relative minimum of a function whose partial derivatives $f_{x_1}, f_{x_2}, \ldots, f_{x_n}$ all exist is that

$$f_{x_1} = 0, f_{x_2} = 0, \ldots, f_{x_n} = 0 \qquad \textbf{(15.26)}$$

The necessary condition requires that all first partial derivatives of f equal 0.

EXAMPLE 22 ▉▉▉▉▉▉▉▉▉▉▉▉▉▉▉▉▉▉▉▉▉▉▉▉▉

To locate any *candidates* for relative extreme points on

$$f(x_1, x_2, x_3) = x_1^2 - 2x_1x_2 + 2x_2^2 + 2x_1x_3 + 4x_3^2 - 2x_3$$

the first partial derivatives are found

$$f_{x_1} = 2x_1 - 2x_2 + x_3$$
$$f_{x_2} = -2x_1 + 4x_2$$
$$f_{x_3} = 2x_1 + 8x_3 - 2$$

Since all three derivatives must equal 0, the three equations

$$2x_1 - 2x_2 + x_3 = 0$$
$$-2x_1 + 4x_2 \qquad = 0$$
$$2x_1 \qquad + 8x_3 = 2$$

must be solved simultaneously. When the system is solved the critical values

$$x_1 = -1, \; x_2 = -\tfrac{1}{2}, \; \text{and} \; x_3 = \tfrac{1}{2}$$

are identified. Because

$$f(-1, -\tfrac{1}{2}, \tfrac{1}{2}) = -\tfrac{1}{2}$$

we can state that the critical point $(-1, -\tfrac{1}{2}, \tfrac{1}{2}, -\tfrac{1}{2})$ is a candidate for a relative extreme point.

Sufficient Conditions

As with functions containing one or two independent variables, the test of critical points requires the use of second derivatives. Specifically, the test utilizes a *hessian matrix,* which is a matrix of second partial derivatives having the form

$$\mathbf{H} = \begin{pmatrix} f_{x_1x_1} & f_{x_1x_2} & f_{x_1x_3} & \cdots & f_{x_1x_n} \\ f_{x_2x_1} & f_{x_2x_2} & f_{x_2x_3} & \cdots & f_{x_2x_n} \\ \cdots & \cdots & \cdots & \cdots & \cdots \\ f_{x_nx_1} & f_{x_nx_2} & f_{x_nx_3} & \cdots & f_{x_nx_n} \end{pmatrix}$$

Given the function $f(x_1, x_2, x_3 \cdots x_n)$, the hessian matrix is square, of dimension $(n \times n)$. The principal diagonal consists of the *pure* second partial derivatives and the nondiagonal elements are *mixed* partial derivatives. The matrix is also symmetric about the principal diagonal when the second partial derivatives are continuous. Under such circumstances the mixed partial derivatives taken with respect to the same two variables are equal. That is, $f_{x_ix_j} = f_{x_jx_i}$.

For an $(n \times n)$ hessian matrix, a set of n submatrices can be identified. The first of these is the (1×1) submatrix consisting of the element located in row 1 and column 1, $f_{x_1x_1}$. Let's denote this matrix as $\mathbf{H}_1$, where

$$\mathbf{H}_1 = (f_{x_1x_1})$$

The second submatrix is the (2×2) matrix

$$\mathbf{H}_2 = \begin{pmatrix} f_{x_1x_1} & f_{x_1x_2} \\ f_{x_2x_1} & f_{x_2x_2} \end{pmatrix}$$

The third submatrix is the (3×3) matrix

$$\mathbf{H}_3 = \begin{pmatrix} f_{x_1x_1} & f_{x_1x_2} & f_{x_1x_3} \\ f_{x_2x_1} & f_{x_2x_2} & f_{x_2x_3} \\ f_{x_3x_1} & f_{x_3x_2} & f_{x_3x_3} \end{pmatrix}$$

The nth submatrix is the hessian matrix itself, or $\mathbf{H}_n = \mathbf{H}$.

The determinants of these submatrices are called *principal minors.* These can be denoted as $|\mathbf{H}_i|$ where $\mathbf{H}_i$ represents the ith submatrix.

SUFFICIENT CONDITION FOR RELATIVE EXTREMA

Given critical values $x_1 = a_1, \; x_2 = a_2, \; x_3 = a_3, \; \ldots, \; x_n = a_n$ for which

$$f_{x_1} = f_{x_2} = f_{x_3} = \ldots = f_{x_n} = 0$$

and all second-order derivatives are continuous,

I A *relative maximum* exists if the principal minors (*evaluated at the critical values*) alternate in sign with the odd-numbered principal minors negative and the even-numbered principal minors positive. That is,

$$|\mathbf{H}_1| < 0, \ |\mathbf{H}_2| > 0, \ |\mathbf{H}_3| < 0, \ \ldots$$

II A *relative minimum* exists if the principal minors (*evaluated at the critical values*) are all positive. That is,

$$|\mathbf{H}_1| > 0, \ |\mathbf{H}_2| > 0, \ |\mathbf{H}_3| > 0, \ \ldots$$

III If neither of the first two conditions is satisfied, no conclusion can be drawn regarding the critical point. Further analysis in the neighborhood of the critical point is required to determine its nature.

EXAMPLE 23

Continuing Example 22, the hessian matrix is

$$\mathbf{H} = \begin{pmatrix} 2 & -2 & 2 \\ -2 & 4 & 0 \\ 2 & 0 & 8 \end{pmatrix}$$

The submatrices and corresponding values of the principal minors are

$$\mathbf{H}_1 = (2) \qquad\qquad |\mathbf{H}_1| = 2$$

$$\mathbf{H}_2 = \begin{pmatrix} 2 & -2 \\ -2 & 4 \end{pmatrix} \qquad\qquad |\mathbf{H}_2| = 4$$

$$\mathbf{H}_3 = \begin{pmatrix} 2 & -2 & 0 \\ -2 & 4 & 0 \\ 2 & 0 & 8 \end{pmatrix} \qquad |\mathbf{H}_3| = 16$$

Since the principal minors $|\mathbf{H}_1|$, $|\mathbf{H}_2|$, and $|\mathbf{H}_3|$ are all positive, we conclude that a relative minimum occurs at the critical point $(-1, -\frac{1}{2}, \frac{1}{2}, -\frac{1}{2})$.

EXAMPLE 24

Given the function

$$f(x_1, x_2, x_3) = -2x_1^3 + 6x_1x_3 + 2x_2 - x_2^2 - 6x_3^2 + 5$$

the first partial derivatives are found and set equal to 0, as follows:

$$\begin{aligned} f_{x_1} &= -6x_1^2 + 6x_3 = 0 \\ f_{x_2} &= 2 - 2x_2 = 0 \\ f_{x_3} &= 6x_1 - 12x_3 = 0 \end{aligned}$$

If these equations are solved simultaneously, critical values occur when $x_1 = 0$, $x_2 = 1$, and $x_3 = 0$, and also when $x_1 = \frac{1}{2}$, $x_2 = 1$, and $x_3 = \frac{1}{4}$. If the corresponding values of $f(x_1, x_2, x_3)$ are computed, we can state that critical points occur at $(0, 1, 0, 6)$ and $(\frac{1}{2}, 1, \frac{1}{4}, 6\frac{1}{4})$.

To test the nature of these critical points, second partial derivatives are identified and combined into the hessian matrix

$$
\mathbf{H} = \begin{pmatrix} -12x_1 & 0 & 6 \\ 0 & -2 & 0 \\ 6 & 0 & -12 \end{pmatrix}
$$

At $(0, 1, 0, 6)$

$$\mathbf{H}_1 = (0) \qquad \text{and} \qquad |\mathbf{H}_1| = 0$$

$$\mathbf{H}_2 = \begin{pmatrix} 0 & 0 \\ 0 & -2 \end{pmatrix} \qquad \text{and} \qquad |\mathbf{H}_2| = 0$$

$$\mathbf{H}_3 = \begin{pmatrix} 0 & 0 & 6 \\ 0 & -2 & 0 \\ 6 & 0 & -12 \end{pmatrix} \qquad \text{and} \qquad |\mathbf{H}_3| = 72$$

These principal minors do not satisfy the requirements for either a relative maximum or relative minimum; thus, no conclusions can be reached regarding the critical point $(0, 1, 0, 6)$.

At $(\tfrac{1}{2}, 1, \tfrac{1}{4}, 6\tfrac{1}{4})$

$$\mathbf{H}_1 = (-6) \qquad \text{and} \qquad |\mathbf{H}_1| = -6$$

$$\mathbf{H}_2 = \begin{pmatrix} -6 & 0 \\ 0 & -2 \end{pmatrix} \qquad \text{and} \qquad |\mathbf{H}_2| = 12$$

$$\mathbf{H}_3 = \begin{pmatrix} -6 & 0 & 6 \\ 0 & -2 & 0 \\ 6 & 0 & -12 \end{pmatrix} \qquad \text{and} \qquad |\mathbf{H}_3| = -72$$

Since $|\mathbf{H}_1| < 0$, $|\mathbf{H}_2| > 0$, and $|\mathbf{H}_3| < 0$, we can conclude that a relative maximum occurs at $(\tfrac{1}{2}, 1, \tfrac{1}{4}, 6\tfrac{1}{4})$.

Section 15.5 Follow-up Exercises

For the following functions, locate any critical points and determine their nature.

1 $f(x_1, x_2, x_3) = x_1 - 4x_1x_2 - x_2^2 + 5x_3^2 - 2x_2x_3$

2 $f(x_1, x_2, x_3) = 10x_1^2 + 15x_2^2 + 5x_3^2 - 60x_1 + 90x_2 - 40x_3 + 15,000$

3 $f(x_1, x_2, x_3) = 2x_1^2 + x_1x_2 + 4x_2^2 + x_1x_3 + x_3^2 + 2$

4 $f(x_1, x_2, x_3) = x_1^2 - 3x_1x_2 + 3x_2^2 + 4x_2x_3 + 6x_3^2$

5 $f(x_1, x_2, x_3) = 25 - x_1^2 - x_2^2 - x_3^2$

6 $f(x_1, x_2, x_3, x_4) = 8x_2^3 + 4x_1^2 + 2x_2^2 + 5x_3^2 + 3.5x_4^2 - 24x_1 + 20x_3 - 75$

7 **Pricing Model** A firm manufactures three competing microcomputers. Demand functions for each of the three computers are

$$
\begin{aligned}
q_1 &= 4{,}000 - 2p_1 + p_2 + p_3 \\
q_2 &= 6{,}000 + p_1 - 3p_2 + p_3 \\
q_3 &= 5{,}000 + p_1 + p_2 - 2p_3
\end{aligned}
$$

where q_i is the estimated demand (in units per year) for computer i and p_i is the price of the ith computer (in dollars per unit).

(*a*) Determine the prices which will result in maximum total revenue from the three computers. Verify that you have, in fact, identified a relative maximum.

(*b*) What quantities should be produced if these prices are charged?

(*c*) What is the maximum total revenue?

   8 Joint Cost Model A firm manufactures three products. The joint cost function is

$$C = f(q_1, q_2, q_3)$$
$$= 10q_1^2 + 30q_2^2 + 20q_3^2 - 400q_1 - 900q_2 - 1{,}000q_3 + 750{,}000$$

where C is the total cost (in dollars) of producing q_1, q_2, and q_3 units of products 1, 2, and 3, respectively.

(*a*) Determine the quantities which result in a minimum total cost. Confirm that the critical point is a relative minimum.

(*b*) What is the expected minimum total cost?

15.6 OPTIMIZATION SUBJECT TO CONSTRAINTS (OPTIONAL)

Our discussion of calculus-based optimization methods has focused upon *unconstrained optimization.* Many applications of mathematical modeling involve the optimization of an *objective function* subject to certain constraining conditions, or more simply, *constraints.* These constraints represent restrictions that can influence the degree to which an objective function is optimized. Constraints may reflect such restrictions as limited resources (e.g., labor, materials, or capital), limited demand for products, sales goals, etc. Problems having this structure are considered to be *constrained optimization problems.* We examined a linear subset of these problems when we studied linear programming (Chaps. 7 and 8). In this section we will examine a method for solving certain nonlinear constrained optimization problems.

The Lagrange Multiplier Method (Equality Constraint)

Consider the constrained optimization problem.

> Maximize (or minimize) $y = f(x_1, x_2)$
> subject to $g(x_1, x_2) = k$ **(15.27)**

In Eq. (15.27), f is the objective function and $g(x_1, x_2) = k$ is an *equality* constraint.

   One way of solving this type of problem is to combine the information in Eq. (15.27) into the composite function

> $$L(x_1, x_2, \lambda) = f(x_1, x_2) - \lambda[g(x_1, x_2) - k]$$ **(15.28)**

This composite function is called the *lagrangian function,* and the variable λ (lambda) is referred to as the *Lagrange multiplier.* The lagrangian function is composed of the objective function and a linear multiple of the constraint equation. Notice in the lagrangian function that λ can equal any value and the term $\lambda[g(x_1, x_2) - k]$ will equal 0, provided that (x_1, x_2) are values which satisfy the constraint. Thus, the value of the newly formed lagrangian function L will equal the value of the original objective function f.

The creation of the lagrangian function ingeniously transforms the original constrained problem into an unconstrained problem which can be solved by procedures very similar to those discussed in the last section. That is, to solve the original problem, Eq. (15.27), partial derivatives of $L(x_1, x_2, \lambda)$ are found with respect to x_1, x_2, and λ and are then set equal to 0.

NECESSARY CONDITIONS FOR RELATIVE EXTREMA

$$L_{x_1} = 0$$
$$L_{x_2} = 0 \qquad\qquad \textbf{(15.29)}$$
$$L_\lambda = 0$$

EXAMPLE 25

Consider the problem

$$\text{Maximize} \quad f(x_1, x_2) = 25 - x_1^2 - x_2^2$$
$$\text{subject to} \quad 2x_1 + x_2 = 4$$

The Lagrange multiplier method transforms this problem into the unconstrained form

$$L(x_1, x_2, \lambda) = 25 - x_1^2 - x_2^2 - \lambda(2x_1 + x_2 - 4)$$

First partial derivatives are identified as

$$L_{x_1} = -2x_1 - 2\lambda$$
$$L_{x_2} = -2x_2 - \lambda$$
$$L_\lambda = -2x_1 - x_2 + 4$$

Critical values are found by setting the three partial derivatives equal to zero and solving simultaneously.

$$-2x_1 - 2\lambda \quad\ = 0 \qquad\qquad \textbf{(15.30)}$$

$$-2x_2 - \lambda = 0 \qquad\qquad \textbf{(15.31)}$$

$$-2x_1 - x_2 + 4 = 0 \qquad\qquad \textbf{(15.32)}$$

Multiplying both sides of Eq. (15.31) by -2 gives

$$4x_2 + 2\lambda = 0$$

Adding this to Eq. (15.30),

$$4x_2 + 2\lambda = 0$$
$$\underline{-2x_1 - 2\lambda = 0} \qquad\qquad \textbf{(15.30)}$$
$$-2x_1 + 4x_2 = 0 \qquad\qquad \textbf{(15.33)}$$

Solving for x_1 in Eq. (15.33) yields

$$4x_2 = 2x_1$$
$$2x_2 = x_1 \qquad\qquad \textbf{(15.34)}.$$

If this value for x_1 is substituted into Eq. (15.32)

$$-2(2x_2) - x_2 + 4 = 0$$
$$-5x_2 = -4$$
$$x_2 = \tfrac{4}{5} = 0.8$$

If this value is substituted into Eq. (15.34), $x_1 = 1.6$. Also, substituting $x_2 = 0.8$ into Eq. (15.31) yields $\lambda = -1.6$. Thus, $x_1 = 1.6$, $x_2 = 0.8$, and $\lambda = -1.6$ are critical values on the lagrangian function. These values for x_1 and x_2 also represent the only candidate points for a relative maximum (or minimum).

Sufficient Condition

To assess the behavior of $L(x_1, x_2, \lambda)$ at any critical values, the *bordered hessian matrix* $\mathbf{H}_B$ must be determined, where

$$\mathbf{H}_B = \begin{pmatrix} 0 & g_{x_1} & g_{x_2} \\ g_{x_1} & L_{x_1 x_1} & L_{x_1 x_2} \\ g_{x_2} & L_{x_2 x_1} & L_{x_2 x_2} \end{pmatrix}$$

and g_{x_i} represents the partial derivative of the left side of the constraint taken with respect to x_i.

SUFFICIENT CONDITIONS FOR RELATIVE EXTREMA

Given critical values $x_1 = a_1$, $x_2 = a_2$, and $\lambda = \lambda^*$ for which $L_{x_1} = L_{x_2} = L_\lambda = 0$, $|\mathbf{H}_B|$ is evaluated at the critical values.

I   A *relative maximum* exists if $|\mathbf{H}_B| > 0$.

II A *relative minimum* exists if $|\mathbf{H}_B| < 0$.

EXAMPLE 26

To determine the behavior of

$$L(x_1, x_2, \lambda) = 25 - x_1^2 - x_2^2 - \lambda(2x_1 + x_2 - 4)$$

at $x_1 = 1.6$, $x_2 = 0.8$, and $\lambda = -1.6$, we form the bordered hessian matrix

$$\mathbf{H}_B = \begin{pmatrix} 0 & 2 & 1 \\ 2 & -2 & 0 \\ 1 & 0 & -2 \end{pmatrix}$$

If we use methods from Chap. 6 to find the determinant we will find that

$$|\mathbf{H}_B| = 10 > 0$$

which implies that $L(x_1, x_2, \lambda)$ achieves a relative maximum when $x_1 = 1.6$, $x_2 = 0.8$, and $\lambda = -1.6$. If these values are substituted into the lagrangian function,

$$L(1.6, 0.8, -1.6) = 25 - (1.6)^2 - (0.8)^2 - (-1.6)[2(1.6) + 0.8 - 4]$$
$$= 25 - 2.56 - 0.64 + 1.6(0) = 21.8.$$

Therefore $L(x_1, x_2, \lambda)$ achieves a maximum value of 21.8. This is also the maximum value for $f(x_1, x_2)$ in the original constrained optimization problem of Example 25.

Figure 15.23 is a graphic portrayal of this problem. You may remember that the surface representing $f(x_1, x_2) = 25 - x_1^2 - x_2^2$ is the same as shown earlier in Fig. 15.4. Without the constraint, the relative maximum would occur at (0, 0, 25). The constraint $2x_1 + x_2 = 4$ requires that the only values which can be considered lie on the intersection of the plane *ABCD* and the surface representing f. Given the points of intersection (*MN*) between the surface $f(x_1, x_2)$ and the plane *ABCD*, the maximum value for f occurs at (1.6, 0.8, 21.8).

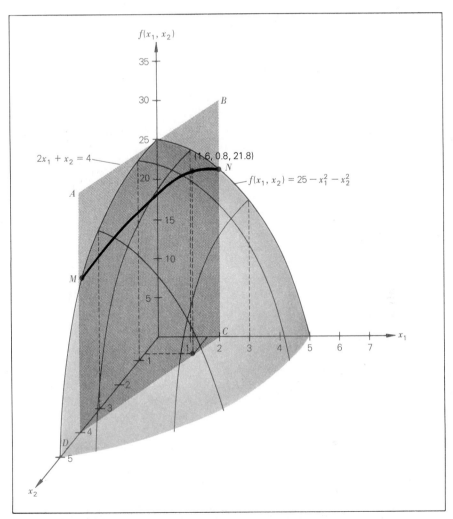

FIGURE 15.23
Constrained optimization problem.

n-Variable Single-Equality Constraint Case

Given a problem of the form

> Maximize (or minimize) $y = f(x_1, x_2, \ldots, x_n)$
> subject to $g(x_1, x_2, \ldots, x_n) = k$ (15.35)

the Lagrange multiplier method is just slightly different from the two independent variable case. The corresponding lagrangian function is

$$L(x_1, x_2, \ldots, x_n, \lambda) = f(x_1, x_2, \ldots, x_n) - \lambda[g(x_1, x_2, \ldots, x_n) - k]$$

(15.36)

NECESSARY CONDITION FOR RELATIVE EXTREMA

$$L_{x_1} = 0$$
$$L_{x_2} = 0$$
$$\cdot$$
$$\cdot$$
$$\cdot$$
$$L_x = 0$$
$$L_\lambda = 0$$

(15.37)

where $L_{x_1}, L_{x_2}, \ldots, L_{x_n}, L_\lambda$ all exist.

The bordered hessian matrix for the n-variable case has the form

$$\mathbf{H}_B = \begin{pmatrix} 0 & g_{x_1} & g_{x_2} & \cdots & g_{x_n} \\ g_{x_1} & L_{x_1 x_1} & L_{x_1 x_2} & \cdots & L_{x_1 x_n} \\ g_{x_2} & L_{x_2 x_1} & L_{x_2 x_2} & \cdots & L_{x_2 x_n} \\ \cdots & \cdots & \cdots & \cdots & \cdots \\ g_{x_n} & L_{x_n x_1} & L_{x_n x_2} & \cdots & L_{x_n x_n} \end{pmatrix}$$

(15.38)

Given the bordered hessian in Eq. (15.38), various submatrices and their **bordered principal minors** are defined as follows:

$$|\mathbf{H}_{B_2}| = \begin{vmatrix} 0 & g_{x_1} & g_{x_2} \\ g_{x_1} & L_{x_1 x_1} & L_{x_1 x_2} \\ g_{x_2} & L_{x_2 x_1} & L_{x_2 x_2} \end{vmatrix}$$

$$|\mathbf{H}_{B_3}| = \begin{vmatrix} 0 & g_{x_1} & g_{x_2} & g_{x_3} \\ g_{x_1} & L_{x_1 x_1} & L_{x_1 x_2} & L_{x_1 x_3} \\ g_{x_2} & L_{x_2 x_1} & L_{x_2 x_2} & L_{x_2 x_3} \\ g_{x_3} & L_{x_3 x_1} & L_{x_3 x_2} & L_{x_3 x_3} \end{vmatrix}$$

$$|\mathbf{H}_B| = \begin{vmatrix} 0 & g_{x_1} & g_{x_2} & \cdots & g_{x_n} \\ g_{x_1} & L_{x_1 x_1} & L_{x_1 x_2} & \cdots & L_{x_1 x_n} \\ g_{x_2} & L_{x_2 x_1} & L_{x_2 x_2} & \cdots & L_{x_2 x_n} \\ \cdots & \cdots & \cdots & \cdots & \cdots \\ g_{x_n} & L_{x_n x_1} & L_{x_n x_2} & \cdots & L_{x_n x_n} \end{vmatrix}$$

SUFFICIENT CONDITIONS FOR RELATIVE EXTREMA

Given critical values $x_1 = a_1, x_2 = a_2, \ldots, x_n = a_n$, and $\lambda = \lambda^*$ for which

$$L_{x_1} = L_{x_2} = \cdots = L_{x_n} = L_\lambda = 0$$

$|\mathbf{H}_B|$ is evaluated at the critical values.

I A *relative maximum* exists if

$$|\mathbf{H}_{B_2}| > 0, |\mathbf{H}_{B_3}| < 0, |\mathbf{H}_{B_4}| > 0, \ldots$$

II A *relative minimum* exists if

$$|\mathbf{H}_{B_2}| < 0, |\mathbf{H}_{B_3}| < 0, |\mathbf{H}_{B_4}| < 0, \ldots$$

EXAMPLE 27

Given the problem

$$\text{Maximize} \quad f(x_1, x_2, x_3) = 5x_1x_2x_3$$
$$\text{subject to} \quad x_1 + 2x_2 + 3x_3 = 24$$

the corresponding lagrangian function is

$$L(x_1, x_2, x_3, \lambda) = 5x_1x_2x_3 - \lambda(x_1 + 2x_2 + 3x_3 - 24)$$

To locate any critical values, the first partial derivatives are found and set equal to 0.

$$\begin{aligned}
L_{x_1} &= 5x_2x_3 - \lambda & = 0 \\
L_{x_2} &= 5x_1x_3 - 2\lambda & = 0 \\
L_{x_3} &= 5x_1x_2 - 3\lambda & = 0 \\
L_\lambda &= -x_1 - 2x_2 - 3x_3 + 24 & = 0
\end{aligned}$$

These four equations can be rewritten as

$$5x_2x_3 = \lambda \tag{15.39}$$

$$5x_1x_3 = 2\lambda \tag{15.40}$$

$$5x_1x_2 = 3\lambda \tag{15.41}$$

$$x_1 + 2x_2 + 3x_3 = 24 \tag{15.42}$$

If both sides of Eq. (15.39) are divided by the corresponding side of Eq. (15.40),

$$\frac{5x_2x_3}{5x_1x_3} = \frac{\lambda}{2\lambda} \quad \text{or} \quad \frac{x_2}{x_1} = \frac{1}{2}$$

Thus

$$x_2 = \frac{x_1}{2} \tag{15.43}$$

In a similar manner, both sides of Eq. (15.39) can be divided by both sides of Eq. (15.41):

$$\frac{5x_2x_3}{5x_1x_2} = \frac{\lambda}{3\lambda} \quad \text{or} \quad \frac{x_3}{x_1} = \frac{1}{3}$$

and

$$x_3 = \frac{x_1}{3} \tag{15.44}$$

Substituting Eqs. (15.43) and (15.44) into Eq. (15.42),

$$x_1 + 2\frac{x_1}{2} + 3\frac{x_1}{3} = 24$$

$$3x_1 = 24$$

$$x_1 = 8$$

If this value is substituted into Eqs. (15.43), (15.44), and (15.39), critical values are identified for $L(x_1, x_2, x_3, \lambda)$ as $x_1 = 8$, $x_2 = 4$, $x_3 = \frac{8}{3}$, and $\lambda = \frac{160}{3}$, or $53\frac{1}{3}$.

To test the nature of this critical point the bordered hessian is identified as

$$\mathbf{H}_B = \begin{pmatrix} 0 & 1 & 2 & 3 \\ 1 & 0 & 5x_3 & 5x_2 \\ 2 & 5x_3 & 0 & 5x_1 \\ 3 & 5x_2 & 5x_1 & 0 \end{pmatrix}$$

Evaluated at the critical values,

$$\mathbf{H}_B = \begin{pmatrix} 0 & 1 & 2 & 3 \\ 1 & 0 & \frac{40}{3} & 20 \\ 2 & \frac{40}{3} & 0 & 40 \\ 3 & 20 & 40 & 0 \end{pmatrix}$$

The bordered principal minors are

$$|\mathbf{H}_{B_2}| = \begin{vmatrix} 0 & 1 & 2 \\ 1 & 0 & \frac{40}{3} \\ 2 & \frac{40}{3} & 0 \end{vmatrix} = \frac{160}{3}$$

$$|\mathbf{H}_{B_3}| = \begin{vmatrix} 0 & 1 & 2 & 3 \\ 1 & 0 & \frac{40}{3} & 20 \\ 2 & \frac{40}{3} & 0 & 40 \\ 3 & 20 & 40 & 0 \end{vmatrix} = -4,800$$

Since $|\mathbf{H}_{B_2}| > 0$ and $|\mathbf{H}_{B_3}| < 0$, we can conclude that a relative maximum occurs for $L(x_1, x_2, x_3, \lambda)$ [and also for $f(x_1, x_2, x_3)$] when $x_1 = 8$, $x_2 = 4$, $x_3 = \frac{8}{3}$ and $\lambda = \frac{160}{3}$. The constrained maximum value is

$$5x_1x_2x_3 = 5(8)(4)(\tfrac{8}{3})$$

$$= \frac{1,280}{3} = 426\tfrac{2}{3}$$

Interpreting λ

Lambda is more than just an artificial creation allowing for the solution of constrained optimization problems. It has an interpretation which can be very useful. Given the generalized lagrangian function of Eq. (15.36),

$$\boxed{\frac{\partial L}{\partial k} = L_k = \lambda} \tag{15.45}$$

Thus, λ can be interpreted as the instantaneous rate of change in the value of the lagrangian function with respect to a change in the right-hand side constant k of the constraint equation. The value of $\lambda = \frac{160}{3}$ in the optimal solution to the previous example suggests that if the right-hand side constant, 24, *increases* (decreases) by 1 unit, the optimal value for $f(x_1, x_2, x_3)$ will *increase* (decrease) by approximately $\frac{160}{3}$ units from the current maximum of $426\frac{2}{3}$.

The economic interpretation of λ can be of particular value in problems where the constraint(s) represent such things as limited resources. If there is an ability to provide additional resources, the λ values can offer guidance in allocating such resources.*

Extensions

The Lagrange approach can be extended to the case of multiple constraints and the case of constraint sets which include inequality as well as equality constraint types. This material, however, is beyond the scope of this text.

Section 15.6 Follow-up Exercises

In Exercises 1 to 8, examine the function for relative extrema and test for the nature of any extrema.

1 $f(x_1, x_2) = -3x_1^2 - 2x_2^2 + 20x_1x_2$ subject to $x_1 + x_2 = 100$
2 $f(x_1, x_2) = x_1x_2$ subject to $x_1 + x_2 = 6$
3 $f(x_1, x_2) = x_1^2 + 3x_1x_2 - 6x_2$ subject to $x_1 + x_2 = 42$
4 $f(x_1, x_2) = 5x_1^2 + 6x_2^2 - x_1x_2$ subject to $x_1 + 2x_2 = 24$
5 $f(x_1, x_2) = 12x_1x_2 - 3x_2^2 - x_1^2$ subject to $x_1 + x_2 = 16$
6 $f(x_1, x_2, x_3) = x_1^2 + x_2^2 + x_3^2$ subject to $x_1 - x_2 + 2x_3 = 6$
7 $f(x_1, x_2, x_3) = x_1^2 + x_1x_2 + 2x_2^2 + x_3^2$ subject to $x_1 - 3x_2 - 4x_3 = 16$
8 $f(x_1, x_2, x_3) = x_1x_2x_3$ subject to $x_1 + 2x_2 + 3x_3 = 18$
9 A company has received an order for 200 units of one of its products. The order will be supplied from the combined production of its two plants. The joint cost function for production of this particular product is

$$C = f(q_1, q_2) = 2q_1^2 + q_1q_2 + q_2^2 + 500$$

where q_1 and q_2 equal the quantities produced at plants 1 and 2, respectively. If the objective is to minimize total costs subject to the requirement that 200 units be supplied from the two plants, what quantities should be supplied by each plant?

10 A factory manufactures two types of products. The joint cost function is

$$C = f(x_1, x_2) = x_1^2 + 2x_2^2 - x_1x_2$$

where C is the weekly production cost stated in thousands of dollars and x_1 and x_2 equal the quantities produced of the two products each week. If combined weekly production should equal 16 units, what quantities of each product will result in minimum total costs?

KEY TERMS AND CONCEPTS

bivariate function   591
bordered hessian matrix   638
bordered principal minors   640
constrained optimization   636
functions of several variables   591

hessian matrix   633
hypersurface   632
lagrangian function   636
Lagrange multiplier   636
least-squares model   627

---

* For those of you who studied linear programming in Chaps. 7 and 8, λ is equivalent to a *shadow price*.

IMPORTANT FORMULAS

$$D(x^*, y^*) = f_{xx}(x^*, y^*)f_{yy}(x^*, y^*) - [f_{xy}(x^*, y^*)]^2 \qquad (15.13)$$

$$L(x_1, x_2, \lambda) = f(x_1, x_2) - \lambda[g(x_1, x_2) - k] \qquad (15.28)$$

$$L(x_1, x_2, \ldots, x_n, \lambda) = f(x_1, x_2, \ldots, x_n) - \lambda[g(x_1, x_2, \ldots, x_n) - k] \qquad (15.36)$$

ADDITIONAL EXERCISES

Exercises 1 to 14 are related to Sec. 15.2.
Determine f_x and f_y for the following functions.

1 $f(x, y) = 4x^3 - 3x^2y + y^2$
2 $f(x, y) = 5x^2y^3 - 3x^3y$
3 $f(x, y) = (5x^3 - 2y^3)^4$
4 $f(x, y) = \sqrt[3]{4xy^3} - 10$
5 $f(x, y) = (x^2 - y)/3xy^2$
6 $f(x, y) = 3x^2(x - y^2)^4$
7 $f(x, y) = e^{4xy}$
8 $f(x, y) = e^{x/y^2}$

Find all second-order partial derivatives for the following functions.

9 $f(x, y) = 10x^2y$
10 $f(x, y) = 5x^2 - 2xy + 3y^2$
11 $f(x, y) = \ln xy$
12 $f(x, y) = e^{x^2+y^2}$

*13 **Cross Elasticity of Demand**   Example 30 in Chap. 14 (page 581) discussed the elasticity of demand. Given a demand function of the form $q = f(p)$, the elasticity of demand η was defined as

$$\eta = -\frac{dq/q}{dp/p} = -\frac{dq}{dp} \cdot \frac{p}{q}$$

The elasticity of demand is the ratio of the percentage change in quantity demanded to the percentage change in price.

When demand for a product is dependent upon its price as well as the prices of other products, the *cross elasticity of demand* for product i with respect to a change in the price of product j is defined as

$$\eta_{ij} = \frac{\Delta q_i/q_i}{\Delta p_j/p_j}$$

$$= \frac{\partial q_i/q_i}{\partial p_j/p_j}$$

$$= \frac{\partial q_i}{\partial p_j} \cdot \frac{p_j}{q_i}$$

This measure is the ratio of the percentage change in the demand for product i to the percentage change in the price of product j, all other prices held constant.

Given the demand function

$$q_1 = f(p_1, p_2) = 60{,}000 - 0.1p_1^2 - p_1 + 0.5p_2^2 - 2p_2$$

assume that current prices are $p_1 = 50$ and $p_2 = 80$.

(a) Determine the cross elasticity of demand η_{12}.

(b) Determine the elasticity of demand η_{11}.

(c) Interpret the difference in meaning between η_{12} and η_{11}.

*14   Given the discussion in Exercise 13, suppose the demand function for a product is

$$q_2 = f(p_1, p_2, p_3) = 100{,}000 - p_1^2 - 1.5p_2^2 - 2p_3^2$$

If current prices are $p_1 = 40$, $p_2 = 20$, and $p_3 = 50$,

(a) Determine η_{21}, η_{22}, and η_{23}.

(b) Interpret the meaning of the answers in part (a).

Exercises 15 to 19 are related to Sec. 15.3.

For the following functions, determine the location of all critical points and their nature.

15    $f(x, y) = x^2/2 + 2y^2 - 20x - 40y + 100$

16    $f(x, y) = -3x^2 - 2y^2 + 45x - 30y - 50$

17    $f(x, y) = 3x^2 + y^2 + 3xy - 60x - 32y + 200$

18    $f(x, y) = x^2 + xy + y^2 - 3x$

19    $f(x, y) = xy - x^3 - y^2$

Exercises 20 to 24 are related to Sec. 15.4.

20   A firm sells two products. The annual total revenue R behaves as a function of the number of units sold. Specifically,

$$R = 400x - 4x^2 + 1{,}960y - 8y^2$$

where x and y equal, respectively, the number of units sold of each product. The cost of producing the two products is

$$C = 100 + 2x^2 + 4y^2 + 2xy$$

(a) Determine the number of units which should be produced and sold in order to maximize annual profit.

(b) What does total revenue equal?

(c) What do total costs equal?

(d) What is the maximum profit?

21   A firm sells two products. The demand functions for the two products are

$$q_1 = 110 - 4p_1 - p_2$$
$$q_2 = 90 - 2p_1 - 3p_2$$

where p_j equals the price of product j in dollars and q_j equals the demand (in thousands of units) for product j.

(*a*) Determine the prices which should be charged for each product in order to maximize total revenue from the two products.

(*b*) How many units will be demanded of each product at these prices?

(*c*) What is the maximum total revenue expected to equal?

22 Given the four data points (1, 2.5), (−2, 17.5), (4, −12.5), and (−1, 12.5), determine the equation of the line of best fit using the least-squares model.

23 Given the data points (2, 2), (−3, 17), and (10, −22), determine the equation of the line of best fit using the least squares model.

*24 A rectangular container is being designed which is to have a volume of 8,000 cubic inches. The objective is to minimize the amount of material used in constructing the container. Thus, the surface area is to be minimized. If x, y, and z represent the dimensions of the container (in inches), determine the dimensions which minimize the surface area. (*Hint:* $V = xyz$.)

Exercises 25 to 28 are related to Sec. 15.5.

For the following functions, locate any critical points and determine their nature.

25 $f(x_1, x_2, x_3) = x_1^2 + x_2^2 + x_3^2 - 4x_1 - 8x_2 - 12x_3 + 56$

26 $f(x_1, x_2, x_3) = x_1^2 + 3x_2^2 + 3x_3^2 + 2x_1x_2 + 4x_2x_3 + 2x_1x_3$

27 $f(x_1, x_2, x_3) = x_1^2 + x_2^2 + x_3^2 + x_1x_2 + x_1x_3 + 4x_1 - 4x_2 + 8x_3$

28 $f(x_1, x_2, x_3) = 200 - x_1^2 - x_2^2 - 2x_3^2 + 20x_1 + 10x_2 + 20x_3$

Exercises 29 to 35 are related to Sec. 15.6.

Examine each of the following functions for relative extrema and test for the nature of any extrema. What is the optimal value of λ?

29 $f(x_1, x_2) = 20x_1 + 10x_2 - x_1^2 - x_2^2$ subject to $x_1 + 2x_2 = 10$

30 $f(x_1, x_2) = -x_2^2 - 5x_1^2 + 4x_1x_2 + 16x_1 + 10x_2$ subject to $2x_1 + x_2 = 60$

31 $f(x_1, x_2) = 3x_1^2 + x_2^2 + 3x_1x_2 - 60x_1 - 32x_2 + 400$ subject to $x_1 + x_2 = 10$

32 $f(x_1, x_2) = 2x_2^2 - 6x_1^2$ subject to $2x_1 + x_2 = 4$

33 A cylindrical container is to be designed to hold 12 ounces, or 26 cubic inches, of liquid. Determine the dimensions (height and radius) which result in minimum surface area for the container. What is the minimum surface area? (Assume the container has both a top and bottom.)

34 A firm estimates that its monthly profit is a function of the amount of money it spends on TV and radio advertising per month. The profit function is

$$P = \frac{80x}{5 + x} + \frac{40y}{10 + y} - 2x - 2y$$

where P equals the monthly profit (in thousands of dollars) and x and y equal the monthly advertising expenditure for TV and radio, respectively (both in thousands of dollars). If the monthly advertising budget is $25,000, determine the amount which should be allocated to each medium in order to maximize monthly profit. What is the optimal value for λ? Interpret the meaning of this value.

*35 A warehouse is to be constructed which will have a volume of 850,000 cubic feet. The warehouse is to have a rectangular foundation of dimensions x feet by y feet and height of z feet. Construction costs are estimated based upon floor and ceiling area as well as wall area. The estimated costs are $6 per square foot of wall area, $8 per square foot of floor area, and $6 per square foot of ceiling area.

(*a*) Formulate the cost function for constructing the warehouse.

(*b*) Determine the building dimensions which will result in minimum construction costs.

(*c*) What is the minimum cost?

CHAPTER TEST

1 Give two interpretations of f_x.

2 What is a *trace*?

3 Determine f_x and f_y if

$$f(x, y) = 5x^3 - 4y^2 + 5x^2y$$

4 Determine all second-order partial derivatives for the function

$$f(x, y) = 4x^5 + 6x^3 - 3x^2y^2$$

5 Given the function

$$f(x, y) = 3x^2 - 4xy + 3y^2 + 8x - 17y + 5$$

(*a*) Locate any critical points and determine their nature.
(*b*) What is $f(x^*, y^*)$?

6 A researcher at a college of agriculture estimated that annual profit at a local farm can be described by the function

$$P = 1{,}200x + 1{,}600y - 2x^2 - 4y^2 - 4xy$$

where P equals annual profit in dollars, x equals the number of acres planted with soybeans, and y equals the number of acres planted with corn. Determine the number of acres of each crop which should be planted if the objective is to maximize annual profit. What is the expected maximum profit?

7 Given the function

$$f(x_1, x_2) = -4x_1^3 + 3x_2^2 - 4x_1x_2$$
$$\text{subject to} \qquad x_1 - 2x_2 = 20$$

formulate the lagrangian function.

MINICASE

BACK-ORDER INVENTORY MODEL

A variation of the classic EOQ model (Chap. 13 Minicase on page 543) allows for the possibility of shortages of inventory items. In this model, an inventory may be depleted while demand for the item continues to exist. This leads to shortages of the inventory item and the model assumes that these items can be "back-ordered." When the next replenishment supply arrives, the back-ordered demand is filled first and the remaining items are placed in inventory. This type of inventory management is common for vendors such as those in the home furnishings industry. Although vendors incur additional costs by allowing shortages, the hope is to reduce carrying costs (by maintaining less inventory) and ordering costs (by ordering less frequently and in larger quantities).

Figure 15.24 illustrates a typical inventory cycle for this model. Constant demand results in a linear depletion of inventory from a maximum level of L. After t_1 time units, the inventory is depleted. Demand continues for a time t_2 before the replenishment supply of q units arrives. During t_2 the continued demand for the item results in a shortage of S units. Thus, upon arrival of the replenishment supply, S units must be allocated to cover the shortage.

If

- D = *annual demand in units*
- C_o = *ordering cost per order*
- C_h = *carrying cost per item per year*
- C_s = *shortage cost per item per year*
- S = *maximum shortage (in units)*
- q = *order quantity*

the relevant cost function is

$$TC = \frac{\text{annual ordering}}{\text{cost}} + \frac{\text{annual carrying}}{\text{cost}} + \frac{\text{annual shortage}}{\text{cost}}$$

or

$$TC = f(q, S) = \frac{D}{q}\,C_o + \frac{(q-S)^2}{2q}\,C_h + \frac{S^2 C_s}{2q} \tag{15.46}$$

Requirements:

(*a*) If $D = 600,000$, $C_o = \$100$, $C_h = \$0.25$, and $C_s = \$2$, determine the values of q and S which minimize total annual ordering, carrying, and shortage costs. What is the minimum cost? What is the maximum inventory level?

(*b*) Using Eq. (15.46), show that the general expressions for q and S which result in minimum annual inventory cost are

$$q^* = \sqrt{\frac{2DC_o}{C_h}\left(\frac{C_h + C_s}{C_s}\right)}$$

and

$$S^* = \sqrt{\frac{2C_o D C_h}{C_h C_s + C_s^2}}$$

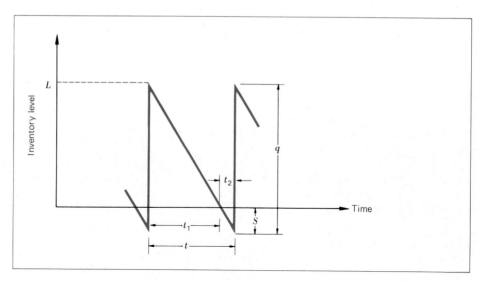

FIGURE 15.24
Classic EOQ
model: inven-
tory cycle with
backorders.

16

INTEGRAL CALCULUS: AN INTRODUCTION

CHAPTER OBJECTIVES

- Introduce the nature and methods of integral calculus

- Present selected rules of integration and illustrate their use

- Illustrate other methods of integration which may be appropriate when basic rules are not

In this chapter we will introduce a second major area of study within the calculus—*integral calculus*. As was mentioned at the beginning of Chap. 11, differential calculus is useful in considering rates of change and tangent slopes. An important concern of integral calculus is the determination of areas which occur between curves and other defined boundaries. Also, if the derivative of an unknown function is known, integral calculus may provide a way of determining the original function.

As we begin this new area of study, it will be of value to know where we are headed. First, integral calculus comprises a major area of study within the calculus. We will devote two chapters to this material. The purpose is to survey the area in such a way that you have a feeling for the concerns and methods of integral calculus, how integral calculus relates to differential calculus, and where it can be applied.

In this chapter the nature of integral calculus will be introduced first by relating it to derivatives. As there were rules for finding derivatives in differential calculus, there are rules for finding *integrals* in integral calculus. The more commonly applied rules will be presented in Secs. 16.2 and 16.3. Section 16.4 discusses *differential equations*. Finally, Sec. 16.5 discusses procedures for finding integrals when the rules in Secs. 16.2 and 16.3 are not applicable. Chapter 17 will focus upon the applications of integral calculus.

16.1 ANTIDERIVATIVES

The Antiderivative Concept

Given a function f, we are acquainted with how to find the derivative f'. There may be occasions in which we are given the derivative f' and wish to determine the original function f. Since the process of finding the original function is the reverse of differentiation, f is said to be an *antiderivative* of f'.

Consider the derivative

$$f'(x) = 4 \qquad\qquad (16.1)$$

By using a trial-and-error approach, it is not very difficult to conclude that the function

$$f(x) = 4x \qquad\qquad (16.2)$$

has a derivative of the form of Eq. (16.1). Another function having the same derivative is

$$f(x) = 4x + 1$$

In fact, any function having the form

$$f(x) = 4x + C \qquad\qquad (16.3)$$

where C is any constant, will have the same derivative. Thus, given the derivative in Eq. (16.1), our conclusion is that the original function was one of the *family* of functions characterized by Eq. (16.3). This family of functions is a set of linear functions whose members all have a slope of $+4$ but different y intercepts C. Figure 16.1 illustrates selected members of this family of functions.

We can also state that the function

$$f(x) = 4x + C$$

is the *antiderivative* of

$$f'(x) = 4$$

EXAMPLE 1

Find the antiderivative of $f'(x) = 0$.

SOLUTION

We know that the derivative of any constant function is 0. Therefore the antiderivative is $f(x) = C$.

EXAMPLE 2

Find the antiderivative of $f'(x) = 2x - 5$.

SOLUTION

Using a trial-and-error approach and working with each term separately, you should conclude that the antiderivative is

$$f(x) = x^2 - 5x + C$$

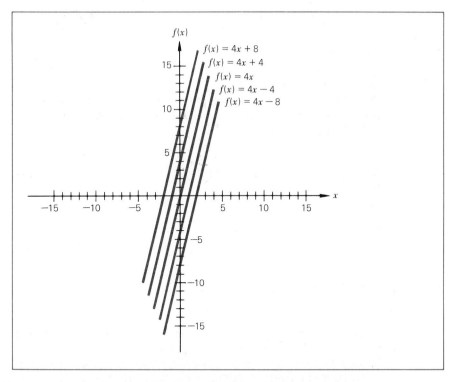

$f(x)$

$f(x) = 4x + 8$
$f(x) = 4x + 4$
$f(x) = 4x$
$f(x) = 4x - 4$
$f(x) = 4x - 8$

FIGURE 16.1

NOTE

An easy check on your antiderivative f is to differentiate it to determine f'.

With additional information it may be possible to determine the precise function from which f' was derived. Assume for the original example we are told that $f'(x) = 4$ *and* one point on the original function is (2, 6). Since the coordinates of this point must satisfy the equation of the original function, we can solve for the y coordinate of the y intercept C by substituting $x = 2$ and $f(x) = 6$ into Eq. (16.3), or

$$6 = 4(2) + C$$
$$-2 = C$$

Therefore, the specific member of the family of functions characterized by Eq. (16.3) is

$$f(x) = 4x - 2$$

EXAMPLE 3

Assume in Example 1 that one point on the function f is $(-2, 5)$. Determine the specific function from which f' was derived.

SOLUTION

The antiderivative describing the family of possible functions was

$$f(x) = C$$

Substituting $x = -2$ and $f(x) = 5$ into this equation gives

$$5 = C$$

Thus, the specific function is $f(x) = 5$.

EXAMPLE 4 ▨▨▨▨▨▨▨▨▨▨▨▨▨▨▨▨▨▨▨▨▨▨▨▨

Assume in Example 2 that one point on the function f is $(2, 20)$. Determine the specific function from which f' was derived.

SOLUTION

The antiderivative describing the family of possible functions was

$$f(x) = x^2 - 5x + C$$

Substituting $x = 2$ and $f(x) = 20$ into this equation, we have

$$
\begin{aligned}
20 &= 2^2 - 5(2) + C \\
20 &= -6 + C \\
26 &= C
\end{aligned}
$$

Thus the original function is

$$f(x) = x^2 - 5x + 26$$

Revenue and Cost Functions

In Chap. 13 we discussed the "marginal approach" for determining the profit-maximizing level of output. We stated that an expression for marginal revenue (MR) is the derivative of the total revenue function where the independent variable is the level of output. Similarly, we said that an expression for marginal cost (MC) is the derivative of the total cost function. If we have an expression for either marginal revenue or marginal cost, the respective antiderivatives will be the total revenue and total cost functions.

EXAMPLE 5 ▨▨▨▨▨▨▨▨▨▨▨▨▨▨▨▨▨▨▨▨▨▨▨▨

Marginal Revenue The marginal revenue function for a company's product is

$$MR = 50{,}000 - x$$

where x equals the number of units produced and sold. If total revenue equals 0 when no units are sold, determine the total revenue function for the product.

SOLUTION

Because the marginal revenue function is the derivative of the total revenue function, the total revenue function is the antiderivative of MR. Using a trial-and-error approach gives

$$R(x) = 50{,}000x - \frac{x^2}{2} + C \tag{16.4}$$

Since we are told that $R(0) = 0$, substitution of $x = 0$ and $R = 0$ into Eq. (16.4) yields

$$0 = 50,000(0) - \frac{0^2}{2} + C$$

or
$$0 = C$$

Thus, the total revenue function for the company's product is

$$R(x) = 50,000x - \frac{x^2}{2}$$

EXAMPLE 6

Marginal Cost   The function describing the marginal cost of producing a product is

$$MC = x + 100$$

where x equals the number of units produced. It is also known that total cost equals $40,000 when $x = 100$. Determine the total cost function.

SOLUTION

To determine the total cost function, we must first find the antiderivative of the marginal cost function, or

$$C(x) = \frac{x^2}{2} + 100x + C \tag{16.5}$$

Given that $C(100) = 40,000$, we can solve for the value of C, which happens to represent the fixed cost.

$$40,000 = \frac{(100)^2}{2} + 100(100) + C$$

$$40,000 = 5,000 + 10,000 + C$$

or
$$25,000 = C$$

The specific function representing the total cost of producing the product is

$$C(x) = \frac{x^2}{2} + 100x + 25,000$$

Section 16.1 Follow-up Exercises

In Exercises 1 to 16, find the antiderivative of the given function.

1 $f'(x) = 40$
2 $f'(x) = -10$
3 $f'(x) = \frac{1}{2}$
4 $f'(x) = \sqrt{2}$
5 $f'(x) = 5x$
6 $f'(x) = -7x$
7 $f'(x) = x^2$
8 $f'(x) = x^2/2$
9 $f'(x) = x^3/3$
10 $f'(x) = x^4$
11 $f'(x) = x^2 - 6x$
12 $f'(x) = x^3 - x^2 + x$
13 $f'(x) = x^2 + 3x + 1$
14 $f'(x) = x^5$

15   $f'(x) = x^4/2$ 16 $f'(x) = \sqrt{2x}$

In Exercises 17 to 26, determine f given f' and a point which satisfies f.

17   $f'(x) = 15,\ (1, 10)$ 18 $f'(x) = -2x + 1,\ (3, 20)$
19   $f'(x) = 20x,\ (-2, 50)$ 20 $f'(x) = x^2,\ (-4, 16)$
21   $f'(x) = 4x^3,\ (2, 45)$ 22 $f'(x) = x^3,\ (0, 10)$
23   $f'(x) = x^2 - 5x,\ (3, 25)$ 24 $f'(x) = x^2 - 3x + 2,\ (-1, 21)$
25   $f'(x) = -x^2 + 5x,\ (2, -15)$ 26 $f'(x) = 5x^4,\ (-3, -10)$
27   The marginal revenue function for a company's product is

$$MR = 60,000 - 3x$$

where x equals the number of units sold. If total revenue equals 0 when no units are sold, determine the total revenue function for the product.

28   The function describing the marginal cost (in dollars) of producing a product is

$$MC = 4x + 1,500$$

where x equals the number of units produced. It is known that total cost equals \$40,200 when 10 units are produced. Determine the total cost function.

29   The function describing the *marginal profit* from producing and selling a product is

$$MP = -6x + 750$$

where x equals the number of units and MP is the marginal profit measured in dollars. When 100 units are produced and sold, *total profit* equals \$25,000. Determine the total profit function.

30   The function describing the marginal profit from producing and selling a product is

$$MP = -4x + 350$$

where x equals the number of units and MP is the marginal profit measured in dollars. When 200 units are produced and sold, total profit (which is negative) equals $-\$35,000$. Determine the total profit function.

16.2   RULES OF INTEGRATION

Fortunately, we need not resort to a trial-and-error approach whenever we wish to find an antiderivative. As with differentiation, a set of rules has been developed for finding antiderivatives. If a function has a particular form, a rule may be available which allows one to determine its antiderivative very easily.

Integration

The process of finding antiderivatives is more frequently called *integration.* And the family of functions obtained through this process is called the *indefinite integral.* The notation

$$\int f(x)\ dx \tag{16.6}$$

is often used to indicate the indefinite integral of the function f. The symbol $\int$ is the *integral sign, f* is the *integrand,* or the function for which we want to find the indefinite integral, and dx, as we will deal with it, indicates the variable with respect to which the integration process is performed. Two verbal descriptions of Eq. (16.6) are "integrate the function f with respect to the variable x" or "find the indefinite integral of f with respect to x."

NOTE

Keep in mind that finding an indefinite integral is the same as finding an antiderivative.

In Example 2 we found that the antiderivative of $2x - 5$ is $x^2 - 5x + C$. We can denote this, using integral notation, as

$$\int (2x - 5)\, dx = x^2 - 5x + C$$

A more formal definition of the indefinite integral follows.

DEFINITION: INDEFINITE INTEGRAL

Given that f is a continuous function,

$$\int f(x)\, dx = F(x) + C \qquad\qquad \textbf{(16.7)}$$

if $F'(x) = f(x)$.

In this definition C is termed the *constant of integration.* Again, C reflects the indefinite nature of finding the antiderivative, or indefinite integral.

Rules of Integration

Following are a set of rules for finding the indefinite integral of some functions common in business and economics applications.

RULE 1: CONSTANT FUNCTIONS

$$\int k\, dx = kx + C \qquad \text{where } k \text{ is a real-valued constant.}$$

Example 7 illustrates this rule.

EXAMPLE 7

(a) $\displaystyle\int (-2)\, dx = -2x + C$

(b) $\displaystyle\int \frac{3}{2}\, dx = \frac{3}{2} x + C$

(c) $\displaystyle\int \sqrt{2}\, dx = \sqrt{2} x + C$

(d) $\int 0\,dx = (0)x + C = C$

RULE 2: POWER RULE

$$\int x^n\,dx = \frac{x^{n+1}}{n+1} + C \qquad n \neq -1$$

This rule is analogous to the power rule of differentiation. *Note that this rule is not valid when $n = -1$.* We will treat this exception shortly. Verbally, the rule states that when the integrand is x raised to some real-valued power, increase the exponent of x by 1, divide by the new exponent, and add the constant of integration. Example 8 provides several illustrations of this rule.

EXAMPLE 8

(a) $\int x\,dx = \dfrac{x^2}{2} + C$

(b) $\int x^2\,dx = \dfrac{x^3}{3} + C$

(c) $\int \sqrt{x}\,dx = \int x^{1/2}\,dx = \dfrac{x^{3/2}}{\frac{3}{2}} + C$

$$= \frac{2}{3}x^{3/2} + C$$

(d) $\int \dfrac{1}{x^3}\,dx = \int x^{-3}\,dx = \dfrac{x^{-2}}{-2} + C$

$$= \frac{-1}{2x^2} + C$$

NOTE

Do not forget the built-in checking mechanism. It takes only a few seconds and may save you from careless errors. Find the derivative of the indefinite integrals found above and see if they equal the respective integrands. Some algebraic manipulation may be needed to verify these results.

RULE 3

$$\int kf(x)\,dx = k \int f(x)\,dx \qquad \text{where } k \text{ is a real-valued constant}$$

Verbally, this rule states that the indefinite integral of a constant k times a function f is found by multiplying the constant by the indefinite integral of f. Another way of viewing this rule is to say that whenever a *constant* can be factored from the integrand, the constant may also be factored outside the integral. Example 9 provides some illustrations of this rule.

EXAMPLE 9

(a) $\int 5x \, dx = 5 \int x \, dx$

$$= 5 \left(\frac{x^2}{2} + C_1 \right)$$

$$= \frac{5x^2}{2} + 5C_1$$

$$= \frac{5x^2}{2} + C$$

Check If $f(x) = \frac{5x^2}{2} + C$, $f'(x) = \frac{5}{2}(2x) = 5x$ ✔

NOTE

With indefinite integrals we always include the constant of integration. In using Rule 3, the algebra suggests that any constant k factored out of the integral will be multiplied by the constant of integration (e.g., the $5C_1$ term in this example). This multiplication is unnecessary. We simply need a constant of integration to indicate the "indefinite nature" of the integral. Thus, the convention is to add C and not a multiple of C. In the last step the $5C_1$ term is rewritten as just C, since C can represent any constant as well as $5C_1$.

(b) $\int \frac{x^2}{2} \, dx = \int \frac{1}{2} x^2 \, dx$

$$= \frac{1}{2} \int x^2 \, dx$$

$$= \frac{1}{2} \frac{x^3}{3} + C$$

$$= \frac{x^3}{6} + C$$

Check If $f(x) = \frac{x^3}{6} + C$, $f'(x) = \frac{3x^2}{6} = \frac{x^2}{2}$ ✔

(c) $\int \frac{3}{\sqrt{x}} \, dx = \int 3x^{-1/2} \, dx$

$$= 3 \int x^{-1/2} \, dx$$

$$= 3 \frac{x^{1/2}}{\frac{1}{2}} + C$$

$$= 6x^{1/2} + C$$

Check　　If $f(x) = 6x^{1/2} + C$, $f'(x) = 6(\frac{1}{2})x^{-1/2}$

$$= \frac{3}{x^{1/2}}$$

$$= \frac{3}{\sqrt{x}} \quad ✔$$

RULE 4

If $\int f(x)\, dx$ and $\int g(x)\, dx$ exist, then

$$\int [f(x) \pm g(x)]\, dx = \int f(x)\, dx \pm \int g(x)\, dx$$

The integral of the sum (difference) of two functions is the sum (difference) of their respective integrals.

EXAMPLE 10

(a) $\displaystyle \int (3x - 6)\, dx = \int 3x\, dx - \int 6\, dx$

$$= \frac{3x^2}{2} + C_1 - (6x + C_2)$$

$$= \frac{3x^2}{2} - 6x + C$$

Note again that even though the two integrals technically result in separate constants of integration, these constants may be considered together as one.

Check　　If $f(x) = \dfrac{3x^2}{2} - 6x + C$, $f'(x) = 3x - 6$ ✔

(b) $\displaystyle \int (4x^2 - 7x + 6)\, dx = \int 4x^2\, dx - \int 7x\, dx + \int 6\, dx$

$$= \frac{4x^3}{3} - \frac{7x^2}{2} + 6x + C$$

Check　　If $f(x) = \dfrac{4x^3}{3} - \dfrac{7x^2}{2} + 6x + C$, $f'(x) = \dfrac{12x^2}{3} - \dfrac{14x}{2} + 6$

$$= 4x^2 - 7x + 6 \quad ✔$$

Section 16.2 Follow-up Exercises

For Exercises 1 to 20, find the indefinite integral (if possible).

1　$\displaystyle \int 50\, dx$ 　　　　　　　　　　　　2　$\displaystyle \int -25\, dx$

3　$\displaystyle \int dx/2$ 　　　　　　　　　　　　4　$\displaystyle \int dx$

5　$\displaystyle \int 8x\, dx$ 　　　　　　　　　　　6　$\displaystyle \int (x/2)\, dx$

7 $\int (5x - 3)\, dx$ 8 $\int (10 - 2x)\, dx$

9 $\int (x^2 - 3x + 5)\, dx$ 10 $\int (8x^2 - x/2 + 3)\, dx$

11 $\int \sqrt[3]{x}\, dx$ 12 $\int (4/\sqrt[4]{x})\, dx$

13 $\int dx/x^3$ 14 $\int (-5/\sqrt[3]{x^2})\, dx$

15 $\int (ax^3 + bx^2 + cx + d)\, dx$ 16 $\int (mx + b)\, dx$

17 $\int (a/bx^n)\, dx$ 18 $\int \sqrt[b]{x}\, dx$

19 $\int dx/x^n$ 20 $\int (a/\sqrt[b]{x})\, dx$

16.3 ADDITIONAL RULES OF INTEGRATION

This section presents additional rules of integration and illustrates their application.

RULE 5: POWER-RULE EXCEPTION

$$\int x^{-1}\, dx = \ln x + C$$

This is the exception associated with Rule 2 (the power rule) where $n = -1$ for x^n. Remember our differentiation rules? If $f(x) = \ln x$, $f'(x) = 1/x = x^{-1}$.

RULE 6

$$\int e^x\, dx = e^x + C$$

RULE 7

$$\int [f(x)]^n f'(x)\, dx = \frac{[f(x)]^{n+1}}{n + 1} + C$$

where $n \neq -1$

This rule is similar to the power rule (Rule 2). In fact, the power rule is the special case of this rule where $f(x) = x$. If the integrand consists of the product of a function f raised to a power n and the derivative of f, the indefinite integral is found by increasing the exponent of f by 1 and dividing by the new exponent.

EXAMPLE 11

Evaluate $\int (5x - 3)^3 (5)\, dx$.

SOLUTION

When an integrand is identified which contains a function raised to a power, you should immediately think of Rule 7. The first step is to determine the function f. In this case, the function which is raised to the third power is

$$f(x) = 5x - 3$$

Once f has been found, f' should be determined. In this case

$$f'(x) = 5$$

If the integrand has the form $[f(x)]^n f'(x)$, then Rule 7 applies. The integrand in this example *does* have the required form, and

$$\int \underbrace{(5x-3)^3}_{f(x)} \underbrace{(5)}_{f'(x)} \, dx = \frac{(5x-3)^4}{4} + C$$

Check   If $f(x) = \dfrac{(5x-3)^4}{4}$, $f'(x) = \dfrac{4}{4}(5x-3)^3(5)$

$$= (5x-3)^3(5) \ \ \blacktriangleright$$

EXAMPLE 12

Evaluate $\int \sqrt{2x^2 - 6}\,(4)\, dx$.

SOLUTION

The integrand can be rewritten as

$$\int (2x^2 - 6)^{1/2}(4)\, dx$$

Referring to Rule 7, we have

$$f(x) = 2x^2 - 6 \quad \text{and} \quad f'(x) = 4x$$

For Rule 7 to apply, $(2x^2 - 6)^{1/2}$ should be multiplied by f', or $4x$, in the integrand. Since the other factor in the integrand is 4 and not $4x$, we cannot evaluate the integral by using Rule 7.

EXAMPLE 13

Evaluate $\int (x^2 - 2x)^5(x - 1)\, dx$.

SOLUTION

For this integral

$$f(x) = x^2 - 2x \quad \text{and} \quad f'(x) = 2x - 2$$

Again it seems that the integrand is not in the proper form. To apply Rule 7, the second factor in the integrand should be $2x - 2$, and not $x - 1$. However, recalling Rule 3 and using some algebraic manipulations, we get

$$\int (x^2 - 2x)^5(x - 1)\, dx = \frac{2}{2}\int (x^2 - 2x)^5(x - 1)\, dx$$

$$= \frac{1}{2} \int (x^2 - 2x)^5(2)(x - 1) \, dx$$

$$= \frac{1}{2} \int (x^2 - 2x)^5(2x - 2) \, dx \qquad \qquad \textbf{(16.8)}$$

What we have done is manipulate the integrand into the proper form. Rule 3 indicated that *constants* can be factored from inside to outside the integral sign. Similarly, we can move a constant which is a factor from outside the integral sign to inside. We multiplied the integrand by 2 and offset this multiplication by multiplying the integral by $\frac{1}{2}$. Effectively, we have simply multiplied the original integral by $\frac{2}{2}$, or 1. Thus, we have changed the appearance of the original integral but not its value.

Evaluating the integral in Eq. (16.8) gives

$$\int (x^2 - 2x)^5(x - 1) \, dx = \frac{1}{2} \int \overbrace{(x^2 - 2x)^5}^{f(x)}\overbrace{(2x - 2)}^{f'(x)} \, dx$$

$$= \frac{1}{2}\frac{(x^2 - 2x)^6}{6} + C$$

$$= \frac{(x^2 - 2x)^6}{12} + C$$

Check   If $f(x) = \dfrac{(x^2 - 2x)^6}{12}$, $f'(x) = \dfrac{6}{12}(x^2 - 2x)^5(2x - 2)$

$$= \frac{6(x^2 - 2x)^5(2)(x - 1)}{12}$$

$$= (x^2 - 2x)^5(x - 1) \quad \large\checkmark$$

EXAMPLE 14

Evaluate $\int (x^4 - 2x^2)^4(4x^2 - 4) \, dx$.

SOLUTION

For this integral

$$f(x) = x^4 - 2x^2 \qquad \text{and} \qquad f'(x) = 4x^3 - 4x$$

The integrand is not quite in the form of Rule 7. And, there is great temptation to perform the following operations.

$$\int (x^4 - 2x^2)^4(4x^2 - 4) \, dx = \frac{x}{x} \int (x^4 - 2x^2)^4(4x^2 - 4) \, dx$$

$$= \frac{1}{x} \int (x^4 - 2x^2)^4(4x^3 - 4x) \, dx$$

However, we have not discussed any property which allows us to factor *variables* through an integral sign. Constants yes; variables no! Therefore, given our current rules, we cannot evaluate the integral.

RULE 8

$$\int f'(x)e^{f(x)}\, dx = e^{f(x)} + C$$

This rule, as with the previous rule, requires that the integrand be in a very specific form. Rule 6 is actually the special case of this rule when $f(x) = x$.

EXAMPLE 15

Evaluate $\int 2xe^{x^2}\, dx$.

SOLUTION

When an integrand is identified which contains e raised to a power that is a function of x, you should immediately think of Rule 8. As with Rule 7, the next step is to see if the integrand has the form required to apply Rule 8. For this integrand

$$f(x) = x^2 \qquad \text{and} \qquad f'(x) = 2x$$

Refer to Rule 8: the integrand has the appropriate form, and

$$\int \overbrace{2x}^{f'(x)}\ \overbrace{e^{x^2}}^{f(x)}\, dx = e^{x^2} + C$$

Check If $f(x) = e^{x^2}$, $f'(x) = e^{x^2}(2x)$ ✔

EXAMPLE 16

Evaluate $\int x^2 e^{3x^3}\, dx$.

SOLUTION

Referring to Rule 8, for this integrand we have

$$f(x) = 3x^3 \qquad \text{and} \qquad f'(x) = 9x^2$$

The integrand is currently not in a form which is suitable for using Rule 8. However,

$$\int x^2 e^{3x^3}\, dx = \frac{9}{9} \int x^2 e^{3x^3}\, dx$$

$$= \frac{1}{9} \int 9x^2 e^{3x^3}\, dx$$

$$= \frac{1}{9} e^{3x^3} + C$$

Check If $f(x) = \frac{1}{9}e^{3x^3} + C$, $f'(x) = \frac{1}{9}e^{3x^3}(9x^2) = x^2 e^{3x^3}$ ✔

RULE 9

$$\int \frac{f'(x)}{f(x)}\, dx = \ln f(x) + C$$

EXAMPLE 17

Evaluate $\displaystyle\int \frac{6x}{3x^2 - 10}\, dx$.

SOLUTION

Referring to Rule 9, we have

$$f(x) = 3x^2 - 10 \quad\text{and}\quad f'(x) = 6x$$

Since the integrand has the form required by Rule 9,

$$\int \frac{6x\, dx}{3x^2 - 10} = \ln(3x^2 - 10) + C$$

Check If $f(x) = \ln(3x^2 - 10) + C$, $f'(x) = \dfrac{6x}{3x^2 - 10}$ ✔

EXAMPLE 18

Evaluate $\displaystyle\int \frac{x - 1}{4x^2 - 8x + 10}\, dx$.

SOLUTION

Referring to Rule 9, we have

$$f(x) = 4x^2 - 8x + 10 \quad\text{and}\quad f'(x) = 8x - 8$$

At first glance, the form of the integrand does not seem to comply with that required by Rule 9. However, an algebraic manipulation allows us to rewrite the integrand in the required form, or

$$\int \frac{x - 1}{4x^2 - 8x + 10}\, dx = \frac{8}{8}\int \frac{x - 1}{4x^2 - 8x + 10}\, dx$$

$$= \frac{1}{8}\int \frac{8(x - 1)}{4x^2 - 8x + 10}\, dx$$

$$= \frac{1}{8}\int \frac{8x - 8}{4x^2 - 8x + 10}\, dx$$

$$= \frac{1}{8}\ln(4x^2 - 8x + 10) + C$$

Check If $f(x) = \frac{1}{8}\ln(4x^2 - 8x + 10) + C$,

$$f'(x) = \frac{1}{8}\left[\frac{8x - 8}{4x^2 - 8x + 10}\right] = \frac{x - 1}{4x^2 - 8x + 10} \quad ✔$$

Section 16.3 Follow-up Exercises

In the following exercises, find the indefinite integral (if possible).

1 $\displaystyle\int (x + 25)^4\, dx$

2 $\displaystyle\int \sqrt{x - 15}\, dx$

3 $\displaystyle\int (x^2 - 8)^5(2x)\, dx$

4 $\displaystyle\int (x^3 - 10)^3(3x^2)\, dx$

5 $\displaystyle\int (4x^3 - 10)^3(x^2)\, dx$

6 $\displaystyle\int (x^2 - 5)^{3/2}(x)\, dx$

7 $\displaystyle\int (2x^2 - 4x)^4(x - 1)\, dx$

8 $\displaystyle\int (x^2/4 - x/2)^5(x - 1)\, dx$

9 $\displaystyle\int \frac{2x}{\sqrt{x^2 - 1}}\, dx$

10 $\displaystyle\int \frac{x^2}{(x^3 - 15)^3}\, dx$

11 $\displaystyle\int (4x^3 - 3x^2)^5(x)\, dx$

12 $\displaystyle\int x^3\sqrt{x^2 - 1}\, dx$

13 $\displaystyle\int e^{x^3}\, dx$

14 $\displaystyle\int e^{x-1}\, dx$

15 $\displaystyle\int e^{2x}\, dx$

16 $\displaystyle\int 2x e^{x^2}\, dx$

17 $\displaystyle\int e^{ax}\, dx$

18 $\displaystyle\int (x - 2)e^{x^2 - 4x}\, dx$

19 $\displaystyle\int \frac{x}{x^2 - 5}\, dx$

20 $\displaystyle\int \frac{-2x}{100 - x^2}\, dx$

21 $\displaystyle\int \frac{12}{6x - 5}\, dx$

22 $\displaystyle\int \frac{x^3 - 1}{x^4 - 4x}\, dx$

23 $\displaystyle\int \frac{dx}{ax + b}$

24 $\displaystyle\int \frac{ax - 1}{ax^2 - 2x}\, dx$

16.4 DIFFERENTIAL EQUATIONS

A *differential equation* is an equation which involves derivatives and/or differentials.* In Sec. 16.1 we examined differential equations (without calling them by that name) when going from a derivative f' to the corresponding antiderivative f. We *solved* the differential equation when we found the antiderivative. In this section we will expand upon this topic using the rules of integration to assist in the solution process.

Classifications of Differential Equations

Again, a differential equation is an equation which includes derivatives of one or more functions. If a differential equation involves derivatives of a function of one independent variable, it is called an *ordinary differential equation.* The following equation is an example, where the independent variable is x.

$$\frac{dy}{dx} = 5x - 2 \qquad (16.9)$$

If a differential equation includes partial derivatives of functions of two or more independent variables, it is called a *partial differential equation.* The following equation is an example of a partial differential equation.

$$\frac{\partial^2 z}{\partial x^2} + \frac{\partial z}{\partial x} + 2x - y = 0 \qquad (16.10)$$

---

* We have regularly used notation such as dy/dx. Separately, dy and dx are called *differentials,* reflecting instantaneous changes in y and x, respectively.

This equation also could be written alternatively using the notation of Chap. 15 as

$$f_{xx} + f_x + 2x - y = 0 \qquad \textbf{(16.11)}$$

Differential equations are also classified by their *order,* which is the order of the highest-order derivative appearing in the equation. Equation (16.9) is a first-order, ordinary differential equation. Equation (16.10) is a second-order, partial differential equation.

Another way of classifying differential equations is by their *degree.* The degree is the *power* of the highest-order derivative in the differential equation. Each of the previous differential equations is of *first degree.* Equation (16.12) is an ordinary differential equation of first order and second degree.

$$\left(\frac{dy}{dx}\right)^2 - 10 = y \qquad \textbf{(16.12)}$$

EXAMPLE 19

Classify each of the following differential equations, by type, order, and degree.
(a) $dy/dx = x^2 - 2x + 1$
(b) $d^2y/dx^2 - (dy/dx) = x$
(c) $d^2y/dx^2 - (dy/dx)^3 + 2x = 0$
(d) $\partial z/\partial x - \partial z/\partial y = 0$
(e) $\partial^2 z/\partial x^2 + (\partial z/\partial x)^2 - \partial^2 z/\partial y^2 = 0$

SOLUTION

(a) This is an ordinary differential equation of first order and first degree.
(b) This is an ordinary differential equation of second order and first degree.
(c) This is an ordinary differential equation of second order and first degree (dy/dx is not the highest-order derivative).
(d) This is a partial differential equation of first order and first degree.
(e) This is a partial differential equation of second order and first degree.

Solutions of Ordinary Differential Equations

In this section we will focus on the solutions to ordinary differential equations. A solution to a differential equation is a function not containing derivatives or differentials which satisfies the original differential equation.

Solutions to differential equations can be classified into *general solutions* and *particular solutions.* A general solution is one which contains arbitrary constants of integration. A particular solution is one which is obtained from the general solution. For particular solutions specific values are assigned to the constants of integration based on *initial conditions* or *boundary conditions.*

Consider the differential equation

$$\frac{dy}{dx} = 3x^2 - 2x + 5$$

The *general solution* to this differential equation is found by integrating the equation, or

$$y = f(x) = \frac{3x^3}{3} - \frac{2x^2}{2} + 5x + C$$

$$= x^3 - x^2 + 5x + C$$

Given the *initial condition* that $f(0) = 15$, the *particular solution* is derived by substituting these values into the general solution and solving for C.

$$15 = 0^3 - 0^2 + 50 + C$$

or $\qquad 15 = C$

The particular solution to the differential equation is

$$f(x) = x^3 - x^2 + 5x + 15$$

EXAMPLE 20

Given the differential equation

$$f''(x) = \frac{d^2y}{dx^2} = x - 5 \qquad (16.13)$$

and the *boundary conditions* $f'(2) = 4$ and $f(0) = 10$, determine the general solution and particular solution.

SOLUTION

The given equation is an ordinary differential equation of *second* order and *first* degree. If the equation is integrated, the result is

$$f'(x) = \frac{dy}{dx} = \frac{x^2}{2} - 5x + C_1 \qquad (16.14)$$

which is also a differential equation because it contains the derivative dy/dx. Thus, to rid the equation of any derivatives we must integrate Eq. (16.14).

$$f(x) = y = \frac{x^3}{6} - \frac{5x^2}{2} + C_1 x + C_2 \qquad (16.15)$$

Equation (16.15) is the *general* solution to the original differential equation. Notice the use of subscripts on the constants of integration to distinguish them from one another.

NOTE

The general solution of an *n*th-order differential equation will contain *n* constants of integration

To obtain the particular solution, the boundary conditions must be substituted into Eqs. (16.14) and (16.15). Starting with Eq. (16.14) and the condition that $f'(2) = 4$,

$$4 = \frac{(2)^2}{2} - 5(2) + C_1$$

$$4 = -8 + C_1$$

and

$$12 = C_1$$

If this value is substituted into Eq. (16.15), along with the other boundary condition information $f(0) = 10$,

$$10 = \frac{0^3}{6} - \frac{5(0)^2}{2} + 12(0) + C_2$$

or

$$10 = C_2$$

Therefore the particular solution is

$$f(x) = \frac{x^3}{6} - \frac{5x^2}{2} + 12x + 10$$

In Chap. 14 exponential growth and exponential decay functions were discussed. Exponential growth functions have the general form

$$\boxed{V = V_0 e^{kt}} \tag{16.16}$$

where V_0 equals the value of the function when $t = 0$ and k is a positive constant. It was demonstrated in Example 14 of that chapter (page 565) that these functions are characterized by a constant percentage rate of growth k, and

$$\frac{dV}{dt} = kV_0 e^{kt}$$

or

$$\boxed{\frac{dV}{dt} = kV} \tag{16.17}$$

Equation (16.17) is a differential equation; the general solution to Eq. (16.17) is expressed by Eq. (16.16), where V_0 and k are constants.

Empirical research frequently involves observations of a process (e.g., bacteria growth, population growth or decay, and radioactivity decay) over time. The gathered data often reflect values of the function at different points in time and measures of *rates of change* in the value of the function. It is from these types of data that the actual functional relationship can be derived. Stated more simply, research frequently results in differential equations which describe, partially, the relationships among variables. The solution to these differential equations results in a complete description of the functional relationships.

EXAMPLE 21

Species Growth The population of a rare species of fish is believed to be growing exponentially. When first identified and classified the population was estimated at 50,000. Five years later the population was estimated to equal 75,000. *If P equals the population of this species at time t, where t is measured in years,* the population growth occurs at a rate described by the differential equation

$$\frac{dP}{dt} = kP = kP_0 e^{kt}$$

Integrating this equation,

$$\int \frac{dP}{dt} = \int kP_0 e^{kt}$$

$$= P_0 \int k e^{kt}$$

Or the general solution is

$$P = P_0 e^{kt}$$

where P_0 and k are constants. To determine the specific value of P_0 we utilize the initial condition which states that $P = 50{,}000$ when $t = 0$,

$$50{,}000 = P_0 e^{k(0)}$$
or
$$50{,}000 = P_0$$

The value of k can be found by substituting the boundary condition ($P = 75{,}000$ when $t = 5$) along with the $P_0 = 50{,}000$ into the general solution.

$$75{,}000 = 50{,}000\ e^{k(5)}$$
$$1.5 = e^{5k}$$

If the natural logarithm of both sides of the equation is found,

$$\ln 1.5 = 5k$$

From Table 2 (inside the back cover)

$$\ln 1.5 = 0.4055$$
$$0.4055 = 5k$$
and
$$0.0811 = k$$

Thus, the particular function describing the growth function is

$$P = 50{,}000\ e^{0.0811t}$$

An exponential decay process is characterized by a constant percent decrease in value over time. The general function describing these functions is

$$\boxed{V = V_0 e^{-kt}} \tag{16.18}$$

where V equals the value of the function at time t, V_0 equals the value of the function at $t = 0$, and k is the percentage rate of decay. The rate of change in the value of the function with respect to a change in time is

$$\frac{dV}{dt} = -kV_0 e^{-kt}$$

or
$$\boxed{\frac{dV}{dt} = -kV} \tag{16.19}$$

Equation (16.19) is a differential equation for which the general solution is Eq. (16.18).

EXAMPLE 22

Drug Absorption   A particular prescription drug was administered to a person in a dosage of 100 milligrams. The amount of the drug contained in the bloodstream diminishes over time as described by an exponential decay function. After 6 hours, a blood sample reveals that the amount in the system is 40 milligrams. If V equals the amount of the drug in the bloodstream after t hours and V_0 equals the amount in the bloodstream at $t = 0$, the decay occurs at a rate described by the function

$$\frac{dV}{dt} = -kV = -kV_0e^{-kt}$$

The general solution to this differential equation is

$$V = V_0e^{-kt}$$

If the initial condition ($V = 100$ at $t = 0$) is substituted into this equation, V_0 is identified as 100 and

$$V = 100e^{-kt}$$

Substituting the boundary condition ($V = 40$ when $t = 6$)

$$40 = 100e^{-k(6)}$$

or

$$0.4 = e^{-6k}$$

Taking the natural logarithm of both sides of the equation,

$$\ln(0.4) = -6k$$

From Table 2,

$$\ln(0.4) = -0.9163$$

and

$$-0.9163 = -6k$$

$$0.1527 = k$$

Thus, the particular function describing the drug level decay function is

$$V = 100e^{-0.1527t}$$

Extension of Differential Equations

This discussion has revealed the "tip of the iceberg" regarding the topic of differential equations. We have examined only the simplest of cases. This topic frequently is the focus of an entire one-term course. The objective for us has been to introduce this topic and relate it to integral calculus.

Section 16.4 Follow-up Exercises

In Exercises 1 to 8, classify each differential equation by type, order, and degree.

1 $dy/dx = x^3 - 2x^2 + 5x$

2 $dy/dx - d^2y/dx^2 = x + 5$

3 $(d^2y/dx^2)^3 = x^3 - dy/dx$

4 $d^2y/dx^2 = (dy/dx)^4 - x^3$

5 $5(\partial z/\partial x) - 2(\partial z/\partial y) = 10$

6 $\partial^2 z/\partial x^2 - \partial z/\partial x = \partial^2 z/\partial y^2$

7 $\partial^2 z/\partial x^2 + 3(\partial z/\partial x)^3 = x^2 - 5x$

8 $3(\partial^2 z/\partial x^2)^2 + 6(\partial z/\partial x)^3 = 2x^3 - 4$

In Exercises 9 to 18, find the general solution for the differential equation.

9 $dy/dx = x^4 - 2x + 5$
10 $dy/dx = 3x^2 - 6x - 10$
11 $dy/dx = 1/x$
12 $dy/dx = (2x)(x^2 - 5)^4$
13 $dy/dx = x/(5x^2 - 10)$
14 $dy/dx = 6xe^{3x^2}$
15 $d^2y/dx^2 = x - 3$
16 $6x = 24x^2 + d^2y/dx^2$
17 $2(d^2y/dx^2) + x^3 = d^2y/dx^2 + 2x - 16$
18 $d^2y/dx^2 = e^x$

In Exercises 19 to 26, find the general and particular solutions for the differential equation.

19 $dy/dx = x, f(0) = -5$
20 $dy/dx = 3x^2 - 2x + 5, f(0) = 10$
21 $dy/dx = x^2 - 2x + 3, f(1) = 2.5$
22 $dy/dx = (6x)(3x^2 - 1), f(1) = 20$
23 $d^2y/dx^2 = 6x - 18; f'(3) = -10, f(2) = 50$
24 $d^2y/dx^2 = 15; f'(1) = 20, f(2) = -10$
25 $d^2y/dx^2 = 25e^{5x}; f'(0) = 4, f(0) = -2$
26 $5 - d^2y/dx^2 = 24x; f'(0) = -2, f(-1) = 8$

27 The population of a newly discovered species of rabbit appears to be growing exponentially. When first identified in a South American country the population was estimated at 500. Two years later the population was estimated to equal 1,250. Determine the exponential growth function which describes the population P as a function of time t, measured in years since the discovery of the species.

28 The population of an endangered species of Alaskan elk appears to be declining at an exponential rate. When the decline was first suspected the elk population was estimated to equal 2,500. Ten years later the population was estimated to equal 1,500. Determine the exponential decay function which describes the elk population as a function of time t, measured in years since the decline was first suspected.

16.5 OTHER TECHNIQUES OF INTEGRATION (OPTIONAL)

The nine integration rules presented in Secs. 16.2 and 16.3 apply only to a subset of the functions which might be integrated. This subset includes some of the more common functions used in business and economics applications. A natural question is, What happens when our rules do not apply? This section discusses two techniques which can be employed when the other rules do not apply and when the structure of the integrand is of an appropriate form. We will also discuss the use of special tables of integration formulas.

Integration by Parts

Recall the product rule of differentiation from Chap. 12. This rule stated that if

$$f(x) = u(x)v(x)$$

then

$$f'(x) = v(x)u'(x) + u(x)v'(x)$$

We can write this rule in a slightly different form as

$$\frac{d}{dx}[u(x)v(x)] = v(x)u'(x) + u(x)v'(x)$$

If we integrate both sides of this equation, the result is

$$u(x)v(x) = \int v(x)u'(x)\, dx + \int u(x)v'(x)\, dx$$

And, rewriting this equation, we get the *integration-by-parts formula.*

INTEGRATION-BY-PARTS FORMULA

$$\int u(x)v'(x)\, dx = u(x)v(x) - \int v(x)u'(x)\, dx \quad \text{(16.20)}$$

This equation expresses a relationship which can be used to determine integrals where the integrand has the form $u(x)v'(x)$.

The integration-by-parts procedure is a trial-and-error method which may or may not be successful for a given integrand. If the integrand is in the form of a product and the other integration rules do not apply, the following procedure can be attempted.

TRIAL-AND-ERROR INTEGRATION-BY-PARTS PROCEDURES

I Define two functions u and v and determine whether the integrand has the form $u(x)v'(x)$.

II If two functions are found such that $u(x)v'(x)$ equals the integrand, attempt to find the integral by evaluating the right side of Eq. (16.20). The key is whether you can evaluate $\int v(x)u'(x)\, dx$.

The following examples illustrate the approach.

EXAMPLE 23

Determine $\int xe^x\, dx$.

SOLUTION

Our first observation should be that the integrand is in a product form. The temptation is to try to use Rule 8, which applies for integrals of the form $\int f'(x)e^{f(x)}\, dx$. With the exponent $f(x)$ defined as x, $f'(x) = 1$ and the integrand is not in an appropriate form to apply Rule 8.

Let's try to define two functions u and v such that the integrand has the form $u(x)v'(x)$.

NOTE

A hint is to examine the factors of the integrand to determine if one of them has the form of the derivative of another function.

Let's define v' as equaling x and u as equaling e^x so that the integrand has the form

$$\int \overbrace{x}^{v'(x)}\,\overbrace{e^x}^{u(x)}\, dx$$

With these definitions we can determine v by integrating v' and u' by differentiating u, or

$$v'(x) = x \text{ suggests that } v(x) = \frac{x^2}{2}$$

and
$$u(x) = e^x \text{ suggests that } u'(x) = e^x$$

With u, v, and their derivatives defined, we substitute into Eq. (16.20):

$$\int \overbrace{xe^x}^{u(x)v'(x)} dx = \overbrace{e^x \frac{x^2}{2}}^{u(x)\ v(x)} - \int \overbrace{\frac{x^2}{2} e^x}^{v(x)u'(x)} dx$$

An examination of $\int (x^2/2)e^x\, dx$ suggests that this integral may be as difficult to evaluate as the original integral.

So, let's backtrack and start again. Let's redefine v' and u such that $v'(x) = e^x$ and $u(x) = x$:

$$\int \frac{u(x)}{x}\ \frac{v'(x)}{e^x}\, dx$$

Given these definitions,

$$u(x) = x \text{ suggests that } u'(x) = 1$$
$$v'(x) = e^x \text{ suggests that } v(x) = e^x$$

Substituting into Eq. (16.20) yields

$$\int \overbrace{xe^x}^{u(x)v'(x)} dx = \overbrace{xe^x}^{u(x)v(x)} - \int \overbrace{e^x(1)}^{v(x)u'(x)} dx$$

$$= xe^x - \int e^x\, dx$$

Because $\int e^x\, dx = e^x$,

$$\int xe^x\, dx = xe^x - e^x + C$$

Check Differentiating this answer as a check, we find

$$\frac{d}{dx}[xe^x - e^x + C] = (1)e^x + e^x x - e^x$$

$$= xe^x \ ✔$$

EXAMPLE 24

Determine $\int x^2 \ln x\, dx$.

SOLUTION

If we let $u(x) = \ln x$ and $v'(x) = x^2$, then

$$u'(x) = \frac{1}{x} \quad \text{and} \quad v(x) = \int x^2\, dx = \frac{x^3}{3}$$

Substituting into Eq. (16.20) gives

$$\int x^2 \ln x \, dx = (\ln x) \left(\frac{x^3}{3}\right) - \int \frac{x^3}{3} \frac{1}{x} \, dx$$

$$= \frac{x^3}{3} \ln x - \int \frac{x^2}{3} \, dx$$

$$= \frac{x^3}{3} \ln x - \frac{x^3}{9} + C$$

Check   Checking this answer by differentiating, we get

$$\frac{d}{dx}\left[\frac{x^3}{3} \ln x - \frac{x^3}{9} + C\right] = \frac{3x^2}{3} \ln x + \frac{1}{x} \frac{x^3}{3} - \frac{3x^2}{9}$$

$$= x^2 \ln x + \frac{x^2}{3} - \frac{x^2}{3}$$

$$= x^2 \ln x \quad \text{✔}$$

EXAMPLE 25

Determine $\int \ln x \, dx$.

SOLUTION

Although the integrand is not in the form of a product, we can imagine it to have the form

$$\int \ln x(1) \, dx$$

Letting $u(x) = \ln x$ and $v'(x) = 1$, we have

$$u'(x) = \frac{1}{x}$$

and

$$v(x) = \int 1 \, dx$$

$$= x$$

Substituting into Eq. (16.20) yields

$$\int \ln x \, dx = (\ln x)(x) - \int x \frac{1}{x} \, dx$$

$$= x \ln x - \int dx$$

$$= x \ln x - x + C$$

Check   This answer can be checked by differentiating, or

$$\frac{d}{dx}[x \ln x - x + C] = (1) \ln x + \frac{1}{x} x - 1$$

$$= \ln x + 1 - 1$$

$$= \ln x \quad \text{✔}$$

Integration by parts is often time-consuming, given the trial-and-error approach required. You are again reminded to first examine the integrand carefully to determine whether our other rules apply before you try this procedure.

Integration by Partial Fractions

Rational functions have the form of a quotient of two polynomials. Many rational functions exist which cannot be integrated by the rules (specifically, Rule 9) presented earlier. When this occurs, one possibility is that the rational function can be restated in an equivalent form consisting of more elementary functions. The following example illustrates the decomposition of a rational function into equivalent *partial fractions.*

$$f(x) = \frac{x + 3}{x^2 + 3x + 2} = \frac{2}{x + 1} - \frac{1}{x + 2}$$

Verify that the rational function

$$f(x) = \frac{x + 3}{x^2 + 3x + 2}$$

cannot be integrated using Rule 9. However, the equivalent partial fractions can be integrated. Thus,

$$\int \frac{x + 3}{x^2 + 3x + 2} \, dx = \int \frac{2}{x + 1} \, dx - \int \frac{dx}{x + 2}$$

$$= 2 \ln (x + 1) - \ln (x + 2) + C$$

$$= \ln \left[\frac{(x + 1)^2}{(x + 2)} \right] + C$$

This technique for integrating rational functions is called the *method of partial fractions.*

Let's discuss the process of decomposing a rational function into equivalent partial fractions. To apply the method of partial fractions, the rational function must have the form of a *proper fraction.* A rational function is a proper fraction if the degree of the numerator polynomial is lower than the degree of the denominator polynomial.

ALGEBRA FLASHBACK

The degree of a term is the sum of the exponents on the variables contained in the term. For example, the degree of $5x^2yz^3$ is 6. The degree of a polynomial is the degree of the term of highest degree in the polynomial. For example, the degree of the polynomial

$$2x^3 - 4x^2 + x - 10$$

is 3.

The rational function $f(x) = x^2/(5x^3 - 2x + 1)$ is in the form of a proper fraction. In an *improper fraction,* the degree of the numerator polynomial is the same or higher than that for the denominator polynomial. The rational function

$f(x) = x^3/(3x^2 - 10)$ is in the form of an improper fraction. Improper fractions can be reduced to the algebraic sum of a polynomial and a proper fraction by performing long division of the numerator and denominator functions. To illustrate, the improper fraction

$$\frac{x^3 - 2x}{x - 1}$$

can be divided as follows:

$$
\begin{array}{r}
x^2 + x - 1 \\
x - 1 \overline{\smash{)}\,x^3 - 2x} \\
\underline{x^3 - x^2} \\
x^2 - 2x \\
\underline{x^2 - x} \\
-x \\
-x + 1 \\
\underline{-1}
\end{array}
$$

Thus, long division results in

$$\frac{x^3 - 2x}{x - 1} = x^2 + x - 1 + \frac{-1}{x - 1}$$

If our objective is to integrate

$$f(x) = \frac{x^3 - 2x}{x - 1}$$

we could do so as follows:

$$\int \frac{x^3 - 2x}{x - 1}\, dx = \int \left(x^2 + x - 1 + \frac{-1}{x - 1} \right) dx$$

$$= \int (x^2 + x - 1)\, dx - \int \frac{dx}{x - 1}$$

$$= \frac{x^3}{3} + \frac{x^2}{2} - x - \ln (x - 1) + C$$

Given a proper fraction, the decomposition into equivalent partial fractions requires that the denominator be factored. In general, for each factor of the denominator there is a corresponding partial fraction. The form of each factor determines the form of the equivalent partial fraction. Table 16.1 summarizes some of the possibilities.

TABLE 16.1

	FORM OF FACTOR	FORM OF THE CORRESPONDING PARTIAL FRACTION
1	Unique linear factor $ax + b$	$\dfrac{A}{ax + b}$, A constant
2	Repeated linear factor $(ax + b)^n$	$\dfrac{A_1}{ax + b} + \dfrac{A_2}{(ax + b)^2} + \cdots + \dfrac{A_n}{(ax + b)^n}$
3	Unique quadratic factor $ax^2 + bx + c$	$\dfrac{Ax + B}{ax^2 + bx + c}$, A and B constants

EXAMPLE 26 ████████████████████████████████████

Earlier we stated that

$$f(x) = \frac{x + 3}{x^2 + 3x + 2} = \frac{2}{x + 1} - \frac{1}{x + 2}$$

Let's derive these partial fractions. The first step is to try and factor the denominator of f. Because

$$x^2 + 3x + 2 = (x + 1)(x + 2)$$

the denominator can be factored into two *linear* factors. According to Table 16.1, the decomposition of f should result in *two* (one for each factor) partial fractions, or

$$\frac{x + 3}{(x + 1)(x + 2)} = \frac{A_1}{x + 1} + \frac{A_2}{x + 2} \qquad \text{(16.21)}$$

To solve for the constants A_1 and A_2, the two fractions on the right side of Eq. (16.21) are combined over the common denominator $(x + 1)(x + 2)$ yielding

$$\frac{x + 3}{(x + 1)(x + 2)} = \frac{A_1(x + 2) + A_2(x + 1)}{(x + 1)(x + 2)}$$

or

$$\frac{x + 3}{(x + 1)(x + 2)} = \frac{(A_1 + A_2)x + 2A_1 + A_2}{(x + 1)(x + 2)}$$

For the two sides of this equation to be equal, A_1 and A_2 must be such that

$$A_1 + A_2 = 1$$

and

$$2A_1 + A_2 = 3$$

Solving these equations, $A_1 = 2$ and $A_2 = -1$. If these values are substituted into Eq. (16.21), the result is

$$\frac{x + 3}{(x + 1)(x + 2)} = \frac{2}{x + 1} - \frac{1}{x + 2}$$

which is the result shown earlier.

EXAMPLE 27 ████████████████████████████████████

Using the method of partial fractions, find the indefinite integral

$$\int \frac{5x + 8}{x^2 + 4x + 4} \, dx$$

SOLUTION

The first step is to verify that Rules 7 and 9 do not apply. Once convinced of this, we attempt to factor the denominator. Because

$$x^2 + 4x + 4 = (x + 2)^2$$

Table 16.1 indicates that the integrand can be decomposed into the general partial fractions

$$\frac{5x + 8}{(x + 2)^2} = \frac{A_1}{x + 2} + \frac{A_2}{(x + 2)^2} \qquad \text{(16.22)}$$

To solve for A_1 and A_2, the two partial fractions on the right side of Eq. (16.22) are combined over the common denominator $(x + 2)^2$, yielding

$$\frac{5x + 8}{(x + 2)^2} = \frac{A_1(x + 2) + A_2}{(x + 2)^2}$$

or

$$\frac{5x + 8}{(x + 2)^2} = \frac{A_1x + 2A_1 + A_2}{(x + 2)^2}$$

For the two sides of this equation to be equal, A_1 and A_2 must be chosen such that

$$A_1 = 5$$

and

$$2A_1 + A_2 = 8$$

Since $A_1 = 5$,

$$2(5) + A_2 = 8$$
$$A_2 = -2$$

Substituting these values into Eq. (16.22)

$$\frac{5x + 8}{(x + 2)^2} = \frac{5}{x + 2} - \frac{2}{(x + 2)^2}$$

Therefore

$$\int \frac{5x + 8}{(x + 2)^2} \, dx = \int \frac{5}{x + 2} \, dx - \int \frac{2}{(x + 2)^2} \, dx$$

$$= 5 \int \frac{dx}{x + 2} - 2 \int (x + 2)^{-2} \, dx$$

$$= 5 \ln (x + 2) - 2 \frac{(x + 2)^{-1}}{-1} + C$$

$$= 5 \ln (x + 2) + \frac{2}{(x + 2)} + C$$

EXAMPLE 28

Using the method of partial fractions, find the indefinite integral

$$\int \frac{2x^2 - 1}{x^3 + x^2} \, dx$$

SOLUTION

The first step is to verify that Rule 9 does not apply for this integrand. Once convinced of this, we attempt to factor the denominator. Because

$$x^3 + x^2 = x^2(x + 1)$$

we conclude that it has two factors: the quadratic factor x^2 and the linear factor $(x + 1)$. According to Table 16.1 the integrand can be decomposed into the general partial fractions

$$\frac{2x^2 - 1}{x^2(x + 1)} = \frac{A_1x + B_1}{x^2} + \frac{A_2}{x + 1} \qquad \textbf{(16.23)}$$

To solve for the constants A_1, B_1, and A_2, the two partial fractions on the right side of Eq. (16.23) are combined over the common denominator $x^2(x + 1)$, yielding

$$\frac{2x^2 - 1}{x^2(x + 1)} = \frac{(A_1 x + B_1)(x + 1) + A_2 x^2}{x^2(x + 1)}$$

$$= \frac{A_1 x^2 + A_1 x + B_1 x + B_1 + A_2 x^2}{x^2(x + 1)}$$

or

$$\frac{2x^2 - 1}{x^2(x + 1)} = \frac{(A_1 + A_2)x^2 + (A_1 + B_1)x + B_1}{x^2(x + 1)}$$

For the two sides of this equation to be equal, A_1, A_2, and B_1 must be such that

$$A_1 + A_2 = 2$$
$$A_1 + B_1 = 0$$

and

$$B_1 = -1$$

Substituting the value $B_1 = -1$ into the second equation yields $A_1 = 1$. And, substituting this value into the first equation results in $A_2 = 1$.

Therefore,

$$\frac{2x^2 - 1}{x^2(x + 1)} = \frac{x - 1}{x^2} + \frac{1}{x + 1}$$

and

$$\int \frac{2x^2 - 1}{x^3 + x^2} \, dx = \int \frac{x - 1}{x^2} \, dx + \int \frac{dx}{x + 1}$$

Although the integrand of the first partial fraction is not in an appropriate form to apply Rule 9,

$$\frac{x - 1}{x^2} = \frac{x}{x^2} - \frac{1}{x^2}$$

$$= \frac{1}{x} - \frac{1}{x^2}$$

Therefore,

$$\int \frac{(2x^2 - 1)}{x^3 + x^2} \, dx = \int \frac{dx}{x} - \int \frac{dx}{x^2} + \int \frac{dx}{x + 1}$$

$$= \ln x + \frac{1}{x} + \ln (x + 1) + C$$

Tables of Integrals

For cases where our rules and other procedures are inadequate for determining indefinite integrals, special tables of integrals are available which may contain literally hundreds of integration formulas. Each formula applies to an integrand which has a particular functional form. To use the tables, you match the form of your integrand with the corresponding general form in the table. Once the appropriate formula has been identified, the indefinite integral follows directly from the formula.

Table 16.2 illustrates some sample integration formulas for natural logarithms and exponential forms of an integrand.

TABLE 16.2

1 $\displaystyle\int \ln x \, dx = x \ln x - x + C$

2 $\displaystyle\int x \ln x \, dx = \frac{x^2}{2} \ln x - \frac{x^2}{4} + C$

3 $\displaystyle\int x^2 \ln x \, dx = \frac{x^3}{3} \ln x - \frac{x^3}{9} + C$

4 $\displaystyle\int x^n \ln ax \, dx = \frac{x^{n+1}}{n+1} \ln ax - \frac{x^{n+1}}{(n+1)^2} + C \qquad n \neq -1$

5 $\displaystyle\int (\ln x)^2 \, dx = x(\ln x)^2 - 2x \ln x + 2x + C$

6 $\displaystyle\int (\ln x)^n \, dx = x(\ln x)^n - n \int (\ln x)^{n-1} \, dx + C \qquad n \neq -1$

7 $\displaystyle\int \frac{(\ln x)^n}{x} \, dx = \frac{1}{n+1} (\ln x)^{n+1} + C \qquad n \neq -1$

8 $\displaystyle\int x^n \ln x \, dx = x^{n+1} \left[\frac{\ln x}{n+1} - \frac{1}{(n+1)^2} \right] + C \qquad n \neq -1$

9 $\displaystyle\int e^{-x} \, dx = -e^{-x} + C$

10 $\displaystyle\int e^{ax} \, dx = \frac{e^{ax}}{a} + C$

11 $\displaystyle\int xe^{ax} \, dx = \frac{e^{ax}}{a^2} (ax - 1) + C$

12 $\displaystyle\int \frac{dx}{1 + e^x} = x - \ln (1 + e^x) = \ln \frac{e^x}{1 + e^x} + C$

13 $\displaystyle\int \frac{dx}{a + be^{px}} = \frac{x}{a} - \frac{1}{ap} \ln (a + be^{px}) + C$

EXAMPLE 29

According to formula (4) in Table 16.2.

$$\int x^3 \ln 5x \, dx = \frac{x^{3+1}}{3+1} \ln 5x - \frac{x^{3+1}}{(3+1)^2} + C$$

$$= \frac{x^4}{4} \ln 5x - \frac{x^4}{16} + C$$

We can check this result, as before, by differentiating.

$$\frac{d}{dx} \left(\frac{x^4}{4} \ln 5x - \frac{x^4}{16} + C \right) = \left(\frac{4x^3}{4} \ln 5x + \frac{1}{x} \frac{x^4}{4} \right) - \frac{4x^3}{16}$$

$$= x^3 \ln 5x + \frac{x^3}{4} - \frac{x^3}{4}$$

$$= x^3 \ln 5x$$

which was the original integrand.

EXAMPLE 30

According to formula (7),

$$\int \frac{(\ln x)^5}{x} \, dx = \frac{1}{5 + 1} (\ln x)^{5+1} + C$$

$$= \frac{(\ln x)^6}{6} + C$$

To check this result,

$$\frac{d}{dx} \left[\frac{(\ln x)^6}{6} + C \right] = \frac{1}{6} [6(\ln x)^5] \frac{1}{x}$$

$$= \frac{(\ln x)^5}{x}$$

which was the original integrand.

EXAMPLE 31

According to formula (10),

$$\int e^{-5x} \, dx = \frac{e^{-5x}}{-5} + C$$

To check this result,

$$\frac{d}{dx} \left(\frac{e^{-5x}}{-5} + C \right) = -\frac{1}{5} (-5) e^{-5x}$$

$$= e^{-5x}$$

Section 16.5 Follow-up Exercises

In Exercises 1 to 14 determine the indefinite integral (if possible) using integration by parts.

1 $\int x e^{-x} \, dx$

2 $\int 5x e^x \, dx$

3 $\int x \sqrt[3]{x + 1} \, dx$

4 $\int x \sqrt{x + 1} \, dx$

5 $\int x e^{2x} \, dx$

6 $\int x e^{-2x} \, dx$

7 $\int (x + 4) \ln x \, dx$

8 $\int x^2 \ln 5x \, dx$

9 $\int x(x + 2)^4 \, dx$

10 $\int x(x - 4)^5 \, dx$

11 $\int \frac{x \, dx}{\sqrt{x - 3}}$

12 $\int \frac{x}{(x - 3)^2} \, dx$

13 $\int (\ln x / x^2) \, dx$

14 $\int (2x + 5)(x + 1)^{1/2} \, dx$

In Exercises 15 to 22, use the method of partial fractions to find the indefinite integral.

15 $\displaystyle\int \frac{5 - x}{x^2 + 5x + 6}\, dx$

16 $\displaystyle\int \frac{5x - 7}{x^2 - 2x - 15}\, dx$

17 $\displaystyle\int \frac{7 - 2x}{x^2 - 2x + 1}\, dx$

18 $\displaystyle\int \frac{10x + 25}{x^2 + 6x + 9}\, dx$

19 $\displaystyle\int \frac{5x^2 - 2x + 64}{x^3 - 16x}\, dx$

20 $\displaystyle\int \frac{x - 3}{x^3 + 2x^2}\, dx$

21 $\displaystyle\int \frac{4x^2 - 2x - 6}{x^3 - x}\, dx$

22 $\displaystyle\int \frac{36 - 9x - 5x^2}{x^3 - 9x}\, dx$

In Exercises 23 to 36, determine the indefinite integral (if possible) using Table 16.2.

23 $\displaystyle\int x^4 \ln 10x\, dx$

24 $\displaystyle\int \frac{\ln 4x}{x^2}\, dx$

25 $\displaystyle\int \frac{\ln x}{x^3}\, dx$

26 $\displaystyle\int (\ln x)^4\, dx$

27 $\displaystyle\int (\ln x)^2\, dx$

28 $\displaystyle\int \frac{(\ln x)^3}{x}\, dx$

29 $\displaystyle\int x^4 \ln x\, dx$

30 $\displaystyle\int \frac{\ln x}{x^5}\, dx$

31 $\displaystyle\int e^{2.5x}\, dx$

32 $\displaystyle\int e^{-2x}\, dx$

33 $\displaystyle\int x e^{5x}\, dx$

34 $\displaystyle\int \frac{x}{e^{3x}}\, dx$

35 $\displaystyle\int \frac{dx}{5 + 3e^{2x}}$

36 $\displaystyle\int \frac{dx}{10 - 2e^x}$

KEY TERMS AND CONCEPTS

antiderivative   652
constant of integration   657
differential equation   666
indefinite integral   656
integral sign   656
integrand   656
integration   656

integration by parts   673
method of partial fractions   676
ordinary differential
  equations   666
partial differential equations   666
solutions of ordinary differential
  equations   667

IMPORTANT FORMULAS

$\displaystyle\int k\, dx = kx + c \qquad k \text{ real}$ **(Rule 1)**

$\displaystyle\int x^n\, dx = \frac{x^{n+1}}{n + 1} + C \qquad n \neq -1$ **(Rule 2)**

$\displaystyle\int k f(x)\, dx = k \int f(x)\, dx \qquad k \text{ real}$ **(Rule 3)**

$$\int [f(x) \pm g(x)]\, dx = \int f(x)\, dx \pm \int g(x)\, dx \qquad \text{(Rule 4)}$$

$$\int x^{-1}\, dx = \ln x + C \qquad \text{(Rule 5)}$$

$$\int e^x\, dx = e^x + C \qquad \text{(Rule 6)}$$

$$\int [f(x)]^n f'(x)\, dx = \frac{[f(x)]^{n+1}}{n+1} + C \qquad n \neq -1 \qquad \text{(Rule 7)}$$

$$\int f'(x) e^{f(x)}\, dx = e^{f(x)} + C \qquad \text{(Rule 8)}$$

$$\int \frac{f'(x)}{f(x)}\, dx = \ln f(x) + C \qquad \text{(Rule 9)}$$

ADDITIONAL EXERCISES

Exercises 1 to 9 are related to Sec. 16.1.
Find the antiderivative of the following functions.

1   $f'(x) = -5$ 2 $f'(x) = \sqrt{e}$
3   $f'(x) = x/3$ 4 $f'(x) = x/4 - 5$
5   $f'(x) = 3x^2 - 4x + 8$ 6 $f'(x) = 2x^3 - x^2 + 2x - 4$

For the following exercises, determine f given f' and a point which satisfies f.

7   $f'(x) = 8$, (2, 20)   8 $f'(x) = x^2 + 3x - 6$, (1, 0)
9   $f'(x) = -4x^3/3 + x^2 + 2x + 1$, $(-1, \frac{1}{3})$

Exercises 10 to 35 are related to Secs. 16.2 and 16.3.
For the following exercises, find the indefinite integral (if possible).

10   $\int 33\, dx$ 11 $\int -12\, dx$

12   $\int 9x\, dx$ 13 $\int (-x + 1)\, dx$

14   $\int (-5x + 3)\, dx$ 15 $\int (x/2 + 7)\, dx$

16   $\int (2x^3 - 4x^2)\, dx$ 17 $\int (x^4/5 + 3x^3 - 5)\, dx$

18   $\int (x - 1/x^3)\, dx$ 19 $\int (x + 3)^4\, dx$

20   $\int (2x^4 + 4x^3 - x^2 + 6x - 7)\, dx$ 21 $\int (ax^4 + bx^3 + cx^2 + dx + e)\, dx$

22　$\displaystyle\int \sqrt{x^5}\, dx$

23　$\displaystyle\int \sqrt[4]{1/x}\, dx$

24　$\displaystyle\int (4x^2 + 5)^{1/2}(8x)\, dx$

25　$\displaystyle\int (x^2 + 3e^x + 2)\, dx$

26　$\displaystyle\int (\sqrt{x} + \sqrt[5]{x})\, dx$

27　$\displaystyle\int (x^2 + 1)(2x)\, dx$

28　$\displaystyle\int (3x^2 - 2)^3(x)\, dx$

29　$\displaystyle\int (2x^3 - x^2)^2(3x^2 - x)\, dx$

30　$\displaystyle\int \frac{-x}{3 - x^2/2}\, dx$

31　$\displaystyle\int \frac{2 - x}{x^3}\, dx$

32　$\displaystyle\int \frac{7}{x - 3}\, dx$

33　$\displaystyle\int (e^{8x} + 2)\, dx$

34　$\displaystyle\int \frac{2x}{\sqrt{x^2 + 3}}\, dx$

35　$\displaystyle\int \frac{x}{(x^2 + 4)^3}\, dx$

Exercises 36 to 49 are related to Sec. 16.4.

Classify the following differential equations by type, order, and degree.

36　$dy/dx = 3x^4 - 5x^2 - 10$
37　$(d^2y/dx^2)^3 - (d^2y/dx^2) = x^2 - (dy/dx)$
38　$(\partial z/\partial x)^2 = x - 2y$
39　$\partial^2 z/\partial x^2 = \partial z/\partial x - 2x$
40　$d^2y/dx^2 = (dy/dx)^4 - x$
41　$\partial z/\partial y = (\partial^2 z/\partial y^2)^3 - y + 3x$

Find the general solution for each of the following differential equations.

42　$dy/dx = x^3 - 3x$
43　$dy/dx = x/(x^2 - 3) - 6x^2 e^{2x^3 - 4}$
44　$d^2y/dx^2 = x/6 - 20$
45　$x^2 - 2x = d^2y/dx^2 + 3$

For each of the following differential equations, find the general and particular solutions.

46　$dy/dx = -2x + 4,\ f(2) = 10$
47　$dy/dx = 4x^3 - 3x^2,\ f(-1) = 5$
48　$d^2y/dx^2 = x^2/12 - 6x$
　　$f'(2) = 20$
　　$f(2) = 40$
49　$48x = 4 - (d^2y/dx^2)$
　　$f'(1) = 25$
　　$f(2) = 81$

Exercises 50 to 66 are related to Sec. 16.5.

Find the indefinite integral (if possible) using integration by parts.

50　$\displaystyle\int x \ln x\, dx$

51　$\displaystyle\int xe^{ax}\, dx$

52　$\displaystyle\int e^x(x + 1)^2\, dx$

53　$\displaystyle\int xe^{-3x}\, dx$

54　$\displaystyle\int x^2 e^x\, dx$

Find the indefinite integral (if possible) using the method of partial fractions.

55　$\displaystyle\int \frac{10 - 2x}{x^2 - 5x - 4}\, dx$

56　$\displaystyle\int \frac{3x - 5}{x^2 + 2x - 15}\, dx$

57　$\displaystyle\int \frac{3x^2 - x + 5}{x^3 - 4x}\, dx$

58　$\displaystyle\int \frac{x - 5}{x^3 - 9x}\, dx$

Find the indefinite integral (if possible) using Table 16.2.

59 $\displaystyle\int 3e^{-5x}\, dx$

60 $\displaystyle\int \frac{xe^{-3x}}{2}\, dx$

61 $\displaystyle\int \frac{dx}{5 + 2e^{3x}}$

62 $\displaystyle\int x^5 \ln x\, dx$

63 $\displaystyle\int \frac{(\ln x)^4}{x}\, dx$

64 $\displaystyle\int x^5 \ln 3x\, dx$

65 $\displaystyle\int \frac{(\ln x)^2}{2}\, dx$

66 $\displaystyle\int -2(\ln x)^3\, dx$

CHAPTER TEST

1   Given $f'(x) = 4x^3 - 2x - 10$ and the point $(5, 100)$ which satisfies f, determine f.

2   Find the following indefinite integrals.

(a) $\displaystyle\int \frac{dx}{\sqrt[3]{x^5}}$

(b) $\displaystyle\int (x^4 - 10)^7 x^3 \, dx$

(c) $\displaystyle\int e^{-10x} \, dx$

3   Find the general and particular solutions for the differential equation $5 - x = d^2y/dx^2$, where $f(3) = 24$ and $f'(2) = 5$.

4   The marginal revenue function for a company's product is

$$MR = 120,000 - 12x$$

where x equals the number of units sold. If total revenue equals 0 when 0 units are sold, determine the total revenue function.

5   Using integration by parts, find the indefinite integral $\displaystyle\int xe^{10x} \, dx$.

6   Use the method of partial fractions to find the indefinite integral $\displaystyle\int \frac{20x - 10}{x^2 - x - 6} \, dx$

17

INTEGRAL CALCULUS: APPLICATIONS

CHAPTER OBJECTIVES

- Introduce the definite integral
- Illustrate the relationships which exist between the definite integral and areas
- Provide a wide variety of applications of integral calculus
- Illustrate the relationship between integral calculus and probability theory

This chapter will focus on the application of integral calculus. In particular, we will discuss the *definite integral,* the use of definite integrals in calculating areas beneath and between curves, several applications utilizing integral calculus, and the application of integral calculus to probability theory.

17.1 DEFINITE INTEGRALS

In this section we will introduce the definite integral which forms the basis for many applications of integral calculus.

The Definite Integral

The *definite integral* can be interpreted both as an area and as a limit. Consider the graph of the function $f(x) = x^2$, $x \geq 0$, shown in Fig. 17.1. Assume that we wish to determine the shaded area A under the curve between $x = 1$ and $x = 3$. One approach is to *approximate* the area by computing the areas of a set of rectangles which are contained within the shaded area. In Fig. 17.2 two rectangles have been drawn within the area of interest. The width of each rectangle equals 1, and the heights are respectively $f(1)$ and $f(2)$. Using the sum of the areas of the two rectangles to approximate the area of interest, we have

$$A^* = f(1) \cdot (1) + f(2) \cdot (1)$$
$$= (1)(1) + (4)(1) = 5$$

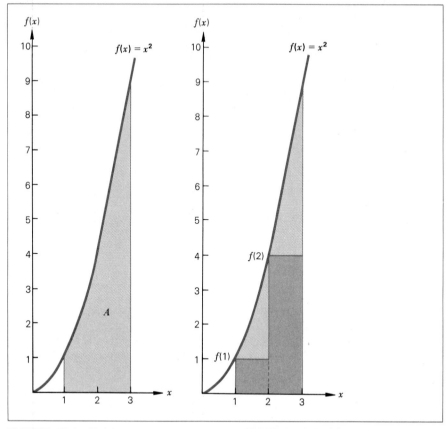

FIGURE 17.1 (left)   **FIGURE 17.2 (right)**
Approximation using two rectangles.

where A^* is the approximate area. Note that this approximation *underestimates* the actual area. The error introduced is represented by the more lightly shaded areas.

In Fig. 17.3 four rectangles have been drawn within the area of interest. The width of each rectangle equals $\frac{1}{2}$, and the total area of the four rectangles is computed by using the equation

$$A^* = f(1) \cdot (0.5) + f(1.5) \cdot (0.5) + f(2) \cdot (0.5) + f(2.5) \cdot (0.5)$$
$$= (1)(0.5) + (2.25)(0.5) + (4)(0.5) + (6.25)(0.5)$$
$$= 0.5 + 1.125 + 2.0 + 3.125 = 6.75$$

Compared with Fig. 17.2, the use of four rectangles rather than two results in a better approximation of the actual area. The more lightly shaded area is smaller in Fig. 17.3.

In Fig. 17.4 eight rectangles have been drawn, each having a width equal to 0.25. The area of these rectangles is computed by using the equation

$$A^* = f(1) \cdot (0.25) + f(1.25) \cdot (0.25) + \cdots + f(2.75) \cdot (0.25)$$
$$= (1)(0.25) + (1.5625)(0.25) + \cdots + (7.5625)(0.25) = 7.6781$$

Observe that this approximation is better than the others. In fact, if we continue

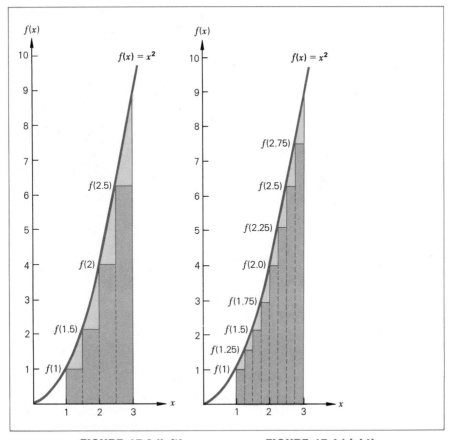

FIGURE 17.3 (left)
Approximation using four rectangles.

FIGURE 17.4 (right)
Approximation using eight rectangles.

to subdivide the interval between $x = 1$ and $x = 3$, making the base of each rectangle smaller and smaller, the approximation will come closer and closer to the actual area (which we will determine later to equal $8\frac{2}{3}$).

Let's now look at this process in a more general sense. Consider the function in Fig. 17.5. Suppose we are interested in determining the area beneath the curve but above the x axis between $x = a$ and $x = b$. Further suppose that the interval has been subdivided into n rectangles. Assume that the width of rectangle i is Δx_i and the height is $f(x_i)$. It is not necessary to assume that the width of each rectangle is the same. We can approximate the area of interest by summing the areas of the n rectangles, or

$$A^* = f(x_1)\Delta x_1 + f(x_2)\Delta x_2 + \cdots + f(x_n)\Delta x_n$$

$$= \sum_{i=1}^{n} f(x_i)\Delta x_i$$

As we observed for the function $f(x) = x^2$, the approximation becomes more and more accurate as the width of the rectangles becomes smaller and smaller, and hence concurrently with the number of rectangles becoming larger and larger. We can formalize this observation by stating that when the limit exists,

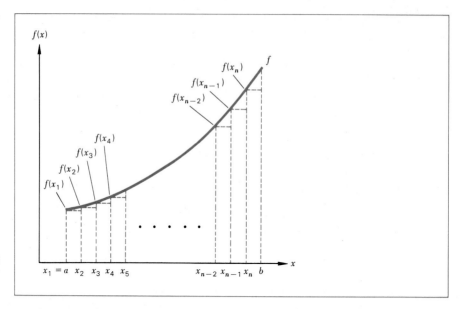

FIGURE 17.5
Area approximation using n rectangles.

$$\lim_{n \to \infty} \sum_{i=1}^{n} f(x_i)\Delta x_i = A \qquad (17.1)$$

That is, the actual area under the curve A is the limiting value of the sum of the areas of the n rectangles as the number of rectangles approaches infinity and the width of each approaches 0.

Just as the summation sign Σ applies when the sum of discrete elements is desired, the definite integral implies summation for continuous functions.

DEFINITION: DEFINITE INTEGRAL

If f is a bounded function on the interval $[a, b]$ we shall define the **definite integral** of f as

$$\int_a^b f(x)\ dx = \lim_{n \to \infty} \sum_{i=1}^{n} f(x_i)\Delta x_i = A \qquad (17.2)$$

provided this limit exists as the size of all the intervals in the subdivision approach zero and hence the number of intervals n approaches infinity.

The left side of Eq. (17.2) presents the notation of the *definite integral.* The values a and b which appear, respectively, below and above the integral sign are called the **limits of integration.** The *lower limit of integration* is a, and the *upper limit of integration* is b. The notation $\int_a^b f(x)\ dx$ can be verbalized as "*the definite* *integral of f between a lower limit x = a and an upper limit x = b," or more simply "the integral of f between a and b."*

Evaluating Definite Integrals

The evaluation of definite integrals is facilitated by the following important theorem.

FUNDAMENTAL THEOREM OF INTEGRAL CALCULUS

If a function f is continuous over an interval and F is any anti-derivative of f, then for any points $x = a$ and $x = b$ on the interval, where $a \le b$,

$$\int_{a}^{b} f(x)\ dx = F(b) - F(a) \qquad (17.3)$$

According to the fundamental theorem of integral calculus, the definite integral can be evaluated by (1) determining the indefinite integral $F(x) + C$ and (2) computing $F(b) - F(a)$, sometimes denoted by $F(x)\Big]_{a}^{b}$. As you will see in the following example, there is no need to include the constant of integration in evaluating definite integrals.

EXAMPLE 1

To evaluate $\displaystyle\int_{0}^{3} x^2\ dx$, the indefinite integral is

$$F(x) = \int x^2\ dx$$

$$= \frac{x^3}{3} + C$$

Now

$$\int_{0}^{3} x^2\ dx = \left(\frac{x^3}{3} + C\right)\Big]_{0}^{3} = \left(\frac{3^3}{3} + C\right) - \left(\frac{0^3}{3} + C\right)$$

$$= 9 + C - C$$

$$= 9$$

When evaluating definite integrals, always subtract the value of the indefinite integral at the lower limit of integration from the value at the upper limit of integration. The constant of integration will always drop out in this computation, as it did in this example. Thus, there is no need to include the constant in evaluating definite integrals.

EXAMPLE 2

To evaluate $\displaystyle\int_{1}^{4} (2x^2 - 4x + 5)\ dx$

$$F(x) = \int (2x^2 - 4x + 5)\, dx$$

$$= \frac{2x^3}{3} - \frac{4x^2}{2} + 5x$$

$$= \frac{2x^3}{3} - 2x^2 + 5x$$

Therefore,

$$\int_1^4 (2x^2 - 4x + 5)\, dx = \frac{2x^3}{3} - 2x^2 + 5x \Big]_1^4$$

$$= \left[\frac{2(4)^3}{3} - 2(4)^2 + 5(4)\right] - \left[\frac{2(1)^3}{3} - 2(1)^2 + 5(1)\right]$$

$$= (\tfrac{128}{3} - 32 + 20) - (\tfrac{2}{3} - 2 + 5) = 30\tfrac{2}{3} - 3\tfrac{2}{3} = 27$$

EXAMPLE 3

To evaluate $\displaystyle\int_{-2}^1 e^x\, dx$

$$F(x) = \int e^x\, dx$$

$$= e^x$$

Therefore,

$$\int_{-2}^1 e^x\, dx = e^x \Big]_{-2}^1$$

$$= e^1 - e^{-2}$$

or, from Table 1,

$$= 2.7183 - 0.1353$$

$$= 2.5830$$

EXAMPLE 4

To evaluate $\displaystyle\int_2^4 \frac{x\, dx}{x^2 - 1}$

$$F(x) = \int \frac{x\, dx}{x^2 - 1}$$

$$= \frac{1}{2} \int \frac{2x\, dx}{x^2 - 1}$$

And, by Rule 9,

$$F(x) = \frac{1}{2} \ln (x^2 - 1)$$

Therefore,

$$\int_2^4 \frac{x\, dx}{x^2 - 1} = \frac{1}{2} \ln (x^2 - 1) \Big]_2^4$$

$$= \frac{1}{2} \ln (16 - 1) - \frac{1}{2} \ln (4 - 1)$$

$$= \frac{1}{2} \ln 15 - \frac{1}{2} \ln 3$$

From Table 2,

$$\int_2^4 \frac{x\, dx}{x^2 - 1} = \frac{1}{2} (2.7081) - \frac{1}{2} (1.0986)$$

$$= 1.35405 - 0.5493 = 0.80475$$

Properties of Definite Integrals

There are several properties which can be of assistance when evaluating definite integrals. These follow, along with examples to illustrate.

PROPERTY 1

If f is defined and continuous on the interval (a, b),

$$\int_a^b f(x)\, dx = -\int_b^a f(x)\, dx \qquad \text{(17.4)}$$

EXAMPLE 5

Consider the function $f(x) = 4x^3$.

$$\int_{-2}^{1} 4x^3\, dx = x^4 \Big]_{-2}^{1}$$

$$= (1)^4 - (-2)^4 = 1 - 16 = -15$$

$$\int_{1}^{-2} 4x^3\, dx = x^4 \Big]_{1}^{-2}$$

$$= (-2)^4 - (1)^4 = 16 - 1 = 15$$

Thus, $\quad\displaystyle\int_{-2}^{1} 4x^3\, dx = -\int_{1}^{-2} 4x^3\, dx$

PROPERTY 2

$$\int_a^a f(x)\, dx = 0 \qquad \text{(17.5)}$$

EXAMPLE 6

$$\int_{10}^{10} e^x\, dx = e^x \Big]_{10}^{10}$$

$$= e^{10} - e^{10}$$

$$= 0$$

PROPERTY 3

If f is continuous on the interval (a, c) and $a < b < c$,

$$\int_a^b f(x)\, dx + \int_b^c f(x)\, dx = \int_a^c f(x)\, dx \qquad \text{(17.6)}$$

EXAMPLE 7

Show that

$$\int_0^4 3x^2\, dx = \int_0^2 3x^2\, dx + \int_2^4 3x^2\, dx$$

SOLUTION

$$\int_0^4 3x^2 \, dx = x^3 \Big]_0^4$$

$$= (4)^3 - (0)^3 = 64$$

$$\int_0^2 3x^2 \, dx + \int_2^4 3x^2 \, dx = x^3 \Big]_0^2 + x^3 \Big]_2^4$$

$$= [(2)^3 - (0)^3] + [(4)^3 - (2)^3] = (8 - 0) + (64 - 8) = 64.$$

EXERCISE

Show that

$$\int_0^4 3x^2 \, dx = \int_0^1 3x^2 \, dx + \int_1^4 3x^2 \, dx$$

PROPERTY 4

$$\int_a^b cf(x) \, dx = c \int_a^b f(x) \, dx \qquad (17.7)$$

where c is constant.

EXAMPLE 8

Show that for the function in Example 7,

$$\int_0^4 3x^2 \, dx = 3 \int_0^4 x^2 \, dx$$

SOLUTION

In Example 7, $\int_0^4 3x^2 \, dx$ was determined to equal 64. We need to evaluate $3 \int_0^4 x^2 \, dx$.

$$3 \int_0^4 x^2 \, dx = 3 \frac{x^3}{3} \Big]_0^4$$

$$= 3 \left[\frac{(4)^3}{3} - \frac{(0)^3}{3} \right] = 3 \left(\frac{64}{3} \right) = 64$$

PROPERTY 5

If $\int_a^b f(x) \, dx$ and $\int_a^b g(x) \, dx$ exist,

$$\int_a^b [f(x) \pm g(x)] \, dx = \int_a^b f(x) \, dx \pm \int_a^b g(x) \, dx \qquad (17.8)$$

EXAMPLE 9 ▮▮▮▮▮▮▮▮▮▮▮▮▮▮▮▮▮▮▮▮▮▮▮▮▮▮▮▮▮▮▮▮▮

Suppose we wish to evaluate

$$\int_2^4 (4x - 5)\, dx + \int_2^4 (5 - 6x)\, dx$$

Because the limits of integration are the same, Eq. (17.8) indicates that the integrands can be combined algebraically using one definite integral, or

$$\int_2^4 (4x - 5)\, dx + \int_2^4 (5 - 6x)\, dx = \int_2^4 [(4x - 5) + (5 - 6x)]\, dx$$

$$= \int_2^4 (-2x)\, dx$$

$$= -x^2 \Big]_2^4$$

$$= [-(4)^2] - [-(2)^2]$$

$$= -16 + 4 = -12$$

EXERCISE ▮▮▮▮▮▮▮▮▮▮▮▮▮▮▮▮▮▮▮▮▮▮▮▮▮▮▮▮▮

Evaluate

$$\int_2^4 (4x - 5)\, dx + \int_2^4 (5 - 6x)\, dx$$

using the two definite integrals and verify that their sum equals −12.

Section 17.1 Follow-up Exercises

1. $\displaystyle \int_0^3 x\, dx$

2. $\displaystyle \int_1^2 (x - 1)\, dx$

3. $\displaystyle \int_3^5 dx$

4. $\displaystyle \int_{-2}^3 5\, dx$

5. $\displaystyle \int_{-1}^1 2x\, dx$

6. $\displaystyle \int_{-2}^2 -x\, dx$

7. $\displaystyle \int_0^3 (x^2 - 2x)\, dx$

8. $\displaystyle \int_0^6 (4x^3 - 3x^2)\, dx$

9. $\displaystyle \int_0^{64} \sqrt{x}\, dx$

10. $\displaystyle \int_{-2}^0 e^x\, dx$

11. $\displaystyle \int_2^6 \frac{dx}{x}$

12. $\displaystyle \int_3^4 \frac{4\, dx}{x}$

13. $\displaystyle \int_{-2}^1 (2x)e^{x^2}\, dx$

14. $\displaystyle \int_{-2}^{-1} (3x^2)e^{x^3}\, dx$

15. $\displaystyle \int_4^2 x\, dx$

16. $\displaystyle \int_{-2}^{-1} 4\, dx$

17. $\displaystyle \int_b^b 2x\, dx$

18. $\displaystyle \int_c^c x^3\, dx$

19 $\displaystyle\int_0^1 (mx + b)\, dx$ 20 $\displaystyle\int_0^3 (ax^2 + bx + c)\, dx$

21 $\displaystyle\int_9^{16} \sqrt{x}\, dx$ 22 $\displaystyle\int_5^8 \frac{2x}{x^2 - 4}\, dx$

23 $\displaystyle\int_1^2 (x^2 - 2x + 1)\, dx - \int_1^2 (3x^2 - 2x + 1)\, dx$

24 $\displaystyle\int_0^2 (5x^2 - x + 2)\, dx + \int_0^2 (3x^2 + 2x - 3)\, dx$

25 $\displaystyle\int_1^2 (6x^3 - 8x^2)\, dx - \int_1^2 (2x^3 + 5x^2 + 10)\, dx$

26 $\displaystyle\int_{-2}^1 (5x^2 - 2x + 1)\, dx - \int_{-2}^1 (2x^2 + 2x - 1)\, dx$

27 $\displaystyle\int_2^4 (x - 3)\, dx - \int_4^2 (3x + 5)\, dx$

28 $\displaystyle\int_3^5 (x^2 - 5)\, dx + \int_5^3 (-4x^2 + 10)\, dx$

17.2 DEFINITE INTEGRALS AND AREAS

One of the practical applications of integral calculus is that definite integrals can be used to compute areas. These may represent areas which are bounded by curves representing functions and/or the coordinate axes. In Sec. 17.3 we will examine situations where such areas hold particular meaning in an applied problem.

Areas between a Function and the x Axis

Definite integrals can be used to compute the area between the curve representing a function and the x axis. Several different situations may occur. The treatment of these varies and is now discussed.

CASE 1: ($f(x) > 0$)

When the value of a continuous function f is positive over the interval $a \leq x \leq b$ —that is, the graph of f lies above the x axis—the area which is bounded by f, the x axis, $x = a$, and $x = b$ is determined by

$$\int_a^b f(x)\, dx$$

Figure 17.6 illustrates the situation.

EXAMPLE 10

Determine the area beneath $f(x) = x^2$ and above the x axis between $x = 1$ and $x = 3$.

SOLUTION

This area was illustrated earlier in Fig. 17.1. The area is computed as

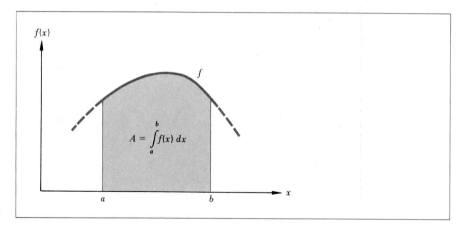

FIGURE 17.6

$$A = \int_{1}^{3} x^2 \, dx$$

$$= \frac{x^3}{3}\Bigg]_{1}^{3}$$

$$= \frac{3^3}{3} - \frac{1^3}{3} = 9 - \tfrac{1}{3} = 8\tfrac{2}{3}$$

The (exact) area equals $8\tfrac{2}{3}$ *square* units.

EXAMPLE 11

Determine the area indicated in Fig. 17.7.

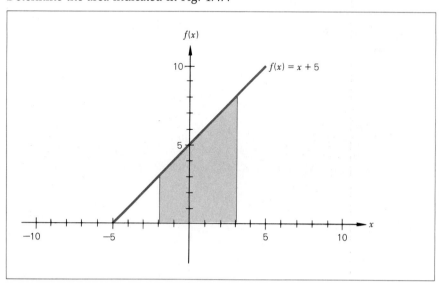

FIGURE 17.7

SOLUTION

Let's anticipate the answer by using familiar formulas for computing the area of a rectangle and a triangle. As shown in Fig. 17.8, the area of interest can be thought of as

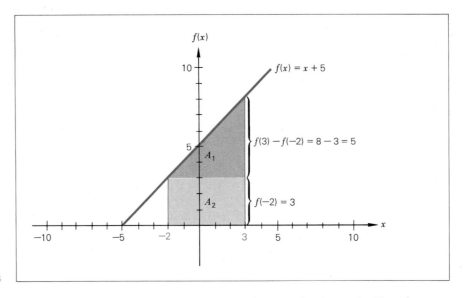

FIGURE 17.8

being composed of a rectangle of area A_2 and a triangle of area A_1. Therefore,

$$A = A_1 + A_2$$
$$= \tfrac{1}{2}bh + lw$$
$$= \tfrac{1}{2}(5)(5) + (5)(3) = 12.5 + 15 = 27.5 \text{ square units}$$

Using the definite integral,

$$A = \int_{-2}^{3} (x + 5) \, dx$$

$$= \frac{x^2}{2} + 5x \Bigg]_{-2}^{3}$$

$$= \left[\frac{(3)^2}{2} + 5(3) \right] - \left[\frac{(-2)^2}{2} + 5(-2) \right]$$

$$= (\tfrac{9}{2} + 15) - (2 - 10) = 19.5 - (-8) = 27.5 \text{ square units}$$

CASE 2: ($f(x) < 0$)

When the value of a continuous function f is negative over the interval $a \le x \le b$—that is, the graph of f lies below the x axis—the area which is bounded by f, the x axis, $x = a$, and $x = b$ is determined by

$$\int_{a}^{b} f(x) \, dx$$

However, the definite integral evaluates the area as *negative* when it lies below the x axis. Because area is *positive*, the area will be computed as

$$- \int_{a}^{b} f(x) \, dx$$

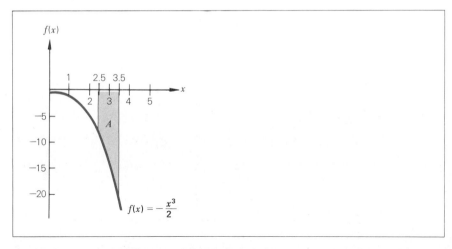

FIGURE 17.9

EXERCISE 12

Determine the area indicated in Fig. 17.9.

SOLUTION

Because f is a negative function,

$$A = -\int_{2.5}^{3.5} -\frac{x^3}{2}\, dx$$

$$= -\left[-\frac{x^4}{8}\right]_{2.5}^{3.5}$$

$$= -\left\{\left[-\frac{(3.5)^4}{8}\right] - \left[\frac{-(2.5)^4}{8}\right]\right\}$$

$$= -[-18.7578 - (-4.8828)] = -[-13.875] = 13.875 \text{ square units}$$

CASE 3: ($f(x) < 0$ and $f(x) > 0$)

When the value of a continuous function f is positive over part of the interval $a \le x \le b$ and negative over the remainder of the interval—part of the area between f and the x axis is above the x axis and part is below the x axis—then $\int_a^b f(x)\, dx$ calculates the *net area*. That is, areas above the x axis are evaluated as positive, and those below are evaluated as negative. The two are combined algebraically to yield the net value.

EXAMPLE 13

Evaluate $\int_0^{15} (x - 5)\, dx$ to determine the *net* area, shown in Fig. 17.10.

SOLUTION

Again, we can anticipate the answer using the formula for the area of a triangle. Remem-

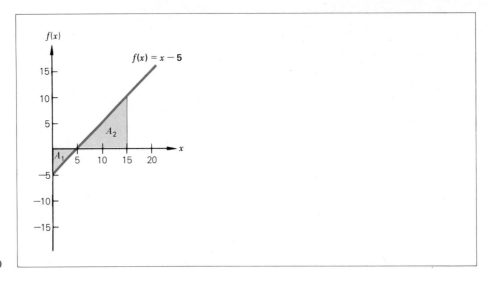

FIGURE 17.10

bering that the area below the x axis will be evaluated as negative when we integrate, we have

$$A = -A_1 + A_2$$
$$= -\tfrac{1}{2}(5)(5) + \tfrac{1}{2}(10)(10)$$
$$= -12.5 + 50$$
$$= 37.5 \text{ square units}$$

Evaluating the definite integral,

$$A = \int_0^{15} (x - 5)\, dx$$

$$= \frac{x^2}{2} - 5x\bigg]_0^{15}$$

$$= \left[\frac{(15)^2}{2} - 5(15)\right] - \left[\frac{0^2}{2} - 5(0)\right]$$

$$= (112.5 - 75) - 0$$
$$= 37.5 \text{ square units}$$

Finding Areas between Curves

The following examples illustrate procedures for determining areas between curves.

EXAMPLE 14

Determine the shaded area between f and g indicated in Fig. 17.11.

SOLUTION

In order to determine the area A, it is necessary to examine the composition of the area. The area cannot be determined by integrating only one of the functions. One way of de-

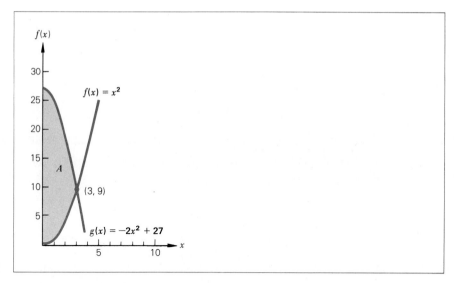

FIGURE 17.11

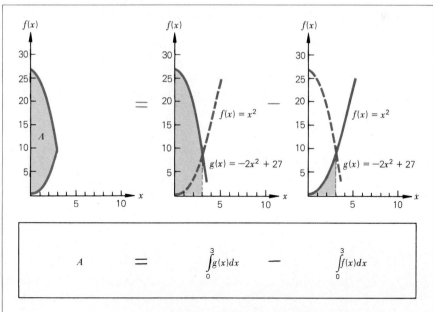

FIGURE 17.12

termining A is shown in Fig. 17.12. If g is integrated between $x = 0$ and $x = 3$, the resulting area includes A, but it also includes an additional area which is not part of A. Having overestimated A, we need to subtract the *surplus*. The surplus area happens to be the area under f between $x = 0$ and $x = 3$. Thus, A can be determined as

$$A = \int_0^3 g(x)\ dx - \int_0^3 f(x)\ dx$$

or

$$A = \int_0^3 (-2x^2 + 27)\ dx - \int_0^3 x^2\ dx$$

Using Property 5,

$$A = \int_0^3 (-3x^2 + 27)\, dx$$

$$= -x^3 + 27x \Big]_0^3$$

$$= [-(3)^3 + 27(3)] - [-(0)^3 + 27(0)] = -27 + 81 - 0 = 54 \text{ square units}$$

EXAMPLE 15

Referring to Fig. 17.13, determine the combination of integrals which would compute the size of (*a*) area A_1, (*b*) area A_2, (*c*) area A_3.

SOLUTION

This example presents no actual numbers. It really is an exercise in the logic of formulating combinations of definite integrals to define areas.

(*a*) The upper boundary on A_1 is determined by f. If f is integrated between $x = 0$ and $x = a$, the result is an area including A_1 plus a surplus area. The surplus area can be determined by integrating g between $x = 0$ and $x = a$. Thus,

$$A_1 = \int_0^a f(x)\, dx - \int_0^a g(x)\, dx$$

This is illustrated graphically in Fig. 17.14*a*.

(*b*) The upper boundary on A_2 is determined by g up until $x = a$ and by f when $a \leq x \leq b$. If g is integrated between $x = 0$ and $x = a$, the resulting area is a portion of A_2. The remaining portion of A_2 can be determined by integrating f between $x = a$ and $x = b$. Thus,

$$A_2 = \int_0^a g(x)\, dx + \int_a^b f(x)\, dx$$

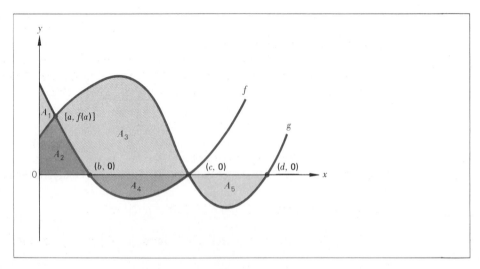

FIGURE 17.13

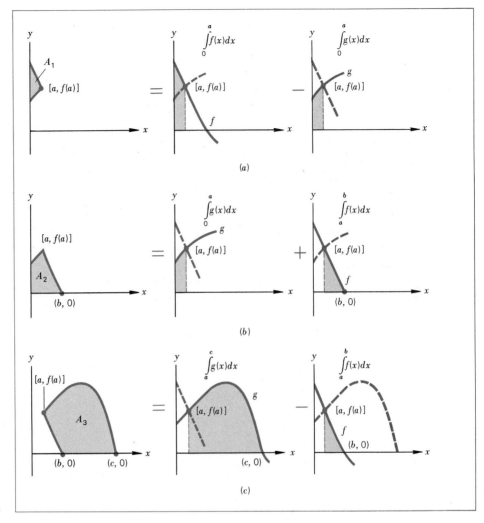

FIGURE 17.14

This is illustrated graphically in Fig. 17.14b.

(c) The upper boundary on A_3 is determined entirely by g. If we integrate g between $x = a$ and $x = c$, the resulting area includes A_3 plus a surplus area. The surplus area can be determined by integrating f between $x = a$ and $x = b$. Thus,

$$A_3 = \int_a^c g(x)\,dx - \int_a^b f(x)\,dx$$

This is illustrated graphically in Fig. 17.14c.

Verify for yourself in Fig. 17.13 that

$$A_4 = -\int_b^c f(x)\,dx \quad \text{and} \quad A_5 = -\int_c^d g(x)\,dx$$

NOTE

A suggestion in using definite integrals to compute areas is always to draw a sketch of the functions involved. Having a picture of the areas of interest makes it easier to identify pertinent boundaries and to understand the logic required to define the areas.

Section 17.2 Follow-up Exercises

In Exercises 1 to 10, (a) sketch f and (b) determine the size of the area between f and the x axis over the indicated interval.

1 $f(x) = -2x + 8$, between $x = 1$ and $x = 3$
2 $f(x) = x^2$, between $x = 6$ and $x = 10$
3 $f(x) = 2x^3$, between $x = 1$ and $x = 3$
4 $f(x) = 3x^2$, between $x = -2$ and $x = 2$
5 $f(x) = 10 - x^2$, between $x = -1$ and $x = 3$
6 $f(x) = e^x$, between $x = 1$ and $x = 4$
7 $f(x) = -x^3$, between $x = 2$ and $x = 3$
8 $f(x) = 40x - x^2$, between $x = 0$ and $x = 20$
9 $f(x) = xe^{x^2}$, between $x = 1$ and $x = 2$
10 $f(x) = \dfrac{1}{x}$, between $x = 2$ and $x = 10$

11 Referring to Fig. 17.15, determine the combinations of definite integrals which would compute the area of (a) A_1, (b) A_2, (c) A_3, (d) A_4, (e) A_5.

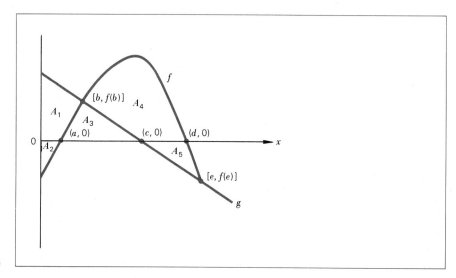

FIGURE 17.15

12 Referring to Fig. 17.16, determine the combinations of definite integrals which would compute the area of (a) A_1, (b) A_2, (c) A_3.

13 Given $f(x) = x^2/2$ and $g(x) = 24 - x^2$, (a) sketch the two functions. (b) For $x \geq 0$, determine the area bounded by the two functions and the y axis.

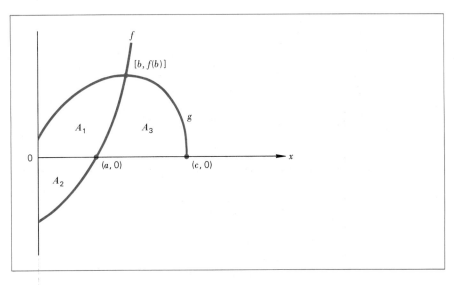

FIGURE 17.16

14   Given $f(x) = 2x + 2$ and $g(x) = 14 - x$, (*a*) sketch the two functions. (*b*) For $x \geq 0$, determine the area bounded by the two functions and the y axis.

15   Given $f(x) = x^2 - 20x$ and $g(x) = -x^2 + 20x$, (*a*) sketch the two functions. (*b*) Determine the area bounded by the two functions between $x = 0$ and $x = 20$.

16   Given $f(x) = x^2$ and $g(x) = x + 6$, for $x \geq 0$ determine the area bounded on three sides by the two functions and the y axis.

17.3 APPLICATIONS OF INTEGRAL CALCULUS

The following examples illustrate sample applications of integral calculus.

EXAMPLE 16

Revenue   In Chap. 16 we discussed how the total revenue function can be determined by integrating the marginal revenue function. As a simple extension of this concept, assume that the price of a product is constant at a value of $10 per unit, or the marginal revenue function is

$$MR = f(x)$$
$$= 10$$

where x equals the number of units sold. Total revenue from selling x units can be determined by integrating the marginal revenue function between 0 and x. For example, the total revenue from selling 1,500 units can be computed as

$$\int_0^{1,500} 10 \, dx = 10x \Big]_0^{1,500}$$
$$= 10(1,500)$$
$$= \$15,000$$

This is a rather elaborate procedure for calculating total revenue since we simply could have multiplied price by quantity sold to determine the same result. However, it does illustrate how the area beneath the marginal revenue function (Fig. 17.17) can be inter-

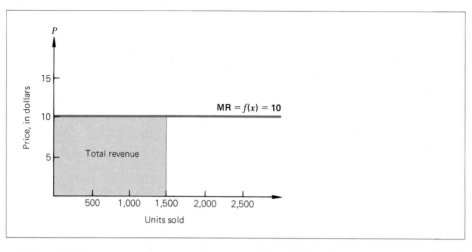

FIGURE 17.17

preted as total revenue or incremental revenue. The additional revenue associated with increasing sales from 1,500 to 1,800 units can be computed as

$$\int_{1,500}^{1,800} 10 \ dx = 10x \Big]_{1,500}^{1,800}$$
$$= \$18,000 - \$15,000$$
$$= \$3,000$$

EXAMPLE 17

Maintenance Expenditures   An automobile manufacturer estimates that the annual rate of expenditure $r(t)$ for maintenance on one of its models is represented by the function

$$r(t) = 100 + 10t^2$$

where t is the age of the automobile stated in years and r(t) is measured in dollars per year. This function suggests that when the car is 1 year old, maintenance expenses are being incurred at a rate of

$$r(1) = 100 + 10(1)^2$$
$$= \$110 \text{ per year}$$

When the car is 3 years old, maintenance costs are being incurred at a rate of

$$r(3) = 100 + 10(3)^2$$
$$= \$190 \text{ per year}$$

As would be anticipated, the older the automobile, the more maintenance is required. Figure 17.18 illustrates the sketch of the rate of expenditure function.

The area under this curve between any two values of t is a measure of the expected maintenance cost during that time interval. The expected maintenance expenditures during the automobile's first 5 years are computed as

$$\int_0^5 (100 + 10t^2) \ dt = 100t + \frac{10t^3}{3} \Big]_0^5$$

$$= 100(5) + \frac{10(5)^3}{3} = 500 + 416.67 = \$916.67$$

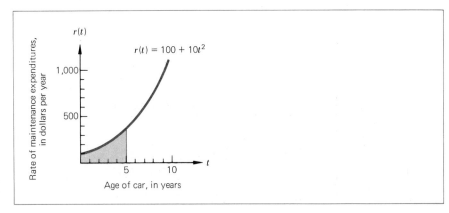

FIGURE 17.18
Rate of expend-
iture function.

Of these expenditures, those expected to be incurred *during the fifth year* are estimated as

$$\int_{4}^{5} (100 + 10t^2) \, dt = 100t + \frac{10t^3}{3} \Big]_{4}^{5}$$

$$= 916.67 - \left[100(4) + \frac{10(4)^3}{3} \right]$$

$$= 916.67 - (400 + 213.33) = \$303.34$$

EXAMPLE 18

Fund Raising   A state civic organization is conducting its annual fund raising campaign for its summer camp program for the disadvantaged. Campaign expenditures will be in-curred at a rate of \$10,000 per day. From past experience it is known that contributions will be high during the early stages of the campaign and will tend to fall off as the campaign continues. The function describing the rate at which contributions are received is

$$c(t) = -100t^2 + 20,000$$

where t represents the day of the campaign, and c(t) is measured in dollars per day.
    The organization wishes to maximize the net proceeds from the campaign.
(*a*) Determine how long the campaign should be conducted in order to maximize net proceeds.
(*b*) What are total campaign expenditures expected to equal?
(*c*) What are total contributions expected to equal?
(*d*) What are the net proceeds (total contributions less total expenditures) expected to equal?

SOLUTION

(*a*) The function which describes the rate at which expenditures *e*(*t*) are incurred is

$$e(t) = 10,000$$

Figure 17.19 illustrates the two functions. As long as the rate at which contributions are made exceeds the rate of expenditures for the campaign, net proceeds are positive. Refer to Fig. 17.19. Net proceeds will be positive up until the time when the graphs of the two

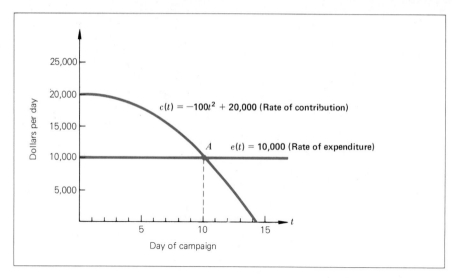

FIGURE 17.19
Fund-raising
contributions
and expenditure
functions.

functions intersect. Beyond this point, the rate of expenditure exceeds the rate of contribution. That is, contributions would be coming in at a rate of less than $10,000 per day.

The two functions intersect when

$$c(t) = e(t)$$

or when

$$-100t^2 + 20,000 = 10,000$$
$$-100t^2 = -10,000$$
$$t^2 = 100$$
$$t = 10 \text{ days}$$

(*b*) Total campaign expenditures are represented by the area under *e* between $t = 0$ and $t = 10$. This could be found by integrating *e* between these limits or more simply by multiplying:

$$E = (\$10,000 \text{ per day})(10 \text{ days})$$
$$= \$100,000$$

(*c*) Total contributions during the 10 days are represented by the area under *c* between $t = 0$ and $t = 10$, or

$$C = \int_0^{10} (-100t^2 + 20,000)\, dt$$

$$= -100\frac{t^3}{3} + 20,000t \Bigg]_0^{10}$$

$$= \frac{-100(10)^3}{3} + 20,000(10)$$

$$= -33,333.33 + 200,000 = \$166,666.67$$

(*d*) Net proceeds are expected to equal

$$C - E = \$166,666.67 - \$100,000$$
$$= \$66,666.67$$

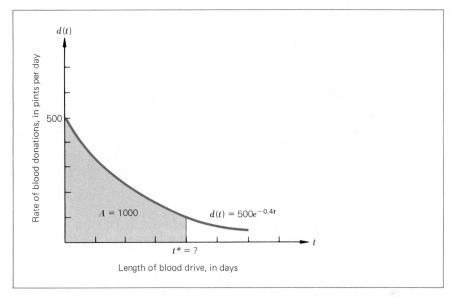

FIGURE 17.20
Determining
upper limit of
integration.

EXAMPLE 19

Blood Bank Management   A hospital blood bank conducts an annual blood drive to replenish its inventory of blood. The hospital estimates that blood will be donated at a rate of $d(t)$ pints per day where

$$d(t) = 500e^{-0.4t}$$

and *t equals the length of the blood drive in days*. If the goal of the blood drive is 1,000 pints, when will the hospital reach its goal?

SOLUTION

In this problem the area between the graph of d and the t axis represents total donations of blood in pints. Unlike previous applications, the desired area is known; the unknown is the upper limit of integration, as shown in Fig. 17.20. The hospital will reach its goal when

$$\int_0^{t^*} 500e^{-0.4t}\, dt = 1,000$$

Rewriting the integrand,

$$\int_0^{t^*} -1,250(-0.4)e^{-0.4t}\, dt = 1,000$$

or $$-1,250 \int_0^{t^*} -0.4e^{-0.4t}\, dt = 1,000$$

Evaluating the definite integral and solving for t^*,

$$-1,250[e^{-0.4t}]_0^{t^*} = 1,000$$
$$-1,250[e^{-0.4t^*} - e^{-0.4(0)}] = 1,000$$

$$-1{,}250[e^{-0.4t^*} - 1] = 1{,}000$$
$$-1{,}250e^{-0.4t^*} + 1{,}250 = 1{,}000$$
$$-1{,}250e^{-0.4t^*} = -250$$
$$e^{-0.4t^*} = \frac{-250}{-1250}$$
$$e^{-0.4t^*} = 0.2$$

Taking the natural logarithm of both sides of the equation (using Table 2),

$$-0.4t^* = -1.6094$$
$$t^* = \frac{-1.6094}{-0.4}$$

or

$$t^* = 4.0235$$

Thus, the hospital will reach its goal in approximately 4 days.

EXAMPLE 20

Nuclear Power An electric company has proposed building a nuclear power plant on the outskirts of a major metropolitan area. As might be expected, public opinion is divided and discussions have been heated. One lobbyist group opposing the construction of the plant has presented some disputed data regarding the consequences of a catastrophic accident at the proposed plant. The lobbyist group estimates that the rate at which deaths would occur within the metropolitan area because of radioactive fallout is described by the function

$$r(t) = 200{,}000e^{-0.1t}$$

where *r(t) represents the rate of deaths in persons per hour and t represents time elapsed since the accident, measured in hours. Note:* Although the dispute in this example is quite real, the data are all contrived!

The population of the metropolitan area is 1.5 million persons.
(a) Determine the expected number of deaths 1 hour after a major accident.
(b) How long would it take for all people in the metropolitan area to succumb to the effects of the radioactivity?

SOLUTION

(a) Figure 17.21 presents a sketch of *r*. The area beneath this function between any two points t_1 and t_2 is a measure of the expected number of deaths during that time interval. Thus, the number of deaths expected during the first hour would be computed as

$$\int_0^1 200{,}000e^{-0.1t} \, dt = \int_0^1 -2{,}000{,}000(-0.1)e^{-0.1t} \, dt$$
$$= -2{,}000{,}000 \int_0^1 (-0.1)e^{-0.1t} \, dt$$
$$= -2{,}000{,}000e^{-0.1t} \Big]_0^1$$

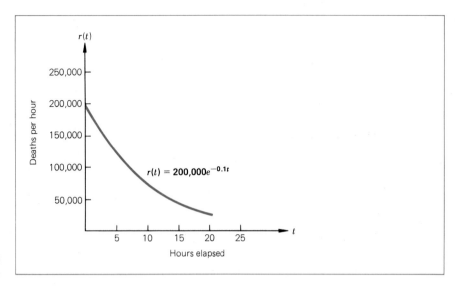

FIGURE 17.21
Rate of deaths.

$$= -2,000,000e^{-0.1} + 2,000,000e^0$$
$$= -2,000,000(e^{-0.1} - e^0)$$
$$= -2,000,000(0.9048 - 1)$$
$$= -2,000,000(-0.0952) = 190,400 \text{ people}$$

(b) As morbid as it is, the entire population would succumb after t^* hours, where

$$\int_0^{t^*} 200,000e^{-0.1t} \, dt = 1,500,000$$

or when

$$-2,000,000e^{-0.1t} \Big]_0^{t^*} = 1,500,000$$

Solving for t^*, we get

$$-2,000,000e^{-0.1t^*} + 2,000,000 = 1,500,000$$
$$-2,000,000e^{-0.1t^*} = -500,000$$
$$e^{-0.1t^*} = 0.25$$

If the natural logarithm (Table 2) is found for both sides of the equation,

$$-0.1t = -1.3863$$

or

$$t = 13.863 \text{ hours}$$

EXAMPLE 21

Consumer's Surplus   One way of measuring the value or utility that a product holds for a consumer is the price that he or she is willing to pay for it. Economists contend that consumers actually receive bonus or surplus value from the products they purchase according to the way in which the marketplace operates.

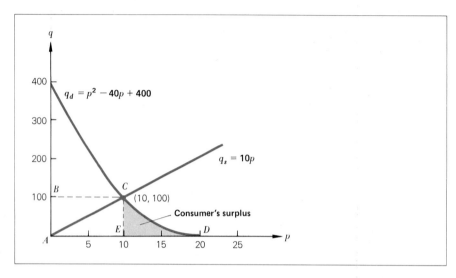

FIGURE 17.22
Consumer's
surplus.

Figure 17.22 portrays the supply and demand functions for a product. Equilibrium occurs when a price of $10 is charged and demand equals 100 units. If dollars are used to represent the value of this product to consumers, our accounting practices would suggest that the total revenue ($10 · 100 units = $1,000) is a measure of the *economic value* of this product. The area of rectangle *ABCE* represents this measure of value.

However, if you consider the nature of the demand function, there would have been a demand for the product at prices higher than $10. That is, there would have been con-sumers willing to pay almost $20 for the product. And, additional consumers would have been drawn into the market at prices between $10 and $20. If we assume that the price these people would be willing to pay is a measure of the utility the product holds for them, they actually receive a bonus when the market price is $10. Refer again to Fig. 17.22. Economists would claim that a measure of the actual utility of the product is the area *ABCDE*. And when the market is in equilibrium, the extra utility received by con-sumers, referred to as the *consumer's surplus,* is represented by the shaded area *CDE*. This area can be found as

$$\int_{10}^{20} (p^2 - 40p + 400)\, dp = \frac{p^3}{3} - 20p^2 + 400p \Big]_{10}^{20}$$

$$= \left[\frac{(20)^3}{3} - 20(20)^2 + 400(20) \right]$$

$$- \left[\frac{(10)^3}{3} - 20(10)^2 + 400(10) \right]$$

$$= 2{,}666.67 - 2{,}333.33 = \$333.34$$

Our accounting methods would value the utility of the product at $1,000. Economists would contend that the actual utility is $1,333.34, or that the consumer's surplus equals $333.34. This measure of added, or bonus, utility applies particularly to those consumers who would have been willing to pay more than $10.

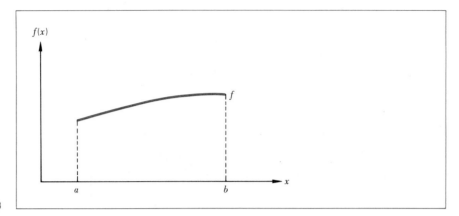

FIGURE 17.23

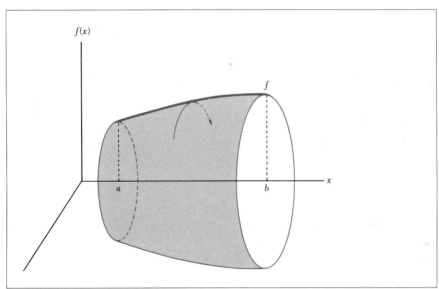

FIGURE 17.24
Surface of revo-
lution.

EXAMPLE 22

Volume of a Solid of Revolution   Consider the function f in Fig. 17.23. If the half-plane bounded by f, the x axis, and the lines $x = a$ and $x = b$ is rotated about the x axis one full revolution, a *surface of revolution* is formed. Each point on f sweeps a circular path. The composite sweep of all points f on the interval $a \leq x \leq b$ is the surface of revolution shown in Fig. 17.24.

Corresponding to the surface of revolution is a *solid of revolution.* This is the volume which the plane sweeps out as the graph of f is rotated about the x axis. Suppose that we wish to determine the volume of the solid of revolution. We might estimate the volume by forming an approximate solid of revolution consisting of a set of right circular cylinders as shown in Fig. 17.25. In this figure the interval $a \leq x \leq b$ has been subdivided into equal subintervals of width Δx. The height of each of the right cylinders is Δx. The radius of each right cylinder is $f(x_i)$ where x_i is the left-hand value of x for subinterval i.

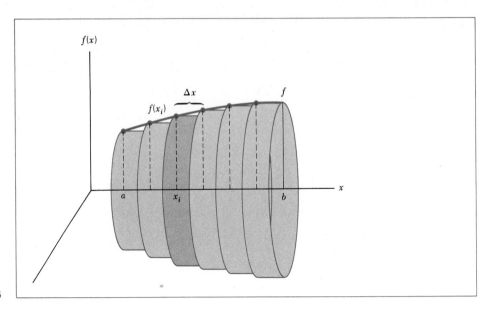

FIGURE 17.25

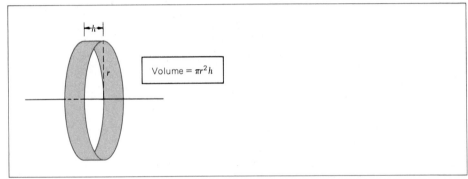

FIGURE 17.26
Circular
cylinder of
height h and
radius r.

Volume $= \pi r^2 h$

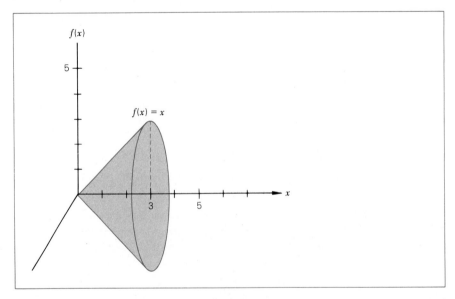

FIGURE 17.27

$f(x) = x$

As shown in Fig. 17.26, the volume of a right cylinder having radius r and height h is

$$V = \pi r^2 h$$

where π (pi) = 3.14 . . . . . For each right cylinder in Fig. 17.25, the volume is

$$V_i = \pi [f(x_i)]^2 \, \Delta x$$

If the interval $a \leq x \leq b$ has been divided into n subintervals, the estimated volume of the solid of revolution is

$$V = \sum_{i=1}^{n} V_i = \sum_{i=1}^{n} \pi [f(x_i)]^2 \, \Delta x$$

The estimate will become more accurate as the interval $a \leq x \leq b$ is subdivided into a greater number of subintervals, with Δx approaching 0.

DEFINITION: VOLUME OF SOLID OF REVOLUTION

Given a function f which is continuous over the interval $a \leq x \leq b$, the volume of the solid of revolution generated as the function is rotated one revolution about the x axis is defined by

$$V = \lim_{n \to \infty} \sum_{i=1}^{n} \pi [f(x_i)]^2 \, \Delta x$$

When the limit exists, it can be shown that

$$V = \int_{a}^{b} \pi [f(x)]^2 \, dx \tag{17.9}$$

Given the function $f(x) = x$, suppose we wish to determine the volume of the solid of revolution generated as the graph of f, between $x = 0$ and $x = 3$, is rotated about the x axis. This solid of revolution is shown in Fig. 17.27. The volume is

$$V = \int_{0}^{3} \pi (x)^2 \, dx$$

$$= \pi \frac{(x)^3}{3} \Bigg]_{0}^{3}$$

$$= \pi \left[\frac{(3)^3}{3} - \frac{(0)^3}{3} \right]$$

$$= 9\pi$$

$$\doteq 28.26 \text{ cubic units}$$

Section 17.3 Follow-up Exercises

1   The marginal revenue function for a firm's product is

$$MR = -0.04x + 10$$

where x equals the number of units sold.

(a) Determine the total revenue from selling 200 units of the product.

(b) What is the added revenue associated with an increase in sales from 100 to 200 units?

2   A manufacturer of jet engines estimates that the rate at which maintenance costs are incurred on its engines is a function of the number of hours of operation of the engine. For one engine used on commercial aircraft, the function is

$$r(x) = 60 + 0.040x^2$$

where x equals the number of hours of operation and $r(x)$ equals the rate at which repair costs are incurred in dollars per hour of operation.

(a) Determine the rate at which costs are being incurred after 100 hours of operation.

(b) What are total maintenance costs expected to equal during the first 100 hours of operation?

3   A company specializing in a mail-order sales approach is beginning a promotional campaign. Advertising expenditures will cost the firm $5,950 per day. Marketing specialists estimate that the rate at which profit (exclusive of advertising costs) will be generated from the promotion campaign decreases over the length of the campaign. Specifically, the rate $r(t)$ for this campaign is estimated by the function

$$r(t) = -50t^2 + 10,000$$

where t represents the day of the campaign and $r(t)$ is measured in dollars per day. In order to maximize *net* profit, the firm should conduct the campaign as long as $r(t)$ exceeds the daily advertising cost.

(a) Graph the function $r(t)$ and the function $c(t) = 5,950$ which describes the rate at which advertising expenses are incurred.

(b) How long should the campaign be conducted?

(c) What are total advertising expenditures expected to equal during the campaign?

(d) What *net* profit will be expected?

4   Rework Example 18, assuming that campaign expenditures will be incurred at a rate of $5,000 per day and that

$$c(t) = -10t^2 + 9,000$$

5   Rework Example 20, assuming that $r(t) = 200,000e^{-0.05t}$.

6   Rework Example 20, assuming that the population equals 800,000 and $r(t) = 100,000e^{-0.1t}$.

7   You are given the demand function

$$q_d = p^2 - 30p + 200$$

and the supply function

$$q_s = 5p$$

where p is stated in dollars, q_d and q_s are stated in units, and $0 \le p \le 9$.

(a) Sketch the two functions.

(b) Determine the equilibrium price and quantity.

(c) Determine the value of the consumer's surplus if the market is in equilibrium.

8   **Energy Conservation**   A small business is considering buying an energy-saving device which will reduce its consumption of fuel. The device will cost $32,000. Engineer-

ing estimates suggest that savings from using the device will occur at a rate of $s(t)$ dollars per year where

$$s(t) = 20,000e^{-0.5t}$$

and t equals time measured in years. Determine how long it will take for the firm to recover the cost of the device (that is, when the accumulated fuel savings equal the purchase cost).

9   Blood Bank Management   A hospital blood bank conducts an annual blood drive to replenish its inventory of blood. The hospital estimates that blood will be donated at a rate of $d(t)$ pints per day where

$$d(t) = 300e^{-0.1t}$$

and t equals the length of the blood drive in days. If the goal for the blood drive is 2,000 pints, when will the hospital reach its goal?

10   Forest Management   The demand for commercial forestland timber has been increasing rapidly over the past three to four decades. The function describing the rate of demand for timber is

$$d(t) = 20 + 0.003t^2$$

where $d(t)$ is stated in billions of cubic feet per year and t equals time in years ($t = 0$ corresponds to January 1, 1970).
(a) Determine the rate of demand at the beginning of 1975.
(b) Determine the rate of demand at the beginning of 1990.
(c) Determine the *total* demand for timber during the period 1970 through 1989. (*Hint:* Integrate $d(t)$ between $t = 0$ and $t = 20$.)

11   Solid Waste Management   The rate $w(t)$ at which solid waste is being generated in a major United States city is described by the function

$$w(t) = 0.5e^{0.025t}$$

where $w(t)$ is stated in billions of tons per year and t equals time measured in years ($t = 0$ corresponds to January 1, 1970).
(a) Determine the rate at which solid waste is expected to be generated at the beginning of 1990.
(b) What total tonnage is expected to be generated during the 20-year period from 1970 through 1989?

12   Epidemic Control   A health research center specializes in the study of epidemics. They estimate that for one particular type of epidemic which occurred in one region of the country the rate at which new people were afflicted was described by the function

$$r(t) = 50e^{0.2t} - 40$$

where $r(t)$ is the rate of new afflictions, measured in people per day, and t equals time since the beginning of the epidemic, measured in days. How many persons were afflicted during the first 20 days?

13   Learning Curves   People in the manufacturing industries have observed in many instances that employees assigned to a new job or task become more efficient with experience. That is, as the employee repeats the task, he or she becomes more familiar with the operations, motions, and equipment required to perform the job. Some companies have enough experience with job training that they can project how quickly an employee will learn a job. Very often a *learning curve* can be constructed which estimates the rate at which a job is performed as a function of the number of times the job has been performed by an employee.

The *learning curve* for a particular job has been defined as

$$h(x) = \frac{20}{x} + 4 \qquad x > 0$$

where $h(x)$ equals the production rate measured in hours per unit and x equals the unit produced.

(a) Determine the production rate $h(x)$ at the time of the 10th unit ($x = 10$).

(b) Integrating the learning curve over a specified interval provides an estimate of the total number of production hours required over the corresponding range of output. Determine the total number of hours expected for producing the first 20 units by integrating $h(x)$ between $x = 1$ and $x = 20$.

(c) Sketch h.

(d) Is there any limit suggested as to how efficient an employee can become at this job?

14 Producer's Surplus Example 21 discussed the notion of consumer's surplus, which represents what economists believe to be a measure of the added utility consumers enjoy when the market is in equilibrium. Economists also suggest that producers receive a bonus or added utility when the market is in equilibrium. Figure 17.28 repeats the supply and demand functions presented in Example 21.

If you focus on the supply function q_s, it indicates that certain suppliers would be willing to supply units at prices less than the equilibrium price of $10. When the market price is $10, these suppliers earn more than they otherwise would have. If each supplier sells at the price he or she is willing to, the total revenue received would be represented by area ACD. Since total revenue at equilibrium is represented by $ABCD$, the shaded area represents a measure of the added value to suppliers. This added value is referred to as *producer's surplus*.

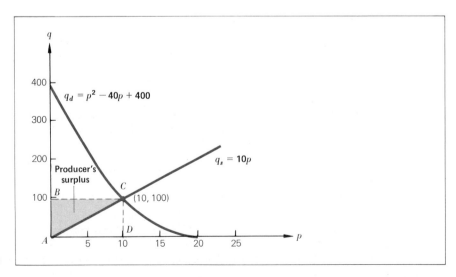

FIGURE 17.28

(a) Determine the producer's surplus in Example 21.

(b) Determine the producer's surplus for the functions described in Exercise 7.

    15   Given the function $f(x) = -x^2 + 9$, find the volume of the solid of revolution between $x = 0$ and $x = 3$ is f is rotated about the x axis.

    16   Given the function $f(x) = -x - 2$, find the volume of the solid of revolution between $x = -2$ and $x = 5$ if f is rotated about the x axis.

17.4   INTEGRAL CALCULUS AND PROBABILITY (OPTIONAL)

A mathematical function which determines the probability of each possible outcome of an experiment is called a *probability density function (pdf)*. Compared with probability distributions which display each outcome and its probability, density functions can be thought of as the mathematical functions used to compute the probability. If x is a continuous random variable, its density function f must satisfy the two conditions

1 $f(x) \geq 0$ for all x.

2 The area under the graph of f equals 1.

The first condition prohibits negative probabilities for any event while the second condition guarantees that the events are mutually exclusive and collectively exhaustive.

    The probability that a random variable x assumes a value in the interval between a and b, where $a < b$, equals the area under the density function between $x = a$ and $x = b$. Applying the definite integral, the probability that x will assume a value between $x = a$ and $x = b$ equals $\int_a^b f(x)\, dx$, or

$$P(a \leq x \leq b) = \int_a^b f(x)\, dx$$

    The density function for normally distributed variables was presented in Eq. (9.22). Technically, if we wanted to determine the probability that a normally distributed variable x, having a mean μ and standard deviation σ, will assume a value between $x = a$ and $x = b$, $a < b$, we could determine the probability by integrating the density function, or

$$P(a \leq x \leq b) = \int_a^b \frac{1}{\sqrt{2\pi}\sigma} e^{-1/2[(x-\mu)/\sigma]^2}\, dx$$

Fortunately, the equivalent conversion to the standard normal distribution and the availability of tables such as Table 9.24 eliminate any need to perform what appears to be a cumbersome integration.

EXAMPLE 23

Consider the probability density function for the random variable x

$$f(x) = \frac{2 + x}{30} \qquad 0 \leq x \leq 6$$

Determine the probability that x will assume a value between 2 and 5.

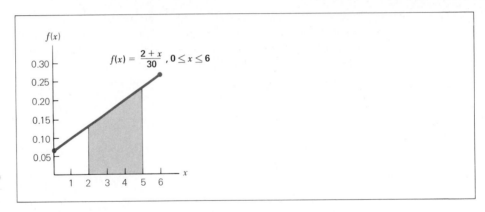

SOLUTION

The density function and the area of interest are illustrated in Fig. 17.29. The probability is computed as

$$P(2 \le x \le 5) = \int_2^5 \frac{2+x}{30} \, dx$$

$$= \frac{x}{15} + \frac{x^2}{60} \Big]_2^5$$

$$= \left(\frac{5}{15} + \frac{5^2}{60} \right) - \left(\frac{2}{15} + \frac{2^2}{60} \right)$$

$$= \frac{5}{15} + \frac{25}{60} - \frac{2}{15} - \frac{4}{60}$$

$$= \frac{20 + 25 - 8 - 4}{60} = \frac{33}{60} = .55$$

EXAMPLE 24

A 3-hour examination is given to all prospective salespeople of a national retail chain. The time x in hours required to complete the examination has been found to be random with a density function

$$f(x) = \frac{-x^2 + 10x}{36} \qquad 0 \le x \le 3$$

Determine the probability that someone will complete the test in 1 hour or less.

SOLUTION

The density function and area of interest are shown in Fig. 17.30. The probability is computed as

$$P(0 \le x \le 1) = \int_0^1 \frac{-x^2 + 10x}{36} \, dx$$

$$= \frac{-x^3}{108} + \frac{10x^2}{72} \Big]_0^1$$

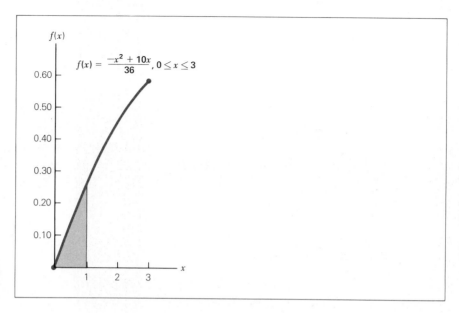

FIGURE 17.30
Probability density function.

$$= \frac{-(1)^3}{108} + \frac{10(1)^2}{72} = \frac{-1}{108} + \frac{10}{72} = -.009 + .139 = .13$$

Section 17.4 Follow-up Exercises

1   The probability density function for a continuous random variable x is

$$f(x) = \frac{5 - x}{4.5} \qquad 2 \le x \le 5$$

What is the probability that the random variable will assume a value greater than 3? Less than 2?

2   The probability density function for a continuous random variable x is

$$f(x) = \frac{x^2 - 10x + 25}{39} \qquad 0 \le x \le 3$$

Determine the probability that the random variable will assume a value greater than 2. Less than 1?

3   The probability density function for a continuous random variable x is

$$f(x) = \frac{1 + 2x}{36} \qquad 2 \le x \le 6$$

Determine the probability that the random variable will assume a value between 2 and 4.

KEY TERMS AND CONCEPTS

definite integral   689
fundamental theorem of integral
  calculus   693

limits of integration (lower and
  upper)   692
probability density function   721

IMPORTANT FORMULAS

$$\int_a^b f(x)\,dx = F(b) - F(a) \tag{17.3}$$

$$\int_a^b f(x)\,dx = -\int_b^a f(x)\,dx \tag{17.4}$$

$$\int_a^a f(x)\,dx = 0 \tag{17.5}$$

$$\int_a^b f(x)\,dx + \int_b^c f(x)\,dx = \int_a^c f(x)\,dx \tag{17.6}$$

$$\int_a^b cf(x)\,dx = c\int_a^b f(x)\,dx \tag{17.7}$$

$$\int_a^b [f(x) \pm g(x)]\,dx = \int_a^b f(x)\,dx \pm \int_a^b g(x)\,dx \tag{17.8}$$

ADDITIONAL EXERCISES

Exercises 1 to 15 are related to Sec. 17.1.

1 $\displaystyle\int_0^1 (x^2 - 3e^x - 2)\,dx =$ 2 $\displaystyle\int_1^3 (4x^2 + 5)\,dx =$

3 $\displaystyle\int_{-2}^2 (6x + 7)\,dx =$ 4 $\displaystyle\int_{-1}^0 3x^2\,dx =$

5 $\displaystyle\int_0^1 (-2x^5 + 3x^4)\,dx =$ 6 $\displaystyle\int_{-1}^1 (x - 3)/x^3\,dx =$

7 $\displaystyle\int_1^2 (x^2/2 - 2x)\,dx =$ 8 $\displaystyle\int_{-3}^0 3x^2 e^{x^3}\,dx =$

9 $\displaystyle\int_{-3}^3 (-5xe^{x^2+2}\,dx =$ 10 $\displaystyle\int_2^3 \frac{6x}{3x^2 - 7}\,dx =$

11 $\displaystyle\int_0^1 x^{1/2}(1 + x)\,dx =$ 12 $\displaystyle\int_{-4}^0 e^{-1-6x}\,dx =$

13 $\displaystyle\int_0^2 (x^2 - 2x + 1)\,dx - \int_0^2 (x^2 + 2x + 1)\,dx =$

14 $\displaystyle\int_2^5 (x - 5)\,dx + \int_2^5 (x^2 - x + 5)\,dx =$

15 $\displaystyle\int_{-2}^1 (3x^2 - 2x)\,dx - \int_1^{-2} (x^2 + x - 5)\,dx =$

Exercises 16 to 22 are related to Sec. 17.2.
In Exercises 16 to 19, (a) sketch f and (b) determine the size of the area between f and the x axis over the indicated interval.

16 $f(x) = 5 + 2x$, between $x = 3$ and $x = 5$
17 $f(x) = e^{2x}$, between $x = 0$ and $x = 2.5$
18 $f(x) = x^2$, between $x = 2$ and $x = 4$
19 $f(x) = \ln(x + 1)$, between $x = 4$ and $x = 8$

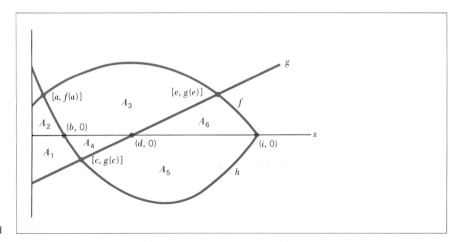

FIGURE 17.31

20 Given $f(x) = x^2 + 4$ and $g(x) = x + 6$, for $x \geq 0$, determine the size of the area bounded on three sides by the two functions and the y axis.

21 Given $f(x) = x^2$ and $g(x) = -x^2 + 8$, determine the size of the finite area which is bounded by the two functions (a sketch will help).

22 Given the functions in Fig. 17.31, determine the combinations of definite integrals necessary to compute (a) $A_1 + A_2$, (b) A_3, (c) $A_5 + A_6$.

Exercises 23 to 31 are related to Sec. 17.3.

23 The marginal revenue function for a firm's product is

$$MR = f(x) = 17.5$$

where x equals the number of units sold. Using a definite integral, determine the total revenue associated with selling 500 units.

24 The marginal revenue function for a firm's product is

$$MR = -0.04x + 10,$$

where x equals the number of units sold. What is the additional revenue if sales increase from 100 units to 200 units?

25 A manufacturer of a special-purpose piece of industrial equipment estimates that the annual rate of expenditure $r(t)$ for maintenance is represented by the function

$$r(t) = 1,000 + 25t^2$$

where t is the age of the machine in years and $r(t)$ is measured in dollars per year. (a) Determine the rate at which maintenance costs are being incurred when the machine is 2 years old. (b) What are total maintenance costs expected to equal during the first 3 years?

26 **Oil Consumption** In 1976 the amount of oil used in a particular region of the United States was 5 billion barrels. The demand for oil was growing at an exponential rate of 10 percent per year. The function describing annual rate of consumption $c(t)$ at time t is

$$c(t) = 5e^{0.1t}$$

where t is measured in years, $t = 0$ corresponds to January 1, 1976, and $c(t)$ is measured in billions of barrels per year. If the demand for oil continues to grow at this rate, how much oil is expected to be consumed in the 20-year period January 1, 1976, to January 1, 1996?

*27 **Velocity and Acceleration** Given the function $s(t)$ which describes the position of a moving object as a function of time t, the velocity function is $v(t) = s'(t)$, and the acceleration function is $a(t) = v'(t) = s''(t)$.

An object in free fall experiences a constant downward acceleration of 32 feet per square second. The acceleration function for a particular object is $a(t) = -32$. The initial velocity of the object thrown from ground level is 80 feet per second.

(a) Determine the function $v(t)$ which describes the velocity of the object at time t.
(b) Determine the velocity at $t = 2$.
(c) Determine the function $s(t)$ which describes the height of the object at time t.
(d) What is the height at $t = 1$?

28 The demand for a product has been decreasing exponentially. The annual rate of demand $d(t)$ is

$$d(t) = 250,000e^{-0.15t}$$

where $t = 0$ corresponds to January 1, 1977. The demand continues to decrease at the same rate.

(a) Determine the annual rate of demand at $t = 4$.
(b) How many total units are expected to be demanded over the time interval 1977 through 1986 ($t = 0$ to $t = 10$)?

29 A state has projected that the cost of unemployment compensation will be at a rate of $5e^{0.05t}$ million dollars per year t years from now. (a) Compute total unemployment compensation over the next 5 years. (b) How long will it be until total benefits paid out equal $200 million?

30 Given the function $f(t) = 2e^{0.5t}$, find the volume of the solid of revolution between $t = 0$ and $t = 5$. Sketch the solid of revolution.

31 A microcomputer manufacturer estimates that sales of its microcomputer systems will be at the rate of $\sqrt{1.2t + 10}$ thousand units per year t years from now. (a) At what rate are sales expected to be 10 years from now? (b) What are total sales expected to be over the next 10 years?

Exercises 32 to 33 are related to Sec. 17.4.

32 The probability density function for a continuous random variable is

$$f(x) = \tfrac{3}{4}(4x - x^2 - 3) \qquad 1 \le x \le 3$$

Determine the probability that the random variable will assume a value less than 2. Greater than 1.5?

33 The probability density function for a continuous random variable x is

$$f(x) = \frac{-x^3 + 80}{256} \qquad 0 \le x \le 4$$

What is the probability that the random variable will assume a value between 2 and 4?

CHAPTER TEST

1   Evaluate (a) $\int_0^4 (x^2 - 3x + 1)\, dx$ and (b) $\int_2^4 e^{x/2}\, dx$.

2   Given $f(x) = x^2$ and $g(x) = 8 + 2x$, (a) sketch the two functions. (b) For $x \geq 0$ determine the area bounded by the two functions and the y axis.

3   An automobile manufacturer estimates that the annual rate of expenditure $r(t)$ for maintenance on one of its models is represented by the function

$$r(t) = 120 + 8t^2$$

where t is the age of the automobile stated in years and $r(t)$ is measured in dollars per year.
(a) At what annual rate are maintenance costs being incurred when the car is 4 years old?
(b) What are total maintenance costs expected to equal during the first 3 years?

4   The probability density function for a continuous random variable is

$$f(x) = \frac{2 + x}{30} \qquad 0 \leq x \leq 6$$

Determine the probability that x will assume a value greater than 2?

MINICASE

THE SOCIAL SECURITY DILEMMA: A PROBLEM OF SOLVENCY

In the late 1970s, the U.S. government and its citizens (especially the more senior members) became greatly concerned about the Social Security program and its survival. The biggest problem was the growth in the population eligible for Social Security benefits. Disbursements from the Social Security trust fund reached a point where they outpaced income. The trust fund had a balance of approximately $24 billion at the beginning of 1980.

Economists confirmed that the rate of disbursement of benefits was increasing in a *linear* manner. One "think tank" projected that disbursements would be at an annual rate of $122.5 billion at the beginning of 1980. At the beginning of 1985 they estimated that disbursements would be occurring at an annual rate of $230 billion. This same group confirmed that the rate of income generation was increasing in a linear manner. They projected that income would be generated at an annual rate of $117.5 billion at the beginning of 1980 and at an annual rate of $222.5 billion at the beginning of 1985.

Required:
(1) Formulate the linear function which estimates the rate of disbursements as a function of time. Formulate the linear function which estimates the rate of income generation as a function of time. Sketch the two functions.

(2) Assuming the economists' assumptions are valid, determine when the trust fund will go broke (i.e., when the $24 billion balance will be consumed). Assume that the $24 billion figure has been normalized to account for interest income on the trust fund balance as well as on income from Social Security contributions.

(3) If the economists' assumptions are valid, what is the projected deficit at the beginning of 1985?

(4) A number of possible remedies have been proposed. One senator has suggested transferring $5 billion per year from a Medicare trust fund in order to delay bankruptcy. How long would it take for the trust fund to go broke if such a transfer can be arranged?

(5) Another proposal has suggested sharp reductions in benefits for those retiring at age 62. If this plan is implemented, economists project that disbursements at the beginning of 1985 would be reduced to an annual rate of $217.5 billion (a linear trend is still assumed). Assuming that the rate of income generation remains the same, when will the rate of disbursements equal the rate of income generation? Would the fund go broke under this proposal?

(6) A final proposal suggested increasing the Social Security taxation rate, resulting in increased income for the trust fund. If increased as proposed, economists estimate that the rate of income generation would be at an annual rate of $230 billion at the beginning of 1985 (linear trend still assumed). Assuming that the rate of disbursement remains the same as originally estimated, when will the rate of disbursements equal the rate of income generation? Would the fund go broke under this proposal?

18

MATHEMATICS OF FINANCE

CHAPTER OBJECTIVES

■ Provide an understanding of the time value of money

■ Provide an understanding of the mathematics of interest computations for single payment and annuity cash flow structures

■ Understand the nature of and computations related to mortgage loans

■ Introduce cost-benefit analysis and related considerations

This chapter is concerned with interest rates and their effects on the value of money. Interest rates have widespread influence over decisions made by businesses and by us in our personal lives. Corporations pay millions of dollars in interest each year for the use of money they have borrowed. We earn money on sums we have invested in savings accounts, certificates of deposit, and money market funds. We also pay for the use of money which we have borrowed for school loans, mortages, or credit card purchases.

The interest concept also has applications that are not related to money. Population growth, for example, may be characterized by an "interest rate," or rate of growth.

We will first examine the nature of interest and its computation. Then we will discuss several different investment situations and computations related to each. Next, a special section will discuss computations related to mortgages. Finally, the last section will discuss cost-benefit analysis.

18.1 INTEREST AND ITS COMPUTATION

Simple Interest

Interest is a fee which is paid for having the use of money. We pay interest on mortgages for having the use of the bank's money. We use the bank's money to pay a contractor or person from whom we are purchasing a home. Similarly, the bank pays us interest on money invested in savings accounts or certificates of deposit (CD's) because it has temporary access to our money. The amount of money that is lent or invested is called the *principal.* Interest is usually paid in proportion to the principal and the period of time over which the money is used. The *interest rate* specifies the rate at which interest accumulates. The interest rate is typically stated as a *percentage of the principal* per period of time, for example, 18 percent per year or 1.5 percent per month.

Interest that is paid solely on the amount of the principal is called *simple interest.* Simple interest is usually associated with loans or investments which are short-term in nature. The computation of simple interest is based on the following formula:

Simple interest = principal × interest rate per time period
$$\times \text{ number of time periods}$$

or
$$I = Pin \tag{18.1}$$

where
$$I = \text{simple interest (in dollars)}$$
$$P = \text{principal (in dollars)}$$
$$i = \text{interest rate per time period}$$
$$n = \text{number of time periods of loan}$$

It is essential that the time periods for i and n be consistent with each other. That is, if i is expressed as a percentage per year, n should be expressed in number of years. Similarly, if i is expressed as a percentage per month, n must be stated in number of months.

EXAMPLE 1

A credit union has issued a 3-year loan of $5,000. Simple interest is charged at a rate of 10 percent per year. The principal plus interest is to be repaid at the end of the third year. Compute the interest for the 3-year period. What amount will be repaid at the end of the third year?

SOLUTION

Using the variable definitions from Eq. (18.1), we get $P = \$5,000$, $i = 0.10$ per year, and $n = 3$ years. Therefore

$$I = (\$5,000)(0.10)(3)$$
$$= \$1,500$$

The amount to be repaid is the principal *plus* the accumulated interest, or

$$A = P + I$$
$$= \$5,000 + \$1,500 = \$6,500$$

EXAMPLE 2

A person "lends" $10,000 to a corporation by purchasing a bond from the corporation. Simple interest is computed quarterly at a rate of 3 percent per quarter, and a check for the interest is mailed each quarter to all bondholders. The bonds expire at the end of 5 years, and the final check includes the original principal plus interest earned during the last quarter. Compute the interest earned each quarter and the total interest which will be earned over the 5-year life of the bonds.

SOLUTION

In this problem $P = \$10,000$, $i = 0.03$ per quarter, and the period of the loan is 5 years. Since the time period for i is a quarter (of a year), we must consider 5 years as 20 quarters. And since we are interested in the amount of interest earned over one quarter, we must let $n = 1$. Therefore, quarterly interest equals

$$I = (\$10,000)(0.03)(1)$$
$$= \$300$$

To compute total interest over the 5-year period, we multiply the per-quarter interest of $300 by the number of quarters, 20, to obtain

$$\text{Total interest} = \$300 \times 20 = \$6,000$$

Compound Interest

A common procedure for computing interest is by *compounding interest.* Under this procedure, the interest is reinvested. The interest earned each period is added to the principal for purposes of computing interest for the next period. The amount of interest computed using this procedure is called the **compound interest.**

A simple example will illustrate this procedure. Assume that we have deposited $8,000 in a credit union which pays interest of 8 percent per year *compounded* quarterly. Assume that we want to determine the amount of money we will have on deposit at the end of 1 year if all interest is left in the savings account. At the end of the first quarter, interest is computed as

$$I_1 = (\$8,000)(0.08)(0.25)$$
$$= \$160$$

Note that n was defined as 0.25 *year.* With the interest left in the account, the principal on which interest is earned in the second quarter is the original principal plus $160 interest earned during the first quarter, or

$$P_2 = P_1 + I_1 = \$8,160$$

Interest earned during the second quarter is

$$I_2 = (\$8,160)(0.08)(0.25)$$
$$= \$163.20$$

Table 18.1 summarizes the computations for the four quarters. Note that for each quarter the accumulated principal plus interest is referred to as the **compound amount.** Notice that total interest earned during the four quarters equals $659.46.

Two conclusions should soon become apparent. For a stated interest rate i:

1 *Compound interest is greater than simple interest.* This is because interest which has been earned subsequently earns interest itself.

TABLE 18.1

QUARTER	(P) PRINCIPAL	(I) INTEREST	(S = P + I) COMPOUND AMOUNT
1	$8,000.00	$160.00	$8,000.00 + $160.00 = $8,160.00
2	8 160.00	163.20	8,160.00 + 163.20 = 8,323.20
3	8,323.20	166.46	8,323.20 + 166.46 = 8,489.66
4	8,489.66	169.79	8,489.66 + 169.79 = 8,659.46

2 *The more frequently interest is compounded, the greater the interest earned.* That is, a bank deposit having interest compounded monthly will earn more interest than an equal deposit having the same interest compounded quarterly.

In the last example, simple interest for the year would have been equal to

$$I = (\$8,000)(0.08)(1)$$
$$= \$640$$

The difference between the simple interest and the compound interest $659.46 - $640.00 = $19.46. Compound interest exceeds simple interest in this example by almost $20 over the 1-year period.

Section 18.1 Follow-up Exercises

1 A company has issued a 5-year loan of $30,000 to a new vice president to finance a home improvement project. The terms of the loan are that it is to be paid back in full at the end of 5 years with simple interest computed at the rate of 10 percent per year. Determine the interest which must be paid on the loan for the 5-year period.

2 A student has received a $10,000 loan from a wealthy aunt in order to finance his 4-year college program. The terms are that the student repay his aunt in full at the end of 10 years with simple interest computed at a rate of 4 percent per year. Determine the interest which must be paid on the 10-year loan.

3 An elderly woman has purchased $80,000 worth of corporate bonds. The bonds expire in 10 years, and simple interest is computed semiannually at a rate of 6 percent per 6-month period. Interest checks are mailed to bondholders every 6 months. Determine the interest the woman can expect to earn every 6 months. How much interest can she expect over the 10-year period?

4 A major airline is planning to purchase new airplanes. It wants to borrow $100 million by issuing bonds. The bonds are for a 5-year period with simple interest computed quarterly at a rate of 3 percent per quarter. Interest is to be paid each quarter to bondholders. How much will the airline have to pay in quarterly interest? How much interest will they pay over the 5-year period?

5 A $10,000 certificate of deposit earns interest of 12 percent per year, compounded semiannually. Complete the following table with regard to semiannual compounding. What is total interest over the 2-year period?

SEMIANNUAL PERIOD	(P) PRINCIPAL	(I) INTEREST	(S = P + I) COMPOUND AMOUNT
1	$10,000	$600	$10,600.00
2			
3			
4			

6 The sum of $500,000 has been placed in an investment which earns interest at the rate of 12 percent per year, compounded quarterly. Complete the following table with regard to quarterly compounding. What is total interest for the year?

QUARTER	(P) PRINCIPAL	(I) INTEREST	(S = P + I) COMPOUND AMOUNT
1	$500,000	$15,000	$515,000
2			
3			
4			

7 Refer to Exercise 5.
(*a*) Determine the compound amount after 2 years if interest is compounded quarterly instead of semiannually.
(*b*) Under which compounding plan, semiannually or quarterly, is total interest higher? By how much?
  8 Refer to Exercise 6.
(*a*) Determine the compound amount after 1 year if interest is compounded semiannually instead of quarterly.
(*b*) Under which compounding plan is total interest higher? By how much?

18.2 SINGLE-PAYMENT COMPUTATIONS

This section discusses the relationship between a sum of money at the present time and its value at some time in the future. The assumption in this and the remaining sections is that any interest is computed on a compounding basis.

Compound Amount

Assume that a sum of money is invested and that it earns interest which is compounded. One question related to such an investment is, What will the value of the investment be at some point in the future? The value of the investment is the original investment (principal) plus any earned interest. In our example illustrating calculations of compound interest in Sec. 18.1, we called this the *compound amount.* Given any principal invested at the beginning of a time period, the compound amount at the end of the period was calculated as

$$S = P + iP \qquad\qquad (18.2)$$

Let's redefine our variables and then develop a generalized formula which can be used to calculate the compound amount. Let

$P = principal\ (dollars)$
$i = interest\ rate\ per\ compounding\ period$
$n = number\ of\ compounding\ periods\ (number\ of\ periods$
   $\quad in\ which\ the\ principal\ has\ earned\ interest)$
$S = compound\ amount$

A *period,* for purposes of these definitions, may be any unit of time. If interest is compounded annually, a year is the appropriate period. If it is compounded monthly, a month is the appropriate period. It is again important to emphasize that *the definition of a period must be the same for both i and n.*

Suppose there has been an investment of P dollars which will earn interest at the rate of i percent per compounding period. From Eq. (18.2) we determined that the compound amount after one period is

$$S = P + iP$$

Factoring P from the terms on the right side of the equation, we can restate the compound amount as

$$S = P(1 + i) \qquad \text{(18.3)}$$

If we are interested in determining the compound amount after two periods, it may be computed using the equation

$$\begin{matrix} \text{Compound amount} \\ \text{after two periods} \end{matrix} = \begin{matrix} \text{compound amount} \\ \text{after one period} \end{matrix}$$
$$+ \begin{matrix} \text{interest earned} \\ \text{during the second period} \end{matrix}$$

or $\qquad S = P(1 + i) + i[P(1 + i)]$

Factoring P and $1 + i$ from both terms on the right side of the equation gives us

$$S = P(1 + i)(1 + i)$$

or $\qquad S = P(1 + i)^2 \qquad \text{(18.4)}$

Similarly, if we wish to determine the compound amount after three periods, it may be computed using the equation

$$\begin{matrix} \text{Compound amount} \\ \text{after three periods} \end{matrix} = \begin{matrix} \text{compound amount} \\ \text{after two periods} \end{matrix}$$
$$+ \begin{matrix} \text{interest earned} \\ \text{during the third period} \end{matrix}$$

or $\qquad S = P(1 + i)^2 + i[P(1 + i)^2]$

Factoring P and $(1 + i)^2$ from the terms on the right side of the equation, we have

$$S = P(1 + i)^2(1 + i)$$

or $\qquad S = P(1 + i)^3 \qquad \text{(18.5)}$

The compound-amount formulas developed so far are summarized below:

COMPOUND AMOUNT FORMULAS

Compound amount after one period = $P(1 + i)$.
Compound amount after two periods = $P(1 + i)^2$.
Compound amount after three periods = $P(1 + i)^3$.

And the pattern continues so that the following definition is possible.

DEFINITION: COMPOUND AMOUNT

If an amount of money P earns interest compounded at a rate of i percent per period, it will grow after n periods to the compound amount S, where

$$S = P(1 + i)^n \qquad (18.6)$$

Equation (18.6) is often referred to as the *compound-amount formula.* This relationship may be portrayed graphically as in Fig. 18.1.

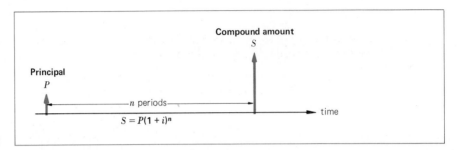

FIGURE 18.1

EXAMPLE 3

Suppose that $1,000 is invested in a savings bank which earns interest at a rate of 8 percent per year compounded annually. If all interest is left in the account, what will the account balance be after 10 years?

SOLUTION

In all these examples we will assume that the investment is made at the very beginning of a compounding period. By using Eq. (18.6), the compound amount after 10 years (periods) is

$$S = \$1,000(1 + 0.08)^{10}$$

The question now becomes, How do we evaluate $(1 + 0.08)^{10}$? Among possible alternatives are:

1 Sit close to a pencil sharpener, load up on paper, and use a brute-force hand calculation approach.

2 Use an electronic calculator.

3 Rewrite the equation by finding the logarithm of both sides and solving for the log of S.

4 Use an electronic calculator with financial functions (e.g., Texas Instruments Business Analyst-II)

Since these kinds of computations are fairly common, especially for banking and financial institutions and not everyone has an electronic calculator with financial functions, sets of tables are available which provide values of $(1 + i)^n$ for given values of i and n. For your convenience Table I on page T.0 (after page 769) provides values of $(1 + i)^n$ values. The expression $(1 + i)^n$ is called the *compound-amount factor.*
For our problem we simply find the column associated with an interest rate per period of 8 percent and the row corresponding to 10 compounding periods. Figure 18.2 is an ex-

n	i .08
1	1.08000
2	1.16640
3	1.25971
4	1.36049
5	1.46933
6	1.58687
7	1.71382
8	1.85093
9	1.99900
10	2.15892
11	2.33164
12	2.51817
13	2.71962
14	2.93719

FIGURE 18.2
Excerpt From
Table I.

cerpt from these tables. The value of $(1 + 0.08)^{10}$ is 2.15892. Therefore

$$S = (\$1,000)(2.15892)$$
$$= \$2,158.92$$

The \$1,000 investment will grow to \$2,158.92, meaning that interest of \$1,158.92 will be earned.

EXAMPLE 4

A long-term investment of \$250,000 has been made by a medium-sized company. The interest rate is 12 percent per year, and interest is compounded quarterly. If all interest is reinvested at the same *rate* of interest, what will the value of the investment be after 8 years?

NOTE

In almost all cases, the interest rate in a problem will be stated as an annual interest rate or as the interest rate per compounding period. When the former case occurs, the interest rate per compounding period is computed by the formula

$$i = \frac{\text{interest rate per year}}{\text{number of compounding periods per year}}$$

SOLUTION

In the compound-amount formula, Eq. (18.6), i is defined as the interest rate per compounding period and n as the number of compounding periods. In this problem compounding occurs every quarter of a year. The interest rate per quarter equals the annual interest rate divided by the number of compounding periods per year, or

$$i = \frac{0.12}{4} = 0.03$$

The number of compounding periods over the 8-year period is $8 \times 4 = 32$. Therefore

$$S = \$250,000(1 + 0.03)^{32}$$

From Table I, $(1 + 0.03)^{32} = 2.57508$, and

$$S = \$250,000(2.57508) = \$643,770$$

Over the 8-year period interest of $\$643,770 - \$250,000$, or $\$393,770$, is expected to be earned.

Present Value

The compound-amount formula

$$S = P(1 + i)^n$$

is an equation involving four variables—S, P, i, and n. And given the values of any three of these four, the equation can be solved for the remaining variable. To illustrate this point, suppose that a person can invest money in a savings account at the rate of 10 percent per year compounded quarterly. Assume that the person wishes to deposit a lump sum at the beginning of the year and have that sum grow to $\$20,000$ over the next 10 years. The question becomes, How much money should be deposited at the beginning of the year? Since we are given values for S, i, and n, we need to solve the equation for P. Doing this, we have

$$P = \frac{S}{(1 + i)^n} \qquad (18.7)$$

For the situation mentioned, $S = \$20,000$, $n = 40$ (10×4 compounding periods over the 10 years), and $i = 0.10/4 = 0.025$. The problem is illustrated in Fig. 18.3.

From Table I, we have $(1 + 0.025)^{40} = 2.68506$ and

$$P = \frac{\$20,000}{2.68506}$$

$$= \$7,448.62$$

In order to accumulate $\$20,000$ after 10 years, $\$7,448.62$ will have to be deposited.

Some kind soul, having used Eq. (18.7) without the benefit of an electronic calculator, concluded that multiplication by large decimal numbers is easier than division by such numbers. When it was recognized that Eq. (18.7) can be rewritten in the product form of Eq. (18.7a),

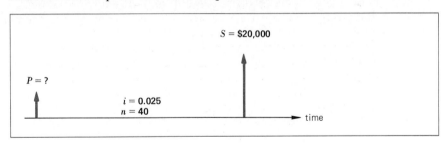

FIGURE 18.3
Present-value
problem.

$$P = \left[\frac{1}{(1 + i)^n} \right] S \qquad (18.7a)$$

tables were constructed for values of $1/(1 + i)^n$, or $(1 + i)^{-n}$. The factor in brackets is called the *present-value factor.* Table II (on page T.4) presents selected values for this. The values in these tables are simply the reciprocal values for those in Table I.

To solve the same problem using Table II, the appropriate value is found for $i = 0.025$ and $n = 40$. Thus

$$P = (0.37243)(\$20,000)$$
$$= \$7,448.60$$

Note that this answer is not *exactly* the same as computed with Table I—they are different by $0.02. This is due to rounding differences for the values in the two tables.

If you are wondering which table to use for these types of problems, you may use *either* one. In the following examples, Table II will be used.

EXAMPLE 5

A young man has recently received an inheritance of $200,000. He wants to take a portion of his inheritance and invest it for his later years. His goal is to accumulate $300,000 in 15 years. How much of the inheritance should be invested if the money will earn 12 percent per year compounded semiannually? How much interest will be earned over the 15 years?

SOLUTION

For this problem $S = \$300,000$, $n = 30$, and $i = 0.12/2 = 0.06$. Using Eq. (18.7a) and the appropriate value from Table II, we get

$$P = (0.17411)(\$300,000)$$
$$= \$52,233$$

Over the 15-year period, interest of $300,000 - \$52,233$, or $247,767 will be earned.

In these applications P can be considered to be the *present value* of S. That is, P and S can be considered as *equivalent* if you consider the interest which can be earned on P during n compounding periods. In Example 5, $52,233 at the time of the inheritance is considered to be the present value of $300,000 at 15 years hence. It is considered the present value because if the $52,233 is invested at that point and if it earns 12 percent per year compounded semiannually, it will grow to a value of $300,000 in 15 years.

The present-value concept implies that a dollar in hand today is not equivalent to a dollar in hand at some point in the future. We can understand this in an *investment sense* from the preceding discussions. As consumers, we can also appreciate this idea by observing the effects of inflation on prices over time. Businesses often have to evaluate proposed projects which will generate cash flows in different periods. Today, $20,000 of revenue is not equivalent to

$20,000 in revenue 10 years from now. Thus, businesses very often use the present-value concept to translate all cash flows associated with a project into equivalent dollars at one common time. We will examine this in greater detail in Sec. 18.5.

Other Applications of the Compound-Amount Formula

The following examples illustrate other applications of the compound-amount formula. They illustrate problems in which the parameters i and n are unknown.

EXAMPLE 6

When a sum of money is invested, there may be a desire to know how long it will take for the principal to grow by a given percentage. Suppose we want to know how long it will take for an investment P to double itself, given that it receives compound interest of i percent per compounding period. If an investment doubles, the ratio of the compound amount S to the principal P is 2, or

$$\frac{S}{P} = 2$$

Given the compound-amount formula

$$S = P(1 + i)^n$$

if both sides are divided by P, we get

$$\frac{S}{P} = (1 + i)^n$$

Because the ratio of S/P equals the compound-amount factor, an investment will double, when

$$(1 + i)^n = 2$$

Given the interest rate per compounding period for the investment, the number of compounding periods required would be found by selecting the appropriate column of Table I and determining the value of n for which $(1 + i)^n = 2$.

EXAMPLE 7

A lump sum of money is invested at a rate of 10 percent per year compounded quarterly. How long will it take the investment to double? To triple? To *increase by* 50 percent?

SOLUTION

For this investment the interest rate per compounding period is $0.10/4 = 0.025$. Referring to the column in Table I which corresponds to $i = 2.5$ percent, we read down, looking for a compound-amount factor equal to 2. There is no value of n for which $(1 + 0.025)^n$ equals exactly 2. However, for $n = 28$ the compound-amount factor equals 1.99650, and for $n = 29$ the compound-amount factor equals 2.04641. This suggests that after 28 quarters (or 7 years) the sum will almost have doubled in value. After 29 quarters ($7\frac{1}{4}$ years) the initial sum will have grown to slightly more than double its original value.

The sum will triple when $S/P = 3$ or when $(1 + 0.025)^n = 3$. Examining the same column in Table I, we find that the investment will be slightly less than triple in value after 11 years [for $n = 44$, $(1 + 0.025)^{44} = 2.96381$] and slightly more than triple after 11.25 years [for $n = 45$, $(1 + 0.025)^{45} = 3.03790$].

For an investment to *increase by* 50 percent

$$S = P + 0.5P$$

or

$$S = 1.5P$$

and

$$\frac{S}{P} = 1.5$$

Refer again to Table I. An investment will increase by slightly less than 50 percent after 4 years [$(1 + 0.025)^{16} = 1.48451$] and by slightly more than 50 percent after $4\frac{1}{4}$ years [$(1 + 0.025)^{17} = 1.52162$].

EXAMPLE 8

College Enrollments   The board of regents of a Southern state is planning the future college-level needs for the state. They have observed that the number of students attending state-operated schools—junior colleges, 4-year schools, and the state university—has been increasing at the rate of 7 percent per year. There are currently 80,000 students enrolled in the various schools. Assuming continued growth at the same rate, how long will it take for enrollments to reach 200,000 students?

SOLUTION

Defining current enrollments as $P = 80,000$ and future enrollments as $S = 200,000$, we have

$$\frac{S}{P} = \frac{200,000}{80,000}$$

$$= 2.5$$

Therefore, from Table I with $i = 7$ percent,

$$(1 + 0.07)^{13} = 2.40985 \qquad \text{at } n = 13$$
$$(1 + 0.07)^{14} = 2.57853 \qquad \text{at } n = 14$$

Enrollments will have increased beyond the 200,000 level after 14 years.

EXAMPLE 9

A person wishes to invest $10,000 and wants the investment to grow to $20,000 over the next 10 years. At what annual interest rate would the $10,000 have to be invested for this growth to occur, assuming annual compounding?

SOLUTION

In this problem S, P, and n are specified, and the unknown is the interest rate i. Substituting the known parameters into the compound amount formula gives

$$20{,}000 = 10{,}000(1 + i)^{10}$$

or

$$\frac{20{,}000}{10{,}000} = (1 + i)^{10}$$

$$2 = (1 + i)^{10}$$

To determine the interest rate, return to Table I and focus upon the row of values associated with $n = 10$. Read across the row until a value of 2 is found in the table. There is no compound-amount factor which equals 2 exactly, however,

$$(1 + 0.07)^{10} = 1.96715 \qquad \text{when } i = 7 \text{ percent}$$
$$(1 + 0.08)^{10} = 2.15892 \qquad \text{when } i = 8 \text{ percent}$$

The original investment will grow to $20,000 over the 10 years if it is invested at an interest rate between 7 and 8 percent. A process called *interpolation* can be used to approximate the exact interest rate required. We will not devote time to this topic in this text.

Effective Interest Rates

Interest rates are typically stated as annual percentages. The stated annual rate is usually referred to as the *nominal rate*. We have seen that when interest is compounded semiannually, quarterly, and monthly, the interest earned during a year is greater than if compounded annually. When compounding is done more frequently than annually, an *effective annual interest rate* can be determined. This is the interest rate compounded annually which is equivalent to a nominal rate compounded more frequently than annually. The two rates would be considered equivalent if both result in the same compound amount.

Let r equal the effective annual interest rate, i the nominal annual interest rate, and m the number of compounding periods per year. The equivalence between the two rates suggests that if a principal P is invested for n years, the two compound amounts would be the same, or

$$P(1 + r)^n = P\left(1 + \frac{i}{m}\right)^{nm}$$

Dividing both sides of the equation by P results in

$$(1 + r)^n = \left(1 + \frac{i}{m}\right)^{nm}$$

Taking the nth root of both sides results in

$$1 + r = \left(1 + \frac{i}{m}\right)^{m}$$

and, by rearranging, the effective annual interest rate can be computed as

$$r = \left(1 + \frac{i}{m}\right)^{m} - 1 \tag{18.8}$$

In Example 4 the investment was made with a nominal interest rate of 12 percent per year compounded quarterly. For this investment $i = 0.12$ and $m = 4$. The effective annual interest rate is

$$r = \left(1 + \frac{0.12}{4}\right)^4 - 1$$
$$= (1 + 0.03)^4 - 1$$

From Table I we can determine that $(1 + 0.03)^4 = 1.12551$. Thus,

$$r = 1.12551 - 1$$
$$= 0.12551$$

The effective annual rate is 12.551 percent.

Section 18.2 Follow-up Exercises

1   A sum of $1,000 is invested in a savings account which pays interest at a rate of 8 percent per year compounded annually. If the amount is kept on deposit for 8 years, what will the compound amount equal? How much interest will be earned during the 8 years?

2   A sum of $5,000 is invested in a savings account which pays interest at a rate of 10 percent per year compounded annually. If the amount is kept on deposit for 12 years, what will the compound amount equal? How much interest will be earned during the 12 years?

3   A company invests $750,000 in a money market fund which is expected to yield interest at a rate of 12 percent per year compounded quarterly. If the interest rate projections are valid, to what amount should the $750,000 grow over the next 10 years? How much interest will be earned during this period?

4   A university endowment fund has invested $2 million in United States government certificates of deposit. Interest of 14 percent per year, compounded semiannually, will be earned for 10 years. To what amount will the investment grow during this period? How much interest will be earned?

5   The compound-amount factor $(1 + i)^n$ is the amount to which $1 would grow after n periods if it earns compound interest of i percent per period. Determine the compound amount and the interest earned if $1 is invested for 5 years at 12 percent per year (a) compounded semiannually, (b) compounded quarterly, and (c) compounded monthly.

6   Compute the compound amount and interest if $1 million is invested under the different conditions mentioned in Exercise 5.

7   The number of students at a local university is currently 24,000. Enrollments have been growing at a rate of 4 percent per year. If enrollments continue at the same rate, what is the student population expected to be 10 years from now?

8   A sales representative for the college division of a large publisher had sales of 30,000 books this past year. Her sales have been increasing at the rate of 9 percent per year. If her sales continue to grow at this rate, how many books should she expect to sell 3 years from now?

9   Consumer prices have been increasing at an average rate of 8 percent per year compounded quarterly. The base price on a particular model Chevrolet is $7,500. If prices on this model increase at the same rate as other consumer prices, what will the expected base price of this same model be 5 years from now?

10   If consumer prices are increasing at the rate of 10 percent per year compounded semiannually, an item which costs $2.25 today will cost what amount in 10 years?

11   If a savings account awards interest of 8 percent per year compounded quarterly, what amount must be deposited today in order to accumulate $20,000 after 6 years? How much interest will be earned during these 6 years?

12   If a credit union awards interest of 8 percent per year compounded semiannually, what amount must be deposited today in order to accumulate $25,000 after 10 years? How much interest will be earned during these 10 years?

13   What sum must be deposited today at 10 percent per year compounded.quarterly if the goal is to have a compound amount of $50,000 5 years from today? How much interest will be earned during this period?

14   What sum must be deposited today at 7 percent per year compounded annually if the goal is to have a compound amount of $100,000 20 years from today? How much interest will be earned during this period?

15   A sum of $30,000 earns interest at a rate of 12 percent per year compounded semiannually. How long will it take for the investment to grow to $75,000?

16   A sum of $15,000 earns interest at a rate of 9 percent per year compounded annually. How long will it take for the investment to grow to $50,000?

17   The nominal interest rate on an investment is 16 percent per year. Determine the effective annual interest rate if (*a*) interest is compounded semiannually, (*b*) interest is compounded quarterly.

18   The nominal interest rate on an investment is 8 percent per year. Determine the effective annual interest rate if (*a*) interest is compounded semiannually, (*b*) interest is compounded quarterly.

19   If $300,000 is to grow to $500,000 over a 6-year period, at what annual rate of interest must it be invested, given that interest is compounded semiannually?

20   If $2,000 is to grow to $5,000 over an 8-year period, at what annual rate of interest must it be invested, given that interest is compounded annually?

18.3   ANNUITIES AND THEIR FUTURE VALUE

An *annuity* is a series of periodic payments. Examples of annuities include regular deposits to a savings account, monthly car, mortgage, or insurance payments, and periodic payments to a person from a retirement fund. Although an annuity may vary in dollar amount, *we will assume that an annuity involves a series of equal payments. We will also assume that the payments are all made at the end of a compounding period.* One may certainly argue that the end of one period coincides with the beginning of the next period. The important point is that the payment does not qualify for interest in the previous period but will earn full interest during the next period. Figure 18.4 illustrates a series of payments R, each of which equals $1,000. These might represent year-end deposits in a savings account or quarterly tax payments by a self-employed person to the IRS.

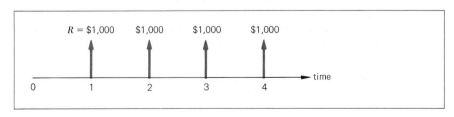

FIGURE 18.4
Annuity.

The Sum of an Annuity

Just as we had an interest in determining the future value of a lump-sum investment in Sec. 18.2, there is often some benefit in determining the future value or sum of an annuity. Example 10 illustrates a problem of this type.

EXAMPLE 10 ▰▰▰▰▰▰▰▰▰▰▰▰▰▰▰▰▰▰▰▰▰▰▰▰

A person plans to deposit $1,000 in a tax exempt savings plan at the end of this year and an equal sum at the end of each following year. If interest is expected to be earned at the rate of 6 percent per year compounded annually, to what sum will the investment grow at the time of the fourth deposit?

SOLUTION

Figure 18.5 illustrates the annuity and the timing of the deposits. Let S_n equal the sum to which the deposits will have grown *at the time of the nth deposit*. We can determine the value of S_n by applying the compound-amount formula to *each* deposit, determining its value at the time of the nth deposit. These compound amounts may be summed for the four deposits to determine S_4. Figure 18.6 summarizes these calculations.

Note that the first deposit earns interest for 3 years while the fourth deposit earns no interest. Of the $4,374.72, the interest which has been earned on the first three deposits is $374.62.

The procedure used to determine S in Example 10 is manageable but impractical when the number of payments becomes large. Let's see if we can develop a simpler approach to determine S_n. Note in Example 10 that S_4 was determined by the sum

$$S_4 = 1,000 + 1,000(1 + 0.06) + 1,000(1 + 0.06)^2 \\ + 1,000(1 + 0.06)^3 \tag{18.9}$$

Let

$$R = amount\ of\ an\ annuity$$
$$i = interest\ rate\ per\ period$$
$$n = number\ of\ annuity\ payments\ (also\ the$$
$$number\ of\ compounding\ periods)$$
$$S_n = sum\ (future\ value)\ of\ the\ annuity\ after\ n\ periods\ (payments)$$

If we wish to determine the sum S_n that a series of deposits R (made at the end of each period) will grow to after n periods, first examine Eq. (18.9) for the four-period case. The comparable expression for the n-period case is

$$S_n = R + R(1 + i) + R(1 + i)^2 + \cdots + R(1 + i)^{n-1}$$

Factoring R from the terms on the right side gives

$$S_n = R[1 + (1 + i) + (1 + i)^2 + \cdots + (1 + i)^{n-1}] \tag{18.10}$$

Multiplying both sides of the equation by $(1 + i)$ yields

$$(1 + i)S_n = (1 + i)R[1 + (1 + i) + (1 + i)^2 + \cdots + (1 + i)^{n-1}]$$

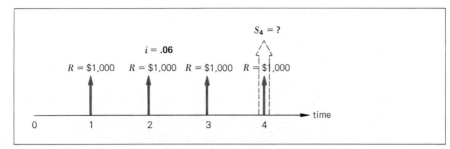

FIGURE 18.5
Annuity and its
future value.

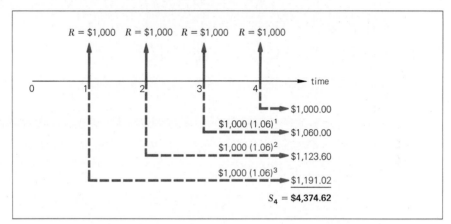

FIGURE 18.6
Calculating
future value
of each pay-
ment R.

which simplifies to

$$S_n + iS_n = R[(1 + i) + (1 + i)^2 + (1 + i)^3 + \cdots + (1 + i)^n] \quad \textbf{(18.11)}$$

Subtracting Eq. (18.10) from (18.11) results in

$$iS_n = R(1 + i)^n - R$$

or

$$iS_n = R[(1 + i)^n - 1]$$

Solving for S_n, we get

$$S_n = R\left[\frac{(1 + i)^n - 1}{i}\right] \quad \textbf{(18.12)}$$

The expression in brackets is called the *series compound-amount factor.* As with
the compound-amount factor, tables have been constructed which contain values of this factor for different values of i and n. Table III (on page T.8) contains
selected values for this factor.

EXAMPLE 11 ▬▬▬▬▬▬▬▬▬▬▬▬▬▬▬▬▬▬▬▬▬▬▬

Re-solve Example 10 using Eq. (18.12).

SOLUTION

Since $i = 0.06$ and $n = 4$, the appropriate entry in Table III is 4.37461. Substituting this
value and $R = \$1,000$ into Eq. (18.12) yields

$$S_4 = \$1,000(4.37462)$$
$$= \$4374.62$$

which is the same answer as before.

NOTE

An assumption in this section is that interest is computed at the time of each payment. Annual payments earn interest compounded annually, quarterly payments earn interest compounded quarterly, and so forth. Differences between the timing of payments and interest computation (e.g., annual deposits to an account which earns interest compounded quarterly) can be handled by means other than those discussed in this chapter.

EXAMPLE 12

A 12-year-old wants to begin saving for college. She plans to deposit \$50 in a savings account at the end of each quarter for the next 6 years. Interest is earned at a rate of 8 percent per year compounded quarterly. What should her account balance be 6 years from now? How much interest will she earn?

SOLUTION

In this problem $R = \$50$, $i = 0.08/4 = 0.02$, and $n = $ (6 years)(4 quarters per year) $= 24$ compounding periods. The appropriate entry in Table III is 30.42186. Substituting into Eq. (18.12), we have

$$S_{24} = \$50(30.42186)$$
$$= \$1521.09$$

Over the 6-year period she will make 24 deposits of \$50 for a total of \$1,200. Interest for the period will be \$1521.09 − \$1,200.00 = \$321.09.

Determining the Size of an Annuity

As with the compound-amount formula, Eq. (18.12) can be solved for any of the four parameters, given values for the other three. For example, we might have a goal of accumulating a particular sum of money by some future time. If the rate of interest which can be earned is known, the question becomes, What amount should be deposited each period in order to reach the goal?

To solve such a problem, Eq. (18.12) can be solved for R, or

$$R = \frac{S_n}{[(1 + i)^n - 1]/i}$$

This can be rewritten as

$$R = S_n \left[\frac{i}{(1 + i)^n - 1} \right] \qquad (18.13)$$

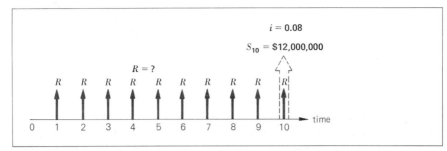

FIGURE 18.7
Determining the
size of an
annuity.

where the expression in brackets is the reciprocal of the series compound amount factor. This factor is often called the *sinking fund factor.* This is because the series of deposits used to accumulate some future sum of money is often called a *sinking fund.* Values for the sinking fund factor are found in Table IV (on page T.12).

EXAMPLE 13

A corporation wants to establish a sinking fund beginning at the end of this year. Annual deposits will be made at the end of this year and for the following 9 years. If deposits earn interest at the rate of 8 percent per year compounded annually, how much money must be deposited each year in order to have $12 million at the time of the tenth deposit? How much interest will be earned?

SOLUTION

Figure 18.7 indicates the situation for this problem. In this problem $S_{10} = 12 million, $i = 0.08$, and $n = 10$. The appropriate sinking fund factor in Table IV is 0.06903. Substituting into Eq. (18.13) gives

$$R = \$12,000,000(0.06903)$$
$$= \$828,360$$

Since 10 deposits of $828,360 will be made during this period, total deposits will equal $8,283,600. Because these deposits plus accumulated interest will equal $12 million, interest of $12,000,000 − $8,283,600 = $3,716,400 will be earned.

EXAMPLE 14

Assume in the last example that the corporation is going to make quarterly deposits and that interest is earned at the rate of 8 percent per year compounded quarterly. How much money should be deposited each quarter? How much less will the company have to deposit over the 10-year period as compared with annual deposits and annual compounding?

SOLUTION

For this problem $S_{40} = 12 million, $i = 0.08/4 = 0.02$, and $n = 40$. The appropriate sinking fund factor in Table IV is 0.01656. Substituting into Eq. (18.13) yields

$$R = \$12,000,000(0.01656)$$
$$= \$198,720$$

Since there will be 40 deposits of $198,720, total deposits over the 10-year period will equal $7,948,800. Compared with annual deposits and annual compounding in Example 13, total deposits required to accumulate the $12 million will be $8,283,600 − $7,948,800 = $334,800 less under the quarterly plan.

Section 18.3 Follow-up Exercises

1   A person wishes to deposit $2,500 per year in a savings account which earns interest of 10 percent per year compounded annually. Assume the first deposit is made at the end of this current year and additional deposits at the end of each following year.
(a) To what sum will the investment grow at the time of the 20th deposit?
(b) How much interest will be earned?

2   A company wants to deposit $500,000 per year in an investment which earns interest of 12 percent per year compounded annually. Assume the first deposit is made at the end of the current year and additional deposits at the end of each following year.
(a) To what sum will the investment grow at the time of the 10th deposit?
(b) How much interest will be earned?

3   A mother wishes to set up a savings account for her son's education. She plans on investing $250 when her son is 6 months old and every 6 months after. The account earns interest of 8 percent per year, compounded semiannually.
(a) To what amount will the account grow by the time of her son's eighteenth birthday?
(b) How much interest will be earned during this period?

4   A local university is planning to invest $50,000 every 3 months in an investment which earns interest at the rate of 12 percent per year compounded quarterly. The first investment will be at the end of this current quarter.
(a) To what sum will the investment grow at the end of 10 years?
(b) How much interest will be earned during this period?

5   A person wants to deposit $10,000 per year for 5 years. If interest is earned at the rate of 14 percent per year, compute the amount to which the deposits will grow by the end of the 5 years if:
(a) Deposits of $10,000 are made at the end of each year with interest compounded annually.
(b) Deposits of $5,000 are made at the end of each 6-month period with interest compounded semiannually.
(c) Deposits of $2,500 are made at the end of every quarter with interest compounded quarterly.

6   A corporation wants to deposit $10 million per year for 10 years. If interest is earned at the rate of 12 percent per year, compute the amount to which the deposits will grow if:
(a) Deposits of $10 million are made at the end of each year with interest compounded annually.
(b) Deposits of $5 million are made at the end of each 6-month period with interest compounded semiannually.
(c) Deposits of $2.5 million are made at the end of each quarter with interest compounded quarterly.

7   How much money must be deposited at the end of each year if the objective is to

accumulate $20,000 by the time of the fifth deposit? Assume interest is earned at the rate of 10 percent per year compounded annually. How much interest will be earned on the deposits?

8 How much money must be deposited at the end of each quarter if the objective is to accumulate $800,000 after 5 years? Assume interest is earned at the rate of 10 percent per year compounded quarterly. How much interest will be earned?

9 A family wants to begin saving for a trip to Europe. The trip is planned for 3 years from now, and the family wants to accumulate $10,000 for the trip. If 12 deposits are made quarterly to an account which earns interest at the rate of 8 percent per year compounded quarterly, how much should each deposit equal? How much interest will be earned on their deposits?

10 A major city wants to establish a sinking fund to pay off debts of $50 million which come due in 5 years. The city can earn interest at the rate of 9 percent per year compounded semiannually. If the first deposit is made 6 months from now, what semi-annual deposit will be required to accumulate the $50 million? How much interest will be earned on these deposits?

18.4 ANNUITIES AND THEIR PRESENT VALUE

Just as there are problems relating annuities and their equivalent future value, there are applications which relate an annuity to its present-value equivalent. For example, we may be interested in determining the size of a deposit which will generate a series of payments (an annuity) for college, retirement years, and so forth. Or, given that a loan has been made, we may be interested in determining the series of payments (annuity) necessary to repay the loan with interest. This section discusses problems of these types.

The Present Value of an Annuity

The *present value of an annuity* is an amount of money today which is equivalent to a series of equal payments in the future. Assume you have won a lottery and lottery officials give you the choice of having a lump-sum payment today or a series of payments at the end of each of the next 5 years. The two alternatives would be considered equivalent (in a monetary sense) if by investing the lump sum today you could generate (with accumulated interest) annual withdrawals equal to the five installments offered by the lottery officials. *An assumption is that the final withdrawal would deplete the investment completely.* Consider the following example.

EXAMPLE 15 ▰▰▰▰▰▰▰▰▰▰▰▰▰▰▰▰▰▰▰▰▰▰▰▰▰▰▰▰

Lottery A person recently won a state lottery. The terms of the lottery are that the winner will receive annual payments of $20,000 at the end of this year and each of the following 3 years. If the winner could invest money today at the rate of 8 percent per year compounded annually, what is the present value of the four payments?

SOLUTION

Figure 18.8 illustrates the situation. If A is defined as the present value of the annuity, we might determine the value of A by computing the present value of each $20,000 payment. Applying Eq. (18.7a) and using values from Table II, we find the sum of the four

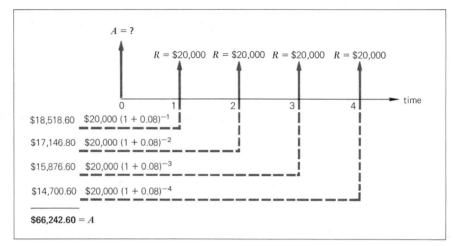

FIGURE 18.8
Calculating
present value
of each pay-
ment R.

present values is $66,242.60. We can conclude that a deposit today of $66,242.60 which earns interest at the rate of 8 percent per year compounded annually could generate a series of four withdrawals of $20,000 at the end of each of the next four years.

As with the future value of an annuity, the approach of summing the present values of each payment is possible but impractical. A more general and efficient method of determining the present value of an annuity follows.
    Let

R = amount of an annuity
i = interest rate per period
n = number of annuity payments (also, the number of compounding periods)
A = present value of the annuity

Equation (18.12), which determines the future value or sum of an annuity, is restated below.

$$S_n = R\frac{(1 + i)^n - 1}{i}$$ **(18.12)**

Looking at Fig. 18.9, we can think of S_n as being the equivalent future value of the annuity. If we know the value of S_n, the present value A of the annuity should simply be the present value of S_n, or

$$A = S_n(1 + i)^{-n}$$

Substituting the expression for S_n from Eq. (18.12) yields

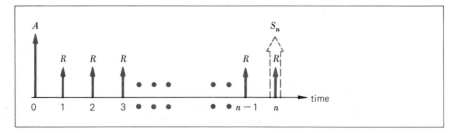

FIGURE 18.9

$$A = R\frac{(1 + i)^n - 1}{i}(1 + i)^{-n} \tag{18.13}$$

or

$$\boxed{A = R\left[\frac{(1 + i)^n - 1}{i(1 + i)^n}\right]} \tag{18.14}$$

Equation (18.14) can be used to compute the present value A of an annuity consisting of n equal payments R, each made at the end of n periods. The expression in brackets is referred to as the *series present-worth factor*, and selected values for this factor are contained in Table V (on page T.16).

EXAMPLE 16

Rework Example 15 using Equation (18.14).

SOLUTION

Since $i = 0.08$ and $n = 4$, the appropriate value from Table V is 3.31213. Substituting this value and $R = \$20,000$ into Eq. (18.14) yields

$$A = \$20,000(3.31213)$$
$$= \$66,242.60$$

EXAMPLE 17

Parents of a teenage girl want to deposit a sum of money which will earn interest at the rate of 9 percent per year compounded semiannually. The deposit will be used to generate a series of eight semiannual payments of \$2,500 beginning 6 months after the deposit. These payments will be used to help finance their daughter's college education. What amount must be deposited to achieve their goal? How much interest will be earned on this deposit?

SOLUTION

For this problem, $R = \$2,500$, $i = 0.09/2 = 0.045$, and $n = 8$. The appropriate value of the series present-worth factor is 6.59589. Substituting into Eq. (18.14) gives

$$A = (\$2,500)(6.59589)$$
$$= \$16,489.73$$

Since the \$16,489.73 will generate eight payments totaling \$20,000, interest of \$20,000 − \$16,489.73 or \$3,510.27 will be earned.

Determining the Size of the Annuity

There are problems in which we may be given the present value of an annuity and need to determine the size of the corresponding annuity. For example, given a loan of \$10,000 which is received today, what quarterly payments must be made to repay the loan in 5 years if interest is charged at the rate of 10 percent per year, compounded quarterly? The process of repaying a loan by installment payments is referred to as *amortizing a loan.*

For the loan example, the quarterly payments can be calculated by solving for R in Eq. (18.14). Solving for R, we get

$$R = \frac{A}{[(1 + i)^n - 1]/[i(1 + i)^n]}$$

or
$$R = A\left[\frac{i(1 + i)^n}{(1 + i)^n - 1}\right] \qquad (18.15)$$

The expression in brackets is sometimes called the *capital-recovery factor.* Table VI (on page T.20) contains selected values for this factor.

EXAMPLE 18

Determine the quarterly payment necessary to repay the previously mentioned $10,000 loan. How much interest will be paid on the loan?

SOLUTION

For this problem $A = \$10,000$, $i = 0.10/4 = 0.025$, and $n = 20$. The corresponding factor in Table VI is 0.06415. Substituting into Eq. (18.15) gives

$$R = \$10,000(0.06415)$$
$$= \$641.50$$

There will be 20 payments totaling $12,830; thus interest will equal $2,830 on the loan.

EXAMPLE 19

Retirement Planning   An employee has contributed with her employer to a retirement plan. At the date of her retirement, the total retirement benefits are $250,000. The retirement program provides for investment of this sum at an interest rate of 12 percent per year compounded semiannually. Semiannual disbursements will be made for 30 years to the employee or, in the event of her death, to her heirs. What semiannual payment should be generated? How much interest will be earned on the $250,000 over the 30 years?

SOLUTION

For this problem $A = \$250,000$, $i = 0.12/2 = 0.06$, and $n = 60$. The appropriate value from Table VI is 0.06188. Substituting into Eq. (18.15), we get

$$R = \$250,000(0.06188)$$
$$= \$928,200.$$

Total payments over the 30 years will equal $928,200. Thus, interest of $928,200 − $250,000, or $678,200, will be earned over the 30 years.

Mortgages

Sooner or later, many of us succumb to the "American dream" of owning a home. However, with the growth of interest rates this dream is becoming one realized by fewer and fewer people. Aside from the numerous pleasures of home ownership, there is *at least* one time during each month when we cringe from the effects of owning a home. That time is when we sign a check for the monthly mortgage payment. And whether we realize it or not, we spend an incredible amount of money to realize our dream.

Given a mortgage loan, many homeowners do not realize how the amount of their mortgage payment is calculated. It is calculated in the same way as were the loan payments in the last section. That is, they are calculated by using Eq. (18.15). Interest is typically compounded monthly, and the interest rate per compounding period can equal unusual fractions or decimal answers. If the annual interest rate is 8.5 percent, the value of i is $0.085/12 = \frac{17}{24}$ of a percent, or 0.0070833. Obviously Table VI cannot be used for these interest rates.

Table VII (on page T.24) is an extension of Table VI designed specifically for determining mortgage payments. Note that the interest rates are stated as annual percentages.

EXAMPLE 20

A person pays $100,000 for a new house. A down payment of $30,000 leaves a mortgage of $70,000 with interest computed at 13.5 percent per year compounded monthly. Determine the monthly mortgage payment if the loan is to be repaid over (a) 20 years, (b) 25 years, and (c) 30 years. (d) Compute total interest under the three different loan periods.

SOLUTION

(a) From Table VII, the monthly payment per dollar of mortgage is 0.01207375 (corresponding to $n = 20 \times 12 = 240$ payments). Therefore

$$R = \$70,000(0.01207375)$$
$$= \$845.16$$

(b) For 25 years (or 300 monthly payments),

$$R = \$70,000(0.01165645)$$
$$= \$815.95$$

(c) For 30 years (or 360 monthly payments)

$$R = \$70,000(0.01145412)$$
$$= \$801.79$$

(d) Total payments are

$$(240)(\$845.16) = \$202,838.40 \quad \text{for 20 years}$$
$$(300)(\$815.95) = \$244,785.00 \quad \text{for 25 years}$$
$$(360)(\$801.79) = \$288,644.40 \quad \text{for 30 years}$$

Because these payments are all repaying a $70,000 loan, interest on the loan is

$$\$202,838.40 - \$70,000 = \$132,838.40 \quad \text{for 20 years}$$
$$\$244,785.00 - \$70,000 = \$174,785.00 \quad \text{for 25 years}$$
$$\$288,644.40 - \$70,000 = \$218,644.40 \quad \text{for 30 years}$$

EXAMPLE 21

In the previous problem, determine the effects of a decrease in the interest rate to 13 percent (a) on monthly payments for the 25-year mortgage, (b) on total interest for the 25-year mortgage.

SOLUTION

(*a*) For $i = 13.00$ and 25 years,

$$R = (0.01127835)(70{,}000)$$
$$= \$789.50$$

Therefore, monthly payments are less by an amount

$$\$815.95 - \$789.50 = \$26.40$$

(*b*) Total payments over the 25 years will equal

$$300(789.50) = \$236{,}850$$

The total interest is \$166,850, which is \$7,935 less than with the 13.5 percent mortgage.

EXAMPLE 22

Maximum Affordable Loan A couple estimates that they can afford a monthly mortgage of \$750. Current mortgage interest rates are 16.5 percent. If a 30-year mortgage is obtainable, what is the maximum mortgage loan this couple can afford?

SOLUTION

The formula for computing the monthly mortgage payment is

$$\text{Monthly payment} = \left(\begin{array}{c}\text{mortgage loan} \\ \text{amount}\end{array}\right)\left(\begin{array}{c}\text{monthly payment per} \\ \text{dollar of mortgage loan,} \\ \text{Table VII}\end{array}\right)$$

or

$$\boxed{R = A\left(\begin{array}{c}\text{Table VII} \\ \text{factor}\end{array}\right)} \qquad (18.16)$$

In this problem, A is the unknown. If Eq. (18.16) is rearranged,

$$A = \frac{R}{\text{Table VII factor}}$$

$$= \frac{750}{0.01385148} = \$54{,}145.84$$

Section 18.4 Follow-up Exercises

1 Determine the present value of a series of 20 annual payments of \$7,500 each which begins 1 year from today. Assume interest of 8 percent per year compounded annually.

2 Determine the present value of a series of 25 annual payments of \$1,000 each which begins 1 year from today. Assume interest of 9 percent per year compounded annually.

3 Determine the present value of a series of 25 semiannual payments of \$2,000 each which begins in 6 months. Assume interest of 12 percent per year compounded semiannually.

4 Determine the present value of a series of 36 quarterly payments of $5,000 each which begins in 3 months. Assume interest of 12 percent per year compounded quarterly.

5 A person wants to buy a life insurance policy which would yield a large enough sum of money to provide for 25 annual payments of $20,000 to surviving members of the family. The payments would begin 1 year from the time of death. It is assumed that interest could be earned on the sum received from the policy at a rate of 10 percent per year compounded annually.

(*a*) What amount of insurance should be taken out so as to ensure the desired annuity?

(*b*) How much interest will be earned on the policy benefits over the 25-year period?

6 Assume in Exercise 5 that semiannual payments of $10,000 are desired over the 25-year period, and interest is compounded semiannually.

(*a*) What amount of insurance should be taken out?

(*b*) How does this amount compare with that for Exercise 5?

(*c*) How much interest will be earned on the policy benefits?

(*d*) How does this compare with that for Exercise 5?

7 Given $100,000 today, determine the equivalent series of 10 annual payments which could be generated beginning in 1 year. Assume interest is 14 percent compounded annually.

8 Given $5 million today, determine the equivalent series of 20 annual payments which could be generated beginning in 1 year. Assume interest of 11 percent compounded annually.

9 Given $750,000 today, determine the equivalent series of 40 quarterly payments which could be generated beginning in 3 months. Assume interest of 10 percent per year compounded quarterly.

10 Given $10 million today, determine the equivalent series of 20 semiannual payments which could be generated beginning in 6 months. Assume interest of 12 percent per year compounded semiannually.

11 (*a*) Determine the monthly car payment necessary to repay a $5,000 automobile loan if interest is computed at 18 percent per year compounded monthly. Assume the period of the loan is 3 years.

(*b*) How much interest will be paid over the 3-year period?

12 (*a*) Determine the quarterly payment necessary to repay a $20,000 loan if interest is computed at the rate of 14 percent per year compounded quarterly. Assume the loan is to be repaid in 10 years.

(*b*) How much interest will be paid over the 10-year period?

For Exercises 13–16 compute the monthly mortgage payment, total payments, and total interest.

13 Mortgage loan of $60,000 at 12 percent per year for 25 years

14 Mortgage loan of $100,000 at 14.5 percent per year for 30 years

15 Mortgage loan of $80,000 at 12.5 percent per year for 20 years

16 Mortgage loan of $200,000 at 16.5 percent per year for 30 years

17 to 20 Rework Exercises 13–16 computing the difference between the amount of the monthly mortgage payment and the *total* interest paid if the interest rate increases by 1 percent.

21 A couple estimates that they can afford a mortgage payment of $650 per month.

They can obtain a 25-year mortgage at an interest rate of 15.00 percent. What is the largest mortgage loan they can afford?

22 A couple estimates that they can afford a mortgage payment of $800 per month. They can obtain a 30-year mortgage at an interest rate of 14.75 percent. What is the largest mortgage loan they can afford?

18.5 COST-BENEFIT ANALYSIS

When organizations evaluate the financial feasibility of investment decisions, the time value of money is an essential consideration. This is particularly true when a project involves cash flow patterns which extend over a number of years. This section will discuss one way in which such multiperiod investments can be evaluated.

Discounted Cash Flow

Consider an investment decision characterized by the cash flow pattern shown in Fig. 18.10. An initial investment of $50,000 is expected to generate a net (after expenses) return of $15,000 at the end of 1 year and an equal return at the end of the following 3 years. Thus, a $50,000 investment is expected to return $60,000 over a 4-year period. Because the cash inflows occur over a 4-year period, the dollars during the different periods cannot be considered equivalent. To evaluate this project properly, the time value of the different cash flows must be accounted for.

One approach to evaluating a project like this is to translate all cash flows into equivalent dollars at a common base period. This is called a ***discounted cash flow method.*** For example, this project might be evaluated by restating all cash flows in terms of their equivalent values at $t = 0$, the time of the investment. The original $50,000 is stated in terms of dollars at $t = 0$. However, each of the $15,000 cash inflows must be restated in terms of their equivalent values at $t = 0$.

In order to discount all cash flows to a common base period, an interest rate must be assumed for the intervening period. Frequently this interest rate is an assumed minimum desired rate of return on investments. For example, management might state that a minimum desired rate of return on all investments is 10 percent per year. How this figure is obtained by management is another issue in itself. Sometimes it is a reflection of the known rate of return which can be earned on alternative investments (e.g., bonds, money market funds, etc.).

Let's assume that the minimum desired rate of return for the project in Fig. 18.10 is 8 percent per year. Our discounted cash flow analysis will compute the ***net present value (NPV)*** of all cash flows for the project. The net present value is the algebraic sum of the present value of all cash flows associated with a project; cash *inflows* are treated as positive cash flows and cash *outflows* as negative cash

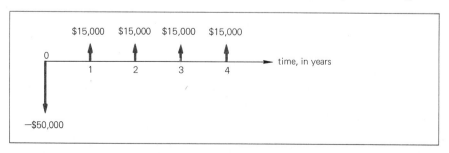

FIGURE 18.10
Net cash flows.

flows. *If the net present value of all cash flows is **positive** at the assumed minimum rate of return, the actual rate of return from the project exceeds the minimum desired rate of return. If the net present value for all cash flows is **negative,** the actual rate of return from the project is less than the minimum desired rate of return.*

In our example, we discount the four $15,000 figures at 8 percent. By computing the present value of these figures, we are, in effect, determining the amount of money we would have to invest today ($t = 0$) at 8 percent in order to generate those four cash flows. Given that the net cash return values are equal, we can treat this as the computation of the present value of an annuity. Using Table V and Eq. (18.14), with $n = 4$ and $i = 0.08$,

$$A = 15,000(3.31213)$$
$$= \$49,681.95$$

This value suggests that an investment of $49,681.95 would generate an annual payment of $15,000 at the end of each of the following 4 years. In this example, an investment of $50,000 is required.

The net present value for this project combines the present values of all cash flows at $t = 0$, or

$$\boxed{\text{NPV} = \frac{\text{present value}}{\text{of cash inflows}} - \frac{\text{present value}}{\text{of cash outflows}}} \qquad (18.17)$$

Thus,

$$\text{NPV} = \$49,681.80 - \$50,000$$
$$= -\$318.20$$

This negative value indicates that the project will result in a rate of return less than the minimum desired return of 8 percent per year, compounded annually.

EXAMPLE 23 ▰▰▰▰▰▰▰▰▰▰▰▰▰▰▰▰▰▰▰▰▰▰▰▰▰▰▰▰▰▰▰▰▰▰▰

Nonuniform Cash Flow Patterns   The previous example resulted in net cash inflows which were equal over 4 years. The cash flow patterns for most investments tend to be irregular, both with regard to amount of money and timing of cash flows. Consider the cash flow pattern illustrated in Fig. 18.11. For this investment project, a $1 million investment results in no cash flow during the first year. However, at the end of each of the following 5 years the investment generates a stream of positive net returns. These returns are not equal to one another, increasing to a maximum of $450,000 at the end of the fourth year and decreasing finally to $100,000 at the end of the sixth year.

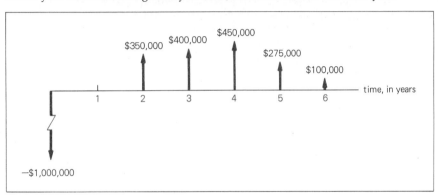

FIGURE 18.11
Net cash flows.

Suppose that the minimum desired return on investments is 12 percent. In order to evaluate the desirability of this project, we must discount all cash flows to their equivalent values at $t = 0$. In contrast with the previous example, each net return figure must be discounted separately. The present value of each is computed as shown in the following table.

n	NET RETURN	PRESENT-VALUE FACTOR $(1 + 0.12)^{-n}$	PRESENT VALUE
2	$350,000	0.79719	$ 279.016.50
3	400,000	0.71178	284,712.00
4	450,000	0.63552	285,984.00
5	275,000	0.56743	156,043.25
6	100,000	0.50663	50,663.00
			$1,056,418.75

The net present value of all cash flows is

$$NPV = \$1,056,418.75 - \$1,000,000 = \$56,418.75$$

Because the net present value is positive, this project will result in a rate of return which exceeds the minimum desired rate of return of 12 percent per year, compounded annually. Another way of viewing this is that $1,056,418.75, invested at 12 percent per year, will generate the indicated net returns; this investment only requires $1,000,000.

Extensions of Discounted Cash Flow Analysis

The net-present-value approach is one of a variety of methods available to evaluate long range investment decisions. Although this analysis allows one to determine if a project satisfies the minimum desired rate of return criterion, it does not provide a measure of the exact rate of return. Knowing the actual rate of return is desirable, especially if there is a set of competing investment opportunities which differ with respect to amount of investment and investment time horizon. Methods for computing the actual rate of return are simple extensions of the net-present-value technique. The actual rate of return from a project is the one which results in a net present value of 0. This can be found using a trial-and-error approach. The net present value of a project is computed using different interest rates until the NPV equals (approximately) 0.

Another consideration in evaluating such projects is the impact of taxes. Although some organizations evaluate projects on a *before-tax* basis, most find that the best analysis is on an *after-tax* basis. Considering investment credits as well as a variety of possible depreciation methods, an after-tax analysis usually is most appropriate.

Section 18.5 Follow-up Exercises

In Exercises 1 to 6, determine whether the investment project depicted by the cash flow diagram satisfies the minimum desired rate of return criterion. What is the NPV at the indicated interest rate?

1 Cash flow depicted in Fig. 18.12, 10 percent per year minimum rate of return.
2 Cash flow depicted in Fig. 18.13, 8 percent per year minimum rate of return.
3 Cash flow depicted in Fig. 18.14, 12 percent per year minimum rate of return.
4 Cash flow depicted in Fig. 18.15, 9 percent per year minimum rate of return.

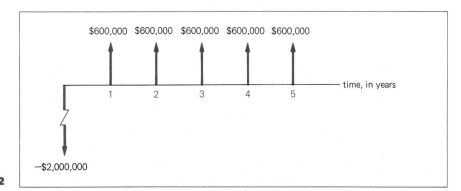

FIGURE 18.12

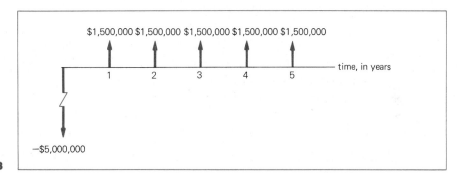

FIGURE 18.13

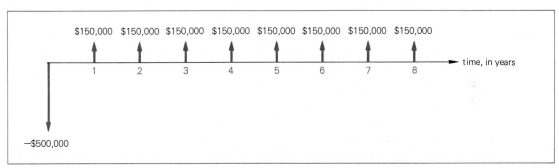

FIGURE 18.14
(above)

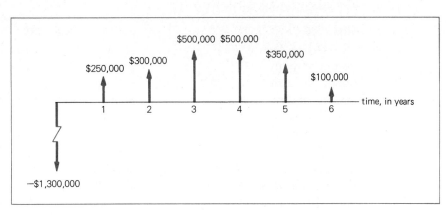

FIGURE 18.15
(right)

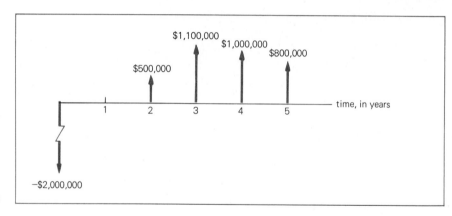

FIGURE 18.16

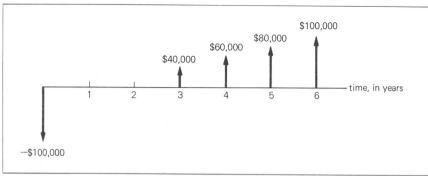

FIGURE 18.17

5   Cash flow depicted in Fig. 18.16, 10 percent per year minimum rate of return.
6   Cash flow depicted in Fig. 18.17, 14 percent per year minimum rate of return.
*7 Estimate the actual rate of return generated by the project depicted in Fig. 18.12.
*8 Estimate the actual rate of return generated by the project depicted in Fig. 18.13.

KEY TERMS AND CONCEPTS

IMPORTANT FORMULAS

$$I = Pin \tag{18.1}$$

$$S = P(1 + i)^n \tag{18.6}$$

$$P = \frac{1}{(1 + i)^n} S \tag{18.7a}$$

$$r = \left(1 + \frac{i}{m}\right)^m - 1 \tag{18.8}$$

$$S_n = R \frac{(1 + i)^n - 1}{i} \tag{18.12}$$

$$R = S_n \frac{i}{(1 + i)^n - 1} \tag{18.13}$$

$$A = R \frac{(1 + i)^n - 1}{i(1 + i)^n} \tag{18.14}$$

$$R = A \frac{i(1 + i)^n}{(1 + i)^n - 1} \tag{18.15}$$

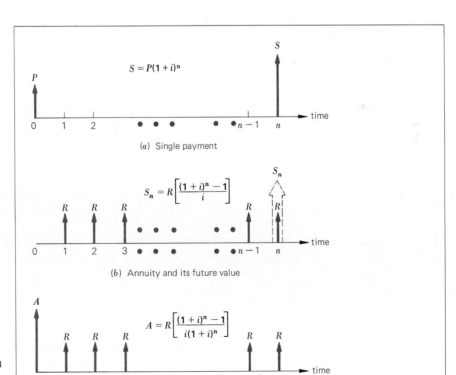

FIGURE 18.18 Summary of single payment and annuity cash flow situations.

ADDITIONAL EXERCISES

Exercises 1 to 11 are related to Sec. 18.2.

1   Sales of personal computers costing less than $1,000 were estimated to equal $336 million in 1982. One analyst estimates that sales will grow at a rate of 60 percent per year over the next 5 years. Predict annual sales for the year 1987. (Since our tables only go up as high as 20 percent, approximate the answer by assuming growth at a rate of 60 percent per year compounded quarterly.)

2   **Fire Protection**   The number of fires reported each year in a major United States city has been increasing at a rate of 5 percent per year. The number of fires reported for the year 1980 was 12,000. If the number of fires continues to increase at the same rate, how many will be expected in 1990?

3   A sum of $2 million has been invested at an interest rate of 18 percent per year. If the investment is made for a period of 10 years, determine the compound amount if interest is compounded (*a*) annually, (*b*) semiannually, (*c*) quarterly, (*d*) bimonthly.

4   Prices for a particular commodity have been increasing at an annual rate of 8 percent compounded annually. The current price of the commodity is $25. What was the price of the same item 4 years ago?

5   A sum of money will be deposited today at 9 percent per year. The goal is to have this sum grow to $50,000 in 8 years. What sum must be deposited if interest is compounded (*a*) annually, (*b*) semiannually?

6   **Real Estate**   Real estate prices within a state have been increasing at an average rate of 12 percent per year. How long will it take for current prices to increase by 50 percent if prices continue to increase at the same rate?

7   **Alcoholism**   A state health agency has gathered data on the number of known alcoholics in the state. The number is currently 60,000. Data indicate that this number has been increasing at a rate of 2.5 percent per year and is expected to increase at the same rate in the future. How long will it take for the number of alcoholics in the state to reach a level of 90,000?

8   **Public Utilities**   A major water utility estimates that the average daily consumption of water within a certain city is 30 million gallons. It has projected that the average daily consumption will equal 40 million gallons in 5 years. What annual rate of growth has the utility used in making its estimate of future consumption?

9   If compounding is done annually, at what interest rate must a sum be invested if it is to double in value over the next 9 years?

10   The nominal interest rate on an investment is 14 percent per year. Determine the effective annual interest rate if interest is compounded (*a*) semiannually, (*b*) quarterly.

11   The nominal interest rate on an investment is 10 percent per year. Determine the effective annual interest rate if interest is compounded (*a*) semiannually, (*b*) quarterly.

Exercises 12 to 17 are related to Sec. 18.3.

12   Quarterly deposits of $5,000 are to be made in an account which earns interest at the rate of 10 percent per year compounded quarterly. To what sum will the investment grow by the time of the twentieth deposit? How much interest will be earned during this period?

13   A person wishes to deposit $1,000 per year for 10 years. If interest is earned at the rate of 16 percent per year, compute the amount that the deposits will grow to by the end of 10 years if:

(*a*) Deposits of $1,000 are made at the end of each year with interest compounded annually.

(*b*) Deposits of $500 are made at the end of each 6-month period with interest compounded semiannually.

(*c*) Deposits of $250 are made at the end of every quarter with interest compounded quarterly.

14 How much money must be deposited at the end of each 6-month period if the objective is to accumulate $20,000 by the time of the eighth deposit? Assume that interest is earned at the rate of 9 percent per year compounded semiannually. How much interest will be earned on these deposits?

15 A small community wants to establish a sinking fund to pay off debts of $5 million associated with the construction of a sewage treatment plant. The community can earn interest at the rate of 12 percent per year compounded quarterly. The debt comes due in 6 years. If the first deposit is made 3 months from now, what quarterly deposit will be required to accumulate the $5 million? How much interest will be earned on these deposits?

16 Interest can be earned on a savings account at the rate of 8 percent per year compounded annually. A person wishes to make deposits of $1,000 at the end of each year. How long will it take for the deposits and accumulated interest to grow to a sum which will exceed $10,000?

17 Interest can be earned on a savings account at the rate of 10 percent per year compounded quarterly. If deposits of $10,000 are made at the end of each quarter, how long will it take for the deposits and accumulated interest to grow to a sum which exceeds $500,000?

Exercises 18 to 26 are related to Sec. 18.4.

18 Determine the present value of a series of 20 quarterly payments of $1,500 each which begins in 3 months. Assume interest is 10 percent per year compounded quarterly.

19 A person recently won a state lottery. The terms of the lottery are that the winner will receive annual payments of $10,000 at the end of this year and each of the following 19 years. If money can be invested today at the rate of 13 percent per year compounded annually, what is the present value of the 20 lottery payments?

20 Given $500,000 today, determine the equivalent series of 36 semiannual payments which could be generated beginning in 6 months. Assume interest can be earned at a rate of 14 percent per year compounded semiannually.

21 (*a*) Determine the monthly car payment necessary to repay a $4,000 automobile loan if interest is computed at 18 percent per year compounded monthly. Assume the period of the loan is 3 years. (*b*) How much interest will be paid over the 3-year period?

22 A lump sum of $100,000 is invested at the rate of 15 percent per year compounded annually. How many annual withdrawals of $10,000 can be made (assume that the first withdrawal occurs in one year)?

23 A family has inherited $50,000. If they choose to invest the $50,000 at 12 percent per year compounded quarterly, how many quarterly withdrawals of $5,000 can be made (assume that the first withdrawal is 3 months after the investment is made)?

24 Determine the monthly mortgage payment, total payments, and total interest on a 25-year mortgage loan of $40,000 if the interest rate is 16.5 percent per year.

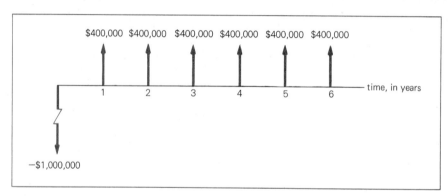

FIGURE 18.19

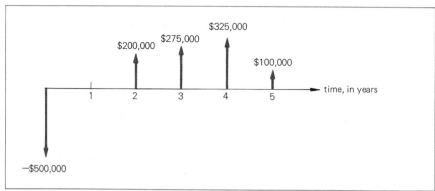

FIGURE 18.20

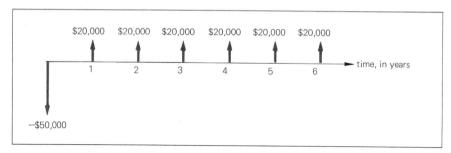

FIGURE 18.21

25 Determine the monthly mortgage payment, total payments, and total interest on a 30-year mortgage loan of $50,000 if the interest rate is 17.25 percent per year.

26 A person estimates that she can afford a mortgage payment of $750 per month. If she can obtain a 25-year mortgage at an interest rate of 16.75 percent, what is the largest mortgage she can afford?

Exercises 27 to 30 are related to Sec. 18.5.

27 Determine whether the investment project depicted in Fig. 18.19 has a rate of return greater than or equal to 14 percent per year. What is the NPV at this interest rate?

28 Determine whether the investment project depicted in Fig. 18.20 has a rate of return greater than or equal to 11 percent per year. What is the NPV at this interest rate?

*29 Estimate the actual rate of return generated by the project depicted in Fig. 18.21.

*30 Estimate the actual rate of return generated by the project depicted in Fig. 18.22.

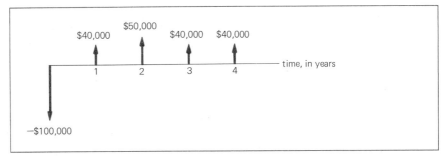

FIGURE 18.22

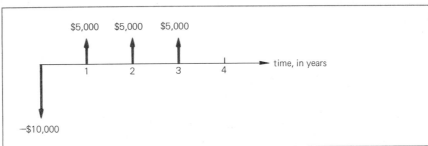

FIGURE 18.23

CHAPTER TEST

1 A principal of $20,000 has been invested at an interest rate of 8 percent per year compounded semiannually. If the principal is invested for 8 years, determine the compound amount at the end of this period.

2 Real estate prices in one locality have been increasing at a rate of 8 percent per year compounded annually. A house which sells for $100,000 today would have sold for what price 3 years ago?

3 Quarterly deposits of $2,500 are to be made in an account which earns interest at the rate of 12 percent per year compounded quarterly.
(*a*) To what sum will the investment grow by the time of the fortieth deposit?
(*b*) How much interest will be earned during this period?

4 A sinking fund is to be established to repay debts totaling $20,000. The debts come due in 5 years. If interest can be earned at the rate of 10 percent per year compounded semiannually, what semiannual deposit will be required to accumulate the $20,000 (assume the first deposit is made in 6 months)? How much interest will be earned on these deposits?

5 Given $25,000 today, determine the equivalent series of 12 annual payments which could be generated beginning in 1 year. Assume interest of 9 percent per year compounded annually.

6 The nominal interest rate on an investment is 18 percent per year. Determine the effective annual interest rate if interest is compounded quarterly.

7 A mortgage loan of $80,000 is available at an annual interest rate of 17.50 percent. What is the difference between the monthly mortgage payments if the loan is for 20 years versus 30 years?

8 Does the investment project depicted in Fig. 18.23 have a rate of return greater than or equal to 10 percent? What is the NPV at this interest rate?

MINICASE

XYZ CORPORATION

The XYZ Corporation is considering three alternative investments characterized by the data shown in the accompanying table. Notice that the three investments have equal initial cash outlays, equal lifetimes, and equal dollar returns. Note that the patterns of dollar returns are different for the three investments.

	Alternative		
	1	2	3
Initial investment	$180,000	$180,000	$180,000
Cash inflows:*	$ 80,000	$120,000	$ 40,000
	80,000	80,000	80,000
	80,000	40,000	120,000
Total cash inflows	$240,000	$240,000	$240,000

* Assume that cash inflows occur at the end of each year.

Required:
(*a*) XYZ Corporation has a minimum desired rate of return on investments of 15 percent. Determine the NPV of each of these investments and determine which meet the rate of return criterion.
(*b*) Use *linear interpolation* to estimate the actual rates of return for the three investment alternatives. Linear interpolation is a trial-and-error method of estimating actual rates of return when such rates are different from those available from tables (or calculators). To illustrate, we used the discounted cash flow method to conclude that the investment portrayed in Fig. 18.10 resulted in a rate of return less than 8 percent per year. Our basis for this conclusion was that the NPV for the investment at 8 percent per year was −$318.20.

Remember, the actual rate of return on an investment is one which results in a NPV of 0. For the investment in Fig. 18.10, the next lowest interest rate available from our tables is 7 percent. If the NPV is computed at a 7 percent rate, you will find that it equals +$808.15. We can conclude from this that the actual rate of return is between 7 and 8 percent per year. Linear interpolation assumes that interest rates are proportionate to NPV dollars. For this example, the actual interest rate lies somewhere between

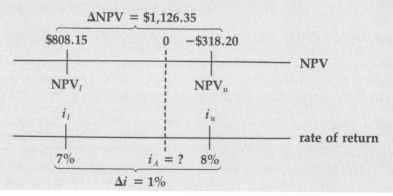

7 and 8 percent, in proportion to the location of a NPV of 0 (located between the NPV of $808.15 at 7 percent and the NPV of −$318.20 at 8 percent).

Given the lower interest rate i_l and upper interest rate i_u which bound the actual rate of return, and their respective net present values NPV_l and NPV_u, one method of estimating the actual rate of return is

$$i_A = i_l + \frac{NPV_l}{\Delta NPV} \Delta i$$

For this example, the estimated actual rate of return is

$$i_A = 0.07 + \frac{808.15}{1126.35} 0.01 = 0.07 + 0.717(0.01)$$

$$= 0.07717$$

The actual interest rate is approximately 7.717 percent.

TABLE I

COMPOUND-AMOUNT FACTOR $(1 + i)^n$

n:	0.01 (1%)	0.015 (1½%)	0.02 (2%)	0.025 (2½%)	0.03 (3%)	0.035 (3½%)
			i			
1	1.01000	1.01500	1.02000	1.02500	1.03000	1.03500
2	1.02010	1.03022	1.04040	1.05062	1.06090	1.07122
3	1.03030	1.04568	1.06121	1.07689	1.09273	1.10872
4	1.04060	1.06136	1.08243	1.10381	1.12551	1.14752
5	1.05101	1.07728	1.10408	1.13141	1.15927	1.18769
6	1.06152	1.09344	1.12616	1.15969	1.19405	1.22926
7	1.07214	1.10984	1.14869	1.18869	1.22987	1.27228
8	1.08286	1.12649	1.17166	1.21840	1.26677	1.31681
9	1.09369	1.14339	1.19509	1.24886	1.30477	1.36290
10	1.10462	1.16054	1.21899	1.28008	1.34392	1.41060
11	1.11567	1.17795	1.24337	1.31209	1.38423	1.45997
12	1.12683	1.19562	1.26824	1.34489	1.42576	1.51107
13	1.13809	1.21355	1.29361	1.37851	1.46853	1.56396
14	1.14947	1.23176	1.31948	1.41297	1.51259	1.61869
15	1.16097	1.25023	1.34587	1.44830	1.55797	1.67535
16	1.17258	1.26899	1.37279	1.48451	1.60471	1.73399
17	1.18430	1.28802	1.40024	1.52162	1.65285	1.79468
18	1.19615	1.30734	1.42825	1.55966	1.70243	1.85749
19	1.20811	1.32695	1.45681	1.59865	1.75351	1.92250
20	1.22019	1.34686	1.48595	1.63862	1.80611	1.98979
21	1.23239	1.36706	1.51567	1.67958	1.86029	2.05943
22	1.24472	1.38756	1.54598	1.72157	1.91610	2.13151
23	1.25716	1.40838	1.57690	1.76461	1.97359	2.20611
24	1.26973	1.42950	1.60844	1.80873	2.03279	2.28333
25	1.28243	1.45095	1.64061	1.85394	2.09378	2.36324
26	1.29526	1.47271	1.67342	1.90029	2.15659	2.44596
27	1.30821	1.49480	1.70689	1.94780	2.22129	2.53157
28	1.32129	1.51722	1.74102	1.99650	2.28793	2.62017
29	1.33450	1.53998	1.77584	2.04641	2.35657	2.71188
30	1.34785	1.56308	1.81136	2.09757	2.42726	2.80679
31	1.36133	1.58653	1.84759	2.15001	2.50008	2.90503
32	1.37494	1.61032	1.88454	2.20376	2.57508	3.00671
33	1.38869	1.63448	1.92223	2.25885	2.65234	3.11194
34	1.40258	1.65900	1.96068	2.31532	2.73191	3.22086
35	1.41660	1.68388	1.99989	2.37321	2.81386	3.33359
36	1.43077	1.70914	2.03989	2.43254	2.89828	3.45027
37	1.44508	1.73478	2.08069	2.49335	2.98523	3.57103
38	1.45953	1.76080	2.12230	2.55568	3.07478	3.69601
39	1.47412	1.78721	2.16474	2.61957	3.16703	3.82537
40	1.48886	1.81402	2.20804	2.68506	3.26204	3.95926
41	1.50375	1.84123	2.25220	2.75219	3.35990	4.09783
42	1.51879	1.86885	2.29724	2.82100	3.46070	4.24126
43	1.53398	1.89688	2.34319	2.89152	3.56452	4.38970
44	1.54932	1.92533	2.39005	2.96381	3.67145	4.54334
45	1.56481	1.95421	2.43785	3.03790	3.78160	4.70236
46	1.58046	1.98353	2.48661	3.11385	3.89504	4.86694
47	1.59626	2.01328	2.53634	3.19170	4.01190	5.03728
48	1.61223	2.04348	2.58707	3.27149	4.13225	5.21359
49	1.62835	2.07413	2.63881	3.35328	4.25622	5.39606
50	1.64463	2.10524	2.69159	3.43711	4.38391	5.58493
51	1.66108	2.13682	2.74542	3.52304	4.51542	5.78040
52	1.67769	2.16887	2.80033	3.61111	4.65089	5.98271
53	1.69447	2.20141	2.85633	3.70139	4.79041	6.19211
54	1.71141	2.23443	2.91346	3.79392	4.93412	6.40883
55	1.72852	2.26794	2.97173	3.88877	5.08215	6.63314
56	1.74581	2.30196	3.03117	3.98599	5.23461	6.86530
57	1.76327	2.33649	3.09179	4.08564	5.39165	7.10559
58	1.78090	2.37154	3.15362	4.18778	5.55340	7.35428
59	1.79871	2.40711	3.21670	4.29248	5.72000	7.61168
60	1.81670	2.44322	3.28103	4.39979	5.89160	7.87809

TABLE I
(Continued)

n	0.04 (4%)	0.045 (4½%)	0.05 (5%)	0.06 (6%)	0.07 (7%)	0.08 (8%)
1	1.04000	1.04500	1.05000	1.06000	1.07000	1.08000
2	1.08160	1.09202	1.10250	1.12360	1.14490	1.16640
3	1.12486	1.14117	1.15762	1.19102	1.22504	1.25971
4	1.16986	1.19252	1.21551	1.26248	1.31080	1.36049
5	1.21665	1.24618	1.27628	1.33823	1.40255	1.46933
6	1.26532	1.30226	1.34010	1.41852	1.50073	1.58687
7	1.31593	1.36086	1.40710	1.50363	1.60578	1.71382
8	1.36857	1.42210	1.47746	1.59385	1.71819	1.85093
9	1.42331	1.48610	1.55133	1.68948	1.83846	1.99900
10	1.48024	1.55297	1.62889	1.79085	1.96715	2.15892
11	1.53945	1.62285	1.71034	1.89830	2.10485	2.33164
12	1.60103	1.69588	1.79586	2.01220	2.25219	2.51817
13	1.66507	1.77220	1.88565	2.13293	2.40985	2.71962
14	1.73168	1.85194	1.97993	2.26090	2.57853	2.93719
15	1.80094	1.93528	2.07893	2.39656	2.75903	3.17217
16	1.87298	2.02237	2.18287	2.54035	2.95216	3.42594
17	1.94790	2.11338	2.29202	2.69277	3.15882	3.70002
18	2.02582	2.20848	2.40662	2.85434	3.37993	3.99602
19	2.10685	2.30786	2.52695	3.02560	3.61653	4.31570
20	2.19112	2.41171	2.65330	3.20714	3.86968	4.66096
21	2.27877	2.52024	2.78596	3.39956	4.14056	5.03383
22	2.36992	2.63365	2.92526	3.60354	4.43040	5.43654
23	2.46472	2.75217	3.07152	3.81975	4.74053	5.87146
24	2.56330	2.87601	3.22510	4.04893	5.07237	6.34118
25	2.66584	3.00543	3.38635	4.29187	5.42743	6.84848
26	2.77247	3.14068	3.55567	4.54938	5.80735	7.39635
27	2.88337	3.28201	3.73346	4.82235	6.21387	7.98806
28	2.99870	3.42970	3.92013	5.11169	6.64884	8.62711
29	3.11865	3.58404	4.11614	5.41839	7.11426	9.31727
30	3.24340	3.74532	4.32194	5.74349	7.61226	10.06266
31	3.37313	3.91386	4.53804	6.08810	8.14511	10.86767
32	3.50806	4.08998	4.76494	6.45339	8.71527	11.73708
33	3.64838	4.27403	5.00319	6.84059	9.32534	12.67605
34	3.79432	4.46636	5.25335	7.25103	9.97811	13.69013
35	3.94609	4.66735	5.51602	7.68609	10.67658	14.78534
36	4.10393	4.87738	5.79182	8.14725	11.42394	15.96817
37	4.26809	5.09686	6.08141	8.63609	12.22362	17.24563
38	4.43881	5.32622	6.38548	9.15425	13.07927	18.62528
39	4.61637	5.56590	6.70475	9.70351	13.99482	20.11530
40	4.80102	5.81636	7.03999	10.28572	14.97446	21.72452
41	4.99306	6.07810	7.39199	10.90286	16.02267	23.46248
42	5.19278	6.35162	7.76159	11.55703	17.14426	25.33948
43	5.40050	6.63744	8.14967	12.25045	18.34435	27.36664
44	5.61652	6.93612	8.55715	12.98548	19.62846	29.55597
45	5.84118	7.24825	8.98501	13.76461	21.00245	31.92045
46	6.07482	7.57442	9.43426	14.59049	22.47262	34.47409
47	6.31782	7.91527	9.90597	15.46592	24.04571	37.23201
48	6.57053	8.27146	10.40127	16.39387	25.72891	40.21057
49	6.83335	8.64367	10.92133	17.37750	27.52993	43.42742
50	7.10668	9.03264	11.46740	18.42015	29.45703	46.90161
51	7.39095	9.43910	12.04077	19.52536	31.51902	50.65374
52	7.68659	9.86386	12.64281	20.69689	33.72535	54.70604
53	7.99405	10.30774	13.27495	21.93870	36.08612	59.08252
54	8.31381	10.77159	13.93870	23.25502	38.61215	63.80913
55	8.64637	11.25631	14.63563	24.65032	41.31500	68.91386
56	8.99222	11.76284	15.36741	26.12934	44.20705	74.42696
57	9.35191	12.29217	16.13578	27.69710	47.30155	80.38112
58	9.72599	12.84532	16.94257	29.35893	50.61265	86.81161
59	10.11503	13.42336	17.78970	31.12046	54.15554	93.75654
60	10.51963	14.02741	18.67919	32.98769	57.94643	101.25706

TABLE I
(Continued)

n:	0.09 (9%)	0.10 (10%)	0.11 (11%)	0.12 (12%)	0.13 (13%)	0.14 (14%)
1	1.09000	1.10000	1.11000	1.12000	1.13000	1.14000
2	1.18810	1.21000	1.23210	1.25440	1.27690	1.29960
3	1.29503	1.33100	1.36763	1.40493	1.44290	1.48154
4	1.41158	1.46410	1.51807	1.57352	1.63047	1.68896
5	1.53862	1.61051	1.68506	1.76234	1.84244	1.92541
6	1.67710	1.77156	1.87041	1.97382	2.08195	2.19497
7	1.82804	1.94872	2.07616	2.21068	2.35261	2.50227
8	1.99256	2.14359	2.30454	2.47596	2.65844	2.85259
9	2.17189	2.35795	2.55804	2.77308	3.00404	3.25195
10	2.36736	2.59374	2.83942	3.10585	3.39457	3.70722
11	2.58043	2.85312	3.15176	3.47855	3.83586	4.22623
12	2.81266	3.13843	3.49845	3.89598	4.33452	4.81790
13	3.06580	3.45227	3.88328	4.36349	4.89801	5.49241
14	3.34173	3.79750	4.31044	4.88711	5.53475	6.26135
15	3.64248	4.17725	4.78459	5.47357	6.25427	7.13794
16	3.97031	4.59497	5.31089	6.13039	7.06733	8.13725
17	4.32763	5.05447	5.89509	6.86604	7.98608	9.27646
18	4.71712	5.55992	6.54355	7.68997	9.02427	10.57517
19	5.14166	6.11591	7.26334	8.61276	10.19742	12.05569
20	5.60441	6.72750	8.06231	9.64629	11.52309	13.74349
21	6.10881	7.40025	8.94917	10.80385	13.02109	15.66758
22	6.65860	8.14027	9.93357	12.10031	14.71383	17.86104
23	7.25787	8.95430	11.02627	13.55235	16.62663	20.36158
24	7.91108	9.84973	12.23916	15.17863	18.78809	23.21221
25	8.62308	10.83471	13.58546	17.00006	21.23054	26.46192
26	9.39916	11.91818	15.07986	19.04007	23.99051	30.16658
27	10.24508	13.10999	16.73865	21.32488	27.10928	34.38991
28	11.16714	14.42099	18.57990	23.88387	30.63349	39.20449
29	12.17218	15.86309	20.62369	26.74993	34.61584	44.69312
30	13.26768	17.44940	22.89230	29.95992	39.11590	50.95016
31	14.46177	19.19434	25.41045	33.55511	44.20096	58.08318
32	15.76333	21.11378	28.20560	37.58173	49.94709	66.21483
33	17.18203	23.22515	31.30821	42.09153	56.44021	75.48490
34	18.72841	25.54767	34.75212	47.14252	63.77744	86.05279
35	20.41397	28.10244	38.57485	52.79962	72.06851	98.10018
36	22.25123	30.91268	42.81808	59.13557	81.43741	111.83420
37	24.25384	34.00395	47.52807	66.23184	92.02428	127.49099
38	26.43668	37.40434	52.75616	74.17966	103.98743	145.33973
39	28.81598	41.14478	58.55934	83.08122	117.50580	165.68729
40	31.40942	45.25926	65.00087	93.05097	132.78155	188.88351
41	34.23627	49.78518	72.15096	104.21709	150.04315	215.32721
42	37.31753	54.76370	80.08757	116.72314	169.54876	245.47301
43	40.67611	60.24007	88.89720	130.72991	191.59010	279.83924
44	44.33696	66.26408	98.67589	146.41750	216.49682	319.01673
45	48.32729	72.89048	109.53024	163.98760	244.64140	363.67907
46	52.67674	80.17953	121.57857	183.66612	276.44478	414.59414
47	57.41765	88.19749	134.95221	205.70605	312.38261	472.63732
48	62.58524	97.01723	149.79695	230.39078	352.99234	538.80655
49	68.21791	106.71896	166.27462	258.03767	398.88135	614.23946
50	74.35752	117.39085	184.56483	289.00219	450.73593	700.23299
51	81.04970	129.12994	204.86696	323.68245	509.33160	798.26561
52	88.34417	142.04293	227.40232	362.52435	575.54470	910.02279
53	96.29514	156.24723	252.41658	406.02727	650.36551	1037.42598
54	104.96171	171.87195	280.18240	454.75054	734.91303	1182.66562
55	114.40826	189.05914	311.00247	509.32061	830.45173	1348.23881
56	124.70501	207.96506	345.21274	570.43908	938.41045	1536.99224
57	135.92846	228.76156	383.18614	638.89177	1060.40381	1752.17115
58	148.16202	251.63772	425.33661	715.55878	1198.25630	1997.47512
59	161.49660	276.80149	472.12364	801.42583	1354.02962	2277.12163
60	176.03129	304.48164	524.05724	897.59693	1530.05347	2595.91866

TABLE I
(Continued)

n	0.15 (15%)	0.16 (16%)	0.17 (17%)	0.18 (18%)	0.19 (19%)	0.20 (20%)
1	1.15000	1.16000	1.17000	1.18000	1.19000	1.20000
2	1.32250	1.34560	1.36890	1.39240	1.41610	1.44000
3	1.52087	1.56090	1.60161	1.64303	1.68516	1.72800
4	1.74901	1.81064	1.87389	1.93878	2.00534	2.07360
5	2.01136	2.10034	2.19245	2.28776	2.38635	2.48832
6	2.31306	2.43640	2.56516	2.69955	2.83976	2.98598
7	2.66002	2.82622	3.00124	3.18547	3.37932	3.58318
8	3.05902	3.27841	3.51145	3.75886	4.02139	4.29982
9	3.51788	3.80296	4.10840	4.43545	4.78545	5.15978
10	4.04556	4.41144	4.80683	5.23384	5.69468	6.19174
11	4.65239	5.11726	5.62399	6.17593	6.77667	7.43008
12	5.35025	5.93603	6.58007	7.28759	8.06424	8.91610
13	6.15279	6.88579	7.69868	8.59936	9.59645	10.69932
14	7.07571	7.98752	9.00745	10.14724	11.41977	12.83918
15	8.13706	9.26552	10.53872	11.97375	13.58953	15.40702
16	9.35762	10.74800	12.33030	14.12902	16.17154	18.48843
17	10.76126	12.46768	14.42646	16.67225	19.24413	22.18611
18	12.37545	14.46251	16.87895	19.67325	22.90052	26.62333
19	14.23177	16.77652	19.74838	23.21444	27.25162	31.94800
20	16.36654	19.46076	23.10560	27.39303	32.42942	38.33760
21	18.82152	22.57448	27.03355	32.32378	38.59101	46.00512
22	21.64475	26.18640	31.62925	38.14206	45.92331	55.20614
23	24.89146	30.37622	37.00623	45.00763	54.64873	66.24737
24	28.62518	35.23642	43.29729	53.10901	65.03199	79.49685
25	32.91895	40.87424	50.65783	62.66863	77.38807	95.39622
26	37.85680	47.41412	59.26966	73.94898	92.09181	114.47546
27	43.53531	55.00038	69.34550	87.25980	109.58925	137.37055
28	50.06561	63.80044	81.13423	102.96656	130.41121	164.84466
29	57.57545	74.00851	94.92705	121.50054	155.18934	197.81359
30	66.21177	85.84988	111.06465	143.37064	184.67531	237.37631
31	76.14354	99.58586	129.94564	169.17735	219.76362	284.85158
32	87.56507	115.51959	152.03640	199.62928	261.51871	341.82189
33	100.69983	134.00273	177.88259	235.56255	311.20726	410.18627
34	115.80480	155.44317	208.12263	277.96381	370.33664	492.22352
35	133.17552	180.31407	243.50347	327.99729	440.70061	590.66823
36	153.15185	209.16432	284.89906	387.03680	524.43372	708.80187
37	176.12463	242.63062	333.33191	456.70343	624.07613	850.56225
38	202.54332	281.45151	389.99833	538.91004	742.65059	1020.67470
39	232.92482	326.48376	456.29805	635.91385	883.75421	1224.80964
40	267.86355	378.72116	533.86871	750.37834	1051.66751	1469.77157
41	308.04308	439.31654	624.62639	885.44645	1251.48433	1763.72588
42	354.24954	509.60719	730.81288	1044.82681	1489.26636	2116.47106
43	407.38697	591.14434	855.05107	1232.89563	1772.22696	2539.76527
44	468.49502	685.72744	1000.40975	1454.81685	2108.95009	3047.71832
45	538.76927	795.44383	1170.47941	1716.68388	2509.65060	3657.26199
46	619.58466	922.71484	1369.46091	2025.68698	2986.48422	4388.71439
47	712.52236	1070.34921	1602.26927	2390.31063	3553.91622	5266.45726
48	819.40071	1241.60509	1874.65504	2820.56655	4229.16030	6319.74872
49	942.31082	1440.26190	2193.34640	3328.26853	5032.70076	7583.69846
50	1083.65744	1670.70380	2566.21528	3927.35686	5988.91390	9100.43815
51	1246.20606	1938.01641	3002.47188	4634.28109	7126.80754	10920.52578
52	1433.13697	2248.09904	3512.89210	5468.45169	8480.90098	13104.63094
53	1648.10751	2607.79488	4110.08376	6452.77300	10092.27216	15725.55712
54	1895.32364	3025.04207	4808.79800	7614.27214	12009.80387	18870.66855
55	2179.62218	3509.04880	5626.29366	8984.84112	14291.66661	22644.80226
56	2506.56551	4070.49660	6582.76358	10602.11252	17007.08327	27173.76271
57	2882.55034	4721.77606	7701.83339	12510.49278	20238.42909	32608.51525
58	3314.93289	5477.26023	9011.14507	14762.38148	24083.73061	39130.21830
59	3812.17282	6353.62187	10543.03973	17419.61014	28659.63943	46956.26196
60	4383.99875	7370.20137	12335.35648	20555.13997	34104.97092	56347.51435

TABLE II
PRESENT-VALUE FACTOR $(1 + i)^{-n}$

n	0.01 (1%)	0.015 ($1\frac{1}{2}$%)	0.02 (2%)	0.025 ($2\frac{1}{2}$%)	0.03 (3%)	0.035 ($3\frac{1}{2}$%)
1	0.99010	0.98522	0.98039	0.97561	0.97087	0.96618
2	0.98030	0.97066	0.96117	0.95181	0.94260	0.93351
3	0.97059	0.95632	0.94232	0.92860	0.91514	0.90194
4	0.96098	0.94218	0.92385	0.90595	0.88849	0.87144
5	0.95147	0.92826	0.90573	0.88385	0.86261	0.84197
6	0.94205	0.91454	0.88797	0.86230	0.83748	0.81350
7	0.93272	0.90103	0.87056	0.84127	0.81309	0.78599
8	0.92348	0.88771	0.85349	0.82075	0.78941	0.75941
9	0.91434	0.87459	0.83676	0.80073	0.76642	0.73373
10	0.90529	0.86167	0.82035	0.78120	0.74409	0.70892
11	0.89632	0.84893	0.80426	0.76214	0.72242	0.68495
12	0.88745	0.83639	0.78849	0.74356	0.70138	0.66178
13	0.87866	0.82403	0.77303	0.72542	0.68095	0.63940
14	0.86996	0.81185	0.75788	0.70773	0.66112	0.61778
15	0.86135	0.79985	0.74301	0.69047	0.64186	0.59689
16	0.85282	0.78803	0.72845	0.67362	0.62317	0.57671
17	0.84438	0.77639	0.71416	0.65720	0.60502	0.55720
18	0.83602	0.76491	0.70016	0.64117	0.58739	0.53836
19	0.82774	0.75361	0.68643	0.62553	0.57029	0.52016
20	0.81954	0.74247	0.67297	0.61027	0.55368	0.50257
21	0.81143	0.73150	0.65978	0.59539	0.53755	0.48557
22	0.80340	0.72069	0.64684	0.58086	0.52189	0.46915
23	0.79544	0.71004	0.63416	0.56670	0.50669	0.45329
24	0.78757	0.69954	0.62172	0.55288	0.49193	0.43796
25	0.77977	0.68921	0.60953	0.53939	0.47761	0.42315
26	0.77205	0.67902	0.59758	0.52623	0.46369	0.40884
27	0.76440	0.66899	0.58586	0.51340	0.45019	0.39501
28	0.75684	0.65910	0.57437	0.50088	0.43708	0.38165
29	0.74934	0.64936	0.56311	0.48866	0.42435	0.36875
30	0.74192	0.63976	0.55207	0.47674	0.41199	0.35628
31	0.73458	0.63031	0.54125	0.46511	0.39999	0.34423
32	0.72730	0.62099	0.53063	0.45377	0.38834	0.33259
33	0.72010	0.61182	0.52023	0.44270	0.37703	0.32134
34	0.71297	0.60277	0.51003	0.43191	0.36604	0.31048
35	0.70591	0.59387	0.50003	0.42137	0.35538	0.29998
36	0.69892	0.58509	0.49022	0.41109	0.34503	0.28983
37	0.69200	0.57644	0.48061	0.40107	0.33498	0.28003
38	0.68515	0.56792	0.47119	0.39128	0.32523	0.27056
39	0.67837	0.55953	0.46195	0.38174	0.31575	0.26141
40	0.67165	0.55126	0.45289	0.37243	0.30656	0.25257
41	0.66500	0.54312	0.44401	0.36335	0.29763	0.24403
42	0.65842	0.53509	0.43530	0.35448	0.28896	0.23578
43	0.65190	0.52718	0.42677	0.34584	0.28054	0.22781
44	0.64545	0.51939	0.41840	0.33740	0.27237	0.22010
45	0.63905	0.51171	0.41020	0.32917	0.26444	0.21266
46	0.63273	0.50415	0.40215	0.32115	0.25674	0.20547
47	0.62646	0.49670	0.39427	0.31331	0.24926	0.19852
48	0.62026	0.48936	0.38654	0.30567	0.24200	0.19181
49	0.61412	0.48213	0.37896	0.29822	0.23495	0.18532
50	0.60804	0.47500	0.37153	0.29094	0.22811	0.17905
51	0.60202	0.46798	0.36424	0.28385	0.22146	0.17300
52	0.59606	0.46107	0.35710	0.27692	0.21501	0.16715
53	0.59016	0.45426	0.35010	0.27017	0.20875	0.16150
54	0.58431	0.44754	0.34323	0.26358	0.20267	0.15603
55	0.57853	0.44093	0.33650	0.25715	0.19677	0.15076
56	0.57280	0.43441	0.32991	0.25088	0.19104	0.14566
57	0.56713	0.42799	0.32344	0.24476	0.18547	0.14073
58	0.56151	0.42167	0.31710	0.23879	0.18007	0.13598
59	0.55595	0.41544	0.31088	0.23297	0.17483	0.13138
60	0.55045	0.40930	0.30478	0.22728	0.16973	0.12693

TABLE II
(Continued)

n	0.04 (4%)	0.045 (4½%)	0.05 (5%)	0.06 (6%)	0.07 (7%)	0.08 (8%)
1	0.96154	0.95694	0.95238	0.94340	0.93458	0.92593
2	0.92456	0.91573	0.90703	0.89000	0.87344	0.85734
3	0.88900	0.87630	0.86384	0.83962	0.81630	0.79383
4	0.85480	0.83856	0.82270	0.79209	0.76290	0.73503
5	0.82193	0.80245	0.78353	0.74726	0.71299	0.68058
6	0.79031	0.76790	0.74622	0.70496	0.66634	0.63017
7	0.75992	0.73483	0.71068	0.66506	0.62275	0.58349
8	0.73069	0.70319	0.67684	0.62741	0.58201	0.54027
9	0.70259	0.67290	0.64461	0.59190	0.54393	0.50025
10	0.67556	0.64393	0.61391	0.55839	0.50835	0.46319
11	0.64958	0.61620	0.58468	0.52679	0.47509	0.42888
12	0.62460	0.58966	0.55684	0.49697	0.44401	0.39711
13	0.60057	0.56427	0.53032	0.46884	0.41496	0.36770
14	0.57748	0.53997	0.50507	0.44230	0.38782	0.34046
15	0.55526	0.51672	0.48102	0.41727	0.36245	0.31524
16	0.53391	0.49447	0.45811	0.39365	0.33873	0.29189
17	0.51337	0.47318	0.43630	0.37136	0.31657	0.27027
18	0.49363	0.45280	0.41552	0.35034	0.29586	0.25025
19	0.47464	0.43330	0.39573	0.33051	0.27651	0.23171
20	0.45639	0.41464	0.37689	0.31180	0.25842	0.21455
21	0.43883	0.39679	0.35894	0.29416	0.24151	0.19866
22	0.42196	0.37970	0.34185	0.27751	0.22571	0.18394
23	0.40573	0.36335	0.32557	0.26180	0.21095	0.17032
24	0.39012	0.34770	0.31007	0.24698	0.19715	0.15770
25	0.37512	0.33273	0.29530	0.23300	0.18425	0.14602
26	0.36069	0.31840	0.28124	0.21981	0.17220	0.13520
27	0.34682	0.30469	0.26785	0.20737	0.16093	0.12519
28	0.33348	0.29157	0.25509	0.19563	0.15040	0.11591
29	0.32065	0.27902	0.24295	0.18456	0.14056	0.10733
30	0.30832	0.26700	0.23138	0.17411	0.13137	0.09938
31	0.29646	0.25550	0.22036	0.16425	0.12277	0.09202
32	0.28506	0.24450	0.20987	0.15496	0.11474	0.08520
33	0.27409	0.23397	0.19987	0.14619	0.10723	0.07889
34	0.26355	0.22390	0.19035	0.13791	0.10022	0.07305
35	0.25342	0.21425	0.18129	0.13011	0.09366	0.06763
36	0.24367	0.20503	0.17266	0.12274	0.08754	0.06262
37	0.23430	0.19620	0.16444	0.11579	0.08181	0.05799
38	0.22529	0.18775	0.15661	0.10924	0.07646	0.05369
39	0.21662	0.17967	0.14915	0.10306	0.07146	0.04971
40	0.20829	0.17193	0.14205	0.09722	0.06678	0.04603
41	0.20028	0.16453	0.13528	0.09172	0.06241	0.04262
42	0.19257	0.15744	0.12884	0.08653	0.05833	0.03946
43	0.18517	0.15066	0.12270	0.08163	0.05451	0.03654
44	0.17805	0.14417	0.11686	0.07701	0.05095	0.03383
45	0.17120	0.13796	0.11130	0.07265	0.04761	0.03133
46	0.16461	0.13202	0.10600	0.06854	0.04450	0.02901
47	0.15828	0.12634	0.10095	0.06466	0.04159	0.02686
48	0.15219	0.12090	0.09614	0.06100	0.03837	0.02487
49	0.14634	0.11569	0.09156	0.05755	0.03632	0.02303
50	0.14071	0.11071	0.08720	0.05429	0.03395	0.02132
51	0.13530	0.10594	0.08305	0.05122	0.03173	0.01974
52	0.13010	0.10138	0.07910	0.04832	0.02965	0.01828
53	0.12509	0.09701	0.07533	0.04558	0.02771	0.01693
54	0.12028	0.09284	0.07174	0.04300	0.02590	0.01567
55	0.11566	0.08884	0.06833	0.04057	0.02420	0.01451
56	0.11121	0.08501	0.06507	0.03827	0.02262	0.01344
57	0.10693	0.08135	0.06197	0.03610	0.02114	0.01244
58	0.10282	0.07785	0.05902	0.03406	0.01976	0.01152
59	0.09886	0.07450	0.05621	0.03213	0.01847	0.01067
60	0.09506	0.07129	0.05354	0.03031	0.01726	0.00988

TABLE II
(Continued)

n	0.09 (9%)	0.10 (10%)	0.11 (11%)	0.12 (12%)	0.13 (13%)	0.14 (14%)
				i		
1	0.91743	0.90909	0.90090	0.89286	0.88496	0.87719
2	0.84168	0.82645	0.81162	0.79719	0.78315	0.76947
3	0.77218	0.75131	0.73119	0.71178	0.69305	0.67497
4	0.70843	0.68301	0.65873	0.63552	0.61332	0.59208
5	0.64993	0.62092	0.59345	0.56743	0.54276	0.51937
6	0.59627	0.56447	0.53464	0.50663	0.48032	0.45559
7	0.54703	0.51316	0.48166	0.45235	0.42506	0.39964
8	0.50187	0.46651	0.43393	0.40388	0.37616	0.35056
9	0.46043	0.42410	0.39092	0.36061	0.33288	0.30751
10	0.42241	0.38554	0.35218	0.32197	0.29459	0.26974
11	0.38753	0.35049	0.31728	0.28748	0.26070	0.23662
12	0.35553	0.31863	0.28584	0.25668	0.23071	0.20756
13	0.32618	0.28966	0.25751	0.22917	0.20416	0.18207
14	0.29925	0.26333	0.23199	0.20462	0.18068	0.15971
15	0.27454	0.23939	0.20900	0.18270	0.15989	0.14010
16	0.25187	0.21763	0.18829	0.16312	0.14150	0.12289
17	0.23107	0.19784	0.16963	0.14564	0.12522	0.10780
18	0.21199	0.17986	0.15282	0.13004	0.11081	0.09456
19	0.19449	0.16351	0.13768	0.11611	0.09806	0.08295
20	0.17843	0.14864	0.12403	0.10367	0.08678	0.07276
21	0.16370	0.13513	0.11174	0.09256	0.07680	0.06383
22	0.15018	0.12285	0.10067	0.08264	0.06796	0.05599
23	0.13778	0.11168	0.09069	0.07379	0.06014	0.04911
24	0.12640	0.10153	0.08170	0.06588	0.05323	0.04308
25	0.11597	0.09230	0.07361	0.05882	0.04710	0.03779
26	0.10639	0.08391	0.06631	0.05252	0.04168	0.03315
27	0.09761	0.07628	0.05974	0.04689	0.03689	0.02908
28	0.08955	0.06934	0.05382	0.04187	0.03264	0.02551
29	0.08215	0.06304	0.04849	0.03738	0.02889	0.02237
30	0.07537	0.05731	0.04368	0.03338	0.02557	0.01963
31	0.06915	0.05210	0.03935	0.02980	0.02262	0.01722
32	0.06344	0.04736	0.03545	0.02661	0.02002	0.01510
33	0.05820	0.04306	0.03194	0.02376	0.01772	0.01325
34	0.05339	0.03914	0.02878	0.02121	0.01568	0.01162
35	0.04899	0.03558	0.02592	0.01894	0.01388	0.01019
36	0.04494	0.03235	0.02335	0.01691	0.01228	0.00894
37	0.04123	0.02941	0.02104	0.01510	0.01087	0.00784
38	0.03783	0.02673	0.01896	0.01348	0.00962	0.00688
39	0.03470	0.02430	0.01708	0.01204	0.00851	0.00604
40	0.03184	0.02209	0.01538	0.01075	0.00753	0.00529
41	0.02921	0.02009	0.01386	0.00960	0.00666	0.00464
42	0.02680	0.01826	0.01249	0.00857	0.00590	0.00407
43	0.02458	0.01660	0.01125	0.00765	0.00522	0.00357
44	0.02255	0.01509	0.01013	0.00683	0.00462	0.00313
45	0.02069	0.01372	0.00913	0.00610	0.00409	0.00275
46	0.01898	0.01247	0.00823	0.00544	0.00362	0.00241
47	0.01742	0.01134	0.00741	0.00486	0.00320	0.00212
48	0.01598	0.01031	0.00668	0.00434	0.00283	0.00186
49	0.01466	0.00937	0.00601	0.00388	0.00251	0.00163
50	0.01345	0.00852	0.00542	0.00346	0.00222	0.00143
51	0.01234	0.00774	0.00488	0.00309	0.00196	0.00125
52	0.01132	0.00704	0.00440	0.00276	0.00174	0.00110
53	0.01038	0.00640	0.00396	0.00246	0.00154	0.00096
54	0.00953	0.00582	0.00357	0.00220	0.00136	0.00085
55	0.00874	0.00529	0.00322	0.00196	0.00120	0.00074
56	0.00802	0.00481	0.00290	0.00175	0.00107	0.00065
57	0.00736	0.00437	0.00261	0.00157	0.00094	0.00057
58	0.00675	0.00397	0.00235	0.00140	0.00083	0.00050
59	0.00619	0.00361	0.00212	0.00125	0.00074	0.00044
60	0.00568	0.00328	0.00191	0.00111	0.00065	0.00039

TABLE II
(Continued)

n	0.15 (15%)	0.16 (16%)	0.17 (17%)	0.18 (18%)	0.19 (19%)	0.20 (20%)
1	0.86957	0.86207	0.85470	0.84746	0.84034	0.83333
2	0.75614	0.74316	0.73051	0.71818	0.70616	0.69444
3	0.65752	0.64066	0.62437	0.60863	0.59342	0.57870
4	0.57175	0.55229	0.53365	0.51579	0.49867	0.48225
5	0.49718	0.47611	0.45611	0.43711	0.41905	0.40188
6	0.43233	0.41044	0.38984	0.37043	0.35214	0.33490
7	0.37594	0.35383	0.33320	0.31393	0.29592	0.27908
8	0.32690	0.30503	0.28478	0.26604	0.24867	0.23257
9	0.28426	0.26295	0.24340	0.22546	0.20897	0.19381
10	0.24718	0.22668	0.20804	0.19106	0.17560	0.16151
11	0.21494	0.19542	0.17781	0.16192	0.14757	0.13459
12	0.18691	0.16846	0.15197	0.13722	0.12400	0.11216
13	0.16253	0.14523	0.12989	0.11629	0.10421	0.09346
14	0.14133	0.12520	0.11102	0.09855	0.08757	0.07789
15	0.12289	0.10793	0.09489	0.08352	0.07359	0.06491
16	0.10686	0.09304	0.08110	0.07078	0.06184	0.05409
17	0.09293	0.08021	0.06932	0.05998	0.05196	0.04507
18	0.08081	0.06914	0.05925	0.05083	0.04367	0.03756
19	0.07027	0.05961	0.05064	0.04308	0.03670	0.03130
20	0.06110	0.05139	0.04328	0.03651	0.03084	0.02608
21	0.05313	0.04430	0.03699	0.03094	0.02591	0.02174
22	0.04620	0.03819	0.03162	0.02622	0.02178	0.01811
23	0.04017	0.03292	0.02702	0.02222	0.01830	0.01509
24	0.03493	0.02838	0.02310	0.01883	0.01538	0.01258
25	0.03038	0.02447	0.01974	0.01596	0.01292	0.01048
26	0.02642	0.02109	0.01687	0.01352	0.01086	0.00874
27	0.02297	0.01818	0.01442	0.01146	0.00912	0.00728
28	0.01997	0.01567	0.01233	0.00971	0.00767	0.00607
29	0.01737	0.01351	0.01053	0.00823	0.00644	0.00506
30	0.01510	0.01165	0.00900	0.00697	0.00541	0.00421
31	0.01313	0.01004	0.00770	0.00591	0.00455	0.00351
32	0.01142	0.00866	0.00658	0.00501	0.00382	0.00293
33	0.00993	0.00746	0.00562	0.00425	0.00321	0.00244
34	0.00864	0.00643	0.00480	0.00360	0.00270	0.00203
35	0.00751	0.00555	0.00411	0.00305	0.00227	0.00169
36	0.00653	0.00478	0.00351	0.00258	0.00191	0.00141
37	0.00568	0.00412	0.00300	0.00219	0.00160	0.00118
38	0.00494	0.00355	0.00256	0.00186	0.00135	0.00098
39	0.00429	0.00306	0.00219	0.00157	0.00113	0.00082
40	0.00373	0.00264	0.00187	0.00133	0.00095	0.00068
41	0.00325	0.00228	0.00160	0.00113	0.00080	0.00057
42	0.00282	0.00196	0.00137	0.00096	0.00067	0.00047
43	0.00245	0.00169	0.00117	0.00081	0.00056	0.00039
44	0.00213	0.00146	0.00100	0.00069	0.00047	0.00033
45	0.00186	0.00126	0.00085	0.00058	0.00040	0.00027
46	0.00161	0.00108	0.00073	0.00049	0.00033	0.00023
47	0.00140	0.00093	0.00062	0.00042	0.00028	0.00019
48	0.00122	0.00081	0.00053	0.00035	0.00024	0.00016
49	0.00106	0.00069	0.00046	0.00030	0.00020	0.00013
50	0.00092	0.00060	0.00039	0.00025	0.00017	0.00011
51	0.00080	0.00052	0.00033	0.00022	0.00014	0.00009
52	0.00070	0.00044	0.00028	0.00018	0.00012	0.00008
53	0.00061	0.00038	0.00024	0.00015	0.00010	0.00006
54	0.00053	0.00033	0.00021	0.00013	0.00008	0.00005
55	0.00046	0.00028	0.00018	0.00011	0.00007	0.00004
56	0.00040	0.00025	0.00015	0.00009	0.00006	0.00004
57	0.00035	0.00021	0.00013	0.00008	0.00005	0.00003
58	0.00030	0.00018	0.00011	0.00007	0.00004	0.00003
59	0.00026	0.00016	0.00009	0.00006	0.00003	0.00002
60	0.00023	0.00014	0.00008	0.00005	0.00003	0.00002

TABLE III

SERIES COMPOUND-AMOUNT FACTOR

n	0.01 (1%)	0.015 (1½%)	0.02 (2%)	0.025 (2½%)	0.03 (3%)	0.035 (3½%)
1	1.00000	1.00000	1.00000	1.00000	1.00000	1.00000
2	2.01000	2.01500	2.02000	2.02500	2.03000	2.03500
3	3.03010	3.04522	3.06040	3.07562	3.09090	3.10622
4	4.06040	4.09090	4.12161	4.15252	4.18363	4.21494
5	5.10101	5.15227	5.20404	5.25633	5.30914	5.36247
6	6.15202	6.22955	6.30812	6.38774	6.46841	6.55015
7	7.21354	7.32299	7.43428	7.54743	7.66246	7.77941
8	8.28567	8.43284	8.58297	8.73612	8.89234	9.05169
9	9.36853	9.55933	9.75463	9.95452	10.15911	10.36850
10	10.46221	10.70272	10.94972	11.20338	11.46388	11.73139
11	11.56683	11.86326	12.16872	12.48347	12.80780	13.14199
12	12.68250	13.04121	13.41209	13.79555	14.19203	14.60196
13	13.80933	14.23683	14.68033	15.14044	15.61779	16.11303
14	14.94742	15.45038	15.97394	16.51895	17.08632	17.67699
15	16.09690	16.68214	17.29342	17.93193	18.59891	19.29568
16	17.25786	17.93237	18.63929	19.38022	20.15688	20.97103
17	18.43044	19.20136	20.01207	20.86473	21.76159	22.70502
18	19.61475	20.48938	21.41231	22.38635	23.41444	24.49969
19	20.81090	21.79672	22.84056	23.94601	25.11687	26.35718
20	22.01900	23.12367	24.29737	25.54466	26.87037	28.27968
21	23.23919	24.47052	25.78332	27.18327	28.67649	30.26947
22	24.47159	25.83758	27.29898	28.86286	30.53678	32.32890
23	25.71630	27.22514	28.84496	30.58443	32.45288	34.46041
24	26.97346	28.63352	30.42186	32.34904	34.42647	36.66653
25	28.24320	30.06302	32.03030	34.15776	36.45926	38.94986
26	29.52563	31.51397	33.67091	36.01171	38.55304	41.31310
27	30.82089	32.98668	35.34432	37.91200	40.70963	43.75906
28	32.12910	34.48148	37.05121	39.85980	42.93092	46.29063
29	33.45039	35.99870	38.79223	41.85630	45.21885	48.91080
30	34.78489	37.53868	40.56808	43.90270	47.57542	51.62268
31	36.13274	39.10176	42.37944	46.00027	50.00268	54.42947
32	37.49407	40.68829	44.22703	48.15028	52.50276	57.33450
33	38.86901	42.29861	46.11157	50.35403	55.07784	60.34121
34	40.25770	43.93309	48.03380	52.61289	57.73018	63.45315
35	41.66028	45.59209	49.99448	54.92821	60.46208	66.67401
36	43.07688	47.27597	51.99437	57.30141	63.27594	70.00760
37	44.50765	48.98511	54.03425	59.73395	66.17422	73.45787
38	45.95272	50.71989	56.11494	62.22730	69.15945	77.02889
39	47.41225	52.48068	58.23724	64.78298	72.23423	80.72491
40	48.88637	54.26789	60.40198	67.40255	75.40126	84.55028
41	50.37524	56.08191	62.61002	70.08762	78.66330	88.50954
42	51.87899	57.92314	64.86222	72.83981	82.02320	92.60737
43	53.39778	59.79199	67.15947	75.66080	85.48389	96.84863
44	54.93176	61.68887	69.50266	78.55232	89.04841	101.23833
45	56.48107	63.61420	71.89271	81.51613	92.71986	105.78167
46	58.04589	65.56841	74.33056	84.55403	96.50146	110.48403
47	59.62634	67.55194	76.81718	87.66789	100.39650	115.35097
48	61.22261	69.56522	79.35352	90.85958	104.40840	120.38826
49	62.83483	71.60870	81.94059	94.13107	108.54065	125.60185
50	64.46318	73.68283	84.57940	97.48435	112.79687	130.99791
51	66.10781	75.78807	87.27099	100.92146	117.18077	136.58284
52	67.76889	77.92489	90.01641	104.44449	121.69620	142.36324
53	69.44658	80.09376	92.81674	108.05561	126.34708	148.34595
54	71.14105	82.29517	95.67307	111.75700	131.13749	154.53806
55	72.85246	84.52960	98.58653	115.55092	136.07162	160.94689
56	74.58098	86.79754	101.55826	119.43969	141.15377	167.58003
57	76.32679	89.09951	104.58943	123.42569	146.38838	174.44533
58	78.09006	91.43600	107.68122	127.51133	151.78003	181.55092
59	79.87096	93.80754	110.83484	131.69911	157.33343	188.90520
60	81.66967	96.21465	114.05154	135.99159	163.05344	196.51688

TABLE III
(*Continued*)

n	0.04 (4%)	0.045 (4½%)	0.05 (5%)	0.06 (6%)	0.07 (7%)	0.08 (8%)
1	1.00000	1.00000	1.00000	1.00000	1.00000	1.00000
2	2.04000	2.04500	2.05000	2.06000	2.07000	2.08000
3	3.12160	3.13702	3.15250	3.18360	3.21490	3.24640
4	4.24646	4.27819	4.31012	4.37462	4.43994	4.50611
5	5.41632	5.47071	5.52563	5.63709	5.75074	5.86660
6	6.63298	6.71689	6.80191	6.97532	7.15329	7.33593
7	7.89829	8.01915	8.14201	8.39384	8.65402	8.92280
8	9.21423	9.38001	9.54911	9.89747	10.25980	10.63663
9	10.58280	10.80211	11.02656	11.49132	11.97799	12.48756
10	12.00611	12.28821	12.57789	13.18079	13.81645	14.48656
11	13.48635	13.84118	14.20679	14.97164	15.78360	16.64549
12	15.02581	15.46403	15.91713	16.86994	17.88845	18.97713
13	16.62684	17.15991	17.71298	18.88214	20.14064	21.49530
14	18.29191	18.93211	19.59863	21.01507	22.55049	24.21492
15	20.02359	20.78405	21.57856	23.27597	25.12902	27.15211
16	21.82453	22.71934	23.65749	25.67253	27.88805	30.32428
17	23.69751	24.74171	25.84037	28.21288	30.84022	33.75023
18	25.64541	26.85508	28.13238	30.90565	33.99903	37.45024
19	27.67123	29.06356	30.53900	33.75999	37.37896	41.44626
20	29.77808	31.37142	33.06595	36.78559	40.99549	45.76196
21	31.96920	33.78314	35.71925	39.99273	44.86518	50.42292
22	34.24797	36.30338	38.50521	43.39229	49.00574	55.45676
23	36.61789	38.93703	41.43048	46.99583	53.43614	60.89330
24	39.08260	41.68920	44.50200	50.81558	58.17667	66.76476
25	41.64591	44.56521	47.72710	54.86451	63.24904	73.10594
26	44.31174	47.57064	51.11345	59.15638	68.67647	79.95442
27	47.08421	50.71132	54.66913	63.70577	74.48382	87.35077
28	49.96758	53.99333	58.40258	68.52811	80.69769	95.33883
29	52.96629	57.42303	62.32271	73.63980	87.34653	103.96594
30	56.08494	61.00707	66.43885	79.05819	94.46079	113.28321
31	59.32834	64.75239	70.76079	84.80168	102.07304	123.34587
32	62.70147	68.66625	75.29883	90.88978	110.21815	134.21354
33	66.20953	72.75623	80.06377	97.34316	118.93343	145.95062
34	69.85791	77.03026	85.06696	104.18375	128.25876	158.62667
35	73.65222	81.49662	90.32031	111.43478	138.23688	172.31680
36	77.59831	86.16397	95.83632	119.12087	148.91346	187.10215
37	81.70225	91.04134	101.62814	127.26812	160.33740	203.07032
38	85.97034	96.13820	107.70955	135.90421	172.56102	220.31595
39	90.40915	101.46442	114.09502	145.05846	185.64029	238.94122
40	95.02552	107.03032	120.79977	154.76197	199.63511	259.05652
41	99.82654	112.84669	127.83976	165.04768	214.60957	280.78104
42	104.81960	118.92479	135.23175	175.95054	230.63224	304.24352
43	110.01238	125.27640	142.99334	187.50758	247.77650	329.58301
44	115.41288	131.91384	151.14301	199.75803	266.12085	356.94965
45	121.02939	138.84997	159.70016	212.74351	285.74931	386.50562
46	126.87057	146.09821	168.68516	226.50812	306.75176	418.42607
47	132.94539	153.67263	178.11942	241.09861	329.22439	452.90015
48	139.26321	161.58790	188.02539	256.56453	353.27009	490.13216
49	145.83373	169.85936	198.42666	272.95840	378.99900	530.34274
50	152.66708	178.50303	209.34800	290.33590	406.52893	573.77016
51	159.77377	187.53566	220.81540	308.75606	435.98595	620.67177
52	167.16472	196.97477	232.85617	328.28142	467.50497	671.32551
53	174.85131	206.83863	245.49897	348.97831	501.23032	726.03155
54	182.84536	217.14637	258.77392	370.91701	537.31644	785.11408
55	191.15917	227.91796	272.71262	394.17203	575.92859	848.92320
56	199.80554	239.17427	287.34825	418.82235	617.24359	917.83706
57	208.79776	250.93711	302.71566	444.95169	661.45065	992.26402
58	218.14967	263.22928	318.85144	472.64879	708.75219	1072.64514
59	227.87566	276.07460	335.79402	502.00772	759.36484	1159.45676
60	237.99069	289.49795	353.58372	533.12818	813.52038	1253.21330

TABLE III
(Continued)

n				i		
	0.09 (9%)	0.10 (10%)	0.11 (11%)	0.12 (12%)	0.13 (13%)	0.14 (14%)
1	1.00000	1.00000	1.00000	1.00000	1.00000	1.00000
2	2.09000	2.10000	2.11000	2.12000	2.13000	2.14000
3	3.27810	3.31000	3.34210	3.37440	3.40690	3.43960
4	4.57313	4.64100	4.70973	4.77933	4.84980	4.92114
5	5.98471	6.10510	6.22780	6.35285	6.48027	6.61010
6	7.52333	7.71561	7.91286	8.11519	8.32271	8.53552
7	9.20043	9.48717	9.78327	10.08901	10.40466	10.73049
8	11.02847	11.43589	11.85943	12.29969	12.75726	13.23276
9	13.02104	13.57948	14.16397	14.77566	15.41571	16.08535
10	15.19293	15.93742	16.72201	17.54874	18.41975	19.33730
11	17.56029	18.53117	19.56143	20.65458	21.81432	23.04452
12	20.14072	21.38428	22.71319	24.13313	25.65018	27.27075
13	22.95338	24.52271	26.21164	28.02911	29.98470	32.08865
14	26.01919	27.97498	30.09492	32.39260	34.88271	37.58107
15	29.36092	31.77248	34.40536	37.27971	40.41746	43.84251
16	33.00340	35.94973	39.18995	42.75328	46.67173	50.98035
17	36.97370	40.54470	44.50084	48.88367	53.73906	59.11760
18	41.30134	45.59917	50.39594	55.74971	61.72514	68.39407
19	46.01846	51.15909	56.93949	63.43968	70.74941	78.96923
20	51.16012	57.27500	64.20283	72.05244	80.94683	91.02493
21	56.76453	64.00250	72.26514	81.69874	92.46992	104.76842
22	62.87334	71.40275	81.21431	92.50258	105.49101	120.43600
23	69.53194	79.54302	91.14788	104.60289	120.20484	138.29704
24	76.78981	88.49733	102.17415	118.15524	136.83147	158.65862
25	84.70090	98.34706	114.41331	133.33387	155.61956	181.87083
26	93.32398	109.18177	127.99877	150.33393	176.85010	208.33274
27	102.72313	121.09994	143.07864	169.37401	200.84061	238.49933
28	112.96822	134.20994	159.81729	190.69889	227.94989	272.88923
29	124.13536	148.63093	178.39719	214.58275	258.58338	312.09373
30	136.30754	164.49402	199.02088	241.33268	293.19922	356.78685
31	149.57522	181.94342	221.91317	271.29261	332.31511	407.73701
32	164.03699	201.13777	247.32362	304.84772	376.51608	465.82019
33	179.80032	222.25154	275.52922	342.42945	426.46317	532.03501
34	196.98234	245.47670	306.83744	384.52098	482.90338	607.51991
35	215.71075	271.02437	341.58955	431.66350	546.68082	693.57270
36	236.12472	299.12681	380.16441	484.46312	618.74933	791.67288
37	258.37595	330.03949	422.98249	543.59869	700.18674	903.50708
38	282.62978	364.04343	470.51056	609.83053	792.21101	1030.99808
39	309.06646	401.44778	523.26673	684.01020	896.19845	1176.33781
40	337.88245	442.59256	581.82607	767.09142	1013.70424	1342.02510
41	369.29187	487.85181	646.82693	860.14239	1146.48579	1530.90861
42	403.52813	537.63699	718.97790	964.35948	1296.52895	1746.23582
43	440.84566	592.40069	799.06547	1081.08262	1466.07771	1991.70883
44	481.52177	652.64076	887.96267	1211.81253	1657.66781	2271 54807
45	525.85873	718.90484	986.63856	1358.23003	1874.16463	2590.56480
46	574.18602	791.79532	1096.16880	1522.21764	2118.80603	2954.24387
47	626.86276	871.97485	1217.74737	1705.88375	2395.25082	3368.83801
48	684.28041	960.17234	1352.69958	1911.58980	2707.63342	3841.47534
49	746.86565	1057.18957	1502.49653	2141.98058	3060.62577	4380.28188
50	815.08356	1163.90853	1668.77115	2400.01825	3459.50712	4994.52135
51	889.44108	1281.29938	1853.33598	2689.02044	3910.24304	5694.75433
52	970.49077	1410.42932	2058.20294	3012.70289	4419.57464	6493.01994
53	1058.83494	1552.47225	2285.60526	3375.22724	4995.11934	7403.04273
54	1155.13009	1708.71948	2538.02184	3781.25451	5645.48485	8440.46872
55	1260.09180	1880.59142	2818.20424	4236.00505	6380.39789	9623.13434
56	1374.50006	2069.65057	3129.20671	4745.32565	7210.84961	10971.37314
57	1499.20506	2277.61562	3474.41944	5315.76473	8149.26006	12508.36538
58	1635.13352	2506.37719	3857.60558	5954.65650	9209.66387	14260.53654
59	1783.29553	2758.01490	4282.94220	6670.21528	10407.92017	16258.01165
60	1944.79213	3034.81640	4755.06584	7471.64111	11761.94979	18535.13328

TABLE III
(Continued)

n	0.15 (15%)	0.16 (16%)	0.17 (17%)	0.18 (18%)	0.19 (19%)	0.20 (20%)
1	1.00000	1.00000	1.00000	1.00000	1.00000	1.00000
2	2.15000	2.16000	2.17000	2.18000	2.19000	2.20000
3	3.47250	3.50560	3.53890	3.57240	3.60610	3.64000
4	4.99337	5.06650	5.14051	5.21543	5.29126	5.36800
5	6.74238	6.87714	7.01440	7.15421	7.29660	7.44160
6	8.75374	8.97748	9.20685	9.44197	9.68295	9.92992
7	11.06680	11.41387	11.77201	12.14152	12.52271	12.91590
8	13.72682	14.24009	14.77325	15.32700	15.90203	16.49908
9	16.78584	17.51851	18.28471	19.08585	19.92341	20.79890
10	20.30372	21.32147	22.39311	23.52131	24.70886	25.95868
11	24.34928	25.73290	27.19994	28.75514	30.40355	32.15042
12	29.00167	30.85017	32.82393	34.93107	37.18022	39.58050
13	34.35192	36.78620	39.40399	42.21866	45.24446	48.49660
14	40.50471	43.67199	47.10267	50.81802	54.84091	59.19592
15	47.58041	51.65951	56.11013	60.96527	66.26068	72.03511
16	55.71747	60.92503	66.64885	72.93901	79.85021	87.44213
17	65.07509	71.67303	78.97915	87.06804	96.02175	105.93056
18	75.83636	84.14072	93.40561	103.74028	115.26588	128.11667
19	88.21181	98.60323	110.28456	123.41353	138.16640	154.74000
20	102.44358	115.37975	130.03294	146.62797	165.41802	186.68800
21	118.81012	134.84051	153.13854	174.02100	197.84744	225.02560
22	137.63164	157.41499	180.17209	206.34479	236.43846	271.03072
23	159.27638	183.60138	211.80134	244.48685	282.36176	326.23686
24	184.16784	213.97761	248.80757	289.49448	337.01050	392.48424
25	212.79302	249.21402	292.10486	342.60349	402.04249	471.98108
26	245.71197	290.08827	342.76268	405.27211	479.43056	567.37730
27	283.56877	337.50239	402.03234	479.22109	571.52237	681.85276
28	327.10408	392.50277	471.37783	566.48089	681.11162	819.22331
29	377.16969	456.30322	552.51207	669.44745	811.52283	984.06797
30	434.74515	530.31172	647.43912	790.94799	966.71217	1181.88157
31	500.95692	616.16161	758.50377	934.31863	1151.38748	1419.25788
32	577.10046	715.74746	888.44941	1103.49598	1371.15110	1704.10946
33	664.66552	831.26706	1040.48581	1303.12526	1632.66981	2045.93136
34	765.36535	965.26979	1218.36839	1538.68781	1943.87708	2456.11762
35	881.17016	1120.71295	1426.49102	1816.65161	2314.21372	2948.34115
36	1014.34568	1301.02703	1669.99450	2144.64890	2754.91433	3539.00937
37	1167.49753	1510.19135	1954.89356	2531.68570	3279.34805	4247.81125
38	1343.62216	1752.82197	2288.22547	2988.38913	3903.42418	5098.37350
39	1546.16549	2034.27348	2678.22379	3527.29918	4646.07477	6119.04820
40	1779.09031	2360.75724	3134.52184	4163.21303	5529.82898	7343.85784
41	2046.95385	2739.47840	3668.39055	4913.59137	6581.49649	8813.62941
42	2354.99693	3178.79494	4293.01695	5799.03782	7832.98082	10577.35529
43	2709.24647	3688.40213	5023.82983	6843.86463	9322.24718	12693.82635
44	3116.63344	4279.54648	5878.88090	8076.76026	11094.47414	15233.59162
45	3585.12846	4965.27391	6879.29065	9531.57711	13203.42423	18281.30994
46	4123.89773	5760.71774	8049.77006	11248.26098	15713.07483	21938.57193
47	4743.48239	6683.43257	9419.23097	13273.94796	18699.55905	26327.28631
48	5456.00475	7753.78179	11021.50024	15664.25859	22253.47527	31593.74358
49	6275.40546	8995.38687	12896.15528	18484.82514	26482.63557	37913.49229
50	7217.71628	10435.64877	15089.50167	21813.09367	31515.33633	45497.19075
51	8301.37372	12106.35258	17655.71696	25740.45053	37504.25023	54597.62890
52	9547.57978	14044.36899	20658.18884	30374.73162	44631.05777	65518.15468
53	10980.71674	16292.46803	24171.08094	35843.18331	53111.95875	78622.78562
54	12628.82425	18900.26291	28281.16470	42295.95631	63204.23091	94348.34274
55	14524.14789	21925.30498	33089.96270	49910.22844	75214.03479	113219.01129
56	16703.77008	25434.35377	38716.25636	58895.06957	89505.70140	135863.81354
57	19210.33559	29504.85038	45299.01994	69497.18209	106512.78466	163037.57625
58	22092.88593	34226.62644	53000.85333	82007.67486	126751.21375	195646.09150
59	25407.81882	39703.88667	62011.99840	96770.05634	150834.94436	234776.30980
60	29219.99164	46057.50853	72555.03813	114189.66648	179494.58379	281723.57177

TABLE IV

SINKING FUND FACTOR $\dfrac{i}{(1 + i)^n - 1}$

n	0.01 (1%)	0.015 (1½%)	0.02 (2%)	0.025 (2½%)	0.03 (3%)	0.035 (3½%)
1	1.00000	1.00000	1.00000	1.00000	1.00000	1.00000
2	0.49751	0.49628	0.49505	0.49383	0.49261	0.49140
3	0.33002	0.32838	0.32675	0.32514	0.32353	0.32193
4	0.24628	0.24444	0.24262	0.24082	0.23903	0.23725
5	0.19604	0.19409	0.19216	0.19025	0.18835	0.18648
6	0.16255	0.16053	0.15853	0.15655	0.15460	0.15267
7	0.13863	0.13656	0.13451	0.13250	0.13051	0.12854
8	0.12069	0.11858	0.11651	0.11447	0.11246	0.11048
9	0.10674	0.10461	0.10252	0.10046	0.09843	0.09645
10	0.09558	0.09343	0.09133	0.08926	0.08723	0.08524
11	0.08645	0.08429	0.08218	0.08011	0.07808	0.07609
12	0.07885	0.07668	0.07456	0.07249	0.07046	0.06848
13	0.07241	0.07024	0.06812	0.06605	0.06403	0.06206
14	0.06690	0.06472	0.06260	0.06054	0.05853	0.05657
15	0.06212	0.05994	0.05783	0.05577	0.05377	0.05183
16	0.05794	0.05577	0.05365	0.05160	0.04961	0.04768
17	0.05426	0.05208	0.04997	0.04793	0.04595	0.04404
18	0.05098	0.04881	0.04670	0.04467	0.04271	0.04082
19	0.04805	0.04588	0.04378	0.04176	0.03981	0.03794
20	0.04542	0.04325	0.04116	0.03915	0.03722	0.03536
21	0.04303	0.04087	0.03878	0.03679	0.03487	0.03304
22	0.04086	0.03870	0.03663	0.03465	0.03275	0.03093
23	0.03889	0.03673	0.03467	0.03270	0.03081	0.02902
24	0.03707	0.03492	0.03287	0.03091	0.02905	0.02727
25	0.03541	0.03326	0.03122	0.02928	0.02743	0.02567
26	0.03387	0.03173	0.02970	0.02777	0.02594	0.02421
27	0.03245	0.03032	0.02829	0.02638	0.02456	0.02285
28	0.03112	0.02900	0.02699	0.02509	0.02329	0.02160
29	0.02990	0.02778	0.02578	0.02389	0.02211	0.02045
30	0.02875	0.02664	0.02465	0.02278	0.02102	0.01937
31	0.02768	0.02557	0.02360	0.02174	0.02000	0.01837
32	0.02667	0.02458	0.02261	0.02077	0.01905	0.01744
33	0.02573	0.02364	0.02169	0.01986	0.01816	0.01657
34	0.02484	0.02276	0.02082	0.01901	0.01732	0.01576
35	0.02400	0.02193	0.02000	0.01821	0.01654	0.01500
36	0.02321	0.02115	0.01923	0.01745	0.01580	0.01428
37	0.02247	0.02041	0.01851	0.01674	0.01511	0.01361
38	0.02176	0.01972	0.01782	0.01607	0.01446	0.01298
39	0.02109	0.01905	0.01717	0.01544	0.01384	0.01239
40	0.02046	0.01843	0.01656	0.01484	0.01326	0.01183
41	0.01985	0.01783	0.01597	0.01427	0.01271	0.01130
42	0.01928	0.01726	0.01542	0.01373	0.01219	0.01080
43	0.01873	0.01672	0.01489	0.01322	0.01170	0.01033
44	0.01820	0.01621	0.01439	0.01273	0.01123	0.00988
45	0.01771	0.01572	0.01391	0.01227	0.01079	0.00945
46	0.01723	0.01525	0.01345	0.01183	0.01036	0.00905
47	0.01677	0.01480	0.01302	0.01141	0.00996	0.00867
48	0.01633	0.01437	0.01260	0.01101	0.00958	0.00831
49	0.01591	0.01396	0.01220	0.01062	0.00921	0.00796
50	0.01551	0.01357	0.01182	0.01026	0.00887	0.00763
51	0.01513	0.01319	0.01146	0.00991	0.00853	0.00732
52	0.01476	0.01283	0.01111	0.00957	0.00822	0.00702
53	0.01440	0.01249	0.01077	0.00925	0.00791	0.00674
54	0.01406	0.01215	0.01045	0.00895	0.00763	0.00647
55	0.01373	0.01183	0.01014	0.00865	0.00735	0.00621
56	0.01341	0.01152	0.00985	0.00837	0.00708	0.00597
57	0.01310	0.01122	0.00956	0.00810	0.00683	0.00573
58	0.01281	0.01094	0.00929	0.00784	0.00659	0.00551
59	0.01252	0.01066	0.00902	0.00759	0.00636	0.00529
60	0.01224	0.01039	0.00877	0.00735	0.00613	0.00509

TABLE IV
(Continued)

n	0.04 (4%)	0.045 (4½%)	0.05 (5%)	0.06 (6%)	0.07 (7%)	0.08 (8%)
1	1.00000	1.00000	1.00000	1.00000	1.00000	1.00000
2	0.49020	0.48900	0.48780	0.48544	0.48309	0.48077
3	0.32035	0.31877	0.31721	0.31411	0.31105	0.30803
4	0.23549	0.23374	0.23201	0.22859	0.22523	0.22192
5	0.18463	0.18279	0.18097	0.17740	0.17389	0.17046
6	0.15076	0.14888	0.14702	0.14336	0.13980	0.13632
7	0.12661	0.12470	0.12282	0.11914	0.11555	0.11207
8	0.10853	0.10661	0.10472	0.10104	0.09747	0.09401
9	0.09449	0.09257	0.09069	0.08702	0.08349	0.08008
10	0.08329	0.08138	0.07950	0.07587	0.07238	0.06903
11	0.07415	0.07225	0.07039	0.06679	0.06336	0.06008
12	0.06655	0.06467	0.06283	0.05928	0.05590	0.05270
13	0.06014	0.05828	0.05646	0.05296	0.04965	0.04652
14	0.05467	0.05282	0.05102	0.04758	0.04434	0.04130
15	0.04994	0.04811	0.04634	0.04296	0.03979	0.03683
16	0.04582	0.04402	0.04227	0.03895	0.03586	0.03298
17	0.04220	0.04042	0.03870	0.03544	0.03243	0.02963
18	0.03899	0.03724	0.03555	0.03236	0.02941	0.02670
19	0.03614	0.03441	0.03275	0.02962	0.02675	0.02413
20	0.03358	0.03188	0.03024	0.02718	0.02439	0.02185
21	0.03128	0.02960	0.02800	0.02500	0.02229	0.01983
22	0.02920	0.02755	0.02597	0.02305	0.02041	0.01803
23	0.02731	0.02568	0.02414	0.02128	0.01871	0.01642
24	0.02559	0.02399	0.02247	0.01968	0.01719	0.01498
25	0.02401	0.02244	0.02095	0.01823	0.01581	0.01368
26	0.02257	0.02102	0.01956	0.01690	0.01456	0.01251
27	0.02124	0.01972	0.01829	0.01570	0.01343	0.01145
28	0.02001	0.01852	0.01712	0.01459	0.01239	0.01049
29	0.01888	0.01741	0.01605	0.01358	0.01145	0.00962
30	0.01783	0.01639	0.01505	0.01265	0.01059	0.00883
31	0.01686	0.01544	0.01413	0.01179	0.00980	0.00811
32	0.01595	0.01456	0.01328	0.01100	0.00907	0.00745
33	0.01510	0.01374	0.01249	0.01027	0.00841	0.00685
34	0.01431	0.01298	0.01176	0.00960	0.00780	0.00630
35	0.01358	0.01227	0.01107	0.00897	0.00723	0.00580
36	0.01289	0.01161	0.01043	0.00839	0.00672	0.00534
37	0.01224	0.01098	0.00984	0.00786	0.00624	0.00492
38	0.01163	0.01040	0.00928	0.00736	0.00580	0.00454
39	0.01106	0.00986	0.00876	0.00689	0.00539	0.00419
40	0.01052	0.00934	0.00828	0.00646	0.00501	0.00386
41	0.01002	0.00886	0.00782	0.00606	0.00466	0.00356
42	0.00954	0.00841	0.00739	0.00568	0.00434	0.00329
43	0.00909	0.00798	0.00699	0.00533	0.00404	0.00303
44	0.00866	0.00758	0.00662	0.00501	0.00376	0.00280
45	0.00826	0.00720	0.00626	0.00470	0.00350	0.00259
46	0.00788	0.00684	0.00593	0.00441	0.00326	0.00239
47	0.00752	0.00651	0.00561	0.00415	0.00304	0.00221
48	0.00718	0.00619	0.00532	0.00390	0.00283	0.00204
49	0.00686	0.00589	0.00504	0.00366	0.00264	0.00189
50	0.00655	0.00560	0.00478	0.00344	0.00246	0.00174
51	0.00626	0.00533	0.00453	0.00324	0.00229	0.00161
52	0.00598	0.00508	0.00429	0.00305	0.00214	0.00149
53	0.00572	0.00483	0.00407	0.00287	0.00200	0.00138
54	0.00547	0.00461	0.00386	0.00270	0.00186	0.00127
55	0.00523	0.00439	0.00367	0.00254	0.00174	0.00118
56	0.00500	0.00418	0.00348	0.00239	0.00162	0.00109
57	0.00479	0.00399	0.00330	0.00225	0.00151	0.00101
58	0.00458	0.00380	0.00314	0.00212	0.00141	0.00093
59	0.00439	0.00362	0.00298	0.00199	0.00132	0.00086
60	0.00420	0.00345	0.00283	0.00188	0.00123	0.00080

TABLE IV
(Continued)

n	0.09 (9%)	0.10 (10%)	0.11 (11%)	0.12 (12%)	0.13 (13%)	0.14 (14%)
				i		
1	1.00000	1.00000	1.00000	1.00000	1.00000	1.00000
2	0.47847	0.47619	0.47393	0.47170	0.46948	0.46729
3	0.30505	0.30211	0.29921	0.29635	0.29352	0.29073
4	0.21867	0.21547	0.21233	0.20923	0.20619	0.20320
5	0.16709	0.16380	0.16057	0.15741	0.15431	0.15128
6	0.13292	0.12961	0.12638	0.12323	0.12015	0.11716
7	0.10869	0.10541	0.10222	0.09912	0.09611	0.09319
8	0.09067	0.08744	0.08432	0.08130	0.07839	0.07557
9	0.07680	0.07364	0.07060	0.06768	0.06487	0.06217
10	0.06582	0.06275	0.05980	0.05698	0.05429	0.05171
11	0.05695	0.05396	0.05112	0.04842	0.04584	0.04339
12	0.04965	0.04676	0.04403	0.04144	0.03899	0.03667
13	0.04357	0.04078	0.03815	0.03568	0.03335	0.03116
14	0.03843	0.03575	0.03323	0.03087	0.02867	0.02661
15	0.03406	0.03147	0.02907	0.02682	0.02474	0.02281
16	0.03030	0.02782	0.02552	0.02339	0.02143	0.01962
17	0.02705	0.02466	0.02247	0.02046	0.01861	0.01692
18	0.02421	0.02193	0.01984	0.01794	0.01620	0.01462
19	0.02173	0.01955	0.01756	0.01576	0.01413	0.01266
20	0.01955	0.01746	0.01558	0.01388	0.01235	0.01099
21	0.01762	0.01562	0.01384	0.01224	0.01081	0.00954
22	0.01590	0.01401	0.01231	0.01081	0.00948	0.00830
23	0.01438	0.01257	0.01097	0.00956	0.00832	0.00723
24	0.01302	0.01130	0.00979	0.00846	0.00731	0.00630
25	0.01181	0.01017	0.00874	0.00750	0.00643	0.00550
26	0.01072	0.00916	0.00781	0.00665	0.00565	0.00480
27	0.00973	0.00826	0.00699	0.00590	0.00498	0.00419
28	0.00885	0.00745	0.00626	0.00524	0.00439	0.00366
29	0.00806	0.00673	0.00561	0.00466	0.00387	0.00320
30	0.00734	0.00608	0.00502	0.00414	0.00341	0.00280
31	0.00669	0.00550	0.00451	0.00369	0.00301	0.00245
32	0.00610	0.00497	0.00404	0.00328	0.00266	0.00215
33	0.00556	0.00450	0.00363	0.00292	0.00234	0.00188
34	0.00508	0.00407	0.00326	0.00260	0.00207	0.00165
35	0.00464	0.00369	0.00293	0.00232	0.00183	0.00144
36	0.00424	0.00334	0.00263	0.00206	0.00162	0.00126
37	0.00387	0.00303	0.00236	0.00184	0.00143	0.00111
38	0.00354	0.00275	0.00213	0.00164	0.00126	0.00097
39	0.00324	0.00249	0.00191	0.00146	0.00112	0.00085
40	0.00296	0.00226	0.00172	0.00130	0.00099	0.00075
41	0.00271	0.00205	0.00155	0.00116	0.00087	0.00065
42	0.00248	0.00186	0.00139	0.00104	0.00077	0.00057
43	0.00227	0.00169	0.00125	0.00092	0.00068	0.00050
44	0.00208	0.00153	0.00113	0.00083	0.00060	0.00044
45	0.00190	0.00139	0.00101	0.00074	0.00053	0.00039
46	0.00174	0.00126	0.00091	0.00066	0.00047	0.00034
47	0.00160	0.00115	0.00082	0.00059	0.00042	0.00030
48	0.00146	0.00104	0.00074	0.00052	0.00037	0.00026
49	0.00134	0.00095	0.00067	0.00047	0.00033	0.00023
50	0.00123	0.00086	0.00060	0.00042	0.00029	0.00020
51	0.00112	0.00078	0.00054	0.00037	0.00026	0.00018
52	0.00103	0.00071	0.00049	0.00033	0.00023	0.00015
53	0.00094	0.00064	0.00044	0.00030	0.00020	0.00014
54	0.00087	0.00059	0.00039	0.00026	0.00018	0.00012
55	0.00079	0.00053	0.00035	0.00024	0.00016	0.00010
56	0.00073	0.00048	0.00032	0.00021	0.00014	0.00009
57	0.00067	0.00044	0.00029	0.00019	0.00012	0.00008
58	0.00061	0.00040	0.00026	0.00017	0.00011	0.00007
59	0.00056	0.00036	0.00023	0.00015	0.00010	0.00006
60	0.00051	0.00033	0.00021	0.00013	0.00009	0.00005

TABLE IV
(*Continued*)

n	0.15 (15%)	0.16 (16%)	0.17 (17%)	0.18 (18%)	0.19 (19%)	0.20 (20%)
1	1.00000	1.00000	1.00000	1.00000	1.00000	1.00000
2	0.46512	0.46296	0.46083	0.45872	0.45662	0.45455
3	0.28798	0.28526	0.28257	0.27992	0.27731	0.27473
4	0.20027	0.19738	0.19453	0.19174	0.18899	0.18629
5	0.14832	0.14541	0.14256	0.13978	0.13705	0.13438
6	0.11424	0.11139	0.10861	0.10591	0.10327	0.10071
7	0.09036	0.08761	0.08495	0.08236	0.07985	0.07742
8	0.07285	0.07022	0.06769	0.06524	0.06289	0.06061
9	0.05957	0.05708	0.05469	0.05239	0.05019	0.04808
10	0.04925	0.04690	0.04466	0.04251	0.04047	0.03852
11	0.04107	0.03886	0.03676	0.03478	0.03289	0.03110
12	0.03448	0.03241	0.03047	0.02863	0.02690	0.02526
13	0.02911	0.02718	0.02538	0.02369	0.02210	0.02062
14	0.02469	0.02290	0.02123	0.01968	0.01823	0.01689
15	0.02102	0.01936	0.01782	0.01640	0.01509	0.01388
16	0.01795	0.01641	0.01500	0.01371	0.01252	0.01144
17	0.01537	0.01395	0.01266	0.01149	0.01041	0.00944
18	0.01319	0.01188	0.01071	0.00964	0.00868	0.00781
19	0.01134	0.01014	0.00907	0.00810	0.00724	0.00646
20	0.00976	0.00867	0.00769	0.00682	0.00605	0.00536
21	0.00842	0.00742	0.00653	0.00575	0.00505	0.00444
22	0.00727	0.00635	0.00555	0.00485	0.00423	0.00369
23	0.00628	0.00545	0.00472	0.00409	0.00354	0.00307
24	0.00543	0.00467	0.00402	0.00345	0.00297	0.00255
25	0.00470	0.00401	0.00342	0.00292	0.00249	0.00212
26	0.00407	0.00345	0.00292	0.00247	0.00209	0.00176
27	0.00353	0.00296	0.00249	0.00209	0.00175	0.00147
28	0.00306	0.00255	0.00212	0.00177	0.00147	0.00122
29	0.00265	0.00219	0.00181	0.00149	0.00123	0.00102
30	0.00230	0.00189	0.00154	0.00126	0.00103	0.00085
31	0.00200	0.00162	0.00132	0.00107	0.00087	0.00070
32	0.00173	0.00140	0.00113	0.00091	0.00073	0.00059
33	0.00150	0.00120	0.00096	0.00077	0.00061	0.00049
34	0.00131	0.00104	0.00082	0.00065	0.00051	0.00041
35	0.00113	0.00089	0.00070	0.00055	0.00043	0.00034
36	0.00099	0.00077	0.00060	0.00047	0.00036	0.00028
37	0.00086	0.00066	0.00051	0.00039	0.00030	0.00024
38	0.00074	0.00057	0.00044	0.00033	0.00026	0.00020
39	0.00065	0.00049	0.00037	0.00028	0.00022	0.00016
40	0.00056	0.00042	0.00032	0.00024	0.00018	0.00014
41	0.00049	0.00037	0.00027	0.00020	0.00015	0.00011
42	0.00042	0.00031	0.00023	0.00017	0.00013	0.00009
43	0.00037	0.00027	0.00020	0.00015	0.00011	0.00008
44	0.00032	0.00023	0.00017	0.00012	0.00009	0.00007
45	0.00028	0.00020	0.00015	0.00010	0.00008	0.00005
46	0.00024	0.00017	0.00012	0.00009	0.00006	0.00005
47	0.00021	0.00015	0.00011	0.00008	0.00005	0.00004
48	0.00018	0.00013	0.00009	0.00006	0.00004	0.00003
49	0.00016	0.00011	0.00008	0.00005	0.00004	0.00003
50	0.00014	0.00010	0.00007	0.00005	0.00003	0.00002
51	0.00012	0.00008	0.00006	0.00004	0.00003	0.00002
52	0.00010	0.00007	0.00005	0.00003	0.00002	0.00002
53	0.00009	0.00006	0.00004	0.00003	0.00002	0.00001
54	0.00008	0.00005	0.00004	0.00002	0.00002	0.00001
55	0.00007	0.00005	0.00003	0.00002	0.00001	0.00001
56	0.00006	0.00004	0.00003	0.00002	0.00001	0.00001
57	0.00005	0.00003	0.00002	0.00001	0.00001	0.00001
58	0.00005	0.00003	0.00002	0.00001	0.00001	0.00001
59	0.00004	0.00003	0.00002	0.00001	0.00001	0.00000
60	0.00003	0.00002	0.00001	0.00001	0.00001	0.00000

TABLE V

SERIES PRESENT-WORTH FACTOR $\dfrac{(1 + i)^n - 1}{i(1 + i)^n}$

n	0.01 (1%)	0.015 (1½%)	0.02 (2%)	0.025 (2½%)	0.03 (3%)	0.035 (3½%)
1	0.99010	0.98522	0.98039	0.97561	0.97087	0.96618
2	1.97040	1.95588	1.94156	1.92742	1.91347	1.89969
3	2.94099	2.91220	2.88388	2.85602	2.82861	2.80164
4	3.90197	3.85438	3.80773	3.76197	3.71710	3.67308
5	4.85343	4.78264	4.71346	4.64583	4.57971	4.51505
6	5.79548	5.69719	5.60143	5.50813	5.41719	5.32855
7	6.72819	6.59821	6.47199	6.34939	6.23028	6.11454
8	7.65168	7.48593	7.32548	7.17014	7.01969	6.87396
9	8.56602	8.36052	8.16224	7.97087	7.78611	7.60769
10	9.47130	9.22218	8.98259	8.75206	8.53020	8.31661
11	10.36763	10.07112	9.78685	9.51421	9.25262	9.00155
12	11.25508	10.90751	10.57534	10.25776	9.95400	9.66333
13	12.13374	11.73153	11.34837	10.98318	10.63496	10.30274
14	13.00370	12.54338	12.10625	11.69091	11.29607	10.92052
15	13.86505	13.34323	12.84926	12.38138	11.93794	11.51741
16	14.71787	14.13126	13.57771	13.05500	12.56110	12.09412
17	15.56225	14.90765	14.29187	13.71220	13.16612	12.65132
18	16.39827	15.67256	14.99203	14.35336	13.75351	13.18968
19	17.22601	16.42617	15.67846	14.97889	14.32380	13.70984
20	18.04555	17.16864	16.35143	15.58916	14.87747	14.21240
21	18.85698	17.90014	17.01121	16.18455	15.41502	14.69797
22	19.66038	18.62082	17.65805	16.76541	15.93692	15.16712
23	20.45582	19.33086	18.29220	17.33211	16.44361	15.62041
24	21.24339	20.03041	18.91393	17.88499	16.93554	16.05837
25	22.02316	20.71961	19.52346	18.42438	17.41315	16.48151
26	22.79520	21.39863	20.12104	18.95061	17.87684	16.89035
27	23.55961	22.06762	20.70690	19.46401	18.32703	17.28536
28	24.31644	22.72672	21.28127	19.96489	18.76411	17.66702
29	25.06579	23.37€08	21.84438	20.45355	19.18845	18.03577
30	25.80771	24.01584	22.39646	20.93029	19.60044	18.39205
31	26.54229	24.64615	22.93770	21.39541	20.00043	18.73628
32	27.26959	25.26714	23.46833	21.84918	20.38877	19.06887
33	27.98969	25.87895	23.98856	22.29188	20.76579	19.39021
34	28.70267	26.48173	24.49859	22.72379	21.13184	19.70068
35	29.40858	27.07559	24.99862	23.14516	21.48722	20.00066
36	30.10751	27.66068	25.48884	23.55625	21.83225	20.29049
37	30.79951	28.23713	25.96945	23.95732	22.16724	20.57053
38	31.48466	28.80505	26.44064	24.34860	22.49246	20.84109
39	32.16303	29.36458	26.90259	24.73034	22.80822	21.10250
40	32.83469	29.91585	27.35548	25.10278	23.11477	21.35507
41	33.49969	30.45896	27.79949	25.46612	23.41240	21.59910
42	34.15811	30.99405	28.23479	25.82061	23.70136	21.83486
43	34.81001	31.52123	28.66156	26.16645	23.98190	22.06269
44	35.45545	32.04062	29.07996	26.50385	24.25427	22.28279
45	36.09451	32.55234	29.49016	26.83302	24.51871	22.49545
46	36.72724	33.05649	29.89231	27.15417	24.77545	22.70092
47	37.35370	33.55319	30.28658	27.46748	25.02471	22.89944
48	37.97396	34.04255	30.67312	27.77315	25.26671	23.09124
49	38.58808	34.52468	31.05208	28.07137	25.50166	23.27656
50	39.19612	34.99969	31.42361	28.36231	25.72976	23.45562
51	39.79814	35.46767	31.78785	28.64616	25.95123	23.62862
52	40.39419	35.92874	32.14495	28.92308	26.16624	23.79576
53	40.98435	36.38300	32.49505	29.19325	26.37499	23.95726
54	41.56866	36.83054	32.83828	29.45683	26.57766	24.11330
55	42.14719	37.27147	33.17479	29.71398	26.77443	24.26405
56	42.71999	37.70588	33.50469	29.96486	26.96546	24.40971
57	43.28712	38.13387	33.82813	30.20962	27.15094	24.55045
58	43.84863	38.55554	34.14523	30.44841	27.33101	24.68642
59	44.40459	38.97097	34.45610	30.68137	27.50583	24.81780
60	44.95504	39.38027	34.76089	30.90866	27.67556	24.94473

TABLE V
(Continued)

n	0.04 (4%)	0.045 (4½%)	0.05 (5%)	0.06 (6%)	0.07 (7%)	0.08 (8%)
1	0.96154	0.95694	0.95238	0.94340	0.93458	0.92593
2	1.88609	1.87267	1.85941	1.83339	1.80802	1.78326
3	2.77509	2.74896	2.72325	2.67301	2.62432	2.57710
4	3.62990	3.58753	3.54595	3.46511	3.38721	3.31213
5	4.45182	4.38998	4.32948	4.21236	4.10020	3.99271
6	5.24214	5.15787	5.07569	4.91732	4.76654	4.62288
7	6.00205	5.89270	5.78637	5.58238	5.38929	5.20637
8	6.73274	6.59589	6.46321	6.20979	5.97130	5.74664
9	7.43533	7.26879	7.10782	6.80169	6.51523	6.24689
10	8.11090	7.91272	7.72173	7.36009	7.02358	6.71008
11	8.76048	8.52892	8.30641	7.88687	7.49867	7.13896
12	9.38507	9.11858	8.86325	8.38384	7.94269	7.53608
13	9.98565	9.68285	9.39357	8.85268	8.35765	7.90378
14	10.56312	10.22283	9.89864	9.29498	8.74547	8.24424
15	11.11839	10.73955	10.37966	9.71225	9.10791	8.55948
16	11.65230	11.23402	10.83777	10.10590	9.44665	8.85137
17	12.16567	11.70719	11.27407	10.47726	9.76322	9.12164
18	12.65930	12.15999	11.68959	10.82760	10.05909	9.37189
19	13.13394	12.59329	12.08532	11.15812	10.33560	9.60360
20	13.59033	13.00794	12.46221	11.46992	10.59401	9.81815
21	14.02916	13.40472	12.82115	11.76408	10.83553	10.01680
22	14.45112	13.78442	13.16300	12.04158	11.06124	10.20074
23	14.85684	14.14777	13.48857	12.30338	11.27219	10.37106
24	15.24696	14.49548	13.79864	12.55036	11.46933	10.52876
25	15.62208	14.82821	14.09394	12.78336	11.65358	10.67478
26	15.98277	15.14661	14.37519	13.00317	11.82578	10.80998
27	16.32959	15.45130	14.64303	13.21053	11.98671	10.93516
28	16.66306	15.74287	14.89813	13.40616	12.13711	11.05108
29	16.98371	16.02189	15.14107	13.59072	12.27767	11.15841
30	17.29203	16.28889	15.37245	13.76483	12.40904	11.25778
31	17.58849	16.54439	15.59281	13.92909	12.53181	11.34980
32	17.87355	16.78889	15.80268	14.08404	12.64656	11.43500
33	18.14765	17.02286	16.00255	14.23023	12.75379	11.51389
34	18.41120	17.24676	16.19290	14.36814	12.85401	11.58693
35	18.66461	17.46101	16.37419	14.49825	12.94767	11.65457
36	18.90828	17.66604	16.54685	14.62099	13.03521	11.71719
37	19.14258	17.86224	16.71129	14.73678	13.11702	11.77518
38	19.36786	18.04999	16.86789	14.84602	13.19347	11.82887
39	19.58448	18.22966	17.01704	14.94907	13.26493	11.87858
40	19.79277	18.40158	17.15909	15.04630	13.33171	11.92461
41	19.99305	18.56611	17.29437	15.13802	13.39412	11.96723
42	20.18563	18.72355	17.42321	15.22454	13.45245	12.00670
43	20.37079	18.87421	17.54591	15.30617	13.50696	12.04324
44	20.54884	19.01838	17.66277	15.38318	13.55791	12.07707
45	20.72004	19.15635	17.77407	15.45583	13.60552	12.10840
46	20.88465	19.28837	17.88007	15.52437	13.65002	12.13741
47	21.04294	19.41471	17.98102	15.58903	13.69161	12.16427
48	21.19513	19.53561	18.07716	15.65003	13.73047	12.18914
49	21.34147	19.65130	18.16872	15.70757	13.76680	12.21216
50	21.48218	19.76201	18.25593	15.76186	13.80075	12.23348
51	21.61749	19.86795	18.33898	15.81308	13.83247	12.25323
52	21.74758	19.96933	18.41807	15.86139	13.86212	12.27151
53	21.87267	20.06634	18.49340	15.90697	13.88984	12.28843
54	21.99296	20.15918	18.56515	15.94998	13.91573	12.30410
55	22.10861	20.24802	18.63347	15.99054	13.93994	12.31861
56	22.21982	20.33303	18.69854	16.02881	13.96256	12.33205
57	22.32675	20.41439	18.76052	16.06492	13.98370	12.34449
58	22.42957	20.49224	18.81954	16.09898	14.00346	12.35601
59	22.52843	20.56673	18.87575	16.13111	14.02192	12.36668
60	22.62349	20.63802	18.92929	16.16143	14.03918	12.37655

TABLE V
(Continued)

n	0.09 (9%)	0.10 (10%)	0.11 (11%)	0.12 (12%)	0.13 (13%)	0.14 (14%)
1	0.91743	0.90909	0.90090	0.89286	0.88496	0.87719
2	1.75911	1.73554	1.71252	1.69005	1.66810	1.64666
3	2.53129	2.48685	2.44371	2.40183	2.36115	2.32163
4	3.23972	3.16987	3.10245	3.03735	2.97447	2.91371
5	3.88965	3.79079	3.69590	3.60478	3.51723	3.43308
6	4.48592	4.35526	4.23054	4.11141	3.99755	3.88867
7	5.03295	4.86842	4.71220	4.56376	4.42261	4.28830
8	5.53482	5.33493	5.14612	4.96764	4.79877	4.63886
9	5.99525	5.75902	5.53705	5.32825	5.13166	4.94637
10	6.41766	6.14457	5.88923	5.65022	5.42624	5.21612
11	6.80519	6.49506	6.20652	5.93770	5.68694	5.45273
12	7.16073	6.81369	6.49236	6.19437	5.91765	5.66029
13	7.48690	7.10336	6.74987	6.42355	6.12181	5.84236
14	7.78615	7.36669	6.98187	6.62817	6.30249	6.00207
15	8.06069	7.60608	7.19087	6.81086	6.46238	6.14217
16	8.31256	7.82371	7.37916	6.97399	6.60388	6.26506
17	8.54363	8.02155	7.54879	7.11963	6.72909	6.37286
18	8.75563	8.20141	7.70162	7.24967	6.83991	6.46742
19	8.95011	8.36492	7.83929	7.36578	6.93797	6.55037
20	9.12855	8.51356	7.96333	7.46944	7.02475	6.62313
21	9.29224	8.64869	8.07507	7.56200	7.10155	6.68696
22	9.44243	8.77154	8.17574	7.64465	7.16951	6.74294
23	9.58021	8.88322	8.26643	7.71843	7.22966	6.79206
24	9.70661	8.98474	8.34814	7.78432	7.28288	6.83514
25	9.82258	9.07704	8.42174	7.84314	7.32998	6.87293
26	9.92897	9.16095	8.48806	7.89566	7.37167	6.90608
27	10.02658	9.23722	8.54780	7.94255	7.40856	6.93515
28	10.11613	9.30657	8.60162	7.98442	7.44120	6.96066
29	10.19828	9.36961	8.65011	8.02181	7.47009	6.98304
30	10.27365	9.42691	8.69379	8.05518	7.49565	7.00266
31	10.34280	9.47901	8.73315	8.08499	7.51828	7.01988
32	10.40624	9.52638	8.76860	8.11159	7.53830	7.03498
33	10.46444	9.56943	8.80054	8.13535	7.55602	7.04823
34	10.51784	9.60857	8.82932	8.15656	7.57170	7.05985
35	10.56682	9.64416	8.85524	8.17550	7.58557	7.07005
36	10.61176	9.67651	8.87859	8.19241	7.59785	7.07899
37	10.65299	9.70592	8.89963	8.20751	7.60872	7.08683
38	10.69082	9.73265	8.91859	8.22099	7.61833	7.09371
39	10.72552	9.75696	8.93567	8.23303	7.62684	7.09975
40	10.75736	9.77905	8.95105	8.24378	7.63438	7.10504
41	10.78657	9.79914	8.96491	8.25337	7.64104	7.10969
42	10.81337	9.81740	8.97740	8.26194	7.64694	7.11376
43	10.83795	9.83400	8.98865	8.26959	7.65216	7.11733
44	10.86051	9.84909	8.99878	8.27642	7.65678	7.12047
45	10.88120	9.86281	9.00791	8.28252	7.66086	7.12322
46	10.90018	9.87528	9.01614	8.28796	7.66448	6.12563
47	10.91760	9.88662	9.02355	8.29282	7.66768	7.12774
48	10.93358	9.89693	9.03022	8.29716	7.67052	7.12960
49	10.94823	9.90630	9.03624	8.30104	7.67302	7.13123
50	10.96168	9.91481	9.04165	8.30450	7.67524	7.13266
51	10.97402	9.92256	9.04653	8.30759	7.67720	7.13391
52	10.98534	9.92960	9.05093	8.31035	7.67894	7.13501
53	10.99573	9.93600	9.05489	8.31281	7.68048	7.13597
54	11.00525	9.94182	9.05846	9.31501	7.68184	7.13682
55	11.01399	9.94711	9.06168	8.31697	7.68304	7.13756
56	11.02201	9.95191	9.06457	8.31872	7.68411	7.13821
57	11.02937	9.95629	9.06718	8.32029	7.68505	7.13878
58	11.03612	9.96026	9.06954	8.32169	7.68589	7.13928
59	11.04231	9.96387	9.07165	8.32294	7.68663	7.13972
60	11.04799	9.96716	9.07356	8.32405	7.68728	7.14011

TABLE V
(Continued)

n	0.15 (15%)	0.16 (16%)	0.17 (17%)	0.18 (18%)	0.19 (19%)	0.20 (20%)
1	0.86957	0.86207	0.85470	0.84746	0.84034	0.83333
2	1.62571	1.60523	1.58521	1.56564	1.54650	1.52778
3	2.28323	2.24589	2.20958	2.17427	2.13992	2.10648
4	2.85498	2.79818	2.74324	2.69006	2.63859	2.58873
5	3.35216	3.27429	3.19935	3.12717	3.05763	2.99061
6	3.78448	3.68474	3.58918	3.49760	3.40978	3.32551
7	4.16042	4.03857	3.92238	3.81153	3.70570	3.60459
8	4.48732	4.34359	4.20716	4.07757	3.95437	3.83716
9	4.77158	4.60654	4.45057	4.30302	4.16333	4.03097
10	5.01877	4.83323	4.65860	4.49409	4.33893	4.19247
11	5.23371	5.02864	4.83641	4.65601	4.48650	4.32706
12	5.42062	5.19711	4.98839	4.79322	4.61050	4.43922
13	5.58315	5.34233	5.11828	4.90951	4.71471	4.53268
14	5.72448	5.46753	5.22930	5.00806	4.80228	4.61057
15	5.84737	5.57546	5.32419	5.09158	4.87586	4.67547
16	5.95423	5.66850	5.40529	5.16235	4.93770	4.72956
17	6.04716	5.74870	5.47461	5.22233	4.98966	4.77463
18	6.12797	5.81785	5.53385	5.27316	5.03333	4.81219
19	6.19823	5.87746	5.58449	5.31624	5.07003	4.84350
20	6.25933	5.92884	5.62777	5.35275	5.10086	4.86958
21	6.31246	5.97314	5.66476	5.38368	5.12677	4.89132
22	6.35866	6.01133	5.69637	5.40990	5.14855	4.90943
23	6.39884	6.04425	5.72340	5.43212	5.16685	4.92453
24	6.43377	6.07263	5.74649	5.45095	5.18223	4.93710
25	6.46415	6.09709	5.76623	5.46691	5.19515	4.94759
26	6.49056	6.11818	5.78311	5.48043	5.20601	4.95632
27	6.51353	6.13636	5.79753	5.49189	5.21513	4.96360
28	6.53351	6.15204	5.80985	5.50160	5.22280	4.96967
29	6.55088	6.16555	5.82039	5.50983	5.22924	4.97472
30	6.56598	6.17720	5.82939	5.51681	5.23466	4.97894
31	6.57911	6.18724	5.83709	5.52272	5.23921	4.98245
32	6.59053	6.19590	5.84366	5.52773	5.24303	4.98537
33	6.60046	6.20336	5.84928	5.53197	5.24625	4.98781
34	6.60910	6.20979	5.85409	5.53557	5.24895	4.98984
35	6.61661	6.21534	5.85820	5.53862	5.25122	4.99154
36	6.62314	6.22012	5.86171	5.54120	5.25312	4.99295
37	6.62881	6.22424	5.86471	5.54339	5.25472	4.99412
38	6.63375	6.22779	5.86727	5.54525	5.25607	4.99510
39	6.63805	6.23086	5.86946	5.54682	5.25720	4.99592
40	6.64178	6.23350	5.87133	5.54815	5.25815	4.99660
41	6.64502	6.23577	5.87294	5.54928	5.25895	4.99717
42	6.64785	6.23774	5.87430	5.55024	5.25962	4.99764
43	6.65030	6.23943	5.87547	5.55105	5.26019	4.99803
44	6.65244	6.24089	5.87647	5.55174	5.26066	4.99836
45	6.65429	6.24214	5.87733	5.55232	5.26106	4.99863
46	6.65591	6.24323	5.87806	5.55281	5.26140	4.99886
47	6.65731	6.24416	5.87868	5.55323	5.26168	4.99905
48	6.65853	6.24497	5.87922	5.55359	5.26191	4.99921
49	6.65959	6.24566	5.87967	5.55389	5.26211	4.99934
50	6.66051	6.24626	5.88006	5.55414	5.26228	4.99945
51	6.66132	6.24678	5.88039	5.55436	5.26242	4.99954
52	6.66201	6.24722	5.88068	5.55454	5.26254	4.99962
53	6.66262	6.24760	5.88092	5.55469	5.26264	4.99968
54	6.66315	6.24793	5.88113	5.55483	5.26272	4.99974
55	6.66361	6.24822	5.88131	5.55494	5.26279	4.99978
56	6.66401	6.24846	5.88146	5.55503	5.26285	4.99982
57	6.66435	6.24868	5.88159	5.55511	5.26290	4.99985
58	6.66466	6.24886	5.88170	5.55518	5.26294	4.99987
59	6.66492	6.24902	5.88180	5.55524	5.26297	4.99989
60	6.66515	6.24915	5.88188	5.55529	5.26300	4.99991

TABLE VI

CAPITAL-RECOVERY FACTOR $\dfrac{i(1+i)^n}{(1+i)^n - 1}$

n	0.01 (1%)	0.015 (1.5%)	0.02 (2%)	0.025 ($2\frac{1}{2}$%)	0.03 (3%)	0.035 ($3\frac{1}{2}$%)
1	1.01000	1.01500	1.02000	1.02500	1.03000	1.03500
2	0.50751	0.51128	0.51505	0.51883	0.52261	0.52640
3	0.34002	0.34338	0.34675	0.35014	0.35353	0.35693
4	0.25628	0.25944	0.26262	0.26582	0.26903	0.27225
5	0.20604	0.20909	0.21216	0.21525	0.21835	0.22148
6	0.17255	0.17553	0.17853	0.18155	0.18460	0.18767
7	0.14863	0.15156	0.15451	0.15750	0.16051	0.16354
8	0.13069	0.13358	0.13651	0.13947	0.14246	0.14548
9	0.11674	0.11961	0.12252	0.12546	0.12843	0.13145
10	0.10558	0.10843	0.11133	0.11426	0.11723	0.12024
11	0.09645	0.09929	0.10218	0.10511	0.10808	0.11109
12	0.08885	0.09168	0.09456	0.09749	0.10046	0.10348
13	0.08241	0.08524	0.08812	0.09105	0.09403	0.09706
14	0.07690	0.07972	0.08260	0.08554	0.08853	0.09157
15	0.07212	0.07494	0.07783	0.08077	0.08377	0.08683
16	0.06794	0.07077	0.07365	0.07660	0.07961	0.08268
17	0.06426	0.06708	0.06997	0.07293	0.07595	0.07904
18	0.06098	0.06381	0.06670	0.06967	0.07271	0.07582
19	0.05805	0.06088	0.06378	0.06676	0.06981	0.07294
20	0.05542	0.05825	0.06116	0.06415	0.06722	0.07036
21	0.05303	0.05587	0.05878	0.06179	0.06487	0.06804
22	0.05086	0.05370	0.05663	0.05965	0.06275	0.06593
23	0.04889	0.05173	0.05467	0.05770	0.06081	0.06402
24	0.04707	0.04992	0.05287	0.05591	0.05905	0.06227
25	0.04541	0.04826	0.05122	0.05428	0.05743	0.06067
26	0.04387	0.04673	0.04970	0.05277	0.05594	0.05921
27	0.04245	0.04532	0.04829	0.05138	0.05456	0.05785
28	0.04112	0.04400	0.04699	0.05009	0.05329	0.05660
29	0.03990	0.04278	0.04578	0.04889	0.05211	0.05545
30	0.03875	0.04164	0.04465	0.04778	0.05102	0.05437
31	0.03768	0.04057	0.04360	0.04674	0.05000	0.05337
32	0.03667	0.03958	0.04261	0.04577	0.04905	0.05244
33	0.03573	0.03864	0.04169	0.04486	0.04816	0.05157
34	0.03484	0.03776	0.04082	0.04401	0.04732	0.05076
35	0.03400	0.03693	0.04000	0.04321	0.04654	0.05000
36	0.03321	0.03615	0.03923	0.04245	0.04580	0.04928
37	0.03247	0.03541	0.03851	0.04174	0.04511	0.04861
38	0.03176	0.03472	0.03782	0.04107	0.04446	0.04798
39	0.03109	0.03405	0.03717	0.04044	0.04384	0.04739
40	0.03046	0.03343	0.03656	0.03984	0.04326	0.04683
41	0.02985	0.03283	0.03597	0.03927	0.04271	0.04630
42	0.02928	0.03226	0.03542	0.03873	0.04219	0.04580
43	0.02873	0.03172	0.03489	0.03822	0.04170	0.04533
44	0.02820	0.03121	0.03439	0.03773	0.04123	0.04488
45	0.02771	0.03072	0.03391	0.03727	0.04079	0.04445
46	0.02723	0.03025	0.03345	0.03683	0.04036	0.04405
47	0.02677	0.02980	0.03302	0.03641	0.03996	0.04367
48	0.02633	0.02937	0.03260	0.03601	0.03958	0.04331
49	0.02591	0.02896	0.03220	0.03562	0.03921	0.04296
50	0.02551	0.02857	0.03182	0.03526	0.03887	0.04263
51	0.02513	0.02819	0.03146	0.03491	0.03853	0.04232
52	0.02476	0.02783	0.03111	0.03457	0.03822	0.04202
53	0.02440	0.02749	0.03077	0.03425	0.03791	0.04174
54	0.02406	0.02715	0.03045	0.03395	0.03763	0.04147
55	0.02373	0.02683	0.03014	0.03365	0.03735	0.04121
56	0.02341	0.02652	0.02985	0.03337	0.03708	0.04097
57	0.02310	0.02622	0.02956	0.03310	0.03683	0.04073
58	0.02281	0.02594	0.02929	0.03284	0.03659	0.04051
59	0.02252	0.02566	0.02902	0.03259	0.03636	0.04029
60	0.02224	0.02539	0.02877	0.03235	0.03613	0.04009

TABLE VI
(Continued)

			i			
n	0.04 (4%)	0.045 (4½%)	0.05 (5%)	0.06 (6%)	0.07 (7%)	0.08 (8%)
1	1.04000	1.04500	1.05000	1.06000	1.07000	1.08000
2	0.53020	0.53400	0.53780	0.54544	0.55309	0.56077
3	0.36035	0.36377	0.36721	0.37411	0.38105	0.38803
4	0.27549	0.27874	0.28201	0.28859	0.29523	0.30192
5	0.22463	0.22779	0.23097	0.23740	0.24389	0.25046
6	0.19076	0.19388	0.19702	0.20336	0.20980	0.21632
7	0.16661	0.16970	0.17282	0.17914	0.18555	0.19207
8	0.14853	0.15161	0.15472	0.16104	0.16747	0.17401
9	0.13449	0.13757	0.14069	0.14702	0.15349	0.16008
10	0.12329	0.12638	0.12950	0.13587	0.14238	0.14903
11	0.11415	0.11725	0.12039	0.12679	0.13336	0.14008
12	0.10655	0.10967	0.11283	0.11928	0.12590	0.13270
13	0.10014	0.10328	0.10646	0.11296	0.11965	0.12652
14	0.09467	0.09782	0.10102	0.10758	0.11434	0.12130
15	0.08994	0.09311	0.09634	0.10296	0.10979	0.11683
16	0.08582	0.08902	0.09227	0.09895	0.10586	0.11298
17	0.08220	0.08542	0.08870	0.09544	0.10243	0.10963
18	0.07899	0.08224	0.08555	0.09236	0.09941	0.10670
19	0.07614	0.07941	0.08275	0.08962	0.09675	0.10413
20	0.07358	0.07688	0.08024	0.08718	0.09439	0.10185
21	0.07128	0.07460	0.07800	0.08500	0.09229	0.09983
22	0.06920	0.07255	0.07597	0.08305	0.09041	0.09803
23	0.06731	0.07068	0.07414	0.08128	0.08871	0.09642
24	0.06559	0.06899	0.07247	0.07968	0.08719	0.09498
25	0.06401	0.06744	0.07095	0.07823	0.08581	0.09368
26	0.06257	0.06602	0.06956	0.07690	0.08456	0.09251
27	0.06124	0.06472	0.06829	0.07570	0.08343	0.09145
28	0.06001	0.06352	0.06712	0.07459	0.08239	0.09049
29	0.05888	0.06241	0.06605	0.07358	0.08145	0.08962
30	0.05783	0.06139	0.06505	0.07265	0.08059	0.08883
31	0.05686	0.06044	0.06413	0.07179	0.07980	0.08811
32	0.05595	0.05956	0.06328	0.07100	0.07907	0.08745
33	0.05510	0.05874	0.06249	0.07027	0.07841	0.08685
34	0.05431	0.05798	0.06176	0.06960	0.07780	0.08630
35	0.05358	0.05727	0.06107	0.06897	0.07723	0.08580
36	0.05289	0.05661	0.06043	0.06839	0.07672	0.08534
37	0.05224	0.05598	0.05984	0.06786	0.07624	0.08492
38	0.05163	0.05540	0.05928	0.06736	0.07580	0.08454
39	0.05106	0.05486	0.05876	0.06689	0.07539	0.08419
40	0.05052	0.05434	0.05828	0.06646	0.07501	0.08386
41	0.05002	0.05386	0.05782	0.06606	0.07466	0.08356
42	0.04954	0.05341	0.05739	0.06568	0.07434	0.08329
43	0.04909	0.05298	0.05699	0.06533	0.07404	0.08303
44	0.04866	0.05258	0.05662	0.06501	0.07376	0.08280
45	0.04826	0.05220	0.05626	0.06470	0.07350	0.08259
46	0.04788	0.05184	0.05593	0.06441	0.07326	0.08239
47	0.04752	0.05151	0.05561	0.06415	0.07304	0.08221
48	0.04718	0.05119	0.05532	0.06390	0.07283	0.08204
49	0.04686	0.05089	0.05504	0.06366	0.07264	0.08189
50	0.04655	0.05060	0.05478	0.06344	0.07246	0.08174
51	0.04626	0.05033	0.05453	0.06324	0.07229	0.08161
52	0.04598	0.05008	0.05429	0.06305	0.07214	0.08149
53	0.04572	0.04983	0.05407	0.06287	0.07200	0.08138
54	0.04547	0.04961	0.05386	0.06270	0.07186	0.08127
55	0.04523	0.04939	0.05367	0.06254	0.07174	0.08118
56	0.04500	0.04918	0.05348	0.06239	0.07162	0.08109
57	0.04479	0.04899	0.05330	0.06225	0.07151	0.08101
58	0.04458	0.04880	0.05314	0.06212	0.07141	0.08093
59	0.04439	0.04862	0.05298	0.06199	0.07132	0.08086
60	0.04420	0.04845	0.05283	0.06188	0.07123	0.08080

TABLE VI
(Continued)

n	0.09 (9%)	0.10 (10%)	0.11 (11%)	0.12 (12%)	0.13 (13%)	0.14 (14%)
1	1.09000	1.10000	1.11000	1.12000	1.13000	1.14000
2	0.56847	0.57619	0.58393	0.59170	0.59948	0.60729
3	0.39505	0.40211	0.40921	0.41635	0.42352	0.43073
4	0.30867	0.31547	0.32233	0.32923	0.33619	0.34320
5	0.25709	0.26380	0.27057	0.27741	0.28431	0.29128
6	0.22292	0.22961	0.23638	0.24323	0.25015	0.25716
7	0.19869	0.20541	0.21222	0.21912	0.22611	0.23319
8	0.18067	0.18744	0.19432	0.20130	0.20839	0.21557
9	0.16680	0.17364	0.18060	0.18768	0.19487	0.20217
10	0.15582	0.16275	0.16980	0.17698	0.18429	0.19171
11	0.14695	0.15396	0.16112	0.16842	0.17584	0.18339
12	0.13965	0.14676	0.15403	0.16144	0.16899	0.17667
13	0.13357	0.14078	0.14815	0.15568	0.16335	0.17116
14	0.12843	0.13575	0.14323	0.15087	0.15867	0.16661
15	0.12406	0.13147	0.13907	0.14682	0.15474	0.16281
16	0.12030	0.12782	0.13552	0.14339	0.15143	0.15962
17	0.11705	0.12466	0.13247	0.14046	0.14861	0.15692
18	0.11421	0.12193	0.12984	0.13794	0.14620	0.15462
19	0.11173	0.11955	0.12756	0.13576	0.14413	0.15266
20	0.10955	0.11746	0.12558	0.13388	0.14235	0.15099
21	0.10762	0.11562	0.12384	0.13224	0.14081	0.14954
22	0.10590	0.11401	0.12231	0.13081	0.13948	0.14830
23	0.10438	0.11257	0.12097	0.12956	0.13832	0.14723
24	0.10302	0.11130	0.11979	0.12846	0.13731	0.14630
25	0.10181	0.11017	0.11874	0.12750	0.13643	0.14550
26	0.10072	0.10916	0.11781	0.12665	0.13565	0.14480
27	0.09973	0.10826	0.11699	0.12590	0.13498	0.14419
28	0.09885	0.10745	0.11626	0.12524	0.13439	0.14366
29	0.09806	0.10673	0.11561	0.12466	0.13387	0.14320
30	0.09734	0.10608	0.11502	0.12414	0.13341	0.14280
31	0.09669	0.10550	0.11451	0.12369	0.13301	0.14245
32	0.09610	0.10497	0.11404	0.12328	0.13266	0.14215
33	0.09556	0.10450	0.11363	0.12292	0.13234	0.14188
34	0.09508	0.10407	0.11326	0.12260	0.13207	0.14165
35	0.09464	0.10369	0.11293	0.12232	0.13183	0.14144
36	0.09424	0.10334	0.11263	0.12206	0.13162	0.14126
37	0.09387	0.10303	0.11236	0.12184	0.13143	0.14111
38	0.09354	0.10275	0.11213	0.12164	0.13126	0.14097
39	0.09324	0.10249	0.11191	0.12146	0.13112	0.14085
40	0.09296	0.10226	0.11172	0.12130	0.13099	0.14075
41	0.09271	0.10205	0.11155	0.12116	0.13087	0.14065
42	0.09248	0.10186	0.11139	0.12104	0.13077	0.14057
43	0.09227	0.10169	0.11125	0.12092	0.13068	0.14050
44	0.09208	0.10153	0.11113	0.12083	0.13060	0.14044
45	0.09190	0.10139	0.11101	0.12074	0.13053	0.14039
46	0.09174	0.10126	0.11091	0.12066	0.13047	0.14034
47	0.09160	0.10115	0.11082	0.12059	0.13042	0.14030
48	0.09146	0.10104	0.11074	0.12052	0.13037	0.14026
49	0.09134	0.10095	0.11067	0.12047	0.13033	0.14023
50	0.09123	0.10086	0.11060	0.12042	0.13029	0.14020
51	0.09112	0.10078	0.11054	0.12037	0.13026	0.14018
52	0.09103	0.10071	0.11049	0.12033	0.13023	0.14015
53	0.09094	0.10064	0.11044	0.12030	0.13020	0.14014
54	0.09087	0.10059	0.11039	0.12026	0.13018	0.14012
55	0.09079	0.10053	0.11035	0.12024	0.13016	0.14010
56	0.09073	0.10048	0.11032	0.12021	0.13014	0.14009
57	0.09067	0.10044	0.11029	0.12019	0.13012	0.14008
58	0.09061	0.10040	0.11026	0.12017	0.13011	0.14007
59	0.09056	0.10036	0.11023	0.12015	0.13010	0.14006
60	0.09051	0.10033	0.11021	0.12013	0.13009	0.14005

TABLE VI
(Continued)

n	0.15 (15%)	0.16 (16%)	0.17 (17%)	0.18 (18%)	0.19 (19%)	0.20 (20%)
			i			
1	1.15000	1.16000	1.17000	1.18000	1.19000	1.20000
2	0.61512	0.62296	0.63083	0.63872	0.64662	0.65455
3	0.43798	0.44526	0.45257	0.45992	0.46731	0.47473
4	0.35027	0.35738	0.36453	0.37174	0.37899	0.38629
5	0.29832	0.30541	0.31256	0.31978	0.32705	0.33438
6	0.26424	0.27139	0.27861	0.28591	0.29327	0.30071
7	0.24036	0.24761	0.25495	0.26236	0.26985	0.27742
8	0.22285	0.23022	0.23769	0.24524	0.25289	0.26061
9	0.20957	0.21708	0.22469	0.23239	0.24019	0.24808
10	0.19925	0.20690	0.21466	0.22251	0.23047	0.23852
11	0.19107	0.19886	0.20676	0.21478	0.22289	0.23110
12	0.18448	0.19241	0.20047	0.20863	0.21690	0.22526
13	0.17911	0.18718	0.19538	0.20369	0.21210	0.22062
14	0.17469	0.18290	0.19123	0.19968	0.20823	0.21689
15	0.17102	0.17936	0.18782	0.19640	0.20509	0.21388
16	0.16795	0.17641	0.18500	0.19371	0.20252	0.21144
17	0.16537	0.17395	0.18266	0.19149	0.20041	0.20944
18	0.16319	0.17188	0.18071	0.18964	0.19868	0.20781
19	0.16134	0.17014	0.17907	0.18810	0.19724	0.20646
20	0.15976	0.16867	0.17769	0.18682	0.19605	0.20536
21	0.15842	0.16742	0.17653	0.18575	0.19505	0.20444
22	0.15727	0.16635	0.17555	0.18485	0.19423	0.20369
23	0.15628	0.16545	0.17472	0.18409	0.19354	0.20307
24	0.15543	0.16467	0.17402	0.18345	0.19297	0.20255
25	0.15470	0.16401	0.17342	0.18292	0.19249	0.20212
26	0.15407	0.16345	0.17292	0.18247	0.19209	0.20176
27	0.15353	0.16296	0.17249	0.18209	0.19175	0.20147
28	0.15306	0.16255	0.17212	0.18177	0.19147	0.20122
29	0.15265	0.16219	0.17181	0.18149	0.19123	0.20102
30	0.15230	0.16189	0.17154	0.18126	0.19103	0.20085
31	0.15200	0.16162	0.17132	0.18107	0.19087	0.20070
32	0.15173	0.16140	0.17113	0.18091	0.19073	0.20059
33	0.15150	0.16120	0.17096	0.18077	0.19061	0.20049
34	0.15131	0.16104	0.17082	0.18065	0.19051	0.20041
35	0.15113	0.16089	0.17070	0.18055	0.19043	0.20034
36	0.15099	0.16077	0.17060	0.18047	0.19036	0.20028
37	0.15086	0.16066	0.17051	0.18039	0.19030	0.20024
38	0.15074	0.16057	0.17044	0.18033	0.19026	0.20020
39	0.15065	0.16049	0.17037	0.18028	0.19022	0.20016
40	0.15056	0.16042	0.17032	0.18024	0.19018	0.20014
41	0.15049	0.16037	0.17027	0.18020	0.19015	0.20011
42	0.15042	0.16031	0.17023	0.18017	0.19013	0.20009
43	0.15037	0.16027	0.17020	0.18015	0.19011	0.20008
44	0.15032	0.16023	0.17017	0.18012	0.19009	0.20007
45	0.15028	0.16020	0.17015	0.18010	0.19008	0.20005
46	0.15024	0.16017	0.17012	0.18009	0.19006	0.20005
47	0.15021	0.16015	0.17011	0.18008	0.19005	0.20004
48	0.15018	0.16013	0.17009	0.18006	0.19004	0.20003
49	0.15016	0.16011	0.17008	0.18005	0.19004	0.20003
50	0.15014	0.16010	0.17007	0.18005	0.19003	0.20002
51	0.15012	0.16008	0.17006	0.18004	0.19003	0.20002
52	0.15010	0.16007	0.17005	0.18003	0.19002	0.20002
53	0.15009	0.16006	0.17004	0.18003	0.19002	0.20001
54	0.15008	0.16005	0.17004	0.18002	0.19002	0.20001
55	0.15007	0.16005	0.17003	0.18002	0.19001	0.20001
56	0.15006	0.16004	0.17003	0.18002	0.19001	0.20001
57	0.15005	0.16003	0.17002	0.18001	0.19001	0.20001
58	0.15005	0.16003	0.17002	0.18001	0.19001	0.20001
59	0.15004	0.16003	0.17002	0.18001	0.19001	0.20000
60	0.15003	0.16002	0.17001	0.18001	0.19001	0.20000

TABLE VII
MONTHLY PAYMENT PER DOLLAR OF MORTGAGE LOAN

ANNUAL INTEREST RATE	Mortgage Period			
	15 YEARS (180 PAYMENTS)	20 YEARS (240 PAYMENTS)	25 YEARS (300 PAYMENTS)	30 YEARS (360 PAYMENTS)
7.50	0.00927012	0.00805593	0.00738991	0.00699214
7.75	0.00941276	0.00820948	0.00755329	0.00716412
8.00	0.00955652	0.00836440	0.00771816	0.00733764
8.25	0.00970140	0.00852065	0.00788450	0.00751266
8.50	0.00984740	0.00867823	0.00805227	0.00768913
8.75	0.00999448	0.00883710	0.00822143	0.00786700
9.00	0.01014266	0.00899725	0.00839196	0.00804622
9.25	0.01029192	0.00915866	0.00856381	0.00822675
9.50	0.01044224	0.00932131	0.00873696	0.00840854
9.75	0.01059362	0.00948516	0.00891137	0.00859154
10.00	0.01074605	0.00965021	0.00908700	0.00877572
10.25	0.01089951	0.00981643	0.00926383	0.00896101
10.50	0.01105399	0.00998380	0.00944182	0.00914739
10.75	0.01120948	0.01015229	0.00962093	0.00933481
11.00	0.01136597	0.01032188	0.00980113	0.00952323
11.25	0.01152345	0.01049256	0.00998240	0.00971261
11.50	0.01168190	0.01066430	0.01016469	0.00990291
11.75	0.01184131	0.01083707	0.01034798	0.01009410
12.00	0.01200168	0.01101086	0.01053224	0.01028613
12.25	0.01216299	0.01118565	0.01071744	0.01047896
12.50	0.01232522	0.01136140	0.01090354	0.01067258
12.75	0.01248837	0.01153817	0.01109052	0.01086693
13.00	0.01265242	0.01171576	0.01127835	0.01106200
13.25	0.01281736	0.01189431	0.01146700	0.01125774
13.50	0.01298319	0.01207375	0.01165645	0.01145412
13.75	0.01314987	0.01225405	0.01184666	0.01165113
14.00	0.01331741	0.01243521	0.01203761	0.01884872
14.25	0.01348580	0.01261719	0.01222928	0.01204687
14.50	0.01365501	0.01279998	0.01242163	0.01224556
14.75	0.01382504	0.01298355	0.01261465	0.01244476
15.00	0.01399587	0.01316790	0.01280831	0.01264444
15.25	0.01416750	0.01335299	0.01300258	0.01284459
15.50	0.01433990	0.01353881	0.01319745	0.01304517
15.75	0.01451308	0.01372534	0.01339290	0.01324617
16.00	0.01468701	0.01391256	0.01358889	0.01344757
16.25	0.01486168	0.01410046	0.01378541	0.01364935
16.50	0.01503709	0.01428901	0.01398245	0.01385148
16.75	0.01521321	0.01447820	0.01417998	0.01405396
17.00	0.01539004	0.01466801	0.01437797	0.01425675
17.25	0.01556757	0.01485842	0.01457641	0.01445986
17.50	0.01574578	0.01504942	0.01477530	0.01466325
17.75	0.01592467	0.01524099	0.01497460	0.01486692
18.00	0.01610421	0.01543312	0.01517430	0.01507085
18.25	0.01628440	0.01562578	0.01537439	0.01527503
18.50	0.01646523	0.01581897	0.01557484	0.01547945
18.75	0.01664669	0.01601266	0.01577565	0.01568408
19.00	0.01682876	0.01620685	0.01597680	0.01588892
19.25	0.01701143	0.01640152	0.01617827	0.01609397
19.50	0.01719470	0.01659665	0.01638006	0.01629920
19.75	0.01737855	0.01679223	0.01658215	0.01650461
20.00	0.01756297	0.01698825	0.01678452	0.01671019

APPENDIX A
SUMMATION NOTATION

The Greek letter Σ (sigma) is the mathematical symbol which denotes the summation or addition operation. It provides a type of "shorthand" notation for representing addition. The expression

$$\sum_{j=l}^{u} f(j) \qquad\qquad \textbf{(B.1)}$$

is read "summation of $f(j)$ where j goes from l to u". To the right of Σ is the general function or expression being added. The letter j beneath Σ is the summation index. The summation index increments one unit at a time from a lower limit l to an upper limit u. For each value of j, $f(j)$ is evaluated and added to the other values of $f(j)$.

Suppose that we wanted to add the positive integers 1 through 10. One way of denoting this is by the expression

$$\sum_{j=1}^{10} j$$

The longhand equivalent of this expression is

$$1 + 2 + 3 + 4 + 5 + 6 + 7 + 8 + 9 + 10$$

The following are other examples of summation notation:

$$\sum_{j=5}^{8} j^2 = (5)^2 + (6)^2 + (7)^2 + (8)^2 = 174$$

$$\sum_{i=1}^{4} (i^3 - 1) = [(1)^3 - 1] + [(2)^3 - 1] + [(3)^3 - 1] + [(4)^3 - 1] = 96$$

$$\sum_{i=1}^{3} (-3i) = (-3)(1) + (-3)(2) + (-3)(3) = -18$$

$$\sum_{j=1}^{5} x_j = x_1 + x_2 + x_3 + x_4 + x_5$$

Note that the name of the index is not restricted to j.

Summation notation can provide considerable efficiency in expressing the summation operation. It is a convenient way of representing systems of equations. And it has particular value when a computer can be used to perform computations.

SELECTED ANSWERS: FOLLOW-UP EXERCISES AND CHAPTER TESTS

Chapter 1

Sec. 1.2   1 5^4;   3 $(3)^2(-2)^3$;   5 $(-x)^3$;   7 $a^2b^3c^2$;
9   $2^7 = 128$;   11 x^8;   13 x^5y^4;   15 x^6;   17 x^{14};   19 a^{12};
21   $27x^6$;   23 $1/a^4$;   25   8;   27 x^2;   29 $\frac{1}{8}$;   31   3;
33   1;   35 x^3/y^3;   37 x^8/y^4;   39 a^8b^4/c^{12}

Sec. 1.2 (Continued)   1 $13x$;   3 $5y^3 + 2y^2 - 4y$;
5   $25x^3y^2 - 25xy^3$;   7   0;   9 $21x^4y^2$;   11 $-8a^{10}$;
13   $-2x^4 + 2x^2y$;   15 $x^4y - 2x^3y^2 + x^2y^3$;   17 $a^2 + 2ab + b^2$;
19   $a^2 - 2ab + b^2$;   21 $x^3 - 6x^2 + 12x - 8$;   23 $4xy$;
25   $-3/y$;   27 $5x - 8$;   29 $-4a^2 + 3a - 2$;   31 $2x^5 + 3x^2 - 4x$

Sec. 1.3   1 $2a(x - 4a^2)$;   3 $2xy(2x^2 - 3y^2 + 4xy)$;
5   $3a(3a^2 - 5a - 9)$;   7   cannot be factored;   9 $(p + 12)(p - 3)$;
11   $(r + 1)(r - 22)$;   13   cannot be factored;   15 $(6m - 1)(m - 3)$;
17   $(2x + 1)(4x - 3)$;   19 $(x^2 + 9)(x + 3)(x - 3)$;
21   $(9x^2 + 25)(3x + 5)(3x - 5)$;   23   cannot be factored;
25   $(1 + 2x)(1 - 2x + 4x^2)$;   27 $x^2(x - 2)(x + 1)$

Sec. 1.4   1 $\frac{11}{30}$;   3 $\frac{1}{8}$;   5 $(x - 2)/x^2$;   7 $(x^2 + 7x)/(x^2 - 4)$;
9   $(10x^2 - 2)/x^2$;   11 $(3a^2 + 3a - 5)/(a^2 + 2a + 1)$;   13 -3;
15   $1/3a^2b$;   17 $\frac{7}{15}$;   19 $2a^3b^2/3c^2$;   21 $(x - 4)/(x^2 - 5x - 4)$

Sec. 1.5   1 $a^{17/6}$;   3 $x^{31/30}$;   5 $a^{5/4}$;   7 $-27x^2$;   9 $a^{4/3}$;
11   25;   13 $-a$;   15 $-2x^2$;   17 $12x^3$;   19 $5\sqrt{7}$;
21   $7\sqrt{2}$;   23 $4\sqrt{x} - x\sqrt{x}$;   25   4;   27 $\frac{8}{3}$;   29 $25x/7y^2$;
31   $\sqrt[3]{x^2}$;   33 $\sqrt[5]{(ab)^3}$;   35 $1/\sqrt{x}$;   37 $\frac{1}{2}$;   39 $(45x)^{1/2}$;
41   $x^{3/4}$;   43 $x^{5/3}$;   45 x^2

Sec. 1.6   1   6;   3   6;   5 -10;   7 -3;   9   3.5;   11 ± 6;
13   4, 1;   15   5, -2;   17   no roots;   19   4, $-\frac{1}{2}$;   21 $\frac{5}{4}$, $-\frac{3}{2}$;
23   $x \geq -10$;   25   no solution;   27 $x \leq 4$;   29 $x \geq -6$;
31   $-36 \leq x \leq -4$;   33   no solution

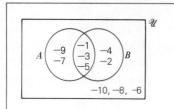

Sec. 1.7,
Exercise 17

Sec. 1.7   **1** $A = \{a \mid a$ is a nonnegative even integer less than 21$\}$;
3 $V = \{v \mid v$ is a vowel$\}$;   **5** $C = \{c \mid c = x^3$ where $x = 1, 2, 3,$ or 4$\}$;
7 $B = \{1, 2, 3, 4\}$;   **9** $B = \{-3\}$;   **11** $B' = \{2, 4, 6, 8, 9, 10\}$;
13 $S = \{6, 8, 11, 14\}$;   **15** $A \subset \mathcal{U}, B \subset \mathcal{U}, C \subset \mathcal{U}, A \subset C, B \subset C$;
17 see figure

Sec. 1.8   **1** $A = B$;
3 (a)–(c) $\{-1, -2, -3, -4, -5, -6, -7, -8, -9\}$,
(d) $\{-1, -3, -5, -7, -9\}$, (e) $\varnothing$, (f) $\{-2, -4, -6, -8\}$

Sec. 1.9   **1** (b) 450, (c) 250, (d) 650;
3 (b) 725, (c) 225, (d) 775;   **5** (a) 0.15, (b) 0.02, (c) 0.03,
(d) 0.04, (e) 0.30, (f) 0.33

Chapter Test   **1** $(2x - 3)(x - 3)$;   **2** $\frac{47}{60}$;   **3** $14xz/5y$;
4 $x^{14}y^{10}z^{20}$;   **5** $\sqrt[5]{(ab)^4}$;   **6** no roots;   **7** $2 \leq x \leq 13$;
8 (a) $\{2, 4, 6, 8\}$, (b) $\{2\}$, (c) $\{-2, 0, 1, 2, 3\}$
9 area 1: respondents who neither smoke nor drink
       area 2: respondents who only smoke
       area 3: respondents who smoke and drink
       area 4: respondents who only drink

Chapter 2

Sec. 2.1   **1** (a) 5, (b) 17, (c) -3, (d) $-4p + 5$;
3 (a) 4, (b) 34, (c) 14, (d) $3p^2 - p + 4$;
5 (a) -1, (b) -64, (c) 1, (d) $(p - 1)^3$;   **7** (a)–(d) 10;
9 8, $a^2 + 2ab + b^2 - 2a - 2b + 5$;   **11** all real numbers;
13 $|x| \leq 5$;   **15** $x \neq 3$;   **17** all real numbers;   **19** $x \leq -2$ except
$x \neq 3$, and $x > 2$;   **21** $0 \leq x \leq 20{,}000$ and $50{,}000 \leq C(x) \leq 550{,}000$;
23 $0 \leq p \leq 5{,}000$ and $0 \leq q \leq 150{,}000$;   **25** $10 \leq x \leq 200$ and
$45 \leq p \leq 425$;   **27** $200 \leq k \leq 1{,}500$ and $19 \leq c \leq 123$;
29 (a) 57, (b) 22, (c) $a^2 - 2ab + 5b^2 + 5$;   **31** (a) 106, (b) 15

Sec. 2.2 **1** constant;   **3** linear;   **5** rational;   **7** quadratic;
9 constant;   **11** logarithmic;   **13** polynomial;
15 logarithmic;   **17** rational;   **19** all real numbers;
21 $g(x)$ defined, $1h(x) \neq 0$;   **23** $(a)x^2 + 8x + 16$, (b) 4, (c) 25;
25 (a)–(c) 497;   **27** $f(x)$ not defined, $x = g(y) = -4y/3$;
29 $y = f(x) = 20/x^2$, $x = g(y) = \sqrt{20/y}$;   **31** $q = f(p) = 4p - 400$,
$p = h(q) = \dfrac{q}{4} + 100$

Sec. 2.3 **1, 3, 5, 7,** and **9** see figures;   **11** $a, b,$ and d are functions

Chapter Test **1** $24, a^2 + 2ab + b^2 - 2a - 2b + 9$;   **2** $x \geq -2$ except
$x \neq -1, x \neq 0, x \neq 3$;   **4** $y - 4x^2 + 3x - 1 = 0$;
5 (a) $(x^2 + 10x + 25)/(-2x - 9)$, (b) $-\frac{9}{5}$;   **6** (a) polynomial, (b) constant;   **7** see figure

Chapter 3

Sec. 3.1 **1** linear;   **3** linear;   **5** nonlinear;   **7** linear;
9 linear;   **11** $S = \{(x, y) | 3x + 7y = 21\}$;
13 (b) $(12, -4)$, $(0, 5)$, $(6\frac{2}{3}, 0)$;   **15** (a) $4x + 2y = 120$, (b) 15, (c) 30
units of A, 60 units of B;   **17** (a) $(1, 1, 1, -9.5)$, (b) $(0, -15, 1, -2)$,
(c) $(16, 0, 0, 0)$, $(0, -16, 0, 0)$, $(0, 0, -5\frac{2}{3}, 0)$, $(0, 0, 0, -8)$;
19 (a) $4x + 5y = 120$, (b) 20, (c) 50

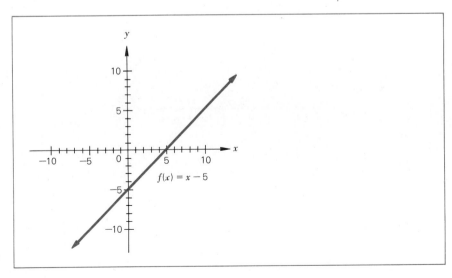

Sec. 2.3,
Exercise 1

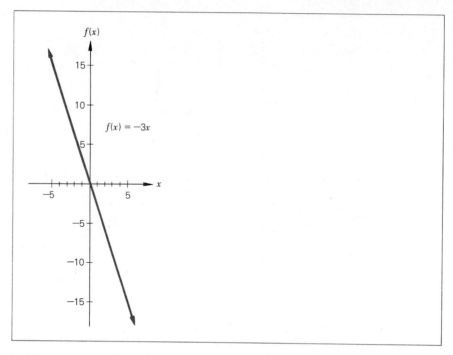

Sec. 2.3,
Exercise 3

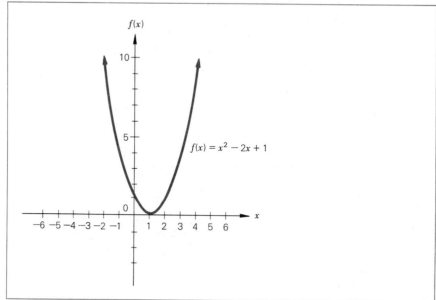

Sec. 2.3,
Exercise 5

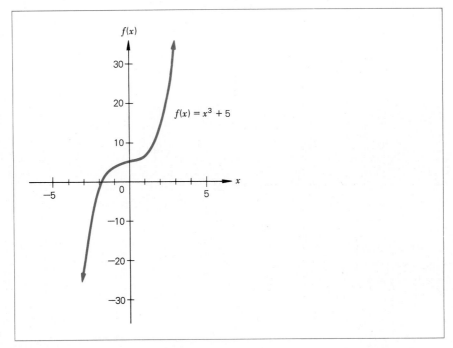

Sec. 2.3,
Exercise 7

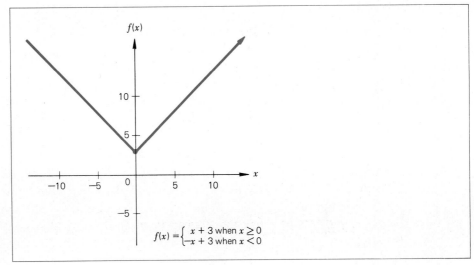

Sec. 2.3,
Exercise 9

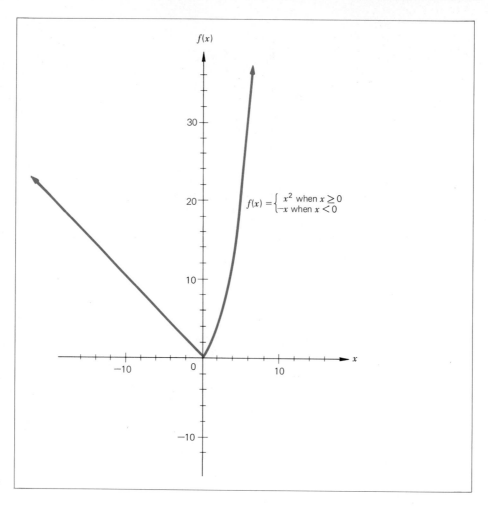

$$f(x) = \begin{cases} x^2 & \text{when } x \geq 0 \\ -x & \text{when } x < 0 \end{cases}$$

Chap. 2,
Chapter Test,
Problem 7

Sec. 3.2   **1** $(8, 0), (0, -6)$;   **3** $(-9, 0), (0, 6)$;   **5** $(8, 0)$, no y intercept;   **7** $(8, 0), (0, -8)$;   **9** $(0, 0), (0, 0)$;   **11**   see figure;
13   see figure;   **15**   see figure;   **17**   see figure;   **19**   see figure;
21 $y = 0, x = 0$;   **23** $m = 4$; for every unit that x increases, y increases 4
units;   **25** $m = -4$;   **27** $m = 0$;   **29** $m = (d - b)/(c - a)$

Sec. 3.3   **1** $y = \dfrac{x}{2} - 6, m = \frac{1}{2}, y$ intercept at $(0, -6)$;

3 $y = x - 10, m = 1, (0, -10)$;   **5** $y = 10 - x, m = -1, (0, 10)$;
7 $y = -x/2, m = -\frac{1}{2}, (0, 0)$;   **9** (b) $m = 0.25, (0, 8.8)$, (d) 11.05 million;
11 (a) $m = \frac{5}{9}, (0, -\frac{160}{9})$, (b) Celsius temperature increases by $\frac{5}{9}$ of a degree
for each increase in temperature by 1 degree Fahrenheit; 0°F equals $-\frac{160}{9}$°C,
(c) F $= \frac{9}{5}$ C $+ 32, m = \frac{9}{5}, (0, 32)$, Fahrenheit temperature increases by $\frac{9}{5}$ of a
degree for each increase in temperature by 1 degree Celsius; 0°C equals 32°F

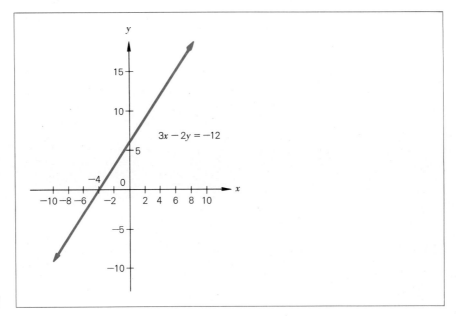

$3x - 2y = -12$

Sec. 3.2,
Exercise 11

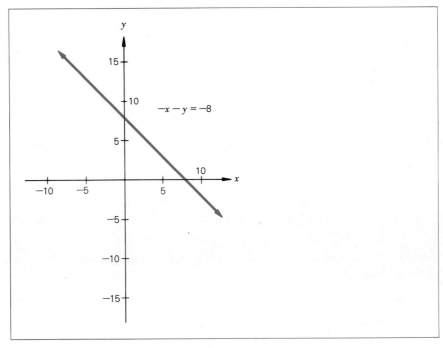

$-x - y = -8$

Sec. 3.2,
Exercise 13

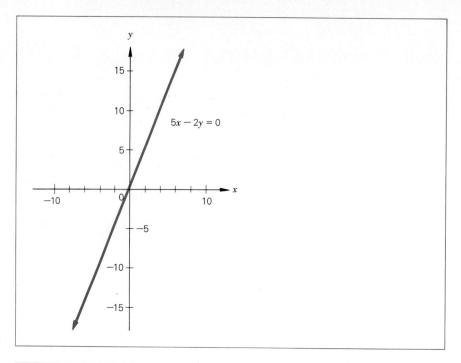

Sec. 3.2,
Exercise 15

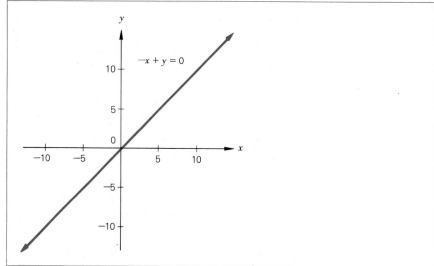

Sec. 3.2,
Exercise 17

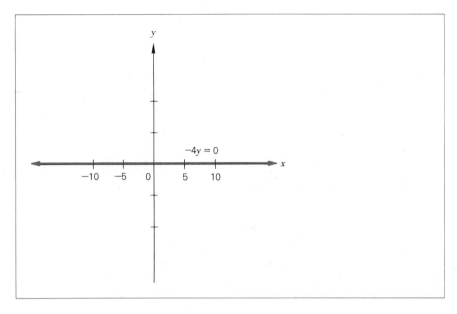

Sec. 3.2,
Exercise 19

Sec. 3.4 1 $y = 3x + 5$;   3 $y = \dfrac{x}{2} - 3$;   5 $y = 2.8x + \tfrac{1}{2}$;   7 no

slope-intercept form, $x = 0$;   9 $y = -2x$;   11 $y = -\dfrac{x}{4} - \tfrac{9}{2}$;

13 $y = -ax + (2a + 4)$;   15 $y = -4x - 14$;   17 $y = -4x - 1$;
19 no-slope intercept form, $x = a$;   21 not colinear;   23 $y = x - 2$;
25 $F = \tfrac{9}{5}C + 32$

Sec. 3.5 1 $A(0, 4, 0)$, $B(3, 4, 0)$, $C(3, 0, 0)$, $D(-6, 0, 0)$, $E(-6, 0, 6)$,
$F(-6, -2, 6)$, $G(0, -2, 6)$, $H(0, 0, 6)$, $I(0, -2, 0)$;   3 $(\tfrac{15}{2}, 0, 0)$,
$(0, -5, 0)$, $(0, 0, 15)$;   5 see figure

Sec. 3.6 1 emergency airlift;   3 $8A + 5.5B + 65C = 600$;
5 $25,000x_1 + 18,000x_2 + 15,000x_3 = 10,000,000$

Chapter Test 1 (a) $(10, 0)$, $(0, -6)$, (b) see figure;
2 (a) $y = \tfrac{7}{3}x - 20$, (b) $m = \tfrac{7}{3}$, $(0, -20)$, (c) for each unit increase in x, y
increases $\tfrac{7}{3}$ units;
3 (a) $y = 3x + 2$, (b) $m = 3$, $(0, 2)$;   4 $y = -\tfrac{1}{4}x - \tfrac{1}{2}$;
5 $3,000x_1 + 4,000x_2 + 1,000x_3 + 1,500x_4 = 300,000$

Chapter 4

Sec. 4.2 1 unique;   3 no solution;   5 $(2, 1)$;   7 no solution;

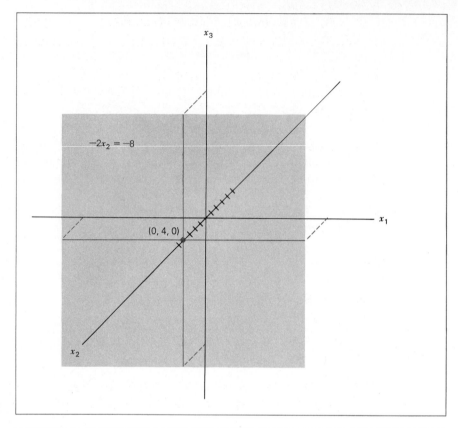

Sec. 3.5,
Exercise 5

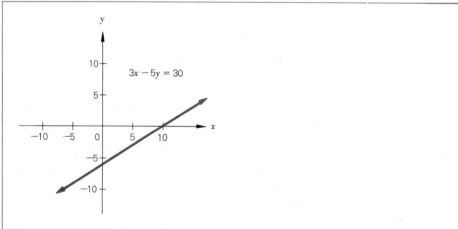

Chap. 3,
Chapter Test,
Problem 1(b)

9 $(3, -5)$;   **11** infinite number of solutions;   **13** $(-2, -1)$;
15 infinite;   **17** $(-1, 3)$;   **19** $(3, 1)$;   **21** no solution

Sec. 4.3 1 $(2, -1, 1)$;   **3** infinite;   **5** $(2, 1, -3)$;   **7** no solution;
9 no solution;   **11** infinite;   **13** $(3, 2, 1)$;   **15** x_1 arbitrary,
$$x_2 = \frac{x_1}{4} + \frac{25}{4}, \; x_3 = -\frac{5x_1}{4} + 13\tfrac{3}{4};$$
17 x_1, x_2 arbitrary, $x_3 = -\tfrac{2}{3}x_1 + \tfrac{5}{3}x_2 - \tfrac{7}{3}$, x_1, x_3 arbitrary, $x_2 = \tfrac{2}{5}x_1 + \tfrac{3}{5}x_2 + \tfrac{7}{5}$;
19 (a) unique, no solution, or infinite, (b) infinite or none, (c) all 3
possibilities, (d) all 3, (e) all 3

Sec. 4.4 1 $(4, -6)$;   **3** $(-2, 1)$;   **5** infinite;   **7** no solution;
9 no solution;   **11** $(1, 2, -1)$;   **13** infinite

Chapter Test 1 $(1, -1)$;   **2** $(3, -5)$;
3 (a) unique, none, or infinite, (b) none or infinite;
4 no solution;   **5** $(3, -4, 3)$;
6 (a) no solution, (b) $x_1 = 4, x_2 = -2, x_3 = 1, x_4 = 3$

Chapter 5

Sec. 5.1 1 $y = f(x_1, x_2, x_3, x_4, x_5) = a_1x_1 + a_2x_2 + a_3x_3 + a_4x_4 + a_5x_5 + b$;
3 $y = 5x_1 + 3x_2 + 25$ when $x_1 + x_2 \le 50$, $y = 7.5x_1 + 5.5x_2 - 100$ when
$x_1 + x_2 > 50$;
5 (a) $R = 400x_1 + 1{,}000x_2 + 1{,}750x_3$,
(b) $C = 300x_1 + 600x_2 + 1{,}020x_3 + 25{,}000{,}000$,
(c) $P = 100x_1 + 400x_2 + 730x_3 - 25{,}000{,}000$ (d) $300{,}000$;
7 $f_1(x) = 588.24x + 78{,}528.4$, $f_2(x) = 884.62x + 40{,}000$

Sec. 5.2 1 $V = f(t) = 50{,}000 - 6{,}250t$;   **3** $V = f(t) = 400{,}000 - 20{,}000t$;
5 (a) $R = 0.75n + 21$, (b) percentage of arrests when no plainclothes officers are assigned;
7 (a) $q = f(p) = -750p + 58{,}750$, (b) 5, (c) for each dollar increase in
price demand decreases by 750 units, (d) see figure;
9 (a) $q = f(p) = 17{,}500p - 51{,}250$, (b) 11.79, (c) for each dollar increase
in price, quantity supplied will increase by 17,500 units, (d) no supply will
be offered at price below 2.93, (e) see figure;
11 (a) $y = f(t) = 1{,}876{,}868t + 49{,}250{,}405$, (b) $49{,}250{,}405$, (c) $68{,}019{,}085$

Sec. 5.3 1 7,500 units;   **3** 35;   **5** (a) 20, (b) $-37{,}500$;
7 (a) 8, (b) 12;
9 (a) $16{,}666\tfrac{2}{3}$ lines, (b) $37{,}500$ in-house, $40{,}000$ outside, (c) 1.375/line;
11 If output $< 24{,}000$ units, purchase from supplier at 10/unit; if output-
$> 24{,}000$, buy more highly automated equipment (see figure)

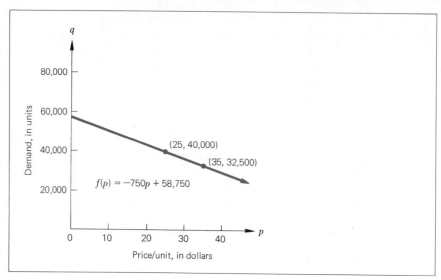

Sec. 5.2,
Exercise 7(*d*)

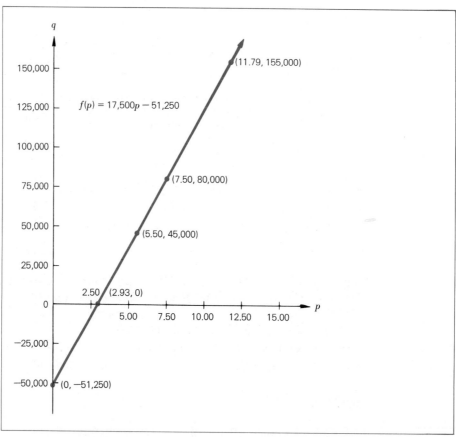

Sec. 5.2,
Exercise 9(*e*)

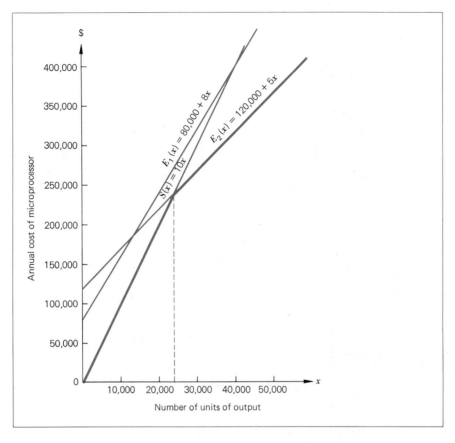

Sec. 5.4   **1** $p = \$625$, $q = 28{,}750$;   **3** $p = \$131.25$, $q = 5{,}937.5$ (thousands);   **5** $p = \$675$, $q = 26{,}250$;   **7** $y = f(x) = 3.5x + 40$;
9 $x_1 = 100$, $x_2 = x_3 = 200$;   **11** $x_1 = \$180{,}000$, $x_2 = \$120{,}000$, $x_3 = \$200{,}000$

Chapter Test   **1**   (a) $g = 2.42 + 0.06t$,   (b) $t = 9.67$ (or sometime between 1982 and 1983,   (c) 2.84,   (d) the cumulative grade point average increases 0.06 per year;
2   (a) $P = 25x - 100{,}000$,   (b) 10,000 units;
3   (a) $66\tfrac{2}{3}$ persons,   (b) 133.34 persons;   **4** $p = \$20$, $q = 70{,}000$;
5 $6A + 2B + 2C = 80$, $7A + 4B + C = 60$, $5A + 5B + 3C = 100$

Chapter 6

Sec. 6.2   **1** (3×1), $\begin{pmatrix} 6 \\ -8 \\ 2 \end{pmatrix}$;   **3** (1×4), $(0\ 4\ -5\ 1)$;

5 (3 × 3), $\begin{pmatrix} 1 & 0 & 0 \\ 0 & 1 & 0 \\ 0 & 0 & 1 \end{pmatrix}$;   7 $\begin{pmatrix} 2 & 0 & 0 & 0 \\ 0 & 4 & 0 & 0 \end{pmatrix}$

Sec. 6.3 1 $\begin{pmatrix} -3 & -9 \\ -8 & -10 \end{pmatrix}$;   3 $\begin{pmatrix} 1 & 4 \\ -4 & 4 \end{pmatrix}$;   5 (2);   7 inner product

not defined;   9 $(ax + by)$;   11 $\begin{pmatrix} 8 & 24 \\ -5 & -12 \end{pmatrix}$;   13 $(2 \quad -3)$;

15 $\begin{pmatrix} 1 & -2 & 1 \\ 0 & 3 & 0 \end{pmatrix}$;   17 cannot be multiplied;   19 $\begin{pmatrix} 5 & 4 & 3 \\ -3 & -4 & -4 \\ 2 & -2 & -1 \end{pmatrix}$;

21 $\begin{pmatrix} a_{11}x_1 + a_{12}x_2 \\ a_{21}x_1 + a_{22}x_2 \end{pmatrix}$;   23 $\begin{pmatrix} 1 & -1 \\ 2 & 3 \end{pmatrix}\begin{pmatrix} x \\ y \end{pmatrix} = \begin{pmatrix} 5 \\ -10 \end{pmatrix}$;

25 $\begin{pmatrix} 1 & -2 & 1 \\ 3 & -1 & -2 \end{pmatrix}\begin{pmatrix} x_1 \\ x_2 \\ x_3 \end{pmatrix} = \begin{pmatrix} 12 \\ 5 \end{pmatrix}$;   27 $\begin{pmatrix} a & b \\ d & e \\ g & h \end{pmatrix}\begin{pmatrix} x_1 \\ x_2 \end{pmatrix} = \begin{pmatrix} c \\ f \\ i \end{pmatrix}$;

29 $\begin{pmatrix} a_1 & a_2 & a_3 \\ a_4 & a_5 & a_6 \end{pmatrix}\begin{pmatrix} x^2 \\ x \\ 1 \end{pmatrix} = \begin{pmatrix} b_1 \\ b_2 \end{pmatrix}$

Sec. 6.4 1 -2;   3 14;   5 1;   7 -68;   9 0;   11 $\begin{pmatrix} 4 & -1 \\ 2 & 3 \end{pmatrix}$;

13 $\begin{pmatrix} 1 & 0 \\ 0 & 1 \end{pmatrix}$;   15 $\begin{pmatrix} -8 & -2 & 4 \\ -16 & 8 & 0 \\ 16 & -12 & -8 \end{pmatrix}$;   17 $\begin{pmatrix} 1 & 0 & -1 \\ 0 & 0 & 0 \\ -1 & 0 & 1 \end{pmatrix}$;

19 14;   21 1;   23 -32;   25 0;   27 -196

Sec. 6.5 1 $\begin{pmatrix} 3 & -1 \\ 2 & -1 \end{pmatrix}$;   3 no inverse;   5 $\begin{pmatrix} 1 & 0 \\ 0 & 1 \end{pmatrix}$;

7 $\frac{1}{8}\begin{pmatrix} -3 & 6 & 1 \\ 3 & 2 & -1 \\ -1 & -6 & 3 \end{pmatrix}$;   9 $\begin{pmatrix} 5 & -7 \\ -2 & 3 \end{pmatrix}$;   11 no inverse;

13 $x_1 = 2$, $x_2 = 3$;   15 $x_1 = 10$, $x_2 = 5$;
17 $x_1 = 20$, $x_2 = 10$, $x_3 = 30$;   19 either no solution or an infinite
number;   21 $x_1 = 1$, $x_2 = 5$, $x_3 = 0$;
23 $2x_1 + 2x_2 + 3x_3 = 3$
     $x_2 + x_3 = 2$
     $x_1 + x_2 + x_3 = 4$

Sec. 6.6 1 Democrat—96,850, Republican—98,850, Independent—104,300
(projected winner);
3 (a) brand 3 will eventually have entire market, (b) brands 2 and 3 will
eventually share the market equally;

5　$p_N = 23\frac{1}{3}$ (millions), $P_s = 46\frac{2}{3}$ (millions);

7

$$
\begin{array}{c}
\text{To} \\
\begin{array}{cccc} A & B & C & D \end{array} \\
\text{From}\
\begin{array}{c} A \\ B \\ C \\ D \end{array}
\begin{pmatrix}
0 & 0 & 1 & 0 \\
1 & 0 & 1 & 0 \\
1 & 1 & 0 & 1 \\
0 & 0 & 1 & 0
\end{pmatrix} \\
\text{Adjaceney matrix}
\end{array}
\qquad
\begin{array}{c}
\text{To} \\
\begin{array}{cccc} A & B & C & D \end{array} \\
\text{From}\
\begin{array}{c} A \\ B \\ C \\ D \end{array}
\begin{pmatrix}
1 & 1 & 0 & 1 \\
1 & 1 & 1 & 1 \\
1 & 0 & 3 & 0 \\
1 & 1 & 0 & 1
\end{pmatrix} \\
\text{One-stop service}
\end{array}
$$

Chapter Test　1　$\begin{pmatrix} 1 & 6 \\ -3 & -2 \\ 0 & 4 \\ 5 & 9 \end{pmatrix}$;　2　$ae + bf + cg + dh$;

3　(a) not possible,　(b) $\begin{pmatrix} -11 & -22 \\ 2 & -1 \\ 26 & 9 \end{pmatrix}$,　(c) not possible;

4　$\begin{pmatrix} 1 & 0 & 0 & -1 \\ 0 & 1 & 1 & 0 \\ 0 & 0 & 1 & 1 \\ 0 & 0 & 0 & 1 \end{pmatrix} \begin{pmatrix} x_1 \\ x_2 \\ x_3 \\ x_4 \end{pmatrix} = \begin{pmatrix} 20 \\ 15 \\ 18 \\ 9 \end{pmatrix}$;　5　-30;　6　no inverse;

7　$3x_1 + 7x_2 = 15$
$\quad 2x_1 + 5x_2 = 11$

Chapter 7

Sec. 7.2　1　(a) add the constraints
$x_1 \geq 22$, $x_2 \geq 18$, $x_3 \geq 25$, $x_4 \geq 15$, $x_5 \geq 40$ (note that this is redundant),
$x_6 \geq 12$,　(b) $x_4 \geq x_3$ or $x_4 - x_3 \geq 0$,　(c) $x_3 + x_6 \geq 40$;
3　if x_j = no. of ounces of food j,
Minimize $z = 0.15x_1 + 0.10x_2 + 0.12x_3$
subject to
$$
\begin{aligned}
30x_1 + 20x_2 + 40x_3 &\geq 300 \\
10x_1 + 15x_2 + 5x_3 &\geq 120 \\
40x_1 + 30x_2 + 20x_3 &\geq 210 \\
x_1 + x_2 + x_3 &\geq 7.5 \\
x_1, x_2, x_3 &\geq 0
\end{aligned}
$$

5　Minimize $z = 50x_{11} + 40x_{12} + 35x_{13} + 30x_{21} + 45x_{22} + 40x_{23}$
subject to
$$
\begin{aligned}
x_{11} + x_{12} + x_{13} &\leq 1{,}000 \\
x_{21} + x_{22} + x_{23} &\leq 1{,}400 \\
x_{11} + x_{21} &= 800 \\
x_{12} + x_{22} &= 750 \\
x_{13} + x_{23} &= 650 \\
x_{11}, x_{12}, x_{13}, x_{21}, x_{22}, x_{23} &\geq 0
\end{aligned}
$$

7　(a) $x_1 + x_2 + x_3 \geq 40$,　(b) $x_1 \leq 2x_3$ or $x_1 - 2x_3 \leq 0$,　(c) $x_2 = x_3$ or
$x_2 - x_3 = 0$;

9 x_{ij} = no. of pounds of component i used in blend j.

Minimize $z = .70x_{11} + .85x_{12} + 1.25x_{13} + .55x_{21} + .70x_{22} + 1.10x_{23} + .65x_{31} + .80x_{32} + 1.20x_{33} + .45x_{41} + .60x_{42} + 1.00x_{43}$

subject to

$$
\begin{aligned}
x_{11} + x_{12} + x_{13} &\leq 30{,}000 \\
x_{21} + x_{22} + x_{23} &\leq 40{,}000 \\
x_{31} + x_{32} + x_{33} &\leq 25{,}000 \\
x_{41} + x_{42} + x_{43} &\leq 20{,}000 \\
x_{11} + x_{21} + x_{31} + x_{41} &\geq 40{,}000 \\
-.3x_{11} + .7x_{21} - .3x_{31} - .3x_{41} &\geq 0 \\
- .2x_{13} + .8x_{23} - .2x_{33} - .2x_{43} &\leq 0 \\
- .2x_{13} - .2x_{23} + .8x_{33} - .2x_{43} &= 0 \\
- .4x_{13} - .4x_{23} - .4x_{33} + .6x_{43} &\geq 0 \\
-.1x_{11} - .1x_{21} - .1x_{31} + .9x_{41} &\leq 0 \\
x_{ij} &\geq 0 \text{ for all} \\
&\quad i \text{ and } j
\end{aligned}
$$

Sec. 7.3   **1, 3, 5, 7,** and **9**   see figures;   **11** $z = 144$, $x_1 = 16$, $x_2 = 0$;
13 $z = 270$, $x_1 = 3$, $x_2 = 9$;   **15** $z = 360$, $x_1 = 18$, $x_2 = 12$;
17   alternative optimal solutions, $z = 240$ when $x_1 = 5$ and $x_2 = 0$ *or* $x_1 = 12$ and $x_2 = 6$;
19   alternative optimal solutions, $z = 20$ when $x_1 = .8$ and $x_2 = 4$ *or* when $x_1 = 1\frac{1}{3}$ and $x_2 = 3\frac{1}{3}$;

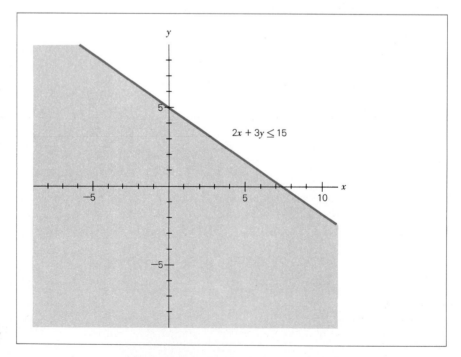

Sec. 7.3,
Exercise 1

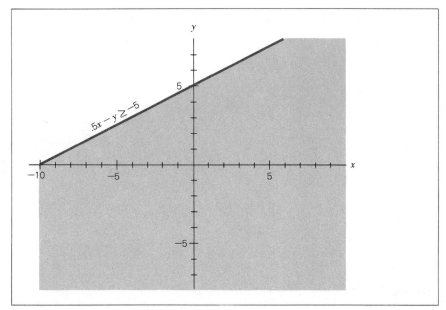

Sec. 7.3,
Exercise 3

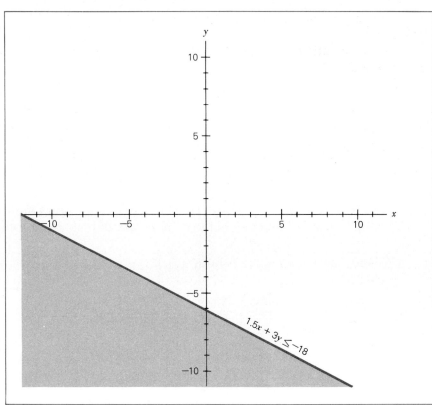

Sec. 7.3,
Exercise 5

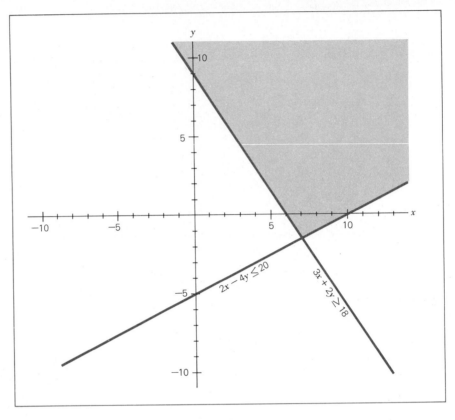

Sec. 7.3,
Exercise 7

21   no feasible solution;

23   (a) Maximize $z = 3x_1 + 4x_2$
subject to $2x_1 + 3x_2 \leq 60$
$4x_1 + 2x_2 \leq 80$
$x_1, x_2 \geq 0$

(b) $z = 85$ when $x_1 = 15$ and $x_2 = 10$;   (c) 15 units of product A and 10 units of product B should be produced. 100% use of both departments.

Sec. 7.4   1   Minimize $z = 0.10x_1 + 0.15x_2 + 0.12x_3 + MA_1 + MA_2 + MA_3 + MA_4$

subject to $50x_1 + 30x_2 + 20x_3 - E_1 + A_1 = 290$
$20x_1 + 10x_2 + 30x_3 - E_2 + A_2 = 200$
$10x_1 + 50x_2 + 20x_3 - E_3 + A_3 = 210$
$x_1 + x_2 + x_3 - E_4 + A_4 = 9$
$x_1, x_2, x_3, E_1, E_2, E_3, E_4, A_1, A_2, A_3, A_4 \geq 0$

3   Maximize $z = 4.4x_1 + 3.8x_2 + 4.1x_3 + 3.5x_4 + 5.1x_5 + 3.2x_6 - MA_8 - MA_9$

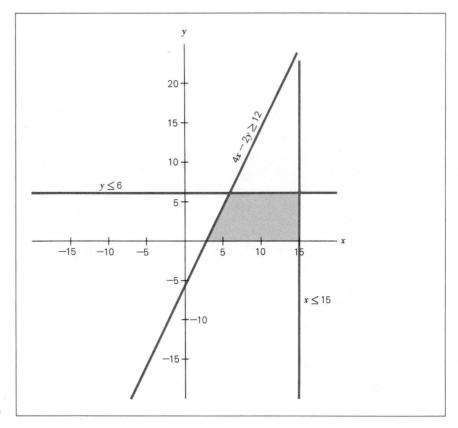

Sec. 7.3,
Exercise 9

subject to
$$
\begin{aligned}
x_1 + x_2 + x_3 + x_4 + x_5 + x_6 + S_1 &= 1000 \\
x_1 \qquad\qquad\qquad\qquad\qquad + S_2 &= 220 \\
x_2 \qquad\qquad\qquad\qquad + S_3 &= 180 \\
x_3 \qquad\qquad\qquad + S_4 &= 250 \\
x_4 \qquad\qquad + S_5 &= 150 \\
x_5 \qquad + S_6 &= 400 \\
x_6 \qquad + S_7 &= 120 \\
x_5 \quad - E_8 + A_8 &= 200 \\
x_1 + x_2 \qquad\qquad - E_9 + A_9 &= 300 \\
x_1, x_2, x_3, x_4, x_5, x_6, S_1, S_2, S_3, S_4, S_5, S_6, S_7, E_8, E_9, A_8, A_9 &\geq 0
\end{aligned}
$$

5   Minimize $z = 3x_1 - 5x_2 + 2x_3 + 7x_4 + MA_1 + MA_2 + MA_3 + MA_5$

subject to
$$
\begin{aligned}
x_1 + x_2 + x_3 + x_4 - E_1 + A_1 &= 25 \\
x_1 - 3x_2 \qquad + 2x_4 - E_2 + A_2 &= 20 \\
3x_1 \qquad\qquad - 4x_4 \qquad\qquad + A_3 &= 10 \\
5x_1 - x_2 + 3x_3 + 8x_4 \qquad\qquad + S_4 &= 125 \\
x_1 \qquad\qquad\qquad\qquad - E_5 + A_5 &= 5 \\
x_3 \qquad\qquad\qquad + S_6 &= 30 \\
x_1, x_2, x_3, x_4, E_1, A_1, E_2, A_2, A_3, S_4, E_5, A_5, S_6 &\geq 0
\end{aligned}
$$

11 z minimized at 660 when $x_2 = 35$, $x_3 = 30$, and $S_3 = 5$. *Shadow Prices:* constraint 1, 6.333; constraint 2, 0.333; constraint 3, 0.

Sensitivity Analysis on Objective Function Coefficients:
nonbasic variable C_1, delta = 11, upper limit = 13.

BASIC VARIABLES	LOWER DELTA	UPPER DELTA	LOWER LIMIT	UPPER LIMIT
c_2	−14.67	4.00	−2.67	16.00
c_3	−2.00	no limit	6.00	no limit

Right-hand-side constants:

CONSTRAINT	LOWER DELTA	UPPER DELTA	LOWER LIMIT	UPPER LIMIT
1	−84.00	1.818	16.00	101.818
2	−180	20	−100	100
3	−5.00	no limit	295	no limit

13 z minimized at \$3,925 when $x_{11} = 300$, $x_{12} = 100$, $x_{13} = 500$, $x_{22} = 350$, and $x_{24} = 350$

Chapter Test   1   see figure;

2   Maximize $z = 20A + 10B + 50C + 25D + 2E$
subject to
$$A \geq 20$$
$$B \geq 10$$
$$A + B + C + D + E \leq 75$$
$$C - E = 0$$
$$A, B, C, D, E \geq 0$$

3   alternative optimal solutions; $z = 36$ when $x_1 = 12$ and $x_2 = 6$ *or* when $x_1 = 8$ and $x_2 = 8$;

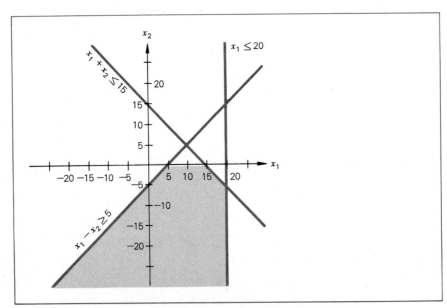

Chap. 7,
Chapter Test,
Problem 1

5 Minimize $z = 10x_1 + 5x_2 + 15x_3 + MA_2 + MA_3 + MA_4$
subject to
$$x_1 + x_2 + x_3 + S_1 = 40$$
$$x_1 - 5x_2 + 4x_3 - E_2 + A_2 = 25$$
$$-2x_1 + 3x_3 - E_3 + A_3 = 10$$
$$x_1 + x_2 + A_4 = 24$$
$$x_1, x_2, x_3, S_1, E_2, A_2, E_3, A_3, A_4 \geq 0$$

Chapter 8

Sec. 8.1 **1** (a) $5x_1 + 4x_2 + S_1 = 48$
$$2x_1 + 5x_2 + S_2 = 26$$
$$x_1, x_2, S_1, S_2 \geq 0$$

(b)

SOLUTION	VARIABLE SET EQUAL TO ZERO	VALUE OF OTHER VARIABLES	z
1	x_1, x_2	$S_1 = 48, S_2 = 26$	0
2	x_1, S_1	$S_2 = -34, x_2 = 12$	
3	x_1, S_2	$S_1 = 27.2, x_2 = 5.2$	52
4	x_2, S_1	$x_1 = 9.6, S_2 = 6.8$	134.4
5	x_2, S_2	$x_1 = 13, S_1 = -17$	
6	S_1, S_2	$x_1 = 8, x_2 = 2$	132

(c) feasible solutions 1, 3, 4, and 6,   (e) maximum of 134.4 reached when $x_1 = 9.6$, $S_2 = 6.8$, and $x_2 = S_1 = 0$;

3

BASIC VARIABLES	z	x_1	x_2	S_1	S_2	b_i	ROW NO.	r_i
	1	-4	-2	0	0	0	(0)	
S_1	0	1	1	1	0	50	(1)	50
S_2	0	⑥	0	0	1	240	(2)	40*
	1	0	-2	0	$\frac{2}{3}$	160	(0)	
S_1	0	0	①	1	$-\frac{1}{6}$	10	(1)	10*
x_1	0	1	0	0	$\frac{1}{6}$	40	(2)	
	1	0	0	2	$\frac{1}{3}$	180	(0)	
x_2	0	0	1	1	$-\frac{1}{6}$	10	(1)	
x_1	0	1	0	0	$\frac{1}{6}$	40	(2)	

z maximized at value of 180 when $x_1 = 40$ and $x_2 = 10$.

5

BASIC VARIABLES	z	x_1	x_2	S_1	S_2	S_3	b_i	ROW NO.	r_i
	1	-10	-12	0	0	0	0	(0)	
S_1	0	1	1	1	0	0	150	(1)	150
S_2	0	3	⑥	0	1	0	300	(2)	50*
S_3	0	4	2	0	0	1	160	(3)	80
	1	-4	0	0	2	0	600	(0)	
S_1	0	$\frac{1}{2}$	0	1	$-\frac{1}{6}$	0	100	(1)	200
x_2	0	$\frac{1}{2}$	1	0	$\frac{1}{6}$	0	50	(2)	100
S_3	0	③	0	0	$-\frac{1}{3}$	1	60	(3)	20*
	1	0	0	0	$\frac{14}{9}$	$\frac{4}{3}$	680	(0)	
S_1	0	0	0	1	$-\frac{1}{9}$	$-\frac{1}{6}$	90	(1)	
x_2	0	0	1	0	$\frac{2}{9}$	$-\frac{1}{6}$	40	(2)	
x_1	0	1	0	0	$-\frac{1}{9}$	$\frac{1}{3}$	20	(3)	

z maximized at value of 680 when $x_1 = 20$, $x_2 = 40$, and $S_1 = 90$.

7

BASIC VARIABLES	z	x_1	x_2	x_3	S_1	S_2	S_3	b_i	ROW NO.	r_i
	1	−10	−3	−4	0	0	0	0	(0)	
S_1	0	⑧	2	3	1	0	0	400	(1)	50*
S_2	0	4	3	0	0	1	0	200	(2)	50
S_3	0	0	0	1	0	0	1	40	(3)	
	1	0	$-\frac{1}{2}$	$-\frac{1}{4}$	$\frac{5}{4}$	0	0	500	(0)	
x_1	0	1	$\frac{1}{4}$	$\frac{3}{8}$	$\frac{1}{8}$	0	0	50	(1)	200
S_2	0	0	②	$-\frac{3}{2}$	$-\frac{1}{2}$	1	0	0	(2)	0*
S_3	0	0	0	1	0	0	1	40	(3)	
	1	0	0	$-\frac{5}{8}$	$\frac{9}{8}$	$\frac{1}{4}$	0	500	(0)	
x_1	0	1	0	$\frac{9}{16}$	$\frac{3}{16}$	$-\frac{1}{8}$	0	50	(1)	
x_2	0	0	1	$-\frac{3}{4}$	$-\frac{1}{4}$	$\frac{1}{2}$	0	0	(2)	
S_3	0	0	0	①	0	0	1	40	(3)	40*
	1	0	0	0	$\frac{9}{8}$	$\frac{1}{4}$	$\frac{5}{8}$	525	(0)	
x_1	0	1	0	0	$\frac{3}{16}$	$-\frac{1}{8}$	$-\frac{9}{16}$	525	(1)	
x_2	0	0	1	0	$-\frac{1}{4}$	$\frac{1}{2}$	$\frac{3}{4}$	30	(2)	
x_3	0	0	0	1	0	0	1	40	(3)	

z maximized at value of 525 when $x_1 = 27.5$, $x_2 = 30$, and $x_3 = 40$.

9

	z	x_1	x_2	E_1	A_1	S_2	E_3	A_3	b_i	ROW NO.	r_i
	1	−3	−6	0	$-M$	0	0	$-M$	0	(0)	
A_1	0	4	1	−1	1	0	0	0	20	(1)	
S_2	0	1	1	0	0	1	0	0	20	(2)	
A_3	0	1	1	0	0	0	−1	−1	10	(3)	
	1	$5M-3$	$2M-6$	$-M$	0	0	$-M$	0	$30M$	(0)	
A_1	0	4	1	−1	1	0	0	0	20	(1)	5*
S_2	0	1	1	0	0	1	0	0	20	(2)	20
A_3	0	1	1	0	0	0	−1	1	10	(3)	20
	1	0	$\dfrac{3M-21}{4}$	$\dfrac{M-3}{4}$	$\dfrac{3-5M}{4}$	0	$-M$	0	$15+5M$	(0)	
x_1	0	1	$\frac{1}{4}$	$-\frac{1}{4}$	$\frac{1}{4}$	0	0	0	5	(1)	20
S_2	0	0	$\frac{3}{4}$	$\frac{1}{4}$	$-\frac{1}{4}$	1	0	0	15	(2)	20
A_3	0	0	$\frac{3}{4}$	$\frac{1}{4}$	$-\frac{1}{4}$	0	−1	1	5	(3)	$\frac{20}{3}$*
	1	0	0	1	$-M-1$	0	−7	$7-M$	50	(0)	
x_1	0	1	0	$-\frac{1}{3}$	$\frac{1}{3}$	0	$\frac{1}{3}$	$-\frac{1}{3}$	$\frac{10}{3}$	(1)	
S_2	0	0	0	0	0	1	1	−1	10	(2)	
x_2	0	0	1	$\frac{1}{3}$	$-\frac{1}{3}$	0	$-\frac{4}{3}$	$\frac{4}{3}$	$\frac{20}{3}$	(3)	20*
	1	0	−3	0	$-M$	0	−3	$3-M$	30	(0)	
x_1	0	1	1	0	0	0	−1	1	10	(1)	
S_2	0	0	0	0	0	1	1	−1	10	(2)	
E_1	0	0	3	1	−1	0	−4	4	20	(3)	

z minimized at value of 30 when $x_1 = 10$, $S_2 = 10$, and $E_1 = 20$.

11 When $a_{ik} = 0$ for a row, the corresponding basic variable will retain the same value as units of the new basic variable are entered. When $a_{ik} < 0$, the corresponding basic variable will *increase* as units of the new basic variable are introduced. Thus for $a_{ik} \le 0$, the corresponding basic variable will *never* be driven to a value of zero.

Sec. 8.2 1

BASIC VARIABLES	z	x_1	x_2	S_1	S_2	b_i	ROW NO.	r_i
	1	-4	-2	0	0	0	(0)	
S_1	0	1	1	1	0	15	(1)	15
S_2	0	②	1	0	1	20	(2)	10*
	1	0	0	0	2	40	(0)	
S_1	0	0	①	1	$-\frac{1}{2}$	5	(1)	$\frac{5}{2}$*
x_1	0	1	$\frac{1}{2}$	0	$\frac{1}{2}$	10	(2)	5

Optimal solution exists when $x_1 = 10$ and $S_1 = 5$, resulting in $z = 40$. However, row (0) coefficient of zero for x_2 indicates that an alternative optimal solution exists.

BASIC VARIABLES	z	x_1	x_2	S_1	S_2	b_i	ROW NO.	r_i
	1	0	0	0	2	40	(0)	
x_2	0	0	1	2	-1	$\frac{5}{2}$	(1)	
x_1	0	1	0	-1	1	$8\frac{3}{4}$	(2)	

Alternative optimal solution occurs when $x_1 = 8.75$, $x_2 = 2.5$, and $z = 40$.

3 Alternative optimal solution occurs when $x_1 = 4$, $x_2 = 8$, and $z = 48$ *or* when $x_1 = 8$ and $S_1 = 12$;

5 no feasible solution exists

Sec. 8.3 1 Minimize $z = 45y_1 + 30y_2 + 50y_3$
subject to $y_1 + 4y_2 - y_3 \geq 3$
$y_1 + 5y_2 + 3y_3 \geq 4$
$y_1 - 3y_2 - 4y_3 \geq 2$
$y_1, y_2, y_3 \geq 0$

3 Minimize $z = 60y_1 + 25y_2 + 35y_3$
subject to $5y_1 + y_2 \geq 20$
$-3y_1 + y_2 - y_3 \geq 15$
$10y_1 + y_2 + 4y_3 \geq 18$
$4y_1 + 7y_3 = 10$
$y_1 \geq 0$
y_2 unrestricted
$y_3 \leq 0$

5 Maximize $z = 45y_1 + 24y_2 + 20y_3$
subject to $y_1 + 3y_2 \leq 4$
$y_1 + 5y_2 \leq 5$
$y_1 + 7y_3 = 2$
$y_1 - 2y_2 - 5y_3 \leq 3$
$y_1 + 3y_3 = 1$
y_1 unrestricted
$y_2 \leq 0$
$y_3 \geq 0$

7 (a) Minimize $z = 32y_1 + 24y_2$
subject to $2y_1 + 3y_2 \geq 5$
$\qquad\qquad 4y_1 + 2y_2 \geq 3$
$\qquad\qquad\quad y_1, y_2 \geq 0$

(b)

BASIC VARIABLES	z	x_1	x_2	S_1	S_2	b_i	ROW NO.	r_i
	1	-5	-3	0	0	0	(0)	
S_1	0	2	4	1	0	32	(1)	16
S_2	0	③	2	0	1	24	(2)	8*
	1	0	0	$\frac{1}{3}$	$\boxed{0}$	$\boxed{\frac{5}{3}}$	40	(0)
S_1	0	0	$\frac{8}{3}$	1	-2	16	(1)
x_1	0	1	$\frac{2}{3}$	0	$\frac{1}{3}$	8	(2)

z maximized at value of 40 when $x_1 = 8$ and $S_1 = 16$.

(c) The two boxed values under S_1 and S_2 in row (0) of the optimal primal tableau indicate that in the optimal dual solution $y_1 = 0$ and $y_2 = \frac{5}{3}$. When substituted into the dual objective function, the minimum value for z is 40.

Chapter Test **1** $\quad 4x_1 - 2x_2 + x_3 + S_1 = 25$
$\qquad\qquad -x_1 - 3x_2 + S_2 \qquad = 10$
$\qquad\qquad -2x_1 - 3x_3 + A_3 \qquad = 20$
$\qquad\qquad x_1, x_2, x_3, S_1, S_2, A_3 \geq 0$

2 Maximum reached when $x_1 = 4$, $x_2 = 8$, and $z = 272$;

3 (a)

BASIC VARIABLES	z	x_1	x_2	E_1	A_1	A_2	b_i	ROW NO.
	1	$3M - 5$	-4	$-M$	0	0	$25M$	(0)
A_1	0	1	1	-1	1	0	10	(1)
A_2	0	2	-1	0	0	1	15	(2)

(b) A_2 will leave first,   (c) x_1 will enter first;
5 Maximize $z = 25y_1 + 10y_2 + 48y_3 + 12y_4$
subject to $y_1 + 4y_2 + \ y_3 \qquad\quad \leq 8$
$\qquad\qquad y_1 - 5y_2 - \ y_3 + y_4 \leq 5$
$\qquad\qquad y_1 \qquad\quad + 2y_3 \qquad = 6$
$\qquad\qquad\qquad\qquad y_1$ unrestricted
$\qquad\qquad\qquad\qquad y_2 \geq 0$
$\qquad\qquad\qquad\qquad y_3, y_4 \leq 0$

Chapter 9

Sec. 9.1 **1** $4! = 24$;   **3** 6720;   **5** 1;   **7** 252;
9 $10! = 3,628,800$;   **11** 56;   **13** 220

Sec. 9.2 **1** (a) 0.47, (b) 0.30, (c) 0.04, (d) 0.30;   **3** (a) 0.20,
(b) 0.70, (c) 0.667, (d) $\frac{100}{101}$;

5 0.20, 4 to 1;   7 (a) 0.20, (b) 0.95, (c) 0.75;

9 (a) $\frac{8}{52}$, (b) $\frac{12}{52}$, (c) $\frac{16}{52}$, (d) $\frac{32}{52}$;   11 (a) 0.0012, (b) 0.288, (c) 0.9312;

13 1,024/311,875,200;   15 (a) 120/5,040, (b) $\frac{620}{5,040}$, (c) $\frac{300}{5,040}$

Sec. 9.3 1   NO. OF HEADS

x	$p(x)$
0	$\frac{1}{8}$
1	$\frac{3}{8}$
2	$\frac{3}{8}$
3	$\frac{1}{8}$

3 (a) $\mu = 33.6$, (b) $\sigma = 10.85$;   5 $\mu_{x_1} = 500$, $\sigma_{x_1} = 0$, $\mu_{x_2} = 500$,
$\sigma_{x_2} = 284.60$;   7 \$11.08;   9 stock 12, \$110;
11 \$67.80, EVPI = \$2.60.

Sec. 9.4 1 a, c, and g are Bernoulli processes;   3 $\frac{25}{216}$, $\frac{1125}{1296}$;
5 $P(x = 0) = 0.00001$, $P(x = 1) = 0.00045$, $P(x = 2) = 0.0081$,
$P(x = 3) = 0.0792$, $P(x = 4) = 0.32805$, $P(x = 5) = 0.59049$;   7 0.38228,
0.25000 (probability of passing not the same);
9 0.0009765, 0.0880803;   11 $\mu = 2.0$, $\sigma = 1.26911$

Sec. 9.5 1 (a) 0.1151, (b) 0.8413, (c) 0.1832, (d) 0.9786;
3 (a) 0.9495, (b) 0.5478, (c) 0.2221, (d) 0.0317;   5 0.0808, 0.0047;
7 0.6826, 0.0228;   9 0.3085, 0.0668

Chapter Test 2 (a) 120, (b) 20;   3 $\frac{24}{132,600}$;   4 (a) $\frac{12}{26}$, (b) $\frac{18}{34}$;

5 (a)

		STOCK ACTION			
	6	7	8	9	10
6	12	9	6	3	0
7	12	14	11	8	5
DEMAND 8	12	14	16	13	10
9	12	14	16	18	15
10	12	14	16	18	20

(b) stock 7, (c) \$12.50;   6 0.234375;   7 (a) 0.4207, (b) 0.1078

Chapter 10

Sec. 10.2 1 not quadratic;   3 quadratic, $a = -\frac{1}{100}$, $b = 0$, $c = 0$;
5 quadratic, $a = \frac{1}{5}$, $b = -\frac{2}{5}$, $c = \frac{4}{5}$;   7 quadratic, $a = 4$, $b = -1$,
$c = 1$;   9 down, (0, 0), (0, 0), (0, 0);   11 up, (0, 6), no x intercepts,

(.2, 5.8);   **13**   down, (0, -9), (-3, 0), (-3, 0);   **15**   up, (0, -5), (2.5, 0) and (-2, 0), (.25, -5.0625);   **19** $y = -3x^2 + 2x$

Sec. 10.3   **1** $R = g(p) = 400,000p - 2,000p^2$, down (0, 0), $g(20) = \$7,200,000$, $f(20) = 360,000$ units;

3 $R = h(q) = -.0005q^2 + 200q$;

5   (a) $q_s = 2.5p^2 - 6,250$,   (c) 50,   (d) 7,812.5 units;

7   (a) $q_d = 3p^2 - 240p + 4,800$, 675 units;   **9** $p = 75$, $q = 5,225$;

11   (a) $S = f(x) = 3x^2 - 124x + 1,444$,   (b) $x = 20.67$ (miles to right of zero)

Sec. 10.4   **1**   (a) third degree,   (b) as $x \to \infty$, $f(x) \to -\infty$; as $x \to -\infty$, $f(x) \to \infty$;

3   (a) sixth degree,   (b) as $x \to \infty$, $f(x) \to \infty$; as $x \to -\infty$, $f(x) \to \infty$;

5   (a) fifth degree,   (b) as $x \to \infty$, $f(x) \to \infty$; as $x \to -\infty$, $f(x) \to -\infty$;

7   (a) fourth degree,   (b) as $x \to \infty$, $f(x) \to \infty$; as $x \to -\infty$, $f(x) \to \infty$

Chapter Test   **1**   (a) up,   (b) (0, 25),   (c) (-5, 0),   (d) (-5, 0), (e) see sketch;   **2** $R = 400,000p - 30p^2$;

3 $400a + 20b + c = 400$
$625a + 25b + c = 850$
$900a + 30b + c = 1,400$;

4   (a) ninth degree,   (b) as $x \to \infty$, $f(x) \to \infty$; as $x \to -\infty$, $f(x) \to -\infty$

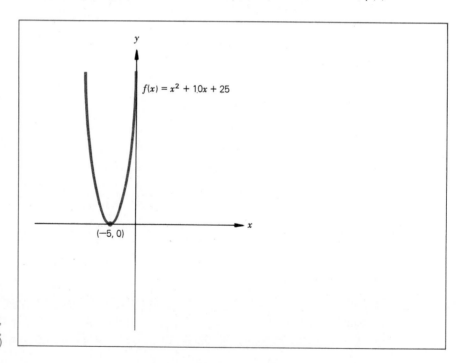

Chapter 11

Sec. 11.1 **1** 12; **3** 10; **5** limit does not exist; **7** 16;
9 −5; **11** limit does not exist

Sec. 11.1 (Continued) **1** 1; **3** −1; **5** 2; **7** 125; **9** 3,900;
11 −9; **13** −8; **15** $4c^3 - 3c^2 + 10$;
17 0, horizontal asymptote at $y = 0$, vertical asymptote at $x = 0$;
19 $\frac{1}{4}$, horizontal asymptote at $y = \frac{1}{4}$, vertical asymptote at $x = -25$;
21 no limit, no asymptotes; **23** continuous; **25** continuous;
27 discontinuous at $x = -6$; **29** discontinuous at $x = -3$ and 7;
31 discontinuous at $x = -3, 0,$ and 2

Sec. 11.2 **1** 10; **3** 0; **5** $\frac{5}{21}$;
7 (a) 96 ft/sec, 64 ft/sec, 0 ft/sec, (b) 8 sec;
9 \$5.75 million/year, \$6 million/year, \$5.5 million/year, \$5 million/year;
11 1.1 billion ft³/year, 0.933 billion ft³/year, 1.35 billion ft³/year;
13 (a) $4x + 2\Delta x$, (b) 8; **15** (a) $40x + 20\Delta x + 6$, (b) 86;
17 (a) $3x^2 + 3x\Delta x + \Delta x^2$, (b) 13; **19** (a) $-1/x(x + \Delta x)$, (b) $-\frac{1}{3}$

Sec. 11.3 **1** (a) 2, (b) 2, 2; **3** (a) $16x$, (b) $-16, 32$;
5 (a) $6x$, (b) $-6, 12$; **7** (a) $2x - 2$, (b) $-4, 2$;
9 (a) $-3/x^2$, (b) $-3, -\frac{3}{4}$; **11** (a) $3x^2$, (b) 3, 12;
13 (a) $3x^2 - 6x$, (b) 9, 0; **15** (a) $-2, -18$, (c) $\frac{1}{4}$;
17 (a) 20, 20, (c) no values for x; **19** (a) 0, 0, (c) all values of x;
21 (a) $-16, 0$, (c) $x = 2, -2$;
23 (a) 14, (b) 20, 27, (c) $f(2) = 13, f(2.5) = 21, f(3) = 31$

Sec. 11.4 **1** 0; **3** $3x^2 - 4$; **5** $\frac{3}{5}x^{-2/5} = \dfrac{3}{5x^{2/5}} = \dfrac{3}{5\sqrt[5]{x^2}}$; **7** $10x^9$;

9 $2x^5 - 2$; **11** $-10/x^3$; **13** $1 + \dfrac{1}{2\sqrt{x^3}} = 1 + \dfrac{1}{2x\sqrt{x}}$;

15 $8x^7 - 12x^5 + 30x^4 - 36x^2$; **17** $7.5x^4 - 2x^3 + 0.75x^2 + 60x - 10$;
19 $(1 + x^2)/(1 - x^2)^2$; **21** $(-20x^4 + 6x)/(4x^5 - 3x^2 + 1)^2$;
23 $-60x^2(1 - 4x^3)^4$; **25** $-15x^2/2\sqrt{1 - 5x^3}$;

27 $-x/(x^2 - 1)^{3/2} = -x/(x^2 - 1)\sqrt{x^2 - 1}$; **29** $\dfrac{2}{3[x^2(5x - 1)]^{1/3}} \dfrac{(5x^2 - 2x)}{(5x - 1)^2}$;

31 $\dfrac{(9 - 2x^2)[-15x^5(1 - x^3)^4 + 3x^2(1 - x^3)^5] - 4x^4(1 - x^3)^5}{3(9 - 2x^2)^2 \left[\dfrac{(1 - x^3)^5 x^3}{9 - 2x^2}\right]^{2/3}}$;

33 $2ax + b$; **35** $3a_3x^2 + 3a_2x^2 + a_1$; **37** (a) 10, (b) none;

39 (a) -2, (b) $\pm\sqrt{6}$;   41 (a) $4a_2 + a_1$, (b) $-a_1/2a_2$;

43 (a) $\frac{4}{9}$, (b) 0;   45 (a) 17, (b) $-\frac{13}{2}$;

47 (a) 40 (hundreds) ft/sec, (b) 750 (hundreds) ft/sec, $3{,}000$ (hundreds) ft/sec;

49 (a) -48 ft/sec, (b) -32 ft/sec, (c) -128 ft/sec

Sec. 11.5 1 (a) $0, 0$, (b) $0, 0$;   3 (a) $8x - 1, 8$, (b) $7, 8$;

5 (a) $15x^2, 30x$, (b) $15, 30$;   7 (a) $x^3 - x^2 + 10, 3x^2 - 2x$, (b) $10, 1$;

9 (a) $-1/x^2, 2/x^3$, (b) $-1, 2$;   11 (a) -128 ft/sec, (b) -32 ft/sec;

13 $f'(x) = 48x^2 - 8x, f''(x) = 96x - 8, f'''(x) = 96, f^{IV}(x) = 0$;

15 $f'(x) = m, f''(x) = 0$;

17 $f'(x) = 5x^4 - 20x^3 - 60x, f''(x) = 20x^3 - 60x^2 - 60, f'''(x) = 60x^2 - 120x,$
$f^{IV}(x) = 120x - 120, f^V(x) = 120, f^{VI}(x) = 0$;

19 $f'(x) = 3a_3x^2 + 2a_2x, f''(x) = 6a_3x + 2a_2, f'''(x) = 6a_3, f^{IV}(x) = 0$

Sec. 11.6 1 -15;   3 $4x^3 - 4x$;   5 $-45x^8 + 105x^6 - 75x^4 + 15x^2$;

7 $\dfrac{\sqrt{2}}{2}$;   9 $(10x - 10)(x^2 - 2x - 3)^4$;   11 $1/12(x^2 - 2x + 1), x \neq 1$;

13 $1/(14x + 7), x \neq -\frac{1}{2}$;   15 $1/10(2x - 6)^4, x \neq 3$;

17 $1/(2a_2y + a_1)$;   19 $1/(15y^2 - 4y + 1)$;

21 $3x^2\sqrt{x^2 - 1}(1 - x^3)^2 + \frac{1}{2}(x^2 - 1)^{-1/2}(2x)(x^3)(1 - x^3)^2$
$+ 2(1 - x^3)(-3x^2)(x^3)\sqrt{x^2 - 1}$;

23 $5x^4(x^2 - 3x)^{1/3}(x - 5)^4 + \frac{1}{3}(x^2 - 3x)^{-2/3}(2x - 3)x^5(x - 5)^4$
$+ 4(x - 5)^3x^5(x^2 - 3x)^{1/3}$;

25 $750x^5$;   27 $24x^{23}$

Chapter Test 1 (a) 5, (b) 2;   2 none;   3 $-6x + 1$;

4 (a) $-8x^{-7/5}/5$, (b) $8x^7 - 28x^3 - 2x$,
(c) $\{(x^3 + 5)^2(-2x) - (12 - x^2)[2(x^3 + 5)(3x^2)]\}/(x^3 + 5)^4$;

5 $x = 1$;   6 $f'(x) = x^2 - 4x + 5, f''(x) = 2x - 4, f'''(x) = 2, f^{IV}(x) = 0$;

7 $8x(x^2 - 15)^3 - 4x$;   8 $\frac{1}{10}$

Chapter 12

Sec. 12.1 1 (a) decreasing, (b)–(d) function decreasing for all x;

3 (a) decreasing, (b) $x > \frac{5}{2}$, (c) $x < \frac{5}{2}$, (d) $x = \frac{5}{2}$;

5 (a) neither, (b) $x > 1$ and $x < 0$, (c) $0 < x < 1$, (d) $x = 0, 1$;

7 (a) neither, (b) $x > 1$ and $-1 < x < 0$, (c) $0 < x < 1$ and $x < -1$,
(d) $x = 0, 1, -1$;

9 (a) function undefined at $x = 1$, (b) $x > 5$, (c) none, (d) $x = 5$;

11 down, down;   13 up, up;   15 f undefined, up;

17 down, up;

19 (a) all values of x, (b) none, (c) and (d) linear function;

21   (a) $x > -b/2a$,   (b) $x < -b/2a$,   (c) all values of x,   (d) none;
23   (a) $x \neq 0$,   (b) none,   (c) $x > 0$,   (d) $x < 0$;   **25** 3;
27 5, -3;   **29** 5;   **31** no inflection points;
33   (a) $a < x < b, c < x < d, x > e$,   (b) $b < x < c, d < x < e$,
(c) $x = b, c, d, e$;
35   (a) $a_1 < x < a_2, a_3 < x < a_5, x > a_7$,   (b) $a_2 < x < a_3, a_5 < x < a_7$,
(c) $x = a_2, a_3, a_5, a_7$,   (d) same as (b),   (e) same as (a)

Sec. 12.2   **1**   relative min at $(4, -70)$;
3   inflection point at $(0, -25)$;
5   inflection point at $(0, 12)$;
7   relative max at $(0, 0)$, relative min at $(-3, -\frac{81}{4})$ and at $(3, -\frac{81}{4})$;
9   relative min at $(0.5, -3.125)$, relative max at $(-4, 88)$;
11   relative min at $(0, 0)$, relative max at $(-5, \frac{125}{6})$;
13   inflection point at $(2.5, 0)$;
15   inflection point at $(6, 0)$;
17   relative max at $(1, \frac{1}{2})$, relative min at $(-1, -\frac{1}{2})$;
19   relative min at $\left(-b/2a, -\dfrac{b^2}{4a} + c\right)$

Sec. 12.3   **1**   absolute max at $(6, 53)$, absolute min at $(1, 3)$;
3   absolute max at $(0, 0)$, absolute min at $(8, -256)$;
5   absolute max at $(5, 595)$, absolute min at $(1, -25\frac{4}{5})$;
7   absolute max at $(2, 18\frac{2}{3})$, absolute min at $(0, 0)$;
9   absolute max at $(16, 4)$, absolute min at $(1, 1)$

Chapter Test   **1** $x < 4$;   **2**   see figure;   **3**   min at $(7, -129\frac{2}{3})$, max at
$(-3, 37)$;   **4** $x = \pm\sqrt{2}$;   **5**   max at $(1, 1\frac{1}{6})$, min at $(-1, -2\frac{1}{6})$;
6   see figure

Chapter 13

Sec. 13.1   **1**   (a) \$87.50,   (b) \$76,562.50;
3   (a) 250,000 units,   (b) \$624,750,000;
5   (a) \$24.00,   (b) \$72,000,000,   (c) 3,000,000;

Chap. 12,
Chapter Test,
Problem 2

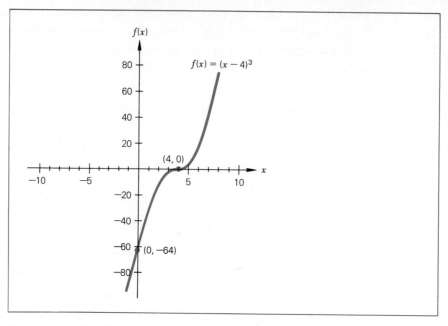

7 (*a*) 75, (*b*) \$751,282.60, (*c*) \$2.60 higher;

9 (*a*) $q = 1{,}200$, (*b*) \$2,000,413.33, (*c*) \$3.45 higher;

11 (*a*) 1,183.20, (*b*) \$8,091.60, (*c*) \$9,573,990.60;

13 (*a*) \$9.00, (*b*) \$2,940,000; **15** (*a*) 42,000, (*b*) \$552, (*c*) \$8,470,000

Sec. 13.2 **1** (*a*) 400 units, (*b*) \$79,500; **3** cannot use marginal
approach; **5** (*a*) 2,500, (*b*) \$22,500

Sec. 13.3 **1** 45' by 45'; **3** $x = 150$, $y = 75$, $A = 11{,}250$ sq. meters;
5 $x = 900$, $y = 600$, $A = 540{,}000$ ft²; **7** $x = 63\frac{2}{3}$;
9 (*a*) 70,710.68 miles, (*b*) \$0.324, (*c*) \$7,757.36;
11 (*a*) $p = 100 - x$, (*b*) $0 \le x \le 100$, (*c*) $R = 5000 + 50x - x^2$, (*d*) 25,
(*e*) 75, (*f*) \$5,625, (*g*) \$75, (*h*) no;
13 $x = 11.54$

Chapter Test **1** $R = 50{,}000p - 7.5p^2$;
2 (*a*) $P = -5x^2 + 350x - 5{,}000$, (*b*) $x = 35$ hundreds, (*c*) \$1,125 hundreds;
3 (*a*) 316.23' by 316.23', (*b*) \$12,649.20; **4** (*a*) $q = 200$, (*b*) \$50,200

Chapter 14

Sec. 14.1 **1** *a*, *b*, *c*, and *e* are exponential functions;
5 $f(0) = 1$, $f(-2) = \frac{1}{3}$, $f(2) = 3$; **7** $f(0) = 1$, $f(-2) = e$, $f(2) = 1/e$;
9 $f(0) = 1$, $f(-2) = e^2$, $f(2) = e^2$;

11 $f(0) = 0$, $f(-2) = 10(1 - e^{-4}) = 9.817$, $f(2) = 10(1 - e^4) = -535.98$;
19 $f(x) = e^{0.69x^2}$;   21 $f(x) = e^{0.405x}$;   23 $f(t) = 10e^{1.2t}$;
25 $f(t) = -2e^{4.5t}$

Sec. 14.2 1 (a) $S = 250,000e^{0.15t}$, (b) \$455,525, \$1,120,425;
3 approximately 4.6 years to double; approximately 9.33 years to quadruple;
5 (a) $P = f(t) = 40e^{.032t}$, where $t = 0$ corresponds to Jan. 1, 1975, (b) 64.644
million, 89.02 million;
7 (a) 5,466.3 tons/day, (b) approximately 11.5 years;
9 approximately 13.8 years;
11 approximately 13.8 years (sometime during late 1993);
13 (a) 10.878%, 19.782%, (b) .6

Sec. 14.3 1 e^x;   3 $20xe^{x^2}$;   5 $375e^{3x}$;   7 $4e^{x^2} + 8x^2e^{x^2}$;
9 $(xe^x - e^x)/x^2$;   11 $3e^{3x}$;   13 no critical points;   15 relative
min at $(-13.9, 460)$;   17 relative min at $(0, 22,026)$;   19 relative max at
$(-5.8, 3,080.5)$;
21 (a) approximately 105 days, (b) \$2,460,000, 87.75%;
23 6 months, \$43.7875 millions;   25 (a) 500, (b) \$183,900

Sec. 14.4 1 $\log_2 16 = 4$;   3 $\log_6 216 = 3$;   5 $\log_2 \frac{1}{16} = -4$;
7 $\log_{.5} 16 = -4$;   9 $\log_{.1} 1000 = -3$;   11 $2^7 = 128$;
13 $3^4 = 81$;   15 $5^3 = 125$;   17 $0.2^{-2} = 25$;   19 $e^{4.6052} = 100$;
21 2.3026;   23 5.8579;   25 6.1633;   27 -1.8971;
29 5.0751;   31 $x = 2.7183$;   33 $x = 1$;   35 $x = 1.5415$;
37 $x = .9986$;   39 $x = \pm 2.0933$;
45 (a) $(e^{c/a} - b, 0)$, (b) $(0, a \ln b - c)$;   47 $1/x$;   49 $2x/(x^2 - 3)$;
51 $2x \ln x + x$;   53 $10(\ln x - 1)/(\ln x)^2$;   55 $\dfrac{\ln 3x - (x - 1)/x}{(\ln 3x)^2}$;
57 relative max at $(\frac{1}{3}, 1.3026)$;   59 relative max at $(1, -\frac{1}{2})$;
61 relative min at $(1, 4.5)$ and relative max at $(4, 6.4548)$; relative min at
$(.6065, -.1839)$

Sec. 14.5 1 (a) 6, (b) \$4.72;   3 $\eta = 4.2962$;
5 (a) $P = 10^5 e^{.45t}$, (b) 1.54 hours, (c) 2.44 hours;
7 (a) 2.13 hours, (b) 4.27 hours;   9 $k = .0000693$

Chapter Test 1 82.1;   2 \$40,552, \$30,552;   3 $\log_4 65,536 = 8$;
4 relative max at $(0, e^3)$;   5 relative min at $(.3679, -.3679)$;
6 $N = 1,500,000(1 - e^{-.06x}) - 5000x$

Chapter 15

Sec. 15.2   **1** $f_x = 10x$, $f_y = -18y^2$;   **3** $f_x = 20x - 3y$,
$f_y = -3x + 10y$;   **5** $f_x = 3x^2y^2$, $f_y = 2x^3y$;   **7** $f_x = 6x - y$,
$f_y = -x + 30y^2$;   **9** $f_x = -1/x^2y$, $f_y = -1/xy^2$;
11 $f_x = 15x^2 + 4xy^5 - 15y$, $f_y = 10x^2y^4 - 15x - 36y^5$;
13 $f_x = 3(x - y)^2$, $f_y = -3(x - y)^2$;   **15** $f_x = x/\sqrt{x^2 - y^2}$,
$f_y = -y/\sqrt{x^2 - y^2}$;   **17** $f_x = \ln{(y - 1)}/(x + 5)$, $f_y = \ln{(x + 5)}/(y - 1)$;
19 $f_x = 15x^2e^{5x^3-2y^2}$, $f_y = -4ye^{5x^3-2y^2}$;   **21** $f_{xx} = 6$, $f_{yy} = -30y$,
$f_{xy} = f_{yx} = 0$;   **23** $f_{xx} = 6x$, $f_{yy} = 14$, $f_{xy} = f_{yx} = -3$;   **25** $f_{xx} = 6xy^2$,
$f_{yy} = 2x^3$, $f_{xy} = f_{yx} = 6x^2y$;   **27** $f_{xx} = f_{yy} = f_{xy} = f_{yx} = e^{x+y}$;
29 $f_{xx} = y^2e^{xy}$, $f_{yy} = x^2e^{xy}$, $f_{xy} = f_{yx} = e^{xy} + xye^{xy}$;
31 (a) 88,000, (b) +1,800, (c) actual change +1,900, (d) projected change
$= +7,900$, actual $= +8,100$;
33 (a) 116,000, (b) −1,500, (c) 1,900, (d) better spent on radio;
35 (a) $f_{p_1} = -p_1$, $f_{p_2} = 2p_2$, $f_{p_3} = -.8p_3$, (b) $f_{p_1} = -30$, $f_{p_2} = 20$, $f_{p_3} = -16$,
(c) products 1 and 3 appear to be complementary while product 2 seems to
be competing

Sec. 15.3   **1** saddle point at $(-10, 10, -310)$;
3 saddle point at $(0, 2, -12)$ and relative max at $(5, 2, -32\frac{5}{6})$;
5 relative min at $(1, 3.5, -20.75)$;
7 relative min at $(1, -3, -1)$ and saddle point at $(-1, -3, 3)$;
9 saddle point at $(0, 0, 0)$, relative min at $(1, 1, -1)$;
11 saddle point at $(1.414, -.707, -8.15)$

Sec. 15.4   **1** (a) $x = 2,000$ (thousands of \$), $y = 2,000$ (thousands of \$),
(b) 100,000,000;   **3** (a) $p_1 = p_2 = 10$, (b) $q_1 = 60$ (thousands), $q_2 = 40$
(thousands), (c) \$1,000,000;   **5** $x = -3.75$, $y = 10$;   **7** $y = -3x + 8$

Sec. 15.5   **1** no conclusion about critical point located at $(-.15, .25, .05,$
$-0.075)$;   **3** relative min at $(0, 0, 0, 2)$;   **5** relative max at $(0, 0, 0, 25)$;
7 (a) $p_1 = \$9,666.67$, $p_2 = \$7,500$, $p_3 = \$9,833.34$, (b) $q_1 = 2,000$, $q_2 = 3,000$,
$q_3 = 2,500$, (c) \$66,416,690

Sec. 15.6   **1** relative max at $(48, 52, 37,600)$, $\lambda = 752$;
3 relative min at $(33, 9, 1,926)$, $\lambda = -93$;
5 relative max at $(9, 7, 528)$, $\lambda = 66$;

Chapter Test   **1** (a) instantaneous change in $f(x, y)$ given a change in x, y
assumed to be held constant, (b) f_x represents a general expression for the
tangent slope of the family of traces which are parallel to the xz plane;

2 given $z = f(x, y)$, a trace is the graphical representation of $f(x, y)$ when one variable is held constant;

3 $f_x = 15x^2 + 10xy$
$f_y = -8y + 5x^2$

4 $f_{xx} = 80x^3 + 36x - 6y^2$
$f_{yy} = -6x^2$
$f_{xy} = -12xy$
$f_{yx} = -12xy$

5 (a) relative minimum when $x = 1$ and $y = 3.5$,   (b) $f(1, 3.5) = -20.75$;

6 200 acres of soybeans
100 acres of corn
$200,000;

7 $L(x_1, x_2, \lambda) = -4x_1^3 + 3x_2^2 - 4x_1x_2 - \lambda(x_1 - 2x_2 - 20)$

Chapter 16

Sec. 16.1   1 $40x + C$;   3 $\dfrac{x}{2} + C$;   5 $\dfrac{5x^2}{2} + C$;   7 $\dfrac{x^3}{3} + C$;

9 $\dfrac{x^4}{12} + C$;   11 $\dfrac{x^3}{3} - 3x^2 + C$;   13 $\dfrac{x^3}{3} + \dfrac{3x^2}{2} + x + C$;

15 $\dfrac{x^5}{10} + C$;   17 $f(x) = 15x - 5$;   19 $f(x) = 10x^2 + 10$;

21 $f(x) = x^4 + 29$ 23 $f(x) = \dfrac{x^3}{3} - \dfrac{5x^2}{2} + 38.5$;

25 $f(x) = \dfrac{-x^3}{3} + \dfrac{5x^2}{2} - 22\frac{1}{3}$;   27 $R = 60,000x - \dfrac{3x^2}{2}$;

29 $P = -3x^2 + 750x - 20,000$

Sec. 16.2   1 $50x + C$;   3 $\dfrac{x}{2} + C$;   5 $4x^2 + C$;   7 $\dfrac{5x^2}{2} - 3x + C$;

9 $\dfrac{x^3}{3} - \dfrac{3x^2}{2} + 5x + C$;   11 $\dfrac{3}{4}x^{4/3} + C$;   13 $-\dfrac{1}{2x^2} + C$;

15 $\dfrac{ax^4}{4} + \dfrac{bx^3}{3} + \dfrac{cx^2}{2} + dx + C$;   17 $\dfrac{a}{b}\dfrac{x^{1-n}}{(1-n)} + C, n \neq 1$;

19 $\dfrac{x^{1-n}}{1-n} + C, n \neq 1$

Sec. 16.3   1 $\dfrac{(x + 25)^5}{5} + C$;   3 $\dfrac{(x^2 - 8)^6}{6} + C$;   5 $\dfrac{(4x^3 - 10)^4}{48} + C$;

7 $\dfrac{(2x^2 - 4x)^5}{20} + C$;   9 $2\sqrt{x^2 - 1} + C$;   11 cannot be done;

13 cannot be done;   15 $e^{2x}/2 + C$;   17 $e^{ax}/a + C$;

19 $\frac{1}{2} \ln (x^2 - 5) + C$;　　　**21** $2 \ln (6x - 5) + C$;　　　**23** $\frac{1}{a} \ln (ax + b) + C$

Sec. 16.4　1 ordinary, first order, first degree;
3 ordinary, second order, third degree;
5 partial, first order, first degree;　　**7** partial, second order, first degree;
9 $y = \frac{x^5}{5} - x^2 + 5x + C$;　　**11** $y = \ln x + C$;　　**13** $y = \frac{\ln (5x^2 - 10)}{10} + C$;

15 $y = \frac{x^3}{6} - \frac{3x^2}{2} + C_1 x + C_2$;　　**17** $y = -\frac{x^5}{20} + \frac{x^3}{3} - 8x^2 + C_1 x + C_2$;

19 $y = \frac{x^2}{2} + C, y = \frac{x^2}{2} - 5$;

21 $y = \frac{x^3}{3} - x^2 + 3x + C, y = \frac{x^3}{3} - x^2 + 3x + \frac{1}{6}$;

23 $y = x^3 - 9x^2 + C_1 x + C_2, y = x^3 - 9x^2 + 17x + 44$;
25 $y = e^{5x} + C_1 x + C_2, y = e^{5x} - x - 3$;　　**27** $P = 500e^{.45815t}$

Sec. 16.5　1 $-xe^{-x} - e^{-x} + C$;　　**3** $\frac{3x(x + 1)^{4/3}}{4} - \frac{9(x + 1)^{7/3}}{28} + C$;

5 $\frac{x(e^{2x})}{2} - \frac{e^{2x}}{4} + C$;　　**7** $\left(\frac{x^2}{2} + 4x\right) \ln x - \frac{x^2}{4} - 4x + C$;

9 $\frac{x(x + 2)^5}{5} - \frac{(x + 2)^6}{30} + C$;　　**11** $2x(x - 3)^{1/2} - \frac{4}{3}(x - 3)^{3/2} + C$;

13 $\frac{-\ln x}{x} - \frac{1}{x} + C$;　　**15** $-8 \ln (x + 3) + 7 \ln (x + 2) + C$;

17 $-2 \ln (x - 1) - \frac{5}{(x - 1)} + C$;

19 $-4 \ln x + 4.75 \ln (x + 4) + 4.25 \ln (x - 4) + C$;

21 $6 \ln x - 2 \ln (x - 1) + C$;　　**23** $\frac{x^5}{5} \ln (10x) - \frac{x^5}{25} + C$;

25 $\left[\frac{\ln x}{-2} - \frac{1}{4}\right] \bigg/ x^2 + C$;　　**27** $x (\ln x)^2 - 2x \ln x + 2x + C$;

29 $x^5 \left[\frac{\ln x}{5} - \frac{1}{25}\right] + C$;　　**31** $\frac{e^{2.5x}}{2.5} + C$;　　**33** $\frac{e^{5x}}{25} (5x - 1) + C$;

35 $\frac{x}{5} - \frac{1}{10} \ln (5 + 3e^{2x}) + C$

Chapter Test　1 $f(x) = x^4 - x^2 - 10x - 450$;

2 (a) $-\frac{3}{2}x^{2/3} + C$,　(b) $\frac{(x^4 - 10)^8}{32} + C$,　(c) $-e^{-10x}/10 + C$;

3 $y = \frac{5x^2}{2} - \frac{x^3}{6} + C_1 x + C_2, y = \frac{5x^2}{2} - \frac{x^3}{6} - 3x + 15$;

4 $R = 120,000x - 6x^2$;   **5** $\dfrac{xe^{10x}}{10} - \dfrac{e^{10x}}{100} + C$;

6 $10 \ln (x - 3) + 10 \ln (x + 2) + C$

Chapter 17

Sec. 17.1 **1** $\frac{9}{2}$;   **3** 2;   **5** 0;   **7** 0;   **9** $341\frac{1}{3}$;   **11** 1.0987;

13 $-51.8797+$ **15** -6;   **17** 0;   **19** $\dfrac{m}{2} + b$;   **21** $24\frac{2}{3}$;

23 $-4\frac{2}{3}$;   **25** $-25\frac{1}{3}$;   **27** 28

Sec. 17.2 **1** 8;   **3** 40;   **5** $30\frac{2}{3}$;   **7** 16.25;   **9** 25.9425;

11 (a) $\displaystyle\int_0^b g(x)\,dx - \int_a^b f(x)\,dx$, (b) $-\displaystyle\int_0^a f(x)\,dx$,

(c) $\displaystyle\int_a^b f(x)\,dx + \int_b^c g(x)\,dx$, (d) $\displaystyle\int_b^d f(x)\,dx - \int_b^c g(x)\,dx$, (e) $-\displaystyle\int_c^e g(x)\,dx +$

$\displaystyle\int_d^e f(x)\,dx$;   **13** 64;   **15** $2,666\frac{2}{3}$

Sec. 17.3 **1** (a) \$1,200, (b) \$400;

3 (b) 9 days, (c) \$53,550, (d) \$24,300;

5 (a) 195,200, (b) 9.4 hours;   **7** (b) $p = 5$, $q = 75$, (c) \$166.67;

9 11 days;   **11** (a) .82435 million tons, (b) 12.974 million tons;

13 (a) 6 hours/unit, (b) 135.914 hours, (c) 4 hours/unit;

15 406.944 units^3

Sec. 17.4 **1** 0.444, 0.888;   **3** 0.3888

Chapter Test **1** (a) $\frac{4}{3}$, (b) 9.3416;   **2** (b) $26\frac{2}{3}$;

3 (a) \$248/year, (b) \$432;   **4** 0.800

Chapter 18

Sec. 18.1 **1** \$15,000;   **3** \$4,800, \$96,000;

5

SEMIANNUAL PERIOD	(P) PRINCIPAL	(I) INTEREST	S = P + I COMPOUND AMOUNT
1	\$10,000	\$600	\$10,600
2	10,600	636	11,236
3	11,236	674.16	11,910.16
4	11,910.16	714.61	12,624.77

Total interest = \$2624.77.

7   (a) $12,667.70,   (b) quarterly, by $42.93

Sec. 18.2   1 $1,850.93, $850.93;   3 $2,446,530, $1,696,530;
5   (a) $1.79085 (or $1.79), $0.79,   (b) $1.80611 (or $1.81), $0.81,
(c) $1.81670 (or $1.82), $0.82;
7   35,525.76 or 35,526;   9 $11,144.63;   11 $12,434.40, $7,565.60;
13   $30,513.50, $19,486.50;   15   between 15 and 16 (semiannual) periods;   17   (a) 0.16640,   (b) 0.16986;   19   between 8 and 9%

Sec. 18.3   1   (a) $143,187.50,   (b) $93,187.50;
3   (a) $19,399.58,   (b) $10,399.58;
5   (a) $66,101,   (b) $69,082.25,   (c) $70,699.20;   7 $3,276, $3,620;
9   $745.60, $1,052.80

Sec. 18.4   1 $73,636.13;   3 $25,566.72;
5   (a) $181,540.80,   (b) $318,459.20;   7 $19,171;   9 $29,880;
11   (a) $180.75,   (b) $1,507;   13 $631.93, $189,579, $129,579;
15   $908.91, $218,138.40, $138,138.40;   17 $44.77, $13,431;
19   $56.99, $13,677.60;   21 $50,748.30

Sec. 18.5   1 $274,474, yes;   3 $245,146, yes;   5 $419,412, yes;
7   between 15 and 16%

Chapter Test   1 $37,459.60;   2 $79,383;
3   (a) $188,503.15;   (b) $88,503.15;   4 $1,590, $4,100;   5 $3,491.25;
6   .19252 or 19.252%;   7 $30.89;   8   yes, $2434.25

INDEX

x	e^x	e^{-x}	x	e^x	e^{-x}	x	e^x	e^{-x}
4.900	134.29	0.0074	6.650	772.78	0.0013	8.400	4447.1	0.0002
4.950	141.17	0.0071	6.700	812.41	0.0012	8.450	4675.1	0.0002
5.000	148.41	0.0067	6.750	854.06	0.0012	8.500	4914.8	0.0002
5.050	156.02	0.0064	6.800	897.85	0.0011	8.550	5166.8	0.0002
5.100	164.02	0.0061	6.850	943.88	0.0011	8.600	5431.7	0.0002
5.150	172.43	0.0058	6.900	992.27	0.0010	8.650	5710.1	0.0002
5.200	181.27	0.0055	6.950	1043.1	0.0010	8.700	6002.9	0.0002
5.250	190.57	0.0052	7.000	1096.6	0.0009	8.750	6310.7	0.0002
5.300	200.34	0.0050	7.050	1152.9	0.0009	8.800	6634.2	0.0002
5.350	210.61	0.0047	7.100	1212.0	0.0008	8.850	6974.4	0.0001
5.400	221.41	0.0045	7.150	1274.1	0.0008	8.900	7332.0	0.0001
5.450	232.76	0.0043	7.200	1339.4	0.0007	8.950	7707.9	0.0001
5.500	244.69	0.0041	7.250	1408.1	0.0007	9.000	8103.1	0.0001
5.550	257.24	0.0039	7.300	1480.3	0.0007	9.050	8518.5	0.0001
5.600	270.43	0.0037	7.350	1556.2	0.0006	9.100	8955.3	0.0001
5.650	284.29	0.0035	7.400	1636.0	0.0006	9.150	9414.4	0.0001
5.700	298.87	0.0033	7.450	1719.9	0.0006	9.200	9897.1	0.0001
5.750	314.19	0.0032	7.500	1808.0	0.0006	9.250	10405.	0.0001
5.800	330.30	0.0030	7.550	1900.7	0.0005	9.300	10938.	0.0001
5.850	347.23	0.0029	7.600	1998.8	0.0005	9.350	11499.	0.0001
5.900	365.04	0.0027	7.650	2100.6	0.0005	9.400	12088.	0.0001
5.950	383.75	0.0026	7.700	2208.3	0.0005	9.450	12708.	0.0001
6.000	403.43	0.0025	7.750	2321.6	0.0004	9.500	13360.	0.0001
6.050	424.11	0.0024	7.800	2440.6	0.0004	9.550	14045.	0.0001
6.100	445.86	0.0022	7.850	2565.7	0.0004	9.600	14765.	0.0001
6.150	468.72	0.0021	7.900	2697.3	0.0004	9.650	15522.	0.0001
6.200	492.75	0.0020	7.950	2835.6	0.0004	9.700	16318.	0.0001
6.250	518.01	0.0019	8.000	2981.0	0.0003	9.750	17154.	0.0001
6.300	544.57	0.0018	8.050	3133.8	0.0003	9.800	18034.	0.0001
6.350	572.49	0.0017	8.100	3294.5	0.0003	9.850	18958.	0.0001
6.400	601.85	0.0017	8.150	3463.4	0.0003	9.900	19930.	0.0001
6.450	632.70	0.0016	8.200	3641.0	0.0003	9.950	20952.	0.0000
6.500	665.14	0.0015	8.250	3827.6	0.0003	10.000	22026.	0.0000
6.550	699.24	0.0014	8.300	4023.9	0.0002			
6.600	735.10	0.0014	8.350	4230.2	0.0002			

TABLE 2
NATURAL LOGARITHMS

x	ln x	x	ln x	x	ln x	x	ln x
0.050	−2.9957	0.900	−0.1054	1.750	0.5596	2.600	0.9555
0.100	−2.3026	0.950	−0.0513	1.800	0.5878	2.650	0.9745
0.150	−1.8971	1.000	−0.0000	1.850	0.6152	2.700	0.9932
0.200	−1.6094	1.050	0.0488	1.900	0.6418	2.750	1.0116
0.250	−1.3863	1.100	0.0953	1.950	0.6678	2.800	1.0296
0.300	−1.2040	1.150	0.1398	2.000	0.6932	2.850	1.0473
0.350	−1.0498	1.200	0.1823	2.050	0.7178	2.900	1.0647
0.400	−0.9163	1.250	0.2231	2.100	0.7419	2.950	1.0818
0.450	−0.7985	1.300	0.2624	2.150	0.7655	3.000	1.0986
0.500	−0.6932	1.350	0.3001	2.200	0.7884	3.050	1.1151
0.550	−0.5978	1.400	0.3365	2.250	0.8109	3.100	1.1314
0.600	−0.5108	1.450	0.3716	2.300	0.8329	3.150	1.1474
0.650	−0.4308	1.500	0.4055	2.350	0.8544	3.200	1.1631
0.700	−0.3567	1.550	0.4382	2.400	0.8755	3.250	1.1786
0.750	−0.2877	1.600	0.4700	2.450	0.8961	3.300	1.1939
0.800	−0.2231	1.650	0.5008	2.500	0.9163	3.350	1.2089
0.850	−0.1625	1.700	0.5306	2.550	0.9361	3.400	1.2238